A People's Tragedy

A People's Tragedy

The Russian Revolution 1891–1924

ORLANDO FIGES

THE BODLEY HEAD
LONDON

Published by The Bodley Head 2014

2 4 6 8 10 9 7 5 3 1

Copyright © Orlando Figes 2014, 1996

Orlando Figes has asserted his right under the Copyright, Designs
and Patents Act 1988 to be identified as the author of this work

First published in Great Britain in 1996 by Jonathan Cape

Published in 1997 by Pimlico

The Bodley Head
20 Vauxhall Bridge Road,
London SW1V 2SA

www.bodleyhead.co.uk
www.vintage-books.co.uk

Addresses for companies within The Random House Group Limited can be found at:
www.randomhouse.co.uk/offices.htm

The Random House Group Limited Reg. No. 954009

A CIP catalogue record for this book
is available from the British Library

Maps by James Sinclair

ISBN 9781847922915

The Random House Group Limited supports the Forest Stewardship
Council® (FSC®), the leading international forest-certification organisation.
Our books carrying the FSC label are printed on FSC®-certified paper.
FSC is the only forest-certification scheme supported by the leading
environmental organisations, including Greenpeace.
Our paper procurement policy can be found at:
www.randomhouse.co.uk/environment

Printed and bound in Great Britain by Clays Ltd, St Ives PLC

For Stephanie

Contents

PART TWO THE CRISIS OF AUTHORITY (1891–1917)

PART THREE RUSSIA IN REVOLUTION (FEBRUARY 1917–MARCH 1918)

PART FOUR THE CIVIL WAR AND THE MAKING OF THE SOVIET SYSTEM (1918–24)

Illustrations

Photographic Credits

Bakhmeteff Archive, Columbia University: 58; California Museum of Photography, University of California, Riverside: 20. Hoover Institution of War, Revolution and Peace, Stanford, California: 82–4; *Life on the Russian Country Estate. A Social and Cultural history,* by Priscilla Roosevelt (Yale University Press, 1995): 26; Museum of the Revolution, Moscow: 7, 15, 36, 52, 61–2, 77–8, 90; Photokhronika Tass, Moscow: 107; private collections: 10, 32, 97; *Russian in Original Photographs 1860–1920,* by Marvin Lyons (Routledge & Kegan Paul, London, 1977): 25, 47; *Russie, 1904–1924: La Révolution est là,* (Baschet, Paris, 1978): 80; *Russian Century, The,* by Brian Moynahan (Chatto & Windus, London, 1994): 13, 28 (courtesy of Slava Katamidze Collection/Endeavour Group, London), 46 (Courtesy of the Endeavour Group, London); Russian State Archive of Film and Photographic Documents, Krasnogorsk: 18–19, 21–3, 35, 37–8, 40, 45, 48, 51, 59–60, 65–71, 73–6, 79, 81, 85–93, 98–106; Russian State Military History Archive, Moscow: 29; Saltykov-Shchedrin Library, St Petersburg: 12; State Archive of Film and Photographic Documents, St Petersburg: 1–6, 8–9, 11, 14, 16–17, 24, 27, 30–1, 34, 39, 41–4, 49–50, 53–7, 63–4, 72, 94–6; Tula District Museum: 33.

Preface

These days we call so many things a 'revolution' — a change in the government's policies on sport, a technological innovation, or even a new trend in marketing — that it may be hard for the reader of this book to take on board the vast scale of its subject at the start. The Russian Revolution was, at least in terms of its effects, one of the biggest events in the history of the world. Within a generation of the establishment of Soviet power, one-third of humanity was living under regimes modelled upon it. The revolution of 1917 has defined the shape of the contemporary world, and we are only now emerging from its shadow. It was not so much a single revolution — the compact eruption of 1917 so often depicted in the history books — as a whole complex of different *revolutions* which exploded in the middle of the First World War and set off a chain reaction of more revolutions, civil, ethnic and national wars. By the time that it was over, it had blown apart — and then put back together — an empire covering one-sixth of the surface of the globe. At the risk of appearing callous, the easiest way to convey the revolution's scope is to list the ways in which it wasted human life: tens of thousands were killed by the bombs and bullets of the revolutionaries, and at least an equal number by the repressions of the tsarist regime, before 1917; thousands died in the street fighting of that year; hundreds of thousands from the Terror of the Reds — and an equal number from the Terror of the Whites, if one counts the victims of their pogroms against Jews — during the years that followed; more than a million perished in the fighting of the civil war, including civilians in the rear; and yet more people died from hunger, cold and disease than from all these put together.

All of which, I suppose, is by way of an apology for the vast size of this book — the first attempt at a comprehensive history of the entire revolutionary period in a single volume. Its narrative begins in the 1890s, when the revolutionary crisis really started, and more specifically in 1891, when the public's reaction to the famine crisis set it for the first time on a collision course with the tsarist autocracy. And our story ends in 1924, with the death of Lenin, by which time the revolution had come full circle and the basic institutions, if not all the practices, of the Stalinist regime were in place. This is to give to the revolution a much longer lifespan than is customary. But it seems to me that, with one or two exceptions, previous histories of the revolution have been too narrowly focused on the events of 1917, and that this has made the range of its possible outcomes appear much more limited than they actually were. It was by no means inevitable that the revolution should have ended in the Bolshevik dictatorship, although looking only at that fateful year would lead one towards this conclusion. There were a number of decisive moments, both before and during 1917, when Russia might have followed a more democratic course. It is the aim of *A People's Tragedy*, by looking at the revolution in the *longue durée*, to explain why it did not at each of these in turn. As its title is intended to suggest, the book rests on the proposition that Russia's democratic failure was deeply rooted in its political culture and social history. Many of the themes of the four introductory chapters in Part One — the absence of a state-based counter-balance to the despotism of the Tsar; the isolation and fragility of liberal civil society; the backwardness and violence of the Russian village that drove so many peasants to go and seek a better life in the industrial towns; and the strange fanaticism of the Russian radical intelligentsia — will reappear as constant themes in the narrative of Parts Two, Three and Four.

Although politics are never far away, this is, I suppose, a social history in the sense that its main focus is the common people. I have tried to present the major social forces — the peasantry, the working class, the soldiers and the national minorities — as the participants in their own revolutionary drama rather than as 'victims' of the revolution. This is not to deny that there were many victims. Nor is it to adopt the 'bottom-up' approach so fashionable these days among the 'revisionist' historians of Soviet Russia. It would be absurd — and in Russia's case obscene — to imply that a people gets the rulers it deserves. But it is to argue that the sort of politicized 'top-down' histories of the Russian Revolution which used to be written in the Cold War era, in which the common people appeared as the passive objects of the evil machinations of the Bolsheviks, are no longer adequate. We now have a rich and growing literature, based upon research in the newly opened archives, on the social life of the Russian peasantry, the workers, the soldiers and the sailors, the provincial towns, the Cossacks and the non-Russian regions of the Empire during the revolutionary period. These monographs have given us a much more complex and convincing picture of the relationship between the party and the people than the one presented in the older 'top-down' version. They have shown that instead of a single abstract revolution imposed by the Bolsheviks on the whole of Russia, it was as often shaped by local passions and interests. *A People's Tragedy* is an attempt to synthesize this reappraisal and to push the argument one stage further. It attempts to show, as its title indicates, that what began as a people's revolution contained the seeds of its own degeneration into violence and dictatorship. The same social forces which brought about the triumph of the Bolshevik regime became its main victims.

Finally, the narrative of *A People's Tragedy* weaves between the private and the public spheres. Wherever possible, I have tried to emphasize the human aspect of its great events by listening to the voices of individual people whose lives became caught up in the storm. Their diaries, letters and other private writings feature prominently in this book. More substantially, the personal histories of several figures have been interwoven through the narrative. Some of these figures are well known (Maxim Gorky, General Brusilov and Prince Lvov), while others are unknown even to historians (the peasant reformer Sergei Semenov and the soldier-commissar Dmitry Os'kin). But all of them had hopes and aspirations, fears and disappointments, that were typical of the revolutionary experience as a whole. In following the fortunes of these figures, my aim has been to convey the chaos of these years, as it must have been felt by ordinary men and women. I have tried to present the revolution not as a march of abstract social forces and ideologies but as a human event of complicated individual tragedies. It was a story, by and large, of people, like the figures in this book, setting out with high ideals to achieve one thing, only to find out later that the outcome was quite different. This, again, is why I chose to call the book *A People's Tragedy*. For it is not just about the tragic turning-point in the history of a people. It is also about the ways in which the tragedy of the revolution engulfed the destinies of those who lived through it.

* * *

This book has taken over six years to write and it owes a great debt to many people.

Above all, I must thank Stephanie Palmer, who has had to endure far more in the way of selfish office hours, weekends and holidays spoilt by homework and generally impossible behaviour by her husband than she had any right to expect. In return I received from her love and support in much greater measure than I deserved. Stephanie looked after me through the dark years of debilitating illness in the early stages of this book, and, in addition to her own heavy work burdens, took on more than her fair share of child-care for our daughters, Lydia and Alice, after they were born in 1993. I dedicate this book to her in gratitude.

Neil Belton at Jonathan Cape has played a huge part in the writing of this book. Neil is any writer's dream of an editor. He read every chapter in every draft, and commented on them in long and detailed letters of the finest prose. His criticisms were always on the mark, his knowledge of the subject constantly surprising, and his enthusiasm was inspiring. If there is any one reader to whom this book is addressed, it is to him.

The second draft was also read by Boris Kolonitskii during the course of our various meetings in Cambridge and St Petersburg. I am very grateful to him for his many comments, all of which resulted in improvements to the text, and hope that, although it has so far been one-sided, this may be the start of a lasting intellectual partnership.

I owe a great debt to two amazing women. One is my mother, Eva Figes, a past master of the art of narrative who always gave me good advice on how to practise it. The other is my agent, Deborah Rogers, who did me a great service in brokering the marriage with Cape.

At Cape two other people merit special thanks. Dan Franklin navigated the book through its final stages with sensitivity and intelligence. And Liz Cowen went through the whole text line by line suggesting improvements with meticulous care. I am deeply grateful to them both.

For their assistance in the preparation of the final text I should also like to thank Claire Farrimond, who helped to check the notes, and Laura Pieters Cordy, who worked overtime to enter the corrections to the text. Thanks are also due to Ian Agnew, who drew the splendid maps.

The past six years have been an exciting time for historical research in Russia. I should like to thank the staff of the many Russian archives and libraries in which the research for this book was completed. I owe a great debt to the knowledge and advice of far too many archivists to name individually, but the one exception is Vladimir Barakhov, Director of the Gorky Archive, who was more than generous with his time.

Many institutions have helped me in the research for this book. I am grateful to the British Academy, the Leverhulme Trust, and — although the Fellowship could not be taken up — to the Woodrow Wilson Center in Washington for their generous support. My own Cambridge college, Trinity, which is as generous as it is rich, has also been of enormous assistance, giving me both grants and study leave. Among the Holy and Undivided Fellows of the college special thanks are due to my teaching colleagues, Boyd Hilton and John Lonsdale, for covering for me in my frequent absences; to the inimitable Anil Seal for being a supporter; and, above all, to Raj Chandavarkar, for being such a clever critic and loyal friend. Finally, in the History Faculty, I am, as always, grateful to Quentin Skinner for his efforts on my behalf.

The best thing about Cambridge University is the quality of its students, and in the course of the past six years I have had the privilege of teaching some of the brightest in my special subject on the Russian Revolution. This book is in no small measure the result of that experience. Many were the occasions when I rushed back from the lecture hall to write down the ideas I had picked up from discussions with my students. If they cannot be acknowledged in the notes, then I only hope that those who read this book will take it as a tribute of my gratitude to them.

Cambridge
November 1995

Glossary

ataman	Cossack chieftain
Black Hundreds	extremist right-wing paramilitary groups and proto-parties (for the origin of the term see page 196)
Bund	Jewish social democratic organization
burzhooi	popular term for a bourgeois or other social enemy (see page 523)
Cheka	Soviet secret police 1917–22 (later transformed into the OGPU, the NKVD and the KGB); the Cheka's full title was the All-Russian Extraordinary Commission for Struggle against Counter-Revolution and Sabotage
Defensists	socialist supporters of the war campaign (1914–18) for national defence; the Menshevik and SR parties were split between Defensists and Internationalists
desyatina	measurement of land area, equivalent to 1.09 hectares or 2.7 acres
Duma	the state Duma was the elected lower house of the Russian parliament 1906–17; the municipal dumas were elected town councils
guberniia	province (subdivided into uezdy and volosti)
Internationalists	socialists opposed to the war campaign (1914–18) who campaigned for immediate peace through international socialist collaboration; the Menshevik and SR parties were split between Defensists and Internationalists
Kadets	Constitutional Democratic Party
kolkhoz	collective farm
Komuch	anti-Bolshevik government established in Samara during the summer of 1918; its full title was the Committee of Members of the Constituent Assembly
Krug	Cossack assembly
kulak	capitalist peasant (see page 91)
mir	village commune
NEP	New Economic Policy (1921–9)

obshchina	peasant land commune
Octobrists	liberal-conservative political party
pud	measurement of weight, equivalent to 16.38 kg
SDs	Social Democrats: Marxist party (known in full as the Russian Social Democratic Labour Party); split into Menshevik and Bolshevik factions after 1903
skhod	communal or village assembly
sovkhoz	Soviet farm
SRs	Socialist Revolutionaries: non-Marxist revolutionary party (PSR); split into Right and Left SRs during 1917
Stavka	army headquarters
uezd	district (sub-division of *guberniia*)
versta	measurement of distance, equivalent to 0.66 miles
voisko	Cossack self-governing community
volia	freedom; autonomy
volost	rural township and basic administrative unit usually comprising several villages
zemstvo	elected assembly of local government dominated by the gentry at the provincial and district level (1864–1917); a volost-level zemstvo was finally established in 1917 but was soon supplanted by the Soviets.

Note on Dates

Until February 1918 Russia adhered to the Julian (Old Style) calendar, which ran thirteen days behind the Gregorian (New Style) calendar in use in Western Europe. The Soviet government switched to the New Style calendar at midnight on 31 January 1918: the next day was declared 14 February. Dates relating to domestic events are given in the Old Style up until 31 January 1918; and in the New Style after that. Dates relating to international events (e.g. diplomatic negotiations and military battles in the First World War) are given in the New Style throughout the book.

NB The term 'the Ukraine' has been used throughout this book, rather than the currently correct but ahistorical 'Ukraine'.

Maps

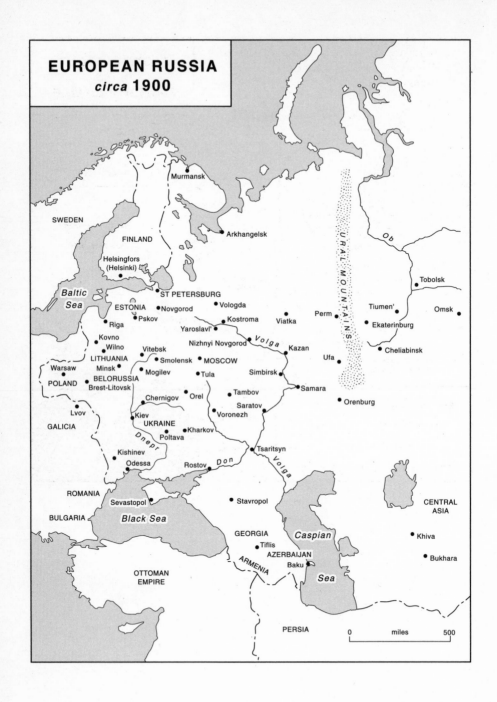

EUROPEAN RUSSIA
circa 1900

SWEDEN

FINLAND

Murmansk

Arkhangelsk

Helsingfors
(Helsinki)

*Baltic
Sea*

ST PETERSBURG

ESTONIA • Novgorod • Vologda

Riga • Pskov • Kostroma • Viatka Perm

Yaroslavl' Ekaterinburg

Kovno
Wilno • Vitebsk Nizhnyi Novgorod *Volga* Kazan

LITHUANIA • Smolensk • MOSCOW Ufa

Warsaw • Minsk • Mogilev • Tula Simbirsk

POLAND BELORUSSIA

Brest-Litovsk Chernigov • Orel • Tambov Samara

Saratov

Lvov Kiev UKRAINE Voronezh Orenburg

GALICIA Poltava • Kharkov

Dnepr

Kishinev Tsaritsyn

Odessa Rostov *Don* *Volga*

ROMANIA

Sevastopol Stavropol

BULGARIA *Black Sea*

GEORGIA *Caspian*

Tiflis

AZERBAIJAN

ARMENIA Baku *Sea*

OTTOMAN
EMPIRE

U R A L   M O U N T A I N S

Ob

Tobolsk

Tiumen' Omsk

Cheliabinsk

CENTRAL
ASIA

Khiva

Bukhara

PERSIA

0   miles   500

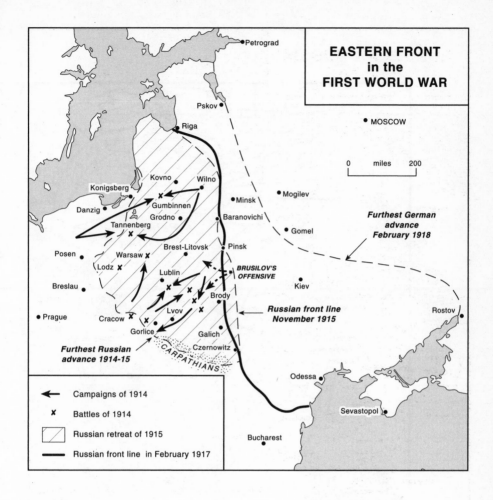

**EASTERN FRONT
in the
FIRST WORLD WAR**

Petrograd

Pskov

Riga

• MOSCOW

Kovno
Wilno

Konigsberg

Minsk
Mogilev

Gumbinnen

Danzig

Grodno

Baranovichi

Tannenberg
×

Gomel

Brest-Litovsk
Pinsk

Posen

Warsaw ×

*Furthest German
advance
February 1918*

Breslau

Lodz ×

Lublin

***BRUSILOV'S
OFFENSIVE***

Kiev

Rostov

Prague

Cracow

Lvov

Brody

*Russian front line
November 1915*

×

×

Gorlice

Galich

Czernowitz

*Furthest Russian
advance 1914-15*

CARPATHIANS

Odessa

Sevastopol

Bucharest

0   miles   200

⟵   Campaigns of 1914

×   Battles of 1914

▨   Russian retreat of 1915

——   Russian front line in February 1917

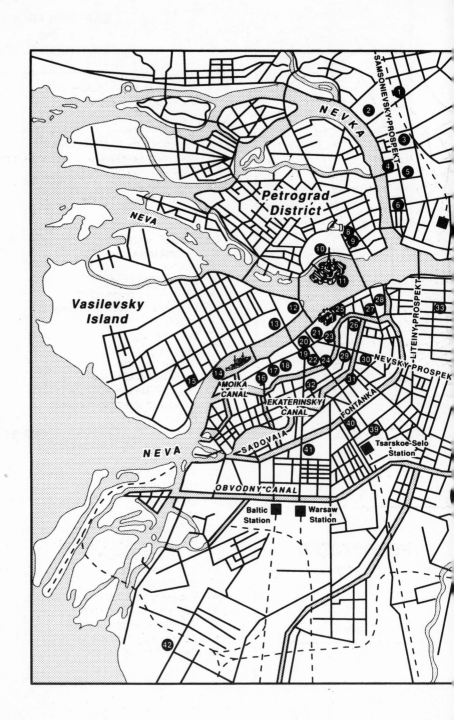

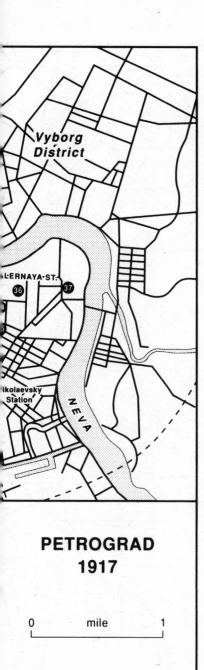

PETROGRAD
1917

0   mile   1

Gorky's house
1   Russian Renault factory
2   New Lessner factory
3   Moscow Regiment
4   Erickson factory
5   First Machine-Gun Regiment
6   Bolshevik headquarters, Vyborg District
7   Kresty Prison
8   Cirque Moderne
9   Kshesinskaya Mansion
10   Arsenal
11   Peter and Paul Fortress
12   Stock Exchange
13   Petersburg University
14   *Aurora*
15   Finland Regiment
16   Central telegraph office
17   Petrograd telegraph agency
18   Post office
19   War Ministry
20   Admiralty
21   Palace Square
22   St Isaac's Cathedral
23   General Staff headquarters
24   Petrograd telephone station
25   Winter Palace
26   *Pravda* editorial offices and printing plant
27   Pavlovsky Regiment
28   Mars Field
29   Kazan Cathedral
30   City Duma
31   State Bank
32   Marinsky Palace
33   Lithuanian Regiment
34   Preobrazhensky Regiment
35   Volynsky Regiment
36   Tauride Palace
37   Smolny Institute
38   Znamenskaya Square
39   Semenovsky Regiment
40   Petrograd electric station
41   Petrograd Regiment
42   Putilov factory

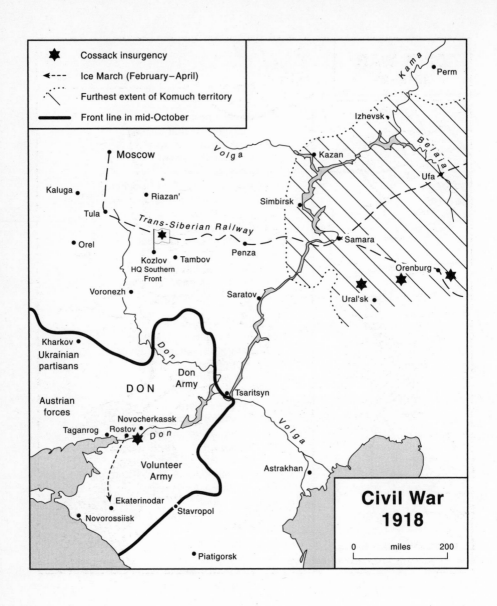

Civil War 1918

Legend:
- ★ Cossack insurgency
- ←--- Ice March (February–April)
- ⋯⋯ Furthest extent of Komuch territory
- ▬▬ Front line in mid-October

Moscow
Kaluga
Riazan'
Tula
Orel
Kozlov
HQ Southern Front
Tambov
Penza
Voronezh
Saratov
Kharkov
Ukrainian partisans
DON
Don Army
Austrian forces
Taganrog
Rostov
Novocherkassk
Don
Volunteer Army
Ekaterinodar
Novorossiisk
Stavropol
Piatigorsk
Tsaritsyn
Astrakhan
Volga
Trans-Siberian Railway
Simbirsk
Kazan
Izhevsk
Perm
Kama
Belaia
Ufa
Samara
Orenburg
Ural'sk

0   miles   200

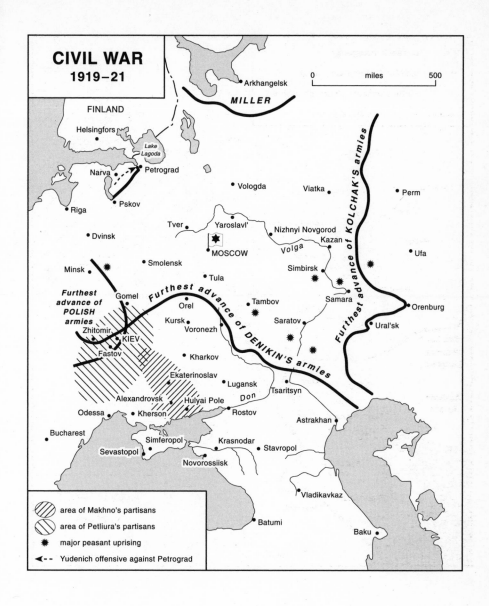

CIVIL WAR
1919–21

0   miles   500

Arkhangelsk

MILLER

FINLAND

Helsingfors

Lake Lagoda

Narva

Petrograd

Riga

Pskov

Dvinsk

Vologda

Viatka

Perm

Tver

Yaroslavl'

Nizhnyi Novgorod

Kazan

Ufa

MOSCOW

Volga

Minsk

Smolensk

Simbirsk

Furthest advance of KOLCHAK'S armies

Furthest advance of **POLISH armies**

Gomel

Tula

Orel

Tambov

Samara

Orenburg

Zhitomir

Kursk

Voronezh

Saratov

Ural'sk

KIEV

Furthest advance of DENIKIN'S armies

Fastov

Kharkov

Ekaterinoslav

Lugansk

Alexandrovsk

Hulyai Pole

Don

Tsaritsyn

Odessa

Kherson

Rostov

Astrakhan

Bucharest

Simferopol

Krasnodar

Stavropol

Sevastopol

Novorossiisk

Vladikavkaz

Batumi

Baku

area of Makhno's partisans

area of Petliura's partisans

major peasant uprising

Yudenich offensive against Petrograd

Part One

RUSSIA UNDER THE
OLD REGIME

I The Dynasty

i The Tsar and His People

On a wet and windy morning in February 1913 St Petersburg celebrated three hundred years of Romanov rule over Russia. People had been talking about the great event for weeks, and everyone agreed that nothing quite so splendid would ever be seen again in their lifetimes. The majestic power of the dynasty would be displayed, as never before, in an extravaganza of pageantry. As the jubilee approached, dignitaries from far-flung parts of the Russian Empire filled the capital's grand hotels: princes from Poland and the Baltic lands; high priests from Georgia and Armenia; mullahs and tribal chiefs from Central Asia; the Emir of Bukhara and the Khan of Khiva. The city bustled with sightseers from the provinces, and the usual well-dressed promenaders around the Winter Palace now found themselves outnumbered by the unwashed masses — peasants and workers in their tunics and caps, rag-bundled women with kerchiefs on their heads. Nevsky Prospekt experienced the worst traffic jams in its history as trams and horse-drawn carriages, cars and sleighs, converged on it. The main streets were decked out in the imperial colours of white, blue and red; statues were dressed in garlands and ribbons; and portraits of the tsars, stretching back to Mikhail, the founder of the dynasty, hung on the façades of banks and stores. Above the tram-lines were strung chains of coloured lights, which lit up at night with the words 'God Save the Tsar' or a Romanov double-headed eagle and the dates 1613–1913. Out-of-towners, many of whom had never seen electric light, stared up and scratched their heads in wonderment. There were columns, arcs and obelisks of light. In front of the Kazan Cathedral stood a white pavilion filled with incense, bromeliads and palms, shivering in the Russian winter air.

The rituals began with a solemn thanksgiving in the Kazan Cathedral led by the Patriarch of Antioch, who had come from Greece especially for the occasion, the three Russian Metropolitans and fifty priests from St Petersburg. The imperial family drove out from the Winter Palace in open carriages accompanied by two squadrons of His Majesty's Own Horseguards and Cossack riders in black caftans and red Caucasian caps. It was the first time the Tsar had ridden in public view since the 1905 Revolution, and the police were taking no chances. The route was lined by the Imperial Guards gorgeously turned out in their feathered shakos and scarlet uniforms. Military bands thumped out the national anthem and the soldiers boomed 'Oorah!' as the cavalcade passed by. Outside the cathedral religious processions from various parts of the city had been converging from early in the morning. The vast crowd, a forest of crosses, icons and banners, knelt down as one as the carriages approached. Inside the cathedral stood Russia's ruling class: grand dukes and princes, members of the court, senators, ministers, state councillors, Duma parliamentarians, senior Civil Servants, generals and admirals, provincial governors, city mayors, zemstvo leaders, and marshals of the nobility. Hardly a breast without a row of shining medals or a diamond star; hardly a pair of legs without a sword. Everything sparkled in the candlelight — the silver iconostasis, the priests' bejewelled mitres, and the crystal cross. In the middle of the ceremony two doves flew down from the darkness of the dome and hovered for several moments over the heads of the Tsar and his son. Carried away by religious exaltation, Nicholas interpreted it as a symbol of God's blessing on the House of Romanov.

Meanwhile, in the workers' districts factories were closed for a public holiday. The poor queued outside municipal canteens, where free meals were served to mark the anniversary. Pawnshops were beset by crowds after rumours spread of a special dispensation allowing people to redeem their valuables without interest payments; when these rumours turned out to be false, the crowds became angry and several pawnshops had their windows smashed. Women gathered outside the city's jails in the hope that their loved ones would be among the 2,000 prisoners released under the amnesty to celebrate the tercentenary.

During the afternoon huge crowds walked into the city centre for the long-awaited *son et lumière*. Stalls along the way sold mugs of beer and pies, Romanov flags and souvenirs. There were fairs and concerts in the parks. As darkness fell, the Nevsky Prospekt became one solid mass of people. Every face turned upwards as the sky was lit up in a blaze of colour by fireworks and lights that criss-crossed the city, sweeping over roofs to land for a moment on significant monuments. The golden spire of the Admiralty burned like a torch against the black sky, and the Winter Palace was brilliantly illuminated with three huge portraits of Nicholas II, Peter the Great and Mikhail Romanov.

The imperial family remained in the capital for another week of ritual self-congratulation. There were pompous receptions at the Winter Palace where long lines of genuflecting dignitaries filed through the state rooms to present themselves to Nicholas and Alexandra in the concert hall. There was a sumptuous ball in the Noblemen's Assembly attended by the imperial couple and their eldest daughter, Olga, in one of her first social engagements. She danced the polonaise with Prince Saltykov, who caused a stir by forgetting to take off his hat. At the Marinsky Theatre there was a gala performance of Glinka's patriotic opera, *A Life for the Tsar*, which retold the legend of the peasant Susanin, who had saved the life of the first Romanov Tsar. The tiers of boxes 'blazed with jewels and tiaras', according to Meriel Buchanan, the British Ambassador's daughter, and the stalls were filled with the scarlet uniforms of the court officials, who swayed in unison 'like a field of poppies' as they rose to greet the arrival of the Tsar. Mathilde Kshesinskaya, Nicholas's former mistress, came out of retirement to dance the mazurkas in the second act. But the sensation of the evening was the silent appearance of the tenor, Leonid Sobinov, standing in for Shaliapin, who walked across the stage at the head of a religious procession dressed as Mikhail Romanov. It was the first (and the last) occasion in the history of the imperial theatre when the figure of a Romanov Tsar was represented on the stage.[1]

Three months later, during an usually hot May, the imperial family went on a Romanov pilgrimage around the towns of ancient Muscovy associated with the foundation of the dynasty. They followed the route taken by Mikhail Romanov, the first Romanov Tsar, from his home at Kostroma on the Volga to Moscow after his election to the Russian throne in 1613. The imperial touring party arrived at Kostroma in a flotilla of steamboats. The river bank was packed with townspeople and peasants, the men all dressed in tunics and caps, the women in the traditional light blue and white headscarfs of Kostroma. Hundreds of sightseers had waded waist deep into the river to get closer to the royal visitors. Nicholas visited the Ipatiev monastery, where Mikhail had taken refuge from the Polish invaders and from the civil wars that had raged through Muscovy on the eve of his assumption of the throne. He received a peasant delegation from the lands that had belonged to the monastery and posed for a photograph with the descendants of the boyars who had travelled from Moscow in 1613 to offer the crown to the Romanovs.

From Kostroma the touring party went on to Vladimir, Nizhnyi Novgorod and Yaroslavl'. They travelled in the beautifully furnished imperial train, complete with mahogany-panelled rooms, soft velvet armchairs, writing desk and grand piano. The bathroom even had a special device to prevent His Imperial Majesty's bathwater from spilling when the train was moving. There was no railway between Vladimir and the small monastery town of Suzdal, so the entourage had to make the journey along dusty country roads in a fleet of thirty open-top Renaults. In the villages old peasant men and women bent down on their knees as the cars sped past. In front of their modest wooden huts, barely noticed by the travellers, they had set up little tables laid with flowers, bread and salt, the traditional Russian offerings to strangers.

The royal pilgrimage climaxed with a triumphant entry into Moscow, the old Russian capital, where the first Romanov Tsar had been crowned, followed by another round of pageantry and gastronomy. The ball in the Assembly of the Moscow Nobility was particularly lavish, far beyond the wildest dreams of Hollywood. A lift was installed specially so the royal waltzers need not tire themselves by climbing to the ballroom on the second floor. The imperial touring party arrived in Moscow by train and was greeted by a vast delegation of dignitaries at the Alexandrovsky Station. The Tsar rode alone on a white horse, sixty feet ahead of his Cossack escort and the rest of the imperial cavalcade, through huge cheering crowds to the Kremlin. The decorations along Tverskaya Street, bathed in brilliant sunshine, were even more magnificent than in St Petersburg. Maroon velvet banners with Romanov emblems spanned the boulevard. Buildings were draped in colourful flags and pennants, and covered in lights which lit up at night to reveal even more inventive emblems than those on the Nevsky Prospekt. Garlanded statues of the Tsar stood in shop windows and on the balconies of private apartments. People showered the procession with confetti. The Tsar dismounted in Red Square, where religious processions from all parts of the city had converged to meet him, and walked through lines of chanting priests into the Uspensky Cathedral for prayers. The Empress and the Tsarevich Alexis were also to walk the last few hundred yards. But Alexis was struck down once again by his haemophilia and had to be carried by a Cossack bodyguard. As the procession paused, Count Kokovtsov, the Prime Minister, heard from the crowd 'exclamations of sorrow at the sight of this poor helpless child, the heir to the throne of the Romanovs'.[2]

*   *   *

The Romanov dynasty presented to the world a brilliant image of monarchical power and opulence during its tercentenary. This was no simple propaganda exercise. The rituals of homage to the dynasty and the glorification of its history were, to be sure, meant to inspire reverence and popular support for the principle of autocracy. But their aim was also to *reinvent* the past, to recount the epic of the 'popular Tsar', so as to invest the monarchy with a mythical historical legitimacy and an image of enduring permanence at this anxious time when its right to rule was being challenged by Russia's emerging democracy. The Romanovs were retreating to the past, hoping it would save them from the future.

The cult of seventeenth-century Muscovy was the key to this self-reinvention, and the *leitmotiv* of the jubilee. Three perceived principles of Muscovite tsardom appealed to the Romanovs in their final years. The first was the notion of patrimonialism whereby the Tsar was deemed literally to own the whole of Russia as his private fiefdom (*votchina*) in the manner of a medieval lord. In the first national census of 1897 Nicholas described himself as a 'landowner'. Until the second half of the eighteenth century this idea had set Russia apart from the West, where an independent landowning class emerged as a counter-balance to the monarchy. The second principle from Muscovy was the idea of personal rule: as the embodiment of God on earth, the Tsar's will should be unrestrained by laws or bureaucracy and he should be left to rule the country according to his own consciousness of duty and right. This too had distinguished the Byzantine tradition of despotism from the Western absolutist state. Conservatives, such as Konstantin Pobedonostsev, tutor and leading ideologist to both Nicholas and Alexander, the last two Tsars, argued that this religious autocracy was uniquely suited to the Russian national spirit, that a god-like autocrat was needed to restrain the anarchic instincts of the Russian people.* Lastly, there was the idea of a mystical union between the Tsar and the Orthodox people, who loved and obeyed him as a father and a god. It was a fantasy of paternal rule, of a golden age of popular autocracy, free from the complications of a modern state.

The last two tsars had obvious motives for holding on so firmly to this archaic vision. Indeed, in so far as they believed that their power and prestige were being undermined by 'modernity' in all its forms — secular beliefs, Western constitutional ideologies and the new urban classes — it was only logical for them to seek to put the clock back to some distant golden age. It was in the eighteenth century and the reign of Peter the Great — 'Your Peter' as Nicholas called him speaking with officials — that the rot, in their view, had begun to set in. There were two opposing models of autocracy in Russia: the Petrine and the Muscovite. Emulating Western absolutism, the Petrine model sought to systematize the power of the crown through legal norms and bureaucratic institutions. This was deemed a limitation on the Tsar's powers in that even he would henceforth be obliged to obey his own laws. The Tsar who did not was a despot. The Petrine tradition also implied a shift in the focus of power from the divine person of the Tsar to the abstract concept of the autocratic state. Nicholas disliked this, above all. Like his father, Alexander III, he had been taught to uphold the principles of personal rule, keeping power at the court, and to distrust the bureaucracy as a sort of 'wall' that broke the natural bond between the Tsar and his people. This distrust may be explained by the fact that during the nineteenth century the imperial bureaucracy had begun to emerge as a force for modernization and reform. It became increasingly independent of the court and closer to public opinion, which, in the view of conservatives, was bound to lead to revolutionary demands for a constitution. Alexander II's assassination in 1881 (after two decades of cautious reform) seemed to confirm their view that the time had come to stop the rot. Alexander III (who once claimed that he 'despised the bureaucracy and drank champagne to its obliteration')[3] instituted a return to personal forms of autocratic rule, both in

---

* Bertrand Russell used a similar idea when, in an attempt to explain the Russian Revolution to Lady Ottoline Morrell, he remarked that, terrible though Bolshevik despotism was, it seemed the right sort of government for Russia: 'If you ask yourself how Dostoevsky's characters should be governed, you will understand.'

central and local government. And where the father led the son was bound to follow.

Nicholas's model of the autocracy was almost entirely Muscovite. His favourite Tsar was Alexei Mikhailovich (1645–76), after whom he named his son the Tsarevich. He emulated his tranquil piety, which it was said had given him the conviction to rule Russia through his own religious conscience. Nicholas often liked to justify his policies on the grounds that the idea had 'come to him' from God. According to Count Witte, one of his most enlightened ministers, Nicholas believed that 'people do not influence events, that God directs everything, and that the Tsar, as God's anointed, should not take advice from anyone but follow only his divine inspiration'. Such was Nicholas's admiration for the semi-Asiatic customs of the Middle Ages that he tried to introduce them at his court. He ordered the retention of the old Slavonic forms of spelling in official documents and publications long after they had been phased out in literary Russian. He talked of *Rus'*, the old Muscovite term for the core lands of Russia, instead of *Rossiia*, a term for the Empire which had been adopted since Peter the Great. He disliked the title *Gosudar Imperator* (Sovereign Emperor), also introduced by Peter, since it implied that the autocrat was no more than the first servant of the abstract state (the *gosudarstvo*), and much preferred the older title *Tsar* (derived from the Greek term *kaisar*), which went back to the Byzantine era and carried religious connotations of paternal rule. He even toyed with the idea of making all his courtiers wear long caftans, like those of the ancient Muscovite boyars (it was only the cost that discouraged him). The Minister of the Interior, D. S. Sipiagin, who had given him the idea, had his own offices decorated in the Muscovite style. On one occasion he received the Tsar, who came dressed as Alexei, with all the rituals of the seventeenth-century court, complete with a traditional Russian feast and a gypsy orchestra. Nicholas encouraged the Russian courtly fashion — which had begun in his father's reign — for seventeenth-century costume balls. In 1903 he himself gave one of the most lavish. The guests appeared in replicas of court dress from Alexei's reign and danced medieval Russian dances. Photographs of all the guests, each identified by their respective court ranks from the seventeenth and the twentieth centuries, were published in two richly produced albums. Nicholas appeared in a replica of the processional robe worn by Alexei, and Alexandra in the gown and headdress worn by his Tsarina Natalia.[4]

Nicholas made no secret of the fact that he much preferred Moscow to St Petersburg. The old 'holy city', with its thousand onion domes, stood for the Eastern and Byzantine traditions which lay at the heart of his Muscovite world-view. Untouched by the West, Moscow retained the 'national style' so favoured by the last two Tsars. Both considered Petersburg, with its classical architectural style, its Western shops and bourgeoisie, alien to Russia. They tried to Muscovitize it by building churches in the Byzantine style — a fashion started under Nicholas I — and adding archaic architectural features to its cityscape. Alexander III, for example, commissioned a Temple of Christ's Resurrection, which was built in the old Moscow style, to consecrate the site on the Catherine Canal where his father had been assassinated in 1881. With its onion domes, colourful mosaics and ornate decorations, it presented a bizarre contrast with the other great cathedrals of the city, the Kazan Cathedral and St Isaac's, which were both built in the classical style. Nicholas refashioned buildings in the neo-Byzantine manner. The School Council of the Holy Synod was remodelled as the Alexander Nevsky Temple-Monument by embellishing its classical façade with Muscovite motifs and adding to its flat roof five onion domes and a triangular steeple. More buildings were built in the old Russian style to mark the Romanov jubilee. The Tercentenary Cathedral, near the Moscow Station, for example, was built in explicit imitation of the seventeenth-century Rostov church style. The Fedorov Village, built by Nicholas at Tsarskoe Selo, just outside the capital, elaborately recreated a seventeenth-century Kremlin and Cathedral.[5] It was a sort of Muscovite theme park.

Nicholas and his father Alexander visited Moscow often and used it increasingly for ritualistic displays of homage to the dynasty. The coronation of the Tsar, which traditionally took place in Moscow, became an important symbolic event — much more so than it had been in the past. Nicholas made a habit of visiting Moscow at Easter — something no Tsar had done for more than fifty years. He convinced himself that only in Moscow and the provinces would he find his spiritual communion with the ordinary Russian people. 'United in prayer with my people', he wrote to Moscow's Governor-General in 1900, shortly after his first Easter visit to the old capital, 'I draw new strength for serving Russia, for her well-being and glory'.[6] After 1906, when St Petersburg became the seat of the Duma, Nicholas looked even more towards Moscow and the provinces as a base on which to build his 'popular autocracy' as a rival to the parliament. With the support of the simple Russian people — represented increasingly by Grigorii Rasputin — he would reassert the power of the throne, which for too long had been forced to retreat before the bureaucracy and society.

The tercentenary jubilee marked the culmination of this Muscovite heritage industry. It was a dynastic celebration, centred on the symbols of the Tsar, with those of the state pushed firmly into the background. The squabble between Rasputin, the scandalous peasant 'holy man' whose influence had come to dominate the court, and Mikhail Rodzianko, President of the Duma, during the service in the Kazan Cathedral was symbolic in this respect. Rodzianko had taken offence because the members of the Duma were to be seated at the back, far behind the places reserved for the state councillors and senators. This, he complained to the master of ceremonies, was 'not in accordance with the dignity' of the parliament. 'If the jubilee was intended to be a truly national rejoicing, it should not be overlooked that in 1613 it was an assembly of the people and not a group of officials that elected Mikhail Romanov Tsar of Russia.' Rodzianko's point was taken and the Duma places were duly exchanged for those of the senators. But when he arrived to take his own place he found it occupied by a dark bearded man in peasant dress, whom he immediately recognized as Rasputin. The two men confronted each other in a heated exchange, the one insisting on the sanctity of his position as President of the country's elected parliament, the other claiming the support of the Tsar himself, until a sergeant-at-arms was called to restore the peace. With a heavy groan, Rasputin slunk away towards the exit, where he was helped on with his sable coat and shown to a waiting carriage.[7]

The Prime Minister was equally outraged by the court's contemptuous attitude towards the government during the jubilee rituals. Ministers were expected to provide their own transport and accommodation whilst they accompanied the royal party on its tour of the provinces. 'The current attitude', recalled Count Kokovtsov:

> seemed to suggest that the government was a barrier between the people and their Tsar, whom they regarded with blind devotion because he was anointed by God ... The Tsar's closest friends at court became persuaded that the Sovereign could do anything by relying upon the unbounded love and utter loyalty of the people. The ministers of the government, on the other hand, did not hold to this sort of autocracy; nor did the Duma, which steadily sought control of the executive power. Both were of the opinion that the Sovereign should recognize that conditions had changed since the day the Romanovs became Tsars of Moscow and lords of the Russian domain.

The Prime Minister tried in vain to tell the Tsar that he could not save his throne by trying to adopt 'the halo of the "Muscovite Tsar" ruling Russia as his own patrimony'.[8]

The communion between the Tsar and his people was the central theme of the jubilee. The cult of the peasant Ivan Susanin was supposed to reinforce the message that the simple people loved the Tsar. Susanin had lived on the Romanov estate in Kostroma. Legend had it that, at the cost of his own life, he saved Mikhail Romanov's by misleading the Poles who had come to kill him on the eve of his assumption of the throne. From the nineteenth century he was officially promoted as a national hero and celebrated in patriotic poems and operas such as Glinka's *A Life for the Tsar*. During the tercentenary celebrations *A Life* was performed throughout the country by amateur companies, schools and regiments. The penny press and popular pamphlets retold the Susanin myth *ad nauseam*. It was said to symbolize the people's devotion and their duty to the Tsar. One army newspaper told its readers that Susanin had shown every soldier how to fulfil his oath to the Tsar. The image of the seventeenth-century peasant hero was reproduced everywhere during the jubilee, most notably at the base of the Romanov Monument in Kostroma, where a female figure representing Russia blessed a kneeling Susanin. During his tour of Kostroma Nicholas was even presented with a delegation of Potemkin-peasants purporting to be descendants of Susanin.[9]

According to the jubilee propaganda, the election of the Romanovs in 1613 was a crucial moment of national awakening, the first real act of the Russian nation state. The 'entire land' was said to have participated in the election, thus providing a popular mandate for the dynasty, although it had been widely accepted by historians in the nineteenth century that the election owed more to the machinations of a few powerful boyars than to the ordinary people. Through their election, it was claimed, the Romanovs had come to personify the will of the nation. 'The spirit of Russia is incarnate in her Tsar,' wrote one propagandist. 'The Tsar stands to the people as their highest conception of the destiny and ideals of the nation.' Russia, in short, was the Romanovs. 'In every soul there is something Romanov,' declared the newspaper *Novoe vremia*. 'Something from the soul and spirit of the House that has reigned for 300 years.'[10]

Nicholas Romanov, Russia incarnate: that was the cult promoted by the jubilee. It sought to build on the Tsar's religious status in the popular consciousness. Russia had a long tradition of saintly princes — rulers who were canonized for laying down their lives *pro patria et fides* — stretching back to the tenth century. In the mind of the ordinary peasant the Tsar was not just a kingly ruler but a god on earth. He thought of him as a father-figure (the *Tsar Batiushka*, or Father-Tsar, of folk tales) who knew all the peasants personally by name, understood their problems in all their minute details, and, if it were not for the evil boyars, the noble officials, who surrounded him, would satisfy their demands in a Golden Manifesto giving them the land. Hence the peasant tradition of sending direct appeals to the Tsar — a tradition that (like the monarchic psyche it reflected in the common people) continued well into the Soviet era when similar petitions were sent to Lenin and Stalin. This 'naive' peasant myth of the Good Tsar could sometimes be used to legitimize peasant rebellions, especially when a long-awaited government reform failed to satisfy the people's expectations. Pugachev, the Cossack rebel leader of the 1770s, proclaimed himself Tsar Peter III; while the peasant rebels after 1861 also rose up in the name of the True Tsar when the serf emancipation of that year failed to satisfy the grievances of the peasantry. But in general the myth of the Good Tsar worked to the benefit of the crown, and as the revolutionary crisis deepened Nicholas's propagandists relied increasingly upon it.

The propaganda of the tercentenary was the final flourish of this legend. It depicted Nicholas as a godfather to his subjects, intimately acquainted with each of them and caring for their every need. He was praised for his modest lifestyle and his simple tastes, his accessibility to the common people, his kindness and his wisdom. A popular biography of Nicholas was commissioned especially for the jubilee, the first ever published of a living Tsar. It portrayed him as the 'father of his people, over whose needs he keeps an earnest and compassionate watch'. He was said to devote 'special care and attention to the welfare and moral development' of the peasants, whose huts he frequently entered 'to see how they live and to partake of their milk and black bread'. At official functions he 'talked genially' with the peasants, who then 'crossed themselves and felt happier for the rest of their lives'. He shared the people's simple habits and pursuits, wore a peasant blouse and ate humble peasant dishes such as borscht and blinies. During the jubilee the Tsar was photographed in symbolic acts of homage to the people, such as inspecting a new type of plough or tasting the rations of his soldiers. Such images were calculated to reinforce the popular myth that nothing, however trivial, in the people's daily lives escaped the attention of the Tsar and that his influence was everywhere. 'Thousands of invisible threads centre in the Tsar's heart,' wrote the royal biographer; 'and these threads stretch to the huts of the poor and the palaces of the rich. And that is the reason why the Russian people always acclaims its Tsar with such fervent enthusiasm, whether in St Petersburg in the Marinsky Theatre . . . or on his way through the towns and villages.'[11]

*   *   *

'Now you can see for yourself what cowards those state ministers are,' the Empress Alexandra told a lady-in-waiting shortly after the jubilee. 'They are constantly frightening the Emperor with threats of revolution and here — you see it for yourself — we need merely to show ourselves and at once their hearts are ours.' If the rituals of the jubilee were intended to create the illusion of a mighty and stable dynasty, then they had convinced few people except the court itself. The Romanovs became victims of their own propaganda. Nicholas, in particular, returned from his tour of the provinces confirmed in the self-delusion that 'My people love me.' It aroused a fresh desire to travel in the Russian interior. He talked of a boat trip down the Volga, a visit to the Caucasus and Siberia. Emboldened by the belief in his own popularity, he began to look for ways of moving one step closer towards the system of personal rule which he so admired in ancient Muscovy. Encouraged by his more reactionary ministers, he even considered dissolving the Duma altogether or turning it into a purely consultative body such as the Land Assembly (Zemskii Sobor) of the sixteenth and seventeenth centuries.

Foreign observers friendly to the monarchy were just as easily swept along by the rosy rhetoric. 'No hope seems too confident or too bright,' the London *Times* pronounced on the Romanovs' future in a special edition on the jubilee. Convinced of the people's devotion to the Tsar, it reported that a series of postage stamps with portraits of the Romanov rulers had been issued to mark the tercentenary but had been withdrawn when some royalist post-office clerks refused to impress the obliterating postmark on these hallowed visages. 'These loyal and eminently respectable scruples', concluded *The Times*, 'are typical of the mind of the vast masses of the Russian people.' Such sentiments were echoed by the British Foreign Office. 'Nothing could exceed the affection and devotion to the person of the Emperor displayed by the population wherever His Majesty appeared. There is no doubt that in this strong attachment of the masses ... to the person of the Emperor lies the great strength of the Russian autocracy.'[12]

In fact, the jubilee took place in the midst of a profound social and political crisis — some would even say a revolutionary one. Its celebrations were set against a backdrop of several decades of growing violence, human suffering and repression, which had set the Tsar's people against his regime. None of the wounds of the 1905 Revolution had yet healed; and some of them had festered and become worse. The great peasant problem remained unresolved, despite belated efforts at land reform; and in fact, if anything, the landed gentry had become even more opposed to the idea of concessions to the peasants since the 1905 Revolution, when crowds had attacked their estates. There had also been a resurgence of industrial strikes, much more militant than their predecessors in the early 1900s, with the Bolsheviks steadily gaining ground at the expense of their more moderate rivals, the Mensheviks, among the labour organizations. And as for the aspirations of the liberals, which had seemed so near in 1905, they were now becoming a more distant prospect as the court and its supporters blocked all the Duma's liberal reforms and (with the Beiliss trial of 1913, which even after the Dreyfus Affair shocked the whole of Europe with its medieval persecution of an innocent Jew on trumped-up charges of the ritual murder of a Christian boy) trampled on their fragile ideal of civil rights. There was, in short, a widening gulf of mistrust not just between the court and society — a gulf epitomized by the Rasputin scandal — but also between the court and many of its own traditional supporters in the Civil Service, the Church and the army, as the Tsar resisted their own demands for reform. Just as the Romanovs were honouring themselves and flattering themselves with the fantastic belief that they might rule for another three centuries, outside their own narrow court circles there was a growing sense of impending crisis and catastrophe. This sense of despair was best voiced by the poets of this so-called 'Silver Age' of Russian literature — Blok and Belyi above all — who depicted Russia as living on a volcano. In the words of Blok:

> And over Russia I see a quiet
> Far-spreading fire consume all.

How are we to explain the dynasty's collapse? Collapse is certainly the right word to use. For the Romanov regime fell under the weight of its own internal contradictions. It was not overthrown. As in all modern revolutions, the first cracks appeared at the top. The revolution did not start with the labour movement — so long the preoccupation of left-wing historians in the West. Nor did it start with the breakaway of the nationalist movements on the periphery: as with the collapse of the Soviet Empire that was built on the ruins of the Romanovs', nationalist revolt was a consequence of the crisis in the centre rather than its cause. A more convincing case could be made for saying that it was all started by the peasant revolution on the land, which in some places began as early as 1902, three years before the 1905 Revolution, and indeed that it was bound to be in so far as Russia was overwhelmingly a peasant society. But while the peasant problem, like that of the workers and nationalities, introduced fundamental structural weaknesses into the social system of the old regime, it did not determine its politics; and it was with politics that the problem lay. There is no reason to suppose that the tsarist regime was doomed to collapse in the way that Marxist determinists once claimed from their narrow focus on its 'social contradictions'. It could have been saved by reform. But there is the rub. For Russia's last two tsars lacked the will for real reform. True, in 1905, when the Tsar was nearly toppled from his throne, he was forced reluctantly to concede reforms; but once that threat had passed he realigned himself with the supporters of reaction. This is the fatal weakness in the argument of those historians on the Right who paint a rosy image of the Tsarist Empire on the eve of the First World War. They claim that the tsarist system was being reformed, or 'modernized', along Western liberal lines. But the last two tsars and their more reactionary supporters — in the gentry, the Church and Rightist political circles — were at best ambiguous towards the idea of 'modernization'. They knew, for example, that they needed a modern industrial economy in order to compete with the Western powers; yet at the same time they were deeply hostile to the political demands and social transformations of the urban industrial order. Instead of embracing reform they adhered obstinately to their own archaic vision of autocracy. It was their tragedy that just as Russia was entering the twentieth century they were trying to return it to the seventeenth.

Here, then, were the roots of the revolution, in the growing conflict between a society rapidly becoming more educated, more urban and more complex, and a fossilized autocracy that would not concede its political demands. That conflict first became acute (indeed revolutionary) following the famine of 1891, as the government floundered in the crisis and liberal society became politicized as it launched its own relief campaign; and it is there that the narrative of Part Two commences. But before that we must look more closely at the main protagonists of the conflict, starting with the Tsar.

ii The Miniaturist

Four years before the tercentenary the brilliant sculptor, Prince P. N. Trubetskoi, had completed an equestrian statue of the former Tsar Alexander III which stood in Znamenskaya Square opposite the Nikolaevsky Station in St Petersburg. It was such an ingenious and formidable representation of autocracy in human form that after the revolution the Bolsheviks decided to leave it in place as a fearful reminder of the old regime; and there it remained until the 1930s.* The huge bronze figure of Alexander sat rigidly astride a ponderous horse of massive architectural proportions, its four thick legs fixed like pillars to the ground. The rider and horse had been made to appear so heavy and solid that it seemed impossible for them to move. Many people took this to be a symbol of the autocracy's own inertia, and there was a perhaps not-altogether unintentional element of irony in this. Workers were quick to recognize the statue's funny side. They christened it the 'Hippopotamus' and recited the witty lines:

> Here stands a chest of drawers,
> On the chest a hippopotamus
> And on the hippopotamus sits an idiot.

Even the Grand Duke Vladimir Alexandrovich, President of the Academy of Arts and the late Tsar's brother, denounced the statue as a caricature. It was certainly a cruel twist of fate that Trubetskoi had chosen to build the statue in equestrian form, since Alexander III had always been afraid of horses. His difficulties with them had grown in his final years as he put on weight. It became almost impossible to find a horse that he could be persuaded to mount.[13]

      Nicholas was oblivious to such ironies. For him, the Trubetskoi statue symbolized the power and solidity of the autocracy during his father's reign. He

---

* After more than fifty years in storage the statue was returned to the city's streets in 1994. Ironically, the horse now stands in front of the former Lenin Museum, where it has taken the place of the armoured car which, in April 1917, brought Lenin from the Finland Station.

ordered an even larger statue of Alexander to be built for Moscow, his favoured capital, in time for the tercentenary. It took two years to construct the awesome monument, which Nicholas himself unveiled amidst great ceremony during the jubilee celebrations. Unlike its Petersburg brother, which had combined a good representational likeness of the Tsar with a strong symbolic point, the new statue had no pretensions to artistic merit. The Tsar's giant figure was a mannequin without human expression, a monolithic incarnation of autocratic power. It sat straight-backed on its throne, hands on knees, encumbered with all the symbols of tsarist authority — the crown, the sceptre and orb, the imperial robe and full military dress — staring out towards the Kremlin, its back to the cathedral, in the manner of a pharaoh with nothing to think about except the source of his own illimitable power.[14]

Since Alexander's death, in 1894, Nicholas had developed an almost mystical reverence towards the memory of his father. He thought of him as the true autocrat. Alexander had ruled over Russia like a medieval lord over his private patrimony. He had centralized power in his hands and commanded his ministers like a general at war. He even looked like an autocrat should look — a giant of a man, six feet three inches tall, his stern face framed by an imposing black beard. This was a man who liked to amuse his drinking companions by crashing through locked doors and bending silver roubles in his 'vice-like imperial thumb'. Out of earshot in a private corner of his palace he played the trumpet with similar boisterousness. Legend has it that in 1888 he had even saved his family from certain death by supporting on his Herculean shoulders the collapsed steel roof of the dining carriage in the imperial train, which had been derailed by revolutionaries on its way to the Crimea. His only weakness, it seems, was his fatal addiction to liquor. When he fell ill with kidney disease the Empress forbade him to drink. But he got round this by having a special pair of boots made with hidden compartments large enough to carry a flask of cognac. General P. A. Cherevin, one of his favourite companions, recalled, 'When the Tsaritsa was beside us, we sat quietly and played like good children. But whenever she went off a little, we would exchange glances. And then — one, two, three! We'd pull out our flasks, take a swig and then it would be as if nothing had happened. He [Alexander] was greatly pleased with this amusement. It was like a game. We named it "Necessity is the mother of invention." "One, two, three. Necessity, Cherevin?" — "Invention, Your Majesty." "One, two and three" — and we'd swig.'[15]

Nicholas grew up in the shadow of this boozy colossus, acutely aware of his own inferiority. Being naturally shy and juvenile in appearance, his parents continued to treat him like a little child ('Nicky' was his family name) long after he had outgrown his teenage years. Nicholas retained many of his childish tastes and pursuits. The diaries he wrote in his early twenties are full of silly little notes about games and pranks. In 1894, at the age of twenty-six, for example, less than a month before his accession to the throne, he recorded an epic chestnut battle with Prince George of Greece in the royal park: 'We started in front of the house and ended up on the roof.' A few days later he wrote of another battle, this time with pine cones. Alexander, who knew nothing of physical or emotional complexes, considered his son a weakling and something of an imbecile. He called him 'girlie' and thought there was little point in preparing him for the tasks of government. When Count Witte, his Minister of Finance, suggested that the time had come to instruct the heir to the throne in the affairs of state, Alexander seemed surprised. 'Tell me,' he asked the Minister, 'have you ever spoken to his Imperial Highness, the Grand Duke Tsarevich?' Witte admitted that he had. 'Then don't tell me you never noticed that the Grand Duke is a dunce!'[16]

Through his education Nicholas had all the talents and charms of an English public schoolboy. He danced gracefully, rode beautifully, was a very good shot and excelled in several other sports. He spoke English like an Oxford professor, and French and German well. His manners were, almost needless to say, impeccable. His cousin and boyhood friend, the Grand Duke Alexander, supposed him to be 'the most polite man in Europe'. But of the practical knowledge required to govern a country the size of Russia — and a country, moreover, in a pre-revolutionary situation — Nicholas possessed almost nothing. His principal tutor, an English gentleman by the name of Mr Heath, painted well in water-colours, and was extremely fond of the outdoor life. But he lacked the advantage of a university education and knew nothing about Russia except for a few basic words of its language. From V. O. Kliuchevsky, the distinguished historian, Nicholas learned something of the history of his country, but nothing of its contemporary problems. When Pobedonostsev tried to instruct him in the workings of the state, he became 'actively absorbed in picking his nose'. Politics bored Nicholas. He was always more at home in the company of officers and society women than ministers and politicians.[17]

Less than sanguine about his son's ability to learn the art of kingship from books, Alexander enrolled him in the officer corps of the Guards in the hope that the army would build up his character and teach him something of the world. Nicholas loved the military life. The comradely spirit of the officers' mess, more like a gentleman's club than a military barracks, would remain with him for the rest of his life as a fond memory of the days before he had been weighed down by the burdens of office. It was then that he had fallen in love with the ballerina Mathilde Kshesinskaia. His rank of Colonel in the Preobrazhensky Guards, awarded to him by his father, remained a source of immense pride. He refused to take a higher rank, even during the First World

War when he assumed the position of Supreme Commander. This damaged his prestige in the army, where he became known as 'Colonel Romanov'.

In 1890 Alexander sent his son on a grand tour of Siberia, Japan, Indo-China, Egypt and Greece. The journey was intended to broaden the heir's political education. But the nature of his travelling suite (the usual complement of dim and hedonistic Guards officers) largely precluded this. During the tour Nicholas filled his diary with the same banal and trivial entries with which he usually filled his diary at home: terse notes on the weather, the distances covered each day, the times of landfall and departure, the company at meals, and so on. It seems that nothing in his travels had encouraged him to broaden his outlook and observations on life. The one lasting effect of the tour was unfortunate. At Otsu in Japan he narrowly escaped an attempt on his life by a deranged terrorist. The experience left him with an ingrained hatred of the Japanese (he called them 'monkeys', *makaki*), and it is often argued that this made him vulnerable to the influence of those at his court who promoted the disastrous war with Japan in 1904–5.

Had Alexander lived three score years and ten then the fate of the Russian Empire might have been very different. But as fortune would have it, he died from kidney disease in 1894 at the age of only forty-nine. As the crowd of relatives, physicians and courtiers gathered around the death-bed of the great autocrat, Nicholas burst into tears and exclaimed pathetically to his cousin, Alexander, 'What is going to happen to me and to all of Russia? I am not prepared to be a Tsar. I never wanted to become one. I know nothing of the business of ruling. I have no idea of even how to talk to the ministers.'[18] Louis XVI, with whom Nicholas had much in common, made a strikingly similar remark when he first learned in 1775 that he was to be the King of France.

The reign of Russia's last Tsar began disastrously. A few days after the coronation, in May 1896, a celebratory fair was organized on the Khodynka Field, a military training ground just outside Moscow. By the early morning some half a million people had already assembled, expecting to receive from their new Tsar gifts of souvenir tankards and biscuits embossed with the date and the occasion. Vast quantities of free beer and sausage were to be distributed. As more people arrived, a rumour went round that there would not be enough gifts for everyone. The crowd surged forward. People tripped and stumbled into the military ditches, where they were suffocated and crushed to death. Within minutes, 1,400 people had been killed and 600 wounded. Yet the Tsar was persuaded to continue with the celebrations. In the evening, while the corpses were carted away, he even attended a ball given by the French Ambassador, the Marquis de Montebello. During the next few days the rest of the scheduled festivities — banquets, balls and concerts — went ahead as if nothing had happened. Public opinion was outraged. Nicholas tried to atone by appointing a former Minister of Justice to look into the causes of the catastrophe. But when the Minister found that the Grand Duke Sergius, Governor-General of Moscow and the husband of the Empress's sister, was to blame, the other Grand Dukes protested furiously. They said it would undermine the principles of autocracy to admit in public the fault of a member of the imperial family. The affair was closed. But it was seen as a bad omen for the new reign and deepened the growing divide between the court and society. Nicholas, who increasingly believed himself to be ill-fated, would later look back at this incident as the start of all his troubles.[19]

Throughout his reign Nicholas gave the impression of being unable to cope with the task of ruling a vast Empire in the grips of a deepening revolutionary crisis. True, only a genius could have coped with it. And Nicholas was certainly no genius.* Had circumstances and his own inclinations been different, he might have saved his dynasty by moving away from autocratic rule towards a constitutional regime during the first decade of his reign, while there was still hope of appeasing the liberals and isolating the revolutionary movement. Nicholas had many of the personal qualities required to be a good constitutional monarch. In England, where one needed only to be a 'good man' in order to be a good king, he would have made an admirable sovereign. He was certainly no dimmer than his look-alike cousin, George V, who was a model of the constitutional king. Nicholas was mild-mannered, had an excellent memory and a perfect sense of decorum, all of which made him potentially ideal for the largely ceremonial tasks of a constitutional monarch. But Nicholas had not been born to that role: he was the Emperor and Autocrat of All the Russias.† Family tradition and pressure from the crown's traditional allies compelled him not only to reign, but to rule. It would not do for a Romanov to play the role of a ceremonial monarch, leaving the actual business of government to the bureaucracy. Nor would it do to retreat before the demands of the liberals. The Romanov way, in the face of political opposition, was to assert the 'divine authority' of the absolute monarch, to trust in the 'historic bond between the Tsar and the people', and to rule with

---

* There used to be a nice Soviet joke that the Supreme Soviet had decided to award the Order of the Red Banner to Nicholas II posthumously 'for his services to the revolution'. The last Tsar's achievement, it was said, was to have brought about a revolutionary situation.

† The full titles of Nicholas II were: Emperor and Autocrat of All the Russias; Tsar of Moscow, Kiev, Vladimir, Novgorod, Kazan, Astrakhan, Poland, Siberia, the Tauric Chersonese and Georgia; Lord of Pskov; Grand Prince of Smolensk, Lithuania, Volhynia, Podolia and Finland; Prince of Estonia, Livonia, Courland and Semigalia, Samogatia, Belostok, Karelia, Tver, Yugria, Perm, Viatka, Bulgaria and other lands; Lord and Grand Prince of Nizhnyi Novgorod and Chernigov; Ruler of Riazan, Polotsk, Rostov, Yaroslavl', Belo-Ozero, Udoria, Obdoria, Kondia, Vitebsk, Mstislavl and all the Northern Lands; Lord and Sovereign of the Iverian, Kartalinian and Kabardinian lands and of the Armenian provinces; Hereditary Lord and Suzerain of the Circassian Princes and Highland Princes and others; Lord of Turkestan; Heir to the Throne of Norway; Duke of Schleswig-Holstein, Stormarn, the Dithmarschen and Oldenburg.

force and resolution. In spite of her Anglo-German background, the Empress adopted with a vengeance all the medieval traditions of Byzantine despotism, and constantly urged her mild-mannered husband to be more like Ivan the Terrible and Peter the Great. The veneration which Nicholas felt for his father, and his own growing ambition to rule in the manner of his Muscovite ancestors, made it inevitable that he would endeavour to play the part of a true autocrat. As he warned the liberal nobles of Tver shortly after his coronation, he saw it as his duty before God to 'maintain the principle of autocracy just as firmly and unflinchingly as it was preserved by my unforgettable dead father'.[20]

But Nicholas had been blessed with neither his father's strength of character nor his intelligence. That was Nicholas's tragedy. With his limitations, he could only play at the part of an autocrat, meddling in (and, in the process, disrupting) the work of government without bringing to it any leadership. He was far too mild-mannered and shy to command any real authority among his subordinates. Being only five feet seven inches tall and feminine in stature, he didn't even look the part of an autocrat. Domineering figures, like his mother, the Empress Maria Fedorovna, his uncles, the four Grand Dukes, and his ex-tutor, Konstantin Pobedonostsev, towered over him during the early years of his reign. Later his wife would 'wear the trousers', as she once put it in a letter to him.

Yet it would be mistaken to assume, as so many historians have done, that Nicholas's failure stemmed from a fundamental 'weakness of will'. The generally accepted wisdom has been that Nicholas was a passive victim of history who became increasingly mystical and indifferent towards his own fate as he realized his growing powerlessness against the revolution. This interpretation owes much to the observations of his revolutionary enemies, who dominated the early literature on him. Viktor Chernov, the Social Revolutionary leader, for example, argued that Nicholas had met adversity with 'a kind of stubborn passivity, as if he wished to escape from life ... He seemed not a man, but a poor copy of one.' Trotsky similarly portrayed the last Tsar as opposing 'only a dumb indifference' to the 'historic flood' that flowed ever closer to the gates of his palace. There is of course an element of truth in all this. Frustrated in his ambitions to rule as he thought a true autocrat should, Nicholas increasingly retreated into the private and equally damaged realm of his family. Yet this covert admission of political failure was not made for want of trying. Beneath his docile exterior Nicholas had a strong sense of his duty to uphold the principles of autocracy. As he grew in confidence during his reign he developed an intense desire to rule, like his Muscovite ancestors, on the basis of his own religious conscience. He stubbornly defended his autocratic prerogatives against the encroachments of his ambitious ministers and even his own wife, whose persistent demands (often in Rasputin's name) he did his best to ignore and resist. It was not a 'weakness of will' that was the undoing of the last Tsar but, on the contrary, a wilful determination to rule from the throne, despite the fact that he clearly lacked the necessary qualities to do so.[21]

A complete inability to handle and command his subordinates was one obvious deficiency. Throughout his life Nicholas was burdened by a quite unnatural sense of decorum. He hid his emotions and feelings behind a mask of passive reserve which gave the impression of indifference to those, like Chernov and Trotsky, who observed him from a distance. He tactfully agreed with everyone who spoke to him rather than suffer the embarrassment of having to contradict them. This gave rise to the witticism, which went round the salons of St Petersburg, that the most powerful man in Russia was the last man to have spoken to the Tsar. Nicholas was too polite to confront his ministers with complaints about their work, so he left it to others to inform them of their discharge. Count Witte recalled his own dismissal as President of the Council of Ministers: 'We [Nicholas and Witte] talked for two solid hours. He shook my hand. He embraced me. He wished me all the luck in the world. I returned home beside myself with happiness and found a written order for my dismissal lying on my desk.' Witte believed that the Tsar derived some curious satisfaction from tormenting his ministers in this way. 'Our Tsar', he wrote in his memoirs, 'is an Oriental, a hundred per cent Byzantine.' Such unpredictable behaviour gave rise to feelings of insecurity within the ruling circles. Damaging rumours began to circulate that the Tsar was involved in various court conspiracies, or, even worse, that he did not know his own mind and had become the unwitting tool of dark and hidden forces behind the scenes. The fact that Nicholas relied on a kitchen cabinet of reactionary advisers (including Pobedonostsev, Procurator-General of the Holy Synod, and the notorious newspaper editor, Prince Meshchersky, whose homosexual lovers were promoted to prominent positions at court) merely added fuel to this conspiracy theory — as of course in later years Rasputin did.

What Nicholas lacked in leadership he made up for by hard work. He was an industrious and conscientious monarch, especially during the first half of his reign, diligently sitting at his desk until he had finished his daily administrative duties. All this he did in the manner of a clerk — the 'Chief Clerk of the Empire' — devoting all his energies to the routine minutiae of his office without ever stopping to consider the broader policy issues. Whereas his father had been briefed on only the major questions of policy and had delegated most of his minor executive functions to his subordinates, Nicholas proved quite incapable of dealing with anything but the most trivial matters. He personally attended to such things as the budget for repairs at an agricultural training school, and the appointment of provincial midwives. It was evident that he found real comfort in these minor bureaucratic routines: they created the illusion of a smoothly functioning government and gave him a sense of purpose. Every day he carefully recorded in his diary the time and duration of his meetings with his ministers and his other official activities, along with terse notes on the weather, the time of his morning coffee, the company at tea, and so on. These routines became a sort of ritual: at the same time every day he performed the same functions, so much so that his officials often joked that one could set one's watch by him. To the petty-minded Nicholas, it seemed that the role of the true autocrat, ruling in person from the throne, was precisely to concern himself with every minor detail in the administration of his vast lands. He spent hours, for example, dealing with the petitions to the Chancellery: hundreds of these came in every month, many of them from peasants with rude names (e.g. serf nicknames such as 'Smelly' or 'Ugly' that had been formalized as their surnames) which they could not change without the Tsar's consent. Nicholas proved unable to rise above such petty tasks. He grew increasingly jealous of his ministers' bureaucratic functions, which he confused with the exercise of power, and resented having to delegate authority to them since he saw it as a usurpation of his own autocratic powers. So protective was he of his petty executive prerogatives that he even refused to appoint a private secretary, preferring instead to deal with his own correspondence. Even such simple instructions as the summoning of an official or the readying of a motor car were written out in a note and sealed in an envelope by the Tsar's own gentle hand. It never occurred to him that an autocrat might be more usefully employed in resolving the larger questions of state. His mind was that of a miniaturist, well attuned to the smallest details of administration yet entirely incapable of synthesizing them into general principles of government. As Pobedonostsev once said of him, 'He only understands the significance of some isolated fact, without connection with the rest, without appreciating the interrelation of all other pertinent facts, events, trends, occurrences. He sticks to his insignificant, petty point of view.'[22]

To defend his autocratic prerogatives Nicholas believed that he needed to keep his officials weak and divided. The more powerful a minister became, the more Nicholas grew jealous of his powers. Able prime ministers, such as Count Witte and Petr Stolypin, who alone could have saved the tsarist regime, were forced out in this fog of mistrust. Only grey mediocrities, such as the 'old man' Ivan Goremykin, survived long in the highest office. Goremykin's success was put down by the British commentator Bernard Pares to the fact that he was 'acceptable' to both the Tsar and the Tsarina 'for his attitude of a butler, taking instructions to the other servants'. Indeed, as befits a Tsar who ruled over Russia like a medieval lord, Nicholas regarded his ministers as the servants of his own private household rather than officials of the state. True, he no longer addressed them with the familiar *tyi* (the 'you' reserved for animals, serfs and children). But he did expect unthinking devotion from them and placed loyalty far above competence in his estimation of his ministers. Even Count Witte, who was anything but humble in his normal demeanour, found himself standing to attention in the presence of the Tsar, his thumbs in line with the seams of his trousers, as if he were some private steward.

Nicholas exploited the rivalries and divisions between his different ministries. He would balance the views of the one against the other in order to retain the upper hand. This made for little coherence in government, but in so far as it bolstered his position it did not appear to bother him. Apart from a short time in 1901, Nicholas consistently refused to co-ordinate the work of the different ministries by chairing meetings of the Council of Ministers: it seems he was afraid that powerful factions might be formed there which would force him to adopt policies of which he disapproved. He preferred to see his ministers on a one-to-one basis, which had the effect of keeping them divided but was a recipe for chaos and confusion. These audiences could be extremely frustrating for ministers, for while Nicholas invariably gave the impression that he agreed with a minister's proposals, he could never be trusted to support them against those of another minister. Sustained and general debates on policy were thus extremely rare. If a minister talked too long on politics, the Tsar would make clear that he was bored and change the conversation to the weather or some other more agreeable topic. Aware that the Tsar found their reports dull, ministers consciously shortened them. Some even scrapped them altogether and amused him instead with anecdotes and gossip.[23]

The result of all this was to deprive the government of effective leadership or co-ordination during the final years of the tsarist regime. Nicholas was the source of all the problems. If there was a vacuum of power at the centre of the ruling system, then he was the empty space. In a sense, Russia gained in him the worst of both worlds: a Tsar determined to rule from the throne yet quite incapable of exercising power. This was 'autocracy without an autocrat'. Perhaps nobody could have fulfilled the role which Nicholas had set himself: the work of government had become much too vast and complex for a single man; autocracy itself was out of date. But Nicholas was mistaken to try in the first place. Instead of delegating power he indulged in a fantasy of absolute power. So jealous was he of his own prerogatives that he tried to bypass the state institutions altogether and centre power on the court. Yet none of his amiable but dim-witted courtiers was remotely capable of providing him with sound advice on how to rule the country, coming as they did from a narrow circle of aristocratic Guards officers who knew nothing of the Russia beyond St Petersburg's fashionable streets. Most of them were contemptuous of Russia, speaking French not Russian and spending more time in Nice or Biarritz than on their landed estates in the provinces. Under the court's growing domination, Nicholas's government was unable to create coherent policies to deal with the mounting problems of society which were leading inexorably towards revolution. During its final years, especially after Stolypin's downfall in 1911, the government drifted dangerously as one sycophantic mediocrity after another was appointed Prime Minister by the Tsar. Nicholas himself spent more and more time away from his office. Government business had to be delayed for weeks at a time, while he went off on hunting trips, yachting parties and family holidays to the Crimea. But in the apparently secure refuge of his family another tragedy was unfolding.

iii The Heir

The Empress Alexandra found the jubilee celebrations a strain. She dragged herself with difficulty to all the public functions, but often left early with obvious signs of distress. At the magnificent ball given by the Moscow nobility she felt so ill that she could scarcely keep her feet. When the Emperor came to her rescue, it was just in time to lead her away and prevent her from fainting in public. During the gala performance at the Marinsky Theatre she appeared pale and sombre. Sitting in the adjacent box, Meriel Buchanan, the British Ambassador's daughter, observed how the fan she was holding trembled in her hands, and how her laboured breathing:

> made the diamonds which covered the bodice of her gown rise and fall, flashing and trembling with a thousand uneasy sparks of light. Presently, it seemed that this emotion or distress mastered her completely, and with a few whispered words to the Emperor she rose and withdrew to the back of the box, to be no more seen that evening. A little wave of resentment rippled over the theatre.[24]

The fact was that the Empress had not appeared in public on more than a dozen occasions during the previous decade. Since the birth of her haemophiliac son, the Tsarevich Alexis, in 1904, she had secluded herself at the Alexander Palace at Tsarskoe Selo and other imperial residences away from the capital. It had been hoped that she would use the opportunity of the tercentenary to improve her public image. Having turned her back on society, she had come to be seen as cold and arrogant, while her dependence on the 'holy man' Rasputin had long been a matter of political concern because of his growing domination of the court. Yet shortly before the jubilee the illness of her son had taken a turn for the worse, and this was constantly on her mind during the celebrations. To make matters worse, Tatyana, her second daughter, had fallen ill with typhoid after drinking the infected water of the capital.

Alexandra did her best to conceal her inner anguish from the public. But she lacked the heart to go out and win their sympathy.

Alexandra was a stranger to Russia when she became its Empress. Since the eighteenth century, it had become the custom for Romanov rulers to marry foreign princesses. By the end of the nineteenth, inter-marriage had made the Romanovs an integral part of the family of European crowned heads. Their opponents liked to call them the 'Gottorp-Holstein' dynasty, which in genealogical terms was not far from the truth. Most statesmen shared the view that the balance of power in Europe would be secured by these dynastic ties. So there was reason to welcome the engagement in April 1894 of the Tsarevich Nicholas to Princess Alexandra, or Alix for short, daughter of the Grand Duke of Hesse-Darmstadt and Princess Alice of England. It was expected that the Princess would have plenty of time to prepare herself for the role of Empress. But Alexander III died only six months later, and the 22-year-old woman suddenly found herself on the Russian throne.

Although in later years she was to be cursed by her subjects as 'the German woman', Alexandra was in fact in many ways the quintessential English woman. After the death of her mother, in 1878, she had been brought up in England by her grandmother, Queen Victoria, whose strict morals, attitudes and tastes, not to speak of her tenacity of purpose, she had assimilated. Alexandra spoke and wrote with Nicholas in English. Russian she spoke poorly, with a heavy English accent, only to servants, officials and the clergy. Her housekeeping at the Alexander Palace was austerely Victorian. Factory-produced furniture was ordered from Maples, the English middle-class department store, in preference to the fine imperial furniture which much better suited the classic Empire style of the Alexander Palace. Her four daughters shared a bedroom, sleeping on narrow camp-beds; the Empress herself was known to change the sheets. Cold baths were taken every day. It was in many ways the modest ambition of Nicholas and Alexandra to lead the lifestyle of the English middle class. They spoke the cosy domestic language of the Victorian bourgeoisie: 'Hubby' and 'Wifey' were their nicknames for each other.[25] But the Empress was wrong to assume, as she did from her knowledge of the English court, that such a lifestyle, which in England was a result of the monarch's steady retreat from the domain of executive power, might be enjoyed by a Russian autocrat.

From the beginning, Alexandra gave the impression of resenting the public role which her position obliged her to play. She appeared only rarely at court and social functions and, being naturally shy, adopted a pose of reserve in her first appearances, which made her seem awkward and unsympathetic. She gained a reputation for coldness and hauteur, two very un-Russian vices. 'No one liked the Tsarina,' wrote the literary hostess Zinaida Gippius. 'Her sharp face, beautiful, but ill-tempered and depressed, with thin, tightly pressed lips, did not please; her German, angular height did not please.' Learning of her granddaughter's unpopularity, Queen Victoria wrote to her with some advice:

> There is no harder craft than our craft of ruling. I have ruled for more than fifty years in my own country, which I have known since childhood, and, nevertheless, every day I think about what I need to do to retain and strengthen the love of my subjects. How much harder is your situation. You find yourself in a foreign country, a country which you do not know at all, where the customs, the way of thinking and the people themselves are completely alien to you, and nevertheless it is your first duty to win their love and respect.

Alexandra replied with an arrogance suggesting her reputation was deserved:

> You are mistaken, my dear grandmama; Russia is not England. Here we do not need to earn the love of the people. The Russian people revere their Tsars as divine beings, from whom all charity and fortune derive. As far as St Petersburg society is concerned, that is something which one may wholly disregard. The opinions of those who make up this society and their mocking have no significance whatsoever.

The contents of this correspondence soon became known in St Petersburg circles, resulting in the complete breakdown of relations between the leaders of high society and the Empress. She steadily reduced her public appearances and limited her circle of friends to those from whom she could expect a slavish devotion. Here lay the roots of her paranoic insistence on dividing court and society into 'friends' and 'enemies', which was to bring the monarchy to the brink of catastrophe.[26]

   The unpopularity of the Empress would not have mattered so much had she not taken it upon herself to play an active political role. From her letter to Queen Victoria it was clear that the mystical attractions of Byzantine despotism had taken early possession of her. Even more than her mild-mannered husband, Alexandra believed that Russia could still be ruled — and indeed had to be — as it had been ruled by the medieval tsars. She saw the country as the private fiefdom of the crown: Russia existed for the benefit of the dynasty rather than the other way round. Government ministers were the private servants of the Tsar, not public servants of the state. In her bossy way she set out to organize the state as if it was part of her personal household. She constantly urged her husband to be more forceful and to assert his autocratic will. 'Be more autocratic than Peter the Great', she would tell her husband, 'and sterner than Ivan the Terrible.' She wanted him to rule, like the medieval tsars, on the basis of his own religious convictions and without regard for the constraints of the law. 'You and Russia are one and the same,' she would tell him as she pushed him this way and that according to her own ambitions, vanities, fears and jealousies. It was the Tsarina and Rasputin who — at least so the public thought — became the real rulers of tsarist Russia during the final catastrophic years. Alexandra liked to compare herself with Catherine the Great. But in fact her role was much more reminiscent of Marie Antoinette, the last queen of *ancien-régime* France, whose portrait hung over her writing desk in the Alexander Palace.[27]

Alexandra made it her mission to give the Romanov dynasty a healthy son and heir. But she gave birth to four daughters in succession. In desperation she turned to Dr Philippe, a practitioner of 'astral medicine', who had been introduced to the imperial family in 1901 during their visit to France. He convinced her she was pregnant with a son, and she duly expanded until a medical examination revealed that it was no more than a sympathetic pregnancy. Philippe was a charlatan (he had been fined three times in France for posing as a regular practitioner) and left Russia in disgrace. But the episode had revealed the Empress's susceptibility to bogus forms of mysticism. One could have predicted this from the emotional nature of her conversion to Orthodoxy. After the cold and spartan spiritual world of north German Protestantism, she was ravished by the solemn rituals, the chanted prayers and the soulful singing of the Russian Church. With all the fervour of the newly converted, she came to believe in the power of prayer and of divine miracles. And when, in 1904, she finally gave birth to a son, she was convinced it had been due to the intercession of St Seraphim, a pious old man of the Russian countryside, who in 1903 had been somewhat irregularly canonized on the Tsar's insistence.

The Tsarevich Alexis grew up into a playful little boy. But it was soon discovered that he suffered from haemophilia, at that time incurable and in most cases fatal. The disease was hereditary in the House of Hesse (one of Alexandra's uncles, one of her brothers and three of her nephews died from it) and there was no doubt that the Empress had transmitted it. Had the Romanovs been more prudent they might have stopped Nicholas from marrying her; but then haemophilia was so common in the royal houses of Europe that it had become something of an occupational hazard. Alexandra looked upon the illness as a punishment from God and, to atone for her sin, devoted herself to religion and the duties of motherhood. Had the nature of her son's illness not been kept a secret, she might have won as a mother that measure of sympathy from the public which she so utterly failed to attract from it as an Empress. Alexandra constantly watched over the boy lest he should fall and bring on the deadly internal bleeding from which the victims of haemophilia can suffer. There was no way he could lead the life of a normal child, since the slightest accident could start the bleeding. A sailor by the name of Derevenko was appointed to go with him wherever he went and to carry him when, as was often the case, he could not walk. Alexandra consulted numerous doctors, but a cure was beyond their science. She became convinced that only a miracle could save her son, and strove to make herself worthy of God's favour by donating money to churches, performing good works and spending endless hours in prayer. 'Every time the Tsarina saw him with red cheeks, or heard his merry laugh, or watched his frolics,' recalled Pierre Gilliard, the Tsarevich's tutor, 'her heart would fill with an immense hope, and she would say: "God has heard me. He has pitied my sorrow at last." Then the disease would suddenly swoop down on the boy, stretch him once more on his bed of pain and take him to the gates of death.'[28]

It was her desperate need to find a miracle cure that brought Rasputin into her life and into the life of Russia. Grigorii Rasputin was born into a relatively wealthy peasant family in the village of Pokrovskoe in western Siberia. Until recently it was thought that he had been born in the early 1860s; but it is now known that he was younger than people assumed — he was in fact born in 1869. Little more is known about Rasputin's early years. A commission set up by the Provisional Government in 1917 interviewed a number of his fellow villagers, who remembered him as a dirty and unruly boy. Later he became known as a drunkard, a lecher and a horse thief, which was almost certainly how he acquired his surname, from the word *rasputnyi*, meaning 'dissolute'.* At some point he repented and joined a group of pilgrims on their way to the nearby monastery of Verkhoturye, where he stayed for three months before returning to Pokrovskoe, a much changed man. He had renounced alcohol and meat, learned to read and write a little, and become religious and reclusive. The main cause of his conversion seems to have been the 'holy man' or *starets* Makarii, a monk at the Verkhoturye Monastery, whose spiritual powers, like those of the *starets* Zosima in Dostoevsky's *Brothers Karamazov,* had attracted disciples from all over the region. Makarii had been received by the Tsar and the Tsarina, who were always on the lookout for Men of God among the simple folk, and it was Makarii's example that Rasputin later claimed had inspired him. There is no question of Rasputin ever having been Makarii's disciple: he had never received the formal education needed to become a monk, and indeed seemed quite incapable of it. When the post of the Tsar's confessor fell vacant in 1910, Alexandra insisted on Rasputin being trained for ordination so that he could take up the job. But it soon became clear that he was unable to read anything but the most basic parts of the Scriptures. The capacity for learning by heart, which was essential for the priesthood, proved quite beyond him (Rasputin's

---

* It was common for fellow villagers to address one another by nicknames describing their characteristics: 'Clever', 'Calf', 'Wolf', 'Heart', and so on.

memory was in fact so poor that often he even forgot the names of his friends; so he gave them nicknames, such as 'Beauty' or 'Governor', which were easier to recall). In any case, it was not exactly the Orthodox faith that Rasputin brought with him from the wilds of Siberia to St Petersburg. His strange hybrid of mysticism and eroticism had more similarities with the practices of the Khlysty, an outlawed sect he would certainly have encountered at Verkhoturye, even if the frequent accusations that he was himself a member of the sect were never proved conclusively. The Khlysty believed that sin was the first step towards redemption. At their nocturnal meetings they danced naked to achieve a state of frenzy and engaged in flagellation and group sex. Indeed there was a lot in common between the views of the Khlysty and the semi-pagan beliefs of the Russian peasantry, which Rasputin's mysticism reflected. The Russian peasant believed that the sinner could be as intimate with God as the pious man; and perhaps even more intimate.[29]

At the age of twenty-eight, or so Rasputin later claimed, he saw an apparition of the Holy Mother and went on a pilgrimage to Jerusalem. There is no record of this pilgrimage, and it is more likely that he merely joined the trail of peasant wanderers, wise men and prophets, who for centuries had walked the length and breadth of Russia living off the alms of the villagers. He developed an aura of spiritual authority and a gift for preaching which soon attracted the attention of some of Russia's leading clergymen. In 1903 he appeared for the first time in St Petersburg sponsored by the Archimandrite Theophan, Alexandra's confessor, Bishop Hermogen of Saratov, and the celebrated Father John of Kronstadt, who was also a close friend of the royal family. The Orthodox Church was looking for holy men, like Rasputin, who came from the common people, to revive its waning influence among the urban masses and increase its prestige at Nicholas's court.

It was also a time when the court and social circles of St Petersburg were steeped in alternative forms of religion. In the salons of the aristocracy and the drawing-rooms of the middle classes there was a ferment of curiosity about all forms of spiritualism and theosophy, the occult and the supernatural. Séances and ouija boards were all the rage. In part, this reflected a hedonistic quest for new forms of belief and experience. But it was also part of a more general and profound sense of moral disequilibrium, which was echoed in the works of writers such as Blok and Belyi and was symptomatic of European culture during the decade before 1914. Various holy men and spiritualists had established themselves in the palaces of Russia's great and good long before Rasputin came on to the scene. Their success cleared the way for him. He was presented at parties and soirées as a man of God, a sinner and repentant, who had been graced with extraordinary powers of clairvoyance and healing. His disgusting physical appearance merely added piquancy to his moral charms.

Dressed in a peasant blouse and baggy trousers, his greasy black hair hung down to his shoulders, his beard was encrusted with old bits of food, and his hands and body were never washed. He carried a strong body odour, which many people compared to that of a goat. But it was his eyes that caught his audience's attention. Their penetrating brilliance and hypnotic power made a lasting impression. Some people even claimed that Rasputin was able to make his pupils expand and contract at will.[30]

It was as a healer for their son that Rasputin was first introduced to the Tsar and the Tsarina in November 1905. From the beginning, he seemed to possess some mysterious power by which he could check the internal bleeding. He prophesied that Alexis would not die, and that the disease would disappear when he reached the age of thirteen. Alexandra persuaded herself that God had sent Rasputin in answer to her prayers, and his visits to the palace grew more frequent as she came increasingly to rely upon him. It confirmed the prejudices of both Alexandra and Nicholas that a simple Russian peasant who was close to God should be able to do what was beyond all the doctors.

In the many books on this subject there is no final word on the secret of Rasputin's gift of healing. It is widely testified that his presence had a remarkably soothing effect on both children and animals, and this might well have helped to stop Alexis's bleeding. It is also known that he had been trained in the art of hypnotism, which may have the power to effect a physical change such as the contraction of the blood vessels. Rasputin himself once confessed to his secretary, Aron Simanovich, that he sometimes used Tibetan drugs or whatever else came to hand, and that sometimes he merely pretended to use remedies or mumbled nonsensical words while he prayed. This is reminiscent of faith healing and it may be that Rasputin's most remarkable feat can be credited to such methods. In October 1912 the Tsarevich suffered a particularly bad bout of bleeding after accompanying his mother on a carriage ride near Spala, the imperial hunting estate in eastern Poland. The doctors were unable to do anything to prevent a large and painful tumour from forming in his groin, and they told the imperial family to prepare for his imminent death. It was generally thought that only a miracle, such as the spontaneous reabsorption of the tumour, could save the boy. The situation was considered so grave that medical bulletins on the condition of the patient were published for the first time in the national press, though no mention was made of the nature of his illness. Prayer services were held in churches across the land and Alexis was given the last sacraments, as he lay racked with pain. In desperation, Alexandra sent a telegram to Rasputin, who was at his home in Pokrovskoe. According to the testimony of his daughter, he said some prayers and then went to the local telegram office, where he wired the Empress: 'God has seen your tears and heard your prayers. Do not grieve. The little one will not die.' Within hours, the patient had undergone a sudden recovery: the bleeding had stopped, his temperature had fallen and the flabber-gasted doctors confirmed that the danger had passed. Those who are sceptical of the power of prayer to heal through the medium of a telegraph cable may want to put this down to remarkable coincidence. But Alexandra was convinced otherwise, and after the 'Spala miracle' Rasputin's position at her court became unassailable.[31]

Rasputin's status at court brought him immense power and prestige. He became a *maître de requêtes*, accepting bribes, gifts and sexual favours from those who came to him in the hope that he would use his influence on their behalf. During the First World War, when his political influence was at its zenith, he developed a lucrative system of placements in the government, the Church and the Civil Service, all of which he boasted were under his control. For the hundreds of lesser mortals who queued outside his apartment every day — women begging for military exemption for their sons and husbands, people looking for somewhere to live — he would simply take a scrap of paper, put a cross on the letter head, and in his semi-literate scrawl write to some official: 'My dear and valued friend. Do this for me, Grigorii.' One such note was brought to the head of the court secretariat by a pretty young girl whom Rasputin clearly liked. 'Fix it up for her. She is all right. Grigorii.' When the official asked her what she wanted, the girl replied that she wanted to become a prima donna in the Imperial Opera.[32]

It has often been assumed that because he accepted bribes Rasputin was motivated by financial gain. This is not quite true. He took no pleasure in the accumulation of money, which he spent or gave away as quickly as he earned it. What excited him was power. Rasputin was the supreme egotist. He always had to be the centre of attention. He loved to boast of his connections at the court. 'I can do anything,' he often said, and from this the exaggerated rumours spread of his political omnipotence. The gifts he received from his wealthy patrons were important to him not because they were valuable but because they confirmed his personal influence. 'Look, this carpet is worth 400 roubles,' he once boasted to a friend, 'a Grand Duchess sent it to me for blessing her marriage. And do you see, I've got a golden cross? The Tsar gave it to me.' Above all, Rasputin liked the status which his position gave him and also the power it gave him, no more than a peasant, over men and women of a higher social class. He delighted in being rude to the well-born ladies who sat at his feet. He would dip his dirty finger into a dish of jam and turn to one and say, 'Humble yourself, lick it clean!' The first time he was received by Varvara Uexküll, the wealthy socialite, he attacked her for her expensive taste in art: 'What's this, little mother, pictures on the wall like a real museum? I'll bet you could feed five villages of starving people with what's hanging on a single wall.' When Uexküll introduced him to her guests, he stared intently at each woman, took her hands, and asked questions such as: 'Are you married?', 'Where is your husband?', 'Why did you come alone?', 'Had you been here together, I could have looked you over, seen how you eat and live.' He calculated that such insolence made him even more attractive to the guilt-ridden aristocrats who patronized him. Rich but dissatisfied society ladies were particularly attracted to this charismatic peasant. Many of them got a curious sexual excitement from being humiliated by him. Indeed the pleasure he gained from such sexual conquests probably had as much to do with the psychological domination of his victims as it did with the gratification of his physical desires. He told women that they could gain salvation through the annihilation of their pride, which entailed giving themselves up to him. One woman confessed that the first time she made love to him her orgasm was so violent that she fainted. Perhaps his potency as a lover also had a physical explanation. Rasputin's assassin and alleged homosexual lover, Felix Yusupov, claimed that his prowess was explained by a large wart strategically situated on his penis, which was of exceptional size. On the other hand, there is evidence to suggest that Rasputin was in fact impotent and that while he lay naked with many women, he had sex with very few of them. In short, he was a great lecher but not a great lover. When Rasputin was medically examined after being stabbed in a failed murder attempt in 1914, his genitals were found to be so small and shrivelled that the doctor wondered whether he was capable of the sexual act at all. Rasputin himself had once boasted to the monk Iliodor that he could lie with women without feeling passion because his 'penis did not function'.[33]

As Rasputin's power grew so did the legends of his crimes and misdemeanours. There were damaging stories of his sexual advances, some of them unwanted, including rape. Even the Tsar's sister, Olga Alexandrovna, was rumoured to have found herself the victim of his wandering hands. There were the drunken orgies, the days spent in bath-houses with prostitutes, and the nights spent carousing in restaurants and brothels. The most famous scandal took place at the Yar, a well-known gipsy restaurant, in March 1915. Rasputin had gone there with two journalists and three prostitutes. He became drunk, tried to grab the gypsy girls, and began to boast loudly of his sexual exploits with the Empress. 'See this belt?' he bellowed. 'It's her majesty's own work, I can make her do anything. Yes, I Grishka Rasputin. I could make the old girl dance like this if I wished' — and he made a gesture of the sexual act. By now, everyone was looking at Rasputin and several people asked if he really was the famous holy man. Rasputin dropped his pants and waved his penis at the spectators. The British agent, Bruce Lockhart, who was in the restaurant downstairs, heard 'wild shrieks of women, broken glass and banging doors'. The waiters rushed about, the police were called, but no one dared evict the holy man. Telephone calls to increasingly high officials finally reached the Chief of the Corps of Gendarmes, who ordered Rasputin's arrest. He was led away and imprisoned for the night. But the next morning orders came down from the Tsar for his release.[34]

What made these rumours so damaging politically was the widespread belief, which Rasputin himself encouraged, that he was the Tsarina's lover. There were even rumours of the Empress and Rasputin engaging in wild orgies with the Tsar and Anna Vyrubova, her lady-in-waiting, who was said to be a lesbian. Similar pornographic tales about Marie Antoinette and the 'impotent Louis' circulated on the eve of the French Revolution. There was no evidence for any of these rumours. True, there was the infamous letter from the Empress to Rasputin, leaked to the press in 1912, in which she had written: 'I kiss your hands and lay my head upon your blessed shoulders. I feel so joyful then. Then all I want is to sleep, sleep for ever on your shoulder, in your embrace.'[35] But, given virtually everything else we know of the Empress, it would be a travesty to read this as a love letter. She was a loyal and devoted wife and mother who had turned to Rasputin in spiritual distress. In any case, she was probably too narrow-minded to take a lover.

Nevertheless, it was the fact that the rumours existed, rather than their truth, which caused such alarm to the Tsar's supporters. They tried to convince him of Rasputin's evil influence and to get him expelled from the court. But, although Nicholas knew of his misdemeanours, he would not remove Rasputin so long as the Empress continued to believe that he, and only he, could help their dying son. Rasputin's calming effect on the Empress was too much appreciated by her henpecked husband, who once let slip in an unguarded moment: 'Better one Rasputin than ten fits of hysterics every day.' The Archimandrite Theophan, who had helped to bring Rasputin to St Petersburg, found himself expelled from the capital in 1910 after he tried to acquaint the Empress with the scandalous nature of her Holy Man's behaviour. The monk Iliodor and Bishop Hermogen were imprisoned in remote monasteries in 1911, after confronting Rasputin with a long chronicle of his misdeeds and calling on him to repent. It was Iliodor, in revenge, who then leaked to the press the Empress's letters to Rasputin. The Tsar stopped the press printing any more stories about Rasputin, in spite of the pledge he had given in the wake of the 1905 Revolution to abolish preliminary censorship. This effectively silenced the Church, coming as it did with the appointment of Vladimir Sabler, a close ally of Rasputin's, as Procurator-General of the Holy Synod.[36]

Politicians were no more successful in their efforts to bring Rasputin down. They presented evidence of his sins to the Tsar, but Nicholas again refused to act. Why was he so tolerant of Rasputin? The answer surely lies in his belief that Rasputin was a simple man, a peasant, from 'the people', and that God had sent him to save the Romanov dynasty. Rasputin confirmed his prejudices and flattered his fantasies of a popular autocracy. He was a symbol of the Tsar's belief in the Byzantine trinity — God, Tsar, and People — which he thought would help him to recast the regime in the mould of seventeenth-century Muscovy. 'He is just a good, religious, simple-minded Russian,' Nicholas once said to one of his courtiers. 'When I am in trouble or plagued by doubts, I like to have a talk with him and invariably feel at peace with myself afterwards.' Rasputin consciously played on this fantasy by addressing his royal patrons in the folksy terms *batiushka-Tsar* and *matiushka-Tsarina* ('Father-Tsar' and 'Mother-Tsarina') instead of 'Your Imperial Majesty'. Nicholas believed that only simple people — people who were untainted by their connections with the political factions of St Petersburg — were capable of telling him the truth and of giving him disinterested advice. For nearly twenty years he received direct reports from Anatoly Klopov, a clerk in the Ministry of Finance. Rasputin fitted into the same category. As the embodiment of Nicholas's ideal of the loyal Russian people, he could do no wrong. Nicholas discounted the rumours about him on the grounds that anyone shown such favour at court, especially a simple peasant like Rasputin, was bound to attract jealous criticisms. Moreover, he clearly considered Rasputin a family matter and looked upon such criticisms as an infringement of his private patrimony. When the Prime Minister, Stolypin, for example, gave him a dossier of secret police reports on Rasputin's indiscretions, the Tsar made it clear that he regarded this unsolicited warning as a grave breach of etiquette: 'I know, Petr Arkadevich, that you are sincerely devoted to me. Perhaps everything you say is true. But I ask you never again to speak to me about Rasputin. There is in any case nothing I can do.' The President of the Duma got no further when he presented an even more damaging dossier based on the materials of Iliodor and the Holy Synod. Nicholas, though clearly disturbed by the evidence, told Rodzianko: 'Rasputin is a simple peasant who can relieve the sufferings of my son by a strange power. The Tsarina's reliance upon him is a matter for the family, and I will allow no one to meddle in my affairs.'[37] It seems that the Tsar, in his obstinate adherence to the principles of autocracy, considered any questioning of his judgement an act of disloyalty.

And so the Rasputin affair went unresolved. More and more it poisoned the monarchy's relations with society and its traditional pillars of support in the court, the bureaucracy, the Church and the army. The episode has often been compared to the Diamond Necklace Affair, a similar scandal that irreparably damaged the reputation of Marie Antoinette on the eve of the French Revolution, and that is about the sum of it. By the time of Rasputin's eventual murder, in December 1916, the Romanov dynasty was on the verge of collapse.

2 Unstable Pillars

i Bureaucrats and Dressing-Gowns

On the first morning of 1883 the readers of *Government News* (*Pravitel'stvennyi vestnik*) opened their newspaper to learn that A. A. Polovtsov had been appointed Imperial Secretary. It was hardly the sort of announcement to make anyone choke on their breakfast. At the age of fifty-one, Polovtsov had all the right credentials for this top Civil Service job. The son of a noble landowner, he had married the heiress to a banking fortune, graduated from the élite School of Law, and steadily risen through the ranks of the imperial bureaucracy. He was, by all accounts, refined, cultured and well mannered; Witte even thought him a little vain. Polovtsov was confident and perfectly at ease in the aristocratic circles of St Petersburg, counting several grand dukes among his closest friends. He even belonged to the Imperial Yacht Club, the after-hours headquarters of Russia's ruling élite, where on New Year's Eve he had been told of his promotion.[1] In short, Alexander Alexandrovich was a model representative of that small and privileged tribe who administered the affairs of the imperial state.

The Russian imperial bureaucracy was an élite caste set above the rest of society. In this sense it was not unlike the Communist bureaucracy that was to succeed it. The tsarist system was based upon a strict social hierarchy. At its apex was the court; below that, its pillars of support in the civil and military service, and the Church, made up by the members of the first two estates; and at the bottom of the social order, the peasantry. There was a close link between the autocracy and this rigid pyramid of social estates (nobles, clergy, merchantry and peasants), which were ranked in accordance with their service to the state. It was a fixed social hierarchy with each estate demarcated by specific legal rights and duties. Nicholas compared it with the patrimonial system. 'I conceive of Russia as a landed estate,' he declared in 1902, 'of which the proprietor is the Tsar, the administrator is the nobility, and the workers are the peasantry.' He could not have chosen a more archaic metaphor for society at the turn of the twentieth century.

Despite the rapid progress of commerce and industry during the last decades of the nineteenth century, Russia's ruling élite still came predominantly from the old landed aristocracy. Noblemen accounted for 71 per cent of the

top four Civil Service ranks (i.e. above the rank of civil councillor) in the census
of 1897. True, the doors of the Civil Service were being opened to the sons of
commoners, so long as they had a university degree or a high-school diploma
with honours. True, too, the gap was growing, both in terms of social background
and in terms of ethos, between the service nobles and the farming gentry. Many
of the service nobles had sold their estates, moving permanently into the city,
or indeed had never owned land, having been ennobled for their service to the
state. In other words, the Civil Service was becoming just as much a path to
nobility as nobility was to the Civil Service. It also had its own élite values,
which only the crudest Marxist would seek to portray as synonymous with the
'class interests' of the landed nobles. Nevertheless, the aphorism of the writer
Iurii Samarin, that 'the bureaucrat is just a nobleman in uniform, and the
nobleman just a bureaucrat in a dressing-gown', remained generally true in 1900.
Russia was still an old agrarian kingdom and its ruling élite was still dominated
by the richest landowning families. These were the Stroganovs, the Dolgorukovs,
the Sheremetevs, the Obolenskys, the Volkonskys, and so on, powerful dynasties
which had stood near the summit of the Muscovite state during its great
territorial expansion between the fifteenth and the eighteenth centuries and had
been rewarded with lavish endowments of fertile land, mainly in the south of
Russia and the Ukraine.[2] Dependence on the state for their wealth, and indeed
for most of their employment, had prevented the Russian aristocracy from
developing into an independent landowning class counter-balancing the monarchy
in the way that they had done in most of Europe since the sixteenth century.

As readers of Gogol will know, the imperial Civil Service was obsessed
by rank and hierarchy. An elaborate set of rules, spelled out in 869 paragraphs
of Volume I of the Code of Laws, distinguished between fourteen different Civil
Service ranks, each with its own appropriate uniform and title (all of them
translations from the German). Polovtsov, for example, on his appointment as
Imperial Secretary, received the dark-blue ribbon and the silver star of the Order
of the White Eagle. Like all Civil Servants in the top two ranks, he was to be
addressed as 'Your High Excellency'; those in ranks 3 and 4 were to be addressed
as 'Your Excellency'; and so on down the scale, with those in the bottom ranks
(9 to 14) addressed simply as 'Your Honour'. The *chinovnik*, or Civil Servant,
was acutely aware of these status symbols. The progression from white to black
trousers, the switch from a red to a blue ribbon, or the simple addition of a stripe,
were ritual events of immense significance in his well-ordered life. Promotion was
determined by the Table of Ranks established in 1722 by Peter the Great. An
official could hold only those posts at or below his own personal rank. In 1856
standard intervals were set for promotion: one rank every three years from ranks
14 to 8; and one every four years from ranks 8 to 5. The top four ranks, which
brought with them a hereditary title, were appointed directly by the Tsar. This

meant that, barring some heinous sin, even the most average bureaucrat could expect to rise automatically with age, becoming, say, a civil councillor by the age of sixty-five. The system encouraged the sort of time-serving mediocrity which writers like Gogol portrayed as the essence of officialdom in nineteenth-century Russia. By the end of the century, however, this system of automatic advancement was falling into disuse as merit became more important than age.[3]

Still, the top ranks in St Petersburg were dominated by a very small élite of noble families. This was a tiny political world in which everyone knew each other. All the people who mattered lived in the fashionable residential streets around the Nevsky and the Liteiny Prospekts. They were closely connected through marriage and friendship. Most of them patronized the same élite schools (the Corps des Pages, the School of Guards Sub-Ensigns and Cavalry Junkers, the Alexander Lycée and the School of Law) and their sons joined the same élite regiments (the Chevaliers Gardes, the Horse Guards, the Emperor's Own Life Guard Hussar Regiment and the Preobrazhensky), from which they could be certain of a fast lane to the top of the civil or military service. Social connections were essential in this world, as Polovtsov's diary reveals, for much of the real business of politics was done at balls and banquets, in private salons and drawing-rooms, in the restaurant of the Evropeiskaya Hotel and the bar of the Imperial Yacht Club. This was an exclusive world but not a stuffy one. The St Petersburg aristocracy was far too cosmopolitan to be really snobbish. 'Petersburg was not Vienna,' as Dominic Lieven reminds us in his magisterial study of the Russian ruling élite, and there was always a place in its aristocratic circles for charmers and eccentrics. Take, for example, Prince Alexei Lobanov-Rostovsky, one of Nicholas II's better foreign ministers, an octogenarian *grand seigneur*, collector of Hebrew books and French mistresses, who 'sparkled in salons' and 'attended church in his dressing-gown'; or Prince M. I. Khilkov, a 'scion of one of Russia's oldest aristocratic families', who worked for a number of years as an engine driver in South America and as a shipwright in Liverpool before becoming Russia's Minister of Communications.[4]

Despite its talents, the bureaucracy never really became an effective tool in the hands of the autocracy. There were three main reasons for this. First, its dependence on the nobility became a source of weakness as the noble estate fell into decline during the later nineteenth century. There was an increasing shortfall in expertise (especially in the industrial field) to meet the demands of the modern state. The gap might have been bridged by recruiting Civil Servants from the new industrial middle classes. But the ruling élite was far too committed to its own archaic vision of the tsarist order, in which the gentry had pride of place, and feared the democratic threat posed by these new classes. Second, the apparatus was too poorly financed (it was very difficult to collect enough taxes in such a vast and poor peasant country) so that the ministries, and still more local government, never really had the resources they needed either to control or reform society. Finally, there were too many overlapping jurisdictions and divisions between the different ministries. This was a result of the way the state had developed, with each ministry growing as a separate, almost *ad hoc*, extension of the autocrat's own powers. The agencies of government were never properly systematized, nor their work co-ordinated, arguably because it was in the Tsar's best interests to keep them weak and dependent upon him. Each Tsar would patronize a different set of agencies in a given policy field, often simply bypassing those set up by his predecessors. The result was bureaucratic chaos and confusion. Each ministry was left to develop on its own without a cabinet-like body to co-ordinate the work between them. The two major ministries (Finance and Interior) recruited people through their own clientèles in the élite families and schools. They competed with each other for resources, for control of policy and for influence over lesser ministries and local government. There was no clear distinction between the functions of the different agencies, nor between the status of different laws — *nakaz, ukaz, ustav, zakon, polozhenie, ulozhenie, gramota* and *manifest*, to name just a few — so that the Tsar's personal intervention was constantly required to unhook these knots of competing jurisdiction and legislation. From the perspective of the individual, the effect of this confusion was to make the regime appear arbitrary: it was never clear where the real power lay, whether one law would be overridden by special regulations from the Tsar, or whether the police would respect the law at all. Some complacent philosophers argued on this basis that there was in fact no real autocracy. 'There is an autocracy of policeman and land captains, of governors, department heads, and ministers,' wrote Prince Sergei Trubetskoi in 1900. 'But a unitary tsarist autocracy, in the proper sense of the word, does not and cannot exist.' To the less privileged it was this arbitrariness (what the Russians cursed as *proizvol*) that made the regime's power feel so oppressive. There were no clear principles or regulations which enabled the individual to challenge authority or the state.[5]

This was, in effect, a bureaucracy that failed to develop into a coherent political force which, like the Prussian bureaucracy analysed by Max Weber, was capable of serving as a tool of reform and modernization. Rather than a 'rational' bureaucratic system as distilled in Weber's ideal type — one based on fixed institutional relations, clear functional divisions, regular procedures, legal principles — Russia had a hybrid state which combined elements of the Prussian system with an older patrimonialism that left the Civil Service subject to the patronage and intervention of the court and thus prevented the complete emergence of a professional bureaucratic ethos.

It did not have to be this way. There was a time, in the mid-nineteenth century, when the imperial bureaucracy could have fulfilled its potential as a creative and modernizing force. After all, the ideals of the 'enlightened bureaucrats', so aptly named by W. Bruce Lincoln, shaped the Great Reforms of the 1860s. Here was a new class of career Civil Servants, mostly sons of landless nobles and mixed marriages (*raznochintsy*) who had entered the profession through the widening channels of higher education in the 1830s and 1840s. They were upright and serious-minded men, like Karenin in Tolstoy's *Anna Karenina,* who talked earnestly, if slightly pedantically, about 'progress' and statistics; scoffed at the amateur aristocrats in high office, such as Count Vronsky, Anna's lover, who encroached on their field of expertise; and believed in the bureaucracy's mission to civilize and reform Russia along Western lines. Most of them stopped short of the liberal demand for a state based upon the rule of law with civil liberties and a parliament: their understanding of the *Rechtsstaat* was really no more than a bureaucratic state functioning on the basis of rational procedures and general laws. But they called for greater openness in the work of government, what they termed *glasnost,* as a public check against the abuse of power and a means of involving experts from society in debates about reform. Progressive officials moved in the circles of the liberal intelligentsia in the capital and were dubbed the 'Party of St Petersburg Progress'. They were seen regularly at the salon of the Grand Duchess Elena Pavlovna, and enjoyed the patronage of the Grand Duke Konstantin, who, as President of the State Council, did much to promote reformist officials in the government circles of Alexander II. They also had close ties with public bodies, such as the Imperial Geographic Society, from which they commissioned statistical surveys in preparation for the great reforming legislation of the 1860s.[6]

The Great Reforms were the high-water mark of this bureaucratic enlightenment. They were conceived as a modernizing process — which in Russia meant a Westernizing one — with the aim of strengthening the state after its defeat in the Crimean War. Limited freedoms and reforms were granted in the hope of activating society and creating a dynamic economy without altering the basic political framework of the autocracy. In this sense they were similar in conception to the *perestroika* of Mikhail Gorbachev a century later. In 1861 the serfs were *de jure* (if not *de facto*) emancipated from their landlord's tyranny and given some of the rights of a citizen. They were still tied to the village commune, which enforced the old patriarchal order, deprived of the right to own the land individually, and remained legally inferior to the nobles and other estates. But the groundwork had at least been laid for the development of peasant agriculture. A second major reform of 1864 saw the establishment of local assemblies of self-government, called the zemstvos, in most Russian provinces. To preserve the domination of the landed nobles, they were set up only at the provincial and district level; below that, at the volost and the village level, the peasant communes were left to rule themselves with only minimal supervision by the gentry. The judicial reforms of the same year set up an independent legal system with public jury trials for all estates except the peasants (who remained under the jurisdiction of local customary law). There were also new laws relaxing censorship (1865), giving more autonomy to universities (1863), reforming primary schools (1864) and modernizing the military (1863–75). Boris Chicherin (with the benefit of hindsight) summed up their progressive ideals:

> to remodel completely the enormous state, which had been entrusted to [Alexander's] care, to abolish an age-old order founded on slavery, to replace it with civic decency and freedom, to establish justice in a country which had never known the meaning of legality, to redesign the entire adminis-tration, to introduce freedom of the press in the context of untrammelled authority, to call new forces to life at every turn and set them on firm legal foundations, to put a repressed and humiliated society on its feet and to give it the chance to flex its muscles.[7]

Had the liberal spirit of the 1860s continued to pervade the work of government, Russia might have become a Western-style society based upon individual property and liberty upheld by the rule of law. The revolution need not have occurred. To be sure, it would still have been a slow and painful progress. The peasantry, in particular, would have remained a revolutionary threat so long as they were excluded from property and civil rights. The old patriarchal system in the countryside, which even after Emancipation preserved the hegemony of the nobles, called out for replacement with a modern system in which the peasants had a greater stake. But there was at least, within the ruling élite, a growing awareness of what was needed — and indeed of what it would cost — for this social transformation to succeed. The problem was, however, that the élite was increasingly divided over the desirability of this transformation. And as a result of these divisions it failed to develop a coherent strategy to deal with the challenges of modernization.

On the one hand were the reformists, the 'Men of 1864' like Polovtsov, who broadly accepted the need for a bourgeois social order (even at the expense of the nobility), the need for the concession of political freedoms (especially in local government), and the need for a *Rechtsstaat* (which increasingly they under-stood to mean not just a state based on universal laws but one based on the rule of law itself). By the end of the 1870s this reformist vision had developed into demands for a constitution. Enlightened statesmen openly argued that the tasks of government in the modern age had become too complex for the Tsar and his bureaucrats to tackle alone, and that the loyal and educated public had to be brought into the work of government. In January 1881 Alexander II instructed his Minister of the Interior, Count Loris-Melikov, to draw up plans for a limited constitution which would give invited figures from the public an advisory role in legislation. 'The throne', argued the Minister of Finance, A. A. Abaza, during the debates on these proposals, 'cannot rest exclusively on a million bayonets and an army of officials.' Such reformist sentiments were commonplace among the officials in the Ministry of Finance. Being responsible for industrialization, they were the first to see the need to sweep away obstacles to bourgeois enterprise and initiative. Many of them, moreover, like Polovtsov, who had married into a banking family, were themselves drawn from the 'new Russia' of commerce and industry. Witte, the great reforming Finance Minister of the 1890s, who had worked for twenty years in railroad management (to begin with as a lowly ticket clerk) before entering government service, argued that the tsarist system could avoid a revolution only by transforming Russia into a modern industrial society where 'personal and public initiatives' were encouraged by a rule-of-law state with guarantees of civil liberties.[8]

On the other hand were the supporters of the traditional tsarist order. It was no accident that their strongest base was the Ministry of the Interior, since its officials were drawn almost exclusively from 'old Russia', noble officers and landowners, who believed most rigidly in the *Polizeistaat*. The only way, they argued, to prevent a revolution was to rule Russia with an iron hand. This meant defending the autocratic principle (both in central and local government), the unchecked powers of the police, the hegemony of the nobility and the moral domination of the Church, against the liberal and secular challenges of the urban-industrial order. Conceding constitutions and political rights would only serve to weaken the state, argued P. N. Durnovo and Viacheslav von Plehve, the two great Ministers of the Interior during Witte's time at the Ministry of Finance, because the liberal middle classes who would come to power as a result had no authority among the masses and were even despised by them. Only when economic progress had removed the threat of a social revolution would the time be ripe for political reforms. Russia's backwardness necessitated such a strategy (economic liberalism plus autocracy). For as Durnovo argued (not without reason): 'One cannot in the course of a few weeks introduce North American or English systems into Russia.'[9] That was to be one of the lessons of 1917.

The arguments of the reactionaries were greatly strengthened by the tragic assassination of Alexander II in March 1881. The new Tsar was persuaded by his tutor and adviser, the Procurator of the Holy Synod, Konstantin Pobedonostsev, that continuing with the liberal reforms would only help to produce more revolutionaries like the ones who had murdered his father. Alexander III soon abandoned the project for a constitution, claiming he did not want a government of 'troublesome brawlers and lawyers'; forced the resignation of his reformist ministers (Abaza from Finance, Loris-Melikov from the Interior, and Dmitry Miliutin from War); and proclaimed a Manifesto reasserting the principles of autocracy.[10] This was the signal for a series of counter-reforms during Alexander III's reign. Their purpose was to centralize control and roll back the rights of local government, to reassert the personal rule of the Tsar through the police and his direct agents, and to reinforce the patriarchal order — headed by the nobility — in the countryside. Nothing was more likely to bring about a revolution. For at the same time the liberal classes of provincial society were coming to the view that their common interests and identity entailed defending the rights of local government against the very centralizing bureaucracy upon which the new Tsar staked so much.

ii The Thin Veneer of Civilization

When Prince Sergei Urusov was appointed Governor of Bessarabia in May 1903 the first thing he did was to purchase a guidebook of the area. This south-western province of the Empire, wedged between the Black Sea and Romania, was totally unknown to the former graduate of Moscow University, thrice-elected Marshal of the Kaluga Nobility. 'I knew as little of Bessarabia', he would later admit, 'as I did of New Zealand, or even less.'

Three weeks later, after stopping in the capital for a briefing with the Tsar, he set off by train from Moscow to Kishinev, the capital of Bessarabia, some 900 miles away. The journey took two nights and three long days, the train chugging ever slower as it moved deeper and deeper into the Ukrainian countryside. Alone in his special compartment, Urusov used the time to study his guidebook in preparation for his first exchanges with the civic dignitaries he expected to meet on his arrival. He had written to the Vice-Governor, asking him to keep the reception party small. But as his train pulled into the station at Bendery, the first major town of the province, he saw through his carriage window a platform crowded with people and what looked like a full orchestral band. At the centre, cordoned off by a ring of policemen, stood the Vice-Governor in full dress uniform and the city's mayor with the chain of office bearing a platter of bread and salt. This was how the new Governor had always been welcomed in Bessarabia and no exception would be made for Urusov. In Kishinev, an hour and a half later, His Excellency the Governor was driven through the city in an open carriage drawn by six white horses. 'Men, women and children stood in crowded ranks on the sidewalks,' Urusov recalled. 'They bowed, waved their handkerchiefs, and some of them even went down on their knees. I was quite struck by the latter, not having been used to such scenes.' After a brief stop at the cathedral, where God's blessing was invoked for the work that lay ahead of him, Urusov was driven to the Governor's house, an imposing neo-classical palace in the centre of the city, from which he would rule as the Tsar's viceroy over this distant corner of the Russian Empire.[11]

With a population of 120,000 people, Kishinev was a typical provincial city. The administrative centre, situated in the 'upper city' on a hill, was a formal grid of broad and straight paved streets bordered by poplars and white acacias. The main boulevard, the Alexandrov, was particularly elegant, its pavements wide enough for horse-drawn trams to run along their edges. In addition to the Governor's House, it boasted a number of large stone buildings, offices and churches, which in Urusov's judgement 'would have made no unfavourable impression even in the streets of St Petersburg'. Yet not a stone's throw from these elegant neo-classical façades, in the 'lower city' straggling down the hillside, was a totally different world — a world of narrow and unpaved winding streets, muddy in the spring and dusty in the summer; of wooden shanties and overcrowded hovels which served as the homes and shops for the Russian, Jewish and Moldavian workers; a world of pigs and cows grazing in the alleys, of open sewers and piles of rubbish on the public squares; a world where cholera epidemics struck on average one year in every three. These were the two faces of every Russian city: the one of imperial power and European civilization, the other of poverty and squalor of Asiatic proportions.[12]

One could hardly blame Urusov for seeing his appointment as a kind of exile. Many governors felt the same. Accustomed to the cosmopolitan world of the capital cities, they were bound to find provincial society dull and narrow by comparison. The civic culture of provincial Russia was, even at the end of the nineteenth century, still in the early stages of development compared with the societies of the West. Most of Russia's cities had evolved historically as administrative or military outposts of the tsarist state rather than as commercial or cultural centres in their own right. Typically they comprised a small nobility, mostly employed in the local Civil Service, and a large mass of petty traders, artisans and labourers. But there was no real 'bourgeoisie' or 'middle class' in the Western sense. The burghers, who in Western Europe had advanced civilization since the Renaissance, were largely missing in peasant Russia. The professions were too weak and dependent on the state to assert their autonomy until the last decades of the nineteenth century. The artisans and merchants were too divided among themselves (they were historically and legally two separate estates) and too divorced from the educated classes to provide the Russian cities with their missing *Bürgertum*. In short, Russia seemed to bear out Petr Struve's dictum: 'the further to the East one goes in Europe, the weaker in politics, the more cowardly, and the baser becomes the bourgeoisie'.[13]

As anyone familiar with Chekhov's plays will know, the cultural life of the average provincial town was extremely dull and parochial. At least that is how the intelligentsia — steeped in the culture of Western Europe — saw (with some disgust) the backward life of the Russian provinces. Listen to the brother of the *Three Sisters* describing the place in which they lived:

> This town's been in existence for two hundred years; a hundred thousand people live in it, but there's not one who's any different from all the others! There's never been a scholar or an artist or a saint in this place, never a single man sufficiently outstanding to make you feel passionately that you wanted to emulate him. People here do nothing but eat, drink and sleep. Then they die and some more take their places, and they eat, drink and sleep, too — and just to introduce a bit of variety into their lives, so as to avoid getting completely stupid with boredom, they indulge in their disgusting gossip and vodka and gambling and law-suits.

Kishinev was in this respect a very average town. It had twelve schools, two theatres and an open-air music hall, but no library or gallery. The social centre of the town was the Nobleman's Club. It was here, according to Urusov, that 'the general character of Kishinev society found its most conspicuous reflection. The club rooms were always full. The habitués of the club would gather around the card-tables from as early as 2 p.m., not leaving until 3 or 4 a.m. in winter; and in summer not until 6 or 7 a.m.' In Kishinev, as in most provincial towns, the social habits of the nobility had much more in common with those of the local merchants than with the aristocrats of St Petersburg. Stolypin's daughter, for example, recalled that in Saratov, where her father was once Governor, the wives of noblemen 'dressed so informally that on invitations it was necessary to specify "evening dress requested". Even then, they would sometimes appear at balls in dressing-gowns.'[14]

In a society such as this the provincial Governor inevitably played the role of a major celebrity. The high point of any social event was the moment when His Excellency arrived to grace the company with his presence. To receive an invitation to the annual ball at the Governor's house was to have made it to the top of provincial society. Prince Urusov, being a modest sort of man, was taken aback by the god-like esteem in which he was held by the local residents: 'According to Kishinev convention, I was to go out exclusively in a carriage, escorted by a mounted guard, with the Chief of Police in the van. To walk or to go out shopping was on my part a grave breach of etiquette.' But other governors, less modest than himself, took advantage of their lofty status to behave like petty autocrats. One provincial Governor, for example, ordered the police to stop all the traffic whenever he passed through the town. Another would not allow the play to begin before he arrived at the local theatre. To lovers of liberty the provincial Governor was the very personification of tsarist oppression and despotism. Gorky could find no better way to condemn Tolstoy's authoritarianism than to compare him to a governor.[15]

The office Urusov assumed went back to the medieval era, although its exact form was altered many times. In a country as vast and difficult to govern as Russia the tasks of tax collection and maintaining law and order were obviously beyond the capabilities of the tiny medieval state. So they were farmed out to governors, plenipotentiaries of the Tsar, who in exchange for their service to the state were allowed to 'feed' themselves at the expense of the districts they ruled (usually with a great deal of violence and venality). The inability of the state to build up an effective system of provincial administration secured the power of these governors. Even in the nineteenth century, when the bureaucracy did extend its agencies to the provinces, the governors were never entirely integrated into the centralized state apparatus.

The provincial governors were in charge of the local police, for whom they were technically answerable to the Ministry of the Interior. They also served as chairmen on the provincial boards whose work fell within the domain of the other ministries, such as Justice, Finance and Transportation. This fragmentation of executive power increasingly obliged the governors to negotiate, persuade and compromise — to play the part of a modern politician — during the later nineteenth century. Nevertheless, because of their close connections with the court, they could still ignore the demands of the ministries in St Petersburg — and indeed often did so when they deemed that these clashed with the interests of the noble estate, from which all the provincial governors were drawn. Stolypin's local government reforms, for example, which he tried to introduce after 1906, were effectively resisted by the governors who saw them as a challenge to the domination of the nobility. A. A. Khvostov, one of Stolypin's successors at the Ministry of the Interior, complained that it was 'virtually impossible' to prevent the governors from sabotaging the work of his ministry because of their 'lofty protectors' at the court: 'one has an aunt who is friendly with the Empress, another a gentleman-in-waiting for a relative, and a third a cousin who is an Imperial Master of the Horse.' The governors' extraordinary power stemmed from the fact that they were the Tsar's personal viceroys: they embodied the autocratic principle in the provinces. Russia's last two tsars were particularly adamant against the idea of subordinating the governors to the bureaucracy because they saw them as their most loyal supporters and because, in the words of Richard Robbins, 'as the personal representatives of the Sovereign, the governors helped keep the emperors from becoming dependent on their ministers and gave [them] a direct connection to the provinces and the people'. Two of Alexander III's counter-reforms, in 1890 and 1892, greatly increased the governors' powers over the zemstvos and municipal bodies. Like his son, Alexander saw this as a way of moving closer to the fantasy of ruling Russia directly from the throne. But the result was confusion in the provincial administration: the governors, the agencies of the central ministries and the elected local bodies were all set against each other.[16]

The power of the imperial government effectively stopped at the eighty-nine provincial capitals where the governors had their offices. Below that there was no real state administration to speak of. Neither the uezd or district towns nor the volost or rural townships had any standing government officials. There was only a series of magistrates who would appear from time to time on some specific mission, usually to collect taxes or sort out a local conflict, and then disappear once again. The affairs of peasant Russia, where 85 per cent of the population lived, were entirely unknown to the city bureaucrats. 'We knew as much about the Tula countryside', confessed Prince Lvov, leader of the Tula zemstvo in the 1890s, 'as we knew about Central Africa.'[17]

The crucial weakness of the tsarist system was the *under-government* of the localities. This vital fact is all too often clouded by the revolutionaries' mythic image of an all-powerful old regime. Nothing could be further from the truth. For every 1,000 inhabitants of the Russian Empire there were only 4 state officials at the turn of the century, compared with 7.3 in England and Wales, 12.6 in Germany and 17.6 in France. The regular police, as opposed to the political branch, was extremely small by European standards. Russia's expenditure on the police *per capita* of the population was less than half of that in Italy or France and less than one quarter of that in Prussia. For a rural population of 100 million people, Russia in 1900 had no more than 1,852 police sergeants and 6,874 police constables. The average constable was responsible for policing 50,000 people in dozens of settlements stretched across nearly 2,000 square miles. Many of them did not even have a horse and cart. True, from 1903 the constables were aided by the peasant constables, some 40,000 of whom were appointed. But these were notoriously unreliable and, in any case, did very little to reduce the mounting burdens on the police. Without its own effective organs in the countryside, the central bureaucracy was assigning more and more tasks to the local police: not just the maintenance of law and order but also the collection of taxes, the implementation of government laws and military decrees, the enforcement of health and safety regulations, the inspection of public roads and buildings, the collection of statistics, and the general supervision of 'public morals' (e.g. making sure that the peasants washed their beards). The police, in short, were being used as a sort of catch-all executive organ. They were often the only agents of the state with whom the peasants ever came into contact.[18]

Russia's general backwardness — its small tax-base and poor communications — largely accounts for this under-government. The legacy of serfdom also played a part. Until 1861 the serfs had been under the jurisdiction of their noble owners and, provided they paid their taxes, the state did not intervene in the relations between them. Only after the Emancipation — and then very slowly — did the tsarist government come round to the problem of how to extend its influence to its new 'citizens' in the villages and of how to shape a policy to help the development of peasant agriculture.

Initially, in the 1860s, the regime left the affairs of the country districts in the hands of the local nobles. They dominated the zemstvo assemblies and accounted for nearly three-quarters of the provincial zemstvo boards. The noble assemblies and their elected marshals were left with broad administrative powers, especially at the district level (uezd) where they were virtually the only agents upon whom the tsarist regime could rely. Moreover, the new magistrates (*mirovye posredniki*) were given broad judicial powers, not unlike those of their predecessors under serfdom, including the right to flog the peasants for minor crimes and misdemeanours.

It was logical for the tsarist regime to seek to base its power in the provinces on the landed nobility, its closest ally. But this was a dangerous strategy, and the danger grew as time went on. The landed nobility was in severe economic decline during the years of agricultural depression in the late nineteenth century, and was turning to the zemstvos to defend its local agrarian interests against the centralizing and industrializing bureaucracy of St Petersburg. In the years leading up to 1905 this resistance was expressed in mainly liberal terms: it was seen as the defence of 'provincial society', a term which was now used for the first time and consciously broadened to include the interests of the peasantry. This liberal zemstvo movement culminated in the political demand for more autonomy for local government, for a national parliament and a constitution. Here was the start of the revolution: not in the socialist or labour movements but — as in France in the 1780s — in the aspirations of the regime's oldest ally, the provincial nobility.

The Emancipation came as a rude shock not just to the economy but also to the whole of the provincial civilization of the gentry. Deprived of their serfs, most of the landed nobles went into terminal decline. Very few were able to respond to the new challenges of the commercial world in which as farmers — and less often industrialists and merchants — they were henceforth obliged to survive. The whole of the period between 1861 and 1917 could be presented as the slow death of the old agrarian élite upon which the tsarist system had always relied.

From Gogol to Chekhov, the figure of the impoverished noble landowner was a perennial of nineteenth-century Russian literature. He was a cultural obsession. Chekhov's play *The Cherry Orchard* (1903) was particularly, and subtly, resonant with the familiar themes of a decaying gentry: the elegant but loss-making estate is sold off to a self-made businessman, the son of a serf on the very same estate, who chops down the orchard to build houses. Most of the squires, like the Ranevskys in Chekhov's play, proved incapable of transforming their landed estates into viable commercial farms once the Emancipation had deprived them of the prop of free serf labour and forced them into the capitalist world. They could not follow in the footsteps of the Prussian Junkers. The old Russian serf economy had never been run, in the main, with the intention of making profits. Nobles gained prestige (and sometimes high office) from the number of serfs they owned — whence the story of Chichikov in Gogol's *Dead Souls* (1842), who travels around the estates of Russia buying up the lists of deceased serfs (or 'souls' as they were then called) whose death had not yet been registered — and from the ostentation of their manor houses rather than the success of their farms. Most seigneurial demesnes were farmed by the serfs with the same tools and primitive methods as they used on their own household plots. Many of the squires squandered the small income from their estates on expensive luxuries imported from Europe rather than investing it in their farms. Few appeared to understand that income was not profit.

By the middle of the nineteenth century many of the squires had fallen hopelessly into debt. By 1859, one-third of the estates and two-thirds of the serfs owned by the landed nobles had been mortgaged to the state and aristocratic banks. This, more than anything, helped the government to force Emancipation through against considerable opposition from the gentry. Not that the conditions of the liberation were unfavourable to the landowners: they received good money for the (often inferior) land which they chose to transfer to the peasants.* But now the squires were on their own, deprived of the free labour of the serfs and their tools and animals. They could no longer live a life of ease: their survival depended on the market place. They had to pay for tools and labour and learn the difference between profit and loss. Yet there was almost nothing in their backgrounds to prepare them for the challenge of capitalism. Most of them knew next to nothing about agriculture or accounting and went on spending in the same old lavish way, furnishing their manor houses in the French Empire style and sending their sons to the most expensive schools. Once again their debts increased, forcing them to lease or sell off first one or two and then more and more chunks of land. Between 1861 and 1900 more than 40 per cent of the gentry's land was sold to the peasants, whose growing land hunger, due to a population boom, led to a seven-fold increase in land values. There was a similar rise in rental values and, by 1900, two-thirds of the gentry's arable land had been rented out to the peasants. It was ironic that the depression of agricultural prices during the 1880s and the 1890s, which forced the peasants

* Under the terms of the Emancipation the serfs were forced to pay for their newly acquired land through a mortgage arrangement with the state, which paid the gentry for it in full and directly. Thus, in effect, the serfs bought their freedom by paying off their masters' debts.

to increase the land they ploughed, also made it more profitable for the squires to rent out or sell their land rather than cultivate it. Yet despite these speculative profits, by the turn of the century most of the squires found they could no longer afford to live in the manner to which they had grown accustomed. Their neo-classical manor houses, with their Italian paintings and their libraries, their ballrooms and their formal gardens, slowly fell into decay.[19]

Not all the squires went willingly to the wall. Many of them made a go of running their estates as commercial enterprises, and it was from these circles that the liberal zemstvo men emerged to challenge the autocracy during the last decades of the century.

Prince G. E. Lvov (1861–1925) — who was to become the first Prime Minister of democratic Russia in 1917 — typified these men. The Lvovs were one of the oldest noble Russian families. They traced their roots back thirty-one generations to Rurik himself, the ninth-century founder of the Russian 'state'. Popovka, the ancestral home of the Lvovs, was in Tula province, less than 120 miles — but on Russia's primitive roads at least two days' travel by coach — from Moscow. The Tolstoy estate at Yasnaya Polyana was only a few miles away, and the Lvovs counted the great writer as one of their closest friends. The manor house at Popovka was rather grand for what, at only 1,000 acres, was a small estate by Russian standards. It was a two-storey residence, built in the Empire style of the 1820s, with over twenty rooms, each with a high ceiling, double-doors and windows, overlooking a formal garden planted with roses and classical statues at the front. There was a park behind the house with a large white-stone chapel, an artificial lake, an orangery, a birch avenue and an orchard. The domestic regime was fairly standard for the nineteenth-century provincial gentry. There was an English governess called 'Miss Jenny' (English was the first language Lvov learned to read). Lvov's father was a reform-liberal, a man of 1864, and spent all his money on his children's education. The five sons — though not the only daughter — were all sent off to the best Moscow schools. Luxuries were minimal by the spendthrift standards of the Russian noble class: the standard First Empire mahogany furniture; one or two Flemish eighteenth-century landscapes; a few dogs for the autumn hunt; and an English carriage with pedigree horses; but very little to impress the much grander Tolstoys.

Yet, even so, by the end of the 1870s, the Lvovs had managed to clock up massive debts well in excess of 150,000 roubles. 'With the abolition of serfdom,' recalled Lvov, 'we soon fell into the category of landowners who did not have the means to live in the manner to which their circle had become accustomed.' The family had to sell off its two other landed estates, one in Chernigov for 30,000 roubles, the other in Kostroma for slightly less, as well as a beer factory in Briansk and the Lvovs' apartment in Moscow. But this still left them heavily in debt. They now had to choose between selling Popovka or making it profitable as a farm. Despite their inexperience, and the onset of the worst depression in agriculture for a century, the Lvovs had no doubts about opting for the latter. 'The idea of giving up the home of our ancestors was unthinkable,' Lvov wrote later. The farm at Popovka had become so run down from decades of neglect that when the Lvovs first returned there to run it even the peasants from the neighbouring villages shook their heads and pitied them. They offered to help them restore the farm buildings and clear the forest of weeds from the fields. The four eldest brothers took charge of the farm — their father was too old and ill to work — while Georgii studied law at Moscow University and returned to Popovka during the holidays. The family laid off the servants, leaving all the housework to Georgii's sister, and lived like peasants on rye bread and cabbage soup. Later Lvov would look back at this time as a source of his own emancipation — his own personal revolution — from the landowners' culture of the tsarist order. 'It separated us from the upper crust and made us democratic. I began to feel uncomfortable in the company of aristocrats and always felt much closer to the peasants.' Gradually, by their own hard labour in the fields, the Lvovs restored the farm. They learned about farming methods from their peasant neighbours and from agricultural textbooks purchased in Moscow by Georgii. The soil turned out to be good for growing clover and, by switching to it from rye, they even began to make impressive profits. By the late 1880s Popovka was saved, all its debts had been repaid, and the newly graduated Georgii returned to transform it into a commercial farm. He even planted an orchard and built a canning factory near the estate to make apple purée for the Moscow market.[20] What could be a more fitting counter to Chekhov's vision of the gentry in decline?

Prince Lvov became a leading member of the Tula zemstvo during the early 1890s. The ideals and limitations which he shared with the liberal 'zemstvo men' were to leave their imprint on the government he led between March and July 1917. Prince Lvov was not the sort of man whom one would expect to find at the head of a revolutionary government. As a boy he had dreamed of 'becoming a forester and of living on my own in the woods'. This mystical aspect of his character — a sort of Tolstoyan naturalism — was never extinguished. Ekaterina Kuskova said that 'in one conversation he could speak with feeling about mysticism and then turn at once to the price of potatoes'. By temperament he was much better suited to the intimate circles (*kruzhki*) of the zemstvo activists than to the cut-throat world of modern party politics. The Prince was shy and modest, gentle and withdrawn, and quite incapable of commanding people by anything other than a purely moral authority. None of these were virtues in the eyes of more ambitious politicians, who found him 'passive', 'grey' and 'cold'. Lvov's sad and noble face, which rarely showed signs of emotion or excitement, made him appear even more remote. The metropolitan and arrogant élite considered Lvov parochial and dim — the liberal leader Pavel Miliukov, for example, called him 'simple-minded' (*shliapa*) — and this largely accounts for Lvov's poor reputation, even neglect, in the history books. But this is both to misunderstand and to underestimate Lvov. He had a practical political mind — one formed by years of zemstvo work dedicated to improving rural conditions — and not a theoretical one like Miliukov's. The liberal V. A. Obolensky, who knew Lvov well, claimed that he 'never once heard him make a remark of a theoretical nature. The "ideologies" of the intelligentsia were completely alien to him.' Yet this practicality — what Obolensky called his 'native wit' — did not necessarily make Lvov an inferior politician. He had a sound grasp of technical matters, bags of common sense and a rare ability to judge people — all good political qualities.[21]

Lvov was not just an unlikely revolutionary: he was also a reluctant one. His ideals were derived from the Great Reforms — he was born symbolically in 1861 — and, in his heart, he was always to remain a liberal monarchist. He believed it was the calling of the noble class to dedicate itself to the service of the people. This sort of paternal populism was commonplace among the zemstvo men. They were well-meaning and dedicated public servants, of the sort who fill the pages of Tolstoy and Chekhov, who dreamt of bringing civilization to the dark and backward countryside. As the liberal (and thus guilt-ridden) sons of ex-serf-owners, many of them no doubt felt that, in this way, they were helping to repay their debts to the peasants. Some were ready to make considerable personal sacrifices. Lvov, for example, spent three months a year travelling around the villages inspecting schools and courts. He used some of the profits from the estate at Popovka to build a school and install an improved water system for the nearby villages. Under his leadership in the 1890s, the Tula zemstvo became one of the most progressive in the whole country. It established schools and libraries; set up hospitals and lunatic asylums; built new roads and bridges; provided veterinary and agronomic services for the peasantry; invested in local trades and industries; financed insurance schemes and rural credit; and, in the best liberal tradition, completed ambitious statistical surveys in preparation for further reforms. It was a model of the liberal zemstvo mission: to overcome the backwardness and apathy of provincial life and integrate the peasantry, as 'citizens', into the life of 'the nation'.

The optimistic expectations of the zemstvo liberals were, it is almost needless to say, never realized. Theirs was a vast undertaking, quite beyond the limited capabilities of the zemstvos. There were some achievements, especially in primary education, which were reflected in the general increase of zemstvo expenditure from 15 million roubles per annum in 1868 to 96 million per annum by the turn of the century. However, the overall level of spending was not very high, considering the zemstvos' wide range of responsibilities; and the proportion of local to state taxation (about 15 per cent) remained very low compared with most of Europe (where it was over 50 per cent).[22] There was, moreover, a fundamental problem — one which undermined the whole liberal project — of how to involve the peasants in the zemstvo's work. The peasants after the Emancipation were kept isolated in their village communes without legal rights equal to the nobility's or even the right to elect delegates directly to the district zemstvo. They saw the zemstvo as an institution of the gentry and paid its taxes reluctantly.

But an even more intractable problem for the zemstvos was the growing opposition of the central government to their work under the last two tsars. Alexander III looked upon the zemstvos as a dangerous breeding place of liberalism. Most of his bureaucrats agreed with him. Polovtsov, for example, thought that the zemstvos had 'brought a whole new breed of urban types — writers, money-lenders, clerks, and the like — into the countryside who were quite alien to the peasantry'. The government was very concerned about the 70,000 professional employees of the zemstvos — teachers, doctors, statisticians and agronomists — who were known collectively as the Third Element. In contrast to the first two zemstvo Elements (the administrators and elected deputies), who were drawn mainly from the landed nobility, these professionals often came from peasant or lower-class backgrounds and this gave their politics a democratic and radical edge. As their numbers increased in the 1880s and 1890s, so they sought to broaden the zemstvos' social mission. In effect they transformed them from organs for the gentry into organs mainly for the peasantry. Ambitious projects for agricultural reform and improvements in health and sanitation were advanced in the wake of the great famine which struck rural Russia in the early 1890s. Liberal landowners like Lvov went along with them. But the large and more conservative landowners were very hostile to the increased taxes which such projects would demand — after more than a decade of agricultural depression many of them were in dire financial straits — and campaigned against the Third Element. They found a natural and powerful ally in the Ministry of the Interior, which since the start of Alexander's reign had campaigned to curtail the democratic tendencies of local government. Successive Ministers of the Interior and their police chiefs portrayed the Third Element as revolutionaries — 'cohorts of the sans-culottes' in the words of Plehve, Director of the Police Department and later Minister of the Interior — who were using their positions in the zemstvos to stir up the peasantry.

In response to their pressure, a statute was passed in 1890 which increased the landed nobles' domination of the zemstvos by disenfranchising Jews and peasant landowners from elections to these assemblies. It also brought the zemstvos' work under the tight control of a new provincial bureau, headed by the provincial governor and subordinated to the Ministry of the Interior, which was given a wide veto over the appointment of zemstvo personnel, the zemstvos' budgets and publications, as well as most of their daily resolutions. Armed with these sweeping powers, the Ministry and its provincial agents constantly obstructed the zemstvos' work. They imposed stringent limits on their budgets on the grounds that some of their expenditures were unnecessary. Some of this was extremely petty. The Perm zemstvo, for example, had its budget capped for commissioning a portrait of Dr Litvinov, the long-serving director of the provincial lunatic asylum. The Suzdal zemstvo was similarly punished for using fifty roubles from a reserve fund to help pay for the building of a library. The police also blocked the zemstvos' work. They arrested statisticians and agronomists as 'revolutionaries' and prevented them from travelling into the countryside. They raided the zemstvo institutions — including hospitals and lunatic asylums — in search of 'political suspects'. They even arrested local noblewomen for teaching peasant children how to read and write in their spare time.[23]

The counter-reforms of Alexander's reign, of which the 1890 Statute was a cornerstone, were essentially an attempt to restore the autocratic principle to local government. The provincial governor, whose powers over the zemstvos and the municipal bodies had been greatly increased by the counter-reforms, was to play the role of a tsar in miniature. The same idea lay behind the institution of the land captains (*zemskie nachal'niki*) as a result of another counter-reform in 1889. They remained the central agents of the tsarist regime in the countryside until 1917, although after the 1905 Revolution their powers were considerably diluted. Appointed by the provincial governors and subordinated to the Ministry of the Interior, the 2,000 land captains, mainly from the gentry, were given a wide range of executive and judicial powers over the peasants, to whom they were known as the 'little tsars'. Their powers included the right to overturn the decisions of the village assemblies, to discharge elected peasant officials, and to decide judicial disputes. Until 1904 they could even order the public flogging of the peasants for minor misdemeanours, such as (and most commonly) for trespassing on the gentry's land or for failing to pay their taxes. It is hard to overstress the psychological impact of this public flogging — decades after the Emancipation — on the peasant mind. The peasant writer Sergei Semenov* (1868–1922), whom we shall encounter throughout this book, wrote that his fellow peasants saw the land captains as 'a return to the days of serfdom, when the master squire had lorded it over the village'. Semen* Kanatchikov, another peasant-son we shall encounter, also voiced the resentment caused by the captains' feudal treatment of the peasantry. One peasant, who had been arrested for failing to remove his hat and bow before the land captain while he delivered a lecture to

---

* Semenov is pronounced Semyónov and Semen is Semyón.

the village, asked Kanatchikov: 'What's a poor peasant to a gentleman? Why he's worse than a dog. At least a dog can bite, but the peasant is meek and humble and tolerates everything.'

Worried by the damage the land captains were causing to the image of the regime in the countryside, many of the more liberal bureaucrats — and even some of the conservatives — pressed for their abolition during the first decade of Nicholas's reign. They pointed to the low calibre of the land captains — who were often retired army officers or the lesser sons of the local squires too dim to advance within the regular bureaucracy — and warned that their readiness to resort to the whip might provoke the peasants to rebel. But Nicholas would not hear a word against them. He saw the land captains as the 'knight servitors' of his personal power in the countryside. They would give him a direct link with the peasantry — a link which the 'wall' of the bureaucracy had blocked — and help to realize his dream of a popular autocracy in the Muscovite style. Through their power he sought to restore the traditional order of society, with the landed gentry at its head, thereby counteracting the democratic trends of the modern world.[24]

The counter-reforms of Alexander's reign were a vital turning point in the pre-history of the revolution. They set the tsarist regime and Russian society on the path of growing conflict and, to a certain extent, determined the outcome of events between 1905 and 1917. The autocratic reaction against the zemstvos — like the gentry's reaction against democracy with which it became associated — had both the intention and the effect of excluding the mass of the people from the realm of politics. The liberal dream of the 'Men of 1864' — of turning the peasants into citizens and broadening the base of local government — was undermined as the court and its allies sought to reassert the old paternal system, headed by the Tsar, his clergy and his knights, in which the peasants, like children or savages, were deemed too primitive to play an active part. The demise of the liberal agenda did not become fully clear until the defeat of Prime Minister Stolypin's reforms — above all his project to establish a volost zemstvo dominated by the peasantry — between 1906 and 1911. But its likely consequences were clear long before that. As their pioneers had often pointed out, the zemstvos were the one institution capable of providing a political base for the regime in the countryside. Had they been allowed to integrate the peasants into the system of local politics, then perhaps the old divide between the 'two Russias' (in Herzen's famous phrase), between official Russia and peasant Russia, might at least have been narrowed if not bridged. That divide defined the whole course of the revolution. Without a stake in the old ruling system, the peasants in 1917 had no hesitation in sweeping away the entire state, thereby creating the political vacuum for the Bolshevik seizure of power. Tsarism in this sense undermined itself; but it also created the basic conditions for the triumph of Bolshevism.

iii Remnants of a Feudal Army

'I promise and do hereby swear before the Almighty God, before His Holy Gospels, to serve His Imperial Majesty, the Supreme Autocrat, truly and faithfully, to obey him in all things, and to defend his dynasty, without sparing my body, until the last drop of my blood.' Every soldier took this oath of allegiance upon entering the imperial army. Significantly, it was to the Tsar and the preservation of his dynasty rather than to the state or even to the nation that the soldier swore his loyalty. Every soldier had to renew this oath on the coronation of each new Tsar. The Russian army belonged to the Tsar in person; its officers and soldiers were in effect in vassalage to him.[25]

The patrimonial principle survived longer in the army than in any other institution of the Russian state. Nothing was closer to the Romanov court or more important to it than the military. The power of the Empire was founded on it, and the needs of the army and the navy always took precedence in the formulation of tsarist policies. All the most important reforms in Russian history had been motivated by the need to catch up and compete in war with the Empire's rivals in the west and south: Peter the Great's reforms had been brought about by the wars with Sweden and the Ottomans; those of Alexander II by military defeat in the Crimea.

The court was steeped in the ethos of the military. Since the late eighteenth century it had become the custom of the tsars to play soldiers with their families. The royal household was run like a huge army staff, with the Tsar as the Supreme Commander, all his courtiers divided by rank, and his sons, who were enrolled in the Guards, subjected from an early age to the sort of cruel humiliations which they would encounter in the officers' mess, so as to inculcate the principles of discipline and subordination which it was thought they would need in order to rule. Nicholas himself had a passion for the Guards. His fondest memories were of his youthful and carefree days as Colonel in the Preobrazhensky Regiment. He had a weakness for military parades and spared no expense on gold braid for his soldiers. He even restored some of the more archaic and operatic embellishments to the uniforms of the élite Guards regiments which Alexander III had thought better to abolish in the interests of economy. Nicholas was constantly making fussy alterations to the uniforms of his favourite units — an extra button here, another tassel there — as if he was still playing with the toy soldiers of his boyhood. All his daughters, as well as his son, were enrolled in Guards regiments. On namedays and birthdays they wore their uniforms and received delegations of their officers. They appeared at military parades and reviews, troop departures, flag presentations, regimental dinners, battle anniversaries and other ceremonies. The Guards officers of the Imperial Suite, who accompanied them everywhere they went, were treated almost as extended members of the Romanov family. No other group was as close or as loyal to the person of the Tsar.[26]

Many historians have depicted the army as a stalwart buttress of the tsarist regime. That was also the view of most observers until the revolution. Major Von Tettau from the German General Staff wrote in 1903, for example, that the Russian soldier 'is full of selflessnesss and loyalty to his duty' in a way 'that is scarcely to be found in any other army of the world'. He did 'everything with a will' and was always 'unassuming, satisfied and jolly — even after labour and deprivation'.[27] But in fact there were growing tensions between the military — in every rank — and the Romanov regime.

For the country's military leaders the root of the problem lay in the army's dismal record in the nineteenth century, which many of them came to blame on the policies of the government. Defeat in the Crimean War (1853–6), followed by a costly campaign against Turkey (1877–8), and then the humiliation of defeat by the Japanese — the first time a major European power had lost to an Asian country — in 1904–5, left the army and the navy demoralized. The causes of Russia's military weakness were partly economic: her industrial resources failed to match up to her military commitments in an age of increasing competition between empires. But this incompetence also had a political source: during the later nineteenth century the army had gradually lost its place at the top of government spending priorities. The Crimean defeat had discredited the armed services and highlighted the need to divert resources from the military to the modernization of the economy. The Ministry of War lost the favoured position it had held in the government system of Nicholas I (1825–55) and became overshadowed by the Ministries of Finance and the Interior, which from this point on received between them the lion's share of state expenditure. Between 1881 and 1902 the military's share of the budget dropped from 30 per cent to 18 per cent. Ten years before the First World War the Russian army was spending only 57 per cent of the amount spent on each soldier in the German army, and only 63 per cent of that spent in the Austrian. In short, the Russian soldier went to war worse trained, worse equipped and more poorly serviced than his enemy. The army was so short of cash that it relied largely on its own internal economy to clothe and feed itself. Soldiers grew their own food and tobacco, and repaired their own uniforms and boots. They even earned money for the regiment by going off to work as seasonal labourers on landed estates, in factories and mines near their garrisons. Many soldiers spent more time growing vegetables or repairing boots than they did learning how to handle their guns. By reducing the military budget, the tsarist regime created an army of farmers and cobblers.

The demoralization of the army was also connected to its increasing role in the suppression of civilian protests. The Russian Empire was covered with a network of garrisons. Their job was to provide more or less instant military assistance for the provincial governors or the police to deal with unrest. Between 1883 and 1903 the troops were called out nearly 1,500 times. Officers complained bitterly that this police duty was beneath the dignity of a professional soldier, and that it distracted the army from its proper military purpose. They also warned of the damaging effect it was likely to have on the army's discipline. History proved them right. The vast majority of the private soldiers were peasants, and their morale was heavily influenced by the news they received from their villages. When the army was called out to put down the peasant uprisings of 1905–6 many of the units, especially in the peasant-dominated infantry, refused to obey and mutinied in support of the revolution. There were over 400 mutinies between the autumn of 1905 and the summer of 1906. The army was brought to the brink of collapse, and it took years to restore a semblance of order.[28]

Many of these mutinies were part of a general pr[...] [...] [...] conditions prevailing in the army. Tolstoy, who had serve[...] the Crimean War, described them in his last novel *Ha[...]* soldiers, in particular, objected to the way their officers addressed them with the familiar 'you' (*tyi*) — normally used for animals and children — rather than the polite 'you' (*vyi*). It was how the masters had once addressed their serfs; and since most of the officers were nobles, and most of the soldiers were sons of former serfs, this mode of address symbolized the continuation of the old feudal world inside the army. The first thing a recruit did on joining the army was to learn the different titles of his officers: 'Your Honour' up to the rank of colonel; 'Your Excellency' for generals; and 'Your Radiance' or 'Most High Radiance' for titled officers. Colonels and generals were to be greeted not just with the simple hand salute but by halting and standing sideways to attention while the officer passed by for a strictly prescribed number of paces. The soldier was trained to answer his superiors in regulation phrases of deference: 'Not at all, Your Honour'; 'Happy to serve you, Your Excellency.' Any deviations were likely to be punished. Soldiers could expect to be punched in the face, hit in the mouth with the butt of a rifle and sometimes even flogged for relatively minor misdemeanours. Officers were allowed to use a wide range of abusive terms — such as 'scum' and 'scoundrel' — to humiliate their soldiers and keep them in their place. Even whilst off-duty the common soldier was deprived of the rights of a normal citizen. He could not smoke in public places, go to restaurants or theatres, ride in trams, or occupy a seat in a first- or second-class

railway carriage. Civic parks displayed the sign: DOGS AND SOLDIERS FORBIDDEN
TO ENTER. The determination of the soldiery to throw off this 'army serfdom'
and gain the dignity of citizenship was to become a major story of the
revolution.[29]

     It was not just the peasant infantry who joined the mutinies after 1905.
Even some of the Cossack cavalry — who since the start of the nineteenth
century had been a model of loyalty to the Tsar — joined the rebellions. The
Cossacks had specific grievances. Since the sixteenth century they had developed
as an élite military caste, which in the nineteenth century came under the control
of the Ministry of War. In exchange for their military service, the Cossacks were
granted generous tracts of fertile land — mainly on the southern borders they
were to defend (the Don and Kuban) and the eastern steppes — as well as
considerable political freedom for their self-governing communities (*voiskos*, from
the word for 'war'). However, during the last decades of the nineteenth century the
costs of equipping themselves for the cavalry, of buying saddles, harnesses and
military-grade horses, as they were obliged to in the charters of their estate,
became increasingly burdensome. Many Cossack farmers, already struggling in
the depression, had to sell part of their livestock to meet their obligations and
equip their sons to join. The *voiskos* demanded more and more concessions —
both economic and political — as the price of their military service. They began
to raise the flag of 'Cossack nationalism' — a parochial and nasty form of local
patriotism based on the idea of the Cossacks' ethnic superiority to the Russian
peasantry, and the memory of a distant and largely mythic past when the
Cossacks had been left to rule themselves through their 'ancient' assemblies of
elders and their elected atamans.[30]

     The government's treatment of the army provoked growing resentment
among Russia's military élite. The fiercest opposition came from the new generation of so-called military professionals emerging within the officer corps and
the Ministry of War itself during the last decades of the old regime. Many of
them were graduates from the Junker military schools, which had been opened
up and revitalized in the wake of the Crimean defeat to provide a means for the
sons of non-nobles to rise to the senior ranks. Career officers dedicated to
the modernization of the armed services, they were bitterly critical of the archaic
military doctrines of the élite academies and the General Staff. To them the
main priorities of the court seemed to be the appointment of aristocrats loyal
to the Tsar to the top command posts and the pouring of resources into what
had become in the modern age a largely ornamental cavalry. They argued, by
contrast, that more attention needed to be paid to the new technologies —
heavy artillery, machine-guns, motor transportation, trench design and avi-
ation — which were bound to be decisive in coming wars. The strains of

modernization on the politics of the autocracy were just as apparent in the military as they were in all the other institutions of the old regime.

Alexei Brusilov (1853–1926) typified the new professional outlook. He was perhaps the most talented commander produced by the old regime in its final decades; and yet, after 1917, he did more than any other to secure the victory of the Bolsheviks. For this he would later come to be vilified as a 'traitor to Russia' by the White Russian émigrés. But the whole of his extraordinary career — from his long service as a general in the imperial army to his time as the commander of Kerensky's army in 1917 and finally to his years as a senior adviser in the Red Army — was dedicated to the military defence of his country. In many ways the bitter life of Brusilov, which we shall be tracing throughout this book, symbolized the tragedy of his class.

There was nothing in Brusilov's background or early years to suggest the revolutionary path he would later take. Even physically, with his handsome fox-like features and his fine moustache, he cut the figure of a typical nineteenth-century tsarist general. One friend described him as a 'man of average height with gentle features and a natural easy-going manner but with such an air of commanding dignity that, when one looks at him, one feels duty-bound to love him and at the same time to fear him'. Brusilov came from an old Russian noble family with a long tradition of military service. One of his ancestors in the eighteenth century had distinguished himself in the battle for the Ukraine against the Poles — a feat he would emulate in 1920 — and for this the family had been given a large amount of fertile land in the Ukraine. At the age of nineteen Brusilov graduated from the Corps des Pages, the most élite of all the military academies, where officers were trained for the Imperial Guards. He joined the Dragoons of the Tver Regiment in the Caucasus and fought there with distinction, winning several medals, in the war against Turkey in 1877–8, before returning to St Petersburg and enrolling in the School of Guards Sub-Ensigns and Cavalry Junkers, where he rose to become one of Russia's top cavalry experts. Not surprisingly, given such a background, he instinctively shared the basic attitudes and prejudices of his peers. He was a monarchist, a Great Russian nationalist, a stern disciplinarian with his soldiers and a patriarch with his family. Above all, he was a devout, even mystical, believer in the Orthodox faith. It was this, according to his wife, that gave him his legendary calmness and self-belief even at moments of impending disaster for his troops.[31]

But Brusilov's views were broader and more intelligent than those of the average Guards officer. Although by training a cavalryman, he was among the first to recognize the declining military significance of the horse in an age of modern warfare dominated by the artillery, railways, telephones and motor transportation. 'We were too well supplied with cavalry,' he would later recall in his memoirs, 'especially when trench fighting took the place of open warfare.'[32]

He believed that everything had to be subordinated to the goal of preparing the imperial army for a modern war. This meant inevitably sacrificing the archaic domination of the cavalry, and if necessary even the dynastic interests of the court, for the good of defending the Russian Fatherland. While he was by instinct a monarchist, he placed the army above politics, and his allegiance to the Tsar weakened as he saw it undermined and destroyed by the leadership of the court.

Brusilov's disaffection with the monarchy was to conclude in 1917 when he threw in his lot with the revolution. But the roots of this conversion went back to the 1900s, when, like many of the new professionals, he came to see the court's domination of the military as a major obstacle to its reform and modernization in readiness for the European war that, with every passing year, seemed more likely to break out on Russia's western borders. The critical turning point was the failure of the General Staff to learn the lessons of the disastrous defeat in the Japanese war of 1904–5. Like many officers, he bitterly resented the way the military had been forced into this campaign, 6,000 miles away and virtually without preparation, by a small clique at court. The war in the Far East had led to the run-down of the country's defences in the west. When, in 1909, he assumed the command of the Fourteenth Army in the crucial Warsaw border region, Brusilov found a state of 'utter chaos and disorganization in all our forces':

> In the event of mobilization there would have been no clothes or boots for the men called up, and the lorries would have broken down as soon as they were put on the roads. We had machine-guns, but only eight per regiment, and they had no carriages, so that in case of war they would have had to be mounted on country carts. There were no howitzer batteries, and we knew that we were very short of ammunition, whether for field artillery or for rifles. I [later] learnt that the state of affairs was everywhere the same as with the XIV Army. At that moment it would have been utterly impossible to make war, even if Germany had thought of seizing Poland or the Baltic provinces.[33]

Very few Russian soldiers received training for trench warfare. The senior generals continued to believe that the cavalry was destined to play the key role in any forthcoming war, just as it had done in the eighteenth century. They dismissed Brusilov's attempts to involve the soldiers in mock artillery battles as a waste of ammunition. Their notion of training was to march the men up and down in parades and reviews: these were nice to look at and gave them the impression of military discipline and precision, but as a preparation for a modern war they had no value whatsoever. Brusilov believed that such archaic practices were due to the domination of the General Staff by the court and the aristocracy. These people even seemed to think that whole divisions of the infantry could be commanded by dullards and fools so long as they had gone through one of the élite military schools reserved for noblemen. Attitudes like these alienated the new career soldiers from the Junker schools, who, unlike the prodigal sons of the General Staff, had often made it through the ranks by competence alone. It was not coincidental that, like Brusilov, more than a few of them would later join the Reds.

The grievances of the military professionals gradually forced them into politics. The emergence of the Duma after 1905 gave them an organ through which to express their opposition to the court's leadership of the military. Many of the more progressive among them, like A. A. Polivanov, the Assistant Minister of War, joined forces with liberal politicians in the Duma, such as Alexander Guchkov, who, whilst arguing for increased spending on the army and especially the navy, wanted this connected with military reforms, including the transfer of certain controls from the court to the Duma and the government. Slowly but surely, the Tsar was losing his authority over the most talented elements of the military élite. Nicholas tried to reassert his influence by appointing the elegant and eminently loyal courtier, V. A. Sukhomlinov, to the post of War Minister in 1908. In the naval staff crisis of the following year he made a great show of forcing the Duma and the government to recognize his exclusive control of the military command (see pages 225–6). Yet it was almost certainly too late for the Tsar to win back the hearts and minds of the military professionals like Brusilov. They were already looking to the Duma and its broader vision of reform to restore the strength of their beloved army. Here were the roots of the wartime coalition which helped to bring about the downfall of the Tsar.

iv Not-So-Holy Russia

> God grant health to the Orthodox Tsar
> Grand Prince Mikhail Fedorovich
> May he hold the Muscovite tsardom
> And all the Holyrussian land.

According to popular song, Mikhail Romanov had been blessed by his father, the Metropolitan Filaret, in 1619 with this prayer, six years after ascending the Russian throne. The myth of the 'Holyrussian land' was the founding idea of the Muscovite tsardom as it was developed by the Romanovs from the start of the seventeenth century. The foundation of their dynasty, as it was presented in the propaganda of the 1913 jubilee, symbolized the awakening of a new

Russian national consciousness based on the defence of Orthodoxy. Mikhail Romanov, so the legend went, had been elected by the entire Russian people following the civil war and Polish intervention during the Time of Troubles (1598–1613). The 'Holyrussian land' was thus reunited behind the Romanov dynasty, and Mikhail saved Orthodox Russia from the Catholics. From this point on, the idea of 'Holy Russia', of a stronghold for the defence of Orthodoxy, became the fundamental legitimizing myth of the dynasty.

Not that the idea of Holy Russia lacked a popular base. Folksongs and Cossack epics had talked of the Holy Russian land since at least the seventeenth century. It was only natural that Christianity should become a symbol of popular self-identification for the Slavs on this flat Eurasian land-mass so regularly threatened by Mongol and Tatar invasion. To be a Russian was to be Christian and a member of the Orthodox faith. Indeed it was telling that the phrase 'Holy Russia' (*Sviataia Rus'*) could only be applied to this older term for Russia, from which the very word for a Russian (*russkii*) derived; it was impossible to say *Sviataia Rossiia*, since *Rossiia*, the newer term for Russia, was connected only with the imperial state.* Even more suggestive is the fact that the word in Russian for a peasant (*krest'ianin*), which in all other European languages stemmed from the idea of the country or the land, was coupled with the word for a Christian (*khrist'ianin*).

But where the popular myth of Holy Russia had sanctified the people and their customs, the official one sanctified the state in the person of the Tsar. Moscow became the 'Third Rome', heir to the legacy of Byzantium, the last capital of Orthodoxy; and Russia became a 'holy land' singled out by God for humanity's salvation. This messianic mission gave the tsars a unique religious role: to preach the True Word and fight heresies across the world. The image of the tsar was not just of a king, mortal as a man but ruling with a divine right, as in the Western medieval tradition; he was fabricated as a God on earth, divinely ordained as a ruler and saintly as a man. There was a long tradition in Russia of canonizing princes who had laid down their lives *pro patria et fides*, as Michael Cherniavsky has shown in his superb study of Russian myths. The tsars used Church laws, as no Western rulers did, to persecute their political opponents. The whole of Russia became transformed into a sort of vast monastery, under the rule of a tsar-archimandrite, where all heresies were rooted out.[34]

It was only gradually from the eighteenth century that this religious base of tsarist power was replaced by a secular one. Peter the Great sought to reform the relations between Church and state on Western absolutist lines. In an effort to subordinate it to the state, the Church's administration was transferred from the patriarchate to the Holy Synod, a body of laymen and clergy

* The difference between *Rus* and *Rossiia* was similar to that between 'England' and 'Britain'.

appointed by the Tsar. By the nineteenth century its secular representative, the Procurator-General, had in effect attained the status of minister for ecclesiastical affairs with control of episcopal appointments, religious education and most of the Church's finances, although not of questions of theological dogma. The Holy Synod remained, for the most part, a faithful tool in the hands of the Tsar. It was in the Church's interests not to rock the boat: during the latter half of the eighteenth century it had lost much of its land to the state and it now relied on it for funding to support 100,000 parish clergy and their families.* Still, it would be wrong to portray the Church as a submissive organ of the state. The tsarist system relied on the Church just as much as the Church relied on it: theirs was a mutual dependence. In a vast peasant country like Russia, where most of the population was illiterate, the Church was an essential propaganda weapon and a means of social control.[35]

The priests were called upon to denounce from the pulpit all forms of dissent and opposition to the Tsar, and to inform the police about subversive elements within their parish, even if they had obtained the information through the confessional. They were burdened with petty administrative duties: helping the police to control vagrants; reading out imperial manifestos and decrees; providing the authorities with statistics on births, deaths and marriages registered in parish books, and so on. Through 41,000 parish schools the Orthodox clergy were also expected to teach the peasant children to show loyalty, deference and obedience not just to the Tsar and his officials but also to their elders and betters. Here is a section of the basic school catechism prepared by the Holy Synod:

Q. How should we show our respect for the Tsar?
A. 1. We should feel complete loyalty to the Tsar and be prepared to lay down our lives for him. 2. We should without objection fulfil his commands and be obedient to the authorities appointed by him. 3. We should pray for his health and salvation, and also for that of all the Ruling House.
Q. What should we think of those who violate their duty toward their Sovereign?
A. They are guilty not only before the Sovereign, but also before God. The Word of God says, 'Whosoever therefore resisteth the power, resisteth the ordinance of God.' (Rom. 13: 2)[36]

For its part the Church was given a pre-eminent position in the moral order of the old regime. It alone was allowed to proselytize and do missionary

---

* Unlike their Catholic counterparts, Russian Orthodox priests were allowed to marry. Only the monastic clergy were not.

work in the Empire. The regime's policies of Russification helped to promote the Orthodox cause: in Poland and the Baltic, for example, 40,000 Catholics and Lutherans were converted to the Orthodox Church, albeit only nominally, during the reign of Alexander III. The Church applied a wide range of legal pressures against the dissident religious sects, especially the Old Believers.* Until 1905, it remained an offence for anyone in the Orthodox Church to convert from it to another faith or to publish attacks on it. All books on religion and philosophy had to pass through the Church's censors. There was, moreover, a whole range of moral and social issues where the Church's influence remained dominant and sometimes even took precedence over the secular authorities. Cases of adultery, incest, bestiality and blasphemy were tried in the Church's courts. Convictions resulted in the application of exclusively religious, not to say medieval, punishments, such as penance and incarceration in a monastery, since the state left such questions in the Church's hands and abstained from formulating its own punishments. Over divorce, too, the Church's influence remained dominant. The only way to attain a divorce was on the grounds of adultery through the ecclesiastical courts, which was a difficult and often painful process. Attempts to liberalize the divorce laws, and to shift the whole issue to the criminal courts, were successfully blocked in the late nineteenth century by a Church which was becoming more doctrinaire on matters of private sexuality and which, in upholding the old patriarchal order, forged a natural alliance with the last two tsars in their struggle against the modern liberal world. In short, late imperial Russia was still very much an Orthodox state.[37]

But was it still holy? That was the question that worried the leaders of the Church. And it was from this concern that many of the more liberal Orthodox clergy called for a reform in Church–state relations during the last decades of the old regime. After 1917 there were many shell-shocked Christians — Brusilov was a typical example — who argued that the revolution had been caused by the decline of the Church's influence. This of course was a simplistic view. Yet there is no doubt that the social revolution was closely connected with the secularization of society, and to a large extent dependent on it.

Urbanization was the root cause. The growth of the cities far outstripped the pace of church-building in them, with the result that millions of

---

* The Old Believers rejected the liturgical reforms of Patriarch Nikon during the 1660s as well as the government that enforced them. Fleeing persecution, most of them settled in the remote areas of Siberia, where they remain to this day. At the turn of the century there were estimated to be as many as eighteen million Old Believers. The other main religious sects, closer in spirit to Evangelicalism, were the *Stundists* (Baptists), the *Dukhobortsy* ('Fighters for the Spirit') and the *Molokane* (Milk-Drinkers). They had about one million followers between them. Many of these sects had a radical tradition of dissent, which is both explained by and helps to explain their persecution by the state.

workers, having been uprooted from the village with its church, were consigned to live in a state of Godlessness. The industrial suburb of Orekhovo-Zuevo, just outside Moscow, for example, had only one church for 40,000 residents at the turn of the century. Iuzovka, the mining capital of the Donbass, today called Donetsk, had only two for 20,000. But it was not just a question of bricks. The Church also failed to find an urban mission, to address the new problems of city life in the way that, for example, Methodism had done during the British industrial revolution. The Orthodox clergy proved incapable of creating a popular religion for the world of factories and tenements. Those who tried, such as Father Gapon, the radical preacher of St Petersburg who led the workers' march to the Winter Palace in January 1905, were soon disavowed by the Church's conservative leaders, who would have nothing to do with religiously inspired calls for social reform.[38]

The experience of urbanization was an added pressure towards secular-ization. Young peasants who migrated to the cities left behind them the old oral culture of the village, in which the priests and peasant elders were dominant, and joined an urban culture where the written word was dominant and where the Church was forced to compete with the new socialist ideologies. One peasant who made this leap was Semen Kanatchikov during his progress through the school of industry and into the ranks of the Bolsheviks. In his memoirs he recalled how his apostasy was slowly nurtured in the 1890s when he left his native village for Moscow and went to work in a machine-building factory where socialists often agitated. To begin with, he was somewhat afraid of these 'students' because 'they didn't believe in God and might be able to shake my faith as well, which could have resulted in eternal hellish torments in the next world'. But he also admired them 'because they were so free, so independent, so well informed about everything, and because there was nobody and nothing on earth that they feared'. As the country boy grew in confidence and sought to emulate their individualism, so he became more influenced by them. Stories of corrupt priests and 'miracles'-cum-frauds began to shake 'the moral foundations with which I had lived and grown up'. One young worker 'proved' to him that God had not created man by showing that, if one filled a box with earth and kept it warm, worms and insects would eventually appear in it. This sort of vulgarized pre-Darwinian science, which was widely found in the left-wing pamphlets of that time, had a tremendous impact on young workers like Kanatchikov. 'Now my emancipation from my old prejudices moved forward at an accelerated tempo,' he later wrote. 'I stopped going to the priest for "confession", no longer attended church, and began to eat "forbidden" food during Lenten fast days. However, for a long time to come I didn't abandon the habit of crossing myself, especially when I returned to the village for holidays.'[39]

And what about the countryside itself? This was the bedrock of 'Holy

Russia', the supposed stronghold of the Church. The religiosity of the Russian peasant has been one of the most enduring myths — along with the depth of the Russian soul — in the history of Russia. But in reality the Russian peasant had never been more than semi-detached with the Orthodox religion. Only a thin coat of Christianity had been painted over his ancient pagan folk-culture. To be sure, the Russian peasant displayed a great deal of external devotion. He crossed himself continually, pronounced the Lord's name in every other sentence, regularly went to church, always observed the Lenten fast, never worked on religious holidays, and was even known from time to time to go on pilgrimage to holy shrines. Slavophile intellectuals, like Dostoevsky or Solzhenitsyn, might wish to see this as a sign of the peasant's deep attachment to the Orthodox faith. And it is certainly true that most of the peasants thought of themselves as Orthodox. If one could go into a Russian village at the turn of the century and ask its inhabitants who they were, one would probably receive the reply: 'We are Orthodox and from here.' But the peasants' religion was far from the bookish Christianity of the clergy. They mixed pagan cults and superstitions, magic and sorcery, with their adherence to Orthodox beliefs. This was the peasants' own vernacular religion shaped to fit the needs of their precarious farming lives.

Being illiterate, the average peasant knew very little of the Gospels. The Lord's Prayer and the Ten Commandments were unknown to him. But he did vaguely understand the concepts of heaven and hell, and no doubt hoped that his lifelong observance of the church rituals would somehow save his soul. He conceived of God as a real human being, not as an abstract spirit. Gorky described one peasant he encountered in a village near Kazan, who:

> pictured God as a large, handsome old man, the kindly, clever master of the universe who could not conquer evil only because: 'He cannot be everywhere at once, too many men have been born for that. But he will succeed, you see. But I can't understand Christ at all! He serves no purpose as far as I'm concerned. There is God and that's enough. But now there's another! The son, they say. So what if he's God's son. God isn't dead, not that I know of.'

The icon was the focus of the peasant's faith. He followed the Bible stories from the icons in his church and believed that icons had magical powers. The corner in the peasant's hut, where he positioned the family icon, was, like the stove, a holy place. It sheltered the souls of his deceased ancestors and protected the household from evil spirits. Whenever the peasant entered or left his house he was supposed to take off his hat, bow and cross himself in front of it. And yet, as Belinsky pointed out to Gogol, the peasant also found another use for this sacred object. 'He says of the icon: "It's good for praying — and you can cover the pots with it too." '[40]

The peasant shared in the Church's cult of the saints in a similarly down-to-earth fashion, adding to it his own pagan gods and spirits connected with the agricultural world. There were Vlas (the patron saint of cattle), Frol and Lavr (the saints of horses), Elijah (the saint of thunder and rain), Muchenitsa Paraskeva (the saint of flax and yarn), as well as countless other spirits and deities — household, river, forest, mountain, lakeland and marine — called on by midwives, healers, witch doctors, bloodletters, bonesetters, sorcerers and witches through their charms and prayers. The peasants were proverbially superstitious. They believed that their lives were plagued by demons and evil spirits who cast their spells on the crops and the cattle, made women infertile, caused misfortune and illness, and brought back the souls of the dead to haunt them. The spells could only be exorcised by a priest or some other gifted person with the help of icons, candles, herbs and primitive alchemy. This was a strange religious world which, despite much good research in recent years, we can never hope to understand in full.[41]

The position of the parish priest, who lived on the constantly shifting border between the official religion of the Church and the paganism of the peasants, was precarious. By all accounts, the peasants did not hold their priests in high esteem.* The Russian peasants looked upon their local priests, in the words of one contemporary, not so much as 'spiritual guides or advisers but as a class of tradesmen with wholesale and retail dealings in sacraments'. Unable to support themselves on the meagre subsidies they received from the state, or from the farming of their own small chapel plots, the clergy relied heavily on collecting peasant fees for their services: two roubles for a wedding; a hen for a blessing of the crops; a few bottles of vodka for a funeral; and so on. The crippling poverty of the peasants and the proverbial greed of the priests often made this bargaining process long and heated. Peasant brides would be left standing in the church for hours, or the dead left unburied for several days, while the peasants and the priest haggled over the fee. Such shameless (though often necessary) bargaining by the clergy was bound to harm the prestige of the Church. The low educational level of many of the priests, their tendency to corruption and drunkenness, their well-known connections with the police and their general subservience to the local gentry, all added to the low esteem in which they were held. 'Everywhere', wrote a nineteenth-century parish priest, 'from the most resplendent drawing rooms to smoky peasant huts, people

---

* When one compares this with the respect and deference shown by the peasants of Catholic Europe towards their priests then one begins to understand why peasant Russia had a revolution and, say, peasant Spain a counter-revolution.

disparage the clergy with the most vicious mockery, with words of the most profound scorn and infinite disgust.'[42]

This was hardly a position of strength from which the Church could hope to defend its peasant flock from the insidious secular culture of the modern city. Towards the end of the nineteenth century a growing number of Orthodox clergy came to realize this. They were worried about the falling rate of church attendance which they blamed for the rise of 'hooliganism', violent attacks on landed property and other social evils in the countryside. It was from this concern for the Christian guidance of the peasants that calls were increasingly made for a radical reform of the Church. They were first voiced by the generation of liberal clergymen who had emerged from the seminaries during the middle decades of the century. Better educated and more conscientious than their predecessors, these 'clerical liberals' were inspired by the Great Reforms of the 1860s. They talked of revitalizing the life of the parish and of instilling a 'conscious' Christianity into the minds of the peasants. This they thought they could achieve by bringing the parish church closer to the peasants' lives: parishioners should have more control of their local church; there should be more parish schools; and parish priests should be allowed to concentrate on religious and pastoral affairs instead of being burdened with petty bureaucratic tasks. By the turn of the century, as it became clear that the Church could not be revitalized until it was liberated from its obligations to the state, the demands of the liberal clergy had developed into a broader movement for the wholesale reform of the Church's relations with the tsarist state. This movement climaxed in 1905 with calls from a broad cross-section of the clergy for a Church Council (*Sobor*) to replace the Holy Synod. Many also called for the decentralization of ecclesiastical power from St Petersburg and the monastic hierarchy to the dioceses and indeed from there to the parishes. While it would be wrong to claim that this movement was part of the 1905 democratic revolution, there were certainly parallels between the clergy's demands for church reform and the liberals' demands for political reform. Like the zemstvo men, the liberal clergy wanted more self-government so that they could better serve society in their local communities.[43]

This was much further than the conservatives within the ecclesiastical hierarchy were prepared to go. While they supported the general notion of self-government for the Church, they were not prepared to see the authority of the appointed bishops or the monastic clergy weakened in any way. Even less were they inclined to accept the argument put forward by the Prime Minister, Count Witte, on proposing the Law of Religious Toleration in 1905, that ending discrimination against the rivals of Orthodoxy would not harm the Church provided it embraced the reforms that would revive its own religious life. The senior hierarchs of the Church might have flirted for a while with the heady ideas of self-government being bandied about by their liberal brethren, but Witte's insistence on making religious toleration the price of such autonomy (a policy motivated by the prospect of wooing important commercial groups in the Old Believer and Jewish communities) was guaranteed to drive them back into the arms of reaction. After 1905 they allied themselves with the court and extreme Rightist organizations, such as the Union of the Russian People, in opposing all further attempts by the liberals to reform the Church and extend religious toleration. The old alliance of 'Autocracy, Orthodoxy and Nationality' was thus revived against the threat of a liberal moral order. This clash of ideologies was one of the most decisive in shaping Russian history between 1905 and 1917.

With the liberal clergy defeated, the Church was left in a state of terminal division and weakness. The central ideological pillar of the tsarist regime was at last beginning to crumble. Rasputin's rise to power within the Church signalled its own final fall from grace. 'The Most Holy Synod has never sunk so low!' one former minister told the French Ambassador in February 1916. 'If they wanted to destroy all respect for religion, all religious faith, they would not go about it in any other way. What will be left of the Orthodox Church before long? When Tsarism, in danger, seeks its support, it will find there is nothing left.'[44]

v Prison of Peoples

The collapse of the tsarist system, like that of its successor, was intimately connected with the growth of nationalist movements in the non-Russian parts of the Empire. In neither the tsarist case nor in the Soviet were these movements the direct cause of the collapse. Rather they developed in reaction to it, at first putting forward moderate proposals for autonomy and then, only when Russia's impotence became clear, pushing on to the demand for complete independence. But, in both cases, the old regime was weakened by the growth of nationalist aspirations during the decades of gradual decline which led to its final downfall.

From the post-Soviet perspective, all this may seem obvious. National-ism today is such a potent force that we are inclined to believe that it is, and always has been, part of human nature. But, as the late Ernest Gellner warned us, 'having a nation is not an inherent attribute of humanity'. The development of a mass national consciousness did not occur in most of Eastern Europe until the final decades of the nineteenth century. It was contingent on many other factors associated with the rise of a modern civil society: the transition from an agrarian society and polity to an urban and industrial one; the shift from a folk to a national culture through the development of schooling, mass literacy and communication; and an increase in the mobility of the population which not only made it more aware of its own ethnic differences and disadvantages, compared with other groups in the broader world, but also resulted in its literate sons and grandsons joining the leadership of the embryonic nation. In short, the failure of the tsarist system to cope with the growth of nationalism was yet another reflection of its failure to cope with the challenges of the modern world.[45]

So new were these national movements that, even after the Polish uprisings of the nineteenth century, they took the tsarist regime largely by surprise when they appeared as a political force during the 1905 Revolution. Neither of the two mainstream Russian schools of thought could handle the conceptual problems thrown up by the rise of nationalism. Both the conservatives and the liberals were entrapped by the fact that Russia had become an Empire before it had become a nation: for it obliged them as patriots to identify with Russia's imperial claims. For right-wing supporters of autocracy the non-Russian lands were simply the possessions of the Tsar. The Russian Empire was indivisible, just as the Tsar's power was divine. Even Brusilov, who in 1917 would throw in his lot with the Republic, could not give up the idea of the Russian Empire, and it was this that made him join the Reds, whose regime was destined to preserve it. Since, moreover, in the Rightists' view Orthodoxy was the basis of the Russian nation, the Ukrainians and the Belorussians were not separate peoples but 'Little' and 'White' Russians; yet by the same token, the Poles, the Muslims and the Jews could never be assimilated into the Russian nation, or given equal rights to the Russian people, but had to be kept within the Empire in a sort of permanent apartheid. Hence the supporters of autocracy had no conceptual means of dealing with the problems of nationalism: for even to recognize the validity of the claims of the non-Russians would be to undermine the racial basis of their own ruling ideology. And yet the liberals were equally unable to meet the challenges of nationalism. They subordinated the question of national rights to the struggle for civil and religious freedoms, in the belief that once these had been achieved the problem of nationalism would somehow disappear. Some liberals were prepared to talk of a Russian federation in which the non-Russians would be granted some rights of self-rule and cultural freedoms, but none of them was ready to concede that the aspirations of the non-Russian peoples might legitimately be extended to the demand for an independent state. Even Prince Lvov could not understand the Ukrainian claims to nationhood: in his view the Ukrainians were Little Russian peasants who had different customs and a different dialect from the Great Russians of the north.

Only the socialist parties in Russia embraced the ideas of national autonomy and independence, although even they tended to subordinate the national question to the broader democratic struggle within Russia. It is hardly surprising, then, that the national movements for liberation should have formed such a central part of the revolutionary movement as a whole. Indeed this was the pretext for their persecution by the Right: simply to be a Pole or, even worse, a Jew was to be a revolutionary in their eyes. This socialistic aspect of the nationalist movements is worth underlining. For the late twentieth-century reader might be tempted to assume, on the basis of the collapse of Communism and the rise of nationalism in Eastern Europe, that they must have been opposed to socialist goals. What is striking about the nationalist movements within the Russian Empire is that their most successful political variants were nearly always socialist in form: Joseph Pilsudski's Polish Socialist Party led the national movement in Poland; the Socialist Party became the national party of the Finns; the Baltic movements were led by socialists; the Ukrainian Socialist Revolutionaries were the leading Ukrainian national party; the Mensheviks led the Georgian national movement; and the Dashnak socialists the Armenian one. This was in part because the main ethnic conflict also tended to run along social lines: Estonian and Latvian peasants against German landlords and merchants; Ukrainian peasants against Polish or Russian landlords and officials; Azeri workers, or Georgian peasants, against the Armenian bourgeoisie; Kazakh and Kirghiz pastoralists against Russian farmers; and so on. Parties which appealed exclusively to nationalism effectively deprived themselves of mass support; whereas those which successfully combined the national with the social struggle had an almost unstoppable democratic force. In this sense it is worth repeating, given the understandably bad press which nationalism has received in the twentieth century, that for the subject peoples of the Tsarist Empire, as indeed of the Soviet Empire, nationalism was a means of human liberation from oppression and foreign domination. Lenin himself acknowledged this when, paraphrasing the Marquis de Custine, he called Imperial Russia a 'prison of peoples'.[46]

*   *   *

Most of the national movements in the Tsarist Empire began with the growth of a literary cultural nationalism in the middle decades of the nineteenth century. Romantic writers, students and artists, alienated by the life of the cities, travelled to the countryside for refreshment and inspiration. They idealized the simple rustic lifestyle of their peasant countrymen and added folk themes to their works in an effort to create a 'national style'. This appropriation of the native culture — of folksongs and folklore, local customs and dialects, peasant crafts and costumes — was more than a passing fashion for the pastoral. It was part of a broader project by a newly conscious urban middle class: the creation of a set of ethnic symbols as the basis of their own national ethos and identity. This was their 'imagined community'. The urban intelligentsia did not so much observe peasant life as reinvent and mythologize it in their own image. The folk culture of the countryside, which they believed was the ancient origin of their nation, was in fact often little more than the product of their own fertile imagination. It was increasingly the urban middle classes, rather than the peasants, who dressed up in folk costumes when they went to church, and who filled their homes with furniture and tableware in the 'peasant style'. It was they who flocked to the ethnographic and folk museums which were opened in cities throughout Eastern Europe around the turn of the century.* But if instead of these museums they had gone into the villages themselves, to observe this folk culture, so to speak, in its native habitat, they would have found it was disappearing fast. The old handicrafts were dying out under competition from cheaper industry. The peasants were increasingly wearing the same manufactured clothes as the urban workers, buying the same food in tins and jars, the same factory furniture, household utensils and linen. It was only the urban middle classes who could afford to buy the old handicrafts.[47]

The essentially bourgeois character of this kind of nationalism was clearly visible in Finland. The Grand Duchy of Finland enjoyed more self-rule and autonomy than any other part of the Tsarist Empire because on its capture from Sweden in 1808–9 the Russians confirmed the same rights and privileges that had been granted to the Finns by the more liberal Swedes. These cultural freedoms enabled the growth of a small but nationally conscious native intelligentsia, which took its inspiration from the publication of such Finnish folk-epics as the *Kalevala*, and which, from the 1860s, became increasingly unified through the national campaign for the Finnish language to be put on an equal footing with the historically dominant Swedish.[48]

In the Baltic provinces there was a similar cultural movement based around the campaign for native language rights in schools and universities, literary publications and official life. It was directed less against the Russians than the Germans (in Estonia and Latvia) or the Poles (in Lithuania), who had dominated these regions before their conquest by the Russians in the eighteenth century. Here the native languages had survived only in the remote rural areas (the native élites had been assimilated into the dominant linguistic culture). They were really no more than peasant dialects, closely related but locally varied, not unlike the Gaelic of the Irish and the Scots. During the nineteenth century linguists and ethnographers collected together and standardized these dialects in the form of a written language with a settled grammar and orthography. Ironically, even if the peasants could have read this 'national language', most of them would have found it hard to understand, since it was usually either based on just one of the dominant dialects or was an artificial construction, a sort of

---

* Warsaw established the first Ethnographic Museum in 1888. It was followed by Sarajevo in 1888, Helsinki in 1893, Prague and Lvov in 1895, Belgrade in 1901, St Petersburg in 1902, and Krakov in 1905.

peasant Esperanto, made up from all the different dialects. Nevertheless, this creation of a literary native language, and the publication of a national literature and history written in its prose, helped to start the process of nation-building and made it possible, in future decades, to educate the peasantry in this emergent national culture. In Estonia the cultural landmarks of this national renaissance were the publication of the epic poem *Kalevipoeg* by Kreutzwald in 1857, and the foundation, in the same year, of an Estonian-language newspaper, *Postimees*, aimed at peasant readers. In Latvia there was also a native-language newspaper, *Balss* (*The Voice*), from 1878, which, like the Latvian Association, was committed to the idea of uniting the peoples of the two provinces of Livonia and Kurland — which then comprised the territory of Latvia — to form a single Latvian nation. Finally, in Lithuania, which for so long had been dominated by the Poles, a national written language was also developed during the latter half of the nineteenth century (just to spite the Poles it was based on the Czech alphabet) and a native literature began to appear.[49]

As on the Baltic, so in post-partition Poland, the nation was an idea and not yet a place. Poland existed only in the imagination and in the memory of the historic Polish kingdom which had existed before its defeat and subjugation to the great powers of Eastern Europe towards the end of the eighteenth century. Its spirit was expressed in the poetry of Adam Mickiewicz, in the patriotic hymns of the Catholic Church, and — or so at least the patriots claimed (for he was half-French) — in the music of Chopin. This cultural nationalism was a comfort for the Poles, and a substitute for politics. Very few people were engaged in public life, even fewer in open dissent against Russia. Censorship and the constant danger of arrest forced the literate population to withdraw into the world of poetry (as in Russia, literature in Poland served as a metaphor for politics). The 1830 Polish uprising, even the great 1863 uprising, were the work of a relatively small nationalist minority, mostly students, officers, priests and the more liberal noble landowners. Neither won much support from the peasantry, who had little concept of themselves as Poles and who, in any case, were much more interested in gaining their own land and freedom from the nobles than in fighting for a cause led by noblemen and intellectuals.[50]

This first and primarily cultural expression of aspiring nationhood was nowhere more in evidence than in the Ukraine, no doubt in part due to the fact that of all the Empire's subject nationalities the Ukrainians were the closest culturally to the Russians. The Russians called the Ukraine 'Little Russia', and made it illegal to print the word 'Ukraine'. Kiev, the Ukrainian capital, was the tenth-century founding place of Russian Christianity. The cultural differences between Russia and the Ukraine — mainly in language, land rights and customs — had really only developed between the thirteenth and seventeenth centuries, when the western Ukraine fell under Polish-Lithuanian domination.

Thus the Ukrainian nationalists had their work cut out to make a case for these distinctions as the basis of a separate national culture.

They took inspiration from the Ukrainian national movement in neighbouring Galicia. As part of the Austro-Hungarian Empire, Galicia had been granted relatively liberal rights of self-government. This had allowed the Ukrainians, or 'Ruthenians' (dog-Latin for 'Russians') as they were known by the Austrians, to promote their own Ukrainian language in primary schools and public life, to publish native-language newspapers and books, and to advance the study of Ukrainian history and folk culture. Galicia became a sort of 'Ukrainian Piedmont' for the rest of the national movement in tsarist Ukraine: a forcing-house of national consciousness and an oasis of freedom for nationalist intellectuals. Lviv, its capital, also known as Lemberg (by the Germans) and as Lvov (by the Russians), was a thriving centre of Ukrainian culture. Although subjects of the Tsar, both the composer Lysenko and the historian Hrushevsky had found their nation in Galicia. The nationalist intellectuals who pioneered the Ukrainian literary language in the middle decades of the nineteenth century all borrowed terms from the Galician dialect, which they considered the most advanced, although later, as they tried to reach the peasantry with newspapers and books, they were forced to base it on the Poltavan folk idiom, which, as the dialect of the central Ukraine, was the most commonly understood. The seminal texts of this national literary renaissance were published by the Brotherhood of Saints Cyril and Methodius prior to its dissolution by the tsarist authorites in 1847. The romantic poetry of Taras Shevchenko, which played the same role as Mickiewicz's poetry in Poland in shaping the intelligentsia's national consciousness, was the most important of these. Ukrainian-language publications continued to appear, despite the legal restrictions on them. Many were published by the Kiev section of the Russian Geographical Society, whose increasingly nationalist members devoted themselves to the study of Ukrainian folk culture, language and history.[51]

In the non-European sectors of the Empire this cultural stage of the national movements was much slower to take off. The Armenian intelligentsia had welcomed the extension of tsarist rule to the eastern half of their country after the Russian defeat of Persia in 1827. They now had a Christian ruler to protect them from the Turks, and, or so they hoped, to free the larger half of the Armenian people who remained subjects of the Ottoman Empire. The defence of Armenian culture remained centred on the Gregorian Church and its schools, which, at least until the Russification campaign of the 1880s, aligned the Armenians with the Russians as fellow Christians against the Turks. In neighbouring Georgia, by contrast, language rather than religion was the key to the evolution of national identity. The Georgian Church, unlike the Armenian, had been merged with the Russian Orthodox; while the Georgian social system, the historic product of a specific type of feudalism, had been, albeit imperfectly, assimilated into the Russian system of estates during the half-century following Georgia's annexation in 1801. The Georgian nobles, ruined by the Emancipation of their serfs in the 1860s, dominated the intelligentsia. Theirs was a nostalgic nationalism: the romantic poetry of Chavchavadze and Baratashvili lamented the lost greatness of the Georgian kingdoms in the Middle Ages. Finally, in Azerbaijan, conquered by Russia in the 1800s, the emergence of a national consciousness was complicated by the domination of Islam, which tended towards supranational forms and blocked the growth of a secular culture and a written language for the masses. To begin with, ironically, it was the Russians who encouraged the Azeris' secular culture to develop, promoting the plays of Akhundzada, the 'Tatar Molière', and commissioning histories of the Azeri folk culture and language, as a way of weakening the influence of the Muslim powers to the south.[52]

Here, more than anywhere, the incipient nationalist intelligentsia found its ability to influence the peasant masses hampered by the general backwardness of society. This was a problem throughout the Tsarist Empire. Isolated in their remote settlements, without schools or communications with the broader world, the vast majority of the peasants had no concept of their nationality. Theirs was a local culture dominated by tradition and the spoken word. It was confined to a small and narrow world: the village and its fields, the parish church, the landowner's manor and the local market. Beyond that was a foreign country. In Estonia, for example, the peasants simply called themselves *maarahvas*, meaning 'country people', while they understood the term *saks* (from Saxon — i.e. German) to mean simply a landlord or a master; it was only in the late nineteenth century, when the Tallinn intellectuals spread their influence into the villages, that these terms took on a new ethnic meaning. Much the same was true in Poland. 'I did not know that I was a Pole till I began to read books and papers,' recalled one peasant in the 1920s. The people of his region, not far from Warsaw on the Vistula, called themselves Mazurians rather than Poles.[53]

In Belorussia and the northern Ukraine there was so much ethnic and religious intermingling — in an area the size of Cambridgeshire there might be a mixture of Belorussian, Ukrainian, Russian, Polish, Jewish and Lithuanian settlements — that it was difficult for anything more than a localized form of ethnic identity to take root in the popular consciousness. One British diplomat — though no doubt a great imperialist and therefore somewhat contemptuous of the claims of small peasant nations like the Ukraine — concluded that this was still the case as late as 1918:

Were one to ask the average peasant in the Ukraine his nationality he would answer that he is Greek Orthodox; if pressed to say whether he is a Great Russian, a Pole, or an Ukrainian, he would probably reply that he is a peasant; and if one insisted on knowing what language he spoke, he would say that he talked 'the local tongue'. One might perhaps get him to call himself by a proper national name and say that he is 'russki', but this declaration would hardly yet prejudge the question of an Ukrainian relationship; he simply does not think of nationality in the terms familiar to the intelligentsia. Again, if one tried to find out to what state he desires to belong — whether he wants to be ruled by an All-Russian or a separate Ukrainian government — one would find that in his opinion all governments alike are a nuisance, and it would be best if the 'Christian peasant folk' were left to themselves.

Such localized forms of identity were even more marked in the Muslim regions of the Caucasus (among the Chechens, Daghestanis and Azeris) as well as in much of Central Asia where tribal fiefdoms remained dominant, despite the superimposition of tsarist administrative structures.[54]

Clearly, then, the process of exposing the peasantry to this emergent national culture, centred in the cities, and of getting them to think in national terms, depended upon the general opening up of their narrow village culture to the outside world. This was a pan-European phenomenon during the latter half of the nineteenth century, as Eugen Weber has shown in his splendid book *Peasants into Frenchmen*. It was contingent on the extension of state education in the countryside, on the growth of rural institutions, such as clubs and societies, markets and co-operatives, peasant unions and mass-based parties, which were integrated at the national level, and on the penetration of roads and railways, postal services and telegraphs, newspapers and journals, into the remote rural areas.

In Poland, for example, the development of a national consciousness among the mass of the peasantry followed the spread of rural schooling and rural institutions such as the co-operatives, and the increased movement of the peasants into towns. In Georgia the rise of popular nationalism was linked to similar processes. The Georgian peasants were becoming increasingly integrated into the market economy, selling cereals, fruit, wine and tobacco to Armenian traders, while Tiflis itself, once a predominantly Armenian city, developed a Georgian working class from the poorer and immigrant peasants. As in Tiflis, so in Baku, the domination of Armenian merchants and industrialists served as a focus for the growing national and class consciousness of the immigrant Azeri peasants who flooded into the oil-industrial suburbs of Baku during the last decades of the century. In the Tatar regions of the Volga the origins of pan-Turkic nationalism were to be found in the Jadidist movement, which advocated the secular education of the native masses in opposition to the old élite schooling provided by the Muslim religious leaders. By 1900 the Volga Jadidists controlled over a thousand primary schools. Meanwhile, in the Kazan Teachers' School and at Kazan University, there were the makings of a native and increasingly rebellious Tatar intelligentsia, although Kazan itself was mainly Russian.[55]

In the western Ukraine (Galicia) the development of the peasants' national consciousness went hand in hand with the formation of a network of rural institutions such as reading clubs, credit unions, co-operative stores, choirs, insurance agencies, volunteer fire departments and gymnastic societies, which were linked with the national movement. The Ukrainian-language newspaper *Baktivshchyna* ('Fatherland') was the nationalists' main route into the village: it attracted a mass peasant readership through its close attention to local affairs which it mixed with a subtle propaganda for the national cause. The readers of *Baktivshchyna*, like the members of the reading clubs and the other primary institutions of the national movement, were mainly the new and 'conscious type' of peasants — young and literate, thrifty and sober, and, above all, self-improving — who emerged from the parish schools around the turn of the century. They formed the village cohort of the national movement, together with the local priests, cantors and teachers, who slowly took over local govern-ment from the local mayors and their (mainly Jewish) henchmen in the villages, most of whom had been appointed by the Polish landowners. In this sense the national movement was thoroughly democratic: it brought politics to the village.[56]

The most remarkable thing about the Ukrainian national movement, both under Austrian and tsarist rule, was that it remained based on the peasants. Most nationalist movements are centred on the towns. In the Constituent Assembly elections of November 1917 — the first democratic elections in the country's history — 71 per cent of the Ukrainian peasants voted for the nationalists. In the end, of course, when it came to the naked power struggles of 1917–21, this would be the national movement's fundamental weakness: the history of almost every country shows that the peasants are too weak politically to sustain a revolutionary regime without the support of the towns. But in the earlier period, when the main concern of the national movement was to build up a popular base, this distinctive peasant character was a source of strength. Ninety per cent of the Ukrainian people lived in rural areas. The towns of the Ukraine were dominated by the Russians, the Jews and the Poles; and even those few Ukrainians who lived there, mostly professionals and administrators, easily became Russified. Thus to be a Ukrainian meant in effect to be a peasant (i.e. doubly disadvantaged). Indeed this was symbolized by the fact that the original Ukrainian word for 'citizen' (*hromadjanyn*), which in all other European languages is derived from the word for a city, was based on the word for the village assembly (*hromada*). The Ukrainian national movement developed as a peasant movement against the influence of the 'foreign' towns. Nationalist agitators blamed all the evils which the peasants associated with towns — the oppression of the state, the wealth and privilege of the nobility, the greed and swindling of usurers and merchants — on the Russians, Poles and Jews who lived there. They contrasted the pure and simple lifestyle of the Ukrainian village with the corruption of this alien urban world; and as the influence of the latter grew, with the penetration of capitalism, of factory-made goods and city fashions, into the Ukrainian countryside, so they were able to present this as a threat to the 'national way of life'. More and more traditional crafts would be pushed aside, they said, by manufactured goods. The 'honest' Ukrainian shopkeeper would be superseded by the 'cheating' Jewish one. The co-operative movement, which became the backbone of the Ukrainian nationalist organization in the countryside, was developed with the aim — and the rhetoric — of protecting the simple peasants from exploitation by the Jewish traders and money-men.[57]

But it would be unfair to suggest that the nationalists' appeal to the peasantry was based solely on xenophobia and hatred of the towns. The peasant land struggle, for example, was intertwined with the nationalist movement in the Ukraine, where three-quarters of the landowners were either Russians or Poles. It is no coincidence that the peasant revolution on the land erupted first, in 1902, in those regions around Poltava province where the Ukrainian nationalist movement was also most advanced. The national movement strengthened and politicized the peasant-landlord conflict. It linked the struggle of an individual village to the national liberation movement of the whole of the Ukrainian people against a foreign class of landowners and officials. How did the nationalists make this link? Let's take two examples of their rhetoric. One concerns the peasants' conflict with the landowners over the forests and pasture lands. During the Emancipation in the Ukraine the landowners had enclosed the woods and pastures as their private property, thus depriving the peasants of their traditional rights of access to these lands, granted under serfdom, for timber and grazing. By helping the peasants in their long and bitter struggles for the restoration of these rights, the nationalists were able to involve them in their own broader political movement. Indeed it is telling that much of the romantic, nationalist folk culture of this period played on the theme of the forests and the pastures as a primal symbol of the native soil: nothing would have stirred up more the passions and emotions of the peasantry. A second example concerns the causes of rural poverty. Nationalist agitators explained their poverty to the peasants in the broader context of the semi-colonial exploitation of the Ukraine. They told them that more than half its agricultural surplus was exported to Russia or abroad; and that the Ukrainian peasant was poor because of the high taxes on Russian goods, such as kerosene, vodka and matches, which forced him to sell most of his foodstuffs in order to provide for his basic household needs. The peasant would be better off in an independent Ukraine. Through their exposure to such arguments, the Ukrainian peasants increasingly interpreted their own economic struggles in a broader national context — and as a result they gained both strength and unity. One recent scholar has found, for example, that the peasants would co-ordinate their voting patterns throughout a whole district in order to secure the defeat of the more powerful Polish-Jewish or Russian candidates in local government elections.[58]

The nationalist struggle for language rights was also a liberation movement for the peasants. Unless the peasants could understand the language of the government and the courts, they had no direct access to political or civil rights. Unless they could learn to read in their own tongue, they had no hope of social betterment. And unless they could understand their priests, they had reason to fear for their souls. The public use of their native language was not just a matter of necessity, however. It became an issue of personal pride and dignity for the Ukrainian peasant, and this gave the nationalists a profound base of emotional support. As Trotsky himself later acknowledged, looking back on the events of 1917: 'This political awakening of the peasantry could not have taken place otherwise ... than through their own native language — with all the consequences ensuing in regard to schools, courts, self-administration. To oppose this would have been to try to drive the peasants back into non-existence.'[59]

* * *

The rise of these nationalist movements need not have spelled the end of the Russian Empire. Not even the most advanced of them had developed as a mass-based political movement before the reign of the last Tsar. Most of them were still mainly limited to cultural goals, which were not necessarily incompatible with the continuation of imperial rule. There was no historical law stating that this cultural nationalism had to evolve into fully fledged national independence movements against Russia. Indeed it was clear that many of the nationalist leaders saw that their country's interests would best be served by preserving the union with Russia, albeit with looser ties and more autonomy. But tsarist ideology would not tolerate such autonomy — its ruling motto of 'Autocracy, Orthodoxy, and Nationality' meant subordinating the non-Russian peoples to Russia's cultural domination. More than anything else, it was this policy of Russification, pursued increasingly by the last two tsars, that politicized the nationalist movements and turned them into enemies of Russia. By 1905 nationalist parties had emerged as a major revolutionary force in most of the non-Russian borderlands. By its failure to come to terms with nationalism, the tsarist regime had created another instrument of its own destruction. The same was true of its clumsy handling of the liberal movement before 1905: by repressing this moderate opposition it helped to create a revolutionary one. Sir John Maynard, who as an Englishman writing in the twilight of the British Empire was in a good position to appreciate the dangers of colonial nationalism, went so far as to say that half the causes of the Russian Revolution resided in the policies of the last two tsars towards their non-Russian subjects.[60]

There was nothing new in the policy of Russification. It had always been a central aim of the tsarist imperial philosophy to assimilate the non-Russian peoples into the Russian cultural and political system, to turn them into 'true Christians, loyal subjects, and good Russians', although different tsars laid different emphases on the three principles of the policy. There was an ethnic hierarchy — parallel to the social one — within the tsarist ruling system that ranked the different nationalities in accordance with their loyalty to the Tsar and gave each a different set of legal rights and privileges. At the top were the Russians and the Baltic Germans, who between them occupied the dominant positions in the court and the civil and military services. Below them were the Poles, the Ukrainians, the Georgians, the Armenians, and so on. The Empire's five million Jews, at the bottom of its ethnic hierarchy, were subject to a comprehensive range of legal disabilities and discriminations which by the end of the nineteenth century embraced some 1,400 different statutes and regulations as well as thousands of lesser rules, provisions and judicial interpretations. They — alone of all the ethnic groups — were forbidden to own land, to enter the Civil Service, or to serve as officers in the army; there were strict quotas on Jewish admissions into higher schools and universities; and, apart from a few exceptions, the Jews were forced by law to live within the fifteen provinces of the western Ukraine, Belorussia, Lithuania and Poland which made up the Pale of Settlement. This was a tsarist version of the Hindu caste system, with the Jews in the role of the Untouchables.[61]

As the regime's fears about nationalism grew, however, during the later nineteenth century, so its policies of Russification were gradually intensified. One cause for anxiety was that the Russians were losing their demographic domination as a result of the Empire's territorial expansion into Asia, especially, with its high birth-rates and overpopulation. The census of 1897 showed that the Russians accounted for only 44 per cent of the Empire's population and that, even more alarmingly, they were one of the slowest-growing ethnic groups.[62] The Slavophile nationalists, who were responsible for shaping the Russification campaigns of the last two tsars, argued that in this age of growing nationalism and imperial competition the Russian Empire would eventually break up unless something was done to preserve the cultural domination of the Russians. In short, they argued that Russian nationalism should be mobilized as a political force and consolidated at the heart of the tsarist ruling system as a counterweight to the centrifugal forces of the non-Russian nationalities.

Along with the persecution of their religion, the banning of the non-Russians' native language from schools, literature, streets signs, courts, and public offices, was the most conspicuous and the most oppressive of the Russification policies pursued after 1881. The language ban was particularly clumsy. One of its effects was to block the path for the growing native-language intelligentsia to make its way up through the education system and bureaucracy, so that it was drawn increasingly into the nationalist and revolutionary opposition. Trying to stamp out the native language was not just an insulting and demoralizing policy as far as the non-Russians were concerned; it was ridiculous as well. Polish students at Warsaw University, for example, had to suffer the absurd indignity of studying their own native literature in Russian translation. High-school students could be expelled for speaking in Polish in their dormitories, as the Bolshevik leader and founder of the Cheka, Felix Dzerzhinsky, discovered. Even Anton Denikin, the future leader of the Whites, who as a Russian in a Warsaw district high school during the mid-1880s was obliged to monitor the conversations of his Polish classmates, thought that the policy was 'unrealistically harsh' and always wrote down 'nothing to report'. But if forbidding high-school students to speak in Polish was merely harsh (at least they had learned to speak in Russian), to do the same to railway porters (most of whom had never learned Russian, which as 'public officials' they were ordered to speak) was to enter into the cruelly surreal. This was not the only act of bureaucratic madness. In 1907 the medical committee in Kiev Province refused to allow cholera epidemic notices to be published in Ukrainian with the result that many of the peasants, who could not read Russian, died from drinking infected water.[63]

Of all the non-Russian nationalities, the Jews suffered the most from this Great Russian chauvinist backlash during the last years of tsarism. The Jews were widely, if mistakenly, blamed for the assassination of Alexander II in 1881. They were the victims of hundreds of pogroms throughout the Ukraine in that year. Contrary to the old and well-established myth, none of these pogroms — and there were to be many more (e.g. in Kishinev in 1903 and throughout the Empire in 1905–6) — was ever instigated by the government. True, the authorities were slow to restore order and few pogromists were ever brought to trial. But this was not part of a conspiracy, just a reflection of the authorities' ineffectiveness and their general hostility to Jews. During the 1880s, at a time when both the German and the Austrian Empires were beginning to dismantle their legal restrictions on the Jews, the tsarist regime was continuing to add to its own cumbersome structure of institutionalized anti-Semitism. The last two tsars were vocal anti-Semites — both associated the Jews with the threats of urban modernity, capitalism and socialism — and it became fashionable in official circles to repeat their racial prejudices. Nicholas II, in particular, was increasingly inclined to see the anti-Jewish pogroms of his reign as an act of patriotism and loyalty by the 'good and simple Russian folk'. Indeed, at the time of the Beiliss Affair in 1911–13, when a Jew was dragged through the Kiev courts on trumped-up charges of ritual murder, Nicholas was clearly looking to use the widespread anti-Semitism within the population at large, drummed up by extremist nationalist groups such as his own beloved Union of the Russian People, as a banner to rally the masses against the opponents of his faltering regime (see pages 241–6).[64]

Hardly surprising, then, that such a large and prominent part in the revolutionary movement should have been played by the Jews.* Even Witte, speaking in the wake of the Kishinev pogrom in 1903, was forced to admit that if the Jews 'comprise about 50 per cent of the membership in the revolutionary parties' then this was 'the fault of our government. The Jews are too oppressed.' The Jewish Bund was Russia's first mass-based Marxist party. Established in 1897, it had 35,000 members by 1905. It declared the Jews to be a 'nation' and demanded full national autonomy for them, with Yiddish as the official language, within a Russian federation. Such demands were rejected by the Russian Marxists (including Iulii Martov and Leon Trotsky, who were themselves Jews), who put class interests above nationalist ones and who, in any case, were deeply hostile to the Jewish nationalism of the Bundists (Georgii Plekhanov accused them of being Zionists who were afraid of sea-sickness). The result was that the two Marxist movements went their separate ways. There was also a large Zionist movement, which the tsarist regime had allowed to grow after the early 1880s because it advocated Jewish emigration in reponse to the pogroms; although it too was banned in 1903 on the grounds that inside Russia it served as a vehicle for Jewish nationalism.[65]

It was not just the Jews who were turning to nationalism in response to the growing discrimination against them at the turn of the century. Throughout the Empire the effect of the Russification campaign was to drive the non-Russians into the new anti-tsarist parties. Virtually the whole of the Finnish population rallied to the Young Finns, the Social Democrats and the Party of Active Resistance, against the imposition of Russian rule and military conscription, in contravention of Finland's rights of self-rule, after 1899. In the Baltic provinces the native population turned to the Social Democrats to defend their national rights against the tsarist state. In Poland they turned to the Polish Socialist Party, which argued that the Polish problem could only be solved by the combination of a social and a national revolution. In the Ukraine it was the Revolutionary Ukrainian Party, established in 1902, which made the early running in the national and social revolution, playing a key role in the peasant

---

* Although, of course, it must never be forgotten that while many revolutionaries were Jews, relatively few Jews were revolutionaries. It was a myth of the anti-Semites that all the Jews were Bolsheviks. In fact, as far as one can tell from the elections to the Constituent Assembly in 1917, most of the Jewish population favoured the Zionist and democratic socialist parties. As the Chief Rabbi of Moscow once remarked, not without his usual Jewish humour: 'The Trotskys make the revolutions and the Bronsteins pay the bills.' (Melamed, 'St Paul and Leon Trotsky', 8.)

uprisings of 1902, although it was quickly overshadowed by the Ukrainian National Party and the Ukrainian Social Democrats. In Georgia the Social Democrats led the national revolution, which was both anti-Russian and socialist, in 1904–6. Even the Armenians, who had always been the most loyal to their Russian masters, rallied to the Dashnaks after 1903 in opposition to the Russification of their local schools. In short, the whole of the Tsarist Empire was ripe for collapse on the eve of the 1905 Revolution. Its peoples wanted to escape.

3 Icons and Cockroaches

i A World Apart

Early one morning in March 1888 Mikhail Romas left Kazan and sailed thirty miles down the Volga River as far as the village of Krasnovidovo. There he hoped to change the life of the peasants by setting up a co-operative store. Romas was a Populist, a member of the clandestine People's Right group, who had recently returned from twelve years in prison and exile for trying to organize the peasants. Siberia had not made him change his views. At Krasnovidovo he aimed to rescue the villagers from the clutches of the local merchants by selling them cheap manufactured goods and organizing them into a gardeners' co-operative selling fruit and vegetables direct to Kazan.

He took with him Alexei Peshkov, later to become known as the writer Maxim Gorky (1868–1936), who was then, at the age of twenty, already known as an 'old man' (Tolstoy once said of him that he seemed 'to have been born a grown-up'). In his first eight years Gorky had experienced more human suffering than the literary Count would see in the whole of his eight decades. His grandfather's household in Nizhnyi Novgorod where he had been brought up after the death of his father, was, as he described it in *My Childhood*, a microcosm of provincial Russia — a place of poverty, cruelty and cholera, where the men took to the bottle in a big way and the women found solace in God. By the age of nine, Gorky had already been put out to work, scavenging for rags, bones and nails, and occasionally thieving timber from the banks of the Volga. Then his mother had died and his grandfather had sent him out into the world to fend for himself. Like countless other abandoned orphans, Gorky had roamed around the booming industrial towns of the Volga, a shoeless street urchin dressed in rags. He had worked as a dish washer on a steamboat, as a stevedore, a watchman, a cobbler's assistant, an apprentice draughtsman, an icon painter, and finally as a baker in Kazan, where Romas had found him and taken pity on the lad after he had tried to kill himself by shooting himself in the chest.

Krasnovidovo was set on a steep hill overlooking the Volga River. At the top of the hill was a church with a light-blue onion dome, and below it a row of log huts stretching down towards the river. Beyond these were the kitchen gardens, the bath-houses and the rickety animal sheds, and then the dark ploughed fields which 'gently rolled away towards the blue ridge of the forest on the horizon'. It was a relatively wealthy village. Its proximity to Kazan had made it a centre of production for the market and its most successful farmers had come to enjoy a modicum of comfort. Their well-built huts had boarded roofs and colourful ornamentation, with animal designs on their wooden shutters and window-frames. Inside them one would find an assortment of factory-made items from Russia's burgeoning industries: iron pots and pans, samovars, curtains, mirrors, bedsteads, kerosene lamps, accordions, and so on. Slowly but surely, like the rest of peasant Russia, Krasnovidovo was being drawn into the market economy.[1]

This put it in the front line of the Populists' battle for the peasantry. Central to their philosophy was the idea that the egalitarian customs of the peasant commune could serve as a model for the socialist reorganization of society. If the village was protected against the intrusions of capitalism, Russia, they believed, could move directly towards the socialist utopia without going through the 'bourgeois stage of development' — with all the negative features which that entailed — as had happened in Western Europe. The ancient village commune would be preserved as the basis of Russian communism.

Responding to the calls of the Populist leaders to 'Go to the People', thousands of radical students, Mikhail Romas among them, poured into the countryside during the 1870s in the naive belief that they could win over the peasantry to their revolutionary cause. Finding in the world of the village a reflection of their own romantic aspirations, they convinced themselves that they would find in the ordinary peasants soul-mates and allies in their socialist struggle. Some of them tried to dress and talk like peasants, so much did they identify themselves with their 'simple way of life'. One of them, a Jew, even converted to Orthodoxy in the belief that this would bring him closer to the 'peasant soul'. These romantics conceived of the village as a collective and harmonious community that testified to the basic socialist instincts of the Russian people. Among the peasantry, wrote one of the Populist leaders, 'there is more attentiveness to the worth of the individual man, less indifference to what my neighbour is like and what I appear like to my neighbour'. Such was their idealized view of the peasants that many Populists even contended that in sexual matters they were more moral and celibate than the corrupted urban population. So, for example, they believed that prostitution did not exist among the peasants (even though the majority of urban prostitutes were originally peasant women); that there was no rape or sexual assault in the village (despite the peasant custom of *snokhachestvo* which gave the household patriarchs a sexual claim on their daughters-in-law in the absence of their husbands); and that whereas syphilis (which was endemic throughout Russia) might have been venereal in the depraved cities, in the villages it was caused more innocently by the peasant custom of sharing wooden spoons and bowls.[2]

These romantic missionaries were shattered by the reality they encountered in the countryside. Most of the students were met by a cautious suspicion or hostility on the part of the peasantry, and were soon arrested by the police. Looking back on the experience from prison and exile, moderate Populists such as Romas were convinced that the basic problem had been the peasantry's isolation from the rest of society. Through the centuries of serfdom the only outsiders they had met had been the gentry and state officials, so it was hardly surprising that they were wary of the student agitators. What was needed now was years of patient work to build up the bonds of trust between the peasants and the Populist intelligentsia. Hence Romas had come to Krasnovidovo.

His efforts were in vain. From the start the villagers were suspicious of his co-operative. They could not understand why its prices were so much cheaper than the other retail outlets. The richest peasants, who were closely linked with the established merchants, intimidated Romas and his allies. They filled one of his firewood logs with gunpowder, causing a minor explosion. They threatened the poorer peasants who began to show an interest in the co-operative; and brutally murdered one of his assistants, a poor peasant from the village, leaving his horribly mutilated body in several pieces along the river bank. Finally, they blew up the co-operative (along with half the rest of the village) by setting light to the kerosene store. Romas's enemies blamed him and Gorky for the fire, and set the angry peasants on them. But the 'heretics' fought themselves free and fled for their lives.

Romas accepted defeat philosophically, putting it down to the ignorance of the villagers. He refused to give up his belief in the peasants' socialist potential and when, fifteen years later, Gorky met him again, he had already served another ten-year sentence of exile in Siberia for his involvement in the Populist movement. But for Gorky the experience was a bitter disillusionment. It led him to the conclusion that, however good they may be on their own, the peasants left all that was fine behind them when they 'gathered in one grey mass':

> Some dog-like desire to please the strong ones in the village took possession of them, and then it disgusted me to look at them. They would howl wildly at each other, ready for a fight — and they would fight, over any trifle. At these moments they were terrifying and they seemed capable of destroying the very church where only the previous evening they had gathered humbly and submissively, like sheep in a fold.[3]

The 'noble savage' whom the Populists had seen in the simple peasant was, as Gorky now concluded, no more than a romantic illusion. And the more he experienced the everyday life of the peasants, the more he denounced them as savage and barbaric.*

Such misunderstandings were a constant theme in the history of relations between educated and peasant Russia — the 'Two Russias', as Herzen once called them. The Populists, though perhaps the most conspicuous, were not the only people to impose their own ideals on the peasants. Virtually every trend of Russian social thought fell into the same trap. As Dostoevsky wrote:

> We, the lovers of 'the people', regard them as part of a theory, and it seems that none us really likes them as they actually are but only as each of us has imagined them. Moreover, should the Russian people, at some future time, turn out to be not what we imagined, then we, despite our love of them, would immediately renounce them without regret.[4]

Long before the Populists came on to the scene, Slavophile writers had argued for the moral superiority of the 'ancient' peasant commune over modern Western values. 'A commune', wrote Konstantin Aksakov, 'is a union of the people who have renounced their egoism, their individuality, and who express their common accord; this is an act of love, a noble Christian act.' Similar virtues were attributed to the peasants by the great romantic writers of the nineteenth century. Dostoevsky, for example, claimed that the simple Russian peasant — the 'kitchen muzhik' as he once called him in a famous dispute — lived on a higher moral plane than the more sophisticated citizens of Western Europe. The peasants, he had written in his *Diary of a Writer*, were truly Christian and long-suffering. It was they who would 'show us a new road, a new way out of all our apparently insoluble difficulties. For it will not be St Petersburg that finally settles the Russian destiny . . . Light and salvation will come from below.' Tolstoy also saw the simple peasant as a natural sage. Thus it is from the peasants that Prince Levin learns how to live in *Anna Karenina*; just as in *War and Peace* it is from Karataev, a humble Russian peasant, that Pierre Bezukhov comes to understand the spiritual meaning of life. Karataev's character — spontaneous, direct and unselfconscious — was a projection of Tolstoy's own moral philosophy. He lived in harmony with the world and humanity.[5]

These romantic visions of the peasantry were constantly undone by contact with reality, often with devastating consequences for their bearers. The Populists, who invested much of themselves in their conception of the peasants, suffered the most in this respect, since the disintegration of that conception

---

* At the age of twenty-three Gorky was beaten unconscious by a group of peasants when he tried to intervene on behalf of a peasant woman, who had been stripped naked and horsewhipped by her husband and a howling mob after being found guilty of adultery.

threatened to undermine not only their radical beliefs but also their own self-identity. The writer Gleb Uspensky, to cite an extreme and tragic example, drove himself insane after years of trying to reconcile his romantic view of the peasants with the ugly reality of human relations which he was forced to observe in the countryside. Many of the 'realist' writers of the 1860s, who described the darker side of the countryside, ended up as alcoholics. There was a general sense of *Angst* amongst the liberal educated classes whenever the hard facts of peasant life disturbed their idealized images of it. Witness the storm of debate caused by the unflattering portrait of village life in Chekhov's *Peasants* (1897), the short story of a sick Moscow waiter who returns with his wife to his native village, only to find that his poverty-stricken family resents him for bringing another set of mouths to feed. Or the even greater public outrage at the publication of Bunin's novella *The Village* (1910), which spared nothing in its dark portrayal of peasant poverty and cruelty. 'What stunned the Russian reader in this book', a contemporary critic remarked, 'was not the depiction of the [peasants'] material, cultural and legal poverty . . . but the realization that there was no escape from it . . . The most that the Russian peasant, as depicted by Bunin, was capable of achieving . . . was only the awareness of his hopeless savagery, of being doomed.'[6]

Gorky wrote about *The Village* that it had forced society to think 'seriously not just about the peasant but about the grave question of whether Russia was to be or not to be?'[7] The enigma of the peasant stood at the heart of the problem of Russia's national self-identity. The 'Peasant Question' was the starting point of all those interminable debates (they fill the largely unread pages of nineteenth-century Russian novels) about the future of Russia itself.

Russia was still a peasant country at the turn of the twentieth century: 80 per cent of the population was classified as belonging to the peasantry; and most of the rest traced their roots back to it. Scratch a Russian townsman and one found a peasant. Most of the workers in the cities' factories and workshops, laundries and kitchens, bath-houses and shops, were either immigrants from the countryside or the children of such immigrants, who still returned to their farms for harvest and sent money back to their villages. Restaurants employed vast armies of peasant waiters, while the houses of the wealthy relied on peasant domestics in numbers that made European visitors gasp. The vendors on the city streets were mostly peasants by origin, as were the cabmen, doormen, hauliers, builders, gardeners, dustmen, draymen, hawkers, beggars, thieves and prostitutes. Russia's towns and cities all remained essentially 'peasant' in their social composition and character. Only a few miles from any city centre one would find oneself already in the backwoods, where there were bandits living in the forests, where roads turned into muddy bogs in spring, and where the external signs of life in the remote hamlets had remained essentially unchanged since the Middle Ages. Yet, despite living so close to the peasants, the educated classes of the cities knew next to nothing about their world. It was as exotic and alien to them as the natives of Africa were to their distant colonial rulers. And in this mutual incomprehension, in the cultural gulf between the 'Two Russias', lay the roots of the social revolution and its tragic destiny.

✻   ✻   ✻

The isolation of the peasantry from the rest of society was manifested at almost every level — legal, political, economic, cultural, social and geographic. The peasants inhabited three-quarters of a million rural settlements scattered across one-sixth of the world's surface. They rarely came across anything beyond the narrow confines of their own village and its fields, the parish church, the squire's manor and the local market. The village community was the centre of this small and isolated world. Indeed, the old peasant term for it (the *mir*) also carried the meaning in Russian of 'world', 'peace' and 'universe'. The *mir* was governed by an assembly of peasant elders which, alongside the land commune (*obshchina*), regulated virtually every aspect of village and agrarian life. Its powers of self-government had been considerably broadened by the Emancipation, when it took over most of the administrative, police and judicial functions of the landlords and became the basic unit of rural administration (*obshchestva*) subordinate to the rudimentary organs of state administration in the volost township. It controlled the land transferred to the peasants from the landlords during the Emancipation and was made collectively responsible for the payment of redemption dues on the land. In most parts of Russia the arable land was kept in communal tenure and every few years the *mir* would redistribute the hundreds of arable strips between the peasant households according to the number of workers or 'eaters' in each. It also set the common patterns of cultivation and grazing on the stubble necessitated by the open-field system of strip-farming;* managed the woods and communal pasture lands; hired village watchmen and shepherds; collected taxes; carried out the recruitment of soldiers; saw to the repair of roads, bridges and communal buildings; established charity and other welfare schemes; organized village holidays; maintained public order; arbitrated minor disputes; and administered justice in accordance with local custom.

The *mir* could engender strong feelings of communal solidarity among the peasants, bound as they were by their common ties to the village and to the land. This was reflected in many peasant sayings: 'What one man can't bear, the *mir* can'; 'No one is greater than the *mir*'; and so on.[8] The existence of such ties can be found in peasant communities throughout the world. They bear

---

* Since there were no hedges between the strips or the fields it was essential for every household to sow the same crops at the same time (e.g. a three-field rotation of winter/spring/fallow), otherwise the cattle left to graze on the stubble of one strip would trample on the crops of the neighbouring strip.

witness not so much to the 'natural collectivism' of the Russian people, so
beloved by the Slavophiles and the Populists, as to the functional logic of peasant
self-organization in the struggle for survival against the harsh realities of nature
and powerful external enemies, such as the landlords and the state. Indeed,
beneath the cloak of communal solidarity observed by outsiders, fellow villagers
continued to struggle between themselves for individual advantage. The village
was a hotbed of intrigue, vendettas, greed, dishonesty, meanness, and sometimes
gruesome acts of violence by one peasant neighbour against another; it was not
the haven of communal harmony that intellectuals from the city imagined it to
be. It was simply that the individual interests of the peasants were often best
served by collective activity. The brevity of the agricultural season in Russia,
from the thaw and the start of the spring ploughing in April to the first snows
in early November, made some form of labour co-operation essential so that
the major tasks of the agricultural cycle could be completed in brief bursts of
intense activity. That is why the traditional peasant household tended to be
much larger than its European counterpart, often containing more than a dozen
members with the wives and families of two or three brothers living under the
same roof as their parents. Statistical studies consistently highlighted the economic advantages of the bigger households (a higher proportion of adult male
labourers, more land and livestock per head and so on) and these had much to
do with the benefits of labour co-operation. The difficulties of small-scale
peasant farming, which in the vast majority of households was carried out with
only one horse and a tiny store of seed and tools, also made simple forms of
neighbourly co-operation, such as borrowing and lending, advantageous to all
parties. Finally, there were many worthwhile projects that could only be done
by the village as a whole, such as clearing woods and swamp-lands, constructing
barns, building roads and bridges, and organizing irrigation schemes.

The village assembly, or *skhod*, where these decisions were taken, was
attended by the peasant household elders and usually held on a public holiday
in the street or in a meadow, since few villages had a big enough building to
accommodate the whole meeting. There was no formal procedure as such. The
peasants stood around in loose groups, drinking, smoking and debating different
subjects of local interest, until the village elder, having mingled in the crowd
and ascertained the feelings of the dominant peasants, called for the meeting to
vote on a series of resolutions. Voting was done by shouting, or by standing in
groups, and all the resolutions were passed unanimously, for when opinion was
divided the minority always submitted to the majority, or, as the peasants put
it, to the 'will of the *mir*'. Romantic observers took this self-imposed conformity
as a sign of social harmony. In Aksakov's words, the commune expressed its
will as one, like a 'moral choir'. But in fact the decision-making was usually
dominated by a small clique of the oldest household heads, who were often also

the most successful farmers, and the rest of the villagers tended to follow their lead. The unanimity of the *mir* was not the reflection of some natural peasant harmony, but an imposed conformity set from above by the patriarchal elders of the village.

Some observers of peasant life (and this was to include the Bolsheviks) described these dominant patriarchs as 'commune-eaters' (*miroyedy*) or 'kulaks'.* These were the so-called 'rich' and 'cunning' peasants, 'petty-capitalist entre-preneurs', 'usurers', 'parasites' and 'strongmen', whom the rest of the villagers feared and whose greed and individualism would eventually lead to the commune's destruction. 'At the village assemblies', wrote one jurist in the early 1900s, 'the only people to participate are the loud-mouths and the lackeys of the rich. The honest working peasants do not attend, realising that their presence is useless.'[9]

But this too was by and large the outcome of looking at the peasants not for what they were but for the proof of some abstract theory, in this case the Marxist one. The dominant peasants within the village were, on the whole, the oldest patriarchs, who were often but not necessarily the heads of the richest households too. The late nineteenth-century Russian village still retained many of the features of what anthropologists would call a 'traditional society'. Although capitalism was certainly developing in Russia as a whole, apart from in a few specific regions it had yet to penetrate the village, where indeed the purpose of the commune was to limit its effects. The domination of the peasant patriarchs was not based on capitalist exploitation but on the fact that, by and large, this was still an oral culture, where the customs of the past, passed down through the generations, served as a model for the collective actions of the village in the present and the future: 'Our grandfathers did it this way, and so shall we.' In this sort of culture the old men were invariably deemed to be the most important people in the village — they had the most experience of farming and knew the most about the land — and their opinion was usually decisive. Old women, too, were respected for their expertise in handicrafts, medicine and magic. This was by and large a conservative culture. True, as the social anthropol-ogist Jack Goody's many works have shown, there are ways in which an oral culture may produce an informal dynamism: since no one knew for sure what their grandfathers did, the peasant elders could remake tradition in every gener-

---

* The term 'kulak', derived from the word for a 'fist', was originally used by the peasants to delineate exploitative elements (usurers, sub-renters of land, wheeler-dealers and so on) from the farming peasantry. An entrepreneurial peasant farmer, in their view, could not be a kulak, even if he hired labour. The Bolsheviks, by contrast, misused the term in a Marxist sense to describe any wealthy peasant. They made it synonymous with 'capitalist' on the false assumption that the use of hired labour in peasant farming was a form of 'capitalism'. Under Stalin, the term 'kulak' was employed against the smallholding peasantry as a whole. Through collectivization the regime set about the 'destruction of the kulaks as a class'.

ation to fit in with their changing needs. But on the whole the peasant patriarchs had an inbred mistrust of any ideas from the world outside their own experience. They aimed to preserve the village traditions and to defend them against progress. The 'old way of life' was always deemed to be better than the new. There was, they believed, a peasant utopia in the distant past, long before the gentry and the state had imposed their domination on the village.

Of course, it was true that there were broader forces leading to the decline of this patriarchal world. The money economy was slowly penetrating into remote rural areas. Urban manufactures were replacing the old peasant handicrafts. New technologies were becoming available to the enterprising peasant. Railways, roads, postal services and telegraphs were opening up the village to the outside world. Hospitals and schools, reading clubs and libraries, local government and political parties, were all moving closer to the peasantry. The growth of rural schooling, in particular, was giving rise to a new generation of 'conscious' peasant men and women — young and literate, thrifty and sober, self-improving and individualistic — who sought to overturn the old village world.

We can see it first in the fragmentation of the patriarchal household during the later nineteenth century. There was a sharp rise in the rate of household partitions following the Emancipation. Between 1861 and 1884 the annual rate of partitions rose from 82,000 to 140,000 households. Over 40 per cent of all peasant households were divided in these years. As a result, the average household size in central Russia declined from 9.5 members to 6.8. The peasants were moving from the traditional extended family to the modern nuclear one. Such partitions made little economic sense — the newly partitioned households, like the ones from which they had split, were left with much less livestock, tools and labour than before — and this was a cause of considerable anxiety to the tsarist government, which for moral and social reasons as much as for economic ones saw the peasantry's livelihood as dependent upon the survival of the patriarchal family. But it was the individualistic aspirations of the younger peasants that maintained the pressure for these partitions, in spite of their economic costs. Peasant sons and their young wives, fed up with the tyranny of the household elder, were breaking away to set up their own farms rather than wait until his death (when they themselves might be forty or fifty) to take his place at the household head. Their new farms might be small and weak but at least they were working for themselves. 'In the small family', explained one young peasant in the 1880s, 'everyone works for himself, everyone earns for himself; but if the family is large, then he doesn't end up with anything for himself.' The rate of partitioning was directly related to the involvement of the peasantry in off-farm employment as labourers. Once the younger peasants were earning wages there was a marked increase in disputes between them and their household elders over money and property. Peasant sons would refuse to send their wages home, or would set up their own farm rather than share their earnings in the household fund. They made the distinction between their own private earnings off the farm and the family's common property from its collective labour on it.[10] It was a sign of their own growing sense of individual worth: 'I earn money therefore I am.'

The growing literacy of the younger peasants was another source of their aspiring individualism. Literacy in Russia rose from 21 per cent of the Empire's population in 1897 to 40 per cent on the eve of the First World War. The highest rural rates were among young men in those regions closest to the cities. Nine out of ten peasant recruits into the imperial army from the two provinces of Petersburg and Moscow were considered literate by 1904. These peasant youths were the main beneficiaries of the boom in rural schooling during the last decades of the old regime. The number of primary schools quadrupled (from 25,000 to 100,000) between 1878 and 1911; and well over half the peasant children of school age (eight to eleven) were enrolled in primary schools by the latter date.[11]

The link between literacy and revolutions is a well-known historical phenomenon. The three great revolutions of modern European history — the English, the French and the Russian — all took place in societies where the rate of literacy was approaching 50 per cent. The local activists of the Russian Revolution were drawn mainly from this newly literate generation. Ironically, in its belated efforts to educate the common people, the tsarist regime was helping to dig its own grave.

Literacy has a profound effect on the peasant mind and community. It promotes abstract thought and enables the peasant to master new skills and technologies, which in turn help him to accept the concept of progress that fuels change in the modern world. It also weakens the village's patriarchal order by breaking down the barriers between it and the outside world, and by shifting power within the village to those with access to the written word. The young and literate peasant was much better equipped than his father to deal with the new agricultural technologies of the late nineteenth century; with the accounting methods of the money system; with written contracts, land deeds and loan agreements; and with the whole new world of administration — from the simple recording of clock-time and dates, to the reading of official documents and the formulation of village resolutions and petitions to the higher authorities — into which they entered after 1861. The status of the young and literate peasant rose as the market and bureaucracy filtered down to the village level and the peasant community relied more upon leaders with the skills which this new society demanded.

The written word divided the village into two generational groups. The older and illiterate generation feared and mistrusted too much education ('You can't eat books') and tried to limit its corrosive effects on the traditional culture of the village. They were worried by the urban-individualistic ways — the fashions and haircuts, the growing disrespect for peasant elders, and the dangerous political ideas — which the young picked up from their reading. As an inspector of church schools — who was clearly sympathetic to these concerns — wrote in 1911:

> The only thing observed [as a result of schooling] is a heightened interest in tasteless and useless dandyism. In many areas, the normal peasant dress is being replaced by urban styles, which cut deeply into the peasants' skimpy budget, hindering major improvements to other, far more important sides of peasant life ... Family ties, the very foundation of the well-being of state and society, have been deeply shaken. Complaints about insubordination to parents and elders are ubiquitous. Young men and adolescents often verbally abuse their elders and even beat them; they file complaints in the courts and remove from the home whatever [possessions] they can. It seems that parents have lost all authority over their children.[12]

On the other hand, the younger peasants — and with the explosion of the rural population they were fast becoming the majority (65 per cent of the rural population was aged under thirty by 1897)[13] — placed education at the top of their list of priorities. It was the key to their social betterment. This cultural divide was to be a major feature of the peasant revolution. One part of it was progressive and reforming: it sought to bring the village closer to the influences of the modern urban world. But another part of the peasant revolution was restorationist: it tried to defend the traditional village against these very influences. We shall see how these two conflicting forces affected the life of a single village when we turn to the story of Sergei Semenov and the revolution in Andreevskoe.

Nevertheless, despite these modernizing forces, the basic structure of peasant politics remained essentially patriarchal. Indeed the upholders of the patriarchal order had a whole range of social controls with which to stem the tide of modernity. In every aspect of the peasants' lives, from their material culture to their legal customs, there was a relentless conformity. The peasants all wore the same basic clothes. Even their hairstyles were the same — the men with their hair parted down the middle and cut underneath a bowl, the women's hair plaited, until they were married, and then covered with a scarf. The peasants in the traditional village were not supposed to assert their individual identity, as the people of the city did, by a particular fashion of dress. They had very little sense of privacy. All household members ate their meals from a common pot and slept together in one room. Lack of private spaces, not to speak of fertility rites, dictated that the sexual act was kept at least partly in the public domain. It was still a common practice in some parts of Russia for a peasant bride to be deflowered before the whole village; and if the groom proved impotent, his place could be taken by an older man, or by the finger of the matchmaker. Modesty had very little place in the peasant world. Toilets were in the open air. Peasant women were constantly baring their breasts, either to inspect and fondle them or to nurse their babies, while peasant men were quite unselfconscious about playing with their genitals. Urban doctors were shocked by the peasant customs of spitting into a person's eye to get rid of sties, of feeding children mouth to mouth, and of calming baby boys by sucking on their penis.[14]

The huts of the peasants, both in their external aspect and in their internal layout and furnishings, conformed to the same rigid pattern that governed the rest of their lives. Throughout Russia, in fact, there were only three basic types of peasant housing: the northern *izba*, or log hut, with the living quarters and outbuildings all contained under one roof around a quadrangle; the southern *izba*, with the outbuildings separate from the living quarters; and the Ukrainian *khata*, again a separate building made of wood or clay, but with a thatched roof. Every hut contained the same basic elements: a cooking space, where the stove was located, upon which the peasants (despite the cockroaches) liked to sleep; a 'red'* or 'holy' corner, where the icons were hung, guests were entertained, and the family ate around a whitewashed table; and a sleeping area, where in winter it was common to find goats, foals and calves bedded down in the straw alongside the humans. The moist warmth and smell of the animals, the black fumes of the kerosene lamps, and the pungent odour of the home-cured tobacco, which the peasants smoked rolled up in newspaper, combined to create a unique, noxious atmosphere. 'The doors are kept vigorously closed, windows are hermetically sealed and the atmosphere cannot be described,' wrote an English Quaker from one Volga village. 'Its poisonous quality can only be realised by experience.' Given such unsanitary conditions, it is hardly surprising that even as late as the 1900s one in four peasant babies died before the age of one. Those who survived could expect to live in poor health for an average of about thirty-five years.[15] Peasant life in Russia really was nasty, brutish and short.

It was also cramped by strict conformity to the social mores of the village. Dissident behaviour brought upon its perpetrators various punishments, such as village fines, ostracism, or some sort of public humiliation. The most common form of humiliation was 'rough music', or *charivari*, as it was known in

---

* The Russian word for red (*krasnyi*) is connected with the word for beautiful (*krasivyi*), a fact of powerful symbolic significance for the revolutionary movement.

southern Europe, where the villagers made a rumpus outside the house of the guilty person until he or she appeared and surrendered to the crowd, who would then subject him or her to public shame or even violent punishment. Adulterous wives and horse-thieves suffered the most brutal punishments. It was not uncommon for cheating wives to be stripped naked and beaten by their husbands, or tied to the end of a wagon and dragged naked through the village. Horse-thieves could be castrated, beaten, branded with hot irons, or hacked to death with sickles. Other transgressors were known to have had their eyes pulled out, nails hammered into their body, legs and arms cut off, or stakes driven down their throat. A favourite punishment was to raise the victim on a pulley with his feet and hands tied together and to drop him so that the vertebrae in his back were broken; this was repeated several times until he was reduced to a spineless sack. In another form of torture the naked victim was wrapped in a wet sack, a pillow was tied around his torso, and his stomach beaten with hammers, logs and stones, so that his internal organs were crushed without leaving any external marks on his body.[16]

It is difficult to say where this barbarism came from — whether it was the culture of the Russian peasants, or the harsh environment in which they lived. During the revolution and civil war the peasantry developed even more gruesome forms of killing and torture. They mutilated the bodies of their victims, cut off their heads and disgorged their internal organs. Revolution and civil war are extreme situations, and there is no guarantee that anyone else, regardless of their nationality, would not act in a similar fashion given the same circumstances. But it is surely right to ask, as Gorky did in his famous essay 'On the Russian Peasantry' (1922), whether in fact the revolution had not merely brought out, as he put it, 'the exceptional cruelty of the Russian people'? This was a cruelty made by history. Long after serfdom had been abolished the land captains exercised their right to flog the peasants for petty crimes. Liberals rightly warned about the psychological effects of this brutality. One physician, addressing the Kazan Medical Society in 1895, said that it 'not only debases but even hardens and brutalizes human nature'. Chekhov, who was also a practising physician, denounced corporal punishment, adding that 'it coarsens and brutalizes not only the offenders but also those who execute the punishments and those who are present at it'.[17] The violence and cruelty which the old regime inflicted on the peasant was transformed into a peasant violence which not only disfigured daily village life, but which also rebounded against the regime in the terrible violence of the revolution.

If the Russian village was a violent place, the peasant household was even worse. For centuries the peasants had claimed the right to beat their wives. Russian peasant proverbs were full of advice on the wisdom of such beatings:

IMAGES OF AUTOCRACY

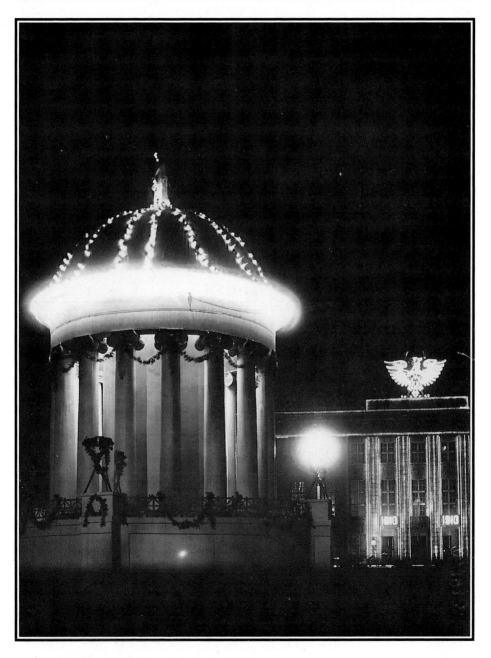

1 St Petersburg illuminated for the Romanov tercentenary in 1913. This electric display of state power was the biggest light show in tsarist history.

2 The imperial family rides from the Winter Palace to the Kazan Cathedral for the opening ceremony of the tercentenary.

3 Nicholas II rides in public view for the first time since the 1905 Revolution.

4 The famous Yeliseev store on Nevsky Prospekt is decorated for the tercentenary.

5 Guards officers greeting the imperial family at the Kazan Cathedral. Note the icons, the religious banners, and the crosses of the onlookers.

6 Townspeople and peasants come to see the Tsar in Kostroma during the tercentenary provincial tour.

7 The court ball of 1903 was a landmark in the cult of ancient Muscovy. Each guest dressed in the seventeenth-century costume of his twentieth-century rank. The Tsar and Tsarina are standing in the centre of the front row.

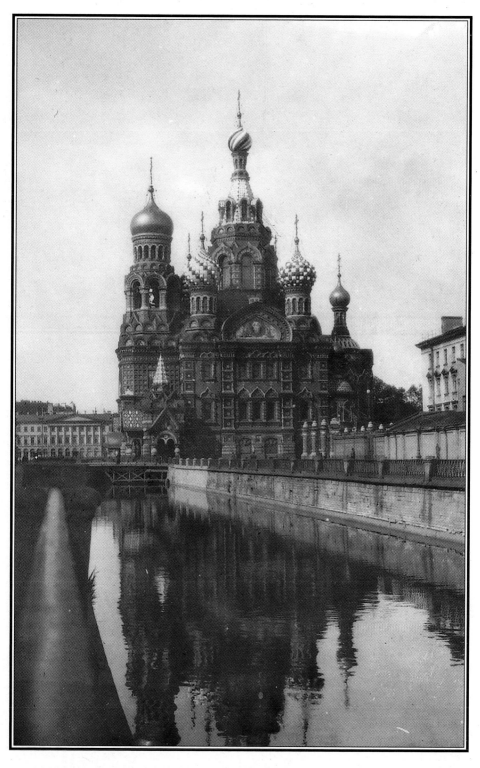

8 The Temple of Christ's Resurrection on the Catherine Canal – a hideous example of the last tsars' efforts to 'Muscovitize' St Petersburg.

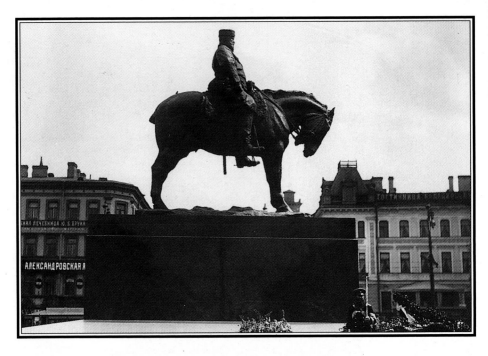

9 Trubetskoi's bronze statue of Alexander III on Znamenskaia Square in St Petersburg. The workers called it 'the hippopotamus'.

10 The Moscow statue of Alexander III – with its back to the Cathedral of Christ the Saviour – at its opening ceremony in 1913.

11 The imperial family (*right to left*): Olga, Tatyana, Nicholas, Alexandra, Maria, Alexis and Anastasia.

12 Rasputin with his admirers. Anna Vyrubova, the closest friend of both Rasputin and the Empress, is standing fifth from left.

13 The Tsarevich Alexis with his playmate and protector, the sailor Derevenko. After the February Revolution Derevenko joined the Bolsheviks.

'Hit your wife with the butt of the axe, get down and see if she's breathing. If she is, she's shamming and wants some more.'

'The more you beat the old woman, the tastier the soup will be.'

'Beat your wife like a fur coat, then there'll be less noise.'

'A wife is nice twice: when she's brought into the house [as a bride] and when she's carried out of it to her grave.'

Popular proverbs also put a high value on the beating of men: 'For a man that has been beaten you have to offer two unbeaten ones, and even then you may not clinch the bargain.' There were even peasant sayings to suggest that a good life was not complete without violence: 'Oh, it's a jolly life, only there's no one to beat.' Fighting was a favourite pastime of the peasants. At Christmas, Epiphany and Shrovetide there were huge and often fatal fist-fights between different sections of the village, sometimes even between villages, the women and children included, accompanied by heavy bouts of drinking. Petty village disputes frequently ended in fights. 'Just because of a broken earthenware pot, worth about 12 kopecks,' Gorky wrote from his time at Krasnovidovo, 'three families fought with sticks, an old woman's arm got broken and a young boy had his skull cracked. Quarrels like this happened every week.'[18] This was a culture in which life was cheap and, however one explains the origins of this violence, it was to play a major part in the revolution.

Many people explained the violence of the peasant world by the weakness of the legal order and the general lawlessness of the state. The Emancipation had liberated the serfs from the judicial tyranny of their landlords but it had not incorporated them in the world ruled by law, which included the rest of society. Excluded from the written law administered through the civil courts, the newly liberated peasants were kept in a sort of legal apartheid after 1861. The tsarist regime looked upon them as a cross between savages and children, and subjected them to magistrates appointed from the gentry. Their legal rights were confined to the peasant-class courts, which operated on the basis of local custom. The peasants were deprived of many civil rights taken for granted by the members of other social estates. Until 1906, they did not have the right to own their allotments. Legal restrictions severely limited their mobility. Peasants could not leave the village commune without paying off their share of the collective tax burden or of the redemption payments on the land gained from the nobles during the Emancipation. For a household to separate from the commune, a complex bureaucratic procedure was necessary, requiring the consent of at least two-thirds of the village assembly, and this was difficult to obtain.* Even a peasant wanting to leave the village for a few weeks on migrant labour could not do so without first obtaining an internal passport from the commune's elders (who were usually opposed to such migration on the grounds that it weakened the patriarchal household and increased the tax burden on the rest of the village). Statistics show that the issuing of passports was heavily restricted, despite the demands of industrialization and commercial agriculture for such migrant labour.[19] The peasants remained tied to the land and, although serfdom had been abolished, it enjoyed a vigorous afterlife in the regulation of the peasant. Deprived of the consciousness and the legal rights of citizenship, it is hardly surprising that the peasants respected neither the state's law nor its authority when its coercive power over them was removed in 1905 and again in 1917.

*   *   *

It is mistaken to suppose, as so many historians do, that the Russian peasantry had no moral order or ideology at all to substitute for the tsarist state. Richard Pipes, for example, in his recent history of the revolution, portrays the peasants as primitive and ignorant people who could only play a destructive role in the revolution and who were therefore ripe for manipulation by the Bolsheviks. Yet, as we shall see, during 1917–18 the peasants proved themselves quite capable of restructuring the whole of rural society, from the system of land relations and local trade to education and justice, and in so doing they often revealed a remarkable political sophistication, which did not well up from a moral vacuum. The ideals of the peasant revolution had their roots in a long tradition of peasant dreaming and utopian philosophy. Through peasant proverbs, myths, tales, songs and customary law, a distinctive ideology emerges which expressed itself in the peasants' actions throughout the revolutionary years from 1902 to 1921. That ideology had been shaped by centuries of opposition to the tsarist state. As Herzen put it, for hundreds of years the peasant's 'whole life has been one long, dumb, passive opposition to the existing order of things: he has endured oppression, he has groaned under it; but he has never accepted anything that goes on outside the life of the commune'.[20] It was in this cultural confrontation, in the way that the peasant looked at the world outside his village, that the revolution had its roots.

Let us look more closely at this peasant world-view as expressed in customary law. Contrary to the view of some historians, peasant customary law

---

* Even in communes with hereditary tenure (mainly in the north-west and the Ukraine) it was hardly easier. There the household wishing to separate had either to pay off its share of the communal tax debt in full (a near-impossible task for the vast majority of the peasants) or find another household willing to take over the tax burden in return for its land allotment. Since the taxes usually exceeded the cost of rented land outside the commune, it was difficult to find a household willing to do this.

contained a fairly comprehensive set of moral concepts. True, these were not always applied uniformly. The peasant-class courts often functioned in a random manner, deciding cases on the basis of the litigants' reputations and connections, or on the basis of which side was prepared to bribe the elected judges with the most vodka. Yet, amidst all this chaos, there could be discerned some pragmatic concepts of justice, arising from the peasants' daily lives, which had crystallized into more-or-less universal legal norms, albeit with minor regional variations.

Three legal ideas, in particular, shaped the peasant revolutionary mind. The first was the concept of family ownership. The assets of the peasant household (the livestock, the tools, the crops, the buildings and their contents, but not the land beneath them) were regarded as the common property of the family.* Every member of the household was deemed to have an equal right to use these assets, including those not yet born. The patriarch of the household, the *bol'shak*, it is true, had an authoritarian influence over the running of the farm and the disposal of its assets. But customary law made it clear that he was expected to act with the consent of the other adult members of the family and that, on his death, he could not bequeath any part of the household property, which was to remain in the common ownership of the family under a new *bol'shak* (usually the eldest son). If the *bol'shak* mismanaged the family farm, or was too often drunk and violent, the commune could replace him under customary law with another household member. The only way the family property could be divided was through the partition of an extended household into smaller units, according to the methods set out by local customary law. In all regions of Russia this stipulated that the property was to be divided on an equal basis between all the adult males, with provision being made for the elderly and unmarried women.[21] The principles of family ownership and egalitarian partition were deeply ingrained in Russian peasant culture. This helps to explain the failure of the Stolypin land reforms (1906–17), which, as part of their programme to create a stratum of well-to-do capitalist farmers, attempted to convert the family property of the peasant household into the private property of the *bol'shak*, thus enabling him to bequeath it to one or more of his sons.† The peasant revolution of 1917 made a clean sweep of these reforms, returning to the traditional legal principles of family ownership.

The peasant family farm was organized and defined according to the

---

* The one major exception was the peasant wife's dowry and other personal effects (e.g. clothing and domestic utensils), which were regarded as her private property and could be passed on to her daughter.

† Whereas the partitioning of household property was entirely controlled by local customary law, Stolypin's new laws of inheritance came under the Civil Code. Cases concerning peasant inheritance of land were thus heard in the civil (i.e. non-peasant) courts — the first major instance of the peasantry being integrated into the national legal system.

labour principle, the second major peasant legal concept. Membership of
the household was defined by active participation in the life of the farm (or,
as the peasants put it, 'eating from the common pot') rather than by blood or
kinship ties. An outsider adopted by the family who lived and worked on the
farm was usually viewed as a full member of the household with equal rights to
those of the blood relatives, whereas a son of the family who left the village
to earn his living elsewhere eventually ceased to be seen as a household member.
This same attachment of rights to labour could be seen on the land as well.*
The peasants believed in a sacred link between land and labour. The land
belonged to no one but God, and could not be bought or sold. But every family
had the right to support itself from the land on the basis of its own labour,
and the commune was there to ensure its equal distribution between them.[22] On
this basis — that the land should be in the hands of those who tilled it — the
squires did not hold their land rightfully and the hungry peasants were justified
in their struggle to take it from them. A constant battle was fought between the
written law of the state, framed to defend the property rights of the landowners,
and the customary law of the peasants, used by them to defend their own
transgressions of those property rights. Under customary law, for example, no
one thought it wrong when a peasant stole wood from the landlord's forest,
since the landlord had more wood than he could personally use and, as the
proverb said, 'God grew the forest for everyone.' The state categorized as 'crimes'
a whole range of activities which peasant custom did not: poaching and grazing
livestock on the squire's land; gathering mushrooms and berries from his forest;
picking fruit from his orchards; fishing in his ponds, and so on. Customary law
was a tool which the peasants used to subvert a legal order that in their view
maintained the unjust domination of the landowners and the biggest landowner
of all: the state.† It is no coincidence that the revolutionary land legislation of
1917–18 based itself on the labour principles found in customary law.

The subjective approach to the law — judging the merits of a case
according to the social and economic position of the parties concerned — was
the third specific aspect of the peasantry's legal thinking which had an affinity
with the revolution. It was echoed in the Bolshevik concept of 'revolutionary
justice', the guiding principle of the People's Courts of 1917–18, according to

---

* For example, under customary law a peasant found guilty of tilling another man's land was
always compensated for his labour, though the bulk of the harvest went to the land's rightful
holder. The peasants, in the words of one observer, 'looked on the right to own the product of
one's own labour on the land with an almost religious respect' and by custom this had to be
balanced against the formal right of land tenure (Efimenko, *Issledovaniia*, 2, 143).

† This was partly the reason why peasants had so few scruples about perjuring themselves in
court and, indeed, why they tended to sympathize with convicted criminals. It was common for
peasants to give away food to gangs of prisoners as they passed through the villages on their way
to Siberia.

which a man's social class was taken as the decisive factor in determining his guilt or innocence. The peasants considered stealing from a rich man, especially by the poor, a much less serious offence than stealing from a man who could barely feed himself and his family.* In the peasants' view it was even justified, as we have seen, to kill someone guilty of a serious offence against the community. And to murder a stranger from outside the village was clearly not as bad as killing a fellow villager. Similarly, whereas deceiving a neighbour was seen by the peasants as obviously immoral, cheating on a landlord or a government official was not subject to any moral censure; such 'cunning' was just one of the many everyday forms of passive resistance used by peasants to subvert an unjust established order.[23] Within the context of peasant society this subjective approach was not without its own logic, since the peasants viewed justice in terms of its direct practical effects on their own communities rather than in general or abstract terms. But it could often result in the sort of muddled thinking that made people call the peasants 'dark'. In *The Criminal*, for example, Chekhov tells the true story of a peasant who was brought to court for stealing a bolt from the railway tracks to use as a weight on his fishing tackle. He fails to understand his guilt and in trying to justify himself repeatedly talks of 'we' (the peasants of his village): 'Bah! Look how many years we have been removing bolts, and God preserve us, and here you are talking about a crash, people killed. We do not remove all of them — we always leave some. We do not act without thinking. We do understand.'

Here, in this moral subjectivity, was the root of the peasant's instinctive anarchism. He lived outside the realm of the state's laws — and that is where he chose to stay. Centuries of serfdom had bred within the peasant a profound mistrust of all authority outside his own village. What he wanted was *volia*, the ancient peasant concept of freedom and autonomy without restraints from the powers that be. 'For hundreds of years', wrote Gorky, 'the Russian peasant has dreamt of a state with no right to influence the will of the individual and his freedom of action, a state without power over man.' That peasant dream was kept alive by subversive tales of Stenka Razin and Emelian Pugachev, those peasant revolutionaries of the seventeenth and eighteenth centuries, whose mythical images continued as late as the 1900s to be seen by the peasants flying as ravens across the Volga announcing the advent of utopia. And there were equally fabulous tales of a 'Kingdom of Opona', somewhere on the edge of the flat earth, where the peasants lived happily, undisturbed by gentry or state. Groups of peasants even set out on expeditions in the far north in the hope of finding this arcadia.[24]

---

* This was connected with the religious belief of the peasants that to be poor was to be virtuous.

As the state attempted to extend its bureaucratic control into the countryside during the late nineteenth century, the peasants sought to defend their autonomy by developing ever more subtle forms of passive resistance to it. What they did, in effect, was to set up a dual structure of administration in the villages: a formal one, with its face to the state, which remained inactive and inefficient; and an informal one, with its face to the peasants, which was quite the opposite. The village elders and tax collectors elected to serve in the organs of state administration in the villages (*obshchestva*) and the volost townships (*upravy*) were, in the words of one frustrated official, 'highly unreliable and unsatisfactory', many of them having been deliberately chosen for their incompetence in order to sabotage government work. There were even cases where the peasants elected the village idiot as their elder.[25] Meanwhile, the real centre of power remained in the *mir*, in the old village assembly dominated by the patriarchs. The power of the tsarist state never really penetrated the village, and this remained its fundamental weakness until 1917, when the power of the state was removed altogether and the village gained its *volia*.

The educated classes had always feared that a peasant *volia* would soon degenerate into anarchic licence and violent revenge against figures of authority. Belinsky wrote in 1837: 'Our people understand freedom as *volia*, and *volia* for the people means to make mischief. The liberated Russian nation will not head for the parliament but will run for the tavern to drink liquor, smash glasses, and hang the nobility, whose only guilt is to shave their beards and wear a frock-coat instead of a peasant tunic.'[26] The revolution would, in all too many ways, fulfil Belinsky's prophecy.

ii The Quest to Banish the Past

As a young girl in the 1900s the writer Nina Berberova used to observe the peasants as they came to consult her grandfather in his study on the family estate near Tver. 'They were of two kinds,' she recalled, 'and it seemed to me that they were two completely different breeds':

Some muzhiks [peasants] were demure, well bred, important-looking, with greasy hair, fat paunches, and shiny faces. They were dressed in embroidered shirts and caftans of fine cloth. These were the ones who were later called kulaks. They ... felled trees for new homes in the thick woods that only recently had been Grandfather's. They walked in the church with collection trays and placed candles before the Saint-Mary-Appease-My-Grief icon. But what kind of grief could they have? The Peasants' Credit Bank gave them credit. In their houses, which I sometimes visited, there were geraniums on the window sills and the smell of rich buns from the ovens. Their sons grew into energetic and ambitious men, began new lives for themselves, and created a new class in embryo for Russia.

The other muzhiks wore bast sandals, dressed in rags, bowed fawningly, never went further than the doors, and had faces that had lost all human expression . . . They were undersized, and often lay in ditches near the state-owned wine shop. Their children did not grow because they were underfed. Their consumptive wives seemed always to be in the final month of pregnancy, the infants were covered with weeping eczema, and in their homes, which I also visited, broken windows were stopped up with rags, and calves and hens were kept in the corners. There was a sour stench.[27]

The differences between rich and poor peasants had been widely debated since the 1870s, when the whole issue of rural poverty and its causes had first come to the shocked attention of the Russian public. To Marxists and many liberals it was axiomatic that the peasantry should be divided into two separate classes — the one of entrepreneurial farmers, the other of landless labourers — as capitalism took root in the Russian countryside. But the Populists, who dreamt of a united peasantry leading Russia directly towards socialism, denied this process was taking place at all. Each side produced a library of statistics to prove or disprove that capitalism was leading to the disintegration of the peasantry, and historians today still dispute their significance.

There were, it is true, growing inequalities between the richest and the poorest sections of the peasantry. At one extreme there was a small but growing class of wealthy peasant entrepreneurs; at the other an impoverished peasantry increasingly forced to abandon its farms and join the army of migrant wage-labourers in agriculture, mining, transport and industry. The young Lenin set out to prove in the 1890s that these two extremes were the result of capitalist development. But this is not necessarily true.

The major differences in the living standards of the peasantry were in fact geographic. Commercial farming had taken root in a circular band of regions around the periphery of the old Muscovite centre of Russia during the nineteenth century. In parts of the Baltic the Emancipation of the serfs in 1817 had enabled the local landowners, with access to the Western grain markets, to turn their estates into capitalist farms worked by wage-labourers. In the western Ukraine, too, the nobles had established huge sugar-beet farms. Meanwhile, in the fertile regions of south Russia, the Kuban and the northern Caucasus a wealthy stratum of mixed farmers had emerged from the peasants and the Cossacks. The same was true in western Siberia, where the building of the Trans-Siberian Railway had made it possible for the smallholders to grow rich producing cereals and dairy products for the market. These regions accounted for the national rise in peasant living standards — reflected in their increased spending-power — which recent historians have detected and used to refute the old historical orthodoxy that the peasants were becoming increasingly impoverished before 1917.[28] What was emerging, in fact, was a growing divergence in the economic position of the peasantry between the new and relatively affluent areas of commercial farming in the west, the south and the east, on the one hand, and, on the other, the old and increasingly overpopulated central agricultural zone, where the majority of the gentry's estates were located, and where backward farming methods were unable to maintain all of the peasants on the land. It is no coincidence that after 1917 the richer agricultural regions became strongholds of counter-revolution, whereas the impoverished central zone remained loyal to the revolution.

In the central agricultural zone of Russia there were few signs of commercialism and the main inequalities in the living standards of the peasants were explained by local differences in the quality of the soil or by historic legacies stretching back to the days of serfdom. So, for example, villages made up of former state peasants (i.e. peasants settled on state land) tended to be more land-rich than villages of former serfs. The market economy was weak in these regions and most peasants were engaged in a natural system of production. They sold a small amount of produce and perhaps some handicrafts, the product of their winter labours, in order to pay off their taxes and buy a few household goods, but otherwise their production was geared towards the basic food requirements of the family. According to a zemstvo survey of the 1880s, two out of three peasant households in the central Russian province of Tambov were unable to feed themselves without getting into debt. 'In our village', recalled Semenov, 'only five or six families managed to survive the whole year on their own. As for the rest, some got by until the Mikhailov holiday [in early November], some until Christmas, and some until Shrovetide, but then they had to borrow to buy grain.' It was the tragedy of millions of peasants that constant debt and taxes forced them to sell off their grain in the autumn, when supplies were plentiful and prices were low, only to buy it back in the hungry spring, when prices were at their peak. Every volost township had its handful of usurers and merchants — the peasants called them 'kulaks' — who bought up the peasants' grain cheaply in the autumn and, six months later, sold it back to them at twice the price. Theirs was a hard and cruel greed, the sort to be found, as one contemporary put it, in 'a thoroughly uneducated man who has made his way from poverty to wealth and has come to consider money-making, by whatever means, as the only pursuit to which a rational being should devote himself.' Whole villages were indebted to these 'kulaks', and many were forced to sell part of their land to repay them. If this was 'capitalism', as the Bolsheviks insisted, it was of a primitive kind.[29]

The number of 'capitalist' peasants (those employing permanent wage-labour) was probably no more than I per cent.[30] That more of them did not emerge had much to do with the periodic redistribution of the communal allotment land; and with the fact that the richest peasant farms, which also tended to have the most members, customarily divided their property when the adult sons were married and ready to set up new family households of their own.* In other words, the peasants failed to become capitalists because they rarely held on to their property for more than a generation.

Nor did peasant poverty have much to do with the development of capitalism. The basic problem in the central agricultural zone was that the peasantry's egalitarian customs gave them little incentive to produce anything other than babies. The birth-rate in Russia (at about fifty births for every 1,000 people every year) was nearly twice the European average during the second half of the nineteenth century, and the highest rates of all were in the areas of communal tenure where the holding of land was fixed according to family size. The astronomical rise of the peasant population (from 50 to 79 million during 1861–1897) resulted in a growing shortage of land. By the turn of the century 7 per cent of the peasant households had no land at all, while one in five had only a tiny plot of less than one *desyatina* (2.7 acres). This may seem odd in a country the size of Russia. But in central Russia, where most of the peasantry lived, the density of the population was similar to that of Western Europe. The average peasant allotment, at 2.6 *desyatiny* in 1900, was comparable in size to the typical smallholding in France or Germany. But Russian peasant farming was much less intensive, with grain yields at barely half the level reached in the rest of Europe. The light wooden scratch plough used by the majority of Russian peasants with a single horse, or a pair of oxen, was similar to the *aratrum* used in the Roman Empire and vastly inferior to the heavy iron ploughs used in Western Europe with a four- or six-horse team. The small hand sickle was still being used on most peasant farms in Russia on the eve of the First World War, more than a half-century after it had been replaced by the scythe and the heavy reaping hook in the West. Sowing, threshing and winnowing were all done by hand, long after they had been mechanized elsewhere. The application of manure, let alone of chemical fertilizers, was far behind European standards. And the

---

* So, for example, a study in Tula province found that 62 per cent of the peasant households with four or more horses had partitioned their property between 1899 and 1911, compared with only 23 per cent of those with one horse (Shanin, *Awkward Class*, 83). Statisticians such as A. V. Chayanov believed that the life-cycle of the peasant household largely explained economic inequalities within the village. The newly partitioned household, consisting of a married couple and one or two children, tended to have only a small plot of land and very little livestock. But as the children grew up and began to contribute as workers to the family economy, the household was able to accumulate more land and livestock, until it partitioned itself. Chayanov argued that the statistical surveys used by the Marxists to show the economic differentiation of the peasantry were in fact no more than 'snapshots' of the peasant households at different stages of this life-cycle.

advanced field rotations, root crops alternating with cereals, which had been introduced into Western Europe during the agricultural revolution of the eighteenth century, were still largely unknown in backward peasant Russia.[31]

Under these circumstances, lacking the capital to modernize their farms, the only way for the peasants to feed the growing number of mouths was to bring more land under the plough. The easiest way to achieve this within the three-field system was by reducing the size of the fallow land — and thousands of villages did just that. But the long-term effect was only to make the situation worse, since the soil was exhausted by being overworked, while livestock herds (the main source of fertilizer) were reduced because of the shortage of fallow and other pasture lands. By the turn of the century one in three peasant households did not even have a horse.[32] To cultivate their land they had to hire horses or else attach themselves to the plough. There is no sadder symbol of the crippling poverty in which millions of peasants were forced to live than the image of a peasant and his son struggling to drag a plough through the mud.

The most tempting solution to the peasantry's hunger for land could be seen every day from their villages — in the form of the squire's estate. 'Every single peasant', wrote Prince Lvov, 'believed from the very bottom of his soul that one day, sooner or later, the squire's land would belong to him.' One-third of the arable land in Russia was owned by nobles in the 1870s. By 1905 this proportion had declined to 22 per cent, mainly as a result of peasant communal purchases (the peasant share of landownership had increased in these years from 58 per cent to 68 per cent). Moreover, by this time about one-third of the gentry land was rented out to the peasantry. Yet this should not deceive us into thinking, as so many right-wing historians have claimed, that there was no land problem. Most of the peasants who rented land from the gentry did so under the pressure of poverty rather than of wealth: with the rapid rise of the peasant population they had come to depend on renting extra land to feed themselves and their families. For this reason, they were often prepared to pay a much higher rent than the land was worth in strictly economic terms. It was the readiness of the peasant family to work itself into the ground in order to feed itself that fuelled the seven-fold increase in rental values, on which the late-nineteenth-century gentry lived.[33]

There was a clear geographic pattern in peasant–gentry land relations which helps to explain the distinctive distribution of agrarian violence during the revolution. The peasant war against the squires, both in 1905 and 1917, was concentrated in an arc of provinces around the southern edge of the central agricultural zone (from Samara and Saratov in the south-east, through Tambov, Voronezh, Kursk, Kharkov, Chernigov, Ekaterinoslav, Kherson and Poltava, as far as Kiev and Podolia in the south-west). These were regions of peasant overpopulation and large-scale landownership by the gentry. Land rents were high and wages low. They were also regions where the fertile soil and the relatively long growing season favoured the development of commercial farming in wheat, sugar-beet and other crops suitable for mechanization. In other words, the peasants of these transitional regions were caught in the worst of all possible worlds: between the old pre-capitalist system of agriculture in the centre, and the emergent system of commercial farming at the periphery. As long as the landowners continued to lease out their land to them, albeit at exorbitant prices, then the peasants could just about survive. With the depression of world agricultural prices between 1878 and 1896 most of the landowners had done just that. But then cereal prices rose, freight transportation became cheaper, and, encouraged by the prospect of high profits, many landowners returned to their estates to transform them into commercial farms. Between 1900 and 1914 the amount of arable farmed by the landowning gentry in Russia increased by almost a third, and in these transitional regions the increase was considerably more. In Poltava province, for example, which saw the first wave of real peasant violence in 1902, the amount of land farmed by the squires almost doubled in these years. Land previously leased out to the peasants — and upon which the peasants had relied in order to feed their families — was withdrawn from them, or else rented under even more exploitative conditions. These often involved a switch from money rent to rental payments by labour on the squire's estate (*otrabotka*) which the peasants saw as a new type of serfdom. Moreover, many of these large-scale commercial farms were mechanized with the introduction of harvesters and threshing machines so that the need for peasant labour — and thus the wage level — was further reduced. Many peasant families dependent on seasonal labour were forced off the land altogether.[34]

During the last decades of the old regime millions of peasants were gradually driven off the land by poverty or by some other misfortune, such as a fire or the death of an adult worker, which to the poor family, up to its neck in debt, was enough to make all the difference between survival and catastrophe. Drink was also a growing cause of peasant debt and ruination. Semenov described a whole class of heavy drinkers in Andreevskoe: 'The adults were always thin and looked down and out; the children were rickety, with swollen necks from scrofula, big frightened eyes in pale anaemic faces, and inflated bellies on spindly legs.'[35]

Some of these poor peasants managed to scrape a living through local trades, such as weaving, carpentry, pottery, shoe-making, timber-felling and carting, although many of these handicrafts were being squeezed out by factory competition. Others migrated to Siberia, where land was made available to the colonists. Over a million peasants, especially from the Ukraine, made this trek during the decade following the famine of 1891. But the vast majority joined the army of migrant labourers who every spring made their way along the country's muddy roads by foot or in carts, sailed down its swollen rivers in home-made rowing-boats or stowed away on steamers, and travelled across Russia by rail in unheated carriages or clinging to the roofs of trains. This nomadic host, some nine million strong by the turn of the century,[36] headed for the Easter holiday markets where men were hired for ploughing on the large commercial estates. Later in the summer they were followed by reinforcements for the harvest. And then they dispersed throughout Russia in search of winter work on the railways, in dockyards, mines, construction sites, workshops and factories, only to repeat the whole cycle the following spring.

Every year, in body and spirit, these peasant migrants were taken further away from their villages and drawn into the new world of Russia's industrial revolution. In the last half-century of the old regime the Empire's urban population quadrupled, from 7 to 28 million. Most of the increase was accounted for by peasants flooding into the cities in search of work. First came the young peasant men, many of them no more than boys, followed by the married men, then unmarried girls, and finally married women and children. By 1914 three out of four people living in St Petersburg were registered as peasants by birth, compared with less than one-third fifty years before. Half the city's population of 2.2 million people had arrived in the previous twenty years.[37] The effect of this massive peasant in-migration was even more pronounced in Moscow. The crowds of peasants in the streets, the numerous outdoor markets (there was even one on Red Square), the unpaved streets, the wooden housing, and the livestock that roamed freely around the workers' quarters, gave large sections of the city a rural feel. Moscow is still nicknamed the 'Big Village'.

☀   ☀   ☀

Semen Kanatchikov (1879–1940) was just one of the millions of peasants to make this transition from the village to the city during the industrial boom of the 1890s. Many years later, as a minor grandee in the Bolshevik government, he recalled the experience in his memoirs. He was born to a poor peasant family in the village of Gusevo in the Volokolamsk district of Moscow province. His father had been born a serf and, although he had tried to improve his lot by renting land, dabbling in trade and teaching himself to read, he had lived on the margins of poverty like most of the peasants in his district. Every winter he left the village to work as a labourer in the city, leaving his sick and feeble wife, who had lost all but four of her eighteen children, to run the farm on her own. Years of disappointment had turned him into a heavy drinker, and when he was drunk he would beat his wife and children. And yet, like many Russians, he mixed heavy drinking with a deep fear of God; and wanted nothing more than for his son to become a 'good peasant'. The young Kanatchikov found life unbearable. After his mother's premature death, for which he blamed his father, he resolved to run away. 'I wanted to rid myself of the monotony of village life as quickly as possible,' he later wrote, 'to free myself from my father's despotism and tutelage, to begin to live a self-reliant and independent life.'[38] It was not long before poverty forced his father to give in to his requests. At the age of sixteen Kanatchikov finally left for Moscow, where his father had arranged for him to work as an apprentice in the Gustav List metal factory. There, like thousands of other peasant immigrants, he would begin to redefine himself both as a worker and as a 'comrade' in the revolutionary movement.

Kanatchikov's motives for wanting to leave the village were typical of his generation. The dull routines of peasant life and the isolation of the village were a heavy burden for young men like him. It became even more difficult once they had learned to read, for the stories of city life in newspapers and pamphlets could only strengthen their awareness of these restrictions. Virtually any employment in the city seemed exciting and desirable compared with the hardships of peasant life. 'All the healthy and able young men ran away from our village to Moscow and took whatever jobs they could find,' recalled Semenov. 'We eagerly awaited the time when we would be old enough to find something in Moscow and could leave our native village.' Andreevskoe, Semenov's village, was, like Gusevo, close to Moscow, and the city was a magnet for the young peasants. 'The proximity of our village to Moscow', Semenov wrote to a friend in 1888, 'has made our peasants sick of the land. The desire for a social life, for fashionable dress, for drinking, for the pursuit of an easier life — all this weighs very heavily on them. They do not care any longer for farming. Everyone is trying as hard as he can to liberate himself from it and find an easier means of existence.'[39]

The desire for social betterment was very often synonymous with the desire to leave the village and find a job outside agriculture. Becoming a clerk or a shop assistant was seen by the younger peasants as a move up in the world. For young peasant women, in particular, who found themselves at the bottom of the patriarchal pile, working as a domestic servant in the city (which is what most of them did) offered them a better and more independent life. Many social commentators noted such aspirations. A study of rural schoolchildren in the 1900s, for example, found that nearly half of them wanted to pursue an 'educated profession' in the city, whereas less than 2 per cent wanted to follow in the footsteps of their peasant parents. 'I want to be a shop assistant', remarked one village schoolboy, 'because I do not like to walk in the mud. I want to be like those people who are cleanly dressed and work as shop assistants.'[40] Parents and educators became alarmed that many peasant boys, in particular, once they learned how to read and write, refused to do agricultural work and tried to distinguish themselves from the rest of the village by swaggering around in raffish city clothes.

If social ambition was often the primary motive of those peasants who went to the towns, more commonly, as in Kanatchikov's case, it was an unexpected consequence of a move enforced by poverty. But either way the experience of the city transformed the way most peasants thought — of the world, of themselves, and of the village life they had left behind. On the whole, it had the effect of making them think in secular, more rational and more humanistic terms, which brought them closer to the socialist intelligentsia, and to reject and even despise village culture, with its superstitions and its dark and backward ways. That was the Russia of 'icons and cockroaches', to cite Trotsky's phrase, whereas the city, and (for many of them) the urban culture of the revolutionary movement, stood for progress, enlightenment and human liberation. The rank and file of the Bolshevik Party were recruited from peasants, like Kanatchikov. The mistrust and indeed contempt which they were to show for the peasantry, once in power, can be explained by this social fact. For they associated the dismal peasant world with their own unhappy past, and it was a vital impulse of their own emerging personal and class identity, as well as of their commitment to the revolution, that this world should be abolished.

Kanatchikov's father had arranged an apprenticeship for him at the Gustav List factory through a neighbour from Gusevo who had gone to work there several years before. Most immigrants relied on such contacts to get themselves settled in the city. The peasants of one village or region would form an association (either an *artel'* or a *zemliachestvo*) to secure factory jobs and living quarters for their countrymen. Whole factories and areas of the city were 'colonized' by the peasants of one locality or another, especially if they all shared some valuable regional craft, and it was not unusual for employers to use such organizations to recruit workers. The industrial suburb of Sormovo near Nizhnyi Novgorod, for example, where one of the country's largest engineering works was located, recruited all its workers from a handful of surrounding villages, where metal-working was an established handicraft. Through such associations the peasant immigrants were able to maintain ties with their native villages. Most of them supplemented their factory incomes by holding on to their land allotment in the commune and returning to their village in the summer to help their families with the harvest. The factories suffered much disruption at harvest time.* Other peasants regularly sent home money to their families. In this way they were able to keep one foot in the village, whilst their economic position in

---

* According to a survey of 1881, over 90 per cent of the workforce in textiles and 71 per cent of all industrial workers returned to their villages during the summer. The proportion declined towards the turn of the century as the urban workforce became more settled. Factories adapted to the situation by stopping work during the agricultural season, or by moving to the countryside. The government encouraged the latter, fearing the build-up of an urban working class. Only 40 per cent of the Empire's industrial workers lived in the cities at the turn of the century.

the city was still insecure. Indeed in some industrial regions, such as the Urals and the mining areas of the south, it was common for the workers to live in their villages, where their families kept a vegetable plot, and commute to the factories and mines.

Many of these immigrants continued to see themselves as essentially peasants, and looked on industrial work as a means of 'raiding' the cash economy to support their family farms. They maintained their peasant appearance — wearing their traditional home-made cotton-print blouses rather than manufactured ones, having their hair cut 'under a bowl' rather than in the new urban styles, and refusing to shave off their beards. 'They lived in crowded, dirty conditions and behaved stingily, denying themselves everything in order to accumulate more money for the village,' Kanatchikov recalled. 'On holidays they attended mass and visited their countrymen, and their conversations were mostly about grain, land, the harvest and livestock.' When they had saved up enough money they would go back to their village and buy up a small piece of land. Others, however, like Kanatchikov, preferred to see their future as urban workers. They regarded their land in the village as a temporary fall-back whilst they set themselves up in the city.[41]

It was through an *artel'* of fifteen immigrant workers that Kanatchikov found a 'corner' of a room in a 'large, smelly house inhabited by all kinds of poor folk'. The fifteen men who shared the room bought food and paid for a cook collectively. Every day at noon they hurried home from the factory to eat cabbage soup — just as the peasants did, 'from a common bowl with wooden spoons'. Kanatchikov slept in a small cot with another apprentice. His windowless 'corner' was dirty and full of 'bed bugs and fleas and the stench of "humanity"'. But in fact he was lucky to be in a private room at all. Many workers had to make do with a narrow plank-bed in the factory barracks, where hundreds of men, women and children slept together in rows, with nothing but their own dirty clothes for bedding. In these barracks, which Gorky compared with the 'dwellings of a prehistoric people', there were neither washing nor cooking facilities, so the workers had to visit the bath-house and eat in canteens. There were whole families living in such conditions. They tried as best they could to get a little privacy by hanging a curtain around their plank-beds. Others, even less fortunate, were forced to live in the flophouse or eat and sleep by the sides of their machines. Such was the demand for accommodation that workers thought nothing of spending half their income on rent. Landlords divided rooms, hallways, cellars and kitchens to maximize their profits. Speculative developers rushed to build high tenements, which in turn were quickly sub-divided. Sixteen people lived in the average apartment in St Petersburg, six in every room, according to a survey of 1904. In the workers' districts the figures were higher. The city council could have relieved the housing crisis by building suburbs and developing cheap transportation, but pressure from the landlords in the centre blocked all such plans.[42]

Like most of Russia's industrial cities, St Petersburg had developed without any proper planning. Factories had been built in the central residential districts and allowed to discharge their industrial waste into rivers and canals. The domestic water supply was a breeding ground for typhus and cholera, as the Tsar's own daughter, the Grand Duchess Tatyana Nikolaevna, discovered to her cost when she contracted it during the tercentenary celebrations in the capital. The death rate in this City of Tsars was the highest of any European capital, including Constantinople, with a cholera epidemic on average once in every three years. In the workers' districts fewer than one in three apartments had a toilet or running water. Excrement piled high in the back yards until wooden carts came to collect it at night. Water was fetched in buckets from street pumps and wells and had to be boiled before it was safe to drink. Throughout the city — on house-fronts, inside tramcars, and in hundreds of public places — there were placards in bold red letters warning people not to drink the water, though thirsty workers, and especially those who had recently arrived from the countryside, paid very little attention to them. Nothing of any real consequence was done to improve the city's water and sewage systems, which remained a national scandal even after 30,000 residents had been struck down by cholera in 1908–9. There was a good deal of talk about building a pipeline to Lake Lagoda, but the project remained on the drawing board until 1917.[43]

From his first day at the factory the young Kanatchikov was acutely conscious of his awkward and rustic appearance: 'The skilled workers looked down on me with scorn, pinched me by the ear, pulled me by the hair, called me a "green country bumpkin" and other insulting names.' These labour aristocrats became a model for Kanatchikov as he sought to assimilate himself into this new working-class culture. He envied their fashionable dress, with their trouser cuffs left out over their shiny leather boots, their white 'fantasia' shirts tucked into their trousers, and their collars fastened with lace. They smelt of soap and eau de Cologne, cut their hair 'in the Polish style' (i.e. with a parting down one side rather than in the middle as the peasants wore their hair), and on Sundays dressed in suits and bowler hats. The pride which they took in their physical appearance seemed to convey 'their consciousness of their own worth'; and it was precisely this sense of dignity that Kanatchikov set out to achieve.[44]

But for the moment, he found himself at the bottom of the factory hierarchy, an unskilled worker, labouring for six days every week, from 6 a.m. to 7p.m., for a measly wage of 1.5 roubles a week. Russia's late-flowering industrial revolution depended on cheap labourers from the countryside like Kanatchikov. This was its principal advantage over the older industrial powers, in which organized labour had won better pay and working conditions. As

Count Witte put it in 1900, the Russian worker, 'raised in the frugal habits of rural life', was 'much more easily satisfied' than his counterpart in Europe or North America, so that 'low wages appeared as a fortunate gift to Russian enterprise'. Indeed, as the factories became more mechanized, employers were able to exploit the even cheaper labour of women and children. By 1914 women represented 33 per cent of the industrial workforce in Russia, compared to 20 per cent in 1885, and in certain sectors, such as textiles and food processing, women workers were in the majority. The factory took a heavy toll on their health, additionally burdened, as so many of them were, with bawling babies and alcoholic husbands. 'One cannot help but note the premature decrepitude of the factory women,' a senior doctor wrote in 1913. 'A woman worker of fifty sees and hears poorly, her head trembles, her shoulders are sharply hunched over. She looks about seventy. It is obvious that only dire need keeps her at the factory, forcing her to work beyond her strength. While in the West, elderly workers have pensions, our women workers can expect nothing better than to live out their last days as lavatory attendants.'[45]

The tsarist government was reluctant to better the lot of the workers through factory legislation. This was one of its biggest mistakes, for the build-up of a large and discontented working class in the cities was to be one of the principal causes of its downfall. Part of the problem was that influential reactionaries, like Pobedonostsev, the Procurator-General of the Holy Synod and close adviser to the last two tsars, refused to recognize the 'labour question' at all, since in their view Russia was still (and should remain) an agrarian society. In other words the workers should be treated as no more than peasants. Others feared that passing such reforms would only raise the workers' expectations. But the main concern was that so much of Russian industry remained in the hands of foreign owners,* and, if their labour costs were to rise, they might take their capital elsewhere. The gains made by British workers in the 1840s, and by German workers in the 1880s, remained out of reach of Russian workers at the turn of the century. The two most important factory laws — one in 1885 prohibiting the night-time employment of women and children, and the other in 1897 restricting the working day to eleven and a half hours — had to be wrenched from the government, after major strikes. But even these reforms left major loopholes. The small artisanal trades and sweatshops, which probably employed the majority of the country's workers, were excluded from all such protective legislation. The inspectorates, charged with ensuring that the factories complied with the regulations, lacked effective powers, and employers ignored them with impunity. Working areas were filled with noxious fumes and left

---

* The percentage of foreign shareholding in joint-stock companies rose from 25 per cent in 1890 to about 40 per cent on the eve of the First World War.

unventilated. Shopfloors were crammed with dangerous machinery, so that accidents occurred frequently. Yet most workers were denied a legal right to insurance and, if they lost an eye or a limb, could expect no more than a few roubles' compensation.

'The factory owner is an absolute sovereign and legislator whom no laws constrain,' declared Professor Yanzhul, a leading proponent of factory regulation during the 1880s. Indeed, by hiring workers on private contracts, employers could bypass most of the government's labour legislation. All sorts of clauses were inserted into workers' contracts, depriving them of legal rights. Long after such fines had been outlawed, many workers continued to have their pay docked for low productivity, breakages and petty infringements of the factory rules (sometimes amounting to no more than going to the toilet during working hours). Some employers had their workers degradingly searched for stolen goods whenever they left the factory gates, while others had them flogged for misdemeanours. Others forbade their workers to wear hats, or to turn up for work in their best clothes, as a way of teaching them their proper place. This sort of 'serf regime' was bitterly resented by the workers as an affront to their personal dignity. 'We are not even recognized as people,' one complained, 'but we are considered as things which can be thrown out at any moment.' Another lamented that 'outside Russia even horses get to rest. But our workers' existence is worse than a horse's.'[46] As they developed their own sense of self-worth, these workers demanded more respectful treatment by their employers. They wanted them to call them by the polite 'you' (*vyi*) instead of the familiar one (*tyi*), which they associated with the old serf regime. They wanted to be treated as 'citizens'. It was often this issue of respectful treatment, rather than the bread-and-butter question of wages, which fuelled workers' strikes and demonstrations.

Historians have searched exhaustively for the roots of this labour militancy. The size of the factories, the levels of skill and literacy, the movement of wages and prices, the number of years spent living in the city, and the influence of the revolutionary intelligentsia — all these factors have been examined in microscopic detail in countless monographs, each hoping to discover the crucial mix that explained the take-off of the 'workers' revolution'. The main argument among historians concerns the effects of urbanization. Some have argued that it was the most urbanized workers, those with the highest levels of skill and literacy, who became the foot soldiers of the revolution.[47] But others have argued that the recent immigrants — those who had been 'snatched from the plough and hurled straight into the factory furnace', as Trotsky once put it — tended to be the most violent, often adapting the spontaneous forms of rebellion associated with the countryside (*buntarstvo*) to the new and hostile industrial environment in which they found themselves.[48]

Now there is no doubt that the peasant immigrants added a volatile and often belligerent element to the urban working class. Labour unrest during the early decades of industrialization tended to take the form of spontaneous outbreaks of violence, such as riots, pogroms, looting and machine-breaking, the sort of actions one might expect from an uprooted but disorganized peasant mass struggling to adapt to the new world of the city and the discipline of the factory. Some of these 'pre-industrial' forms of violence became permanent features of the landscape of labour unrest. A good example is the common workers' practice during strikes and demonstrations of 'carting out' their factory boss or foreman in a wheelbarrow and dumping him in a cesspool or a canal. Nevertheless, it is going too far to suggest that such 'primitive' forms of industrial protest, or the raw recruits behind them, were the crucial factor in the rise of labour militancy.[49] During the 1890s strikes became the principal form of industrial protest and they required the sort of disciplined organization that only the most urbanized workers, with their higher levels of skills and literacy, could provide. In this context, the peasant immigrants were unlikely to play a leading role. Indeed, they were often reluctant to join strikes at all. With a piece of land in the village, to which they could return when times got hard, they had less inclination to take the risks which a strike entailed, compared with those workers who had broken their ties with the village and depended exclusively on their factory wage. The latter stood at the forefront of the labour movement.

Here Russia stood in stark contrast to Europe, where the most skilled and literate workers tended to be the least revolutionary and were being integrated into the wider democratic movement. There were few signs of such a moderate 'labour aristocracy' emerging in Russia. The print workers, with their high rates of pay and their close ties with the intelligentsia, were the most likely candidates for such a role. Yet even they stood firmly behind the Marxist and Social Revolutionary parties. Had they been able to develop their own legal trade unions, then these workers might have made enough gains from the status quo not to demand its overthrow. They might then have gone down the path of moderate reform taken by the European labour movements. But the Russian political situation naturally pushed them towards extremes. Unable to develop their own independent organizations, they were forced to rely upon the leadership of the revolutionary underground. To a large extent, then, the workers' revolutionary movement was created by the tsarist regime.

Militancy is nothing if not a set of attitudes and emotions. And as Kanatchikov's story illustrates, the roots of the workers' militancy were essentially psychological. His personality changed as he adapted himself to the lifestyle of the city and acquired new skills. Mastering the precision techniques of the pattern-makers, the élite machine-construction workers who drafted and moulded the metal parts, gave him confidence in his own powers. It also paid him more money, which gave him a greater sense of his own worth. Learning to read and talking to the other workers exposed him to the secular modes of thought and new 'scientific' theories, such as Darwinism and Marxism, which weakened his belief in religion. In other ways, too, the young Kanatchikov was struggling to break free from the influence of the village. He was repelled by the 'hooliganism' of his co-inhabitants in the *artel'*, by their heavy drinking, their fighting and their rough peasant manners. He moved into a room on his own, swore a solemn oath never to drink anything stronger than tea, and set out on a rigorous course of self-improvement to wipe out all traces of his humble peasant roots. He sought to make a new image for himself, to emulate 'those young urban metalworkers', as he put it, 'who earned an independent living and didn't ruin themselves with vodka'. He saved up to get his hair cut in the Polish style and to buy a stylish jacket with mother-of-pearl buttons, and a cap with a velvet band, such as the labour aristocrats wore. He bought a suit, with a watch for the waistcoat pocket, a straw hat and a pair of fancy shoes, for Sundays. For fifteen kopecks, he even bought a *Self-Teacher of Dance and Good Manners*, which warned him not to wipe his nose with his napkin and told him how to eat such delicacies as artichoke and asparagus, although, as he later admitted, he 'did not even know if these things belonged to the animal, vegetable, or mineral world'.[50]

Self-improvement was a natural enough aspiration among skilled workers, like Kanatchikov, who were anxious to rise above their peasant origins and attain the status in society which their growing sense of dignity made them feel they deserved. Many harboured dreams of marrying into the petty-bourgeoisie and of setting themselves up in a small shop or business. They read the boulevard dailies, such as the *Petersburg Sheet* (*Peterburgskii listok*), which espoused the Victorian ideals of self-help, guided its readers in questions of good taste and decorum, and entertained them with sensational stories about the glamorous and the rich.

It was only to be expected that this search for respectability should be accompanied by a certain priggishness on the part of the labour élite, a fussy concern to set themselves apart from the 'dark' mass of the peasant-workers by conducting themselves in a sober and 'cultured' way.* But among those peasant-workers, like Kanatchikov, who would later join the Bolsheviks, this prudishness was often reflected in an extreme form. Their sobriety became a militant puritanism, as if by their prim and ascetic manners, by their tea-drinking and self-discipline, they could banish their peasant past completely. 'We were of the

---

* Here lay the roots of that peculiar Russian concept of *kul'turnost'*, the state of having good manners, rather than being well educated, as in the Western concept of the term 'cultured', from which it is derived. This etymological twist could only have happened in a country like Russia, which was struggling to rid itself of its peasant past and attain the external trappings, if not the deeper moral sensibilities, of Western civilization.

opinion that no conscious Socialist should ever drink vodka,' recalled one such Bolshevik. 'We even condemned smoking. We propagated morality in the strictest sense of the word.' It was for this reason that so many rank-and-file Bolsheviks abstained from romantic attachments, although in Kanatchikov's case this may have had more to do with his own dismal failure with women. The worker-revolutionaries, he later admitted, 'developed a negative attitude toward the family, toward marriage, and even toward women'. They saw themselves as 'doomed' men, their fate tied wholly to the cause of the revolution, which could only be compromised by 'contact with girls'. So strait-laced were these pioneering proletarians that people often mistook them for the Pashkovites, a pious Bible sect. Even the police sometimes became confused when they were instructed to increase their surveillance of 'revolutionary' workers who drank only tea.[51]

* * *

It was through his tea-drinking friends that the young Kanatchikov first became involved in the underground 'study circles' (*kruzhki*) devoted to the reading of socialist tracts and the education of the workers. In the early days most of these circles had been organized by Populist students, but by the late 1890s, when Kanatchikov moved to St Petersburg and joined a circle there, the Marxists were making the running. For him, as for many other 'conscious' workers, the circle's main attraction was the opening it gave him to a new world of learning. Through it he was introduced to the writings of Pushkin and Nekrasov, to books on science, history, arithmetic and grammar, to the theatre and to serious concerts, as well as to the popular Marxist tracts of the day. All this gave him the sense of being raised to a higher cultural level than most workers, who spent their leisure time in the tavern. But he and his comrades were still ill at ease in the company of the liberal middle classes who patronized their groups. Occasionally, as Kanatchikov recalls, they would be taken 'for display' to fashionable bourgeois homes:

> Our intelligentsia guide would introduce us in a loud voice, emphasizing the words: 'conscious workers'. Then we were regaled with tea and all manner of strange snacks that we were afraid to touch, lest we make some embarrassing blunder. Our conversations with such liberals had a very strained character. They would interrogate us about this or that book we had read, question us about how the mass of workers lived, what they thought, whether they were interested in a constitution. Some would ask us if we'd read Marx. Any stupidity that we uttered in our confusion would be met with condescending approval.

On leaving these parties, Kanatchikov and his friends 'would breathe a sigh of relief and laugh at our hosts' lack of understanding about our lives'. While on the surface they agreed with their student mentors that the liberals might be useful to the revolutionary cause, 'a kind of hostility toward them, a feeling of distrust, was constantly growing inside us'.[52] It was precisely this feeling of distrust, the workers' awareness that their own aspirations were not the same as the liberals', that hastened the downfall of the Provisional Government in 1917.

Kanatchikov's conception of socialism was extremely malleable at this stage. And the same was true of most workers. They found it difficult to take on board complex or abstract ideas, but they were receptive to propaganda in the form of simple pamphlet stories highlighting the exploitation of the workers in their daily lives. Gorky's stories were very popular. Since escaping from Krasnovidovo, he had roamed across the country doing various casual jobs, until he had met the novelist and critic V. G. Korolenko, who had encouraged him to write. By the mid-1890s Gorky had become a national celebrity, the first real writer of any quality to emerge from the urban underworld of migratory labourers, vagabonds and thieves, which his stories represented with vividness and compassion. Dressed like a simple worker, with his walrus moustache and his strongly chiselled face, Gorky was received as a phenomenon in the salons of the radical intelligentsia. The workers could easily identify themselves with his stories, because they drew on the concerns that filled their everyday lives and, like the writer's pseudonym, captured their own spirit of defiance and revolt (*gor'kii* means 'bitter' in Russian). Moreover, Gorky's obvious sympathy for the industrial worker, and his equal antipathy to the 'backward' peasant Russia of the past, gave workers like Kanatchikov, who were trying to break free from their own roots, a new set of moral values and ideals. In a famous passage in *My Childhood* (1913), for example, Gorky asked himself why he had recorded all the incidents of cruelty and suffering which had filled his early years; and he gave an answer with which many workers, like Kanatchikov, would have sympathized:

When I try to recall those vile abominations of that barbarous life in Russia, at times I find myself asking the question: is it worth while recording them? And with ever stronger conviction I find the answer is yes, because that was the real loathsome truth and to this day it is still valid. It is that truth which must be known down to the very roots, so that by tearing them up it can be completely erased from the memory, from the soul of man, from our whole oppressive and shameful life.

All the characters in Gorky's stories were divided into good or bad — both defined in terms of their social class — with little shading or variation. This moral absolutism also appealed to the workers' growing class and revolutionary consciousness. But, perhaps above all, it was the spirit of revolt in Gorky's writing that made it so inspiring. 'The Stormy Petrel' (1895), his bombastic eulogy to the romantic revolutionary hero, disguised in the form of a falcon flying above the foamy waves, became the revolutionaries' hymn and was circulated through the underground in hundreds of printed, typed and hand-written copies. Like most workers, Kanatchikov had learned it by heart:

> Intrepid petrel, even though you die,
> Yet in the song of the bold and firm in spirit,
> You'll always live as an example,
> A proud summons — to freedom and light![53]

The workers also liked to read stories about the popular struggle for liberation in foreign lands. 'Whether it was the Albigenses battling against the Inquisition, the Garibaldians, or the Bulgarian nationalists, we saw them all as our kindred spirits,' wrote Kanatchikov. It did not matter that these foreign heroes had fought very different battles from their own, since the workers were quick to reinterpret these stories in the Russian context. Indeed the censorship of literature about Russia's own historic 'revolutionaries', such as Pugachev or the Decembrists, obliged them to look abroad for inspiration. In that good old Russian tradition of reading between the lines they seized upon the Netherlanders' struggle against the Inquisition as a stirring example of the spirit and organization they would need in their own struggle against the police. It was the stories' emotional content, their romantic depiction of the rebel as a fighter for freedom and justice, that made them so inspiring. From them, Kanatchikov wrote, 'we learned the meaning of selflessness, the capacity to sacrifice oneself in the name of the common good'.[54] By identifying themselves with the fearless champions of human emancipation everywhere, they became converted to the revolution.

The special attraction of Marxism stemmed from the importance it gave to the role of the working class and to the idea of progress. The popular Marxist pamphlets of the late 1890s, which for the first time attracted large numbers of workers like Kanatchikov to the cause, drove home the lessons of the famine crisis of 1891: that the peasants were doomed to die out as a result of economic progress; that they were a relic of Russia's backward past who would be swept away by industry; and that the Populists' belief in the commune (to which many of the peasant-workers still adhered) was no longer tenable. Only Marxism could explain to workers why their peasant parents had become so poor, and why they had been forced into the cities. There was thus a close link between Kanatchikov's attachment to the Marxist exaltation of industrialization and progress and his own psychological rejection of his peasant past. Like many workers from the countryside, Kanatchikov invested much of his own personality in the ideal of liberation through industry. He found 'poetry' in 'the rumblings and the puffings' of the factory. To workers like him Marxism appeared as a modern 'science' that explained in simple black-and-white terms why their world was structured the way that it was, and how it could be transformed.

Many people have argued that Marxism acted like a religion, at least in its popular form. But workers like Kanatchikov believed with the utmost seriousness that the teachings of Marx were a science, on a par with the natural sciences; and to claim that their belief was really nothing more than a form of religious faith is unfair to them. There was, however, an obvious dogmatism in the outlook of many such workers, which could easily be mistaken for religious zealotry. It manifested itself in that air of disdain which many workers, having reached the uplands of Marxist understanding, showed towards those who had not yet ascended to such heights. One 'comrade', for example, arrogantly told a police officer, who was in the process of arresting him, that he was a 'fool' because he had 'never read Marx' and did 'not even know what politics and economics [were]'.[55] This dogmatism had much to do with the relative scarcity of alternative political ideas, which might at least have caused the workers to regard the Marxist doctrine with a little more reserve and scepticism. But it also had its roots in the way most of these workers had been educated in philosophy. When people learn as adults what children are normally taught in schools, they often find it difficult to progress beyond the simplest abstract ideas. These tend to lodge deep in their minds, making them resistant to the subsequent absorption of knowledge on a more sophisticated level. They see the world in black-and-white terms because their narrow learning obscures any other coloration. Marxism had much the same effect on workers like Kanatchikov. It gave them a simple solution to the problems of 'capitalism' and backwardness without requiring that they think independently.

For a worker to commit himself to the militant labour movement was to invite persecution. Once the local police got wind of his activities he would soon find himself dismissed from his factory as a troublemaker. Yet because of the huge demand for skilled labour during the industrial boom, workers like Kanatchikov were easily able to find jobs again. They roamed from factory to factory, organizing illegal workers' clubs and associations, until the police caught up with them and again forced them to move on. Faced with a life on the run, the weak-willed militant might have chosen to return to the security of his native village. But for workers like Kanatchikov this was unthinkable. They had already committed themselves to the revolutionary movement, and their identity was invested in it. To return to the backwardness of the village would undermine their hard-won sense of themselves. The only alternative was to join the revolutionary movement underground. The comradeship which they found there partly compensated for the rootlessness which many of them must have felt as they moved from town to town. The party organization became the worker's 'family home and hearth', as Kanatchikov put it. His 'comrades in struggle' took 'the place of his brothers, sisters, father and mother'. Belonging to this secret community, moreover, had its own romantic appeal, as another Bolshevik worker explained: 'The constant danger of arrest, the secrecy of our meetings and the awareness that I was no longer just a grain of sand, no longer just another one of the workers, but a member of an organization that was dangerous and threatening to the government and to the rich — all this was new and exciting.'[56]

This sense of belonging to the party and of being a part of its historic mission acted as a solvent on the social divisions between the workers and the Marxist intelligentsia. Comradeship was, initially, more powerful than class. Yet increasingly the relationship between the two was marked by tension and distrust. The workers were beginning to organize themselves. The strikes of the mid-1890s were the first real breakthrough by the independent labour movement. Most of them were led by the skilled workers themselves, though the Marxist intelligentsia in the Social Democratic Party played an important subsidiary role in spreading the propaganda that helped to make the strikes so widespread and effective. At this stage the Marxists were still committed to the idea of mass agitation for strikes. But towards the end of the decade many began to claim that the labour movement, with its narrow focus on bread-and-butter issues, was not strong enough by itself to bring down the tsarist regime. They demanded a broader political movement, in which the discipline and organization of the Social Democrats, rather than the workers themselves, would play the leading role. Here was the root of the conflict between the economic goals of the labour movement and the political ambitions of the revolutionary intelligentsia, a conflict that would split the whole Marxist movement in Russia.

With one foot in the factory and the other in the revolutionary underground, Kanatchikov now had to choose between them. On the eve of the 1905 Revolution, as we learn from the last proud sentence of his memoirs, he left the factory and became a full-time 'professional revolutionary' in the Bolshevik Party.

4 Red Ink

i Inside the Fortress

At the mouth of the Neva River, directly opposite the Winter Palace, stands the Fortress of Peter and Paul. Constructed in 1703 by Peter the Great as a bastion against the Swedish fleet, it was the first building in St Petersburg, and for several years served as the capital of his vast Empire. Once the rest of the city had been constructed — on the bones of the serfs who died building it — the tiny island fortress ceased to be the seat of tsarist rule, but it continued to symbolize its awesome power. The tombs of the tsars were kept in its cathedral, whose golden spire rose like a needle above the centre of the capital. And inside the thick stone walls and beneath the eight towers of the fortress was concealed the most infamous of all the regime's political prisons. Its list of inmates reads like a roll of honour of the Russian radical and revolutionary movements: Radishchev; the Decembrists; the Petrashevtsy; Kropotkin; Chernyshevsky; Bakunin; Tkachev; Nechaev; Populists and Marxists; workers and students — they all suffered in its damp and gloomy cells. In its two centuries as a jail not a single prisoner ever escaped from the fortress, although many found a different form of deliverance through suicide or insanity.

This 'Russian Bastille' not only held captive dangerous subversives; it captured the popular imagination. Folksongs and ballads portrayed the fortress as a living hell. Legends abounded of how its prisoners were tortured, of how they languished in dark and vermin-ridden dungeons, or were driven mad by its tomb-like silence (enforced as part of the prison regime). Tales were told of prisoners kept in cells so small that they could neither stand nor lie down but had to curl up like a ball; after a while their bodies became twisted and deformed. There were stories of secret executions, of prisoners being forced to dig their own graves on the frozen river at night before being drowned beneath the ice. In the minds of the common people the fortress became a monstrous symbol of the despotism under which they lived, a symbol of their fears and lack of freedom, and the fact that it was located right in the middle of St Petersburg, that people daily passed by its secret horrors, only made it seem more terrible.

In fact, conditions in the prison were not as bad as people believed. Compared with the conditions which the tyrannies of the twentieth century have provided for their victims, the fortress was like a comfortable hotel. Most of the inmates had access to food and tobacco, books and writing paper, and could receive letters from their relatives. The Bolshevik, Nikolai Bauman, was even allowed to read Marx's *Capital* during his stay in the prison. Several classics of Russian literature were composed in the silence of its cells, including Dostoevsky's story *The Little Hero*, Gorky's play *The Children of the Sun*, and Chernyshevsky's novel *What Is To Be Done?*, which became a seminal text of the revolutionary movement.* The public image of the prison — crammed full to bursting point with tens of thousands of long-term inmates — could not have been further from the truth. There were never more than a hundred prisoners there at any time, and after 1908 never more than thirty. Few stayed more than a month or so before being transferred to provincial jails. In February 1917, when the fortress was finally taken by the crowd, the anti-climactic reality of liberating a mere nineteen prisoners (all of them mutinous soldiers imprisoned only the previous day) was not allowed to intrude on the revolutionaries' mythic expectations. The event was portrayed as Freedom's triumph over Despotism.

This reinvention of the fortress was a vital aspect of the revolutionaries' demonology. If the tsarist regime was to be depicted as cruel and oppressive, secretive and arbitrary in its penal powers, then the fortress was a perfect symbol of those sins. During the latter half of the nineteenth century, as in reality it became more benign, its prison regime was described in the writings of its former inmates with increasingly exaggerated horror. There was a fashion for gothic prison memoirs during the last decades of the old regime, and these tales fed the public's appetite for revolutionary martyrs. As Gorky put it, when once asked why he had refused to add his memoirs to the pile: 'Every Russian who has ever sat in jail, if only for a month, as a "political", or who has spent a year in exile, considers it his holy duty to bestow on Russia his memoirs of how he has suffered.'[1]

To its critics the Peter and Paul Fortress was a microcosm of the tsarist system. Russia, remarked the Marquis de Custine after visiting the fortress in the 1830s, is 'in itself a prison; a prison whose vast size only makes it the more formidable'. The basic structure of the tsarist police state had been built up under Nicholas I after the Decembrist uprising of 1825, when a small coterie of liberal noblemen had conspired — as Pushkin put it, 'between the claret and champagne' — to impose a constitution on the monarchy after Alexander I's death. Nicholas introduced sweeping laws — including a new code of censorship in 1826 that (uniquely in Europe at the time) obliged all printed matter to gain clearance from the censor *before* publication — to stamp out all political dissent.

---

* Chernyshevsky's novel was published while he was still in the Peter and Paul Fortress — only to be subsequently banned!

The Third Section, or secret police, established that year, had — and this was once again unique in Europe — the power to detain and even send into administrative exile in Siberia anyone *suspected* of 'political crimes'. No other country in the world had two kinds of police — one to protect the interests of the state, the other to protect its people.

Yet it was not until the late nineteenth century, with the arrival of telegraphs and telephones, that the machinery of the police state became really efficient. The Okhrana, which took over the functions of the Third Section in 1881, fought what can only be described as a secret war, using special powers outside the law, to stamp out revolutionaries. It had thousands of agents and informers, many of them posing as revolutionaries, who reported on conditions in the factories, the universities, the army and the institutions of the state itself. House porters filed daily reports to the police. Hundreds of bureaucrats were employed in a 'Black Office' to read people's intercepted mail. 'The whole of St Petersburg is aware that its letters are read by the police,' complained Countess Vorontsova to Nicholas II. There was a huge list of activities — from putting on a concert or opening a shop to consulting the works of Darwin — for which even the most high-born citizen required a licence from the police. Indeed, from the perspective of the individual, it could be said that the single greatest difference between Russia and the West, both under Tsarism and Communism, was that in Western Europe citizens were generally free to do as they pleased so long as their activities had not been specifically prohibited by the state, while the people of Russia were not free to do anything unless the state had given them specific permission to do it. No subject of the Tsar, regardless of his rank or class, could sleep securely in his bed in the knowledge that his house would not be subject to a search, or he himself to arrest.[2]

This constant battle with the police state engendered a special kind of mentality among its opponents. One can draw a straight line from the penal rigours of the tsarist regime to the terrorism of the revolutionaries and indeed to the police state of the Bolsheviks. As Flaubert put it, 'inside every revolutionary there is a policeman'. Felix Dzerzhinsky (1877–1926), the founding father of the Cheka, was a classic case in point. By 1917 he had spent the best part of his adult life in jails and penal exile, including the last three in the Orel prison, notorious for its sadistic tortures, where, as the leader of a hunger strike, he was singled out for punishment (his body was said to be covered with scars). Once installed in power, he was to copy many of these torture methods during the Red Terror. Yet Dzerzhinsky was only one of many poachers turned gamekeepers. By 1917, the average Bolshevik Party activist had spent nearly four years in tsarist jails or exile; the average Menshevik nearly five. Prison hardened the revolutionaries. It prepared them for 'the struggle', giving them a private reason to hate the old regime and to seek revenge against its representatives. Kanatchikov, who spent several years in tsarist jails, claimed that for Bolshevized workers like himself prison acted as a form of 'natural selection': 'the weak in spirit left the revolution, and often life, but the strong and steadfast were toughened and prepared for future battles'. Many years later, in 1923, Kanatchikov was told that one of the judges who had sentenced him to jail in 1910 had been shot by the Bolsheviks. 'When I heard this', Kanatchikov confessed, 'it gave me great satisfaction'.[3]

Justifying violence in the name of revolution was not exclusive to the revolutionaries. Among the educated élite there was a general cult of revolution-ism. The Russian 'intelligentsia' (a Russian word by derivation) was less a class than a state of mind: it meant by definition a stance of radical and uncomprom-ising opposition to the tsarist regime, and a willingness to take part in the struggle for its overthrow. The history of the revolutionary movement is the history of the intelligentsia. Most of the revolutionary leaders were first and foremost intellectuals. Their heads were full of European literature and history, especially the history of the French Revolutions of 1789 and 1848. 'I think', recalled Lydia Dan, a Menshevik, 'that as people we were much more out of books than out of real life.'[4] No other single group of intellectuals has had such a huge impact on the twentieth-century world.

Those who thought of themselves as *intelligenty* (students, writers, pro-fessionals, etc.) had a special set of ethics, and shared codes of dress and language, notions of honour and comradeship, not to mention salons and coffee-houses, clubs and social circles, newspapers and journals, which set them apart as a sort of sub-culture from the rest of the privileged society from which most of them had sprung. Many of them even shared a distinct 'look' — unkempt, long-haired, bearded and bespectacled — which became the hallmark of left-wingers and revolutionaries across the world.* The philosopher Nikolai Berdyaev once compared the Russian intelligentsia to a 'monastic order' or 'religious sect'; and there was much in their mentality akin to Christianity. Take, for example, their rejection of the existing order as sinful and corrupt; or their self-image as the righteous champions of the 'people's cause'; or indeed their almost mystical belief in the existence of absolute truth. The radical intelligentsia had a religious veneration for the revolutionary literary canon. Ariadna Tyrkova-Williams recalls, for example, how in the 1880s her teenage sister 'used to smuggle a volume of revolutionary verses into Church during afternoon prayers and, while

---

* Lydia Dan's father had a nice way of poking fun at these self-conscious radicals. Boys, he said, did not cut their hair on the grounds that they did not have time; but women cut their hair short also to save time. Women went to university on the grounds that this was a mark of progress; but men dropped out of the education system on the grounds that this was also progressive.

the others read from the Bible, she would recite their summons to revolt and terror'.[5]

        This self-conscious tradition stemmed from the Decembrists. Their execution in 1826 produced the first martyrs of 'the movement'. Younger generations took romantic inspiration from the self-sacrifice of these noble Jacobins. From that point on — and here was born the cult of opposition — it became the fashion for the sons of noblemen to shun careers in the Civil Service 'out of principle'. It was seen as a moral betrayal to let oneself be used, as Chicherin put it, 'as a direct tool of a government which was repressing mercilessly every thought and all enlightenment'. Bloody-minded opposition to the tsarist state and all its officials, however petty, was a matter of honour. Consider the story of Anatolii Dubois, a student of the University of St Petersburg in 1902, who refused ('on principle') to shake the hand of a police sergeant who, whilst registering his new address, had engaged him in a friendly conversation and had offered to shake hands as a parting gesture. A police report was made to the rector of the university and Dubois was expelled — only to join the revolutionary movement and get himself arrested in 1903. It was a typical example of the tsarist police state, by a stupid act of repression, forcing a middle-class dissident into the revolutionary underground out of which the terrorist tradition developed (Lenin's own story was very similar). The radical intelligentsia contemptuously rejected any act of compromise with 'the regime': only violent struggle could bring about its end. Liberalism was denounced as a weak half-measure. The law was despised as a tool of the state: it was said to be morally inferior to the peasants' ancient customs and to the interests of social justice — which justified breaking the law. This was the shaky moral foundation of the revolutionary sentiment that gripped the minds of the educated middle classes during the later nineteenth century. Vera Figner, who was herself a terrorist, spoke of a 'cult of the bomb and the gun' in which 'murder and the scaffold took on a magnetic charm'. Within the intelligentsia's circles it was deemed a matter of 'good taste' to sympathize with the terrorists and many wealthy citizens donated large sums of money to them.[6]

        It is impossible to understand this political extremism without first considering the cultural isolation of the Russian intelligentsia. This tiny élite was isolated from official Russia by its politics, and from peasant Russia by its education. Both chasms were unbridgeable. But, perhaps even more importantly, it was cut off from the European cultural world which it sought to emulate. The consequence, as Isaiah Berlin has so elegantly argued, was that ideas imported from the West (as nearly all ideas in Russia were) tended to become frozen into abstract dogmas once the Russian intelligentsia took them up. Whereas in Europe new ideas were forced to compete against other doctrines and attitudes, with the result that people tended towards healthy scepticism about claims to absolute truth, and a climate of pluralism developed, in Russia there was a cultural void. The censor forbade all political expression, so that when ideas were introduced there they easily assumed the status of holy dogma, a panacea for all the world's ills, beyond questioning or indeed the need to test them in real life. One European intellectual fashion would spread through St Petersburg after another — Hegelianism in the 1840s, Darwinism in the 1860s, Marxism in the 1890s — and each was viewed in turn as a final truth.[7] There was much that was endearing in this strangely Russian search for absolutes — such as the passion for big ideas that gave the literature of nineteenth-century Russia its unique character and power — and yet the underside of this idealism was a badgering didacticism, a moral dogmatism and intolerance, which in its own way was just as harmful as the censorship it opposed. Convinced that their own ideas were the key to the future of the world, that the fate of humanity rested on the outcome of their own doctrinal struggles, the Russian intelligentsia divided up the world into the forces of 'progress' and 'reaction', friends and enemies of the people's cause, leaving no room for doubters in between. Here were the origins of the totalitarian world-view. Although neither would have liked to admit it, there was much in common between Lenin and Tolstoy.

Guilt was the psychological inspiration of the revolution. Nearly all of these radical intellectuals were acutely conscious of their wealth and privilege. 'We have come to realise', the radical thinker Nikolai Mikhailovsky wrote, 'that our awareness of the universal truth could only have been reached at the cost of the age-old suffering of the people. We are the people's debtors and this debt weighs down on our conscience.' As the children of noblemen brought up by serf domestics on the estate, many of them felt a special personal sense of guilt, since, as Marc Raeff has pointed out, these 'little masters' had usually been allowed to treat their serf nannies and 'uncles' (whose job it had been to play with them) with cruel contempt.* Later in life these conscience-stricken nobles would seek to repay their debt to 'the people' by serving them in the revolution. If only, they thought, they could bring about the people's liberation, then their own original sin — that of being born into privilege — would be redeemed. Nineteenth-century Russian literature was dominated by the theme of repentance for the sin of privilege. Take, for example, Prince Levin in Tolstoy's *Anna Karenina*, who works alongside the peasants in his fields and dreams of giving them the profits of his farm so as to bring about a 'bloodless revolution': 'in place of poverty there would be wealth and happiness for all; in place of hostility, concord and a bond of common interest'.[8]

---

* These peasant nannies and domestic servants would not even be called by their proper names but by a pet name such as Masha or Vanka. They were thus denied the most basic recognition of a personality.

The first step towards this reconciliation was to immerse oneself in the people's daily lives. The romantic interest in folk culture which swept through Europe in the nineteenth century was felt nowhere more keenly than among the Russian intelligentsia. As Blok wrote (with just a touch of irony) in 1908:

> the intelligentsia cram their bookcases with anthologies of Russian folk-songs, epics, legends, incantations, dirges; they investigate Russian mythology, wedding and funeral rites; they grieve for the people; go to the people; are filled with high hopes; fall into despair; they even give up their lives, face execution or starve to death for the people's cause.

Riddled with the guilt of privilege, the intelligentsia worshipped at the altar of 'the people'. They believed profoundly in their mission of service to the people, just as their noble fathers had believed in their duty of service to the state. And in their world-view the 'good of the people' was the highest interest, to which all other principles, such as law or morals, were subordinate. Here was the root of the revolutionaries' maxim that any means could be justified in the interests of the revolution.

For all too many of these high-born revolutionaries, the main attraction of 'the cause' lay not so much in the satisfaction which they might derive from seeing the people's daily lives improved, as in their own romantic search for a sense of 'wholeness' which might give higher meaning to their lives and end their alienation from the world. This was certainly the case with Mikhail Bakunin, the founding father of Russian Anarchism, as Aileen Kelly has so brilliantly shown in her biography of him. It was, as she puts it, his own need 'to identify with a meaningful collective entity' that led this wealthy nobleman to sublimate his (quite enormous) ego in the abstract notion of the people's cause. The history of the revolutionary movement is to a large extent the prosopography of such noble and bourgeois intellectuals seeking this sense of belonging. They thought they had found it in the clan-like atmosphere of the revolutionary underground.

As for their commitment to 'the people', it was essentially abstract. They loved Man but were not so sure of individual men. M. V. Petrashevsky, the utopian theorist, summed it up when he proclaimed: 'unable to find anything either in women or in men worthy of my adherence, I have turned to devote myself to the service of humanity'. In this idealized abstraction of 'the people' there was not a little of that snobbish contempt which aristocrats are inclined to nurture for the habits of the common man. How else can one explain the authoritarian attitudes of such revolutionaries as Bakunin, Speshnev, Tkachev, Plekhanov and Lenin, if not by their noble origins? It was as if they saw the people as agents of their abstract doctrines rather than as suffering individuals with their own complex needs and ideals. Ironically, the interests of 'the cause' sometimes meant that the people's conditions had to deteriorate even further, to bring about the final cataclysm. 'The worse, the better,' as Chernyshevsky often said (meaning the worse things became, the better it was for the revolution). He had advocated, for example, the emancipation of the serfs *without* land in 1861 on the grounds that this would have resulted 'in an immediate catastrophe'.[9]*

In this contempt for the living conditions of the common people were the roots of the authoritarianism to which the revolution had such a tragic propensity. Its leaders sought to liberate 'the people' according to their own abstract notions of Truth and Justice. But if the people were unwilling to be led in that direction, or became too chaotic to control, then they would have to be forced to be free.

*　*　*

Literature in modern Russia always was a surrogate for politics. Nowhere else was Shelley's maxim — that 'poets are the unofficial legislators of the world' — so tragically relevant as in Russia. In the absence of credible politicians, the Russian public looked to its writers for moral leadership in the fight against autocracy. 'That is why', Vissarion Belinsky wrote to Gogol in 1847, 'so much attention is given to every liberal literary trend, even in the case of inferior talent, and why the popularity of even great writers rapidly declines when they enlist in the service of autocracy.' Throughout the eighteenth and nineteenth centuries the intelligentsia had shaped its social codes and conventions according to literary models and the morals drawn from them by literary critics.[10] Russian literary criticism, which Belinsky founded, served as a vehicle for political ideas, albeit in an Aesopian language that repaid careful reading between the lines. All the early revolutionary theorists (Herzen, Belinsky, Dobroliubov, Chernyshevsky) wrote mainly about literature. It was through the literary journals of the 1850s, such as Herzen's *The Bell* and Chernyshevsky's *The Contemporary*, which mixed literature with social comment, that the basic ideas of the revolutionary movement were first publicized to a mass audience. No other culture attached such status to the high-brow periodical. These 'thick' literary journals were read and discussed by virtually the whole of educated society.† There was nothing like it in the West, where freedom of expression resulted in widespread political apathy.

---

* It was a doctrine that Lenin was to follow. During the famine of 1891 he opposed the idea of humanitarian relief on the grounds that the famine would force millions of destitute peasants to flee to the cities and join the ranks of the proletariat: this would bring the revolution one step closer.

† The 'thick' literary journals had a similar influence in the Soviet period with publications such as *Novyi Mir*, which had a readership of tens of millions. They were also vehicles for political ideas in a system where open political debate had been banned.

The *Edinburgh Review*, which was perhaps the nearest equivalent in the nineteenth century, was read by only a tiny élite.

From Belinsky on, the self-imposed mission of Russian literature was both social and didactic: to highlight the motive forces of society and to lead the people towards a new and democratic life. No other literature gave such prominence to the social novel: it dominated the literary canon from the 1840s and Dostoevsky's *Poor Folk* to the 1900s and Gorky's *Mother*. (The latter in turn became the model for the reincarnation of the social novel in its Sovietized version of Socialist Realism.) As a form of moral instruction, the social novel nearly always contained a 'positive hero' who embodied the virtues of the New Man. A commitment to the people's cause, often at the expense of great self-sacrifice, was an essential attribute of such fictional heroes. Characters interested in the aesthetic, or in pursuits unconnected with the cause, were 'superfluous men', alienated from society.

The most heroic of these positive heroes was Rakhmetev in Chernyshevsky's dreadful novel *What Is To Be Done?* (1862). This monolithic titan, who was to serve as a model for a whole generation of revolutionaries (including Lenin), renounces all the pleasures of life in order to harden his superhuman will and make himself insensible to the human suffering which the coming revolution is bound to create. He is a puritan and an ascetic: on one occasion he even sleeps on a bed of nails in order to stifle his sexual urges. He trains his body by gymnastics and lifting weights. He eats nothing but raw steak. He trains his mind in a similar way, reading 'only the essential' (politics and science) for days and nights on end until he has absorbed the wisdom of humankind. Only then does the revolutionary hero set out on his mission to 'work for the benefit of the people'. Nothing diverts him from the cause, not even the amorous attentions of a young and beautiful widow, whom he rejects. The life he leads is rigorous and disciplined: it proceeds like clockwork, with so much time for reading every day, so much time for exercise and so on. Yet (and here is the message of the story) it is only through such selfless dedication that the New Man is able to transcend the alienated existence of the old 'superfluous man'. He finds salvation through politics.[11]

Allowing the publication of Chernyshevsky's novel was one of the biggest mistakes the tsarist censor ever made: for it converted more people to the cause of the revolution than all the works of Marx and Engels put together (Marx himself learned Russian in order to read it). Plekhanov, the 'founder of Russian Marxism', said that from that novel 'we have all drawn moral strength and faith in a better future'. The revolutionary theorist Tkachev called it the 'gospel' of the movement; Kropotkin the 'banner of Russian youth'. One young revolutionary of the 1860s claimed that there were only three great men in history: Jesus Christ, St Paul and Chernyshevsky. Lenin, whose own ascetic lifestyle bore a disturbing resemblance to Rakhmetev's, read the novel five times in one summer. He later acknowledged that it had been crucial in converting him to the revolutionary movement. 'It completely reshaped me,' he told Valentinov in 1904. 'This is a book that changes one for a whole lifetime.' Chernyshevsky's importance, in Lenin's view, was that he had 'not only showed that every right-thinking and really honest man must be a revolutionary, but also — and this is his greatest merit — what a revolutionary *must be like*'. Rakhmetev, with his superhuman will and selfless dedication to the cause, was the perfect model of the Bolshevik.[12]

Chernyshevsky's hero was also an inspiration to the nihilistic students of the 1860s. His asceticism, his belief in science, and his rejection of the old moral order appealed to them. Their 'nihilism' entailed a youthful rebellion against the artistic dabbling of their father's generation (the 'men of the forties'); a militant utilitarianism, materialism and belief in progress through the application of scientific methods to society; and a general questioning of all authority, moral and religious, which was manifested in a revolutionary passion to destroy. Dmitry Pisarev, one of the student idols of the 1860s, urged his followers to hit out right and left at all institutions, on the grounds that whatever collapsed from their blows was not worth preserving. As Bakunin put it, since the old Russia was rotten to the core, it was 'a creative urge' to destroy it. These were the angry young men of their day. Many of them came from relatively humble backgrounds — the sons of priests, such as Chernyshevsky, or of mixed social origins (*raznochintsy*) — so that their sense of Russia's worthlessness was reinforced by their own feelings of underprivilege. Chernyshevsky, for example, often expressed a deep hatred and feeling of shame for the backwardness of Saratov province where he had grown up. 'It would be better', he once wrote, 'not to be born at all than to be born a Russian.' There was a long tradition of national self-hatred among the Russian intelligentsia, stemming from the fact that they were so cut off from the ordinary people and had always modelled themselves on the West.[13]

These restless youths found another mirror of their attitudes in Bazarov, the young hero of Turgenev's novel *Fathers and Sons* (1862). Turgenev (a 'man of the forties') had intended him as a monstrous caricature of the nihilists, whom he regarded as narrowly materialist, morally slippery and artistically philistine, although later he would pretend otherwise. There was a striking resemblance between Bazarov and the student idol Pisarev. Yet such was the gulf of misunderstanding between the fathers and sons of real life that the young radicals took his faults as virtues and acclaimed Bazarov as their ideal man.

The manifesto of these juvenile Jacobins was written by Zaichnevsky, an imprisoned student agitator, in 1862. *Young Russia*, as it was called in imitation of *Young Italy*, had little else in common with Mazzini's creed. It advocated the violent seizure of power by a small but well-disciplined group of conspirators, followed by the establishment of a revolutionary dictatorship which would carry out the socialist transformation of society and exterminate all its enemies, including democrats and any socialists who opposed it. The manifesto could have passed for a description of what the Bolsheviks actually did (they later claimed Zaichnevsky as their own). It planned to nationalize the land and industry, to bring all children under the care of the state, and to fix the elections to a newly convened constituent assembly to ensure that the government side won. This would be 'a bloody revolution' but, Zaichnesvky claimed, 'we are not afraid of it, even though we know that a river of blood will flow and that many innocent victims will perish'. In one of the most chilling passages of the Russian revolutionary canon, he weighed up the likely costs:

> Soon, very soon, the day will come when we shall unfurl the great banner of the future, the red flag, and with a mighty cry of 'Long Live the Russian Social and Democratic Republic!' we shall move against the Winter Palace to exterminate all its inhabitants. It may be that it will be sufficient to kill only the imperial family, i.e. about 100 people; but it may also happen, and this is more likely, that the whole imperial party will rise as one man behind the Tsar, because for them it will be a matter of life and death. If this should happen, then with faith in ourselves and our strength, in the support of the people, and in the glorious future of Russia — whose fate it is to be the first country to bring about the triumph of socialism — we shall raise the battle-cry: 'To your axes!' and we shall kill the imperial party with no more mercy than they show for us now. We shall kill them in the squares, if the dirty swine ever dare to appear there; kill them in their houses; kill them in the narrow streets of the towns; kill them in the avenues of the capitals; kill them in the villages. Remember: anyone who is not with us is our enemy, and every method may be used to exterminate our enemies.[14]

This new spirit of violence and hatred was even more pronounced in the writings of Sergei Nechaev. Lenin placed a high value on them as a theory of revolutionary conspiracy. Born in 1847 into a serf family, Nechaev was the first revolutionary theorist in Russia to emerge from the lower classes rather than the intelligentsia. Put out to factory work from the age of nine, he taught himself to read and write and then qualified, in 1866, as an instructor of religion. His propaganda among the students and workers of St Petersburg during the late 1860s was dominated by the theme of class revenge. 'Nechaev', wrote Vera Zasulich, a Populist who would later become a Menshevik, 'was not a product of our intelligentsia milieu. He was alien to it. It was not opinions, derived from contact with this milieu, which underlay his revolutionary energy, but burning hatred, and not only hatred against the government . . . but against all of society, all educated strata, all these gentlefolk, rich and poor, conservative, liberal and radical.' He was, in short, a Bolshevik before the Bolsheviks.

Nechaev is principally remembered for the *Revolutionary Catechism*, written either by him or possibly by Bakunin in collaboration with him in 1869. Its twenty-six articles, setting out the principles of the professional revolutionary, might have served as the Bolshevik oath. The morals of that party owed as much to Nechaev as they did to Marx. Ruthless discipline and dedication were the key themes of the *Catechism*. Its essential message was that only 'Tsarist methods' — i.e. the methods of the police state — were capable of defeating the tsarist regime. Its first article read:

The revolutionary is a dedicated man. He has no personal feelings, no private affairs, no emotions, no attachments, no property, and no name. Everything in him is subordinated towards a single exclusive attachment, a single thought and a single passion — the revolution.

Rejecting all morality, the revolutionary must be ready 'to destroy everyone who stands in his way'. He must harden himself to all suffering: 'All the soft and tender feelings of the family, friendship and love, even all gratitude and honour, must be stifled, and in their place there must be the cold and single-minded passion for the work of the revolution.' The revolutionary was to relate to members of society in accordance with their designated purpose in the revolution. So, for example, the ruling élites were to be 'executed without delay'; the rich exploited for the benefit of the cause; and the democrats compromised and used to create disorder. Even the lower-ranking party comrades were to be thought of as 'portions of a common fund of revolutionary capital' which each leader was to expend 'as he thinks fit'.

One comrade who proved to be expendable was Ivan Ivanov. Together with three of his fellow-conspirators Nechaev murdered him after he refused to carry out Necheev's dictatorial orders as the leader of a revolutionary student group. The brutality of the killing, which Dostoevsky used in *The Possessed* as the basis for Shatov's murder scene,* led to a widespread feeling of moral revulsion, even among the socialists. Bakunin (who had formerly been Nechaev's mentor)

---

* Dostoevsky, who had himself belonged to the Petrashevsky revolutionary circle in the 1850s, used this novel to attack the mentality of the revolutionaries, especially the nihilists. Petr Verkhovensky, its central character, is clearly based upon Nechaev. At one point in the novel he says that it would be justified to kill a million people in the struggle against despotism because in the course of a hundred years the despots would kill many more.

wrote to a London friend in 1870, eight months after Ivanov's murder, warning him not to help the Russian fugitive:

> N. does not stop at anything... Deeply impressed by the [police repressions] which destroyed the secret organization in Russia, he came to the conclusion that if he was to form a strong organization he would have to base it on the principles of Machiavelli and the motto of the Jesuits: 'Violence for the body, lies for the soul!' Truth, mutual trust, solidarity — these can only exist among the dozen comrades who make up the inner sanctum of the Society. All the rest are no more than a blind instrument, expendable by these dozen men. It is allowed, indeed a duty, to cheat them, compromise them, and steal from them; it is even allowed to have them killed.[15]

The police did eventually catch up with Nechaev. In 1872 he was arrested in Switzerland and extradited to Russia, where he was imprisoned in solitary confinement in the Peter and Paul Fortress. Nothing more was heard of him — he was assumed to have died — until eight years later when a group of terrorists suddenly received a letter from him containing a plan for his escape. By the sheer force of his personality Nechaev had won over his own guards and had (literally) set up an underground revolutionary cell in the dungeons of this tsarist bastion. These guards had smuggled out the letter. Later, when they were brought to trial, they chose to go to jail themselves rather than denounce their leader. Yet it was already too late for Nechaev (he died in the fortress the following year). Since his imprisonment the climate had changed and the new creed, Populism, had turned away from his putschist tactics and begun to look instead to mass propaganda and education as a means of igniting a social revolution.

Populism was less a doctrine than a set of sentiments and attitudes. At its root was the intelligentsia's adoration of the simple folk, and a belief in their wisdom and goodness. The cult was expressed as much in literature as it was in politics and social theories. Although the term was only really used from the 1870s onwards, the three basic principles of Populism — the primacy of liberty and democracy, the idealization of the peasantry and the belief that Russia's path to socialism was autochthonous and separate from that of the West — were common to a long tradition of Russian thought beginning in the 1840s with the radical Slavophiles and Herzen and culminating half a century later with the formation of the Social Revolutionary Party.

Disillusioned with bourgeois Europe after the failure of the 1848 Revolutions, Herzen pinned his hopes on peasant Russia — Young Russia, as he called it — to lead the way to socialism. The peasant commune was the bearer of this messianic mission. Herzen saw it as the indestructible repository of Russia's ancient freedoms, an organic symbol of her authentic condition before the imposition of the tsarist state and its 'German' civilization. This was of course a romantic vision: it stemmed from the same craving for a simple fraternal life, unspoilt by modern civilization, and from the same belief in the 'noble savage', which had inspired intellectuals since Rousseau. The commune, argued Herzen, already contained the socialist ideals towards which the rest of Europe — the Old (and 'dying') Europe — was still striving. It was democratic and egalitarian, based on the sharing of the land; it fostered a spirit of community and social harmony among the peasants; and through its ancient customs it expressed a deeper sense of social justice and morality than the Western legal tradition, based on the defence of private property. The commune, in short, offered Russia the chance to move directly towards socialism without first experiencing the painful effects of capitalism.

Herzen's theory of revolution came down to one central proposition: since the source of all freedom was in the people, and the source of all oppression in the tsarist state, Russia could only be liberated through a genuine social revolution. This would have to be a democratic revolution, one that came from below and was based on the will of the people. It would also have to be a total revolution, one that overturned the alien civilization upon which the tsarist system had been based, since the Russian people were too oppressed to be satisfied by the 'half-freedoms' of political reform. This had important implications for the methods of the revolutionaries; and it was here that Herzen left his imprint on the later Populist movement. No minority had the right to enforce its abstract ideals on the people. There was to be no more talk of conspiracy and seizing power — which was bound to end in tyranny and terror. Instead of breaking down the tsarist prison walls it would merely 'give them a new function, as if a plan for a jail could be used for a free existence'.[16] The only democratic means of revolution were education and propaganda to help the people understand their own best interests and to prepare them gradually for the tasks of power.

Democratic as this ideal was, it raised a huge dilemma for the Populists (and later for the Marxists). If the revolution was to come from the people themselves then what should the revolutionary leaders do if the people rejected the revolution? What if the peasants proved conservative? Or if the workers were more interested in sharing the benefits of capitalism than in trying to overthrow it? All the revolutionary parties — none of which numbered more than a few hundred at this stage — were divided on this question: where should they draw the line between the rank and file and the leadership, between democracy and dictatorship, within the party? Among the Populists there were, on the one hand, those such as Plekhanov and Pavel Axelrod, who argued that there was no alternative but to wait until propaganda and education had prepared the ground for a mass social movement. The revolution could not otherwise be justified as democratic and was likely to end in a new dictatorship. The Mensheviks in the Social Democratic Party later espoused the same principles. But, on the other hand, Populists like Tkachev argued that to wait indefinitely for a social revolution, and in the meantime to condemn all forms of revolt and terrorism by its élite vanguard, was to run the risk of allowing the tsarist order to stabilize itself through the advance of capitalism. Only by seizing power first and establishing a revolutionary dictatorship was it possible to secure the necessary political conditions for the transition to socialism. This idea also had its followers in the Social Democratic Party: it became the guiding principle of Lenin's theory of revolution.

This was the dilemma the Populists faced after the collapse of the 'To the People' movement. During the 'mad summer' of 1874 thousands of students left their lecture halls to 'go to the people'. There was no real organization, although many of these missionaries belonged to the circles of Lavrov and Chaikovsky, which believed in spreading propaganda among the peasants in preparation for the inevitable revolution. Dressed like peasants or petty traders, these young idealists flooded into the countryside with the aim of 'serving the people' by teaching them how to read and write, by taking jobs as simple labourers, and by helping them to understand the causes of their suffering. Guilt and the desire for self-sacrifice played a large role in this revolutionary passion play. The students were acutely conscious of the need to repay their 'debt to the people'. They embraced the idea of living with the peasants and sharing in their sufferings. They were ready to run the risks of catching cholera, or of being arrested and sent to jail. Some even welcomed the idea of becoming a martyr 'for the people': it would make them into heroes. 'You will be washing pots and plucking chickens,' one of these fictionalized students Mariana is told in Turgenev's novel *Virgin Soil*. 'And, who knows, maybe you will save your country in that way.' The peasants, however, met these childish crusaders with mistrust and hostility. They found their urban manners and doctrines alien; and while they did not understand their propaganda, they understood enough to know that it was dangerous. 'Socialism', one of the Populists later wrote, 'bounced off the peasants like peas from a wall. They listened to our people as they do to the priest — respectfully but without the slightest effect on their thinking or their actions.' Most of the radicals were soon rounded up by the police, sometimes tipped off by the local peasants.[17]

This sobering encounter with the common people led the Populists to turn away disillusioned from propaganda and the social revolution. 'We cannot change the thinking of even one in six hundred peasants, let alone of one in sixty,' Stepniak wrote to Lavrov in 1876. 'Everyone is beginning to realize the need for organization ... A revolt has to be organized.'[18] The result was the emergence of a more centralized party structure than the loose circles of the early 1870s. It took the name of Land and Liberty (*Zemlia i Volia*), established that year, which turned away from open propaganda to underground conspiracy and political work. On 6 December 1876 it organized the first public demonstration in Russian history.

The wheel was turning full circle: having rejected Jacobinism in favour of a social revolution, the Populists were now returning to the Jacobin methods of conspiracy, terrorism and coups in the name of the people. The writings of Petr Tkachev marked the crucial watershed. They formed a bridge between the Jacobin tradition of Nechaev, the classic Populist tradition of Land and Liberty, and the Marxist tradition of Lenin. The Bolshevik leader owed more to Tkachev than to any other single Russian theorist. Born in 1844 into a minor gentry family, Tkachev had spent several years in the Peter and Paul Fortress after being arrested for his role in the student strikes of 1861. During the late 1860s he had fallen under Nechaev's spell — for which he spent another term in jail, followed by exile in Switzerland. It was there that, albeit crudely, he began to adopt the sociology of Marx, which led him away from Populism. In the mid-1870s he developed a violent critique of the 'To the People' movement. He claimed that propaganda could not bring about a revolution because the laws of social progress (to which Russia, like the rest of Europe, was subordinate) meant that the richer peasants would always support the regime. He argued instead for a seizure of power by the revolutionary vanguard, which would then set up a dictatorship and begin the construction of socialism. Tkachev claimed that the time was ripe for this putsch, which should take place as soon as possible, since as yet there was no real social force prepared to side with the government but there would soon be with the development of capitalism and the bourgeoisie. In a passage which Lenin was to echo in October 1917, Tkachev raised the battlecry: 'This is why we cannot wait. This is why we claim that a revolution is indispensable, and indispensable now, *at this very moment*. We cannot allow any postponement. It is *now* or — perhaps very soon — *never*.' To carry through this *coup d'état* Tkachev made it clear that there had to be an élitist and conspiratorial party, which, like an army, was highly disciplined and centralized. Here too Lenin was to echo him.[19]

Returning to the methods of the Jacobins, however, meant that the Populists, like their predecessors, were forced to engage in a hopeless war against the tsarist police state. A vicious cycle started of increasing repression by the police and counter-terror by the Populists. The turning point came in 1878, when Vera Zasulich, one of the leaders of Land and Liberty, shot and wounded General F. F. Trepov, the Governor of St Petersburg, as a reprisal for his order to have a student prisoner flogged who — in a typical gesture of defiance — had refused to take off his hat in the Governor's presence. Zasulich was hailed as a martyr for justice by the democratic intelligentsia, and was acquitted by a liberal court. This was the signal for a wave of terror, whose aim was to undermine the autocracy and to force it to make political concessions. Two provincial governors were killed. Six failed attempts were made on the Tsar, including a bomb on the imperial train and a huge explosion in the Winter Palace. Finally, on 1 March 1881, as Alexander was driving in his carriage through St Petersburg, he was killed by a bomb.

The widespread revulsion felt even amongst the revolutionaries to this wave of terrorism led to a split in Land and Liberty. One branch, calling itself the People's Will (*Narodnaia Volia*), espoused the ideals of Tkachev and stayed loyal to the tactics of terrorism leading to the violent seizure of power. Formed in 1879, this faction carried out the murder of the Tsar. Many of its leaders were later arrested — several of them executed — in the repressions that followed the assassination. But the campaign of terror which it had started was carried on by several other smaller groups in the 1880s. One of them included Lenin's elder brother, Alexander Ul'ianov, who was executed after a failed plot to assassinate Alexander III on the sixth anniversary of his father's death. The supposed aim of the campaign was to destabilize the state and provide a spark for a popular rebellion. But it soon degenerated — as all terror does — into violence for violence's sake. It has been estimated that over 17,000 people were killed or wounded by terrorists during the last twenty years of the tsarist regime — more than five times the number of people killed in Northern Ireland during the twenty-five years of 'the troubles'.[20] Some of the terror was little more than criminal violence for personal gain. All the revolutionary parties financed themselves at least partly by robberies (which they euphemistically termed 'expropriations'), mainly of banks and trains, and there was little to stop those who did the stealing from pocketing the proceeds. This was bad enough for the moral climate of the revolutionary parties. But it was not nearly as damaging as the cumulative effect of years of killing, which resulted in a cynicism, an indifference and callousness, to the victims of their cause.

The rival branch of Land and Liberty called itself the Black Partition (*Chernyi Peredel*) — a peasant term for the revolution on the land. It was formed in 1880 by three future leading lights of the Social Democratic Party — Plekhanov, Axelrod and Zasulich — who would all convert to Marxism during the early 1880s. They rejected the use of terror, claiming it was bound to end in failure and renewed repression. They argued that only a social revolution, coming from the people themselves, could be both successful and democratic. The failure after Alexander's assassination to extract political concessions seemed to prove the correctness of their first claim; while the growth of the urban working class gave them new grounds for hope on the second. This was the real beginning of the Marxist movement in Russia.

ii Marx Comes to Russia

In March 1872 a heavy tome of political economy, written in German, landed on the desk of the tsarist censor. Its author was well known for his socialist theories and all his previous books had been banned. The publishers had no right to expect a different fate for this new work. It was an uncompromising critique of the modern factory system and, although the censorship laws had been liberalized in 1865, there was still a clear ban on any work expounding 'the harmful doctrines of socialism and communism', or rousing 'enmity between one class and another'. The new laws were strict enough to ban such dangerous books as Spinoza's *Ethics*, Hobbes's *Leviathan*, Voltaire's *Philosophy of History* and Lecky's *History of European Morals*. And yet this German *magnum opus* — 674 pages of dense statistical analysis — was deemed much too difficult and abstruse to be seditious. 'It is possible to state with certainty', concluded the first of the two censors, 'that very few people in Russia will read it, and even fewer will understand it.' Moreover, added the second, since the author attacked the British factory system, his critique was not applicable to Russia, where the 'capitalist exploitation' of which he spoke had never been experienced. Neither censor thought it necessary to prevent the publication of this 'strictly scientific work'.[21]

Thus Marx's *Capital* was launched in Russia. It was the book's first foreign publication, just five years after the original Hamburg edition and fifteen before its first English publication. Contrary to everyone's expectations, the author's as well as the censors', it led to revolution earlier in Russia than in any of the Western societies to which it had been addressed.

The tsarist censors soon realized their mistake. Ten months later they took their revenge on Nikolai Poliakov, Marx's first Russian publisher, by putting him on trial for his next 'subversive' publication, a collection of Diderot's stories, which were confiscated and burned by the police, forcing Poliakov out of business. But it was too late. *Capital* was an instant hit. Its first print run of 3,000 copies was sold out within the year (the first German edition of 1,000 copies, by comparison, took over five years to sell). Marx himself acknowledged that in Russia his masterpiece was 'read and valued more than anywhere'. Slavophiles and Populists both welcomed the book as an exposé of the horrors of the Western capitalist system, which they wanted Russia to avoid. Marx's sociology and view of history, if not yet his politics, spread like a wild craze during the later 1870s. Among students it was 'almost improper' not to be a Marxist. 'Nobody dares to raise a voice against Karl Marx these days', complained one liberal, 'without bringing down the wrath of his youthful admirers.'[22]

After the collapse of the 'To the People' movement, with its false idealization of the Russian peasant, the Marxist message seemed like salvation to the radical intelligentsia. All their hopes for a social revolution could now be switched to the industrial working class. There was clearly no more mileage in the idea of a peasant revolutionary movement; and from the 1880s work among the peasants was condescendingly described by the Marxists as 'small deeds' (i.e. the sort of charity work favoured by the gentry and zemstvo types). The famine crisis of 1891 seemed to underline the backwardness of the peasantry. It showed that they were doomed to die out, both as individuals and as a class, under the wheels of economic development. The peasants were a relic of Russia's savage past — its *Aziatchina* or Asiatic way of life — which would inevitably be swept away by the progress of industry. Their cultural backwardness was symbolized by stories that during the cholera epidemic after the famine peasants had attacked the very doctors who were trying to inoculate them because they thought that their medicines were some strange poison. During the 1890s social science publications boomed — whole libraries were filled by the volumes of statistics published in these years; their aim was to find the causes of the famine crisis in the Marxist laws of economic development.

The 'scientific' nature of Marxist theory intoxicated the Russian radical mind, already steeped in the rationalism and materialism of the 1860s. Marx's historical dialectic seemed to do for society what Darwin had done for humanity: provide a logical theory of evolutionary development. It was 'serious' and 'objective', a comprehensive system that would explain the social world. It was in this sense an answer to that quintessential Russian quest for a knowledge that was absolute. Marxism, moreover, was optimistic. It showed that progress lay in industry, that there was meaning in the chaos of history, and that through the working class, through the conscious striving of humanity, socialism would become the end of history. This message had a special appeal to the Russian intelligentsia, painfully aware as they were of their country's backwardness, since it implied that Russia would inevitably become more like the advanced countries of the West — Germany, in particular, whose Social Democratic Party was a model for the rest of the Marxist movement in Europe. The Populist belief in Russia's 'separate path', which had seemed to consign her to perpetual peasant-hood, could thus be dismissed as romantic and devoid of scientific content.

The idea that Marxism could bring Russia closer to the West was perhaps its principal appeal. Marxism was seen as a 'path of reason', in the words of Lydia Dan, lighting up the way to modernity, enlightenment and civilization. As Valentinov, another veteran of the Marxist movement, recalled in the 1950s:

> We seized on Marxism because we were attracted by its sociological and economic *optimism*, its strong belief, buttressed by facts and figures, that the development of the economy, the development of capitalism, by demoralizing and eroding the foundations of the old society, was creating new

social forces (including us) which would certainly sweep away the autocratic regime together with its abominations. With the optimism of youth we had been searching for a formula that offered hope, and we found it in Marxism. We were also attracted by its *European* nature. Marxism came from Europe. It did not smell and taste of home-grown mould and provincialism, but was new, fresh, and exciting. Marxism held out a promise that we would not stay a semi-Asiatic country, but would become part of the West with its culture, institutions and attributes of a free political system. The West was our guiding light.

Petr Struve, one of the leading Marxist theorists, said he had subscribed to the doctrine because it offered a 'scientific solution' to Russia's twin problems of liberation from autocracy and the misery of backwardness. His famous words of 1894 — 'No, let us admit our lack of culture and enroll in the school of capitalism' — became one of the mottoes of the movement. Lenin echoed it in 1921. Here perhaps, as Leo Haimson has suggested, was the intellectual root of the movement's attraction to the Jews.* Whereas Populism offered an archaic vision of peasant Russia — a land of pogroms and discrimination against the Jews — Marxism offered a modern and Western vision. It promised to assimilate the Jews into a movement of universal human liberation — not just the liberation of the peasantry — based on the principles of internationalism.[23]

Until the middle of the 1890s it was hard to distinguish between the Populists and Marxists in Russia. Even the police (normally well informed in such matters) often confused them. The Populists adopted Marx's sociology, translated and distributed his works, and, in the final years of his life, even gained the support of Marx himself. The Marxists equally borrowed from the Populists' rhetoric and tactics and, at least inside Russia, if not in exile, were forced to work alongside them. The revolutionary underground was not large enough for the two factions to fall out: they were forced to share their printing presses and work together in the factories and clubs. There was great fluidity and co-operation between the various workers' groups — Plekhanov's Emancipation of Labour, the Workers' Section of the People's Will, the student-organized Workers' Circles, the Polish Marxist Party and the first groupings of Social Democrats — which all combined elements from Marx and the Populists in their propaganda.

This was the context in which the young Lenin, or Ul'ianov, as he was

---

* Jews played a prominent role in the Social Democratic movement, providing many of its most important leaders (Axelrod, Deich, Martov, Trotsky, Kamenev and Zinoviev, just to name a few). In 1905 the Social Democratic Party in Russia had 8,400 members. The Bund, by contrast, the Jewish workers' party of the Pale, had 35,000 members.

then known,* entered revolutionary politics. Contrary to the Soviet myth, which had Lenin a fully fledged Marxist theorist in his nappies, the leader of the Bolshevik Revolution came to politics quite late. At the age of sixteen he was still religious and showed no interest in politics at all. Classics and literature were his main studies at the gymnasium in Simbirsk. There, by one of those curious historical ironies, Lenin's headmaster was Fedor Kerensky, the father of his arch-rival in 1917. During Lenin's final year at the gymnasium (1887) Kerensky wrote a report on the future Bolshevik describing him as a model student, never giving 'cause for dissatisfaction, by word or by deed, to the school authorities'. This he put down to the 'moral' nature of his upbringing. 'Religion and discipline', wrote the headmaster, 'were the basis of this upbringing, the fruits of which are apparent in Ul'ianov's behaviour.' So far there was nothing to suggest that Lenin was set to become a revolutionary; on the contrary, all the indications were that he would follow in his father's footsteps and make a distinguished career in the tsarist bureaucracy.

Ilya Ul'ianov, Lenin's father, was a typical gentleman-liberal of the type that his son would come to despise. There is no basis to the myth, advanced by Nadezhda Krupskaya in 1938, that he exerted a revolutionary influence on his children. Anna Ul'ianova, Lenin's sister, recalls that he was a religious man, that he greatly admired Alexander II's reforms of the 1860s, and that he saw it as his job to protect the young from radicalism. He was the Inspector of Schools for Simbirsk Province, an important office which entitled him to be addressed as 'Your Excellency'. This noble background was a source of embarrassment to Lenin's Soviet hagiographers. They chose to dwell instead on the humble origins of his paternal grandfather, Nikolai Ul'ianov, the son of a serf who had worked as a tailor in the lower Volga town of Astrakhan. But here too there was a problem: Nikolai was partly Kalmyk, and his wife Anna wholly so (Lenin's face had obvious Mongol features), and this was inconvenient to a Stalinist regime peddling its own brand of Great Russian chauvinism. Lenin's ancestry on his mother's side was even more embarrassing. Maria Alexandrovna, Lenin's mother, was the daughter of Alexander Blank, a baptized Jew who rose to become a wealthy doctor and landowner in Kazan. He was the son of Moishe Blank, a Jewish merchant from Volhynia who had married a Swedish woman by the name of Anna Ostedt. Lenin's Jewish ancestry was always hidden by the Soviet author-ities, despite an appeal by Anna Ul'ianova, in a letter to Stalin in 1932, suggest-ing that 'this fact could be used to combat anti-Semitism'. 'Absolutely not one word about this letter!' was Stalin's categorical imperative. Alexander Blank married Anna Groschopf, the daughter of a well-to-do Lutheran family from

---

* The alias and pseudonym 'Lenin' was probably derived from the River Lena in Siberia. Lenin first used it in 1901.

Germany and with this newly acquired wealth launched his distinguished medical career, rising to become a police doctor and medical inspector in one of the largest state arms factories. In 1847, having attained the rank of State Councillor, he retired to his estate at Kokushkino and registered himself as a nobleman.[24]

Lenin's non-Russian ethnic antecedents — Mongol, Jewish, Swedish and German — may partly explain his often expressed contempt for Russia and the Russians, although to conclude, as the late Dmitry Volkogonov did, that Lenin's 'cruel policies' towards the Russian people were derived from his 'foreign' origins is quite unjustified (one might say the same of the equally 'foreign' Romanovs). He often used the phrase 'Russian idiots'. He complained that the Russians were 'too soft' for the tasks of the revolution. And indeed many of its most important tasks were to be entrusted to the non-Russians (Latvians and Jews in particular) in the party. Yet paradoxically — and Lenin's character was full of such paradoxes — he was in many ways a typical Russian nobleman. He was fond of the Blank estate, where he spent a long time in his youth. When young he was proud to describe himself as 'a squire's son'. He once even signed himself before the police as 'Hereditary Nobleman Vladimir Ul'ianov'. In his private life Lenin was the epitome of the heartless squire whom his government would one day destroy. In 1891, at the height of the famine, he sued his peasant neighbours for causing damage to the family estate. And while he condemned in his early writings the practices of 'gentry capitalism', he himself was living handsomely on its profits, drawing nearly all his income from the rents and interest derived from the sale of his mother's estate.[25]

Lenin's noble background was one key to his domineering personality. This is something that has often been ignored by his biographers. Valentinov, who lived with Lenin in Geneva during 1904, recalls how he found a rare and deeply hidden source of sentiment in the Bolshevik leader. Having read Herzen's *My Past and Thoughts*, a work that frequently waxes lyrical on the subject of the Russian countryside, Valentinov had become homesick for his long-abandoned family estate in Tambov province. He told Lenin of these feelings and found him clearly sympathetic. Lenin began asking him about the arrangement of the flower-beds, but their conversation was soon interrupted by a fellow Bolshevik, Olminsky, who, having heard the last part of Valentinov's confession, attacked him for his 'schoolgirl' sentiments: 'Listen to the landowner's son giving himself away!' According to Valentinov, Lenin rounded on Olminsky:

> Well, what about me, if it comes to that? I too used to live on a country estate which belonged to my grandfather. In a sense, I too am a scion of the landed gentry. This is all many years ago, but I still haven't forgotten the pleasant aspects of life on our estate. I have forgotten neither its lime trees nor its flowers. So go on, put me to death. I remember with pleasure how

I used to loll about in haystacks, although I had not made them, how I used to eat strawberries and raspberries, although I had not planted them, and how I used to drink fresh milk, although I had not milked the cows. So am I . . . unworthy to be called a revolutionary?

It was not just Lenin's emotions which were rooted in his noble past. So too were many of his political attitudes: his dogmatic outlook and domineering manner; his intolerance of any form of criticism from subordinates; and his tendency to look upon the masses as no more than the human material needed for his own revolutionary plans. As Gorky put it in 1917, 'Lenin is a "leader" and a Russian nobleman, not without certain psychological traits of this extinct class, and therefore he considers himself justified in performing with the Russian people a cruel experiment which is doomed to failure.'[26]

While, of course, it is all too easy to impose the Lenin of 1917 on that of the early 1890s, it is clear that many of the characteristics which he would display in power were already visible at this early stage. Witness, for example, Lenin's callous attitude to the suffering of the peasants during the famine of 1891 — his idea that aid should be denied to them to hasten the revolutionary crisis. Thirty years later he would show the same indifference to their suffering — which he was now in a position to exploit politically — during the famine of 1921.

The charmed life of the Ul'ianovs came to an abrupt halt in 1887, when Lenin's elder brother Alexander was executed for his involvement in the abortive plot to kill the Tsar. Alexander was generally thought to be the most gifted of the Ul'ianov children, the one most likely to leave his mark on the world. Whereas the young Vladimir had a cruel and angry streak — he often told lies and cheated at games — Alexander was honest and kind, serious and hard-working. In 1883 he entered St Petersburg University to read science and seemed set on becoming a biologist. But after his father's sudden death, in 1886, Alexander fell in with a group of student terrorists who modelled themselves on the People's Will. All of them were squires' sons, and many of them Poles, including ironically Joseph Pilsudski, who would later become the ruler of Poland and an arch-enemy of Lenin's regime. They conspired to blow up the Tsar's carriage on 1 March 1887, the sixth anniversary of Alexander II's assassination, when there would be a procession from the Winter Palace to a special memorial service at St Isaac's Cathedral. Alexander put his scientific education into practice by designing and making the bombs. But the plot was discovered by the police and the conspirators were arrested (one of them launched one of Alexander's bombs whilst they were inside the police station but the home-made device failed to go off). The seventy-two conspirators were imprisoned in the Peter and Paul Fortress — fifteen of them were later brought to trial.

Alexander, as one of the ring-leaders, realized that his fate was already sealed, and from the dock made a brave speech justifying the use of terrorism. He and four others were executed.

There is a legend that on hearing of his brother's death Lenin remarked to his sister Maria: 'No, we shall not take that road, our road must be different.' The implication is that Lenin was already committed to the Marxist cause — the 'we' of the quotation — with its rejection of terror. But this is absurd. Maria at the time was only nine and thus hardly likely to recall the words accurately when she made this claim in 1924. And while it is true that Alexander's execution was a catalyst to Lenin's involvement in the revolutionary movement, his first inclination was, like his brother's, towards the tradition of the People's Will. Lenin's Marxism, which developed slowly after 1889, remained infused with the Jacobin spirit of the terrorists and their belief in the overwhelming importance of the seizure of power.

In 1887 Lenin enrolled as a law student at Kazan University. There, as the brother of a revolutionary martyr, he was drawn into yet another clandestine group modelling itself on the People's Will. Most of the group was arrested that December during student demonstrations. Lenin was singled out for punishment, no doubt partly because of his name, and, along with thirty-nine others, was expelled from the university. This effectively ended Lenin's chance of making a successful career for himself within the existing social order, and it is reasonable to suppose that much of his hatred for that order stemmed from this experience of rejection. Lenin was nothing if not ambitious. Having failed to make a name for himself as a lawyer, he now set about trying to make one for himself as a revolutionary opponent of the law. Until 1890, when he was readmitted to take his law exams, he lived the life of an idle squire on his mother's estate at Kokushkino. He read law, tried unsuccessfully to run his own farm (which his mother had bought for him in the hope that he would make good), and immersed himself in radical books.

Chernyshevsky was his first and greatest love. It was through reading him that Lenin was converted into a revolutionary — long before he read any Marx. Indeed, by the time he came to Marxism, Lenin was already forearmed with the ideas not just of Chernyshevsky but also of Tkachev and the People's Will, and it was these that made for the distinctive features of his 'Leninist' approach to Marx. All the main components of Lenin's doctrine — the stress on the need for a disciplined revolutionary vanguard; the belief that action (the 'subjective factor') could alter the objective course of history (and in particular that seizure of the state apparatus could bring about a social revolution); his defence of Jacobin methods of dictatorship; his contempt for liberals and democrats (and indeed for socialists who compromised with them) — all these stemmed not so much from Marx as from the Russian revolutionary tradition.

Lenin used the ideas of Chernyshevsky, Nechaev, Tkachev and the People's Will to inject a distinctly Russian dose of conspiratorial politics into a Marxist dialectic that would otherwise have remained passive — content to wait for the revolution to mature through the development of objective conditions rather than eager to bring it about through political action. It was not Marxism that made Lenin a revolutionary but Lenin who made Marxism revolutionary.

Gradually, between 1889 and 1894, Lenin moved towards the Marxist mainstream. But only temporarily. To begin with, like many provincial revolutionaries, he merely added Marx's sociology to the putschist tactics of the People's Will. The goal of the revolutionary movement was still the seizure of power but the arena for this struggle was to be transferred from the peasantry to the working class. Then, in his first major published work, *The Development of Capitalism in Russia* (1899), he squared the lessons of Marx's work — that a capitalist stage of development was necessary before a socialist revolution — with his own preference for such a revolution in the immediate future through the bizarre (not to say preposterous) thesis that peasant Russia was already in the throes of capitalism, classifying no less than one-fifth of its peasant households as 'capitalist' and over half the peasants as 'proletarians'. This was Tkachev dressed up as Marx. It was only after his arrival in St Petersburg, during the autumn of 1893, that Lenin came round to the standard Marxist view — the view that Russia was only at the start of its capitalist stage and that to bring this to its maturity there had to be a democratic movement uniting the workers with the bourgeoisie in the struggle against autocracy. No more talk of a *coup d'état* or of terror. It was only after the establishment of a 'bourgeois democracy', granting freedoms of speech and association for the organization of the workers, that the second and socialist phase of the revolution could begin.

Plekhanov's influence was paramount here. It was he who had first mapped out this two-stage revolutionary strategy. With it the Russian Marxists at last had an answer to the problem of how to bring about a post-capitalist society in a pre-capitalist one. After so many years of fruitless terror, it gave them grounds for their belief that in forsaking the seizure of power — which, as Plekhanov put it, could only lead to a 'despotism in Communist form' — they could still advance towards socialism. Lenin, in his own words, fell 'in love' with Plekhanov, as did all the Marxists in St Petersburg. Although Plekhanov lived in exile, his works made him their undisputed leader and sage. No other Russian Marxist had such a high standing in the European movement. His most famous work of 1895 — a stunningly reductionist interpretation of the Marxist world-view published under the pseudonym of Beltov and, like Marx's *Capital*, slipped past the Russian censors with the esoteric title *On the Question of Developing a Monistic View of History* — 'made people into Marxists overnight'. He was the Moses of the Marxists. His works, in Potresov's words, brought 'the ten commandments of Marxism down from Mount Sinai and handed them to the Russian young'.[27]

At first, Lenin made a bad impression on the Marxists in St Petersburg. Many of them were repelled by this short and stocky figure with his egg-shaped, balding head, small piercing eyes, dry sarcastic laugh, brusqueness and acerbity. Lenin was a newcomer and his musty and 'provincial' appearance was distinctly unimpressive. Potresov described him at their first meeting as a 'typical middle-aged tradesman from some northern Yaroslavl' province'.* But through his conscientious dedication and self-discipline, his iron logic and practicality, Lenin soon emerged as a natural leader — a clear man of action — among the Petersburg intellectuals. Many people thought he was a decent man — Lenin could be charming when he wanted and he was nearly always personally decent in his comradely relations — and not a few people fell in love with him. One of these was his future wife, Nadezhda Krupskaya, whom Lenin met around this time as a fellow propagandist in St Petersburg.[28]

The purpose of their propaganda was the education of a vanguard of 'conscious' workers — Russian Bebels like Kanatchikov, who would organize the working class for the coming revolution. But education did not necessarily make the workers revolutionary. On the contrary, as Kanatchikov soon discovered, most of the skilled and educated workers were more inclined to improve their lot within the capitalist system than seek to overthrow it. There was a growing tension between the mainly economic concerns of the workers and the political aims of those activists and intellectuals who would be their leaders. The Marxists were thus faced with the same dilemma which the Populists had confronted in relation to the peasantry after the mid-1870s: what should they do when the masses failed to respond to their propaganda? Whereas the Populists had been driven to isolated terrorism, the Marxists found a temporary solution to this problem in the switch from propaganda to mass agitation† as a means of organizing — and in the process politicizing — the working class through specific labour struggles. The new strategy was pioneered in the Vilno strikes of 1893, where the Marxist intelligentsia, instead of preaching to the Jewish workers, participated in the strikes and even learned Yiddish to gain their support. Two of the Wilno Social Democrats, Arkadii Kremer and Yuli Martov, explained their strategy in an influential pamphlet, *On Agitation*, written in 1895: through their involvement in organized strikes the workers would learn to appreciate the need for a broader political campaign, one led by the Social

---

* The merchants of Yaroslavl' had a long-established reputation, stretching back to the Middle Ages, for being much more cunning than the rest.

† For the Marxists of the 1890s 'propaganda' meant the gradual education of the workers in small study groups with the goal of inculcating in them a general understanding of the movement and class consciousness. 'Agitation' meant a mass campaign on specific labour and political issues.

Democrats, since the tsarist authorities would not tolerate a legal trade union movement. In St Petersburg the new plan was taken up by the short-lived but windily titled Union of Struggle for the Emancipation of the Working Class. It was organized in 1895 by a small group of Marxist intellectuals, Martov and Lenin prominent among them, who were arrested almost at once. However, its local activists could claim some credit for the big but unsuccessful textile strike of 1896, when over 30,000 workers came out in protest.

After a year in prison Lenin was sentenced to three years' exile in Siberia (1897–1900). Unlike the 'politicals' of his own regime, Lenin was allowed to live in considerable comfort. For 'health reasons' he was allowed to choose where he would live, and he chose a remote village called Shushenskoe in the southern Minusinsk region, which was well known for its tolerable climate. He took several crates of books and even a hunting gun with him, and kept in constant touch with his comrades. To enable Krupskaya to accompany him he agreed to marry her. The wedding took place in a church, since the Russian government did not recognize civil marriages, although neither bride nor bridegroom ever referred to this embarrassing episode in their later writings.[29]

During Lenin's exile the workers' movement in Russia became increasingly dominated by the new trend of 'Economism'. The Economists advocated concentrating on purely economic goals. Their aim was to improve the workers' conditions within the capitalist system rather than seeking to destroy it. To begin with, it was the workers and local factory activists who expressed this view. They believed that the workers should be left alone to run their own affairs, free from the direction of the socialist intelligentsia. But increasingly the same ideas were taken up by the so-called Legal Marxists. Kuskova and Struve, their best-known leaders, were brilliant theorists. Influenced by Eduard Bernstein's Revisionism, which was convulsing the German workers' movement at the time, as well as by neo-Kantian ideas, they sought to challenge many of the basic Marxist doctrines. Like Bernstein, they denied that capitalism was leading to a worsening of the workers' conditions. On the contrary, capitalism could be reconciled with socialism under a democratic system. The two would eventually converge. This meant that the workers should focus their efforts on reform rather than revolution. They should work within the law, in collaboration with the bourgeoisie rather than underground and in violent conflict with it.

For Plekhanov and his followers in Russia, Economism, like Bernstein's heresy, represented a betrayal of the Marxist movement's commitment to the goal of revolution. Instead of revolutionary socialism, it threatened to construct an evolutionary version. Instead of the 'dictatorship of the proletariat' there would be a parliamentary democracy. Perhaps in Germany, where the Social Democrats could now work within the Reichstag, this new moderation had a certain logic. But in Russia there were no such openings — indeed the new Tsar had made clear his commitment to tightening the grip of autocracy — and so the strategy of revolution had to be maintained at all costs. This necessity seemed all the more urgent given the developments in Russian politics during the latter 1890s. In the wake of the famine crisis, which politicized society, Neo-Populism, Zemstvo Liberalism and Legal Marxism converged, and together had the makings of a national movement for constitutional reform (see pages 161–5). If this movement was allowed to grow and win supporters from the workers and peasants, it would have the effect of putting back the revolution for at least a generation — and perhaps for good — while driving the revolutionary Marxists to the outer margins of politics.

The exiled Lenin was thrown into a rage by the 'heresy'. Krupskaya recalled that during 1899, after reading the works of Kuskova and Kautsky, Lenin became depressed and lost weight and sleep.[30] The ideological struggle became a profound personal crisis for him. He had embraced Marxism as the surest way to revolution — a revolution that some would say he saw increasingly as an extension of his own power and personality. Yet here was Marxism being stripped of all its revolutionary meaning and transformed into little more than the wishy-washy type of social liberalism of which no doubt his father would have approved. Lenin led the attack on Economism with the sort of violence that would later become the trademark of his rhetoric. Its tactics, he argued, would destroy socialism and the revolution, which could only succeed under the centralized political leadership of a disciplined vanguard party in the mould of the People's Will.

Lenin's views were shared at the time by many Russian Marxists — those who called themselves the 'Politicals'. They sought to organize a centralized party which would take up the leadership of the workers' movement and direct it towards political ends.* 'Subconsciously', Lydia Dan recalled, 'many of us associated such a party with what the People's Will had been.' Although they admired the German Social Democrats, it seemed impossible to construct such an open and democratic party in Russia's illegal conditions. If the police regime was to be defeated, the party had to be equally centralized and disciplined. It had to mirror the tsarist state. The quickest way to build such a party was to base it on the running of an underground newspaper, which, in the words of Lydia Dan, 'could be both a collective agitator and a collective organizer'. This was the inspiration of *Iskra* (*The Spark*) which Lenin established with Martov in 1900 on his return from exile. Its title echoed the Decembrist poet whose words

---

* The First Congress of the Russian Social Democratic Labour Party was held in 1898. This founding moment in the history of the party, which in nineteen years would come to rule the largest country in the world, was attended by no more than nine socialists! They met secretly in the town of Minsk, passed a declaration of standard Marxist goals, and then, almost to a man, were arrested by the police.

appeared on its masthead: 'Out of this spark will come a conflagration.' *Iskra* was not so much a source of news as the command centre of the Social Democrats in their political and ideological struggles against the Economists. Its editorial board — Plekhanov, Axelrod and Zasulich in Geneva; Lenin, Potresov and Martov now in Munich — was in effect the first central committee of the party. Published in Munich, then London and Geneva, it was smuggled into Russia by a network of agents who formed the nucleus of the party's organization in the years to come.

In his polemics against the Economists Lenin came out with a pamphlet that was to become the primer of his own party through the revolution of 1917 and the founding text of international Leninism. It was entirely fitting that its title, *What Is To Be Done?*, should have been taken from Chernyshevsky's famous novel. For the professional revolutionary outlined by Lenin in these pages bore a close resemblance to Rakhmetev, Chernyshevsky's disciplined and self-denying militant of the people's cause; while his insistence on a tightly disciplined and centralized party was an echo of the Russian Jacobin tradition of which Chernyshevsky was an ornament. Lenin's strident prose style, which was imitated by all the great dictators and revolutionaries of the twentieth century, emerged for the first time in *What Is To Be Done?* It had a barking, military rhythm, a manic violence and decisiveness, with cumulative cadences of action or abuse, and opponents lumped together by synecdoche ('Messrs Bernstein, Martynov, etc'). Here is a typical passage from the opening section, in which Lenin sets out the battle lines between the *Iskra*-ites and the 'Bernsteinians':

He who does not deliberately close his eyes cannot fail to see that the new 'critical' trend in socialism is nothing more or less than a new variety of *opportunism*. And if we judge people, not by the glittering uniforms they don or by the high-sounding appellations they give themselves, but by their actions and by what they actually advocate, it will be clear that 'freedom of criticism' means freedom for an opportunist trend in Social Democracy, freedom to convert Social Democracy into a democratic party of reform, freedom to introduce bourgeois ideas and bourgeois elements into socialism.

'Freedom' is a grand word, but under the banner of freedom for industry the most predatory wars were waged, under the banner of freedom for labour, the working people were robbed. The modern use of the term 'freedom of criticism' contains the same inherent falsehood. Those who are really convinced that they have made progress in science would not demand freedom for the new views to continue side by side with the old, but the substitution of the new views for the old. The cry heard today,

'Long live freedom of criticism', is too strongly reminiscent of the fable of the empty barrel.

We are marching in a compact group along a precipitous and difficult path, firmly holding each other by the hand. We are surrounded on all sides by enemies, and we have to advance almost constantly under their fire. We have combined, by a freely adopted decision, for the purpose of fighting the enemy, and not of retreating into the neighbouring marsh, the inhabitants of which, from the very outset, have reproached us with having separated ourselves into an exclusive group and with having chosen the path of struggle instead of the path of conciliation. And now some among us begin to cry out: Let us go into the marsh! And when we begin to shame them, they retort: What backward people you are! Are you not ashamed to deny us the liberty to invite you to take a better road! Oh, yes, gentlemen! You are free not only to invite us, but to go yourselves wherever you will, even into the marsh. In fact, we think that the marsh is your proper place, and we are prepared to render *you* every assistance to get there. Only let go of our hands, don't clutch at us and don't besmirch the grand word freedom, for we too are 'free' to go where we please, free to fight not only against the marsh, but also against those who are turning towards the marsh!

When it first appeared, in March 1902, Lenin's pamphlet seemed to voice the general viewpoint of the *Iskra*-ites. They all wanted a centralized party: it seemed essential in a police state like Russia. The dictatorial implications of *What Is To Be Done?* — that the party's rank and file would be forced to obey, in military fashion, the commands of the leadership — were as yet not fully realized. 'None of us could imagine', Lydia Dan recalled, 'that there could be a party that might arrest its own members. There was the thought or the certainty that if a party was truly centralized, each member would submit naturally to the instructions or directives.'[31]

It was only at the Second Party Congress, which met in Brussels the following year, that the implications of Lenin's catechism for the party began to emerge. The result was a split in the party and the formation of two distinct Social Democratic factions — the Bolsheviks and the Mensheviks. The immediate cause of the split may seem really quite trivial. Even those inside the party did not at first realize the historic importance which it would later come to assume. It arose over the precise wording of Article One of the Party Statute, in which party membership was defined. Lenin wanted membership limited to those who participated in one of the party's organizations; whereas Martov, while recognizing the need for a nucleus of disciplined activists, wanted anyone who recognized the Party Programme and was willing to obey its leadership to be admitted. Beneath the surface of this semantic dispute lay two opposing views of the party's role. On the one hand, Lenin was proposing a centralized and conspiratorial party of professional revolutionaries in the tradition of the People's Will. He had a profound mistrust of the revolutionary potential of the masses, who he believed, without the leadership of an élite party vanguard, would inevitably become diverted by the bread-and-butter issues of Economism. 'Socialist consciousness', he had written in *What Is To Be Done?*, 'cannot exist among the workers. This can be introduced only from without.' This mistrust of democracy was to form the basis of Lenin's centralist approach to the trade unions, the soviets and all the other mass-based organizations after 1917. The masses should in his view be no more than instruments of the party. This was pointed out by Lenin's critics, who warned that such a centralized party would lead to dictatorship. Socialism, in their view, was unattainable without democracy, which necessitated a broad-based party arising directly from the culture and the consciousness of the working class. Martov's view on Article One was at first upheld by 28 votes to 23. But two factions which supported it — the 5 Bundist delegates (who had been denied their demand for autonomy within the party) followed by the 2 Economists (who had been defeated by the *Iskra*-ites) — then walked out of the Congress, leaving Lenin with a slender majority. It was on this basis that his faction was christened the 'Bolsheviks' ('Majoritarians') and their opponents the 'Mensheviks' ('Minoritarians'). With hindsight it is clear that the Mensheviks were very foolish to allow the adoption of these names. It saddled them with the permanent image of a minority party, which was to be an important disadvantage in their rivalry with the Bolsheviks.

Lenin seized this opportunity to assert his control of the Central Committee and its organ, *Iskra*, by ejecting the three 'Menshevik' veterans — Zasulich, Axelrod and Potresov — from its editorial board. Lenin's conspiratorial methods hardened the divide between the two factions. Their clash was at first much more to do with personalities, style and emotions than with the articulation of distinctive ideologies. The Mensheviks were outraged by Lenin's shoddy treatment of the three ousted editors — he had called them *Iskra*'s 'least productive members' — and in solidarity with them Martov now refused to serve with Lenin and Plekhanov on the new editorial board. They accused Lenin of trying to become the dictator of the party — one talked of his needing to wield a 'baton' like the one used by army commanders to instil discipline in the ranks — and set themselves up as the defenders of democracy in the party. Lenin's own intransigence, his refusal to patch up his differences with the Mensheviks (differences which, by his own admission, were 'in substance . . . very unimportant'), and his readiness, once provoked, to admit to his belief that there had to be a dictator of the party to discipline the 'wavering elements in our midst', merely heightened the emotional tensions. The meeting broke down in petty squabbles, with each side accusing the other of having 'started it', or of having 'betrayed' the other. People took sides on the basis of hurt feelings and outraged sensibilities and established bonds of loyalty. Lydia Dan recalls that she took Martov's side not so much because she thought that he was right but because:

> I felt that I had to support him. And many others felt that way. Martov was poorly suited to be a leader. But he had an inexhaustible charm that attracted people. It was frequently difficult to account for why they followed him. He himself said, 'I have the nasty privilege of being liked by people.' And, naturally, if something like a schism occurred, Martov would be noble, Martov would be honourable, while Lenin . . . well, Lenin's influence was enormous, but still . . . For my own part, it was very tragic to have to say that all my sympathies for Lenin (which were considerable) were based upon misunderstanding.[32]

For several years the incipient political differences between the Mensheviks and the Bolsheviks continued to be masked by personal factors. No doubt it was in part because the two factions all lived together — sometimes literally — in small exile communities, so that their arguments over party dogma often became entangled in squabbles over money and lovers. But Lenin's personality was the crucial issue. Bolshevism was defined by a personal pledge of loyalty to him; and Menshevism, though to a lesser extent, by opposition to him. Valentinov, on his arrival in Geneva in 1904, was shocked by the 'atmosphere of worship [of Lenin] which people calling themselves Bolsheviks had created' there. Lenin reinforced this divide by his violent attack on the Mensheviks in his pamphlet *One Step Forward, Two Steps Back* (1904). He now called them 'traitors' to the Marxist cause. None of his Bolshevik lieutenants was even allowed to talk to any of the Menshevik leaders without gaining his prior approval.[33]

Only very slowly, during and after 1905, were the differences between the two factions spelled out in political terms. In fact for a long time (right up until 1918) the rank and file Social Democrats, particularly on the Menshevik side, sought to stitch the party together again. This was especially so in the provinces, where the party's forces were simply too small to afford such factional disputes. Here they continued to work together in united SD organizations. But gradually, as the party was forced to confront the dilemmas of real politics, during the 1905 Revolution and then in the Duma period, so its two factions demarcated themselves both in terms of their different ideologies, their strategies and tactics, and in terms of their ever more diverse political styles and cultures.

Menshevism remained a loose movement — high on morals, low on discipline. There was no real Menshevik leader, in the sense that the Bolsheviks had one, and indeed it was a part of Menshevik ideology to deny the need for one. Only slowly and reluctantly were the Mensheviks dragged towards the type of formal party structure which their rivals had from the start. Their spirit remained that of the friendly and informal circles (*kruzhki*) of the 1890s, what Lenin mocked as 'the loose Oblomov gowns and slippers' of the movement's salad days. But the Mensheviks were genuinely more democratic, both in their policies and in their composition, than the Bolsheviks. They tended to attract a broader range of people — more non-Russians, especially Jews and Georgians, more diverse types of workers, petty merchants and members of the intelligentsia — whereas the followers of the Bolsheviks tended to come from a narrower range (the vast majority were Great Russian workers and uprooted peasants). This broader social base may partly explain the Mensheviks' inclination towards compromise and conciliation with the liberal bourgeoisie. This was certainly the main distinction between them and the Bolsheviks, who, under Lenin's guidance, became increasingly intransigent in their opposition to democracy. Yet this demarcation — much as it may have been linked with social differences — was essentially an ethical one. The Mensheviks were democrats by instinct, and their actions as revolutionaries were always held back by the moral scruples which this entailed. This was not true of the Bolsheviks. They were simpler and younger men, militant peasant-workers like Kanatchikov; doers rather than thinkers. They were attracted by Lenin's discipline and firm leadership of the party, by his simple slogans, and by his belief in immediate action to bring down the tsarist regime rather than waiting, as the Mensheviks advised, for it to be eroded by the development of capitalism. This, above all, was what Lenin offered them: the idea that something *could* be done.

Part Two

THE CRISIS OF AUTHORITY
(1891–1917)

5 First Blood

i Patriots and Liberators

After a year of meteorological disasters the peasants of the Volga region found themselves facing starvation in the summer of 1891. As they surveyed their ruined crops, they might have been forgiven for believing that God had singled them out for particular punishment. The seeds they had planted the previous autumn barely had time to germinate before the frosts arrived. There had been precious little snow to protect the young plants in the winter, when the temperature averaged 30 degrees below zero. Spring brought with it dusty winds that blew away the topsoil and then, as early as April, the long dry summer began. In Tsaritsyn there had been no rain for 96 consecutive days, in Saratov none for 88, and in Orenburg none for more than 100. Wells and ponds dried up, the scorched earth cracked, forests went prematurely brown, and cattle died by the roadsides. The peasants pinned their last hopes on the harvest. But the crops that survived turned out to be small and burned by the sun. In Voronezh the harvest of rye was less than 0.1 *pud* (1.6 kg) per inhabitant, compared with a normal yield of 15 *pud*. 'Here we are getting ready to go hungry,' wrote Count Vorontsov-Dashkov to the Tsar from Tambov province on 3 July. 'The peasants' winter crops have failed completely and the situation demands immediate aid.'

By the autumn the area threatened by famine had spread to seventeen provinces, from the Ural mountains to the Black Sea, an area double the size of France with a population of thirty-six million people. Travellers in the region painted a picture of growing despair, as the peasants weakened and took to their huts. Those who had the strength packed up their meagre belongings and fled wherever they could, jamming the roads with their carts. Those who remained lived on 'famine bread' made from rye husks mixed with the weed goosefoot, moss and tree bark, which made the loaves turn yellow and bitter. The peasants stripped the thatch from the roofs of their huts and used it to feed their horses: people may go hungry for a long time but unfed horses simply die, and if this happened there would be no harvest the next year. And then, almost inevitably, cholera and typhus struck, killing half a million people by the end of 1892.

The government struggled to deal with the crisis as best as it could.

But its bureaucracy was far too slow and clumsy, and the transport system proved unable to cope. Politically, its handling of the crisis was disastrous, giving rise to the general impression of official carelessness and callousness. There were widespread rumours, for example, of the obstinate bureaucracy holding back food deliveries until it had received 'statistical proof' that the population for which they were intended had no other means of feeding itself: by which time it was often too late. Then there were stories of the relief schemes set up by the government to employ the destitute peasantry in public works: all too often it turned out that the peasants to be employed had already taken to their death-beds. There were reports of cholera victims being forced to leave their homes and being packed off to quarantine centres miles away from their villages, so that the peasants became hysterical wherever the medical authorities appeared and riots broke out which had to be put down by troops. But by far the greatest public outrage was caused by the government's postponement of a proposed ban on cereal exports until the middle of August, several weeks into the crisis. It had given a month's warning of the ban, so that cereal merchants rushed to fulfil their foreign contracts, and foodstuffs which could have been used for the starving peasants vanished abroad. The ban had been opposed by Vyshnegradsky, the Minister of Finance, whose economic policies (which essentially consisted of raising taxes on consumer goods so that the peasants would be forced to sell more grain) were seen by the public as the main cause of the famine. As the government slogan went: 'Even if we starve we will export grain.'[1]

Such cynicism did not seem unjustified. All along, the government had been refusing to admit the existence of a 'famine' (*golod*), preferring instead to speak euphemistically of a 'poor harvest' (*neurozhai*). The reactionary daily *Moscow News* had even warned that it would be an act of disloyalty to use the more 'alarmist term', since it would give rise to a 'dangerous hubbub' from which only the revolutionaries could gain. Newspapers were forbidden to print reports on the 'famine', although many did in all but name. This was enough to convince the liberal public, shocked and concerned by the rumours of the crisis, that there was a government conspiracy to conceal the truth. Gossip now began to paint the situation in the blackest terms. Alexandra Bogdanovich, the St Petersburg salon hostess, noted in her diary on 3 December:

> Now they are saying that Durnovo [the Minister of the Interior] already knew of the famine in May and should have forced Vyshnegradsky to ban exports then. Verkhovsky says that the export of wheat was only banned when Abaza [Chairman of the Department of State Economy] had been able to sell his own wheat for a good price. They say that in Simbirsk province all the children have died from starvation; they sent children's

clothes there but all were returned — there is no one to wear them. Indignation is growing in all quarters.

Even General Kutaisov, a Senator and State Councillor, was heard to complain that 'there would not have been a famine, if the government had not got itself into such a terrible mess'.[2]

Unable to cope with the crisis, the government bowed to the inevitable and, on 17 November, issued an imperial order calling on the public to form voluntary organizations to help with famine relief. Politically, this was to prove a historic moment, for it opened the door to a powerful new wave of public activity and debate which the government could not control and which quickly turned from the philanthropic to the political. The 'dangerous hubbub' that *Moscow News* had feared was growing louder and louder.

The public response to the famine was tremendous. 'People of the most varied persuasions and temperaments threw themselves into the cause,' recalled Vasilii Maklakov. 'Many forsook their usual occupations and went about setting up canteens and, during the epidemics, helping the doctors. In this work not a few lost forever their positions and their health.' The zemstvos were the first off the mark, having already established their own provincial networks to distribute food and medicine. Prince Lvov, who was at that time chairman of the Tula provincial zemstvo, threw himself into the relief campaign as if it was a matter of his own life and death. It was a mark of his love for the peasants, with whom he had lived and worked for the previous ten years, that he should risk his own life to save theirs. And how romantic that at such a time, whilst working in a soup kitchen in Tambov province, he should meet and fall in love with his future wife. Such elevated feelings of compassion for the peasants were by no means unusual among progressive landowners of his sort. Hundreds of committees were formed by nobles and 'public men' to help raise money for the famine victims. Doctors volunteered for medical teams. Thousands of well-meaning citizens rushed to join the relief campaigns organized by the Free Economic Society and other voluntary bodies. Impassioned speeches were made at public meetings. Newspapers printed appeals in bold print on their front pages. And the students volunteered for relief work in a new 'Going to the People'.[3]

Among these volunteers was Anton Chekhov, who was a doctor as well as a playwright. He put aside his writing to work for his district zemstvo near Moscow. In August 1892 he wrote to a friend:

I have been appointed a cholera doctor, and my district encompasses twenty-five villages, four factories and a monastery. I am organizing things, setting up shelters and so on, and I'm lonely, because everything that has to do with cholera is alien to me, and the work, which requires constant trips, talks and fuss and bustle, tires me out. There is no time to write. I abandoned literature long ago, and I'm poor and broke because I thought it desirable for myself and my independence to refuse the renumeration cholera doctors receive . . . The peasants are crude, unsanitary and mistrustful, but the thought that our labours will not be in vain makes it all unnoticeable.[4]

Tolstoy also gave up his writing to join the relief campaign. With his two eldest daughters he organized hundreds of canteens in the famine region, while Sonya, his wife, raised money from abroad. 'I cannot describe in simple words the utter destitution and suffering of these people,' he wrote to her at the end of October 1891. According to the peasant Sergei Semenov, who was a follower of Tolstoy and who joined him in his relief campaign, the great writer was so overcome by his experience of the peasants' suffering that his beard went grey, his hair became thinner and he lost a great deal of weight. The guilt-ridden Count blamed the famine crisis on the social order, the Orthodox Church* and the government. 'Everything has happened because of our own sin,' he wrote to a friend in December. 'We have cut ourselves off from our own brothers, and there is only one remedy — by repentance, by changing our lives, and by destroying the walls between us and the people.' Tolstoy broadened his condemnation of social inequality in his essay 'The Kingdom of God' (1892) and in the press. His message struck a deep chord in the moral conscience of the liberal public, plagued as they were by feelings of guilt on account of their privilege and alienation from the peasantry. Semenov captured this sense of shame when he wrote of the relief campaign:

> With every day the need and misery of the peasants grew. The scenes of starvation were deeply distressing, and it was all the more disturbing to see that amidst all this suffering and death there were sprawling huge estates, beautiful and well-furnished manors, and that the grand old life of the squires, with its jolly hunts and balls, its banquets and its concerts, carried on as usual.[5]

For the guilt-ridden liberal public, serving 'the people' through the relief campaign was a means of paying off their 'debt' to them. And they now turned to Tolstoy as their moral leader and their champion against the sins of the old regime. His condemnation of the government turned him into a public hero, a

---

* The Orthodox Church, which had recently excommunicated Tolstoy, forbade the starving peasants to accept food from his relief campaign.

man of integrity whose word could be trusted as the truth on a subject which the regime had tried so hard to conceal.

Russian society had been activated and politicized by the famine crisis, its social conscience had been stung, and the old bureaucratic system had been discredited. Public mistrust of the government did not diminish once the crisis had passed, but strengthened as the representatives of civil society continued to press for a greater role in the administration of the nation's affairs. The famine, it was said, had proved the culpability and incompetence of the old regime, and there was now a growing expectation that wider circles of society would have to be drawn into its work if another catastrophe was to be avoided. The zemstvos, which had spent the past decade battling to expand their activities in the face of growing bureaucratic opposition, were now strengthened by widespread support from the liberal public for their work in agronomy, public health and education. The liberal Moscow merchants and industrialists, who had rallied behind the relief campaign, now began to question the government's policies of industrialization, which seemed so ruinous for the peasantry, the main buyers of their manufactures. From the middle of the 1890s they too supported the various projects of the zemstvos and municipal bodies to revive the rural economy. Physicians, teachers and engineers, who had all been forced to organize themselves as a result of their involvement in the relief campaign, now began to demand more professional autonomy and influence over public policy; and when they failed to make any advances they began to campaign for political reforms. In the press, in the 'thick journals', in the universities, and in learned and philanthropic societies, the debates on the causes of the famine — and on the reforms needed to prevent its recurrence — continued to rage throughout the 1890s, long after the immediate crisis had passed.[6]

The socialist opposition, which had been largely dormant in the 1880s, sprang back into life with a renewed vigour as a result of these debates. There was a revival of the Populist movement (later rechristened Neo-Populism), culminating in 1901 with the establishment of the Socialist Revolutionary Party. Under the leadership of Viktor Chernov (1873–1952), a law graduate from Moscow University who had been imprisoned in the Peter and Paul Fortress for his role in the student movement, it embraced the new Marxist sociology whilst still adhering to the Populist belief that all the workers and peasants alike — what it called the 'labouring people' — were united by their poverty and their opposition to the regime. Briefly, then, in the wake of the famine, there was growing unity between the Marxists and the Neo-Populists as they put aside their differences about the development of capitalism (which the SRs now accepted as a fact) and concentrated on the democratic struggle. Lydia Dan, from the Marxist side, recalled this as a 'new era . . . when it was not so much the struggle for socialism that was important for us as the political struggle . . . [which] could and should become nationwide'.[7]

Marxism as a social science was fast becoming the national creed: it alone seemed to explain the causes of the famine. Universities and learned societies were swept along by the new intellectual fashion. Even such well-established institutions as the Free Economic Society fell under the influence of the Marxists, who produced libraries of social statistics, dressed up as studies of the causes of the great starvation, to prove the truth of Marx's economic laws. Socialists who had previously wavered in their Marxism were now completely converted in the wake of the famine crisis, when, it seemed to them, there was no more hope in the Populist faith in the peasantry. Petr Struve (1870–1944), who had previously thought of himself as a political liberal, found his Marxist passions stirred by the crisis: it 'made much more of a Marxist out of me than the reading of Marx's *Capital*'. Martov also recalled how the crisis had turned him into a Marxist: 'It suddenly became clear to me how superficial and groundless the whole of my revolutionism had been until then, and how my subjective political romanticism was dwarfed before the philosophical and sociological heights of Marxism.'[8] Even the young Lenin only became converted to the Marxist mainstream in the wake of the famine crisis.

In short, the whole of society had been politicized and radicalized as a result of the famine crisis. The conflict between the population and the regime had been set in motion — and there was now no turning back. In the words of Lydia Dan, the famine had been a vital landmark in the history of the revolution because it had shown to the youth of her generation 'that the Russian system was completely bankrupt. It felt as though Russia was on the brink of something.'[9]

*   *   *

This political awakening of the public was part of the broader social changes that lie at the root of the revolution. From the 1890s can be dated the emergence of a civil society, a public sphere and an ethic, all in opposition to the tsarist state. The time was passing when, in the words of Miliukov, the autocracy had been 'the only organized force' in Russia and had been able to dominate a weak and divided society. Now that relationship was being reversed. The institutions of society were becoming more independent and organized, while the tsarist state was steadily becoming weaker and less able to control them. The famine crisis was the crucial turning-point in this process, the moment when Russian society first became politically aware of itself and its powers, of its duties to 'the people', and of the potential it had to govern itself. It was the moment, in a sense, when Russia first became a 'nation'.

Profound social changes were pulling this public culture on to the political scene. The old hierarchy of social estates (*sosloviia*), which the autocracy had created to organize society around its own needs, was breaking down as a new and much more mobile social system began to take shape. Men born as peasants, even as serfs, rose to establish themselves as merchants and landowners, teachers, doctors, engineers, writers, publishers and patrons of the arts. The sons and daughters of noblemen entered the liberal professions. Merchants became noblemen. Marriages between the estates became commonplace. Overall, people neither could nor wanted any longer to define themselves in the old and rigid terms.[10]

This new civil society was too complicated to be described in crude terms of 'class'. For one thing, it was defined much less by social position than by politics and culture. The world-view of the intelligentsia — based on the notion of public service and the liberal values of the West — defined its identity. The intelligentsia had always been made up of people from diverse social backgrounds, and had claimed to stand for 'the nation' as a whole. And this universalist tradition shaped the ethics and the language of this nascent public sphere. Educated liberals talked of serving the 'public good' (*obshchestvennost'*), expressed as 'society' or 'the nation', as opposed to the old noble ethic of service to the tsarist state. They called their politicians 'public men' (*obshchestvennye deiateli*). And indeed it was an important part of the whole rhetorical process of defining this 'political nation' — which meant setting it apart from the 'alien' tsarist state — that its leaders should be honoured with a generic name that made them patriots of the people's cause. A national political culture based on the ideals and institutions of the intelligentsia was coalescing in Russia. An active public was emerging in opposition to the old regime and demanding the rights of an independent citizenry. The spread of higher education, of public opinion and activity, shaped this emerging public culture. Between 1860 and 1914 the number of university students in Russia grew from 5,000 to 69,000 (45 per cent of them women); the number of daily newspapers rose from 13 to 856; and the number of public bodies from 250 to over 16,000.[11]

These were the signs of a new middle stratum between the aristocracy and the peasants and the working class. But it was much too fragile in social terms to deserve the robust title of a 'middle class'. The industrial 'bourgeoisie', which in the West had led the way in the forging of a middle-class identity, was too weak and dependent on the state, too fragmented by regional and ethnic divisions, and too isolated from the educated élite, to play the same role in tsarist Russia, although this was the belated aim of the liberal Moscow businessmen of the Riabushinsky circle in the 1900s.[12] Indeed an awareness of its own fragility and isolation was a crucial aspect of the self-identity of this fledgling 'census society' (*tsenzovoe obshchestvo*). As the liberal and educated public became more conscious of itself and of its leading role in politics, so it also grew more conscious of the huge and frightening gulf — a gulf revealed by the famine — separating it from the hungry masses. As in South Africa under apartheid, there was always a time-bomb of violent revolution ticking in the cupboard of liberal politics.

Two main groups stood in the forefront of this public campaign during the decade leading up to the Revolution of 1905: the liberal 'zemstvo men' and the students.

The 'zemstvo men' were unlikely pioneers of the revolution. Most of them were noble landowners, progressive and practical men like Prince Lvov, who simply wanted the monarchy to play a positive role in improving the life of its subjects. They sought to increase the influence of the zemstvos in the framing of government legislation, but the notion of leading a broad opposition movement was repugnant to them. Prince Lvov's mentor, D. N. Shipov, who organized the zemstvos at a national level, was himself a devoted monarchist and flatly opposed the liberal demand for a constitution. The whole purpose of his work was to strengthen the autocracy by bringing the Tsar closer to his people, organized through the zemstvos and a consultative parliament. In many ways he was trying to create from below the same popular autocracy which Nicholas was aiming to impose from above in the last years of his reign. Central to his liberal Slavophilism was the notion of Russia as 'a locally self-governing land with an autocratic Sovereign at its head'. He believed in the ancient communion between the Tsar and his people, a union which, in his view, had been broken only by the 'autocracy of the bureaucracy'.[13]

There was plenty of ground, then, for the autocracy to reach an accommodation with the 'zemstvo men'. But, as so often during its inexorable downfall, the old regime chose repression instead of compromise and thus *created* the political hostility of the zemstvos. The chief architect of this suicidal policy was the all-powerful Ministry of the Interior, which regarded the zemstvos as dangerous havens for revolutionaries and subjected them to a relentless campaign of persecution. Armed with the statute of 1890, the provincial governors capped the zemstvos' budgets, censored their publications and removed or arrested the elected members of their boards.

The famine crisis brought a temporary halt to this conflict, for the government relied on the zemstvos as agencies of food and medical relief. But, by expanding their activities, the crisis also encouraged the zemstvos to reassert their own demands for autonomy and reform. The lead was taken by the zemstvo professionals — the teachers, doctors, statisticians and agronomists commonly known as the Third Element — whose radical influence on the zemstvo assemblies was increased as a result of their direct participation in the relief campaigns. They were followed by many landowners, who blamed the famine on the government's failure to protect the nation's farmers and were worried that the destitute peasants would seize their estates. They now rallied behind the zemstvos to defend the agrarian interests of provincial society against the industrializing bureaucracy of St Petersburg. The more liberal nobles, like Prince Lvov, went on to demand the creation of an all-class zemstvo at the volost level (which they believed would help to integrate the peasants into local government) and the convocation of a national assembly. This was the inspiration behind the Tver Address, presented to Nicholas II on his accession to the throne by the country's most progressive zemstvo leaders. In a speech that infuriated public opinion the new Tsar denounced such 'senseless dreams' and emphasized his 'firm and unflinching' adherence to the 'principle of autocracy'. Within days, the Ministry of the Interior resumed its persecution of the zemstvos. Shipov's All-Zemstvo Organization was banned soon after its foundation in 1896, forcing the reluctant revolutionary into the arms of the more radical constitutionalists. Together they formed *Beseda* (Symposium) in 1899, a clandestine discussion circle of liberal 'zemstvo men', including some of the grandest names of the Russian aristocracy, as well as Prince Lvov, which met in the Moscow palace of the Dolgorukov princes. To begin with, *Beseda* confined its discussion to zemstvo affairs. But in 1900 the government once again stepped up its campaign of persecution, ordering the dismissal of hundreds of liberals from the zemstvos' elected boards, and this inevitably forced the genteel symposium to confront political questions. Over the next two years it would become the leading force in the constitutional movement, as a wide range of public men, from civic leaders to the captains of industry, rallied behind its call for reform.[14]

The universities had been the organizational centre of opposition to the tsarist regime since the 1860s. In the Russian language the words 'student' and 'revolutionary' were almost synonymous. Like everyone else, the students had been politicized by the sheer scale of human misery which the famine exposed. The lecture-rooms became hotbeds of socialist agitation and there was a new mood of rebelliousness against the university authorities, which since 1884 had been under police control. Alexander Kerensky (1881–1970) recalls the camaraderie of the dormitory at St Petersburg University: 'The students lived as a friendly, closely united community, with its own favourite men as leaders in matters of communal concern ... If something exceptional happened in the country that touched and hurt the moral feelings of youth, if some order of the educational authorities touched our corporate pride, then all the students rose as one man.'[15]

Kerensky's early life had many similarities with that of Lenin, who would become his arch-rival in 1917. He was born in the same town of Simbirsk eleven years after Lenin. His father was the headmaster of Lenin's gymnasium and an acquaintance of Lenin's father, who was the Chief Inspector of Schools in Simbirsk. In 1889 Kerensky's father was promoted to the same post in

Tashkent, where the young Kerensky went to school. As with the adolescent Lenin, there was 'nothing at this stage to suggest the future career of Kerensky as a minister of the revolution', one of his teachers recalled. 'He happily complied with the strict discipline of the school, went enthusiastically to church,* and even sang in the church choir.' At the age of fourteen, Kerensky's heart was set on an acting career. He even signed a letter to his parents: 'The future Artist of the Imperial Theatre. A. Kerensky'.[16] His belief in his destiny — which would drive his actions in 1917 — had clearly taken root at an early age. Kerensky never made it into the theatre, although as an actor on the revolutionary stage he was to prove as self-dramatizing as any provincial thespian. In 1899 he went up to St Petersburg University to read history and philology, the subjects his father had studied there, although in the second year he switched to law. This too set the pattern for the future: changing from history to law is, obviously, the move of a careerist.

In the year Kerensky matriculated the students at St Petersburg became embroiled in a series of campus demonstrations. On 8 February it was customary for the students to mark the anniversary of the foundation of the university by holding celebrations in the city centre. But in 1899 the government was in no mood for a student street party and banned the event. When some students tried to defy the ban by marching into the city they found their way blocked by police, who beat them with whips. Greatly agitated, the students began a protest strike, which spread to other universities. Their grievances were still not political; they would have been satisfied by an official apology for the brutality of the police and the restoration of the academic and student freedoms removed from the universities in 1884. This, at least, was the finding of a commission appointed later to look into the troubles. Instead the government arrested the student leaders and threatened future demonstrators with military conscription. The students were outraged and, encouraged by socialist agitators, began to condemn the political system root and branch. Even Kerensky, who until this point had been more interested in the theatre than in politics, joined the campus protest. 'Last year's insult has not been forgotten, and cannot be,' he wrote to his parents in February 1900. 'The repressions were uncivilized, that is what disturbs us, and those who ordered them (i.e. the ministers) do not deserve respect!'[17] Once again, the heavy-handed tactics of the government turned a minor protest into a full-blown opposition movement.

The following November there were fresh student demonstrations at Kiev and other universities. Bogolepov, the Minister of Education, responded in January 1901 by enlisting more than 200 student leaders into the army. One month later a student called Karpovich shot Bogolepov in the neck, fatally

---

* As he would throughout his life.

wounding him in the first of a new wave of terrorist actions. The public were generally unmoved by the murder (Kerensky and his student comrades even saw Karpovich as a saint); its outrage was provoked by Bogolepov's repressions. 'I feel, you see,' wrote Gorky to Bryusov, 'that to send students into the army is disgusting, it is a flagrant crime against individual freedom, an idiotic measure of power-sated scoundrels.' On 4 March, two days after Bogolepov's death, Gorky took part in a massive demonstration in St Petersburg. The capital came to a standstill as 3,000 students converged in front of the Kazan Cathedral. Red flags were unfurled, the Marseillaise was sung, and Gorky made a speech condemning the government's actions. In the crowd were a large number of bourgeois liberals sympathetic to the students and dozens of present and future luminaries of the revolutionary movement. Suddenly, a squadron of mounted Cossacks appeared from behind the cathedral and charged into the crowd, hitting out on all sides with their batons. Struve was one of those struck. As people scrambled for cover some of the crowd broke into the cathedral itself, where a service was in progress. Thirteen people were killed, hundreds came away with bloodied faces and, in all, some 1,500 students were imprisoned, many of them in the Peter and Paul Fortress. It was the first time that such a large number of respectable bourgeois citizens had found themselves within its famous penitentiary walls. The students' parents and friends visited them daily with lavish food hampers. A well-known tobacco manufacturer, whose son had been jailed, sent 10,000 de-luxe cigarettes and repeated the gift at regular intervals. Thousands of books arrived, allowing the students to catch up with their long-neglected studies, although, according to one of the students, they spent most of their time in chess tournaments and concerts. The whole adventure was described by him as 'a kind of student picnic'.[18]

For many of the students this was their first shocking confrontation with the coercive power of the state. It was to prove a radicalizing experience. Thousands of students joined the SR Party, whose Combat Organization took the lead in a campaign of terror which soon claimed the life of D. S. Sipiagin, the Minister of the Interior. Others joined the Social Democrats. But the real home of the democratic students was the Union of Liberation, established in 1903. It was the brainchild of Struve, one of a small but influential group of liberal defectors from the Marxist movement at the turn of the century. He argued that a violent social revolution would be disastrous for Russia. What it needed was a period of social and political evolution on European lines, during which the workers campaigned for their rights within the capitalist system and the whole democracy was united in a constitutional movement. This was the message of Struve's journal *Osvobozhdenie* (Liberation), published in Germany, which had inspired the foundation of the Union. Antagonized by the campaign of police persecution organized by Plehve, Sipiagin's successor at the Ministry of the

Interior, the Union gradually moved to the left and, in 1904, embraced the programme of a constitution based on universal suffrage, self-determination for the nationalities, and far-reaching social reforms.

✳   ✳   ✳

It was at this moment that Russia went to war with Japan. Plehve is often said to have planned this as 'a little victorious war to stem the revolution'. But its origins were more complex — and its consequences just the opposite. Russia's economic penetration of the Far East, made possible by the construction of the Trans-Siberian Railway during the 1890s, was bound to bring her into conflict with Japan, which had ambitions in Korea and Manchuria. But a war could have been avoided if Russia's foreign policy had been in competent hands. Instead it was left to a narrow court cabal, led by Alexander Bezobrazov, a well-connected speculator with lumber interests in Korea, and this group of lobbyists persuaded the Tsar to reject the Japanese offer of a compromise, thus making war unavoidable. That Nicholas had decided to take a personal interest in the matter only made things worse; unfortunately foreign policy was the one area of government where the Tsar felt competent to lead from the front. Because he had toured the Far East in his youth, he even believed himself to be something of an expert on the region. General Kuropatkin, the Minister of War, believed that Nicholas wanted to extend his Empire across the whole of Asia, conquering not only Manchuria and Korea but also Tibet, Afghanistan and Persia. Most of his ministers encouraged such ambitions. It was a way of flattering the Tsar — who after all had very few talents. Nicholas's cousin, the Kaiser Wilhelm, also played along with his imperial fantasies, since he wished to divert Russia from the Balkans. On one occasion he had cabled the Tsar from his yacht: 'The Admiral of the Atlantic greets the Admiral of the Pacific.'[19]

When the war began, in January 1904, with the Japanese attack on the Russian fleet at Port Arthur in Manchuria, the Tsar and his advisers took victory for granted. Kuropatkin claimed he would need only two Russian soldiers for every three Japanese, so superior were they to the Asians. Government posters portrayed the Japanese as puny little monkeys, slit-eyed and yellow-skinned, running in panic from the giant white fist of a robust Russian soldier. Another displayed a swarm of spider-like 'Japs', faces twisted in fear, struggling to escape from underneath a huge Cossack hat. The caption read 'Catch them by the hatful!' This patriotic mood, with its racist overtones, swept through liberal society. Prince S. N. Trubetskoi, the distinguished Professor of Philosophy at Moscow University and a founding member of *Beseda*, contended that Russia was defending the whole of European civilization against 'the yellow danger, the new hordes of Mongols armed by modern technology'. The academic leaders of Kiev University described the war as a Christian crusade against the 'insolent Mongols'. Even the Legal Marxist Struve felt obliged to bow to the patriotic mood, urging his followers to rally behind the nation and *its* armed forces whilst continuing to oppose the autocracy.* The provincial zemstvos went even further in their patriotic efforts. To help the Red Cross on the Manchurian Front thirteen of them formed a combined medical brigade of 360 doctors and nurses led by Prince Lvov. It was the first time the zemstvos had been allowed to organize themselves at a national level. The Prince pleaded with the Tsar to let the brigade go and so moved him by his own patriotic sentiments that Nicholas ended up hugging him and kissing him and wishing him well. The mission, which won high praise from the military leaders, turned Lvov into a national hero and enabled the zemstvos to wrap themselves in the national flag.[20]

Had the war been won, the regime might have been able to make political capital from this patriotic upsurge. The ancient bond between the tsarist state and Russian nationalism could be used to create powerful emotions when the enemy came from the heathen East. The Mongol invasion, which the Muscovite state had been formed to repel, had left a powerful mark on the Russian psyche. It was expressed in a deep anxiety about the mixed Eurasian roots of the people and its culture, which made it easy for an educated liberal such as Trubetskoi to convince himself that this war was nothing less than a defence of Russia's European identity against the Asian hordes. And it was only a short step from this to the view that the Christian tsarist state was the champion of that identity.

But winning the war was far harder than Russia's rulers imagined. The military turned out to be poorly equipped with modern weaponry, and there were terrible logistical problems in running a war from 6,000 miles away. The biggest problem was the sheer incompetence of the High Command, which stuck rigidly to the military doctrines of the nineteenth century and wasted thousands of Russian lives by ordering hopeless bayonet charges against well-entrenched artillery positions. The Commander-in-Chief himself, Admiral Alexeev, knew almost nothing about the art of war. Afraid of horses, he had to suffer the indignity of inspecting his cavalry on foot. Alexeev's promotion had been largely due to the patronage of the Grand Duke Alexis, whom he once rescued from the French police after the Grand Duke had been involved in a drunken brawl in a Marseille brothel. Alexeev had offered himself up for arrest, claiming that the *maîtresse* of the brothel had confused his name with that of the Grand Duke.[21]

As the war went from bad to worse, the liberal opposition revived, accusing the government of incompetence in its handling of the campaign. There was plenty of evidence to support the charge, including the futile despatch of

---

* For this Struve was treated by the government as a defeatist. He was even approached by a Japanese spy.

the Baltic Fleet on a seven-month trip around the world to relieve Port Arthur. The only shots the squadron fired hit some English fishing trawlers in the North Sea, which the commander had mistaken for Japanese torpedo boats. The case went to international arbitration (the Dogger Bank Inquiry) and Russia was forced to pay damages of £65,000. Even the country's leading entrepreneurs, who had in the past relied on the state for protection, now joined in the chorus of criticism as they suffered the economic dislocations of the war. A. I. Guchkov (1862–1936), a wealthy Moscow industrialist who fought for the Boers against the British and ran a field hospital in Manchuria, was particularly critical of the monarchy for its failure to equip the military with the tools of modern warfare. The future leader of the Octobrist Party was echoed by much of the press, which blamed the bureaucratic system for Russia's military decline. The gossip in the salons was cruel. On the news that the Tsar had sent the troops icons to boost their morale, General Dragomirov quipped: 'The Japanese are beating us with machine-guns, but never mind: we'll beat them with icons.' The autocracy had shown itself incapable of defending the national interest and joining the opposition now came to be seen, in the words of one official, as something 'noble and patriotic'.[22]

So unpopular had the government become that in July 1904, when Plehve, its Minister of the Interior, was blown to pieces by a bomb planted by the SR Combat Organization (which had already made several attempts on his life), there was hardly a word of public regret.* And such was the 'cult of the bomb and the gun' that the public looked upon these terrorists as champions of freedom. In Warsaw, Plehve's murder was celebrated by crowds in the street. 'The most striking aspect of the present situation', noted Count Aerenthal, the Austro-Hungarian Ambassador to St Petersburg:

> is the total indifference of society to an event that constituted a heavy blow to the principles of the government. One could hardly have expected sympathy for a minister who because of his authoritarian bent must have made many enemies. But a certain degree of human compassion, or at least concern and anxiety with respect to the immediate future, would be natural. Not a trace of this is to be found ... I have found only totally indifferent people or people so cynical that they say that no other outcome was to be expected. People are prepared to say that further catastrophes similar to Plehve's murder will be necessary in order to bring about a change of mind on the part of the highest authority.[23]

---

* It was organized by Boris Savinkov (1879–1925), who was later to become a minister in the Provisional Government.

The citizens of Russia were after their rulers' blood.

The opposition now rallied behind the campaign for a national zemstvo assembly. The liberal 'zemstvo men' had been calling for this since 1902, but Plehve always stood in their way. Now there were hopeful signs. Plehve's murder had deeply shocked the Tsar and, although his natural inclination had been to replace him with another hardliner, the bad news from the Front and the strength of the opposition at home had convinced him of the need to appoint a man enjoying the 'confidence of society'. The new Minister of the Interior, Prince Sviatopolk-Mirsky (or Mirsky for short) was made for the role. Liberal, good-natured and decent, he was a typical product of the enlightened bureaucracy that espoused the ideals of the *Rechtsstaat*. He spoke of the need to strengthen the rule of law, to end the despotism of the police, and to break down the barriers of mistrust between the government and society. He called himself a 'zemstvo man' — in the sense that as a bureaucrat he saw his primary duty as to serve the public rather than the Tsar — and sought to conciliate the zemstvo liberals. They took his appointment, on 25 August, as a cue to revive their campaign for a national assembly.

Such expectations placed Mirsky in an impossible situation. 'I am afraid', wrote his wife in her diary on 22 September, 'that so much is expected from Pepka [Mirsky] and yet so little will be possible; the only thing he can do is to act in accordance with his conscience, so God willing.' The Minister was trapped between the demands of the liberals and the stubborn determination of the Tsar to stand firm on the principle of autocracy. He was not the last to be caught in this way. If there is a single, repetitive theme in the history of Russia during the last twenty years of the old regime, it is that of the need for reform and the failure of successive governments to achieve it in the face of the Tsar's opposition. Not that sweeping reforms would have been necessary: most of the liberals would have been satisfied by such moderate changes as the convocation of a consultative assembly, the expansion of local self-government and greater civil rights, which need not have undermined the monarchy. But Nicholas was opposed to the idea of any limitation upon his autocratic prerogatives. Naively perhaps, Mirsky continued through gentle persuasion to try and bring the Tsar round to the idea of reform. But Nicholas was impervious to reason, and the Minister's frustration grew. On one occasion, when Mirsky explained that the whole of the country was clamouring for a national zemstvo assembly, the Tsar replied: 'Yes, it is needed, then they will be able to look into the veterinary problem.' When Mirsky explained that the issue was the right of elected representatives to participate in the work of government, and warned that, if nothing was conceded, there would soon be a revolution, the Tsar remained silent. 'He lets everything unpleasant run off him', the exasperated Minister complained later to his wife.[24]

Mirsky initially thought to give the zemstvo assembly his official approval on the understanding that it would confine itself to local affairs. But when it produced a revised agenda that included discussion of a legislative parliament, he tried to have it postponed, or moved to the provinces, where it would attract less attention. But the 'zemstvo men' stood firm and the mild-mannered Mirsky at last gave way, allowing the assembly to meet in private quarters in the capital — 'for a cup of tea', as he put it. On 6–9 November 1904, 103 zemstvo representatives assembled in various residences, including the apartment of Vladimir Nabokov, father of the future novelist. Shipov was elected chairman, Prince Lvov and Petrunkevich vice-chairmen. It was, in effect, the first national assembly in Russian history. People compared it with the French *Etats Generaux* of 1789, and, despite Mirsky's ban on publicity, more than 5,000 congratulatory telegrams arrived from all over the country. Civic bodies and associations held meetings to support its resolutions, which condemned the existing state of affairs and called, in all but name, for a constitution. Even the Provincial Marshals of the Nobility, normally the most conservative of gentry office-holders, held a congress to support the idea of a national assembly. Professional organizations held public banquets, modelled on the Paris banquet campaign that preceded the Revolution of 1848, where speakers called for political reforms and toasts were proposed to the future constitution. Gorky was at the biggest of these in St Petersburg on 20 November, and the following morning he wrote to his wife in Yalta:

I have just returned from the banquet in the Pavlova Hall. There were more than 600 diners — writers, lawyers, 'zemstvo men', in general, the intelligentsia ... Outspoken speeches were made and people chanted in unison 'Down with the autocracy!', 'Long live the Constituent Assembly!', and 'Give us a constitution!' ... A resolution was passed unanimously calling for a Constituent Assembly elected by universal suffrage. It was all very heated and very democratic ... For the first time a woman even stood up to speak. She said that universal suffrage would give the vote to policemen, but no one had yet mentioned women. All this time they have struggled alongside the men — yet now people have forgotten about them. Shame! Her speech was very good.[25]

Mirsky presented the Tsar with a carefully worded digest of the zemstvo assembly's resolutions, in the hope of winning him over to a programme of moderate reforms. The most controversial recommendation was the one for elected zemstvo representatives to sit on the State Council. But it also declared, in terms that must have offended the Supreme Autocrat, that the 'old patrimonial order' with its 'notions of personal rule' had been dead since the 1860s. Russia was no longer 'the personal property and fiefdom of its ruler', but an 'an impersonal state with its own body politic', its own 'public interest' and 'public opinion', which made it 'separate from the person of the ruler'. It was no doubt this challenge to his cherished ideals of patrimonialism that convinced the Tsar, under pressure from the Empress and his court advisers, to reject the most progressive parts of Mirsky's draft decree. 'I will never agree to the representative form of government', Nicholas proclaimed, 'because I consider it harmful to the people whom God thas entrusted to me.' The decree, which was finally passed on 12 December, promised to strengthen the rule of law, to ease restrictions on the press and to expand the rights of the zemstvos. But it said nothing on the all-important subject of a parliamentary body, on which concessions were essential if a revolution was to be averted. Hearing of its contents, Mirsky at once fell into despair. 'Everything has failed,' he said despondently to one of his colleagues. 'Let us build jails.'[26]

ii 'There is no Tsar'

Snow had fallen in the night and St Petersburg awoke to an eerie silence on that Sunday morning, 9 January 1905. Soon after dawn the workers and their families congregated in churches to pray for a peaceful end to the day. Later, 150,000 of them would march in columns from various quarters of the city and converge in front of the Winter Palace, where their leader, a priest called Father Gapon, was to present a Humble and Loyal Address to the Tsar begging him to improve the conditions of the workers. Singing hymns and carrying icons and crosses, they formed something more like a religious procession than a workers' demonstration. Bystanders took off their hats and crossed themselves as they passed. And yet there was no doubt that the marchers' lives were in danger. During the night 12,000 troops had been posted in the city to prevent them from reaching the palace. Many of the marchers had been up all night preparing themselves for death. One of them, Ivan Vasilev, left a note for his wife as he left her asleep with his young son in the small hours of the morning:

> Niusha!
> If I fail to return and am killed, Niusha, do not cry. You'll get along somehow to begin with, and then you'll find work at a factory. Bring up Vaniura and tell him I died a martyr for the people's freedom and happiness. I shall have died, if such be the case, for our own happiness as well . . .
> Your loving father and husband, Vania
> P.S. Niusha, if I die, you'll know of it from one of my comrades; otherwise,

I'll write to you or come to see you. I kiss you, farewell. Regards to father,
our brothers and all our relations.

Farewell, your Vania[27]

He never returned.

It was ironic but somehow fitting that the 1905 Revolution should
have been started by an organization dreamed up by the tsarist regime itself. No
one believed more than Father Gapon in the bond between Tsar and people. As
a student at the St Petersburg Theological Academy he had made a name for
himself as a preacher in the workers' districts of the city. He told the urban
poor who flocked to his church that the Tsar, their paternal guardian, had a
holy obligation to care for them, his most humble subjects. Gapon's popularity
attracted the attention of S.V. Zubatov, Chief of the Moscow Okhrana, who
since 1900 had been organizing his own police-sponsored trade unions with the
blessing of the Grand Duke Sergei, Governor-General of Moscow. Zubatov
began his remarkable career as a schoolboy terrorist in the Populist underground,
but soon became disillusioned with the revolutionary movement and turned
police informer. The rest of his life he devoted to the Okhrana and its campaign
against the revolutionaries.

Zubatov acknowledged that the workers had real and legitimate grievances, and that these could make them into a revolutionary threat. If they were
left to the mercy of their factory employers, the workers were almost bound to
come under the influence of the socialists. But if, as he advocated, the government
set up its own workers' organizations, the initiative would lie with the Tsar's
loyal servants. Zubatov's unions aimed to satisfy the workers' demands for
education, mutual aid and organization, whilst serving as a channel for monarchist
propaganda. To his masters at court, they offered the prospect of a popular
autocracy, where the Tsar could appear as the workers' paternal guardian, protecting them from the greed of their bosses and the 'alien' contamination of the
revolutionaries. It was the old imperial strategy of divide and rule: the workers
would be used to weaken the main threats to the autocracy — the industrial
bourgeoisie and the socialist intelligentsia.

By 1903, when Gapon began to organize his own workers' clubs and
tea-rooms under the patronage of the police, Zubatov's star was already falling.
In the previous year he had organized a march of 50,000 workers to commemorate the Emancipation of the serfs. Although the march was peaceful and utterly
loyalist in its intentions, grave concerns were expressed about its unprecedented
size and about Zubatov's ability to contain it and indeed his movement in
general. Such doubts were confirmed in July 1903, when one of Zubatov's unions
became involved in a general strike in Odessa. Zubatov was dismissed and
his experiment abruptly terminated. But his supporters now joined Gapon's

organization, which sought to establish similar unions under the patronage of the Church. Once again the movement was radicalized from below, as growing numbers of workers joined it to campaign for their own reform agenda. It had begun as a cultural mission for tea-drinking for 'respectable' workers. There were evenings of dancing, concerts and lectures on various forms of self-help. Meetings began with the Lord's Prayer and ended with the national anthem. But the movement was soon transformed into an independent labour union, the Assembly of Russian Factory and Mill Workers, which, despite its loyal surface, demanded radical reforms, including the establishment of a government responsible to the people, a progressive income tax, trade union rights, and an eight-hour day.[28]

The reform programme would have required the complete restructuring of the state, yet said nothing about how this was to be achieved. Gapon himself was completely ignorant of political theory: he could not even pronounce the word 'constitutionalism'. He saw himself as a man of destiny sent by God for the deliverance of the workers. Driven by vanity and restless ambition, he never stopped to think that he might be raising their expectations too high. He told his followers in simple terms, with arguments drawn from the Bible, that the Tsar was obliged before God to satisfy their demands if 'the people' went directly to him. He consciously drew on the myth of the benevolent Tsar — 'The Tsar wants justice but the boyars resist' — that had fuelled and legitimized so many protest movements in Russian history. On 3–8 January 1905, when 120,000 workers went on strike in St Petersburg and began to speak about going to the Tsar in order to 'seek truth and justice', Gapon took up their cause. Encouraged by the Liberation Movement, he drew up a list of demands to be presented to the Tsar in a mass demonstration scheduled for the following Sunday. Supplicating and sentimental, the petition moved to tears whole crowds of workers. It began:

SIRE

We, the workers and inhabitants of St Petersburg, of various estates, our wives, our children, and our aged, helpless parents, come to THEE, O SIRE to seek justice and protection. We are impoverished; we are oppressed, overburdened with excessive toil, contemptuously treated . . . We are suffocating in despotism and lawlessness. O SIRE we have no strength left, and our endurance is at an end. We have reached that frightful moment when death is better than the prolongation of our unbearable sufferings . . .[29]

On 7 January the government ordered Gapon to call off the march and posted notices in the city centre warning of 'resolute measures' against any gatherings on the streets. Aware of the imminent tragedy, Gorky led a delegation of intellectuals to the offices of Witte and Mirsky in a vain effort to get them to negotiate with the demonstrators. But the government, which continued to entertain the illusion that it could control Gapon, was confident that force would not be required. Nicholas thought so little of the danger that he even left the capital for his palace at Tsarskoe Selo and another quiet weekend of country walks and games of dominoes. But by then the workers were far too determined to be put off by simple prohibitions. At a series of mass rallies Gapon worked them up into a hysterical religious fervour, using all the oratorical tricks of the fundamentalist preacher:

> *Gapon*: Do the police and soldiers dare stop us from passing, comrades?
> *Hundreds of voices in unison*: They do not dare.
> *Gapon*: Comrades, it is better for us to die for our demands than live as
>   we have lived until now.
> *Voices*: We will die.
> *Gapon*: Do you swear to die?
> *Voices*: We swear!
> *Gapon*: Let the ones who swear raise their hands . . .

And hundreds of people raised their hands and with their fingers made the sign of the cross.

Despite their private fears, the workers put their faith in the Tsar receiving them: they saw him as a man of God, and knew their cause was just. The soldiers would surely not fire on a peaceful demonstration. To boost the marchers' spirits it was even said that refreshments had been prepared for them inside the Winter Palace and that a parade would be held to celebrate the great occasion.[30]

Church bells rang and their golden domes sparkled in the sun on that Sunday morning as the long columns marched across the ice towards the centre of the city. In the front ranks were the women and children, dressed in their Sunday best, who had been placed there to deter the soldiers from shooting. At the head of the largest column was the bearded figure of Father Gapon in a long white cassock carrying a crucifix. Behind him was a portrait of the Tsar and a large white banner with the words: 'Soldiers do not shoot at the people!' Red flags had been banned.

As the column approached the Narva Gates it was suddenly charged by a squadron of cavalry. Some of the marchers scattered but others continued to advance towards the lines of infantry, whose rifles were pointing directly at them. Two warning salvoes were fired into the air, and then at close range a third volley was aimed at the unarmed crowd. People screamed and fell to the ground but the soldiers, now panicking themselves, continued to fire steadily into the mass of people. Forty people were killed and hundreds wounded as they tried to flee. Gapon was knocked down in the rush. But he got up and, staring in disbelief at the carnage around him, was heard to say over and over again: 'There is no God any longer. There is no Tsar.'[31]

There were similar massacres in other parts of the city. At the Troitsky Bridge, near the Peter and Paul Fortress, the marchers were mown down by gunfire and sabred by the Cossack cavalry. Gorky, who was in the crowd, recalls the death of one worker:

> The dragoon circled round him and, shrieking like a woman, waved his sabre in the air . . . Swooping down from his dancing horse . . . he slashed him across the face, cutting him open from the eyes to the chin. I remember the strangely enlarged eyes of the worker and . . . the murderer's face, blushed from the cold and excitement, his teeth clenched in a grin and the hairs of his moustache standing up on his elevated lip. Brandishing his tarnished shaft of steel he let out another shriek and, with a wheeze, spat at the dead man through his teeth.[32]

Stunned and confused, the survivors made their way to Nevsky Prospekt in a last desperate bid to reach the Palace Square. The sunshine had brought out more than the usual number of Sunday afternoon promenaders, and many of them were to witness the shocking events that followed. A huge body of cavalry and several cannons had been posted in front of the palace to prevent the marchers from moving on to the square. But the crowd, some 60,000 of them, continued to build up, swollen by students and onlookers. As news of the massacres reached them, they began to push forward, jeering at the soldiers. Some of the Guards of the Preobrazhensky Regiment were ordered to clear the crowds around the Alexandrovsky Gardens, using whips and the flats of their sabres. But when this proved unsuccessful they took up firing positions. Seeing the rifles pointed at them, the demonstrators fell to their knees, took off their caps and crossed themselves in supplication. Suddenly, a bugle sounded and the soldiers fired into the crowd. A young girl, who had climbed up on to an iron fence to get a better view, was crucified to it by the hail of bullets. A small boy, who had mounted the equestrian statue of Prince Przewalski, was hurled into the air by a volley of artillery. Other children were hit and fell from the trees where they had been perching.

When the firing finally stopped and the survivors looked around at the dead and wounded bodies on the ground there was one vital moment, the turning-point of the whole revolution, when their mood suddenly changed from disbelief to anger. 'I observed the faces around me', recalled a Bolshevik in the crowd, 'and I detected neither fear nor panic. No, the reverend and almost prayerful expressions were replaced by hostility and even hatred. I saw these looks of hatred and vengeance on literally every face — old and young, men and women.

The revolution had been truly born, and it had been born in the very core, in the very bowels of the people.' In that one vital moment the popular myth of a Good Tsar which had sustained the regime through the centuries was suddenly destroyed. Only moments after the shooting had ceased an old man turned to a boy of fourteen and said to him, with his voice full of anger: 'Remember, son, remember and swear to repay the Tsar. You saw how much blood he spilled, did you see? Then swear, son, swear!'[33]

Later, as the Sunday promenaders hurried home in a state of shock, the workers went on a rampage through the fashionable streets around the Winter Palace. They smashed windows, beat up policemen, threw rocks at the soldiers, and broke into the houses of the well-to-do. As darkness fell, the crowds began to build barricades in front of the Kazan Cathedral using benches, telegraph poles and furniture taken from buildings. More barricades were built in the workers' districts. Gangs went round looting liquor and gun shops. The streets were momentarily in the hands of the mob and the first red flags appeared. But these revolutionaries had no leaders and by midnight most of them had gone home.

Gapon, meanwhile, had taken refuge in Gorky's apartment. His beard was cut off, his hair cropped short and his face made up by one of Gorky's theatrical friends, who, according to the writer, 'did not quite understand the tragedy of the moment and made him look like a hairdresser or a salesman in a fashionable shop'. That evening Gorky took the revolutionary priest to a meeting at the Free Economic Society in order to dispel the growing rumours of his death. Practically the whole of the St Petersburg intelligentsia was crammed into the small building on Zabalkansky Avenue. They were outraged by the news that 'thousands' of people had been slaughtered (the true figures were probably in the region of 200 killed and 800 wounded). 'Peaceful means have failed,' the disguised figure shouted. 'Now we must go over to other means.' He appealed for money to help the 'workers' party' in its 'struggle for freedom'. Suddenly, chaos broke out in the hall as people recognized Gapon. But the priest managed to escape through a back door and returned to Gorky's apartment. There he wrote an address to his 'Comrade Workers' in which he urged them to 'tear up all portraits of the blood-sucking Tsar and say to him: Be Thou damned with all Thine August Reptilian Progeny!' Hours later, in a new disguise, Gapon fled to Finland and then abroad.[34]*

* At the end of January Gapon turned up in Geneva, where he fell in with the revolutionaries in exile. Their theoretical disputes were above him and, seduced by international fame, he soon left for London to write his autobiography. Having made himself a celebrity, Gapon had no more use for the revolutionary movement. In December he returned to Russia, where he supported the Witte government and even co-operated with the secret police against the socialists. In March 1906, for reasons that are unclear, he was brutally murdered by agents of the secret police, including his closest associate, who on 9 January had rescued him from the massacre at the Narva Gates.

That night Gorky wrote to his separated wife, Ekaterina, in Nizhnyi Novgorod: 'And so, my friend, the Russian Revolution has begun: I send you my sincere congratulations. People have died — but don't let that trouble you — only blood can change the colour of history.'[35]

Two days later he was arrested, along with the other members of the deputation to Witte and Mirsky on 8 January (they had foolishly left their visiting cards). All of them were charged (quite ridiculously, though it showed the extent of the regime's fears) with belonging to a 'revolutionary convention' which had planned to seize power and establish a 'provisional government'. They were imprisoned in the Peter and Paul Fortress.[36]

* * *

The events of 'Bloody Sunday', as 9 January became known, brought Gorky closer to the Bolsheviks. Gorky had first met Lenin in 1902 and had quickly fallen into a love-hate relationship with him. He had since been active in attracting funds for the Social Democrats from rich industrialists, such as Savva Morozov, who clearly saw the writing on the wall ('These days it is necessary to be friends with one's enemies,' Morozov had once said to the Bolshevik Krasin). Gorky's relationship with the Bolsheviks was never easy or straightforward. As with many intellectuals, his commitment to the revolution was romantic and idealist. He saw it as a vast struggle of the human spirit for freedom, brotherhood and spiritual improvement. His was essentially a humanist view, one which placed the individual at its heart, and he could never quite bring himself to accept the iron discipline or the narrow dogmatism of the Bolsheviks. 'I belong to none of our parties', he once wrote to the painter Repin, 'and I am glad of it. For this is freedom, and man is greatly in need of that.' The gipsies, gamblers, beggars and swindlers who filled the pages of his stories were all struggling in their own small way for individual freedom and dignity: they were not the representatives of an organized 'proletariat'. People struggled, classes did not struggle, that was Gorky's view. Gorky, in his own words, 'could admire but not like' wooden dogmatists like Lenin who tried to compress life's diversity into their abstract theory. Being fully human meant, in his view, 'loving passionately and painfully the living, sinning, and — forgive me — pitiful Russian'.[37] It was almost a Christian view of human redemption through revolution (and Gorky flirted with Christianity). Such ideas were common among the radical intelligentsia. Witness the writings of Merezhkovsky (on 'Christianity without Christ'), Solovyov (on 'Godmanhood') and Bogdanov (on 'God-Building'), with whom Gorky was closely linked. During and after 1917 this contradiction between the party and the human goals of the revolution would bring Gorky into conflict with the Bolsheviks. But for the moment, in 1905, they were brought together by their common view that the workers' movement had to be radicalized. This was why Gorky, in his letter to Ekaterina, had seen some good in Bloody Sunday; the effect of the massacre would be to radicalize the mood on the streets. The workers needed something like this to shake them out of their naïve belief in the existence of a benevolent Tsar. Only blood could change the colour of history. Now it was time to organize the workers and to move them away from their attachment to the liberals towards socialist goals.

There was a huge wave of strikes during the weeks after Bloody Sunday. In January alone, more than 400,000 workers downed tools across the country. It was the largest ever labour protest in Russian history. But the strikes were not really organized; they were more like a spontaneous outburst of anger; and the workers' demands were often not even formulated until after the strike had begun. The socialist parties were still much too weak to play a leading role. Their main leaders — Lenin, Martov, Trotsky, Plekhanov and Chernov — were all in exile, and although they were undoubtedly excited by what they agreed was the long-awaited start of the revolution, very few of them were in a hurry to leave the comfortable environment of their coffee houses in Geneva or Paris for the dangerous and harsh existence awaiting them back in Russia. It was only later during 1905 that they began to return and the workers rallied to the left-wing parties as they became more politicized.*

In the meantime the running continued to be made by the liberal and democratic opposition. Educated society was outraged by the massacre of Bloody Sunday. The student Kerensky, who had witnessed the shooting on Nevsky Prospekt, went home that evening and wrote a furious protest letter to his schoolfriends in the Guards. Two weeks later he wrote to his parents in Tashkent:

> I am sorry not to have written to you earlier, but we have been living here in such a state of shock that it was impossible to write. Oh, 'these awful days' in Peter will remain for ever in the memory of everybody who lived through them. Now there is silence, but it is the silence before the storm. Both sides are preparing and reviewing their own forces. Only one side can prevail. Either the demands of society will be satisfied (i.e. a freely elected legislature of people's representatives) or there will be a bloody and terrible conflict, no doubt ending in the victory of the reaction.

Alexander Pasternak, a twelve-year-old schoolboy and brother of the poet to be, was so disturbed by the shootings that he declared himself to be a 'wholehearted revolutionary' and marched with his friends through his affluent St Petersburg

---

* The Bolsheviks and Mensheviks probably had something in the region of 10,000 members each by the end of 1905, although at this early stage party membership was not clearly defined. There are no reliable figures for SR party membership in 1905. But in November 1906 there were 50,000 members, compared with a total of 40,000 members for the two Marxist factions.

neighbourhood shouting, 'We are Social Democrats!' Students across the country went on strike and turned their campuses into centres of political agitation. At Moscow University 3,000 students held a rally, at which they burned a portrait of the Tsar and hung red flags on the faculty buildings. By the end of February the government had been forced to close down virtually all the institutions of higher learning until the end of the academic year. Even the theological academies were affected by student disorders.[38]

Meanwhile, the zemstvo constitutionalists revived their campaign and at their Second National Congress in April called for the convocation of a Constituent Assembly. Professional unions organized themselves at a national level into a Union of Unions to rally their members behind the liberal cause. The Unions of Writers, Lawyers, Professors and Engineers were the first such unions to be formed. They were later joined (despite the opposition of some reluctant males in the leadership of the Union of Unions) by a Women's Union for Equality which campaigned for voting rights. Semi-professional groups, such as the Pharmaceutical Assistants, the Clerks and Book-keepers, and the Railway Workers and Employees, also established affiliated unions. Their participation in the Union of Unions gave the intelligentsia a direct link with the masses.* Hundreds of zemstvos, city councils and voluntary bodies sent petitions to the government demanding political reforms. The press publicized them and highlighted other grievances in a way that gave the public anger a single national voice. 'We can no longer live like this,' declared the headline of a leading liberal newspaper on 21 May, and soon everyone was repeating the phrase.[39]

The literary intelligentsia also sought to play a leading role. 'We have to serve the people,' Gorky admonished a fellow writer who had turned his back on politics. 'The blood of the people is being spilt, the blood of the workers, everywhere the regime is cynically killing the best people — the young Rus' — and you write only about yourself.' Like most of Russia's intellectuals, Gorky threw himself into politics and journalism. He had been released from the Peter and Paul Fortress after a European-wide campaign, joined by (among others) Auguste Rodin, Anatole France and Marie Curie, which lent the weight of Western opinion to the democratic cause against autocracy. Shortly after his release, on 5 March, he wrote to Tolstoy criticizing him for not involving himself more in politics:

In these grim times when blood is flowing on the soil of your country, and when hundreds and thousands of decent, honest people are dying for

---

* Since the professions had taken the lead in forming these unions, other blue-collar unions, even in Communist Russia, continued to be called 'professional unions' (*profsoiuzy*) rather than trade or industrial unions.

the right to live like human beings, instead of cattle, you whose word is heeded by the whole world, you find it possible merely to repeat once again the fundamental idea behind your philosophy: 'Moral perfection of individuals — this is the meaning and aim of life for all people'. But just think, Lev Nikolaevich, is it possible for a man to occupy himself with morally perfecting his character at a time when men and women are being shot down in the streets?[40]

The social engagement of the writer, in which Gorky passionately believed, and which at the time of the famine crisis had made Tolstoy the country's moral conscience, was now becoming rather harder for some, like Tolstoy, to maintain. For it now obliged them to support a revolution that might itself spill the people's blood. Gorky would later come to share these doubts; but for now they were suppressed in the urgency of the revolutionary moment.

The mood of rebellion soon spread to the countryside. Seeing the government's weakness, the peasants took their chance and organized rent strikes to force the landowners to increase their wages as labourers. They trespassed on the gentry's land, felled their trees and cut their hay. By the early summer, when it became clear that the harvest had failed once again, they began to launch full-scale attacks on their estates, seizing property and setting fire to the manors, forcing the landowners to flee. Witnesses spoke of the night sky lit up by the blaze of burning manors and of lines of horse-drawn carts moving along the roads, loaded with plundered property. There was a good deal of vandalism — 'culture smashing' — as the peasants set out to destroy anything that smacked of superfluous wealth. They burned libraries, destroyed antiques and left shit on the Oriental carpets. Some villagers even took the paintings and statues, the Bohemian crystal and the English porcelain, the satin dresses and powdered wigs, which they then divided among themselves, along with the livestock, the grain and the tools. In one village the peasants broke up a grand piano, which they had hauled away from the manor, and shared out the ivory keys. Nearly 3,000 manors were destroyed (15 per cent of the total) during the Jacquerie of 1905–6. Most of the violence was concentrated in the central agricultural zone, where peasant poverty was most acute and the largest estates were located. Once the local squires had been 'smoked out', the peasants retreated into their own communal world. Local officials were replaced by the peasants, conservative priests driven out, and government laws and tax demands ignored.[41]

The struggle for the land was not the only form of peasant revolution in 1905–6, although because of the gentry's fears it was the main concern of official records (and has thus since dominated the historiography). Alongside the violence on the land there grew up a whole range of peasant unions, agricultural societies and co-operatives. They were generally more moderate and sophisticated in their aims and methods than the majority of traditional village communes, and they tended to attract the sort of young and 'conscious' peasants who had emerged with the spread of rural schools. Many of the peasant unions, in particular, had close connections with the local teachers and the rural intelligentsia. For these reasons, they tended to develop in the largest villages, where there were more cultural institutions, such as schools and reading-rooms, and where the peasantry was most exposed to the influence of the outside world (e.g. in the form of markets and railways, state officials and police). Some of these organizations became famous throughout Russia for establishing what were in effect independent peasant republics (for example, the Sumy Republic in Kharkov province). They espoused the ideals of political reform, of a constitution and a parliament, and of better education for the peasants, in addition to land reform. Their aim was to end the 'dark' and 'backward' ways of the villages, to bring them the benefits of the modern world, and to end their isolation by integrating them into national politics.[42]

Sergei Semenov, peasant, local writer and Tolstoyan from the village of Andreevskoe, was among the founders of the Markovo Republic, one of the most famous and impressive examples of progressive peasant politics during the 1905 Revolution. For the best part of a year, whilst the tsarist state was paralysed, the 'Republic' instituted a sophisticated system of 'peasant rule' in several volosts of the Volokolamsk district. It was formed by a group of activists, teachers and peasants (among them Semenov) from Markovo and other nearby villages, who had been meeting since 1901 in the reading-clubs and tea-rooms of the region to discuss the Moscow newspapers. They organized the Peasant Union, which provided the political structure of the Markovo Republic. In October 1905 a general meeting of the peasants passed a resolution calling for a radical overhaul of the whole political system. Its demands included the convocation of a national parliament, secret and universal adult suffrage, equal civil rights for the peasantry, progressive taxes, land for the landless, free and universal education, freedom of movement and a political amnesty. The peasants declared that they would not obey the existing authorities, nor pay their taxes, nor provide any army recruits, until their demands were satisfied. They elected a 'Republican Government', headed by a 'President' (one of the local commune's elders), and declared their allegiance to the Peasant Union. Local branches of the union were established — Semenov set up one in Andreevskoe — which effectively ran the villages. Rents were controlled. Agronomic measures were introduced. The volost authorities were democratized and the church schools 'nationalized'. The tsarist regime was powerless — there was no land captain and only one police sergeant in the volost — and could only watch with increasing frustration as this 'free territory' of peasant self-rule, under eighty miles from Moscow itself, continued to spread and to grow in fame. A professor from Chicago, who had read about the Republic in the US newspapers, arrived in Markovo to lend it his support. For several months the authorities tried unsuccessfully to defeat the Republic by political means. It dismissed the elected volost elder, one of the Republic's leaders, called Ryzhkov. But the Schweikian peasants counteracted this by refusing to elect a successor, while Ryzhkov declared that to his sorrow he could not relinquish his powers, because there was no one to whom he could hand them. It was only in July 1906, six months after the revolution had been put down in the cities, that this peasant republic was finally destroyed. Ryzhkov was removed by a police trick. All the villages were then raided and their leaders, Semenov among them, rounded up and imprisoned in Moscow. During his eight months as the leader of the Peasant Union in Andreevskoe, Semenov had established a new village school, an agricultural society, two co-operatives, a reading club, and, remarkably, a peasant theatre.[43]

The local gentry appealed for help against the peasants, and the government sent in the troops. From January to October the army was used no fewer than 2,700 times to put down peasant uprisings, accelerating the breakdown of army discipline which had begun with the despatch of the troops to Manchuria.[44] It was the growing threat of a mutinous revolution at home combined with the prospect of defeat abroad — signalled by the navy's humiliation at Tsushima in May 1905 — which forced the Tsar to sue for peace with Japan. It proved impossible — as it would again in 1917 — to conduct a foreign war in the midst of a domestic social revolution. The vast majority of the infantry were peasants, and resented being used to suppress agrarian discontent. Whole units refused to carry out orders and mutinies spread through the ranks; even the Cossack cavalry was affected. And then, on 14 June, the unrest spread to the Black Sea Fleet.

It all began with a piece of maggoty meat, which the ship's doctor on board the battleship *Potemkin* declared was fit to eat. When the sailors complained to the captain, he had their spokesman, Vakulenchuk, shot. The crew rebelled, murdered seven officers and raised the red flag. A small group of active revolutionaries leading the mutiny hoped it would spread to the rest of the fleet. They sailed overnight to Odessa, where striking workers had been in a virtual state of war with the city government for the past two weeks. There they placed Vakulenchuk's body, surrounded by a guard of honour, at the foot of a set of marble steps (later immortalized by Eisenstein's film) leading from the harbour to the city. During the next day thousands of people gathered on the harbour front, placing wreaths around the bier of the martyred revolutionary and offering food to the sailors. As night approached troops were sent in to quell the crowd. Moving down the steps, they fired indiscriminately into the hemmed-in civilians below. Hundreds of people jumped into the sea. By dawn, when the massacre finally ended, 2,000 people had been killed and 3,000 wounded. The *Potemkin* set sail from Odessa but, without the support of the rest of the fleet, it was eventually forced to surrender. On 25 June the sailors docked at Constanza in Romania and exchanged the *Potemkin* for safe refuge.[45] In itself, the mutiny had been a minor threat. But it was a major embarrassment to the regime, for it showed the world that the revolution had spread to the heart of its own military machine.

The subject nationalities of the Empire had been equally quick to take advantage of the regime's temporary weakness. The strikes and protests which followed the Bloody Sunday revolt in St Petersburg were especially intense in the non-Russian borderlands — Latvia and Poland in particular — where social and political tensions were reinforced by a widespread hatred of Russian rule. In Riga up to 15,000 workers marched through the city on 13 January in protest against the tsarist regime and the ruthlessness of the Russian Governor-General, A. N. Meller-Zakomelsky. He gave further cruel evidence of this when he ordered his soldiers to fire on the crowd. Seventy were killed and 200 injured. Meller-Zakomelsky was proud of the way his men had handled the situation and wrote to the Tsar suggesting that if more local authorities were willing to act with such decisiveness there would be no further trouble. In the ten Polish provinces there were more strikes in the spring and summer of 1905 than in the rest of the Empire combined. The textile city of Lodz was particularly turbulent: in mid-June, weeks before anything like it happened in Russia, barricades went up, and there were five days of street-fighting between workers and police. Warsaw was even more violent: up to 100,000 workers took part in demonstrations after Bloody Sunday. Russian troops fired at the crowds, killing ninety-three people, and a state of siege was declared. Later in the summer news of Russia's defeat by Japan was met by further demonstrations in the Polish capital with such slogans as 'Down with Tsarism!', 'Long Live an Independent Socialist Poland!' and 'Long Live Japan!'[46] Nationalists everywhere welcomed Russia's defeat in the belief that it would bring down the Tsar and thus pave the way for their own autonomy. Pilsudski, the leader of the Polish Socialists, had even gone to Japan to discuss Polish action against Russia's war effort.

In many of these non-Russian lands virtually the whole of the population became involved in the national liberation movement. In Finland, for example, where the imposition of Russian rule had destroyed the autonomy of the Grand Duchy, there was a mass campaign of passive resistance led by the nationalist intelligentsia. Nearly everyone joined it, including the Finnish Swedes, who had enjoyed many privileges under Russia's domination which they were likely to lose under Finnish rule. The Russian Governor-General, an imperialist hardliner by the name of Bobrikov, was assassinated in 1904, and by the following year Finland was engaged in a full-scale war of passive resistance against St Petersburg. In Georgia the Mensheviks led this national revolution. Theirs was the first Marxist national-liberation movement in history to enjoy the support of the peasantry: between 1904 and 1906 it effectively replaced the tsarist state in western Georgia.

*   *   *

With the Russian Empire teetering on the brink of collapse, the tsarist regime responded to the crisis with its usual incompetence and obstinacy. Witte called it a 'mixture of cowardice, blindness and stupidity'. The basic problem was that Nicholas himself remained totally oblivious to the extremity of the situation. While the country sank deeper into chaos he continued to fill his diary with terse and trivial notes on the weather, the company at tea and the number of birds he had shot that day. His advisers convinced him that foreign agents had been responsible for the demonstration on Bloody Sunday and he duly filled the prisons with suitable political suspects. A carefully picked delegation of 'reliable' workers was summoned to Tsarskoe Selo, where they were lined up like children to hear a short address from the Tsar, in which he blamed the workers for allowing themselves to be deceived by 'foreign revolutionaries' but promised to 'forgive them their sins' because he believed in their 'unshakeable devotion' to him. Meanwhile, the liberal Mirsky was replaced as Minister of the Interior by the decent but malleable A. G. Bulygin, who in effect took orders from his own deputy and chief of police, D. F. Trepov, a strict disciplinarian from the Horse Guards whom Nicholas liked for his straightforward, soldierly approach, and whom he had therefore allowed to become a dominant force at court. When Bulygin suggested that political concessions might be needed to calm the country, Nicholas was taken aback and told the Minister: 'One would think you are afraid a revolution will break out.' 'Your Majesty,' came the reply, 'the revolution has already begun.'[47]

The remark must have been enough to make Nicholas a little uncomfortable, for he soon made promises of political reform. On 18 February he issued an Imperial Manifesto and Decree, which, while condemning the disorders, acknowledged the shortcomings of the bureaucracy and summoned the 'well-meaning people of all estates' to unite behind the throne and send in ideas for 'improvements in the state organization'. Bulygin was instructed to draw up proposals for a national assembly. The Manifesto was a tactical manoeuvre, its sole purpose to buy time; there was no sign that it came from the heart. The educated circles on the whole remained sceptical. 'The main aim of this Manifesto', Kerensky wrote to his parents on 18 February, 'is to calm and silence the revolutionary movement that has just begun so that all the forces of the government can be consolidated for one purpose in the future: to prevent any of its promises from being delivered.' Indeed it was typical of the Tsar's obstinate adherence to the archaic principles of patrimonial autocracy that at such a moment he should have attempted to shift the blame for the crisis on to the bureaucracy while at the same time appealing to the direct bond between himself and his subjects. If the people had grievances, or so his Manifesto had implied, they should bring them directly to him and they would be satisfied.

And indeed in the following weeks tens of thousands of reform petitions were sent in to the Tsar from village assemblies, army regiments, towns and factories. Like the *cahiers*, the letters of grievance of 1789, they gave expression to the evolving language of political and social democracy. But their demands were far too radical for Nicholas. Most of them called for a national parliament with sovereign rights of legislation. Yet the sort of assembly which the Tsar had in mind — and which Bulygin finally presented for his signature on 6 August — was a purely consultative one elected on a limited franchise to ensure the domination of the nobles. This was to be a king's parliament, like the *Zemskii Sobor* of the seventeeth century, which was compatible with the preservation of the Tsar's own personal rule. Its main purpose, as Nicholas saw it, would be to inform him of his subjects' needs and thus enable him to rule on their behalf without the mediation of the self-aggrandizing bureaucracy.[48]

The Bulygin Duma was yet another example of too little too late. Six months earlier it would have been welcomed, and enabled the government to regain the political initiative. But now all but the most moderate reformers found it quite unsatisfactory. The liberal newspapers, having carefully scrutinized the complex provisions of the new electoral law, claimed that less than 1 per cent of St Petersburg's adult residents would qualify for the vote, while in many provincial cities the proportion would be even tinier. Despite their criticisms, the liberals chose not to boycott the Duma elections. But the Social Democrats and the radicals in the Union of Unions were now more determined than ever to use mass civil disobedience to pressurize the government into making further concessions. The culmination of their efforts was the general strike of September and October, the first general strike in history, which forced the reluctant government to concede real political reforms.

During 1905 there was a marked increase in the level of organization and militancy of the workers' strikes and protests. This was partly the result of the socialists taking over the labour movement. But it was also — and probably much more so — the result of the workers themselves becoming more class conscious and violent as their conflicts with employers and police became more bitter and intense. Gorky noted the workers' growing aggression after witnessing a clash on Znamenskaya Square in St Petersburg in early September. An officer struck a soldier in the street, and an angry crowd of workers gathered to defend the soldier. They tore the epaulettes from the officer's uniform and, so Gorky thought, would have killed him too had it not been for the timely intervention of the police and Cossacks. 'The crowd conducted itself with remarkable simplicity and openness,' Gorky wrote to Ekaterina, 'they said and chanted everything they wanted right there and then in front of the police and in general displayed a great deal of moral strength and even tact. There is a world of difference between this crowd and the supplicant people of 9 January.'[49]

Not all the violence in the cities was the result of the growing militancy of the labour movement. There was a marked increase in all forms of violence, from muggings and murders to drunken riots and vandalism, as law and order broke down. Indeed, as the police withdrew from the scene, so the public added to the violence by forming groups of vigilantes and lynching criminals in the streets. Every day the press reported dozens of these cases of 'mob law' (*samosud*), along with robberies and murders. Mobs of a different kind went round the streets beating up students and well-dressed passers-by. There were pogroms against Jews. In short, the whole country seemed locked into a downward spiral of violence and anarchy. As the US Consul in Batumi reported:

[Russia] is permeated with sedition and reeking with revolution, racial hatred and warfare, murder, incendiarism, brigandage, robbery and crime of every kind . . . As far as can be seen we are on the high road to complete anarchy and social chaos . . . One of the worst signs is that the public under this long reign of anarchy and crime is growing callous and the news of the murder of an acquaintance or friend is, by the bulk of the population, received with indifference whilst cases of brigandage are looked upon as being quite in the ordinary course of events.[50]

Because of the preoccupation of many historians with the organized labour movement — and their seduction by the Soviet myth of the armed workers on the barricades — the role of this everyday criminal violence in the revolutionary crowd has been either ignored or, even more misleadingly, confused with the violence of industrial war. Yet the closer one looks at the crowds on the streets, the harder it becomes to distinguish clearly between organized forms of protest — the marching workers with banners and songs — and criminal acts of looting and violence. The one could easily — and often did — break down into the other. It was not just a question of 'hooligans' or criminals joining in labour protests or taking advantage of the chaos they created to vandalize, assault and loot. Such acts seem to have been an integral element of labour militancy, a means of asserting the power of the plebeian crowd and of despoiling and destroying symbols of wealth and privilege. What the frightened middle classes termed 'hooliganism' — mob attacks on the well-to-do and on figures of authority, looting and vandalism, drunken brawling and rioting — could just as easily be categorized as 'revolutionary acts'. And in part that is what they were: the revolutionary violence of 1905–17 was expressed in just these sorts of act. It was driven by the same feelings of hatred for the rich and all figures of authority, by the same desire of the poor and the powerless to assert themselves and claim the streets as their own. From the perspective of the propertied there was very little to distinguish between the 'rough' and 'rude' behaviour of the 'hooligans' — their cocky way of dressing, their drunkenness and vulgar language, their 'insolence' and 'licence' — and the behaviour of the revolutionary crowd.[51] Even the most organized labour protests could, on the slightest provocation, break down into violence and looting. It was to become a major problem for all the revolutionary parties, the Bolsheviks in particular, who tried to use the violence of the crowd for their own political ends. Such violence was a double-edged sword and could lead to anarchy rather than controlled revolutionary force. This was the lesson the Bolsheviks would learn during the July and October Days in 1917 — outbursts of violence which were far removed from the Soviet image of heroic proletarian power.

If, however, there was some genuine inspiration for the Soviet myth of the factory worker, gun in hand, fighting for the revolution on the barricades, then that was the general strike of 1905. For it was the classic example of a spontaneous yet disciplined uprising of the working class. It began on 20 September with a walk-out by the Moscow printers — the most educated group of workers — for better pay and conditions. The strikers made contact with the students and held a mass street demonstration, which was attacked by the police. The workers threw stones at the police, smashed shop windows, over-turned benches and knocked down trees to make barricades. By the start of October the printers of St Petersburg and several other cities had come out in solidarity with their comrades: middle-class homes went without their newspapers for several weeks. Then the railway workers came out on strike. The Union of Railway Employees and Workers was affiliated to the Union of Unions, which had been discussing the idea of a general political strike to further its campaign for political reform since the summer. By 10 October virtually the entire railway network had come to a halt. Millions of other workers — factory, shop and transport workers, bank and office employees, hospital staff, students, lecturers, even the actors of the Imperial Theatre in St Petersburg — came out in support of what had become in effect a national strike against the autocracy. The cities were brought to a standstill. All transport stopped. The lights went out at night. Telegraphs and telephones ceased to work. Shops were closed and their windows boarded up. Food became scarce. Robberies and looting exploded out of control. The gentry and the bourgeoisie took fright at the breakdown of law and order. When the Moscow water system began to malfunction there was panic; rumours spread that the strikers had deliberately contaminated the water. Workers, students and professionals joined together in demonstrations against the authori-ties. Many ended in the hasty building of barricades and in violent clashes with the police and Cossacks. The political demands of the demonstrators were remarkably uniform — the convocation of a constituent assembly elected by universal suffrage — which was a sign of the co-ordinating role played by the Union of Unions as well as the increased discipline and organization of the workers themselves.[52]

This last had much to do with the Petersburg Soviet. The word 'soviet' means 'council' in Russian and the Petersburg Soviet was really no more than an *ad hoc* council of workers established to direct the general strike. It owed its origins partly to the Union of Unions, which first came up with the idea, and partly to the Mensheviks, who took the lead in organizing the workers at factory level. On 17 October 562 factory deputies, most of them metalworkers, assembled in the building of the Free Economic Society and elected an executive of fifty members, including seven delegates from each of the three main socialist parties (Mensheviks, Bolsheviks and SRs). From the beginning it assumed the status and form — which it would assume again in 1917 — of a workers' government and an alternative source of power to the tsarist authorities. It organized the strikes, published its own newspaper, *Izvestiia*, which the workers eagerly read, established a militia, saw to the distribution of food supplies, and by its example inspired workers in fifty other cities to set up Soviets of their own. The Mensheviks dominated the Petersburg Soviet. They saw it as the embodiment of their ideology. The Bolsheviks, by contrast, were mistrustful of working-class initiatives and hostile to the idea of the Soviet as an independent workers' council, although this no doubt had something to do with the fact that they themselves had very little influence over it. Not even Lenin, who returned from exile in early November, got to speak in the Soviet, although there is still a desk in the building that housed the workers' council with a plaque on it claiming that he did.[53]

The nominal chairman of the Soviet Executive was the lawyer (and future Menshevik) G. S. Khrustalev-Nosar. But Leon Trotsky was the real force behind it. He framed its resolutions and wrote the editorials for *Izvestiia*. After Khrustalev-Nosar's arrest on 26 November, he also became its chairman. Trotsky had been the first of the major socialist leaders to return from exile after Bloody . Sunday. He lived under various guises, including that of a patient in an eye hospital, where he had written revolutionary proclamations from his bed as the nurses gave him foot-baths. During the general strike he had emerged in the Soviet under the name of Yanovsky, the village where he was born. His support for a working-class insurrection and his brilliant journalistic attacks on the liberals had certainly brought him closer to the Bolshevik wing of the Social Democrats since the great party schism of 1903. Yet in essence he remained a revolutionary Menshevik and, as George Denike later recalled, it was he more than anyone else who 'stood for Menshevism' at this stage.[54]

※   ※   ※

The Tsar's advisers now looked to Count Witte to save the country from disaster. Yet Nicholas himself remained quite impassive. He spent most of his time that autumn hunting. 'The tragic aspect of the situation', remarked a courtier in his diary on 1 October, 'is that the Tsar is living in an utter fool's paradise, thinking that He is as strong and all-powerful as before.' On 9 October Witte was finally received in the Winter Palace. With brutal frankness he told Nicholas that the country was on the verge of a cataclysmic revolution which would 'sweep away a thousand years of history'. The Tsar had one of two choices: either to appoint a military dictator or introduce major reforms. Witte outlined the needed reforms in a memorandum arguing for a Manifesto, which he had brought with him: the granting of civil liberties; a constitutional order; cabinet government; and a legislative Duma elected on a democratic franchise. It was in effect the political programme of the Liberation Movement. His aim was clearly to isolate the Left by pacifying the liberals. He stressed that repression could only be a temporary solution, and a risky one at that, for the loyalty of the armed services was in doubt and if they were used to put down the general strike they might fall apart altogether. Most of the Tsar's senior military advisers agreed with Witte, as did Trepov, the Governor of St Petersburg, whose influence at court was now paramount. Nicholas remained unconvinced and asked his uncle, the Grand Duke Nikolai, to assume the role of dictator. But the Grand Duke, an excitable and outspoken man, took out a revolver and threatened to shoot himself there and then if the Tsar refused to endorse Witte's memorandum. The Empress would henceforth always blame the Grand Duke for Russia's 'constitution'. His *coup de théâtre* was certainly the decisive factor in her husband's change of mind, for the Grand Duke was the one man capable of playing the role of dictator and it was only when he took the side of reform that it finally dawned on the Tsar that repression was no longer an option and he agreed to sign the Manifesto. 'My dear Mama,' he wrote to the Empress Maria two days later on 19 October, 'you can't imagine what I went through before that moment ... From all over Russia they cried for it, they begged for it, and around me many — very many — held the same views ... There was no other way out than to cross oneself and give what everyone was asking for.'[55]

From the start, then, the Tsar was reluctant in the extreme to play the role of a constitutional monarch. The image of Nicholas as an 'enlightened Tsar' who 'introduced democracy to Russia' could not be further from the truth, although it is one that apologists for the tsarist regime as well as peddlers of nostalgia in post-Soviet Russia would have us accept. For an autocrat like Nicholas, who saw himself as ruling from the throne in the good old Byzantine tradition, there could have been no deeper humiliation than to be forced by a bureaucrat like Witte (who was merely a 'businessman' and, moreover, a former 'railway clerk') to grant his subjects the rights of citizenship. Not even the eventual act of abdication in 1917 — which he said he had signed so as not to be forced to relinquish his coronation oath to uphold the principles of autocracy — was such a bitter pill to him. Witte later claimed that the court set out to use his Manifesto as a temporary concession and that it had always intended to return to its old autocratic ways once the danger passed.[56] He was almost certainly correct. By the spring of 1906 the Tsar was already going back on the promises he made the previous October, claiming that the Manifesto had not in fact placed any limits on his own autocratic prerogatives, only on the bureaucracy.

The Manifesto's proclamation was met with jubilation in the streets. Despite the rainy weather, huge numbers of people converged in front of the Winter Palace with a large red flag bearing the inscription 'Freedom of Assembly'. As they must have been aware, they had at last managed to do what their fellow subjects had failed to do on 9 January. Bloody Sunday had not been in vain, after all. In Moscow 50,000 people gathered in front of the Bolshoi Theatre. Officers and society ladies wore red armbands and sang the Marseillaise in solidarity with the workers and students. The general strike was called off, a partial political amnesty was proclaimed, and there was a euphoric sense that Russia was now entering a new era of Western constitutionalism The whole country, in the words of one liberal, 'buzzed like a huge garden full of bees on a hot summer's day'.[57] The newspapers were filled with daring editorials and hideous caricatures of the country's rulers, as the old censorship laws ceased to function. There was a sudden boom in pornography, as the limits of the new laws were tested. In Kiev, Warsaw and other capitals of the Empire, a flood of new publications appeared in the language of the local population as Russification policies were suspended. Political meetings were held in the streets, in squares and in parks, in all public places, as people no longer feared arrest. A new and foreign-sounding word was now invented — *mitingovanie* — to describe the craze for meetings displayed by these newborn citizens. Nevsky Prospekt became a sort of Speakers' Corner, a people's parliament on the street, where orators would stand on barrels, or cling to lamp-posts, and huge crowds would instantly gather to listen to them and grab the leaflets which they handed out. Socialist leaders returned from exile. New political parties were formed. People talked of a new Russia being born. These were the first heady days of freedom.

iii A Parting of Ways

It was in October 1905 that Prince Lvov, the 'liberal zemstvo man', enrolled as a member of the Kadets. The decision had not been an easy one for him to make, for Lvov, by nature, was not a 'party man'. His political outlook was

EVERYDAY LIFE UNDER THE TSARS

14 The city mayors of Russia in St Petersburg for the tercentenary in 1913.

15 The upholders of the patriarchal order in the countryside: a group of volost elders in 1912.

16 A newspaper kiosk in St Petersburg, 1910. There was a boom in newspapers and pamphlets as literacy expanded and censorship was relaxed following the 1905 Revolution.

17 A grocery store in St Petersburg, circa 1900. Note the icon in the top-left corner, a sign of the omnipresence of the Church.

18-19 A society of extreme rich and poor. *Above*: dinner at a ball given by Countess Shuvalov in her splendid palace on the Fontanka Canal in St Petersburg at the beginning of 1914. *Below*: a soup kitchen for the unemployed in pre-war St Petersburg.

20 Peasants of a northern Russian village, mid-1890s. Note the lack of shoes and the uniformity of their clothing and their houses.

21-2 Peasant women were expected to do heavy labour in addition to their domestic duties. *Above*: a peasant's two daughters help him thresh the wheat. *Below*: peasant women haul a barge on the Sura River under the eye of a labour contractor.

23 Serfdom was still within living memory. Twin brothers, former serfs, from Chernigov province, 1914.

24 A typical Russian peasant household – two brothers, one widowed, each with four children – from the Volokolamsk district, circa 1910.

25 A meeting of village elders, 1910. Most village meetings were less orderly than this.

26 A religious procession in Smolensk province. Not all the peasants were equally devoted to the Orthodox Church.

27 The living space of four Moscow workers in the Sukon–Butikovy factory dormitory before 1917.

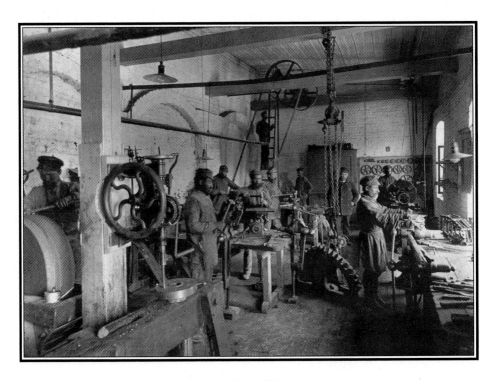

28 Inside a Moscow engineering works, circa 1910.

essentially practical — that is what had drawn him into zemstvo affairs — and he could not easily confine himself to the political dogma of any one party. His knowledge of party politics was almost non-existent. He regularly confused the SDs with the SRs and, according to his friends, did not even know the main points of the Kadet programme. 'In all my years of acquaintance with Prince Lvov', recalled V. A. Obolensky, 'I never once heard him discuss an abstract theoretical point.' The Prince was a 'sceptical Kadet', as Miliukov, the party's leader, once put it. He was always on the edge of the party's platform and rarely took part in its debates. Yet his opinions were eagerly sought by the Kadet party leaders and he himself was frequently called on to act as a mediator between them. (It was his practical common sense, his experience of local politics, and his detachment from factional squabbles, that would eventually make Lvov the favoured candidate to become the Prime Minister of the Provisional Government in March 1917.)[58]

Of all the political parties which sprang up in the wake of the October Manifesto, the Constitutional Democrats, or Kadets for short, was the obvious one for Lvov to join. It was full of liberal zemstvo men who, like him, had come to the party through the Liberation Movement. The agenda of the movement was in the forefront of the Kadet party programme passed at its founding congress in October 1905. The manifesto concentrated almost exclusively on political reforms — a legislative parliament elected on the basis of universal suffrage, guarantees of civil rights, the democratization of local government, and more autonomy for Poland and Finland — not least because the left and right wings of the party were so divided on social issues, the land question above all. But perhaps this concentration was to be expected in a party so dominated by the professional intelligentsia, a party of professors, academics, lawyers, writers, journalists, teachers, doctors, officials and liberal zemstvo men. Of its estimated 100,000 members, nobles made up at least 60 per cent. Its central committee was a veritable 'faculty' of scholars: 21 of its 47 members were university professors, including its chairman, Pavel Miliukov (1859–1943), who was the outstanding historian of his day. These were the 'men of the eighties' — all now in their forties. They had a strong sense of public duty and Western-liberal values, but very little idea of mass politics. In the true tradition of the nineteenth-century intelligentsia they liked to think of themselves as the leaders of 'the people', standing above narrow party or class interests, yet they themselves made very little effort to win the people over to their cause.[59] For in their hearts, as in their dinner-party conversations, they were both afraid and contemptuous of the masses.

Among the other liberal groups to emerge at this time, the most important was the Octobrist Party. It took its name from the October Manifesto of 1905, which it saw as the basis for an era of compromise and co-operation between the government and public forces and the creation of a new legal order. It attracted some 20,000 members, most of them landowners, businessmen and officials of one sort or another, who favoured moderate political reforms but opposed universal suffrage as a challenge to the monarchy, not to mention to their own positions in central and local government.[60] If the Kadets were 'liberal-radicals', in the sense that they kept at least one foot in the democratic opposition, the Octobrists were 'conservative-liberals', in the sense that they were prepared to work for reform only within the existing order and only in order to strengthen it.

Lvov himself might have been tempted to join the Octobrists, for D. N. Shipov, his old political mentor and friend from the national zemstvo movement was one of the party's principal founders, while Alexander Guchkov, a comrade-in-arms from the relief campaign in Manchuria, became its leader. But the bitter reform struggle of the previous ten years had taught him not to trust so blindly in the willingness of the Tsar to deliver the promises he had made in his Manifesto. The Prince preferred to remain with the Kadets in a stance of scepticism and half-opposition to the government, rather than join the Octobrists in declarations of loyal support.

This was, in truth, the main dilemma that the liberals faced after the October Manifesto — whether to support or oppose the government. So far the revolution had been a broad assault by the whole nation united against the autocracy. But now the Manifesto held out the prospect of a new constitutional order in which both monarchy and society might — just might — develop along European lines. The situation was delicately balanced. There was always the danger that the Tsar might renege on his constitutional promises, or that the masses might become impatient with the gradual process of political reform and look instead to a violent social revolution. Much would depend on the role of the liberals, who had so far led the opposition movement and who were now strategically placed between the rulers and the ruled. Their task was bound to be difficult, for they had to appear both moderate (so as not to alarm the former) and at the same time radical (so as not to alienate the latter).

Witte, who was charged with forming the first cabinet government in October, offered several portfolios to the liberals. Shipov was offered the Ministry of Agriculture, Guchkov the Ministry of Trade and Industry, the liberal jurist A. F. Koni was selected for the Ministry of Justice, and E. N. Trubetskoi for Education. Prince Urusov, whom we encountered as the Governor of Bessarabia (see pages 42–5), and who sympathized with the Kadets, was considered for the all-important post of Minister of the Interior (although he was soon rejected on the grounds that, while 'decent' and even 'fairly intelligent', he 'was not a commanding personality'). Two other Kadets, Miliukov and Lvov, were also offered ministerial posts. But not one of these 'public men' agreed to join Witte's government, which in the end had to be made up of tsarist bureaucrats and appointees lacking public confidence.[61]

It is a commonplace that by their refusal to join Witte's cabinet the liberals threw away their best chance to steer the tsarist regime towards constitutional reform. But this is unfair. The ostensible reason for the breakdown of negotiations was the liberals' refusal to work with P. N. Durnovo, a man of known rightist views and a scandalous past,* who had, it seems, been promised the post of Minister of the Interior, and who was now suddenly offered it in preference to Urusov. But the Kadets were also doubtful that Witte would be able to deliver on the promises of the October Manifesto in view of the Tsar's hostility to reform. They were afraid of compromising themselves by joining a government which might be powerless against the autocracy. Their fears were partly conditioned by their own habitual mistrust of the government and their natural predilection towards opposition. 'No enemies on the Left' — that had been their rallying cry during the struggles of 1904–5. And the triumph of October had only confirmed their commitment to the policy of mass agitation from below. Their doubts were hardly groundless. Witte himself had expressed the fear that the court might be using him as a temporary expedient, and this had come out in his conversations with the Kadets. On one occasion Miliukov had asked him point blank why he would not commit himself to a constitution: Witte had been forced to admit that he could not 'because the Tsar does not wish it'.[62] Since the Premier could not guarantee that the Manifesto would be carried out, it was not unreasonable for the liberals to conclude that their energies might be better spent in opposition rather than in fruitless collaboration with the government.

In any case, it soon became clear that the 'liberal moment' would be very brief. Only hours after the declaration of the October Manifesto there was renewed fighting on the streets as the country became polarized between Left and Right. This violence was in many ways a foretaste of the conflicts of 1917. It showed that social divisions were already far too deep for a merely liberal settlement. On 18 October, the day the Manifesto was proclaimed, some of the jubilant Moscow crowds resolved to march on the city's main jail, the Butyrka, to demonstrate for the immediate release of all political prisoners. The protest passed off peacefully and 140 prisoners were released. But on their way back to the city centre the demonstrators were attacked by a large and well-armed mob carrying national flags and a portrait of the Tsar. There was a similar clash

---

* In 1893, when he was working in the Department of Police, Durnovo had ordered his agents to steal the Spanish Ambassador's correspondence with his prostitute mistress, with whom Durnovo was also in love. The Ambassador complained to Alexander III, who ordered Durnovo's immediate dismissal. But after Alexander's death he somehow managed to revive his career.

outside the Taganka jail, where one of the prisoners who had just been released, the Bolshevik activist N. E. Bauman, was beaten to death.

For the extreme Rightists this was to be the start of a street war against the revolutionaries. Several Rightist groups had been established since the start of 1905. There was the Russian Monarchist Party, established by V. A. Gringmut, the reactionary editor of _Moscow News_, in February, which called for the restoration of a strong autocracy, martial law, dictatorship and the suppression of the Jews, who, it was claimed, were mainly the 'instigators' of all the disorders. Then there was the Russian Assembly, led by Prince Golitsyn and made up mainly of right-wing Civil Servants and officers in St Petersburg, which opposed the introduction of Western parliamentary institutions, and espoused the old formula of Autocracy, Orthodoxy and Nationality.

But by far the most important was the Union of the Russian People, which was established in October by two minor government officials, A. I. Dubrovin and V. M. Purishkevich, as a movement to mobilize the masses against the forces of the Left. It was an early Russian version of the Fascist movement. Anti-liberal, anti-socialist and above all anti-Semitic, it spoke of the restoration of the popular autocracy which it believed had existed before Russia was taken over by the Jews and intellectuals. The Tsar and his supporters at the court, who shared this fantasy, patronized the Union, as did several leading Churchmen, including Father John of Kronstadt, a close friend of the royal family, Bishop Hermogen and the monk Iliodor. Nicholas himself wore the Union's badge and wished its leaders 'total success' in their efforts to unify the 'loyal Russians' behind the autocracy. Acting on the Tsar's instructions, the Ministry of the Interior financed its newspapers and secretly channelled arms to it. The Union itself was appalled, however, by what it saw as the Tsar's own weakness and his feeble failure to suppress the Left. It resolved to do this for him by forming paramilitary groups and confronting the revolutionaries in the street. The Black Hundreds,* as the democrats called them, marched with patriotic banners, icons, crosses and portraits of the Tsar, knives and knuckle-dusters in their pockets. By the end of 1906 there were 1,000 branches of the Union with a combined total of up to 300,000 members.[63] As with the Fascist movements of inter-war Europe, most of their support came from those embittered _lumpen_ elements who had either lost — or were afraid of losing — their petty status in the social hierarchy as a result of modernization and reform: uprooted peasants forced into the towns as casual labourers; small shopkeepers and artisans squeezed by competition from big business; low-ranking officials and policemen, the threat

---

* The name was a derogatory one, adapted from the term 'White Hundreds', which was used in medieval Russia for the privileged caste of nobles and wealthy merchants. The lower-class types who joined the Black Hundreds were not in this class, hence their ironic nomenclature.

to whose power from the new democratic institutions rankled; and pub patriots of all kinds disturbed by the sight of 'upstart' workers, students and Jews challenging the God-given power of the Tsar. Fighting revolution in the streets was their way of revenging themselves, a means of putting the clock back and restoring the social and racial hierarchy. Their gangs were also joined by common criminals — thousands of whom had been released under the October amnesty — who saw in them an opportunity for looting and violence. Often encouraged by the police, the Black Hundreds marched through the streets beating up anyone they suspected of democratic sympathies. Sometimes they forced their victims to kneel in homage before a portrait of the Tsar, or dragged them into churches and made them kiss the imperial flag.

The worst violence was reserved for the Jews. There were 690 documented pogroms — with over 3,000 reported murders — during the two weeks following the declaration of the October Manifesto. The Rightist groups played a leading role in these pogroms, either by inciting the crowd against the Jews or by planning them from the start. The worst pogrom took place in Odessa, where 800 Jews were murdered, 5,000 wounded and more than 100,000 made homeless. An official investigation ordered by Witte revealed that the police had not only organized, armed and supplied the crowd with vodka, but had helped it root out the Jews from their hiding places and taken part in the killings. The police headquarters in St Petersburg even had its own secret printing press, which produced thousands of pamphlets accusing the Jews of trying to ruin Russia and calling upon the people to 'tear them to pieces and kill them'. Trepov, the virtual dictator of the country, had personally edited the pamphlets. Durnovo, the Minister of the Interior, subsidized them to the tune of 70,000 roubles. But when Witte called for the prosecution of the police chief responsible, the Tsar intervened to protect him. Nicholas was evidently pleased with the pogroms. He agreed with the anti-Semites that the revolution was largely the work of Jews, and naively regarded the pogroms as a justified form of revenge by his 'loyal subjects'. He made this clear in a letter to his mother on 27 October:

My Dearest Mama . . .

I'll begin by saying that the whole situation is better than it was a week ago . . . In the first days after the Manifesto the subversive elements raised their heads, but a strong reaction set in quickly and a whole mass of loyal people suddenly made their power felt. The result was obvious, and what one would expect in our country. The impertinence of the socialists and revolutionaries had angered the people once more; and because nine-tenths of the trouble-makers are Jews, the people's whole anger turned against them. That's how the pogroms happened. It is amazing how they took place *simultaneously* in all the towns of Russia and Siberia . . . Cases as far

apart as in Tomsk, Simferopol, Tver and Odessa show clearly what an
infuriated mob can do: they surrounded the houses where revolutionaries
had taken refuge, set fire to them and killed everybody trying to escape.[64]

What was emerging was the start of the counter-revolution which would culmi-
nate in the civil war. From this point on anti-Semitism became one of the
principal weapons used by the court and its supporters to rally the 'loyal people'
behind them in their struggle against the revolution and the emerging liberal
order.

For the revolutionaries Bauman's murder was a powerful reminder of
the regime's bloody habits. Overnight the Bolshevik became a martyr of the
revolution. Later, under the Soviet regime, his name would be given to streets,
schools, factories, and even a whole district of Moscow. But in fact Bauman was
quite unworthy of such inflated honours. He was fond of practical jokes, and
on one occasion had been so malicious to a sensitive party comrade, drawing a
cruel cartoon of her as the Virgin Mary with a baby in her womb and a question
mark asking who the baby looked like, that she was driven to hang herself.
Many Social Democrats, including Martov, wanted Bauman expelled from the
party. But Lenin disagreed on the grounds that he was a good party worker and
that that was all that mattered in the end. The scandal continued to divide the
party — it was one of the many personal clashes which came to define the ethical
distinctions between the Bolsheviks and the Mensheviks after 1903 — until
Bauman himself was arrested and imprisoned in the Taganka jail. Death
cleansed Bauman of his sins. Through his martyrdom the Bolsheviks were able,
for the first time, to play on the sympathies of a mass audience. For in the
highly charged atmosphere of late October 1905 people from across the whole
of the democratic spectrum saw in Bauman's corpse a symbol of the fate awaiting
the revolution if they did not unite against reaction. And they turned out in
their tens of thousands for his funeral.

If there was one thing the Bolsheviks really mastered, that was the art
of burying their dead. Six herculean leather-clad comrades carried Bauman's
coffin, draped in a scarlet pall, through the streets of Moscow. At their head
was a Bolshevik dressed in Jesuitical-black with a palm branch in his hand which
he swung from side to side in time with the music and his own slow steps. The
party leaders followed with wreaths, red flags and heavy velvet banners, bearing
the slogans of their struggle in ornate gold. They were flanked by an armed
militia of students and workers. And behind them row upon row of mourners,
some 100,000 in all, marched ten abreast in military formation. This religious-
like procession continued all day, stopping at various points in the city to pick
up reinforcements. As it passed the Conservatory it was joined by a student
orchestra, which played, over and over again, the funeral dirge of the revolution:

'You Fell Victim to a Fateful Struggle'. The measured heaviness of the marchers, their melancholy music and their military organization filled the streets with dark menace. As night fell, thousands of torches were lit, making the red flags glow. The graveside orations were emotional, defiant and uplifting. Bauman's widow called on the crowds to avenge her husband's death and, as they made their way back to the city centre, sporadic fighting broke out with Black Hundred gangs.[65]

By this stage the Bolsheviks were already planning an armed insurrection. Their resolve was stiffened by Lenin's return from Geneva at the start of November, for he was insistent on the need to launch a revolt. Since Bloody Sunday much of his correspondence from Switzerland had been dominated by detailed instructions on how to build barricades and how to fight the Cossacks using bombs and pistols. The Petersburg Soviet was also preparing for a show-down with the government. During November it supported a series of strikes which were distinguished by their militancy. Under Trotsky's leadership and the influence of the street crowds, which at least in Petersburg were starting to show signs of readiness for a socialist revolution, many of the Mensheviks moved away from their broad alliance with the liberals and embraced the idea of an armed revolt to assert the 'hegemony of the working class'. There was little prospect of success, but this was buried under all the emotion. Some of the Social Democrats were carried away by their own rhetoric of defiance — after all, it made them popular with the angry workers — and somehow talk slid into actual plans of action. Others took the view that it would be better to go down with a fight than not to try and seize power at all. In the words of one Menshevik, 'we were certain in our hearts that defeat was inevitable. But we were all young and seized with revolutionary enthusiasm and to us it seemed better to perish in a struggle than to be paralysed without even engaging in one. *The honour of the Revolution was at stake.*' Indeed for Lenin (the 'Jacobin') it did not even matter if the putsch should fail. 'Victory?!', he was heard to say in mid-November. 'That for us is not the point at all! . . . We should not harbour any illusions, we are realists, and let no one imagine that we have to win. For that we are still too weak. The point is not about victory but about giving the regime a shake and attracting the masses to the movement. That is the whole point. And to say that because we cannot win we should not stage an insurrection — that is simply the talk of cowards. And we have nothing to do with them!'[66]

The turning-point came on 3 December with the arrest of the Peters-burg Soviet leaders. Despite their own poor preparations and the absence of any clear signs of mass support, the Moscow Social Democrats declared a general strike and began to distribute arms to the workers. There were feverish prep-arations — some of them quite comical. A group of Petersburg Social Democrats became involved, for example, in a hare-brained scheme to develop a 'chemical compound that, if sprinkled on a policeman, would supposedly make him lose consciousness immediately so that you could grab his weapon'. Gorky lent a hand with the preparations. He converted his Moscow apartment into the headquarters of the insurrection and, dressed in a black leather tunic and knee-high military boots, supervised the operations like a Bolshevik commissar. Bombs were made in his study and food was prepared and sent from his kitchens to the workers and students on the barricades. 'The whole of Moscow has become a battleground,' he wrote to his publisher on 10 December. 'The windows have all lost their glass. What's going on in the suburbs and factories I don't know, but from all directions there is the sound of gun-fire. No doubt the authorities will win, but their victory will be a pyrrhic one and it will teach the public an excellent lesson. It will be costly. Today we saw three wounded officers pass our windows. One of them was dead.'[67]

Ironically, with just a little more strategic planning, the insurgents might have taken Moscow, although in the end, given the lack of nationwide support and the collapse of the army mutinies, the authorities were bound to prevail. By 12 December the rebel militias had gained control of all the railway stations and several districts of the city. Barricades went up in the major streets. Students and well-dressed citizens, incensed by the deployment of artillery against the workers and unarmed crowds, joined in building the barricades from telegraph poles, broken fences, iron gates, overturned trams, lamp-posts, market stalls, doors ripped out of houses, and whatever else came to hand. What had started as a working-class strike was now turning into a general street war against the authorities. The police and the troops would dismantle the barricades at night, only to find them rebuilt in the morning. The outer ring of boulevards which encircles the centre of Moscow became one vast battlefield, with troops and artillery concentrated in the major squares and the rebels controlling most of the streets in between. At this moment, had they struck towards the Kremlin, the rebels might have won. But their plans were largely dictated by the goals of the workers themselves, who preferred to concentrate on the defence of their own rebel strongholds. In the Presnia district, for example, the centre of the textile industry and the home of the most militant workers, there was certainly no thought of marching on the centre. Instead the rebels turned Presnia into a workers' republic, with its own police and a revolutionary council, which in many ways anticipated the future system of the Soviets.

By 15 December the tide was already turning against the rebels. Long-awaited reinforcements from St Peterbsurg arrived in the form of the Semenovsky Regiment and began to bombard the Presnia district, shelling buildings indiscriminately. The Prokhorov cotton mill and the Schmidt furniture factory, which, thanks to their Left-inclined owners, had been turned into fortresses of the uprising in Presnia, were bombarded for two days and nights, despite Schmidt's readiness to negotiate a surrender. Much of the Presnia district was destroyed. House fires burned out of control. By the time the uprising was crushed, more than a thousand people had been killed, most of them civilians caught in the crossfire or in burning buildings. During the weeks that followed the authorities launched a brutal crackdown with mass arrests and summary executions. Workers' children were rounded up in barracks and beaten by police to 'teach them a lesson'. The prisons filled up, militant workers lost their jobs, and the socialist parties were forced underground. Slowly, through terror, order was restored.[68]

The Moscow uprising failed to raise the banner of social revolution, but it did act as a red rag to the bull of counter-revolution. Witte told Polovtsov in April 1906 that after the success of the Moscow repressions he lost all his influence over the Tsar and, despite his protestations, Durnovo was allowed to 'carry out a brutal and excessive, and often totally unjustified, series of repressive measures'. Throughout the country the socialists were rounded up and imprisoned, or forced into exile or underground. Semen Kanatchikov, who had played a leading part in the Bolshevik revolutionary organizations of Moscow and Petrograd during 1905, was arrested and imprisoned no fewer than three times between 1906 and 1910, whereupon he was sentenced to a life term of exile in Siberia. The newly won freedoms of the socialist parties were now lost as the old police regime was restored. Between 1906 and 1909 over 5,000 'politicals' were sentenced to death, and a further 38,000 were either imprisoned or sent into penal servitude. In the Baltic lands punitive army units went through the towns and villages. During a six-month campaign of terror, starting in December, they executed 1,200 people, destroyed tens of thousands of buildings, and flogged thousands of workers and peasants. The Tsar was delighted with the operation and praised its commanding officer for 'acting splendidly'. In Russia itself the regime did not hesitate to launch a war of terror against its own people. In the areas of peasant revolt whole villages were destroyed by the army and thousands of peasants were imprisoned. When there was no more room in the county jails, orders were given to shoot the guilty peasants instead. 'Arrests alone will not achieve our goals,' Durnovo wrote to his provincial governors in December. 'It is impossible to judge hundreds of thousands of people. I propose to shoot the rioters and in cases of resistance to burn their homes.' The regime aimed to break the spirits of the peasants by humiliating and beating them into submission. Whole communities were forced to take off their hats and scarves and prostrate themselves like serfs before the Cossack troops. Interrogating officers then rode on horses through the villagers, whipping them on the back whenever their answers displeased them, until they gave up their rebel leaders for summary execution. Liberally plied with vodka, the Cossacks committed terrible atrocities against the peasant population. Women and girls were raped in front of their menfolk. Hundreds of peasants were hanged from the trees without any pretence of a trial. In all it has been estimated that the tsarist regime executed 15,000 people, shot or wounded at least 20,000 and deported or exiled 45,000, between mid-October and the opening of the first State Duma in April 1906.[69] It was hardly a promising start to the new parliamentary order.

During the suppression of the Moscow uprising Gorky's flat was raided by the Black Hundred gangs and he was forced to flee under cover to Finland. 'I am staying near a waterfall, deep in the woods on the shores of Lake Saimaa,' he wrote to his separated wife Ekaterina on 6 January. 'It's beautiful here, like a fairy tale.'[70] Given the new political climate it would have been suicidal for Gorky to return to Russia. The government was doing its best to slander the writer's name. Witte even paid a correspondent of the London *Daily Telegraph* — a newspaper not known for its fairness to the Left — to spread the libel that Gorky was an anti-Semite. Nothing could have been further from the truth. Gorky despised the popular anti-Semitism of his day, seeing it as a symptom of Russia's backwardness. The fact that pogroms were often an expression of the people's own revolutionary impulses was to become one of his own anxieties about the revolution.

In the spring of 1906 Gorky set sail for America with his common-law wife, the actress Marya Andreeva. At first he was welcomed in the Land of the Free as a champion of the struggle against tyrannical monarchs. To the Americans, as to the French, Gorky appeared as a modern version of their own republican heroes. Cheering crowds greeted his ship as it docked in New York and Mark Twain spoke at a banquet in his honour. But the arms of the tsarist police were very long indeed, and when the American press was informed by them that the woman travelling with Gorky was not his wife there was public outrage. Newspapers accused Gorky of spreading licentious anarchism in the Land of the Righteous. Twain refused to appear with him again, and angry protesters stopped him from making any more public speeches. Returning to their hotel one evening, Gorky and Andreeva discovered that their luggage had been packed and was waiting for them in the lobby. The manager explained that he could not risk the good reputation of his establishment by giving them a bed for the night. No other hotel in Manhattan would put up the immoral couple and they were forced to find sanctuary in the home of the Martins, a broad-minded couple in Staten Island.[71]

*   *   *

What were the lessons of 1905? Although the tsarist regime had been shaken, it was not brought down. The reasons for this were clear enough. First, the various opposition movements — the urban public and the workers, the peasant revolution, the mutinies in the armed services, and the national independence movements — had all followed their own separate rhythms and failed to combine politically. This would be different in February 1917, when the Duma and the

Soviet performed the essential role of co-ordination. Second, the armed forces remained loyal, despite the rash of mutinies, and helped the regime to stabilize itself. This too would be different in future — for in February 1917 the crucial units of the army and the navy quickly went over to the people's side. Third, following the victory of October there was a fatal split within the revolutionary camp between the liberals and democrats, who, on the one hand, were mainly interested in political reforms, and the socialists and their followers, who wanted to push on to a social revolution. By issuing the October Manifesto the tsarist regime succeeded in driving a wedge between the liberals and the socialists. Never again would the Russian masses support the constitutional democratic movement as they did in 1905.

'The reaction is triumphant — but its victory cannot last long,' Gorky wrote to a friend before leaving for New York. And indeed, although the regime succeeded in restoring order, it could not hope to put the clock back. 1905 changed society for good. It was a formative experience for all those who had lived through it. Many of the younger comrades of 1905 were the elders of 1917. They were inspired by its memory and instructed by its lessons. The writer Boris Pasternak (1890–1960) summed up its importance for his generation in the poem '1905':

> This night of guns,
> Put asleep
> By a strike.
> This night —
> Was our childhood
> And the youth of our teachers.[72]

The Russian people — and many of the non-Russians too — won new political freedoms in 1905 and these could not be simply withdrawn once the regime had regained its grip on power. The boom in newspapers and journals, the convocation of the Duma, the formation of political parties and the growth of public institutions — all these ensured that politics would no longer be the state's exclusive preserve but would have to be openly discussed, even if the real levers of power remained firmly in the hands of the Tsar.

Once they had tasted these new freedoms, the mass of the people could never again put their trust in the Tsar. Fear alone kept them in their place. Bernard Pares cites a conversation he had with a Russian peasant in 1907. The Englishman had asked him what he thought had been the main change in the country during the past five years. After some thought the peasant replied: 'Five years ago there was a belief [in the Tsar] as well as fear. Now the belief is all gone and only the fear remains.'[73]

It was not just a change in public mood that ruled out a return to the pre-revolutionary order. Too many of the regime's own institutional supports had lost the will for power. Even the prisons, the last resort of the autocracy, were now infected by the new liberal spirit. When, in August 1905, Miliukov, the Kadet leader, was imprisoned in the Kresty jail, he found that even the prison governor showed 'all the symptoms of liberalism. He acquainted me with the prison system and discussed with me ways of organizing the prisoners' labour, entertainment and the running of the prison library.' Trotsky found the prison regime at the Peter and Paul Fortress equally lenient:

> The cells were not locked during the day, and we could take our walks all together. For hours at a time we would go into raptures over playing leap-frog. My wife came to visit me twice a week. The officials on duty winked at our exchange of letters and manuscripts. One of them, a middle-aged man, was especially well disposed towards us. At his request I presented him with a copy of my book and my photograph with an inscription. 'My daughters are all college students,' he whispered delightedly, as he winked mysteriously at me. I met him later under the Soviet, and did what I could for him in those years of famine.

His jailers in this top security penitentiary allowed him to receive the latest socialist tracts, along with a pile of French and German novels, which he read with 'the same sense of physical delight that the gourmet has in sipping choice wines or in inhaling the fragrant smoke of a fine cigar'. He even managed to write a history of the Petersburg Soviet and several other pieces of revolutionary propaganda during his stay. 'I feel splendid,' he liked to joke with his visitors. 'I sit and work and feel perfectly sure that I cannot be arrested.' When he left the Fortress it was, as he later recalled, 'with a slight tinge of regret'. There is a photograph of Trotsky in his cell. Dressed in a black suit, a stiff-collared white shirt and well-polished shoes, this could have been, in the words of Isaac Deutscher, 'a prosperous western European *fin-de-siècle* intellectual, just about to attend a somewhat formal reception, rather than . . . a revolutionary awaiting trial in the Peter and Paul Fortress. Only the austerity of the bare wall and the peephole in the door offer a hint of the real background.'[74]

With his usual panache Trotsky transformed the trial of the fifty-one Soviet leaders into a brilliant propaganda exercise against the tsarist regime. The trial began in October 1906. Every day the court was besieged with petitions, letters, boxes of food and flowers sent by well-wishers for the defendants. The court-room began to resemble a florists' shop. The defendants and their supporters in the public gallery wore flowers in their buttonholes and dresses. The dock was covered in blooms. The judge did not have the courage to remove this fragrant demonstration and the demoralized court attendants were obliged to cope as best they could with the growing barrage of deliveries. At one stage the defendants rose to pay homage to one of their comrades, who had been executed shortly before the trial. Even the prosecuting attorneys felt obliged to stand for a minute's silence.

Trotsky was called to speak for the defence. He turned the dock into a revolutionary tribune, sermonizing to the court on the justice of the workers' uprising and occasionally pointing an accusatory finger towards the judge behind him. His speech turned the prosecution on its head: the Soviet leaders had not misled the workers into the insurrection but had followed them to it; if they were guilty of treason then so were thousands of workers, who would also have to be tried. The political order against which they had risen was not a 'form of government', argued Trotsky, but an 'automaton for mass murder . . . And if you tell me that the pogroms, the arson and the violence . . . represent the form of government of the Russian Empire, then — yes, then I recognize, together with the prosecution, that in October and November we were arming ourselves against the form of government of the Russian Empire.'[75] When he left the dock there was an outburst of emotion. The defence lawyers crowded around him wanting to shake his hand.* They had won a clear moral victory. On 2 November the jury delivered its verdict: all but fifteen of the Soviet leaders were acquitted. But Trotsky and fourteen others were exiled to the Arctic Circle.

For the peasants and the workers these new political liberties were of little direct interest. None of their own demands for social reform had been met. The experience of 1905 taught them to look to the social revolution and not to follow the political lead of the liberals. Their disillusionment became even deeper with the failures of the Duma years. There was a growing gulf, which had been exposed by the polarization of the opposition movement after the October Manifesto, between the constitutional ideals of the liberal propertied classes and the socio-economic grievances of the mass of workers and peasants: a general parting of the ways between the political and the social revolutions.

The workers returned to their factories to find that the old work regime was still in place. Having had their bosses briefly on the run, the brutal conditions must now have seemed even more intolerable to them. With the suppression of the socialist movement the working-class organizations were besieged and isolated. And yet the number of politicized workers ready and willing to join them grew with every month.

For their part, the peasants had been frustrated but not defeated in their struggle for the gentry's land. When the squires returned to their estates,

---

* Among them, ironically, was A.A. Zarudny, who in 1917, as the Minister of Justice in Kerensky's government, would imprison Trotsky on charges of state treason.

they noticed a change in the peasants' mood. Their old deference was gone, replaced by a sullen rudeness in their behaviour towards their masters. 'Instead of the peasants' previous courtesy, their friendliness and humility,' one landowner remarked on returning to his estate in Samara in 1906, 'there was only hatred on their faces, and the manner of their greetings was such as to underline their rudeness.' Another landowner remarked on returning to his Tula estate in 1908:

> Externally everything appeared to have returned to normal. But something essential, something irreparable had occurred within the people themselves. A general feeling of fear had undermined all trust. After a lifetime of security — no one ever locked their doors and windows in the evening — the nobles concerned themselves with weapons and personally made the rounds to test their security measures.

Many nobles complained of a rise in peasant crime, vandalism and 'hooliganism'. They would find farm buildings and machines smashed, or would have to deal with distraught daughters who had been harassed by the villagers. This new militant assertiveness and impatience with the nobles was reflected in village songs, such as this one from 1912:

> At night I strut around,
> And rich men don't get in my way.
> Just let some rich guy try,
> And I'll screw his head on upside-down.[76]

The revolution luridly exposed the peasants' deep hatred of the gentry. They resented having to give back the land they had briefly taken in the 'days of freedom'. Through hostile looks and petty acts of vandalism they were letting it be known that the land was 'theirs' and that as soon as the old regime was weakened once more they would again reclaim it.

The provincial squires, many of whom supported the liberal reform movement in 1904–5, now became, for the most part, inactive or stalwart supporters of reaction. Many of them took fright from the peasant violence and sold their estates to move back to the city: between 1906 and 1914 the gentry sold one-fifth of its land to the peasants; and in the most rebellious regions in 1905–6 the proportion was nearer one-third. But among the majority who chose to remain on the land there was a hardening resolution to defend their property rights. They called loudly for the restoration of law and order. Some local squires hired their own private armies to protect their estates from vandalism and arson. Many of the largest, in particular, joined the United Nobility and the other landowners' organizations established after 1905. This 'gentry reaction' was reflected in the changing nature of the zemstvos, which were transformed from liberal institutions into pillars of conservatism. In their liberal days the zemstvos had sought to improve conditions for the peasantry, but after 1905 they became increasingly focused on the gentry's narrowest concerns. Even the liberal-minded Prince Lvov was voted off the provincial board of the Tula zemstvo during the winter of 1905–6, and had to stand again as an urban delegate. Count Bobrinsky, the leader of the United Nobility, and ironically Lvov's brother-in-law, condemned him as a 'dangerous liberal'.[77]

The squires were not the only gentlemen who feared the lower classes more and more. Propertied society in general had been forced to confront the frightening reality of a violent revolution, and the prospect of it erupting again — no doubt with still more violence — filled its members with horror. The next revolution, it now seemed clear, would not be a bloodless celebration of Liberty, Fraternity and Equality. It would come as a terrible storm, a violent explosion of suppressed anger and hatred from the dispossessed, which would sweep away the old civilization. Here was the awesome vision of poets such as Blok and Belyi, who portrayed Russia after 1905 as an active and unstable volcano.

Such fears were reflected in the darkening mood of bourgeois language towards the 'mob' in the wake of 1905. In place of the earlier benign view of the urban poor as a 'colourful lot, worthy of compassion', there was now a growing fear of what Belyi called the 'many-thousand human swarm'. The boulevard press and periodicals fed on this growing bourgeois moral panic — reminiscent of our own concerns today about the rise of an 'underclass' — and editorialized on the breakdown of the social order, juvenile crime and delinquency, violent attacks on the well-to-do, disrespect towards authority, and even working-class promiscuity. All 'rough' behaviour by the lower classes was increasingly seen as aggressive and condemned as 'hooliganism' — as indeed were organized labour protests which liberal society in previous years had viewed with some sympathy. In other words, there was no longer any clear distinction in the minds of the respectable classes between criminal hooliganism and violent but justifiable protest. The Revolution of 1905 was now roundly condemned as a form of 'madness', a 'psychic epidemic', in the words of one psychologist, which had merely stirred up the 'base instincts' of the mob. There was less compassion for the poor on the part of this frightened bourgeoisie, and this was reflected in the falling rate of their contributions to charity.[78]

As the liberal conscience of their class, the Kadets agonized over the dilemmas which this growing threat of violence raised for their support of the revolution. On the one hand, they had been drawn into an alliance with the street, if only because there were no political alternatives. And as they themselves proclaimed, there were 'No enemies on the Left'. But, on the other hand, most of the Kadets were bourgeois, both in terms of their social status and in terms of their general world-view, and as such they were terrified of any further violence from the streets. As E. N. Trubetskoi warned in November:

> The wave of anarchy that is advancing from all sides, and that at the present time threatens the legal government, would quickly sweep away any revolutionary government: the embittered masses would then turn against the real or presumed culprits; they would seek the destruction of the entire intelligentsia; they would begin indiscriminately to slaughter anyone who wears German clothes [i.e. is well-dressed].[79]

Most of the Kadets now came to the conclusion that they did not want a revolution after all. They were intelligent enough to realize that they themselves would be its next victims. At its second conference in February 1906 the Kadet Party condemned the strikes, the Moscow uprising and the land seizures of the previous autumn. It then breathed a sigh of relief: its dishonest marriage with the revolution had at last been brought to an end.

This turning away from the masses was nowhere more marked than within the intelligentsia. The defeat of the 1905 Revolution and the threat of a new and more violent social revolution evoked a wide range of responses from the writers and publicists who had always championed the 'people's cause'. Many became disillusioned and gave up politics for comfortable careers in law and business. They settled down, grew fat and complacent, and looked back with embarrassment at their left-wing student days. Others abandoned political debate for aesthetic pursuits, Bohemian lifestyles, discussions about language and sexuality, or esoteric mystical philosophies. This was the heyday of exotic and pretentious intellectualism. The religious idealism of Vladimir Solovyov gained a particular hold over the Symbolist poets, such as Blok, Merezhkovsky and Belyi, as well as philosophers such as S. L. Frank, Sergei Bulgakov and Berdyaev, who rejected the materialism of the Marxist intelligentsia and sought to reassert the primacy of moral and spiritual values. Common to all of these trends was a deep sense of unease about the prospects for liberal progress in Russia.

There was a general feeling that Russian civilization was doomed. In Belyi's novel *Petersburg* (1913) one of the characters is a bomb. Fear and loathing of the 'dark' masses lay at the root of this cultural pessimism. 'The people' had lost their abstract purity: in 1905 they had behaved as ordinary people, driven by envy, hatred and greed. One could not build a new civilization on such foundations. Even Gorky, the self-proclaimed champion of the common man, expressed his deepest fears forcefully. 'You are right 666 times over,' he wrote to a literary friend in July 1905, '[the revolution] is giving birth to real barbarians, just like those that ravaged Rome.'[80] From this point on, Gorky was plagued by the fear — and after 1917 by the terrible realization — that the 'people's revolution' for which he had struggled all his life would destroy Russian civilization.

Many of these themes came together in *Vekhi* (*Landmarks*), a collection of essays published in 1909 by a group of philosophers critical of the radical intelligentsia and its role in the 1905 Revolution. The essays caused a storm of controversy — not least because their writers all had had spotless intelligentsia (i.e. politically radical) credentials — which in itself was symptomatic of the intelligentsia's new mood of doubt and self-questioning. Much of the uproar was caused by their portrayal — echoed by Boris Savinkov's novel *The Pale Horse* (1909) — of the revolutionary as a crippled personality driven to pathological destruction, amoral violence and cruelty, and the pursuit of personal power. The cult of the revolutionary hero was so intrinsic to the intelligentsia's self-identity that such debunking was bound to throw it into existential crisis. In one of the *Vekhi* essays Struve condemned the intelligentsia for its failure to recognize the need to co-operate with the state in the construction of a legal order after the October Manifesto. Until the intelligentsia abandoned its habits of revolutionary opposition and sought instead to teach the masses respect for the law, the tsarist state would remain the only real protection against the threat of anarchy.

Frank and Berdyaev argued that the atheist and materialist attitudes of the intelligentsia had tempted it to subordinate absolute truths and moral values to 'the good of the people'. On this utilitarian principle the revolutionaries would end by dividing society into victims and oppressors, and out of a great love for humanity would be a born a great hatred and desire for vengeance against particular men. B. A. Kistiakovsky condemned the tendency of the radical intelligentsia to dismiss the 'formality' of law as inferior to the inner justice of 'the people'. The law, argued Kistiakovsky, was an absolute value, the only real guarantee of freedom, and any attempt to subordinate it to the interests of the revolution was bound to end in despotism. Another essayist, A. S. Izgoev, ridiculed the infantile Leftism of the students, who blamed the government for every ill, and adopted the most extreme views in the belief that it made them more 'noble'. Finally, M. O. Gershenzon summed up the duties that now confronted the endangered intelligentsia:

The intelligentsia should stop dreaming of the liberation of the people — we should fear the people more than all the executions carried out by the government, and hail this government which alone, with its bayonets and its prisons, still protects us from the fury of the masses.[81]

* * *

In the long run the Bolsheviks were the real victors of the 1905 Revolution. Not that they came out from it any stronger than their main rivals; in many ways they suffered relatively more from the repressions after 1905 and, but for the financial support of wealthy patrons such as Gorky, might well not have survived the next twelve years. The few openings that remained for the socialist press and the trade unions were better exploited by the Mensheviks, whose dominant right wing (the so-called Liquidators) ceased all underground activities in order to concentrate on developing legal organizations. By 1910 not a single underground newspaper was still in print in Russia. Of the 10,000 Social Democrats who remained in the country, fewer than 10 per cent were Bolsheviks. Mass arrests, the exile of its leaders and constant surveillance by the police reduced the Bolsheviks to a tiny underground sect. The Okhrana's infiltration of their party was such that several of Lenin's most trusted lieutenants turned out to be police spies, including both secretaries of the Petersburg Committee and the head of the Bolshevik faction in the Fourth Duma, Roman Malinovsky.

Nor were the Bolsheviks immune to the factional splits that crippled all the socialist parties after 1905, despite the Soviet (and anti-Soviet) myth of a unified party under Lenin's command. As with the Mensheviks and SRs, the most heated argument among the Bolsheviks concerned the use of legal and illegal methods. All Bolsheviks were agreed on the primacy of the revolutionary underground. But some, like Lenin, also wanted to exploit the available legal channels, such as the Duma and the trade unions, if only as a 'front' for their own mass agitation; whereas others, like Bogdanov, Lenin's co-founder of the Bolshevik faction, argued that this would only encourage the workers to believe in 'constitutional illusions'. The conflict was mixed up with two other issues: the Bolsheviks' controversial use of 'expropriations' (i.e. bank robberies) to finance their activities; and the desire of many Bolsheviks, especially among the rank and file, for the two Social Democratic factions to mend their differences and reunite.

Yet the consequences of 1905 were set to divide the Mensheviks and Bolsheviks even more than the Party Congress of 1903. It was only after 1905 that the rival wings of the Social Democratic movement emerged as two distinctive parties, each with its own political culture, system of ethics, philosophy and methods. Lenin's tactical shifts made all the difference. The basic tenets of the Bolshevik political philosophy had already been formed by 1903, but it was only after 1905, as Lenin digested the practical lessons of the failed revolution, that its unique strategic features began to emerge. Hence Lenin's reference, fifteen years later, to the 1905 Revolution as a 'dress rehearsal' for the Bolshevik seizure of power.[82]

As Lenin later came to see it, three things had been made clear by 1905: the bankruptcy of the 'bourgeoisie' and its liberal parties as a revolutionary force; the immense revolutionary potential of the peasantry; and the capacity of the nationalist movements in the borderlands to weaken the Empire fatally. He argued for a break with the orthodox Marxist assumption, held as a matter of faith by most of the Mensheviks, that a backward country like Russia would have to go through a 'bourgeois-democratic revolution', accompanied by several decades of capitalist development, before its working class would be sufficiently advanced to take power and install a socialist system. It was not true, Lenin claimed, that the workers would have to follow the lead of the liberal 'bourgeoisie' in overthrowing Tsarism, since they could form a revolutionary government of their own in alliance with the peasants and the national minorities. This concept of working-class autonomy was to become a powerful weapon in the hands of the Bolsheviks. When the workers renewed their strikes and protests after 1912 they turned increasingly to the leadership of the Bolsheviks, whose support for militant action against the 'bourgeoisie' matched their own growing sense of working-class solidarity in the wake of 1905.

Trotsky advanced a similar idea in his theory of the 'permanent revolution' which he had taken from the Marxist theoretician Parvus and developed from his analysis of the 1905 Revolution, *Results and Prospects*. Although still a Menshevik (pride prevented him from joining Lenin's party), Trotsky's theory fitted better with the revolutionary Bolshevism which he would espouse in 1917 than with the mainstream of Menshevism, as voiced by Plekhanov and Axelrod, which insisted that the bourgeois revolution was a prerequisite of real socialism.* The Russian bourgeoisie, Trotsky said, had shown itself to be incapable of leading the democratic revolution. And yet this feebleness of capitalism's own agents would make it possible for the working class to carry out its revolution earlier than in the more advanced countries of the West. Here was historical paradox raised to the level of strategy. To begin with, the Russian Revolution would have to win the support of the peasants, the vast majority of the population, by allowing them to seize the gentry's estates. But as the revolution moved towards socialism, and the resistance of the 'petty-bourgeois' peasantry increased, further advance would depend on the spread of revolution to the industrial countries of the West, without whose support the socialist order would not be able to sustain itself. 'Workers of the World Unite!'

In this aspect of his theory — and in this alone — Trotsky remained a Menshevik. For the one thing which united all the various strains of the Menshevik credo after 1905 was the belief that in the absence of a socialist revolution in the West the revolutionary struggle of the Russian working class

---

* F. I. Dan and E. I. Martynov had also broken with this old Menshevik view (which went back to the 1880s). Their theory of the 'unbroken revolution', which they advanced in the newspaper *Nachalo* during the autumn of 1905, differed little from that of the 'permanent revolution'.

was bound to fail without the support, or at least the neutrality, of the bourgeoisie. This, in the view of the Mensheviks, demanded a flexible approach to
the liberal parties after 1905; it was in their mutual interests to campaign
for the dismantling of the despotic state and the establishment of a democracy.
The years in which the Duma operated would serve as the last test for this
experiment in political reform.

6 Last Hopes

i Parliaments and Peasants

The State Duma finally opened on 27 April 1906. It was a hot and sunny day, one of many in an exceptional Russian spring, and it was with some discomfort that Vladimir Obolensky, the elected deputy for the district of Yalta, squeezed himself into his old tail-coat and set off by carriage for the Winter Palace, where the new parliamentarians were to be received in the Coronation Hall. The Tsar and the Duma deputies regarded each other with the utmost suspicion, both being reluctant to share its power with the other. So the whole occasion was marked by a hostile posturing from each side, as if all the pomp and ceremony, the bowing and genuflections, were really delicate manœuvres in a beautifully camouflaged battle.

Nicholas had already scored the first victory in having the deputies come to him, not he to the Duma, for the opening ceremony. Indeed it was not until February 1916, in the midst of a grave political crisis, that the Tsar finally deigned to make an appearance in the Tauride Palace, the seat of the Duma. And as if to underline this royal supremacy, the Coronation Hall of the Winter Palace was sumptuously furnished to greet the parliamentary deputies. The throne was draped in ermine with the crown, the sceptre, the seal and the orb placed at its feet on four little camp-stools. The miraculous icon of Christ was placed, like a holy protector, before it, and solemnly guarded by a retinue of high priests. The deep basses of the choir, dressed in cassocks of crimson and gold, sang verse after verse of 'God Save the Tsar', as if on purpose to keep the congregation standing, until, at the height of the fanfare's crescendo, the royal procession arrived.

On one side of the hall stood the great and the good of autocratic Russia: state councillors, senators, ministers, admirals, generals and members of the court, all of them turned out in their brilliant dress uniforms dripping with medals and golden braid. Facing them were the parliamentary leaders of the new democratic Russia, a motley collection of peasants in cotton shirts and tunics, professional men in lounge suits, monks and priests in black, Ukrainians, Poles, Tatars and others in colourful national costumes, and a small number of nobles in evening dress. 'The two hostile sides stood confronting each other', recalled

Obolensky. 'The old and grey court dignitaries, keepers of etiquette and tradition, looked across in a haughty manner, though not without fear and confusion, at the "people off the street", whom the revolution had swept into the palace, and quietly whispered to one another. The other side looked across at them with no less disdain or contempt.' One of the socialist deputies, a tall man in a worker's blouse, scrutinized the throne and the courtiers around it with obvious disgust. As the Tsar and his entourage entered the hall, he lurched forward and stared at them with an anguished expression of hatred. For a moment it was feared that he might throw a bomb.

The court side of the hall resounded with orchestrated cheers as the Tsar approached the throne. But the Duma deputies remained completely silent. 'It was', Obolensky recalled, 'a natural expression of our feelings towards the monarch, who in the twelve years of his reign had managed to destroy all the prestige enjoyed by his predecessors.' The feeling was mutual: not once did the Tsar glance towards the Duma side of the hall. Sitting on his throne he delivered a short and perfunctory speech in which he promised to uphold the principles of autocracy 'with unwavering firmness' and, in a tone of obvious insincerity, greeted the Duma deputies as 'the best people' of his Empire. With that, he got up to leave. The parliamentary era had begun. As the royal procession filed out of the hall, tears could be seen on the face of the Tsar's mother, the Dowager Empress. It had been a 'terrible ceremony', she later confided to the Minister of Finance. For several days she had been unable to calm herself from the shock of seeing so many commoners inside the palace. 'They looked at us as upon their enemies and I could not stop myself from looking at certain faces, so much did they seem to reflect a strange hatred for us all.'[1]

This ceremonial confrontation was only a foretaste of the war to come. The whole period of Russian political history between the two revolutions of 1905 and February 1917 could be characterized as a battle between the royalist and parliamentary forces. To begin with, when the country was still emerging from the revolutionary crisis, the court was forced to concede ground to the Duma. But as the memory of 1905 passed, it tried to roll back its powers and restore the old autocracy.

The constitutional reforms of 1905–6 were ambiguous enough to give both sides grounds for hope. Nicholas had never accepted the October Manifesto as a necessary limitation upon his own autocratic prerogatives. He had reluctantly granted the Manifesto under pressure from Witte in order to save his throne. But at no time had he sworn to act upon it as a 'constitution' (the crucial word had nowhere been mentioned) and therefore, at least in his own mind, his coronation oath to uphold the principles of autocracy remained in force. The Tsar's sovereignty was in his view still handed to him directly from God. The mystical basis of the Tsar's power — which put it beyond any challenge —

remained intact. There was nothing in the new Fundamental Laws (passed in April 1906) to suggest that from now on the Tsar's authority should be deemed to derive from the people, as in Western constitutional theories.

In this sense, Miliukov was correct to insist (against the advice of most of his Kadet colleagues) that Russia would not have a real constitution until the Tsar had specifically acknowledged one in the form of a new oath of allegiance. For until then Nicholas was bound to feel no real obligation to uphold the constitutional principles of his own Manifesto, and there was nothing the Duma could do to prevent him from returning to the old autocratic ways once the revolutionary crisis had passed. Indeed the Fundamental Laws were deliberately framed to fulfil the promises of the October Manifesto whilst preserving the Tsar's prerogatives. They forced the new constitutional liberties into the old legal framework of the autocracy. The Tsar even explicitly retained the title of 'Autocrat', albeit only with the prefix 'Supreme' in place of the former 'Unlimited'. Nicholas took this to mean business as usual. As he saw it, the limitations imposed by the Fundamental Laws applied only to the tsarist *administration*, not to his own rights of unfettered rule. Indeed, in so far as the bureaucracy was viewed as a 'wall' between himself and the people, he could even comfort himself with the thought that the reforms would strengthen his personal powers.

And the Tsar held most of the trump cards in the post-1905 system. He was the supreme commander of the armed services and retained the exclusive right to declare war and to make peace. He could dissolve the Duma, and did so twice when its conduct failed to please him. According to Article 87 of the Fundamental Laws he could also legislate by emergency decree when the Duma was not in session, and his government used this loophole to bypass parliamentary opposition. The Duma Electoral Law established an indirect system of voting by estates heavily weighted in favour of the crown's traditional allies, the nobility and the peasants (still quite mistakenly assumed to be monarchists at heart). The government (the Council of Ministers) was appointed exclusively by the Tsar, while the Duma had a veto over its bills. But there was no effective parliamentary sanction against the abuses of the executive, which remained subordinate to the crown (as in the German system) rather than to parliament (as in the English). There was nothing the Duma could do, for example, to prevent the government from subsidizing Rightist newspapers and organizations, which were known to incite pogroms and which even tried to assassinate prominent liberal Duma leaders. The Ministry of the Interior and the police, both of which retained close ties with the court, were quite beyond the Duma's control. Thanks to their sweeping and arbitrary powers, the civil rights and freedoms contained in the October Manifesto remained little more than empty promises. Indeed there is no more accurate reflection of the Duma's true position than the fact that whenever it met in the Tauride Palace a group of plain-clothes policemen could be seen on the pavement outside waiting for those deputies to emerge whom they had been assigned to follow and keep under surveillance.[2]

The Duma was a legislative parliament. Yet it could not enact its own laws. Its legislative proposals could not become effective until they received the endorsement of both the Tsar and the State Council, an old consultative assembly of mostly reactionary nobles, half of them elected by the zemstvos, half of them appointed by the Tsar, which was transformed into the upper house, with equal legislative powers to the Duma itself, by a statute of February 1906. The State Council met in the splendid hall of the Marinsky Palace. Its elderly members, most of them retired bureaucrats and generals, sat (or dozed) in its comfortable velvet armchairs whilst stately footmen in white livery moved silently about serving tea and coffee. The State Council was more like an English gentleman's club than a parliamentary chamber (since it emulated the House of Lords this was perhaps a mark of its success). Its debates were not exactly heated since most of the councillors shared the same royalist attitudes, while some of the octogenarians — of which there were more than a few — had clearly lost most of their critical faculties. At the end of one debate, for example, a General Stürler announced that he intended to vote with the majority. When it was explained to him that no majority had yet been formed since the voting had only just begun, he replied with irritation: 'I still insist that I am with the majority!' Nevertheless, it would be mistaken to present the State Council as either ridiculous or benign. The domination of the United Nobility — to which one-third of the councillors belonged — ensured that it would act as a force of reaction, and it voted down all the liberal Duma bills. It was not for nothing that the State Council became known as the 'graveyard of Duma hopes'.[3]

And yet on that first day, when the Duma deputies took their seats in the Tauride Palace, there was nothing but hope in their hearts. Seated on the Kadet benches, Obolensky found himself next to Prince Lvov, who was 'full of optimism' about the new parliamentary era. 'Don't believe the rumours that the government will close us down,' Lvov told him with confidence. 'You'll see everything will be all right. I know from the best sources that the government is ready to make concessions.'[4] Most of the Duma members shared his naive faith that Russia had at last won its 'House of Commons' and would now move towards joining the club of Western liberal parliamentary states. The time for tyrants was passing. Tomorrow belonged to the people. This was the 'Duma of National Hopes'.

No one believed that the Tsar would dare to dissolve the Duma and risk a storm of criticism from the liberal public at home and abroad. It was confidently assumed that Russia's dependence on Western finance, renewed in 1906 with the biggest foreign loan in its history, would force him to retain the liberal structure of the state. That Nicholas despised 'public opinion', and had no legal obligation to respect it, was forgotten. So too was the fact that Witte, the architect of the new parliamentary order, had just been replaced by Ivan Goremykin, an old-fashioned reactionary and favourite of the court who regarded the Duma as an unnecessary obstacle to his government. The young parliamentarians innocently believed that, so long as they had 'the people' behind them, they would be able to force the Tsar to concede a fully sovereign parliament. Russia would follow the path of France after 1789, from the Estates-General to the Constituent Assembly.

The Tauride Palace was the birthplace, the citadel and the burial ground of Russian democracy. Until February 1917 it was the seat of the Duma. During the first weeks of the revolution it housed both the Provisional Government (which moved to the Marinsky Palace on 7 March) and the Petrograd Soviet (which moved to the Smolny Institute in July). Then, for a day, 6 January 1918, it played host to the first fully democratic parliament in Russia's history — the Constituent Assembly — until it was closed down by the Bolsheviks. No other building on Russian soil has ever been the scene of such turbulent political drama. How incongruous, then, that the palace should have been so graceful and serene. It was built in 1783 by Catherine the Great for one of her favourites, Grigorii Potemkin, who assumed the title of Prince of Tauride after his conquest of the Crimea. Designed in the style of a pantheon, decorated with Doric pillars and classical statues, it was a peaceful suburban refuge from the noise of the capital and was surrounded by its own private park and lakes. The Catherine Hall, where the deputies assembled, had semi-circular rows of seats and a dais at one end bearing Repin's portrait of Nicholas II. Behind the dais were three large bay windows looking out on to a landscaped vista that could have been painted by Watteau.

To this elegant palace the peasant Duma deputies brought the political culture of their village barns. 'It was enough to take a look at this motley mob of "deputies"', remarked one shocked senior official, 'to feel horror at the sight of Russia's first representative body. It was a gathering of savages. It seemed as if the Russian Land had sent to Petersburg everything that was barbarian in it.' Hundreds of peasant petitioners came to the Tauride Palace from every corner of Russia: some to appeal about a decision of their local court; some to complain about their taxes; others simply to check up on the activities of their elected delegates. Sergei Semenov found himself among them. He had been sent by a meeting of the peasants in his volost of Andreevskoe with a mandate on the land reforms which, as he recalled, 'I was supposed to make sure the Duma passed.' The musty smell of the peasants' cheap tobacco and their farmyard clothes filled the long corridors of the palace. The floors were covered with the chewed husks of their sunflower seeds, which they spat out regardless of public notices that most of them could not read. Some peasant deputies got drunk in taverns, became involved in brawls, and when attempts were made to arrest them claimed immunity as Duma members. Two were even found selling 'entrance tickets' to the Tauride Palace. It turned out that they had been convicted for petty thefts and swindles, for which they should have been disqualified from standing for election.[5]

Partly because of this village element, the Duma proceedings had a decidedly informal air. The English journalist Maurice Baring compared the sessions to 'a meeting of acquaintances in a club or a café'.[6] A deputy might begin to speak from his seat and continue to address the hall as he strolled up to the tribune. He might break off his speech in mid-sentence to talk to the President or offer a brief explanation of some detail. Sometimes the deputies at the back of the hall would engage in a private debate of their own, and when the President called for order would move out into the corridor. It was as if the politics of the street, or rather of the field, had been brought inside the parliament building. Perhaps the Duma was bound to be disorganized: this, after all, was Russia's first parliamentary experience; and there were many similar conventions — the National Assembly of 1789 or the Frankfurt Parliament of 1848 immediately come to mind — where novice politicians made a hash of things. And yet it seems that the Russians were by nature especially ill-prepared for the disciplines of parliamentary practice. Even today, in the post-Communist Duma, a similar informality is on display, verging on the manners of the beer-house. Russian democracy can be rather like the Russians themselves: chaotic and disorganized.

Most of the peasant deputies, about a hundred in all, sat with the Trudovik group (Labour), a loosely knit agrarian party, whose main plank was the need for a radical solution of the land question through the compulsory expropriation of all the gentry's property. This made it the obvious choice of the peasants once their usual party of choice, the SRs, had decided, along with the SDs, to boycott the Duma elections. The Kadets were the biggest party in the Duma, with 179 deputies (including Obolensky and Lvov) out of a total of 478. This was a gross exaggeration of their true level of support in the country, since the Kadets had won much of the vote that would otherwise have gone to the SRs and SDs. But their electoral success had none the less given them a sense of their own legitimacy as spokesmen for 'the people'. Inspired by this historic role — and a little frightened of it lest they should fail to match the radical expectations of the masses — the Kadets adopted a militant posture of opposition to the government which set the tone for the Duma's short and troubled existence.

From its opening session, the Duma was turned into a revolutionary tribune. It became a rhetorical battering ram against the fortress of autocracy. On that first day the deputies arrived at the Tauride Palace in a militant mood and at once began to condemn the repressive violence of the government (no condemnation was made of the left-wing terror). They had come by steamboat down the Neva from the Winter Palace and as they passed the Kresty jail they saw the prisoners waving to them through the bars of their windows. The deputies waved their hats in reply and the symbolism of that moment — the thought that they were being carried into the new parliamentary era thanks to the sacrifices of these 'politicals' — brought tears to many eyes. As they took up their seats in the Catherine Hall, the Kadet leader Petrunkevich called on the delegates 'to devote our first thought and our first free word to those who have sacrificed their own freedom for the liberation of our dear Russia. The prisons are full but Free Russia demands the liberation of all political prisoners.' His words struck a deep emotional chord among the deputies. Almost to a man they rose to their feet and, turning to the ministers who had come to watch the opening session, cried out, 'Amnesty! Amnesty!'[7]

According to the Fundamental Laws, the granting of political amnesties remained the exclusive prerogative of the Tsar. But the aim of the deputies was to force the crown to concede its executive powers to the Duma and, since this seemed a suitable place to start, they included it in their list of demands. These they presented as an Address to the Throne, which also included the appointment of a government responsible to the Duma, the abolition of the State Council, radical land reform and universal male suffrage. For two weeks there was silence, as the crown considered how to respond to these *ultra vires* demands. There were various attempts to neutralize the liberals by co-opting their leaders into the government. But, believing they stood on the brink of a second and decisive revolution, they stood firm. Then on 14 May the government finally passed down its first two bills for the Duma's approval: one for a new laundry, the other for a greenhouse at the University of Dorpat. It was a clear declaration of legislative war. The government was obviously unwilling to co-operate with the Duma. It would not even acknowledge its reform demands.

From this point on it could only be a matter of time before the Duma was dissolved. A battle of nerves ensued as the parliamentarians continued to show their defiance in a series of radical speeches from the tribune of the Tauride Palace. The tension was such that many deputies later claimed to have lost weight in these weeks, though the hot June weather probably helped. From the government's point of view, the revolutionary mood in the country was still a threat — the peasant war on the manors had revived in the spring with a ferocity equal to the previous autumn's, while the SR terrorist campaign had still not been quelled — and the Duma's militant stance was bound to encourage it.

The crux of the matter was the Duma's determination to appease the peasants with radical land reform. Both the Kadets and the Trudoviks were loudly advocating the compulsory expropriation of all the gentry's surplus land (the former with compensation and the latter without). There had been a time, during the 'Great Fear' of 1905, when many landowners might have been prepared to accept some form of expropriation in order to save their skins. 'If we do not make some concessions,' one besieged squire had argued before his local council of nobles, 'the revolution will come from below and fires will flare up everywhere from one end of the country to the other.' Even Trepov had once said to Witte: 'I myself am a landowner and I would be glad to relinquish half of my land if I were convinced that under these conditions I could keep the remainder.' But as the revolutionary tide receded, the landowners became less inclined to compromise. The Tsar spoke for them when he said, 'What belongs to the landowner belongs to him.' The provincial zemstvos, once strongholds of the liberal opposition, now became bastions of law and order. The United Nobility, which was formed to defend property rights, had powerful supporters in the court, the State Council and the Civil Service. It led the campaign against the Duma's reform proposals on the grounds that granting additional land to the peasants would not help solve their problems, since these were caused by the inefficiencies of the communal system and not by the shortage of land. The argument was strongly coloured by recent experience: having always viewed the commune as the bulwark of the old rural order, these conservatives had learned in 1905 that it could easily become the organizing mechanism of the peasant revolution. 'In other countries there is much less land per capita than in Russia,' declared Prince A. P. Urusov to a meeting of landowners in May 1906, 'yet there is no talk of land shortage because the concept of property is clear in the minds of the people. But we have the commune — which is to say that the principle of socialism has destroyed this concept. The result is that nowhere else do we see such unceremonious destruction of property as we see in Russia.'[8] The abolition of the commune and the creation of a peasant landowning class were now seized upon by the gentry as an alternative to the Duma's radical land reform.

On 8 July the Duma was finally dissolved, seventy-two days after its convocation. New elections were called for a second Duma session the following February. The Premier Goremykin was replaced by Stolypin, a well-known advocate of the commune's abolition and a proven executor of repressive measures to restore order in the countryside. The liberals were outraged by the dissolution. Prince Lvov, who had been so confident that it would not happen, now wrote of his 'anger at this blatant attack on the parliamentary principle', although as a landowner he had opposed the Duma's land reform. The dissolution transformed Lvov from a moderate liberal into a radical. He was among those Kadets who, as a protest against it, fled to the Finnish resort town of Vyborg, where they signed a manifesto calling on 'the people' to rise up against the government by refusing to pay any more taxes or to give any more recruits to the army.* The Vyborg Manifesto was a typical example of the Kadets' militant posturing since the opening of the Duma. As for 'the people', they were clearly not listening to these liberals. For their Manifesto was greeted with universal indifference. And so the government could now take repressive measures with a quiet mind to silence its brave but naive liberal critics. More than 100 leading Kadets were brought to trial and suspended from the Duma for their part in the Vyborg Manifesto. The Kadets who took their places in the second and third Dumas were on the whole much less radical — and less talented — than those who had sat in the first. Living under the shadow of their party's 'Vyborg complex', they pursued a more conservative line, keeping well within the confines of the tsarist laws, in the defence of the Duma.[9] Never again would the Kadets place their trust in the support of 'the people'. Nor would they claim to represent them. From this point on, they would consciously become what in fact they had been all along: the natural party of the bourgeoisie. Liberalism and the people went their separate ways.

ii The Statesman

Few figures in Russian history have aroused so much controversy as Petr Arkadevich Stolypin (1862–1911), Russia's Prime Minister from 1906 until his assassination five years later. The socialists condemned him as one of the last bloody defenders of the tsarist order. He gave his name to the hangman's noose ('Stolypin's neckties') administered by the military field courts to quell the peasant revolution on the land. The railway cars that were used to carry the 'politicals' to Siberia were called 'Stolypin carriages' (as they still were when they went to the Gulags). After 1917 the most hardened followers of the Tsar would come to denounce Stolypin as an upstart bureaucrat whose dangerous reform policies had only served to undermine the sacred principles of autocracy. But to his admirers — and there are many of them in post-Soviet Russia — Stolypin was the greatest statesman Russia ever had, the one man who could have saved the country from the revolution and the civil war. His reforms, they argue, given enough time, would have transformed Russia into a liberal capitalist society, but they were cut short by his death and the war. A popular tale relates that when the Tsar was signing his abdication order he said that if Stolypin had still been alive, this would never have come about. But this of course is a very big 'if'. Could one man have saved the Tsar? The truth is that Nicholas himself

---

* Lvov was taken ill on the way to Vyborg and had to return to St Petersburg. So he never signed the Manifesto, although he clearly sympathized with it.

had been sympathetic to Stolypin's opponents on the Right; and, frustrated by this royalist reaction, his reforms were doomed long before his death.

Stolypin's fate had in it much that was tragic. Yet his failure had as much to do with the weaknesses of his own personality as it did with the opposition he encountered from both the Left and the Right in Russia. His story is in many ways similar to that of Mikhail Gorbachev. Both were brave, intelligent and single-minded statesmen committed to the liberal reform of an old and decaying authoritarian system of which they themselves were products. Both trod a narrow path between the powerful vested interests of the old ruling élites and the radical opposition of the democrats. They failed in their different ways to see that the two opposing sides were set on a collision course, and that trying to mediate between them could only create enemies in both camps whilst winning few friends. Trained in the monolithic world of bureaucratic politics, both men failed to appreciate that their reforms could only succeed if they gained the support of a mass-based party or some other broad community of interests. They tried to impose their reforms from above, bureaucratically, without attempting to build a popular base, and that, more than anything else, is the key to their political demise.

In his appearance and background Stolypin was typical of that charmed circle of aristocrats that dominated the imperial bureaucracy. Tall, bearded and distinguished, he had considerable personal charm. The Englishman Bernard Pares compared him to 'a big naive friendly bear'.[10] Stolypin came from an ancient noble family which had served the tsars since the sixteenth century and, as a reward for their service, had accumulated huge estates in several provinces. Stolypin's great-aunt was related to Lermontov and his parents were friends of Gogol and Tolstoy. During his childhood the family had travelled extensively in Europe, and he himself was fluent in French, German and English by the time he enrolled, in 1881, at the Physical-Mathematical Faculty of St Petersburg University.

In one important respect, however, Stolypin was different from the rest of the ruling élite: he had not made his way up the ranks of the St Petersburg bureaucracy but had been appointed head of the government directly from the provinces. This was to become a dangerous source of friction with his rivals. Stolypin's political outlook was directly shaped by his provincial experience. Even as Prime Minister he remained in essence a country squire, whose primary interest was in agriculture and local administration. His first thirteen years in office (1889–1902) had been spent as Marshal of the Kovno Nobility, a Polish-Lithuanian province where his wife, O. B. Neidgardt, owned an estate. It was here that Stolypin first became preoccupied with the problems of Russian peasant farming. The Kovno region, like most of the west of the Russian Empire, had never experienced the communal system. The peasants owned their plots of land privately and their farming techniques, as in neighbouring Prussia, were much more efficient than those of the peasants in central Russia where the communal system prevailed. The contrast was strengthened for him in 1903, when Stolypin became Governor of Saratov, a land-extensive province with the communal system. Its peasants were among the poorest and the most rebellious in the whole of the country. In 1905–6 more of the gentry's property was destroyed in Saratov than in any other province of the Empire. Stolypin's daughter recalled the sight of 'the steppe lit up at night by the burning manor houses' and long lines of carts moving along the red horizon like 'a peasant army coming back from its wars'.[11] All this confirmed Stolypin's conviction — which he brought with him to St Petersburg and made the cornerstone of his agrarian reform — that the land question would not be resolved and the threat of revolution averted until the communal system was abolished and a stable landowning class of peasants created, which would have an equal stake in the status quo to that of the gentry.

Largely as a result of his resolute measures to restore order in Saratov, Stolypin was appointed Minister of the Interior in April 1906. The following July he became Prime Minister, or Chairman of the Council of Ministers. The Tsar wanted a 'strong man' to deal with the country in crisis and stories of Stolypin's personal bravery circulated freely around the capital. Unlike other provincial governors, who had barricaded themselves into their official residences or fled their posts in terror during the recent upheavals, Stolypin visited the most rebellious villages in Saratov and, in confronting the radical agitators, put to good use what his daughter referred to as 'his country gentleman's knowledge of how to dominate peasants'. In one village he persuaded a would-be assassin to lay down his gun by opening his coat to the man and challenging him in front of the crowd to shoot him in cold blood. On another occasion, whilst addressing a village meeting, he became aware of a peasant agitator standing beside him with apparently dangerous intentions. Stolypin broke off his speech and, turning to the agitator, told him to hand him his overcoat. The peasant obediently took the overcoat from the hand of a courier and passed it to the Governor.[12] With one arrogant gesture, Stolypin had managed to assert his mastery — the mastery of a squire — over his peasant adversary. This vignette said a great deal about the nature of power in Russia.

These were not isolated examples of Stolypin's personal bravery. During his premiership there were several attempts on his life, including a bomb blast at his house which killed several servants and wounded one of his daughters. He was not deterred. He wore a bullet-proof vest and surrounded himself with security men — but he seemed to expect nonetheless that he would eventually die violently. The first line of his will, written shortly after he had become Prime Minister, read: 'Bury me where I am assassinated.'[13]

'I am fighting on two fronts,' Stolypin told Bernard Pares in 1906. 'I am fighting against revolution, but for reform. You may say that such a position is beyond human strength and you might be right.' In this, as in all his public statements, there was a certain amount of self-dramatization. Stolypin was nothing if not vain. He liked to picture himself as a man of destiny, fighting in the name of progress against all the odds. His appearances in the Duma always contained an element of theatre. He liked to play to the gallery, making the most of his shortness of breath and the natural spasms in his speech (the result of an unsuccessful operation) to evoke sympathy from the deputies. He encouraged the legend that he had been wounded in a duel.[14]

Nevertheless, the task he had set himself would truly require an almost Herculean effort. His first aim was simply to restore order. This he accomplished by measures that earned him opprobrium from the liberals. Hundreds of radical newspapers and trade unions were closed down, while nearly 60,000 political detainees were executed, sentenced to penal servitude or exiled without trial during his first three years in office. Thousands of peasants were tried in military field courts. Yet repression alone, as Stolypin well knew, was not enough to strengthen the established order and so he simultaneously mapped out a comprehensive programme of reforms to conciliate the opposition and seize the initiative for the state. He introduced reforms to dismantle the commune and give the peasants property rights and full civil equality; to modernize local government on the basis of citizenship and property rather than membership of an estate; to improve the local courts and regulate the police; to protect civil liberties and end discrimination against the Jews; to provide for universal and compulsory primary schooling; and, among many others, to improve the conditions of the factory workers. In each of these there was a clear political motive: to strengthen the government. Perhaps in this sense, like his hero Bismarck, Stolypin should be described, as Leontovitsch once suggested, as a 'conservative liberal'.[15] For the whole purpose of his reforms was not to create a democratic order, as such, but to strengthen the tsarist system.

The same statist instrumentalism determined Stolypin's attitude towards the Duma. He saw it as an appendage to the state, a public body to endorse government policies, but not to check or direct the administration. His constitutional model was more Prussian than English. Sovereignty was to remain with the monarch and his executive, and was never to be conceded to parliament. The Second Duma, which convened in February 1907, was tolerated by Stolypin only in so far as it did what he wanted. His administration had done its best to influence the elections and secure the return of its allies, the Octobrists, who had declared themselves a 'party of state order'. But the 54 elected Octobrists, even if supported by the 98 Kadets and the 60 other Centrist and Rightist deputies, were hardly enough to give the government a workable majority against the huge bloc of 222 socialists (65 SDs, 37 SRs, 16 Popular Socialists and 104 Trudoviks) now that all the parties of the Left had ended their boycott of the Duma. The 25-year-old Georgian Menshevik, Irakli Tsereteli, who would lead the Soviet in 1917, soon became the hero of this so-called 'Duma of National Anger' through his fiery and radical speeches condemning the policies of the government. Nor could Stolypin rely on the peasants to be their usual humble selves. One peasant deputy, from Stolypin's own Saratov province, caused a great sensation during the debate on the land reforms when he said to a delegate of the nobility: 'We know about your property, for we were your property once. My uncle was exchanged for a greyhound.'[16]

With little prospect of finding support for his reforms, Stolypin had no qualms about dissolving the Duma and changing the electoral law so that when the next assembly convened it would be dominated by conservative elements. The electoral weight of the peasants, the workers and the national minorities was drastically reduced, while the representation of the gentry was even more exaggerated. When the Third Duma assembled in November 1907 the pro-government parties (Octobrists, Rightists and Nationalists) controlled 287 of the 443 seats. The Kadets and the socialists were reduced to small and fragmented minorities. Even Prince Lvov, the mildest of liberals, could not find a seat. This, at last, was a Duma with which Stolypin could do business. It was, he believed, a parliament dominated by 'responsible' and 'statesmanlike' people, who would be able to see the need for a new and constructive partnership between state and nation for the purpose of gradual reform. The radicals called it a 'Duma of Lords and Lackeys'.

Yet even this 'king's parliament' proved too hard for Stolypin to manage, as he found himself under growing pressure from both Left and Right. The electoral decree of 3 June was technically an infringement of the Fundamental Laws and the liberals were quick to denounce it as a *coup d'état*. Even the Octobrists, the new law's chief beneficiaries, felt uncomfortable with it and aimed to atone for their 'illegal' gains by trying to defend and expand the Duma's powers.

Alexander Guchkov, their leader, had special ambitions for the Duma in the military field. As an industrialist who had served as a Red Cross official in the war against Japan, he could see both the military need and the economic advantage of a big rearmaments programme. The Octobrists were increasingly committed to a policy of imperial expansion, but in their view this could only be achieved if responsibility for the military was shifted from the court to the institutions of the state. There was no point spending more money on the army without at the same time reforming its command, which was dominated by the aristocracy and the military doctrines of the eighteenth century. Russia needed heavy artillery, not more elegant Horseguards. In this conviction

Guchkov was supported by the 'military professionals', such as General Brusilov and Stolypin's own Assistant Minister of War, A.A. Polivanov. Guchkov was Chairman of the Duma's Committee of Imperial Defence, which had a veto over the military budget, and he used this position to launch an attack on the court's supreme command. In 1909 the Duma threatened to refuse the navy credits unless its strategic planning agency, the Naval General Staff, came under the control of the Ministry rather than the court. Nicholas was furious. He saw in this ultimatum a brazen attempt by the Duma to wrest military command from the crown, and used his veto to block its Naval General Staff Bill. The fact that Stolypin and his Council of Ministers had supported the bill made matters worse, since now there was a fundamental conflict of interests, with the government taking the view that it should control the armed forces and the court and its allies insisting that this was the sole right of the Tsar. Stolypin offered to resign, and Nicholas was pressed by his more reactionary allies to accept his resignation. But at this moment, having restored the country to a kind of order, Stolypin was indispensable and the royalists had to be satisfied with the lesser triumph of forcing him to reconfirm the Tsar's exclusive prerogatives in the military sphere.[17]

Beneath the technicalities of the naval staff crisis lay a fundamental problem that was to undermine Stolypin's efforts to save the tsarist system by reforming it. As far as the Tsar was concerned, Stolypin's political programme threatened to shift the balance of power from the court to the state institutions. The Naval General Staff Bill was an obvious signal of this intention. Stolypin stood foursquare in the Petrine tradition of bureaucratic modernization so detested by Nicholas. Everything in his Prime Minister's conduct was intended to break with the old patrimonial system. Whereas previous chief ministers had been treated as little more than household servants by the Tsar, Stolypin deliberately avoided the court and preferred to spend his weekends at home with his family, as a Western Prime Minister would, rather than on hunting parties with the Tsar and his lackeys. Stolypin viewed the state as a neutral and universal agent of reform and modernization which would protect Russia's imperial interests. In his view, the state stood above the interests of the aristocracy — even above the dynasty itself — which negated the notion of a social order based on the old estate rankings. Everyone, from the peasant to the prince, was a citizen (so long as he owned property). This essentially Western view of the state was a direct challenge to the Muscovite ideology so favoured by the Tsar and his courtiers, who imagined the autocracy as a steep and mystically sanctioned pyramid of patrimonial power based on a strict social hierarchy headed by the nobility. If Stolypin's reforms were allowed to succeed, then the Tsar's personal rule would be overshadowed by the institutions of his state, while the traditional social order would be undermined.

Such fears were fuelled by the old élite groups who all had their own reasons to oppose Stolypin's reforms and who now rallied to the defence of the Tsar's autocratic prerogatives. This legitimist bloc was brought together by the naval staff crisis, which presented an obvious threat to the crown's traditional rights. It had powerful institutional support within court circles, the State Council, the United Nobility, the Orthodox Church, the Union of the Russian People, the police and certain sections of the bureaucracy and, although it operated through informal channels, was strong enough to defeat virtually all Stolypin's political innovations.

His proposal to expand the state system of primary education was defeated by reactionaries in the Church, who had their own interest in the schools. The same fate awaited his legislation to ease discrimination against religious minorities, the Old Believers and the Jews in particular. His efforts to curb the illegal behaviour of the bureaucracy and the police were doomed, since he never had full control of either. The provincial governors, with their family ties at court, constantly sabotaged his reforms, while senior bureaucrats in St Petersburg intrigued against him. As for the actual control of the police, Stolypin was virtually powerless. The Empress's own candidate, General P. G. Kurlov, was appointed chief of the secret police, over Stolypin's protests. Kurlov used his position to divert large sums of government money to extremist Rightist groups and newspapers. He placed Stolypin himself under surveillance, intercepted his mail, and kept the Empress informed about his intentions, especially with regard to her favourite Rasputin. When Stolypin was finally assassinated, in August 1911, rumours immediately began to circulate that Kurlov had commissioned the murder. To this day, the rumours have never been proved. But they tell us a good deal about the public perception of the relations between Stolypin and his enemies on the Right.

The United Nobility was by far the most vociferous of these groups. It had been formed in the wake of the 1905 Revolution to defend the gentry's property rights and its domination of rural politics. Stolypin's local government reforms threatened the latter by giving the peasants, as landowners, representation in the zemstvos equal to that of the nobles. They also proposed to abolish the peasant-class courts, bringing the peasants fully into the system of civil law. Stolypin saw these reforms as essential for the success of his land reform programme (see pages 232–41). The new class of conservative peasant land-owners which he hoped to create would not support the existing order unless they were made citizens with equal political and legal rights to those enjoyed by other estates. 'First of all,' Stolypin said, 'we have to create a citizen, a small landowner, and then the peasant problem will be solved.'

The provincial gentry, however, interpreted this inclusive gesture as a threat to their own privileged position in the rural social and political order.

Stolypin was proposing to establish a new tier of zemstvo representation at the volost level, in which the franchise would be based on property rather than birth. He was also planning to increase the powers of the zemstvos and abolish the land captains, who had previously ruled the roost in the countryside. The effect of all this, as the outraged squires pointed out, would be to end their ancient domination of the system of rural government. The local zemstvos would be transformed from gentry into peasant organs, since for every squire at the volost level there would be several hundred newly-enfranchised peasant smallholders. The squires accused Stolypin of trying to undermine 'provincial society' (i.e. themselves) through bureaucratic centralization, and on this basis rallied their forces against him in the Duma, the State Council, the United Nobility and among their allies at court. Too vain to suffer certain defeat, Stolypin gave up the battle. The system of rural administration, by far the weakest link in the tsarist state, stayed in the hands of 20,000 nobles, a tiny and outdated social group which, thanks to its supporters in high places, was able to fend off all reform in defence of its own narrow interests. Had Stolypin succeeded in broadening the social base of local government in the countryside, then perhaps in 1917 it would not have collapsed so disastrously and Soviet power might never have filled the subsequent political vacuum as successfully as it did.

Much the same clash of interests lay behind the famous western zemstvo crisis of 1911, which marked Stolypin's final demise. With the decline of the Octobrists, as a result of the naval staff crisis and the rightward shift of the landowning squires, Stolypin was obliged to tailor his policies to the other main government party in the Duma, the Nationalists, which had been established in 1909 with strong support among the Russian landowners of the nine Polish provinces. The party, in the words of its historian Robert Edelman, was 'not so much a party of nationalism as a party of the dominant Russian nationality in a multinational Empire'.[18] The zemstvos had never been established in these western provinces, since most of the landowners were Poles and the Polish Rebellion of 1863 was still fresh in the memory of Alexander II. But the Nationalist Party campaigned for a western zemstvo bill, arguing that Russia's imperial interests in these crucial borderlands could be guaranteed by a complex voting procedure based on nationality as well as property. Stolypin knew this western region from his days in Kovno. The peasant smallholders, who were mainly Russian, Ukrainian and Belorussian, were among the most advanced in the Empire and he expected them to develop rapidly into yeoman farmers under his agrarian reforms. If they were given the largest share of the vote in the zemstvos, as planned by the lower property franchise of his Western Zemstvo Bill, they might become the model yeoman-citizens of the Russian imperial state.

An area formerly dominated by Polish landowners would be ruled by Russians,* albeit of peasant origin.

The bill was passed by the Duma but defeated in the State Council, where the gentry's fundamentalists were unwilling to see the privileges of the noble estate (even its Polish element) sacrificed to ensure the domination of Russian interests; the fact that the Poles were aristocrats should in their view take precedence over the fact that the peasants were Russian. Their opposition was encouraged by Trepov and Durnovo, favourites at court, who sought to use this opportunity to bring down their rival. They ensured the bill's defeat by persuading the Tsar to go behind Stolypin's back and issue a statement encouraging the deputies to vote as their 'conscience' dictated (i.e. implying they should vote against the government). It was a clear vote of no confidence in Stolypin engineered by the court and its camp followers on the Right. But there was still one glimmer of hope. Nicholas had second thoughts about his role in the plot and promised Stolypin that if the bill was reintroduced, he would support its passage through the upper chamber. Stolypin, however, was not a man to compromise. He was unaccustomed to opposition and was poorly versed in the skills of the modern politician, skills which might have enabled him to negotiate a way through. Rather than wait for a second reading of the bill he chose to make a firm stand on the first, realizing in any case that his career was probably finished. He threatened to resign unless the Tsar prorogued the Duma and the State Council and passed the bill by emergency decree under Article 87 of the Fundamental Laws. He also demanded that Durnovo and Trepov should be expelled from the capital. After four days of consideration Nicholas finally agreed to Stolypin's demands. On 14 March, with the two chambers closed, he promulgated the Western Zemstvo Bill and ordered Durnovo and Trepov to leave St Petersburg until the end of the year. It had taken several hours of persuasion by his mother, the eminently sensible Dowager Empress, to get the Tsar to go against the advice of his wife (who was at the centre of the plot against Stolypin). When he received Stolypin at the Gatchina Palace his face was 'red from weeping'.[19]

Stolypin had prevailed by sheer force of character. But his high-handed tactics in the western zemstvo crisis alienated almost everyone and his political fortunes now declined rapidly. The Tsar had been deeply humiliated by his own Prime Minister and, spurred on by his royalist cronies, now sought revenge. The liberals were outraged by Stolypin's contemptuous treatment of the Duma. Guchkov resigned from its presidency and the Octobrists moved into opposition; the Nationalists were the only Duma faction to support Stolypin in a motion

---

* Like all Great-Russian nationalists, Stolypin counted the Ukrainians and Belorussians as bearers of the Russian national idea.

of censure. Isolated and spurned, Stolypin himself lost all his former confidence, lost sleep and became moody.[20] He sensed that his days were numbered.

At the end of August 1911 Stolypin arrived in Kiev for celebrations to mark the unveiling of a monument to Alexander II. He had long been prepared for a violent death and before he left St Petersburg had entrusted one of his senior aides with a box of secret papers which he ordered to be destroyed should he fail to return. He ignored police warnings of a plot to kill him and travelled to Kiev without bodyguards. He refused even to wear his bullet-proof vest. On I September the Kiev Opera put on a performance of Rimsky-Korsakov's *The Legend of Tsar Sultan*. Nicholas and his four daughters occupied the royal box near the orchestra, while Stolypin sat in the front row of the stalls. During the second interval, while he stood talking with Count Fredericks in front of the orchestra pit, a young man in evening dress approached and, drawing a revolver from under his programme, fired twice at Stolypin. One bullet struck him in the right arm, the other in his chest, where a medal deflected it into his liver. Slowly, as if unaware of what had happened, Stolypin took off his gloves, carefully placed them on the barrier and unbuttoned his jacket, whereupon he saw his waistcoat covered in blood and sank into a chair. In a voice audible to all those around him, he said, 'I am happy to die for the Tsar,' and, on seeing him in the royal box above, lifted his hands and motioned him to withdraw to safety. Nicholas remained standing there and Stolypin, in a last theatrical gesture, blessed him with a sign of the cross. For four days the Prime Minister's condition remained stable. The Tsar continued with the programme of celebrations in Kiev and visited him in hospital. But on 5 September, Stolypin began to slip away. He died that evening. The Tsar came the next morning and said prayers by his bedside. Over and over he repeated the words, 'Forgive me.'[21]

*   *   *

The man who shot Stolypin was D. G. Bogrov, a student-revolutionary turned police informer through financial need. Nobody ever managed to discover which side Bogrov was working for — the Right or the Left — and in a sense that is the real point. For Stolypin had many enemies on either side. Long before Bogrov's bullet killed him, he was politically dead.

Stolypin's political demise must be explained by his failure as a politician. Had he been better versed in 'the art of the possible', perhaps he could have gained more time for himself and his reforms. Stolypin had said that he needed twenty years to transform Russia. But partly through his own fault he had only five. He adhered so rigidly to his own aims and principles that he lost sight of the need to negotiate and compromise with his opponents. He antagonized the old political élites by riding roughshod over their traditional privileges and lost the support of the liberals by suppressing the Duma whenever it stood in his way. This political inflexibility stemmed from his narrow bureaucratic outlook.

He acted as if everything had to be subordinated to the interests of the state, as these were defined by his reforms, and believed that this placed him above the need to involve himself in the dirty business of party manœuvring. He thought he could get his reforms by administrative fiat, and never moved outside the bureacracy to mobilize a broader base of support. Although he acknowledged that the key to his programme was the creation of a conservative peasant landowning class, he never considered the idea of sponsoring the foundation of a smallholders' party. There was a Stolypin but no Stolypinites. And so when Stolypin died his reforms died with him.

According to some historians, the tsarist regime's last real hope was wiped out by the assassin's bullets. Stolypin's reforms, they argue, were its one real chance to reform itself on Western lines. If only they had been given more time, instead of being disrupted by the First World War, then perhaps the Revolution of 1917 would not have taken place. This optimistic view rests on two assumptions: that Stolypin's reforms were succeeding in their aims; and that they were capable of stabilizing Russia's social system after the crisis of 1905. Both assumptions are patently false.

First, the reforms made relatively little headway in moving Russia towards a constitutional parliamentary order. Indeed some of Stolypin's own methods — such as the *coup d'état* of June 1907 and his tactics over the Western Zemstvo Bill — were a flagrant abuse of that system's ideals. True, there were some gains in civil liberties, in the freedom of the press, and in the fact that the Duma itself continued to exist, if only as a symbol and a school for the new culture of constitutionalism, between 1906 and 1914.* But this hardly meant that tsarist Russia was necessarily moving towards some sort of Western liberal normality. The nature of the tsarist regime was the single biggest guarantee of its own political irreformability. The Muscovite ideology of patrimonial autocracy which Nicholas and the Rightists increasingly favoured was deeply hostile to the Western constitutional vision entailed in Stolypin's programme of reforms; and the entrenched powers of the court, together with the vested interests of the Church and the provincial nobility, were quite strong enough to prevent that programme from ever being realized. Once the revolutionary crisis of 1905–7 had passed, the monarchy no longer needed the protection of Stolypin, and increasingly detached itself from his government, paralysed its programme,

---

* This last cultural aspect was a crucial one — and itself a sign of the mountain to be climbed — for the introduction of a constitutional order in a country such as Russia which then (as today) had no real traditions of constitutionalism. Whereas in Western countries the constitution merely had to guarantee the rights of a pre-existing civil society and culture, in Russia it also had to *create* these. It had to educate society — and the state itself — into the values and ideas of liberal constitutionalism.

and began to pursue its own separate agenda, based increasingly after 1912 on the use of Russian nationalism to rally 'the loyal people' behind the throne.

Second, by 1912, if not before, it had already become clear that no package of political reforms could ever resolve the profound social crisis that had caused the first crack in the system during 1905. True, for a while, largely as a result of government repressions, the labour movement subsided and showed signs of greater moderation, enough to give grounds for the Menshevik hope that it might evolve on European lines. But in the two years after 1912 there was a dramatic increase in both the number of industrial strikes and in their level of militancy, culminating in July 1914 with a general strike in St Petersburg, where in the midst of a state visit by the French President there was street fighting and barricades. The workers of the capital cities, according to Leo Haimson's seminal work of thirty years ago, were rapidly turning away from all the democratic parties — including even the Mensheviks — which advocated the adoption of constitutional or gradualist methods, and were moving over to the Bolsheviks, who encouraged direct workers' action and a violent struggle against the regime.[22] Despite all the efforts at political reform, urban Russia on the eve of the First World War found itself on the brink of a new and potentially more violent revolution than the 'dress rehearsal' of 1905.

iii The Wager on the Strong

The exiled peasant returned to his village on a cold April morning in 1908. It had taken him nearly three days by train, horse and cart to travel the one hundred miles from Moscow, and as he neared his birthplace his hopes of finding some improvement made during his two years of absence increased. But the village of Andreevskoe had never been a dynamic sort of place. The currents of modern civilization had somehow passed it by, and as he returned to it now, fresh from the sights of England and France, Sergei Semenov saw only familiar signs of backwardness and decay. The black strips of ploughed land seemed narrower and more ragged than ever, the tussocks in the meadow had grown to the size of small bushes, the woods had been cut down, the cattle allowed to roam freely over the gardens, and weeds sprouted in the main village street. Semenov's neighbour, once a hard-working peasant, had taken to the bottle, while his eight children went without shoes. But what depressed Semenov most was to learn that the elders of the village were the same old patriarchs who had been there when he left. For they would now have even more reason to regard his plans for reform with hostility and mistrust.[23]

Chief among the elders was Grigorii Maliutin, a heavy-built and heavy-drinking septuagenarian, with a big red-blistered face and a long white beard, who had been the dominant elder for as long as anyone could remember. Maliutin was the richest peasant in Andreevskoe, living partly on the profits from his son's soap factory near Moscow, and for his age he was surprisingly strong. Vain and jealous of his power, he was a strict disciplinarian, a village despot of the old school, who still beat his elderly wife and, as the elder of the village, flogged any peasant found guilty of a crime. Most of the villagers lived in fear of him. Maliutin's main ally was another relic from the days of serfdom, Yefim Stepanov, who over the years had made himself rich by scrimping and saving like a miser. He always wore the same old dirty clothes, fed his animals only just enough to keep them alive, and never once gave anything to the beggars outside church. Both men were illiterate Old Believers, and they were united by their fear of change. Their power over the village depended on keeping it sealed off from the modern world. Maliutin made a habit of denouncing every new invention, from the samovar to the sowing machine, as ruinously wasteful. Even to think of them caused him pain.[24]

What could be worse, then, than for them to see the return of their arch-rival Sergei Semenov. Semenov had been born in 1868 into a poor peasant family in Andreevskoe. Like Semen Kanatchikov, whose village of Gusevo was in the same district of Volokolamsk, he was sent out as a young boy to earn his own living in Moscow. His father, like Kanatchikov's, was an alcoholic, and his mother did most of the work on the farm, which did not yield enough to support him. Between the ages of ten and eighteen Semenov roamed from factory to factory, at first in Moscow and then in Petersburg, Poltava and Ekaterinoslav, sending money home to his family and returning to the village at harvest time. He taught himself to read and at the age of eighteen began to write stories of village life. One day he turned up on Tolstoy's doorstep at Yasnaya Polyana. Tolstoy admired Semenov's tales — here was his ideal of the 'peasant writer' — and the two men became life-long friends. Semenov was a quiet and a modest man. 'Small and thin, with a red goatee beard, a sad intelligent face, and a sensitive, almost child-like, shyness, he always dressed like a peasant in a tunic and', according to one of his Moscow friends, 'looked more like a village clerk than a littérateur.' Unlike Kanatchikov, he never hankered for the bright lights of the city. At the age of twenty he returned to Andreevskoe, married a local village girl, and took over the running of his father's farm. His bitter childhood had turned him into a firm believer in reform. 'I was always driven by a burning desire to improve the life of my village, to end its dark and backward ways,' he later wrote. This belief in progress was the source of his commitment to the revolution and — closely connected — to his own self-improvement. He gave up drink and saved up to buy handbooks on agriculture. The Volokolamsk district was fast becoming a major centre of flax cultivation — perhaps the most important form of intensification on the Russian peasant farm — and handsome profits could be made from it. Semenov was in the forefront of this movement. He rented extra land from a nearby squire and grew not only flax but a variety of other market crops with the latest farming methods. He began to campaign for land reform in Andreevskoe, and so came into bitter conflict with Maliutin.[25]

The feud between them had begun with a skeleton. Maliutin's daughter, Vera, had given birth to a baby out of wedlock. Out of shame she murdered it and buried its body in the woods. Somehow the authorities found out and the police arrived in the village to investigate. Maliutin managed to buy them off, and the matter was quietly dropped. But for a long time he accused Semenov of having informed the authorities. With his supporters he began a campaign of intimidation to drive Semenov out of the village. They burned down his barn, killed his livestock, took away his tools and accused him of sorcery. The local church added its voice to this charge. Semenov was an atheist. He refused to receive priests in his house, and on Sundays and other holidays was the only peasant to be seen working in the fields. But even worse, he was also a follower of Tolstoy, who had been excommunicated. In 1902 Semenov was finally convicted of sorcery in the ecclesiastical courts and imprisoned for six months.[26]

On his release, he returned to his village, this time to join the peasant revolutionary struggle. He was among that remarkable group of local peasants, agronomists and teachers, who established the reading clubs, the co-operatives and the peasant unions in Volokolamsk district, culminating in the Markovo Republic of 1905–6 (see pages 183–4). This gave Maliutin a second chance to strike a blow at his rival, and he now informed the police that the village contained a dangerous revolutionary. Semenov was arrested in July 1906, along with the peasant leaders of Markovo, and imprisoned for two months in Moscow before being sent into exile abroad. With Tolstoy's financial help, Semenov spent the next eighteen months touring the countryside of England and France. Seeing the farming methods practised in the West merely strengthened his conviction of the need for a complete overhaul of the communal system in Russia. It burdened the Russian peasants with an inefficient system of land use and stifled their initiative as individual farmers. Under the communal system, the peasants held their land in dozens of narrow arable strips scattered across the village domain. Semenov's own 10 *desyatiny* (27 acres) consisted of over 50 different strips in a dozen different locations. The strips were far too narrow — some of them no more than three feet wide — for modern ploughs and harrows; and far too much time was wasted in moving from one to another. The periodic redistribution of the strips left little incentive to improve the soil, since any benefits from this might be lost in the subsequent reallocation of the strips. There was little prospect of introducing advanced crop-rotations because in the open-field system everyone was obliged to follow the same pattern of cultivation so as to allow the cattle to graze on the stubble simultaneously, and, if only by force of numbers, inertia set in. 'It was my dream', Semenov wrote, 'to set up an enclosed farm of my own with a seven-field rotation and no more narrow strips.'[27]

Having left the village as a revolutionary, he was now returning to it as a pioneer of the government's own policies. His dream had also become that of Stolypin: the dismantling of the commune. But unlike Semenov, who saw this only in agronomic terms, Stolypin also linked it to the creation of a new class of peasant landowners, who, by owning property and growing more wealthy, would learn to respect the rights of the squires and give up their revolutionary aspirations. 'The government', Stolypin told the Duma in 1908, 'has placed its wager, not on the needy and the drunken, but on the sturdy and the strong.'[28] Entrepreneurial peasants like Semenov were now encouraged to break away from the commune and set up their own private enclosed farms. By a Law of 9 November 1906 they were given the right to convert their communal strips of land into private property on fully enclosed farms outside the village (*khutora*) or consolidated holdings within it (*otruba*). The whole village could make this transformation by a vote of two-thirds majority of the household heads. Further legislation followed to speed up the process of land reorganization and to help the separators purchase additional land from the gentry and the state with low-interest credit from the Peasant Land Bank. There was little doubt of the high priority the government gave to this project. This was the first time it had ever really tried to effect a major change in the everyday life of the peasants and the more intelligent ministers and officials knew that, unless a dramatic improvement was made, it was also likely to be the last. Conscious of its historic powerlessness in the countryside, the government pulled out all the bureaucratic stops to facilitate the enclosure process. Four different ministries, hundreds of provincial and district land commissions and thousands of surveyors, agronomists, statisticians and engineers were employed in its administration. The land captains and the other local officials were bombarded with directives from the centre urging them to encourage the separators, and tens of millions of roubles were earmarked to help them. It was as if the regime realized that its own political survival had come to depend on this 'wager on the strong'.

Stolypin could not have wished for a better pioneer than Sergei Semenov. He embodied the spirit of peasant self-improvement and enterprise upon which Stolypin's reforms relied. Like Stolypin, he took a dim view of his neighbours' ways — their disrespect for property, their fear of books and science, their constant drinking and their fighting — which he blamed on the 'serf-like habits of the commune and the Maliutins of this world'.[29]

To the Maliutins of Andreevskoe, who saw no need to change the old communal ways, Semenov was nothing but a trouble-maker. They continued to denounce him as an 'arteist' (atheist) and a 'lootinary' (revolutionary) because he attacked the Church and the Tsar. They tried to block him from attending the village assembly on the grounds that his old and alcoholic father, whom Semenov continued to support, was still legally the household head. Maliutin argued that to invest time and money in reforms would be a waste. 'Our grandfathers did it this way — and so shall we.'

Maliutin's arguments had much to recommend them to the peasantry, who were by their nature wary of reform. There were profound cultural reasons for the peasants to oppose the break-up of the commune, which had been the focus of their lives for centuries. The basic worry was that giving some peasants the right to own part of the communal land, or to hold it privately in perpetuity, would deprive others of their rights of access to this land as their basic means of livelihood. This fear was strongest amongst the junior members of the family, especially the women, for once a household consolidated its land as private property, family ownership ceased to function and the land became the legal property of the household elder. He could bequeath it to one or more of his sons, or sell it altogether, thus depriving the other household members of their inheritance. 'The peasants', declared one official, 'are very hostile to the Law of 9 November,' because 'they fear that the peasant elders will sell up the land and their children will become paupers. They say no one should sell land — let them trade what they like but not land.'[30] Many peasants were afraid that allowing the communal land to become private property would enable the richest members to buy it all up. There was also a widespread fear that the government surveyors, who had been instructed to encourage the process of enclosure, would reward the separators with more than their fair share of the best land.

And indeed the peasants had real cause to wonder just how the old patchwork of strips, which were often intermingled within the commune, could be disentangled at all. On what terms was a good bit of land in one place to be exchanged for a poor one in another? How were they to divide the meadows, the woods and the rivers, which had always been held in common? And if the new enclosed farms were to build their own roads, wouldn't these cut across existing boundaries and private rights of way? The peasants were attached to their land in a very particular sense. Most of them had farmed the same strips for many years, knew their peculiar traits and would not easily be parted from them. No one had ever taught them how to calculate the area of a piece of land by multiplying its width by its length, so they had no reliable means of satisfying themselves that two equal plots were in fact the same size. Their fields were divided 'by eye' or by pacing out the width of the strips and making rough adjustments where their length or the quality of their soil was uneven. They had no doubt that this primitive method, used by their grandfathers, was a good deal more accurate than the complex scientific methods of the government's land surveyors, with their suits, their rulers and their tripods. For one thing, the surveyors could not take into account the detailed variations in the quality of each strip, as the peasants themselves did in endless debates during the land division. Nor could they take into account the various social factors that inevitably influenced the peasants' allocation of the strips: for giving the best land to the most powerful families had become an important means of preserving traditional peasant hierarchies. It was the biggest farmers, with the most to lose from the break-up of the commune, who usually led the campaign against land reform. And it was not hard for them to stir up a general fear of reform among the peasants, for the existing dispensation had become a part of their everyday life, their family histories and the social structure of the village.[31]

All these factors played their part in Semenov's struggle to separate from the commune. To begin with he and his supporters, who were mostly the younger and more literate peasants, tried to persuade the rest of the village to consolidate all their land together, or at least to carry out a communal redivision of the land to reduce the number of narrow strips. But Maliutin and his supporters raised all sorts of objections, and the rest of the peasants were either too fearful of them, or else too fearful of change, to give Semenov and his supporters the two-thirds majority they required to enforce a general consolidation. So Semenov's group now began to campaign for the right to consolidate their own allotments as *otruba*. But again they encountered hostile opposition from Maliutin and the other elders. The village broke down into two warring minority camps — one trying to break away from the commune and the other trying to stop them — whilst the majority of the peasants did not know what to think but tried, like sheep, to stay with the largest group. To frighten Semenov, the elders barred his children from the village school and deprived him of access to the communal pastures and woods. Maliutin's followers beat up his wife, killed his livestock and burned the houses of his supporters. They even threatened to kill the land surveyors when they came to the village; and for eighteen months no surveyor dared re-appear.

Such intimidation was by no means unusual (in many villages troops had to be brought in and martial law imposed to end the violence). It was certainly effective in putting off many potential peasant pioneers. Of the six million individual applications for land consolidation received before 1915, over one-third were subsequently withdrawn by the applicants themselves, largely because of pressure from their neighbours. Of those that were completed (about one million individual consolidations in all), two-thirds had to be forced through by the authorities against the opposition of the commune.[32] And yet, as Semenov was to learn, even with the state on their side, it would need considerable determination by the separators to see the thing through to the end.

Bureaucratically, the fate of Stolypin's reforms was in the hands of the local land captains. They were charged with explaining to the peasants the advantages of the new mode of farming and with approving their petitions to the land commission, the Peasant Land Bank, and other sources of financial support. Semenov's land captain, Makarov, was a liberal and educated noble driven to this relatively humble office by bankruptcy and a tragic love affair. Like the provincial governor, he was quite sympathetic to the enclosure movement. This was unusual. The majority of their colleagues in the provincial bureaucracy were opponents of reform. They saw the enclosures as part of a general campaign by Stolypin to undermine the gentry's domination of the countryside, and tried to block their implementation through inaction and delay. The need to involve the land captain turned out in itself to be a major deterrent to potential separators. For in many areas the captain had played the key role in putting down the agrarian disorders of 1905–7 and peasant mistrust of the captain, as of all government officials, still ran very deep.[33]

But there was still not much that even Makarov could or would do to help Semenov. The Marshal of the Nobility and the other land captains in Volokolamsk were strongly opposed to the reforms, and Makarov was not prepared to step out of line for fear of losing his job. Nor was he brave enough to use his coercive powers and force through Semenov's rights in the face of hostile opposition from his fellow villagers. Indeed he never once came to the village for fear of his life. All this played into the hands of Semenov's opponents, who now stepped up their resistance. Led by Maliutin, they bombarded the local authorities with petty complaints against Semenov. These complaints were cleverly planned to give the authorities an excuse for endless bureaucratic delays over the land reform. They denounced Semenov to the district police for defiling a portrait of the Tsar, so that a detailed investigation had to be carried out before Semenov was deemed worthy enough to own a private plot. They took the question of whether Semenov or his father was to have rights at the village assembly to the volost court, and, when it failed to reach a decision, they took it to the district courts. All of this took up nearly two years. Maliutin also dragged him through the courts with a bogus claim to his allotment land, so that while the case was *sub judice* he would be unable to enclose his strips since he had no clear legal right to them.

Semenov's determination to cut through all these obstacles was quite extraordinary. Most peasants were deterred by far less difficulty, and the enclosure movement lost much of its impetus as a result. The rate of consolidations, after a strong initial spurt, fell sharply after 1909–10. Between 1906 and the eve of the revolution something in the region of 15 per cent of all the peasant households in European Russia consolidated their land as private plots, either in groups or individually, bringing the total of peasant farms in hereditary tenure to somewhere between 27 and 33 per cent.[34] Yet for every household that enclosed its land there was another that had tried and failed, either because of communal resistance or bureaucratic delays, with the result that they lost interest. Most of the separations took place in the west, the south and south-east of the country, where the market was most developed. The separators tended to be either the more market-oriented farmers or, conversely, the poorest peasants, who quickly sold up their private plots and often moved into the cities. The mass of the peasants in the central region of Russia — precisely those who would lead the agrarian revolution of 1917 — were not affected. Stolypin's reform had failed to alter their communal way of life.

In the end, after more than two years of wrangling, the land surveyors arrived in Andreevskoe with armed bodyguards and the final details of the land consolidation were completed. Of the forty-five households which had originally applied to consolidate their strips along with Semenov, only eight remained. To appease their opponents they were forced to make do with a piece of poor scrubland on the edge of the village. Since it had no suitable pasture, they remained dependent on the village commune's permission to graze their cattle on its land. Such compromises were a fact of life. Most of the peasant separators preferred to keep one foot in the village, as they could do if they held an *otrub* (which gave them rights of access to the communal pastures and the woods), rather than run the risks of setting up an enclosed but dangerously isolated *khutor* on their own. The vast majority of Stolypin's land enclosures were consolidations of *otruba*; and the government, despite its preference for *khutora*, had little choice but to give them its blessing.

Despite the continued opposition of the communal peasants, who occasionally vandalized their property, Semenov and his fellow separators gradually turned their scrubland into model private farms. They introduced big square fields with advanced crop rotations, sorted seed, chemical fertilizers and modern tools. Their cereal and flax yields increased by nearly half. They built winter sheds for their cows, imported better livestock breeds from Europe, exported milk to Moscow and established a dairy farmers' union. They also grew fruit and vegetables, which they took by train for sale in Moscow every Saturday. 'My experience over the past three years', Semenov wrote in 1913, 'has convinced me that a bright new future lies ahead of the peasants.'[35] And these newly enclosed farmers were the pioneers of a brief agricultural revolution in Russia before the First World War. To a large extent it was they who accounted for the marked rise in peasant living standards noted by recent historians. The *khutor* farmers, who were generally the strongest of the strong, had three or four horses and perhaps a dozen cows, compared with one of each for most of the communal peasants. They hired labour, bought more land from the gentry and began to set up in business. Here were the winners of the 'wager on the strong'.

But there were others, especially among the *otrubniki*, who failed to make it on their own. Many of their *otruba* were actually smaller than the neighbouring communal allotments, suggesting that they belonged to the weaker peasant households. No doubt some of them had set up on their own with the aim of selling the land and moving into the cities: over one million peasants did just that between 1908 and 1915. But others did attempt to cultivate their enclosed plots, believing that once they were free of the commune they too could become successful farmers. The truth was, of course, that farming an enclosed plot entailed many more costs and risks than the peasants had faced within the village commune, and that trying to do it with inadequate means was bound to end in disaster. The separators had to pay interest on loans from the bank and invest in roads, fencing and water. They also had to provide their own means of transport, tools, timber, pasture and stocks of seed and grain, some of which they would previously have shared with their communal neighbours. The range of communal services which had always made the village the centre of the peasant's life — the church, the school, the shops and small trades, as well as the personal networks between neighbours — was now closed to them, at least partly. By 1917, many of the private farmers had fallen into desperate poverty and were only too ready to liquidate their farms in order to rejoin the commune and share in the division of spoils as it renewed its war on the gentry's estates.

The majority of Western historians have tended to assume — often more on the basis of their own ideological prejudices than empirical evidence — that Stolypin's land reform 'must have been' a success. It is argued that were it not for the First World War, which brought the separations to a halt, the reform might have averted the agrarian revolution by converting the peasants into a class of yeoman landowners. This fits with the view of those historians who stress that tsarist Russia after 1905 *was* becoming stabilized and strengthened as a result of its evolution towards a modern society and that, if it had not been for the war, the revolution would never have happened. The bad old days of autocracy were receding, a parliamentary order was taking shape, and Russia, so the argument goes, was fast becoming a real industrial power with a peasantry that not merely fed itself but, thanks to Stolypin's reforms, was able to export food as well.

In fact, long before 1914, Stolypin's land reforms had ground to a halt. Stolypin had claimed that they would need at least twenty years to transform rural Russia. But even if they had continued at the same rate as they had been progressing before the First World War, it would have taken the best part of a century for the regime to create the strong agrarian bourgeoisie on which it had evidently decided to stake its future. The land enclosure movement, like every other reform of the tsarist regime, came too late.

Part of the problem was the lack of an adequate bureaucratic structure to implement the reforms, so that they suffered endless delays. The government was attempting to transform the peasantry's way of life without any real political leverage in the countryside. Most of the gentry, from the provincial governors down to the local land captains, opposed the reforms and did their best to stop them. Meanwhile, at village level there was no state administration at all, although Stolypin, to be fair, had tried to create a volost zemstvo dominated by the new peasant landowners and it was only the political opposition of the gentry, defending their traditional hegemony over local government, which buried his proposals. The peasant pioneers, like Semenov, thus had no political authority of their own to which they could turn in their uphill struggle to break away from the commune and unless, like him, they showed extraordinary perseverance they had very little hope of succeeding. Without the democratization of local government Stolypin's reforms were doomed to fail.

Perhaps above all the reforms were fated by their sheer ambition. It turned out to be much harder to impose foreign capitalist ways on the backward Russian countryside than the senior bureaucrats, sitting in their offices in St Petersburg, had been prepared to acknowledge. The village commune was an old institution, in many ways quite defunct, but in others still responsive to the basic needs of the peasants, living as they did on the margins of poverty, afraid of taking risks, suspicious of change and hostile to outsiders. Stolypin assumed that the peasants were poor because they had the commune: by getting them to break from it he could improve their lives. But the reverse was closer to the truth: the commune existed *because* the peasants were poor, it served to distribute the burden of their poverty, and as long as they were poor there would be little incentive for them to leave it. For better or worse, the commune's egalitarian customs had come to embody the peasantry's basic notions of social justice and, as the events of 1917 would prove, these were ideals for which they would fight long and hard.

iv For God, Tsar and Fatherland

In the hills overlooking the western districts of Kiev there are some caves where before the revolution children used to play and, on fine Sundays in the summer, families would come with picnics. One day in the spring of 1911 some children found the corpse of a schoolboy in one of the caves. There were forty-seven stab wounds in the head, the neck and the torso, and the boy's clothing was caked dry with blood. Nearby were his school cap and some notebooks, identifying the victim as Andrei Yustshinsky, a thirteen-year-old pupil at the Sofia Ecclesiastical College.

Kiev was outraged by the murder. It filled the city's papers. Because of the large number of wounds on the victim's body some Black Hundred groups said that it had to be a ritual murder by the Jews. At the funeral they distributed leaflets to the mourners in which it was claimed that 'every year before their Passover the Jews torture to death several dozen Christian children in order to get their blood to mix with their matzos'. They called upon the 'Christians to kill all the Jews until not a single Yid is left in Russia'.[36]

The ritual murder theory received spurious backing from the so-called *Protocols of the Elders of Zion*, a forgery by the tsarist police which had first been published in St Petersburg in 1902, and which long before its enormous success in Hitler's Europe provided a popular basis in Russia for the myth that the Jews formed a worldwide conspiracy to deprave and subjugate the Christian nations. But it was only after 1917, when many Russians blamed the calamities of the war and the revolution on the Jews, that the *Protocols* were widely read. A copy was found among the last effects of Nicholas II after his murder in July 1918. But they were published in several editions between 1905 and Andrei's murder, and so the charge of the Black Hundred groups that he had been killed for Jewish ritual ends would have sounded familiar and thus perhaps half convincing to many tens of thousands of citizens. There was, moreover, in these years a large 'scientific' literature on Jewish ritual murders, vampirism and white slavery, which gave the charges of the Black Hundred groups a certain cachet. In short, as Witte put it, anti-Semitism was 'considered fashionable' among the élite.[37]

During the weeks after Andrei's funeral rumours spread through Kiev of an organized ritual murder campaign by the Jewish population of the city. The Rightist press repeated the charge and used it to argue against the granting of civil and religious rights to the Jews. 'The Jewish people', it was claimed by Russian Banner (*Russkoe znamia*), had been transformed by their religion into a 'criminal species of murderers, ritual torturers, and consumers of Christian blood'. Thirty-seven right-wing Duma deputies, including eleven Orthodox priests, signed a petition demanding that the government bring to justice the 'criminal sect of Jews'. The Ministers of Justice (I. G. Shcheglovitov) and the Interior (N. A. Maklakov) were both convinced of the ritual murder theory, as were most of the government and the court, and it was with the personal blessing of the Tsar himself that they now went in search of a Jewish suspect.[38]

The man they finally chose was Mendel Beiliss, a middle-aged clerk in a Jewish-owned factory which happened to be near the caves where Andrei's body had been found. There was nothing unusual about this quiet family man, of average height and build with a short black beard and glasses. He wasn't even particularly religious and rarely attended the synagogue. Yet for the next two years, as he sat in prison awaiting trial, the most terrible portrait of him was built up by the police. Witnesses were paid to testify that they had seen him violently kidnap Andrei, or had heard him confess to the murder and to his participation in secret Jewish cults. The two physicians in charge of the autopsy were forced to change their report in line with the ritual murder theory. An eminent psychiatrist, Professor Sikorsky, was even wheeled on to confirm that, based on the soundest 'anthropological evidence', Andrei's murder was 'typical' of the ritual killings regularly carried out by Jews. The press had a field day with fantastic stories on 'Mendel Beiliss, the Drinker of Christian Blood' and articles by various 'experts' on the historical and scientific background to the case.[39]

Meanwhile, the real cause of Andrei's murder had already been discovered by two junior policemen. Andrei had been the playmate of Yevgeny Cheberiak, whose mother, Vera, was a member of a criminal gang which had recently carried out a series of robberies in Kiev. Stolen goods were stored in her house before being transported to other cities for resale. On one occasion Andrei had discovered their secret cache. In an argument with his friend he had threatened to tell the police, who were already suspicious. When Yevgeny told his mother, the gang took fright, murdered Andrei, and dumped his body in the caves. All this was covered up by the District Attorney in charge of the investigations, a fanatical anti-Semite called Chaplinsky, who was eager to get promotion by satisfying Shcheglovitov with the head of Beiliss. The two junior policemen were dismissed and others with doubts about the case were forced to keep silent. Chaplinsky even concealed the fact that Vera, who would testify at the trial that she had seen Beiliss kidnap Andrei, had poisoned her own son for fear that he might reveal her role in the affair. Yevgeny, after all, was the one witness who could spoil the prosecution case.

In 1917, when the full extent of this conspiracy became known, it emerged that the Minister of Justice and the Tsar himself had both acknowledged Beiliss's innocence long before he came to trial, but they had carried on with the prosecution in the belief that his conviction would be justified in order to 'prove' that the Jewish cult of ritual murder was a fact. By the opening of the trial, in September 1913, the identity of the real murderers had already been disclosed in the liberal press on the basis of information supplied by the two policemen sacked by Chaplinsky. There were large public demonstrations against the trial. Dozens of attorneys, including the young Kerensky, staged a protest at the Petersburg bar, for which they were suspended. Gorky, who was now living in Capri, wrote a passionate appeal against the 'Jewish witch hunt' which was signed by Thomas Mann, Anatole France, H. G. Wells, Thomas Hardy, the heads of all the Oxbridge colleges and dozens of leading politicians throughout Europe. In the United States the Jewish lobby campaigned for the cessation of all financial credits to Russia. But the tsarist government was undaunted by the international scandal and even increased its efforts to get Beiliss convicted. On the eve of his trial a number of key defence witnesses were arrested and sent into secret exile. The judge was received by the Tsar, given a gold watch and promised promotion if there was a 'government victory'. During the trial he repeatedly interrupted the proceedings and instructed the jury, which was packed with peasants from an area notorious for anti-Jewish pogroms, to accept what the prosecution had just told them as 'established fact'. Yet even this was not enough to secure a conviction. The prosecution witnesses — tramps, convicted criminals and prostitutes — all exposed themselves as liars paid by the police. In the five weeks of the trial the name of the defendant was barely mentioned at all, as the prosecution relied entirely on denigrating his religion. 'How can we convict Beiliss', asked one of the jurors, evidently realizing that this was what was expected of them, 'if nothing is even said about him?'[40]

In the end, amidst widespread rejoicing at home and abroad, Beiliss was acquitted. Six months later he emigrated to Palestine and from there went to the United States, where he died in 1934. Charges were never brought against the criminal gang responsible for the murder of Andrei. Vera Cheberiak was asked by the circus to appear in a pantomime about the Beiliss affair — and a pantomime is more or less what the whole thing was. She continued to live in Kiev until 1918, when she was arrested and shot by the Bolsheviks during the Red Terror (one of its few justifiable victims, one might almost say). As for the tsarist government, it continued to act as if nothing had happened, awarding titles, promotions and valuable gifts of money to those who had taken part on 'its side' in the trial. Chaplinsky was promoted to a senior position in the Senate, while the trial judge was appointed Chief Justice of the Appeal Court. In the eyes of the Western world, however, the Beiliss Affair came to symbolize the struggle between the despotism of medieval Russia and the new European-style society of twentieth-century Russia based upon the civil liberties of the Duma era. The tsarist regime, by siding with the former, had committed moral suicide in the eyes of the civilized world.

Why was the monarchy ready to go so far in the Beiliss trial? The answer surely lies in the general political situation. By 1911 the Duma system had broken down. The two main parties willing to work with the government, the Octobrists and the Nationalists, were both deeply divided and, in the elections of 1912 to the Fourth Duma, their share of the vote collapsed. The old centre-right majority had disintegrated and the Duma was weakened as it drifted through a series of fragile alliances, unable to find a working consensus.* Kokovtsov's government (1911–14) ignored the Duma, sending it petty, 'vermicelli', bills. The Tauride Palace gradually emptied as the influence of parliament declined. Meanwhile, the workers' movement, which had been largely dormant

---

* The parties of the Right (the Nationalists and the Rightists) had 154 deputies in the Fourth Duma, those of the Centre (Octobrists and Centre Group) 126, and those of the Left (Kadets, Progressists and Socialists) 152.

since 1906, had revived with a vengeance in April 1912, following the massacre of 500 demonstrating miners on the Lena River in the northern wilderness of Siberia. During the next two years three million workers were involved in 9,000 strikes, and a growing proportion of these were organized under the Bolsheviks' militant slogans in preference to the more cautious leadership of their Menshevik rivals. The Bolsheviks won six of the nine labour curiae in the Duma elections of 1912 and by 1914 had gained control of all the biggest trade unions in Moscow and St Petersburg. Their newspaper, *Pravda*, established in 1912 with financial help from Gorky among others, had the largest circulation of all the socialist press, with about 40,000 copies bought (and many more read) by workers every day.[41]

To the Tsar and his supporters in the court, the Church and Rightist circles, this doubtless seemed both an opportune moment (with the Duma weakened) and a pressing one (with the rise of the militant Left) to roll back the gains of the constitutional era and mobilize the urban masses behind a popular autocracy. Maklakov and Shcheglovitov, the two main government patrons of the Beiliss Affair, had long been pressing the Tsar to close down the Duma altogether, or at least to demote it to the status of a consultative body. It was only Western pressure and the fear of a popular reaction that restrained the Tsar. To these two ministers, in particular, but no doubt to the Tsar as well, who was naive and easily misled, the Beiliss Affair must have appeared as a prime chance (and perhaps the last) to exploit xenophobia for monarchical ends. They must have hoped to mobilize the 'loyal Russian people' behind the defence of the Tsar and the traditional social order against the evils of modernity — the depravity of urban life, the insidious influence of the intelligentsia and the militancy of the Left — which many simple-minded Russians readily associated with the Jews. As the pogroms of 1905–6 had already shown, popular anti-Semitism was a vital weapon in the armoury of the counter-revolution. The Union of the Russian People (URP), which was its leading exponent, had been among the first Black Hundred groups to proclaim the ritual murder charge; and it provided an anti-Jewish claque for the prosecution throughout the Beiliss trial. The Tsar patronized the URP (and the government secretly financed it) in the hope that it might one day become a popular monarchist party capable of taking support away from the socialists. Its manifesto expressed a plebeian mistrust of all the political parties, the intelligentsia and the bureaucracy, which it claimed were obstacles to the 'direct communion between the Tsar and his people'. This was music to Nicholas's ears: he too shared the fantasy of re-establishing the Tsar's personal rule, as it had existed in the seventeenth century. The mystical bond between the Tsar and his people was the *leitmotiv* of the Romanov tercentenary year. Even Rasputin's success was largely based on Nicholas's wilful self-delusion that the 'Holy Man' was 'just a simple peasant'. In short, to enter the highest ruling circles it was becoming necessary to flatter the Tsar's fantasy of a popular autocracy; and expressing support for the URP was the easiest way to achieve this. Leading members of the Church, the court and the government, including the Minister of the Interior Maklakov, all supported the URP.[42]

The URP was nothing if not a Great Russian nationalist movement. Its first declared aim was a 'Great Russia, United and Indivisible'. But the nationalist card was a hazardous one for the tsarist regime to play. Its consequences were so difficult to predict. The concept of 'the nation' played a key role in the politics of 1905–17. Both the monarchists and the Duma parties used it increasingly in their rhetoric, as they competed with each other for popular support. The idea of 'Russia' served as a vital reference point during this era of transition when the old political certainties seemed to be being undermined and yet the new ones had still to be formed. It served as north on the compass Russians used to steer their way through the new politics — much as it does in post-Communist Russia. Every strand of political thought had its own different nationalism. In the case of the URP it was based on racism and xenophobia. The supremacy of the Great Russians was to be defended in the Empire. For the Rightist leaders of the Church it was similarly based on the supremacy of Orthodoxy. But such Great Russian chauvinism was not limited to the Right. All the centre-right parties of the Duma shared the conviction after 1907 that Russia's best interests, as an Empire in increasing rivalry with the Great Powers of the West, depended on the encouragement of popular nationalist sentiment (for how else were they to raise a strong army?) and on the maintenance of Russia's domination over the non-Russian borderlands. Stolypin's government was forced to tailor its programme to meet the demands of this nationalism, especially after 1909 when the support of the Octobrists declined and the government was forced to turn to the Nationalist Party for a majority in the Duma. The detachment of Kholm from Poland (1909), the re-imposition of Russian rule over Finland in most matters (1910), and the measures to guarantee the domination of the Russian minority over the Polish majority in the Western Zemstvo Bill (1911) were all signs of this new official line in Great Russian nationalism. Many of the concessions won by the non-Russians as a result of the 1905 Revolution were taken away again in these years. Stolypin justified his policies on the grounds of imperial defence. After all, he explained to Bernard Pares, the Finnish border was only twenty miles from St Petersburg: and England would hardly tolerate an autonomous state as near as Gravesend.[43]

* * *

The threat of a war in Europe was increasing. The two great Balkan empires, the Ottoman and the Austro-Hungarian, were both breaking apart under pressure from nationalist movements. Germany and Russia were lining up for conflict over the spoils, as each sought to advance its interests in the region. The occupation of Constantinople and the control of the Dardanelles, through which half her foreign trade passed, had been Russia's main imperial ambition since the time of Peter the Great. But she also harboured broader hopes of her own Slavic Empire in the Balkans, hopes raised by the nationalist movements in Serbia, Bulgaria and Bosnia-Herzogovina.

For a long time such pan-Slavist dreams were seen as the stuff of poetry, not practical politics. The country's military and economic weakness demanded a cautious foreign policy. As Polovtsov had put it in 1885, 'Russia needs roads and schools, not victories or honour, otherwise we'll become another Lapland.'[44] It was left to the diplomats to defend Russia's interests in Europe; and this, for the most part, meant conciliating her two powerful neighbours in Berlin and Vienna. The Romanov court had long been in favour of this pro-German policy, partly because of the strong dynastic ties between the ruling families and partly because of their mutual opposition to European liberalism. There was even talk of reviving the old Three Emperors' League.

After 1905, however, foreign policy could no longer be carried out regardless of public opinion. The Duma and the press both took an active interest in imperial matters and increasingly called for a more aggressive policy in defence of Russia's Balkan interests. The Octobrists led the way, seeking to stop the decline of their own political fortunes by sponsoring a nationalist crusade. Guchkov, their leader, condemned the diplomats' decision not to go to war in 1908, when Austria annexed Bosnia-Herzogovina, as a betrayal of Russia's historic mission to defend the Balkan Slavs. The Russian people, he declared, in contrast with the 'flabby indolence of official Russia', was ready for the 'inevitable war with the German races', and it was their patriotic sentiments that 'foreign and indeed our own diplomats must reckon with'. Not to be outdone by such bluster, the right-wing Kadets fashioned their own liberal version of Slavic imperialism. Struve denounced the Bosnian affair as 'a national disgrace'. Russia's destiny, he argued in a celebrated essay of that year, was to extend its civilization 'to the whole of the Black Sea basin'. This was to be achieved (contradictory though it may seem) by a combination of imperial might and the free association of all the Slavic nations — which in his view would look upon Russia as a constitutional haven from Teutonic oppression. Equally anxious to wave the patriotic flag was the liberal business élite of Moscow, led by Alexander Konovalov and the Riabushinskys, who in 1912 established their own Progressist Party on the grounds that the time had come for the bourgeoisie to assume the leadership of the nation. Russia's control of the Black Sea and the shipping routes through the straits was a principal target of their trading ambitions.[45]

Much of this bourgeois patriotism was informed by the idea that Europe was heading unavoidably towards a titanic clash between the Teutons and the Slavs. Pan-Slavism and pan-Germanism were two mutually self-justifying credos: the one could not exist without the other. The fear of Russia united all German patriots, while the fear of Germany did the same in Russia. Germano-phobia ran extremely deep in Russian society. The revolution was partly based on it — both as a reaction against the war and as a rejection of the German-dominated Romanov court. This fear of Germany stemmed in part from the Russians' cultural insecurity — the feeling that they were living on the edge of a backward, semi-Asian society and that everything modern and progressive came to it from the West. There was, as Dominic Lieven has put it, 'an instinctive sense that Germanic arrogance towards the Slavs entailed an implicit denial of the Russian people's own dignity and of their equality with the other leading races of Europe'. The wealth of the Germans in Russia, their prominence in the Civil Service, and the growing domination of German exports in Russia's tra-ditional markets only served to underline this sense of a racial threat. 'In the past twenty years', declared a 1914 editorial in *Novoe vremia*, 'our Western neighbour has held firmly in its teeth the vital sources of our well-being and like a vampire has sucked the blood of the Russian peasant.' Many people feared that the *Drang nach Osten* was part of a broader German plan to annihilate Slavic civilization and concluded that, unless she now made a firm stand on behalf of her Balkan allies, Russia would suffer a long period of imperial decline and subjugation to Germany. This pan-Slavist sentiment grew as the public became frustrated with the government's conciliatory approach towards the 'German aggressors'. *Novoe vremia* led the way, denouncing the government's decision, brought about by pressure from Berlin, to recognize the Bosnian annexation as a 'diplomatic Tsushima'.* The newspaper called on the government to counteract the growing influence of Germany in the Balkans with a Slavic campaign of its own. Numerous Slavic societies were established after 1908. A Slavic Congress was even convened in Prague, where the Russians attempted to persuade their sceptical 'brothers' from the Czech lands that they would be better off under the Tsar. By the Balkan Wars of 1912–13 this pro-Slav sentiment had brought together many elements of Russian society. Hundreds of public organizations declared their support for the Slavs, the capital cities witnessed huge demon-strations, and at a series of political banquets public figures called for a firmer assertion of Russia's imperial power. 'The straits must become ours,' Mikhail Rodzianko, President of the Duma, told the Tsar in March 1913. 'A war will be joyfully welcomed and it will raise the government's prestige.'[46]

There is no doubt that the pressure of public opinion played an

---

* Tsushima was the site of Russia's biggest defeat in the war against Japan.

important part in the complex series of events leading towards Russia's involvement in the First World War. By the beginning of 1914 the mood of pro-Slav belligerence had spread to the court, the officer corps and much of the state itself. Prince G. N. Trubetskoi, placed in charge of the Balkan and Ottoman sections of the Foreign Ministry in the summer of 1912, was a well-known pan-Slavist determined to gain control of Constantinople and its Balkan hinterland. Similar views were held by the Grand Duke Nikolai Nikolaevich, a military man with a powerful influence over the Tsar who in August 1914 was appointed Commander-in-Chief. His father had fought in the Balkan campaigns of 1877–8 and his wife, an ardent Slav patriot, was the daughter of the King of Montenegro. Many generals shared the Grand Duke's Slavic sympathies. Brusilov was a case in point. Concerned by Russia's lack of moral preparation for the coming war, he looked to pan-Slav nationalism as a means of uniting the people behind the army. 'If the Tsar had appealed to all his subjects', he later wrote, 'to combine to save their country from its present peril and deliver all their brother Slavs from the German yoke, public enthusiasm would have been boundless, and his personal popularity would have become unassailable.'[47]

The Tsar himself was slowly coming round to the pan-Slavist camp. By the beginning of 1914 he was of the view that the time had come for a firm stand against Austria, if not against her more powerful ally in Berlin. 'We will not let ourselves be trampled upon,' he told Delcassé in January. Foreign ambassadors explained this new resolve by the pressure of public opinion. But for the moment Nicholas supported the cautious approach of his Foreign Minister, S. D. Sazonov. Recognizing that a war with the Central Powers was almost certainly unavoidable, they sought to delay it by diplomatic means. Russia's army, according to the military experts, would not be ready for war until 1917. Nor was the diplomatic groundwork complete: for while the support of France was assured, that of Britain was not. But by far the most pressing concern was the threat of a revolution if Russia got bogged down in a long and exhausting campaign. The memory of 1904–5 was still fresh, and there was nothing the revolutionary leaders would now welcome more than a war. 'A war between Russia and Austria would be a very useful thing for the revolution,' Lenin told Gorky in 1913, 'but the chances are small that Franz Joseph and Nicky will give us such a treat.'[48]

All this strengthened the arguments of the pro-German faction at court against the headlong drift towards war. In a prophetic memorandum of February 1914 Durnovo warned the Tsar that Russia was too weak to withstand the long war of attrition which the Anglo-German rivalry was likely to produce. A violent social revolution was bound to be the result in Russia, for the liberal intelligentsia lacked the trust of the masses and was thus incapable of holding power for long in a purely political revolution. Durnovo outlined the course of this revolution in remarkably prescient terms:

The trouble will start with the blaming of the Government for all disasters. In the legislative institutions a bitter campaign against the Government will begin, followed by revolutionary agitations throughout the country, with Socialist slogans, capable of arousing and rallying the masses, beginning with the division of the land and succeeded by a division of all valuables and property. The defeated army, having lost its most dependable men, and carried away by the tide of the primitive peasant desire for land, will find itself too demoralized to serve as a bulwark of law and order. The legislative institutions and the intellectual opposition parties, lacking real authority in the eyes of the people, will be powerless to stem the popular tide, aroused by themselves, and Russia will be flung into hopeless anarchy, the issue of which cannot be foreseen.[49]

Caution was the key-word of the pro-German faction at court. But from Germany's point of view, if there was to be a war with Russia, then it was better fought sooner than later. 'Russia grows and grows, and weighs upon us like a nightmare,' the German Chancellor Bethmann Hollweg declared. When the Archduke Ferdinand was assassinated by Serbian nationalists it was not in Germany's interests to restrain its Austrian ally from threatening war against Russia's last real Balkan ally. This threw the delicate balance of Russia's foreign policy into disarray. The Russian press clamoured for war in defence of Serbia and there were large public demonstrations outside the Austrian Embassy in St Petersburg. On 24 July 1914 the Council of Ministers recommended military preparations. Otherwise, argued A. V. Krivoshein, the influential Minister of Agriculture, 'public opinion would fail to understand why, at the critical moment involving Russia's interests, the Imperial Government was reluctant to act boldly'. It was more important 'to believe in the Russian people and its age-old love for the fatherland than any chance preparedness or unpreparedness for war'.[50]

This placed Nicholas in an impossible situation. If he went to war, he ran the risk of defeat and a social revolution; but if he didn't, there might equally be a sudden uprising of patriotic feeling against him which could also result in a complete loss of political control. There was little time to reach a decision, for if Russia was to mobilize its forces it would need a head start on its enemies, who could mobilize theirs very much more quickly. On 28 July Austria finally declared war on Serbia. Nicholas ordered the partial mobilization of his troops and made one last appeal to the Kaiser to forestall the Austrian attack on Belgrade. 'I foresee', he warned, 'that very soon I shall be overwhelmed by the pressure brought upon me and forced to take extreme measures which will lead to war.' Two days later the Kaiser replied, renouncing Germany's neutrality in the Serbian question. Sazonov recommended a general mobilization, realizing that a German declaration of war against Russia was now imminent (it came on

I August). He warned the Tsar that 'unless he yielded to the popular demand for war and unsheathed the sword in Serbia's behalf, he would run the risk of a revolution and perhaps the loss of his throne'. Nicholas went pale. 'Just think of the responsibility you're advising me to assume!' he said to Sazonov. But the force of his Minister's argument was incontrovertible and, reluctantly, the Tsar called for the general mobilization on 31 July.[51]

Brusilov later claimed that the Tsar had been forced to go to war by the strength of his own people's patriotic fervour: 'Had he not done so, public resentment would have turned on him with such ferocity that he would have been tumbled from his throne, and the Revolution, with the support of the whole intelligentsia, would have taken place in 1914 instead of 1917.' This is undoubtedly an overstatement of the case. The middle-class patriots who assembled in front of the Winter Palace to greet the Tsar's declaration of war on Sunday 2 August — clerks, officials, high-school students and housewives — were hardly the people to start a revolution. Many of them, according to foreign observers, had been ordered to turn out by their employers or masters. But on that sunny afternoon, as Nicholas stood on the balcony of his Winter Palace and surveyed in the square below him the vast flag-waving and cheering crowds, who then, as one, knelt down before him and sang the national anthem, the thought must have crossed his mind that the war had at last united his subjects with him and that perhaps, after all, there was some reason for hope. 'You see,' he told his children's tutor shortly after in a state of great emotion, 'there will now be a national movement in Russia like that which took place in the great war of 1812.'[52]

And indeed in those first heady weeks of August there was every outward sign of a national *ralliement*. The workers' strikes came to a halt. Socialists united behind the defence of the Fatherland, while pacifists, defeatists and internationalists were forced into exile. Patriotic demonstrators attacked German shops and offices. They ransacked the German Embassy in Marinskaya Square, smashing the windows and throwing out the furniture, the fine paintings and even the Ambassador's own personal collection of Renaissance sculptures on to a bonfire in the street below. Then, to the cheers of the crowd, they sent two huge bronze horses crashing down from the Embassy roof. In this wave of anti-German feeling people even changed their names to make them sound more Russian: thus, for example, the orientalist Wilhelm Wilhelmovich Struve became Vasilii Vasilievich Struve. Bowing to the strength of this xenophobia, the government also changed the German-sounding name of St Petersburg to the more Slavonic Petrograd. Nicholas welcomed the change. He had never liked St Petersburg, or its Western traditions, and had long been trying to Russify its appearance by adding Muscovite motifs to its classical buildings.

'Everyone has gone out of their minds,' lamented Zinaida Gippius, the poet, philosopher and salon hostess of St Petersburg. 'Why is it that, in general, war is evil yet this war alone is somehow good?' Most of the country's leading writers supported the war, and more than a few even volunteered for the army. There was a common assumption among the intelligentsia, searching as ever for a sense of belonging, that the war would bring about Russia's spiritual renewal by forcing the individual to sacrifice himself for the good of the nation. The meaning of the war, lectured one Moscow Professor of Philosophy, lay 'in the renovation of life through the acceptance of death for one's country'. War should be seen as a kind of 'Final Judgement'. Few intellectuals would have shared the gloomy verdict of Gorky, recently returned from exile abroad: 'One thing is clear: we are entering the first act of a worldwide tragedy.'[53]

The press waxed lyrical on this new-found unity of the Russian people. *Utro Rossii*, the Progressist paper, pronounced that 'there are now neither Rights nor Lefts, neither government nor society, but only one United Russian Nation'. Finally, as if to consummate this *union sacrée*, the Duma dissolved itself in a single session of patriotic pomp on 8 August in order, as its resolution declared, not to burden the government with 'unnecessary politics' during its war effort. 'We shall only get in your way,' Rodzianko, the Duma President, informed the ministers in the Tauride Palace. 'It is therefore better to dismiss us altogether until the end of hostilities.'[54]

But such declarations of loyalty were deceptive. The mass of the people had yet to be touched by the war; and the millions of peasants and workers who departed for the Front felt little of the middle-class patriotism that had done so much to raise the Tsar's hopes. There were no flags or military bands to see them off at the stations and, according to foreign observers, the expression on most of the soldiers' faces was sombre and resigned. It was their terrible experience of war that would ignite the revolution. The Tsar's desperate gamble was destined to bring the destruction of his regime.

7 A War on Three Fronts

i Metal Against Men

General A.A. Brusilov on 10 August 1914:

My Dear, Priceless Little Wife, Nadyushenka!

It was exceedingly hard to part from you, my darling Sunny. But my duty to my country and my Tsar, the great responsibility which has been cast upon me and my love for the military, which I have studied all my life, compel me not to give in to any weakening of the will and to prepare with tripled energy for the bloody test which confronts us.

As yet, thank God, all goes well. This morning we are going by automobile to inspect the brave 4th Rifle Brigade. It presents a fine appearance, excellent officers with their regiment commanders and heads of brigades. Very reliable troops.

The spirit of the soldiers is excellent. They are all animated by a firm belief in the righteousness and honour of their cause and so there is fortunately no ground for nervousness or unease. That is remarkably comforting.

I constantly pray to our Lord Jesus Christ that He may grant us, His Orthodox Christians, victory over the enemy. I myself am in *very* good spirits. Do not worry, my dearest, be brave, have faith and pray for me . . .

I kiss you passionately.

Alexis[1]

To the men who led Russia to war there seemed good cause for optimism in August 1914. The memory of the shameful defeat by Japan had been drowned in the bouts of military expenditure during recent years. By 1914, Russia was spending more than Germany on her armed forces: over one-third of all government expenditures.[2] It is not true, as historians later claimed, that the Russian army was unprepared for war. In manpower and *matériel* it was at least the equal of the German army, and, thanks to the recent improvement of Russia's western railways, took only three days more than its enemy to complete its mobilization. The Schlieffen Plan — which had been counting on Russia taking three weeks longer so that the German forces would be able to knock out France before Russia attacked them — was thus confounded and the Germans became bogged down in fighting on two Fronts. But this also saw the end of the widespread expectation that this would be a short war — 'All over by Christmas', as the saying went — and it was here that Russia's real weakness became exposed. For while Russia might have been ready for a short campaign of up to six months, she had no real contingency plans for a long war of attrition. Few indeed had expected such an ordeal. But whereas the other European powers managed to adapt and improvise, the tsarist system proved much too rigid and unwieldy, too inflexible and set in its ways, too authoritarian and inefficient, to adapt itself to the situation as it changed. The First World War was a titanic test for the states of Europe — and it was one that Tsarism failed in a singular and catastrophic way. Few people foresaw this in the first days of the conflict. It was only in the autumn, when the opening campaigns ended in bloody stalemate and the two opposing armies dug themselves in, that the weaknesses on the Russian side first became apparent.

Brusilov had been placed in command of the Eighth Army on the South-Western Front. With his foxy face and cavalry moustache, his genteel manners and clipped style of speech, he was in many ways the perfect image of the aristocratic general. But he was also a professional and was well versed in the new technology of warfare. To begin with, his name was scarcely known among the troops. He had spent the better part of his career in the élite School for Cavalry Officers. But he would soon win the soldiers' confidence with his brilliant command of them and his tireless efforts on their behalf; and by the autumn of 1916 his name would be famous not just in Russia but throughout the Allied world. As a commander, Brusilov was strictly disciplinarian. He believed that the only guarantee of military success was the army's own internal cohesion. In this respect he made unusually high demands on his men. Drinking, for example, was strictly forbidden, even among the officers. Yet he also worked day and night to make sure that the soldiers were fed, that they were suitably clothed and armed, and he never hesitated to punish any officer found to be corrupt or indigent in the distribution of supplies. He was at ease in conversation with the soldiers, a talent shared by very few generals, and knew how to raise their spirits on the eve of a battle. Some observers thought that his own deep religious conviction that Russia was destined to win the war rubbed off on his men.[3]

The original plan of the Russian high command had been to launch an offensive on the South-Western Front against the weaker Austrian forces, whilst defending the North-Western Front against the stronger Germans. But under pressure from France this plan was changed to an all-out offensive on both Fronts to force the Germans to transfer troops from the theatre in the west and thus relieve the French. The Russian commanders were happy to accede to the French request. Steeped in the military doctrines of the nineteenth century, they believed that a bold attack with plenty of cavalry charges and liberal use of the bayonet would best reflect the bravery of the Russian character. They failed to consider the huge loss of life that such an offensive was likely to entail once it was met with modern artillery and machine-guns.

On the South-Western Front things went well enough. In mid-August the Russians broke through in Galicia, forcing the Austrians to retreat. Brusilov's reputation as a brilliant Front commander was established here. His Eighth Army advanced 220 versts (130 miles) in the course of the following fortnight, capturing Lvov after heavy fighting (210,000 Russians and 300,000 Austrians were killed or wounded). Brusilov wrote to his wife from the Front at Grodek:

> The entire field of battle, for a distance of almost a hundred versts, was piled high with corpses, and there weren't enough people or stretchers to clear them away . . . Even to give drink and food to all those who were suffering proved impossible. This is the painful and seamy side of war . . . But we have to continue our difficult and terrible task for the good of the Fatherland, and I only pray that God may grant me the strength of mind and spirit to fulfil my duty. As I sit here and write to you I can hear in the distance the booming of cannon and guns, pursuing the enemy. Blood is flowing in endless streams, but there is no other way to fight. The more blood flows the better the results and the sooner the war will end. As you see, it's a hard and bitter task but a necessary one for victory. But it weighs terribly on my heart.[4]

On the North-Western Front, by contrast, the Russian advance soon ended in disaster. An ambitious but hastily concocted plan had envisaged the First Army under General von Rennenkampf invading the Junker heartland of East Prussia, while General Samsonov's Second Army advanced from the south-east to meet it near the Masurian Lakes, where they would combine and march on Berlin. The plan called for boldness, tactical precision and sound intelligence of the enemy's movements. None of these qualities was in evidence. On the fifteenth day of mobilization 408 battalions of infantry and 235 squadrons of cavalry moved rapidly west, pushing back the German Eighth Army, which they outnumbered almost two to one. General Prittwitz, the German commander, was thrown into panic and urged a withdrawal to the western banks of the Vistula, abandoning East Prussia to the Russians. Had they followed up their early successes, the Russians might have forced the Germans back. But the Russian commanders delayed their advance and dispersed vital troops and artillery to protect what turned out to be useless fortresses on their flanks and in their rear.

Meanwhile, the demoralized Prittwitz was replaced by Hindenburg and Ludendorff, whose vast superiority over the Russians in tactics and intelligence enabled them to ambush and rout their larger armies. From intercepted wireless transmissions, which the Russians had carelessly sent unciphered, they learned that Rennenkampf's army had stopped for supplies, and gambled on the assumption that it would go no further. Leaving only a small screening force to deceive Rennenkampf, the Germans transferred the rest of their forces south by train to meet Samsonov's advancing army. Had Rennenkampf realized what was happening and attacked, he could have won a decisive victory against the German left and possibly brought the war to an end. But the Russians had only a primitive system of military intelligence and no one had any idea of the German troop movements. Unprepared for the massive forces that lay in ambush for it in the forests near Tannenberg, Samsonov's army was surrounded and destroyed in four of the bloodiest days of carnage the world had ever known until that time. By the end of the battle, on 31 August, the Germans had killed or wounded 70,000 Russians and taken 100,000 prisoners at a loss to themselves of 15,000 men. They named it the Battle of Tannenberg in a symbolic gesture intended to avenge the defeat of the Teutonic Knights at the hands of the Slavs five hundred years before. Unable to bear the humiliation, Samsonov shot himself.

Moving troops back to the north by rail, and with fresh reinforcements from the Western Front, Hindenburg and Ludendorff once again outmanœuvred the Russians in the Battle of the Masurian Lakes. Fearing a second Tannenberg, Rennenkampf now ordered a panic retreat. The Germans joked that he should no longer be called 'von Rennenkampf' but 'Rennen von Kampf' ('flight from the battle'). The cost of his incompetence and cowardice was 60,000 Russian lives.[5]

One of the striking features of this débâcle was the callous response of the Russian commanders to its enormous human cost. It was as if any expression of regret for the needless loss of a quarter of a million men was seen as a sign of weakness in the aristocratic circles at Supreme Headquarters. When the French representative there condoled with the Grand Duke Nikolai over the losses, the Commander-in-Chief casually replied: 'Nous sommes heureux de faire de tels sacrifices pour nos alliées.'[6] By forcing the Germans to withdraw troops from the Western theatre, the Russian advance had in fact helped to stall the Schlieffen Plan and enabled the French to launch their counter-offensive on the Marne. But at what a price!

From the autumn the Eastern Front began to stabilize as the war of mobility gave way to a war of position. Neither side was strong enough to push the enemy back and stalemate resulted. Sweeping offensives like those of the first month were abandoned as the armies discovered the advantages of defensive warfare and dug themselves in. One entrenched machine-gunner was enough to repel a hundred infantrymen, and railways could bring up defenders much faster than the advancing troops could fill gaps in the front line.

It was at this point that Russia's military weaknesses began to make themselves felt. She was not prepared for a war of attrition. Her single greatest asset, her seemingly inexhaustible supply of peasant soldiers, was not such an advantage as her allies had presumed when they had talked of the 'Russian steamroller' trundling unstoppably towards Berlin. It was true that Russia had by far the largest population of any belligerent country, yet she was also the first to suffer from manpower shortages. Because of the high birth-rate in Russia a large proportion of the population was younger than the minimum draft age. The entire pool of recruitable men was only twenty-seven million, and 48 per cent of these were exempt as only sons or the sole adult male workers in their family, or else on account of their ethnic background (Muslims were exempt, for example). Where 12 per cent of the German population and 16 per cent of the French was mobilized for military service, the figure for Russia was only 5 per cent.

More serious still was the weakness of the Russian reserves. The Russians had adopted the German reserve system. After three years of active duty from the age of twenty-one, recruits spent seven years in the First Levy reserves, followed by eight in the Second and five in the National Militia. To save money the army gave little formal training beyond the First Levy. Yet the casualties of 1914 were so much greater than anyone had ever expected (about 1.8 million) that the army soon found itself having to call on the untrained men of the Second Levy. The Battle of Przemysl in October was the last with which Brusilov could fight with 'an army that had been properly taught and trained before the war':

After hardly three months of war the greater part of our regular, professional officers and trained men had vanished, leaving only skeleton forces which had to be hastily filled with men wretchedly instructed who were sent to me from the depots . . . From this period onwards the professional character of our forces disappeared, and the army became more and more like a sort of badly trained militia . . . The men sent to replace casualties generally knew nothing except how to march . . . many could not even load their rifles and, as for their shooting, the less said about it the better . . . Such people could not really be considered soldiers at all.[7]

The soldier of the Russian army was, for the most part, a stranger to the sentiment of patriotism. Perhaps, to a certain extent, he could identify with the war as a defence of the Tsar, or of his religion, but defence of the

Russian nation, especially if he himself was not Russian, meant very little to him. He was a peasant with little direct knowledge of the world outside his village, and his sense of himself as a 'Russian' was only very weakly developed. He thought of himself as a native of his local region and, as long as the enemy did not threaten to invade that area, saw little reason to fight with him. 'We are Tambov men,' the reluctant recruits would proclaim. 'The Germans will not get as far as that.' A farm agent from Smolensk, who served in the rear garrisons, heard such comments from the peasant soldiers during the first weeks of the war:

> 'What devil has brought this war on us? We are butting into other people's business.'
> 'We have talked it over among ourselves; if the Germans want payment, it would be better to pay ten roubles a head than to kill people.'
> 'Is it not all the same what Tsar we live under? It cannot be worse under the German one.'
> 'Let them go and fight themselves. Wait a while, we will settle accounts with you.'

These sorts of attitudes became more common in the ranks as the war went on, as Brusilov had cause to complain:

> The drafts arriving from the interior of Russia had not the slightest notion of what the war had to do with them. Time after time I asked my men in the trenches why we were at war; the inevitable senseless answer was that a certain Archduke and his wife had been murdered and that consequently the Austrians had tried to humiliate the Serbians. Practically no one knew who these Serbians were; they were equally doubtful as to what a Slav was. Why Germany should want to make war on us because of these Serbians, no one could say ... They had never heard of the ambitions of Germany; they did not even know that such a country existed.[8]

All this hardly boded well for an army whose commanders were intent on marching to Berlin, let alone one that was committed to the capture of Constantinople. The Russian peasant took no pride in his country's imperial gains, being a natural pacifist.

The lack of a clear command structure was one of the army's biggest weaknesses. Military authority was divided between the War Ministry, Supreme Headquarters (Stavka) and the Front commands. Each pursued its own particular ends, so that no clear war plan emerged. 'From the beginning', complained

Brusilov, 'I had never been able to find out anything about our general plan of campaign.' It was, as General Bezobrazov once quipped, all 'order, counter-order and disorder'.[9] The bitter conflicts between the two main Front commands, the North-West and the South-West, were especially damaging. The stubborn refusal of the former to send reinforcements to the latter was a major cause of the collapse of the Carpathian offensive in the winter of 1914–15.

The division between the aristocratic élite of the Cavalry Guards and the new military professionals — Brusilov stood with one foot in each camp — was a major element in these conflicts. The top commanders were drawn from a narrow circle of aristocratic cavalrymen and courtiers with little military expertise. The Supreme Commander himself, the Grand Duke Nikolai, had never taken part in any serious fighting and was little more than a figurehead at Stavka. He entertained foreign visitors, signed the papers put in front of him, and surrounded himself with aides-de-camp, including his brothers, whom he called his 'sleeping pills'. But in strategic matters he failed to lead. At a conference of the Front commands in September he stayed in a separate room from the generals 'so as not to get in their way'. General Yanushkevich, his Chief of Staff, had nothing to recommend him but the personal favour of the Tsar, who had discovered him as a young Guardsman at the palace. He had never even commanded a battalion. Colonel Knox, the British military attaché at Stavka, gained 'the impression of a courtier rather than a soldier'. The whole atmosphere at Stavka, situated at a small Belorussian railway town called Baranovichi, could not have been less warlike. 'We were in the midst of a charming fir wood and everything was quiet and peaceful,' Knox recalled. Senior officers had plenty of time for leisurely conversations, a cigar and a walk in the forest after lunch. Many of them found time to write voluminous diaries or, like Brusilov, long daily letters to their wives.[10]

The same courtly manners were shared by most of the top commanders. Since 1909, when General Sukhomlinov (a perfect example of the military courtier) became War Minister, there had been a deliberate policy of promoting senior officers on the basis of their personal loyalty to the Tsar. Aristocratic but incompetent cavalrymen of the old Suvorov school were favoured over the military professionals, who had a far better understanding of the needs of modern warfare. The Tsar's constant interventions in the appointment of senior officers, sometimes at the insistence of his wife, ensured that connections and allegiance to him would continue to take precedence over military competence. Even in war Nicholas struggled to assert his patrimonial autocracy.

In the spring of 1915 Nicholas paid a visit to Brusilov's army in Galicia and appointed him one of his General-Adjutants. Brusilov assumed that this honour was in recognition of his services in the field, but he was informed by the Tsar himself that in fact it had been awarded for no other reason than that 'he had visited my headquarters and had lunched with me'. News of the honour was suppressed, for the court was not entirely convinced of Brusilov's allegiance (he had criticized the army's leadership). Polivanov, the Deputy War Minister, later admitted to Brusilov's wife that throughout the war 'secret arrangements' had been made to 'hush up' her husband's name lest his military successes should turn him into a focus of public opposition to the court's command of the armed forces. This pathetic tale sums up the way the war was conducted by the Russian ruling élite.[11]

As long as commanders were appointed for their loyalty to the court rather than their abilities there was little prospect of any effective military leadership. The aristocratic generals committed endless blunders (one even had the distinction of ordering his artillery to fire on his own infantry's trenches). They conducted the war after the pattern of a nineteenth-century campaign, asking their men to storm enemy artillery positions regardless of casualties; wasting resources on the expensive and ineffective cavalry; defending useless fortresses in the rear; and neglecting the technological needs of modern artillery war. They scorned the art of building trenches, since they regarded the war of position as beneath contempt. The primitive nature of the Russians' trenches, really no more than graves, caused huge loss of life once the war had developed into a slugging match of heavy artillery bombardment. Brusilov, one of the few army commanders to recognize the vital importance of trench warfare, was amazed by his officers' negligence:

I ordered my army to dig themselves in thoroughly and to construct a system of at least three lines with plenty of communicating trenches. I received a quantity of reports as to the impossibility of carrying out these instructions, but repeated my order explicitly, and was told that it was being obeyed. But when ... I went round the various Army Corps to inspect the work, it transpired that practically nothing had been done, and what little had been done was so completely filled with snow that it was difficult to discover where the trenches had been dug.

'How are you going to get into these lines, supposing the enemy attacks us?' I asked.

'Oh,' they replied, 'we'll clean them out when that happens' ...

In one Army Corps there was a case where neither the Corps Commander, nor the Divisional Commander, nor the Brigadier, nor the Colonel of the Regiment, nor even the officer commanding the Corps Engineers, could tell me where the trenches had been dug.[12]

One of the obvious reasons for the East Prussian débâcle was the Russian army's lack of mobility. Knox compared it to a 'heavy-weight, muscle-bound prize-fighter, who because of his enormous bulk, lacked activity and quickness, and would therefore be at the mercy of a lighter but more wiry and intelligent opponent'. The primitiveness of the Russian railway system ruled out the possibility of following the Germans' example; they moved troops rapidly by train from one part of the Front to another in response to the changing fortunes of war. Russia's military trains could not travel more than 200 miles a day and, in any case, most of them were filled with horses and fodder, such was the preoccupation of the military commanders with the cavalry. Once the army entered German territory it was dependent on captured rolling stock, since Russian trains ran on a different gauge. Russian motor transportation was even more basic. In 1914 there were no more than 679 motor cars (and two motorized ambulances!) for the whole of the army. Military equipment, senior personnel and the wounded had to be moved away from the railhead by peasant carts on muddy country roads. But it was the primitive state of Russia's military communications that really lay at the root of her defeat. Samsonov's Second Army had twenty-five telephones, a few morse-coding machines, a sort of primitive telex called a Hughes apparatus, and a tele-printer capable of printing 1,200 words per hour but which often broke down, which meant that the commander had to move around on horseback to find out what was going on. Telegraphic communications were constantly breaking down between Stavka, the Front commands and the armies, so that orders had to be sent by train or motorbike, which often took days. On the eve of the Battle of Tannenberg the North-West Front commander communicated with Samsonov by sending telegrams to the Warsaw Central Post Office, where an adjutant collected them once a day and took them by car more than sixty miles to Second Army headquarters. Many of these breakdowns in communication were caused by the errors of badly educated soldiers. Too many telephonists were unable to mend a broken line, too many drivers unable to read a map. The telegraphs would suddenly cease to function and an investigation of the lines to the rear would reveal a party of soldiers cooking their tea on a bonfire made of chopped-up telegraph poles.[13]

As the war dragged on through the winter the army began to experience terrible shortages of *matériel*. The breakdown of the supply system in the rear was partly to blame. The transport network could not cope with the massive deliveries of munitions, food, clothing and medical care to the fronts. But the lack of any real pre-war planning was also to blame. Counting on a short campaign, the War Ministry had made no plans for the wartime production of *matériel*, assuming that existing stocks would be enough to see them through. As it turned out, the stocks lasted no longer than the first few weeks of the war.

The problem was particularly acute with regard to munitions. A reserve of seven million shells was expected to last the whole war, enough for a thousand rounds per field gun, or ten days of fighting at 1916 levels. The Russian armaments industry, which could have kept the army well supplied, was deliberately run down by the War Ministry (in the first seven months of 1914 it ordered just 41 rifles), so once shortages became apparent orders had to be placed abroad and delays were inevitable. By the end of the war, there were ten different models of imported rifle, each firing a different type of bullet, in use with the Russian army. Part of the problem was the wastefulness of the soldiers themselves: they used their rifles to prop up improvised roofs over their trenches; chopped them up for firewood; and all too often threw them away, along with the heavy supplies of ammunition, when they were wounded or suddenly forced to retreat. But the crisis would undoubtedly have been less severe if the War Ministry had responded more quickly to the calls of alarm from the generals, instead of dismissing them. In mid-October, when General Karavaev, Chief of the Artillery Department, warned the War Minister that Russia would soon have to sue for peace because of the lack of munitions, Sukhomlinov told him to 'go to the devil and quiet himself'. And yet by the following spring the shortage was such that whole battalions had to be trained without rifles, while many second-line troops at the Front were relying on rifles picked up from the men shot in front of them. Soldiers were told to limit themselves to ten shots a day and in many cases, when the German heavy artillery bombarded their trenches, the Russian gunners were forbidden to return fire. 'Our position is bad,' one soldier wrote to his father, 'and all because we have no ammunition. That's where we've got to, thanks to our ministers of war, making unarmed people face up to the enemy's guns because we don't have any of our own. That's what they have done!'[14]

Brusilov's army, having fought its way to the top of the Carpathian mountains, found itself stuck there for much of the winter without enough ammunition to fight its way down on to the Hungarian plain. 'I was disheartened to learn', he later wrote, 'that the Front Headquarters could hardly promise any improvement before the autumn of 1915, and even in these promises I had no confidence. I therefore no longer aimed at any fresh successes on this front, but attempted merely to hold my ground with as few losses as possible.' But spending the winter in the mountains was a cruel reward for his men, without warm clothes and boots or enough food to see them through the frosts. Brusilov spent the month of December bombarding the War Ministry with demands for winter kit, but his appeals were only part of a growing chorus from all parts of the army and the sad truth was that, having expected the war to be over by Christmas, the Ministry had made no provisions for the huge demand it now encountered. There were not even plans for the mass manufacture of boots and when the Ministry finally looked to its soldiers' footware, it discovered that the whole Russian Empire contained one factory capable of producing tanning extract, and that before 1914 virtually all of the country's tannin had been imported from Germany. New boots had to be ordered from the United States, but meanwhile thousands of soldiers fought barefoot. 'They still haven't given out overcoats,' one frozen soldier wrote to his mother. 'We run around in thin topcoats . . . There is not much to eat and what we get is foul. Perhaps we'd be better off dead!' Another soldier wrote home after the visit of the Tsar to his unit: 'For the Tsar's inspection they prepared one company and collected all the best uniforms from the other regiments for it to wear, leaving the rest of the men in the trenches without boots, knapsacks, bandoliers, trousers, uniforms, hats, or anything else.'[15]

It was not long before the army was ridden with disease. Cholera, typhus, typhoid, scurvy and dysentery epidemics decimated the troops. The unexpectedly high rate of casualties placed the medical services under terrible pressure. Brusilov wrote to his wife after visiting one field hospital in the rear of his army:

Instead of the 200 patients, for which the hospital had been built, there were over 3,000 sick and wounded men. What could four doctors do for them? They worked day and night, ate on their feet, but still couldn't bandage everyone . . . I went around several wards, rooms in vacated houses, where the sick and wounded lay on the floor, on straw, dressed, unwashed and covered in blood. I thanked them on behalf of the Tsar and the Fatherland, and gave out money and St George's crosses, but there was nothing more I could do. I could only try to speed up their evacuation to the rear.

Evacuation, however, was no guarantee of any better treatment. At the Warsaw railway station Rodzianko found 17,000 wounded soldiers lying unattended 'in the cold rain and mud without so much as straw litter'. The Duma President complained angrily to the local medical department, only to find that their 'heartless indifference to the fate of these suffering men' was supported by a host of bureaucratic regulations.[16]

As conditions at the Front worsened and the scale of the slaughter increased, the army's morale and discipline began to fall apart. The war in this sense was the social architect of 1917 as the army gradually turned into one vast revolutionary mob. Part of the problem was the weakening grip of the officers over their men. The army expanded too fast for the officers to retain control (nine million men were called up in the first twelve months of the war). Officer casualties (at 60,000) were meanwhile unusually high, which no doubt owed something to their colourful uniforms and their old-fashioned practice of leading frontal charges. The old officer corps below the level of captain was almost completely wiped out, while a new generation of lower-ranking officers (what in the West would be called NCOs) was hastily trained to replace them. The number of NCOs was never enough — the artisan classes who usually made up this tier of the army were generally weak in Russia — and it was unusual after the first year of the war for a front-line regiment of 3,000 men to have more than a dozen officers. Moreover, 60 per cent of the NCOs came from a peasant background, very few had more than four years' education, and nearly all of them were in their early twenties.[17] The war was thus a great democratizer, opening channels of advancement for millions of peasant sons. Their sympathies lay firmly with the ordinary soldiers, and any hopes that they might form a bridge between the high-born officers and their low-born troops were badly misplaced. This was the radical military cohort — literate, upwardly mobile, socially disoriented and brutalized by war — who would lead the mutiny of February, the revolutionary soldiers' committees, and eventually the drive to Soviet power during 1917. Many of the Red Army's best commanders (e.g. Chapaev, Zhukov and Rokossovsky) had been NCOs in the tsarist army, much as the marshals of Napoleon's wars had begun as subalterns in the king's army. The sergeants of the First World War would become the marshals of the Second.

Dmitry Os'kin (1892–1934), whose story is told throughout this book, was a typical example of this war-created officer class. For a peasant lad like him — literate and bright despite his country-bumpkin looks — the army offered a means of escape from the poverty of the village. In the summer of 1913 he volunteered for the infantry regiment in his local town of Tula, and soon found himself on a training course for NCOs. When the war broke out he was made a platoon commander. Os'kin was a brave and conscientious soldier, thoroughly deserving of the four St George's Crosses he would win in the course of the war.[18] Some part of his character, self-discipline or ambition, compelled him to carry out the commands of his senior officers, despite his 'peasant' animosity towards all figures of authority. Perhaps it was the realization that, unless he established some discipline among his men, they were likely to be slaughtered on the battlefield. Certainly, as the war took its toll on the senior officers, the burden increased on NCOs like him to hold the ranks together.

Os'kin's senior commanders were a swinish lot. On several occasions their reckless orders led his men to the brink of disaster and it was only by his own improvised initiatives that they managed to come out alive. Captain Tsitseron, a gambler, syphilitic and shameless coward, was always in a quandary on the battlefield. Once, when facing some well-entrenched Austrian guns on a hill, he ordered Os'kin's men to cut a way through the rows of barbed wire in full view of their artillery. Crawling forward, they soon came under heavy fire and Os'kin looked up to see countless Russian corpses hanging on the wire. Cursing

Tsitseron, he brought his men back to safety. Captain Samfarov, another of Os'kin's commanders, was an ice-cream glutton, too fat to fit into his uniform, who hid in his private dug-out whenever the shelling began. He liked to 'keep his men on their toes' by ordering midnight attacks, despite the obvious lack of strategic preparations for nocturnal fighting. Once, when such an assault nearly destroyed the whole battalion and Os'kin's men returned the following day in a terrible state, Samfarov had them lined up in their ranks and shouted at them for half an hour because they had failed to polish their boots.[19]

Not all the commanders were so incompetent or cruel. But there was a growing feeling among the soldiers that so much blood need not be spilled, if the officers thought less of themselves and more of the safety of their men. The fact that the mass of the soldiers were peasants, and that many of their officers were noble landowners (often from the same region as their men), added a dimension of social conflict; and this was exacerbated by the 'feudal' customs between the ranks (e.g. the obligation of the soldiers to address their officers by their honorary titles, to clean their boots, run private errands for them, and so on). 'Look at the way our high-up officers live, the landowners whom we have always served,' wrote one peasant soldier to his local newspaper at home. 'They get good food, their families are given everything they need, and although they may live at the Front, they do not live in the trenches where we are but four or five versts away.' For literate and thinking peasants like Os'kin, this was a powerful source of political radicalization, the realization that the war was being fought in very different ways by two very different Russias: the Russia of the rich and the senior officers, and the Russia of the peasants, whose lives were being squandered. Os'kin's diary, April 1915:

> What are we doing in this war? Several hundred men have already passed through my platoon alone and at least half of them have ended up on the fields of battle either killed or wounded. What will they get at the end of the war? . . . My year and a half of military service, with almost a year at the Front, has stopped me from thinking about this, for the task of the platoon commander demands strict discipline and that means, above all, not letting the soldier think freely for himself. But these are the things we must think about.[20]

Others less able to draw political lessons simply voted with their feet. Discipline broke down as soldiers refused to take up positions, cut off their fingers and hands to get themselves discharged, surrendered to the enemy or deserted to the rear. There were drunken outbursts of looting and riots at the recruiting stations as the older reservists, many with families to support, were mobilized. Their despatch to the Front merely accelerated the ferment of rebellion, since they brought bad news from home and sometimes revolutionary propaganda too. The officers responded all too often with more force. Reluctant soldiers were flogged or sent into battle with their own side's artillery aimed at their backs. This internal war between the officers and their men began to overshadow the war itself. 'The officers are trying to break our spirits by terrorizing us,' one soldier wrote to his wife in the spring of 1915. 'They want to make us into lifeless puppets.' Another wrote that a group of officers had 'flogged five men in front of 28,000 troops because they had left their barracks without permission to go and buy bread'.[21]

At this point, after a long winter of demoralization, the army faced the biggest German offensive of the war. With the Western Front bogged down in stalemate, the Germans were pinning their hopes on a decisive breakthrough in the east. It began on the night of 2 May 1915 with a massive four-hour bombardment of the unprepared Third Army near Gorlice. A thousand shells a minute reduced the Russian trenches to rubble. When the German infantry stormed them the following morning they found only a handful of shell-shocked survivors. The rest had all run away. The Russians 'jumped up and ran back weaponless', recalled one German soldier. 'In their grey fur caps and fluttering unbuttoned great coats [they looked] like a flock of sheep in wild confusion.' Without a defensive strategy (Dmitriev, the Third Army commander, had left his headquarters to attend the annual celebration of the Order of the Knights of St George), the Russians were forced into headlong retreat. General Denikin described it as 'one vast tragedy for the Russian army. No cartridges, no shells. Bloody fighting and difficult marches day after day.' Within ten days the Third Army's shattered remnants — a mere 40,000 of its 220,000 troops — had fallen back to the San River, the last natural barrier between the Germans and Przemysl. They prepared to make a stand on its banks, only to find that corrupt officers had sold all the spades, barbed wire and timber needed to build the trenches. Without artillery or supplies of ammunition, they held out as best they could, suffering heavy losses. Many men fought with nothing but bayonets fixed to their empty rifles. But by the end of May they were finally forced to abandon Przemysl. Lvov (Lemberg) was soon to follow, as the Germans approached the borders of Russia itself. It had been, as Knox was to put it, a barrage of 'metal against men'.[22]

The German breakthrough exposed the northern flank of Brusilov's army in the Carpathians. To avoid the danger of being cut off and surrounded, it was forced to retreat and abandon the hard-won heights it had spent the winter desperately defending. 'My dear Nadiushenka,' Brusilov wrote on 11 June:

We have had to give up Przemysl and Lvov. You cannot imagine how painful that is ... I am trying to give the appearance that things really are not so bad, but inside it hurts, my heart is grieving, and my spirits are depressed. Let's suppose, and I am convinced, that we shall regain the land we have just lost and that we shall win the war, it is just a matter of time, but none the less it is terribly painful. One has to show strength of will at such times, not just when everything is going well, that is easy, but when things are bad, so as to encourage the demoralized and those on the brink of losing their morale, of which there are many.[23]

Meanwhile, in mid-July, the Germans also launched an offensive in East Prussia. They pushed north towards Riga, east towards Vilnius and south to join the other German forces advancing through Poland. The 'impregnable' fortresses of Kovno, Grodno, Osowiec, Novogeorgievsk and Ivangorod, which the Russians had placed at the centre of their defensive strategy, filling them up with precious supplies of munitions, were abandoned one by one as the Germans advanced with their heavy artillery. It was yet another example of the Russian military élite trying to fight a twentieth-century conflict with tactics more appropriate to the Crimean War. The huge stone bastions turned out to be useless museums, concrete traps for men and supplies, and Hindenburg and Ludendorff, who had made their names on the Western Front by storming the fortress of Liège, had little difficulty repeating their success in the east. The fortifications at Kovno (Kaunas) were so poor that the Grand Duke Nikolai said the fortress ought to be renamed 'Govno' (the Russian word for 'shit'). Its aged commander, to make matters even worse, had secretly fled the fortress on the eve of its capture. He was finally tracked down to the bar of the Bristol Hotel in Wilno (Vilnius) and sentenced to fifteen years' hard labour.[24]

With all its armies pushed back by the force of German steel, the Russian command had little choice but to order a general retreat. No real plans were made. There were vague romantic notions of repeating the scorched-earth tactics of General Kutuzov which, in Tolstoy's version at least, had so brilliantly entrapped Napoleon's troops in the winter wastelands of Russia. 'The retreat will continue as far — and for as long — as necessary,' the Tsar told Maurice Paléologue at the end of July. 'The Russian people are as unanimous in their will to conquer as they were in 1812.' But in all other respects — the sequence of evacuation, the selection of things to destroy and the planning of strategic positions at which to make a new stand — there were only confusion and panic. Troops destroyed buildings, bridges, animals and crops in a totally random way. This often broke down into pillaging, especially of Jewish property. Hundreds of thousands of refugees, their homes and farms demolished, trudged east along the railway lines with their few belongings piled on to carts, while trains sped past carrying senior officers, their mistresses, and, in the words of one officer, 'all sorts of useless junk, including cages with canaries'. No provision was made for the care of the refugees, most of whom ended up living on station floors and the streets of Russia's cities. 'Sickness, misery and poverty are speading across the whole of Russia,' Krivoshein, the Minister of Agriculture, warned the Council of Ministers in August. 'Starving and ragged masses are sowing panic everywhere. Surely no country ever saved itself by its own destruction.'[25]

The summer months of unending retreat dealt another crippling blow to the troops' morale. It was hard for them to see territory which they had fought and died for so easily sacrificed to the enemy. The destruction of military stores in the rear, full of the clothing and food they had so badly needed, was especially hard to bear. 'Every day', wrote Os'kin, 'we would come across another store of food and munitions in some village or other. They were all just left there and destroyed.' Here was the final damning proof of the military leaders' incompetence. 'They've screwed it all up,' Brusilov overheard one of his soldiers mutter, 'and we've been landed with cleaning up the mess.' Demoraliz- ation in the rear was even more advanced. Nadezhda Brusilova wrote to her husband:

> You are so naive, if you still believe in victory. We in the rear have a much better idea of what is going on and we are already convinced that the Germans will win the war. They will be in Moscow by 1916. This is the catastrophe and collapse of Russia.

There were widespread rumours in the rear about treason in high places, which soon spread to the Front. The German background of the Tsarina and other government figures, and the execution in March 1915 of Colonel Miasoyedov, one of Sukhomlinov's protégés, for spying for Germany seemed to confirm such conspiracy theories. A Bolshevik soldier recalls the efforts of one NCO, for example, to explain to his soldiers the reason for the retreat: 'There are many traitors and spies in the high command of our army, like the War Minister Sukhomlinov, whose fault it is that we don't have any shell, and Miasoyedov, who betrayed the fortresses to the enemy.' When he had finished a soldier-cook drew the conclusion: 'A fish begins to stink from the head. What kind of a Tsar would surround himself with thieves and cheats? It's as clear as day that we're going to lose the war.'[26]

For many soldiers this was the vital psychological moment of the revolution — the moment when their loyalty to the monarchy finally snapped. A government which had dragged them into a war which they could not hope to win, had failed to provide them with adequate weapons and supplies, and now was in league with the enemy was certainly not worthy of further sacrifices. A million men surrendered to the German and Austrian forces during the Great

Retreat, most of them preferring to spend the rest of the war in the enemies' prisoner-of-war camps than vainly trying to fight their superior armies. An unknown number, but certainly tens of thousands, deserted to the rear, where many of them put their guns to a different use and lived from banditry. Even Sergeant Os'kin, who was wounded in the knee and eventually (after being forced to march on his wounded leg) evacuated to a Moscow hospital, felt so humiliated by the Great Retreat that, after his leg had been amputated, he deserted from his regiment and went to a friend's farm in Siberia. But the farm had been burned down by the Cossacks, who had also requisitioned all its cattle for the government and had raped his friend's wife and mother. This was the last straw for Os'kin, who now joined the SR Party underground in Siberia and watched with growing interest the political crisis unfolding as a result of the Great Retreat. In a final desperate effort to raise the morale of the troops, the Chief of Staff General Yanushkevich urged the Tsar to promise that in the event of a Russian victory every loyal soldier would be given 16 *desyatiny* (43 acres) of land. But it was too late for such measures and even Yanushkevich called it 'clutching at straws'. The army was falling apart. By September, when the enemy's advance was finally bogged down in the Russian mud, its front-line forces had been reduced to one-third of their strength at the start of the war.[27]

*　*　*

'It cannot go on like this,' Nicholas wrote in his diary on hearing the news of Warsaw's fall. Three weeks later he took what many people believed at the time was the most fateful decision of his entire reign. On 22 August he dismissed the Grand Duke Nikolai and assumed the supreme command of the army himself. Stavka was moved 200 miles eastward to Mogilev, a dirty and dreary provincial town whose name derives from the word in Russian for a 'grave'. Here the Tsar's regime buried itself.

It seems there were two reasons (both equally flawed) for Nicholas's decision — and it was his decision — to assume the command of the army. First, that at this critical moment the supreme ruler should stand at the head of the armed forces. There was a certain logic to this. Since the war began there had been in effect a dual power system — one led by the Grand Duke and the other by the Tsar — without any real co-ordination between them. However by moving to the Front, Nicholas merely undermined his own authority in the rear, where, in his absence, a sort of bureaucratic anarchy developed with the Tsarina, the ministers and the representatives of the Duma, the zemstvos and the war industries all at loggerheads. Second, the Tsar had hoped that by placing himself at the head of the army, he might help to restore its morale: if the soldiers would not fight for 'Russia', then perhaps they would fight for him. But Nicholas had no experience of military command and, although the important decisions were all taken by his new Chief of Staff, General M. V. Alexeev, who was a gifted strategist, the Tsar's presence had a bad effect overall on morale. For, in the words of Brusilov, 'Everyone knew that Nicholas understood next to nothing about military matters and, although the word "Tsar" still had a magical power over the troops, he utterly lacked the charisma to bring that magic to life. Faced with a group of soldiers, he was nervous and did not know what to say.'[28]

The Council of Ministers, in a unique act of loyal criticism, pleaded with the Tsar to change his mind. 'The decision you have taken', it warned, 'threatens Russia, You, and Your dynasty with the gravest consequences.' But Nicholas would not be dissuaded. No doubt the influence of his wife, who had put him up to this *coup de main*, helped to strengthen his resolve. He may well have seen the move as his last chance to silence the growing public criticism of the war campaign, and the urgent sense that his own throne was threatened drove him on to take what was a huge risk. Coinciding as it did with his decision to close down the Duma, which had been in session since July, it signalled a new resolve on his part to reassert his personal rule. Perhaps he still harboured fantasies that his 'mystical union' with 'the people' would save the country from catastrophe. Krivoshein, for one, thought that the Tsar's decision was 'fully in tune with his spiritual frame of mind and his mystical understanding of his imperial calling'.[29] The support he received from the Tsarina and Rasputin, who encouraged his dreams of personal rule, was in line with this, although their real concern was no doubt in part to get him out of their way. With the Tsar absent at the Front, power in the capital would pass to them.

ii The Mad Chauffeur

The war found Prince Lvov at the head of the Zemstvo Union. As in the war against Japan, the needs of the Front had sparked a patriotic movement of public organization. Civic committees and clubs volunteered helpers to pack up supplies of linen, food and medicine in their hours after work, while hundreds of young women enrolled as nurses and coped as best they could with the legions of wounded and dying. The Tsarina turned part of the Winter Palace into a surgical bandage factory, and the best society ladies turned up in droves to roll up their sleeves and work. Brusilov's wife, Nadezhda, volunteered for the Russian Red Cross in the Ukraine. 'I work day and night', she wrote to him in August 1914, 'and thank God for that, since it keeps me from thinking and makes me feel I am of use.' Kerensky's wife, Olga, who worked in a Belgian hospital, looked back on this as 'one of the happiest periods of my life'.

When I bent down to wash the soldiers' dirty feet, or cleaned and dressed their nasty-smelling and decaying wounds, I experienced an almost religious ecstasy. I bowed before all these soldiers, who had given their lives for Russia. I have never felt such ecstasy.[30]

Here at last, for these idle bourgeois ladies, was a chance to 'serve the people' and thus to redeem their own guilt.

Lvov's Zemstvo Union, established with its sister organization the Union of Towns during the first few weeks of the war, took the lead in most of these activities. It virtually ran the military supply campaign in the absence of any effective governmental grasp of logistics. Russia's war effort, but for Lvov's efforts, would have quickly collapsed altogether. To begin with the Union was supported by the gifts of money and property that poured in from the public. One landowner donated his whole estate, a fertile expanse of 10,000 acres. Peasants delivered cartloads of cabbages, potatoes and homespun linen to its depots in the rear. But it soon became clear that the government itself would have to provide most of the finance, as the failings of its own bureaucracy became apparent and it came to rely on the Union. Increasingly its volunteers took the lead in setting up field canteens and medical units at the Front, evacuating the wounded and giving them hospital care, purchasing military supplies, combating disease, helping refugees and providing support for the poverty-stricken soldiers' families. By 1916 it had grown into a huge national infrastructure, a state within a state, with 8,000 affiliated institutions, several hundred thousand employees (the so-called *zemgussars*) and a budget of two billion roubles. Lvov, at the head of this unofficial government, worked tirelessly from eight in the morning to two or three at night. The queue outside his office stretched into the Moscow streets. As one minister grudgingly acknowledged in the autumn of 1915, he was 'virtually becoming the chairman of a special government. At the Front they talk only of him and say that he has saved the country. He supplies the army, feeds the hungry, cures the sick, establishes barber shops for the soldiers — in a word, he is some kind of a ubiquitous Miur and Mereliz.* One must either end all this or hand over power to him.'[31]

The remark was prophetic. For Lvov was to become the first Prime Minister of democratic Russia in March 1917. His experience in the Zemstvo Union, which demanded administrative boldness and an ability to improvise, equipped him for the role above all else. The civic spirit of the February Revolution had its roots in the wartime activities of the voluntary organizations. It was from these that most of the democratic revolution's leaders, including all but three of the ministers of the First Provisional Government, were to emerge. And yet Lvov had always been a reluctant revolutionary. Had the Tsar liberalized his regime and appointed a government of public confidence, Lvov would not

* The largest department store in Moscow.

have joined the opposition. Politics were of much less interest to him than the direct effect he could have on the lives of 'the people'. It was this desire for practical work that had drawn him into the zemstvo movement during the 1890s and, although he had joined the Kadets, he had never been at ease with the party. In short, he was made for public wartime work.

Lvov's leadership of the Zemstvo Union began with the same essentially practical aims (the good of 'the nation') as he had displayed in the Tula zemstvo (the good of 'the people'). At the heart of Lvov's political being was what one acquaintance described as 'a down-to-earth organic patriotism'. It was rooted in his love of the peasants and his belief in their creative powers as the basic strength of Russia. A similar patriotism lay at the heart of his commitment to the Zemstvo Union. Its duty, as he saw it in 1914, was to reconcile the people with the government by uniting the two behind the war effort. Executive meetings finished with his tenor voice breaking into the national anthem.[32]

By the following autumn, however, even Lvov could no longer stand apart from the growing political opposition to the government and its army command, whose gross mismanagement was being blamed by an angry public for the recent crushing defeats. His own organization had been struggling for some time against constant obstruction by the bureaucracy, and by now he was at the end of his tether. Maklakov, the reactionary Interior Minister of Beiliss trial fame, regarded the Union as little more than a Trojan horse usurping the functions of the government, and had been doing his best to limit its independent powers. He even objected to its labour brigades, some 80,000 strong, which dug trenches and graves in the rear, on the grounds that a public organization should not be allowed to have its own 'army'. Although it had been pointed out that it would be armed with nothing more dangerous than axes and spades, Maklakov stood his ground and ordered Lvov to demobilize the brigades. By September, with the Duma prorogued, the mild-mannered prince was ready to join the fray. 'We are no longer prepared to remain in the passive position of being governed,' he told the Third Zemstvo Union Congress. The Russian people, he went on, were developing into a 'state-like force', and through their service to the nation would earn the right to demand a constitutional system from the government at the end of the war. The work of the public organizations was thus no longer a means of uniting the people behind the Tsar, as he had seen it previously, but a means of transition to self-government by the people.[33]

The Prince's wartime progress along the path of political radicalization was common among the liberal propertied classes. The *union sacrée* of August 1914, when the Duma dissolved itself in a symbolic gesture of patriotic solidarity with the government, had not lasted the winter. The shells crisis and the Miasoyedov scandal saw to that. In fact neither had been as bad in reality as the public perceived them to be — Miasoyedov was no more a German spy than the shortage of shells was solely to blame for the country's military setbacks — yet in a sense that was their real point. For both the shortage of shells and Miasoyedov's tainted reputation became emotive symbols of the regime's treacherous and incompetent handling of the war. 'Respectable Russia' now rallied behind the growing demand for the reconvocation of the Duma and a Ministry which enjoyed public confidence. Miliukov's Kadets were prepared to settle for a three-day Duma session at the end of January to approve the military budget. But the radicals, led by Kerensky, continued the campaign of public criticism. On 11 June Miasoyedov's patron, Sukhomlinov, was finally forced out of office. The disgraced War Minister was summarily arrested and brought before a High Commission of Enquiry, which sentenced him to imprisonment in the Peter and Paul Fortress as a traitor. The dismissal of Maklakov (Interior), Shcheglovitov (Justice) and Sabler (Holy Synod) soon followed, as Nicholas tried to pacify growing public opposition by ditching his most reactionary ministers.

But this was only the start of a summer of political retreat for the Tsar. Calls for reform by the Duma and public organizations were soon joined by those from the liberal business community. The shells crisis and the military defeats of the spring forced the government to set up a Special Council for the Improvement of Artillery Supplies in June. It included three Octobrists from the Duma and the owners of Petrograd's biggest arms firms, as well as officials from the War Ministry. For the liberal business leaders of Moscow this was a slap in the face. Since 1908 they had campaigned aggressively to increase their role in the nation's economy and political life ('The merchant on the move,' as Riabushinsky put it). They had financed their own national newspaper (*Utro Rossii*), established their own political party (the Progressists) and lavishly spent money on the arts (the Tretyakov Gallery and Shekhtel's magnificent *style moderne* buildings, for example, were both commissioned by these industrialists) to advance their own Muscovite version of liberal Manchesterism. The Special Council, from their point of view, was a small coterie of the Petrograd industrial barons and their patrons in government (what would one day come under the title of a 'military-industrial complex') designed to exclude the smaller businesses in the provinces from the lucrative contracts for military production. There was much in the set-up to justify the resentment of the Moscow industrialists. Far too many orders were given to big Petrograd metal firms friendly to the government, while the smaller provincial firms were not properly used. The huge Putilov plant, for example, received 113 million roubles worth of orders for shells — far more than it could deliver on time — at a price six times higher than the average market price. Putilov used the cash to subsidize the loss-making parts of his business, including his own fabulous lifestyle, so that his company eventually went bankrupt and had to be sequestered by the state in 1916.

Medium-sized producers were meanwhile going out of business because, without government orders, they could not afford to buy fuel or raw materials. The Petrograd bureaucracy was indifferent to their fate, as one businessman discovered when he wrote to the War Ministry offering the services of his family factory. A few weeks later he received his letter back with a short note saying it had not been furnished with the required government stamp.

To break down the monopoly of the big munitions producers Moscow's business leaders organized the War Industries Committees. Through their central office, established in July 1915, they succeeded in winning a modest but life-saving share of the government's military orders for their provincial firms. But the committees' real significance was less economic than political. The leaders of the Central War Industries Committees were all liberal critics of the autocracy. Half the ministers of the First Provisional Government of 1917 were to come from their ranks. They sought a greater voice for themselves in the wartime regulation of industry, and more say for their allies in the Duma and other public organizations in the structure of government. There were close connections between these different bodies. Lvov, for example, was the head of the Zemstvo Union, an ex-Duma deputy and a member of the Central War Industries Committee. Through their combined initiatives, these public bodies were able to form an effective political force. They enjoyed the support of several of the more liberal-minded ministers, who had come to realize the need for political change, as well as a number of senior generals, such as Brusilov, who knew from experience the value of their work.[34] Together they embarked on a struggle for power.

Under growing pressure, the Tsar finally agreed to recall the Duma on 19 July 1915. The liberal opposition now had a platform on which to renew its demands for a ministry of national confidence. Two-thirds of the Duma deputies, from the moderate Right to the moderate Left, along with like-minded members of the State Council, formed themselves into a Progressive Bloc to consolidate this campaign. It was a 'tricoloured' union, as one of its members remarked, designed to wrap political reforms in the imperial flag. The Bloc's aim was to prevent the country slipping into revolution (which its well-to-do members feared as much as anyone else) by persuading the Tsar to appoint a new government capable of winning the people's support. Only this, they argued, could lead the country to victory. After four months of unrelieved gloom, with daily reports of defeats at the Front, industrial strikes and growing social chaos, the leaders of the Bloc saw their programme, with some justification, as the last real chance for the regime to find a political solution to its crisis of authority. They bent over backwards to make their proposals acceptable to the Tsar. The calls of the more radical elements — the left-wing Kadets, Kerensky's Trudoviks and the socialists — for a parliamentary government responsible to the Duma were flatly opposed by Miliukov, the Kadet leader and principal architect of the Bloc, despite the risk he thus ran of splitting his party in two. Lvov even pledged that during the war the Bloc would go no further 'on the path of a parliamentary struggle' once a government of confidence had been appointed.[35]

Within the Council of Ministers there was a growing majority in favour of a compromise with the Progressive Bloc. Krivoshein and Polivanov, Sukhomlinov's replacement, led the way. But eight others soon followed, especially after the Tsar had announced his decision to take over the military command, thus leaving the government to the mercy of the Tsarina and Rasputin. On 28 August the 'revolt of the ministers' came to a head with a direct appeal to the Tsar to appoint a new ministry enjoying the confidence of the Duma. Only 'the old man' Goremykin, the discredited Premier, refused to join the demands for reform, blindly convinced to the end of his absolute duty to obey the Tsar. The next day he hurried to Mogilev and urged Nicholas to close down the Duma and sack his disobedient ministers in order to reassert his autocratic power. The Tsarina, who had always believed in her husband's mission to rule 'like Ivan the Terrible', added her own voice, condemning the rebel ministers as 'fiends worse than the Duma' who 'needed smacking'.

It was not hard, by this stage, to convince the Tsar that he should reassert his autocratic authority. That, after all, had probably been his main objective in assuming the supreme command. As he saw it, none of his concessions to the liberal opposition had stemmed the public criticisms of his government, in fact they had only grown louder, and it was time to stop any further erosion of his authority. He deemed it intolerable that at this critical moment for the Empire, when the firm hand of autocracy was needed more than ever, his ministers should think fit to ask him to renounce his personal rule. On 2 September he ordered the dissolution of the Duma and reconfirmed his confidence in the government of his old and faithful servant, Goremykin. When the Premier returned to Petrograd and announced this decision to the Council of Ministers there was uproar. 'Il est fou, ce vieillard,' Sazonov, the Foreign Minister, was heard to say.[36]

There followed a two-day general strike in Petrograd against the Duma's closure. But otherwise the opposition's response was muted. Lvov was elected to lead a delegation of the public organizations to plead with the Tsar to 'place the heavy burden of power upon the shoulders of men made strong by the nation's confidence'. But Nicholas refused to receive them. They were summoned instead to the Ministry of the Interior where they were told that their 'intrusion into state politics' had been presumptuous. The Tsar had made up his mind to rule as an autocrat should, and no counsel, however wise or loyal, could make him change his mind. On 16 September the ministers were summoned to

Mogilev for a final dressing down. 'Show your fist,' the Tsarina had urged her weak-willed husband. 'You are the *Autocrat* and they dare not forget it.' She even implored him to comb his hair with Rasputin's comb in order to strengthen his will.[37] The magic must have worked. For the ministers, having come determined to argue their case for reform, lost their nerve when confronted by the Tsar. The 'revolt of the ministers' was over and the monarchy's final chance to save itself by political means had now been thrown away.

The dissolution of the Duma highlighted the liberals' impotence. Power lay firmly with the Romanov court and, even with ten of the highest government officials on their side, there was nothing, short of revolution, the liberals could do to prevent the Tsar from taking power into his own hands. The Kadet politician, V. A. Maklakov, summed up the liberals' dilemma in a widely quoted article in September. He compared Russia to an automobile being driven down a steep and dangerous hill at uncontrollable speed by a mad chauffeur (Nicholas). Among the passengers there are one's mother (Russia) plus competent drivers, who recognize that they are being driven to inevitable doom. But no one dares grab the steering wheel for fear of causing a fatal accident. The chauffeur knows this and mocks the helplessness and anxiety of the passengers: 'You will not dare touch me,' he tells them. And, indeed, in these terrible circumstances, Maklakov concluded:

> you will not dare touch him, for even if you might risk your own life, you
> are travelling with your mother, and you will not dare endanger your life
> for fear that she too might be killed. So you will leave the steering wheel
> in the hands of the chauffeur. Moreover, you will try not to hinder him —
> you will even help him with advice, warning and assistance. And you will
> be right, for this is what has to be done.[38]

The liberals' paralysis was determined, above all, by their fear of sparking violence on the streets. They were caught between the devil of autocracy and the deep red sea of a social revolution that would undoubtedly drown them too. Miliukov was afraid that if the Duma went into open conflict with the regime and encouraged a popular revolt, as some on the left of his party advocated, it would lead to an 'orgy of the mob'.[39] Pushkin's nightmare of the 'Russian riot, senseless and without mercy' would finally come to pass. Rather than risk this, the liberals played a waiting game: if they could hold out until an Allied victory, new channels for reform would open up. It was not the most dignified stance (a 'revolt on their knees' is how Stalin described it) but, short of moving to the barricades, there was little more that they could do. Essentially, it marked a return to the position of 1906, when the failure of the Vyborg Manifesto to rally the masses in the defence of the Duma had left the liberals high and dry, with nothing more to cling to than the hope of persuading the regime to liberalize itself. Ten years later, with the lessons of Vyborg behind them, they were even more frightened of the masses, who now were hardly more likely — at the height of the war with all its hardships — to limit themselves to the narrow political revolution envisaged by the liberals.

Encouraged by the success of his own show of strength, Nicholas followed it up with a series of further measures to roll back the liberal challenge to his autocracy. The promised Duma session in November, granted to appease the critics of its prorogation in September, was postponed indefinitely. The status of the War Industries Committees was gradually downgraded as the government returned to its old alliance with the big business interests of Petrograd. And, one by one, the main rebel ministers were dismissed. Samarin, the new Procurator of the Holy Synod and a prominent critic of Rasputin, was the first to be forced out, much to the fury of the Church and conservative opinion. Krivoshein, the Agriculture Minister, followed soon after. Next Shcherbatov, the Interior Minister, was replaced by Khvostov, an ally of Rasputin's, distinguished only by the huge size of his belly, who immediately pledged to silence all public criticism of the government. He stepped up police surveillance of the Duma politicians, banned meetings of public organizations, tightened censorship and lavished government funds on the Black Hundred groups, which blamed the Jews for the army's defeats and all the ills of war.

In all these personnel changes the Tsarina's hand was at work. With the Tsar at the Front, she now became the real autocrat (in so far as there was one) in Petrograd. 'Lovy,' she wrote to her husband, 'I am your wall in the rear. I am here, don't laugh at silly old wify, but she has "trousers" on unseen.' The main telephone in the Winter Palace was in her drawing-room, where she sat at her writing desk before a portrait of Marie Antoinette. She liked to boast that she was the first woman in Russia to receive government ministers since Catherine the Great, and in these delusions she was encouraged by Rasputin, who effectively used her as a mouthpiece for his own pretensions to power. Her letters to Nicholas were filled with advice from 'Our Friend', as she liked to call the 'holy' peasant. 'It's not my wisdom', she would write, 'but a certain instinct given by God beyond myself so as to be your help.' Or: 'We, who have been taught to look at all from another side see what the struggle here really is and means — you showing your mastery, proving yourself the Autocrat without which Russia cannot exist.' It seems there was almost no matter of state beyond Rasputin's expertise. She would write to the Tsar with his recommendations on food supply, transport, finance and land reform, although she herself admitted that such things made her own head spin. She even tried to persuade her husband to base his military strategy on what Rasputin had 'seen in the night', although here Nicholas put his foot down.[40]

Most of the Tsarina's ink was used on recommendations for appointments. She saw the world in terms of friends and enemies of the 'hidden cause' waged by Rasputin and herself. Ministers, commanders of the armed forces and members of the court all rose or fell in her favour according to where they stood in relation to the 'cause'. The patronage of Rasputin was the quickest way up the greasy pole — and criticism of him the quickest way down. In the seventeen months of the 'Tsarina's rule', from September 1915 to February 1917, Russia had four Prime Ministers, five Ministers of the Interior, three Foreign Ministers, three War Ministers, three Ministers of Transport and four Ministers of Agriculture. This 'ministerial leapfrog', as it came to be known, not only removed competent men from power, but also disorganized the work of government since no one remained long enough in office to master their responsibilities. Bureaucratic anarchy developed with competing chains of authority: some ministers would defer to the Tsarina or Rasputin, while others remained loyal to the Tsar, or at least to what they thought the Tsar was, although when it came to the crunch he never seemed to know what he stood for and in any case never really dared to oppose his wife. Boris Stürmer, the longest-lasting Prime Minister of the 'Tsarina's rule', who replaced the senile Goremykin in January 1916, was best known as a provincial governor who had been accused of venality, and as an Assistant Minister of Interior who had been charged with incompetence. In Sazonov's memorable phrase, he was 'a man who had left behind a bad memory wherever he had occupied an administrative post'. The affairs of state proved utterly beyond him. He ran to the Tsarina and Rasputin so often for advice that even the extreme monarchist V. M. Purishkevich began to compare this ridiculous figure to Chichikov in Gogol's *Dead Souls*, who, after calling on all the dignitaries of the provincial town, sat for a long time in his carriage wondering who to visit next.[41]

* * *

Perhaps the most damaging change of personnel was the dismissal of Polivanov in March 1916. More than any other man he was responsible for the rebuilding of the Russian army after the terrible losses of the Great Retreat. Major-General Knox, the British military attaché in Russia, thought him 'undoubtedly the ablest military organizer in Russia' and called his dismissal 'a disaster'. Polivanov's crime, in the eyes of the Tsarina, had been his readiness to work with the public organizations in improving army supplies. 'Oh, how I wish you could get rid of Polivanov,' she wrote to her husband in January. 'He is simply a revolutionist.' His friendship with Guchkov, head of the War Industries Committees, was seen by the court with special alarm, since in November the Octobrist leader had invited elected workers' representatives to sit with him on the committees' central governing body. 'I wish you could shut up that rotten war industries committee', the Tsarina implored her husband in March, 'as they prepare simply anti-dynastic questions for their meetings.' As for Guchkov, she asked, 'Could one not hang him?'[42]

The appointment of General Shuvaev, Polivanov's successor, proved beyond doubt that unthinking obedience was now deemed far more important for a Minister of War than military expertise. Shuvaev himself once told Knox that if the Tsar ordered him to jump from the window he would gladly oblige. And when his gross mismanagement of the war led to growing public charges of 'treason in high places', all he could honestly say in self-defence was 'I may be a fool, but I am no traitor.'[43]

With the help of the public organizations Polivanov had greatly improved the supply and morale of the army. Nowhere was this more apparent than on the South-Western Front, where Brusilov had been appointed the Front commander in March. He brought in a new style of military professionalism to the Front headquarters, promoting talented officers such as Klembovsky and Velichko (who along with Brusilov and Polivanov himself would later help inject a similar professionalism into the Red Army). Brusilov was quick to establish a good working relationship with the public organizations, and the effects of this were soon felt on his Front. 'Little by little', he recalled:

> our technical equipment improved; rifles were supplied, of various types perhaps, but anyhow with a sufficiency of cartridges; while ammunition for the artillery, especially the light guns, arrived in abundance ... We had every cause to reckon on being able to defeat the enemy and drive him across our frontier.[44]

Brusilov's optimism marked him out at the Council of War on 15 April, when Russia's Front commanders met with the Tsar at Stavka to plan out the summer's operations. Generals Kuropatkin and Evert, commanders of the North-Western and Western Fronts respectively, were pessimistic about the prospects for an offensive. But Brusilov promised to make things easier for them by launching an attack against the Austrians on his own South-Western Front, despite being warned that no extra men or supplies would be spared from the north. The other commanders were shocked and annoyed by his boldness. 'You have only just been appointed Front commander,' one of them told him as they sat down to dinner, 'and you are lucky enough not to be one of those picked out to take the offensive, and so aren't called upon like them to risk your military reputation. Fancy rushing into such colossal dangers!' But this complacent attitude, so typical of the Tsar's favourite generals, was a long way from Brusilov's own determination and, perhaps naive, optimism. He was sure that God was leading Russia to victory, a faith reflected throughout the war in his letters to his wife. 'I remain convinced', he wrote to her at the height of the Great Retreat, 'that somehow things will work out and we will win the war.'[45]

Nor did the scorn of Brusilov's colleagues take into account the sheer ingenuity of his tactics, which were set to make his offensive, in the words of Norman Stone, the main historian of the Eastern Front, 'the most brilliant victory of the war'.[46] What distinguished Brusilov's military genius was his willingness to learn from the tactical lessons of 1914–15. Ever since the Fronts had become fixed and the war of mobility had given way to the war of position, Europe's generals had attempted to break through the enemy lines by concentrating men and munitions at a single point of the Front. The German breakthrough at Gorlice was a classic example of this 'phalanx' method, which Russia's generals slavishly followed thereafter. Brusilov was the one exception. He argued that the Russians, with their primitive railways, could not hope to concentrate their forces in one place without the enemy learning of it with plenty of time to bring up defensive reserves. As long as the element of surprise continued to be sacrificed on the altar of strength, Russia could not hope to gain a decisive breakthrough. He proposed instead to attack simultaneously at several points along the Front, thus making it difficult for the enemy, even with intelligence of the offensive positions, to guess where defensive reserves would be needed most.

Intensive preparations were made for the offensive. Nothing quite like it had ever been seen before. The key to Brusilov's plan was surprise, so everything was done to safeguard secrecy (even the Tsarina could not find out when or where the attack would begin). Offensive trenches were dug deeper than usual and camouflaged by a novel device of spraying the ground with paint. Assault tunnels were built under the Austrian barbed wire to within a hundred yards of their lines, so that when the assault was launched the first wave of attackers could reach their trenches in one rush. The enemy's positions were carefully studied with the benefit of aerial photography. This enabled Brusilov to build full-scale models of the Austrian trenches and train his assault troops on them. It also meant that when the offensive began the Russians knew the precise location of the Austrian batteries and, in some places, even of individual machine-guns. Despite its inferior numbers, the Russian artillery thus had the one decisive advantage of knowing its targets, and this was to ensure the offensive's initial success.[47]

The offensive began on 4 June, in Brusilov's words, 'with a thunderous artillery barrage all along the South-Western Front'. 'The entire zone of battle was covered by a huge, thick cloud of dust and smoke,' an Austrian officer wrote, which 'allowed the Russians to come over the ruined wire-obstacles in thick waves and into our trenches.' Within forty-eight hours the Russians had broken through the Austrian defences along a fifty-mile front, capturing more than

40,000 prisoners. By day nine the number had risen to 200,000 men, more than half the Habsburg forces on the Eastern Front, and Conrad, the Austrian Chief of Staff, was starting to talk of the need to sue for peace.[48]

If Evert and Kuropatkin had followed up Brusilov's advance with their own promised attacks on the Western and North-Western Fronts, the enemy might have been pushed back and the course of the war changed entirely. Hindenburg later confessed that with a second offensive, 'We [would have been] faced with the menace of a complete collapse.' According to the original war plan, Brusilov's Front was considered secondary to both Evert's and Kuroptakin's. Yet neither of them was prepared to attack. To be fair, their task would have been much harder than Brusilov's. For they would have had to fight the German troops, which were much stronger than the Austro-Hungarian forces whom Brusilov had overcome on the South-Western Front. But their vanity was also a factor: the increased risk of defeat made them all the more afraid of losing their own precious reputations. Perhaps the real blame lay with Stavka. Alexeev had served under Kuropatkin and Evert during the Japanese War and was still too frightened of them to force them to attack. The Tsar also indulged the cowardly generals — they were the favourites of his court — and ignored Brusilov's daily requests to order an offensive. The Tsarina was partly behind this. She bombarded her indecisive husband with Rasputin's 'expert' advice against an offensive in the north 'because', in his words, 'if our successes in the south continue, then they [the Germans] will themselves retreat in the north'.[49]

Such military stupidity was largely to blame for the slow-down of Brusilov's advance. Instead of starting a second offensive Stavka transferred troops from the north to Brusilov's Front. They were not enough to maintain the momentum of his offensive, however, since the Germans, with their position eased by the inactivity of Evert and Kuropatkin, were also able to transfer reinforcements to the south. Conscious of his declining advantage, Brusilov now reverted to orthodox tactics, advancing towards Kovel but fighting, in his own words, 'at a lower pressure . . . to spare my men as far as possible'. Slowly but surely, the Russian advance was grinding to a halt. In eight weeks of fighting Brusilov's armies had captured 425,000 men and a large part of Galicia; the enemy had been forced to withdraw troops from the Western Front, thus relieving pressure on Italy and the French at Verdun; while Romania, for what it was worth, was at last persuaded to join the war on the side of the Russians. Ludendorff called it 'the crisis in the East'. In 1918 he would pay the ultimate compliment to Brusilov's tactics by using them himself on the Western Front.[50]

Coming as it did after a long year of defeat in the east, and of bloody stalemate in the west, Brusilov's offensive turned him overnight into a hero not just in Russia but throughout the Allied countries. Giliarovsky wrote a collection of panegyric poems 'To Brusilov' which sold in their tens of thousands in leaflet form. French and Italian composers dedicated cantatas, marches and songs to the war hero. And throughout Europe people flocked to see the film called *Brusilov*. The General himself later wrote:

> I received hundreds of telegrams congratulating and blessing me from every class of Russian society. Everyone would have his say; peasants, mechanics, aristocrats, the clergy, the intelligentsia, and the children in the schools, all wanted to let me know that the great heart of the country was beating in sympathy with the well-loved soldiers of my victorious armies.

Brusilov had shown that under competent commanders the imperial army was still capable of military success. Had it not been undermined by Stavka, his offensive might have served as the springboard for the restoration of the army's morale — perhaps even one day leading towards its eventual victory. But it is doubtful whether even this would have been enough to save the tsarist regime, such was the extent of the political crisis in the country at large. In any case, with the failure of the offensive it now became clearer than ever, even to a monarchist like Brusilov, that, in his own words, 'Russia could not win the war with its present system of government.'[51] Victory would not stop the revolution; but only a revolution could help bring about victory.

For Brusilov the final damning proof of the old regime's incompetence had come at the start of July, when Alexeev transferred the élite Imperial Guards to his Front in a last desperate bid to save the offensive. These young blue-bloods were described by Knox as 'physically the finest human animals in Europe'. In their dark-green parade uniforms, trimmed with golden braid, each guard stood over six feet tall. But they came with a gormless commander, General Bezobrazov, another favourite of the court, who disobeyed Brusilov's orders and sent them into attack through an exposed swamp. As the warriors waded chest-high through the mud, the German planes flew overhead, raking them with their machine-guns. Knox watched in horror as the planes swooped down to hit their targets and 'the wounded sank slowly into the marsh'.[52] In one stupid action the core of the country's finest fighting force had been lost, and with it the final chance of victory under the old regime.

*   *   *

Brusilov's impatience with the government was increasingly shared by the rest of society as 1916, the third long year of the war, dragged on. Patriotic nobles like Brusilov and Lvov had hoped that a successful war campaign would bring the government and society together and thus forestall the need for radical reforms. They now realized that the opposite was true: radical reforms were a necessary precondition for military success. The growing shortages of food, fuel and basic household goods, the rapid inflation of prices, the breakdown of transport, the widespread corruption of the government and its military suppliers, and the steep increase in crime and social disorder — all these combined with the endless slaughter of the war to create a growing sense of public panic and hysteria. 'More and more', Gorky wrote to a friend in November 1915, 'people are behaving like animals and madmen. They spread stupid rumours and this creates an atmosphere of universal fear which poisons even the intelligent.' Among the propertied classes there was a general feeling that Russia was on the brink of a terrible catastrophe, a violent social explosion, against which the government was totally unprepared to defend them. People spoke of the Tsar and his government with open contempt. The word 'revolution' was on everybody's lips. 'A deluge is approaching,' Guchkov wrote to Alexeev in August 1916, 'and a pitiful, wretched and flabby Government is preparing to face that cataclysm by taking measures only good enough to protect oneself from a shower. It puts on galoshes and opens an umbrella!'[53]

Sensing the coming disaster, the rich and the high-born lost themselves in a last desperate binge of personal pleasure. They drank their stocks of champagne, spent huge sums of money on black-market caviar, sturgeon and other peacetime delicacies, threw lavish parties, deceived their wives and husbands and gambled away fortunes in casinos. Foreigners were shocked by their luxurious lifestyles and, even more so, by the indiscretion with which they flaunted their enjoyment. 'Their wealth and the lavish use they made of it dazzled me after the austere conditions of wartime life in England,' wrote Sir Samuel Hoare, the British intelligence officer in Petrograd. This hysterical hedonism was best expressed in some anonymous satirical verses of early 1916:

> We do not take defeat amiss,
> And victory gives us no delight
> The source of all our cares is this:
> Can we get vodka for tonight.

> The victories we can do without.
> No! Peace and quiet is our line,
> Intrigues and scandal, evenings out
> Trimmed up with women and with wine.

> We only want to know, next day
> What Ministers will be on view,
> Or who takes who to see the play,
> Or who at Cuba's sat next who: . . .

And does Rasputin still prevail
Or do we need another saint,
And is Kshesinskaya quite well,
And how the feast at Shubin's went:

If the Grand Duke took Dina home,
What kind of luck MacDiddie had —
Oh, if a Zeppelin would come.
And smash the whole of Petrograd.[54]

Much of the public hysteria was focused on the court, where a pro-German clique around the Tsarina was widely believed to be conspiring to bring about Russia's defeat. The idea of treason in high places, which started with the Miasoyedov affair and the Great Retreat, gained momentum in 1916 as rumours spread of the existence of a 'Black Bloc' at court, which was said to be seeking a separate peace with Berlin. The growing domination of the Tsarina (the 'German woman'), the anti-war sentiments of Rasputin, the large number of German names at the court, and the Tsar's promotion of Stürmer to the status of a virtual 'dictator' (by June he had assumed the powers of Prime Minister, Minister of the Interior, Foreign Minister and Supreme Minister for State Defence) all helped to fuel speculation. It was widely claimed that the Tsarina and Rasputin were working for the Germans; that they had a direct line to Berlin; and that Nicholas regularly warned his uncle, the Kaiser Wilhelm, of the movements of his troops. Such rumours became even more distorted by the time they reached the Front. Judging from their letters home, demoralized soldiers were prepared to believe that Stürmer had been paid by the Germans to starve the peasants to death; and that Count Fredericks, the Minister of the Imperial Court, had agreed to sell the western half of Russia to the enemy.

Similar credence was given to rumours of various sexual scandals surrounding the Tsarina. Alexandra's 'sexual corruption' became a kind of metaphor for the diseased condition of the tsarist regime. She was said to be a slut, the mistress of Rasputin and the lesbian lover of Anna Vyrubova, her lady-in-waiting, who was said to share her bed with Rasputin and the Tsar. None of these rumours had any basis in fact. Vyrubova was a naive and dim-witted spinster, infatuated with the mystical powers of Rasputin and the cosy domestic lifestyle of the imperial family. In 1917 she was medically certified to be a virgin by a special commission appointed by the Provisional Government to examine the charges against her. As for the Tsarina, she was much too strait-laced to indulge in any sexual act that was not strictly necessary for the reproduction of the dynasty. Nor was there any foundation to the charges of treason against her, although it is possible that German agents picked up information from Rasputin's loud and boastful talk. He regularly dined at the house of a Petrograd banker whom the French Ambassador believed to be the leading German agent in Russia.

The point of these rumours was not their truth or untruth, but their power to mobilize an angry public against the dynasty. In a revolutionary crisis it is perceptions and beliefs that count rather than realities. The demonization of the Romanov court enabled its opponents to point the finger of blame at conspicuous culprits for the people's wartime hardships. Condemning the court as 'German' was a way of defining and legitimizing this revolutionary anger as the patriotic mood of 'the nation', as if all the country's problems were due to the evil influence of a few highly placed foreigners and could be solved by getting rid of them. The February Revolution of 1917 was identified as a patriotic revolution. Anti-German and anti-monarchist attitudes were closely interwoven in the new democratic consciousness which February's leaders sought to cultivate as the basis for Russia's national renewal. In this sense the anti-German riots of June 1915, at the height of the Great Retreat, were the first sign of an upswing in the popular revolutionary mood. Angry Moscow mobs burned and looted German shops and offices. Piano stores were attacked and Bechsteins and Blüthners hurled from the windows. Anyone suspected of being German (which often meant no more than being well dressed) was attacked and robbed. In Red Square crowds shouted insults at the 'German woman' and called for her to be shut up in a convent. There were also calls for the Tsar to abdicate in favour of the Grand Duke Nikolai. The hysterical public was determined to see German sabotage in everything, from the shortage of shells to the corruption of minor officials, and by raising the battle-cry of 'treason in high places' the new pretenders to power became popular national heroes.[55]

It was difficult for the liberals, despite their fear of the masses, to resist this opportunity for political gain. By speaking for 'the nation' against the dynasty they might place themselves once again at the head of the opposition movement. This seemed increasingly important now that the protests against the war and its economic hardships were taking a more radical form, with mass strikes and demonstrations, many of them led by the socialists. 'I am afraid', one Kadet leader told his colleagues in the autumn of 1916, 'that the policy of the government will lead to a situation in which the Duma will be powerless to do anything for the pacification of the masses.' The reports of the secret police made it clear that 'the broad mass of the people' were becoming increasingly hostile to the Duma and were accusing it 'of deliberately refusing to come to the aid of the masses; the most bitter accusations in this respect are levelled not only at the Octobrists, but at the Kadets too'. If the Duma was to avoid becoming obsolete and ineffective, it would have to move closer to the mood of the streets and add its own voice to the revolutionary movement. That was the view of the left Kadets, of Kerensky's Trudoviks, and of a growing number of public figures, including Prince Lvov, who told a meeting of the Progressive Bloc that Russia's only hope of salvation lay in a revolution. 'Abandon all further attempts at constructive collaboration with the present government,' he wrote in December; 'they are all doomed to failure and are only an impediment to our aim. Do not indulge in illusion; turn away from ghosts. There is no longer a government we can recognize.'[56]

Such arguments were strengthened by the continued intransigence of the regime. The appointment in September of A.D. Protopopov as acting Minister of the Interior had raised the hopes of the moderate liberals, men like Miliukov, who still sought to win reforms from the government through conciliation. Protopopov was an Octobrist landowner and textile manufacturer, a member of the Progressive Bloc, and Deputy Chairman of the Duma. His appointment was widely seen as government capitulation to the liberal opposition — one soon to be followed by the appointment of a Duma ministry. But in fact it was no more than a clever political manœuvre by the court. The Duma was due to convene on I November and Protopopov, as a 'Duma man', was seen as the best man to control it. 'Please take Protopopov as Minister of the Interior,' the Tsarina had urged her husband. 'As he is one of the Duma it will make a great effect and shut their mouths.' Protopopov was a fanatical mystic (he once told Kerensky that he ruled with the help of Jesus Christ) and, unknown to the liberals, a protégé of Rasputin (who, as he once told Brusilov, was 'saving Russia from a revolution'). He was ambitious and ridiculously vain — he was clearly overwhelmed by the honour bestowed on him by the Tsar — and was thus unlikely to endanger his own position by making common cause with the opposition. When the real nature of his role became clear — he soon donned the uniform of the Imperial Gendarmerie, an archetypal symbol of tsarist oppression — an old Duma colleague begged him to resign. Protopopov replied: 'How can you ask me to resign? All my life it was my dream to be a Vice-Governor, and here I am a Minister.'[57]

Disillusionment with the new minister set in very quickly. Hope gave way to hatred in Duma circles. Protopopov's obsequiousness to the imperial couple was nauseating. Instead of providing a bridge between the liberal opposition and the government he turned himself into a lackey of the court and was roundly condemned as a traitor to the parliamentary cause. On Rasputin's request, he ordered Sukhomlinov's release from prison — most of the country would have had him hanged for treason — and banned public organizations from meeting without the police in attendance.

By the time the Duma reassembled, on I November, even the moderate Miliukov was finally forced to acknowledge that the time for co-operation with the government was rapidly passing. With the radicals in his own Kadet party calling for open revolt, he now decided to seize the initiative by condemning the government in his opening speech to the Duma. He listed its abuses of power, denouncing each in turn and ending each time with the question: 'Is this folly or treason?' The effect of his speech, as Miliukov later recalled, was 'as if a blister filled with pus had burst and the basic evil, which was known to everyone but had awaited public exposure, had now been pinpointed'. He succeeded in turning the Tauride Palace into the Tribune of the Revolution once again. There were other more fiery speeches in the Duma that day — from Kerensky, for example — but the fact that a statesman as cautious as Miliukov, and one, moreover, with such close connections to Allied diplomats, had openly used the word 'treason' was enough for the public to conclude that treason there had been. This had not been Miliukov's aim. To his own rhetorical question he himself would have answered 'folly'. Yet the public was so charged up with emotion that by the time it read his speech it was almost bound to answer 'treason'. The fact that the speech was banned from the press and had to be read in well-thumbed typescripts passed from hand to hand only further inclined people to read it as being more radical than it was. In some versions of the typescript a particular social grievance would appear inserted into the middle of the speech (for example, claiming that in addition to its other abuses the government treated teachers very badly). 'My speech acquired the reputation of a storm-signal for the revolution,' Miliukov recalled. 'Such was not my intention. But the prevailing mood in the country served as a megaphone for my words.'[58] It was to be a salutary lesson for any future liberals — especially those of 1917 — trying to halt a social revolution by the power of words. Having stoked up his rhetoric in order to help his Duma colleagues let off steam, Miliukov had succeeded in firing the engines of radical protest in the country at large.

What Miliukov had failed to appreciate was the extent to which a revolution had now come to be seen as unstoppable, and even desirable, not just by the radicals but by conservatives too. His own strategy of conciliation and parliamentary struggle, with the aim of reaching a compromise with the government, was rapidly losing ground. As one general at Stavka remarked, there was a 'widespread conviction that something had to be broken and annihilated, a conviction that tormented people and gave them no peace'.[59] Even the Tsar's immediate family were now lining up behind the liberal opposition. On 7 November the Grand Duke Nikolai urged him to let the Duma appoint a government. The Moscow and Petrograd branches of the United Nobility, since 1905 the firmest pillar of the autocracy, gave him similar advice. In short, there was practically no one outside the narrow ruling clique at the court who did not see the need for a fundamental change in the structure of the government.

Yet again Nicholas tried to manœuvre himself out of a corner by making half-hearted concessions. On 8 November Stürmer was dismissed, to the Duma's rejoicing, and A. F. Trepov became the new Prime Minister. Here was a final chance for the liberals to make their peace with the government. For Trepov, who saw himself as a latter-day Stolypin, was determined to win the support of the moderate elements in the Duma by making concessions. Miliukov was ready to accept his olive branch (and no doubt a seat in his cabinet). But the radical and socialist deputies, spurred on by the inflammatory speeches of the Trudovik Kerensky and the Menshevik Nikolai Chkheidze, were determined to bring down the government and called for an alliance with 'the masses' in preparation for a popular revolt.

This was essentially how the Duma remained divided through the following weeks of complex political manœuvring between November and the February Revolution. Miliukov's Kadets, in the words of the secret police, looked on the prospect of a revolution 'with feelings of horror and panic', and 'if the government offered the slightest concession would run to meet it with joy'. Yet the hope of concessions was fading fast. For the Tsarina was flatly opposed to Trepov (she wanted him hanged like Guchkov), while the threat of the radical left was growing all the time. This increasingly gave the initiative to Kerensky and the other Duma radicals, who would open the doors of the Tauride Palace, if not directly to the crowds on the streets, then at least to their more polite representatives. The language of their speeches became increasingly violent, as they sought to express — and thus capture — the mood on the streets. They openly called on the people to overthrow the regime and ridiculed the moderates' calls for calm as a pretext, in the words of Kerensky, to stay in their 'warm armchairs'. Yet they also had cause to worry that the popular mood was passing over their heads too, that the crowds on the streets were becoming contemptuous of the Duma and looking elsewhere for their leaders. For as Vasilii Shulgin, the Nationalist leader, put it, 'no one believes in words any longer'.[60]

From now on it was a question of whether the revolution would start from below or above. The idea of a 'palace coup' had been circulating for some time. Guchkov was at the centre of one such conspiracy. It aimed to seize the imperial train *en route* from Stavka to Tsarskoe Selo and to force the Tsar to abdicate in favour of his son, with the Grand Duke Mikhail, Nicholas's brother, serving as Regent. In this way the conspirators hoped to forestall the social revolution by appointing a new government of confidence. However, with only limited support from the military, the liberals and the imperial family, they put off the plans for their coup until March 1917 — by which time it was too late. A second conspiracy was meanwhile being hatched by Prince Lvov with the help of the Chief of Staff, General Alexeev. They planned to arrest the Tsarina and compel Nicholas to hand over authority to the Grand Duke Nikolai. Lvov would then be appointed as the Premier of a new government of confidence. Several

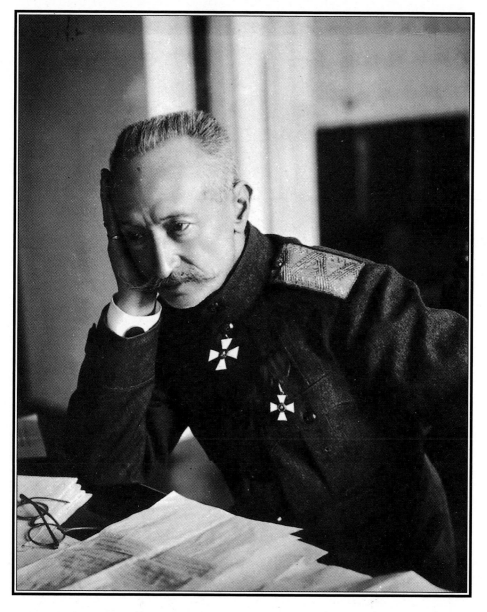

29 General Brusilov in 1917, shortly after his appointment as Commander-in-Chief of the Russian army. One of his subordinates described him as 'a man of average height with gentle features and a natural easy-going manner but with such an air of commanding dignity that, when one looks at him, one feels duty-bound to love him and at the same time to fear him'.

30 Maxim Gorky in 1917. 'It was impossible to argue with Gorky. You couldn't convince him of anything, because he had an astonishing ability: not to listen to what he didn't like, not to respond when a question was asked which he had no answer to' (Nina Berberova). It was no doubt this ability which enabled Gorky to live in Lenin's Russia.

31 Prince G. E. Lvov, democratic Russia's first Prime Minister, in March 1917. During his four months in office Lvov's hair turned white.

32 Sergei Semenov in 1917. The peasant activist was sufficiently well known in his native district of Volokolamsk to warrant this portrait.

33 Dmitry Os'kin (*seated centre*) with the Tula Military Commissariat in 1919. The story of his rise from the peasantry to the senior ranks of the Red Army was later told by Os'kin in two autobiographical volumes of 1926 and 1931. Like Kanatchikov's autobiography, they were part of the Soviet genre of memoirs by the masses.

34 Alexander Kerensky in 1917. This was just one of many portraits of Kerensky circulated to the masses in postcard form as part of the cult of his personality.

35 Lenin harangues the crowd, 1918. The photographer was Petr Otsup, one of the pioneers of the Soviet school of photo-journalism.

36 Trotsky in the Peter and Paul Fortress in 1906. Trotsky was a dapper dresser, even when in jail. Here, in the words of Isaac Deutscher, he looks more like 'a prosperous western European *fin-de-siècle* intellectual just about to attend a somewhat formal reception [than] a revolutionary awaiting trial in the Peter and Paul Fortress. Only the austerity of the bare wall and the peephole in the door offer a hint of the real background.'

37 Alexandra Kollontai in 1921, when she threw her lot in with the Workers'
Opposition. Kollontai's break with Lenin was especially significant because she had
been the only senior Bolshevik to support his *April Theses* from the start.

liberal politicians and generals supported the plan, including Brusilov, who told the Grand Duke: 'If I must choose between the Emperor and Russia, then I march for Russia.' But this plot was also scotched — by the Grand Duke's reluctance to become involved. There were various other conspiracies, some of them originating with the Tsar's distant relatives, to force an abdication in favour of some other Romanov capable of appeasing the Duma. Historians differ widely on these plots, some seeing them as the opening acts of the February Revolution, others as nothing but idle chit-chat. Neither is probably true. For even if the conspirators had been serious in their intentions, and had succeeded in carrying them out, they could hardly have expected to hold on to power for long before they too were swept aside by the revolution on the streets.[61]

The only plot to succeed was the murder of Rasputin. Several efforts had been made to remove him before. Khvostov had tried to have his former patron murdered after being dismissed as Minister of the Interior in January 1916. Trepov had offered him 200,000 roubles in cash to return to Siberia and keep out of politics. But the Tsarina had foiled both plans and, as a result, Rasputin's prestige at court had only risen further. It was this that had finally persuaded a powerful group of conspirators on the fringes of the court to murder Rasputin. The central figure in this plot was Prince Felix Yusupov, a 29-year-old graduate of Oxford, son of the richest woman in Russia, and, although a homosexual, recently married to the Grand Duchess Irina Alexandrovna, daughter of the Tsar's favourite sister. Two other homosexuals in the Romanov court — the Grand Duke Dmitry Pavlovich, a favourite nephew of the Tsar, and the Grand Duke Nikolai Mikhailovich — were also involved. Rasputin had become increasingly involved with the homosexual circles of the high aristocracy. He liked to 'lie with' men as much as with women. Yusupov had approached him after his wedding in the hope that he might 'cure' him from his sexual 'illness'. But Rasputin had tried to seduce him instead. Yusupov turned violently against him and, together with the Grand Dukes Dmitry and Nikolai, plotted his downfall. Along with their own homosexual vendetta (and perhaps in order to conceal it) they had grave political concerns which they voiced to the right-wing Duma leader and outspoken critic of Rasputin, V. M. Purishkevich, who joined them in their plot. They were outraged by Rasputin's influence on the Tsar and by the rumours that because of this Russia would sign a separate peace with Germany. They pledged to 'eliminate' Rasputin and to confine the Tsarina to a mental institution, naively believing that once the Tsar had been freed of their influence, he would see sense and turn himself into a good constitutional king.

Together the three conspirators planned to lure Rasputin to Yusupov's riverside palace on the pretext of meeting his beautiful wife, the Grand Duchess Irina. There they would kill him with poison and sink his body to the bottom of the Neva so that he would be counted as missing rather than dead. The plotters were anything but discreet: half the journalists of Petrograd seem to have known all the details of the murder days before it took place. It is frankly a miracle that, despite the plotters' immunity from police investigation, nothing was done to prevent them.

On the fatal day, 16 December, Rasputin was explicitly warned not to go to the Yusupov palace. He seems to have sensed his fate, for he spent most of the day destroying correspondence, depositing money in his daughter's account and praying. But the worldly attractions of the Grand Duchess Irina were too much for him to resist. Shortly after midnight he arrived in Yusupov's car smelling of cheap soap, his hair greased down and dressed in his most seductive clothes: black velvet trousers, squeaky leather boots and a white silk shirt with a satin-gold waistband given to him by the Tsarina. Yusupov showed his guest to a basement salon, claiming his wife was still entertaining guests in the main part of the palace and would join them later. Rasputin drank several poisoned glasses of his favourite sweet Madeira and helped himself to one or two cyanide-filled gâteaux. But over an hour later neither had taken effect and Yusupov, his patience exhausted, turned to desperate measures. Taking a Browning pistol from his writing desk upstairs, he rejoined the basement party, invited Rasputin to inspect a crystal crucifix standing on a commode, and, as the 'holy man' bent down to do so, shot him in the side. With a wild scream Rasputin fell to the floor. The conspirators presumed he was dead and went off to dispose of his overcoat. But meanwhile he regained consciousness and made his way to a side door that led into a courtyard and out on to the embankment. Purishkevich found him in the courtyard, staggering through the snow towards the outside gate, shouting, 'Felix, Felix, I will tell the Tsarina everything!' Purishkevich fired and missed him twice. But two more shots brought his victim down in a heap and, just to make sure that he was dead, Purishkevich kicked him in the temple. Weighed down with iron chains, Rasputin's corpse was driven to a remote spot of the city and dumped into the Neva, where it was finally washed up on 18 December. For several days thereafter, crowds of women gathered at the spot to collect the 'holy water' from the river sanctified by Rasputin's flesh.[62]

The news of Rasputin's murder was greeted with joy among aristocratic circles. The Grand Duke Dmitry was given a standing ovation when he appeared in the Mikhailovsky Theatre on the evening of 17 December. The Tsarina's sister, the Grand Duchess Elisaveta, wrote to Yusupov's mother offering prayers of thanks for her 'dear son's patriotic act'. She and fifteen other members of the imperial family pleaded with the Tsar not to punish Dmitry. But Nicholas rejected their appeal, replying that 'No one has the right to engage in murder.'[63] Dmitry was exiled to Persia. On special orders from the Tsar, no one was allowed to bid him farewell at the station, and the Grand Duchess Maria Pavlovna was put under house arrest for trying to.

Contrary to the intentions of the conspirators, Rasputin's death drew Nicholas closer to his grief-stricken wife. He was now more determined than ever to resist all advocates of reform. He even banished four dissident grand dukes from Petrograd. As the revolution drew nearer, he retreated more and more into the quiet life of his family at Tsarskoe Selo, cutting off all ties with the outside world and even the rest of the court. There was no customary exchange of gifts between the imperial couple and the Romanovs at the dynasty's final Christmas of 1916.

Rasputin's embalmed body was finally buried outside the palace at Tsarskoe Selo on a freezing January day in 1917. After the February Revolution a group of soldiers exhumed the grave, packed up the corpse in a piano case and took it off to a clearing in the Pargolovo Forest, where they drenched it with kerosene and burned it on top of a pyre. His ashes were scattered in the wind.

iii From the Trenches to the Barricades

Trotsky's boat sailed into New York harbour on a cold and rainy Sunday evening in January 1917. It had been a terrible crossing, seventeen stormy days in a small steamboat from Spain, and the revolutionary leader now looked haggard and tired as he disembarked on the quayside before a waiting crowd of comrades and pressmen. His mood was depressed. Expelled as an anti-war campaigner from France, his adopted home since 1914, he felt that 'the doors of Europe' had been finally 'shut behind' him and that, like his fellow passengers on board the *Montserrat*, a motley bunch of deserters, adventurers and undesirables forced into exile, he would never return. 'This is the last time', he wrote on New Year's Eve as they sailed past Gibraltar, 'that I cast a glance on that old *canaille* Europe.'[64]

It was a mark of the party's frustration that three of the leading Social Democrats — Trotsky, Bukharin and Kollontai — should find themselves together in New York, 5,000 miles from Russia, on the eve of the 1917 Revolution. Nikolai Bukharin had arrived from Oslo during the previous autumn and taken over the editorship of *Novyi mir* (New World), the leading socialist daily of the Russian émigré community. At the age of twenty-nine, he had already established himself as a leading Bolshevik theoretician and squabbled with Lenin on several finer points of party ideology, before leaving Europe with the claim that 'Lenin cannot tolerate any other person with brains.' Short and slight with a boyish, sympathetic face and a thin red beard, he was waiting for Trotsky on the quayside. Unlike the dogmatic Lenin, who had heaped abuse on the left-wing Menshevik, he was keen to include Trotsky in a broad socialist campaign against the war. He had known the Trotskys slightly in Vienna and shared their love for European culture. He greeted them with a bear hug and immediately began to tell them, as Trotsky's wife recalled, 'about a public library which stayed open late at night and which he proposed to show us at once'. Although it was late and the Trotskys were very tired, they were dragged across town 'to admire his great discovery'.[65] Thus began the close but ultimately tragic friendship between Trotsky and Bukharin.

Trotsky saw less of Alexandra Kollontai. She spent much of her time in the New Jersey town of Paterson, where her son had settled to avoid the military draft. This was her second American trip. The year before she had toured the country proselytizing Lenin's views on the war. An ebullient and emotional woman, prone to fall in love with young men and utopian ideas, she had thrown herself into the Bolshevik cause with all the fanaticism of the newly converted. 'Nothing was revolutionary enough for her,' recalled a Trotsky still bitter fourteen years later at her denunciation of him, in a letter to Lenin, as a waverer on the war.[66] Trotsky was closer to the Bolsheviks than Kollontai appreciated, and the motives for his leftward progression from the Mensheviks were similar to her own.

Like many of the exiled revolutionaries, Trotsky and Kollontai were both driven by their commitment to international socialism. Fluent in several European languages and steeped in classical culture, they saw themselves less as Russians — Kollontai was half-Finnish, half-Ukrainian, while Trotsky was a Jew — than as comrades of the international cause. They were equally at home in the British Museum, in the Bibliothèque Nationale in Paris, or in the cafés of Vienna, Zurich and Berlin, as they were in the underground revolutionary cells of St Petersburg. The Russian Revolution was for them no more than a part of the international struggle against capitalism. Germany, the home of Marx and Engels, was the intellectual centre of their world. 'For us', recalled Trotsky, 'the German Social Democracy was mother, teacher and living example. We idealized it from a distance. The names of Bebel and Kautsky were pronounced reverently.'[67]

But the German spell had been abruptly broken in August 1914. The Social Democrats rallied behind the Kaiser in support of the war campaign. For the leaders of the Russian Revolution, who thought of themselves as disciples of the European Marxist tradition, the 'betrayal of the Germans' was, as Bukharin put it, 'the greatest tragedy of our lives'. Lenin, then in Switzerland, had been so convinced of the German comrades' commitment to the international cause that he had at first dismissed the press reports of their support for the war as part of a German plot to deceive the socialists abroad. Trotsky, who had heard the news on his way to Zurich, was shocked by it 'even more than the declaration of war'. As for Kollontai, she had been present in the Reichstag to witness her heroes give their approval to the German military budget. She had watched in disbelief as they lined up one by one, some of them even dressed in army uniforms, to declare their allegiance to the Fatherland. 'I could not believe it,' she wrote in her diary that evening; 'I was convinced that either they had all gone mad, or else I had lost my mind.' After the fatal vote had been taken she had run out in distress into the lobby — only to be accosted by one of the socialist deputies who angrily asked her what a Russian was doing inside the Reichstag building. It had suddenly dawned upon her that the old solidarity of the International had been buried, that the socialist cause had been lost in chauvinism, and 'it seemed to me', she wrote in her diary, 'that all was now lost'.[68]

It was not just their European comrades who had abandoned the international cause. Most Russian socialists had also rallied to the cry of their Fatherland. The Menshevik Party, home and school of both Trotsky and Kollontai, was split between a large Defensist majority, led by the elderly Plekhanov, which supported the Tsar's war effort on the grounds that Russia had the right to defend itself against a foreign aggressor, and a small Internationalist minority, led by Martov, which favoured a democratic peace campaign. The SR Party was similarly divided, with the Defensists placing Allied military victory before revolution, and Internationalists advocating revolution as the only way to end what they saw as an imperialist war in which all the belligerents were equally to blame. These divisions were to cripple both parties during the crucial struggles for power in 1917. At their heart lay a fundamental difference of world-view between those, on the one hand, who acknowledged the legitimacy of nation states and the inevitability of conflict between them, and those, on the other, who placed class divisions above national interests. Feelings on this could run high. Gorky, for example, who considered himself an ardent Internationalist, broke off all relations with his adopted son, Zinovy Peshkov, when he volunteered for the French Legion. Gorky even refused to write to him when his hand was shot off whilst leading an attack on the German positions during his first battle.* To the patriots, the Internationalists' opposition to the war seemed dangerously close to helping the enemy. To the Internationalists, the patriots' call to arms

---

* Zinovy Peshkov (1884–1966) was the brother of Yakov Sverdlov, the Bolshevik leader and first Soviet President. After recovering from his wound, he enlisted in the French military intelligence. He supported Kornilov's movement against the Provisional Government. In 1918 he joined Semenov's anti-Bolshevik army in the Far East and then Kolchak's White government in Omsk. In 1920 he was sent to the Crimea as a French military agent in Wrangel's government and left Russia with Wrangel's army. He later became a close associate of Charles de Gaulle and a prominent French politician. What is strange is that until 1933 Peshkov maintained good relations with Gorky in Russia, and that Gorky knew about his intelligence activities. See Delmas, 'Légionnaire et diplomate'.

seemed tantamount to adopting the slogan 'Workers of the World, Seize Each Other by the Throat!'[69]

The Bolsheviks were the only socialist party to remain broadly united in their opposition to the war, although they too had their own defensists during the early days before Lenin had imposed his views. His opposition to the war was uncompromising. Unlike the Menshevik and SR Internationalists, who sought to bring the war to an end through peaceful demonstration and negotiation, Lenin called on the workers of the world to use their arms against their own governments, to end the war by turning it into a series of civil wars, or revolutions, across the whole of Europe. It was to be a 'war against war'.

For Trotsky and Kollontai, who had both come to see the Russian revolution as part of a European-wide struggle against imperialism, there was an iron logic at the heart of Lenin's slogan which increasingly appealed to their own left-wing Menshevik internationalism. To begin with, in the first year of the war, both had similar doubts about the Bolshevik leader. Whereas Lenin had argued that Russia's defeat would be a 'lesser evil' than that of the more advanced Germany, they opposed the whole idea of military victors and losers. The dispute, though minor in itself, related to a broader difference of opinion. Lenin had recently come to stress the revolutionary potential of nationalist movements within colonial systems, and he argued that Russia's defeat would help to bring about the collapse of the Tsarist Empire. But Trotsky and Kollontai (like Bukharin for that matter) believed that the nation-state would soon become a thing of the past and thus denied it as a revolutionary force. Nor could they quite yet bring themselves to embrace the Leninist call for a 'war against war'. They preferred the pacifist slogans of their old friends and allies among the Menshevik Internationalists. Neither Trotsky nor Kollontai was ready to cut loose from the Mensheviks, whose doubts about Lenin's rigid dogma on party organization they still shared. And while it was true that both were moving towards the Bolsheviks, they still harboured hopes of reuniting the two wings of the SD Party through a broad campaign for peace.

Trotsky had joined Martov in Paris in November 1914 and collaborated with him on *Nashe slovo* (*Our Word*), without doubt the most brilliant pacifist organ in Europe. He represented its views at the Zimmerwald Conference in September 1915, a secret gathering of thirty-eight Internationalists from various countries in a tiny mountain village outside Berne. Its rousing manifesto against the war, passed in opposition to Lenin's civil war resolution, was drawn up by Trotsky himself:

Working men and women! Mothers and fathers! Widows and orphans! Wounded and crippled! To all who are suffering from the war or in consequence of the war, we cry out, over the frontiers, over the smoking battlefields, over the devastated cities and hamlets: 'WORKERS OF THE WORLD UNITE!'[70]

By this stage, Kollontai had already thrown in her lot with Lenin. Her love affair with Alexander Shliapnikov, a handsome worker-Bolshevik twelve years her junior, no doubt had something to do with this. He had joined her in Stockholm in the autumn of 1914 and spent the rest of the war years running errands to Russia for Lenin. Yet perhaps it was not so much this romance as her own emotional commitment to the international cause and to ending the war at all costs that brought her under Lenin's spell. The war's oppressive influence was omnipresent. It seemed to be driving civilization to the edge of an abyss. 'So much blood is spilled, so many crimes are committed every day, every hour,' she wrote in her diary at Christmas 1915:

And the war — it rules over all. Unseen, it decides the fate of each one of us. Before it the individual will is powerless. It was precisely this feeling of helplessness in the face of the war, this sense of the war as an unstoppable force, that had overcome me from the very first days, when I was still in Berlin.

To Kollontai, only Lenin's call for an armed uprising seemed capable of bringing the war to an end. It alone held out the prospect of restoring the power of human will and action over objective forces. 'This is not just "analysis" ', she wrote of Lenin's war *Theses* in her diary. 'This is *action*. This is a political programme . . . Let the barricades answer the war.'[71]

For Trotsky, too, the stress that Lenin placed on the power of proletarian will and action gradually brought him closer to the Bolsheviks. Increasingly it appeared to him that his old friend and teacher Martov and the other Menshevik Internationalists had become trapped in their own analysis of objective conditions — which at that time were all working *against* the revolution — and that they had thus ignored the possibility of cultivating the revolutionary will (the 'subjective' side of the revolution) in order to overcome these. Through excessive study, the Mensheviks had turned themselves into the prisoners of their own social determinism. Their revolutionary slogans were in danger of becoming no more than phrases. What was called for was action, a 'proletarian revolution' across Europe to bring the war to an end. Martov had agreed with this to begin with, raising Trotsky's hopes of a broad anti-war campaign to reunite the left-wing Mensheviks with the Bolshevik Party. Yet by the autumn of 1915, when the Menshevik Defensists joined the war campaign, Martov had already pulled back from the call to arms and adopted more passive and pacifist views in line with the rest of his party. Now Trotsky had nowhere to go but leftwards. It was not, as he later pretended, a straightforward transition. He still harboured typically Menshevik doubts about Lenin's strict centralism and extremism. It was not until July 1917 that he finally joined the Bolshevik Party, and only then, as he put it, because the Bolsheviks were 'becoming less Bolshevik'. Yet he was moving slowly towards the Bolsheviks and surrounding himself with future Bolshevik leaders. All the main contributors to *Nashe slovo*, with the exception of Martov, were to align themselves with Lenin during 1917. Some became commissars in the first Soviet government, such as Kollontai (Social Welfare), Anatoli Lunacharsky (Enlightenment), Vladimir Antonov-Ovseenko (Military Affairs) and Trotsky himself (Foreign Affairs).[72]

For this reason, the trip to New York in 1917 and the collaboration with Bukharin and Kollontai was an important staging post in Trotsky's drift to the left. He rented a three-room apartment in the Bronx which, though cheap by American standards, gave him the unaccustomed luxuries of electric light, a chute for garbage and a telephone. Later there were legends that Trotsky had worked in New York as a dish-washer, as a tailor, and even as an actor. But in fact he scraped a living from émigré journalism and lecturing (in English and German) to half-empty halls on the need for a world revolution. He ate in Jewish delicatessens and made himself unpopular with the waiters by refusing to tip them on the grounds that it was injurious to their dignity. He bought some furniture on an instalment plan, $200 of which remained unpaid when the family left for Russia in the spring. By the time the credit company caught up with him, Trotsky had become Foreign Minister of the largest country in the world.[73]

✵   ✵   ✵

There was a fundamental division within the Bolshevik leadership, one scarcely noticed by historians, between those who spent the war years abroad and those who spent them in Russia. The exiles (e.g. Trotsky, Lunacharsky, Bukharin and Kollontai) tended to be more international and cosmopolitan in their outlook. Steeped in European culture, they were all too aware of Russia's relative backwardness. Many of them had once been Mensheviks, so they understood well the theoretical problems of trying to introduce socialism into Russia without a simultaneous revolution in the more advanced countries of the West. Those Bolsheviks, by contrast, who had spent the war years in Russia (e.g. Stalin and Dzerzhinsky) tended to adopt a more narrow outlook. Many of them came from non-intelligentsia backgrounds and few had any knowledge of Europe, its culture or its languages. Having spent the war in the underground organizations, in prisons, or in Siberian exile, they tended to emerge from it with a fortress-like, embattled mentality towards the party, the country and its relations with the outside world. Many of them harboured xenophobic attitudes — not least towards the Jewish intellectuals in the party (especially Trotsky). After February

1917 many of them implied in their speeches that the returning Bolshevik exiles (although conspicuously not Lenin) had been less than patriotic in the war. Here, in this clash between (if you will) the 'nativists' and the 'cosmopolitans', were the social roots of the party's ideological struggles of the 1920s between 'Socialism in one Country' and 'World Revolution'. It is no coincidence that all Stalin's main allies in his rise to power (Molotov, Voroshilov, Kaganovich, Kalinin, Kirov, Kuibyshev and Ordzhonikidze) had spent the war years in Russia itself; and that most of his victims in the party (Trotsky, Bukharin, Zinoviev, Antonov-Ovseenko) had spent them abroad.

While the revolutionary exiles debated ideology, their beleaguered comrades at home were concerned with more practical problems. Arrests, deportations and exile had crippled the Bolshevik Party in Russia (as well as the underground organizations of the Mensheviks and SRs). Orphaned by their leaders, and with their newspaper *Pravda* suppressed, the Bolshevik organizations had little to guide them. Shliapnikov maintained their last thin line of communication with Lenin, smuggling propaganda into Russia inside the soles of his shoes. It was like returning to the conspiratorial practices of the pre-1905 period. The Bolsheviks in Petrograd numbered fewer than 500 members, once the mass arrests of autumn 1914 had taken their toll. The provincial networks had only a handful of members each. The party's greatest weakness was its shortage of intellectual ability: according to Shliapnikov, there was no one in the capital capable of writing even a leaflet. But there was also the worrying problem of the workers' declining support, both in moral and financial terms, largely as a result of police surveillance and harassment. Trade unions and educational societies were outlawed and militant workers sent into the army. The arrest of five Bolshevik Duma deputies in November 1914 and their trial for sedition the following February evoked little protest from the mass of the workers. Some no doubt had succumbed to the dominant mood of patriotism. But most were afraid of dismissal or, worse, imprisonment, if they should join the 2,000 strikers who came out in support of the deputies. This, after all, was a time when the Black Hundred mobs were encouraged by the police to go round working-class districts singing 'God Save the Tsar' and beat up anyone who failed to take off their hats.[74]

Yet, as the war dragged on and the economic crisis deepened, so the majority of the workers swung back towards the militant Left, resuming the pattern of labour protests begun in 1912–14. It was not so much a crisis of economic decline and stagnation as one of hectic inflationary growth. The war witnessed an industrial boom, mainly to meet the needs of the army. The number of railway workers increased by half a million, the building industry grew by a third, and a million of the poorest peasants, most of them women and youths, poured into the factories, where they could be employed on the mechanized assembly lines at cheaper rates and for longer hours than older and more skilled workers. To pay for its huge war demands the government printed roubles: the money supply increased eightfold between 1914 and 1917. The resulting boom in consumer demand far outstripped the dwindling supply of consumer goods, as manufacturing switched to war production. Workers had too much money in their pockets and not enough to spend it on, so prices rocketed. The ban on vodka sales — a government monopoly which had soaked up roughly 10 per cent of the workers' incomes before 1914 — only worsened this monetary overhang (which we call inflation). Such were the drinking habits of the Russians that it also caused all manner of social abuses, such as the drinking of eau-de-Cologne, methylated spirits, balsams, varnishes, black-market moonshine (*samogon*) and the notorious spirit called *khanja*, made and sold by Chinese workers, which killed hundreds.[75] The vodka ban became a major source of plebeian complaint against the government and resentment against the well-to-do, since expensive wines and liqueurs were not subject to the prohibition. All in all, weighing up the minor gains in sobriety against the major losses in revenue, controls on inflation, public health and political authority, the ban on vodka was nothing less than a disaster, which in no small way contributed to the downfall of the old regime.

But the basic problem was the workers' growing inability to turn their money wages into food. It was a shocking paradox that whereas Russia before the war had exported grain and still been able to feed its urban population, during the war, when all such exports were suspended, it could not always do even this. It was not so much a problem of agricultural production as one of distribution and exchange. Partly it was due to the chronic disruption of transport. Whereas the railways were timetabled to run from east to west in order to supply the army, foodstuffs for the major industrial centres travelled from south to north and, as the army always came first, often ended up rotting in railway sidings waiting for an engine to take them to Moscow or Petrograd. The other part of the problem related to the shift from commercial to peasant farms. The big estates and commercial farms were badly hit by the war. The mobilization of soldiers left them short of hired labour, while the industrial switch to munitions left them short of tools and machines. Overall, agricultural production did not decline but large amounts of estate land were rented out to the better-off peasants, who were less affected by labour shortages (the army on the whole took away only the excess peasant population) and who generally made their own primitive tools. Thus, for example, the private estates of the central agricultural zone reduced their productive area from 21 to 7 million *desyatini* between 1913 and 1916, whereas the region's peasant farms increased theirs from 47 to 64 million *desyatini*. For several years before the agrarian revolution of 1917–18 the demise of the landed gentry's estates and their replacement by the peasant farms was already under way.

This shift towards the smallholding sector led to a decline in the overall rate of marketed grain, since most peasants produced for the needs of their own family farms and usually sold no more than a small proportion of their crops. The growing shortage of consumer goods — and their inflated prices — in the countryside further encouraged these autarkic trends. From 1913 to 1915 the share of peasant grain sold on the market declined from 16 per cent to 9 per cent. With less and less to buy with their money, the peasants increasingly switched from cash crops (wheat, barley and sugar beet) to subsistence crops (rye, oats and potatoes). They ate more, fed their livestock better, stocked up their barns, and turned their grain into vodka rather than sell it on the market for declining profits. Some smallholders also geared their production towards their own domestic handicrafts (wool, hides and cotton), thus making themselves almost self-sufficient. For many peasants, life had never been so good as it was for them at the height of the war. Even their cows were better fed than many of the workers in the city.[76]

In August 1915, the government, concerned by the growing problems of food supply in the cities, established a Special Council with extensive powers to purchase grain at fixed prices through local commissioners. But attempting to control the market only further discouraged the peasants from selling their grain: the unregulated prices of manufactures now rose much faster than the fixed prices of food. It was the so-called 'scissors crisis'. In the Moscow markets, for example, the price of rye went up by 47 per cent in the first two years of the war, while the price of a pair of boots increased by 334 per cent and the price of a box of matches by as much as 500 per cent.[77] An economic war developed as the peasants withdrew their foodstuffs from the market and the government resorted to increasingly coercive measures in an effort to extract supplies from them. In November 1916, with the food supply of the army and the cities reaching a critical level, the government finally introduced a system of compulsory requisitioning similar to that of the Provisional Government. Yet short of building a massive state of terror, such as the Bolsheviks did with their 'Food Dictatorship', it proved impossible to force the grain from the peasants. Only the black-marketeers (who could lay their hands on hard-to-come-by goods) and the soldiers (who could trade their army boots and coats) managed to persuade the peasants to unlock their barns.

From the autumn of 1915 the cities of the north began to experience growing food shortages. Long queues appeared outside the bakeries and meat shops. After a ten-hour shift in their factories women would set up stools and benches to wait in line for pitifully small amounts of bread or sugar. By the following autumn they were bringing their beds to sleep outside the food stores, often because, with so many local shops closed for lack of provisions, they did not have the time to walk across town and return home in one evening. On the eve of 1917 the average working woman in Petrograd was probably spending around forty hours per week in various queues for provisions.[78] The bread queues, in particular, became a sort of political forum or club, where rumours, information and views were exchanged. It was in these queues that the streets began to organize themselves for the coming revolution. The February Revolution was born in the bread queue. It began when a group of women textile workers on the Vyborg side of Petrograd became impatient with waiting in line and went off to rally their menfolk in the neighbouring metal factories for a protest march to the centre of the city.

The economic crisis had the worst effect on the lowest paid. Skilled metal-workers, in great demand at munitions factories, enjoyed an average rise of 30 per cent in their real wages up to 1916. But unskilled workers and petty officials on fixed salaries, such as teachers, clerks and policemen, found their wages falling further and further behind the rising costs of food and housing. Between 1914 and 1916 the calorie intake of unskilled workers fell by a quarter; infant mortality doubled; crime rates tripled; and the number of prostitutes increased by four or five times. From Petrograd, where he had been living since the start of the war, Gorky wrote to Ekaterina in November 1915:

We will soon have a famine. I advise you to buy ten pounds of bread and hide it. In the suburbs of Petrograd you can see well-dressed women begging on the streets. It is very cold. People have nothing to burn in their stoves. Here and there, at night, they tear down the wooden fences. What has happened to the Twentieth Century! What has happened to Civilization! The number of child prostitutes is shocking. On your way somewhere at night you see them shuffling along the sidewalks, just like cockroaches, blue with cold and hungry. Last Tuesday I talked to one of them. I put some money into her hand and hurried away, in tears, in such a state of sadness that I felt like banging my head against a wall. Oh, to hell with it all, how hard it has become to live.[79]

After a year of industrial peace the war between labour and capital resumed in the summer of 1915 with a series of strikes. To begin with they were mostly minor stoppages over pay and conditions, but they gradually grew into larger political strikes as workers came to understand that the only way to end their economic plight was to end the war and change the government. The main anniversaries in the revolutionary calendar — Bloody Sunday on 9 January, International Women's Day on 23 February and Labour Day on 18 April (1 May) — became set dates for strikes and rallies across the country. They usually began with calls for bread, but went on to demand an eight-hour day, an end to the war and the overthrow of the Tsar.

The revolutionary parties played only a secondary role in these strikes. True, some of the biggest and most militant strikes of 1916, at the New Lessner factory in the spring for example, were largely due to the leadership of the Bolshevik Party, whose organization was slowly gaining in strength. Shliapnikov, who returned to Russia in autumn 1916, estimated that the party had as many as 10,000 members at the beginning of 1917, with as many as 3,000 in Petrograd itself. Gorky's apartment on the Kronversky Prospekt was a 'unique central point' of the underground revolutionary organization and Shliapnikov visited it daily for the latest information. The real strike leaders, however, were the skilled and literate workers on the shop-floor, daring young men in their twenties and thirties, such as Kanatchikov, though, unlike him, most of them did not belong to any political party. Although many had seen their real wages rise in the war, they resented the huge war profits of their employers,* and this increasingly defined their sense of class solidarity with the unskilled workers, many of them fresh from the countryside, who followed them into industrial battle.[80] Here were those unnamed leaders of the crowd during the February Days in Petrograd.

There had been a time when such working-class heroes would have rallied behind the Menshevik call to join the Labour Group, an adjunct of the War Industries Committees established in the autumn of 1915. Its aim was to bring the strikes to an end by giving the workers' representatives a chance to sit round a table with their employers and voice their grievances. It was a perfect product of that liberal democratic hope, still so fresh in 1915, that a broad front of all classes might steer the nation towards victory and the government towards reform. There was, it is true, a large number of workers still prepared to try the path of conciliation, especially in the big state munitions factories where the Menshevik influence remained strong. But elsewhere barely half the workers bothered to vote for factory delegates to the Labour Group, although this probably had more to do with their general apathy than any conscious adherence to the calls of the Bolsheviks and the SRs for a boycott of the elections. Either way, their lack of enthusiasm proved justified, as the Labour Group failed to extract either of its main demands — a National Workers' Congress and a system of conciliation boards to arbitrate industrial disputes — from a dominant bloc of employers and bureaucrats who were steadily moving away from the idea of making concessions to the working class. With its policy of conciliation discredited in the eyes of the workers, who now turned increasingly

---

* The big metal factories of Petrograd, to cite the most extreme example, enjoyed a five-fold increase in profits during the war.

towards militant strikes, the Labour Group found itself caught in the widening gap between the two sides of the industrial war. No longer able to stop the strikes, it decided to join them during the autumn of 1916 with a slogan calling for a 'provisional revolutionary government'.[81]

On 17 October the workers of the New Lessner and Russian Renault factories on the Vyborg side of Petrograd downed tools and took to the streets singing revolutionary songs. As they approached the nearby barracks of the 181st Infantry Regiment, the police set upon them with sabres and whips. The soldiers, who had been watching and cheering on the demonstrators through their barrack fences, came out to defend them, throwing rocks and bricks at the police, and only after a training detachment of mounted Cossacks arrived on the scene was order restored. The military authorities arrested 130 soldiers and removed the mutinous regiment from the capital. But the next day more workers came out in solidarity with them and by 19 October as many as 75,000 workers from 63 factories in all parts of the city had joined the political strike.[82]

For the tsarist regime it was an ominous sign of the army's reluctance to control the growing rebellion on the streets. The Petrograd garrison, closest to the sources of revolutionary propaganda, was more reluctant than most. It was filled with older reservists, most of them family men, and wounded evacuees from the Front, perhaps the two most anti-war groups in the entire army, making the regime's decision to rely almost exclusively on it in the event of a revolution all the more ill-conceived. The military authorities clearly had no idea of the soldiers' feelings. The secret police had agents reporting on the political mood in virtually every civilian institution, yet, incredibly, none in the army itself, which was left to the tiny department of army intelligence. Major-General Khabalov, chief of the Petrograd Military District, assured Protopopov that his garrison troops would carry out all commands when he was questioned about their reliability shortly before the February Revolution. He even overruled the Minister of the Interior's recommendation that some unreliable units should be removed from the capital. And yet Colonel Engelhardt, an Octobrist member of the Duma who was soon to replace Khabalov as Military Commissar of the Provisional Government, described the reservists of the Petrograd garrison as nothing less than 'armed mobs'. They were more like 'flammable material than a prop of the regime'. The Rasputin affair, noted Viktor Shklovsky, an instructor in one of the garrison's armoured divisions, had finally broken the soldiers' loyalty to the Tsar. They despised the police — whom they called the 'two-kopeck men' (*semishniki*) because that is what they were thought to receive for each man they arrested — and all looked forward to the revolution as 'an established fact — everyone knew it would come'.[83]

The Petrograd garrison was not the only unreliable part of the army. In many units on the Northern and Western Fronts, and even more so in the army garrisons in the rear, the discipline of the troops was rapidly breaking down. Soldiers were increasingly refusing to take up attacking positions, fraterniz-ing with the enemy, and rejecting the authority of their officers, whom, as peasants eager to return to their farms, they now saw more clearly than ever as their old class enemies, the landowners, in uniform. Only on the South-Western Front, a thousand miles from the revolutionary capital, were there whole army units upon which the tsarist regime could readily rely. But even there Brusilov, the Front commander, regularly received unsigned letters from his men warning him 'that they did not want any more fighting, and that if peace was not concluded shortly, I should be killed'.[84]

As they entered the third and by far the coldest winter of the war, the morale of the soldiers took a sudden turn for the worse. It was no longer a crisis of supplies: if anything, the supply of clothes and munitions had improved since the previous year, thanks to the increase of domestic production and orders from abroad, although the food situation remained as grim as ever. It was now more a crisis of authority, of utter despair and exhaustion: the soldiers could see no end to the slaughter while the present regime remained in command. As one soldier wrote to his wife in November 1916:

Everyone pretends that the war will end soon, that the longed-for peace will arrive, but that is only to keep their spirits up. People are so worn out and destroyed, they have suffered so much, that it's all they can do to stop their hearts from breaking and to keep themselves from losing their mind . . . Maybe I'm wrong, maybe I don't understand the mood of the men and it only seems to me like this because I myself am exhausted and have come to realise in the past few days that I may lose my own mind in all this chaos . . . Liulya, I have written all this to you so that you may understand what sort of a man you love.[85]

Part Three

RUSSIA IN REVOLUTION
(FEBRUARY 1917–MARCH 1918)

8 Glorious February

i The Power of the Streets

It all began with bread. For several weeks the bakeries in Petrograd had been running out, especially in the workers' districts, and long bread queues were beginning to appear. The problem was not shortage of supplies. According to Balk, the city's governor, there was enough flour in the warehouses to feed the population for at least a week when what had started as a series of bread riots turned into a revolution. True, the shops were not full. This was the end of the war's third winter and there was a general feeling of austerity. Buns, pies, cakes and biscuits were no longer baked. 'The shops are not carrying such a full line of articles and provisions,' an Englishman wrote home on 13 February. 'Restaurants no longer have the big fine pastries, owing to the scarcity of sugar.' This, moreover, was the coldest winter Russia had experienced for several years. In Petrograd the average February temperature was fifteen degrees below zero. 'It's as cold here as in Lapland,' Gorky wrote to Ekaterina on the 4th. Arctic frosts and blizzards had brought the railways to a virtual standstill. Factories closed. Thousands of laid-off workers milled around the streets.[1]

It was this that turned the supply problem into a crisis. Because of the breakdown of the transport system, Petrograd was starved of regular supplies of flour and fuel. For want of the one or the other, bakeries were frequently forced to close. Women would queue all night for a loaf of bread, only to be told in the early hours of the morning that there would be none for sale that day. This constant interruption to the bread supply naturally gave rise to rumours in the queues. People said that 'speculators' and 'capitalists' — which in the xenophobic wartime atmosphere usually meant German or Jewish merchants — were deliberately forcing up the bread prices by withholding stocks. Many people blamed the government (wasn't it also full of Germans?). Even educated liberals were inclined to see the shortages as the evil doing of a treasonable government. On 19 February the Petrograd authorities announced that rationing would start from 1 March. Rumours spread that there would soon be no bread stocks at all and the unemployed would be left to starve. In the panic buying that followed the shelves were laid bare, scuffles broke out, and several bakeries had their windows smashed.[2]

On Thursday, 23 February, the temperature in Petrograd rose to a spring-like minus five degrees. People emerged from their winter hibernation to enjoy the sun and join in the hunt for food. Nevsky Prospekt was crowded with shoppers. The mild weather was set to continue until 3 March — by which time the tsarist regime would have collapsed. Not for the first time in Russian history the weather was to play a decisive role.

February 23rd was International Women's Day, an important date in the socialist calendar, and towards noon huge crowds of women began to march towards the city centre to protest for equal rights. Balk described the crowds as 'ladies from society, lots more peasant women, student girls and, compared with the earlier demonstrations, not many workers'. Photographs show the women were in good humour as they marched along the Nevsky Prospekt.

But in the afternoon the mood began to change. Women textile workers from the Vyborg district had come out on strike that morning in protest against the shortages of bread. Joined by their menfolk from the neighbouring metal works, they had marched towards the city centre, drawing in workers from other factories on the way, and in some cases forcing them out, with shouts of 'Bread!' and 'Down with the Tsar!' By the end of the afternoon, some 100,000 workers had come out on strike. There were clashes with the police as the workers tried to cross the Liteiny Bridge, linking the Vyborg side with the city centre. Most of the workers, having been forced back, dispersed and went home, some of them looting shops on the way. But several thousand crossed on the ice and marched towards the Nevsky Prospekt, where they joined the women with cries of 'Bread!' The thickest crowds were around the city Duma. Balk's Cossacks could not clear them and even showed an unwillingness to do so: they would ride up to the women, only to stop short and retreat. Later it emerged that most of the Cossacks were reserves without experience of dealing with crowds, and with horses that were new to the city streets. By some oversight they had not been supplied with their usual whips. It was to prove a fatal mistake by the authorities. For this show of weakness by the Cossacks emboldened the workers over the coming days.[3]

The following morning saw bright sunshine. Workers held factory meetings throughout the city and, urged on by socialist agitators, resolved to march again to the centre. Many armed themselves with knives, spanners, hammers and pieces of iron, partly to fight their way through the squadrons of Cossacks and police who had been brought in overnight to bar their way, and partly to help them loot the well-stocked food shops of the affluent downtown areas. The expedition had the feel of a hungry workers' army going off to war. 'Comrades,' urged one factory agitator, 'if we cannot get a loaf of bread for ourselves in a righteous way, then we must do everything: we must go ahead and solve our problem by force . . . Comrades, arm yourselves with everything possible — bolts, screws, rocks, and go out of the factory and start smashing the first shops you find.'

By mid-morning about 150,000 workers had taken to the streets. They made their way to the bridges connecting the industrial suburbs with the city's administrative centre. Some of them smashed windows, looted shops and overturned trams and carriages. At the Liteiny Bridge a crowd of 40,000 Vyborg workers overran a small brigade of Cossacks, who were clearly unprepared for them. 'But nobody told me there would be a revolution!', a policeman was heard to say as he saw the vast army of workers approach. On the Troitsky Bridge the workers fought their way past mounted police by throwing rocks and ice. The huge crowds converged on the Nevsky Prospekt. The mounted Cossacks were unable to disperse them: they would ride across the street and on to the pavements, forcing the demonstrators to run in all directions; but as soon as they stopped the crowds would reassemble and begin to approach the troops, offering them bread and calling out to them. By this stage, the crowds of workers had been swollen with students, shopkeepers, bank clerks, cabbies, children, well-dressed ladies and gentlemen, who were either sympathizers or just spectators. Balk described the crowds on Nevsky Prospekt as 'consisting of the ordinary people'. There was a holiday mood on the streets, no doubt partly because of the fine weather. One witness compared it to 'an enormous circus'. Arthur Ransome, then the correspondent for the *Daily News*, described the feeling on that day as one of 'rather precarious excitement like a Bank Holiday with thunder in the air'. There was a huge rally on Znamenskaya Square. The equestrian statue of Alexander III, an awesome monument to the principles of autocracy, was conquered by the revolutionary orators. Few in the vast crowd could hear what they were saying, but this did not matter. The people knew what they wanted to hear, and the mere sight of this brave act of free speech — performed from the top of such a monument and in full view of the police — was enough to confirm it in their minds: a revolution was taking place. Later that evening, after the crowds had finally dispersed, the police found the word 'HIPPOPOTA-MUS' — the popular nickname for the statue — engraved in large letters on its plinth.[4]

Emboldened by the absence of vigorous repressive measures, even larger crowds came out on to the streets the following day, Saturday 25 February, in what was virtually a general strike. All the city's major factories ceased to operate, as some 200,000 workers joined the demonstrations. Newspapers failed to appear. Trams and cabs were hard to find. Many shops and restaurants closed their doors. All sorts of people joined the ranks of marching workers heading into the centre of the city. Balk thought the movement 'bore the character of a people's uprising'. Compared to the previous two days, the demonstrations now had a more political flavour. Red flags and banners began to appear, and their slogans were calling not so much for 'Bread!' as for the overthrow of the autocracy. 'Down with the Tsar!' and 'Down with the War!' were now their main demands.

Once again there were clashes with police as the demonstrators tried to cross the bridges connecting the suburbs with the centre of the city. At the Liteiny Bridge the chief of police, Shalfeev, made a last desperate bid to halt the marchers by charging headlong into the crowd. The marchers parted to the sides and then closed ranks to surround Shalfeev, who tried to force his way out by lashing out on all sides with his whip. But the demonstrators dragged him off his horse. One of the workers beat him on the ground with a piece of wood, while another, taking Shalfeev's revolver, shot him in the heart. None of the Cossacks defending the bridge attempted to intervene.

Increasingly this became the pattern — violent clashes with the police combined with efforts to win over the soldiers — as the crowds took over the city centre. The police were 'theirs' — hated agents of the regime. The people called them 'pharaohs' (much as some today might call the police 'pigs') and they had no doubts that the police would fight to the end.* The soldiers, by contrast, were seen as 'ours' — peasants and workers in uniforms — and it was hoped that, if they were ordered to use force against the crowds, they would be as likely to come over to the people's side. Once it became clear that this was so — from the soldiers' hesitation to disperse the demonstrators, from the expressions on the soldiers' faces, and from the odd wink by a soldier to the crowd — the initiative passed to the people's side. It was a crucial psychological moment in the revolution.

The first symbolic battle of this war of nerves was fought out on the Nevsky Prospekt — and won decisively by the people — on the afternoon of the 25th. Part of the crowd was brought to a halt by a squadron of Cossacks blocking their way near the Kazan Cathedral. It was not far from the spot where, twelve years before, on Bloody Sunday 1905, the Horseguards had shot down a similar crowd. A young girl appeared from the ranks of the demonstrators and walked slowly towards the Cossacks. Everyone watched her in nervous silence: surely the Cossacks would not fire at her? From under her cloak the girl brought out a bouquet of red roses and held it out towards the officer. There was a pause. The bouquet was a symbol of both peace and revolution. And then, leaning down from his horse, the officer smiled and took the flowers. With as much relief as jubilation, the crowd burst into a thunderous 'Oorah!'[5] From this moment the people started to speak of the 'comrade Cossacks', a term which at first sounded rather odd.

---

* It was rumoured that Protopopov had promised each policeman 500 roubles for every wound he received from the crowd.

The officers were finding it increasingly difficult to get their men to obey orders. Colonel Khodnev, a commander of the Finland Reserve Regiment, complained bitterly about the Cossacks. They were 'extremely slack and indecisive' and their 'inaction was particularly apparent when they formed an individual patrol or platoon under the command of a young sergeant or a junior lieutenant. More than once I heard them say: "This isn't 1905. We won't carry whips. We won't move against our own kind, against the people." True, there were some soldiers who were still prepared — usually on their own initiative or on the orders of a junior officer when scared or provoked — to take violent measures against the crowd. A platoon of dragoons opened fire near a row of shops at the Gostiny Dvor, killing three and wounding ten, while near the city Duma nine more demonstrators were shot dead. But a growing proportion of the soldiers were either refusing to obey orders to fire, or were deliberately shooting over the heads of the people in the street. Some were even joining them against the police. In one incident on Znamenskaya Square the Cossacks intervened to rescue the crowd when the mounted police, having been frustrated in their efforts to capture a red banner, threatened to charge the people down. The Cossacks, sabres drawn, rode into the crowd and began to attack the mounted police, who then galloped away pursued by the crowd throwing stones. Meanwhile the police commander lay dead on the ground, his body covered with wounds from the Cossacks' sabres and revolver shots.[6]

* * *

Even at this point, on the evening of the 25th, the authorities could still have contained the situation, despite the growing self-assertion of the crowd. The important thing, as the Council of Ministers seemed to sense at its midnight meeting, was to hold back from open conflict with the crowd, which would merely pour fuel on the flames and run the risk of a mutiny among the soldiers in the garrison. There was still some reason to suppose — or at least to act upon the assumption — that the anger of the demonstrators was mainly focused on the shortages of bread and that once this problem had been solved they would become tired of protest and return to work. That had been the outcome of several bread riots in the recent past and, although this one was more ominous, there was no real reason yet to believe that it would end any differently. This was certainly the assumption of the socialist leaders in the capital. Nikolai Sukhanov, perhaps the revolution's most famous memoirist, thought that so far there had only been ' "disorders" — there was still no revolution'. Shliapnikov, the leading Bolshevik in the capital, scoffed at the idea that this was the start of a revolution. 'What revolution?' he asked a local meeting of the party leaders on the 25th. 'Give the workers a pound of bread and the movement will peter out.'[7]

But whatever chances there might have been of containing the disorders were destroyed that evening by the Tsar. Having been informed of the situation at his headquarters in Mogilev, he sent a cable to General Khabalov, Chief of the Petrograd Military District, ordering him to use military force to 'put down the disorders by tomorrow'.[8] There could be no better illustration of the extent to which the Tsar had lost touch with reality. Nor could there be any better guarantee of a revolution. To be fair, Nicholas had been badly advised from the start. He had left the capital for Mogilev on 22 February, after being assured by Protopopov that he had nothing to worry about. Since then the police and Khabalov had played down the seriousness of the situation in their reports to Nicholas: it was embarrassing for them to have to admit that it might be getting out of their control. The Tsar thus had little real idea of the finely balanced nature of the situation, or of the risks involved in using force, when he sent his fatal order to Khabalov. But then it was his job to know — and the job of his advisers to inform him — what was going on in the capital. Only the Tsar could issue the final order to use force against the crowds, and once that order had been issued none of his advisers could challenge it. In other words, if the regime fell because of a breakdown in communications, then one can only say that it deserved to fall.

By Sunday morning, 26 February, the centre of Petrograd had been turned into a militarized camp. Soldiers' pickets and armed policemen stood at the major intersections and strategic buildings; mounted patrols rode through the streets; officers communicated by field telephone; machine-guns, set up in Palace Square, pointed down the Nevsky Prospekt; and in the side streets were military ambulances standing by. During the morning everything was quiet: it was Sunday and people slept in late. But around midday huge crowds of workers once again assembled in the suburbs and marched towards the city centre. As they converged on the Nevsky Prospekt, the police and soldiers fired upon them from several different points. At the junction of the Nevsky and Vladimir Prospekts the Semenovsky Regiment — which had put down the Moscow uprising in 1905 — shot dead several marchers. On the Nevsky, near the Gostiny Dvor, a training detachment of the Pavlovsky Regiment shot a round of blanks and then opened fire on the crowd. The people scattered behind buildings and into shops, re-emerging moments later to throw bricks and pieces of ice at the troops. Dozens of people were wounded or killed. The bloodiest incident took place on Znamenskaya Square, where more than fifty people were shot dead by a training detachment of the Volynsky Regiment. It was a terrible atrocity. An officer, who had been unable to get his young and obviously nervous soldiers to shoot at the demonstrators, grabbed a rifle from one of his men and began to fire wildly at the crowd. Among the dead bodies, which were later piled up around the 'Hippopotamus', were two soldiers from the regiment who had gone over to the side of the people.[9]

This shedding of blood — Russia's second Bloody Sunday — proved a critical turning point. From this moment on the demonstrators knew that they were involved in a life-or-death struggle against the regime. Paradoxically, now that the worst had happened and some of their comrades had been killed, they felt less afraid for their own lives.* As for the soldiers, they were now confronted with a choice between their moral duty to the people and their oath of allegiance to the Tsar. If they followed the former, a full-scale revolution would occur. But if they stuck to their oath of allegiance, then the regime might still manage to survive, as it had done in 1905–6.

After the shooting on the Nevsky Prospekt an angry crowd of demonstrators broke into the barracks of the Pavlovsky Regiment near the Mars Field and shouted at the soldiers that some of their trainees had been firing at the people. Visibly shaken by the news, the 4th Company of the Pavlovskys resolved to march to the Nevsky at once in order to stop the massacre. 'They are shooting at our mothers and our sisters!' was their rallying cry as they mutinied. About a hundred soldiers broke into the arsenal of the barracks and, taking thirty rifles, began to march towards the Nevsky. Almost immediately, they ran into a mounted police patrol on the bank of the Griboyedov Canal. They fired at them, killing one policeman, until they ran out of cartridges, whereupon they decided to return to barracks to bring out the rest of the men. But Khabalov's troops were waiting for them there and, upon the mutineers' arrival, disarmed them and confined them to barracks. Nineteen ringleaders were arrested and imprisoned in the Peter and Paul Fortress. They were to be its last prisoners — at least under the tsarist regime.[10]

But it was too late for repression by this stage. All the prisons in Russia could not have contained the revolutionaries on the streets. The training detachment of the Volynsky Regiment which had been involved in the shooting on Znamenskaya Square had, like their comrades in the Pavlovsky, returned to their barracks during the evening full of doubts and remorse about what they had done. One of the soldiers claimed to have recognized his own mother amongst the people they had killed. All these teenage conscripts were badly shaken by the massacre and it did not take much for their young sergeant, an Os'kin-type peasant called Sergei Kirpichnikov, to talk them into a protest of their own. 'I told them', Kirpichnikov recalled:

that it would be better to die with honour than to obey any further orders to shoot at the crowds: 'Our fathers, mothers, sisters, brothers, and brides

---

* People said the same thing in 1989 after the East German authorities had shot at the demonstrators in Leipzig. Crowds are afraid of the threat of bloodshed but emboldened after it occurs.

are begging for bread,' I said. 'Are we going to kill them? Did you see the blood on the streets today? I say we shouldn't take up positions tomorrow. I myself refuse to go.' And, as one, the soldiers cried out: 'We shall stay with you!'

Having sworn their allegiance to Kirpichnikov, the soldiers were determined to defy their commanding officer when, once again, he ordered them to march against the demonstrators the following morning. At this stage the soldiers did not intend a full-scale mutiny, only a vocal and abusive protest against their officer for having ordered them to fire on the crowds, and a refusal to obey his commands. But when the officer found himself confronted by his angry men he made the fatal error of walking away — and then, even worse, of starting to run across the barracks yard. Sensing their power over him, the soldiers pointed their rifles towards him, and one of them shot him in the back. Suddenly the soldiers were mutineers. They scattered through the barracks, in panic as much as revolutionary fervour, calling on the other soldiers to join their mutiny. Relatively few from the Volynsky joined them but there were many more who were willing in the neighbouring barracks of the Preobrazhensky Regiment, the Lithuanian Regiment and the 6th Engineer Battalion. Fights broke out between loyal and rebel soldiers. The victorious mutineers stormed the regimental arsenals, killed several of their officers and spilled in their thousands on to the streets, where they spread out in all directions, some moving towards the centre of the city, others crossing over to the Vyborg side in order to raise the Moscow Regiment and link up with the workers.[11]

In all these mutinies the decisive role was played by the junior officers, most of whom came from lower-class backgrounds or had democratic sympathies. Fedor Linde (1881–1917), a sergeant in the Finland Regiment, was typical in this respect. He played an unsung but crucial role in turning the tide of the February Revolution. Tall, blond and handsome, Linde was the son of a German chemist and a Polish peasant-woman who had grown up on a small farm near St Petersburg on the Gulf of Finland. There his mother ran a little inn which was popular with the capital's revolutionaries when they wanted to escape the gaze of the police. And it was by socializing with the hotel guests that the teenage Linde, who was by nature a romantic idealist, first became involved in the revolutionary underground. In 1899 he enrolled in the Mathematics Faculty of St Petersburg University, and immediately became a leading light in the student protest movement. During the 1905 Revolution Linde worked alongside the SDs in the capital, and organized the students in an 'academic legion' to spread propaganda to the working class. He was arrested and imprisoned in the Kresty jail, and then forced to go into exile in Europe, before being allowed to return to Russia under the amnesty of 1913 to celebrate the Romanov tercentenary.

The next year he was mobilized by the Finland Regiment, where his courageous leadership of the soldiers soon saw him promoted to sergeant. It was precisely this same quality which distinguished Linde in the mutiny of the February Days. In a letter to the SR Boris Sokolov, written in the spring of 1917, Linde recalled how he persuaded the 5,000 soldiers of the Preobrazhensky Regiment, in whose barracks near the Tauride Palace he was staying at the time, to join the mutiny:

> I don't know what happened to me. I was lying on a couch in the barracks and reading a book by Haldane. I was so absorbed in it that I didn't hear shouts and roars coming from the street. A wild bullet broke the window near my couch ... The Cossacks were firing on defenceless and unarmed crowds, striking people with their whips, crushing the fallen with their horses. And then I saw a young girl trying to evade the galloping horse of a Cossack officer. She was too slow. A severe blow on her head brought her down under the horse's feet. She screamed. It was her inhuman, penetrating scream that caused something in me to snap. I jumped to the table and cried out wildly: 'Friends! Friends! Long live the revolution! To arms! To arms! They are killing innocent people, our brothers and sisters!'
>
> Later they said there was something in my voice that made it impossible to resist my call ... They followed me without realizing where or in the name of what cause they went ... They all joined me in the attack against the Cossacks and police. We killed a few of them. The rest retreated. By night, the fight was over. The revolution had become a reality ... And I, well, I returned that same night to my book by Haldane.[12]

* * *

The mutiny of the Petrograd garrison turned the disorders of the previous four days into a full-scale revolution. The tsarist authorities were virtually deprived of military power in the capital. 'It had now become clear to me', Balk later wrote of the 27th, 'that we had lost all authority.' The spilling of the soldiers on to the streets, moreover, gave a military strength and organization to the revolutionary crowds. Instead of vague and aimless protest they focused on the capture of strategic targets and the armed struggle against the regime. Soldiers and workers fought together for the capture of the Arsenal, where they armed themselves with 40,000 rifles and 30,000 revolvers, followed by the major weapons factories, where at least another 100,000 guns fell into their hands. They occupied the Artillery Department, the telephone exchange and some (though not all) of the railway stations. They spread the mutiny to the remaining barracks (Linde himself led a guard of soldiers from the Preobrazhensky and Lithuanian Regiments to bring out his own Finland Regiment). Thanks to the soldiers and officers like Linde, the first signs of real organization — armed pickets on the bridges and major intersections, barricades, field-telephones and structures of command — began to appear on the streets. Many of the soldiers were also kept busy by the task of arresting — and sometimes beating up or even murdering — their commanding officers. This was a revolution in the ranks.[13]

But the main attention of the insurgents was now focused on the bloody street war against the police. There were hundreds of police snipers hidden on the flat roofs of the buildings, some of them armed with machine-guns, who were firing at the crowds below and at anyone who showed themselves in the windows opposite. Other police snipers had positioned themselves in the belfries of the churches, hoping that the people's respect for religion would prevent them from firing back. The snipers deliberately used smokeless ammunition so the people could not easily tell where the shooting had come from. Suddenly there would be a crack of gunfire, and the crowds would run for cover, leaving little heaps of wounded and dead bodies lying in the streets. Workers and soldiers 'would begin to shoot wildly' at the house from where they thought the firing had come, recalls Viktor Shklovsky, who led a group of fighters against the police, but this usually proved counter-productive. 'The dust rising from where our bullets hit the plaster was taken for return fire,' setting off more shooting and confusion. Many people were killed by 'our own bullets' bouncing off the buildings or by falling masonry.[14]

Even less effective were the motor-cars that went hurtling about the streets filled with soldiers waving red flags and shooting wildly into the air. Virtually every car and lorry had been requisitioned by the crowds, no matter to whom it might belong. Linde and his men commandeered a lorry, upon which they hung a banner with the words: 'The First Revolutionary Flying Squad'. The Grand Duke Gavril Konstantinovich even had his Rolls-Royce requisitioned. It was later seen cruising down the Nevsky Prospekt, with two soldiers lying on the front bonnet, several others riding on the sides, and two with a machine-gun mounted on the roof, although this proved to be of little use since the car was swerving too much for it to be held still and fired properly. Smaller cars, bristling with bayonets, presented an even stranger image. Gorky compared them to 'huge hedgehogs running amok'. Much of the fighting was done from these cars: this was the first revolution on wheels. The vehicles would speed through the streets, pull up alongside a building from which the police were thought to be firing, and start to shoot in the direction of the roof. But since the snipers could see and hear the vehicles coming — what with their horns sounding and their red flags waving — they had plenty of time to conceal themselves. In the end, the only way to defeat them was to climb up and fight them on the roofs. Many snipers were thrown off the roofs — to the cheers of the crowds below. As for the motor-cars, most of them were crashed, since their drivers had no idea how to drive and in any case they were usually drunk. The streets 'resounded' to the noise of car crashes, recalls Shklovsky. 'I don't know how many collisions I saw during those days. Later on the city was jammed with automobiles left by the wayside.'[15]

Much of the crowds' destructive violence was directed against the institutions of the police regime. Armed crowds attacked police stations, setting fire to the buildings and making sure to destroy the police records. Sometimes the contents of the buildings were burned in bonfires on the streets. Gorky, who was charged with the seizure of the Police Headquarters on Kronversky Prospekt, arrived to find it vandalized and most of its records taken or destroyed. Court buildings were similarly targeted by the crowd. Gorky found a crowd of people watching the Palace of Justice go up in flames:

> The roof had already fallen in, the fire crackled between the walls, and red and yellow wisps like wool were creeping out of the windows, throwing a sheaf of paper ashes into the black sky of the night. No one made any attempt to extinguish the fire . . . A tall stooping man in a shaggy sheepskin hat was walking about like a sentinel. He stopped and asked in a dull voice: 'Well — it means that all justice is to be abolished, doesn't it? Punishments all done away with, is that it?' No one answered him.

Last but not least the crowd turned its destructive anger on the prisons, bashing down the gates, opening the cells, and, together with the released prisoners, vandalizing and sometimes burning down the buildings. The destruction of the prisons had a powerful symbolic significance for the revolutionary crowd: it was a sign that the old regime was dead, that the longed-for days of liberty — 'prisonless and crimeless' — were about to come.[16]

No prison was more symbolic than the Peter and Paul Fortress. The crowds were convinced that the fortress was still full of 'politicals', heroes of the revolutionary struggle languishing in its dark and dingy cells: that, after all, was the well-established myth of the revolutionaries' propaganda. There were also rumours that the fortress was being used as a military base by the tsarist military forces (Balk did propose this). On the 28th a huge and angry crowd threatened to storm this 'Russian Bastille'. They brought up lorries with heavy mounted guns ready to fire at its thick stone walls. The fortress commandant telephoned the Duma appealing for help, and Shulgin (for the Duma) and Skobelev (for the Soviet) were sent to negotiate with him. They returned to report that the prison was completely empty — apart from the nineteen mutinous soldiers of the Pavlovsky Regiment who had been imprisoned in it on the 26th — and proposed to calm the crowds by allowing them to send representatives to inspect its cells. But even this was not sufficient to convince the crowds that the fortress was 'for the revolution'. Some of the mutinous soldiers accused Shulgin of working for the counter-revolution. There was some fighting between them and the fortress guards. And then, finally, the red flag was raised above this bastion of the old regime.[17]

*   *   *

The crowds displayed extraordinary levels of self-organization and solidarity during all these actions. 'The entire civil population felt itself to be in one camp against the enemy — the police and the military,' Sukhanov wrote. 'Strangers passing by conversed with each other, asking questions and talking about the news, about clashes with and the diversionary movements of the enemy.' The London *Times* was equally impressed. 'The astounding, and to the stranger unacquainted with the Russian character almost uncanny, orderliness and good nature of the crowds are perhaps the most striking feature of this great Russian Revolution.' People wore red armbands, or tied red ribbons in their buttonholes, to display their support for the revolution. Not to do so was to invite persecution as a 'counter-revolutionary'. Bonfires were lit throughout the city so that people could warm themselves during the long hours of street-fighting. Residents fed the revolutionaries from their kitchens, and allowed them to sleep — in so far as anyone slept — on their floors. Café and restaurant owners fed the soldiers and workers free of charge, or placed boxes outside for passers-by to contribute towards their meals. One café displayed the following sign:

> FELLOW-CITIZENS! In honour of the great days of freedom, I bid you all welcome. Come inside, and eat and drink to your hearts' content.

Shopkeepers turned their shops into bases for the soldiers, and into shelters for the people when the police were firing in the streets. Cab-men declared that they would take 'only the leaders of the revolution'. Students and children ran about with errands — and veteran soldiers obeyed their commands. All sorts of people volunteered to help the doctors deal with the wounded. It was as if the people on the streets had suddenly become united by a vast network of invisible threads; and it was this that secured their victory.[18]

The tsarist authorities assumed that the crowds must have been organized by the socialist parties; but, although their rank and file were present in the crowds, the socialist leaders were quite unprepared to take on this role and, if anything, followed the people. The street generated its own leaders: students, workers and NCOs, like Linde or Kirpichnikov, whose names, for the most part, have remained hidden from the history books. During the first weeks after February their portraits were displayed in shop windows — often with the heading 'Heroes of the Revolution'. There was one of Kirpichnikov in the windows of the Avantso store.[19] But then these people's leaders faded out of view and were forgotten.

Part of this extraordinary crowd cohesion may be explained by geography. There was, for a start, a long-established spatial-cultural code of street demonstrations in the capital with a number of clear points of orientation for the crowd (e.g. the Kazan Cathedral and the Tauride Palace) which stretched back to the student demonstrations of 1899. Petrograd's industrial suburbs, moreover, were physically separated from the affluent governmental downtown by a series of canals and rivers. Marching into the centre thus became an expression of working-class solidarity and self-assertion, a means for the workers to claim the streets as 'theirs'. This may help to explain some of the carnival aspects of the revolutionary crowd: the celebratory vandalism and destruction of symbols of state power and authority, wealth and privilege; the acts of mockery and humiliation, of verbal abuse and threatening behaviour, often ending in wanton acts of violence, which the crowds performed, as if they were some sport, against the well dressed and the well-to-do; the self-assertive body language and dress of the soldiers (wearing their caps back to front, or tilted to one side, or wearing their coats and tunics unbuttoned, contrary to military regulations); women wearing men's clothes (soldiers' headgear, boots and breeches), as if by reversing the sexual codes of dress they were also overturning the social order; and the sexual acts, from kissing and fondling to full intercourse, which people openly performed on the streets in the euphoria of the February Days.[20]

And yet, contrary to Soviet myth, the crowds were far from solidly proletarian, although it is true that the workers took the lead and tended to do much of the street-fighting. Balk described the February Days as a general uprising of the people. Harold Williams of the *Daily Chronicle* thought the crowds on the 24th were 'mostly women and boys' with only a 'sprinkling of workmen'. Robert Wilton of *The Times* reported that on the 26th the fine weather had 'brought everybody out of doors' and that 'crowds of all ages and conditions' had made their way to the Nevsky Prospekt.[21]

Most of the people on the streets were not 'revolutionaries' at all but simply spectators or the in-between types who wavered between acting and spectating. They would cheer the mutinous soldiers as they sped past in their cars, or when a police sniper was thrown from the roofs. They would gather in small groups around the dead bodies and horses, which at this time were still something of a novelty (soon they would become accustomed to them and would walk past them with indifference). They would wear red ribbons, wave red flags and declare their sympathy for 'the revolution'. But they rarely took a part in the fighting themselves, and would usually scatter when the firing began. 'This is the psychology of the crowds', wrote one witness:

everything they see is both fascinating and terrifying. They stare, and they stare, and then suddenly — they run away. Look, here is a well-dressed gentleman, fat with short legs, standing on the corner. The crowd suddenly runs behind the building — and he follows them, running as fast as his little legs allow, his fat belly shaking, and he clearly out of breath. He runs a few yards, looks back at the scene again, and then runs on.

Many of these onlookers were young children. Little boys delighted in playing with the guns that were left lying in the streets. They made sport of throwing cartridges into the bonfires and watching them explode. Dozens of people were accidentally killed. Stinton Jones, an English journalist, witnessed the following scene:

One little boy of about twelve years of age had secured an automatic pistol and, together with a large number of soldiers, was warming himself at one of these fires. Suddenly he pulled the trigger and one of the soldiers fell dead. This so alarmed the boy, who had no idea of the mechanism of the deadly weapon he held, that he kept the trigger pulled back and the automatic pistol proceeded to empty itself. It contained seven bullets, and it was not until they were all discharged that the boy released his hold of the trigger. The result was that three soldiers were killed, and four seriously injured.[22]

From the 27th the nature of the crowds grew much darker. The soldier element dramatically increased, along with the level of violence, as a result of the mutiny. So did the criminal element, and the level of criminality, as a result of the opening of the jails. Both had the effect, as Jones put it:

of clearing the streets of the more serious-minded and nervous citizens. The mobs presented a strange, almost grotesque appearance. Soldiers, workmen, students, hooligans and freed criminals wandered aimlessly about in detached companies, all armed, but with a strange variety of weapons. Here would be a hooligan with an officer's sword fastened over his overcoat, a rifle in one hand and a revolver in the other; there a small boy with a large butcher's knife on his shoulder. Close by a workman would be seen awkwardly holding an officer's sword in one hand and a bayonet in the other. One man had two revolvers, another a rifle in one hand and a tram-line cleaner in the other. A student with two rifles and a belt of machine-gun bullets round his waist was walking beside another with a bayonet tied to the end of a stick. A drunken soldier had only the barrel of a rifle remaining, the stock having been broken off in forcing an entry into some shop. A steady, quiet business man grasped a large rifle and a formidable belt of cartridges.

Some 8,000 prisoners were liberated on the 27th, the vast majority of them common criminals. They had a vested interest — and took the lead — in the destruction of the police stations, along with their records, the Palace of Justice, the court buildings and the prisons. And they were to blame for much of the crime which took over the streets from this time. 'Tonight the city reverberates with the most terrifying noises: broken glass, screams, and gunshots,' wrote the Director of the Hermitage in the early hours of the 28th. Armed gangs looted shops and liquor stores. They broke into the houses of the well-to-do and robbed and raped their inhabitants. Well-dressed passers-by were mugged in the streets. Even wearing spectacles or a white starched collar was enough to mark one out as a *burzhooi*. A retired professor, who had been a Populist for nearly fifty years, came on to the streets on the evening of the 27th to celebrate the 'victory of the revolution' and immediately had his glasses smashed and his gold watch stolen by the very 'people' he had sought to liberate. This was clearly not the bloodless victory of liberty, equality and fraternity which the democratic intelligentsia had so long hoped for — and which they later mythologized as the 'Glorious February Revolution' — but more like a Russian peasant riot, 'senseless and merciless', as Pushkin had predicted, which sought to destroy all signs of privilege. The idea that the February Days were a 'bloodless revolution' — and that the violence of the crowd did not really take off until October — was a liberal myth. The democratic leaders of 1917 needed it to legitimize their own fragile power. In fact many more people were killed by the crowd in February than in the Bolsheviks' October coup. The February Revolution in Helsingfors and Kronstadt was especially violent, with hundreds of naval officers killed gruesomely by the sailors. According to the official figures of the Provisional Government, 1,443 people were killed or wounded in Petrograd alone. But a friend of Prince Lvov's told Claude Anet, the French journalist, that the true figure was up to 1,500 people killed and about 6,000 people wounded.[23]

Gorky took a dim view of all this violence and destruction. On the 28th Sukhanov found him in a gloomy mood:

> For an hour by the clock he snarled and grumbled at the chaos, the disorder, the excesses, at the displays of political ignorance, at the girls driving around the city, God knows where, in God knows whose cars — and forecast that the movement would probably collapse in ruin worthy of our Asiatic savagery.

It seemed to Gorky that all this was just 'chaos' and not a 'revolution' at all. The next day he wrote to Ekaterina:

Too many people are falsely according a revolutionary character to what in fact is no more than a lack of discipline and organization on the part of the crowd ... There is much more here of an absurd than a heroic nature. Looting has started. What will happen? I don't know ... Much blood will be spilled, much more than ever has been spilled before.[24]

These, of course, as Sukhanov noted, 'were the impressions of a man of letters', of a man who hated violence in all its forms. Many people today might be similarly inclined to condemn the 'needless killing' of the crowds. That certainly has been the recent trend among conservative historians of both the Russian and the French Revolutions.[25] But one may prefer Sukhanov's view:

that the excesses, the man-in-the-street's stupidity, vulgarity, and cowardice, the muddles, the motor cars, the girls — all this was only what the revolution could not in any circumstances avoid, and without which nothing similar had *ever* happened anywhere.[26]

This is not to condone the violence but to understand it as the almost unavoidable reaction of a people angry and with much to avenge. It is to recognize that all social revolutions are bound by their nature to spill blood; and that to condemn them for doing so is tantamount to saying that any form of social protest which might end in violence is morally wrong. Of course there are distinctions that need to be made: the blood spilled by the people on the streets is different from the blood spilled by parties, movements, or armies, claiming to be acting in their name; and it must be analysed and judged in different ways.

The crowd violence of the February Days was not orchestrated by any revolutionary party or movement. It was by and large a spontaneous reaction to the bloody repressions of the 26th, and an expression of the people's long-felt hatred for the old regime. Symbols of the old state power were destroyed. Tsarist statues were smashed or beheaded. A movie camera filmed a group of laughing workers throwing the stone head of Alexander II into the air like a football. Police stations, court houses and prisons were attacked. The crowd exacted a violent revenge against the officials of the old regime. Policemen were hunted down, lynched and killed brutally. Sorokin watched a crowd of soldiers beating one policeman with the butts of their revolvers and kicking him in the head with their heels. Another was thrown on to the street from a fourth-floor window, and when his body thumped, lifeless, on to the ground, people rushed to stamp on it and beat it with sticks.

Once it became clear that any further resistance was doomed to failure, many of these policemen tried to give themselves up to the Tauride Palace, where the Duma and the Soviet were struggling to restore order, in the belief that it would be better to be imprisoned by the new government than to be the victim of this 'mob law' on the streets. Others tried to escape the capital, knowing that their chances of survival would be better in the provinces. Two burly policemen were discovered heading for the Finland Station dressed in women's clothes. Only their large size and awkward gait, and the heavy police boots under their skirts, betrayed their identity to the crowd.[27]

ii Reluctant Revolutionaries

'The revolution found us, the party members, fast asleep, just like the Foolish Virgins in the Gospel,' recalled Sergei Mstislavsky, one of the SR leaders, in 1922. Much the same could be said for all the revolutionary parties in the capital. 'There were no authoritative leaders on the spot in any of the parties,' Sukhanov recalled. 'They were all in exile, in prison, or abroad.' Lenin and Martov were in Zurich, Trotsky in New York, Chernov in Paris. Tsereteli, Dan and Gots were in Siberia. Cut off from the pulse of the capital, the leaders failed to sense what Mstislavsky called 'the approaching storm in the ever mounting waves of the February disturbances'. Having spent their whole lives waiting for the revolution, they failed to recognize it when it came. Lenin himself had predicted in January that 'we older men perhaps will not live to see the coming revolution'. Even as late as 26 February, Shliapnikov, the leading Bolshevik in Petrograd, had told a meeting of socialists in Kerensky's flat: 'There is no and will be no revolution. We have to prepare for a long period of reaction.'[28]

In the absence of the major party leaders, the task of leading the revolution fell on to the shoulders of the secondary ones. They were not just second-ranking but also second-rate. Shliapnikov was an experienced trade unionist and party worker underground. But as a politician, in Sukhanov's words, he 'was quite incapable of grasping the essence' of the situation that had been created. His ideas were 'clichés of ancient party resolutions'. Not much more could be said of the Mensheviks in the capital. Chkheidze, the 'Papa' of the revolution, was an amiable and competent but sleepy-headed Georgian, who, in the words of Sukhanov, could not have been 'less suited to be a working-class or party leader, and he never led anyone anywhere'. Skobelev, a Duma deputy from Baku, was a provincial intellectual, designed on a small-town rather than a national scale. As for Sukhanov, he was on the fringes of all the party factions, being much too undecided to declare his views. Like all too many of the socialist leaders, he was always inclined to look at politics as an intellectual rather than as a politician. Trotsky described him as 'a conscientious observer rather than a statesman, a journalist rather than a revolutionist, a rationaliser rather than a journalist — he was capable of standing by a revolutionary conception only up to the time when it was necessary to carry it into action'. N. D. Sokolov was a similarly floating figure, too vague in his beliefs to fit into any party. This bearded lawyer, with his little pince-nez, would have been more at home in a library or a lecture hall than in a revolutionary crowd. Finally, the SRs were no better off for leaders in the capital. Mstislavsky and Filipovsky found themselves as the closest things the Soviet had to 'military men' (Mstislavsky was merely a librarian at the Military Academy but Filipovsky was a naval engineer) thrown into positions of leadership for which they were suited neither by their temperament nor their skills. Zenzinov was a party hack.[29] And as for Kerensky — well more on him below.

These second-ranking leaders chased after events in the February Days. They telephoned from one apartment to another trying to find out what was happening on the streets. Gorky's apartment on the Kronversky served as a central telephone exchange. Leaders would assemble there to share their impressions and make enquiries. Gorky himself had connections throughout Petrograd. It was only on the 27th, when the revolution had already become an established fact, that the party leaders sprang into action and assumed the leadership of the uprising on the streets. It was a classic example of 'We are their leaders, so we must follow them.'

Everything was focused on the Tauride Palace, seat of the Duma and citadel of democracy. By the early afternoon of the 27th a crowd of 25,000 people — many of them soldiers from the nearby Preobrazhensky and Volynsky barracks — had gathered in front of the palace. They were looking for political leaders. The first to appear were the Mensheviks Khrustalev-Nosar (Chairman of the Petrograd Soviet in 1905), and Gvozdev and Bogdanov (leaders of the Workers' Group), escorted by the crowd that had just released them from the Kresty jail. In the palace they met Chkheidze, Skobelev and Kerensky, and then announced to the crowds outside that a 'Provisional Executive Committee of the Soviet of Workers' Deputies' had been established. They appealed to the workers to elect and send their representatives to the first assembly of the Soviet scheduled for that evening. The appeal was printed in a makeshift first issue of *Izvestiia*, the only newspaper to appear that day, and widely circulated in the streets.

Despite its name, there were very few workers among the fifty voting delegates and 200 observers packed into the smoke-filled Room 12 of the Tauride Palace for that first chaotic session of the Soviet. Most of the workers were still on the streets and were either drunk or completely unaware of the Soviet's existence. Their voting places were largely occupied by socialist intellectuals. Sokolov assumed the preliminary chairmanship of the meeting, which immediately proceeded to set up an Executive Committee of 6 Mensheviks, 2 Bolsheviks, 2 SRs and 5 non-party intellectuals. It was not so much a democratic body as a self-appointed one made up of the various socialist factions and then superimposed on the Soviet. The next day, as 600 Soviet deputies were elected by the workers and soldiers of Petrograd, two more representatives from each of the major socialist parties — the Trudoviks, the Popular Socialists, the SRs, the Bund, the Mensheviks, the Inter-District group* and the Bolsheviks — were added to the Executive Committee. The effect was to strengthen its right wing, those who were most opposed to taking power. The voice of the workers, who might well have demanded that they did take power, was not heard. There was not a single factory delegate on the Soviet Executive — and that in a body claiming to represent the working class.

Chkheidze was appointed Chairman with Skobelev and Kerensky Vice-Chairmen. But there was really no order to the meeting. Executive members were summoned every minute to meet delegations outside the hall. Business was constantly interrupted by 'urgent announcements' or 'emergency reports'. All sorts of unelected groups — post and telegraph officials, zemstvo employees, doctors' and teachers' representatives — demanded admission and sometimes got in to declare their allegiance to the Soviet. Then there were the soldiers' delegations, whose demands for the floor to make their reports were warmly welcomed by the delegates. Standing on stools, their rifles in their hands, they told in simple language of what had been happening in their garrisons and declared the allegiance of their regiments to the Soviet. The delegates were so enthralled, greeting each declaration with thunderous applause, that it was re-solved unanimously, without even taking a formal vote, to create a united Soviet henceforth known as the Petrograd Soviet of Workers' and Soldiers' Deputies.

For those who had wanted a genuine workers' Soviet this was the final kiss of death. Organized in their platoons and companies, the soldiers were in a much better position than the workers to elect their delegates to the Soviet. It often turned out, moreover, that a single platoon of a dozen or so soldiers sent its own representative who was on a par with one from a factory with several thousand workers. There was little real control of voting procedures. The blue of the workers' tunics was lost in the sea of grey uniforms when the first combined session of the Soviet assembled in the Catherine Hall on the evening of the 28th. Of the 3,000 delegates, more than two-thirds were servicemen — and this in a city where workers outnumbered soldiers by three or four to one. The fact that most of the soldiers were peasants may help to account for the chaotic nature of these early sessions, along with the general confusion of events.

---

* The Inter-District group, or Mezhraionka, was a left-wing faction of the Social Democrats in Petrograd. It favoured the reunification of the Menshevik and Bolshevik wings of the party. Trotsky and Lunacharsky belonged to it until the summer of 1917, when they joined the Bolsheviks.

'A mass meeting! Anyone who wants to gets up and says whatever he likes,' is how one delegate described the first session. There were no formal agendas, minutes or procedures for decision-making in the Soviet. Every decision was arrived at through open debate, with speakers in different parts of the hall all talking at once, and the resolutions passed by general acclamation, much as at a village assembly. Because such a body was incapable of any constructive work it soon took on a purely symbolic role, with the real decisions being made by the Executive and the socialist party caucuses to which most of its members belonged. The workers and soldiers who had made the revolution had in effect lost their political voice to the socialist intelligentsia, which claimed to speak in their name.[30]

Meanwhile, over in the right wing of the Tauride Palace the Duma members of the Progressive Bloc and the Council of Elders were meeting to decide whether they should obey the Tsar's order of the previous night to prorogue the Duma, or whether they should defy it and place themselves at the head of the revolutionary movement. The radicals and socialists, whose spokesman was Kerensky, urged the latter course. But the more moderate Duma members, and none more than Miliukov, who acted as their 'boss', were clearly terrified by the sight of the crowds. From inside the palace the noise of the 'mobs', as they were inclined to call them, was growing louder and more threatening all the time. For a while these moderates sought to play for time by hiding, as it were, behind the thick volumes of constitutional law. It would be illegal, they pontificated, to usurp the powers of the Tsar by forming a cabinet on their own initiative; but it would be possible to cable the sovereign with a request for his permission to do so. In a strictly legal sense there was some logic to this reasoning: the crowds on the street had no authority to hand over power to the Duma and any government formed on that basis would lack formal legitimacy. But such legal niceties were hardly the point now. This, after all, was a revolution; and all revolutions, by their nature, are illegal. The only real power — the power of violence — now lay in the streets and the refusal of the Duma moderates to recognize this fact was an act of cowardice and short-sightedness. No doubt they were afraid that if they assumed power, the masses in the streets would try to impose on them a socialist programme of reforms and peace. In other words, they were reluctant to place themselves at the head of a revolutionary government, even though a revolution had just taken place. Rodzianko, the Duma President, and, in his own words, 'the fattest man in Russia', still spoke in terms of a 'government of public confidence' (which could mean one appointed by the Tsar) rather than a public or Duma government.

During the afternoon, however, as the Petrograd Soviet began to emerge as a rival contender for power in the left wing of the palace, twelve Duma members from the Progressive Bloc, along with Kerensky and Chkheidze, took

one more cautious step towards the assumption of power. They formed themselves into a 'Temporary Committee of Duma Members for the Restoration of
Order in the Capital and the Establishment of Relations with Individuals and
Institutions'. The length of its name betrayed the timidity of its intentions. This
was a 'private' body of Duma members formed to help 'restore order' in the
capital, not a Duma organ for the assumption of power. It was only later that
night, when the Soviet plenum was in session and reports came in that the
capital was sinking deeper into anarchy, that these reluctant revolutionaries,
having failed in one last effort to persuade the Grand Duke Mikhail to become
dictator, finally seized the initiative and proclaimed themselves in authority.
There was simply no alternative — except Soviet power.[31]

By 28 February, then, two rival centres of power had emerged: in the
right wing of the Tauride Palace there was the Temporary Committee of
the Duma, which had the closest thing to formal power but no authority in the
streets; while in the left wing there was the Soviet, which had the closest thing
to power in the streets but no formal authority.

* * *

Meanwhile, there were still some battles to be fought. Although the crowd had
captured most of the city, there was still a danger that Major-General Khabalov
might crush the uprising with the aid of troops from the Front, as the Tsar had
ordered on the 27th. 'In conventional military terms', Mstislavsky recalled, 'our
situation was quite catastrophic. We had neither artillery, nor machine-guns;
neither commanding officers, nor field communications,' and if Khabalov attacked
with disciplined troops, 'we had as much chance as a snowball in hell.' Everything
depended on the fighting spirit of the mutinous soldiers and their willingness
to carry out the orders of the Soviet. Many of the soldiers seemed much less
interested in fighting for it than in 'joining the people' and getting drunk.
Shklovsky, who was placed in charge of guarding the railway stations, found it
almost impossible to convince the troops coming into Petrograd to assume even
basic guard duties. The entire guard of the Nikolaevsky Station, where the vital
trains from Moscow came in, consisted of a 'one-armed student and an ancient
naval officer in what seemed to be the uniform of an ensign'. At the Tauride
Palace things were rather better. Catherine the Great's graceful palace was now
turned into the military headquarters of Red Petrograd. The Soviet established
a Military Commission, which issued orders to *ad hoc* brigades placed at strategic
points in the city. Hundreds of soldiers had encamped in the corridors of the
Tauride Palace waiting for the order to defend this bastion of the revolution.
Linde, having put aside his volume of Haldane, took up the command of the
guard at the gates. Having been elected by his Finland Regiment to represent it
in the Soviet, he had an extra reason to defend the palace with gun in hand.
Here was the new politician armed. Stocks of food and guns were piled up high

in the rooms and corridors of the palace. In the middle of the Circular Hall there was a sewing machine: nobody knew how it had got there, or what it was supposed to be for. Perhaps someone had been planning for a long war and had thought it might be needed to mend uniforms. Nabokov described the scene inside the palace:

> Soldiers, soldiers, and more soldiers, with tired, dull faces; everywhere were signs of an improvised camp, rubbish, straw; the air was thick like some kind of dense fog, there was a smell of soldiers' boots, cloth, sweat; from somewhere we could hear the hysterical voices of orators addressing a meeting in the Catherine Hall — everywhere crowding and bustling con- fusion.[32]

There were still, moreover, some troublesome pockets of resistance in the capital: in the Winter Palace, in the General Staff building, at the Admiralty and in the Astoria Hotel. Some of the bloodiest fighting of the whole revolution took place in the hotel on the 28th. It was packed with senior officers and their families and, when snipers on its roof opened fire on the crowds below, the revolutionary soldiers brought up three machine-guns on armoured cars and began to fire through all the windows. Meanwhile, armed crowds stormed the building, wrecking the plush interior, looting the wine stores and searching the rooms for 'counter-revolutionaries'. Several dozen officers were shot or bayoneted. There was a long pitched battle amidst the broken chandeliers and mirrors of the vestibule, and at the end of it, according to one eye-witness, 'the revolving door was running in a pool of blood'.[33]

✻ ✻ ✻

The main aim of the leaders in the Tauride Palace — both in the left wing and in the right — was to restore order on the streets. There was a real danger of the revolution degenerating into anarchy. Thousands of drunken workers and soldiers were roaming through the city looting stores, breaking into houses, beating up and robbing people in the streets. The revolutionary struggle against the police and the army officers was breaking down into uncontrolled violence and retribution. 'Unless all this is brought to a halt,' warned one deputy in the Soviet, 'the revolution will end in defeat and shame.'

One cause for concern was the safe and orderly detention of the tsarist ministers and officials. On the evening of the 27th the Council of Ministers had held its last meeting in the Marinsky Palace and formally submitted its resignation to the Tsar. At one stage in the meeting the lights had gone out and it was assumed that the revolutionaries were about to storm the palace. In fact it was just a power-cut and when the lights came back on after a few minutes, several of the ministers were found hiding under the table. None the less, their panic was not without cause. Some 4,000 tsarist government officials were seized by the crowd in the February Days, and the fate of many of them was not one that anyone would envy. The Temporary Committee of the Duma ordered the arrest of all ex-ministers and senior officials, and their delivery to the Duma 'for justice', partly to save them from the horrors of 'mob law'. It was fitting and symbolic that Shcheglovitov, the former Minister of Justice, should have been the first to be brought by the crowds to the Tauride Palace. There he was met by Kerensky, shortly to become the next Minister of Justice, who, clearly aware of the drama of the situation, announced to the prisoner: 'Ivan Grigorievich Shcheglovitov, you are under arrest! Your life is not in danger!' And then with irony added the words: 'Know that the State Duma does not shed blood.' Several ex-ministers even turned themselves in to the Duma rather than run the risk of being captured by the crowds. Protopopov was among these. He tried to save himself by turning evidence against the Tsar and, when this failed, broke down into tears and whined pathetically. Sukhomlinov, the ex-Minister of War, arrived on 1 March with his own armed escort, causing wild excitement among the soldiers. They were only just dissuaded from executing him on the spot. But they did succeed in tearing off his epaulettes as a rejection of the old military order.[34]

All these fallen officials were detained in the Ministerial Pavilion of the Tauride Palace and then transferred to the Peter and Paul Fortress for interrogation and imprisonment. It was one of those small but nicely symbolic ironies of the revolution that the man who was placed in charge of escorting the ministers to the Peter and Paul should have been a man, Viktor Zenzinov, who had himself once been a prisoner there. He recalls what must have been a very strange sensation as he, now a government official, arrived at the prison gates with Shcheglovitov, once the Minister of Justice himself, but now just another 'political':

> We drove through the gates, did a turn or two, went under the arch and came to a stop in front of the door. Just the same guards stood there now as I remembered from seven years before. Then out came to meet us — I could scarcely believe my eyes — Captain Ivanishin, the same Captain Ivanishin, who seven years before had run the Trubetskoi Bastion, where the solitary confinement prisoners were kept and where I had been kept under him in a damp stone cell for six months during 1910 ... Now he was conducting himself politely with me. I have no doubt that Ivanishin recognized me immediately, just as I recognized him, but he did not give any sign of recognition.

On Zenzinov's request, Kerensky ordered the removal of Ivanishin. But the order was not carried out. It was only later, after several weeks, when Ivanishin was found guilty of accepting bribes from the imprisoned ministers, that he was finally dismissed.[35]

A second cause for concern in the Tauride Palace was how to get the troops to return to their barracks. This was essential to restore order. On the 28th the Military Commission — now under the control of the Temporary Committee — ordered the soldiers who had mutinied to return to their garrisons and to recognize the authority of their officers. But the soldiers were afraid that they would be punished for their participation in the mutiny, and demanded guarantees of their immunity before they returned. Most of them mistrusted the Temporary Committee — some of them called it 'counter-revolutionary' because it supported the officers — and turned to the Soviet to protect them. The result was Order Number One, perhaps the most consequential document to be written as a result of the February Revolution. It was a list of the soldiers' demands and conditions for their return to the garrisons. It provided for the establishment of soldiers' committees as a democratic counterbalance to the authority of the officers. It declared that the soldiers would recognize only the authority of the Petrograd Soviet, and that the orders of the Duma's Military Commission would be executed only in so far as they did not conflict with the Soviet's. When they were not on military duty, soldiers were to enjoy the rights of citizens, including the right not to salute their officers. Rudeness by the officers towards the soldiers, including the use of the familiar 'you' (*tyi*), associated with children and serfs, was henceforth to be prohibited as an insult to the soldier's dignity. The honorific titles of the officers, such as 'Your Excellency' and 'Your Honour', which the peasant soldiers, in particular, resented as a remnant of serfdom, were to be replaced by new and democratic forms of address, such as 'Mister General' or 'Mister Colonel'.

The Order was a popular creation in the full sense of the term. Sukhanov watched as Sokolov sat a table:

> surrounded on all sides by soldiers, standing, sitting, and leaning on the table, half dictating and half suggesting to Sokolov what he should write . . . There was no agenda and no discussion of any kind, everyone spoke, and all were completely absorbed in the work, formulating their collective opinion without any voting . . . When the work was finished they put a heading on the sheet: 'Order No. I'.

A few minutes later the Order was read out before the Soviet, then in session in the Catherine Hall, and passed unanimously to the thunderous applause of the soldiers. This crucial document, which did more than anything else to destroy the discipline of the army, and thus in a sense brought the Bolsheviks to power, had taken only a few minutes to pass.[36]

*   *   *

While the Soviet leaders wanted to restore order, most of them had no intention of assuming power. The whole basis of their strategy was to pressurize the Duma leaders into forming a 'bourgeois government'. Thus there arose what Trotsky later called the 'paradox' of February: that a revolution made in the streets resulted in a government made in the salons. This was a recurring pattern throughout the politics of 1917: there were several moments (February, April, July and September) when the Soviet leaders might have taken power, when indeed the crowds came out on to the streets with the express demand that they do just that, but on each occasion they shied away from the responsibilities of government. In this way they missed their chance to resolve the revolution in a democratic and socialist form. The Bolsheviks reaped the benefits.

How are we to explain this political failure? In the context of February, which determined much of the later politics, there were three main lines of reasoning.

First, there was the problem of party dogma. Both the Mensheviks and the SRs adhered rigidly to the belief that in a backward peasant country such as Russia there would have to be a 'bourgeois revolution' (meaning a long period of capitalism and democracy) before Russian society, and the working class in particular, would be sufficiently advanced for the transition to a socialist order. As Plekhanov had once put it, there was not yet enough proletarian yeast in the peasant dough of Russia to make the cake of socialism. In the case of the Mensheviks this belief in the two-stage revolution derived from Marxist theory; and in the case of the SRs it derived largely from the Mensheviks. The belief was based on two further assumptions, which both made abstract sense but fell down when applied to the real world. It was a case of trying to impose nineteenth-century Western dogmas on the realities of twentieth-century Russia. For one thing, it was said that the peasants (and the provinces in general) would not support a socialist government in the cities because they were too attached to what the Mensheviks called their 'petty-bourgeois' notions of small property. As a result, an urban socialist revolution would either be starved out of existence, like the Paris Commune, or, even worse, would be beaten by a peasant counter-revolution, like the Vendée or the European royalist armies of 1849. But in fact the Russian peasants were even more impatient for a social revolution than, arguably, the workers were. All they wanted was the land and, if 'socialism' meant giving the land to the peasants, then they were 'socialists'. This meant, as the SRs should have realized, that the peasants would not join a counter-revolution so long as that entailed — as it was almost bound to in Russia — a restoration of the gentry on the land. It was also said that the masses were too illiterate and inexperienced politically to assume the tasks of government, and that until this was remedied the support and leadership of the educated classes would remain essential. The Soviets, as class-based organs, might play a role in local government but they lacked the means to run the state. What was needed now, as a preparation for the transition to socialism, was for the masses to go through the school of democracy — which for the workers, in particular, meant following the example of the European labour movements — and this could only be achieved within a liberal framework of political freedom. But this too was to impose a Western model of democracy on a country where the base for it was missing. The 'direct democracy' of the Soviets was much closer to the experience of the Russian masses — it was reminiscent of the peasant commune — and it might have served as the starting point for a new and different type of democratic order, one much more decentralized than the liberal democracy of the West, provided the Soviets were somehow combined with the broader representative bodies (e.g. the city dumas, the zemstvos and the Constituent Assembly) in a national political framework.

No doubt the Soviet leaders' rigid adherence to this dogma was in part the result of their own virginity in government. The bourgeois leaders had years of experience of legislative matters, either in the Duma or in the zemstvos. But the socialists had no real experience of government work, only the long and fruitless years of politics in semi-legal opposition and the underground. Furthermore, their party leaders were all still in exile, and it might be thought of as a 'colonels' revolt' if they assumed power. Yet should this really have been such an obstacle? For all their talk of 'principles' and 'ideology', in the end it was their instincts and their temperament that held back the Soviet leaders from taking power. They had spent so long in hostile opposition to all governmental authority that many of them could not suddenly become — or even think of themselves as — statesmen. They clung to the habits and the culture of the revolutionary underground, preferring opposition to government.

Second, the Soviet leaders were afraid that a counter-revolution, perhaps even a civil war, might be the result if they assumed power. The situation was extremely fluid; it was not yet clear whether Alexeev and the Front commanders would carry out the orders of the Tsar to put down the revolution in the capital; nor whether the revolution would spread to the provinces and the forces at the Front. As things turned out, it soon became clear that the Soviet leaders had grossly overestimated the real danger of a counter-revolution. Almost immediately Alexeev called off the planned expedition to put down the revolution in the capital, partly because he was reassured that the Duma leaders rather than the socialists would assume power, and partly because he realized that to use the troops for this would run the risk of the mutiny spreading to the army at the Front. It did not take long, moreover, for the revolution to spread to the

Kronstadt Naval Base, several northern garrisons and Moscow itself. Within a few days the monarchy would fall, along with its provincial apparatus, while the army and the Church would both declare their support for the revolution. Of course none of this was yet clear on 1 March. The speed of events took everyone by surprise. As Iurii Steklov, one of the Soviet leaders, explained in April 1917:

> at the time when this agreement [to form the Provisional Government] was contemplated, it was not at all clear as to whether the revolution would emerge victorious, either in a revolutionary-democratic form or even in a moderate-bourgeois form. Those of you, comrades, who were not here in Petrograd and did not experience this revolutionary fever cannot imagine how we lived . . . We expected from minute to minute that they [troops loyal to the Tsar] would arrive.[37]

Yet it is probably fair to say that in their appraisal of the situation the Soviet leaders once again allowed themselves to be over-influenced by the experience of nineteenth-century Europe. All the socialists were steeped in the history of European revolutions. They interpreted the events of 1905 and 1917 in terms of the history of 1789, 1848 and 1871, and this led them to believe that a counter-revolution must inevitably follow.

Finally, the Soviet leaders were not even certain of their own authority over the masses in the streets. They had been shocked by the violence and the hatred, the anarchic looting and the vandalism displayed by the crowds in the February Days. They were afraid that if they assumed power, that if they themselves became 'the government', all this uncontrolled anger might be redirected against them. Mstislavsky claimed that 'from the first hours of the revolution' the vast majority of the Soviet leaders were united with the members of the Temporary Committee 'by one single characteristic which determined everything else: this was their fear of the masses':

> Oh, how they feared the masses! As I watched our 'socialists' speaking to the crowds . . . I could feel their nauseating fear . . . I felt the inner trembling, and the effort of will it took not to lower their gaze before the trusting, wide-open eyes of the workers and soldiers crowded around them. As recently as yesterday it had been relatively easy to be 'representatives and leaders' of these working masses; peaceable parliamentary socialists could still utter the most bloodcurdling words 'in the name of the proletariat' without even blinking. It became a different story, however, when this theoretical proletariat suddenly appeared here, in the full power of exhausted flesh and mutinous blood. And when the truly elemental nature of this force, so capable of either creation or destruction, became tangible

to even the most insensitive observer — then, almost involuntarily, the pale lips of the 'leaders' began to utter words of peace and compromise in place of yesterday's harangues. They were scared — and who could blame them?[38]

Who indeed? And yet this fear was also symptomatic of a general cowardice when it came to the responsibilities of power. It was an abdication of statesmanship. Years later Tsereteli said that the Soviet leaders in February had been childish and irresponsible. Many of them welcomed the dual power system — the source of Russia's chronic political weaknesses in 1917 — because it placed them in a good position. They were given power without responsibility; while the Provisional Government had responsibility without power.

For the majority of the Soviet leaders there was a special factor making the negotiation of a Duma government a matter of the utmost urgency. On 1 March the left-wing minority of the Soviet Executive (3 Bolsheviks, 2 Left SRs and 1 member of the Inter-District group) demanded the formation of a 'provisional revolutionary government' based on the Soviets. This resolution was supported by the Bolshevik Committee in the Vyborg district, the most proletarian in Petrograd. There was thus a real threat that, unless the Soviet majority imposed a government on the Duma leaders, the streets might impose a government on them.

At around midnight on 1 March a Soviet delegation (Sukhanov, Chkheidze, Sokolov and Steklov) crossed from the left to the right wing of the Tauride Palace to begin negotiations for a government with the Temporary Committee of the Duma. 'There was not the same chaos and confusion here as with us,' Sukhanov recalled, 'but the room nevertheless gave an impression of disorder: it was smoke-filled and dirty, and cigarette butts, bottles, and dirty glasses were scattered about. There were also innumerable plates, both empty and holding foods of all kinds, which made our eyes glitter and our mouths water.' Sukhanov and Miliukov, 'the boss of the right wing', did most of the talking. The enormous Rodzianko, President of the Duma, sulked in a corner drinking soda. Neither Lvov nor Kerensky, the first and the last Prime Minister of the Provisional Government respectively, had a single word to say on its establishment.

Both the Duma and the Soviet sides were pleasantly surprised by the common ground between them. Each had come prepared for a major battle. But in fact there was only one real point of conflict. Miliukov wanted the monarchy retained, albeit with Alexis as Tsar and the Grand Duke Mikhail acting as Regent. Chkheidze pointed out that the idea was 'not only unacceptable, but also utopian, in view of the general hatred of the monarchy amongst the masses of the people'. But Miliukov did not push his point — for which there was little support among the rest of the Duma leaders — and in the end it was agreed to leave the form of government undecided until the convocation of a Constituent Assembly. Other than that there was little to discuss. Everyone agreed on the need to restore order, and on the need to form a Duma government.

The negotiations were completed in the early hours of the morning. The 'bourgeois groups', as Sukhanov put it, would be left to form a government 'on the view that this followed from the general situation and suited the interests of the revolution'. But the Soviet, 'as the only organ wielding any real power', set as the conditions for its support the following principles of government:

1 an immediate amnesty for all political prisoners;
2 the immediate granting of freedom of speech, press and assembly;
3 the immediate abolition of all restrictions based on class, religion and nationality;
4 immediate preparations for the convocation of a Constituent Assembly, elected on the four-tail suffrage (universal, direct, secret and equal), to determine the form of government and the constitution of the country;
5 the abolition of all the police bodies and, in their place, the creation of a people's militia with elected officers responsible to the organs of local self-government;
6 elections to these organs on the four-tail suffrage;
7 a guarantee that the military units having taken part in the revolution would neither be disarmed nor sent to the Front;
8 recognition of full civil rights for the soldiers off-duty.[39]

No mention was made of the two basic issues (the war and the land) where the aims of the Soviet leaders clashed directly with those of the Duma. Given the bitter political conflicts that later emerged on these two issues (leading to the downfall of the first three cabinets), perhaps this was a crucial mistake.

This, then, was the framework of the dual power system. The Soviet would support the Provisional Government only 'in so far as' (*postol'ku poskol'ku*), to cite the famous phrase, it adhered to these Soviet principles; and it would act as the government's 'watchman' to make sure it did. The effect was to paralyse the Provisional Government. For it could do nothing without the support of the Soviet. Yet at the same time the Soviet's conditions created a climate of such uncontrolled freedom that there was a crying need for stronger government. As Lenin put it, Russia had become the 'freest country in the world' — and he was the first to exploit it.

* * *

The new cabinet was picked by Miliukov on 2 March, and published in the newspapers the next day, alongside a Soviet appeal 'To comrades and citizens!'

calling for order and the people's support of the government. To the crowds outside the Tauride Palace the names of their new rulers were mostly unknown. All of them were from the propertied élite. Most of them had been named in the various 'ministries of confidence' proposed by the liberal opposition circles since 1915. Eight of the twelve were deputies of the Fourth Duma (and two more of earlier Dumas); seven were members of either Zemgor or the War Industries Committee; while six belonged to the same Masonic circles,* whose precise role in the February Revolution has long been the subject of historical speculation but little concrete fact.

Prince Lvov, the Prime Minister and the Minister of the Interior, qualified on all these counts. His wartime work in the zemstvos had won him universal respect among the liberal educated classes. It had made him into a truly national figure and this gave the government at least the pretence of being based on something broader than the Duma. Lvov, moreover, was a good team-worker, a man of practical capabilities and without strong party affiliations, and this embodied the coalition spirit for which the government claimed to stand. This was not a government of any one party — it contained elements ranging from the Octobrists to the SRs — but a government of national salvation. This non-party aspect, combined with the general softness of his character, also made Lvov the ideal figure to conciliate between the real power-brokers in his cabinet — Miliukov and Kerensky — who would otherwise have fallen out and split the government from the start. Each of them was prepared to accept Lvov, if only because it stopped the other from becoming the Prime Minister. Yet when Lvov's name was announced to the crowds some of them cried out: 'The privileged class!' One soldier shouted: 'You mean all we did was exchange a tsar for a prince?'

The name of Tereshchenko, the new Minister of Finance, was greeted by the crowds with roars of laughter. 'Who is Tereshchenko?' people asked. And well might they ask. Even the newspapers knew little about him. All they could say was that he came from the Ukraine, was twenty-nine years old and a multi-millionaire. Shingarev, the Minister of Agriculture, had risen from similar obscurity. A provincial doctor and a Kadet member of the Duma, even his closest friends were forced to admit that he was little more than a decent mediocrity. Not much more was known of Konovalov (Trade and Industry), Nekrasov (Transport) or Manuilov (Education), although Guchkov (War and Navy) and Miliukov (Foreign Affairs) were certainly household names and seemed, at first, to meet with general approval.[40]

Only the name of Kerensky, the one socialist in the cabinet, met with the approval of the crowd. 'The mass of the soldiers', Stankevich recalled, 'felt

---

* Lvov, Kerensky, Nekrasov, Tereshchenko, Konovalov and Guchkov.

that Kerensky was "their" minister.' As the Vice-Chairman of the Soviet Executive, he should never have accepted — and even less have asked for — the portfolio of the Ministry of Justice. For it was the Soviet's official policy not to enter the government. Chkheidze had already turned down the offer of the Ministry of Labour. But Kerensky had his heart set on becoming a minister. Young and ambitious (he was still only thirty-five), Kerensky was convinced of his own calling to greatness, and could not bear to see this chance go by. Throughout the previous days he had been a key figure behind the scenes. He alone belonged both to the Soviet Executive and to the Duma's Temporary Committee. He had run from one wing of the Tauride Palace to the other, making himself indispensable to both. Yet it was clear where his sympathies lay: most of his time had been spent in the right wing, and he only rarely came to the Soviet to make some high-sounding speech about the 'people's revolution'. Not once did he venture on to the streets. Although convinced that he was a socialist, Kerensky was in fact a bourgeois radical, a Duma deputy and a democratic lawyer, dressed up as 'a man of the people'. Formally he belonged to the Trudovik Party. Later, when that became the thing to do, he joined the SRs. But in his heart he was not a socialist. In the Duma he always wore a morning coat with a starched dress-shirt and collar. But when he spoke in the Soviet he ripped off his collar and took off his coat to make himself look more 'proletarian'. This was not a revolutionary. It was someone, as Trotsky put it, who merely 'hung around the Revolution'.

Shortly after 2 p.m. on 2 March Kerensky came into the Soviet to deliver what was perhaps the most important speech of his life. He needed the assembly to endorse his decision, taken earlier that morning without its prior approval, to accept the Ministry of Justice. 'Comrades! Do you trust me?' he asked in a voice charged with theatrical pathos. 'We do, we do!' the delegates shouted. 'I speak, comrades, with all my soul, from the bottom of my heart, and if it is needed to prove this, if you do not trust me, then I am ready to die.' A wave of emotion passed through the hall. The delegates broke into prolonged applause, turning into a standing ovation. Seizing this opportunity, Kerensky claimed that he had been obliged to accept the portfolio, since the tsarist ministers 'were in my hands and I could not let them slip'. He told them that his 'first act' as the Minister of Justice had been to order the immediate release of all political prisoners and the arrangement of a hero's welcome for their return to the capital. The delegates were overcome with emotion and greeted this news with thunderous cheers. Now Kerensky turned to ask them whether they approved of his decision to join the government, offering to resign from the Soviet if the answer should be no. But there were wild cries of 'We do! We do!' and, without a formal vote, his actions were endorsed. It was a brilliant *coup de théâtre*. What might have been the moment of his downfall had in fact become the moment of his triumph. Kerensky was now the only politician with a position in both the government and the Soviet. He was the undisputed leader of the people.[41]

This was to be the start of the 'Kerensky cult'. His popularity was truly enormous. 'There is only one name that unites everyone', Gippius wrote on I March, 'and that is the name of Kerensky.' During these first weeks of the revolution the workers in their factories, the sailors on their ships and the soldiers in their barracks would ask the question, 'What has Alexander Fedorovich to say?', and invariably the answer would become the final word on any given issue. Kerensky was the darling of the democratic intelligentsia. 'We loved Kerensky,' recalled Gippius. 'There was something alive, something bird-like and childish in him.' With his pale and young-looking face, his bright, keen eyes and his nervous manner, he was the perfect image of the student radical.

This almost universal adulation cannot be explained in terms of the conventional virtues of a politician. Kerensky had few of these. His career in the Duma had not been especially distinguished: he lacked the stature of Miliukov and the style of Maklakov or Fedor Rodichev. And there were other lawyers better qualified to become the Minister of Justice. But Kerensky was the ideal man for February. As Gippius put it, 'He is the right man in the right place.' For one thing, Kerensky was a great orator — not so much in the parliamentary context, which demanded eloquence and intellectual balance, but in the sense that could appeal to the crowds. His speeches were fiery and emotional. They were not concerned with detailed policies but with moral principles and spiritual values. They often sounded more like the preachings of a priest than the prescripts of a politician. In his youth Kerensky had wanted to become an actor. His speeches were full of dramatic pathos, theatrical gestures and even fainting fits (these were genuine but Kerensky somehow managed to time them to coincide with the climax of his speech). All this tugged on the heart-strings of his listeners. Kerensky expressed and came to stand for the sentiment of national unity, for the people's resurrection, which the February Revolution was supposed to be. He was called the 'poet of freedom'; the 'heart of the nation'; the 'spirit of the people'; the 'saviour of the fatherland'; and the 'first love of the revolution'.[42]

It is perhaps not surprising that such a cult of the personality should have appeared in these first euphoric days of the revolution. People fell in love with 'the revolution', and this rubbed off on its 'leader', Kerensky. The institutions, the psychology, even the language of democracy had yet to be rooted in Russia's virgin political soil. Most of the people still conceived of politics in monarchical terms. This, after all, was a land of Tsars. Even before Nicholas's abdication, the Russian people had their new 'Tsar'.

iii Nicholas the Last

The Tsar's diary, 26 February 1917:

> At ten o'clock I went to Mass. The reports were on time. There were many people at breakfast, including all the foreigners. Wrote to Alix and went for a walk near the chapel by the Bobrisky road. The weather was fine and frosty. After tea I read and talked with Senator Tregubov until dinner. Played dominoes in the evening.

While Petrograd sank into chaos and the monarchy teetered on the verge of collapse, Nicholas carried on with the peaceful routines of his life at Stavka. There, in the words of one of his entourage, 'one day after another passed like two drops of water'. Judging from his letters, he was much more concerned by the fact that two of his daughters had gone down with measles than by the latest reports of rioting in the capital. True, Khabalov had not informed him of the gravity of the situation. But would the truth have made a difference? It is doubtful. On the morning of the 27th a cable arrived from the President of the Duma informing the Tsar of the real situation and pleading with him to 'take immediate steps' because 'tomorrow it will be too late'. Nicholas glanced at the message and, turning to Count Fredericks, exclaimed: 'That fat fellow Rodzianko has again written to me with all kinds of nonsense, which I shan't even bother to answer.'[43]

Since the death of Rasputin, Nicholas had turned his back on the capital and retreated into the quiet daily routines of Stavka and his family life at Tsarskoe Selo. Now more than ever he lived in a world of his own delusions, surrounding himself with lackeys of the court who flattered his fantasies of patrimonial power. During the last weeks of his reign numerous advisers pleaded with him to appoint a new government of confidence responsible to the Duma. But none had been able to penetrate the invisible wall of indifference that Nicholas erected around himself. And yet, beneath this outward appearance of calm, he was clearly in the midst of a deep internal crisis. Kokovtsov, who had not seen the Tsar for a year, found him 'unrecognizable' at the beginning of February. He was convinced that he was 'on the verge of a mental breakdown'. Paléologue was equally shocked by the Tsar's 'grave, drawn features and furtive distant gaze, the impenetrability of his thoughts, and the thoroughly vague and enigmatic quality of his personality'. It confirmed the French Ambassador in his long-held 'notion that Nicholas II feels himself overwhelmed and dominated by events, that he has lost all faith in his mission or his work, and that he has so to speak abdicated inwardly and is now resigned to disaster'.[44] It was as if his mental crisis consisted of the realization that the autocratic path he had followed for the past twenty-two years had finally come to an end, bringing his dynasty to the brink of disaster, and that the advice which everyone now gave him, to save his throne by handing over executive power to the Duma, was something he simply could not do. His whole life had been dedicated to the maintenance of autocracy, and now that he realized it could no longer be maintained, he gave up on life altogether. Here was the root of his notorious fatalism during the days leading up to his abdication.

In the evening of the 27th news finally reached the Tsar of the mutiny in Petrograd. He ordered General Ivanov, whom he now appointed to replace Khabalov as chief of the Petrograd Military District, to lead a force of punitive troops to the capital and establish a dictatorship there. Nicholas himself set out that night by train for Tsarskoe Selo, ignoring Alexeev's objections that this would merely hinder the counter-revolution and could endanger his life. His only concern, it appears, was to be reunited with his wife and children. The imperial train did not go directly northwards because Ivanov's troops were moving on this line but made a large detour to the east, arriving at Malaya Vishera, some 125 miles south-east of the capital, in the early morning of 1 March. There it could proceed no further because the line ahead had been seized by revolutionaries, so it headed west to Pskov, arriving there at 7 p.m. on 1 March. Because of the hasty arrangements, there was no formal ceremony to welcome the Tsar to the town where he was destined to renounce his throne. General Ruszky, Commander of the Northern Front, arrived late to meet him at the station. He was wearing a pair of rubber boots.[45]

By this time, however, several things had happened to undermine the plans for a counter-revolution. For one thing, the last remaining loyalist forces in the capital had singularly failed to organize resistance. General Khabalov clearly lacked the nerve for a serious fight and did almost nothing, although there was still much that he might have done. From the Admiralty, where he and his entourage had bunkered themselves in, there was a straight path to the three main railway stations (the Baltic, the Warsaw and the Nikolaevsky): loyalist troops, brought in from the Front, might have succeeded in fighting their way through. But Khabalov did not even think of this. Drinking cognacs to keep his hands from shaking, he merely wrote out a proclamation in which he declared the obvious — that the city was in a state of siege. But there was no one with the courage, let alone the brushes or the glue, to post up the printed version in the streets. Instead the leaflets were thrown out of the windows of the Admiralty, and most landed in the garden below. The efforts of Khabalov's men to link up with the loyalist forces in the other parts of the city centre ended in a similar farce. One detachment fought its way across to the Winter Palace — only to be ordered back by the palace commandant, outraged by the sight of the soldiers' dirty boots on his newly polished floors. It later turned out that the Grand

Duke Mikhail, who had been in the palace at the time, had ordered the soldiers to be turned away because he had been afraid that they might damage its chinaware. And for that he lost an Empire! Demoralized and unfed for several days, most of the soldiers ran off to the people's side rather than return to the Admiralty.

There was a second development to foil the plans for a counter-revolution on 1 March. Ivanov's troops had arrived in Tsarskoe Selo to find that the mutiny had even spread to the Imperial Guards, who were garrisoned there. Some of Ivanov's own troops had already begun to show signs of disaffection, answering in a 'surly fashion' when addressed by the Empress during a review. Meanwhile, back in Petrograd, the Temporary Committee had resolved that Nicholas would have to abdicate. Early in the morning on 2 March Guchkov and Shulgin departed for Pskov with instructions to impose the abdication and ensure the Law of Succession with Alexei as Tsar and the Grand Duke Mikhail as Regent. Rodzianko, meanwhile, who still had hopes of persuading the Tsar to make concessions, was prevented from going by a Soviet railway blockade.[46]

But the most important development was the decision of General Alexeev, as the acting Commander-in-Chief, to order a halt to the counter-revolutionary expedition. One of the reasons for this crucial decision was the assurance Alexeev had been given by Rodzianko on 1 March that the Duma leaders, rather than the Soviet ones, would form the new government in Petrograd. Alexeev himself had long been party to the palace coup plots of the Progressive Bloc. Instinctively he trusted Rodzianko, and seemed to believe that the liberals might still be prepared to negotiate a political settlement which retained the monarchical basis of Russia. But there was another motive for Alexeev's change of mind: he was afraid that if the army was used to attack the revolutionary capital, it might become engulfed in a general mutiny, leading to the country's defeat in the war. Already, on 1 March, there were mutinies in several northern garrisons, and there was a real danger that they might soon spread to the units at the Front. He preferred to isolate his front-line soldiers from Red Petrograd rather than send them there and run the risk of having them fall under its revolutionary influence. On 1 March Alexeev ordered General Ivanov to halt his expedition against Petrograd. He then sent a cable to the Tsar begging him to let the Duma form a government for the restoration of order. 'A revolution throughout Russia', he warned prophetically, 'would mean a disgraceful termination of the war. One cannot ask the army to fight while there is a revolution in the rear.'[47]

The armed services had always held a special place in Nicholas's heart, and it was the advice of his military chiefs which now persuaded him to abdicate. If on the morning of 1 March Alexeev had considered the appointment of a Duma government sufficient to calm the capital, by the morning of the 2nd he had become convinced that nothing less than the Tsar's abdication would be necessary. During the small hours of the morning, while Nicholas tossed and turned in his bed, unable to sleep, General Ruzsky conversed with Rodzianko in Petrograd through the Hughes Apparatus and learned from him that the capital was in such a state of chaos that only an act of abdication would be enough to satisfy the crowds. Alexeev was stunned by what he read from the transcripts of their conversation. At 9 a.m. he cabled Pskov with orders to wake the Tsar at once — 'ignoring all etiquette' — and to inform him of the contents of the Ruzsky–Rodzianko tapes. It was now clear to him and the other generals at Stavka that Nicholas had no choice but to follow Rodzianko's advice. But he knew the Tsar well enough to realize that he would not agree to abdicate unless urged to do so by his leading generals. Sending a circular telegram to the Front Commanders with a summary of the situation, he asked them to reply to Pskov in line with his view that Nicholas should step down in favour of his son in order to save the army, the war campaign, the nation and the dynasty.[48]

At 10 a.m. Ruzsky came to the Tsar's railway car and handed him the transcripts of his conversation with Rodzianko. Nicholas read them, stood up and looked out of the window. There was a dreadful silence. At last, he returned to his desk, and quietly spoke of his conviction 'that he had been born for misfortune'. The night before, as he lay in his bed, he had come to realize that it was too late for concessions. 'If it is necessary that I should abdicate for the good of Russia, then I am ready for it,' he said. 'But I am afraid that the people will not understand it.' A few minutes later Alexeev's telegram arrived. Ruzsky read it aloud to the Tsar and suggested postponing any decision until he had seen what the other commanders had to say. Nicholas adjourned for lunch. What else could he do? He was a man of habit.

By half-past two the telegrams from the commanders had arrived and Ruzsky was summoned back to the Emperor's car. Nicholas smoked incessantly as he read the cables. All of them agreed with Alexeev on the need for his abdication. Brusilov, who had long been convinced of the damage caused by the Tsar to the army, declared outright that it was now the only way to restore order in the rear and continue the war. The Grand Duke Nikolai implored his nephew 'on his knees' to give up the crown. When he had finished reading Nicholas asked the opinions of his three attendant generals on the imperial train. It was the same. There was a moment of silence before Nicholas spoke. 'I have made up my mind. I have decided to abdicate from the throne in favour of my son Alexei.' He crossed himself, the generals also made the sign of the cross, and then he withdrew to his cabin.[49]

Many of those who were with him on the imperial train were struck by the Tsar's strange lack of emotion during this ordeal. Right to the end he kept up his stiff Edwardian manners and impeccable sense of decorum. Having made the crucial decision to abdicate, he went for his afternoon walk and appeared in the buffet car as usual for evening tea. Not a word was said of the day's events. His courtiers carried on with the normal small-talk on the weather, while liveried servants went round the table pouring tea as if nothing had happened. 'The Tsar sat peacefully and calm,' recalled one of his aides-de-camp. 'He kept up conversation and only his eyes, which were sad, thoughtful and staring into the distance, and his nervous movements when he took a cigarette, betrayed his inner disturbance.'[50]

The truth of the matter was that his abdication probably came as a relief. That night Nicholas would sleep much better than he had done for a long time. As a young man, he had never really wanted to be Tsar. The jovial life of a young Guards officer, followed by the cosy domestic routines of a landed squire, were much more to his liking. But when misfortune had put him on the throne he swore to uphold and pass on to his son the autocratic powers which he had inherited from his beloved and much-feared father. He adhered to this coronation oath with a dogged narrow-mindedness, as if he was terrified that God (or his wife) would punish him if he failed to rule like Ivan the Terrible. As long as he remained Tsar nothing could divert him from this path. For twenty-two years he had ignored the lessons of history, as well as the pleadings of countless advisers, which all pointed to the fact that the only way to save his throne was to grant a government accountable to the people. His motive was always the same: his 'conscience' forbade him to do it. Even as late as January 1917, when the Grand Duke Pavel, in a last desperate bid to avert the catastrophe, urged him to concede a Duma ministry, Nicholas replied: 'I took an oath for Autocracy on the day of my coronation and I must remit this oath in its integrity to my son.'[51] In a way, he probably found it easier to abdicate than to turn himself into a constitutional king. That was Nicholas's tragedy.

Throughout the whole affair Nicholas's main concern was to be reunited with his family. 'In my thoughts I am always with you,' he wrote to Alexandra on 28 February. It was this that led to a final curious twist in the tale of his abdication. During the evening of 2 March, while he waited for Guchkov and Shulgin to arrive from the capital, Nicholas summoned Professor Fedorov, his court physician, and asked him about the prospects for his son's recovery. He told him of Rasputin's prediction that Alexei would be cured by the age of thirteen, which, by an ironic turn of fate, he was due to reach in 1917. Fedorov dispelled any such hopes: there was no medical cure for haemophilia and Alexei could not live much longer. He also expressed his doubts that the Tsar would be allowed to stay with his son once he had renounced the throne, for he would surely be expected to go into exile. On hearing this, Nicholas resolved to abdicate not only for himself but also for his son in favour of his younger brother, the Grand Duke Mikhail. 'I cannot be separated from him,' he told

Guchkov and Shulgin when they arrived. 'I hope you will understand the feelings of a father.'[52]

In legal terms this was quite invalid. The Law of Succession made it clear that the Russian throne was 'not the Emperor's private property nor his patrimony to be disposed of according to his will', but descended automatically to his eldest son. To make matters worse, Mikhail had legally barred himself from the throne by marrying a commoner who had already been divorced. But Guchkov and Shulgin were now more concerned with the fact of the Tsar's abdication than with its strict legality; and in order to achieve it they were ready to make this final concession to his patrimonial will. The Abdication Manifesto, which Nicholas composed in his private car that evening, was technically illegal. Later it was claimed that this might have served as a pretext for his restoration. But at the time it seemed no more than a minor allowance for his natural rights as a father.[53]

News of the Tsar's abdication reached Tsarskoe Selo on the following day. It was left to the Grand Duke Pavel to inform the Empress, since no one else in her entourage could find the courage to do so. He found her with the children, in a nurse's uniform. When he told her the news 'the Empress trembled and bent down her head, as though she were uttering a prayer'. In a calm voice she explained to him that her husband had evidently 'preferred to abdicate the crown rather than break the oath which he had made at his coronation'. Then she burst into tears.[54]

*   *   *

The crowds outside the Tauride Palace met the announcement that Nicholas would abdicate in favour of the Grand Duke Mikhail with an outburst of angry indignation. The Catherine Hall echoed to shouts from the street of 'Long Live the Republic!' and 'Down with the Dynasty!' When Guchkov returned from Pskov he went in triumph to a meeting of railway workers to tell them what had happened. Ending his speech with the rallying call 'Long Live the Emperor Mikhail!', he was at once arrested and threatened with execution by the workers. Throughout the capital crowds attacked supporters and symbols of the tsarist order. A huge demonstration of soldiers marched to the Tauride Palace demanding the overthrow of the dynasty. Politically, it seemed, the monarchy was doomed. Yet inside the palace Miliukov continued to defend its existence in legal terms. It was essential, the professor argued, to preserve the monarchy as a symbol of the state. For only it could give legitimacy and a historic continuity to the transfer of power. This was the triumph of hope over reality. The mood of the crowd clearly made the survival of the monarchy impossible. The masses would not tolerate a new Tsar, and if one was imposed then further disorders would ensue, perhaps even leading to a civil war. The republican ministers, led by Kerensky and Nekrasov, eventually got their way. The Provisional Government resolved to persuade the Grand Duke to refuse the crown and thus bring the dynasty to an end.[55]

It would not take much persuading. Mikhail was a shy and modest man, not much interested in politics, and even less intelligent than his older brother. In different circumstances he might have made a good, if rather dim, constitutional monarch, much like his English cousin, George V. But the rioting in the capital, which he had personally witnessed, had not given him much appetite for monarchical power. He was not in the least bit eager to put his own head on the block — either metaphorically or literally — and was understandably both surprised and annoyed when his brother suddenly and unexpectedly decided to burden him with the crown without even consulting him.

He met the leaders of the Provisional Government on 3 March in the residence of Princess Putiatina, not far from the Winter Palace, where the Grand Duke had taken refuge from the revolution. Lvov and Kerensky put forward the majority point of view in the government that if Mikhail accepted the throne there would be a violent uprising, leading to civil war. Miliukov disagreed, claiming that only the monarchy was recognized by the people as a symbol of authority and that it was now required to save the country from chaos. 'The Provisional Government on its own, without a monarch', he argued, 'is an unseaworthy vessel liable to sink in the ocean of popular unrest.' All this left the Grand Duke rather confused. He asked for an hour to talk in private with Rodzianko. His main concern, according to Rodzianko, was whether the Duma could guarantee his personal safety if he became Tsar. When Rodzianko said that it could not, he finally made up his mind and, returning to the meeting, announced that he had decided to decline the crown. There was a tear in his eye. Kerensky, whose own emotions often got the better of his senses, rushed up to the Grand Duke, shook his hand and congratulated him with these words of astounding self-importance: 'Your Imperial Highness, you have acted nobly and like a patriot. From now on, I shall assume the obligation of making this known and of defending you.'[56]

Two jurists, Nabokov and Nolde, were later summoned to the Putiatina residence to draft the abdication manifesto. This historic document, which brought to an end 300 years of Romanov rule, was written out by them at a school desk in the study of Putiatina's daughter and then copied out in one of her school notebooks. By 6 p.m. the document was ready. Mikhail signed it in the presence of the ministers and Rodzianko. He then turned to embrace Prince Lvov and wished him good fortune as the Prime Minister of the new Russia.[57]

* * *

The end of the monarchy was marked by scenes of rejoicing throughout the Russian Empire. Rapturous crowds assembled in the streets of Petrograd and Moscow. Red flags were hoisted on to the roofs and hung from the windows of nearly every building. In Helsingfors, Kiev, Tiflis and the other non-Russian capitals, where the downfall of the Tsar was associated with the liberation of the nation, national flags were often displayed alongside them. There was hardly a town, however small, that did not celebrate the revolution with jubilant processions, patriotic speeches and the singing of the Marseillaise. Konstantin Paustovsky recalls the night when his little sleepy town, Yefremov in Tula province, first heard of the revolution.

It was one o'clock in the night, a time when Yefremov was usually asleep. Suddenly, at this odd hour, there sounded a short, booming peal of the cathedral bell. Then another, and a third. The pealing grew faster, its noise spread over the town, and soon the bells of all the outlying churches started to ring.

Lights were lit in all the houses. The streets filled with people. The doors of many houses stood open. Strangers, weeping openly, embraced each other. The solemn, exultant whistling of locomotives could be heard from the direction of the station. Somewhere down one street there began, first quietly, then steadily louder, the singing of the Marseillaise:

Ye tyrants quake, your day is over,
Detested now by friend and foe!

The singing brass sounds of a band joined the human voices in the chorus.

The soldiers in the trenches were equally ecstatic, despite the initial confusion caused by the efforts of the officers to withhold the news from the capital. Red flags were raised in the trenches and red ribbons tied to the military trucks, pieces of artillery and the horses. There were parades to celebrate the revolution, military bands played the Marseillaise and soldiers wildly threw their caps into the air. On the naval ships there was a similar outburst of emotion. The red flag was raised on battleships 'as an emblem', in the words of the Helsingfors sailors, 'of our freedom and our unity'.[58]

In the countryside the news of the abdication filtered down more slowly. Some of the more remote villages did not learn about the events in the capital until the end of March, and in some places, such as in Kazan and Mogilev provinces, where the tsarist forces remained dominant, not until April. Many of the peasants were at first confused by the downfall of the Tsar. 'The church was full of crying peasants,' one witness recalled. ' "What will become of us?" they constantly repeated — "They have taken the Tsar away from us?" ' Some of the older peasants, in particular, venerated the Tsar as a god on earth and saw his removal as an attack upon religion — a fact exploited by many priests in their counter-revolutionary agitation. Even among the more ruralized workers the overthrow of the Tsar was sometimes seen as a sin. The American Frank Golder noted in his diary on 15 March:

> Talked with one of the workmen (an old muzhik) of the Navy archives. He said it was a sin to overthrow the Emperor, since God had placed him in power. It may be that the new regime will help people on this earth, but they will surely pay for it in the world to come.

In the villages people at first spoke in muted voices about the 'big events' in the capital. Until the land captains and the police were removed from power, which took place gradually during March and April, the peasants had no guarantee that they would not be arrested if they spoke their minds. But as the weeks went by, they grew in confidence and began to voice their opposition to the Tsar. A survey by the Duma based upon the reports of its provincial agents for the first three months of the revolution summarized this process:

> the widespread myth that the Russian peasant is devoted to the Tsar and that he 'cannot live' without him has been destroyed by the universal joy and the relief of the peasants upon discovering that in reality they can live without the Tsar, without whom they were told they 'could not live' . . . Now the peasants say: 'The Tsar brought himself down and brought us to ruin.'[59]

Once their initial fear had been removed, the peasants welcomed the revolution. The news from the capital was joyously greeted by huge assemblies in the village fields. 'Our village', recalls one peasant, 'burst into life with celebrations. Everyone felt enormous relief, as if a heavy rock had suddenly been lifted from our shoulders.' Another peasant recalled the celebrations in his village on the day it learned of the Tsar's abdication: 'People kissed each other from joy and said that life from now on would be good. Everyone dressed in their best costumes, as they do on a big holiday. The festivities went on for three days.' Many villages held religious processions to thank the Lord for their newly won freedoms, and offered up prayers for the new government. For many peasants, the revolution appeared as a sacred thing, while those who had laid down their lives for the people's freedom were seen by the peasants as modern-day saints. Thus the villagers of Bol'she-Dvorskaya volost in the Tikhvinsk district of Petrograd province held a 'service of thanksgiving for the divine gift of the people's victory and the eternal memory of those holy men who fell in the struggle for freedom'. The parishioners of Osvyshi village in Tver province offered, as they put it, 'fervent prayers to thank the Lord for the divine gift of the people's victory . . . and since this great victory was achieved by sacrifice, we held a requiem for all our fallen brothers'. It was often with the express purpose of reciprocating this sacrifice that many villages sent donations, often amounting to several hundred roubles, to the authorities in Petrograd for the benefit of those who had suffered losses in the February Days.[60]

  The February Revolution was, in its essence, a revolution against monarchy. The new democracy to which it gave birth defined itself by the negation of all things tsarist. In the rhetoric of its leaders the Tsar was equated with the dark oppression of old Russia, while his removal was associated with enlightenment and progress. The symbols and emblems of the revolution — printed in the press and the pamphlet literature — were the images of a broken chain, of the radiant sun appearing from behind the clouds, and of a toppled throne and crown.[61]

  The revolution was accompanied by the nationwide destruction of all signs and symbols of imperial power. During the February Days the crowds in Petrograd tore down the imperial double-headed eagles which hung from many buildings (sometimes even blowing them up with explosives);* removed imperial signs from shopfronts and streets; smashed tsarist statues; took out portraits of the tsars from government buildings (Repin's famous portrait of Nicholas II was torn down from the tribune of the Tauride Palace), and burned all these in bonfires on the streets. The imperial coats of arms on the iron fence around the Winter Palace were covered up with red material — as were all the statues too large to destroy. During March and April many towns held symbolic re-enactments of the February Days, usually known as 'Festivals of Freedom', in which these tsarist emblems and insignia — sometimes reinstalled especially for the event — were torn down once again. In Moscow the elephantine statue of Alexander III was dismantled by a team of workers using ropes and dynamite. In provincial towns statues of the tsars were also destroyed, although here there were sometimes conflicts when these statues had been paid for out of civic funds and had come to represent a certain civic pride. In Vladimir, for example, there was a dispute between the socialists and the merchants over the town's statue of Alexander II. 'After a series of long street debates,' recalls a local resident, 'it was decided to strike a compromise: the statue would not be destroyed but, in order not to offend the revolutionary morals of the people, the figure of the Tsar would be covered up with a large brown sack.' Much of this iconoclasm was carnivalesque. Thus, for example, in the February Days a crowd paraded through the Petrograd streets with a straw effigy of Nicholas II in police uniform which they then burned in a comic ceremony. But such destruction could easily turn

* Several US eagles were also taken down mistakenly.

violent. A eunuch was lynched by the same crowd simply because such effeminate types were thought to be the lackeys of the court.[62]

This symbolic revolution was also enacted on the personal level. People made a conscious effort to distance themselves from the old regime and to identify themselves with the new democracy. Soldiers renounced their hard-won tsarist medals, and often sent them to the Petrograd Soviet so that it could melt them down and put the silver to the use of the people's cause. Hundreds of people with surnames such as Romanov, Nemets (German) or Rasputin, appealed to the Chancellery for the right to have them changed. One such Romanov, Fedor Andreevich, a peasant of Koltovskii village in Penza province, claimed that his surname had become 'a source of shame' and wanted it changed to Lvov — the surname of the Prime Minister.[63]

The revolution was accompanied by a boom of anti-tsarist pamphlets, postcards, plays and films, as the old laws on censorship were removed. The pamphlets, in particular, were hugely popular, some of them selling in their millions. They all traded in the rumours of the war years: that the Empress was working for the Germans; that she was the lover of Rasputin; that the Tsar had given his throne to this 'holy devil', and so on. Most of their titles were sexually suggestive — *The Secrets of the Romanovs; The Gay Days of Rasputin; The Night Orgies of Rasputin* — as was much of their dialogue. In *The Night Orgies*, for example, Protopopov asks Madame Vyrubova if Rasputin has an 'enormous talent'. 'Oh, I know,' she answers, 'an enormous, enormous talent.'[64] Many of the pamphlets were semi-pornographic and were illustrated with cartoons of the royals rolling around in bed with Rasputin. By making the link between the sexual corruption of the court and the diseased condition of Russia explicit, this propaganda played a vital role (still to be investigated by historians) in debunking the myth and the mystique of the Tsar as a divine king. During the course of 1917 it shaped the popular image of the monarchy as an alien force of darkness and corruption, an image which ruled out the possibility of a restoration and thus largely undermined the counter-revolution in the years to come.

So, politically, the monarchy was dead. All its main institutions of support — the bureaucracy, the police, the army and the Church — collapsed virtually overnight. It was a sign of how far they had been weakened, and of how far they had become alienated from the Tsar, during the years before 1917. The Tsar was the lynchpin of the monarchy — he was at the same time, as it were, an officer, a priest, a district governor and a policeman — and once he had been removed the whole system came crashing down. The army commanders soon declared their allegiance to the Provisional Government. Many of them had been linked with its leaders through the opposition movement of the war; while those who were opposed to the revolution knew that it would break the army to resist it. The Church was undermined by its own internal revolution.

In the countryside there was a strong anti-clerical movement: village communities took away the church lands, removed priests from the parishes and refused to pay for religious services. Many of the local priests managed to escape this fate by throwing in their lot with the revolution. But the rest of the Church hierarchy was thrown on to the defensive. The Holy Synod, purged of its Rasputinites, appealed to the priesthood to support the new government. Religious freedoms were introduced. Church schools were transferred to the control of the state. And preparations were made for the separation of Church and state. The provincial apparatus collapsed in most places like a house of cards, and it was only very rarely that armed force was needed to remove it. The people simply took to the streets; the governors, without any military means to suppress the disorders, were forced to resign; and *ad hoc* committees of citzens declared themselves in power. In Moscow the regime fell as a result of no more than two days of street demonstrations. 'There was no shooting in the streets and no barricades,' recalled a jubilant businessman. 'The old regime in Moscow fell by itself, and no one defended it or even tried to.' The police state similarly collapsed — the police being replaced by citizens' militias almost overnight. Even the Okhrana was dissolved, although it was later rumoured that many of its agents had found employment in the new government.[65]

No one really tried to revive the monarchy. It is telling, for example, that none of the White leaders in the civil war embraced monarchism as a cause, despite the efforts of the many monarchists in their ranks. The White leaders all realized that politically it would be suicide for them to do so. For as Trotsky put it with his usual bluntness, 'the country had so radically vomited up the monarchy that it could not ever crawl down the people's throat again'.[66] His prognosis is probably still true, the post-Soviet romance with the tsarist past notwithstanding.*

But if the monarchy was dead politically, it was still alive in a broader sense. The mass of the peasants thought of politics in monarchical terms. They conceived of the state as embodied in the monarch, and projected their ideals of the revolution on to a 'peasant king', or some other authoritarian liberator come to deliver their cherished land and freedom. Here were the roots of the cults of Kerensky, Kornilov and Lenin, all of which were attempts to fill the missing space of the deposed Tsar, or perhaps rather the vacuum left by the myth of the Tsar Deliverer. George Buchanan, the British Ambassador, noted this monarchical mentality during the first days of the revolution, when one soldier said to him: 'Yes, we need a republic, but at its head there should be a good Tsar.' Frank Golder similarly noted such misunderstandings in his diary

---

* According to an opinion poll in 1995, only 7 per cent of the Russian people favoured the return of the monarchy.

on 7 March: 'Stories are being told of soldiers who say they wish a republic like England, or a republic with a Tsar. One soldier said he wanted to elect a President and when asked, "Whom would you elect?" he replied, "The Tsar."' Soldiers' letters voiced the same confusion. 'We want a democratic republic and a Tsar-Batiushka for three years'; 'It would be good if we had a republic with a sensible Tsar.' It seems that the peasants found it difficult to distinguish between the person of the monarch (*gosudar'*) and the abstract institutions of the state (*gosudarstvo*). Their conception of the democratic order was similarly couched in personalized terms. Sometime during March a Menshevik deputy of the Moscow Soviet went to agitate at a regimental meeting near Vladimir. He spoke of the need for peace, of the need for all the land to be given to the peasants, and of the advantages of a republic over monarchy. The soldiers cheered loudly in agreement, and one of them called out, 'We want to elect you as Tsar', whereupon the other soldiers burst into applause. 'I refused the Romanov crown', recalled the Menshevik, 'and went away with a heavy feeling of how easy it would be for any adventurer or demagogue to become the master of this simple and naive people.'[67]

*   *   *

'A miracle has happened', Blok wrote to his mother on 23 March, 'and we may expect more miracles.' People shared a wild excitement and euphoria during the first days of the revolution. It was partly the sense of absolute freedom — 'the extraordinary feeling', as Blok put it in his letter, 'that nothing is forbidden', that 'almost anything might happen'. It was also the fact that everything had happened so quickly: a mighty dynasty, three centuries old, had collapsed within a few days. 'The most striking thing', Blok wrote in his diary on 25 May, 'was the utter unexpectedness of it, like a train crash in the night, like a bridge crumbling beneath your feet, like a house falling down.' There was a strange sense of unreality. People compared the whole experience to 'living through a dream or a fairy tale'. Things happened too fast for daily life to stop and for people to take it all in. 'What was really strange', wrote the artist Yulia Obolenskaya to a friend, 'was getting your parcel with the dried fruit and coffee on the first day of the revolution, while the street outside was wild with joy and gun carriages with red flags were rolling by ... Outside there was a hurricane ... Then suddenly — a ring and a parcel containing blackcurrants!'[68]

This was the 'honeymoon' of the revolution. People fell in love with 'February'. Almost instantly, the history of the revolution was reinvented to suit these democratic ideals and mythic expectations. The 'Glorious February Revolution', as it became known, was said to have been a bloodless affair. 'Just imagine,' one contemporary wrote, 'there was a great revolution in Russia and not a single drop of blood was spilled.' It was also said to be a single national act without opposition. 'Our revolution', one Duma agitator informed the sailors of Helsingfors, 'is the only one in the history of the world to express the spirit of the entire people.' The revolution was portrayed as a spiritual renewal, a moral resurrection of the people. Merezhkovsky called it 'perhaps the most Christian act in the history of the world.' The revolution was itself transformed into a sort of cult. Huge crowds would assemble in the streets to hold prayers and ceremonies in celebration of Glorious February. The burial of the revolution's martyred victims on the second Sunday of the new order (12 March) equally bore the character, although not the rituals, of a religious mass. Many people compared the revolution to an Easter holiday. People in the streets would congratulate each other on the revolution with the Easter blessing: 'Christ has arisen!' (sometimes this was changed to 'Russia has arisen!'). Tsarism was said to have stood for evil and sin (one priest even called it 'the Devil's institution'); it had split the people into rich and poor; but with its downfall, society would be reorganized on the basis of more Christian attitudes. Some idealists even thought that lying and stealing, gambling and swearing, would at once disappear. 'Drunkenness in Russia', declared a peasant congress in Tomsk province, 'was a source of national shame under the old regime. But now in Free and Democratic Russia there can be no place for drunkenness. And therefore the congress looks upon the manufacture of all alcohol as a betrayal of the revolution, and as a betrayal of the Russian democratic republic.' One woman even wrote to the Soviet that the 'Christian mission' of the Russian Revolution should be to abolish all the country's jails, since there was no criminal who could not be reformed. There were many intellectuals who now claimed that the Russian people would learn to live together in a new *sobornost'* — a universal spiritual community — overriding class or party differences. In the words of Tatyana Gippius: 'The atmosphere has been purified . . . Thank God that *sobornost'* triumphs over *partiinost*'.'[69]

It was in this same Christian-populist sense that the revolution was also portrayed as a process of national and patriotic reawakening. People echoed Herzen's view that Tsarism was 'alien' to the simple people. It was the 'Gottorp-Holstein dynasty'. Germans had dominated at the court. The Empress ('the German woman') had betrayed Russia. But the people had arisen, and from this truly national revolution Russia had received a truly national government, behind which it could unite for the defeat of the external enemy. This was to be a 'patriotic revolution'. Or, as someone put it: 'Now we have beaten the Germans here, we will beat them in the field.'[70]

Many of these ideals were expressed by Prince Lvov in his first interview with the free press. 'I believe', he said, 'in the vitality and the wisdom of our great people, as expressed in the national uprising that overthrew the old regime. It is expressed in the universal effort to establish freedom and to defend it against both internal and external foes. I believe in the great heart of the Russian people, filled as it is with love for their neighbours, and am convinced that it is the foundation of our freedom, justice, and truth.'[71] Such high expectations were soon to be dashed.

9 The Freest Country in the World

i A Distant Liberal State

Nothing in his previous experience had quite prepared Prince Lvov for the tasks that lay ahead of him as the Prime Minister of the Provisional Government. Not that he was unaccustomed to the long hours that such high office demanded of him. His wartime work in the Zemstvo Union had prepared him for that and, although now permanently tired, he was quite able to cope with the extra strain. From early in the morning until at least midnight Lvov was to be found in the Marinsky Palace receiving delegations from all over Russia, meeting foreign diplomats, presiding over cabinet meetings, briefing Civil Servants and giving interviews to the press. Nabokov met him in the early days of March and was 'struck by his sombre, despondent appearance, and the tired expression in his eyes'.[1]

Nor could one say that the Prince was unprepared for the massive new burden of administration. It was precisely his administrative talent that had won him the universal respect of the wartime opposition and had put him at the top of virtually everyone's list for the prospective leadership of the country. His practical common sense and easy-going manner made him a good team-worker. Prince Sergei Urusov, the former Governor of Bessarabia we met in Chapter 2, who became Lvov's number two at the Ministry of Interior, said that he was an inspiring manager of people, that he encouraged them to take initiatives and that he skilfully arbitrated disputes between them. Although historians have been quick to disparage Lvov as a statesman — Samuel Hoare described him in 1930 as 'a man better qualified to be the Chairman of the London County Council than to be the chief of an unstable Government in the midst of a great revolution' — he was in fact widely esteemed at the time as one of Russia's ablest leaders. Tsereteli thought he was 'a talented organizer with far more experience of state affairs than any of the socialists'. Gorky considered him one of the 'three genuinely talented politicians in the government', along with Kerensky and Nekrasov.[2]

Yet the Prince was out of place in the new world of party politics. All his previous work had been of the practical, zemstvo kind, where everybody worked together, regardless of class or party interests, for the 'good of the nation'. At first it was hoped that the Provisional Government would be guided by this same spirit. This was to be a wartime government of national confidence and salvation, not a government of any one party or social class, and this was why Lvov, as a genuinely national figure, had been chosen for its leader. But the revolution had opened the floodgates to party politics, left-wing politics in particular, and it was almost inevitable that they would permeate the government's work. It was this which Lvov was unprepared for. His knowledge of party politics was almost non-existent. Even after several months as Prime Minister he could not really tell the difference between the SRs and the Bolsheviks. The general softness of his character, moreover, left him virtually powerless to cope with the hard cut and thrust of party politics. Coming from the old world of gentlemanly zemstvo activity, he was more inclined to search for compromises than either the party leaders of the capital or the irreconcilable conflicts in the country would ever allow. When his ministers clashed over politics (which was very often) Lvov's instinctive reaction was to look for a means of reconciling them through the implementation of 'practical and constructive' policies. This gave him an image of indecisiveness; and it is true that he tended to be swayed by other politicians with a stronger will. Nabokov, who headed the government's Secretariat, recalled endless 'agonizing sessions' of the Council of Ministers in which 'dissension, and the smouldering or obvious hostility of some individuals toward others' prevented any progress. 'I do not recall a single occasion when the Minister-President used a tone of authority or spoke out decisively and definitively . . . He was the very embodiment of passivity.' Bublikov, the Duma politician, ridiculed Lvov, with his 'permanent look of dismay' and his 'constant efforts to be nice to everyone', as 'a walking symbol of the impotence of the Provisional Government'.[3]

Throughout his four-month term of office the one thing that sustained Lvov, in the face of all these political problems, was his unshakeable optimism. (Could anyone have tried to govern Russia in 1917 without believing in miracles?) Lvov was convinced, as he often liked to say, that 'things will turn out in the end'. This optimism was based on his Slavophile and populist belief in the 'wisdom and the goodness of the Russian people'. 'The soul of the Russian people', he declared in a speech in March, 'turned out by its very nature to be a universal democratic soul. It is prepared not only to merge with the democracy of the whole world, but to stand at the head of it and to lead it along the path of human progress according to the principles of liberty, equality, and fraternity.' From his brief acquaintance with the peasants, with his peasant neighbours at Popovka above all, he had naively jumped to the conclusion that all the peasants were just as good. Once the people had been freed from tsarist oppression, he once explained to his secretary, they would learn to rule themselves in the liberal democratic spirit of the West. It had hardly occurred to him, at least not in these early hopeful weeks, that the people's hatred of the propertied élite and their impatience for a social revolution might not drown the country in blood first.[4]

Kerensky recalled one of the first meetings of the Council of Ministers. Prince Lvov arrived late with a sheaf of telegrams from the provinces. They all said more or less the same thing: that the local administration had collapsed and that power now belonged to various *ad hoc* public committees. The ministers sat around for a long time wondering what to do. 'Here we were in the middle of a war, and large areas of the country had passed into the hands of completely unknown people!' Speaking 'with extraordinary confidence', Lvov then summed up the discussion:

> We must forget all about the old administration — any return to it is psychologically quite impossible. But Russia will not go under without it. The administration is gone, but the people remain . . . Gentlemen, we must be patient. We must have faith in the good sense, statesmanship, and loyalty of the peoples of Russia.

'And indeed', recalled Kerensky, 'we had nothing except this faith in the people.'[5]

Lvov's belief in 'the people' was typical of the intelligentsia attitudes that characterized the political philosophy of the first Provisional Government (2 March to 5 May). Not every minister succumbed to such high hopes. Miliukov and Guchkov argued from the start for a powerful state to contain the people's anarchistic instincts and save the country from chaos. But their cold rationalism was always overshadowed by the warmer sentiments of Kerensky, Nekrasov and Lvov. The dominant outlook of the government was shaped by the liberal values of the intelligentsia which, in turn, had emerged from the people's struggle for freedom against autocracy. Two main beliefs stood at the heart of this democratic political culture: an instinctive mistrust of the state as a coercive power; and a belief in local self-rule. From this it followed that a distant liberal state was all that was required to shepherd Russia through to the civilized world of free nations. Russia's liberal leaders talked of ruling 'with' the people rather than 'over' them. They saw themselves as 'classless' — ruling in the interests of 'all the people' rather than one class — and on this universal promise hoped to build up a sense of legitimacy. They presented themselves as the temporary caretakers of a 'neutral state', above party or class interests, until the election of the new sovereign power, the Constituent Assembly, which alone could give a legal sanction to social and political reforms. This, in effect, was to place their trust in the patience of the people to wait for the legal resolution of their problems. It was to place the 'defence of the state' above the class or party interests of the revolution. Yet when that state itself was threatened by unrest, as it was in April, July and October, they were unwilling to use force in its defence. Their decent liberal intentions, and their inbred mistrust of state coercion, prevented them from taking the necessary measures to defend their cherished constitutional freedoms against the threat of extremism. They were determined to dismantle the old police regime, the courts and the penal system — which merely tied their own hands in the struggle against rising crime and violence. Even when this violence was Bolshevik-inspired, they were reluctant to repress it. The Men of February — who in their own minds had been brought to power by a 'bloodless revolution' — would not have the blood of 'the people' on their hands. This weakness, in the end, would bring them down.

The leaders of the Provisional Government saw themselves as re-enacting the French Revolution on Russian soil. They compared themselves to the heroes of 1789. Kerensky, for one, liked to think of himself as a Mirabeau (and later as a Napoleon). The leaders of the 'Great Russian Revolution' looked for precedents for their policies, and for models for their institutions, in the revolutionary history of France. People called the Bolsheviks Jacobins (which is also how they saw themselves). The Bolsheviks, in turn, called the liberals Girondins. And all democrats warned of the dangers of 'counter-revolution' and 'Bonapartism'.* The provincial commissars, the soldiers' committees and army commissars, the provincial committees of public safety and the Constituent Assembly itself — all of them were copied from their French equivalents. The old deferential terms of address were replaced by the terms *grazhdanin* and *grazhdanka* ('citizen' and 'citizeness'). The Marseillaise — which the Russians mispronounced as the Marsiliuza and to which they added their own different words (there was a 'Workers' Marseillaise', a 'Soldiers' Marseillaise' and a 'Peasants' Marseillaise') — became the national anthem of the revolution. It was played at all public assemblies, street demonstrations, concerts and plays.

> We renounce the old world,
> We shake its dust off from our feet.
> We don't need a Golden Idol,
> And we despise the Tsarist Devil.

Bookshops traded heavily in popular histories of the French Revolution. There was a fit of francophilia. France, after all, was Russia's nearest Western ally against Germany — the last bastion of autocracy — and the founding member of the European club of democratic nations which Russia was now entering. Lvov's visiting card was even printed in French — PRINCE GEORGES LWOFF.

---

* For the Social Democrats, steeped in Marx's writings of 1848–52, Bonapartism meant Napoleon III rather than Napoleon I.

MINISTRE-PRESIDENT DU GOUVERNEMENT PROVISOIRE — as if to symbolize this graduation to the civilized Western world.[6]

Yet Russia could not be another France. The constitutional phase of the Russian Revolution — in the classic European tradition of 1789 and 1848 — had already been played out during 1905–14. Political reform had nothing left to offer. Only a fundamental social revolution — one without precedents in European history — was capable of resolving the power questions thrown up by the downfall of the old regime. This was the basic mistake of the Men of February: intoxicated by their own self-image as the heirs of 1789, they were deluded into believing that they could resolve the problems of 1917 by importing Western constitutional practices and policies for which there were no real precedents, nor the necessary cultural base, in Russia.

As if to prove himself the heir of Lafayette, Prince Lvov presided over the passing of a dazzling series of political reforms during the first weeks of the Provisional Government. Russia overnight was effectively transformed into 'the freest country in the world'. Freedoms of assembly, press and speech were granted. Legal restrictions of religion, class and race were removed. There was a general amnesty. Universal adult suffrage was introduced. The police were made accountable to local government. The courts and the penal system were over-hauled. Capital punishment was abolished. Democratic organs of local self-government were established. Preparations were made for the election of a Constituent Assembly. The laws followed upon each other in such rapid succession that it was hard for Russia's new citizens to keep up with them. One day in the second half of March a delegation of women suffragettes came to Lvov's office to campaign for the right of women to vote in local government elections. They were obviously expecting a hard battle. Some of the women had prepared long and passionate speeches. It seemed to them that the fate of half of Russia depended on the success of their mission. But as soon as they met Lvov it became clear that they were pushing at an open door. 'Why shouldn't women vote?' he asked them with candid surprise. 'I don't see what's the problem. Surely, with universal suffrage there can be no reason to exclude women.'[7]

These reforms helped to create a new culture of democracy. It became politically correct to call oneself a 'democrat' — sometimes literally: there was a peasant called Durakov ('Idiot') who changed his surname to Demokratov. Yet in Russia the word 'democracy' was not just a political label. It was also a social one. The Left, in particular, used it to describe the 'common people' as opposed to 'the bourgeoisie'. The language of 1789, once it entered Russia in 1917, soon became translated into the language of class. This was not just a question of semantics. It showed that for the vast mass of the people the ideals of 'democracy' were expressed in terms of a social revolution rather than in terms of political reform. The peasants and the workers were used to seeing power based on social domination and coercion rather than on the exercise of law. They saw the revolution mainly as a chance to gain autonomy and turn the tables on their former masters rather than as a chance to reconstruct the power system on universal legal principles. Retribution, not a constitution: that was the people's first priority.

The revolution of 1917 should really be conceived of as a general crisis of authority. There was a rejection of not just the state but of all figures of authority: judges, policemen, Civil Servants, army and navy officers, priests, teachers, employers, foremen, landowners, village elders, patriarchal fathers and husbands. It was often said at the time — and historians have emphasized this — that only the Soviet had any real authority. Guchkov wrote to Alexeev on 9 March:

> The Provisional Government has no real power of any kind and its orders are carried out only to the extent that is permitted by the Soviet of Workers' and Soldiers' Deputies. The latter controls the most essential levers of power, insofar as the troops, the railways, and the postal and telegraph services are in its hands. One can assert bluntly that the Provisional Government exists only as long as it is allowed to do so by the Soviet.[8]

Certainly, the Soviet had much more power than any other body. It had a virtual monopoly on the means of organized violence, while the mass of the workers and soldiers looked upon it as the only legitimate authority in the land. At almost any moment between February and October the Soviet could have taken power and, although a civil war might well have been the outcome, its support was enough to ensure a victory. And yet even the Soviet, based as it was in Petrograd, had only a very limited control over the revolution in the provinces. There was a breakdown of all central power: local towns and regions declared their 'independence' from the capital; villages declared themselves 'autonomous republics'; nationalities and ethnic groups seized control of territory and declared themselves to be 'independent states'. The social revolution was to be found in this decentralization of power: local communities defended their interests and asserted their autonomy through the election of *ad hoc* committees (public executive committees, municipal committees, revolutionary committees, committees of public organizations, village committees and Soviets), which paid scant regard to the orders of the centre and which passed their own 'laws' to legitimize the local reconstruction of social relations.

The politics of 1917 should thus be understood not so much as a conflict of 'dual power' (*dvoevlastie*) — the division of all power between the government and the Soviet which has so preoccupied historians — but as a deeper problem of the proliferation of a 'multitude of local powers' (*mnogovlastie*).

In the provincial towns there was really no 'dual power' to speak of at all: the liberal and the socialist intelligentsia, which in Petrograd would have been divided between the government and the Soviet, nearly always worked together in the democratic civic committees between February and October (and in many places afterwards too). Russia, in short, was being Balkanized. It was a recurring pattern that whenever the state's power was removed, Russia broke down into anarchy and chaos. It happened after the collapse of the tsarist state, as it did after the collapse of Communism. If 1917 proved anything, it was that Russian society was neither strong enough nor cohesive enough to sustain a democratic revolution. Apart from the state itself, there was nothing holding Russia together.

'Who elected you?' That was the awkward question someone shouted from the crowd when Miliukov announced the establishment of the Provisional Government. The answer, of course, was that nobody had. The Provisional Government was not a democratic government, in the sense that it had been elected by the people, but a government of 'national confidence'. It never had the legitimacy which can only come from the ballot box. Its liberal leaders were excessively concerned by this absence of a mandate, and thought that they might earn more respect by calling themselves 'provisional'. They presented the government as only the temporary guardian of the state until the election of the Constituent Assembly, and always stressed that their legislation was ultimately dependent on the legal sanction of the Assembly. And yet for this reason people questioned why they should obey the government: the word 'provisional' did not command respect.

With hindsight it is difficult not to blame the leaders of the Provisional Government for failing to act more quickly to convene the Constituent Assembly, which alone could have given them the democratic mandate they required. Everyone acknowledged the urgency of its convocation. But the liberal leaders allowed their common sense to become clouded by their high ideals. They were overawed by the solemn importance of their task — to construct a national parliament expressing the 'will of the people' — and insisted on the most detailed legal preparations to ensure the fairest possible franchise. A council of representatives from various political groups was summoned at the end of March. It took two months to agree on the composition of a second Special Council of over sixty members to draft the electoral law and this, in turn, got bogged down in lengthy deliberations on the various options of proportional representation, the fairest possible methods of redrawing the electoral boundaries, and the best ways of organizing elections in the army and the ethnic borderlands.

By the early summer, as chaos spread through the country and the urgent need for a stronger legal authority became clear, there was growing public concern about the slow progress of the Special Council. Some people argued that it would have been quicker to appoint a smaller commission to draft the electoral law. But F. F. Kokoshkin, a Kadet lawyer and the Chairman of the Special Council, defended its careful approach on the grounds that the new electoral law had to live up to the 'wishes and interests of all the population'. There were certainly practical problems that made hasty elections inadvisable: millions of people were on the move and it was not clear how their votes were to be counted. But to a certain extent these reservations had become a pretext for delay. The Kadets, in particular, favoured the postponement of the elections, no doubt because they knew they would lose them. Prince Lvov supported Kokoshkin's procrastination. He, above all, was sold on the ideal of a perfect parliament. 'The Constituent Assembly', Lvov told the Special Council, 'must crown the great Russian revolution. It must lay all the vital foundations for the future order of the free democratic state. It will bear the responsibility for the entire future of Russia. It must be the essence of all the spiritual and mental forces of the people.'[9]

This was surely placing unrealistic expectations on what, in the context, should have aimed to be no more than a makeshift parliament of national salvation. However imperfect, to begin with, such an assembly might have been, it would at least have established a focus, and a base of legitimacy, for Russia's fragile new democracy. There are very few examples in history of a long-lasting revolutionary parliament, and, steeped as they were in the history of Europe, the leaders of the Provisional Government should have been well enough aware of this to keep their expectations in realistic bounds. But they allowed their high ideals to cloud their common sense. Perhaps it was a case of too many lawyers and not enough statesmen. The failure of the government to hold the elections enabled the Bolsheviks to sow serious doubts in the people's minds about its intentions to hold them at all; and this lent weight to their propaganda claims, which were used to justify their own seizure of power, that the government had fallen into the hands of the 'counter-revolution'. Under growing public pressure, the leaders of the Provisional Government announced in mid-June that the elections would finally be held on 17 September. But everyone knew that at the rate things were going this was out of the question, for the register of electors had not been drawn up and the local government organs, which were supposed to do this, had still not been established. By August little progress had been made and the date of the elections was once again postponed until 12 November. But by this time the Bolsheviks had come to power.

ii Expectations

'We are living through wild times', Sergei Semenov wrote to an old friend in the spring of 1917. 'It is hard for the people of our generation to adapt to the new situation. But through this revolution our lives will be purified and things will get better for the young.'[10] The peasant reformer pinned all his hopes on the civilizing mission of the revolution. At last, so he thought, the time had come for the backward Russian village to receive the benefits of the modern world. He welcomed the fall of the old regime in a spirit of optimistic expectation and reconciliation with his mistrustful peasant neighbours in the village commune of Andreevskoe. It was now a full six years since he had ended his long and bitter struggle to separate from them and set up his own private enclosed farm on the outskirts of the village.

During that first hopeful spring Semenov picked up once again from the reforms he had started during 1905. He expanded his work in the agricultural co-operatives; revived the local Peasant Union; opened a 'people's club' in the local market town of Bukholovo; and organized lectures for the peasants on a whole range of progressive subjects, from republican philosophies to the advanced methods of overwintering cows. He even drew up a blueprint for the electrification of the whole of the Volokolamsk district which he presented to the Moscow city duma. Semenov's daughter, Tatiana, recalls her father's renewed hopes and energies during the spring of 1917:

We were amazed by our father's strength — it had literally doubled overnight — and he now looked forward to the future with high expectations. He not only worked in the fields but he also travelled around the villages, looking into every aspect of peasant affairs. He read on everything, and constantly wrote. Sometimes, when we were all asleep, he would still be working in his room. The next morning he was the first up.[11]

The revolution raised Semenov's standing among the villagers of Andreevskoe. It also reduced the power of Grigorii Maliutin, the patriarchal elder of the village commune and arch-enemy of Semenov's reforms. The old power structure upon which Maliutin had depended — the volost elder, the local police and the gentry land captain — was dismantled almost overnight. Within the village the voice of the younger and more progressive farmers was also becoming more dominant, while that of the older peasants, like Maliutin, who saw nothing good in the revolution, was increasingly ignored. The social changes of the past few years lay at the root of this democratization of the village commune. More and more households were being headed by the younger peasants, as a result of household partitions. During the war years, in the absence of their menfolk, many peasant households were headed by women: in many regions up to one-third, and in Andreevskoe itself over a quarter. These younger peasants looked towards Semenov as a champion of reform. He always spoke out at the village assembly against the Church and the patriarchal order. As the most literate peasant in the village, he was also called upon to write its resolutions when the village scribe, a lackey of Maliutin's, refused to 'work for the revolution'. But what really raised Semenov's standing was the success of his long campaign to get six of the poorest villagers released from the army because there was no one else to feed their families. During the autumn of 1916 he had been sentenced to six weeks in jail after Maliutin had denounced him to the authorities for 'encouraging desertion'. But the villagers had refused to let him go and had held him in Andreevskoe, a hostage and hero of the peasant revolution, until the downfall of the old regime. Two weeks later the six peasants all returned home. Maliutin was discredited, and Semenov emerged as the leader of the village.[12]

During that spring Semenov broke up his private enclosed farm and returned to the peasant land commune. Most of Stolypin's peasant pioneers chose to do likewise in 1917. If up to one-third of the peasant households in Russia farmed private holdings on the eve of the revolution, then four years later less than 2 per cent continued to do so. Only the small minority of fully enclosed *khutora* had to be brought back by force. The semi-enclosed *otruba* tended to be much weaker economically and, like Semenov's, generally smaller than the neighbouring communal allotments. The prospect of sharing in the spoils of the commune's 'war on the manors', which started again during the spring, was enough to encourage most of them to return voluntarily.[13]

This return of the separators reflected a general peasant striving for solidarity within the village commune. 'Today, in free Russia, everyone should be equal and united,' declared the peasants of Dubovo-Pobedimov in Bugul'ma. 'The members of the communes should accept all the separators into their family on an equal basis and should cease all oppressive measures against them, since these only play into the hands of the enemies of the people.' The village commune was greatly strengthened as a result of the revolution. It revived from its pre-revolutionary state of torpor and decay to become the main organizing force of the peasant revolution on the land. All the main political organs of the revolution in the countryside — the village committees, the peasant unions and the Soviets — were really no more than the peasant commune in a more revolutionary form. The village commune stood for the ideals of land and freedom which had always inspired the peasants to revolt. It defined a circle of 'insiders' and defended their interests against 'outsiders' — landowners, townsmen, merchants, state officials, even peasants from the neighbouring communes — at a time of great insecurity.

Since the days of serfdom, the land commune had served as a link between its peasant household members (usually within a single village) and a particular landlord's estate. In 1917 it thus provided these villagers with a historical and a moral right to that estate on the often-stated peasant principle: 'Ours was the lord, ours is the land.' During the seizure of the gentry's estates the members of the commune displayed a remarkable degree of solidarity and organization. It was common for the village assembly to pass a resolution compelling all the members of the commune to take part in the march on the manor, or in other forms of peasant resistance, such as rent strikes and boycotts, on the threat of expulsion from the commune. It was a matter of safety in numbers. Contrary to the old Soviet myth, there were very few conflicts within the village between the richer and poorer peasants. But there were a great many conflicts between neighbouring communes, sometimes ending in little village wars, over the control of the estates.[14]

          This is how the revolution on the land took place. At a pre-selected time the church bells rang and the peasants assembled with their carts in the middle of the village. Then they moved off towards the manor, like a peasant army, armed with guns, pitchforks, axes, scythes and spades. The squire and his stewards, if they had not already fled, were arrested or at least forced to sign a resolution conceding all the peasant demands. During the spring these were usually quite moderate: a lowering of land rents; the redistribution of prisoner-of-war labour; or the compulsory sale of grain, tools and livestock to the commune at prices deemed 'fair' by the peasants. The mass confiscation of the gentry's land did not occur until the summer. Most of the peasants were still prepared to wait for the Provisional Government to pass a new land law transferring the estates to them, just as they had once waited for the Tsar to pass a 'Golden Manifesto'. They were afraid to attack the estates before it was clear that the old regime would not be restored, as it had been in 1906–7, with the mass executions of the peasants which had followed. It was really only at the start of May, with the appointment of the SR Chernov as Minister for Agriculture, that the peasants had such a guarantee; and it was from this time that the outright confiscation of the gentry's estates became a nationwide phenomenon. Early May was also the start of the summer agricultural season. If the peasants were to harvest the squire's fields in the autumn, they would need to plough and sow them now.* So there was an obvious motive for the peasants to seize the land from about this time. The nuns of the Panovka Convent in Serdobsk were some of the more unusual victims of this increasing peasant aggression:

A resolution of the Davydovka volost executive committee on 10 April ordered our convent to rent to the peasants 15 *desyatiny* of our spring fields. On 19 May we received a communication from the same committee that, for our own needs, we may keep 15 *desyatiny* of fallow land, but that a further 30 *desyatiny* of land must be given to the peasants of Pleshcheevka

---

* Not surprisingly, many of the squires had left their fields unsown.

village. Now [in mid-June] the peasants are requisitioning grain from our convent: 600 *pud* has been taken for the local villagers at 1 rouble 52 kopecks, but grain from the peasants is requisitioned at 2 roubles 50 kopecks.[15]

The return of soldiers on Easter leave, and indeed of deserters from the army, also had a lot to do with this increased peasant militancy. The peasant soldiers often took the lead in the march on the manors. Sometimes they encouraged the peasantry to indulge in wanton acts of vandalism. They burned the manor houses to drive the squires out; smashed the agricultural machinery (which in recent years had removed much of the need for hired peasant labour); carried away the contents of the barns on their carts; and destroyed or vandalized anything, like paintings, books or sculptures, that smacked of excessive wealth. It was also not uncommon for these soldiers to incite the peasants to attack the squires. In the village of Bor-Polianshchina, in Saratov province, for example, a band of peasants, led by some soldiers, forced their way into the manor house of Prince V. V. Saburov, and hacked him to death with axes and knives. It was a bloody retribution for the role his son had played as the local land captain in 1906, when twelve peasant rebels had been hanged in the village before their screaming wives and children. For three days after the murder the villagers ran riot on the Saburov estate. The manor house, which contained one of the finest private libraries in Russia, was burned to the ground.[16]

The terrified squires bombarded Prince Lvov with pleas for the restoration of law and order. Isolated in their manors, with nothing to protect them from the surrounding sea of hostile peasants, they were quick to accuse his government of doing nothing to stop the growing tide of anarchy that came ever closer to their gates. 'The countryside is falling into chaos, with robberies and arson every day, while you sit doing nothing in your comfortable Petersburg office,' one Tambov squire wrote to him in April. 'Your local committees are powerless to do anything, and even encourage the theft of property. The police are asleep while the peasants rob and burn. The old government knew better how to deal with this peasant scum which you call "the people".'[17]

With letters such as these to deal with, one could hardly blame Lvov for viewing the plight of the squires as a punishment for their 'boorish and brutal behaviour during the centuries of serfdom'. The revolution was the 'revenge of the serfs', he explained one day in June over lunch to some of his ministers. It was the 'result of our — and I speak now as a landowner — of our original sin. If only Russia had been blessed with a real landed aristocracy, like that in England, which had the human decency to treat the peasants as people rather than dogs. Then perhaps things might have been different.'[18] It was a quite remarkable thing for someone of his class and background to say —

a wistful admission, if you like, that the whole of the civilization of the gentry, of which the Prince himself was a scion, had never been more than a thin veneer laid over the top of the brutal exploitation of the peasants, from which the revolution had emerged.

Whatever Lvov might have said in private, it was the policy of his government to defend the property rights of the squires. The land question, as it saw it, had to be resolved by legal means, and this meant preserving the status quo in property relations until a new land law was decided by the Constituent Assembly. Yet the government had no real means to prevent the peasants from taking the law — and the gentry's land — into their own hands. The old police had been dismantled, while the army units in the countryside — even if their peasant recruits agreed to be used for such repressive purposes — were not nearly enough to protect more than a tiny proportion of the gentry's estates. The temporary volost committees, established by the government on 20 March and designed to uphold the existing order, were soon transformed into revolutionary organs which passed their own 'laws' to legitimize the peasant seizures of the gentry's property. The same thing happened with the volost land committees. The Provisional Government had intended these to protect the gentry's legal rights, while regulating agrarian relations until the Constituent Assembly. But they were taken over by the local peasants and soon transformed into revolutionary organs on the land, helping to impose fixed rents on the gentry, to account for their land and property, and to distribute it among the peasantry. In an attempt to prevent this subversion of the land committees, the government cut its grants to them; but the peasant communes merely filled the gap, financing the committees through self-taxation, and the committees continued to grow.

This revolution on the land was given a pseudo-legal endorsement by the peasant assemblies which convened in the spring in most of the central black-soil provinces, as well as the First All-Russian Peasant Assembly on 4–25 May. Nothing did more to undermine the government's authority in the countryside. The SR party activists, who dominated the executives of these assemblies, appealed for the peasants to show patience over the resolution of the land question. But they were soon obliged by the radical mood of the delegates on the floor to sanction the actions of the local communes, and even the seizures of the gentry's land, as an interim solution. The Kazan provincial peasant assembly resolved on 13 May to transfer all the land to the control of the peasant committees. Twelve days later the Samara peasant assembly followed suit in direct defiance of an order from Lvov ordering the provincial commissar to prevent any further peasant land seizures. The peasants believed that these resolutions by their assemblies carried the status of 'laws'. They used them to authorize further seizures of the land in the summer months. They did not understand the difference between a general declaration of principle by their own peasant assembly, which was in effect no more than a public organization, and the full promulgation of a government law. They seemed to believe that, in order to 'socialize' the land, or in order to transfer the land to the control of the communes, it was enough for a peasant assembly to pass a resolution to that effect. Peasant expectations transformed these assemblies into pseudo-government bodies passing 'laws' by simple declaration. And these 'laws' then took precedence over the statutes of the government. 'The local peasantry', complained the Commissar of Nizhnyi Novgorod, 'has got a fixed opinion that all civil laws have lost their force, and that all legal relations ought now to be regulated by peasant organizations.'[19] This was the meaning of the peasant revolution.

* * *

As with the peasants, so with the workers: their expectations rocketed during the spring of 1917. Over half a million workers came out on strike between mid-April and the start of July; and the range of workers was much broader than in any previous strike wave. Artisans and craftsmen, laundry women, dyers, barbers, kitchen workers, waiters, porters, chauffeurs and domestic servants — not just from the two capital cities but from provincial towns throughout the Empire — took their place alongside the veteran strikers, such as the metal and textile workers.[20] Even the prostitutes went on strike.

Most of the strikers' demands were economic. They wanted higher wages to keep up with inflation and more reliable supplies of food. They wanted better conditions at work. The eight-hour day, in particular, had assumed an almost sacramental nature. The workers saw it as a symbol of all their rights and of their victory in the revolution. In many factories it was simply imposed by the workers downing their tools and walking out after the completion of an eight-hour shift. Anxious not to jeopardize production, or intimidated by their workers, most employers soon agreed to honour the eight-hour day (without wage reductions), although mandatory overtime was often introduced in the munitions factories as a way to maintain output levels. As early as 10 March 300 Petrograd factory owners announced their acceptance of the eight-hour day after negotiations with the Soviet, and on this basis it was introduced in most other towns.[21]

Yet in the context of 1917, when the whole structure of the state and capitalism was being redefined, these economic demands were unavoidably politicized. The vicious cycle of strikes and inflation, of higher pay chasing higher prices, led many workers to demand that the state impose more control on the market itself. The workers' struggle to control their own work environment, above all to prevent their employers from running down production to maintain their profits, led them increasingly to demand that the state take over the running of the factories.

There was also a new stress on the workers' own sense of dignity. They were now aware of themselves as 'citizens', and of the fact that they had 'made the revolution' (or had at least played a leading part in it), and they were no longer willing to be treated with any disrespect by either foremen or managers. This was often a spark for violence: offensive factory officials would be symbolically 'carted out', sometimes literally in a wheelbarrow, and then beaten up or thrown into the canal or cesspool. Many strikers demanded respectful treatment. Waiters and waitresses in Petrograd marched with banners bearing the demands:

WE INSIST ON RESPECT FOR WAITERS AS HUMAN BEINGS!
DOWN WITH TIPS: WAITERS ARE CITIZENS!

Domestic servants marched to demand that they should be addressed with the formal 'you', as opposed to the familiar 'you', previously used to address the serfs. Yardmen demanded that their degrading title should now be changed to 'house directors'. Women workers demanded equal pay to men, an end to 'degrading body searches', fully paid maternity leave and the abolition of child labour. As the workers saw it, these were basic issues of morality. Their revolutionary aspirations, as Kanatchikov's story shows, were inextricably linked with their own personal striving for human dignity and individual worth. Many workers spoke of founding a 'new moral life', based on law and individual rights, in which there would be no more drunkenness, swearing, gambling or wife-beating.[22]

Part of the workers' new-found dignity was expressed in a new self-assertiveness. The workers claimed the down-town streets as 'theirs' by holding mass parades and meetings there. The city became a political theatre, as different groups of workers met to discuss their demands. These rallies were a vital aspect of the revolutionary spectacle. They were 'festivals of liberation', to adopt the phrase of Michelle Perrot, which gave the workers a new sense of confidence and collective solidarity. The whole of urban Russia seemed to have been caught up in this sudden craze for political meetings — *mitingovanie* as people called it. Everyone was talking politics. 'You cannot buy a hat or a packet of cigarettes or ride in a cab without being enticed into a political discussion,' complained Harold Williams of the *Daily Chronicle*:

The servants and house porters demand advice as to which party they should vote for in the ward elections. Every wall in the town is placarded with notices of meetings, lectures, congresses, electoral appeals, and announcements, not only in Russian, but in Polish, Lithuanian, Yiddish, and Hebrew ... Two men argue at a street corner and are at once surrounded by an excited crowd. Even at concerts now the music is diluted with political speeches by well-known orators. The Nevsky Prospekt has become a kind of *Quartier Latin*. Book hawkers line the pavement and cry sensational pamphlets about Rasputin and Nicholas, and who is Lenin, and how much land will the peasants get.

Compared with this, remarked John Reed, 'Carlyle's "flood of French speech" was a mere trickle . . . For months in Petrograd, and all over Russia, every street-corner was a public tribune.' It was as if the whole of Russia, having been kept silent for hundreds of years, had to express everything on its mind in as short a time as possible. 'Day and night, across the whole country', Paustovsky wrote, 'a continuous disorderly meeting went on from February until the autumn of 1917.'[23]

This growing political awareness and self-confidence among the workers was reflected in the mushroom growth of labour organizations during 1917. The trade unions and the Soviets resumed from where they had left off in 1905–6. But these were quickly overtaken by the factory committees, an innovation of 1917 which, having been elected on the factory floor, tended to develop faster and be more responsive to the immediate demands of the workers than either the unions or the Soviets, which, being organized at the industrial and city levels respectively, tended to be more bureaucratized. The main aim of the factory committees was to ensure the continuation of production at the plant. Factory closures were a daily occurrence, thousands of workers were being laid off, and many workers suspected their employers of deliberately running down production so as to 'starve out revolution' (or, as the capitalist Riabushin-sky put it, in a phrase that seemed to confirm these fears, it would take 'the bony hand of hunger' to make the workers 'come to their senses'). The committees set themselves up to fight against 'sabotage' by checking up on the work of the management; by taking charge of the supply of raw materials; and by regulating hiring and firing. They took charge of maintaining labour discipline; fought against absenteeism and drunkenness; and organized militias to defend the factory at night. 'Workers' control' was their aim, although by this was meant not so much the workers' direct management of production as their direct supervision of it, including participation on collective boards of management. As Steve Smith has convincingly shown, this did not make them the anarcho-syndicalist organizations depicted by many historians. It was never the aim of the factory committees to turn their plants into worker-communes and there was nothing in their practice to suggest that they rejected either state power or a centrally planned economy. On the contrary, as organs primarily of workers' defence designed to keep their factories running in the face of an economic crisis, they often ended up by demanding the nationalization of their plant. It was this, along with the Mensheviks' domination of the trade unions, that made them the favoured channel of Bolshevik activity in 1917.[24]

No organization better reflected the growing self-assertiveness of the working class than the Red Guards. Like the factory committees, they were an innovation of 1917, and the initiative for their establishment came essentially from below. During the February Revolution a wide range of workers' armed brigades had sprung up to defend the factories. They refused to disarm when the government set up its own militias in the cities. So there was a dual system of police — with the city militias in the middle-class districts and the workers' brigades in the industrial suburbs — which mirrored the dual power structure in Petrograd. Gradually the workers' brigades were, albeit loosely, unified under the direction of the district Soviets. But from the start it was the Bolsheviks who had the dominant influence on them; and it was a Bolshevik, Vladimir Bonch-Bruevich, who first used the term 'Red Guard'. Whereas the Soviet leadership looked upon the Red Guards as a dangerous precedent which threatened to subvert the government, the Bolsheviks, once Lenin had returned, became keen supporters of the arming of the workers and helped to shape the Red Guards' self-image as a workers' army, permanently on alert, to defend 'the revolution' against any threat. The arming of the workers — and by July there were about 20,000 workers in the Red Guards of Petrograd alone — was a vital aspect of their psychology. These were the workers whom Lenin had in mind when he said that the workers were 'to the left' of the Bolsheviks. They were young (over half the Red Guards were under twenty-five), single, highly literate and skilled workers, most of whom had joined the industrial war during the militant strikes of 1912–14, when the Bolsheviks had first gained a hold on the working class of Petrograd and Moscow. Most of them belonged to or at least were sympathetic to one of the maximalist parties — usually the Bolsheviks or the Anarchists — and had an image of themselves as a 'vanguard of the proletariat'.[25]

The Provisional Government was quite unable to contain this rise of labour militancy. It was misguided by the liberal industrial ethic of the War Industries Committees, of which its Minister of Trade and Industry, Konovalov, as well as its Minister of Finance, Tereshchenko, had been leading members. Central to this ethic was the (frankly rather bogus) notion of the government as the guardian of a 'neutral state', above party or class interests, whose role in industry was to mediate and conciliate between labour and capital. The important thing was to keep production going in the interests of the military campaign. The class war was to be stopped to win the war against Germany.

During the first weeks of Konovalov's rule there were some signs of this new spirit of industrial partnership. As part of the agreement on the eight-hour day brokered by Konovalov on 10 March, conciliation boards, composed equally of managers and workers, were established in many factories to resolve disputes without costly strikes. The administration of the railways was handed over to local railway committees in which the workers participated alongside the technicians and officials. Konovalov himself arbitrated many industrial disputes and leant on the employers to make concessions — often compensating them in other ways — in the interests of the war economy. V. G. Groman, the Menshevik economist, even began to draw up the outlines for a 'planned economy' in which the workers, technicians and employers would come together to regulate the economy under the tutelage of the Soviet and the state.[26]

Yet this armistice in the class war did not and could not last for very long. The government's would-be 'neutral' stance was itself a major reason for the resumption of hostilities. For each side suspected it of favouring the other. On the one hand, the workers were encouraged by their early gains — there were reports of some workers receiving a five-fold or six-fold pay increase — and this engendered unrealistic hopes of what it was possible to achieve by industrial action. Their expectations were further increased by the Mensheviks' entry into the government on 5 May (with Skobelev, a Menshevik, the Minister of Labour). It appeared to give them a green light for more strikes and an assurance that they had supporters in the government. Workers came out with new and often excessive strike demands, became disappointed when they lost, and accused the government of backing their employers. It was a disaster for the Mensheviks.

The employers, on the other hand, were becoming increasingly impatient with the workers' claims, and with the government's failure to contain them. They blamed the industrial crisis on the workers' inflationary pay rises, on the reduced length of the working day, and on the constant disruptions to production caused by strikes and factory meetings. They were alarmed by the Menshevik entry into the government: it seemed to signal more regulation and a swing towards the workers' point of view. From the start of May, they began to move away from Konovalov's path of industrial compromise. They closed ranks and began to resist the workers' strike demands, even at the cost of a lock-out and the closure of the factory. Whereas before strikes had been averted by negotiation, now both sides were more ready for a fight, and the resulting strikes were violent and protracted, since neither side could be leant on to back down. The bitter strike at the huge Sormovo plant in Nizhnyi Novgorod, which brought chaos to the country's biggest defence producer throughout preparations for the offensive in June, was the first real sign of this new climate.[27] It put an end to the liberal hopes of spring, and beckoned in a summer of industrial war.

* * *

As the self-proclaimed guardians of the Russian state, the leaders of the Provisional Government were united on one thing: the need, for the time being, to preserve its imperial boundaries intact. It was, as they saw it, their primary duty to preserve the 'unity of the Russian state' until the conclusion of the war and the resolution of the Empire question by the Constituent Assembly. This did not rule out the possibility of conceding, as an interim measure, rights of local self-rule or cultural freedoms to the non-Russian territories. Indeed the liberals thought this was essential. They assumed that the grievances of the non-Russian peoples were essentially the result of tsarist discrimination and oppression, and that they could thus be satisfied with civil and religious equality. They collapsed the question of national rights into the question of individual rights; and believed that on this basis the Russian Empire could be kept together. But defending the 'unity of the Russian state' did rule out, as the Kadets put it, giving in to nationalist pressures that would lead to 'the division of the country into sovereign, independent units'. Even the SR and Menshevik Defensists, who as revolutionaries had declared their support for the principle of national self-determination, lined up behind the Kadet position once they joined them in the government during 1917. As socialists, they still supported federalism; but as patriots, they were reluctant to preside over the break-up of the state in the middle of a war. The SR leader, Mark Vishniak, speaking at the Third SR Congress in May, compared Russia to a huge Switzerland: a decentralized federation, in which the cantons, or republics, would have the maximum national rights (including the right to their own currencies), but with a single unified state.[28]

This position, like that of Gorbachev during *perestroika*, was quite inadequate as a response to the growing pressures of nationalism after February 1917. True, not everywhere were the non-Russians bursting to break out of the Empire. Some of the more peasant-dominated peoples were barely aware of themselves as a 'nation' as opposed to an ethnic group (e.g. the Belorussians, the Lithuanians, the Azeris, and some might argue the Ukrainians). Others were by and large satisfied with civil and religious rights (e.g. the Jews). Others still combined their ethnic and social grievances in a single national-socialist revolution which looked towards Russia for the lead (e.g. Latvians and Georgians). Armenia, for purely nationalist considerations, looked to Russia for protection against the Turks. Yet elsewhere — and in certain classes of these peoples — the collapse of the tsarist system did result in the rise of mass-based nationalist movements which first demanded autonomy from Russia and then, when this was not granted, went on to call for independence.

The emergence of independence movements was partly the result of opportunity. The coercive power of the old state had collapsed; the persuasive power of the Provisional Government was, to say the least, extremely limited; while the Germans and the Austrians, whose armies occupied the western borderlands, were only too ready to help the nationalists set up mini-states they could control and use against Russia. Yet the nationalists were more than 'German agents', even in those countries (e.g. the Ukraine and Lithuania) where independence was achieved with a separate peace and at the price of a German puppet-state. Many of the nationalist parties achieved mass electoral support. In the Ukraine, for example, 71 per cent of the rural vote went to the Ukrainian SRs and the All-Ukrainian Peasant Union during the elections to the Constituent Assembly in November 1917. Socialist parties with a nationalist platform also gained the majority of votes in Estonia, Georgia, Finland and Armenia during elections in 1917.[29]

To be sure, it is not at all clear — and this remains one of the biggest unanswered questions of the Russian Revolution — what this mass support at the ballot box really tells us about the national consciousness of the peasantry, the vast majority of the population in all these societies. As one would expect, the most active and conscious nationalists were drawn from the petit-bourgeoisie, the petit-intelligentsia and the most prosperous and literate peasants, the peasant soldiers in particular.* After all, as we have seen, the growth of a peasant national consciousness was dependent on the spread of rural institutions, such as schools and reading clubs, peasant unions and co-operatives, which exposed the peasants to the national culture of the urban-centred world; and it was among these literate peasant types that these institutions were most developed. In the traditional political culture of the Ukrainian or Georgian countryside one might well expect the mass of the peasants — and even more so the peasant women, who were voting for the first time — to follow the lead of these rural élites and cast their votes for the nationalists. This was one of the main reasons why the SRs did so well in the elections to the Constituent Assembly: many of the village elders had been involved with the SRs in the past and they often recommended that the whole village vote for the SR list; rather than split the village into two all the peasants agreed to vote for the SRs. Second, all the most successful nationalist parties put forward programmes that combined nationalist with socialist demands, and it is not clear that the peasants were aware of the former separately. It is probable, as Ronald Suny has suggested in the case of the Ukraine, that while the peasantry had a 'cultural or ethnic awareness' and preferred 'leaders of their own ethnicity, people who could speak to them in their own language and promised to secure their local interests', they did not conceive of themselves 'as a single nationality' and were 'not yet moved by a passion for the nation'.[30] In other words, they interpreted the nationalists' slogans in terms of their own parochial concerns — the defence of the village, its culture and its lands (against the foreign towns and landed élites) — rather than in the terms of a nation state.

Certainly, the nationalists were most successful where they managed to

---

* The nationalist leadership was also largely derived from these groups. In the Ukraine, for example, the main leaders of the nationalist movement were Vinnichenko (the son of a peasant), Hrushevsky (the son of a minor official), Doroshenko (the son of a military vet), Konovalov and Naumenko (both the sons of teachers), Sadovsky, Efremov, Mikhnovsky, Chekhovsky and Boldochan (all the sons of priests).

persuade the peasants that national autonomy was the best guarantee of their revolution in the villages. Their policy of land nationalization was particularly successful. In many regions the struggle for the land was also the struggle of a native peasantry against a foreign landowning élite, so when the nationalists spoke of the need to 'nationalize the land' it made real and literal sense. In the northern provinces of the Ukraine, where the Ukrainian villages were closely intermingled with the Russian ones, the nationalists were able to mobilize the Ukrainian peasants around the defence of their traditions of hereditary land tenure against the threat of a Russian land reform based on the principles of communal tenure. Mykola Kovalevsky, the leader of the Ukrainian SRs, recalls how their propaganda worked:

> The Russians want to impose a socialization of the land upon you, I said to the peasants, that is to transfer the ownership of the land to the village communes and, in this way, to abolish your private farms; you will no longer be the masters of your own land, but will be workers on communal land.

The nationalist campaign for native language rights was equally meaningful to the peasants: their expectations of social advancement were dependent on learning to read their native language and on being able to use it in public life. So was their movement (in Georgia and the Ukraine) for the nativization (autocephaly) of the Church hierarchy: with services conducted in the native language the priests would be brought closer to the peasants, and more peasants would enter the priesthood. Similarly, the establishment of national army units, the demand of military congresses held by nearly all the main non-Russian soldiers, would not only provide these would-be nation states with a ready-made national army but would also open the door for more non-Russians to rise up into the officer corps.[31]

Whatever its true nature or extent, the appeal of the nationalists was very much stronger than the leaders of the Provisional Government were prepared to allow for. Only in the case of Poland did they make a full retreat before the nationalists, declaring their support for Polish independence from as early as 16 March, and then only because, with Poland occupied by the Germans and the Austrians, there was nothing to be lost by such declarations and, on the contrary, the possibility of winning the support of the Polish population against the Central Powers. Even Brusilov, a Great Russian patriot fighting at that time on disputed Russian-Ukrainian-Polish soil, recognized that 'we had no other choice but to offer Poland its freedom'.[32] But in the two other major conflicts — with the Finnish and Ukrainian nationalists — the Provisional Government refused to make any real concessions; and, largely as a result of this intransigency, these two movements both grew in their mass appeal and, as the government weakened visibly, turned from the demand for more autonomy to the demand for complete independence.

The Finnish problem stemmed from the doubtful basis of Russian rule in Finland after the collapse of the monarchy. The Finns argued, with some justification, that the Tsar had ruled over the Grand Duchy purely on the basis of his personal authority, as the Grand Duke of Finland, with the effect that after his downfall sovereignty should return to the Finnish parliament (Sejm). But in its Manifesto of 7 March the Provisional Government declared itself the full legal inheritor of the Tsar's authority in Finland and, while it restored the Finnish constitution, thereby ending thirteen years of direct Russian rule, it continued to insist that the government in Helsingfors should remain responsible to the Russian Governor-General, rather than the Sejm, until the future status of Finland had been resolved by the Constituent Assembly.

This was the start of a long and complex constitutional wrangle between the Finns (who refused to recognize the sovereignty of the Provisional Government) and the Russians (who refused to recognize the authority of the Sejm). Tokoi's coalition government in Helsingfors, a mixture of federal-minded socialists and liberal-minded nationalists, was based on the policy of negotiating a compromise solution, whereby Finland would gain full internal autonomy in exchange for a Russian veto over its foreign and military policy. Had level heads prevailed, the Provisional Government might have recognized this as a feasible temporary settlement of the conflict. But since the proposal entailed a smaller Finnish army for the Russian military campaign, it feared that this would prove to be the first step towards Finland's departure from the war, and it blocked the progress of the negotiations.

The deadlock continued through the spring, as Tokoi's government came under growing popular pressure to make a unilateral declaration of Finnish independence, while Petrograd saw in this a reason to stand even more firmly against all the Finnish demands. Both positions were largely determined by the fact that the Bolsheviks, who had taken up the Finnish cause in the hope of gaining an ally against the Provisional Government, were building up a powerful base of support among the sailors of Helsingfors, where they controlled their own Soviet organ of the Baltic Fleet (TsentroBalt). Tokoi underlined this Bolshevik threat in the hope of pressurizing the Provisional Government into making concessions. But the government was determined to stand firm. Even Kerensky, speaking like a true Great Russian patriot as the new Minister of War in May, warned the Finns not to try the patience of the 'open-hearted Russian people' by trying to 'deprive them of their rights to their own national territory'.[33]

Relations with Russia reached a crisis in June and July. A resolution of the All-Russian Soviet Congress calling on the Provisional Government to negotiate a treaty of independence with Finland at the end of the war was interpreted by the Sejm as a green light for it to pass its own declaration of independence (*valtalaki*) on 23 June. The *valtalaki* was greeted by nationwide celebrations. People falsely assumed that it had been supported by the 'Russian parliament'. But the Soviet was just as outraged by it as the Provisional Government. The *valtalaki* was a unilateral declaration of Finnish independence, whereas the Soviet resolution had meant it to be the result of bilateral negotiations with the Provisional Government. A Soviet delegation attempted to persuade the Finns to withdraw the *valtalaki* and, when this failed, the Soviet leaders gave their support to the government's decision to put down the Finnish movement by military force. Throughout July the Russians built up their troops on Finnish soil, threatening to use them against the Sejm if it did not withdraw its *valtalaki*. On 21 July the Sejm was dissolved. Most Russian socialists, despite their recognition of Finland's right to self-determination, accepted the need for this repressive measure and blamed it on the tactics of the Sejm. But others, like Gorky, warned that this action was bound to strengthen Finnish resolve, leading to the 'deepening of the conflict' and to the loss of Russia's democratic prestige in the West. In fact the dissolution did much more than that. By ruling out the possibility of a negotiated settlement, it effectively undermined the government in Helsingfors and pushed Finland along the path that would end in civil war, as the struggle for independence became intertwined with a broader social conflict between the liberal propertied classes, hesitant to make the final break with Russia, and an increasingly Bolshevized mass of workers, sailors and landless labourers, eager to declare independent Finland Red.[34]

In the Ukraine the February Revolution had immediately given rise to a nationalist movement based around the Rada, or parliament, established in Kiev on 4 March. While the Rada was ultimately committed to the Ukraine's right of self-determination, it saw its immediate task as the negotiation of cultural freedoms, greater political autonomy, and a radical land reform within a federal Russian state. The issue of land reform was especially important, for although the Rada could be sure of the support of the Ukrainian intelligentsia, it could not be so sure of the peasants, the vast majority of the Ukrainian population, although most of the Ukrainian soldiers, who were simply peasants in uniform, were, it is true, solidly behind the nationalist cause.

In mid-May a Rada delegation presented its demands to the Provisional Government. These demands were moderate — a recognition of the Ukraine's autonomy, a seat for the Ukraine at the peace settlement, a commissar for Ukrainian affairs, separate Ukrainian army units in the rear, and the appointment of Ukrainians to most civil posts — and the Provisional Government could have easily agreed to them without prejudicing the resolution of the Ukrainian question by the Constituent Assembly. But the Russian government and Soviet leaders dismissed the influence of the Rada — its declaration was not published by a single Russian newspaper — and appeared to assume that if they ignored it the whole problem would go away. Prince Lvov tried to bury the issue by setting up a special commission, packed with Russian jurists, which raised complicated legal questions about the legitimacy of every single Rada demand before concluding, predictably enough, that nothing could be resolved until the Constituent Assembly. It was yet another illustration of the Russian liberals using legal postures to hide from politics.

Yet the result of this ostrich-like reaction was merely to strengthen the nationalist cause and to drive it towards the more radical demand for independence from Russia. Urged by the Second Ukrainian Military Congress to make a unilateral declaration of autonomy, the Rada published its First Universal on 10 June. The Universal was a declaration of the Ukraine's freedom modelled on the charters of the seventeenth-century Cossack Hetmans, whom the nationalists claimed to be the founders of the 'Ukrainian nation', and in the context of 1917 it took on a symbolic role equal to the yellow and light blue flag of the Ukraine. The Universal called for the convocation of a Sejm, or sovereign national assembly, and declared the establishment of a General Secretariat, headed by V. K. Vinnichenko, which effectively assumed executive power, replacing the authority of the Provisional Government in the Ukraine. It was only now that the Ukrainian crisis, coinciding as it did with the Finnish declaration of independence, came to the top of the political agenda. Just as the army was about to launch a fresh offensive in the West, Russia was threatened with the loss of two vital regions behind the Front. Lvov immediately accused the Rada of threatening to 'inflict a fatal blow on the state', while *Volia naroda* expressed the general Soviet view that the Universal was 'a stab in the back of the Revolution'.[35]

Yet it was clear that some compromise was needed, and on 28 June the government despatched a three-man delegation (Tereshchenko, Kerensky and Tsereteli) to negotiate with the Rada. On 2 July the two sides reached a makeshift compromise: the Provisional Government broadly recognized the national autonomy of the Ukraine, the popular legitimacy of the Rada and the executive authority of the General Secretariat. This was enough to cool down Ukrainian tempers for the rest of the summer. But it outraged the Russian nationalists in Kiev, Shulgin's chauvinist supporters in particular, who took to fighting the Ukrainians in the streets. The right-wing Kadets in Lvov's cabinet took up the cause of the Russian minority in the Ukraine. They refused to endorse the settlement on the grounds that only the Constituent Assembly had the legal authority to resolve such matters, which was really no more than a pretext for the defence of Russia's imperial interests in the Ukraine. In a conversation with his secretary, Lvov condemned the Kadets for 'behaving like the worst Black

Hundred bastards' on the issue.[36] On 4 July three Kadets resigned from the cabinet. This was the trigger for the start of a protracted political crisis which would end in the collapse of the Provisional Government.

*   *   *

Brusilov to his wife on I March:

> You must know what is happening. I am of course pleased. But I pray to God that this awful crisis, in this awful war, may soon end, so that our external enemy may not reap the benefit of our collapse. The one fortunate circumstance is that it comes at a time of the year when it is very difficult, almost impossible, for the enemy to launch an attack, for this would be a catastrophe. It is all the more important now that we win this war, otherwise it will be the ruin of Russia.

Brusilov's untiring faith in Russia's victorious destiny was now, more than ever, a matter of hope against hope. It was, as he later acknowledged, entirely unrealistic to sustain a lengthy military campaign in the midst of a social revolution. And yet he still believed in the will of the people to continue fighting until the end, and, unlike most of the Tsar's generals, threw in his lot with the revolution in the hope that the defence of Russia's liberty might at last inspire their patriotism. Monarchists accused him of opportunism; and historians have repeated the charge. But Brusilov had long been persuaded, despite his own sympathies for the monarchy, that without a complete change of government Russia could not win the war. 'If I have to choose between Russia and the Tsar,' Brusilov had said in 1916, 'then I choose Russia.'[37]

    The army of Free Russia was in fact much less willing to go on with the war than the optimistic general had presumed. Order Number One gave the mass of the soldiers a new self-pride as 'citizens' on an equal par with the officers, and this soon led to the breakdown of all discipline. The newly established soldiers' committees, although dominated to begin with by the democratic junior officers and the uniformed intelligentsia, soon became the leaders of this revolution in the ranks. They held meetings on strategy and on whether to obey the officers' orders. Some soldiers refused to fight for more than eight hours a day, claiming the same rights as the workers. Many refused to salute their officers, or replaced them with their own elected officers. Intimidation of officers was common. Brusilov himself received many letters from his men threatening to kill him if he ordered an advance. When, in May, Brusilov assumed the Supreme Command and reviewed the units on the Northern Front, where the spirit of mutiny was strongest, he found that hundreds of officers had already fled their posts, while more than a few had even been driven to suicide. 'I remember one case when a group of officers had overheard their soldiers talk in threatening tones of "the need to kill all the officers". One of the youngest officers became so terrified he shot himself that night. He thought it was better to kill himself than to wait until the soldiers murdered him.' Their methods of killing officers were so brutal, with limbs and genitals sometimes cut off or the victims skinned alive, that one can hardly blame the officer.[38]

One young captain wrote to his father on 11 March:

> Between us and the soldiers there is an abyss that one cannot cross. Whatever they might think of us as individuals, we in their eyes remain no more than *barins* (masters). When we talk of 'the people' we have in mind the nation as a whole, but they mean only the common people. In their view what has taken place is not a political but a social revolution, of which we are the losers and they are the winners. They think that things should get better for them and that they should get worse for us. They do not believe us when we talk of our devotion to the soldiers. They say that we were the *barins* in the past, and that now it is their turn to be the *barins* over us. It is their revenge for the long centuries of servitude.

The peasant soldiers clearly did not share their officers' language of 'citizenship'. They did not see the revolution in the same terms of civic rights and duties. Their revolution in the trenches was another version of the social revolution in the countryside. The peasant conscripts naturally assumed that, if only they could overthrow their noble officers, then peace, bread and land would be the result. As one soldier put it at a meeting of his regiment in March to discuss the abdication of the Tsar:

> Haven't you understood? What is going on is a *ryvailooshun*! Don't you know what a *ryvailooshun* is? It's when the people take all the power. And what's the people without us, the soldiers, with our guns? Bah! It's obvious — it means that the power belongs to us. And while we're about it, the country is ours too, and all the land is ours, and if we choose to fight or not is up to us as well. Now do you understand? That's a *ryvailooshun*.[39]

This assertion of 'soldier power' was essential to the spirit of 'trench Bolshevism' which swept through the armed forces in 1917. Brusilov described it thus:

> The soldiers wanted only one thing — peace, so that they could go home, rob the landowners, and live freely without paying any taxes or recognizing any authority. The soldiers veered towards Bolshevism because they believed that this was its programme. They did not have the slightest understanding

of what either Communism, or the International,* or the division into workers and peasants, actually meant, but they imagined themselves at home living without laws or landowners. This anarchistic freedom is what they called 'Bolshevism'.

From the start of the revolution there was a sharp rise in the rate of desertion, especially among the non-Russian soldiers. Perhaps a million soldiers left their units between March and October. Most of these were soldiers 'absent without leave', men who had simply got fed up with fighting or sitting around unfed in the trenches and the garrisons, and had run off to the nearest town, where they ate and got drunk, went to brothels and often terrorized the local population. 'The streets are full of soldiers,' complained a Perm official in mid-March. 'They harass respectable ladies, ride around with prostitutes, and behave in public like hooligans. They know that no one dares to punish them.'[40]

* * *

Russia's war aims occupied the centre-stage of politics during the spring of 1917. Indeed the whole of 1917 could be seen as a political battle between those who saw the revolution as a means of bringing the war to an end and those who saw the war as a means of bringing the revolution to an end. This was not just a political clash, it was also a social one. Left-wing propaganda made it clear that the war was being waged for different class interests. Enormous mistrust and even hatred of the 'bourgeoisie' and the 'imperialist' or 'capitalist' system could be stirred up by the stories of war-profiteering industrialists, merchants, 'kulaks' and black marketeers. Supporters of the war were instantly tarnished with the stigma of placing their own 'imperial' interests above those of the people. 'We see', declared a workers' resolution of the Dinamo factory in Moscow, 'that the senseless slaughter and destruction of the war is essential to no one but the parasite bourgeoisie.'[41]

The Provisional Government had so far shied away from the crucial question of its policy on the war. There were too many conflicting views within the cabinet. Miliukov, with the loose support of Guchkov, saw no reason to give up Russia's imperial ambitions, contained in the 'secret treaties' with the Allies, to gain control of Constantinople. As Russia's new Foreign Minister, he made this clear to the press and embassies abroad. But his views were sharply at odds with the Soviet peace campaign, launched on 14 March with its Appeal to the Peoples of All the World, in which it renounced the war aims of tsarist Russia and called on the peoples of all the belligerent nations to protest against the 'imperialist war'. The Soviet peace campaign was immediately endorsed by a

* According to General Polovtsov, some of the soldiers thought the International was some sort of deity.

series of military congresses; most soldiers declared their allegiance to the Soviet on the basis that it promised peace. Its campaign was also backed by the more liberal ministers in the Provisional Government, once the left-wing idea of a separate peace, favoured in certain Soviet circles, was abandoned, and instead, on 21 March, the Soviet adopted the moderate line of Revolutionary Defensism (national unity for the defence of Russia combined with an international peace campaign for a democratic settlement 'without annexations or indemnities').

On 27 March the Provisional Government came out with its own Declaration of War Aims which was broadly in line with the Soviet peace campaign. But Miliukov told the *Manchester Guardian* that it would not alter Russia's commitment to her imperial allies. This began a bitter political struggle for the control of the Provisional Government's foreign policy. Miliukov was accused in democratic circles of speaking without cabinet authority. He was, in the words of one liberal newspaper, no more than a 'Minister of Personal Opinion'. The Soviet leaders, who saw the declaration of 27 March as a sacred achievement of the revolution, urged the Provisional Government to present it in the form of a diplomatic note to the Allies, which would give it effect as Russia's practical foreign policy, albeit without the approval of her Foreign Minister. After a great deal of fuss, Miliukov was forced to agree to this plan: the endorsement of the Soviet peace programme by a visiting delegation of French and British socialists had undercut his main objection that it would not be acceptable to the Allies. But when he came to despatch the declaration to the foreign embassies he added a covering note of his own in which he stressed, in contravention of the declaration, that Russia was still firmly committed to a 'decisive victory', including, at least by implication, the imperial war aims of the tsarist government.[42]

The effect of the Miliukov Note was like a red rag to the Soviet bull. Gorky, who had helped to write the Soviet Appeal of 14 March, denounced it as part of a 'bourgeois assault on the democracy with the purpose of prolonging the war'. Miliukov's action had, to be sure, greatly strengthened the Soviet message — that only 'the bourgeoisie' stood to gain from the 'imperialist war' — in the minds of the workers and soldiers. On 20 April thousands of armed workers and soldiers came out to demonstrate on the streets of Petrograd. Many of them carried banners with slogans calling for the removal of the 'ten bourgeois ministers', for an end to the war and for the appointment of a new revolutionary government. Linde, who had led the mutiny in February, was outraged by the Miliukov Note. He saw it as a betrayal of the revolution's fundamental promise, to bring the war to a democratic end. Inclined by nature to spontaneous protest (February had proved that), he led a battalion of the Finland Regiment in an armed demonstration to the Marinsky Palace in the expectation that the Soviet would call for the arrest of the government and the establishment of Soviet power.

By the time they reached the palace Linde's street army had been joined by crowds of angry soldiers from the Moscow and Pavlov regiments, so that it had swollen to 25,000 men. Linde's show of force was completely improvised — he had not consulted with anyone — but he was clearly under the illusion that the Soviet Executive (of which he was a member) would give its full approval to his actions. He was mistaken. The Executive had passed a resolution condemning Linde's demonstration on the grounds that it, the Soviet, was not prepared to assume power but, on the contrary, should help the Provisional Government to restore its own authority. It was only the far Left, the Vyborg Bolsheviks and the Anarchists, who had encouraged the demonstrators and had put the wild idea into their heads that they should 'get rid of the bourgeoisie'. The right-wing press immediately condemned Linde as a 'Bolshevik' and depicted his armed demonstration — even though it dispersed peacefully as soon as the Soviet leaders ordered it to — as a bloody attempt to carry out a coup. General Kornilov, the commander of the Petrograd garrison, wanted to disperse the demonstrators with his troops. But the cabinet was reluctant to use force against 'the people', and refused him permission. On 21 April fresh demonstrations took place. Angry protestors surrounded Miliukov's car and pounded it with their fists. Several people were killed when street fights broke out on the Nevsky Prospekt between the demonstrators and a counter-demonstration of right-wing patriots and monarchists.[43] The war question had split the capital into two and brought it to the brink of a bloody civil war.

It was this threat of a civil war that finally spurred the Soviet leaders to join the government and bolster its authority. They had been moving towards the idea of a coalition for some time. Two main factors lay behind this. One was Irakli Tsereteli, the tall and handsome Georgian Menshevik with a pale El Greco-like face, who had returned from Siberian exile in mid-March and at once stamped his authority on the leadership of the Soviet. Tsereteli was, in Lvov's estimation, 'the only true statesman in the Soviet'. In his rigorously intellectual speeches he always appealed to the interests of the state rather than to class or party interests; and their gradual effect was to inculcate in the Soviet leaders a growing sense of their responsibility. They ceased to think and act like revolutionaries and began to see themselves as 'government men'. It was Tsereteli who had shaped the policy of Revolutionary Defensism, which united the Soviet leaders with the liberals on the question of the war and which formed the basis of their coalition. The other factor was the influence of the socialist party rank and file, especially in the provinces, who broadly welcomed the prospect of a coalition with the liberals. For a start, they had never been held back by the same ideological obsession as their party leaders in the capital about the need to form a 'bourgeois government'. They had placed pragmatism before party dogma (what choice did they have with the tiny size of the provincial intelligentsia?) and had joined the liberals in town-hall government from the very first days of the revolution. It was also felt by the rank and file that, if their leaders joined the government, they would gain more leverage over it. Many workers thought that, with the Mensheviks in charge of industry, they would soon gain better pay. Many soldiers thought that, with the SRs in charge of the war, they would soon gain peace.[44]

The establishment of the coalition, like the formation of the government in March, stemmed from the combined efforts of the Soviet leaders and the liberals to restore order on the Petrograd streets. The Soviet leaders were horrified by the violent demonstrations and the prospect of a civil war. It was they who took the lead in stopping the disorders, taking over control of the garrison and prohibiting any further demonstrations on 21 April. Effectively they were already assuming the responsibilities of government. The next day they issued a joint statement with the ministers condemning the Miliukov Note. This resolved the immediate crisis. But Lvov was now determined that the Soviet leaders should join his government to give it popular credibility. Miliukov's presence in the cabinet was the biggest obstacle — working with him would expose the Soviet leaders to the charge from the extreme Left that they supported the 'imperialist war' — and it was this that led them to reject the idea of a coalition on 28 April. But two days later everything was changed with the resignation of Guchkov, the Minister of War and Miliukov's only ally in the cabinet, in protest against the confirmation of the soldiers' rights by a government commission and the Soviet campaign against Miliukov. Lvov, meanwhile, began to plot Miliukov's removal. He promised Tsereteli that he would force Miliukov out of the cabinet if the Soviet leaders agreed to join a coalition government. This, along with Lvov's own threat to resign if Tsereteli did not agree, was enough to convince the Menshevik leader that a coalition was now both possible and essential to end the crisis of authority, which the extreme Right or Left might easily exploit, and it was largely the force of his reasoning that finally persuaded the Soviet Executive to vote in its favour on 2 May by 44 votes to 19.[45]

Three days later the new cabinet was announced. It was agreed, in deference to Menshevik dogma, that the socialists should occupy only a minority of the cabinet posts (they took six out of the sixteen), and that to preserve the liberal conception of the government as a national institution, above party or class interests, they should join the cabinet as private individuals rather than as members of the Soviet. Chernov took Agriculture, Kerensky War, Skobelev Labour, while Tsereteli, whose time was spent mostly in the Soviet, was persuaded to accept the minor post of Posts and Telegraphs, which would allow him to keep one foot in each camp. Chernov called Tsereteli the 'Minister of General Affairs', while Sukhanov dubbed him the 'Commissar of the Government in the Soviet'. It is certainly true that Tsereteli emerged as the central figure of the coalition. Lvov was dependent on him to keep the socialist leaders onside, and he kept him in his 'inner cabinet' (together with the five Minister-Free-masons: Kerensky, Tereshchenko, Nekrasov, Konovalov and Lvov) which decided the general strategy.[46]

The formation of the Coalition, which had been intended to reinforce the democratic centre, had the opposite effect. It accelerated the political and social polarization that led to the outbreak of the civil war in October. On the one hand, most of the provincial rank and file of the Kadets moved with their party leader Miliukov, who had resigned on 4 May, into right-wing opposition against the coalition government. Increasingly they abandoned their liberal self-image as a party of the nation as a whole and began to portray themselves as a party for the defence of bourgeois class interests, property rights, law and order and the Russian Empire. Within the Soviet camp, on the other hand, there was a steady drift towards the Left as the mass of the workers and the peasants became increasingly disillusioned with the failure of the socialists to use their position in the government to speed up the process of social reform or to bring about a democratic peace. The left-wing SRs and Mensheviks, who had been opposed to the coalition, were correct to warn their party colleagues that by entering the government, and by sharing in the blame for its shortcomings, they were bound to lose popular support. For the socialists were henceforth to be 'statesmen', they could no longer act like 'revolutionaries', and this obliged them to resist what they now called the growing 'anarchy' — the peasant seizures of the land, the workers' strikes and the breakdown of army discipline — in the interests of the state. Instead of using their popular mandate to take power for themselves, as they could have done in the April crisis, the Soviet leaders chose instead to lend their support to a liberal government which had already been discredited. They increasingly became seen as the guardians of a 'bourgeois' state, and the initiative for the revolution, for bread, land and peace, was taken up by the Bolsheviks.

iii Lenin's Rage

The Finland Station, on Petrograd's Vyborg side, shortly before midnight on 3 April 1917: workers and soldiers, with red flags and banners, fill the station hall; and there is a military band. The square outside is packed with automobiles and tank-like armoured cars; and the cold night air is blue with smoke. A mounted searchlight sweeps over the faces of the crowd and across the façades of the buildings, momentarily lighting up the tram-lines and the outlines of the city beyond. There is a general buzz of expectation: Lenin's train is due. At last it pulls into the station; a thunderous Marseillaise booms around the hall; and

BETWEEN REVOLUTIONS

38 The Tsar's soldiers fire on the demonstrating workers in front of the Winter Palace, 9 January ('Bloody Sunday') 1905.

39 Demonstrators confront a group of mounted cossacks on the Nevsky Prospekt in 1905.

40 The opening of the State Duma in the Coronation Hall of the Winter Palace, 27 April 1906. The two Russias – autocratic and democratic – confronted each other on either side of the throne. On the left, the appointees of the crown; on the right, the Duma delegates.

41 The Tauride Palace, the citadel of Russia's fragile democracy between 1906 and 1918.

42 Petr Stolypin in 1909. Many things about the Prime Minister – his provincial background and his brilliant intellect – made him an outsider to his own bureaucracy.

43 Patriotic volunteers pack parcels for the Front, Petrograd, 1915. The war campaign activated and politicized the public.

44 The smart set of Petrograd see in the New Year of 1917. Note the anglophilia, the whisky and champagne. This sort of ostentatious hedonism had become quite common among the upper classes; and at a time of enormous wartime hardships it was deeply resented by the workers.

45 Troops pump out a trench on the Northern Front. The poor construction of the trenches, a science which the tsarist Staff had never thought worth learning, was a major cause of the huge Russian losses in the First World War.

46 Cossacks patrol the streets of Petrograd, early February 1917. Recruited from the poorest regions of the Kuban and the Don, they soon joined the revolutionary crowds.

47 A 'pharaon' – the slang name for a policeman – is arrested by a group of soldiers during the February Days in Petrograd.

48-9 The destruction of tsarist symbols. *Above*: a group of Moscow workers playing with the stone head of Alexander II in front of a movie camera. *Below*: a crowd on the Nevsky Prospekt in Petrograd stand around a bonfire with torn-down tsarist emblems during the February Days. Here, too, the display for the camera was an important part of the event.

50 The crowd outside the Tauride Palace, 27 February 1917.

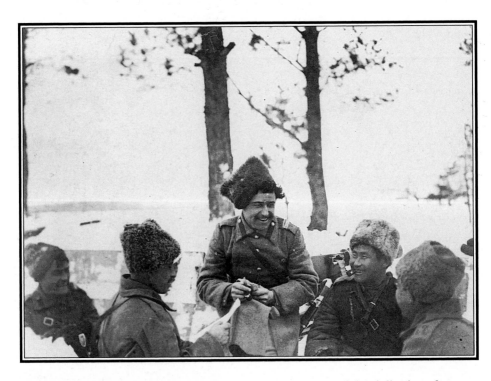

51 Soldiers on the Western Front receive the announcement of the abdication of Nicholas II.

the small and stocky figure of Lenin appears from the carriage, his Swiss wool coat and Homburg hat strangely out of place amidst the welcoming congregation of grey tunics and workers' caps. An armed Bolshevik escort leads him in military formation to the Tsar's former waiting-room, where a Soviet delegation is standing by to greet him, the latest returning hero of the revolutionary struggle, after more than a decade of exile abroad.[47]

For Lenin this was the end of an unexpected journey. The February Revolution had found him in Zurich and, like most of the socialist leaders, it had caught him by surprise. 'It's staggering!' he exclaimed to Krupskaya when he heard the news. 'It's so incredibly unexpected!' Lenin was determined to get back to Russia as soon as possible. But how could he cross the German lines? At first he thought of crossing the North Sea by steamer, as Plekhanov had already done. But the British were hostile to the Russian Marxists: Trotsky and Bukharin had both been detained in England on their way back to Russia from New York. Then he thought of travelling through Germany disguised as a deaf, dumb and blind Swede — until Krupskaya had joked that he was bound to give himself away by muttering abuse against the Mensheviks in his sleep. In a moment of desperation he had even considered hiring a private aeroplane to fly across eastern Europe; but then the thought of the dangers involved put him off this harebrained scheme. When it came to putting himself at physical risk, Lenin always had been something of a coward.*[48]

It was Martov who came up with the idea of exchanging the Russian Marxist exiles in Switzerland for the German citizens interned in Russia. With the help of their Swiss comrades, the Russian exiles made contact with the German authorities, who quickly saw the advantage of letting the Bolsheviks, and other socialist groups opposed to the war, go back to Russia to stir up discord there. They even helped to finance their activities, although this should not necessarily be taken to mean, as many people were later to argue, that the Bolsheviks were German agents.[49] The Provisional Government was not keen on the idea of an exchange — Miliukov was determined to oppose it in view of Lenin's well-known defeatist views — and dragged its heels over the negotiations. Martov and most of the Menshevik exiles were prepared to wait. But Lenin and thirty-one of his comrades were impatient enough to go ahead with the German plan without the sanction of the Russian government. On 27 March they left

---

* Valentinov, who knew Lenin well in Switzerland, wrote: 'He would never have gone on to the streets to fight on the barricades, or stand in the line of fire. Not he, but other, humbler people were to do that . . . Lenin ran headlong even from émigré meetings which seemed likely to end in a scuffle. His rule was to "get away while the going was good" — to use his own words — meaning from any threat of danger. During his stay in Petersburg in 1905–6 he so exaggerated the danger to himself and went to such extremes in his anxiety for self-preservation that one was bound to ask whether he was not simply a man without personal courage.'

on a German train from Gottmadingen on the Swiss border and travelled via Frankfurt, Berlin and Stockholm to Petrograd. The train, which had only one carriage, was 'sealed' in the sense that no inspections of passports or luggage were carried out by the Germans on the way. Lenin worked alone in his own compartment, while his fellow travellers, much to his annoyance, drank and sang in the corridor and the other compartments. Smoking was confined to the lavatory and Lenin ordered that all non-smokers should be issued with a 'first class' pass that gave them priority to use the lavatory over the smokers with their 'second class' passes. As Radek quipped, it seemed from this piece of minor social planning that Lenin was already preparing himself to 'assume the leadership of the revolutionary government'.[50] The 'sealed train' was an early model of Lenin's state dictatorship.

Lenin arrived a stranger to Russia. Apart from a six-month stay in 1905–6, he had spent the previous seventeen years in exile abroad. Most of the workers who turned out to meet him at the Finland Station could never have seen him before.* 'I know very little of Russia,' Lenin once told Gorky. 'Simbirsk, Kazan, Petersburg, exile — that is all I know.' During 1917 he would often claim that the mass of the ordinary people were even further to the Left than the Bolsheviks. Yet he had no experience of them, and knew only what his party agents told him (which was often what he wanted to hear). Between 5 July and the October seizure of power Lenin did not make a single public appearance. He barely set foot in the provinces. The man who was set to become the dictator of Russia had almost no direct knowledge of the way its people lived. Apart from two years as a lawyer, he had never even had a job. He was a 'professional revolutionary', living apart from society and supporting himself from the party's funds and from the income of his mother's estate (which he continued to draw until her death in 1916). According to Gorky, it was this ignorance of everyday work, and the human suffering which it entailed, which had bred in Lenin a 'pitiless contempt, worthy of a nobleman, for the lives of the ordinary people . . . Life in all its complexity is unknown to Lenin. He does not know the ordinary people. He has never lived among them.'[51]

'Well there it is,' Lenin wrote to Kollontai on 2 March. 'This first stage of the revolution (born of the war) will be neither the last, nor confined to Russia.' Lenin was already thinking of a second revolution — a revolution of his own. In his five 'Letters from Afar', written between 7 and 26 March, he mapped out his party's programme for the transition from 'the first to the

---

* Many of the workers who came to greet Lenin may have turned up on the expectation of free beer. Welcoming receptions for returning party leaders had become a regular feature of life in the capital since the revolution, and for many of the workers they had become a pretext for a street party. This was particularly relevant in the case of Lenin's return from exile, since it coincided with the Easter holiday.

second stage of the revolution': no support for the Provisional Government; a clean break with the Mensheviks and the Second International; the arming of the workers; the foundation of Soviet power (the 'democratic dictatorship of the proletariat and the poorest peasants'); and the conclusion of an immediate peace. Lenin boiled all this down into ten punchy theses — his famous April Theses — during the train journey from Switzerland and began to agitate for them upon his arrival at the Finland Station. Brushing aside the formal welcome of the Soviet leaders, the returning exile proclaimed the start of a 'worldwide Socialist revolution!', and then went out into the square, where he climbed on to the bonnet of a car and gave a speech to the waiting crowd. Above all the noise Sukhanov heard only the occasional phrase: ' . . . any part in the shameful imperialist slaughter . . . lies and frauds . . . capitalist pirates . . .' Lenin was then taken off in an armoured car, which proceeded with a military band, workers and soldiers waving red flags, through the Vyborg streets to the Bolshevik headquarters — the palace of Kshesinskaya, the former ballerina and sometime mistress of the Tsar.[52]

On the following day Lenin came with his own armed escort to the Tauride Palace and presented his Theses to a stunned assembly of the Social Democrats. He had turned the Party Programme on its head. Instead of accepting the need for a 'bourgeois stage' of the revolution, as all the Mensheviks and most of the Bolsheviks did, Lenin was calling for a new revolution to transfer power to 'the proletariat and the poorest peasants'. In the present revolutionary conditions, he argued, a parliamentary democracy would be a 'retrograde step' compared with the power of the Soviets, the direct self-rule of the proletariat. Theoretically, the April Theses had their roots in the lessons which Lenin had learned from the failure of the 1905 Revolution: that the Russian bourgeoisie was too feeble on its own to carry out a democratic revolution; and that this would have to be completed by the proletariat instead. The Theses also had their roots in the war, which had led him to conclude that, since the whole of Europe was on the brink of a socialist revolution, the Russian Revolution did not have to confine itself to bourgeois democratic objectives.* But the practical implications of the Theses — that the Bolsheviks should cease to support the February Revolution and should move towards the establishment of the Dictatorship of the Proletariat — went far beyond anything that all but the most extreme left-wingers in the party had ever considered before. It was still not clear whether Lenin envisaged the violent overthrow of the Provisional Government, and, if so, when this should happen. For the moment, he seemed content to limit the party's tasks to mass agitation. The Bolsheviks still lacked a majority

---

* Trotsky had reached the same conclusions, and it is possible that his theory of the 'permanent revolution' partly influenced the April Theses.

in the Soviets; and Russia, as Lenin pointed out, was '*now* the freest of all the belligerent countries in the world'. But the sheer audacity of his speech, coming as it did at a joint SD assembly for the party's reunification, ensured a furious uproar in the hall. The Mensheviks booed and whistled. Tsereteli accused Lenin of ignoring the lessons of Marx and quoted Engels on the dangers of a premature seizure of power. Goldenberg said that the Bolshevik leader had abandoned Marxism altogether so as to occupy the anarchist throne vacated by Bakunin. B. O. Bogdanov condemned the Theses as 'the ravings of a madman'. Even Semen Kanatchikov, the Bolshevik worker we met in Chapter 3, who had come all the way from the Urals to hear Lenin speak, was flabbergasted by what he saw as the 'unrealistic nature of his ideas, which seemed to all of us to go far beyond the realms of what it was possible to achieve'. It seemed that Lenin, having spent so many years in exile abroad, had become out of touch with the realities of political life in Russia. Returning from the Tauride Palace that evening, Skobelev, the Menshevik, assured Prince Lvov: 'Lenin is a has-been.'[53]

Which is just what he might have become, had it not been for one fact: that he was Lenin. All the odds were stacked against him in his struggle for the party to adopt the April Theses. The majority of the Bolsheviks had already pledged their tentative support for the Provisional Government prior to Lenin's arrival (Kollontai was the only major Bolshevik to support the April Theses from the start). Only the Vyborg Committee, the stronghold of Bolshevik extremism in the capital, came out in favour of Soviet power. Stalin and Kamenev, who returned from Siberian exile in mid-March and took over control of *Pravda*, strengthened this cautious approach. Like the Mensheviks, they assumed that the 'bourgeois' stage of the revolution still had a long way to run, that the dual power system was thus necessitated by objective conditions, and that the immediate tasks of the Bolsheviks lay in constructive work within the social democratic movement as a whole. Trotsky later accused them of acting more like a loyal opposition than the representatives of a workers' revolutionary party. The moderate motions of Kamenev and Stalin were adopted at the All-Russian Bolshevik Conference at the end of March: conditional support for the Provisional Government; the continuation of the war; support for the Soviet leaders. The Bolsheviks even agreed to explore the possibilities of reuniting with the Mensheviks. They were already working together, along with the SRs and other socialists, in most of the provincial Soviets. Far away from the factional disputes of their party leaders in the capital, the old camaraderie of the underground remained very strong in the provinces, and Lenin's combative factionalism was strongly resented and resisted by those provincial Bolsheviks who were either unwilling or simply unable to break their ties with the other left-wing groups.[54]

Lenin always liked a fight. It was as if the whole of his life had been a preparation for the struggle that awaited him in 1917. 'That is my life!' he had confessed to Inessa Armand in 1916. 'One fighting campaign after another.' The campaign against the Populists, the campaign against the Economists, the campaign for the organization of the party along centralist lines, the campaign for the boycott of the Duma, the campaign against the Menshevik 'liquidators', the campaign against Bogdanov and Mach, the campaign against the war — these had been the defining moments of his life, and much of his personality had been invested in these political battles. As a private man there was nothing much to Lenin: he gave himself entirely to politics. There was no 'private Lenin' behind the politician. All biographies of the Bolshevik leader become unavoidably discussions of his political ideas and influence. Lenin's personal life was extraordinarily dull. He dressed and lived like a middle-aged provincial clerk, with precisely fixed hours for meals, sleep, work and leisure. He liked everything to be neat and orderly. He was punctilious about his financial accounts, noting on slips of paper everything he spent on food, on train fares, on stationery, and so on. Every morning he tidied his desk. His books were ordered alphabetically. He sewed buttons on to his pin-striped suit, removed stains from it with petrol and kept his bicycle surgically clean.[55]

There was a strong puritanical streak in Lenin's character which later manifested itself in the political culture of his regime. Asceticism was a common trait of the revolutionaries of Lenin's generation. They were all inspired by the self-denying revolutionary hero Rakhmetev in Chernyshevksy's novel *What Is To Be Done?* By suppressing his own sentiments, by denying himself the pleasures of life, Lenin tried to strengthen his resolve and to make himself, like Rakhmetev, insensitive to the suffering of others. This, he believed, was the 'hardness' required by every successful revolutionary: the ability to spill blood for political ends. 'The terrible thing in Lenin', Struve once remarked, 'was that combination in one person of self-castigation, which is the essence of all real asceticism, with the castigation of other people as expressed in abstract social hatred and cold political cruelty.' Even as the leader of the Soviet state Lenin lived the spartan lifestyle of the revolutionary underground. Until March 1918 he and Krupskaya occupied a barely furnished room in the Smolny Institute, a former girls' boarding school, sleeping on two narrow camp-beds and washing themselves with cold water from a bowl. It was more like a prison cell than the suite of the dictator of the biggest country in the world. When the government moved to Moscow they lived with Lenin's sister in a modest three-room apartment within the Kremlin and took their meals in the cafeteria. Like Rakhmetev, Lenin did weight training to build up his muscles. It was all part of the macho culture (the black leather jackets, the militant rhetoric, the belief in action and the cult of violence) that was the essence of Bolshevism. Lenin did not smoke, he did not really drink, and, apart from his romantic friendship with Inessa Armand, he was not interested in beautiful women. Krupskaya called him 'Ilich', his popular name in the party, and he called her 'comrade'. She was more like Lenin's personal secretary than his wife, and it was probably not bad luck that their marriage was childless. Lenin had no place for sentiment in his life. 'I can't listen to music too often,' he once admitted after a performance of Beethoven's Appassionata Sonata. 'It makes me want to say kind, stupid things, and pat the heads of people ... But now you have to beat them on the head, beat them without mercy.'[56]

Lenin's interests in literature were, like everything else, determined by its social and political content. He only bothered with books which he thought might be useful to him. He admired Pushkin for what he simplistically supposed to be his opposition to autocracy, and he liked Nekrasov for his realistic depiction of the oppressed masses. He had read Goethe's *Faust* whilst teaching himself German in Siberia, and had even learned some of Mephistopheles's speeches off by heart; but he never showed any interest in any of Goethe's other works. He refused to read Dostoevsky, dismissing his novel *The Possessed*, which had tried to expose the psychotic nature of the revolutionary, as 'a piece of reactionary filth ... I have absolutely no desire to waste my time on it. I looked through the book and threw it away. I don't read such literature — what good is it to me?'[57]

The root of this philistine approach to life was a burning ambition for power. The Mensheviks joked that it was impossible to compete with a man, such as Lenin, who thought about revolution for twenty-four hours every day. Lenin was driven by an absolute faith in his own historical destiny. He did not doubt for a moment, as he had once put it, that he was the man who was to wield the 'conductor's baton' in the party. This was the message he brought back to Russia in April 1917. Those who had known him before the war noticed a dramatic change in his personality. 'How he had aged,' recalled Roman Gul', who had met him briefly in 1905. 'Lenin's whole appearance had altered. And not only that. There was none of his old geniality, his friendliness or comradely humour, in his relations with other people. The new Lenin that arrived was cynical, secretive and rude, a conspirator "against everyone and everything", trusting no one, suspecting everyone, and determined to launch his drive for power.' Chernov also noted his single-minded drive for power in a brilliant satirical portrait of the Bolshevik leader published in *Delo naroda*:

Lenin possesses an imposing wholeness. He seems to be made of one chunk of granite. And he is all round and polished like a billiard ball. There is nothing you can get hold of him by. He rolls with irrepressible speed. But he could repeat to himself the well-known phrase: 'Je ne sais pas où je vais, mais j'y vais résolument'. Lenin possesses a devotion to the revolutionary cause which permeates his entire being. But to him the revolution is embodied in his person. Lenin possesses an outstanding mind, but it is a ... *mind of one dimension* — more than that, a unilinear mind ... He is a man of one-sided will and consequently a man with a stunned moral sensitivity.[58]

Lenin had never been tolerant of dissent within his party's ranks. Bukharin complained that he 'didn't give a damn for the opinions of others'. Lunacharsky claimed that Lenin deliberately 'surrounded himself with fools' who would not dare question him. During Lenin's struggle for the April Theses this domineering attitude was magnified to almost megalomaniac proportions. Krupskaya called it his 'rage' — the frenzied state of her husband when engaged in clashes with his political rivals — and it was an enraged Lenin whom she had to live with for the next five years. During these fits Lenin acted like a man possessed by hatred and anger. His entire body was seized with extreme nervous tension, and he could neither sleep nor eat. His outward manner became vulgar and coarse. It was hard to believe that this was a cultivated man. He mocked his opponents, both inside and outside the party, in crude and violent language. They were 'blockheads', 'bastards', 'dirty scum', 'prostitutes', 'cunts', 'shits', 'cretins', 'Russian fools', 'windbags', 'stupid hens' and 'silly old maids'. When the rage subsided Lenin would collapse in a state of exhaustion, listlessness and depression, until the rage erupted again. This manic alternation of mood was characteristic of Lenin's psychological make-up. It continued almost unrelentingly between 1917 and 1922, and must have contributed to the brain haemorrhage from which he eventually died.[59]

Much of Lenin's success in 1917 was no doubt explained by his towering domination over the party. No other political party had ever been so closely tied to the personality of a single man. Lenin was the first modern party leader to achieve the status of a god: Stalin, Mussolini, Hitler and Mao Zedong were all his successors in this sense. Being a Bolshevik had come to imply an oath of allegiance to Lenin as both the 'leader' and the 'teacher' of the party. It was this, above all, which distinguished the Bolsheviks from the Mensheviks (who had no clear leader of their own). By comparison with Lenin, all the other leading Bolsheviks were political midgets. Take Zinoviev. He was a brilliant orator but, as his great rival Trotsky put it, he was nothing else. For his speeches to produce results, 'he had to have a tranquillising certainty that he was to be relieved of the political responsibility by a reliable and strong hand. Lenin gave him this certainty.' Or take Kamenev. It was he who led the opposition to the April Theses, and, more than any other Bolshevik, argued the case for a moderate political alternative to Lenin's revolutionary strategy. Yet Kamenev was much too soft to be a real leader. Lunacharsky called him 'flabby'; Stankevich found him 'so gentle that it seemed that he himself was ashamed of his position'; while

George Denike compared him to an old schoolmaster and noted his fondness for wearing slippers. Kamenev was far too weak to stand up against the 'hard men' in the party. He might balk at some of their policies but he always followed them in the end.[60]

Lenin's domination of the party had more to do with the culture of the party than with his own charisma. His oratory was grey. It lacked the brilliant eloquence, the pathos, the humour, the vivid metaphors, the colour or the drama of a speech by Trotsky or Zinoviev. Lenin, moreover, had the handicap of not being able to pronounce his 'r's'.* Yet his speeches had an iron logic, and Lenin had the knack of finding easy slogans, which he crammed into the heads of his listeners by endless repetition. He spoke with his thumbs thrust under his armpits, rocking back and forward on his heels, as if in preparation to launch himself, like a human rocket, into the listening crowd (this is how he was portrayed in the hagiographic portraits painted during the Soviet era). Gorky, who heard Lenin speak for the first time in 1907, thought he 'spoke badly' to start with: 'but after a minute I, like everybody else, was absorbed in his speech. It was the first time I had heard complicated political questions treated so simply. There was no striving after beautiful phrases. He presented every word clearly, and revealed his exact thought with great ease.' Potresov, who had known and worked with Lenin since 1894, explained his appeal by a curious 'hypnotic power':

> Only Lenin was followed unquestioningly as the indisputable leader, as it was only Lenin who was that rare phenomenon, particularly in Russia — a man of iron will and indomitable energy, capable of instilling fanatical faith in the movement and the cause, and possessed of equal faith in himself. Once upon a time I, too, was impressed by this will-power of Lenin's, which seemed to make him into a 'chosen leader'.[61]

And yet it was more than the dominance of Lenin's personality that ensured the victory of his ideas in the party. The Bolshevik rank and file were not simply Lenin's puppets — he had been in exile too long for that — and their initial reservations about his call for a second revolution were strong enough for him to have to do more than simply lay down the party line for them to support it. The idea that the Bolshevik Party in 1917 was a monolithic organization tightly controlled by Lenin is a myth — a myth which used to be propagated by the Soviet establishment, and one which is still believed (for quite different motives) by right-wing historians in the West. In fact the party was quite undisciplined; it had many different factions, both ideological and geo-

---

* Gorbachev had a similar handicap.

graphical; and the leadership, which was itself divided, often proved unable to impose its will on them. Between April and October, and after that in the bitter struggles over Brest-Litovsk, the party was split from top to bottom by a series of ideological conflicts, in which Lenin, at least to begin with, often found himself in a small minority. And if in the end he always got his way, this was due not just to his domination of the party but also to his many political skills, including persuasion, tactful retreat and compromise, threats of resignation and ultimatums, demagogy and appeals to the rank and file.

Three factors worked in Lenin's favour during his struggle for the April Theses — one on the Right, one in the Centre, and one on the Left of the Bolshevik Party. On the Right the effect of the Theses was to impel a number of Bolshevik veterans into the Menshevik camp, where they believed the tenets of orthodox Marxism would be better respected. Some also found refuge in the intermediate group around Gorky's newspaper, *Novaia zhizn'*, of which more later. The Centre, which had rallied around Kamenev to begin with, was gradually won over by Lenin, as he toned down the radical aspects of his April Theses. At the All-Russian Party Conference on 24–9 April he won a majority against Kamenev by accepting that a 'lengthy period of agitation' would be needed before the masses would be ready to follow the Bolsheviks to the next stage of the revolution. He was thus abandoning the call for the immediate overthrow of the Provisional Government which many Bolsheviks had seen as the implication of his April Theses and which they had feared would plunge the country into civil war. Meanwhile, the left wing of the party was strengthened in the spring by the massive enrolment of workers and soldiers as new members. It was these lower-class party members who comprised the majority of the Bolshevik delegates at the April Party Conference — 149 of them in all, representing nearly 80,000 members throughout the country. They tended to be more radical than their party leaders. Knowing little of Marxist theory, they could not understand the need for a 'bourgeois revolution'. Why did their leaders want to reach socialism in two stages when they could get there in one? Hadn't enough blood already been spilled in February? And why should they allow the bourgeoisie to strengthen itself in power, if this was only going to make the task of removing them later even harder? The April Theses, with their call for immediate Soviet power, made more sense to them, and Lenin made a conscious effort to take advantage of this by speaking at numerous local party and factory meetings in the capital. He even swapped his Homburg hat for a worker's cap in an effort to make himself look more 'proletarian'.[62]

The April crisis emphasized Lenin's message among the lower-class rank and file. Miliukov's behaviour seemed to prove his point that peace could not be attained through the 'imperialist' war aims of the Provisional Government. It strengthened the 'us-and-them' mentality of the radical workers and soldiers towards the 'bourgeois ministers'. Some of the Bolsheviks in the party's Petrograd organization attempted to use the demonstrations of 20–1 April as a springboard for the overthrow of the Provisional Government. A Bolshevik activist from the Putilov factory, S. Ia. Bogdatiev, led the demonstrators on to the streets with revolutionary banners. It is not clear what the role of the Bolshevik leadership was in all of this. The later Soviet version was that Bogdatiev and his comrades acted on their own initiative. But some Western historians have claimed that the Central Committee must have authorized their actions and only distanced itself from them when the putsch failed. There is no real evidence for this claim and its basic assumption — that the party was a tightly disciplined body — is in any case unfounded. The Central Committee had all along been opposed to the seizure of power, and the demonstrations evidently took them by surprise. Lenin, it is true, had favoured the idea of turning the demonstrations into a show of strength. But he could not be sure of the party's support, nor of the support of the masses, should this result in a struggle for power, and so he adopted a wait-and-see approach. No doubt if the Provisional Government had been overthrown, he would have claimed the victory. But as soon as order had been restored he condemned the 'adventurism' of the Petersburg 'hot-heads'. His main concern was to appease the centrist elements at the Bolshevik Conference. He told them on 24 April:

> We had only wanted a peaceful reconnaissance of our enemy's forces and not to give battle. But the Petersburg Committee moved 'a wee bit too far to the left'. To move a 'wee bit left' at the moment of action was inept . . . It occurred because of imperfections in our organization. Were there mistakes? Yes, there were. Only those who don't act don't make mistakes. *But to organize well — that's a difficult task.*[63]

Lenin's dilemma was this: if the Bolsheviks tried to seize power before the party or its supporters among the masses were properly organized for it, then they ran the risk of defeat and isolation, like the Paris Commune of 1871, whose fate haunted the Bolshevik leaders throughout 1917 and 1918; but if they failed to keep up with their revolutionary vanguard — the Kronstadt sailors, the Vyborg workers and the Petrograd garrison — then they were in danger of losing their sharpest striking force, which would dissipate itself in fruitless outbursts of anarchic violence. The history of the Bolshevik Party and its factional disputes in 1917 revolved around the problem of how to keep the energies of this revolutionary vanguard in line with the rest of the masses.

The Kronstadt Naval Base, an island of sailor-militants in the Gulf of Finland just off Petrograd, was by far the most rebellious stronghold of this Bolshevik vanguard. The sailors were young trainees who had seen very little military activity during the war. They had spent the previous year cooped up on board their ships with their officers, who treated them with more than the usual sadistic brutality since the normal rules of naval discipline did not apply to trainees. Each ship was a tinderbox of hatred and violence. During the February Days the sailors mutinied with awesome ferocity. Admiral Viren, the Base Commander, was hacked to death with bayonets, and dozens of other officers were murdered, lynched or imprisoned in the island dungeons. The old naval hierarchy was completely destroyed and effective power passed to the Kronstadt Soviet. It was an October in February. The authority of the Provisional Government was never really established, nor was military order restored. Kerensky, the Minister of Justice, proved utterly powerless in his repeated efforts to gain jurisdiction over the imprisoned officers, despite rumours in the bourgeois press that they had been brutally tortured.

The Kronstadt sailors were young (half of them were below the age of twenty-three), almost all of them were literate, and most of them were politicized by the propaganda of the far-left parties. By the start of May the Bolsheviks had recruited over 3,000 members at the naval base. Together with the Anarchists and the SRs, they controlled the Kronstadt Soviet. On 16 May the Soviet declared itself a sovereign power and rejected the authority of the Provisional Government and its appointed Commissar at the naval base. It was, in effect, the unilateral declaration of a 'Kronstadt Soviet Republic'. The Petrograd Soviet denounced the rebels as 'defectors from the revolutionary democracy'. The bourgeoisie of Petrograd was terrified by the thought that they were now at the mercy of this militant fortress, which at any moment might attack the capital. 'In their eyes', recalled Raskolnikov, one of the sailors' Bolshevik leaders, 'Kronstadt was a symbol of savage horror, the devil incarnate, a terrifying spectre of anarchy, a nightmare rebirth of the Paris Commune on Russian soil.' The Kronstadt Bolsheviks had played a major part in framing the 16 May declaration. But their action was not supported by the Bolshevik leaders in the capital.* Lenin was furious with his Kronstadt lieutenants for failing to observe party discipline. It was premature to think of the seizure of power *against* the authority of the Soviet, and he ordered them to call him every day for instructions until the crisis was resolved. Tsereteli was sent by the Petrograd Soviet to negotiate a settlement with the Kronstadt leaders, who agreed to accept the authority of the Provisional Government in return for their own elected Commissar. By 24 May

---

* Trotsky had encouraged the declaration. Speaking in the Kronstadt Soviet on 14 May he had said that what was good for Kronstadt would later be good for any other town: 'You are ahead and the rest have fallen behind.' Trotsky, however, was not yet a member of the Bolshevik Party.

the rebellion was over. Yet the Kronstadt sailors were to remain a threatening source of militancy, as the events of June, July and October were to show.[64]

The other great bastion of Bolshevik militancy was the Vyborg district of Petrograd. The Vyborg party organization had over 5,000 Bolshevik members by the start of May. It was there that the most strike-prone metal factories were located — Russian Renault, Nobel, New Lessner, Erikson, Puzyrev, Vulcan, Phoenix and the Metal Works — and most of them were under the Bolsheviks' sway. These factories contained an inflammable mixture of young and literate metal-workers, who tended to be easily influenced by the Bolsheviks' militant slogans, and the less skilled immigrant workers who had flooded into the cities during the industrial boom of the war, and who consequently had suffered most from the double squeeze of low wages and high rents. Both groups were inclined to engage in violence on the streets. The Vyborg side was also the adopted home of the First Machine-Gun Regiment, the most highly trained and literate and also the most Bolshevized troops in Petrograd, with around 10,000 men and 1,000 machine-guns. During the February Days these machine-gunners had marched from their barracks at Oranienbaum into Petrograd to take part in the mutiny. Militant and self-assertive, they saw themselves as the heroes of the revolution, and refused to return to their barracks so long as the 'bourgeoisie' was 'in power'. In effect, as everyone knew, they were holding the Provisional Government to ransom.[65]

The left-wing Bolsheviks, with their fighting resolve strengthened by these militant groups, advanced the idea of staging an armed demonstration on 10 June as a show of strength against the Provisional Government. The idea originated in the Military Organization, established by the Bolsheviks in the Petrograd garrison, which promised to bring out 60,000 troops. It soon received the backing of the Kronstadt sailors, who staged a dress rehearsal on 4 June with a march past in military ranks to salute the fallen heroes of the February Days. The Petersburg Bolshevik Committee was also showing signs of coming round in favour. They argued that an outlet had to be found for the soldiers and workers to express their anger at the government's preparations for the new offensive in the war campaign, and that if the Bolsheviks failed to lead the demonstration they might turn away from it and dissipate their anger in undirected violence. The party could not afford to waste the energies of its revolutionary vanguard. But the Central Committee was split, with Lenin, Sverdlov and Stalin (who had turned through 180 degrees since Lenin's return to Russia) in favour of the demonstration, and Kamenev, Zinoviev and Nogin against it on the grounds that the party still lacked sufficient mass support to justify the risks of all but calling for the seizure of power. A final decision was put off until 9 June.

By that time a majority of the Central Committee had come round to support the idea of an armed demonstration. On 8 June twenty-eight factories had gone on strike in the capital to protest against the government's attempt to expel the Anarchists from their headquarters in the former tsarist minister Durnovo's villa, on the Vyborg side.* Fifty Kronstadt sailors came armed to defend the Anarchists against the government troops. The capital was on the brink of a bloody confrontation, and the moment seemed ripe for an organized show of force. The Mensheviks later argued that the Bolsheviks were prepared to exploit this opportunity for the seizure of power. Sukhanov even claimed that Lenin had worked out elaborate military plans for a Bolshevik *coup d'état*, right down to the precise role of specific regiments in the seizure of strategic installations. But there is no evidence for this. It is true that at the First All-Russian Soviet Congress on 4 June Lenin had declared his party's readiness 'to assume power at any moment'. But if he was really planning an insurrection, he would hardly have given a public warning of it. Some of the secondary Bolshevik leaders, such as M. Ia. Latsis of the Vyborg Committee, who had close connections with the First Machine-Gun Regiment, certainly wanted to turn the demonstration into a full-scale uprising. But most of the senior leaders seemed to have viewed it as an exploratory test of strength and as a means of putting pressure on the Soviet Congress to take power itself. When the Soviet banned the demonstration on the evening of 9 June, five of the Bolshevik leaders (Lenin, Sverdlov, Zinoviev, Kamenev and Nogin) reconvened to call it off. Their more militant comrades protested furiously. Stalin threatened to resign (an offer that was unfortunately rejected) and accused the Central Committee of 'intolerable wavering'. But Lenin insisted that it was premature for the party to risk everything on a stand *against* the Soviet. The whole of his strategy in 1917, seen not least in the October seizure of power, was to use the cloak of Soviet legitimation to conceal the ambitions of his party. If the armed demonstration had gone ahead, the Bolsheviks would almost certainly have been expelled from the Soviet and the major strategic thrust of his April Theses — mass agitation for Soviet power — would have been undermined altogether.[66]

On 18 June the Soviet sponsored its own demonstration in Petrograd. The aim was to rally mass support behind the slogan of 'revolutionary unity', a by-word for the Soviet's continued participation in the coalition, and, from the viewpoint of those who were becoming more radicalized, probably a more acceptable slogan to the call for unconditional support of the government. The Bolsheviks resolved to take part in the march with banners calling for 'All Power to the Soviets!', and most of the 400,000 marchers who came out did so under

---

* Popular legend had it that the Anarchists had turned the villa into a madhouse, where orgies, sinister plots and witches' sabbaths were held, but when the Procurator arrived he found it in perfect order with part of the garden used as a crèche for the workers' children.

this slogan.[67] Perhaps the supporters of the Soviet leaders had deliberately stayed away, as some of the press later suggested. Or perhaps, as seems more likely, the demonstrators did not understand the ideological differences between the Bolsheviks and the Soviet leaders and marched under the banners of the former on the false assumption that it was a mark of loyalty to the latter. Either way, it was a major propaganda victory for the Bolsheviks and did much to encourage their plans in July for another, far more consequential, armed confrontation with the Provisional Government.

iv Gorky's Despair

Gorky to Ekaterina, 18 June 1917:

> Today's demonstration was a demonstration of the impotence of the loyal democratic forces. Only the 'Bolsheviks' marched. *I despise and hate them more and more.* They are truly Russian idiots. Most of the slogans demanded 'Down with the 10 Bourgeois Ministers!' But there are only eight of them! There were several outbreaks of panic — it was disgusting. Ladies jumped into the canal between the Champs de Mars and the Summer Gardens, waded through the water in their boots, pulled up their skirts, and bared their legs, some of them fat, some of them crooked. The madness continues, but it seems that it is beginning to wear the people out. Although I am a pacifist, I welcome the coming offensive in the hope that it may at least bring some organization to the country, which is becoming incorrigibly lazy and disorganized.[68]

Socialism for Gorky had always been essentially a cultural ideal. It meant for him the building of a humanist civilization based on the principles of democracy and on the development of the people's moral, spiritual and intellectual forces. 'The new political life', he wrote in April, 'demands from us a new structure of the soul.' And yet the revolution, as he saw it, had unleashed an 'anarchic wave of plebeian violence and revenge' which threatened to destroy Russian civilization. There had been no 'social revolution', as Gorky understood the term, but only a 'zoological' outburst of violence and destruction. Instead of heralding a new civilization, the Russian Revolution had brought the country to the brink of a 'new dark age of barbaric chaos', in which the instincts of revenge and hatred would overcome all that was good in the people. The task of the democratic intelligentsia, as he saw it in 1917, was the defence of civilization against the destructive violence of the crowd. It was, in his own Arnoldian terms, a struggle of 'culture against anarchy'.[69]

The violent rejection of everything associated with the old civilization was an integral element of the February Revolution. Symbols of the imperial regime were destroyed, statues of tsarist heroes were smashed, street names were changed. Peasants vandalized manor houses, churches and schools. They burned down libraries and smashed up priceless works of art.

Many romantic socialists saw this iconoclastic violence as a 'natural' (i.e. positive) revolutionary impulse from an oppressed people with much to avenge. Trotsky, for example, spoke in idealistic terms of the revolution, even through the incitement of aggression, arousing the human personality.

> It is natural that persons unaccustomed to revolution and its psychology, or persons who have previously only experienced in the realm of ideas that which has unfolded before them physically, materially, may view with some sorrow, if not disgust, the anarchic wildness and violence which appeared on the surface of the revolutionary events. Yet in that riotous anarchy, even in its most negative manifestations, when the soldier, yesterday's slave, all of a sudden found himself in a first-class railway carriage and tore out the velvet facings to make himself foot-cloths, even in such an act of vandalism the awakening of the personality was expressed. That downtrodden, persecuted Russian peasant, who had been struck in the face and subjected to the vilest curses, found himself, for perhaps the first time in his life, in a first-class carriage and saw the velvet cushions, while on his feet he had stinking rags, and he tore up the velvet, saying that he too had the right to a piece of good silk or velvet.

And there were many left-wing intellectuals who saw the violence in similar terms. Some, like Blok, idealized the burning down of the old Russia as an exorcism of its sinful past, and believed that out of this destruction of the old world a new and more fraternal world, perhaps even a more Christian world, would be created. Hence Blok, in his famous poem 'The Twelve' (written in January 1918), portrayed Christ at the head of the Red Guards. Others, like Voloshin, Mandelstam and Belyi, were rather more ambivalent towards the revolutionary violence, welcoming it, on the one hand, as a just and elemental force, while, on the other, expressing horror at its savage cruelty.[70]

But Gorky saw only darkness in the violence. He was appalled by what, he had no doubts, were its inevitable consequences, the moral corruption of the revolution and the people's descent into barbarism. He was, as always, quite uncompromising and outspoken in his condemnations of the violence in his well-known column, 'Untimely Thoughts', which he published in his newspaper *Novaia zhizn'* during 1917 and 1918. He condemned the boom in royal pornography as 'poisonous filth', whose only real effect was to arouse the 'dark instincts of the mob'. Later, during the Red Terror, he would take up the defence of several Romanovs, including even a Grand Duke, seeing them as the 'poor scapegoats of the Revolution, martyrs to the fanaticism of the times'. He was even more appalled by the 'rise of anti-Semitism, the pogrom mentality of the working class', a class upon which, like all the Marxists, he had placed great faith as a liberating and moral force. Gorky also condemned the vandalism of the peasant revolution. He saw the destruction of the gentry's manors, with their libraries and fine art, as nothing less than an attack on civilization. In March 1917, after hearing rumours that the crowds were about to smash the equestrian statue of Alexander III in Znamenskaya Square, Gorky held a meeting of fifty leading cultural figures in his flat, and out of this was formed a twelve-man commission to campaign for the preservation of all artistic monuments and historic buildings. The 'Gorky Commission' it was often called.[71]

Gorky's own beloved Petersburg, the capital of Russia's Western civilization, was, as he saw it, being destroyed and profaned by 'this Asiatic revolution'. On 14 June he wrote to Ekaterina in Moscow:

> This is no longer a capital, it is a cesspit. No one works, the streets are filthy, there are piles of stinking rubbish in the courtyards . . . It hurts me to say how bad things have become. There is a growing idleness and cowardice in the people, and all those base and criminal instincts which I have fought all my life and which, it seems, are now destroying Russia.[72]

Twentieth-century Russia seemed to be returning to the barbarism of the Middle Ages. Gorky was especially outraged by the spread of lynch law (*samosudy*) in the cities. In December 1917 he claimed to have counted 10,000 cases of summary justice since the collapse of the old regime. It seemed to him that these mob trials — in which the crowd would judge and execute an apprehended criminal on the street — utterly negated the ideals of justice for which the revolution had been fought. The Russian people, having been beaten for hundreds of years, were now beating their own enemies with a morbid sensuality.

> Here is how the democracy tries its sinners. A thief was caught near the Alexandrovsky Market. The crowd there and then beat him up and took a vote — by which death should the thief be punished: drowning or shooting? They decided on drowning and threw the man into the icy water. But with great difficulty he managed to swim out and crawl up on to the shore; one of the crowd then went up to him and shot him.

The middle ages of our history were an epoch of abominable cruelty, but even then if a criminal sentenced to death by a court fell from the gallows, he was allowed to live.

How do the mob trials affect the coming generation?

A thief, beaten half to death, is taken by soldiers to the Moika to be drowned; he is all covered with blood, his face is completely smashed, and one eye has come out. A crowd of children accompanies him; later some of them return from the Moika and, hopping up and down, joyfully shout: 'They sunk him, they drowned him!'

These are our children, the future builders of our life. The life of a man will be cheap in their estimation, but man — one should not forget this! — is the finest and most valuable creation of nature.[73]

Gorky's pessimism was of course the view of a man of letters repulsed by violence in all its forms. He judged the revolution, not in its own terms, but in terms of how far it matched up to his own cultural values and moral ideals. This he made clear in a brave and daring speech, never before published, to commemorate the first anniversary of the February Revolution:

A revolution is only a revolution when it arises as a natural and powerful expression of the people's *creative* force. If, however, the revolution is simply a release of the instincts of the people accumulated through slavery and oppression, then it is not a revolution but just a riot [*bunt*] of malice and hatred, it is incapable of changing our lives but can only lead to bitterness and evil. Can we really say that one year after the Russian Revolution, the people, having been liberated from the violence and oppression of the old police state, have become better, kinder, more intelligent, and more honest people? No, no one could say that. We are still living as we lived under the monarchy, with the same customs, the same prejudices, the same stupidity and the same filth. The greed and the malice which were inculcated in us by the old regime are still within us. People are still robbing and cheating one another, as they have always robbed and cheated one another. The new bureaucrats take bribes just like the old ones did, and they treat the people with even more rudeness and contempt ... The Russian people, having won its freedom, is in its present state incapable of using it for its own good, only for its own harm and the harm of others, and it is in danger of losing everything that it has been fighting for for centuries. It is destroying all the great achievements of its ancestors; gradually the national wealth, the wealth of the land, of industry, of transport, of communications, and of the towns, is being destroyed in the dirt.[74]

There is much that one might admire in Gorky's brave stand against the destruction of the revolution. His despairing voice was an isolated one — which made it all the more noble and tragic. As far as the Left was concerned his 'untimely thoughts' were heretical — they were 'politically incorrect' — because it was the received view that violence and destruction were both natural and even justified by the wider goals of the revolution; and yet Gorky's contacts with the Bolsheviks made them just as unwelcome on the Right. His own circle around *Novaia zhizn'* was not so much a political faction as a loose assortment of disaffected Marxists who had no party they felt they could join. 'I should form my own party,' Gorky wrote to Ekaterina on 19 March, 'but I wouldn't know what to call it. *In this party there is only one member — and that is me.*'[75]

And yet, as Gorky himself acknowledged, his own position was full of prejudices and contradictions which only an intellectual could afford. He made sweeping moral and cultural judgements about the violence of the revolutionary crowd without ever attempting to understand this violence in its historical or social context. In his many writings on the mob trials, for example, he never considered the simple social fact that, with the cities full of crime and violence, and with no police force to uphold the law, these acts of street justice had become the only way for ordinary citizens to protect their property and themselves. Gorky did not really understand the problem; he simply judged it from a moral viewpoint.

Gorky's cultural prejudices were nowhere more apparent than in his efforts to explain the origins of this violence. Of course he saw the need to place it in the context of the legacies of tsarism:

> The conditions in which the Russian people lived in the past could foster in them neither respect for the individual, nor awareness of the citizen's rights, nor a feeling of justice — these were conditions of absolute lawlessness, of the oppression of the individual, of the most shameless lies and bestial cruelty. And one must be amazed that with all these conditions, the people nevertheless retained in themselves quite a few human feelings and some degree of common sense.

And he was the first to stress that the barbarism of the revolution was born in the barbarism of the First World War. The mass slaughter of the trenches and the hardships of the rear had brought out the cruelty and brutishness of people, Gorky explained to Romain Rolland, hardening them to the suffering of their fellow human beings. People had developed a taste for violence and few of them, he maintained, had been shocked by the killing of the February Days. The unwritten rules of civilized behaviour had all been forgotten, the thin veneer of civilization had been stripped away, in the revolutionary explosion.[76]

Yet Gorky was always rather more inclined to explain this violence in terms of the Russian national character than in terms of the context in which it took place. 'The environment in which the tragedy of the Russian Revolution has been and is being played out', he wrote in 1922, 'is an environment of semi-savage people. I explain the cruel manifestations of the revolution in terms of the exceptional cruelty of the Russian people.' He never stopped to think that all social revolutions are, by their very nature, violent. Here Gorky's view was prejudiced by his ardent Westernizing sympathies. It was his belief that all human progress and civilization derived from the West, and that all barbarism derived from the East. Socially, historically and geographically, Russia was caught between Europe and Asia. The Petrine state tradition and the Russian intelligentsia were both Westernizing influences; the peasantry were Asiatic; while the working class was in between, derived as it was from the peasantry yet capable of being civilized under the intelligentsia's guidance. The Russian Revolution, which, Gorky realized in 1917, came essentially from the peasant depths, was an Easternizing and barbaric force. He had no illusions, as Lvov did, about the goodness or the wisdom of the simple Russian people. 'I am turning into a pessimist, and, it seems, a misanthrope,' he wrote to Ekaterina in mid-March. 'In my view the overwhelming majority of the population in Russia is both evil and as stupid as pigs.'[77]

The 'savage instincts' of the Russian peasants, whom Gorky hated with a vengeance, were, in his view, especially to blame for the violence of the revolution. The sole desire of the peasants, Gorky often argued, was to exact a cruel revenge on their former masters, and on all the wealthy and privileged élite, among whom they counted their self-appointed leaders among the intelligentsia. Much of the revolutionary violence in the cities — the mob trials, the anarchic looting and the 'carting out' of the factory bosses — he put down, like many of the Mensheviks, to the sudden influx of unskilled peasant workers into cities during the war. It was as if he refused to believe that the working class, which, like all Marxists, he saw as a force of cultural progress, might behave like peasants or hooligans. And yet he often expressed his own deep fear that the urban culture of the working class was being 'dissolved in the peasant mass', that the world of school and industry was being lost to the barbaric customs of the village.[78]

Gorky blamed the Bolsheviks for much of this. Lenin's April Theses had, as he saw it, called prematurely for a new revolution, and in Russia's state of backwardness this was bound to make it hostage to the peasantry. As he wrote in 1924:

I thought that the Theses sacrificed the small and heroic band of politically educated workers, as well as the truly revolutionary intelligentsia, to the

Russian peasantry. The only active force in Russia would be thrown, like a pinch of salt, into the flat bog of the village, and it would dissolve without a trace, without changing the spirit, the life, the history of the nation.[79]

It seemed to Gorky that the cultural ideals of the socialist intelligentsia were being sacrificed by the Bolsheviks in the interests of their own political ends. The Bolsheviks were guilty of stirring up class hatred and of encouraging the 'nihilistic masses' to destroy the old order root and branch.

  The violent clashes on the Nevsky Prospekt during the demonstrations of 20–1 April, which many people blamed on the Bolsheviks, filled Gorky with a sense of deep revulsion. His 'untimely thoughts' for the 23rd:

> The bright wings of our young freedom are bespattered with innocent blood. Murder and violence are the arguments of despotism ... We must understand that the most terrible enemy of freedom and justice is within us; it is our stupidity, our cruelty, and all that chaos of dark, anarchistic feelings ... Are we capable of understanding this? If we are incapable, if we cannot refrain from the most flagrant use of force on man, then we have no freedom ... Is it possible that the memory of our vile past, the memory of how hundreds and thousands of us were shot in the streets, has implanted in us, too, the calm attitude of the executioner toward the violent death of a man? I cannot find harsh enough words to reproach those who try to prove something with bullets, bayonets, or a fist in the face. Were not these the ... means by which we were kept in shameful slavery? And now, having freed ourselves from slavery externally, we continue to live dominated by the feelings of slaves.[80]

The role of the Bolsheviks in the abortive demonstrations of 10 June also angered him. He wrote to Ekaterina on 14 June:

> I have come to the end of my tether. Physically I am still holding out. But every day my anxiety grows and I think that the crazy politics of Lenin will soon lead us to a civil war. He is completely isolated but his slogans are very popular among the mass of the uneducated workers and some of the soldiers.[81]

It seemed to Gorky that the 'plebeian anger' aroused by the Bolsheviks' militant slogans might all too easily degenerate into a force of destruction and chaos in a peasant country such as Russia, where the mass of the people were 'ignorant and base'. Hatred of the *burzhoois* would soon give way to a senseless pogrom, a class war of retribution, a 'looting of the looters', to adopt the Bolsheviks' own slogan. Distrust of the democratic parties, equally fostered by the Bolsheviks, would soon become a general negation of the intelligentsia and its humanist values.

In a sense it was not just the Bolsheviks but all the political parties which Gorky despaired of in 1917. 'Politics', he wrote on 20 April, 'is the seed-bed of social enmity, evil suspicions, shameless lies, morbid ambitions, and disrespect for the individual. Name anything bad in man, and it is precisely in the soil of political struggle that it grows with abundance.' His *cri de cœur* was based on the belief that the role of the intelligentsia, in which he included the political parties, was to defend the moral and cultural values of the Enlightenment against the destructive violence of the crowd. Its role was to safeguard the revolution as a constructive and creative process of national civilization. Gorky, in this respect, was moving closer to the viewpoint of the liberals and the Soviet leaders, who were just as concerned by the growing tide of anarchy. And like them, during the spring and early summer he was becoming increasingly inclined to view a new offensive on the Front as a galvanizing and disciplining force. For, as Gorky put it on 18 June, 'although I am a pacifist, I welcome the coming offensive in the hope that it may at least bring some organization to the country'.[82] How wrong he would be.

10 The Agony of the Provisional Government

i The Illusion of a Nation

At their first meeting Kerensky made Brusilov the Commander-in-Chief of the Russian army. The new Minister of War had gone down to see Brusilov at his headquarters on the South-Western Front and, after inspecting the troops, had driven with him through the night to the town of Tarnopol. There was a violent storm and the lonely motor-car seemed in constant peril as it trundled along the muddy country roads. Huddled together inside the car, with the rain beating down against the windows and lightning flashing overhead, the two men drew closer together. They started to talk informally, telling each other their private thoughts, as if they were old friends. Both men agreed on the need to launch a summer offensive, and it was this, as he recalled in his memoirs, that made Kerensky decide 'there and then that Brusilov should be given the command of the entire army in time for the opening of the offensive'.[1]

Brusilov's appointment was an act of faith in the fighting capacity of the new revolutionary army. It was, above all, his optimism that had won him the post. 'I needed men who believed that the Russian army was not ruined,' Kerensky later wrote. 'I had no use for people who could not genuinely accept the *fait accompli* of the Revolution, or who doubted that we could rebuild the army's morale in the new psychological atmosphere. I needed men who had lived through the utter folly of the years of war under the old regime and who fully understood the upheaval that had occurred'.[2] Brusilov fitted the bill. He was perhaps the only senior tsarist general to emerge with honour from the war — and one of the first to throw in his lot with the revolution. Like Kerensky, he hoped the defence of liberty might at last inspire the sort of civic patriotism that Russia needed to continue the war.

Brusilov's support for the democracy, and the soldiers' committees in particular, had won him few friends among the rest of the senior generals. They denounced him as an 'opportunist' and a 'traitor' to the army. The General Staff at Stavka received their new commander with open hostility on 22 May. 'I became aware at once, upon my arrival, of their frosty feelings for me,' Brusilov recalled. Instead of the usual mass ovation, to which he had grown accustomed, Brusilov was met at the station at Mogilev by a small and rather formal delegation of sullen-faced generals. To make matters worse, Brusilov at once caused grave offence by failing to receive a group of senior officers, who had come to the station to welcome him, and, in a gesture of democracy, turning instead to shake the hands of the private soldiers. The first soldiers were so confused — it was customary for the generals to salute them — that they dropped their rifles or grasped them clumsily in their left arm whilst shaking hands with their new Commander-in-Chief.[3]

Unlike most of the senior commanders, Brusilov believed in working together with the soldiers' democratic organs. As he saw it, the restoration of the army's morale and the launching of a new offensive could only be achieved in partnership with them. Such optimism in the democratic order contrasted starkly with the scepticism of General Alexeev, the previous Commander-in-Chief, who had so far been doubtful that a successful offensive could be launched with the armed forces in their present revolutionary state. But then Brusilov had always been convinced that God had chosen him to lead Russia's armies to victory. 'Despite all the difficulties,' he wrote to his brother shortly after his arrival at Mogilev, 'I never despair because I know that God has placed this burden on my shoulders and that the fate of the Fatherland lies in His hands. I have a deep faith, as deep as my faith in God Himself, that we shall be victorious in this titanic struggle.'[4]

Ever since the Inter-Allied Conference at Chantilly in November 1915, Russia had been under growing pressure from her Allies to launch a new offensive on the Eastern Front. The Entente leaders wanted 1917 to be the year of final victory, and it was assumed that a combined offensive in the east and the west would be enough to defeat the Central Powers. The legitimacy of the Provisional Government among the Western Powers — and the financial support which it gained from them — rested largely on its declared intention to fulfil this obligation to the Allies. Yet, at the same time, the revolution had increased the already considerable doubts about Russia's fighting capacity. At a meeting of his Front commanders on 18 March Alexeev dismissed the French demand for a new offensive in the spring: the roads were still covered in ice; horses and fodder were in short supply; the reserve units were falling apart; military discipline was breaking down; and the Soviet, which controlled all the essential levers of power, was still reluctant to support anything beyond a purely defensive strategy. Most of the commanders agreed with him that it was impossible to launch a new offensive before June or even July. Brusilov was the only one to support the idea of a spring offensive. In a telegram to the meeting he claimed that his soldiers were eager to fight. It was such an extraordinarily optimistic statement — and no doubt largely the product of his own wishful thinking — that Alexeev asked the Quartermaster-General to check the telegram's authenticity. 'What luck it would be', he scribbled at the bottom of the cable, 'if reality were to justify these hopes.' Coming as it did from the key South-Western Front, where any attack would have to be launched, Brusilov's message certainly helped to bring the cautious Alexeev around to the idea of an earlier offensive during May. He outlined his reasons to Guchkov on 30 March:

> If we fail to go on the attack, we will not escape having to fight but will simply condemn ourselves to fighting at a time and place convenient to the enemy. And if we fail to co-operate with our allies, we cannot expect them to come to our aid when we need it. Disorder in the army will have a no less detrimental effect on defence than it will on offence. *Even if we are not fully confident of success, we should go on the offensive.* Results of unsuccessful defence are worse than those of unsuccessful offence ... The faster we throw our troops into action the sooner their passion for politics will cool. General Brusilov based his support on these considerations ... *It can be said that the less steady the troops, the less successful defence is likely to be; hence the more desirable it is to undertake active operations.*[5]

It was a terrible gamble. There was no guarantee that the risks of attack would be less than those of defence; and even less reason to suppose, as Alexeev and Brusilov had done, that the fighting spirit of the troops could be galvanized by launching an offensive. With hindsight it is clear that the military and political leaders of the Provisional Government were deluded by their own optimism. They grossly underestimated the likely costs of a new offensive. Alexeev, for one, predicted that the Russian losses would be in the region of 6,000 men; but the actual number turned out to be just short of 400,000, and the number of deserters perhaps even greater. This was a huge human price to pay for a piece of wishful thinking. Politically, the costs were even higher. For there is no doubt that the launching — let alone the failure — of the offensive led directly to the summer crisis which culminated in the downfall of the Provisional Government and the Bolshevik seizure of power in October. No doubt the military leaders had assumed that by launching an early offensive they could pre-empt a German attack, which their intelligence had misinformed them was set to take place in the summer. But the Germans had in fact been committed for some time to a 'peace offensive' in the east so that they could release troops for transfer to the west. A defensive strategy thus made much more sense, given the weakness of Russia's army and its rear. But by June, when the offensive was launched, the Russian leaders had become obsessed with the idea of attack — the offensive had come to symbolize the 'national spirit' of the revolution — and they were blind to the possibility that it might end in catastrophe.

More than anything else, the summer offensive swung the soldiers to the Bolsheviks, the only major party which stood uncompromisingly for an immediate end to the war. Had the Provisional Government adopted a similar policy and opened negotiations with the Germans, no doubt the Bolsheviks would never have come to power. Why was this crucial step never taken? The patriotism of the democratic leaders — which for them was virtually synonymous with a commitment to the Allied Powers as democracies — provides part of the answer. Kerensky considered briefly the option of a separate peace, when he took over as Prime Minister after the July Days and the collapse of the offensive; but he rejected it on the grounds, or so he later claimed, that this would make him responsible for Russia's national humiliation. Perhaps one may accuse him and other politicians of a lack of foresight in their rejection of the separate peace option. Five days before the Bolshevik seizure of power, on 20 October, General Verkhovsky, the Minister of War, declared the army unfit to fight. He recommended that the only way to counteract the growing threat of the Bolsheviks was 'by cutting the ground from under them — in other words by raising at once the question of concluding peace'. Yet Kerensky failed to see the Bolshevik danger and once again refused to act. Fourteen years later, Lord Beaverbrook, whilst lunching with Kerensky in London, asked him whether the Provisional Government could have stopped the Bolsheviks by signing a separate peace with Germany. 'Of course,' Kerensky replied, 'we should be in Moscow now.' Astonished by this response, Beaverbrook asked why they had not done this. 'We were too naive,' Kerensky replied.[6]

Hindsight is the luxury of historians. Given the pressures and doctrines of the time it is not hard to understand why the offensive was launched. The leaders of the Provisional Government took Russia's commitments to the Allies in earnest. They would have liked to negotiate a general peace without annexations or indemnities as the saying went; but Russia's military weakness made their bargaining position extremely weak. The Allies were coming round to the view that the war could be won with or without Russia, especially after the entry of the United States in April. They blocked the Stockholm Peace Conference, organized by the Soviet leaders to bring together all the socialist parties in Europe, and dragged their heels on Russian proposals for a revision of the Allied war aims. In this sense, by scotching the international peace campaign, the Allies did their bit to help the Bolsheviks come to power, although this leaves open the question as to whether a general peace could have been achieved.

Paradoxical though it may seem, the leaders of the Provisional Government thus backed an offensive to strengthen their campaign for a general settlement of the conflict. They went to war in order to make peace. That was also the rationale of the Soviet leaders in supporting the offensive. Tsereteli's Revolutionary Defensism, the rallying of the democracy for the needs of national defence, was the main justification for their entry into the Coalition. It might of course be argued that national defence did not demand that an offensive be launched. By supporting the primacy of the needs of the army, as they did in signing the coalition's Declaration of Principles on 5 May, the Soviet leaders were in danger of losing sight of their basic aim — the negotiation of a general peace — and thus laying themselves open to the Bolshevik charge of joining the warmongers. But they were carried away by the hope that the defence of democratic Russia might help to rally the people behind them. They compared Russia's situation with that of France on the eve of the war against Austria in 1792: it seemed to them that a revolutionary war would give birth to a new civic patriotism, just as the defence of the *patrie* had given rise to the national chorus of 'Aux armes, citoyens'. They were quite convinced that a 'national revolution' had taken place, not just a revolt against the old regime, and that through this upsurge of patriotism, through the popular recognition that the interests of 'the nation' stood higher than any class or party interests, they could restore unity and order.

Kerensky, the Minister of War in the coalition government, was cast as the hero of this new civic patriotism. As a popular and above-party figure, he became the embodiment of the coalition's ideal of national unity. The cult of Kerensky, which had first emerged in the February Days, reached its climax with the June offensive, which indeed the cult had helped to bring about. All the nation's hopes and expectations rested on the frail shoulders of Kerensky, 'the first people's minister of war'. Schoolboy poets like Leonid Kannegiser (later to assassinate the Bolshevik Uritsky) portrayed Kerensky as a Russian Bonaparte:

> And if, swirling with pain,
> I fall in the name of Mother Russia,
> And find myself in some deserted field,
> Shot through the chest on the ground,
> Then at the Gates of Heaven,
> In my dying and joyous dreams,
> I will remember — Russia, Liberty,
> Kerensky on a white horse.

Marina Tsvetaeva, who was then herself barely out of school, also felt moved to compare Kerensky with Napoleon:

> And someone, falling on the map,
> Does not sleep in his dreams.
> There came a Bonaparte
> In my country.[7]

Kerensky revelled in this role. He had always seen himself as the leader of the nation, above party or class interests. The adulation went to his head. He became obsessed with the idea of leading the army to glory and of covering himself in honour. He began to model himself on Napoleon. A bust of the French Emperor stood on his desk at the Ministry of War. Although he had never himself been in the army, Kerensky donned a finely tailored khaki tunic, officer's breeches and knee-high leather boots when he became the Minister of War (a semi-military style of dress that many future leaders, including Stalin, would later take from him). The Minister of War took great care over his personal appearance — and it was a huge source of pride for him. Even at the height of the fighting in October, when he appeared before the Cossacks during the battle for Gatchina against the Red Guards, he made sure to wear his 'finest tunic, the one to which the people and the troops had grown so accustomed', and to 'salute, as I always did, slightly casually and with a slight smile'. During his famous tours of the Fronts, Kerensky even wore his right arm in a sling, although there was no record that the arm had ever been hurt (some people joked that he had simply worn it out by too much hand-shaking). It was no doubt a deliberate attempt to suggest that he, like the ordinary soldiers, had been wounded too. Perhaps it was also an attempt to echo the image of Napoleon with his arm tucked into the front of his tunic.[8]

On the eve of his appointment Kerensky had given a melodramatic performance at a Congress of Delegates from the Front. 'I am sorry that I did not die two months ago,' he pronounced with his hand placed solemnly on his heart, 'for then I would have died with the greatest of dreams: that henceforth and forever a new life had dawned for Russia, when we could mutually respect each other and govern our state without whips or clubs.' He appealed to the soldiers to place their 'civic duty' above their own narrow class interests and to strengthen their fighting resolve, since Russia's liberty could only be gained 'as a strong and organized state' and this meant that 'every citizen' had to make a sacrifice for the nation. Under 'the old and hated regime' the soldiery had known how to fulfil their obligations, so why could they not do the same in the name of Freedom? 'Or is it', he asked in a phrase charged with meaning and emotion for the soldiers, 'it it that the free Russian state is in fact a state of rebellious slaves?'[9] There was uproar in the hall. For the soldiers, in their own self-image, had indeed been 'slaves' before Order Number One, and Kerensky now seemed to be asking whether they were worth their freedom, as 'citizens', if they were not prepared to go to war. The phrase 'rebellious slaves' echoed around the country for weeks. It did much to turn the soldiers against Kerensky. But for the patriotic and the propertied it was just the sort of appeal to discipline and duty that they had long been calling for, and they now rallied behind Kerensky and the idea of an offensive at the Front. It was almost as if they sensed that only a victory could save them now.

The liberal press now joined the right in a national chorus of howling headlines calling on the army to 'Take the Offensive!' The Kadet Party took up the national flag. No doubt they hoped that posing as patriots might reverse their alarming electoral decline. In the city Duma elections during May the Kadets had gained less than 20 per cent of the vote. No longer able to compete with the socialists for mass support, they sought to appeal to the middle classes by calling for the defence of the Fatherland and the restoration of order. Patriotism became the basis of their claim to be a party 'above class'. The democratic intelligentsia, which had always been the main social base of the Kadets, largely followed them into the chauvinist camp. The League of Russian Culture, founded by a group of right-wing Kadets in the midst of this patriotic wave, called on all classes to unite behind the banner of Russia. Even Blok, who called himself a socialist, succumbed to the new mood of patriotism, while Gorky welcomed the offensive as a means of 'bringing some organization to the country'. There was a growing feeling that 'Russia' should be put before everything else, even the revolution itself. 'It is not Russia that exists for the revolution,' Dmitry Merezhkovsky wrote, 'but the revolution that exists for Russia.' It was close to the notion of a national-bourgeois Russia advanced by Struve and the *Vekhi* group after 1905; and there was indeed a similar equation of the nation with its middle classes. Propertied patriots subscribed to the Liberty Loan, raised by the government to finance the offensive. N. V. Chaikovsky, President of the Free Economic Society, declared it 'the duty of everyone to the Motherland, to his fellow citizens and the future of Russia, to give his savings for the great cause of freedom'.[10]

This new civic patriotism did not extend beyond the urban middle classes, although the leaders of the Provisional Government deluded themselves that it did. The visit of the Allied socialists — Albert Thomas from France, Emile Vandervelde from Belgium and Arthur Henderson from Britain — was a typical case in point. They had come to Russia to plead with 'the people' not to leave the war; yet very few people bothered to listen to them. Konstantin Paustovsky recalls Thomas speaking in vain from the balcony of the building that was later to become the Moscow Soviet. Thomas spoke in French and the small crowd that had gathered could not understand what he said. 'But everything in his speech could be understood without words. Bobbing up and down on his bowed legs, Thomas showed us graphically what would happen to Russia if it left the war. He twirled his moustaches, like the Kaiser's, narrowed his eyes rapaciously, and jumped up and down choking the throat of an imaginary Russia.' For several minutes the Frenchman continued with this circus act, hurling the body of Russia to the ground and jumping up and down on it, until the crowd began to hiss and boo and laugh. Thomas mistook this for a sign of approval and saluted the crowd with his bowler hat. But the laughter and booing got louder: 'Get that clown off!' one worker cried. Then, at last, someone else appeared on the balcony and diplomatically led him inside.[11]

Some middle-class civilians volunteered for the new shock battalions which were formed to revive the army's morale. Most of these were made up of frightened officers, eager to flee their mutinous regiments. Bernard Pares, who attended several patriotic rallies to encourage these volunteers, compared their hysterical atmosphere to that of a revival meeting. On one occasion he was introduced to the soldiers as 'our English comrade, the Professor', a great war hero, who had won the George Cross by beating the Germans single-handed. This was of course a total invention; but when Pares urged his host to shut up, he was told that such tales were needed to raise the morale of the troops.[12]

One of the best-known volunteer units had been formed by women. The Women's Battalion of Death had been organized by Maria Bochkareva, a truly remarkable woman, who had worked before the war as a foreman on factory building sites. After 1914 she had campaigned to enlist in the army and, having petitioned the Tsar himself, had been allowed to fight under General Gurko. By February 1917, she had risen to the rank of sergeant, having spent two years in the trenches with several wounds and a number of medals to prove it. Concerned by the collapse of military discipline, she appealed to Brusilov to let her form a shock battalion of women in the hope that this would shame the rest of the soldiers into fighting. In fact it was to have the opposite effect: the soldiers viewed its formation as a sign of the government's desperate situation and this strengthened their resolve not to fight; while many soldiers, the Cossacks in particular, refused to fight alongside women. But Brusilov did not anticipate this and saw no reason to object. He was keen on the idea, much debated at that time, of establishing a new army based entirely on volunteer units. He saw it as a means of fighting the war on the basis of patriotic duty, and of breaking down the old divisions between the officers and the troops. Since his own wife was working in the medical services at the Front, he did not see why other women should not also go there to fight. The battalion was hastily formed and blessed by the Patriarch Nikon on Red Square in Moscow before their departure for the Front in June. The women shaved their heads and put on standard army trousers, although one was too fat to fit them and had to go into battle in a skirt.[13]

The army commissars were the other great hope of this civic patriotism. Most of them were junior officers of democratic or socialist persuasion. They enjoyed the confidence of their troops yet also understood the need for military discipline. Linde, the young NCO who had led the mutiny of several regiments during the February Days, was a typical case in point: he became the Commissar of the Special Army during the summer offensive. Dmitry Os'kin, the peasant NCO whom we encountered in Chapter 7, also became a military commissar.

The commissars were instituted by the Soviet on 19 March, and made responsible to the Provisional Government on 6 May. They were meant to smooth relations between the officers and the soldiers' committees and, as such, were seen as the basis for a new patriotic partnership between the democracy and the army.

That, too, was the hope of the Declaration 'On the Rights of Servicemen' issued by Kerensky on 11 May. Kerensky claimed — and he was surely right — that the Russian armed forces were now the 'freest in the world'; and he called on the soldiers to prove 'that there is strength, not weakness, in freedom' in the coming offensive. The Declaration retained the rights of Order Number One, but it also restored the authority of the officers at the Front, including the use of corporal punishment. This was seen in the ruling circles as an essential concession to the military leaders in preparation for the coming offensive. Brusilov was adamant that he would not fight without it. Yet there is no doubt that many soldiers saw the Declaration as an attempt by the government to restore the old system of discipline and this played into the hands of the Bolsheviks. *Pravda* quipped that the Declaration should really be called a 'Declaration on the Rightlessness of Servicemen'.[14]

To raise the morale of the troops Kerensky went on a tour of the Front during May. Here his hysterical oratory reached fever pitch. With his squeaky voice and waving arms, he appealed to the soldiers to make the supreme sacrifice for the glorious future of their Fatherland. At the end of these tirades he would collapse in a state of nervous exhaustion and have to be revived with the aid of valerian spirits. Though these fainting fits were not contrived, or at least not to begin with, they added an extra theatrical effect to Kerensky's performances. Everywhere he was hailed as a hero. Soldiers carried him shoulder-high, pelted him with flowers and threw themselves at his feet. An English nurse watched in amazement as they 'kissed him, his uniform, his car, and the ground on which he walked. Many of them were on their knees praying; others were weeping.'[15] Nothing quite like it had been seen since the days of the Tsar.

Yet all this adulation merely gave Kerensky the false impression that the soldiers were eager to fight. Fifty years later, in his memoirs, he still insisted that a 'healthy mood of patriotism at the Front had become a definite force'.* But this was far from the truth. Kerensky's visits brought him into contact with a very unrepresentative cross-section of the army. The soldiers' meetings which he addressed were mainly attended by the officers, the uniformed intelligentsia and the members of the soldiers' committees. At these meetings Kerensky's

---

* The leaders of the Soviet and the Provisional Government were deceived by the fact that the soldiers, like the common people, expressed extreme hostility to everything 'German'. But the concept of 'German' was for the soldiers a general symbol of everything they hated — the Empress, the treasonable tsarist government, the war and all foreigners — rather than the German soldiers (for whom they often expressed sympathy) on the other side of the front line.

speeches had a mesmerizing effect: they conjured up the sweet illusion of a victorious end to the war with one more heroic heave. Now a weary soldier might well be tempted to believe in this, even if deep down he knew it to be false, simply because he wanted to. But such illusions were soon dispelled once he returned to the trenches. Outside these meetings, moreover, among the vast majority of the rank and file, the mood of the soldiers was much more negative. Kerensky was frequently heckled by such troops during his trips to the Front, yet he never seemed to register the warning that this conveyed. On one occasion near Riga, a soldier was pushed forward by his mates to question the Minister. 'You tell us we must fight the Germans so that the peasants can have the land. But what's the use of us peasants getting land if I am killed and get no land?' Kerensky had no answer — and there was none — but ordered the officer in command of this unit to send the soldier home: 'Let his fellow villagers know that we don't need cowards in the Russian army.' The soldier could not believe his luck, and at once fainted; while the officer scratched his head in disbelief. How many more men would have been sent home on this basis? It was clear that Kerensky saw the soldier as an exception, of whom he could make an example. He did not seem to realize that there were millions of others just like him.[16]

Brusilov, by contrast, was beginning to have second thoughts about the morale of the troops. 'The soldiers are tired,' he wrote to his wife at the end of April, 'and in many ways no longer fit to go on to the offensive.' On taking over the supreme command of the army, he set off on his own tour of the Northern and Western Fronts. In contrast to the soldiers of his own South-Western Front, far removed from the influence of the revolutionary cities, he found the troops in a state of complete demoralization. According to one of his senior aides, Brusilov had to avoid using the words 'offensive' or 'advance' in case the soldiers attacked him. Brusilov was not a natural orator. He would draw the soldiers round him and take off his cap and jacket, holding them — 'democratically' — over his left arm, to create an informal atmosphere. But his speeches failed to convince the soldiers that — as they might have said of Kerensky — 'he is one of us'. On one occasion, for example, whilst addressing a group of particularly Bolshev-ized soldiers near Dvinsk, Brusilov claimed that the Germans had destroyed 'one of the French people's finest properties, the beautiful vineyards that produce champagne'. This of course merely alienated and enraged the soldiers, who began to shout at their Commander-in-Chief: 'Shame on you! You want to spill our blood so that you can drink champagne!' Brusilov became afraid, put his cap back on his head, as if to reassert his old authority, and summoned his protectors to surround him. When the shouts had died down he called on one of the most vociferous soldiers to step forward and state his views. The soldier, a young red-bearded peasant, stood next to Brusilov, leant on his rifle with both arms, and, looking askance at the Commander, delivered a speech in which he claimed that the soldiers had 'had enough of fighting', that 'for three long years the Russian people had spilled their blood for the imperialist and capitalist classes', and that 'if the general wanted to go on fighting for champagne then let him go and spill his own blood'. The troops all cheered; Brusilov was lost for words, and began to leave; and as he did so the soldier, who was evidently a Bolshevik, read out the declaration of the soldiers' committee calling for the conclusion of an immediate peace. The Commander-in-Chief of the Russian army had been upstaged by a simple soldier.[17]

This was only one of many incidents to persuade Brusilov that a new offensive would be ill-advised. On the Northern Front he came across a whole division of men which had driven out its officers and threatened to go home *en masse*:

> When I arrived at their camp I demanded to speak to a delegation of the soldiers: it would have been dangerous to appear before the whole crowd. When these arrived I asked them which party they belonged to, and they replied that before they had been Socialist Revolutionaries, but that now they supported the Bolsheviks. 'What do you want?' I asked them. 'Land and Freedom,' they all cried. 'And what else?' The answer was simple: 'Nothing else!' When I asked them what they wanted now, they said they did not want to fight any more and pleaded to be allowed to go home in order to share out the land their fellow villagers had taken from the squires and live in freedom. And when I asked them: 'What will happen to Mother Russia, if no one wants to defend it, and everyone like you only thinks of themselves?' they replied that it was not their job to think about what should become of the state, and that they had firmly decided to go home.[18]

As Brusilov saw it, the soldiers were so obsessed with the idea of peace that they would have been prepared to support the Tsar himself, so long as he promised to bring the war to an end. This alone, Brusilov claimed, rather than the belief in some abstract 'socialism', explained their attraction to the Bolsheviks. The mass of the soldiers were simple peasants, they wanted land and freedom, and they began to call this 'Bolshevism' because only that party promised peace. This 'trench Bolshevism', as Allan Wildman has called it in his magisterial study of the Russian army during 1917, was not necessarily organized through formal party channels, or even encouraged by the Bolshevik agents. Although both of these were apparent at the Front, neither was as well developed as most of the commanders were apt to assume when they blamed 'the Bolsheviks' or 'Bolshevik agents' for virtually every setback in the field.* It was more a case of tired and angry soldiers picking up the slogans of the Bolshevik press and using these to legitimize their own growing resistance to the war. Few soldiers belonged to any political party during 1917, and of those who did most belonged to the SRs rather than the Bolsheviks.[19]

The soldiers' committees, which many commanders condemned as the principal channel of this trench 'Bolshevism', would discuss the coming offensive and resolve not to fight. 'What's the use of invading Galicia anyway?' one soldier asked. 'Why the hell do we need to take another hilltop,' another added, 'when we can make peace at the bottom?' Many soldiers believed that the Soviet peace plan made further bloodshed pointless. They could not understand why their officers were ordering them to fight when the Soviet leaders had agreed on the need for peace. The question of a democratic peace, 'without annexations or indemnities', was much too complicated for most of them to understand. Many of the troops seemed to be under the impression that *Anneksiia* and *Kontributsiia* ('annexations' and 'indemnities') were two countries in the Balkans.[20]

As the offensive approached, the flood of deserters increased. Knox found the trains from the Front 'constantly stormed' by soldiers on their way home. They travelled on the roofs and hung on to the buffers of the wagons. The actual number of deserters during the offensive was very much higher than the official figure of 170,000. Whole units of deserters took over regions in the rear and lived as bandits. Many of them were family men aged over forty who believed they had been promised a special dispensation to go home for the harvest. In many units it was these older soldiers who led the resistance to the offensive (some of them must have taken part in the mutinies and peasant uprisings of 1905). On the Northern Front thousands ran away from the army and set up their own 'soldiers' republic' at a camp near the Trotters' Racecourse in Petrograd. They paraded through the capital with placards demanding their 'liberation' and were often to be seen in the streets and stations selling cigarettes. Somehow, the leaders of their 'republic' even managed to secure supplies from the government's military depot.[21]

One of the most worrying manifestations of the soldiers' pacifism with which Brusilov had to deal was their fraternization with the enemy troops. It was part of the German campaign to run down the Eastern Front in order to transfer troops to the west. They lured the Russian soldiers from their trenches with vodka, concerts and makeshift brothels set up between the two lines of trenches, and told them, in remarkably similar terms to the Bolshevik propaganda,

---

* Indeed, by blaming 'the Bolsheviks' for every military defeat, the commanders gave the impression that the Bolsheviks were much more influential than they actually were, and this had the effect of making the Bolsheviks even more attractive to the mass of the soldiers.

that they should not shed any more blood to advance the imperial interests of Britain and France. During the Easter break from fighting thousands of Russians abandoned their trenches and crossed with white flags to the enemy lines. Many swam across the Dniester and Dvina rivers so as to join in the fun. German scouts were welcomed as heroes behind the Russian lines. Lieutenant Bauermeister, for example, gained a huge propaganda victory in the Thirty-Third Army Corps south of Galich, precisely the point where the main Russian blow was supposed to be dealt in the June offensive. While the impotent officers fumed with rage, he told the soldiers that Germany did not want to fight any more and that all the blame for the coming offensive should be heaped on the Provisional Government, which was a hireling of the Allied bankers. 'If what you say is true,' the soldiers' delegates replied, 'we'll throw the Government out and bring in a new one that will quickly give the Russian people peace.' The soldiers even agreed to sign an armistice along the whole of their sector. Bauermeister was astonished. He reminded the Russians that they did not have the legal authority to do this. But the soldiers said that, if they chose not to go on fighting, no one had the power to force them to do otherwise. For several weeks the armistice was enforced, right up until the offensive. Guns were taken out of service and white flags were raised along the Russian lines. The flamboyant Bauermeister, dressed in a white cap, became something of a hero. He even managed to speak in a village three miles behind the Russian Front. It was the headquarters of the Seventh Army.[22]

On the eve of the offensive Brusilov warned Kerensky of his growing doubts. Troops were refusing to move up to the Front. Dozens of mutinies had taken place in army garrisons to the rear and even where units were moved up to the trenches three-quarters of the men were likely to desert *en route*. The front-line soldiers had also mutinied when they discovered what lay ahead. Brusilov had been forced to disband a number of his most reliable units. In the Fifth Army on the Northern Front soldiers refused to carry out orders and declared that Lenin was the only authority they would recognize: 23,000 of them had to be transferred to other units or sent to the rear for military trial. But Kerensky ignored all the warnings of his army chief. 'He paid not the slightest attention to my words,' Brusilov recalled, 'and from that moment on, I realized that my own authority as the Commander-in-Chief was quite irrelevant.'[23] Kerensky and his cabinet colleagues had made up their minds: the offensive was to go ahead and there was no room for last-minute doubts.

On 16 June the offensive began with a two-day heavy artillery bombardment. Kerensky hurried from regiment to regiment giving out orders and trying to raise morale. On 18 June the troops moved forward, encouraged by the sight of the German trenches abandoned under fire. The main attack was aimed towards Lvov in the south, while supporting offensives were also launched on the Western and Northern Fronts. For two days the advance continued. The German lines were broken and a glorious 'Triumph for Liberty!' was heralded in the patriotic press. Then, on the third day, the advance came to a halt, the Germans began to counter-attack, and the Russians fled in panic. It was partly a case of the usual military failings: units had been sent into battle without machine-guns; untrained soldiers had been ordered to engage in complex manœuvres using hand grenades and ended up throwing them without first pulling the pins. But the main reason for the fiasco was the simple reluctance of the soldiers to fight. Having advanced two miles, the front-line troops felt they had done their bit and refused to go any further, while those in the second line would not take their places. The advance thus broke down as the men began to run away. In one night alone the shock battalions of the Eleventh Army arrested 12,000 deserters near the town of Volochinsk. Many soldiers turned their guns against their commanding officers rather than fight against the enemy. The retreat degenerated into chaos as soldiers looted shops and stores, raped peasant girls and murdered Jews. The crucial advance towards Lvov soon collapsed when the troops discovered a large store of alcohol in the abandoned town of Koniukhy and stopped there to get drunk. By the time they were fit to resume fighting three days and a hangover later, enemy reinforcements had arrived, and the Russians, suffering heavy losses, were forced to retreat.[24]

Amidst such chaos, even the shock troops stood little chance of success. Bochkareva's Battalion of Death did much better than most. The women volunteers broke through the first two German lines, followed by some of the sheepish male conscripts. But then they came under heavy German fire. The women dispersed in confusion, while most of the men stayed put in the German trenches, where they had found a large supply of liquor and proceeded to get drunk. Despite the shambles around her, Bochkareva battled on. At one point she came across one of her women having sexual intercourse with a soldier in a shell-hole. She ran her through with a bayonet; but the soldier escaped. Eventually, with most of her volunteers killed or wounded, even Bochkareva was forced to retreat.[25] The offensive was over. It was Russia's last.

* * *

The collapse of the offensive dealt a fatal blow to the Provisional Government and the personal authority of its leaders. Hundreds of thousands of soldiers were killed. Millions of square miles of territory were lost. The leaders of the government had gambled everything on the offensive in the hope that it might rally the country behind them in the national defence of democracy. The coalition had been based upon this hope; and it held together as long as there was a chance of military success. But as the collapse of the offensive became clear, so the coalition fell apart.

It had been on the cards for some time. God only knows what Lvov had gone through to keep his government together until at least the start of the offensive. After the socialists' entry into the cabinet, most of the Kadets had moved to the Right. They had given up their old pretence of standing 'above class' and had taken up the defence of property rights, military discipline, law and order and the Russian Empire against the demands of the nationalists. All this had placed them in growing opposition to the socialists, who were under pressure from their own supporters to steer the government's policies further to the Left. Formally, it was the question of Ukrainian autonomy which was to break the coalition and throw the country into crisis. When the government delegation to Kiev conceded a series of autonomous rights to the Rada on 2 July, three Kadet ministers resigned in protest. The Kadets were opposed to granting anything more than cultural freedoms to the 'Little Russians', and insisted that this could only be done by the Constituent Assembly. The concessions of 2 July were thus, in their view, illegal and, as Miliukov put it, amounted to the 'chopping up of Russia under the slogan of self-determination'.[26] The Ukrainian question, however, was only the final straw. The breakdown of the coalition was also caused by fundamental conflicts over domestic social reforms. Foremost among these was Chernov's policy on land, which the Kadets accused of sanctioning the peasant revolution by giving the land committees temporary rights of control over the gentry's estates. Then there was the problem of militant strikes, which the Kadets blamed on the Mensheviks in control of the Ministry of Labour. Old class divisions, which had been papered over in the interests of the offensive, were, it seems, returning with a vengeance.

For Lvov the collapse of this 'national alliance' was a bitter disappointment. More than anyone else, he had stood for the liberal hope of uniting the country. As its figurehead, he had symbolized the government's ideal of constructive work in the interests of the nation. Party politics were a foreign land to him and he was increasingly out of his depth in the factional conflicts of his own cabinet meetings. 'I feel like a piece of driftwood, washed up by the revolutionary waves,' he told his old friend from the Japanese war, General Kuropatkin. He cursed both the Kadets and the socialists for placing class and party interests above those of the nation as a whole. The Kadets, he told his private secretary, had behaved like Great Russian chauvinists over the Ukraine; they could not see that some concessions had to be made, if the state was to be saved. But he was equally fed up with the socialists, who he said were trying to impose the Soviet programme on the Provisional Government. Chernov's policy on the land committees seemed nothing less to him, as a landowner, than a 'Bolshevik programme of organized confiscation'. In his view the general interests of the state were being sacrificed to the particular interests of parties and classes, and Russia, as a result, was moving closer to civil war. He felt politically impotent, caught in the cross-fire between Left and Right, and on

3 July he finally decided to resign.* 'I have reached the end of the road', he told his secretary, 'and so, I'm afraid, has my sort of liberalism.' Later that night he wrote to his parents in a rare mood of dark foreboding:

Sweet Father and Mother,

It was already clear to me about a week ago that there was no way out. Without a doubt the country is heading for a general slaughter, famine, the collapse of the front, where half the soldiers will perish, and the ruin of the urban population. The cultural inheritance of the nation, its people and civilization, will be destroyed. Armies of migrants, then small groups, and then maybe no more than individual people, will roam around the country fighting each other with rifles and then no more than clubs. I will not live to see it, and, I hope, neither will you.[27]

As he wrote these prophetic words, in the midst of the July crisis, the Bolsheviks were preparing for a decisive confrontation with the Provisional Government.

ii A Darker Shade of Red

On the eve of the July uprising the journalist Claude Anet took Joseph Noulens, the new French Ambassador, on an introductory tour of the Russian capital. From the opposite bank of the Neva, outside the French Embassy, he pointed out the Vyborg district, with its factory chimneys and barracks, and explained that the Bolsheviks reigned there as masters: 'If Lenin and Trotsky want to take Petrograd, there is nothing to stop them.' The French Ambassador listened in astonishment: 'How can the government tolerate such a situation?' he asked. 'But what can it do?' replied Anet. 'You must understand that the government has no power but a moral one, and even that seems to me very weak.'[28]

The barracks of the First Machine-Gun Regiment was without a doubt the most menacing bastion of anti-government power on the Vyborg side. With 10,000 men and 1,000 machine-guns, it was by far the largest unit in the capital. Most of its soldiers had been expelled from their front-line units for insubordination and, as highly literate and militant soldiers, were susceptible to the propaganda of both the Bolsheviks and the Anarchists. The regiment's adopted barracks on the Vyborg side nestled among the most strike-prone metal factories of the capital, right next door to the Bolsheviks' headquarters. So

---

* His resignation was not formally announced until 7 July.

important was it to the Bolsheviks that their Military Organization had its own special cell in the regiment.

On 20 June the First Machine-Gun Regiment was ordered to send 500 machine-guns with their crews to the Front, where, it was said, they were badly needed to support the offensive. Since the February Revolution not a single unit of the Petrograd garrison had been transferred to the Front. This had been one of the conditions set by the Petrograd Soviet on the establishment of the Provisional Government. The soldiers believed that they had 'made the revolution' and that they therefore had the right to remain in Petrograd to defend it against a 'counter-revolution'. The Provisional Government was all too aware that it lived at the mercy of the garrison's quarter of a million troops. Until now, it would not have dared to try to remove them from the capital. But by June the presence of these machine-gunners had become a major threat to the government's existence; and one of the main aims of the offensive was undoubtedly to transfer them to the Front. The Foreign Minister, Tereshchenko, admitted as much to the British Ambassador when he claimed in June that the offensive 'will enable us to take measures against the garrison in Petrograd, which is by far the worst and gives a bad example to the others'; while Kerensky repeatedly stressed that it was the aim of the offensive to restore order in the rear.[29] Lvov's private notes, recently discovered in the Russian archives, confirm that during May and June the government was seriously considering removing the capital to Moscow.[30] There were constant rumours that Petrograd was about to be abandoned to the Germans; and many of the 'patriotic' middle classes prayed that they were true (it was a dinner-party commonplace that only the Kaiser could restore order). But if the government's aim was to use the offensive as a pretext to remove the machine-gunners, then this was a very clumsy and a foolish way to go about it. The government could have easily transferred the machine-gunners to the rear, say to some backwater like Tambov province, on the grounds of 'defending the revolution' there. By sending them to the Front, and thus reneging on the Soviet's conditions, it gave credibility to the soldiers' claim — voiced by the Bolshevik and Anarchist agitators in their regiment — that the government was using the offensive to break up the garrison and that it was thus 'counter-revolutionary'. Since the April crisis, the soldiers had viewed the government's efforts to continue the war with growing suspicion — didn't this make them 'imperialists'? — and in this climate of mistrust such conspiracy theories were persuasive.

On 21 June the machine-gunners resolved to overthrow the Provisional Government, if it continued with its threat 'to break up this and other revolutionary regiments' by sending them to the Front. Dozens of other garrison units which had orders to join the offensive passed similar resolutions. The Bolshevik Military Organization encouraged the idea of an armed uprising, and effectively transformed itself into the operational staff for the capture of the capital. But the Central Committee continued to urge restraint. It was the same policy clash as on 10 June, with the ultra-leftist leaders of the Vyborg Committee and the Military Organization keen to ride to power on the violence of the Petrograd vanguard, and the more cautious national leaders of the party afraid that a failed uprising might give rise to an anti-Bolshevik backlash in the country at large. The provinces, they said, were not yet ready for a socialist revolution and the premature seizure of power in the capital was likely to result in a civil war, in which Red Petrograd, like the Paris Commune, would be defeated by the provinces. So argued Lenin himself at a Conference of the Bolshevik Military Organizations on 20 June. He stressed the need to delay the armed uprising, resisting all provocations by the 'counter-revolutionaries', until the offensive was over and the Bolsheviks had won a majority in the Soviet:

> One wrong move on our part can wreck everything ... if we were now able to seize power, it is naive to think that we would be able to hold it ... Even in the Soviets of both capitals, not to speak now of the others, we are an insignificant minority ... This is a basic fact, and it determines the behaviour of our Party ... Events should not be anticipated. Time is on our side.[31]

But Lenin had little control over his lieutenants. On 29 June he departed for a friend's country dacha in Finland complaining of headaches and fatigue. Control of the party slipped out of his hands, as the Military Organization prepared the insurrection. Bolshevik and Anarchist agitators urged the machine-gunners to take to the streets in an armed demonstration on 3 July. A regimental concert in the People's House on the 2nd to bid farewell to the soldiers due to leave for the Front was turned into an anti-government rally, with Trotsky and Lunacharsky (although neither was yet formally a Bolshevik) calling for the transfer of all power to the Soviet. The troops returned to their barracks too excited to sleep. They spent the night and the following morning debating whether to join the uprising. Many were reluctant to come out in force against the orders of the Soviet. But others were eager to join the uprising, seeing in it their last chance to resist the call-up to the Front, or perhaps simply the chance, as one of their slogans proposed, to 'Beat the *burzhoois!*' They elected a Provisional Revolutionary Committee, headed by the Bolshevik, A. I. Semashko, from the Military Organization, which assumed the leadership of the uprising and despatched emissaries to mobilize support from the rest of the garrison units, the factories in Vyborg, and the Kronstadt Naval Base.[32]

During the afternoon a vast grey mass of workers and soldiers moved from the outlying districts to the centre of the city. The streets returned to the look of the February Days, though the mood was now much darker and the composition of the crowd more solidly proletarian. The suits of the middle-class citizens, the beards of the students and the hats of the lady sympathizers, which had all been so visible in February, were no longer to be seen. The marchers carried Bolshevik slogans and were mostly armed, the soldiers with bayonets fixed to their rifles, the workers, brought out by the Red Guards, with belts of bullets wrapped around their torsos like Latin American bandits. A prominent place in the crowd was occupied by soldiers aged over forty who had marched through the city in armed ranks several times before. The demonstrators overturned trams, and set up pickets at various intersections. At one of these pickets, at the fashionable end of the Nevsky Prospekt, the Red Guards mounted a machine-gun. Its minders soon got bored and amused themselves by firing at the *burzhoois* in the streets and houses. Lorries and armoured cars hurtled about the city filled with soldiers firing into the air. Groups of armed men halted passing motor-cars, turned out their terrified passengers, and rode about the streets, their bayonets bristling out in all directions. One official tried to stop the insurgents from confiscating his car by showing them a permit signed by Kerensky. But the soldiers merely laughed, claiming (falsely) that Kerensky had already been arrested: 'You might as well show us a permit with the signature of Nicholas II.'[33]

The crowd as yet lacked leadership or direction. It did not quite know where it should go, or why. It had nothing but a 'mood' — which wasn't enough to make a revolution. The Bolshevik and Anarchist agitators, who had brought out the insurgent army, failed to set it strategic objectives. 'The street itself will organize us,' the Anarchist Bleichman had claimed. There was an assumption that a large enough show of force was bound to bring the government down, and that the detailed questions of power could somehow be left to sort themselves out later. That, after all, was the experience of the February Days.[34]

The bulk of the crowd moved towards the Tauride Palace, as it had done in February. Some became involved in gun fights with loyalist and right-wing forces on their way. There was a smell of civil war. The City Council Building on the Nevsky Prospekt was the scene of especially bloody fighting. The Bolshevik leader, Lunacharsky, watched in horror from inside the building. 'The movement developed spontaneously,' he wrote to his wife on the next day. 'Black Hundreds, hooligans, provocateurs, anarchists and desperate people introduced a large amount of chaos and absurdity to the demonstration.' By the early evening, a solid mass of people had assembled in front of the Tauride Palace. The Soviet leaders were in session debating whether to form a socialist government after the collapse of the coalition, and the crowd no doubt hoped to pressurize them into taking power. 'All Power to the Soviets!' came the roar from the street. The Workers' Section of the Soviet served as a mouthpiece for their demands. That afternoon it had been taken over by the Bolsheviks, who, although still a minority in the Section, had turned up in one solid body for a hastily convened emergency session and — in a premonition of October — provoked the Mensheviks and SRs into walking out by passing a resolution calling for Soviet power. A Special Commission was elected to provide political organization for the crowds outside. But it proved quite ineffective — Sukhanov, who spent the July Days in the Tauride Palace, could not recall any of its activities. The street was thus deprived of any real leverage over the Soviet. Angry demonstrators called out for the arrest of the Soviet leaders, who had 'surrendered to the landlords and the bourgeoisie!' A delegation from the First Machine-Gun Regiment told Chkheidze that it was 'disturbed by rumours that the Executive intended to enter into a new coalition with the reactionary capitalists', and that they 'would not stand for such a policy' because 'they had already suffered enough'. Some of the soldiers penetrated into the Catherine Hall, where they watched the debate. Yet none of them thought to arrest the Soviet leaders, who were quite defenceless. There was no one to tell the soldiers to do it.[35]

As darkness fell, the crowd began to disperse. The uprising seemed to be coming to an end. There were rumours that the Provisional Government had already been arrested. But nothing of the sort had taken place. The remnants of the cabinet were having a meeting in Prince Lvov's apartment. At around 10 p.m. a group of armed workers and soldiers burst into the entrance hall, where they announced to the hall porter that they had come to arrest the Ministers. Tsereteli was summoned to negotiate with them, but before he got to the entrance the insurgents had lost their nerve and run away with his car.[36]

Precisely at this moment the Bolshevik Central Committee was meeting in the Kshesinskaya Mansion to decide on its policy towards the uprising. Although it had so far been urging restraint, afraid to risk all in a premature putsch, there seemed no holding back the movement now. The workers and soldiers had virtually taken over the city, the Kronstadt sailors were on their way, and the vast majority of the rank-and-file Bolsheviks in Petrograd were joining the uprising, leaving the Central Committee on the sidelines. Shortly before midnight it was agreed to call for further demonstrations on the following day. The front page of *Pravda*, which was due to appear with an article by Kamenev and Zinoviev calling for restraint, had to be altered at the final moment and appeared the next morning with a large blank space. Leaflets were hastily printed and distributed in the streets calling for 'organized' demonstrations and a 'new power' based on the Soviet. Meanwhile, a messenger from the Central Committee sped off in a car to Finland to bring Lenin back to the capital.[37]

The exact intentions of the Bolshevik leaders have always been a subject of fierce controversy. Some historians have argued that the Bolsheviks were planning to overthrow the Provisional Government by armed force. Richard Pipes, for example, claims that the July affair was orchestrated from the start by the Bolshevik leaders as 'a power seizure'; it was only when the embarrassing failure of the putsch became clear that they sought to conceal their intentions by depicting the uprising as a 'spontaneous demonstration which they sought to direct into peaceful channels'. This last version of events — as a 'spontaneous demonstration' — was the standard Soviet view. It was supported by the American scholar, Alexander Rabinowitch, in his classic account of the July Days. According to Rabinowitch, the Central Committee only joined the uprising under pressure from its rank and file, and never intended it to go any further than a show of force to pressurize the Soviet into taking power.[38]

The only real piece of evidence in support of the 'failed putsch' thesis comes from Sukhanov's memoirs, written in 1920. Sukhanov claimed that on 7 July Lunacharsky had told him that, on the night of 3–4 July:

> Lenin was definitely planning a *coup d'état*. The Government, which would in fact be in the hands of the Bolshevik Central Committee, would officially be embodied in a 'Soviet' Cabinet made up of eminent and popular Bolsheviks. For the time being three Ministers had been appointed: Lenin, Trotsky and Lunacharsky . . . The *coup d'état* itself was to proceed in this way: the 176th Regiment . . . from Krasnoe Selo* was to arrest the [Soviet] Executive, and at about that time Lenin was to arrive on the scene of action and proclaim the new Government.

Sukhanov himself was the first to acknowledge that 'some elementary facts' told against this version — namely the Bolsheviks' failure to carry through their seizure of power on 4 July, when there were ample opportunities for them to do so. On the face of the evidence, it does appear that the Central Committee had anything but a clear plan. In a manner underestimated by all historians, the events of 4 July were characterized by almost total confusion. The Bolshevik leaders made everything up as they went along. The mass turn-out of 3 July had caught them unprepared, with their leader on vacation in Finland. They were caught in two minds as to whether they should seek to transform the demonstration into the overthrow of the Provisional Government, or whether they should try to limit it to a political demonstration in order to pressurize the Soviet leaders into taking power themselves. When Lenin returned, in the small hours of the morning, the Bolsheviks badgered him for an answer to this question. According to Kalinin, Lenin's tactics were to 'wait and see what happened', leaving open the option of 'throwing regiments into the battle if the correlation of forces should prove favourable'. This may well have been so. But the Bolshevik leader proved utterly unable to make up his own mind if that

---

* Formerly Tsarskoe Selo.

moment had come. Zinoviev, who spent the whole of the 4th by his side, recalled a Lenin hopelessly paralysed by indecision. He kept asking himself if this was the occasion 'to try for power'.[39] Throughout the critical hours of the uprising the Bolshevik leaders continued to sit on the fence waiting to see what would happen. Yet the organized part of the crowd, which had been brought out by the local Bolshevik organizations, would not seize power themselves without specific instructions from them. It was because of this confusion that the demonstrations appeared so badly organized as an attempted putsch — and ended in fiasco.

Tuesday, 4 July, began with an eerie silence over the city. Heavy thunder clouds hung low over the city and the river was dark and sullen. The shops were shut and the streets deserted — a certain sign that trouble was brewing in the workers' quarters. By mid-morning the centre of the city was once again taken over by crowds of workers and soldiers. A motley flotilla of tug-boats, trawlers, barges and gun-boats from the Kronstadt Naval Base was meanwhile mooring near the Nikolaevsky Bridge: 20,000 sailors disembarked, armed to the teeth with rifles and revolvers, along with their own medical teams and several marching bands. This was without doubt the Bolsheviks' chief weapon, if they were planning to seize power. The sailors were spoiling for a fight with the Provisional Government. Ever since February they had been trying to set up their own semi-Anarchist version of Soviet power at Kronstadt. Raskolnikov, the Bolshevik leader of the sailors, said they had come to Petrograd ready 'at any moment to turn the demonstration into an armed uprising'. It was clear, however, that the sailors had no strategic plan — and only a vague idea of what to do once they disembarked. Bernard Pares, who was on the scene, thought most of them had come for a holiday, to walk the streets with their girls, who were very much in evidence throughout the July Days. 'Sailors with scantily-dressed and high-heeled ladies were seen everywhere.'[40]

Looking for leaders, the Kronstadt sailors set off for the Bolshevik headquarters. Led by their bands, which played the Internationale, they marched in armed ranks along the University Embankment, past the Stock Exchange and through the Alexander Park to the Kshesinskaya Mansion, where they amassed in front of the balcony expecting to receive instructions from Lenin. But the Bolshevik leader did not know where he should lead them. At this point it would have been enough for him to give the command, and the sailors would have marched at once to the Tauride, arrested the Soviet leaders, rounded up the cabinet ministers and proclaimed Soviet power. But Lenin was uncharacteristically hesitant, did not want to speak, and when he was finally persuaded to make an appearance on the balcony, gave an ambiguous speech, lasting no more than a few seconds, in which he expressed his confidence in the coming of Soviet power but left the sailors without orders on how to bring it about. He did not even make it clear if he wanted the crowd to continue the demonstration and, according to those who were with him at the time, did not even know himself.[41]

This was to be Lenin's last public speech until the October seizure of power. It was a telling moment, one of the few in his long career when he was faced with the task of leading a revolutionary crowd that was standing before him. Other Bolshevik leaders were much better at handling the crowd. But Lenin's public appearances had been mostly confined to the congress hall. According to his wife, he became very nervous when forced to address a mass gathering.[42] Perhaps at this decisive moment, faced with the raw energy of the street, Lenin lost his nerve. True, what could he say? No doubt he was tongue-tied by the realization that, even if the Bolsheviks won Petrograd, they would still be opposed by the rest of Russia. But none the less his crucial hesitation sealed the fate of the July uprising.

Confused and disappointed by the lack of a clear call for the insurrection to begin, the Kronstadters marched off towards the Tauride Palace, where thousands of armed workers and soldiers were already assembling. On the Nevsky Prospekt they merged with another vast crowd of workers from the Putilov plant, perhaps 20,000 in all. Middle-class Petrograders strolling along the Prospekt looked on in horror at their massed grey ranks. Suddenly, as the column turned into the Liteiny, shots were fired by the Cossacks and cadets from the roof-tops and the upper windows of the buildings, causing the marchers to scatter in panic. Some of the marchers fired back, shooting without aim in all directions, since they did not know where the snipers were hidden. Dozens of their comrades were killed or wounded by their own stray bullets. The rest abandoned their rifles and flags and started to break down the doors and windows of the houses. When the shooting stopped, the leaders of the demonstration tried to restore order by reforming ranks and marching off to an up-beat tune from the military bands. But the equilibrium of the crowd had been upset and, as they marched through the affluent residential streets approaching the Tauride Palace, their columns broke down into a riotous mob, firing wildly into the windows, beating up well-dressed passers-by and looting shops and houses. By 4 p.m. hundreds of people had been wounded or killed; dead horses lay here and there; and the streets were littered with rifles, hats, umbrellas and banners. Gorky, who witnessed the terrible scenes, later wrote to Ekaterina in disgust:

The worst of it all was the crowd, the philistines, the 'worker' and soldier, who is in fact no more than a brute, cowardly and brainless, without an ounce of self-respect and not understanding why he is on the streets, what he is needed for, or who is leading him and where. Whole companies of soldiers threw away their rifles and banners when the shooting began and smashed the shop windows and doors. Is this the revolutionary army of a free people?

It is clear that the crowds on the street had absolutely no idea of what they were doing — it was all a nightmare. Nobody knew the aims of the uprising or its leaders. Were there any leaders at all? I doubt it. Trotsky, Lunacharsky and *tutti grandi* jabbered something or other, but it was all lost to the mood of the crowd.[43]

With 50,000 armed and angry men surrounding the Tauride Palace, there was nothing to prevent a Bolshevik *coup d'état*. V. S. Woytinsky, who was placed in charge of defending the palace, had only eighteen soldiers from the Pavlovsky Regiment at his disposal. There were not even enough soldiers to guard the posts at the entrance to the building, so Woytinsky relied on deception, placing all his men at the huge French windows which spanned the façade of the palace to make it appear as if it was properly defended. To the Soviet leaders inside the palace debating the question of power, it seemed 'completely obvious' that they were about to be stormed. 'At any moment', recalled the Menshevik, Bogdanov, 'the armed mobs could have broken in, wrecked the Tauride Palace, and arrested or shot us if we refused to take the power into our hands.'[44] The Provisional Government, or what remained of it, was equally defenceless. During the morning the cabinet ministers had taken refuge in the building of the General Staff opposite the Winter Palace. Apart from a few dozen Cossacks, there were no available forces willing to defend them. Kerensky had run off to the Front, leaving the Warsaw Station only minutes before his Bolshevik chasers arrived there. The Marinsky Palace, the seat of government power, stood wide open for the taking. The strategic points of the city — the arsenals, the telephone exchange, the supply depots and the railway stations — were all undefended. With a single order from Lenin, the insurgents could easily have taken them as the first step towards the seizure of power.

But that order did not come, and the crowd in front of the Tauride Palace, not quite sure of what it should do, soon lost all its organization. The hand of God, in the form of the weather, also contributed to the collapse of the uprising. At 5 p.m. the storm clouds finally broke and there was a torrential rainstorm. Most of the crowd ran for cover and did not bother to come back. But the unruly elements stayed on. Perhaps because they were soaked by the rain, they lost their self-control and began to fire wildly at the Tauride Palace. This caused the rest of the crowd to scream and stampede in panic: dozens of people were crushed. Some sailors began to penetrate into the palace, climbing in through the open windows. They called for the socialist ministers to come out and explain their reluctance to take power. Chernov was sent out to calm the crowd. But as soon as he appeared on the steps angry shouts were heard from the sailors. The crowd surged forward and seized hold of him, searching him for weapons. One worker raised his fist and shouted at him in anger: 'Take power, you son of a bitch, when it's handed to you!' Several armed men bundled the SR leader into an open car. They declared him under arrest and said they would not release him until the Soviet had taken power. Chernov had gone one better than his old rival, Kerensky. He was now a real 'hostage of the democracy'.

A group of workers broke into the Catherine Hall and interrupted the session: 'Comrade Chernov has been arrested by the mob! They're tearing him to pieces right now! To the rescue! Everyone out into the street!' Chkheidze proposed that Kamenev, Martov and Trotsky should be sent out to rescue the Minister. But Trotsky was the first to get there. Pushing his way through the shouting crowds, he went straight to the car, where the hatless, dishevelled and terrified Chernov sat under arrest in the back seat, and climbed up on to the bonnet. The Kronstadters all knew the figure of Trotsky and waited for his instructions. Had the Bolsheviks planned for the seizure of power, this was surely the moment to urge the sailors on to the storming of the Tauride, the arrest of the Soviet leaders and the proclamation of a socialist government. Raskolnikov, who was standing by Trotsky, asked Chernov's captors where they were planning to take their hostage. 'We don't know,' they answered. 'Wherever you wish, Comrade Raskolnikov. He is at your disposal.' But Trotsky called for Chernov to be released. 'Comrade Kronstadters, pride and glory of the Russian Revolution!', he began in his clear metallic voice; 'you've come to declare your will and show the Soviet that the working class no longer wants to see the bourgeoisie in power. But why hurt your own cause by petty acts of violence against casual individuals? Individuals are not worthy of your attention.' The sailors shouted angrily at Trotsky: they could not understand why Chernov was to be let go, if the aim of their mission was to overthrow the government. But not knowing what to do on their own, they sullenly agreed to release the Minister. 'Citizen Chernov, you are free,' declared Comrade Trotsky, opening the car door and motioning him to get out. Chernov was half-dead and plainly did not understand what was happening to him. He had to be helped out of the car and led, like a frail old man, back into the Tauride Palace.[45] A critical moment had passed, one of the most famous in the history of the revolution, and with it had also passed the initiative for a seizure of power.

According to Sukhanov's account of his conversation with Lunacharsky, the key to the Bolshevik 'plan' for the seizure of power was the 176th Regiment from Krasnoe Selo. It was supposed to arrive at the Tauride Palace and arrest the Soviet leaders. At around 6 o'clock it finally appeared, led by its regimental band. The soldiers were tired and soaked by the rain. With their packs and greatcoats on their shoulders, their mess tins and cooking pots clanging as they walked, they settled themselves in the forecourt of the palace and began to unpack their wet things and prepare their rifles. They had not the slightest idea what they were supposed to do, and only knew that they had been called out to 'defend the revolution'. But where were their leaders? An officer and six men climbed the Tauride steps and asked to see someone from the Soviet. The Menshevik, Dan, came out to greet them. He did not know what the regiment was, or why it had come to the palace, but he soon found a use for it. The 'insurrectionary' soldiers were posted as sentries at various points of the building to protect the Soviet leaders against the insurrection.[46] Having come to demonstrate against the Soviet leaders, they had ended up defending them against the demonstrators. Such things happen in a revolution, when the crowd does not know its leaders.

From this point on, the insurrection was effectively over. By itself, the crowd was unable to bring about political change. The Soviet leaders, discussing the question of whether to assume power, were all the more determined not to be pushed into it by the mob in the street. 'The decision of the revolutionary democracy cannot be dictated by bayonets,' declared Tsereteli.[47] Once the Soviet had resolved not to take power, there was nothing the crowd could do. It did not know how to force the Soviet leaders into changing their minds, or how to complete a Soviet revolution without them. If the Soviet leaders were reluctant to take power, how could they give 'All Power to the Soviet'?

One final event on that day symbolized the powerlessness of the crowd. At around 7 p.m. a group of armed and angry workers from the Putilov plant burst into the Catherine Hall. The Soviet deputies leaped from their seats. Some threw themselves on to the ground in panic. One of the workers, a 'classical sans-culotte' dressed in a blue factory tunic and cap, jumped up on to the speakers' platform. Shaking his rifle in the air, he shouted incoherently at the deputies:

> Comrades! How long must we workers put up with treachery? You're all here debating and making deals with the bourgeoisie and the landlords . . . You're busy betraying the working class. Well, just understand that the working class won't put up with it! There are 30,000 of us all told here from Putilov. We're going to have our way. All power to the Soviets! We have a firm grip on our rifles! Your Kerenskys and Tseretelis are not going to fool us!

Chkheidze, the Soviet chairman, was sitting next to the hysterical worker. He calmly leaned across and placed a piece of paper into his hand. It was a manifesto, printed the evening before, in which it was said that the demonstrators should go home, or be condemned as traitors to the revolution. 'Here, please take this, Comrade,' Chkheidze said to him in an imperious tone. 'It says here what you and your Putilov comrades should do. Please read it carefully and don't interrupt our business.'[48] The confused worker, not knowing what he should do, took the manifesto and left the hall with the rest of the Putilovites. No doubt he was fuming with anger and frustration at his profound humiliation; and yet he was powerless to resist, not because he lacked the guns, but because he lacked the will. Centuries of serfdom and subservience had not prepared him to stand up to his political masters — and in that lay the tragedy of the Russian people as a whole. This was one of the finest scenes of the whole revolution — one of those rare moments in history when the hidden relations of power are flashed up on to the surface of events and the broader course of developments becomes clear.

        As darkness fell, the crowds dispersed. Most of them made their way back home, damp and dejected, to the workers' districts and barracks. The Kronstadt sailors wandered around the city, not knowing where to go. Throughout the night the affluent residential streets reverberated to the sounds of broken windows, sporadic shots and screams, as the last survivors of the failed uprising took out their anger in acts of looting and violence against the *burzhoois*. The Petrograd military headquarters were inundated with telephone calls from terrified shopkeepers, bankers and housewives. In a last desperate act of defiance, 2,000 Kronstadters seized control of the Peter and Paul Fortress. They did not know what to do with the conquered fortress — it was just a symbol of the old regime which it seemed a good idea to capture as a final hostage of the uprising. The sailors slept in the prison's empty cells, and the following day agreed to leave it on condition that they were allowed to make their own way back to Kronstadt, keeping all their weapons.[49]

        By this stage, loyal troops were flocking to defend the Tauride Palace. The Izmailovsky Regiment was the first to arrive, on the evening of the 4th, with a thunderous rendering of the Marseillaise — as if in response to the Internationale of the Kronstadters — from its military band. As they heard the sound of it approaching, the Soviet leaders embraced each other with tears of relief: the siege of the Tauride Palace was finally over. Standing arm in arm, they broke spontaneously into the stirring chorus of 'Aux armes, citoyens'. It was, as Martov angrily muttered, a 'classic scene from the start of a counter-revolution'.[50]

*   *   *

Like most of the loyalist troops, the Izmailovksy Regiment had been turned against the Bolsheviks by leaflets released that evening by the Minister of Justice Pereverzev accusing them of being German agents. On the next day, 5 July, the right-wing press was full of so-called 'evidence' to that effect. Much of it was based on the dubious testimony of a Lieutenant Yermolenko, who claimed to have been told by the Germans, whilst he was a prisoner of war, that Lenin was working for them. There is no doubt that the Germans had financed the Bolshevik Party — the Provisional Government had known that since April. But this did not prove Pereverzev's claim, still repeated by many historians, that the Bolsheviks were German agents. For one thing, the actual amount of German finance was not very great, given the party's financial problems during the summer; and, for another, there is no evidence that the Bolsheviks planned their policies to suit Berlin. Yet the timely release of these charges had an explosive effect, turning many soldiers against the Bolsheviks. Acting under orders from Pereverzev, a large detachment of military cadets ransacked the *Pravda* offices at dawn on 5 July. They only just missed Lenin, who had left for the first of his pre-October hide-outs, the flat of the Bolshevik worker, Sergei Alliluyev,* only minutes before.[51]

Lenin had been given early warning of the treason charges by a secret contact in the Ministry of Justice. Hoping to mitigate the xenophobic reaction which was bound to follow, he called for an end to the demonstrations in an article on the back page of *Pravda*. But it was too late. By the morning of the 5th, the capital was seized with anti-Bolshevik hysteria. The right-wing tabloids bayed for Bolshevik blood, instantly blaming the 'German agents' for the reverses at the Front. It seemed self-evident that the Bolsheviks had planned their uprising to coincide with the German advance. General Polovtsov, who was responsible for the repressions as the head of the Petrograd Military District, later acknowledged that the Bolshevik-baiting contained 'a strong anti-Semitic tendency'; but in the usual way that Russians of his class justified pogroms he put it down 'to the Jews themselves because among the Bolshevik leaders their percentage was not far from a hundred. It was beginning to annoy the soldiers to see that Jews ruled everything, and the remarks I heard in the barracks plainly showed what the soldiers thought about it.'[52]

Early in the morning of 6 July a massive task force of loyalist troops, complete with eight armoured cars and several batteries of heavy artillery, moved up to liberate the Kshesinskaya Mansion. Amidst the anti-Bolshevik hysteria, there had been outrage in the right-wing press at the thought of the unwashed Bolshevik workers and soldiers rummaging through the velvets and silks of Kshesinskaya's boudoir. Not a single shot was fired in the recapture of the ballerina's former mansion. The 500 Bolsheviks still inside surrendered without resistance, despite the large store of weapons at their disposal. The Bolshevik leaders had been too busy burning party files to organize resistance.[53]

Later that day, Pereverzev ordered Lenin's arrest, along with eleven other Bolshevik leaders. They were all charged with high treason. Most of them stayed in the open, risking arrest, and in some cases even giving themselves up. But

---

* His daughter, Nadezhda, would later marry Stalin.

Lenin fled underground — first to a series of safe houses in the capital and then, on 9 July, along with Zinoviev, travelling through the countryside to Finland. Lenin shaved off his beard and wore a worker's tunic and cap to disguise himself. During the following days dozens of houses in the capital were turned over by troops in search of him. Even Gorky's flat was raided. Some 800 Bolsheviks in all were imprisoned, including Kamenev, Lunacharsky, Kollontai and Trotsky — the last not yet a member of the party, though he had declared his allegiance to it.[54] The Peter and Paul Fortress, whose cells had been empty since the February Revolution, once again began to be filled with 'politicals'.

As Lenin travelled into the northern wilderness, it must have seemed to him that the Bolshevik cause was finished. Before leaving the capital he had handed to Kamenev the manuscript of what was later to become *The State and Revolution*, with instructions for it to be published if he should be killed. Lenin was always prone to overestimate the physical danger to himself: in this respect he was something of a coward. It cannot be said that his life was ever at direct risk during his summer on the run: at one point he even stayed with the Chief of Police in Helsingfors, who happened to be a Bolshevik sympathizer. After Lenin's death, during the cult of Lenin, fantastic stories would be told of his personal bravery during countless narrow escapes from the police. But none of them was true. One true incident during this summer, although it hardly spoke of Lenin's courage, took place in a village near Sestoretsk on the Gulf of Finland, where Lenin and Zinoviev spent several weeks sleeping in the hay loft of a party worker. One day they saw two men with guns approaching and assumed that they were the police coming to arrest them. The two leaders of the world revolution dived for cover into a haystack. 'The only thing left to do now', Lenin whispered to Zinoviev, 'is to die an honourable death.' The strangers, however, walked right past: it turned out that they were hunting for ducks.[55]

However, given the frenzied anti-Bolshevik atmosphere, it is not hard to see why Lenin should have been so concerned for his personal safety. This was a time of lynch law, and the tabloid press was full of cartoons showing Lenin on the scaffold. Some of the Bolshevik leaders, Kamenev in particular, wanted Lenin to give himself up and stand trial. They thought he could use his appearance in the courts to reject the treason charges and denounce the authorities. By fleeing abroad, they argued, he risked making the workers suspect that he must have had something to hide. Besides, there was a long tradition of socialists making propaganda from the dock: Trotsky had done it quite brilliantly in 1906; and Lenin's own brother had done it at his trial in 1887. But Lenin was not the sort of man to play the role of a revolutionary martyr: his life was much too important for that. As he saw it, there was no question of getting a fair trial (that, he said, was a 'constitutional illusion'), since the rule of law had been suspended and the state itself had been taken over by the 'counter-revolution'. 'It is not a question of "the courts", but of an episode in the civil war.' Underlying this was a fundamental shift in Lenin's thinking which was to have important consequences. Since the April Theses he had accepted the need to base the party's work on peaceful or political means. But in the wake of the July Days, when, as he saw it, the state had been taken over by 'the military dictatorship', he moved towards the idea of an armed uprising for the seizure of power.[56] Lenin's refusal to appear in the courts was in effect his own declaration of a civil war.

The Soviet leaders were equally fearful of a right-wing backlash and, although they denounced the July uprising and the part the Bolsheviks had played in it, they were also inclined to defend them against the punitive measures of the government. Gorky summed up the ambivalent views of the revolutionary intelligentsia in a letter to Ekaterina on 10 July:

> You will know from the newspapers about the atrocities that have taken place here. My own immediate impression of them is immensely hard to put into words. What has happened and is happening now is repulsively stupid, cowardly and loutish. But it is wrong to assume that everything can be blamed on 'the Bolsheviks' and these so-called German agents, who undoubtedly took no part in the events. The Kadets are to blame here for stirring up trouble, along with the usual philistines and, generally, the whole mass of Petersburg. I am not trying to defend 'the Bolsheviks' — they know themselves there is no justification for what they have done . . .
>
> The Bolshevism of the emotions, which played on the dark instincts of the masses, has mortally wounded itself — and that is good. But the Democracy, England, France and Germany, may see the rout of the Bolsheviks as the defeat of the whole Revolution, and that is desperately bad, for it will deflate the revolutionary mood in the West and endlessly prolong the war . . . I fear that Lenin has come to an awkward end. He of course is not too bad, but his closest comrades, it seems, are truly rogues and scoundrels. They have all been arrested. Now the bourgeois press is after *Novaia zhizn'*, and will probably get it closed down, And then the campaign will start against you and your SRs. The counter-revolution is no longer some idle intention, but a fact. The Kadets stand at its head, people used to intrigue and not ashamed to use such means of struggle.[57]

The Soviet Executive protested against the arrest of the Bolshevik leaders and dismissed the treason charges against them as Black Hundred slander designed to split the revolutionary democracy. The old traditions of socialist camaraderie — in which there were 'no enemies on the Left!' — died hard. Most of the Soviet leaders continued to view the Bolsheviks as 'comrades'. They agreed that the witch-hunt against them was in danger of leading to a right-wing backlash against all socialists in general. As *Novaia zhizn'* put it: 'Today they accuse the Bolsheviks; tomorrow they will cast suspicions on the Soviet; and then they will declare a Holy War Against the Revolution.'[58] The left-wing Mensheviks, many of whom still harboured hopes of reuniting their party with the Bolsheviks, were especially assiduous in their opposition to government repressions; and it was largely due to their efforts that the public trial and commission set up to examine the treason charges lost momentum and came to naught. It was this, more than anything else, that ensured the survival of the Bolsheviks. Because of the reluctance of the Soviet leaders to cut their ties with them, a prime opportunity had been missed to end the Leninist threat once and for all. Twelve months later, when many of these same Soviet leaders sat in Bolshevik jails, they would come to regret it.

The Soviet leaders, in choosing to close ranks with the Bolsheviks, had no doubt overreacted to the threat of a 'counter-revolution'. As in February, they had looked at reality through the distorting prism of history: the shadows of 1849 and 1906 had obscured their vision. It was partly the same fear of counter-revolution which also prevented them, as in February, from taking power themselves. This too would prove a fatal mistake — for only a Soviet government could have filled the power vacuum left by the collapse of the coalition. True, it might not have brought about peace, bread or land; nor could it have ended the spiral into chaos and violence in the country; but at least it would have denied the Bolsheviks the chance to rally mass support under the slogan of 'All Power to the Soviets!' During the July Days the streets had begged the Soviet leaders to take power. Yet the latter had calmly dismissed this as no more than Bolshevik demagogy. It did not occur to them that such calls might express the wishes of the rest of the democracy. After all, as its self-appointed leaders, wasn't it their task to decide that? 'I have been in the provinces and on the Front,' Tsereteli reassured the Soviet deputies on 4 July, 'and I am stating that the authority of the Provisional Government in the country is extremely great.'[59] Their rigid party dogma told the Mensheviks and the SRs that a socialist government could not be formed because the 'bourgeois stage of the revolution' had still not been completed. This higher logic drove these philosophers to the conclusion that a new coalition had to be patched together at all costs and that, if the Kadets still refused to join it, then a bloc would have to be formed with other bourgeois groups. 'The coalition is dead! Long live the coalition!'

The reformation of the coalition became inevitable with Kerensky's appointment as the new Prime Minister. He had returned to the capital on 6 July and, on his own insistence, had been met by a lavish guard of honour, with Cossacks and cavalry lining the streets from the Warsaw Station. This was to be the triumphant entry of a national hero, the man who was said to have saved the country from the Bolshevik menace by rallying loyal troops at the Front. On the next day Prince Lvov resigned and named Kerensky as his successor. For Lvov, it was a great relief. He had already decided to step down, when he had written to his parents on 3 July. He was tired of politics — the burdens of office had turned his hair grey — and he did not have the heart to carry out the repressions demanded in the wake of the July Days. 'The only way to save the country now', Lvov told his old friend T. I. Polner on 9 July, 'is to close down the Soviet and shoot at the people. I cannot do that. But Kerensky can.' Right until the end, the gentle Prince would not use coercion against 'the people'. His life-long faith in their 'goodness and wisdom', however mistaken that may now have seemed, would not allow him to do so. Four days later, he left the capital and retired to a monastery.[60]

Kerensky was hailed as the man to reunite the country and halt the drift towards civil war. He was the only major politician who had a base of popular support yet who was also broadly acceptable to the military leaders and the bourgeoisie. Tsereteli was the senior Soviet leader, to be sure, yet it was precisely this which ruled him out. For if the coalition was to be reformed, it would have to cut its ties with the Soviet programme, or else the Kadets would have nothing to do with it. Kerensky was the ideal figure to bring the coalition back together: as a member of both the Soviet and the Duma circles which had formed the Provisional Government he made a human bridge between the socialist and liberal camps. This placed him in a unique position — and the fate of Russia now seemed to depend upon this one young man. In itself this was a tragic situation, for it was without doubt much too heavy a burden for a man of Kerensky's tender years and rather modest talents.

Kerensky had always liked to see himself as a 'national leader', straddling Right and Left, and his rise to power merely fuelled this vanity. He began to cultivate the image of himself as a man of destiny, summoned by 'the people' to 'save Russia'. This was the high summer of the Kerensky cult. It was engineered with the help of his friends in the Petrograd literary intelligentsia — the Merezhkovskys, Filosofov, Stanislavsky and Nemirovich-Danchenko* — who all eulogized the young Prime Minister as 'the ideal citizen' and the 'embodiment of Russian Liberty'.[61] Success and adulation went to Kerensky's head. He began to strut around with comic self-importance, puffing up his puny chest and striking the pose of a Bonaparte. His offices were transferred to the Winter Palace, where he took over the opulent suite of Alexander III. He slept in the

---

* Dmitrii Merezhkovsky (1865–1941), poet, literary and religious philosopher; Zinaida Gippius (1869–1945), writer and essayist, married to Merezhkovsky; Dmitrii Filosofov (1872–1940), literary critic and co-inhabitant with the Merezhkovskys; Konstantin Stanislavsky (1863–1938), founder, along with Vladimir Nemirovich-Danchenko (1858–1943), of the Moscow Arts Theatre.

Tsar's enormous bed, and had a photo of himself taken sitting behind his swimming-pool-sized desk which he had distributed in postcard form for publicity. Nicholas II's cherished billiard table, which had been packed up for despatch to Tobolsk, was retained by Kerensky for his own amusement. He also kept on the old palace servants, and changed the guards outside his suite several times a day. As he came and left, the red flag on the palace roof was raised and lowered, just as it had been for the tsars. Was this the man who had called himself the 'hostage of democracy'?

The three-week interregnum between the fall of the First Coalition and the formation of the Second certainly saw Kerensky break his ties with the Soviet movement. As the power broker in the party talks, he was prepared to sacrifice most of the Soviet's basic demands — as expressed in the government's own declaration of 8 July — in the interests of persuading the Kadets to rejoin the coalition. On the insistence of the Kadets, he passed decrees imposing tough restrictions on public gatherings, restored the death penalty at the Front and agreed to roll back the influence of the soldiers' committees. The programme of the new coalition, finally formed on 25 July, was no longer to be based on the principles of the Soviet, as had been agreed in February. The nine socialist ministers, though they comprised a majority, entered the cabinet as private individuals rather than Soviet representatives, and thus, in a formal sense at least, were obliged to recognize the sole authority of the Provisional Government. All the socialist ministers, with the exception of Chernov, came from the right wings of their parties and stood much closer to the liberal Duma circles than the Soviet movement itself. Tsereteli, who as the undisputed leader of the Soviet could not accept this erosion of its influence, had no choice but to step aside. Already suffering from TB, he went into semi-retirement. His resignation marked the demise of the Soviet. On 18 July, on the same day that Kerensky's government moved into the Winter Palace, the Soviet was expelled from the Tauride Palace and transferred to the Smolny Institute, a school for the daughters of the nobility, on the outskirts of the capital. It was both a symbol of the Soviet's decline and of the elevation of Kerensky's government to a position where it stood, like its tsarist predecessors, above and apart from the people.

iii The Man on a White Horse

It was generally believed that Linde's own naive idealism had been to blame for his brutal murder. The young commissar had been warned on his arrival at the Front that the deserters were highly dangerous. For several weeks they had been living as bandits, spreading terror throughout the surrounding region of Lutsk, and everyone who knew them agreed that it would be wiser to deploy the Cossacks against their rebel camp. General Krasnov had brought up 500 cavalry-men from reserve and, although there were nearly ten times as many deserters, he was sure that the imposing sight of the Cossacks would be enough to disarm them. But Linde was adamant about the power of the revolutionary word. The Cossacks, he insisted, were a remnant of the tsarist past and, on principle, should not be used against the 'freest army in the world'. 'You see, General, I shall make them listen to sense. One has to know how to talk to the soldiers. It's all a question of psychology.'[62] There was no dissuading the young commissar from his foolish plan — he was carried away by his belief in the power of the revolutionary will — and so he was allowed to go to the camp to try to persuade the deserters to return to battle.

This was not the first time that Linde's overconfidence had got him into trouble. The hotheaded sergeant had twice led his soldiers on to the streets — once in February as a hero of the revolution and once again in the April demonstrations against Miliukov, when he had been condemned as a 'Bolshevik' adventurer attempting to carry out a bloody coup. As a punishment, the Soviet had sent him as a commissar to the Special Army on the Western Front: his skills of leadership of the soldiers were to be employed in the interests of the army command for the coming offensive. Linde took pleasure in his new assignment. The idea of persuading the demoralized soldiers to perform their patriotic duty was perfectly in tune with his own romantic self-image as a revolutionary orator. He quickly became something of a legend on account of his daring missions to those Bolshevized parts of the Front which, by the power of words alone, he seemed to restore to fighting order. Linde was something rare in 1917: a Russian revolutionary with a sense of duty to the nation and the state. He was in this sense a model commissar. 'It is not enough just to achieve freedom,' he explained to a friend on their way to Lutsk. 'Democracy is something that must be defended and fought for.' That was why he had been so determined to make a visit to the deserters' camp: to convince the soldiers of their patriotic duty to defend Russia now that it was free.

The convoy of cars, trucks and mounted Cossacks moved across empty countryside towards the forest, where the rebels had set up their armed camp in a clearing. It was a sunny August afternoon and the fields would normally have been filled with crops, but after three years of wartime neglect they were filled with weeds. Stopping at the edge of the forest, Linde walked on to the camp alone, while a group of officers followed some distance behind, and the mounted Cossacks rode on to surround the camp. The soldiers of the two mutinous regiments, the 443rd and the 444th of the 3rd Infantry Division, were sitting and lying around by their tents in the glade. As the officers approached, they began to stir, rising from the ground like some gigantic prehistoric animal, and prepared their rifles. Linde noticed two distinct groups — one scattered and amorphous containing the bulk of the troops, the other much smaller and more compact, which he realized from their menacing look contained the hardened core of Bolshevized troops. Jumping on to a pile of timber, he began to speak to the former. It was a stirring speech, full of democratic pathos. 'I, who brought the soldiers out to overthrow the tsarist government and to give you freedom, a freedom which is equalled by no other people in the world, demand that you now give me those who have been telling you not to obey the orders of the commanders.' As he spoke, the sound could be heard of German shells flying over the forest, and this added a dramatic effect to Linde's rhetorical fervour. He pointed in the direction of the enemy's guns and called on the soldiers to defend their Fatherland from them. But the soldiers had heard it all before, and years of wheedling propaganda had made them cynical. They had seen too much of the war to believe any more in fine-sounding phrases, especially from this soft-faced youth, with his tailored officer's tunic, his fine breeches and leather boots, and his foreign accent.

Aware that his words were having no effect, Linde began to shout at the men, calling them 'lazy swine' and 'bastards' who did not deserve their freedom. The deserters grew agitated, and several men from the Bolshevik group began to heckle Linde. They called him a German spy and said that his methods were worthy of the old regime. Watching the scene from a distance, General Krasnov could see that something terrible was about to happen, and he sent in a car to rescue the stranded commissar. But Linde was carried away by the power of his own words, intoxicated by his own heroic self-image, and refused to leave. The soldiers moved towards him — and only then did he try to escape. But it was too late. A burly soldier from the Bolshevik group stepped up and thrust the butt of his rifle into Linde's temple; a second shot him to the ground; and a whole crowd of wildly shrieking soldiers then threw themselves on to him, thrusting their bayonets into his body. Fearing for their own lives, Krasnov and the other officers now sought to retreat, but the soldiers, emboldened by their kill, ran after them through the forest, while the Cossacks struggled to restore order. One of the officers, Colonel Girshfeldt, was stripped naked, hanged upside down from a tree and brutally tortured before the mob shot him. Two other officers were also killed before the convoy made it out of the forest to safety.

Linde's body was brought back to Petrograd and given a hero's burial. The democratic press portrayed the 'fallen fighter of the people's cause' as a shining example of the patriotic revolutionary sentiment which the Russian army now so badly needed. Linde was not the first Soviet leader to be killed by the Bolshevized troops. There had been several similar murders during the previous weeks. Even Sokolov, the famous Soviet leader and author of Order Number One, the founding charter of soldiers' rights, had been beaten up and taken hostage by a mob of mutinous soldiers whom he had tried to persuade to return to battle. But Linde's brutal murder, coming as it did at the height of the summer crisis, was seen to be of particular significance. It symbolized the end of the idealistic hopes of the first revolutionary months — the ideal of a free state of citizens, who could be persuaded to fulfil their civic duties to Russia and the revolution. The death of Linde had finally confirmed that the time for persuasion had come to an end. The Russian people were not ready to be citizens, and Kerensky's notorious rebuke that the free Russian state would become 'a state of rebellious slaves' seemed to be vindicated by the growing chaos in the country at large. The Russian army was collapsing and in headlong retreat. On 21 August the Germans captured Riga, and it seemed, as Zinaida Gippius noted in her diary, that 'they could take Petrograd at any moment.' The Empire was falling apart, with self-appointed nationalist governments in Finland and the Ukraine declaring their own independence, while each day brought fresh newspaper reports of militant strikes by workers, of anarchy on the railways, of peasant attacks on the gentry's estates and of crime and disorder in the cities. The lesson of all this, which more and more people were beginning to draw, seemed to be that Russia could only be governed by force. Even Tsereteli was obliged to acknowledge that the summer crisis marked the end of the revolution's 'rose-coloured dreamy youth' and the start of a new and 'grim period' when coercive measures would have to be taken to halt the anarchic tide.[63]

The propertied classes led the call for order. 'The Fatherland in Danger!' became their rallying cry. Hysterical with fear, they gambled vast amounts of money, sold their properties cheaply, and lived wildly for the moment, as if it was the final summer of Russian civilization. Countess Speransky found that in Kiev, 'parties on the river, auto-picnics to châteaux in the neighbourhood, dinners and suppers with gypsy-bands and chorus, bridge and even tangoes, poker, and romances were the order of the day'. The funeral of the seven Cossacks killed by the Bolsheviks during the July Days became a stage for the propertied classes to indulge themselves in a patriotic show of emotion. The funeral began with a sung requiem in St Isaac's Cathedral, followed by a solemn procession through the streets of the capital with each of the seven caskets on a white gilded horse-drawn carriage flanked on either side by liveried Cossacks and incense-waving priests. It was not so much a demonstration of democratic solidarity as a mournful lament for the old regime. There was a growing atmosphere of counter-revolution. Newspapers called for the Bolsheviks to be hanged and the Soviet to be closed down. In the absence of the Bolshevik leaders, Chernov became the new 'German spy' and the *bête noire* of the Right. Bolshevik workers were beaten up by the Black Hundred mobs. Respectable middle-class citizens flocked to the various right-wing groups which blamed Russia's ills on the Jews and called for the restoration of the Tsar, or some other dictator, to save Russia from catastrophe.[64]

As the head of the Russian army, who was thus responsible for the failed offensive, Brusilov soon fell victim to this swing to the Right. He had never been liked at Stavka, where the reactionary generals were suspicious of his democratic leanings, and the failure of the offensive now gave them the chance to step up their campaign for his dismissal. Pressure mounted for his replacement by General Kornilov, a well-known advocate of a return to military discipline in the traditional style. The Kadets even made it a basic condition of their joining Kerensky's government. Although the new Premier had himself been the author of the policies pursued by Brusilov, he was quite prepared to ditch them both if that was the price of power. Brusilov sensed he was about to be dismissed when Kerensky called on him to convene a meeting of all the Front commanders at Stavka on 16 July. He made the mistake of sending only an aide-de-camp to meet Kerensky at the Mogilev station: the train had arrived early and he was still involved in strategic decisions affecting the Front. It was not official protocol for the Supreme Commander to meet the War Minister; but Kerensky, who behaved like a Tsar and had come to expect to be treated like one by his subordinates, flew into a rage and sent an adjutant to Brusilov with orders to come to the station in person. 'The whole thing', Brusilov remarked, 'was petty and ridiculous, particularly in view of the tragic situation at the Front which my Chief of Staff and I had been studying.' But Kerensky was a vain man, obsessed with the trappings of power, and this final breach of etiquette was enough to seal the fate of his Commander-in-Chief. On 18 July Brusilov was dismissed. Hurt by the obvious political motives behind his dismissal, he retired to Moscow for a long-earned rest with his wife, who had fallen ill.[65] It was not until the Bolsheviks came to power that he returned to the army, under quite extraordinary circumstances.

The man who replaced him, General Lavr Kornilov, had already achieved the status of a national saviour in right-wing circles. Small and agile, with a closely shaven head, Mongol moustache and little mousey eyes, Kornilov came from a family of Siberian Cossacks. His father was a smallholder and a soldier, who had risen to become a lower-ranking officer. His mother was allegedly a Buryat. This comparatively plebeian background set Kornilov apart from the rest of Russia's generals, most of whom came from the aristocracy. In the democratic atmosphere of 1917 it was the ideal background for a national military hero. Kornilov's early army career had been spent in Central Asia. He had mastered the Turkic languages of the region and had built up his own bodyguard of Tekke Turkomans, dressed in scarlet robes, who called him their 'Great Boyar'. Kornilov's appointment was hardly merited by his military record. By 1914, at the age of forty-four, he had risen no higher than a divisional commander in the Eighth Army. Brusilov, his army commander, remembered him as a brave and dashing soldier, well loved by his men, yet inclined to disobey orders. He claimed, not without justification, that Kornilov had cultivated his own 'cult of bravery'; and this cult was certainly behind his meteoric rise to fame. In 1915 Kornilov had been wounded and taken prisoner by the Austrians after refusing to obey Brusilov's command to withdraw his division from the Front. The following year he had escaped from prison and, disguised as an Austrian soldier, had made his way back to Russia by foot, where, instead of being court-martialled, he received a hero's welcome.[66]

It was at this time that Kornilov began to attract powerful political backers in the form of Rodzianko and Guchkov. They secured his appointment as Commander of the Petrograd Military District in March 1917. During the April riots Kornilov had threatened to bring his troops on to the street. The Soviet had opposed this and taken control of the garrison, forcing Kornilov to resign. Various right-wing groups were scandalized by the Soviet's interference in army matters, and looked to Kornilov as a champion of their cause. They were united by their opposition to the growing influence of the Soviet over the government, particularly foreign and military matters, in the wake of the April crisis. Miliukov, who had been forced to step down as Foreign Minister, began to flirt with counter-revolutionary ideas. 'It is obvious that the leaders of the Soviet are deliberately leading us to defeat and economic ruin,' he wrote to a friend at the end of June. 'Deep down we both know that the salvation of Russia is to be found in the restoration of the monarchy, and that what has happened during the past two months has clearly shown that the people were incapable of exercising freedom.'[67] Business leaders, increasingly opposed to the policies of Skobelev, the Menshevik Labour Minister, and the gentry, equally hostile to Chernov, the SR Minister of Agriculture, were also beginning to rally behind the anti-Soviet cause. The Officers' Union and the Union of Cossacks campaigned for the abolition of the soldiers' committees and the restoration of military discipline. And all these groups came together through the Republican Centre, a clandestine organization of bourgeois patriots, officers and war veterans formed in May above a bank on the Nevsky Prospekt.[68]

Kornilov was the servant, rather than the master, of these political interests. His own political mind was not very developed. A typical soldier, he was a man of very few words, and of even fewer ideas. 'The heart of a lion, the brains of a sheep' was Alexeev's verdict on him. During his time in prison he had read about the life of Napoleon, and he seemed to believe that he was destined to play a similar role in saving Russia.[69] All that was needed to stem the anarchic tide was a General on a White Horse.

Most of Kornilov's political pronouncements were written for him by Boris Savinkov, Kerensky's Deputy Minister of War. During his youth Savinkov had been a legendary figure — poet, 'freedom fighter' and gambler — in the SR terrorist movement. He was involved in the assassination of several government figures, including Plehve, at the turn of the century. Like many terrorists, however, he had a strong authoritarian streak: 'You are a Lenin, but of the other side,' Kerensky once told him. After a period of exile abroad, Savinkov returned to Russia in 1917 and attached himself to the movement against the Soviet (which he called the 'Council of Rats', Dogs' and Chickens' Deputies').[70] It was he who engineered Kornilov's appointment, first, on 8 July, as Commander of the South-Western Front, and then, ten days later, as Commander-in-Chief.

Other than a well-known advocate of military discipline, it is not clear that Kerensky knew what he was getting in his new Commander. Kerensky harboured Bonapartist ambitions of his own, of course, and no doubt hoped that in Kornilov he might find a strong man to support him. But did he realize that Kornilov and his allies had similar plans to use Kerensky? Brusilov later claimed that he had already been asked by Kerensky if he 'would support him in case it was considered desirable to consummate the Revolution by making him [Kerensky] Dictator'. Brusilov had refused, believing Kerensky to be too 'hysterical' for this role. Kerensky had then asked him if he was prepared to become Dictator himself. But once again Brusilov had refused, comparing the idea to 'building a dam when the river is in flood'. Brusilov's refusal was certainly a factor in Kerensky's decision to replace him with a Commander of more primitive instincts. To secure his appointment, Savinkov had wisely advised Kornilov to stress the role of the commissars as a check on the power of the soldiers' committees at the Stavka conference on 16 July. This was a much more moderate stance than that of Denikin and the other generals, who advocated the immediate abolition of the soldiers' committees, and it would enable Kerensky to appease the Right while salvaging the basic structure of his democratic reforms.[71] Thus Kornilov had given the impression that he might be prepared to fit in with Kerensky's plans.

Yet immediately after his appointment Kornilov began to dictate his own terms to Kerensky. During his brief command of the South-Western Front he had managed to force him to restore the death penalty at the Front (Kornilov had already been practising it on his own authority by ordering all deserters to be shot). Now, as a condition for assuming the Supreme Command, he demanded the extension of the death penalty to the rear, while he, as the head of the army, would consider himself responsible only to his 'conscience and to the nation as a whole'. This was, in effect, a challenge to the authority of the Provisional Government, which Kornilov clearly believed was a captive of the Soviet; and although under pressure from Kerensky he was eventually forced to withdraw this ultimatum, the thrust of his intentions remained clear. During the following days he presented Kerensky with a series of reforms drawn up by Savinkov. The first of these were strictly in the military field: an end to the power of the soldiers' committees; the banning of soldiers' meetings at the Front; and the disbanding of revolutionary regiments. But after 3 August the scope of the reforms was broadened dramatically to include the imposition of martial law throughout the country; the restoration of the death penalty for civilians; the militarization of the railways and the defence industries with a ban on strikes and workers' meetings, under penalty of capital punishment; and compulsory output quotas, with those who failed to meet them instantly sacked.[72] It was, in effect, a demand for the establishment of a military dictatorship.

One of the most enduring myths of the Russian Revolution is the notion that Kornilov was planning a *coup d'état* against the Provisional Government. This was Kerensky's version of events. After his downfall he spent the rest of his long and frustrated life in exile trying to prove it in his voluminous and mendacious memoirs. Soviet historians also pedalled the story because it endorsed Lenin's view that after July the 'military dictatorship' was engaged in a naked struggle for power. But the evidence suggests that Kornilov, far from plotting the overthrow of the Provisional Government, had in fact intended to save it. By pressurizing Kerensky to pass his reforms, he sought to rescue the government from the influence of the Soviet and thus 'save Russia', as he saw it, from the impending catastrophe. Kornilov, in other words, believed that the dictatorship would be 'legitimate' in the sense that Kerensky would support it. It was only when Kerensky began to have his own doubts, on the grounds that the General's plans would undermine his own position, that the 'coup plot' was uncovered by the Prime Minister. Kerensky was determined to play the part of a Bonaparte himself and feared that Kornilov would be a rival. It was, if you like, a question of two men and only one white horse.

None of which is to deny that many of Kornilov's supporters were urging him to do away with the Provisional Government altogether. The Union of Officers, for example, laid plans for a military *coup d'état*, while a 'conference of public men' in mid-August, made up mostly of Kadets and right-wing businessmen, clearly encouraged Kornilov in that direction. At the centre of these rightist circles was Vasilii Zavoiko, a rather shady figure — property speculator, industrial financier, journalist and political intriguer — who, according to General Martynov, acted as Kornilov's 'personal guide, one might even say his mentor, on all state matters'. Zavoiko's plans for a *coup d'état* were so well known that even Whitehall had heard of them: as early as 8 August the Foreign Ministry in London told Buchanan, its Ambassador in Petrograd, that according to its military sources, Zavoiko was plotting the overthrow of the Provisional Government. Nor is it to deny that Kornilov himself had his own ambitions in the political field — the cult of Kornilov, which he helped to generate, was a clear manifestation of this — and he must have been tempted by the constant urgings of his supporters, like Zavoiko, to exploit his enormous popularity in order to install himself as a dictator. The Commander-in-Chief despised Kerensky as 'weak and womanly', and saw his whole administration as hopelessly dependent on the Soviets. Stepun probably summed it up when he described the clash between Kornilov and Kerensky as a clash between two entirely different worlds — the world of the officer corps and the world of the intelligentsia — neither of which could understand the other.[73]

Kornilov's mistrust of the Provisional Government could only have been increased by Kerensky's vacillation over the adoption of his reforms. On 10 August Kornilov turned up uninvited at the Winter Palace with his own personal bodyguard, equipped with two machine-guns, to persuade Kerensky to adopt his proposals. Kornilov was not allowed to address the whole cabinet, but only the inner 'triumvirate' of Kerensky, Tereshchenko and Nekrasov, who warned him not to expect a quick enactment of his reforms, whereupon he and Kerensky became embroiled in a shouting match, with each accusing the other of leading the country to ruin. Over dinner that evening Kornilov told Rodzianko that if Kerensky refused to pass his reforms he would lead the army against him. On the following day he did indeed instruct III Cavalry Corps, including the notorious Savage Division (so named because it was made up of tribal natives from the Caucasus), to move to the region around Velikie Luki, from where it could be despatched to the capital. It was not quite clear whether Krymov's troops were intended to protect the Provisional Government against a possible Bolshevik revolt once it passed Kornilov's reforms, or whether they were meant to threaten it with a military coup should it decide not to pass them after all. The answer is probably both. Kornilov told General Lukomsky that he had 'no intention of going against the Provisional Government' and hoped to 'succeed at the last moment in reaching an agreement with it', but that if he failed to do so 'it might be necessary to strike a blow at the Bolsheviks without their approval'.[74] This was not a confession of his intention to overthrow the government; but it was a threat to rescue it from the Left, even if need be against Kerensky's will.

Yet by the time of Savinkov's visit to Stavka, on 22–4 August, Kornilov was convinced that this would not be necessary. The Deputy War Minister had assured him that Kerensky was about to satisfy his demands within 'the next few days'. He expected that this would lead to the reformation of the Provisional Government as a collective dictatorship — a Council for National Defence, as Kornilov liked to call it — headed by Kerensky himself and including Savinkov, Kornilov and various 'public men' from patriotic circles. Fearing a Bolshevik revolt — which the Soviet forces might join — against the imposition of martial law, Savinkov also asked Kornilov to move III Cavalry Corps from Velikie Luki to Petrograd itself. There were rumours of a Bolshevik coup planned for the end of August and it was agreed that 'merciless' action should be taken against it. On 25 August Kornilov ordered Krymov's troops to occupy the capital, disperse the Soviet and disarm the garrison in the event of a Bolshevik uprising. He thought he was acting on Kerensky's instructions to protect the Provisional Government, not to overthrow it.

But Kerensky was still in two minds. His own political strategy since February had been based on the idea of straddling Right and Left: it was this that had made him the central figure of the coalition and brought him to the verge of his own dictatorship. But the summer crisis and the growing polarization between Right and Left made this increasingly difficult: the political centre, upon which Kerensky aimed to stand, was fast disappearing. The Soviet became distrustful of Kerensky's ability — and indeed his willingness — to defend the achievements of the revolution against the 'counter-revolution'; while the Right reproached him for not being firm enough against the Bolsheviks. Kerensky was unable to decide which way he should turn and, afraid of alienating either side, vacillated hopelessly.

Kornilov's reform proposals forced him to decide between Right and Left. It was a tortuous decision for him. On the one hand, if he refused to go along with Kornilov, the Kadets were likely to leave his fragile coalition. There was also the danger of a military coup, which the Men of February, like Kerensky, were always inclined to overestimate, for throughout their lifetime the army had been against the revolution. On the other hand, if he agreed to pass Kornilov's reforms, he would risk a complete break with the Left and lose his claim to be a 'hostage of the democracy'. The restoration of the death penalty had already seriously tarnished his revolutionary credentials: it was such an emotive issue. The Soviet was fiercely campaigning against Kornilov's proposals and, unlike July, might just endorse a Bolshevik uprising if these proposals were enacted. Besides, Kerensky was doubtful that martial law would even prove effective. Where were the forces to carry out such a plan? How many officers had the courage to execute mutinous soldiers? Who would enforce the militarization of the railways and the factories, shooting workers who dared to go on strike? The whole idea seemed quite impracticable.

In a last desperate bid to rally the nation behind him Kerensky summoned a State Conference in Moscow. It was held in the Bolshoi Theatre on 12–14 August. Kerensky hoped that the conference would reconcile Left and Right and, in an effort to strengthen the political centre, upon which he depended, he assigned a large number of seats to the moderate delegates from the zemstvos and co-operatives. Sergei Semenov attended the conference as a delegate of the latter from Volokolamsk. Kerensky's heart must have sunk, however, at the sight of the opening session. The polarization of Russia was exactly mirrored in the seating arrangements in the auditorium: on the right side of the stalls sat the middle-class parties, the bankers, industrialists and Duma representatives in their frock-coats and starched collars; while on the left, facing them as if in battle, were the Soviet delegates in their workers' tunics and soldiers' uniforms. The scene was reminiscent of the opening of the Duma in 1906; the two Russias had not moved any closer in the intervening years. The Bolsheviks had decided to boycott the conference and called a city-wide strike. The trams did not run and restaurants and cafés were closed, including the theatre's own buffet, so the conference delegates had to serve their own refreshments.

Kerensky had wanted to occupy centre-stage at the conference; but, to his fury, Kornilov stole the show. The General made a triumphant entry into Moscow during the middle of the conference. Middle-class ladies pelted him with flowers at the Alexandrovsky Station. Countess Morozova fell on her knees before him, while the Kadet, Rodichev, called on him to 'Save Russia and a thankful people will crown you.' The Man on a White Horse had arrived. He was carried from the station on the shoulders of some officers and cheered in the street outside by a crowd of right-wing patriots. Seated in an open car, at the head of a motorcade that any twentieth-century dictator would have envied, he then made a pilgrimage to the sacred Iversky shrine, where the tsars had usually prayed on their visits to Moscow. On the following day he entered the conference to a standing ovation from the Right, while the Left sat in stony silence. His speech was a poor one — words were not Kornilov's strength — but it did not seem to matter: it was what he stood for, not what he said, that made him the patriots' hero; and with all his flowery eloquence there was nothing Kerensky could do to stop himself from being eclipsed. His own last speech with which the conference closed went on far too long. The Prime Minister rambled incoherently and seemed to lose his way. It was symbolic of his loosening grip on the country at large, and even Stepun, a loyal supporter, remarked that 'at the very end of his speech one could hear not only the agony of his power, but also of his personality'. It was an embarrassing scene and the audience began to mutter. At one point Kerensky halted for breath and the delegates, as if sensing that the time had come to put him out of his misery, burst into applause and rose from their seats. The conference was over. Kerensky fainted into his chair. He had not finished his sentence.[75]

The Moscow Conference marked Kerensky's moral downfall: the two months between it and the Bolshevik seizure of power were really no more than a long death agony of the Provisional Government. This was the moment when the democratic intelligentsia, which had done so much to create the Cult of Kerensky, finally fell *out* of love with him. 'Kerensky', Gippius wrote in her diary on 14 August, 'is a railway car that has come off the tracks. He wobbles and sways painfully and without the slightest conviction. He is a man near the end;

and it looks like his end will be without honour.' Kerensky was fully aware of his own demise. 'I am a sick man,' he told Savinkov three days later. 'No, not quite. I have died, and am no more. At the Conference I died.'[76] It seemed only a question of time before he succumbed to Kornilov. Under growing pressure he promised Savinkov to pass his reforms, aware that they would reduce him to no more than a figurehead to provide legitimation for the military dictatorship.

But then, suddenly, Kerensky found an unexpected way to save the situation. It came in the form of an intervention by V. N. Lvov, an Octobrist deputy in the Fourth Duma and more recently the Procurator of the Holy Synod, who took it upon himself to act as a mediator between Kerensky and Kornilov. Lvov was one of those numerous characters in Russian history who seem to have escaped from a novel by Gogol or Dostoevsky. A nobleman of no particular talent or profession, he was convinced of his calling to greatness, yet ended up in the 1920s as a pauper and a madman living on the streets of Paris. After his dismissal from the Holy Synod in July, he had fallen in with the right-wing circles urging Kornilov to assume dictatorial powers. It was in this capacity that he approached Kerensky on 22 August and offered to consult, on his behalf, with Kornilov in the hope of smoothing a path towards the creation of a 'strong government'. Kerensky was frequently visited by such self-appointed 'saviours' of the country, and generally gave them little attention. But this one was different. Lvov had warned him that the General Staff was plotting to kill him. Kerensky had of late been much preoccupied with this potential threat. He had even ordered the guards outside his quarters to be changed every hour. Kerensky later claimed that he had not instructed Lvov to negotiate with Kornilov; but this was not Lvov's impression; and it does seem likely that, if only out of fear for his own life, he did instruct him to find out what Kornilov was on about. It is also possible that Kerensky was already planning to use Lvov for what was about to happen.

Lvov arrived in Mogilev on 24 August and presented himself to Kornilov as an emissary from the Premier. Kornilov did not ask for his credentials and this was to prove a fatal mistake (he later said that he had presumed Lvov to be 'an honourable man'). Lvov claimed that he had been instructed to find out the General's views on how to strengthen the government and, on his own initiative, offered three proposals: the assumption of dictatorial powers by Kerensky; a Directory, or collective dictatorship, with Kornilov as a member; or Kornilov's own dictatorship, with Kerensky and Savinkov holding ministerial portfolios. Taking this to mean that Kerensky was offering him power, Kornilov said he preferred the third of these options, but would readily subordinate himself to Kerensky if that was seen to be for the best. He told Lvov to invite Kerensky to come to Mogilev to discuss this issue and because he said he feared for his life in the event of a Bolshevik coup in Petrograd. As soon as the interview was finished, Lvov departed for the capital. Kornilov was clearly under the impression that he had begun a process of negotiation with Kerensky to reform the Provisional Government as a dictatorship.

On the following day, 26 August, Lvov met Kerensky again in the Winter Palace. He claimed that Kornilov was now *demanding* dictatorial powers for himself (he had of course done nothing of the sort) and, on Kerensky's request, listed the three points of his 'ultimatum': the imposition of martial law in Petrograd; the transfer of all civil authority to the Commander-in-Chief; and the resignation of all the ministers, including Kerensky himself, pending the formation of a new cabinet by Kornilov. Kerensky always claimed that when he saw these demands everything instantly became clear: Kornilov was planning a military coup. In fact nothing was clear. For one thing, it might have been asked why Kornilov had chosen to deliver his list of demands through such a nonentity as Lvov. For another, it might have been sensible to check with Kornilov if he really was demanding to be made Dictator. But Kerensky was not concerned with such details. On the contrary, he had suddenly realized — and this is no doubt what he really meant by his lightning-flash of revelation — that as long as everything was kept vague he might succeed in exposing Kornilov as a traitor plotting against the Provisional Government. His own political fortunes would thus be revived as the revolution rallied behind him to defeat his rival.

In order to obtain proof of the 'conspiracy', Kerensky agreed to meet Lvov at the War Ministry later that evening in order to communicate directly with Kornilov through the Hughes Apparatus (a sort of primitive telex machine). Lvov failed to turn up on time, so Kerensky began his own conversation with Kornilov, during which he impersonated the absent Lvov. He asked him to confirm what Lvov had said to him (Kerensky) — without specifying what that was — and repeated the request on Lvov's behalf. Kornilov did so — without knowing what he was being asked to confirm — and urged Kerensky to go to Mogilev at once. Kornilov must have believed that this was simply a prelude to negotiations for the reformation of the government. He had no idea that what he was saying would soon be used by Kerensky to charge him with treason. Later that evening he discussed the situation with General Lukomsky and agreed that Kerensky and Savinkov would have to be included in the cabinet. He also sent out telegrams to various public figures inviting them to come to Mogilev and take part in these negotiations.[77] Hardly the actions of a would-be dictator.

Armed with the transcripts from the Hughes Apparatus and Kornilov's 'demands', as listed by Lvov, Kerensky called a cabinet meeting for midnight, at which he presented the 'counter-revolutionary conspiracy' as an established fact and demanded 'full authority' to deal with the emergency. No doubt he hoped to pose as the champion of free Russia, to declare the revolution in danger and rally the nation behind himself in the struggle against Kornilov. Nekrasov recalled that Kerensky had said: 'I will not give them the revolution' — as if it had been his to give. Savinkov, among others, realized that a misunderstanding had occurred and urged Kerensky to communicate once again with Kornilov to ask him if he confirmed that he had made the three specific 'demands' outlined by Lvov. But Kerensky refused, and the rest of the ministers agreed with him that it was too late for any reconciliation. They resigned *en masse*, thus effectively making Kerensky Dictator — the very thing he had charged Kornilov with plotting to become. With the cabinet adjourned he sent a telegram to Kornilov dismissing him on his own authority; and then, at 4 a.m. on 27th, retired to his suite in the Winter Palace. But Russia's new 'Tsar' was too excited to sleep and, according to Lvov, who had been placed under guard in the adjoining room, paced up and down singing operatic arias.[78]

When Kornilov received the telegram informing him of his dismissal he concluded that Kerensky had already been taken prisoner by the Bolsheviks. Only the full cabinet had the legal authority to dismiss the Commander-in-Chief, whereas the telegram had been signed simply 'Kerensky'. It also made no sense in the light of the agreement he falsely believed he had just concluded over the Hughes Apparatus. Kornilov refused to resign, and ordered Krymov's troops to advance to the capital and place it under martial law. Although this order would later be cited as proof of Kornilov's guilt, it is clear that he gave it on the understanding — and in line with Savinkov's instructions — that Krymov's troops were to rescue the Provisional Government from the Bolsheviks. Various requests were made for clarification of this point through direct communications with Kornilov, and had this been done then the whole crisis might well have been averted. But Kerensky was determined to condemn Kornilov without trial. He was beside himself with excitement and stormed around the palace claiming that Russia was on his side. On Kerensky's orders, a special daytime edition of the press appeared condemning Kornilov as a traitor against the revolution. Kornilov responded with his own appeal to all the Front commanders denouncing the incident with Lvov as a 'grand provocation' by a government that had manifestly fallen under the control of the Bolsheviks and the German General Staff. He, General Kornilov, 'the son of a Cossack', would 'save Russia'.[79]

This at last was mutiny: having been denounced as a rebel, Kornilov chose to rebel. Several senior generals declared their support for him. Now Kerensky had a real 'counter-revolution' to deal with. On 29 August he crowned himself the new Commander-in-Chief, with Alexeev as his Chief of Staff, despite the latter's low opinion of Kerensky ('a nicompoop, buffoon and charlatan').[80] He cabled Krymov with orders to halt the advance of his troops, some of which had already reached the southern suburbs of the capital. The Soviet Executive, which had been divided over whether to support the Revolutionary Dictator, swung around to his defence on news of Krymov's advance. It called on its supporters to arm themselves for a struggle against the 'counter-revolution' and transformed Smolny into a command centre directing operations. It was back to the atmosphere of the Tauride Palace during the February Days, when tired soldiers lay around the Soviet building waiting for the generals to attack.

A special Committee for Struggle Against the Counter-Revolution was set up by the Soviet, with three representatives from each of the Menshevik, SR and Bolshevik Parties, to mobilize forces for the defence of the capital. This marked the political rehabilitation of the Bolsheviks after the July Days — and several prominent Bolshevik leaders, including Trotsky, were released from prison shortly afterwards. The Committee for Struggle represented a united front of the whole Soviet movement. But it was effectively dependent on the military organization of the Bolsheviks, without which, in the words of Sukhanov, it 'could only have passed the time with appeals and idle speeches by orators who had lost their authority'. Only the Bolsheviks had the ability to mobilize and arm the mass of the workers and soldiers, and they now worked in close collaboration with their rivals in the Soviets. Throughout the northern industrial regions *ad hoc* revolutionary committees were formed in line with the Committee for Struggle. Some of them called themselves 'Committees of Public Safety' in emulation of the Jacobins. There was no real leadership of this spontaneous movement. Garrisons placed themselves on alert, and despatched detachments of soldiers to 'defend the revolution'. The Kronstadt sailors, who had last come to Petrograd during the July Days to overthrow the Provisional Government, arrived once again — this time to defend it. The Red Guards and trade unions organized the defence of the factories. Vikzhel, the Railwaymen's Union, set up a bureau to combat Krymov's troops and managed to hold up their progress towards Petrograd by withholding engines and obstructing the line.[81]

Meanwhile, Krymov's troops were harangued by Soviet agitators. They had no desire to overthrow the Provisional Government — Kornilov had instructed them to defend it against the Bolsheviks — and once they were told that it was not in danger from the Left, they soon laid down their arms. Contrary to the Soviet myth, no actual fighting took place in the defeat of Kornilov. What would have been the point? Both sides had gone to defend the Provisional Government, and as soon as this was established they began to fraternize. The Savage Division was persuaded not to fight by a delegation of their own countrymen, the Caucasian Muslims, who happened to be at a Soviet congress in Petrograd at the time. The cavalrymen hoisted a red flag inscribed with 'Land and Freedom', arrested their commanders, and sent a delegation to Petrograd with a pledge of loyalty to the government. The train of the 1st Don Cossack

Division, with which Krymov and his staff were travelling, was halted by railway workers at Luga, where deputies from the Soviet harangued them with propaganda through the carriage windows. There was nothing Krymov could do — the Cossacks were joining the Soviet side in droves. On 30 August he agreed to travel to Petrograd with a government representative and, on the following day, met Kerensky. Krymov tried to explain that he had brought his troops to defend the government. But Kerensky would have none of this, and ordered him to be tried by the military courts. Krymov left in despair and went to a friend's apartment, where he was heard to say: 'The last card for saving the Fatherland has been beaten — life is no longer worth living.' Retiring to a private room, he wrote a short note to Kornilov, and shot himself through the heart.[82]

* * *

Kornilov's revolt was over. On the following day, I September, Alexeev took control at Stavka, and Kornilov himself was placed under house arrest, and then transferred to the Bykhov Monastery, near Mogilev, where he was imprisoned with thirty other officers suspected of having been involved in the 'counter-revolutionary conspiracy'. But if Kerensky had hoped to bolster his own authority by defeating Kornilov, then he achieved precisely the reverse. The Kornilov Affair, as it came to be known, turned out to be a nail in his own coffin. It merely accelerated the social and political polarization which had been eroding the base of the Provisional Government since the early summer, and in this sense brought the revolution closer to its October dénouement.

On the one hand, Kerensky had fatally spoiled his relations with the Right, which by and large remained faithful to Kornilov and condemned Kerensky for betraying his cause. Kornilov became a political martyr for all those who blamed Kerensky's regime for the growing chaos in the country at large. In this respect, the Kornilov Affair had its greatest political impact after it was over. The word 'Kornilovite' began to enter the political vocabulary as an out-and-out opponent of the *Kerenshchina* (Kerensky's rule). The Bykhov Monastery was evidently run by sympathizers with the Kornilov movement, since prison conditions there were extremely relaxed. 'We had the impression that everyone was rather embarrassed at having to act as our "jailors",' Anton Denikin recalled. Kornilov was allowed to retain his faithful Turkoman bodyguards; he issued 'military orders' to the rest of the prison; the officers' families visited twice a day (Denikin's fiancée practically lived in the jail); and there were even secret links with the General Staff, where the Kornilov movement continued to enjoy much support.[83] The Bykhov prisoners were later to become the founding nucleus — and Kornilov and Denikin the leaders — of the Volunteer Army, the major White force of the civil war. It was in Bykhov that the draft programme of the Volunteer Army was written. It was just as much a rejection of Kerensky as it was of the Bolsheviks. Indeed, during the Bolshevik seizure of power none of these elements came to defend the Provisional Government.

Kerensky's standing on the Left, meanwhile, had been equally weakened. The mass of soldiers and workers who had rallied to the defence of the Provisional Government during the Kornilov crisis nevertheless suspected that Kerensky had himself somehow been involved in the Kornilov movement. Many saw the whole affair as a personal feud between the two would-be Napoleons (and in this they were not far wrong). But others believed that Kerensky had been in league with Kornilov, or else had tried to implement his own 'counter-revolutionary' plans through him. This conviction was strengthened by Kerensky's failure to pursue a more democratic course once the crisis was over. For one thing, there was no real enquiry into the affair, and this merely fuelled the popular suspicion that Kerensky had something to hide. His continued support for a coalition with the Kadets (who had clearly been associated with the Kornilov movement) and his appointment of Alexeev (who was widely suspected of having sympathized with it) were seen as added reasons to suspect Kerensky's intentions. The phantom nature of this 'counter-revolution' only made it seem more powerful, a hidden force behind the government, not unlike the shadow of treason which hung over the tsarist regime in 1916.

The mass of the soldiers suspected their officers of having supported Kornilov, and for this reason a sharp deterioration in army discipline resulted. Hundreds of officers were arrested by their men — some of them were executed or brutally killed — for their alleged involvement in the 'counter-revolution'. The soldiers' assemblies passed resolutions for Soviet power and peace. There was a growing consciousness among the rank-and-file troops, which the Kornilov crisis had helped to create, that peace would not be obtained until the nature of the state itself had been changed. They were no longer prepared to trust in the promises of their 'democratic' leaders, and were starting to demand the right to make decisions for themselves. This was reflected in the growing pressure from below for the army congresses to debate the questions of power and peace. But for vast numbers of soldiers there was also a simpler solution — to vote with their feet by deserting the army. In the weeks following the Kornilov crisis the rate of desertion sharply increased, with tens of thousands leaving their units every day. Most of these deserters were peasants, eager to return to their villages, where the harvest season was now in full swing. They often led the attack on the manors and helped to establish local Soviet power; so these weeks also witnessed a sudden upturn in the agrarian movement. Senior commanders began to acknowledge that with such rates of desertion it was impossible to continue the war. The Kornilov movement, which had aimed to save the army, thus ended up by destroying it altogether.

In the big industrial cities there was a similar process of radicalization in the wake of the Kornilov crisis. The Bolsheviks were the principal beneficiaries of this, winning their first majority in the Petrograd Soviet on 31 August. Without the Kornilov movement, they might never have come to power at all. On 4 September Trotsky was finally released from prison, along with two other Bolshevik leaders destined to play a prominent part in the seizure of power, Vladimir Antonov-Ovseenko and P. E. Dybenko. The Bolshevik Military Organization, which had been forced underground after the July Days, could now expand its subversive activities under the guise of its leading role in the Committee for Struggle. Indeed, the Military Revolutionary Committee, which led the Bolshevik seizure of power, was partly modelled on the latter. The Red Guards and the Kronstadt sailors, who were to be the foot-soldiers in October, also emerged strengthened from the struggle against Kornilov. The whole affair was a dress rehearsal for the seizure of power, with the workers, in particular, trained in the art of handling guns. Some 40,000 were armed in the Kornilov crisis, and most of them no doubt retained their weapons after it was over. As Trotsky put it, 'the army that rose against Kornilov was the army-to-be of the October revolution'.[84]

Kerensky's victory over Kornilov was also his own political defeat. He had won dictatorial powers but lost all real authority. 'The prestige of Kerensky and the Provisional Government', wrote Kerensky's wife, 'was completely destroyed by the Kornilov Affair; and he was left almost without supporters.'[85] The five-man Directory, which was established on 1 September and served as a fragile structure for Kerensky's own dictatorship until the power question was resolved at the Democratic Conference in mid-September, was made up of unknown mediocrities.* The only achievement of this *opera buffa* government was to declare Russia a 'republic', though this was formally the prerogative of the Constituent Assembly. It was typical of a government that existed on paper alone: nobody paid any attention to it. Beyond the corridors of the Winter Palace, all Kerensky's decrees were ignored. There was a vacuum of power; and it was now only a question of who would dare to fill it.

iv Hamlets of Democratic Socialism

'On s'engage et puis on voit.' Lenin was fond of citing Napoleon's maxim. It perfectly expressed his own revolutionary philosophy: that revolutions did not make themselves, they had to be made by their leaders. History has long ceased to be the record of the achievements of extraordinary men: we are all social

---

* The 'Directors', apart from Kerensky, were: Tereshchenko (Foreign Affairs); General Verkhovsky (War); Admiral Verderevsky (Marine); and A. M. Nikitin (Posts and Telegraphs).

historians now. Yet the course of history is full of unexpected turns that can only be explained by the actions of great leaders. This is particularly so in the case of revolutions, when the tide of events can be so easily turned. The October seizure of power is a good example: few historical events in the modern era better illustrate the decisive effect of an individual on the course of history. Without Lenin's intervention it would probably never have happened at all — and the history of the twentieth century would have been very different.

Kerensky's role stands out in stark contrast; he was quite unable to control events. Those who were close to him during these final weeks testify to his growing isolation, his weakness of will, his paralytic fear of the Left, and his fatal indecision in taking suitable measures against it. The constant tension and the sleepless nights of 1917 had taken a heavy toll on him — and he now lived with the help of morphine and cocaine. Ekaterina Breshko-Breshkovskaya, the veteran SR and 'grandmother of the revolution', had moved in with Kerensky in the Winter Palace (gossipers called her his 'nanny'). At the end of July the Bolshevik leaders convened in Petrograd for their Sixth Party Conference. She begged Kerensky to arrest them; but he refused, giving the frail excuse that he did not even know where they were meeting. According to David Soskice, Kerensky's private secretary, the grey-haired woman then:

> bowed to the ground before Kerensky and repeated several times in solemn imploring tones: 'I beg thee, Alexander Fedorovich, suppress the Conference, suppress the Bolsheviks. I beg thee to do this, or else they will bring ruin on our country and the revolution.' It was a dramatic scene. To see the grandmother of the Russian Revolution who had passed thirty-eight years of her life in prison and in Siberia in her struggle for liberty, to see that highly cultured and noble woman bowing to the ground in the ancient orthodox manner before the young Kerensky . . . was a thing I shall never forget. I looked at Kerensky. His pale face grew still whiter. His eyes reflected the terrible struggle that was proceeding within him. He was silent for long, and at last he said in a low voice: 'How can I do it?' 'Do it, A.F., I beseech thee', and again Babushka bowed to the ground. Kerensky could stand it no longer. He sprang to his feet and seized the telephone. 'I must learn first where the Conference meets and consult Avksentiev', and rang up the Ministry of the Interior. But Avksentiev was not in his office and the matter had to be adjourned for the time. I fancy to Kerensky's great relief.[86]

The conference went ahead without arrests — and three months later the Bolsheviks came to power.

One of the many remarkable facts about the Bolshevik seizure of power was that it had been expected for so long without anyone taking the measures needed to prevent it: such was the paralysis of the Provisional Government. During the evening of 25 October, as the ministers of the Provisional Government sat in the Winter Palace waiting for the end, many of them were tempted to curse Kerensky for having failed to destroy the Bolshevik Party after the July Days. The legal suppressions against them had certainly failed to reverse their growing influence. But the truth was that the government had neither the means nor the authority to make repressions work against a movement that was starting to grow deep roots in the mass-based organizations.

The social polarization of the summer gave the Bolsheviks their first real mass following as a party which based its main appeal on the plebeian rejection of all superordinate authority. The Kornilov crisis was the critical turning point, for it seemed to confirm their message that neither peace nor radical social change could be obtained through the politics of compromise with the bourgeoisie. The larger factories in the major cities, where the workers' sense of class solidarity was most developed, were the first to go over in large numbers to the Bolsheviks. By the end of May, the party had already gained control of the Central Bureau of the Factory Committees and, although the Menshevik trade unionists remained in the ascendancy until 1918, it also began to get its resolutions passed at important trade union assemblies. Bolshevik activists in the factories tended to be younger, more working class and much more militant than their Menshevik or SR rivals. This made them attractive to those groups of workers — both among the skilled and the unskilled — who were becoming increasingly prepared to engage in violent strikes, not just for better pay and working conditions but also for the control of the factory environment itself. As their network of party cells at the factory level grew, the Bolsheviks began to build up their membership among the working class, and as a result their finances grew through the new members' contributions. By the Sixth Party Conference at the end of July there were probably 200,000 Bolshevik members, rising to perhaps 350,000 on the eve of October, and the vast majority of these were blue-collar workers.[87]

The Bolsheviks made dramatic gains in the city Duma elections of August and September. In Petrograd they increased their share of the popular vote from 20 per cent in May to 33 per cent on 20 August. In Moscow, where the Bolsheviks had polled a mere 11 per cent in June, they swept to victory on 24 September with 51 per cent of the vote, while the SR vote collapsed from 56 per cent to 14 per cent, and the Mensheviks from 12 per cent to 4 per cent. The Kadets, on the other hand, as the only party representing the interests of the bourgeoisie, increased their share of the vote from 17 per cent to 31 per cent. These elections highlighted the political polarization of the country at large — Dan called them the 'civil war returns' — as voters swung to the two

extremes parties with an overt class appeal. The apathy of the uncommitted —
particularly those such as petty clerks, traders and shop assistants, who had no
obvious class allegiance or party to vote for — had much to do with the
Bolshevik success. Six months of fruitless politics and incessant cabinet crises
had not encouraged them to place much faith in the ballot box. The democratic
parties ran low-key campaigns and huge numbers of voters stayed away from
the polling stations. In the Petrograd elections the turn-out was down by a third
since May, while in the Moscow elections it was down by nearly half.[88] This of
course played into the hands of the Bolsheviks, who were far more hungry —
and much better organized — to win power than any other party. How many
Communist take-overs have been based on the apathy of the voters in a
democracy?

A similar swing to the Bolsheviks took place in the Soviets. Here too
grass-roots apathy deprived the Mensheviks and the SRs of their early ascendancy.
They had only themselves to blame. To begin with, the Soviets had been open
and democratic organs, where important decisions were made by the elected
assembly. This made their proceedings somewhat chaotic, but it also gave them
a sense of excitement and popular creativity. As the Soviet leaders became
involved in the responsibilities of government they began to organize the work
of the Soviets along bureaucratic lines, and this alienated the mass of the workers
from them. The assemblies began to decline in frequency and attendance as the
initiative switched to the executives and their quasi-governmental commissions,
whose members were increasingly nominated by the party caucuses. From popular
organs of direct self-rule, the Soviets were thus already beginning to be transformed into complex bureaucratic structures, although this process is more
commonly associated with the period after 1917. At the time, it seemed a
natural development: the workers themselves were deemed to lack the political
experience required to take on the responsibilities of government, while the Soviet
parties, because of their old camaraderie within the revolutionary movement, were
automatically assumed to be exempt from the factional abuse of power which
such centralization made possible. This of course was naive — and merely
played into the hands of the Bolsheviks, the undisputed masters of factional
politics, who increasingly employed such tactics to secure control of the Soviet
executives. In dozens of provincial Soviets the Bolsheviks managed to gain a
majority on the executive, although they were only a minority in the assembly.
This was especially common where a Bolshevik-controlled workers' section was
merged with a section of soldiers or peasants and, because of its 'leading role'
in the revolutionary movement, given more seats on the executive: in the Samara
provincial Soviet, for example, the Bolsheviks made up 75 per cent of the
executive but only 26 per cent of the assembly.[89]

But the Bolsheviks' growing domination of the Soviets was not solely due to their factional scheming: they worked not just from above but also from below. The Soviets' bureaucratization had set them apart from the lives of the ordinary workers, who began to reduce their involvement in the Soviets and either lost all interest in politics or else looked instead to their own *ad hoc* bodies such as the factory committees to take the initiative. This added strength to the Bolshevik campaign, which was largely channelled through these grass-roots organizations, for the recall of the Menshevik and SR leaders from the Soviets as part of Lenin's drive towards Soviet power. The revitalization of the Soviets in the wake of the Kornilov crisis thus coincided with their radicalization from below, as factories and garrisons recalled the pro-coalition Mensheviks and SRs in favour of those Maximalists (Bolsheviks, Anarchists and Left SRs) calling for the assumption of Soviet power.

As early as August, the Bolsheviks had won control of the Soviets in Ivanovo-Voznesentsk (the 'Russian Manchester'), Kronstadt, Ekaterinburg, Samara and Tsaritsyn. But after the Kornilov crisis many other Soviets followed suit: Riga, Saratov and Moscow itself. Even the Petrograd Soviet fell to the Bolsheviks. On 31 August it passed a Bolshevik motion condemning the coalition politics of the Soviet leaders and calling for the establishment of a Soviet government. Half the delegates eligible to vote had not been present at this historic meeting, though some of the Menshevik and SR delegates had voted against their party leaders. The leaders threatened to resign if the vote was not reversed at a second meeting on 9 September. But once again the Bolshevik motion was carried. Trotsky, appearing for the first time after his release from prison, dealt the decisive rhetorical blow by forcing the Soviet leaders to admit that Kerensky, by this stage widely regarded as a 'counter-revolutionary', was still a member of their executive. On 25 September the leadership of the Petrograd Soviet was completely revamped, with the Bolsheviks occupying four of the seven seats on its executive and Trotsky replacing Chkheidze as its Chairman. This was the beginning of the end. In the words of Sukhanov, the Petrograd Soviet was 'now Trotsky's guard, ready at a sign from him to storm the coalition'.[90]

The Bolshevik cause had been greatly strengthened by Trotsky's entry into the party. No one else in the leadership came anywhere near him as a public speaker, and for much of the revolutionary period it was this that made Trotsky, perhaps even more so than Lenin, the best-known Bolshevik leader in the country at large.* Whereas Lenin remained the master strategist of the party, working mainly behind the scenes, Trotsky became its principal source of public

---

* It had largely been personal rivalry that prevented Trotsky from joining the Bolshevik Party earlier, despite the absence of any real ideological differences between himself and Lenin during 1917. He could not bring himself to surrender to 'Lenin's party' — a party which he had been so critical of in the past. As Lenin once replied when asked what still kept him and Trotsky apart: 'Now don't you know? Ambition, ambition, ambition.' (Balabanoff, *My Life*, 175–6.)

inspiration. During the weeks leading up to the seizure of power he spoke almost every night before a packed house at the Cirque Moderne. With his sharp ringing voice, his piercing logic and brilliant wit, he held his listeners spellbound with his denunciations of the Provisional Government. There was a literary, almost Homeric, quality to his oratory (some of his speeches were recorded). It stemmed from the expressive skill of his phrasing, the richness of his imagery, the powerful rhythm and pathos of his speech, and, perhaps above all, the simple style of narration which he used to involve his listeners in the moral drama from which he then drew his political conclusions. He was always careful to use examples and comparisons from the real life of his audience. This gave his speeches a familiarity and earned Trotsky the popular reputation of being 'one of us'.[91] It was this that gave him his extraordinary power to master the crowd, even sometimes when it was extremely hostile. The incident with Chernov during the July Days was a good example, as were the occasions in the civil war, when Trotsky persuaded dangerous bands of deserters from the Red Army to return to the Front against the Whites.

Trotsky brought the Mezhraionka with him into the party. The Mezhraionka, or Inter-District group, was a faction of SD Internationalists with good contacts in the Petrograd garrison. Its importance stemmed less from the size of its following (which was certainly fewer than 4,000 members) than from the stature of its leaders. It was really no more than a collection of brilliant generals without an army. Yet in them the Bolsheviks were to gain some of their most talented organizers, theoreticians, polemicists and agitators: Trotsky, Lunacharsky, Antonov-Ovseenko, Ryazanov, Uritsky, Manuilsky, Pokrovsky, Yoffe and Volodarsky. Many of them were set to play a prominent part in the seizure of power and the later development of the Soviet regime.

The rising fortunes of the Bolsheviks during the summer and autumn were essentially due to the fact that they were the only major political party which stood uncompromisingly for Soviet power.* This point bears emphasizing, for one of the most basic misconceptions of the Russian Revolution is that the Bolsheviks were swept to power on a tide of mass support for the party itself. The October insurrection was a *coup d'état*, actively supported by a small minority of the population (and indeed opposed by several of the Bolshevik leaders themselves). But it took place amidst a social revolution, which was centred on the popular realization of Soviet power as the negation of the state and the direct self-rule of the people, much as in the ancient peasant ideal of *volia*. The political vacuum brought about by this social revolution enabled the Bolsheviks to seize power in the cities and consolidate their dictatorship during the

---

* The Mensheviks and SRs only had minority left-wing factions in favour of a Soviet government, of which more on pages 464–5.

autumn and winter. The slogan 'All Power to the Soviets!' was a useful tool, a banner of popular legitimation covering the nakedness of Lenin's ambition (which was better expressed as All Power to the Party). Later, as the nature of the Bolshevik dictatorship became apparent, the party faced the growing opposition of precisely those groups in society which in 1917 had rallied behind the Soviet slogan.

The popular demand for Soviet power had never expressed itself in a preference for the dictatorship of any particular party. The torrent of resolutions, petitions and declarations from the factories, the army units and the villages in support of a Soviet government after the Kornilov crisis invariably called on all the socialist parties to take part in its establishment, and often displayed a marked impatience with the factional disputes between them. Their political language had basically remained unchanged since 1905: the dominant image within them was that of 'the people', the *narod*, in a struggle for freedom against an oppressive regime, the *Kerenshchina*. The latter, it is true, was now described as 'bourgeois', which no doubt reflected the increased influence of the Marxist agitators and the Bolsheviks in particular. But the basic concept of these resolutions, which these agitators merely articulated in the language of class, remained in essence a popular struggle between 'us' and 'them', the *nizy* and the *verkhi*, or the common people and the privileged élite at the head of the government. Their dominant sentiment was one of anger and frustration that nothing concrete had been gained, neither peace, nor bread, nor land, six months after the February Revolution, and that unless a decisive break was made with the bourgeoisie in the coalition there would only be another winter of stagnation.[92]

What the workers saw in Soviet power, above all, was the chance to control their own factory environment. They wanted to regulate their own shop-floor relations, to set their own wages and working conditions, and combat the 'sabotage', the conspiratorial running-down of production by profit-conscious employers, which many workers blamed for the industrial crisis. In this heightened atmosphere of class war, impatience was growing with the Mensheviks' leadership of the labour movement: their policies of mediating labour disputes and conciliating the employers had failed to stop the rising tide of unemployment. Many workers, especially those under the influence of the Bolsheviks, saw the solution in the sequestration (or nationalization) of their factory by a Workers' State, called 'Soviet Power', which would then set up a management board of workers, technicians and Soviet officials to keep the factory running.* It was part of the growing political consciousness of the workers, the realization that their demands could only be achieved by changing the nature of the state itself.

---

* This was roughly the import of the Bolshevik Decree on Workers' Control passed on 14 November.

This politicization became manifest in the dramatic upsurge of strikes which crippled the country from September onwards. Because of the general effects of inflation, it was far more widespread than previous strike-waves: unskilled labourers and semi-intelligentsia groups, such as hospital, city and clerical workers, were forced to cast aside their usual reluctance to strike in the struggle to keep up with the rising cost of living. Yet because strikes were ineffective — and even counter-productive — in combating inflation, they were often accompanied by broader political demands for the whole economy to be restructured. Industrial strikes, still the most common, were also much more likely to end up in violence. They were no less than a battle for the control of the workplace and the city economy as a whole. The trade unions and factory committees, which tended to have a moderating influence, soon lost control of these militant strikes. They spilled on to the streets and sometimes even ended in bloody conflicts between the workers — armed, trained and organized by the Red Guards — and the government militias. Employers and managers were assaulted; and where they resorted to lock-outs, the factory buildings were stormed and occupied by the workers. Some strikes spread to involve the residents of whole urban districts in attacks on bakeries and shops, house searches and arrests of the *burzhoois* whom the crowd suspected of hoarding food. There was also a steep rise in looting and crime, drunkenness and vandalism, ethnic conflicts and anti-Jewish pogroms during September and October.[93] To the urban propertied classes, these final weeks before the Bolshevik seizure of power appeared like a descent into anarchy.

September also saw a violent upturn in the peasant war against the landed estates. With the approach of the autumn ploughing, the time seemed ripe for a final reckoning with the old agrarian order. The peasants were fed up with waiting for the Provisional Government to deliver on its promises about the land, and most villages now had their own band of soldiers from the army ready to lead them in the march on the manors. The pogrom, or violent sacking of an estate by the mob, became a widespread phenomenon in the central black-soil regions, whereas in previous months the peasant movement had been mainly confined to disputes over rent, the confiscation of cattle and the organized seizure of the arable fields by the village committee. In Tambov province hundreds of manor houses were burned and vandalized — the aim ostensibly being, as the peasants put it, to 'drive the squires out'. This violent wave of destruction seems to have started with the murder of Prince Boris Vyazemsky, the owner of several thousand hectares in the Usman region of Tambov. The local peasants had been demanding since the spring that Vyazemsky lower his rents and return the hundred hectares of prime pasture he had taken from them as a punishment for their part in the revolution of 1905. But on both counts Vyazemsky had refused. On 24 August some 5,000 peasants from the neighbouring villages occupied the estate. Fortified by vodka from the Prince's cellars, and armed with pitchforks and rifles, they repulsed a Cossack detachment, arrested Vyazemsky and organized a kangaroo court which decided to despatch him to the Front, 'so that he can learn to fight as the peasants have done'. But there were also cries of 'Let's kill the Prince, we are sick of him!', and he was murdered by the drunken mob before he even reached the nearby railway station. Vyazemsky's manor house was then destroyed, the livestock and tools divided up and carted back to the villages, and his arable land ploughed by the peasants.[94]

Similar pogroms followed on dozens of other estates, not only in Tambov but also in the neighbouring provinces of Penza, Voronezh, Saratov, Kazan, Orel, Tula and Riazan'. In Penza province some 250 manors (one-fifth of the total) were burned or destroyed in September and October alone. One agronomist left a vivid description of the plundered estates in Saratov province during the autumn of 1917:

As far as the manor buildings are concerned, they have been senselessly destroyed, with only the walls left standing. The windows and doors were the worst to suffer; in the majority of the estates no trace is left of them. All forms of transport have been destroyed or taken. Cumbersome machines like steam-threshers, locomotives, and binders were taken out for no known reason and discarded along the roads and in the fields. The agricultural tools were also taken. Anything that could be used in the peasant households simply disappeared from the estates.

Not even Yasnaya Polyana, Tolstoy's estate in Tula, escaped the wrath of the peasants he had once idolized. Sonya, Tolstoy's widow, who was now old and blind, cabled Kerensky for help, while her daughters packed their father's books and manuscripts into wooden boxes and piled them up in the salon, where they waited in darkness for the plundering mob to come. They had armed themselves with knives and hammers to fight for their lives if need be. But the marauding peasants, seeing the house unlit, assumed it had already been destroyed and moved on to the next estate.[95]

This final reckoning with the squires usually took place at the same time as the establishment of the Soviet in the village or the volost township. The peasants saw the Soviets as the realization of their long-cherished *volia*, the direct self-rule of their villages free from the intervention of the gentry or the state. The village Soviets were really no more than the communes in a more revolutionary form. The Soviet assembly was indistinguishable from the open gathering of the communal *skhod*, except perhaps that the white-bearded patriarchs were now overshadowed by the younger and more literate peasants, such as Semenov, who helped to establish the Soviet in Andreevskoe. The peasant Soviets often behaved like village republics, paying scant regard to the orders of the central state. Many of them employed their own police forces and set up their own courts, while some even had their own flags and emblems. Nearly all of them had their own volunteer militia, or Red Guard, organized by the younger peasants straight out of the army to defend the revolutionary village and its borders.[96]

*   *   *

The mass of workers and peasants were moving inexorably towards their own localist conceptions of Soviet rule. Only a Soviet government could hope to command any real authority in the country at large. This had been the case since the February Revolution. But time and again the Soviet leaders had chosen to ignore it — their dogmatic faith in the need for a 'bourgeois stage of the revolution' had tied them to the hopeless task of trying to keep the coalition going — and every time the streets had arisen to the cry of Soviet power they had chosen to cover their ears. And yet at last, in the wake of the Kornilov crisis, it seemed that the moment had come for the socialist parties to make the decisive break and form a government of their own. The Kadets, the major bourgeois partner of the coalition, had been thoroughly discredited by their support for the 'counter-revolutionary' general; while the socialist parties were being pulled by their own rank-and-file supporters towards Soviet power. The possibility was beginning to emerge during the first half of September that all the major socialist parties, from the Popular Socialists on the right to the Bolsheviks on the left, might come together for the formation of a government based exclusively on the Soviets and the other democratic organizations. It was a unique historical moment, a fleeting chance for the revolution to follow a different course from the one that it did. If this opportunity had been taken, Russia might have become a socialist democracy rather than a Communist dictatorship; and, as a result, the bloody civil war — which by the autumn of 1917 was probably inevitable — might have lasted weeks instead of years.

The three main Soviet parties were all moving towards the idea of a socialist government, or at least a decisive break with the bourgeoisie, in the weeks following the Kornilov crisis. Martov's left-wing Menshevik faction, which favoured an all-socialist government, was steadily gaining supporters among the rank and file of the party. Under their pressure, the Menshevik Central Committee pledged itself to the formation of a 'homogenous democratic government' on 1 September. The Left SRs were also gaining ground, effectively emerging as a separate party after the crisis. Their three major policies — a socialist government based on the Soviet, the immediate confiscation of the gentry's estates and an end to the war — could not have been better tailored to suit the demands of the SR rank and file, the mass of the peasants and soldiers, though such was their disillusionment with Kerensky and Chernov that many of them abandoned the SRs altogether and moved directly to the Bolsheviks. The provincial Soviet in Saratov, home of the SRs, went Bolshevik during September.[97]

The Bolsheviks were also coming round to the idea of a socialist coalition based on the Soviets. Kamenev of course had always been in favour of this. He had been fighting all along to keep the Bolshevik campaign within the Soviet movement and the democratic institutions of the February Revolution. As he saw it, the country was not ripe for a Bolshevik uprising, and any attempt to stage one was bound to end in civil war and the defeat of the party. It would be the Paris Commune all over again. In his view the Bolsheviks had no choice but to continue with the strategy of trying to win support in the Soviets, in the city Dumas, and eventually in the Constituent Assembly through democratic elections. They also had to persuade the Mensheviks and SRs to break with the coalition and join them in a socialist government.

Until the Kornilov crisis, Lenin had been flatly opposed to the idea of any compromise with the Soviet leaders. After the July Days he had given up all hope of coming to power through the Soviets: as he saw it, the Provisional Government had been captured by a 'military dictatorship' engaged in a 'civil war' against the proletariat; the Soviets had lost their revolutionary potential and were being led, 'like sheep to the abattoir', by a group of leaders bent on appeasing the 'counter-revolution'. The only option left was to give up the slogan 'All Power to the Soviets!' and stage an armed uprising to transfer power to the rival proletarian organs under the leadership of the Bolshevik Party. It was revealing of Lenin's attitude towards the Soviets, in whose name his regime was to be founded, that whenever they failed to serve the interests of his party, he was ready to ditch them. It is quite mistaken to argue, as Isaac Deutscher once did, that Lenin was planning to make the Soviet Congress the constitutional source of sovereign power, like the English House of Commons, with the Bolsheviks ruling through this congress in the manner of a Western parliamentary party.* Lenin was no Soviet constitutionalist — and all his actions after October testified to this. The Soviets, in his schema, were always to be subordinated to the party. Even in *The State and Revolution* — supposedly his most 'libertarian' work of political theory, which he completed at this time — Lenin stressed the need for a strong and repressive party state, a Dictatorship of the Proletariat, during the period of transition to the Communist utopia when the 'bourgeois state' was to be smashed. He barely mentioned the Soviets at all.[98]

Yet, in the wake of the Kornilov crisis, which had seen the Soviet leaders

---

* It is interesting how many Marxists of Deutscher's generation (E. H. Carr immediately comes to mind) were inclined to see the Western democratic system as inherently authoritarian and the Soviet regime as inherently democratic. For Deutscher's comments on Lenin's 'Soviet constitutionalism' see *The Prophet Armed*, 290–1.

move to the left, even Lenin was prepared to consider the idea of a compromise with them. Not that he gave up his ultimate aim of a Bolshevik dictatorship. 'Our party', he assured its left wing on 1 September in his article 'On Compromises', 'is striving after political domination *for itself.*' But the leftward move of the Soviets, which worked to the benefit of the party, opened up the prospect of moving once again towards Soviet power through peaceful means. The Bolsheviks, after all, were now likely to be a dominant force in any government based on the Soviets — and it was this that enabled Lenin to consider what, in essence, as he put it, would be 'our return to the pre-July demand of all power to the Soviets'. During the fortnight leading up to the opening of the Democratic Conference, on 14 September, when the power question was to be resolved, Lenin supported Kamenev's efforts to persuade the Mensheviks and SRs to break with the coalition and join the Bolsheviks in a socialist government based on the Soviets. If the Soviet leaders agreed to assume power, the Bolsheviks would give up their campaign for an armed uprising and compete for power within the Soviet movement itself. But Lenin's implication remained clear: if the Soviet leaders refused to do this, the party should prepare for the seizure of power.[99]

The fate of Russia thus depended on the actions of the Soviet leaders at the Democratic Conference. This was the moment when their national leadership was put to the crucial test — and was found wanting. The Conference took place in the Alexandrinsky Theatre, which proved a suitable venue since the meeting ended in farce. Three clear political groupings immediately became apparent: the Right, which favoured a coalition with the Kadets; the Centre, which favoured a coalition with the bourgeoisie but without the Kadets; and the Left, which supported a socialist government, either based on the Soviets or more broadly on the democratic groups represented at the conference. But when it came to the vote there was total confusion. To begin with, the conference passed a resolution (by 766 votes to 688) supporting the general principle of a coalition with the bourgeoisie. But then it passed two further amendments excluding the Kadets from such a coalition. This so angered the Right that they then sided with the Left in a second vote on the original resolution and defeated it by 813 votes to 183. After four days of debate the conference had ended without an opinion on the vital issue for which it had been called. This was neither the first nor the last time in the brief and interrupted history of the Russian democratic movement that the basic skills of parliamentary decision-making proved beyond its leaders; but it was perhaps the most critical in terms of its consequences.

An extraordinary delegation of conference members was hastily convened to resolve the government crisis. It was dominated by the SR and Menshevik leaders in favour of a coalition and, contrary to the clear vote of the conference, immediately opened negotiations with the Kadets. On 24 September agreement was reached, and the following day Kerensky named his cabinet. It was in essence the same political compromise as the Second Coalition of July, with the moderate socialists technically holding a majority of the portfolios and the Kadets in control of the key posts. But the Third Coalition had none of the ministerial talent — slight though that had been — of its predecessor. It was made up of second-rate Kadets and obscure provincial Trudoviks without any real experience of government at the national level. The socialists had wanted to make it responsible to the Preparliament — a bogus and ultimately impotent body appointed by the Democratic Conference in the vain hope of giving the Republic some form of legitimacy until the convocation of the Constituent Assembly (Plekhanov called it 'the little house on chicken's feet'). But the Kadets had forced them to give up this demand as the price for their involvement in the coalition. The Provisional Government was thus to remain *de jure* the sovereign power until the Assembly convened.[100] But would this new *opera buffa* cabinet even last that long? Without *de facto* power, it proved incapable of passing meaningful legislation and only hoped to cling on to office until the November elections. Survival for six weeks — that was the sum of its minuscule ambitions — and yet it lasted only four.

The failure of the Democratic Conference was a public confession of the political bankruptcy of the Soviet leaders. After this final admission of their reluctance to assume power, there was a sudden and sharp collapse in the support for the Mensheviks and SRs. The Menshevik Party had practically ceased to exist in Petrograd by the end of September: the last all-city party conference was unable to meet for lack of a quorum. It was not just their rigid Marxist dogma that had kept the Menshevik leaders within the coalition, but a much more fundamental failure to recognize the social and political forces which had been unfolding during 1917. 'Almost from the outset', writes Leo Haimson, the foremost historian of the Mensheviks, 'they had found themselves valiantly trying to master a chaos that had gradually overwhelmed them. Nothing about the experience had proven familiar, or run according to expectations.' They had failed to see that their own base of support, the industrial workers, was becoming radicalized, and that only a Soviet government could hope to command any real authority among them. Blinded by their own commitment to the state, which had made them defend the coalition principle at all costs, they ceased to act or think like revolutionaries and dismissed the workers' growing radicalism and support for the Bolsheviks as a manifestation of their 'ignorance' and 'imma-turity'; and this confirmed them in their dogmatic belief that the Soviets were not ready for power.[101] The SR leaders were guilty of similar self-deception in their naive belief that the peasantry's demand for a fundamental land reform, upon which the SR Party had been built, could be put off until the end of the war and the resolution of the power question at the Constituent Assembly. The peasants were increasingly indifferent to the outcome of the war and to the form of the national government: all they wanted was peace, land and freedom, as expressed in the *volia* of their own autonomous village committees and Soviets. This would be proved by the ill-fated SR struggle during 1918 to reverse the Treaty of Brest-Litovsk and to rally the Volga peasants behind the defence of the Constituent Assembly, after it had been closed by the Bolsheviks.

The failure of the SRs, like that of the Mensheviks, was above all a failure of leadership. Both parties were hopelessly split on the two fundamental issues of 1917: what to do with the war and where to draw the balance between the political and social revolutions. Their right-wing leaders were Defensist and placed greater stress on the political revolution; while their left-wing comrades were firmly committed to peace and radical social reforms. Given Russia's historical legacy and the huge cultural gulf between the intelligentsia and the masses, there was perhaps no real prospect, at least in 1917, of sustaining a political revolution in the European tradition. But a socialist democracy might just have been stabilized, if the Soviet leaders had agreed to form a coalition with the Bolsheviks in September — and if Lenin had subsequently agreed to respect such a coalition. These, of course, were very big 'ifs'. The Left SRs did eventually form a lonely alliance with the Bolsheviks in October, though by that stage Lenin had no intention of treating them as an equal partner. As for the left-wing Mensheviks, they were hopelessly stranded. Martov, their leader, could not bring himself to join any sort of alliance with his old rival Lenin, although this was the logical outcome of his quarrel with the Defensists, as most of his supporters recognized. A party loyalist to the end, Martov remained on board the sinking ship of Menshevism.

Trotsky described Martov as the 'Hamlet of Democratic Socialism' — and this is just about the sum of it. Like so many of the veteran socialist leaders who found themselves at the head of the Soviet movement in 1917, Martov was much too good an intellectual to be a successful politician. He was always held back by his own integrity and philosophical approach to politics. He tended to choose his allies by the coherence of their general world-view rather than the timeliness or even the practicality of their policies. It was this that made him stick with the Mensheviks rather than switch to a tactical alliance with the Bolsheviks in September: he placed greater importance on the basic Marxist principles of the Mensheviks than on the purely political arguments for such an alliance. This high-minded approach has since won Martov many plaudits among the socialist intelligentsia: even Lenin was said to have confessed in 1921 that his single greatest regret was 'that Martov is not with us. What an amazing comrade he is, what a pure man!' Yet such noble principles are a fatal burden for the revolutionary leader, and in Martov's case they made him soft and indecisive when just the opposite was required.[102]

The same intellectual indecisiveness was characteristic of many of the Soviet leaders in 1917 — and in this sense they could all be described as Hamlets of democratic socialism. Chernov was a similarly tragic figure in the SR Party. Like Martov, he was a brilliant intellectual and party theoretician, yet he utterly lacked the qualities required to become a successful revolutionary leader. He did not have that hardness of inner resolve and will, that single-minded determination to carry his policies through, even if this meant splitting his own party, or indeed that basic instinct to judge when the moment was ripe to strike out for power. That was the crucial difference between a Chernov and a Lenin — and upon that difference the fate of Russia turned.

*   *   *

With Kamenev's plan for a socialist coalition scotched by the failure of the Democratic Conference, Lenin reverted to his campaign in the party for an immediate armed uprising. He had already begun to advocate this in two letters to the Central Committee written from exile in Finland on the eve of the conference. The Bolsheviks, Lenin had argued, 'can and *must* take state power into their own hands'. Can — because the party had already won a majority in the Moscow and Petrograd Soviets, which was 'enough to carry the people with it' in any civil war, provided the party in power proposed an immediate peace and gave the land to the peasants. Must — because if it waited for the convocation of the Constituent Assembly, 'Kerensky and Co.' would take pre-emptive action against the transfer of power, either by giving up Petrograd to the Germans or by delaying the convocation of the Constituent Assembly. The Democratic Conference was to be condemned, since it represented 'only the compromising upper strata of the bourgeoisie. We must not be deceived by the election figures: elections prove nothing ... The majority of the people are on our side.' Reminding his comrades of Marx's dictum that 'insurrection is an art', Lenin had concluded that 'it would be naive to wait for a "formal" majority for the Bolsheviks. No revolution ever waits for *that* ... History will not forgive us if we do not assume power now.'[103]

These two letters reached the Central Committee on 15 September. They were, to say the least, highly inconvenient for the rest of the Bolshevik leaders ('We were all aghast', Bukharin recalled) since the Democratic Conference had just begun and they were still committed to Kamenev's conciliatory tactics. It was even resolved to burn all but one copy of the letters, lest they should fall into the hands of the rank-and-file Bolsheviks and spark a revolt. The Central Committee continued to ignore Lenin's advice and printed instead his earlier articles, in which he had endorsed the Kamenev line. Lenin was beside himself with rage. While he was still afraid to return to Petrograd (Kerensky had ordered

Lenin's arrest at the Democratic Conference), he moved from Finland to the resort town of Vyborg, eighty miles from the capital, to be closer. During the following weeks, he assaulted the Central Committee and the lower-level party organizations with a barrage of impatient letters, full of violent and abusive phrases heavily underlined, in which he urged them to start the armed insurrection at once. He condemned the 'parliamentary tactics' of the Bolshevik leaders; and welcomed the prospect of a civil war ('the sharpest form of the class struggle'), which they were trying to avert on the false assumption that, like the Paris Communards, they were bound to be defeated. On the contrary, Lenin insisted, the antiBolshevik forces would be no more than those aligned behind the Kornilov movement, and any 'rivers of blood' would give 'certain victory' to the party.

Finally, on 29 September, at the high point of his frustration, Lenin scribbled an angry tirade against the Bolshevik leaders, in which he denounced them as *'miserable traitors to the proletarian cause'*. They had wanted to delay the transfer of power until the Soviet Congress, due to convene on 20 October, whereas the moment was already ripe for the seizure of power and any delay would merely enable Kerensky to use military force against them. The workers, Lenin insisted, were solidly behind the Bolshevik cause; the peasants were starting their own war on the manors, thus ruling out the danger of an Eighteenth Brumaire, or a 'petty-bourgeois' counter-revolution, like that of 1849; while the strikes and mutinies in the rest of Europe were 'indisputable symptoms . . . that we are *on the eve of a world revolution*'. To 'miss such a moment and "wait" for the Congress of Soviets would be *utter idiocy*, or *sheer treachery*', and if the Bolsheviks did so they would 'cover themselves with shame and destroy themselves as a party'. As a final ultimatum, he even threatened to resign from the Central Committee, thereby giving himself the freedom to take his campaign for an armed uprising to the Bolshevik rank and file, scheduled to meet at a Party Conference on 17 October. 'For it is my profound conviction that if we "wait" for the Congress of Soviets and let the present moment pass, we shall *ruin* the revolution.'[104] Lenin's infamous 'rage' was reaching fever pitch.

Why was Lenin so insistent on the need for an armed uprising *before* the Congress of Soviets? All the signs were that time was on the side of the Bolsheviks: the country was falling apart; the Soviets were moving to the left; and the forthcoming Congress would almost certainly endorse the Bolshevik call for a transfer of power to the Soviets. Why stage a premature uprising and run the risk of civil war and defeat? Many Bolshevik leaders had stressed the need for the seizure of power to coincide with the Soviet Congress itself. This was the view of Trotsky and several other Bolsheviks in the Petrograd Soviet — and since they were closely informed about the mood in the capital and would have to play a leading role in any uprising, their point of view was highly influential in the party at large. While these leaders doubted that the party had sufficient support to justify an insurrection in its own name, they thought that it might be successfully carried out in the name of the Soviets. Since the Bolsheviks had conducted their campaign on the slogan of Soviet power, it was said that they needed the Congress to legitimize such an uprising and make it appear as the work of the Soviet as a whole, rather than one party. By taking this line, which would have delayed the uprising by no more than a few days, Lenin could have won widespread support in the party against those, such as Kamenev and Zinoviev, who were flatly opposed to the idea of an uprising. But Lenin was adamant — the seizure of power had to be carried out *before* the Congress convened. He continued to insist on this right up until the eve of the Congress itself.

Lenin justified his impatience by the notion that any delay in the seizure of power would enable Kerensky to organize repressive measures against it: Petrograd would be abandoned to the Germans; the seat of government would be moved to Moscow; and the Soviet Congress itself would be banned. This of course was nonsense. Kerensky was quite incapable of such decisive action and, in any case, as Kamenev pointed out, the government was powerless to put any counter-revolutionary intentions into practice. Lenin, it seems from some of his other writings at this time,* was deliberately inventing the danger of a clamp-down by Kerensky in order to strengthen his own arguments for a pre-emptive insurrection, although it is possible that he had become so out of touch with the real situation in Russia, having been in Finland since July, that he himself believed it. There were certainly rumours in the press that the government was planning to evacuate the capital in early October; and these no doubt reinforced his conviction that a civil war had begun, and that military victory would go to the side which dared to strike first. 'On s'engage et puis en voit.'

But there was another motive for wanting the insurrection before the Soviet Congress convened, quite apart from military tactics. If the transfer of power took place by a vote of the Congress itself, the result would almost certainly be a coalition government made up of all the Soviet parties. The Bolsheviks might gain the largest share of the ministerial places, if these were allocated on a proportional basis, but would still have to rule in partnership with at least the left-wing — and possibly all — of the SR and Menshevik parties. This would be a resounding political victory for Kamenev, Lenin's arch rival in the Bolshevik Party, who would no doubt emerge as the central figure in such a coalition. Under his leadership, the centre of power would remain with

---

* During the final days before 25 October Lenin stressed that a military-style coup was bound to succeed, even if only a very small number of disciplined fighters joined it, because Kerensky's forces were so weak.

the Soviet Congress, rather than the party; and there might even be a renewed effort to reunite the Bolsheviks with the Mensheviks. As for Lenin himself, he ran the risk of being kept out of office, either on the insistence of the Mensheviks and SRs or on account of his own unwillingness to co-operate with them. He would thus be consigned to the left-wing margins of his own party. On the other hand, if a Bolshevik seizure of power took place before the Congress convened, then Lenin would emerge as the political master. The Congress majority would probably endorse the Bolshevik action, thereby giving the party the right to form a government of its own. If the Mensheviks and SRs could bring themselves to accept this forcible seizure of power, as a *fait accompli*, then a few minor places for them would no doubt be found in Lenin's cabinet. Otherwise, they would have no choice but to go into opposition, leaving the Bolsheviks in government on their own. Kamenev's coalition efforts would thus be undermined; Lenin would have his Dictatorship of the Proletariat; and although the result would inevitably be to plunge the country into civil war, this was something Lenin himself accepted — and perhaps even welcomed — as a part of the revolutionary process.

Returning to the capital, where he lived under cover in the flat of a party worker, Margarita Fofanova, Lenin convened a secret meeting of the Bolshevik Central Committee on 10 October. The decision to prepare for an armed insurrection was taken at this meeting. It was one of those small ironies, of which there are bound to be many in the history of any revolution, that this historic event took place in the house of the Menshevik, Nikolai Sukhanov. His wife, Galina Flakserman, was a veteran Bolshevik (just imagine their domestic squabbles!) and had told her meddlesome husband not to bother coming home from his office at the Smolny that night, as it seems was his habit. Lenin arrived late and disguised in a wig — Kollontai recalled that 'he looked every bit like a Lutheran minister' — which he doffed for a moment on entering the apartment and then kept adjusting during the meeting: in his haste he had forgotten to pack the powder and, without it, the wig kept slipping off his shiny bald head. Of the twenty-one Central Committee members only twelve were present. The most important decision in the history of the Bolshevik Party — to launch the armed insurrection — was thus taken by a minority of the Central Committee: it passed by ten votes to two (Kamenev and Zinoviev). This, in effect, was a Leninist 'coup' within the Bolshevik Party.* Once again, Lenin had managed to

---

* The Bolshevik Party Conference, scheduled for 17 October, was mysteriously cancelled at about this time — no doubt also on Lenin's insistence. The mood of the party rank and file suggested that it would express powerful opposition to the idea of an armed insurrection. During the following days, Kamenev and Zinoviev spearheaded their opposition to the insurrection with a call for the Party Conference to be convened. We still lack the crucial archival evidence to tell the full story of this internal party struggle. (On this see Rabinowitch, 'Bol'sheviki', 119–20.)

impose his will on the rest of its leaders. Without his decisive personal influence, it is hard to imagine the Bolshevik seizure of power.

In the small hours of the following morning, as the meeting drew to a close, Lenin hastily pencilled its historic resolution on a piece of scrap paper torn from a child's notebook. Although no specific dates or tactics had been set, it recognized 'that an armed uprising [was] inevitable, and the time for it fully ripe', and instructed the party organizations to prepare for it as 'the order of the day'. With the meeting adjourned, Sukhanov's wife brought out the samovar and set the dining table with cheese, salami and black bread. The Bolsheviks at once tucked in.[105] Conspiracy had made them hungry.

11 Lenin's Revolution

i The Art of Insurrection

Some of the revolution's most dramatic scenes were to be played out in a school for the daughters of the nobility. The Smolny Institute, a vast, ochre-coloured, classical palace on the outskirts of the capital, had lain more or less empty since the fall of the Tsar. After the July Days the Soviet Executive had been forced to move its headquarters there from the more prestigious Tauride Palace. From that point on it became, in the words of Sukhanov, the 'internal arena of the revolution'. The Second All-Russian Soviet Congress of October, where Soviet power was proclaimed, took place in the white-colonnaded ballroom, where the schoolgirls had once perfected their waltzes and polkas.

The Smolny had none of the calm architectural grace of the Tauride Palace. Like most girls' academies of the nineteenth century, it was austere and practical, more like a prison than a place to broaden the mind and uplift the spirit. This austerity seemed to reflect the change of mood among its revolutionary squatters. There was a general air of sternness, of sleepless nights and feverish improvisation inside the Smolny. John Reed said that it 'hummed like a gigantic hive'. The outer gates were guarded by surly armed guards, who carefully checked the passes of everyone who entered (Trotsky himself was once refused entry when he could not find his pass). The endless vaulted corridors, dimly lit by electric lamps, were lined with resting soldiers and bundles of newspapers. There was a constant rush of people and the sound of their heavy boots on the stone floors echoed thunderously. The air was thick with cigarette smoke; the floors were covered with rubbish; and everywhere there was the smell of urine. Futile signs were hung up on the walls: 'Comrades, for the sake of your health, preserve cleanliness!' But no one took any notice. The barrack-like classrooms were filled by the offices of the various revolutionary organizations. On their doors, which constantly opened and shut, were still the old enamel plaques naming the classrooms; but over these hung crude paper signs to inform the passer-by of their new occupants: the Executive Committee of the Petrograd Soviet; the Bureau of the Factory Committees; or the caucus of some political party. The centre of life at the Smolny was the ornate chandeliered ballroom, where the uproarious sessions of the Soviet were held; above the dais, where the executive sat, was a blank space on the wall, from which the Tsar's portrait had been removed. Downstairs, in the girls' former refectory, there was always a huge crowd of hungry workers and soldiers; many came to the Smolny for no other reason than to eat. They wolfed down their food, slurped hot tea from tins, and shouted obscenities which the young gentlewomen of the Smolny school could not even have imagined.[1]

With the Bolshevik Central Committee entrenched in Room 36, the Smolny became a physical challenge to the existence of the Provisional Government. The crucial meeting of 10 October had placed an armed uprising on the Bolsheviks' agenda. But they had not set a date. As yet, most of the Bolshevik leaders were still opposed to Lenin's demand for an immediate insurrection, while some put it off to the distant future. 'The resolution of 10 October is one of the best resolutions the Central Committee has ever passed,' declared Mikhail Kalinin, 'but when this uprising will take place is uncertain — perhaps in a year.' The ambivalent mood of the streets was the main cause for concern. Everyone sensed a general fatigue and discontent with the *Kerenshchina*. The war had gone on for far too long, people were fed up queuing half the night for bread, and there was a widespread feeling in the factories and the barracks that the status quo could no longer be endured. But would the Petrograd workers and soldiers 'come out' for an uprising? Many remembered the July Days, the loss of workers' jobs and repressions which followed, and were reluctant to risk another defeat. The Bolshevik Military Organization, which had its pulse on the mood of the capital's slums, repeatedly warned that while the workers and soldiers were thoroughly disgruntled and sympathized with their slogans, they were not yet ready to come out on the party's call, though they might take to the streets on the call of the Soviet if it was in danger.

Unwilling to wait for the All-Russian Soviet Congress, Lenin pinned his hopes on the Northern Regional Congress of Soviets, which met in Petrograd on 11–13 October. As Latsis recalled, 'the plan was that it would declare itself the government, and this would be the start'. Lenin had close ties with the Bolshevik leaders of the Baltic region: it was they who had convened the Northern Regional Congress and arranged for it to be held in Petrograd rather than Helsingfors. Lenin had spent the summer in the Baltic region and had come to see it as a vital launching base for the revolution in Russia as well as the rest of Europe. He was especially impressed by the revolutionary zeal of the Latvians: they made up his personal bodyguard and, during the early days of Soviet rule, the bulk of the leading Chekists and Red Army élite (Latsis, Eiduck, Peters, Smilga). The Bolsheviks in Riga had effectively controlled their Soviet from as early as August, and Lenin now looked towards them to import the principle of Soviet power into Russia.* In a letter to Smilga, one of his closest associates

* So much for the idea that Soviet power was always exported from Russia.

during his summer of exile, Lenin had made it clear that he saw the Petrograd insurrection as a military invasion from the Baltic region. 'It seems to me', he had written on 17 September, 'that we can have completely at our disposal only the troops in Finland and the Baltic Fleet and that only they can play a serious military role.' The Northern Regional Congress was to provide the signal for this invasion. Smilga had organized it at Lenin's urging and had assumed the role of its chairman. The Bolshevik delegates arrived fully armed and clearly assuming that it would become the centre for an uprising. But Lenin was once again frustrated: the majority of the delegates passed Kamenev's cautious resolution to leave the creation of a Soviet government to the All-Russian Congress, due to convene on 20 October. Even in the Baltic, Lenin's own preferred vanguard region, it seems there was no mass support for an insurrection on the call of the party.[2]

The same conclusion was suggested by the evidence presented to a meeting of the Central Committee on 16 October. The representatives of the Bolshevik Military Organization, the Petrograd Soviet, the trade unions and factory committees who attended this meeting all warned of the risks involved in staging an uprising before the Soviet Congress. Krylenko stated the view of the Military Organization that the soldiers' fighting spirit was falling: 'they would have to be stung by something, such as the break-up of the garrison, to come out for an uprising'. Volodarsky from the Petrograd Soviet confirmed the 'general impression . . . that no one is ready to rush out on to the streets but that everyone will come out if the Soviet calls'. Colossal unemployment and the fear of dismissal held the workers back, according to Shmidt of the trade unions. Shliapnikov added that even in the metalworkers' union, where the party's influence was dominant, 'a Bolshevik rising is not popular and rumours of this even produce panic'. Kamenev drew the logical conclusion: 'there is no evidence of any kind that we must begin the fight before the 20th [when the Soviet Congress was due to convene]'. But Lenin was insistent on the need for immediate preparations and saw no reason to hold back in the cautious reports on the mood of the Petrograd masses: in a military *coup d'état*, which is how he conceived of the seizure of power, only a small force was needed, provided it was well armed and disciplined enough. Such was Lenin's towering influence over the rest of the party that he got his way. A counter-resolution by Zinoviev prohibiting the actual staging of an uprising before the Bolshevik delegates to the Soviet Congress had been consulted was defeated by 15 votes to 6, though the closeness of the vote, compared with the 19 to 2 majority in favour of Lenin's much vaguer call for an uprising in the immediate future, does suggest that several Bolshevik leaders had serious apprehensions about the wisdom of an insurrection before the Soviet Congress, albeit not enough to make an open stand against the great dictator.[3] That, after all, would take some courage.

At the end of the meeting Kamenev declared that he could not accept its resolution, which in his view would lead the party to ruin, and submitted his resignation to the Central Committee in order to make his campaign public. He also demanded the convocation of the Party Conference, which Lenin had managed to get postponed: there was little doubt that it would oppose the call for an uprising before the Soviet Congress. On 18 October Kamenev aired his views in Gorky's newspaper, *Novaia zhizn'*. 'At the present', he wrote, 'the instigation of an armed uprising before and independent of the Soviet Congress would be an impermissible and even fatal step for the proletariat and the revolution.' This of course was to let the cat out of the bag: rumours of a Bolshevik coup had been spreading for weeks, and now the conspiracy had finally been exposed. Trotsky was forced to deny the rumours in the Petrograd Soviet, but for once his performance was less than convincing. Lenin was furious and, in a sign of the sort of purges to come, denounced Kamenev and Zinoviev in the Bolshevik press. 'Strike-breaking', 'betrayal', 'blacklegs', 'slanderous lies' and 'crime' — such terms were littered throughout the angry letters he sent on 18 and 19 October. 'Mr Zinoviev and Mr Kamenev' (this was the ultimate insult — they were now no longer even 'comrades') should be 'expelled from the party'.[4] Such were the actions of a tyrant.

By publishing these letters, Lenin was taking the campaign for an uprising into the public domain. He had always based his argument for a preemptive seizure of power (before the Soviet Congress) on the danger — which he either overestimated or (more likely) invented — that the Provisional Government might not allow the Congress to convene. All the local party reports made it clear that, while the Petrograd workers and soldiers would not come out on the call of the party alone, many would do so if the Soviet was threatened. This had been true since the Kornilov crisis, when the popular notion that a 'counter-revolution' still lurked in the shadows of Kerensky's regime had first taken root. If the Bolsheviks were to get their supporters on to the streets once again, they would have to convince them that the Soviet was in danger. Their opponents did this for them.

With the Bolshevik conspiracy public knowledge, the Soviet leaders resolved to delay the Soviet Congress until 25 October. They hoped that the extra five days would give them the chance to muster their supporters from the far-flung provinces. But it merely gave the Bolsheviks the extra time they needed to make the final preparations for their uprising. Moreover, it lent credibility to their charge that the Soviet leaders were planning to ditch the Soviet Congress altogether. It is certainly true that they had regrets about calling it in the first place: when they had done so, at the time of the Democratic Conference, the swing to the Bolsheviks had not yet been fully apparent; but as the Congress approached, they realized that defeat stared them in the face.

Perhaps the Soviet leaders would have been better advised to concentrate their efforts on demanding strong repressive measures to counter the Bolshevik threat. The truth was that, even with a majority at the Soviet Congress, their paper resolutions would not be enough to fend off the bayonets of the Bolsheviks. But the Mensheviks and SRs were precluded from taking such measures by their feelings of comradeship with the Bolshevik Party. They could not forget that only months before they had been fellow-fighters in the revolutionary underground (and could not see that only months ahead they would become the victims of the Bolshevik Terror). They limited themselves to questions aimed at putting the Bolsheviks on the spot. They stamped their feet and demanded that the Bolsheviks declared their plans before the Soviet. 'I want a yes or no answer,' insisted Dan, as if the Bolsheviks were likely to give it.[5]

Kerensky's own conduct was equally short-sighted. During the final weeks of the Provisional Government his behaviour began to resemble that of the last Tsar: both men refused to recognize the revolutionary threat to their own authority. With Nicholas such complacency had stemmed from hopeless despair and fatalistic resignation; but with Kerensky it was rather the result of his own foolish optimism. Kerensky's nationwide popularity during the early days of the revolution had gone to his head. He had come to believe in his own 'providential calling' to lead 'the people' to freedom and, like the Tsar confined to his Winter Palace, was sufficiently removed from their real situation not to question this faith. Like Nicholas, he surrounded himself with devoted admirers who dared not speak their mind; and kept his cabinet weak by constant talk of reshuffles. He had no idea of — or no wish to know — the true extent of his own unpopularity.

No doubt he had not heard the joke circulating round the country during the final weeks of his regime: 'Q: What is the difference between Russia today and at the end of last year? A: Then we had Alexandra Fedorovna [the Empress], but now we have Alexander Fedorovich [Kerensky].' The isolation of the Prime Minister was almost complete. The people's hero of the spring had become their anti-hero by the autumn. There were widespread rumours of his 'moral corruption' (just as there had been of the Romanovs): of his fine living in the Winter Palace; of his love affair with Elena Biriukova, his wife's cousin, who lived with the Kerenskys in the palace; of his constant drunkenness; and of his addiction to morphine and cocaine. Friends and acquaintances would ring Kerensky's wife to express their deepest sympathy. 'I could not understand why they were being so solicitous,' she later recalled, 'but then it turned out that there was some story in the left-wing press that Kerensky had left his wife and had run off with some actress.' It was falsely rumoured that Kerensky was a Jew, which in the climate of anti-Semitism that ran throughout the revolutionary era was highly damaging to his popular image. Kerensky himself recalled that when he fled the Winter Palace, just before the Bolshevik seizure of power, he saw the following ironic graffiti written on a wall: 'Down with the Jew Kerensky, Long Live Trotsky!' It was also rumoured that Kerensky liked to dress in women's clothes. There was much that was rather feminine in Kerensky's physique and gestures (Gippius called him her 'girlish revolutionary'), and this made him appear weak to many of the workers, in particular, who contrasted him unfavourably with the muscular masculinity of the Bolsheviks. Later it was even rumoured that when Kerensky had fled the Winter Palace he had been dressed in the outfit of a nurse.[6]

It was not just on the streets that Kerensky lost his credibility. The Western Allies, who had always been his strongest supporters, also turned against him after the Kornilov crisis. The British Foreign Ministry was clearly taken in by the rumours about his private life. It was under the absurd impression that his secretary, David Soskice, was a German agent and a Bolshevik, and that Kerensky himself was about to conclude a separate peace with Germany. Nabokov, the Provisional Government's representative in London, thought that the British had decided to wash their hands of Kerensky, believing him to be 'on his way out', once Kornilov's reforms had been jettisoned.[7]

Even among the democratic intelligentsia, where he had once been hailed as a popular hero, Kerensky was now reviled. His oldest patron, the poetess and salon hostess Zinaida Gippius, wrote in her diary on 24 October: 'Nobody wants the Bolsheviks, but nobody is prepared to fight for Kerensky either.' This just about sums it up. Brusilov, who since his dismissal as Commander-in-Chief had become an advocate of the need to raise a civilian militia in order to fight the Bolsheviks, found that he could muster neither volunteers nor money to buy mercenaries. Everybody cursed the Bolsheviks but nobody was prepared to do anything about them. The bourgeoisie and the Rightist groups would have nothing more to do with the Provisional Government, and even welcomed its demise. Nobody wanted to defend it, least of all the monarchists. They preferred to let the Bolsheviks seize power, in the belief that they would not last long and would bring the country to such utter ruin that *all* the socialists would be discredited, whereupon the Rightists would impose their own dictatorship.[8]

Kerensky remained oblivious to his declining fortunes. He continued to trust in the support of 'the people' — was he not their hostage? — and refused to take any preventive measures against the Bolshevik threat. No attempt was made to seize control of the Smolny, or to arrest the Bolshevik leaders, or to reinforce the defence of the city, during the first half of October, when such measures stood at least some chance of success. He seemed to believe that any Bolshevik rising would be a repeat of the July Days fiasco. He even began to pray that the Bolsheviks would make a move, in the naive belief that this would give him the chance to deal with them once and for all. 'I would be prepared to offer prayers to produce this uprising,' he told Nabokov on 20 October. 'I have greater forces than necessary. They will be utterly crushed.'[*9]

Confident of victory, Kerensky declared war on the Bolsheviks. He announced his plans to transfer the bulk of the Petrograd garrison to the Northern Front, where the Germans were advancing towards the capital. As on the eve of the July crisis, he no doubt saw in the German threat an excellent excuse to rid the capital of its unruly soldiers; and he must have been counting on the idea that, as in July, the break-up of the garrison would give rise to a badly planned Bolshevik uprising. But this was, of course, a fatal miscalculation. It gave credibility to the Bolshevik charge that there was a 'counter-revolutionary plot' within government circles — a charge which they needed in order to rally support for an immediate uprising. The Bolsheviks claimed that Kerensky was planning to abandon the capital in order to close down the Soviet Congress and kill off the revolution. Such fears reached fever pitch when Rodzianko, the former Duma President, urged Kerensky to do just that in a speech that was widely reported in the press under the headline: 'To hell with Petrograd!'

This was the highly charged political atmosphere in which the Military Revolutionary Committee was able to supersede the authority of the Provisional Government inside the Petrograd garrison and become the leading organizational force of the Bolshevik insurrection. It all happened in a matter of days — and the secret of the MRC's success was in posing as an organ of *Soviet* defence. The MRC was formed in the middle of October, and held its first organizational meeting on the 20th. Like the Soviet Committee for Struggle Against the Counter-Revolution, which had arisen during the Kornilov crisis, it was conceived as an *ad hoc* body of revolutionary defence (as much against the Germans as against the 'counter-revolution'). Its Bureau, which met on the third floor of the Smolny, was made up of three Bolsheviks and two Left SRs, with P. E. Lazimir, a Left SR, as its nominal chairman. This served to give it the appearance of a Soviet organization, which was important because the soldiers would only come out on the call of the Soviet. But in fact the MRC was a Bolshevik organization. Its real leaders were Trotsky, Antonov-Ovseenko, and the Baltic sailor Dybenko, the huge black-bearded lover of Kollontai (who was old enough to be his mother). The role of the Left SRs was what Trotsky called 'camouflage' to conceal the Bolshevik coup plans. The fact that the Left SRs allowed themselves to be used in this way says all that needs to be said about their political naivety. Their strategic decisions were guided by a formless revolutionary spirit

---

* When Kerensky fled the capital on 25 October he left a small fortune in his bank account: the modest size of his last withdrawal, on 24 October, suggests that even at this final hour he was not expecting to be overthrown. His account book is in GARF, f. 1807, op. I, d. 452.

characteristic of students. They were lambs to the Bolshevik wolf. When the MRC resolved to launch the seizure of power, in the small hours of 25 October, the two Left SRs were not even there.

The threat of transfer to the Front immediately sparked a general mutiny in the Petrograd garrison. The bulk of the soldiers refused to obey the orders of the General Staff and switched their allegiance to the MRC, which sent out commissars to replace the unit commanders. Meetings of soldiers expressed their readiness to 'come out' against the Provisional Government if called to do so by the Petrograd Soviet. Even the once loyal Cossack regiments went along with the mutiny, or remained neutral. On 21 October the MRC proclaimed itself the ruling authority of the garrison: it was the first act of the insurrection. The General Staff made a last desperate effort to salvage some of its authority by reaching a compromise with the MRC. But it was too late. The garrison units were already under the effective control of the commissars. On 23 October the MRC extended its power to the Peter and Paul Fortress, whose cannon overlooked the Winter Palace. The Provisional Government had lost effective military control of the capital a full two days before the armed uprising began. This was the essential fact of the whole insurrection: without it one cannot explain the ease of the Bolshevik victory. By 25 October the most important task of any successful revolution — the capture of the garrison in the capital — had already been completed; the Provisional Government was defenceless; and it only remained for the Bolsheviks to walk into the Winter Palace and arrest the ministers.

The remarkable thing about the Bolshevik insurrection is that hardly any of the Bolshevik leaders had wanted it to happen until a few hours before it began. Until late in the evening of 24 October the majority of the Central Committee and the MRC had not envisaged the overthrow of the Provisional Government before the opening of the Soviet Congress the next day. Trotsky, who in Lenin's absence had effectively assumed the leadership of the party, repeatedly stressed the need for discipline and patience. On the morning of the 24th Kerensky had ordered the closure of two Bolshevik newspapers. Trotsky refused to be drawn by this 'provocation': the MRC should be placed on alert; the city's strategic installations should be seized as a defensive measure against any further 'counter-revolutionary' threats; but, as he insisted at a meeting of the Bolshevik Congress delegates in the afternoon, 'it would be a mistake to use even one of the armoured cars which now defend the Winter Palace to arrest the government . . . This is defence, comrades. This is defence.' Later that evening, in the Petrograd Soviet, Trotsky declared — and had good reason to believe — that 'an armed conflict today or tomorrow, on the eve of the Soviet Congress, is not in our plans'.[10]

There were obvious reasons not to force events at this final hour. The

Bolsheviks needed the sanction of the Soviet Congress to give legitimacy to their seizure of power: without it they could certainly not rely on the support of the soldiers and workers, and might even run the risk of having to fight against them. The Soviet delegates were already arriving for the opening of the Congress on the 25th, and from their composition it seemed highly likely that there would be a solid majority in favour of Soviet power. As for the Provisional Government — well, it was looking increasingly provisional, and would no doubt fall at the slightest prod. In the evening of the 24th the Preparliament had effectively passed a motion of no confidence in it. Even Dan and Gots, previously among the most obstinate advocates of the coalition, abandoned Kerensky and called for the establishment of a democratic government committed to peace and radical reforms. They wanted to publicize this as a historic proclamation plastered throughout the capital that same night, in the hope that it might appease the potential insurgents and strengthen the campaign for a peaceful resolution of the power question through the formation of a socialist coalition. Perhaps it was already too late for this: it looked like trying to fend off the Bolshevik guns with paper decrees. Yet, even in these final hours, there was still some basis for hope that agreement might be reached. In the evening of the 24th Kamenev was still rushing around the Smolny trying to win support for a resolution calling on the Congress to form a socialist government of all the Soviet parties; and the SRs and Mensheviks, whose congress delegates met late into the night, were at last coming round to support the plan.

Meanwhile, however, the Bolshevik insurrection was already gaining momentum. Despite Trotsky's call for discipline, it was hard to stop the defensive measures of the MRC from spilling into a general offensive. As darkness fell, armed crowds of Bolshevik workers and soldiers spilled into the centre of the city. The government blockades on the bridges, which controlled the routes from the outlying slums, were taken over by Red Guards. They set up road blocks and patrolled the streets in armoured cars, while late-night theatre-goers hurried home. By the early hours of the morning, Bolshevik forces had seized control of the railway stations, the post and telegraph, the state bank, the telephone exchange and the electricity station. The Red Guards had taken over the local police stations and had begun to assume the functions of the police themselves. Overall, the insurgents had the control of almost all the city with the exception of the central zone around the Winter Palace and St Isaac's Square. Bunkered inside the Winter Palace, Kerensky's ministers did not even have control over their own lights or telephones. One of the Bolshevik engineers engaged in the occupation of the Nikolaevsky Station recalled standing guard by the equestrian statue of Alexander III:

It was a freezing night. One could feel the north wind going through one's bones. On the streets adjacent to the Nikolaevsky Station groups of engineers huddled, shivering from the cold, and peered vigilantly into the shadowy night. The moonlight created a fantastic scene. The hulks of the houses looked like medieval castles, and giant shadows followed the engineers. At this sight the next-to-last Emperor appeared to rein in his horse in horror.[11]

These early successes strengthened Lenin's appeal for the immediate seizure of power. The Bolshevik leaders did not want a repeat of the July Days, when their own initial hesitation in supporting the initiative of the streets had resulted in fiasco. As news reached them of the Bolshevik gains, so pressure mounted to take control of the situation and start the insurrection. Lenin's intervention was decisive. Confined to Fofanova's flat, he had become increasingly frustrated as he watched the day's events unfold. At 6 p.m. he scribbled a desperate appeal to the Petrograd party organizations, urging them to launch an insurrection in the next few hours, and ordered Fofanova to deliver it to the Smolny. The Soviet Congress was due to open the following afternoon, and unless the Bolsheviks had already seized power by then, his whole political strategy would be doomed. By 10 p.m. Lenin could hold back no longer. He donned his wig and a worker's cap, wrapped a bandage around his head, and set off for the Smolny, accompanied by the Finnish Bolshevik, Eino Rakhia. Riding through the Vyborg district in an empty streetcar, Lenin overwhelmed the poor conductress with questions on the latest situation and, discovering that she was a leftist, bullied her with advice on revolutionary action. From the Finland Station the two men continued their journey on foot. Near the Tauride Palace a government patrol stopped them, but, according to Rakhia, mistook Lenin, who was dressed in his worst clothes, for a harmless drunk and let them proceed.[12] One can only wonder how different history would have been if Lenin had been arrested.

Shortly before midnight they finally reached the Smolny. The building was ablaze with lights, like an ocean liner in the dark night sea. Trucks and armoured cars rushed to and fro laden down with Bolshevik troops and guns. Machine-guns had been set up outside the gates, where the Red Guards huddled around a bonfire checking the passes of those wanting to enter the military headquarters of the insurrection. Lenin had arrived without a pass and, in his disguise, was not recognized by the Red Guards; he only succeeded in gaining entry by squeezing through them amidst a crowd. He went at once to Room 36, where the Bolshevik caucus met, and harangued his comrades on the need to start the seizure of power. A meeting of the Central Committee was hastily convened and, although no protocol of it was recorded, the testimonies of those who were there are all agreed that Lenin had a decisive effect in changing the dominant mood from one of defence to one of offence. The Central Committee at last gave the order for the insurrection to begin. A map of the city was brought out and the Bolshevik leaders pored over it, drawing up the main lines of attack and assigning military tasks.

During a break in their deliberations Lenin suggested drawing up a list of the Bolshevik government to be presented to the Soviet Congress the next day. The question arose as to what to call the new government and its members. The term 'Provisional Government' was thought to sound outmoded, whilst calling themselves 'ministers' seemed far too bureaucratic and respectable. The Bolsheviks, after all, liked to see themselves as a fighting organization: they dressed in macho black leather jackets and military boots, whereas most of the other political parties wore ministerial suits.* It was Trotsky who came forward with the idea of calling the ministers 'people's commissars' in emulation of the Jacobins. Everyone liked the suggestion. 'Yes, that's very good,' said Lenin, 'it smells of revolution. And we can call the government itself the "Council of People's Commissars".' Nominations were taken for the various cabinet posts, although with Kerensky not yet overthrown the exercise seemed rather premature and was carried out in a light-hearted manner. Lenin stretched himself out on the floor, relaxed and triumphant. He made several jokes at Kamenev's expense, who had warned that the party could not hold on to power for more than a fortnight. 'Never mind,' Lenin quipped, 'when, in two years' time, we are still in power, then you will be saying that we cannot survive longer than two years.'[13]

✳ ✳ ✳

Few historical events have been more profoundly distorted by myth than those of 25 October 1917. The popular image of the Bolshevik insurrection, as a bloody struggle by the tens of thousands with several thousand fallen heroes, owes more to *October* — Eisenstein's brilliant but largely fictional propaganda film to commemorate the tenth anniversary of the event — than to historical fact. The Great October Socialist Revolution, as it came to be called in Soviet mythology, was in reality such a small-scale event, being in effect no more than a military coup, that it passed unnoticed by the vast majority of the inhabitants of Petrograd. Theatres, restaurants and tram cars functioned much as normal while the Bolsheviks came to power. The whole insurrection could have been completed in six hours, had it not been for the ludicrous incompetence of the insurgents themselves, which made it take an extra fifteen. The legendary 'storming' of the Winter Palace, where Kerensky's cabinet held its final session, was more like a routine house arrest, since most of the forces defending the palace had already left for home, hungry and dejected, before the assault began. The

---

* It was only under Stalin, when the Bolsheviks began to call themselves 'Ministers', that they reverted back to suits.

only real damage to the imperial residence in the whole affair was a chipped cornice and a shattered window on the third floor.

The Bolshevik plan was simple: the garrison soldiers, the Red Guards and the Kronstadt sailors were to capture the Marinsky Palace and disperse the Preparliament; demand the surrender of the Provisional Government and, if it refused, seize control of the Winter Palace on a signal from the Peter and Paul Fortress and the Baltic cruiser *Aurora*. The MRC expected to complete the operations by noon — in time for Lenin to present the seizure of power as a *fait accompli* to the Soviet Congress. At 10 a.m., in anticipation of a speedy victory, the Bolshevik leader was already putting the final touches to his manifesto, 'To the Citizens of Russia!', announcing the overthrow of the Provisional Government and the transfer of power to the MRC.[14]

The first part of the plan went smoothly enough: shortly before noon a group of Bolshevik soldiers and sailors burst into the Marinsky Palace and ordered the deputies to disperse. But after that elementary technical failures forced the MRC to postpone the operations around the Winter Palace until 3 p.m., then 6 p.m., whereafter it ceased to bother with any set deadlines at all. The first major hold-up was the late arrival of the Baltic sailors, without whom the MRC would not go ahead. Then there was another, even more frustrating, problem. The assault on the Winter Palace was due to begin with the heavy field-guns of the Peter and Paul Fortress, but at the final moment these were discovered to be rusty museum pieces which could not be fired. Soldiers were hastily sent out to drag alternative cannons up to the fortress walls, but when these arrived it turned out that there were no suitable shells for them. Even more surreal was the panic created by the seemingly simple task of raising a red lantern to the top of the fortress's flagpole to signal the start of the assault on the palace. When the moment for action arrived, no red lantern could be found. The Bolshevik Commissar of the Fortress, Blagonravov, went out in search of a suitable lamp but got himself lost in the dark and fell into a muddy bog. When he finally returned, the lamp he had brought could not be fixed to the flagpole and was never seen by those who took part in the assault. In any case, it wasn't red.[15]

From Lenin's point of view all these delays were infuriating. It was vital for him to have the seizure of power completed before the opening of the Soviet Congress and, although this too had been delayed, time was rapidly running out. At around 3 p.m. he had told a packed session of the Petrograd Soviet that the Provisional Government had already been overthrown. It was of course a lie — the Ministers were still barricaded inside the Winter Palace — but that was a minor detail: the fact of the seizure of power was to be so important to his political strategy over the next few hours that he was even prepared to invent it. As afternoon turned into evening, he screamed at the MRC commanders to seize the Winter Palace without delay. Podvoisky recalls him pacing around in a small room in the Smolny 'like a lion in a cage. He needed the Winter Palace at any cost . . . he was ready to shoot us.'[16]

In fact the Bolshevik forces which had gathered in the centre of the city by this stage could have walked quite freely into the Winter Palace, since its defence was almost non-existent. With the mutiny of the Petrograd garrison, Kerensky had tried to summon loyal troops from the Northern Front. His order had been dispatched on the night of the 24th with the forged signature of the Soviet leaders, since Kerensky feared the soldiers would not come on the authority of the Provisional Government. By the following morning there was still no sign of the troops and he resolved to go off in search of them. With the railways in Bolshevik hands, he was forced to travel by car; but such was the utter helplessness of the Provisional Government that it did not even have a taxi at its disposal. Military officials were sent out to find a car. They seized a Renault from outside the American Embassy (which later launched a diplomatic protest), while a second car was found at the War Ministry, although it had no fuel and more men had to be sent out to 'borrow' some from the English Hospital. At around 11 a.m. the two cars sped out of the Winter Palace and headed out of the city. Kerensky was seated in the second car, flying the Stars and Stripes, which no doubt helped him past the MRC pickets already beginning to form around the Palace Square.[17]

Kerensky's departure threw the rest of the ministers into a panic (for a while they did not even know where he was). At midday they met in the Malachite Hall and prepared to organize the defence of the palace. But it was a hopeless task. They were totally inexperienced in military operations and spent the best part of the next four hours in a futile and aimless discussion of possible candidates for the post of 'Dictator' (dictator of what?) before settling on the Kadet doctor, and Minister of Welfare, Nikolai Kishkin. The engineer Palchinsky, who was placed in charge of defending the palace, could not even find a plan of the building, or anyone expert in its topography, with the result that one of the side-doors was left unguarded and Bolshevik spies were able to enter it freely. There were already some loyalist forces inside the palace, and others outside who spent the afternoon building barricades out of piles of logs. Kerensky had kept a small number of troops on the ground floor since moving into the palace, and these were now joined by two companies of Cossacks, some young cadets from the military schools and 200 women from the Shock Battalion of Death, in all some 3,000 soldiers. John Reed, one of several foreign journalists to slip past their guard during the afternoon, described the scene:

> At the end of the corridor was a large, ornate room with gilded cornices and enormous crystal lustres . . . On both sides of the parqueted floor lay

rows of dirty mattresses and blankets, upon which occasional soldiers were stretched out; everywhere was a litter of cigarette butts, bits of bread, cloth, and empty bottles with expensive French labels. More and more soldiers . . . moved about in a stale atmosphere of tobacco-smoke and unwashed humanity. One had a bottle of white Burgundy, evidently filched from the cellars of the Palace . . . The place was a huge barrack.[18]

The fighting spirit of the soldiers defending the Winter Palace was extremely weak, however, and the longer they waited for the Bolsheviks to attack the more frightened they became. They were constantly reminded by the propaganda of the enemy that they were vastly outnumbered, and this made it difficult to keep up their morale. Alexander Sinegub, one of the officers in charge, recalls the soldiers smoking, getting drunk and cursing their hopeless situation while the ministers harangued them on the need to maintain discipline. The Cossacks were particularly disgruntled by the idea of having to fight alongside 'women with guns'. There was no real ammunition store inside the palace, while the food supply was not enough to feed all the soldiers even for dinner. As the evening wore on, more and more of these hungry soldiers became demoralized and abandoned the palace: the call of their stomachs was stronger than the call of duty. By the early evening, all but 300 of the troops had laid down their arms and slipped away to the restaurants in the city.[19]

During these final hours of waiting for the inevitable the ministers made a number of futile appeals to the people for help. Although all their telephone lines had been cut, they still had a secret line to the military telegraph office in the attic of the War Ministry building, where, unbeknown to the Bolsheviks, who had occupied the rest of the building, a young officer sat sending out the government's final appeals to various parts of the country (later, when he heard the palace had fallen, he put on his coat and hat and walked calmly out of the building). John Reed, who saw the green baize cabinet table shortly after the ministers' arrest, found it covered in dozens of roughly scribbled drafts, most of them scratched out as their futility became evident. No one, it seems, was prepared to rally to the defence of the Provisional Government. The one attempt to do so, by the deputies of the Petrograd city Duma, was a piece of surreal theatre that ended in farce. Responding to the ministers' appeal for support, the deputies declared their readiness to 'stand in front of the Bolshevik cannon', and marched off in columns of four towards the Winter Palace singing the Marseillaise. The white-bearded figure of Schreider, the Mayor of Petrograd, led this army of salvation, along with Prokopovich, the Minister of Supplies, who carried an umbrella to shelter himself from the rain which was now beginning to fall and a lantern to light up the way. The 300 deputies, dressed in their frock-coats, officers' tunics and dresses, each proudly bore a package of bread and salami for the hungry defenders of the Winter Palace. They were a walking symbol of the decent but doomed old liberal Russia that was about to disappear. The deputies had advanced less than a block from the Duma building when they were halted by a patrol of Bolshevik sailors near the Kazan Square. Schreider bared his breast to their guns and pronounced himself ready to die, if they did not let them pass. But the sailors, no doubt seeing the comical aspect of this impotent protest, threatened to 'spank' them if they did not go home. Prokopovich then climbed on to a box and, waving his umbrella in the air, made a speech: 'Comrades and citizens! Force is being used against us! We cannot have our innocent blood upon the hands of these ignorant men! It is beneath our dignity to be shot down here in the streets . . . Let us return to the Duma and discuss the best means of saving the country and the revolution!' Whereupon the outraged deputies about-turned and marched back up the Nevsky, all the time maintaining a dignified silence in defeat.[20]

Meanwhile, at 6.50 p.m., the MRC delivered its ultimatum to the Winter Palace demanding the surrender of the Provisional Government. The ministers, who were at the time sitting down to a supper of borscht, steamed fish and artichokes, all felt a solemn obligation to be brave and resist for as long as they could, although some were concerned that the palace might be destroyed if the cruiser *Aurora*, anchored alongside the English Embankment,* opened fire at it as had been threatened. They reasoned that the Bolsheviks would be widely condemned if they were made to overthrow them by force; so the ultimatum was refused. For a long time nothing happened — the Bolsheviks were still messing around with faulty field-guns and lanterns in the Peter and Paul Fortress — but at 9.40 p.m. the signal was finally given and one blank round was fired by the *Aurora*. The huge sound of the blast, much louder than a live shot, caused the frightened ministers to drop at once to the floor. The women from the Battalion of Death became hysterical and had to be taken away to a room at the back of the palace, while most of the remaining cadets abandoned their posts. After a short break to allow those who wished to do so to leave the palace, Blagonravov gave the order for the real firing to begin from the Peter and Paul Fortress, the *Aurora* and the Palace Square. Most of the shells from the fortress landed harmlessly in the Neva. George Buchanan, the British Ambassador, who inspected the palace the following day, found only three shrapnel marks on the river side of the building, although 'on the town side the walls were riddled with thousands of bullets from machine guns'.[21]

* The exact 'historic spot' where the *Aurora* was anchored happened to be by a pretty little chapel next to the Nikolaevsky Bridge. Several years later it was decided that this Christian link with the starting place of the Great October Socialist Revolution should be removed — and so the Bolsheviks turned the chapel into a public lavatory!

Just as the bombardment was getting under way, at 10.40 p.m., the Soviet Congress finally opened. The great hall of the Smolny was packed; the delegates stood in the aisles and perched on window-sills. The air was thick with blue tobacco smoke, despite repeated calls from the tribune for 'the comrades' not to smoke. The majority of the delegates were workers and soldiers in their tunics and greatcoats; their unwashed and dirty look contrasted sharply with the clean suits of the old executive members, the Mensheviks and SRs, seated on the platform for the final time. Sukhanov remarked that the 'grey features of the Bolshevik provinces' had a clear preponderance among the Congress delegates. He was shocked by their 'dark', 'morose' and 'primitive' appearance, and thought it reflected a 'crude and ignorant people whose devotion to the revolution was spite and despair, while their "Socialism" was hunger and an unendurable longing for rest'. This of course was a Menshevik speaking, but, even if we ignore his value-laden terms, there is no doubt that the mass of the delegates were indeed less cultured than the urbanized, skilled and educated types who had hitherto made up the majority of the Soviet movement.

The Bolsheviks did not have an absolute majority, as Sukhanov had thought, though with the support of the Left SRs they could push through virtually any motion they liked. Although precise numbers are difficult to determine, the Credentials Committee of the Congress reported that 300 of the 670 delegates were Bolsheviks, 193 SRs (of whom more than half were Left SRs), while 82 were Mensheviks (of whom 14 were Internationalists). Because of the lax regulations for the selection of delegates and their own superior party organization, the Bolsheviks had managed to secure rather more than their fair share of seats. The northern industrial Soviets, where the influence of the Bolsheviks was dominant both in the towns and the semi-industrial villages, sent more representatives than was warranted by their size; whereas those of the Volga and the agricultural south, where the SRs were dominant, sent fewer and in some cases even boycotted the Congress altogether. There was a similar imbalance among the delegates of the armed services, with the Bolshevized north far better represented than the non-Bolshevized south. The Latvians, the most Bolshevized troops of all, made up more than 10 per cent of the delegates.[22]

In accordance with these voting strengths, the old Soviet leaders vacated their seats on the platform; they were replaced by 14 Bolsheviks and 7 Left SRs. The Mensheviks declined to take up the 4 seats allocated to them.

The mandates of the delegates showed an overwhelming majority in favour of a Soviet government. It was up to the Congress to decide how this should be formed. Martov proposed the formation of a united democratic government based upon all the parties in the Soviet: this, he said, was the only way to avert a civil war. The proposal was met with torrents of applause. Even Lunacharsky was forced to admit that the Bolsheviks had nothing against it —

they could not abandon the slogan of Soviet Power — and the proposal was immediately passed by a unanimous vote. But just as it looked as if a socialist coalition was at last about to be formed, a series of Mensheviks and SRs bitterly denounced the violent assault on the Provisional Government. They declared that their parties, or at least the right-wing sections of them, would have nothing to do with this 'criminal venture', which was bound to throw the country into civil war, and walked out of the Congress hall in protest, while the Bolshevik delegates stamped their feet, whistled and hurled abuse at them.[23]

Lenin's planned provocation — the pre-emptive seizure of power — had worked. By walking out of the Congress, the Mensheviks and SRs undermined all hopes of reaching a compromise with the Bolshevik moderates and of forming a coalition government of all the Soviet parties. The path was now clear for the Bolshevik dictatorship, based on the Soviet, which Lenin had no doubt intended all along. In the charged political atmosphere of the time, it is easy to see why the Mensheviks and SRs acted as they did. But it is equally difficult not to draw the conclusion that, by their actions, they merely played into Lenin's hands and thus committed political suicide. Writing in 1921, Sukhanov admitted as much:

> We completely untied the Bolsheviks' hands, making them masters of the whole situation and yielding to them the whole arena of the Revolution. A struggle at the Congress for a united democratic front might have had some success ... But by leaving the Congress, we ourselves gave the Bolsheviks a monopoly of the Soviet, of the masses, and of the Revolution. By our own irrational decision, we ensured the victory of Lenin's whole 'line'.[24]

The immediate effect of their walk-out was to split the opposition forces, leaving Martov and the other left-wing advocates of a coalition isolated. Martov made one more desperate appeal for an all-democratic government. But the mood in the hall was changing. As the mass of the delegates saw it, the Mensheviks and SRs had proved themselves to be 'counter-revolutionaries' by walking out of the Congress; and they were now ready to follow the lead of the Bolsheviks in opposing the whole idea of a compromise with them. Trotsky seized the initiative and, in one of the most often-quoted speeches of the twentieth century, denounced Martov's resolution for a coalition:

> The masses of the people followed our banner and our insurrection was victorious. And now we are told: Renounce your victory, make concessions, compromise. With whom? I ask: With those wretched groups who have left us or who are making this proposal ... No one in Russia is with

them any longer. A compromise is supposed to be made between two equal sides ... But here no compromise is possible. To those who have left and to those who tell us to do this we say: You are miserable bankrupts, your role is played out; go where you ought to go — into the dustbin of history!

In a moment of rage, which he must have agonized over for the rest of his life, Martov shouted, 'Then we'll leave!' and walked in silence towards the exit without looking back. As he did so, a Bolshevik dressed in a black shirt, tied by a leather belt, stepped out into the aisle and said to Martov: 'And we had thought that Martov at least would remain with us.' Visibly shaken by these words, Lenin's old comrade replied: 'One day you will understand the crime in which you are taking part.' And with that he walked out — and into the political wilderness.[25]

It was past two o'clock in the morning and it only remained for Trotsky, who was now clearly doing the work of Lenin, to propose a resolution condemning the 'treacherous' attempts of the Mensheviks and SRs to undermine Soviet power. In effect, this would be to give a Soviet stamp of approval to a Bolshevik dictatorship. The mass of the delegates, who were probably too ignorant to comprehend the political import of what they were doing, raised their hands in support (weren't they in favour of Soviet power?). But the Left SR leaders, who should have known better, were equally fooled; and they too raised their hands in the naive conviction, as their leader, Boris Kamkov, later explained, that 'our place was with the revolution' and that, by going along with the Bolshevik adventure, they might be able to tame it.[26]

Meanwhile, the final assault on the Winter Palace was nearing completion. The loyalist forces had virtually all abandoned the defence of the palace and Bolshevik troops could enter it at will. The ministers, who were now stretched out on sofas, or slouched in chairs, awaiting the end, could hear the sound of running soldiers, shouts and gun shots from the floor below. Finally, some time after 2 a.m., these sounds grew louder: the Bolshevik attackers were climbing the stairs and approaching the door. It was clear that the moment for surrender had arrived. The ministers jumped up and — for some strange reason — grabbed hold of their overcoats, as the door was suddenly flung open and in stepped the small, unassuming figure of Antonov-Ovseenko. 'You are all under arrest,' the Bolshevik leader announced. A register of the ministers was taken. The realization that Kerensky was not present angered the attackers, one of whom shouted: 'Bayonet all the sons of bitches!' But otherwise discipline was maintained. The ministers were led away on foot (no cars were available) to the Peter and Paul Fortress, where they were locked up in dismal conditions for a number of weeks. The Bolshevik escorts had to defend them on the way from several attempts to lynch them on the streets, and it must have been with some relief that the ministers finally reached the safety of their prison. Perhaps some of them were also secretly relieved to be no longer burdened with the near-impossible task of trying to govern Russia. As the door of his cell banged shut, Alexei Nikitin, the deposed Minister of the Interior, found in his pocket a half-forgotten telegram from the Ukrainian Rada. 'I received this yesterday,' he told Antonov-Ovseenko, as he handed him the crumpled piece of paper, 'now it's your problem.'[27]

It fell to Kamenev, ironically enough, to announce the arrest of the ministers to the Soviet Congress. The Bolsheviks cheered as their names were read out. But a large peasant, his face convulsed with rage, got up on behalf of the SRs to denounce the arrest of the socialist ministers. 'Do you know that four comrades, who risked their lives and their freedom fighting against the tyranny of the Tsar, have been flung into the Peter and Paul prison — the historical tomb of Liberty?' There was pandemonium as people shouted out, while Trotsky, gesturing for silence, answered by denouncing them as false 'comrades' and claimed there was no reason 'to handle them with gloves'. After the July Days 'they didn't use much ceremony with us!' Kamenev then announced that the Cyclist Battalion had come over to the 'side of the revolution'. There were reports of more vital troops joining from the Northern Front. And then Lunacharsky read out Lenin's Manifesto 'To All Workers, Soldiers, and Peasants', in which 'Soviet Power' was proclaimed, and its promises on land, bread and peace were announced. The reading of this historic proclamation, which was constantly interrupted by the thunderous cheers of the delegates, played an enormous symbolic role. It provided the illusion that the insurrection was the culmination of a revolution by 'the masses'. When it had been passed, shortly after 5 a.m. on the 26th, the weary but elated delegates emerged from the Tauride Palace. 'The night was yet heavy and chill,' wrote John Reed. 'There was only a faint unearthly pallor stealing over the silent streets, dimming the watch-fires, the shadow of a terrible dawn rising over Russia.'[28]

＊   ＊   ＊

How many people took part in the insurrection? Historians have always been sharply divided on this question, with those on the Left depicting October as a popular revolution driven from below, and those on the Right depicting it as a *coup d'état* without any mass support. At the root of the question is the nature — and thus the 'legitimacy' — of the Soviet system. And in this sense it is one of the fundamental questions of the twentieth century.

The number of active participants in the insurrection was not very large — although of course it must be borne in mind that large numbers were not needed for the task, given the almost complete absence of any military forces in the capital prepared to defend the Provisional Government. Trotsky himself

claimed that 25,000 to 30,000 people 'at the most' were actively involved —
that is about 5 per cent of all the workers and soldiers in the city — and this
broadly tallies with the calculations based on the number of Red Guard units,
Fleet crews and regiments which were mobilized. Most of them were involved
in a limited fashion, such as guarding factories and strategic buildings, manning
the pickets and generally 'standing by'. During the evening of the 25th, there
were probably something in the region of 10,000 to 15,000 people milling
around in the Palace Square; but not all of them were actually involved in the
'storming' of the palace, although many more would later claim that they had
taken part.* Of course, once the palace had been seized, larger crowds of people
did become involved, although, as we shall see, this was largely a question of
looting its wine stores.[29]

The few surviving photographs of the October Days clearly show the
small size of the insurgent force. They depict a handful of Red Guards and
sailors standing around in half-deserted streets. None of the familiar images of
a people's revolution — crowds on the street, barricades and fighting — were
in evidence. The whole insurrection, as Trotsky himself acknowledged, was
carried out as a *coup d'état* with 'a series of small operations, calculated and
prepared in advance'. The immediate vicinity of the Winter Palace was the only
part of the city to be seriously disrupted during 25 October. Elsewhere the life
of Petrograd carried on as normal. Streetcars and taxis ran as usual; the Nevsky
was full of the normal crowds; and during the evening shops, restaurants, theatres
and cinemas even remained open. The Marinsky Theatre went ahead with its
scheduled performance of *Boris Godunov*; while the famous bass Shaliapin sang in
Don Carlos before a packed house at the Narodny Dom. At around 9 p.m. John
Reed was able to dine in the Hotel France, just off Palace Square, although after
his soup the waiter asked him to move into the main dining-room at the back
of the building, since they expected shooting to begin and wanted to put out
the lights in the café. Even the climax of the insurrection passed by largely
unnoticed. Volodya Averbakh was walking home by Gogol Street, not a hundred
yards from Palace Square, at about 11 p.m., just as the Bolsheviks were readying
themselves for their final assault on the Winter Palace. 'The street was completely
deserted,' Averbakh recalled. 'The night was quiet, and the city seemed dead.
We could even hear the echo of our own footsteps on the pavement.'[30]

In the workers' districts things were just as quiet, judging by the local

---

* During the 1930s, when the party carried out a survey of the Red Guard veterans of October,
12 per cent of those responding claimed to have participated in the storming of the palace. On
this calculation, 46,000 people would have been involved in the assault (Startsev, *Ocherki*, 275). It
would be interesting to know the results of a similar survey of the Muscovite intelligentsia during
the defence of the parliament building in August 1991. The number of people claiming to have
been there, alongside Yeltsin on the tank, would probably run into the hundreds of thousands.

494 Russia in Revolution

police reports recently unearthed from the Soviet archives. Asked in the first week of November if there had been any mass armed movements in the October Days, the district police commissars responded, without exception, that there had been none. 'Everything was quiet on the streets,' replied the chief of the Okhtensk police district. 'The streets were empty,' added the police chief of the 3rd Spassky district. In the 1st Vyborg police district, the most Bolshevized part of the city, the police chief made the following report on 25 October: 'the Red Guards helped the police in the maintenance of order, and there were no night-time events to report, apart from the arrest of two drunken and disorderly soldiers, accused of shooting and wounding a man — also, it seems, drunk.'[31] Thus began the Great October Socialist Revolution in the Bolshevik bastion of the Vyborg district.

What about the nature of the crowd during the insurrection? The following incident tells us something about this.

When the Bolsheviks took control of the Winter Palace, they discovered one of the largest wine cellars ever known. During the following days tens of thousands of antique bottles disappeared from the vaults. The Bolshevik workers and soldiers were helping themselves to the Château d'Yquem 1847, the last Tsar's favourite vintage, and selling off the vodka to the crowds outside. The drunken mobs went on the rampage. The Winter Palace was badly vandalized. Shops and liquor stores were looted. Sailors and soldiers went around the well-to-do districts robbing apartments and killing people for sport. Anyone well dressed was an obvious target. Even Uritsky, the Bolshevik leader, narrowly escaped with his life, if not his clothes, when his sleigh was stopped one freezing night on his way home from the Smolny. With his warm overcoat, pince-nez and Jewish-intellectual looks, he had been mistaken for a *burzhooi*.

The Bolsheviks tried in vain to stem the anarchy by sealing off the liquor supply. They appointed a Commissar of the Winter Palace — who was constantly drunk on the job. They posted guards around the cellar — who licensed themselves to sell off the bottles of liquor. They pumped the wine out on to the street — but crowds gathered to drink it from the gutter. They tried to destroy the offending treasure, to transfer it to the Smolny, and even to ship it to Sweden — but all their efforts came to nothing. Hundreds of drunkards were thrown into jail — in one police precinct alone 182 people were arrested on the night of 4 November for drunkenness and looting — until there was no more room in the cells. Machine-guns were set up to deter the looters by firing over their heads — and sometimes at them — but still the looters came. For several weeks the anarchy continued — martial law was even imposed — until, at last, the alcohol ran out with the old year, and the capital woke up with the biggest hangover in history.

The Bolsheviks blamed the 'provocations of the bourgeoisie' for this bacchanalia. It was hard for them to admit that their own supporters, who were supposed to be the 'disciplined vanguard of the proletariat', could have been involved in such anarchic behaviour. But the recently opened records of the MRC show that many of those who had taken part in the seizure of power were the instigators of these drunken riots. Some of them, no doubt, had only taken part in the insurrection *because* of the prospect of loot: the whole uprising for them was a big adventure, a day out in the city with the rest of the lads, and with a licence to rob and kill. This is not to say that the Bolsheviks were simply hooligans and criminals, as many propertied types concluded at the time. But it is to say that the uprising was bound to descend into chaos because the Bolsheviks had at their disposal very few disciplined fighters and because the seizure of power itself, as a violent act, encouraged such actions from the crowd. Similar outbursts of looting and violence were noted in dozens of cities during and after October. Indeed, they were often an integral element of the transfer of power.[32]

All this suggests that the Bolshevik insurrection was not so much the culmination of a social revolution, although of course there were several different social revolutions — in the towns and in the cities, in the countryside, in the armed forces and in the borderlands — and in each of these there were militant forces that had some connections with the Bolsheviks. It was more the result of the degeneration of the urban revolution, and in particular of the workers' movement, as an organized and constructive force, with vandalism, crime, generalized violence and drunken looting as the main expressions of this social breakdown. Gorky, who was, as always, quick to condemn this anarchic violence, was at pains to point out that 'what is going on now is *not a process of social revolution*' but a 'pogrom of greed, hatred and vengeance'.[33] The participants in this destructive violence were not the organized 'working class' but the victims of the breakdown of that class and of the devastation of the war years: the growing army of the urban unemployed; the refugees from the occupied regions, soldiers and sailors, who congregated in the cities; bandits and criminals released from the jails; and the unskilled labourers from the countryside who had always been the most prone to outbursts of anarchic violence in the cities. These were the semi-peasant types whom Gorky had blamed for the urban violence in the spring and to whose support he had ascribed the rising fortunes of the Bolsheviks. He returned to the same theme on the eve of their seizure of power:

All the dark instincts of the crowd irritated by the disintegration of life and by the lies and filth of politics will flare up and fume, poisoning us with anger, hate and revenge; people will kill one another, unable to suppress their own animal stupidity. An unorganized crowd, hardly understanding what it wants, will crawl out into the street, and, using this crowd as a cover, adventurers, thieves, and professional murderers will begin to 'create the history of the Russian Revolution'.[34]

As for the Petrograd workers, they took little part in the insurrection. This was the height of the economic crisis and the fear of losing their jobs was enough to deter the vast majority of them from coming out on to the streets. Hence the factories and the transport system functioned much as normal. The workers, in any case, owed their allegiance to the Soviet rather than the Bolsheviks. Most of them did not know — or even wish to know — the differences of doctrine between the socialist parties. Their own voting patterns were determined by class rather than by party: they tended to vote as their factory had voted in the past, or opted for the party whose candidate seemed most like a worker and spoke the language of class. Among the unskilled, in particular, there was a common belief that the Bolsheviks were a party of 'big men' (from the peasant term *bolshaki*).

So when the leaders of the railwaymen's union, Vikzhel, issued an ultimatum on 29 October demanding that the Bolsheviks begin talks with the other socialist parties for the formation of an all-Soviet government, they received a great deal of support. To the mass of the workers, it seemed that the whole point of the revolution, as expressed at the Soviet Congress, was the formation of a government of the working people as a whole and not just of one party. Hundreds of factories, garrisons, Front and Fleet assemblies sent petitions to Smolny in support of the Vikzhel plan. The Obukhovsky Factory in Petrograd threatened to 'knock the heads of all the party leaders together' if they failed to reach agreement. The workers in Moscow and other provincial cities, where party factionalism was much less pronounced than in the capital, also expressed strong support. There was a general sense that the party leaders, by squabbling between themselves, were betraying the ideals of the revolution and leading the country towards civil war. 'Among the soldiers', declared a petition from the 35th Division, 'there are no Bolsheviks, Mensheviks, or SRs, but only Democrats.'[35]

There were powerful reasons, at least to begin with, for the Bolsheviks to respect Vikzhel's demands. The union's leaders had threatened to bring all the railways to a halt if the inter-party talks did not commence. If this happened the food and fuel supply in the capital, which had already declined to critical levels, would get even worse, looting and rioting would accelerate out of control, and thousands of workers would come out on strike. How long could the Bolsheviks last in this situation? The support of the railways was even more critical for the Bolshevik military campaign on two fronts: against Kerensky's troops on the outskirts of the capital; and in Moscow, where the Bolshevik forces had to fight for power in the streets against loyalist forces.

After his hasty departure from Petrograd on the morning of the 25th,

Kerensky had set up his headquarters at Gatchina, the old imperial residence just outside the city. Most of the army commanders, to whom he appealed for help, were reluctant to become involved in a military adventure against the Bolsheviks: it was bound to be seen by the soldiers as 'counter-revolutionary' and, like the Kornilov crisis, could only hasten the collapse of the army. General Cheremisov, Commander of the Northern Front, even cancelled Kerensky's order for troops on the grounds that the Provisional Government no longer existed. Only General Krasnov put his forces — eighteen Cossack companies — at Kerensky's disposal; while a small force of cadets and officers, organized around the SR-led Committee for the Salvation of Russia and the Revolution, was supposed to rise up in the capital in time for their arrival. The Bolsheviks, however, had even fewer troops prepared to fight than Kerensky. The Petrograd garrison quickly fell apart after the seizure of power, as the mass of the soldiers went on a drunken rampage or fled to their homes in the countryside. The Bolshevik leaders in Petrograd had no direct link with the revolutionary troops at the Front, and even if they had it was doubtful the troops would come out on their call. According to Reed, Lenin was fully prepared for defeat. His best chance lay with the hold-up of Krasnov's troops, situated around Pskov, by the railway workers, as had happened during the Kornilov crisis. Hence the need to respond to the Vikzhel ultimatum.

In Moscow, meanwhile, power hung in the balance for ten days. The MRC forces were engaged in a bloody street war — the opening shots of the civil war — against the military cadets and student volunteers, who remained loyal to the Provisional Government and were organized by the Moscow city Duma and its Committee of Public Safety. The heaviest fighting took place around the Kremlin, and many of the city's greatest architectural treasures were badly damaged. For ordinary Muscovites, too frightened to leave their homes, these were terrible days. Brusilov's flat was caught in the crossfire, and was used by soldiers of both sides to shoot or signal from the windows. The old man himself was badly wounded in the leg when a hand grenade flew in through the window. He had to be stretchered out to receive treatment in a nearby hospital, while 'bombs and bullets continued to fly in all directions. I prayed all the way that none of them would hit my poor old wife, who walked along by my side.'[36] The Moscow Bolsheviks were reluctant fighters — they were much more inclined to resolve the power question through negotiation, as proposed by Vikzhel. Nor were they very good at fighting: the Kremlin was soon lost in the opening battle on the 27th; and two days later the situation had become so bad, with the Bolshevik forces pushed back into the industrial suburbs, that they were frankly glad of the temporary ceasefire enforced by the intervention of Vikzhel. Without victory in Moscow, even Lenin recognized that the Bolsheviks could not retain power on their own. The inter-party talks would have to go ahead.

On 29 October the Central Committee authorized Kamenev to represent the party at the Vikzhel inter-party talks on the platform of Soviet power, as passed at the Second Congress. It was always going to be hard to persuade the right-wing Mensheviks and SRs to accept this, or indeed any partnership with the Bolshevik Party, after their walk-out from the Soviet Congress in protest against the seizure of power. At the opening meeting, confident that the Bolsheviks were on the verge of defeat, they set impossible terms for their involvement in any government: the release of the ministers arrested in the seizure of the Winter Palace; an armistice with Kerensky's troops; the abolition of the MRC; the transfer of the Petrograd garrison to the control of the Duma; and the involvement of Kerensky in the formation of the new administration, which was to exclude Lenin. In short, they were demanding that the clock be put back to 20 October. No wonder Kamenev sounded glum in his report to the Soviet Congress that evening.

On the next day, however, things began to change. Kerensky's offensive had collapsed overnight, much in the manner of Krymov's earlier assault on Petrograd during the Kornilov crisis. Most of Krasnov's Cossacks, who had always been reluctant to fight without infantry support, simply gave up under a barrage from Bolshevik agitators, while the rest were easily repulsed by the Baltic troops on the Pulkovo Heights just outside the city. The Mensheviks and SRs were forced to soften their terms and agreed to take part in a coalition with the Bolsheviks, provided the leadership of the Soviet was broadened to include members from the First Soviet Congress, the city Dumas, the Peasant Soviet (which was still to convene) and the trade unions. Kamenev agreed and even suggested, in a moment of naive credulity, that the Bolsheviks would not insist on the presence of Lenin or Trotsky in the cabinet. But they had different ideas.

From the start, Lenin and Trotsky had been opposed to the Vikzhel talks: only the prospect of military defeat had brought them to the negotiating table. With the defeat of Kerensky, and even the battle in Moscow now beginning to swing back in their favour, with much of the city centre back in Bolshevik hands and the Kremlin itself under heavy bombardment, they set out to undermine the inter-party talks. At a meeting of the Central Committee on 1 November Trotsky condemned the compromise agreed by Kamenev and demanded at least 75 per cent of the cabinet seats for the Bolshevik Party: 'there was no point organizing the insurrection if we don't get the majority'. Lenin advocated leaving the talks altogether, or at least continuing with them only as 'a diplomatic cover for the military operations [in Moscow]'. He even demanded the arrest of the Vikzhel leaders as 'counter-revolutionaries' — a typical provocation designed to wreck the talks, along with the arrest and beating up of the SR leaders, Gots and Zenzinov, by Bolshevik sailors, the closure of the Kadet press, and a series of raids on Menshevik and SR newspaper offices. Despite the objections of several moderate members of the Central Committee, it was agreed to present the Bolshevik platform as an ultimatum to the inter-party talks and abandon them if it was rejected. The SRs and Mensheviks would of course never accept this, as Lenin and Trotsky knew very well. The seizure of power had irrevocably split the socialist movement in Russia, and no amount of negotiation could hope to bridge the gulf. The Vikzhel talks were doomed, and finally broke down on 6 November.[37]

The chances of a coalition were extremely limited. It was almost certainly too late to resolve the power question by political means. The events of 25 October marked the beginning of the civil war. And yet it is hard to avoid the conclusion that this was precisely what Lenin had wanted all along. He believed that the civil war had started back in August, and that the 'talk talk' of all the moderators just got in the way.

Having secured the dictatorship of his party, Lenin turned next to the task of securing his own dictatorship over the party itself. On 2 November the Central Committee was bullied into passing a series of quite astounding resolutions: Kamenev was accused of 'un-Marxist' activities against the October Revolution; his supporters were ordered to withdraw from the Central Committee; and if they failed to submit to the party's policy against the inter-party talks — submitted in the form of an 'Ultimatum from the majority of the Central Committee to the minority' — were threatened with expulsion from the party altogether. Each member of the Central Committee was dragged before Lenin, in his private office, and told to sign the ultimatum or risk expulsion. As Lunacharsky had warned at a meeting of the Petrograd Bolsheviks on 1 November, Lenin's bullying tactics would soon lead to a situation where 'only one man would be left in the Party — the Dictator'. It was a haunting echo of Trotsky's own famous warning, fourteen years before, that the party organization would first substitute itself for the party as a whole, then the Central Committee for the party organization, and then a single dictator for the Central Committee. On 4 November the five-man minority (Kamenev, Zinoviev, Rykov, Miliutin and Nogin) finally resigned from the Central Committee. Their open letter of protest appeared in *Izvestiia* the following day. Alongside it was printed a second letter of protest from five People's Commissars, a third of Lenin's cabinet, four who resigned and six other prominent Bolshevik leaders, in which it was stated that a purely Bolshevik government could be maintained only by means of 'political terror' and that, if this path was taken, it would lead to 'the establishment of an unaccountable regime and to the destruction of the revolution and the country'.[38]

This was without doubt one of the most critical moments in the history of the Bolshevik Party. Though Lenin's revolution had been carried out, the party emerged from it hopelessly divided and isolated from the rest of the revolutionary movement. Few people believed, in its second week, that the Bolshevik regime could survive.

ii The Smolny Autocrats

Five days after the Bolshevik seizure of power, Alexandra Kollontai, the new People's Commissar of Social Welfare, drove up to the entrance of a large government building on Kazan Street. It had formerly housed the Provisional Government's Ministry of Social Welfare, and she was now coming to take possession of it. An old liveried doorman opened the door and examined Kollontai from head to foot. No woman in Russia had ever been appointed to the head of a ministry before, and, as he looked at her now, he might have been excused for thinking that she was just one more impoverished war widow looking for government aid. Kollontai demanded to see the highest-ranking official in the building, but the old man replied that visiting hours were over for the day. When she announced that she was the People's Commissar and demanded to be let in, he merely replied that petitioners were received between one and three and that it was already five. Kollontai tried to force her way through, but the doorman blocked her way and closed the doors in her face.

It was hardly an auspicious start to the new regime. The employees of the Ministry had joined a general Civil Servants' strike in protest against the Bolshevik seizure of power, and when Kollontai returned the next morning with a small detachment of soldiers to take over the building she found it almost deserted. Virtually all the officials had joined the anti-Bolshevik strike, and only the doormen, cleaners and messenger boys, who could not afford to go on strike, had turned up for work as usual. Since it was pointless to try to operate from this vacant building, Kollontai returned to the Smolny and set up office in a small room there. The old doorman in Kazan Street redirected the ragged children and widows, the refugees and ruined peasants who came to plead for aid to the Bolshevik headquarters.

The early weeks of the new regime were frustrated by similar strikes and campaigns of sabotage in all the major ministries and government departments, the banks, the post and telegraph office, the railways administration, the municipal bodies, the law courts, schools, universities and other vital institutions. Although these public employees held diverse political views, virtually all were agreed that the Bolshevik regime was illegal and had to be opposed. Trotsky was greeted with ironic laughter when he arrived at the Ministry of Foreign Affairs and introduced himself to a meeting of the officials as their new Minister; when he ordered them back to work, they left the building in protest. In the Anichkov Palace, where the country's food supply was administered, the Civil

Servants removed all the office furniture and locked away the account books in the palace safe. In the post and telegraph office they walked off with all the directories and piles of telegram blanks (on which some of them would later write their memoirs). The striking officials of the Medical Department even went so far as to remove the nibs from all the pens.[39]

The refusal of the State Bank and the Treasury to honour the new government's cash demands was the most serious threat of all. Without money to pay its supporters, the Bolshevik regime could not hope to survive for long. Sovnarkom (the Council of People's Commissars) had made various requests for the transfer of ten million roubles, but each was refused by the bank officials as illegal. On 7 November the new Commissar of Finance, V. R. Menzhinsky, appeared at the State Bank with a detachment of sailors and demanded the money; but the bankers stood firm and, despite further armed threats, dismissals and ultimatums, continued their strike. Ten days later the Bolsheviks finally seized control of the bank and forced the employees, at the point of a gun, to open the vaults. Five million roubles were removed, taken off to the Smolny in a velvet bag and deposited on Lenin's desk. The whole operation resembled a bank hold-up. The Bolsheviks now took over the State Bank, making it possible for them to dip their hands freely into the nation's coffers; yet none of them had the slightest idea of how such a vast bank worked. 'There were people among us who were acquainted with the banking system from books and manuals,' recalled one of its new directors, 'but there was not a single man among us who knew the technical procedure of the Russian State Bank. We entered the enormous corridors of this bank as if we were penetrating a virgin forest.'[40]

To their opponents, these first stumbling efforts to master the basic institutions of the state symbolized the Bolsheviks' fundamental weakness. Few people thought that the new regime could last. 'Caliphs for an hour' was the verdict of much of the press. The SR leader, Gots, gave the Bolsheviks 'no more than a few days'; Gorky gave them two weeks; Tsereteli up to three; while Nabokov refused to 'believe for one minute in the strength of the Bolshevik regime and expected its early demise'. Many of the less sanguine Bolsheviks were no more optimistic. 'Things are so unstable', wrote Lunacharsky to his wife on 29 October, 'that every time I break off from a letter, I don't even know if it will be my last. I could at any moment be thrown into jail.'[41]

It was not just the opposition of the Civil Service, or the Bolsheviks' own lack of technical expertise in running the complex machinery of the state, which seemed to signal their imminent downfall. The Bolsheviks had no means of feeding the cities or halting the collapse of the economy. They were isolated from the peasants, the vast majority of the population, who were almost bound to vote against them in the forthcoming elections to the Constituent Assembly.

Like the Paris Commune of 1871, Petrograd appeared like a tiny Red island in the middle of a vast Green ocean. The Bolsheviks also had to deal with the censure of the Western powers and the rest of the socialist intelligentsia. Gorky's newspaper, *Novaia zhizn'*, was the most prominent and outspoken mouthpiece of this opposition during the autumn and winter, and it says much for his skills as a politician that it did not fall prey to the Bolshevik censors, like most of the opposition press. Gorky's own column, 'Untimely Thoughts', with its bitter denunciations of the 'new autocracy', must have worn Lenin's indulgent fondness for the writer dangerously thin. Gorky himself often expressed surprise that the paper had not been closed down. 'Lenin and Trotsky', he warned as early as 7 November, 'do not have the slightest idea of the meaning of freedom or the Rights of Man. They have already become poisoned with the filthy venom of power, and this is shown by their shameful attitude towards freedom of speech, the individual, and all those other civil liberties for which the democracy struggled.'[42]

None the less, in spite of their seemingly fatal isolation, the Bolsheviks managed to consolidate their dictatorship during the first three months of the new regime. By the time of its convocation, in January 1918, the Constituent Assembly, upon which the democratic opposition had pinned all its hopes, had already been made powerless by the rise of the one-party state and the spread of local Soviet rule through the provinces. How did the Bolsheviks achieve this? The absence of a serious military opposition during this critical period, when their power was weakest, no doubt helps to explain their success. The great White armies of the Civil War had yet to be formed and the main anti-Bolshevik forces were small Cossack armies engaged in local wars on the periphery of the Empire. Anti-Bolshevik forces in the centre of Russia were almost non-existent. The SRs and the Kadets, the most likely leaders of such a force, were so convinced of the regime's imminent collapse that they neglected to organize against it. Everyone naturally assumed that it would fall through its own internal weaknesses, so no one did anything to help bring this about. The Committee for the Salvation of Russia and the Revolution, organized by the SRs in the first few days after the Bolsheviks' seizure of power, had no real forces behind it; while plans to set up a rival socialist government headed by Chernov at Stavka, the old headquarters of the army, never got off the ground.

But the crux of the Bolshevik success was a two-fold process of state-building and destruction. On the one hand, at the highest levels of the state, they sought to centralize all power in the hands of the party and, by the use of terror, to wipe out all political opposition. At the grass-roots level, on the other, they encouraged the destruction of the old state hierarchies by throwing all power to the local Soviets, the factory organizations, the soldiers' committees and other decentralized forms of class rule. The vacuum of power which this created would help to undermine the democracy at the centre, while the masses themselves would be neutralized by the exercise of power over their old class or ethnic enemies within their own local environment. There was of course no master plan to this — everything was improvised, as it had to be in a revolution; yet Lenin, at least, had an instinctive sense of the general direction, of what he himself called the 'revolutionary dialectic', and in many ways that was the essence of his political genius. Local Soviet rule in the countryside, which was in effect the unfettered power of the village assembly to rule itself and divide the gentry's land, would undermine the need for the Constituent Assembly in the minds of the peasants, and thus destroy the political base of the SRs. The exercise of 'workers' control' through the factory committees would help to dismantle the old industrial infrastructure — what the Bolsheviks called the 'capitalist system' — while shifting the blame for the industrial crisis to the workers themselves. The spread of soldiers' power and of local peace initiatives at the Front, which the Bolsheviks encouraged, would undermine the plans of the old army commanders to mobilize the troops against the new regime and restart the war. And finally, the breakaway of the ethnic borderlands from the Russian Empire, which the Bolsheviks also supported at this time, would complete the fragmentation of the old imperial state and, according to Lenin, hasten the demise of feudal relations.*

No doubt Lenin viewed all these movements as a means to destroy the old political system and thus clear the way for the establishment of his own party's dictatorship. There is of course no proof of this — only the evidence of what actually took place and virtually everything else which we know of his previous thoughts and actions. It is hard to swallow the notion, which some historians on the Left have favoured, that Lenin was a libertarian at heart and encouraged all these localized forms of power in order to construct a new decentralized type of state, as set out in the *State and Revolution*; a plan which was only later blown off-course by the centralizing demands of the civil war. Lenin's conception of the revolutionary state had always been centralist in essence. He merely used the energies of these localist movements to destroy the *ancien régime*, along with the fragile democracy of 1917, while always intending to destroy these movements, in turn, as separate political forces. While he supported the peasants' movement against the gentry's estates, his ultimate aim was to replace the peasant smallholding system with collectivized farms. While he supported the

---

* The Declaration of the Rights of the Nations of Russia, proclaimed on 2 November, granted the non-Russian peoples full rights of self-determination, including the freedom to separate from Russia and form an independent state. Finland was the first to take advantage of this, declaring itself independent on 23 November 1917. It was followed by Lithuania (28 November), Latvia (30 December), the Ukraine (9 January 1918), Estonia (24 February), Transcaucasia (22 April) and Poland (3 November).

calls for 'workers' control', he no doubt did so in the knowledge that it would lead to chaos and thus strengthen the need to return to centralized management methods under the party's control. While he supported soldiers' power in so far as it destroyed the old imperial army, he arguably always intended to construct the Red Army on conventional lines. And while he encouraged the various national independence movements, his eventual aim was to abolish national states altogether. In everything he did, Lenin's ultimate purpose was the pursuit of power. Power for him was not a means — it was the end in itself. To paraphrase George Orwell, he did not establish a dictatorship to safeguard the revolution; he made a revolution to establish the dictatorship.

✻ ✻ ✻

The first priority of the Bolsheviks was the establishment of firm executive control. It took several weeks to break down the resistance of the Civil Service. The strike leaders and some senior Civil Servants were arrested; political commissars were appointed to oversee the bureaucracy; and junior officials willing to serve the Bolshevik rulers were promoted to senior posts. Overall, most Civil Servants in 1918 had been Civil Servants before 1917, especially in the upper echelons of the bureaucracy. But where the old Civil Service was mistrusted (most notably in the Ministry of Foreign Affairs) there was usually a thorough purge.[43] This established a pattern that was to repeat itself throughout the early years of Soviet state-building. It was a marriage of convenience between the Bolsheviks' demand for loyalty and the ambitions of the party's growing rank and file. One of its results was to promote third-rate party hacks, corrupt opportunists and semi-literate elements from the lower classes into positions of real power. This low cultural level of the Soviet bureaucracy was to be a permanent legacy of October which would later come to haunt the Bolshevik leaders.

Because of the Civil Service strike, which made it impossible to set up a system of cabinet rule, the MRC continued to function as the effective government until mid-November. By that time most of the People's Commissars had gained enough control of their respective ministries to enable the transfer of executive authority to Sovnarkom. But Sovnarkom was no ordinary cabinet government. For one thing, there was no clear division between the interests of the party and the government. The meetings of Sovnarkom, which were chaired by Lenin in the Bolshevik headquarters at Smolny, discussed party and government matters interchangeably; Central Committee resolutions were implemented as Soviet decrees. Everything about the early work of Sovnarkom presented a picture of hasty improvisation. Its meetings had no formal agenda and everything was discussed as 'urgent business', while Lenin drew up the appropriate resolutions and, when the moment was right, announced them to the meeting. They were usually passed without discussion, since few dared question Lenin's judgement.

There was, according to many observers, a conspiratorial atmosphere at these meetings. It was as if the Bolsheviks were psychologically unable to make the transition from an underground fighting organization to a responsible party of national government. They could not bring themselves to exchange their leather jackets for ministerial suits. Simon Liberman, who sometimes sat in on the Sovnarkom meetings, recalled that:

> despite all the efforts of an officious secretary to impart to each session the solemn character of a cabinet meeting, we could not help feeling that here we were, attending another sitting of an underground revolutionary committee! For years we had belonged to various underground organizations. All of this seemed so familiar. Many of the commissars remained seated in their topcoats or greatcoats; most of them wore the forbidding leather jackets.[44]

The Bolsheviks never quite succeeded in ridding themselves of their underground habits. Even as late as 1921, Lenin still gave the impression of a party conspirator rather than a statesman. It was of course a common phenomenon — one might call it the Jacobin Syndrome — which in part explains the tendency of the revolutionary state to perpetuate violence and terror. But the Bolsheviks took it one step further than the Jacobins. Theirs was the first of the twentieth-century dictatorships (followed by those of Mussolini, Hitler, Franco and Castro) to glorify its own violent past through propaganda and the adoption of military symbols and emblems. It was as if this cult of violence was central to the Bolshevik self-image, an end in itself rather than the means.

Just as the party came to overshadow the work of Sovnarkom, so Sovnarkom came to overshadow the work of the Soviet Executive. Although the Bolshevik seizure of power had been carried out in the name of the Soviet Congress, Lenin had no intention of ruling through the Congress, or its permanent executive. He did not believe in the principle of parliamentary sovereignty, even when the parliament in question was a Soviet one with, technically at least, an inbuilt Bolshevik majority. In the first weeks after the October coup the Soviet Executive was a real parliamentary brake on Sovnarkom. The Left SRs, the Anarchists and the tiny group of Menshevik Internationalists grouped around Gorky's *Novaia zhizn'*, were a vocal opposition, which, if joined by the Bolshevik moderates, could almost overturn the Leninist majority. In mid-November, when the leaders of the Peasant Soviet, or rather its left wing,* were added to the

---

* The Right SRs had called a Second Congress of Peasant Soviets to rally support against the Bolshevik regime, but it was swamped by left-wing delegates from the soldiers' committees and the lower-level Soviet organizations, causing the Right SRs to walk out in protest. The left-wing leaders then passed a resolution to merge this 'Extraordinary' Congress with the All-Russian Soviet Executive.

Soviet Executive, the potential strength of this opposition was even further increased. On 24 November it actually gained a majority of one for a motion of censure against the Bolshevik closure of the Petrograd City Duma eight days before, although on a recount the decision was reversed.

Yet the merger with the Peasant Soviet was also a critical turning point in the demise of the Soviet Executive as a legislative institution (which was almost certainly what Lenin had intended). To the 108 peasant deputies were added a further 100 delegates from the revolutionary organizations in the army and navy, and half that number again from the trade unions. This more than tripled its size, to 366 members, which was far too many to serve as an effective executive body. The burden of decision-making was thus shifted to Sovnarkom. From mid-November the Soviet Executive began to meet less often (once or twice a week), while Sovnarkom meetings became more frequent (once or twice a day). The volume of legislative acts brought before the Soviet Executive also sharply diminished, as Sovnarkom began to rule by decree. On 4 November Sovnarkom decreed itself the right to pass urgent legislation without approval from the Soviet — a clear breach of the principle of Soviet power. The Bolshevik moderates voted with the opposition against the decree, but it was still passed by two votes in the Soviet Executive. Kamenev resigned as the Chairman of the Soviet Executive and joined the opposition in a concerted effort to defend the sovereignty of the Soviet. But the Leninists pushed on. Sverdlov, who replaced Kamenev, was an ardent advocate of the party dictatorship and faithfully carried out Lenin's instructions to bring it about by centralizing power through Sovnarkom. On 17 November he presented the Soviet Executive with a 'constitutional instruction': while formally reiterating that Sovnarkom was responsible to the Soviet and had to present it with all its legislative acts for approval, it did not specify when this had to be done. Sovnarkom, in other words, could publish a legally binding decree without the prior approval of the Soviet, which increasingly became its practice. On 12 December the Soviet Executive met for the first time in two weeks: during its recess Sovnarkom had begun peace talks with the Central Powers, declared war on the Ukraine and introduced martial law in Petrograd and Moscow. As Sukhanov protested, all these measures had been implemented without discussion in the Soviet. The principle of Soviet power, by which the Bolsheviks claimed their right to rule, had been buried; the Soviet Executive had been reduced to a 'sorry parody of a revolutionary parliament'.[45]

From the first days of the new regime the Bolsheviks had set out to destroy, as 'counter-revolutionaries', all those parties which had opposed the October seizure of power. On 27 October Sovnarkom banned the opposition press. The ban was greeted with outrage. The Bolshevik moderates voted against it in the Soviet Executive on 4 November; the five resignations from the Bolshevik Central Committee that day, followed by an equal number of resignations from

Sovnarkom, were also partly in protest against the ban; while the Printers' Union threatened a national strike unless the freedom of the press was restored. But none of this was enough to prevent the MRC from sending in Bolshevik squads to smash many of the opposition presses, to confiscate their newsprint and arrest their editors. Most of the opposition papers were simply driven underground and soon reappeared with a slightly altered name. The SR paper, *Volia naroda*, reappeared the next day as *Volia*, and later on as *Narod*. The socialist paper, *Den'* (*Day*), appeared as *Morning, Midday, Afternoon, Evening, Night, Midnight*, and so on.[46]

* * *

The opposition parties were sustained by the hope of political salvation through the Constituent Assembly. It was surely the true voice of the democracy. Every citizen was represented by it, regardless of class, whereas the Soviets were only representative of the workers, the peasants and the soldiers. The opposition believed that the Constituent Assembly was bound to be recognized as the highest sovereign power in the land: not even the Bolsheviks would dare to challenge that. In fact, the Bolshevik leaders were divided over their policy towards the Assembly, though we still do not know enough about their internal debates on this matter. Lenin had always been contemptuous of the ballot box and had made it clear as early as the April Theses that he viewed Soviet power as a higher form of democracy than the Constituent Assembly. There was no room for the 'bourgeoisie' in the Soviets and, in Lenin's view, no room for them either in the revolution. But the seizure of power had been partly justified as a measure to ensure the convocation of the Constituent Assembly: a great deal of fuss had been made about how the Provisional Government was planning not to convene it, and about how only a Soviet government could lead the country to the Constituent Assembly. The Bolsheviks could not renege on their promise without losing face. The moderates in the party, moreover, were all, to varying degrees, committed on principle to the Constituent Assembly. Kamenev, for one, was a consistent advocate of the idea that the Bolsheviks should compete for power within it and, like some of the Left SRs, even favoured the notion of combining Soviet power at the local level with the Assembly as a sovereign national parliament.

Given all this, Lenin had little option but to allow the elections to go ahead. Polling started on 12 November and lasted for two weeks, since the vast size of the country made it necessary to stagger the elections. The campaign was vigorous, sometimes violent, and the turn-out high. Most people knew that it was, in effect, a national referendum on the Bolshevik regime. The SRs received 16 million votes (38 per cent of the total), most of them cast by the peasants in the central agricultural zone and Siberia. But the ballot papers had not distinguished between the Left SRs, who supported the Bolshevik seizure of power, and the Right SRs, who did not. The split in the party had taken place too recently for the printing changes to be made, except in one or two places. It is not at all clear, therefore, how much of the SR vote was opposed to the Bolshevik regime, although this was the crucial question of the whole election. The only thing that can be said with relative certainty is that the Left SRs had their main base of support among the younger peasant soldiers, whereas the Right SRs had their stronghold in the older peasants of the village. According to Oliver Radkey, the best authority on this subject, the peasants were more or less split down the middle between the two parties, although the Right SRs probably came out on top in the elections because they retained the bulk of the provincial party organizations and were thus better prepared for the campaign. The traditional voting habits of the peasantry, whereby the whole village assembly resolved to cast its votes for the same party, certainly favoured the Right SRs, since most of the village elders were inclined towards them. But even if the Right SRs did gain most of the peasant vote, they still lacked an outright majority in the Assembly. Only the support of the Mensheviks (who won 3 per cent of the vote), the Kadets (5 per cent) and the Ukrainian SRs (12 per cent) would give them that, though such was the gap between the Russian and the Ukrainian SRs on the question of national independence that even this was open to doubt.[47]

Nevertheless, the election results were a profound setback for the government's claim to rule in the name of the people. The Bolsheviks won just 10 million votes (24 per cent of the total), most of them cast by the soldiers and the workers of the industrial north. In Petrograd and Moscow they won a majority; but in the agricultural south, where their organization was extremely weak, they picked up hardly any votes. The Bolsheviks at once declared the results unfair: local reports on electoral abuses, which were bound to take place in a country as vast and backward as Russia, were rigorously collected and cited as evidence of the need for re-elections. Meanwhile, they stepped up their campaign of intimidation and threats against the defenders of the Assembly. The opening of the Assembly was postponed indefinitely by Sovnarkom on 20 November, just eight days before it was due to convene. On the following day Sovnarkom issued a decree giving electors the right to recall their deputies from all representative bodies, including the Constituent Assembly, provided this was supported by more than half the electorate within a given constituency. This meant, in effect, that Bolshevik activists were given the right to reverse the result of democratic elections by drumming up support in the factories and garrisons. It was obviously aimed against the Kadets, who had done rather well in the cities by rallying the right-of-centre vote. Trotsky defended the bill in the Soviet Executive as a 'painless' alternative to the outright closure of the Assembly in the event of it being opposed to the principle of Soviet power. It was a blatant threat that the Bolsheviks would not tolerate a hostile parliament. 'If the Kadets were to have a majority,' he warned, 'then of course the Constituent Assembly would not be given power.'[48] As a physical reminder of this threat, the MRC burst into the Tauride Palace on 23 November and arrested the Assembly's three electoral commissioners. They were held captive and interrogated in the Smolny for six days, before being dismissed and replaced by the Bolshevik Uritsky.

The opposition parties were outraged by these acts of intimidation. It looked as if the Bolsheviks were slowly coming round to the view that the Assembly should either be postponed into the distant future or closed down altogether in the light of their party's poor performance in the elections. They immediately formed a Union for the Defence of the Constituent Assembly and called on their supporters to demonstrate in front of the Tauride Palace on 28 November with a view to forcing the parliament's opening. Large crowds turned out on that day, though nowhere near as many as the 200,000 claimed by some of the opposition press: a quarter of that number would be a more reasonable estimate, with most of them students, officers and striking Civil Servants, though there were some workers too, such as the printers and skilled artisans. A group of forty-five Assembly deputies, led by Schreider, the indefatigable Mayor of Petrograd, forced their way into the palace through the Bolshevik pickets, the Latvian Riflemen, and proceeded to the first point on the agenda of the parliament, the election of a Presidium. Of course they knew that they lacked the necessary quorum of 400 deputies, but it was at least a symbolic gesture. The next day they found the Tauride Palace surrounded by troops. The crowds were kept away and, although the deputies were once again admitted, they were soon ordered to leave.

The demonstration was immediately branded as a 'counter-revolutionary' act organized by the Kadets. The Kadet Party was outlawed and denounced, in the Jacobin tradition, as 'enemies of the people'. Dozens of its leaders were arrested, including several delegates to the Constituent Assembly: Shingarev, Kokoshkin, Dolgorukov, Panina, Astrov and Rodichev. Revolutionary justice did not recognize parliamentary immunity. Most of them were taken to the Peter and Paul Fortress, where they were kept for three months in fairly reasonable conditions (Dolgorukov found time to catch up with his reading and welcomed the freedom from telephone calls), although Kokoshkin and Shingarev both fell sick, the former with TB, and had to be transferred to the prison hospital (where they were later brutally murdered by a group of Bolshevik sailors). The Left SRs opposed the arrests as an act of terror, while Gorky denounced them as a 'disgrace to the democracy'. But the Bolshevik leaders were clearly intent on destroying the Kadets as the 'organized force of the bourgeois counter-revolution'. It was not so much a ban on a political party, as the declaration of civil war on a whole social class. Justifying the arrests in the Soviet Executive, Lenin called the Kadet Central Committee the 'political staff of the bourgeoisie'. Trotsky even claimed that since the bourgeoisie was already passing away from the scene of history, the Bolsheviks' measures of violence against it were for its own good, since they would help to put it out of its misery even more quickly: 'There is nothing immoral in the proletariat finishing off a class that is collapsing: that is its right.'[49]

The arrests of the supposed 'enemies of the people' did not end with the Kadets. Like the Jacobin Terror, to which the Bolshevik leaders continually appealed for justification, they soon spread into the ranks of the revolutionary movement itself. The Kadets were joined in the Peter and Paul Fortress by a number of SR and Menshevik leaders (Avksentiev, Gots, Sorokin, Argunov), as well as some of the leaders of the Peasant Soviet. Orders were even sent out for the arrest of Tsereteli, Dan and Chernov. By the end of December the prisons were so full of these new 'politicals' that the Bolsheviks began to release common criminals in order to make more room. Some of the richer political prisoners, such as the businessmen Tret'iakov and Konovalov, the former Minister of Trade and Industry, were released for a ransom.[50]

Slowly but surely, the shape of the new police state was starting to emerge. On 5 December the MRC was finally abolished and, two days later, its duties transferred to the Cheka,* the new security organ that one day would become the KGB. From its very inception the Cheka worked outside the law: there was not even a published decree to mark its organization, only the secret minutes of Sovnarkom, to which the Cheka was supposed to be subordinated, although in reality it was virtually beyond political account. Lenin had stressed the need 'for a staunch proletarian Jacobin' to head the new 'Okhrana' and he found that man in Felix Dzerzhinsky, a forty-year-old Pole from the Lithuanian city of Vilnius who had spent half his adult life in various tsarist prisons and who thus perhaps had his own special motive to ensure that all these 'enemies of the people' suffered equally in jail. During his childhood Dzerzhinsky had wanted to be a Jesuit priest and, although he had long ceased to believe in religion, he carried that same fanatical spirit into his campaigns of political persecution. At the Sovnarkom meeting at which it was established he described the task of the Cheka as a merciless war against the internal enemies of the revolution:

We need to send to that front — the most dangerous and cruel of fronts — determined, hard, dedicated comrades ready to do anything in defence of the Revolution. Do not think that I seek forms of revolutionary

* Its full name was the All-Russian Extraordinary Commission for Struggle against Counter-Revolution and Sabotage.

justice; we are not now in need of justice. It is war now — face to face, a fight to the finish. Life or death![51]

One might well ask why the Bolshevik moderates, who were openly opposed to the use of political terror and enjoyed widespread support among the party rank and file, failed to act as a more effective brake on the Leninist zealots. The answer surely lies in the psychological weakness of the moderates and the autocratic status of Lenin among the party leaders after the 'victory' of October.* None of the Bolshevik moderates had either the courage or the capacity for leadership to stand up against Lenin and run the risk of splitting the party. The five who had been brave enough to resign from the Central Committee on 4 November all sooner or later made their peace with Lenin: Zinoviev, who had always been a coward and an opportunist, was the first to recant on 8 November, and was readmitted to the Central Committee; Kamenev, Miliutin, Nogin and Rykov held out three weeks longer. To a greater or lesser extent, the fundamental weakness of all the moderates was their own intellectualism. While it made them uncomfortable with the idea of the Terror, it also deprived them of the means to take their fight against it beyond the realm of words. Lunacharsky was a perfect example. On 2 November he had burst into tears at a Sovnarkom meeting, and subsequently resigned as Commissar of Enlightenment, after hearing reports that the Bolshevik bombardment of the Kremlin had destroyed St Basil's Cathedral during the fighting in Moscow. 'I cannot bear it any longer,' he had written in *Novaia zhizn'*. 'My cup is full. I am powerless to stop this barbarism.' When these reports turned out to be false he had withdrawn his resignation; yet he remained just as frustrated by his impotence against the Bolshevik Terror. Gorky, one of his oldest political friends, who later plagued him with requests to save the country's writers and artists from persecution, summed up the situation of the moderates in a New Year's letter to Ekaterina:

It is clear that Russia is heading for a new and even more savage autocracy. Yesterday I called on the 'Commissar of Justice', a decent enough man but, like all the representatives of 'the authorities', utterly impotent. I pleaded with him to release Vernadsky, it seems without success . . . Lunacharsky's behaviour is astonishingly absurd and ludicrous — he is both a

---

* According to Lozovsky, the Bolshevik trade unionist who had resigned from Sovnarkom on 4 November, the 'hero-worship' of Lenin had become a basic expectation of party discipline. See his open letter of protest against the dictatorial methods of the Leninist wing in *Novaia zhizn'*, 4 November 1917.

comical and a tragic figure. All the Bolsheviks of his ilk have become repulsively pitiable and wretched.[52]

   The Left SRs, who joined Sovnarkom on 12 December, were paralysed by a similar impotence. They had been the only major group not to walk out of the Soviet Congress after the Bolshevik seizure of power, and this had led to their final break with the Right SRs. From that point on, the two were separate parties battling for control of the provincial SR organizations and the Peasant Soviet. Whereas the Right SRs were determined to keep the Bolsheviks isolated and focused all their hopes on the Constituent Assembly, the Left SRs believed that by joining the Bolsheviks in government — and the Cheka — they might be able to curb their worst excesses. Most of the Left SR leaders were still young enough to be excused for such foolish idealism: Steinberg, Karelin and Kalegaev were all in their twenties, while Spiridonova and Kamkov were only thirty-two. The Left SRs were inspired by what they saw as the revolutionary spontaneity of the Soviets. They tried to reconcile extreme libertarianism with the use of extreme terror for the promotion of that ideal. After October they flooded into the local Soviet organs, where they became the dominant party of the radicalized peasants and soldiers. The Decree on Land, which Lenin intro- duced at the Second Soviet Congress on 26 October, was in effect the agrarian programme of the Left SRs, as he himself admitted. It gave *carte blanche* to local peasant communities to seize and redivide all the private land. This was enough to persuade the Left SRs that a concordat with the Bolsheviks might be reached; and in mid-November, after they had led the Peasant Soviet into a merger with the All-Russian Soviet Executive, they began negotiations for their own entry into Sovnarkom. Kalegaev became Commissar of Agriculture; Steinberg the 'impotent' Commissar of Justice visited by Gorky; and five others took on minor posts, including the administration of the country's crumbling post and telegraph network. But the Bolsheviks retained the key government posts, and the Left SRs were really no more than a fig-leaf used by Lenin to conceal the nakedness of his dictatorship. Contrary to their naive expectations, the Left SRs were powerless to moderate the despotic extremes of his policies; and in almost every aspect these turned out to be diametrically opposed to their own revolutionary ideals. The semi-anarchist system of decentralized Soviets which they had envis- aged was impossible to attain within the centralized structure of Lenin's Dictator- ship of the Proletariat; their support for the peasant commune, the organization of the factories on anarcho-syndicalist lines, and the political autonomy of the national minorities were all incompatible with the long-terms goals of Bolshev- ism; and their passionate commitment to civil liberties (Spiridonova had once demanded the destruction of the Peter and Paul Fortress as a symbol of the police state) was hardly reconcilable with the Bolshevik methods of rule.

IMAGES OF 1917

52 The First Provisional Government in the Marinsky Palace. Prince Lvov is seated in the centre, Miliukov is second from the right, while Kerensky is standing behind him. Note that the tsarist portraits (of Alexander II and Alexander III) have not been removed.

53 A rare moment of national unity: the burial of the victims of the February Revolution on the Mars Field in Petrograd, 23 March 1917.

54 A meeting of the Soviet of Soldiers' Deputies in the Catherine Hall of the Tauride Palace.

55 Waiters and waitresses of Petrograd on strike. The main banner reads: 'We insist on respect for waiters as human beings.' The three other banners call for an end to the degrading practice of tipping service staff. This stress on respect for workers as citizens was a prominent feature of many strikes. Note in this context that the strikers are well dressed – they could be mistaken for bourgeois citizens – since this was a demonstration of their dignity.

56 The All-Russian Congress of Peasant Deputies in the People's House in Petrograd, 4 May. A soldiers' delegation (standing in the hall) greets the deputies (on the balconies). In the second balcony on the left are (*from left to right*) the four veteran SR leaders: Viktor Chernov, Vera Figner, Ekaterina Breshko-Breshkovskaya and N. D. Avksentiev.

57 Fedor Linde leads the Finland Regiment to the Marinsky Palace on 20 April to
protest against the continuation of the war for imperial ends.

58 Kerensky cuts a Bonapartist figure during a speech in mid–May to the soldiers of the Front.

59 Metropolitan Nikon blesses the Women's Battalion of Death on Red Square in Moscow before their departure for the Front in June. One of the women was too fat for standard issue trousers and had to go to battle in a skirt.

60 General Kornilov is greeted as a hero by the right-wing members of the Officers' Union on his arrival in Moscow for the State Conference on 12 August.

61 Members of the Women's Battalion of Death await the final assault on the Winter Palace, 25 October 1917. When the *Aurora* fired its first salvo the women became hysterical and had to be confined in a basement room.

62 More of Kerensky's last defenders, barricaded inside the Winter Palace, await the assault of the Bolshevik forces on 25 October.

63 The Smolny Institute, seat of the Soviet and command centre of the Bolshevik Party, in early October.

64 The Red Guard of the Vulkan Factory in Petrograd. Note the ties and suits of many of the guards.

With the Left SRs safely on board, Lenin stepped up his campaign of persecution against the Constituent Assembly. Despite their commitment to democratic freedoms, the Left SRs were just as determined as the Bolsheviks not to allow the principle of parliamentary sovereignty to supersede that of Soviet power. After the events of 28 November many Bolsheviks and Left SRs favoured the idea of driving the Kadets out of the Constituent Assembly, which could then be reorganized around their two parties into a Revolutionary Convention. Bukharin had proposed this in the Central Committee on 29 November. Like the French Convention of 1792, which had replaced the Legislative Assembly, this would be a much more pliant body for the Soviet dictatorship, yet it would preserve all the outward signs of a national parliament in order to appease what Bukharin called the 'constitutional illusions [that] are still alive in the masses'.[53]

Lenin, meanwhile, was coming round to favour the outright abolition of the Constituent Assembly. On 12 December he published his 'Theses' on the subject, in which he argued that Soviet power had cancelled out the need for a 'bourgeois-democratic' Assembly. In any case, it was no longer truly representative because of the split in the SR Party and the leftward shift of the masses since October. The 'class struggle' and the defeat of the 'counter-revolution' demanded the consolidation of Soviet power and, unless the Assembly was ready to recognize this, 'the entire people' would agree that it was 'doomed to political extinction'. It was a declaration of intent to abolish the Assembly, unless the Assembly agreed to abolish itself. Lenin's ultimatum became the policy of the party, and this in turn became the policy of Sovnarkom. Ten days later, at a meeting of the Soviet Executive, the Bolsheviks and Left SRs both demanded the closure of the Constituent Assembly, unless it resolved to subordinate itself to the Soviets at its opening session on 5 January. A Third Soviet Congress was meanwhile convened for 8 January, two weeks earlier than originally planned, so that, as Zinoviev put it, 'the oppressed people may pass sentence on the Constituent Assembly'. Lenin drew up a 'Declaration of the Rights of the Working People' to be passed by the Constituent Assembly at its opening session. This spurious replica of the Rights of Man proclaimed Russia a Republic of Soviets and endorsed all the decrees of Sovnarkom, including the abolition of private landed property, the nationalization of the banks and the introduction of universal labour conscription.[54] It was the death sentence of the Constituent Assembly.

Petrograd was in a state of siege on 5 January, the opening day of the Constituent Assembly. The Bolsheviks had placed the capital under martial law, forbidden public gatherings and flooded the city with troops. Most of them were concentrated near the Tauride Palace, where the Assembly was due to convene. The palace was cordoned off with barricades guarded by Bolshevik pickets. Its forecourt, where Chernov had once been held by the mob, was filled with bivouacs, artillery, machine-guns and field kitchens. It looked like an armed encampment. The Bolsheviks had set up a special military staff and called in their staunchest defenders — the Kronstadt sailors, Latvian Riflemen and Red Guards — to deal with any 'counter-revolutionary' actions by the Union for the Defence of the Constituent Assembly.

The Union had at one stage planned to start an uprising, but since they had no real military forces at their disposal, had abandoned the idea at the final moment in favour of a mass demonstration under the slogan of 'All Power to the Constituent Assembly'. During the morning a sizeable crowd gathered on the Mars Field and, towards noon, began to march in various columns towards the Tauride Palace. Some sources counted 50,000 marchers, but the actual number was probably less. It was certainly not as large as the organizers had hoped: far fewer workers and soldiers turned up than expected, so the crowd was largely made up of the same small active citizenry — students, Civil Servants and middle-class professionals — who had taken part in the earlier march on 28 November. As the demonstrators approached the Liteiny Prospekt they were fired upon by Bolshevik troops, hiding on the rooftops with their machine-guns. Several other columns of marchers, one including workers from the Obukhovsky munitions plant, were also fired on. At least ten people were killed and several dozen wounded.

It was the first time government troops had fired on an unarmed crowd since the February Days. The victims were buried on 9 January, the anniversary of Bloody Sunday, next to the victims of that massacre in the Preobrazhensky Cemetery. The historic parallels did not go unnoticed. Several workers' delegations turned up for the funeral, and one laid a wreath with the inscription: 'To the victims of the Smolny autocrats'. Gorky, who had witnessed both massacres, underlined the parallels in *Novaia zhizn'*. It was the emotional climax of his bitter disillusionment with the revolution:

On 9 January 1905, when the downtrodden, ill-treated soldiers were firing into unarmed and peaceful crowds of workers by order of the tsarist regime, intellectuals and workers ran up to the soldiers — the unwilling murderers — and shouted point-blank in their faces: 'What are you doing, damn you? Who are you killing?' . . .

However, the majority of the Tsar's soldiers answered the reproaches and persuasions with dismal and slavish words: 'We've got our orders. We know nothing, we've got our orders'. And, like machines, they fired at the crowds. Reluctantly, perhaps with a heavy heart, but — they fired.

On 5 January 1918 the unarmed Petersburg democracy — factory and white-collar workers — demonstrated peacefully in honour of the Constituent Assembly.

For almost a hundred years the finest Russians have lived by the idea of a Constituent Assembly ... Rivers of blood have been spilled on the sacrificial altar of this idea, and now the 'People's Commissars' have given the orders to shoot the democracy which demonstrated in honour of this idea ...

Thus, on 5 January, the Petrograd workers were mowed down, unarmed ... They were mowed down from ambush, through cracks in fences, in a cowardly fashion, as if by real murderers.

And just as on 9 January 1905, people who had not lost their conscience and reason asked those who were shooting: 'What are you doing, idiots? Aren't they your own people marching? You can see there are red banners everywhere ...'

And — like the tsarist soldiers — these murderers under orders answered: 'We've got our orders! We've got our orders to shoot.'

I ask the 'People's' Commissars, among whom there must be decent and sensible people: Do they understand that ... they will inevitably end up by strangling the entire Russian democracy and ruining all the conquests of the revolution?

Do they understand this? Or do they think, on the contrary, that 'either we have power or everyone and everything will perish'?[55]

By 4 p.m., when the opening session of the Assembly commenced, the atmosphere in the Tauride Palace was extremely tense. Many of the SR deputies had taken part in the morning's demonstration and were angered by the shootings. To add insult to injury, each of them had been bodily searched by the Bolshevik guards as they entered the palace. Contrary to the claims of the Bolshevik press, not all the arrested deputies had been released for the opening session: Argunov, Avksentiev and Sorokin were even reported as having made speeches in the Tauride Palace, when in fact they were still in the Peter and Paul Fortress. In the Catherine Hall, where the assembly was held, there were almost as many troops as there were delegates. They stood at the back of the hall and sat up in the galleries, drinking vodka and shouting abuse at the SR deputies. Lenin surveyed the scene from the old government loge, where the tsarist ministers had sat during the sessions of the Duma. He gave the impression of a general at the moment before the start of a decisive battle — and that indeed is what it was.

The SRs tried to take the initiative by opening the session with a debate of their own, but the Bolsheviks created such a din that their first speaker, Mikhailov, the oldest member of the Assembly, was unable to make himself heard. Chernov, elected Chairman of the Assembly, made a long and ineffectual speech, as was his usual custom; it did nothing for the reputation of the then only genuinely democratic national parliament in Russia's history as it awaited its execution. Tsereteli then appeared, despite the Bolshevik order for his arrest, and did rather better, denouncing the regime with such a passion that even the hecklers on the Left were forced to shut up and listen. But the Bolsheviks soon after brought the conflict to a head. Raskolnikov, the leader of the Kronstadt sailors, introduced their Declaration of the Rights of the Working People. When this was rejected, by 237 votes against 146, the Bolsheviks declared the Assembly to be in the hands of the 'counter-revolutionaries' and walked out of the hall. A recess was called, while the Bolsheviks and Left SRs discussed what to do. The latter, wavering as usual, wanted to delay the dissolution, but Lenin was adamant: 'the situation is now clear and we can get rid of them'. It was resolved to dissolve the Assembly, although out of deference to the Left SRs, who briefly returned to the session, Lenin instructed the Red Guards not to use violence: when the deputies left, the palace was to be locked up and no one allowed to convene there on the following day. At 2 a.m., having satisfied himself that everything was under control, Lenin returned to the Smolny, and went to bed.[56]

A little over two hours remained before the Assembly was closed down. After the Bolsheviks' departure, various SR speakers made their usual lengthy speeches, while the Red Guards continued to get drunk and heckle from the gallery. Some of them amused themselves by aiming their guns at the speakers. The SRs resolved to use up these final minutes rushing through decrees on land and peace so that the Assembly would at least go under with a symbolic record of popular legislation: they already had an eye to the fast developing civil war, in which they would need to mobilize the support of the democracy for the restoration of the Constituent Assembly. At 2.30 a.m. the Left SRs finally walked out of the hall, unconvinced by the desperate efforts of their old party comrades to push through in minutes what they had failed to do in six months of power under the Provisional Government. The Bolshevik Dybenko then gave the order to the leader of the Red Guards, an anarchist sailor named Zhelezniakov, to bring the meeting to a close. At 4 a.m. he mounted the tribune and, tapping Chernov on the shoulder, announced that 'all those present should leave the assembly hall because the guard is tired'. Chernov replied that the members of the Constituent Assembly were also tired but that this did not prevent them from 'proclaiming a law awaited by all of Russia'. The guards became angry, shouted 'Down with Chernov!', and gathered menacingly with their guns in the main body of the hall. Chernov kept the meeting going for a further twenty minutes; but he had never been noted for his personal bravery before the mob (witness 4 July), and finally agreed to adjourn the meeting until the following afternoon.[57] The only session of the Constituent Assembly had finally ended: it was 4.40 a.m. on 6 January. The delegates sheepishly filed out and the Tauride Palace was then locked up, bringing the twelve-year history of this democratic citadel to a premature end. When the deputies returned the following day, they were denied admission and presented with a decree dissolving the Assembly.

Two days later, on 8 January, the Third Congress of Soviets convened. The Bolsheviks and Left SRs had packed the Congress with their own supporters: nine out of ten delegates came from these two parties. The Congress duly passed all the measures presented to it by the government representatives, including the bogus Declaration of the Rights of the Working People, which effectively served as the first constitution of the Soviet state. This was the only sort of 'parliament' Lenin was ready to work with — one that would rubber-stamp all his decrees.

*　　*　　*

Shortly after the closure of the Constituent Assembly Boris Sokolov asked an SR deputy from the Volga region whether his party would try to defend it by force. 'Do you realize what you are saying?' the deputy replied. 'Do you realize that we are the people's representatives, that we have received the high honour of being elected by the people to write the laws of a new democratic republic? But to defend the Constituent Assembly, to defend us, its members — that is the duty of the people.'[58] Most of the SRs were equally paralysed by the ideal of themselves as the leaders of 'the people', who would somehow come to their rescue. And as a result there was no military campaign to reverse the closure of the Constituent Assembly. No doubt any such campaign would have been doomed from the start, for the democratic leaders of Russia had no real military forces at their disposal. The Union for the Defence of the Constituent Assembly was dominated by SR intellectuals and could only muster the support of a few cadets. But their naive belief in the support of 'the people' was also disturbing, because it betrayed a complete failure to comprehend the revolutionary forces at work and thus boded ill for their chances in the coming civil war.

Sokolov, who was himself a Right SR, thought that the root of his comrades' passivity was their metamorphosis from an underground group of revolutionaries into the leaders of the Provisional Government. This is surely right. Their adopted sense of responsibility for the state (and no doubt a little pride in their new ministerial status) led the Right SRs to reject their old terrorist ways of revolutionary struggle and depend exclusively on parliamentary methods. It was this that had tied them to the Kadets and held them back from forming a purely Soviet government in 1917. 'We must proceed by legal means alone,' was how Sokolov characterized their thinking, 'we must defend the law by the only means permissible to the people's representatives, by parliamentary means.' They were doubtless sincere and held a deep conviction that, by refusing to fight the Bolsheviks using Bolshevik methods, they were saving Russia from the traumas of a civil war. Mark Vishniak, the Right SR and Secretary of the

Constituent Assembly, later acknowledged that their hands had been tied by their own insistence on the need to avoid a civil war at all costs. But there was also a large dose of foolish vanity in all this. The Right SRs were hypnotized by the 'sanctity' and the 'dignity' of the Constituent Assembly, the first democratic parliament in the history of Russia, and by the 'honour' which this bestowed upon them as its representatives. Carried away by such ideals, they deluded themselves into believing that Russia was firmly set on the same democratic path as England or America, and that the 'will of the people' was alone enough to defend its democratic institutions. They placed so much faith in their own democratic methods that they failed to see how the Bolsheviks' undemocratic methods could succeed in the long run.[59]

Yet it was more than a problem of methods: the faith of the Right SRs in 'the people' was itself misplaced. There was no mass reaction to the closure of the Constituent Assembly. The demonstration of 5 January was much smaller and more middle-class than the Right SRs had hoped. Sokolov thought that the dominant mood in the capital was one of passivity. After nearly a year of political conflict, none of which had reversed the economic crisis, people could be excused for a cynical indifference towards politics and politicians. More pressing concerns, such as the daily hunt for food and fuel, occupied most people for most of the time. Even Gorky — a political animal if ever there was one — succumbed to the general mood. On 26 January he wrote to Ekaterina:

> We are living here as the captives of the 'Bolsheviks', as the French call Lenin's venerable henchmen. Life is not much fun! And it's highly annoying, but what can we the people do? There is nothing we can do. 'He who survives will be saved.' We survived the Romanov autocracy, perhaps we'll survive Ul'ianov's. Life has become comic — and tragic. Don't laugh! *Novaia zhizn'* looks like going under. My mood is foul, added to which I am feeling bad physically. There are days when I wake up and don't even want to work. I don't seem to want anything any more, and am paralysed by apathy, which is totally alien to me.[60]

There was an even more profound indifference among the peasantry, the traditional base of support of the SR Party. The SR intelligentsia had always been mistaken in their belief that the peasants shared their veneration for the Constituent Assembly. To the educated peasants, or those who had long been exposed to the propaganda of the SRs, the Assembly perhaps stood as a political symbol of 'the revolution'. But to the mass of the peasants, whose political outlook was limited to the narrow confines of their own village and fields, it was only a distant thing in the city, dominated by the 'chiefs' of the various parties, which they did not understand, and was quite unlike their own political organizations. It was a national parliament, long cherished by the intelligentsia, but the peasants did not share the intelligentsia's conception of the political nation, its language of 'statehood' and 'democracy', of 'civic rights and duties', was alien to them, and when they used this urban rhetoric they attached to it a specific 'peasant' meaning to suit the needs of their own communities.[61] The village Soviets were much closer to the political ideals of the mass of the peasants, being in effect no more than their own village assemblies in a more revolutionary form. Through the village and volost Soviets the peasants were already carrying out their own revolution on the land, and they did not need the sanction of a decree by the Constituent Assembly (or, for that matter, the Soviet Government itself) to complete this. The Right SRs could not understand this fundamental fact: that the autonomy of the peasants through their village Soviets had, from their point of view, reduced the significance of any national parliament, since they had already attained their *volia*, the ancient peasant ideal of self-rule. To be sure, out of habit, or deference to their village elders, the mass of the peasants would cast their votes for the SRs in the elections to the Constituent Assembly. But very few were prepared to fight the SR battle for its restoration, as the dismal failure of the Komuch would prove in the summer of 1918. Virtually all the resolutions from the villages on this question made it clear that they did not want the Assembly to be restored as the 'political master of the Russian land', in the words of one, with a higher authority than the local Soviets. In other words, they did not want to be ruled by a central state. As Sokolov later acknowledged from his experience as an SR propagandist in the army:

> The Constituent Assembly was something totally unknown and unclear to the mass of the front-line soldiers, it was without doubt a *terra incognita*. Their sympathies were clearly with the Soviets. These were the institutions that were near and dear to them, reminding them of their own village assemblies . . . I more than once had occasion to hear the soldiers, some-times even the most intelligent of them, object to the Constituent Assembly. To most of them it was associated with the State Duma, an institution that was remote to them. 'What do we need some Constituent Assembly for, when we already have our Soviets, where our own deputies can meet and decide everything?'[62]

After their defeat in the capital the SRs returned to their old provincial strongholds to rally support for the restoration of democracy. It was to prove a painful lesson in the new realities of provincial life. They found the local peasantry largely indifferent to the closure of the Constituent Assembly and their own party organizations in a state of decay. By basing their party on the support of the peasants, the SRs came to realize that they had built it on sand.

In province after province the Right SRs had lost control of the Soviets to the extreme Left. In the northern and central industrial provinces, where the Bolsheviks and Left SRs could count on the support of most of the workers and garrison soldiers, as well as a large proportion of the semi-industrial peasants, most of the provincial Soviets were in Bolshevik hands, usually through the ballot box, by the end of October, and only in Novgorod, Pskov and Tver did any serious fighting take place. In some of these towns, especially where there was a garrison, the Bolsheviks simply used their military strength to oust the opposition from the Soviet and install their own 'majority'. Further south, in the agricultural provinces, the transfer of power was not generally completed until the New Year and was often quite bloody, with fighting in the streets of the main provincial towns (Orel, Kursk, Voronezh, Astrakhan, Chernigov, Odessa, Kherson, Ekaterinoslav, Sevastopol and others). In most places the extreme Left organized its supporters among the soldiers and workers into an MRC, which seized control of the government institutions after defeating the cadet or Cossack forces loyal to the city Duma. New elections to the ruling Soviet were then held which, in one form or another, were usually rigged. As in Petrograd, the SRs and Mensheviks often played into the hands of the extreme Left by boycotting the Soviet and these 're-elections'. Yet, without real military forces of their own, or a large and active citizenry willing to take up arms in defence of the democracy, they had little option. The political civilization of the provincial towns was not much more advanced than in backward peasant Russia and outside the capital cities there was no real urban middle class to sustain the democratic revolution. That was the tragedy of 1917.

iii Looting the Looters

For the first time in many years General Denikin found himself among ordinary Russians as he sat in a third-class railway carriage, disguised as a Polish nobleman, on his way to the Don:

> Now I was simply a *boorzhui*, who was shoved and cursed, sometimes with malice, sometimes just in passing, but fortunately no one paid any attention to me. Now I saw real life more clearly and was terrified. I saw a boundless hatred of ideas and of people, of everything that was socially or intellectually higher than the crowd, of everything which bore the slightest trace of abundance, even of inanimate objects, which were the signs of some culture strange or inaccessible to the crowd. This feeling expressed hatred accumulated over the centuries, the bitterness of three years of war, and the hysteria generated by the revolutionary leaders.

The future White army leader was not the only refugee from Bolshevik Russia to feel the wrath of the crowd during that terrible winter of 1917–18. The memoir literature is full of similar accounts by princes, countesses, artists, writers and businessmen of the traumatic journeys they had to make through revolutionary Russia in order to flee the Bolshevik regime. They all express the same sense of shock at the rudeness and hostility which they now encountered from the ordinary people: weren't these the brothers and sisters of their nannies and their maids, their cooks and their butlers, who only yesterday had seemed so kind and respectful? It was as if the servant class had all along been wearing a mask of good will which had been blown away by the revolution to reveal the real face of hatred below.

For the vast majority of the Russian people the ending of all social privilege was the basic principle of the revolution. The Russians had a long tradition of social levelling stretching back to the peasant commune. It was expressed in the popular notions of social justice which lay at the heart of the 1917 Revolution. The common belief of the Russian people that surplus wealth was immoral, that property was theft and that manual labour was the only real source of value owed much less to the doctrines of Marx than it did to the egalitarian customs of the village commune. These ideals of social justice had also become a part of that peculiar brand of Christianity which the Russian peasants had made their own. In the Russian peasant mind there was Christian virtue in poverty.* 'The meek shall inherit the earth!' It was this which gave the revolution its quasi-religious status in the popular consciousness: the war on wealth was seen as a purgatory on the way to the gates of a heaven on earth.

If the Bolsheviks had popular appeal in 1917, it was in their promise to end all privilege and replace the unjust social order with a republic of equals. The utopian vision of a universal socialist state was fundamental to the popular idealism of the revolution. One peasant-worker, for example, wrote to the All-Russian Peasant Soviet in May 1917: 'All the people, whether rich or poor, should be provided for; every person should receive his fair and equal ration from a committee so that there is enough for everyone. Not only food but work and living space should be equally divided by committees; everything should be declared public property.' The rejection of all superordinate forms of authority (judges, officers, priests, squires, employers, and so on) was the main driving force of the social revolution. By giving institutional form to this war on privilege, the Bolsheviks were able to draw on the revolutionary energies of those numerous

---

* To the Western mind, it may seem strange that the Bolsheviks should have chosen to call their main peasant newspaper *The Peasant Poor* (*Krest'ianskaia Bednota*). But in fact it was a brilliant example of their propaganda. The Russian peasant saw himself as poor, and, unlike the peasants of the Protestant West, saw nothing shameful in being poor.

elements from the poor who derived pleasure from seeing the rich and mighty destroyed, regardless of whether it brought about any improvement in their own lot. If Soviet power could do little to relieve the misery of the poor, it could at least make the lives of the rich still more miserable than their own — and this was a cause of considerable psychological satisfaction. After 1918, as the revolution's ideals became tarnished and the people became more and more impoverished, the Bolshevik regime was increasingly inclined to base its appeal almost exclusively on these vulgar pleasures of revenge. In an editorial to mark the start of 1919, *Pravda* proudly proclaimed:

> Where are the wealthy, the fashionable ladies, the expensive restaurants and private mansions, the beautiful entrances, the lying newspapers, all the corrupted 'golden life'? All swept away. You can no longer see on the street a rich *barin* [gentleman] in a fur coat reading the *Russkie vedomosti* [a liberal newspaper closed down after October 1917]. There is no *Russkie vedomosti*, no fur coat for the *barin*; he is living in the Ukraine or the Kuban, or else he is exhausted and grown thin from living on a third-class ration; he no longer even has the appearance of a *barin*.[63]

This plebeian war on privilege was in part an extension of the violence and destruction which Gorky had condemned in the wake of the February Revolution. There was the same hatred and mistrust of the propertied classes, the same cruel desire for retribution, and the same urge to destroy the old civilization. To the propertied classes, it all seemed part of the same revolutionary storm. They compared the violence of 1917 to the *Pugachevshchina*, the anarchic wave of peasant destruction — 'senseless and merciless', as Pushkin had described it — which had haunted Russia since the eighteenth century. They talked of the 'dark' and 'savage' instincts of the people, which the Bolsheviks had inflamed, just as their predecessors had talked in the nineteenth century of Pugachev's followers. Yet such crude and value-laden stereotypes probably tell us more about those who used them than they do about those they were meant to describe. It was, in other words, only the social pretensions of those who saw themselves as 'civilized' and 'respectable' which defined the violence of the crowd as 'anarchic', 'dark' and 'savage.' If one looks at the violence in its own terms, there are important distinctions between the war against privilege after October and earlier forms of violence against the propertied classes.

For one thing, the violence after October was articulated and legitimized by a new language of class, and class conflict, which had been developed by the socialist parties during 1917. The old and deferential forms of address for the members of the propertied classes (*gospodin* and *barin*) were phased out of use. They soon became a form of abuse, or of sarcastic mocking, for those who had lost their title and wealth. These were the 'former people' (*byvshchie liudi*), as the Bolsheviks came to call them. The proliferation of egalitarian forms of address — 'comrade' (for party members and workers) and 'citizen' (for all others) — seemed to signify a new republican equality, although of course, in reality, the comrades, to adapt George Orwell's phrase, were rather more equal than the others. The word 'comrade' (*tovarishch*) had long had connotations of brotherhood and solidarity among the most class-conscious industrial workers. It became a badge of proletarian pride, a sign to distinguish and unite the avenging army of the poor in the class war against the rich. This new language of class awakened a sense of dignity and power in the once downtrodden. It was soon reflected in a greater assertiveness in the dress and body-language of the lower classes. Servicemen and workers tilted back their caps and unbuttoned their tunics in a show of cocky defiance. They went around with a pistol sticking out visibly from their belts and behaved in a generally aggressive manner. They spoke rudely to their 'social betters', refused to give up their tram-seats to women, and sat in the theatre, smoking and drinking, with their feet up on the chairs in front of them.

In the minds of the ordinary people, who had never read their Marx, class divisions were based much more on emotion than objective social criteria. The popular term *burzhooi*, for example, had no set class connotations, despite its obvious derivation from the word 'bourgeois'. It was used as a general form of abuse against employers, officers, landowners, priests, merchants, Jews, students, professionals or anyone else well dressed, foreign looking or seemingly well-to-do. Hungry workers condemned the peasants as *burzhoois* because they were thought to be hoarding foodstuffs; while peasants — who often confused the word with *barzhui* (the owners of a barge) and *birzhye* (from the word for the Stock Exchange, *birzh*) — likewise condemned the workers, and all townsmen in general, because they were thought to be hoarding manufactured goods. The *burzhoois*, in other words, were not so much a class as a set of popular scapegoats, or internal enemies, who could be redefined almost at will to account for the breakdown of the market, the hardships of the war and the general inequalities of society. Villagers often described the *burzhooi* as a 'hidden' and 'crafty' enemy of the peasants who was to blame for all their problems: he could be a townsman, a trader or an official. In urban food queues, where endless theories of sabotage were spun to explain the shortage of bread, the words *burzhooi*, 'speculator', 'German' and 'Jew' were virtually synonymous. This was a society at war with itself — only everyone thought they were fighting the *burzhooi*.[64]

The socialist press encouraged such popular attitudes by depicting the *burzhoois* as 'enemies of the people'. The best-selling pamphlet of 1917 — which did more than any other publication to shape the political and class consciousness of the mass of the ordinary people — was *Spiders and Flies* by Wilhelm (not to be confused with Karl) Liebknecht. Several million copies of it were sold in more than twenty different editions sponsored by all the major socialist parties. *Spiders and Flies* divided Russia into two warring species:

> The spiders are the masters, the money-grubbers, the exploiters, the gentry, the wealthy, and the priests, pimps and parasites of all types! . . . The flies are the unhappy workers, who must obey all those laws the capitalist happens to think up — must obey, for the poor man has not even a crumb of bread.*

The rich and educated, by being labelled *burzhooi*, were automatically vilified as antisocial. 'The *burzhooi*', wrote one socialist pamphleteer, 'is someone who thinks only of himself, of his belly. It is someone who is aloof, who is ready to grab anyone by the throat if it involves his money or food.' As the social crisis deepened, the *burzhoois* were increasingly condemned as 'parasites' and 'blood-suckers', and violent calls for their downfall were heard with growing regularity, not just from the extreme left-wing parties but also from the streets, the factories and the barracks. 'We should exterminate all the *burzhooi*', proclaimed one factory worker in January 1918, 'so that the honest Russian people will be able to live more easily.'[65]

The Bolsheviks encouraged this war on privilege — and even made it their own popular *raison d'être*. Lenin had always been an advocate of using mass terror against the enemies of his revolution. In 'How to Organize Competition?', written in December 1917, he called for a 'war to the death against the rich, the idlers and the parasites'. Each village and town should be left to develop its own means of:

> cleansing the Russian land of all vermin, of scoundrel fleas, the bedbug rich and so on. In one place they will put into prison a dozen rich men, a dozen scoundrels, half a dozen workers who shirk on the job . . . In another place they will be put to cleaning latrines. In a third they will be given yellow tickets [such as prostitutes were given] after a term in prison, so that everyone knows they are harmful and can keep an eye on them. In a fourth one out of every ten idlers will be shot. The more variety the better . . . for only practice can devise the best methods of struggle.[66]

On many occasions he stressed that the 'proletarian state' was 'a system of

---

* Right-wing pamphleteers before the war used the image of the spider to depict the Jew 'sucking the blood of the harmless flies (the Russian people) it has caught in its web' (Engelstein, *Keys*, 322–3).

organized violence' against the bourgeoisie: this was what he had always understood by the term 'Dictatorship of the Proletariat'. Licensing popular acts of
plunder and retribution was an integral element of this system, a means
of 'terrorizing the bourgeoisie' into submission to the Proletarian State. Here
were the origins of the Red Terror.

Historians have tended to neglect the connections between this plebeian
war on privilege and the origins of the Red Terror. Most of them have seen the
Terror as exclusively political. They have shown how it was imposed by
the Bolsheviks — either deliberately to build up their power, so that terror
became the fundamental basis of their regime (the view of the Right), or as a
largely pragmatic response to the threats and problems of the civil war (the view
of the Left). Neither is a satisfactory explanation. The Terror erupted from
below. It was an integral element of the social revolution from the start. The
Bolsheviks encouraged but did not create this mass terror. The main institutions
of the Terror were all shaped, at least in part, in response to these pressures
from below. The anarchic plunder of bourgeois, Church and noble property
was legitimized and institutionalized by the Bolshevik decrees of revolutionary
confiscation and taxation, which the local Chekas then enforced through the
arrest of 'bourgeois' and 'counter-revolutionary' hostages. The mob trials of
bourgeois employers, officers, speculators and other 'enemies of the people'
were institutionalized through the People's Courts and the crude system of
'revolutionary justice' which they administered — which in turn became a part
of the Cheka Terror.

The Cheka system, as centrally organized political terror, did not really
take off until the late summer of 1918 (see pages 627–49). During the early
months of the Bolshevik regime, the Cheka system was, like the rest of the state
apparatus, extremely decentralized; and this often meant that social pressures,
such as the desire of the local population to despoil the rich and powerful, or
even the desire of one community to pursue a vendetta against another, could
determine whom the local Cheka bosses chose to arrest or execute. This 'mass
terror' is analysed here, the aim being to understand the social roots of the
Cheka's Terror. For, however much one may condemn it, and however hard it
may be to admit, there is no doubt that the Terror struck a deep chord in the
Russian civil war mentality, and that it had a strange mass appeal. The slogan
'Death to the Bourgeoisie!', which was written on the walls of the Cheka
interrogation rooms, was also the slogan of the street. People even called their
daughters Terrora.

* * *

In January 1918, at a meeting of party agitators on their way to the provinces,
Lenin explained that the plunder of bourgeois property was to be encouraged
as a form of social justice by revenge. It was a question of 'looting the looters'.

Under this slogan, which the Bolsheviks soon made their own, there was an orgy of robbery and violence in the next few months. Gorky described it as a mass pogrom. Armed gangs robbed the propertied — and then robbed each other. Swindlers, thieves and bandits grew rich, as law and order finally vanished. 'They rob artistically,' Gorky wrote in a bitter editorial on 16 March:

> no doubt history will tell of this process of Russia's self-robbery with the greatest inspiration. They rob and sell churches and museums, they sell cannons and rifles, they pilfer army warehouses, they rob the palaces of former grand dukes; everything which can be plundered is plundered, everything which can be sold is sold; in Theodossia the soldiers even traffic in people — they bring Turkish, Armenian and Kurdish women from the Caucasus and sell them for twenty-five roubles apiece. This is very 'original', and we can be proud — there was nothing like it even in the era of the Great French Revolution.[67]

In the provinces the establishment of Soviet power was often accompanied by such acts of looting and violence. Most of it was perpetrated by unruly elements in the crowd, though the local party leaders were often involved, or else urged the crowd on from the sidelines. In Ekaterinoslav the local Bolshevik leader told his followers to 'wrest from the bourgeoisie the millions taken from the masses and cunningly turned into silken under-garments, furs, carpets, gold, furniture, paintings, china. We have to take it and give it to the proletariat and then force the bourgeoisie to work for their rations for the Soviet regime.' In Stavropol the Bolshevized soldiers systematically plundered shops and houses, and arrested hostages from the bourgeoisie; the local Soviet, which shared power with the leaders of the Duma and the zemstvos, was too weak to stop this terror and chose instead to license it as the first step towards the seizure of outright power. The violence soon spread to the surrounding countryside, as the Russian peasant soldiers vented their old class and ethnic hatred of the land-rich Kalmyk pastoralists by setting fire to their houses and killing their families with quite unspeakable brutality (pregnant women had their babies cut out of their wombs). The Kalmyks then retaliated by attacking the Russian peasant farms. It was common for the terror to spiral in this way as long-suppressed ethnic and social conflicts suddenly exploded and there was no neutral power to stop them. In the Don industrial town of Taganrog the Red Guards reaped a savage revenge on the military cadets, mostly bourgeois sons, whom they had defeated in the seizure of power. Fifty cadets, who had surrendered on the promise of an amnesty, were marched off to a metal factory, tied by their hands and feet, and thrown, one by one, into the blast furnace. In Evpatoria, a Crimean coastal town, the Bolshevized sailors were allowed by the

Soviet leaders to go on the rampage: in three days they massacred 800 officers and bourgeois residents. Most of them were killed in a tortuous fashion, with broken arms and legs tied around their head before their bodies were thrown into the sea. Similar massacres took place in Yalta, Theodossia and Sevastopol.[68]

This war against the bourgeoisie was paralleled by a number of Bolshevik decrees sanctioning the 'looting of the looters'. Soviet officials, bearing flimsy warrants, would go round bourgeois houses confiscating typewriters, furniture, clothes and valuables 'for the revolution'. Factories were taken out of private ownership, shares and bonds were annulled, and the law of private inheritance was later abolished. Banks were nationalized and the holders of accounts were restricted to withdrawals of no more than 1,000 roubles per month (a sum that was soon made worthless by hyperinflation). The owners of bank safe deposits were ordered to appear with their keys so that the boxes could be inspected: foreign money, gold and silver, and all other precious items were subject to confiscation. During the first six months of 1918 more than 35,000 deposit boxes were inspected. Countess Meshcherskaia gives a vivid description of the sailor placed in charge of this operation at her local bank:

> Around his chest was wrapped a belt of machine-gun cartridges and from his holster, at his side, one could just make out the handle of his revolver. Young and broad-shouldered, with his eyes wide open from the conscious-ness that he was performing an important task, he tried to make his large and friendly face look menacing by frowning at us. He didn't have the slightest notion about precious jewels but knew only one thing: the state needed gold.

From their opened safe, he took several handfuls of items — jewels, diamond monograms, silver crucifixes and even a Fabergé egg — and piled them up on a table. Several times he paused 'to gaze admiringly at this mountain of booty'.[69]

The Soviets levied their own punitive taxes on the bourgeoisie. This was often the start of the Bolshevik Terror, since the local Chekas were inclined to enforce the payment of these levies by arresting hostages. In Nizhnyi Novgorod, for example, the Soviet imposed a revolutionary levy of twenty-two million roubles, while the Cheka arrested 105 bourgeois citizens and held them hostage until the levy was paid.[70] Many of these taxes were imposed on people quite unable to pay: emigration and inflation had drastically reduced the size and wealth of the Russian bourgeoisie and many of those persecuted as 'the rich' were no more than petty traders or half-impoverished teachers, doctors and clerks. Convinced by their own propaganda that this phantom bourgeoisie must be hiding its wealth, the local Chekas made even more arrests and began to shoot their hostages.

The same happened with the confiscation of Church property. It began with a clumsy attempt by Kollontai, the People's Commissar of Social Welfare, to turn the Alexander Nevsky Monastery into a sanctuary for war invalids. On 19 January she sent a detachment of sailors to occupy this famous holy shrine in the centre of Petrograd. They were met by an angry crowd of worshippers and, in the scuffles that followed, a priest was shot dead. Lenin was furious: the last thing he needed now was open confrontation with the Church, which so far had been careful to keep out of politics. But since Kollontai had already enraged the priesthood, he saw no reason for holding back from the conflict which, as he saw it, would have to come sooner or later. The Decree on the Separation of Church and State was published the next day, 20 January, much earlier than planned. It declared all Church property to be the property of the state. Sanctioned by this licence, Bolshevik squads went round the country's churches and monasteries looting their silver, drinking their wine and terrorizing the priesthood. Patriarch Tikhon, the head of the Church, called on the clergy to resist 'these monsters of the human race' in a pastoral letter anathematizing the Bolshevik regime. Not all the priesthood chose the path of open opposition. Some of the minor clergy, who had welcomed the revolution as a chance to build closer ties with their parish, sought to conciliate the Bolsheviks. The Preobrazhensky Monastery in Viatka, for example, turned itself into a labouring commune with a nursery for workers' children and a workshop where the nuns made clothes and shoes for orphans. But most of the clergy and their congregations followed Tikhon's call, which enabled the Bolsheviks to brand them as 'counter-revolutionaries' and to step up their campaign of looting and terror. The monks of the Alexander Svirsky Monastery in Olonetsk, for example, after trying to resist the Bolshevik squads, were imprisoned — and later executed — by the local Cheka.[71]

One of the most traumatic humiliations suffered by the wealthy classes in these early months of the Soviet regime was the compulsory sharing of all or part of their living space. The Bolsheviks were proud — and stressed it in their propaganda — that they were forcing the wealthy to share their spacious houses with the urban poor. To many people this seemed only fair: the fact that some people had lived in palaces, while others languished in damp and dirty cellars, had become a symbol of the unjust social order of the old regime. Wealthy families often tried their best to find a clean and modest couple to move in with them whom they might be able to persuade to make do with one or two of the smallest rooms in the house. But the vigilance of the buildings committees, which were placed in charge of this process, made it very hard. These committees were usually formed by the old house porters and domestic servants, among whom the desire for revenge could often be very strong. Joining the buildings committee, and even more the party, gave them a licence to turn the tables on their former superiors. They occupied the best rooms in the house and filled them with the finest furniture, while their previous employers were moved into the servants' quarters. Here was a whole world of hidden revolutions in domestic life where the servants and the masters literally changed places. It was a microcosm of the social transformation in the country at large.

'I've spent all my life in the stables,' complained an ex-servant at a political rally in the Cirque Moderne, 'while they live in their beautiful flats and lie on soft couches playing with their poodles. No more of that, I say! It's my turn to play with poodles now: and, as for them, it is their turn to go and work in the stables.' The idea of putting the leisured classes to work was an integral element of the war on social privilege — and the Bolsheviks were quick to institutionalize it. Lenin had promised that the fundamental rule of the Soviet order would be 'He who does not work, neither shall he eat.' The universal conscription of labour was part of the Declaration of Rights of the Working People (which was in effect a Declaration of the Obligations of the Non-Working People) which the Bolsheviks had presented to the Constituent Assembly. Trotsky pioneered the mass conscription of bourgeois labour in the early days of the Red Army, where it was used for non-combatant tasks in the rear, such as digging trenches and cleaning out the barracks. But it soon became a general practice of the city Soviets. Aristocrats, former factory directors, stockbrokers, lawyers, artists, priests and former officials would all be rounded up and forced to do jobs such as clearing the rubbish or snow from the streets. Meanwhile, commissars and groups of idle workers would stand around smoking and watching with obvious pleasure as the well-dressed ladies and gentlemen, none of whom had ever done a single day of manual labour in their lives before, struggled to master their shovels and picks. There was no real economic benefit in these conscriptions of bourgeois labour; their sole purpose was to degrade and physically destroy the genteel classes. As Trotsky put it in a speech that perfectly expressed the mob psychology: 'For centuries our fathers and grandfathers have been cleaning up the dirt and the filth of the ruling classes, but now we will make them clean up our dirt. We must make life so uncomfortable for them that they will lose the desire to remain bourgeois.'[72]

Dispossessed and degraded, the life of these 'former people' soon became an arduous daily struggle. Hours were spent queuing for bread and fuel along with the rest of the urban poor. As inflation rocketed, they were forced to sell their last precious possessions just to feed themselves. Baroness Meyendorff sold a diamond brooch for 5,000 roubles — enough to buy a bag of flour. Mighty scions of the aristocracy were reduced to petty street vendors: Princess Golitsyn sold home-made pies, Baroness Wrangel knitwear, Countess Witte cakes and sweets, while Brusilov's wife sold matches, just like hundreds of wounded veterans from the army her husband had once commanded. A former

Gentleman of the Chamber to the Tsar became the concierge of a museum, where strange creatures were kept in jars of alcoholic spirit; he exchanged this for water and sold the gruesome alcohol on the streets. The flea-markets of Petrograd and Moscow were filled with the former belongings of fallen pluto- crats: icons, paintings, carpets, pianos, gramophones, samovars, morning coats and ball dresses — all could be picked up for the price of a meal or two. The more precious items were snapped up by the *nouveaux riches* of the Soviet regime — commissars and officials, looting soldiers and sailors, petty traders and bandits — as they sought to acquire the status symbols of a ruling class. The new masters of Russia were easily distinguishable by the way they wore their long and dirty hair greased back, by their gold-toothed smiles and their eau-de-cologne smells, and by the way they went around the shops and hotels with dolled-up girls of easy virtue on their arm.

Baron Wrangel recalls one of these *arrivistes rouges*, a Bolshevik soldier 'straight from the plough', purchasing a pearl necklace for his mistress in one of the top jewellers on Nevsky Prospekt. His mistress was a former kitchen-maid, now dressed in sumptuous furs and diamonds, though her face was covered with the scars of smallpox. The country boy was obviously proud to be seen with such a 'fine lady' and demanded to be shown 'the most expensive pearls, shining ones like the *baryni** wear'. He was not satisfied with those the jeweller brought out because, at 75,000 roubles, they were still not expensive enough. He and his mistress were due that evening at a reception in the Winter Palace and had to have the best. The kitchen-maid announced that they would go to the Gostiny Dvor, where 'we are sure to find what I want'. This produced a fit of contemptu- ous laughter from the other customers, a group of former society ladies who had come to sell their diamonds, because the shops there were known to sell cheap imitation jewellery. Realizing that she had made a blunder, the poor girl blushed and tried to recover herself by saying that they would take 'the wretched pearls' after all and come back when the jeweller had found something better.[73]

Many of Russia's fallen rich and mighty sold up everything and either went abroad, though this was very hard, or fled south to the Ukraine and Kuban, or else east to Siberia, where the White Guards had their main bases of power. Others sought refuge on their landed estates in the countryside, hoping that the peasants, whom they had always seen as humble and respectful, would be kinder to them than the Bolshevized workers in the towns. But here too the war against the rich was in full swing, as the peasants, sanctioned by the October Decree on Land, carried out their own seizures of the gentry's land and property.

The equal distribution of all the means of production, the land, the tools and the livestock, had long been the basic ideal of the peasant revolution.

* The ladies of the nobility.

They looked upon this 'Black Repartition' as the Will of God, and believed that the rest of the revolution had also been organized on the same general principles. The All-Russian Soviet was conceived of by the peasants as a kind of giant village commune redistributing all the property in the country. Many peasants were convinced, in the words of one of their more literate representatives, that socialism, of which they had only vaguely heard, 'was some sort of mystical means — mystical because we could not imagine how this would be done — of dividing all the property and the money of the rich; according to our village tailor, this would mean that every peasant household would be given 200,000 roubles. This, it seems, was the biggest number he could think of.'[74]

The peasants themselves had no mystical means of dividing up the land. They did not even have the basic technical means, such as maps and rulers. The land was divided as it always had been, by pacing out the width of the strips, or judging the overall size of the plots by eye, and then allocating them to the peasant households according to the local egalitarian norm. This usually meant the number of eaters, or more rarely the number of adult workers, in each household. Without accurate land-surveying methods, these divisions were inevitably accompanied by arguments, sometimes ending in fist-fights, over who should get what piece of land. But in general terms, given its crucial importance for a peasant community, the land repartition was remarkable for its peaceful-ness — a tribute to the self-organization of the village communes which carried it through.

The confiscated lands of the gentry and the Church were usually divided separately because it was feared that if the revolution was reversed the peasants would be forced to return this land to its former owners. Many communes stipulated that all their household members had to receive a strip of this land in order to share the burden of risk. The gentry themselves, including those who returned to their estates from the cities, were usually left a generous portion of land and tools, enough to turn their estates into a sizeable family farm on a par with the rest of the peasant households. While the peasants were in no doubt that the gentry had to be destroyed as a superordinate class, they also believed that the squires should be allowed to turn themselves into 'peasants' and farm a share of 'God's land', as they put it, with their own family labour. The rights of land and labour, which lay at the heart of the peasant commune, were understood as basic human rights. Indeed, in so far as the 'peasantization' of the squires was in line with the basic peasant ideal of creating a society made up entirely of smallholding family farmers, it was even something to be welcomed. Many landowners, especially the smaller ones, remained on the land after 1917; and they were joined by those, normally resident in the cities, who now sought refuge from the Bolshevik Terror on their estates. As late as the mid-1920s there were still some 10,000 former landlords living on their manors alongside the peasants, a figure equivalent to 10 per cent of the total number of landowners in Russia before 1917.

The Rudnevs, a medium-sized landowning family in Simbirsk province, were a typical example. They had decided to stay on their family estate because, as Semen Rudnev put it, they thought that 'the disturbances of the revolution would be less harsh in the countryside than in the towns [and because] the economic conditions of the village, with its almost natural economy, would also be better'. The turmoil of 1917 largely passed their village by. The Rudnevs spent the summer and autumn in the leisurely manner to which they were accustomed: 'The men went drinking and hunting, guests from Simbirsk came to stay, and we went off to Nazhim and the milk-farm for picnics and mushroom picking.' During the following winter they agreed to the demand of the neighbouring village commune to turn their land and property over to the peasants. They kept a small farm of 20 *desyatiny* (54 acres) near the manor house, where they continued to live. The livestock and tools were auctioned off at bargain prices, though most of the peasants could not afford to feed their new pedigree horses, which kept running back to their former owners for hay. The peasants came to work in the Rudnevs' fields during the spring and were paid in vodka and fruit liqueurs. The harvest was bigger than the peasants' and so the commune ordered the Rudnevs to sell their surplus grain at fixed prices to the village poor. But well before the harvest could be gathered the manor house was ransacked, and the Rudnevs forced to flee, by a local detachment of the Red Guards.[75]

This was a common pattern. Though peasant acts of violence, pillage and arson were not uncommon, it was usually the young demobilized soldiers who took the lead in instigating them. The slogan 'Loot the Looters!' was brought home to the villages by those who returned from the Front and the garrisons, where they had developed a strong sense of militant brotherhood and where they had been exposed to the propaganda of the Bolsheviks. They often formed a paramilitary faction inside the village, not unlike the *fascisti* in rural Italy at this time. They had their own regional organizations, such as the Union of Front-Line Soldiers, or the Union of Wounded Veterans, as well as their own Red Guard detachments, attached to the local Soviet, which could exert a powerful influence on the village and steer it towards more violent forms of action against the gentry. In one particular village of the Kerensky district in Penza province, for example, peasant attacks on the local squires suddenly increased: it was connected to the return of several soldiers, who were then elected to the head of the village Soviet. The war had obviously had a brutalizing effect upon them, for they soon became notorious for their heavy bouts of drinking and sadistic violence. One poor noble widow, who had hitherto lived quite peacefully with the peasants, having already given to them most of her land and livestock, was driven to suicide when the drunken bullies shot her last horse and cow and left her pet dog dead on her doorstep: it had been an act of pure spite.[76]

* * *

The Russians, it might seem, were particularly prone to such cruel and savage acts of revenge. 'I am', wrote Gorky, 'especially distrustful of a Russian when he gets power into his hands. Not long ago a slave, he becomes the most unbridled despot as soon as he has the chance to become his neighbour's master.'[77] Mob trials and lynchings were the most common expression of this popular vengeance, both in the countryside and in the towns. They had taken off as a mass phenomenon in response to the catastrophic rise in crime and the breakdown of law and order during 1917 (when Gorky claimed to have counted over 10,000 cases of mob justice). Since the police and the old criminal courts had virtually disappeared, there was a common feeling that the only way to deal with the problem of crime was by mob trials in the street. Some poor thief would be seized by the crowd, given summary justice and executed on the spot. Gorky witnessed one such instance in the centre of Petrograd, in which even children had taken part in the brutal execution of a thief (see pages 400–1). As the socio-economic crisis deepened, and the popular belief developed that the *burzhoois* were responsible for it, so these mob trials began to assume an overtly class nature. They became a weapon in the war against privilege, focusing less on petty thieves from the urban poor and much more on merchants and shopkeepers, factory owners and employers, army officers, former tsarist officials and other figures of superordinate authority.

The Bolsheviks gave institutional form to the mob trials through the new People's Courts, where 'revolutionary justice' was summarily administered in all criminal cases. The old criminal justice system, with its formal rules of law, was abolished as a relic of the 'bourgeois order'. The twelve elected judges who made up the People's Courts did not have to have any formal legal training — they were to be guided by their 'revolutionary conscience' — and were mainly drawn from the workers, the peasants and the petty officials of the old law courts. Half of them had not been educated beyond primary level, and one in five belonged to the Bolshevik Party. The sessions of the People's Courts were little more than formalized mob trials. There were no set legal procedures or rules of evidence, which in any case hardly featured. Convictions were usually secured on the basis of denunciations, often arising from private vendettas, and sentences tailored to fit the mood of the crowd, which freely voiced its opinions from the public gallery.

The system of revolutionary justice administered by the People's Courts was similar in many ways to the old peasant customary law, with its rough and ready system of an eye for an eye and a tooth for a tooth. Here is the Penal

Code introduced by the People's Court in the village of Lubny, in Tambov province, in May 1918:

> If one strikes another fellow, the sufferer shall strike the offender ten times. If one strikes another fellow causing thereby a wound or a broken bone, the offender shall be deprived of life. If one commits theft or receives stolen articles he shall be deprived of life. If one commits arson and is caught, he shall be deprived of life.

It had long been a basic tenet of peasant legal consciousness that a rich man stealing from the poor was many times more guilty than a poor one stealing from the rich — and this same principle of 'class justice' was applied in the People's Courts. Judgements were reached according to the social status of the accused and their victims. In one People's Court the jurors made it a practice to inspect the hands of the defendant and, if they were clean and soft, to find him guilty. Speculative traders were heavily punished and sometimes even sentenced to death, whereas robbers — and sometimes even murderers — of the rich were often given only a very light sentence, or even acquitted altogether, if they pleaded poverty as the cause of their crime.[78] The looting of the looters had been legalized and, in the process, law as such abolished: there was only lawlessness.

Lenin had always been insistent that the legal system should be used as a weapon of mass terror against the bourgeoisie. The system of mob law which evolved through the People's Courts gave him that weapon of terror. So too did the Revolutionary Tribunals, modelled on their Jacobin namesakes, which dealt with a whole new range of 'crimes against the state'. In February 1918, at the time of the German invasion of Russia, Lenin issued a decree — 'The Socialist Fatherland in Danger!' — ordering the Revolutionary Tribunals to shoot 'on the spot' all 'enemy agents, profiteers, marauders, hooligans and counter-revolutionary agitators'.[79] To his disappointment, the Revolutionary Tribunals turned out to be highly inefficient instruments of the Bolshevik Terror: too many of its judges could be easily bribed, which is hardly surprising given the fact that most of them came directly from the factory floor. But this was only the start of a new state machinery of mass terror, and the work of the tribunals was gradually taken over by the local Chekas, which were not wanting in revolutionary zeal. Latsis, one of the Cheka's leaders, instructed his officials:

> not to look for evidence as proof that the accused has acted or spoken against the Soviets. First you must ask him to what class he belongs, what his social origin is, his education and profession. These are the questions

that must determine the fate of the accused. That is the meaning of the Red Terror.[80]

During its early stages of development the Cheka system was extremely decentralized: each local Cheka organization was a law unto itself. This made the Cheka Terror both random and susceptible to pressures from below. Virtually anyone could be arrested, and almost anything could be construed as 'counter-revolutionary' behaviour. The Cheka's own instructions listed private trading, drunkenness, and even being late for work as 'counter-revolutionary' conduct. But on this basis the whole of the population would have been in jail. Many of the early victims of the Red Terror had been arrested on the basis of no more than a single denunciation by some personal enemy. The Cheka in Omsk complained in April that of the 1,000 cases of 'counter-revolution' so far brought before it, more than 200 had had to be thrown out because the only evidence against the accused had been the hearsay of some person or group of people who, it later turned out, had a private grudge. Some of the less scrupulous Chekas did not let this stop them from securing a conviction. The Penza Department of Justice complained in April, for example, that its prisons were 'full of innocent people arrested by the Cheka on the basis of some false accusation by one person against another'. It was particularly common for someone in debt to denounce his creditor as a 'kulak usurer', and thus a 'counter-revolutionary'.[81] It was one way to cancel your debts.

This is what was happening, then, in the early stages of the Terror, before the Centre took control and redirected it against its own politically defined enemies: sections of society were driving the Terror from below as a means of retribution against those whom they perceived as their own enemies, which in their eyes meant the same thing as 'the enemies of the revolution'. Their ability to do this was of course dependent upon their place in the local Bolshevik power structure. But this hardly means that the Terror was constructed from above. Rather it suggests that there was a close but complicated link between the political and the mass terror. As Dzerzhinsky himself wrote in 1922, all the Cheka did was to 'give a wise direction' to the 'centuries-old hatred of the proletariat for its oppressors', a hatred which might otherwise 'express itself in senseless and bloody episodes'.[82]

Many people foresaw that this mass terror would result in a social holocaust in which not only the bourgeoisie but also many of the common people would be destroyed. Citing the words of the Anarchist sailor Zhelezniakov, that 'for the welfare of the Russian people even a million people could be killed', Gorky warned the readers of *Novaia zhizn'* on 17 January:

a million 'free citizens' could indeed be killed in our country. Even more could be killed. Why shouldn't they be killed? There are many people in Russia and plenty of murderers, but when it comes to prosecuting them, the regime of the People's Commissars encounters certain mysterious obstacles, as it apparently did in the investigation of the foul murder of Shingarev and Kokoshkin.* A wholesale extermination of those who think differently is an old and tested method of Russian governments, from Ivan the Terrible to Nicholas II . . . so why should Vladimir Lenin renounce such a simple method?

Steinberg, the Left SR Commissar for Justice, was another early critic of the Terror, although all his efforts to subordinate the Chekas to the courts proved to be in vain. When, in February, Steinberg first saw the Decree on 'The Socialist Fatherland in Danger!', with its order to shoot 'on the spot' all 'profiteers, hooligans and counter-revolutionaries', he immediately went to Lenin and protested: 'Then why do we bother with a Commissariat of Justice at all? Let's call it frankly the "Commissariat for Social Extermination" and be done with it!' Lenin's face lit up and he replied: 'Well put, that's exactly what it should be; but we can't say that.'[83]

iv Socialism in One Country

Of all the Bolshevik decrees passed in their first days of power none had the same emotional appeal as the Decree on Peace. The revolution had been born of the war — or at least of the yearning that it would end. Russia had been brought to its knees after three long years of total war and its people wanted peace above all else. On 26 October, when Lenin made his immortal announcement to the Soviet Congress that 'We shall now proceed to construct the Socialist order!', the first thing he turned to was the question of peace. This had been the basis of his party's claim to power, the one demand which all the delegates brought with them from their barracks and their factories to the Soviet Congress. When Lenin read out the decree — a bombastic 'Proclamation to the Peoples

---

* The Kadet leaders, Shingarev and Kokoshkin, were arrested by the Bolsheviks and imprisoned in the Peter and Paul Fortress after the demonstrations of 28 November in defence of the Constituent Assembly. They were transferred to the Marinskaya Hospital on 6 January after becoming seriously ill, and were brutally murdered there on the following night by a group of Baltic sailors, who broke into the hospital. The Ministry of Justice later revealed that the murders had taken place with the connivance of the Bolshevik Red Guard and the Commandant of the Hospital, Stefan Basov, who justified the murder on the grounds that there would be 'two less bourgeois mouths to feed'. Basov was brought to trial and convicted, but none of the murderers was ever caught and the Bolshevik leaders, who at first condemned the murders, later sought to justify them as an act of political terror.

of All the Belligerent Nations' proposing a 'just and democratic peace' on the old Soviet formula of no annexations or indemnities — there was an overwhelming wave of emotion in the Smolny hall. 'Suddenly', recalled John Reed, 'by common impulse, we found ourselves on our feet, mumbling together into the smooth lifting unison of the Internationale. A grizzled old soldier was sobbing like a child. Alexandra Kollontai rapidly winked the tears back. The immense sound rolled through the hall, burst windows and doors, and soared into the quiet sky. "The war is ended! The war is ended!" said a young workman near me, his face shining.'[84]

But of course the war had not ended at all. The Decree on Peace was an expression of hope, not a statement of fact. It was one thing to call for peace, another to bring it about. The other belligerent powers had no intention of signing a general peace: both sides were more intent than ever on slogging it out to the bloody end. The Allies had been spurred on by the intervention of the United States, and the Central Powers by the prospect of transferring troops to the west as the Eastern Front was run down. There was no real reason why either should listen to Russia's appeals for peace, especially not now that her military position had been so weakened. She had lost her status among the Great Powers; and her calls for a general peace without annexations or indemnities sounded like the arguments of a loser.

As the Bolsheviks saw it, the peace campaign was inextricably linked with the spread of the revolution to the West. It was this that, in their view, would bring the war to an end — or rather transform it, as Lenin had predicted, into a series of civil wars in which the workers of the world would unite to overthrow their imperialist rulers. The belief in the imminence of a world revolution was central to Bolshevik thinking in the autumn of 1917. As Marxists, it was inconceivable to them that the socialist revolution could survive for long in a backward peasant country like Russia without the support of the proletariat in the advanced industrial countries of the West. Left to themselves, without an industrial base to defend their revolution, and surrounded by a hostile peasantry, the Bolsheviks believed that they were doomed to fail. The October seizure of power had been carried out on the premise, naive though it may sound today, that a worldwide socialist revolution was just around the corner. Every report of a strike or a mutiny in the West was hailed by the Bolsheviks as a certain sign that 'it was starting'.

As long as this expectation remained alive, the Bolsheviks did not need a foreign policy in the conventional sense. All they needed to do was to fan the flames of the world revolution. 'What sort of diplomatic work will we be doing anyway?' Trotsky had said to a friend on hearing of his appointment as Commissar for Foreign Affairs. 'I shall issue a few revolutionary proclamations to the peoples and then shut up shop.' The basic aim of the Soviet peace campaign was to serve as a means of revolutionary propaganda; and in this sense it was not a peace campaign at all. The Decree on Peace was a popular summons to revolution. It called on the peoples of the belligerent countries to revolt against the war and to force their rulers into peace talks. 'This proposal of peace will meet with resistance on the part of the imperialist governments — we don't fool ourselves on that score,' Lenin had warned the Soviet Congress. 'But we hope that revolution will soon break out in all the belligerent countries; and that is why we address ourselves to the workers of France, England and Germany.' As George Kennan once observed, this was the first example of what was later to become known in Soviet foreign policy as 'demonstrative diplomacy' — diplomacy designed not to promote agreements between mutually recognized national governments within the framework of international law, but 'rather to embarrass other governments and stir up opposition among their own people'.*[85]

But what if the world revolution failed to come about? The Bolsheviks would then find themselves without an army, having encouraged its revolutionary destruction, and would be defenceless against the threat of German invasion. The revolution would be defeated and Russia subjected to the Kaiser's imperial rule. As time passed and this scenario became more likely, the Bolsheviks found themselves split down the middle. To those on the left of the party, such as Bukharin, a separate peace with imperialist Germany would represent a betrayal of the international cause, killing off all hopes of a revolution in the West. They favoured the idea of fighting a revolutionary war against the German invaders: this, it was argued, would galvanize the Russian workers and peasants into the defence of the revolution, thereby creating a Red Army in the very process of fighting, and their example would in turn inspire the revolutionary masses abroad.

Lenin, by contrast, was increasingly doubtful both of the chances of fighting such a war and of the likelihood that it might spark a revolution in the West. Though he himself had put forward the idea of a revolutionary war in his April Theses, he now began to doubt that the workers and peasants, who had so far been reluctant to defend Russia, would prove any more willing to defend the Socialist Fatherland. Without an army, the Bolsheviks had no choice but to conclude a separate peace, for if they tried to fight on, the remnants of 'the peasant army, unbearably exhausted by the war, will overthrow the socialist workers' government'. A separate peace with Germany would give the Bolsheviks the 'breathing spell' they needed to consolidate their power base, restore the economy and build up their own revolutionary army. This of course meant giving priority to the policy of strengthening the revolution at home over that

---

* The Soviet anti-nuclear propaganda of the 1970s and 1980s, which was applauded by the anti-nuclear movement in the West, was the last, and in some ways the most successful, example of this 'demonstrative diplomacy'.

of stirring revolution abroad. 'Our tactics', wrote Lenin, 'ought to rest on the principle of how to ensure that the socialist revolution is best able to consolidate itself and survive in one country until such time as other countries join in.' Moreover, in so far as a separate peace in the East would enable the Central Powers to strengthen their campaign in the West and thus prolong the war, such a policy could in itself be seen as a means of *increasing* the chances of a European revolution. For it was surely the continuation of the war, rather than the prospect of a peace, which would intensify the revolutionary crisis, and, although Lenin himself never said so, it was in his party's interests to prolong the slaughter on the battlefields of France and Belgium, even at the risk of helping to bring about a German victory over the Western democracies.

Lenin's view, it must be said, was a much more accurate appraisal of the situation than the naive internationalism of the Bolshevik Left. The Russian army was falling apart, as the peasant soldiers, encouraged by the Bolsheviks, demobilized themselves and went home to their villages to share in the partition of the gentry's land. Even Kerensky's Minister of War, General Verkhovsky, had come to the conclusion that it was impossible to continue the war and Russia had no choice but to sue for peace. There was no reason to suppose that the national consciousness of the peasants had grown any stronger now that Mother Russia had been painted Red. These, after all, were the same people who had failed to see why they should be called up in 1914 because their own particular village had no quarrel with the Germans and, in any case, was not likely to be invaded by them. If anything, such parochial views had been reinforced by the uncertainties of 1917. The peasant and indeed the whole of the social revolution had been largely driven by this petty localism. The Red Guards, who were to become the basis of the new Red Army, were really no more than badly organized partisan units for the defence of the revolution in the separate villages and the separate factories; they were extremely reluctant to leave their own locality and were quite incapable of anything more than petty guerrilla tactics. It was a romantic left-wing fantasy — shared by the Left SRs and Left Communists — to suppose that these guards might sustain, let alone win, a revolutionary war against the German war-machine.

Yet most of the Bolshevik leaders continued to resist Lenin's iron logic. It was hard for them to give up the ideal of a world revolution, especially since so many of them had been drawn to Bolshevism in the first place as a sort of international messianic crusade to liberate the world. For those like Bukharin, and to some extent Trotsky too, who had spent much of their lives in exile in the West, the revolution in Russia was only part — and a minor part at that — of the worldwide struggle between imperialism and socialism. To limit the victory of socialism to one country, let alone a backward one like Russia, seemed to them an admission of defeat. As the prospects of a general peace receded, the Bolsheviks were increasingly divided between the two opposing policies of a revolutionary war or a separate peace with Germany. It was without doubt one of the most critical moments in the history of the party.

* * *

On 13 November Trotsky applied to the German High Command for an armistice with a view to opening talks for a democratic peace. Three days later a Soviet delegation set off from Petrograd for the war-ruined town of Brest-Litovsk, where the German Headquarters were situated, to negotiate the armistice. The purpose of the delegation was propaganda as much as peace: alongside the Bolshevik negotiators, led by Yoffe, Kamenev and Karakhan, it included symbolic representatives from the soldiers, the sailors, the workers, the women and the peasants of Proletarian Russia. The whole preposterous idea was designed to give the impression that the Bolshevik government was filled with elements from the revolutionary democracy.

Actually, the peasant had almost been forgotten, which says a great deal about the peasantry's real place in the Bolshevik schema of the revolution. On their way to the Warsaw Station, Yoffe and Kamenev suddenly realized that their delegation still lacked a peasant representative. As their car sped through the dark and deserted streets of Petrograd, there was consternation at the omission. Suddenly, they turned a corner and spied an old man in a peasant's coat trudging along in the snow with a knapsack on his back. With his long grey beard and his weathered face, he was the archetypal figure of the Russian peasant. Kamenev ordered the car to stop. 'Where are you going, *tovarishch?*' 'To the station, *barin*, I mean *tovarishch*,' the old peasant replied. 'Get in, we'll give you a lift.' The old peasant seemed pleased with this unexpected favour, but as they neared the Warsaw Station, he realized that something was wrong. He had wanted to go to the Nikolaevsky Station, where trains left for Moscow and central Russia. This would not do, thought Kamenev and Yoffe, who began to question the peasant about his politics. 'What party do you belong to?' they asked. 'I'm a Social Revolutionary, comrades. We're all Social Revolutionaries in our village.' 'Left or Right?' they queried further. 'Left, of course, comrades, the leftest you can get.' This was enough to satisfy the Russian peace delegation of the diplomatic credentials of their latest recruit. 'There's no need for you to go to your village,' they told him. 'Come with us to Brest-Litovsk and make peace with the Germans.' The peasant was at first still reluctant, but once he was promised some remuneration quickly changed his mind. Roman Stashkov, a simple villager, was duly recorded in the annals of diplomatic history as the 'plenipotentiary representative of the Russian peasantry'. With his primitive peasant table manners, not unlike Rasputin's, he was to be the centre of attention at the lavish banquets that were laid on for the diplomats. He soon got over the initial embarrassment of not knowing what to do with his fork and began thoroughly to enjoy himself.

What a story he would have to tell when he got back to his village! He particularly enjoyed the fine wines and, on the first night, even drew a smile from the frozen-faced German waiter, when, in response to his question about whether he preferred claret or white wine with his main course, he turned to his neighbour, Prince Ernst von Hohenlohe, and asked: 'Which one is the stronger?'[86]

The first task of the negotiations — the conclusion of a separate armistice — was simple enough. The three main warring parties each had reason to want one: the Germans to release troops to the west, where Ludendorff was pressing for a final 'gambler's throw'; the Austrians to relieve their tired army and civilian population, which were showing signs of growing discontent under the burdens of the war; and the Russians, likewise, to gain a respite as well as time for their peace campaign to spark a revolution in the West. To begin with, the Russian delegation stood firm on the principle of a general armistice: Lenin was hopeful that such a stand might bring the Entente Powers, dragged by their people, to the negotiating table. The Bolshevik policy of encouraging their own soldiers to fraternize and negotiate local armistices at the Front had a similar propagandistic purpose. It was both a means of undercutting the authority of the old (and potentially counter-revolutionary) Russian commanders and of spreading pacifist sentiments among the enemy troops. The Bolsheviks published an enormous quantity of anti-war propaganda in German, Hungarian, Czech and Romanian which they distributed behind enemy lines. General Dukhonin, the acting Commander-in-Chief and a sympathizer with Kornilov, did what he could to oppose these peace initiatives. He even refused to carry out the orders of N. V. Krylenko, the Bolshevik Commissar for War, to open negotiations for a general armistice along the whole of the Front. But Dukhonin, like the old command structure in general, was effectively without power. Krylenko dismissed him and went out to Stavka to replace him. But before he arrived at Mogilev the troops had arrested Dukhonin and savagely beat him to death. It was their revenge for the release of Kornilov from the Bykhov Monastery, and his subsequent flight to the Don, which they believed Dukhonin had ordered. Once Krylenko had gained control of the General Staff, the soldiers continued to negotiate their own local armistices at the Front; but their example failed to spread to the troops in Europe, and on 2 December, with the Entente Powers as determined as ever to continue the war, the Russian delegation was finally forced to accept a one-month separate armistice on the Eastern Front.

The Russians would have much preferred a six-month armistice, as they had suggested. Their strategy was based on playing for time in the hope that the peace campaign might spark a revolution in the West. This was the reason why they had insisted on negotiations for a general peace — not so much because they thought that the Allies might be persuaded to join the talks on these terms (which was extremely doubtful), but because they knew that the effort to persuade them to do so would spin out the talks for a much longer time, giving them the pretext they required to pursue their revolutionary propaganda in the international arena. In replacing Yoffe with Trotsky at the head of the delegation in mid-December, Lenin acknowledged that, without the immediate prospect of a revolution in the West, it was essential to drag out the peace talks for as long as possible. 'To delay the negotiations,' he had told Trotsky on his appointment, 'there must be someone to do the delaying.' And Trotsky, of course, was the obvious choice. With his brilliant rhetorical powers, both in Russian and German, he kept the foreign diplomats and generals spellbound as he subtly switched the focus of the talks from the detailed points of territorial boundaries, where the Russian position was weak, to the general points of principle, where he could run rings around the Germans. Baron Kühlmann, the head of the Kaiser's delegation, who had a typically German weakness for Hegelian philosophizing, was easily drawn into Trotsky's trap. Several days were wasted while the two men crossed swords on the abstract principles of diplomacy. At one point Trotsky halted the talks to give the Baron what he called 'a class in Marxist instruction for beginners'. As they went through the draft treaty's preamble, he even held things up by objecting to the standard phrase that the contracting parties desired to live in peace and friendship. 'I would take the liberty', he said tongue in cheek, 'to propose that the second phrase [about friendship] be deleted ... Such declarations have never yet characterized the real relations between states.'[87]

By the end of December, the German High Command, which had never been keen on Kühlmann's policy of negotiating a general peace, was finally losing patience with the diplomats. The peace talks had broken down in stalemate over Christmas when the Germans had refused to return to Russia the disputed territories of Courland, Lithuania and Poland, where they had important military bases. There was still no sign, moreover, of the Entente Powers coming round to the idea of a general peace. Ludendorff and Hindenburg were both convinced that the Bolsheviks were trying to spin out the negotiations for as long as possible in the hope of stirring a German revolution (there were signs that the loss of spirit which would cripple Germany in 1918 was already beginning to take root). They persuaded the Kaiser, who was also losing patience with Kühlmann, of the need to get tough with the Russians and enforce a separate peace in the east. The prize of this, they stressed, was the chance to transfer troops to the west, where Ludendorff was convinced the war could be won in the spring with enough reinforcements, while opening up the prospect of turning Russia into a German colony.

Eastward expansion, *Der Drang nach Osten*, had long been a central aim of German *Weltpolitik*. Without a colonial empire to challenge Britain or France, Germany looked towards Russia for the resources it needed to become a major imperial power. To Germany's bankers and industrialists, the vast Eurasian landmass was a surrogate Africa in their own backyard. The achievement of Germany's eastern ambitions depended on keeping Russia weak, and on breaking up the Russian Empire. Most of the German leaders had welcomed the Bolshevik seizure of power, despite the Kaiser's dynastic links with the Romanovs. They believed that the Bolsheviks would lead Russia to ruin, that they would allow the break-up of the Empire, and that they would sign a separate peace with Germany. But the German policy of carving up Russia relied even more on the Ukrainian nationalists. The Ukrainian independence movement opened up the prospects of a separate peace with Kiev and the redirection of the Ukraine's rich resources (foodstuffs, iron and coal above all) to the armies of the Central Powers. The Germans had been talking with the would-be leaders of the Ukraine since 1915. During the Christmas recess in the peace negotiations a delegation from the Rada arrived at Brest-Litovsk. Ukrainian nationalists saw the economic subjugation of their country to Berlin as a lesser evil to its political subjugation to Petrograd. Since the end of November, when the Rada had declared the Ukraine independent, the Bolshevik forces had rallied in Kharkov, an industrial city in the eastern Ukraine where the ethnic Russians were in the majority, in preparation (or so, at least it seemed, to the Ukrainian nationalists) for the invasion of Kiev. The Central Powers were the only real force willing to stand by the Rada. They recognized it as the Ukraine's legitimate government, and on 9 February, when the Bolshevik forces — partly in reaction to this — seized Kiev, they signed a separate treaty with the Rada leaders. This treaty effectively turned the Ukraine into a German protectorate, opening the way for its occupation by the Germans and the Austrians, and forcing the Bolsheviks to abandon Kiev after only three weeks and flee eastwards back to Kharkov.

With the Ukrainians detached from the Russians, the Germans greatly strengthened their position at the Brest-Litovsk talks. The prospect of the Ukraine's occupation gave them a powerful military threat that could be used to impose a dictated peace on the Russians; and when peace talks with Russia recommenced at the end of December, they advanced a number of new territorial demands, including the separation of Poland from Russia and the German annexation of Lithuania and most of Latvia. Trotsky called for an adjournment and returned to the Russian capital to confer with the rest of the Bolshevik leaders.

Three clear factions emerged at the decisive meeting of the Central Committee on 11 January. The Bukharin faction, which was the biggest, with 32 votes out of 63 at a special meeting of the party leaders on 8 January, and the support of both the Petrograd and the Moscow Party Committees, favoured fighting a revolutionary war against Germany. This, it was said, was the most likely way to spark an uprising in the West, which was what really mattered. 'We have to look at the socialist republic from the international point of view,' Bukharin argued in the Central Committee. 'Let the Germans strike, let them advance another hundred miles, what interests us is how this affects the international movement.' The Trotsky faction, which was the second biggest, with 16 votes at the meeting on 8 January, was equally concerned not to give up hope of a revolution in the West (there were already signs of a sharp upturn in strikes in Germany and Vienna) but doubted that the peasant guerrilla bands, upon which Bukharin was calling, could seriously withstand a German invasion. Trotsky thus put forward the unusual slogan of 'Neither war nor peace', which was basically designed to play for time. The Soviet delegation would declare the war at an end and walk out of the talks at Brest-Litovsk, but refuse to sign an annexationist peace. If the Germans invaded, which the Bolsheviks could not prevent in any case, then at least it would appear to the rest of the world as a clear act of aggression against a peaceable country.

From Lenin's point of view, at the head of the third and smallest faction, Trotsky's slogan was 'a piece of international political showmanship' which would not stop the Germans advancing. Without an army willing to fight, Russia was in no position to play for time. She had no choice but to sign a separate peace, in which case it was better done sooner than later. 'It is now only a question of how to defend the Fatherland,' Lenin argued with what was for him a rather new tone of patriotic pathos. 'There is no doubt that it will be a shameful peace, but if we embark on a war, our government will be swept away.' There was no point putting the whole of the revolution at risk on the chance (which he himself was now beginning to doubt) that a German revolution might break out. 'Germany is only just pregnant with revolution, but we have already given birth to a completely healthy child.' The reconstruction of Russia and the demands of the civil war both demanded an immediate peace, or as Lenin put it with his usual bluntness: 'The bourgeoisie has to be throttled and for that we need both hands free.'[88]

With only Stalin, Zinoviev and three others behind him in the Central Committee, and a mere fifteen votes at the broader party meeting on 8 January, Lenin was forced to ally with Trotsky against the Bukharin faction. The risk of losing socialist Estonia to the Germans, or of being forced to give in to their demands at the point of a gun, which he saw as the likely outcome of Trotsky's international showmanship, still seemed a price worth paying to prevent what he saw as the suicidal policy of a revolutionary war. Trotsky's mischievous slogan of 'Neither war nor peace' was endorsed by the Central Committee, and Trotsky himself sent back to Brest-Litovsk with orders to spin out the talks.

For three more weeks Trotsky played for time, while the German High Command became more impatient. Then events finally came to a head on 9 February, when a telegram arrived from the Kaiser in Berlin ordering Kühlmann to present the German demands as an ultimatum. If it was not signed by the next day, the German and Austrian armies would be ordered to advance. The

Kaiser had finally been convinced by the German High Command that the peace talks were a waste of time, that the Russians were merely using them to stir up revolt among his troops, and that the treaty with the Rada, signed on the same day as the Kaiser's telegram, opened the door to a military imposition of a separate peace on the Russians through the occupation of the Ukraine. There was clearly no more room for procrastination — and Trotsky was forced to lay down his hand. The next day he told the astounded conference that Russia was 'leaving the war' but refused to sign the German peace treaty. Nothing quite like it had ever been heard before in diplomatic history — a country that acknowledged defeat and declared its intention not to go on fighting but at the same time refused to accept the victor's terms for an end to the war. When Trotsky finished speaking the diplomats sat in silence, dumbfounded by this *coup de théâtre*. Then the silence was at last broken by the scandalized cry of General Max von Hoffman: '*Unerhört!*'[89]

Once the initial shock passed, it was clear to the German High Command that Trotsky's bluff had to be called. Since no peace treaty had been signed, Germany was still at war with Russia, the armistice had come to an end and the way was now open for the German invasion of Russia. Despite his own growing fears of a revolution in Berlin, Kühlmann was forced by pressure from Ludendorff to announce on 16 February that Germany would resume hostilities against Russia on 18 February. Back in the Smolny, on the 17th, the Central Committee met in panic. Lenin's demand that the German treaty should be accepted at once was defeated by six votes to five. Trotsky's policy of waiting for the Germans to launch their attack before signing the peace was adopted instead in the desperate hope that the sight of their troops attacking the defenceless people of Russia might at last inspire the German working classes to rebel.[90]

Sure enough, on the 18th the German troops advanced. Dvinsk and Lutsk were immediately captured without resistance. The last remaining Russian troops fell apart altogether — they were quite indifferent to the call of a revolutionary war — and by the end of the fifth day Hoffman's men had advanced 150 miles. It was as much as the whole German army had advanced in the three previous years of fighting. 'It is the most comical war I have ever known,' Hoffman wrote in his diary. 'It is waged almost exclusively in trains and automobiles. We put a handful of infantry men with machine-guns and one gun on to a train and push them off to the next station; they take it, make prisoners of the Bolsheviks, pick up a few more troops, and go on. This proceeding has, at any rate, the charm of novelty.'[91]

As news came in of the German advance, the Central Committee convened in two emergency sessions on 18 February. Lenin was furious. By refusing to sign the German treaty, his opponents in the Central Committee had merely enabled the enemy to advance. Lenin clearly feared that the Germans were about to capture Petrograd and oust the Bolsheviks from power — and this necessitated sending a telegram accepting the peace at once. When Trotsky and Bukharin proposed to delay this, Lenin was beside himself with rage. But he still lacked enough votes to enforce his policy, which was defeated by seven votes to six at the morning session of the Central Committee. The Bolshevik leadership seemed on the brink of a fatal division as it stared defeat in the face. But during the afternoon, as rumours came in of a German advance into the Ukraine, Trotsky moved round towards Lenin's view. At the evening session of the Central Committee he proposed to ask the Germans to restate their terms. As Lenin rightly saw it, this was a foolish game to play. It was too late now for diplomatic notes, which the Germans would in any case soon dismiss as a ploy for time; only the firm acceptance of their terms for peace would be enough to halt their advance. After three further hours of heated debate the crucial vote was taken on Lenin's proposal to send the Germans an immediate offer of peace. It was passed by the slenderest of margins, by seven votes to five, with Trotsky switching to Lenin's side at the final moment.[92] Though we will probably never find out what went on behind the scenes, it seems that Trotsky's crucial change of mind was largely influenced by the need to avert what could otherwise have turned out to be a fatal division within the party. If Trotsky had joined Bukharin in opposing the peace, Lenin would probably have resigned from the Central Committee, as he had threatened to do, and rallied support from the Bolshevik rank and file. The party would thus have been split and Trotsky, as the leader of its faction against peace, much the weaker for it. Without Lenin, Trotsky's place at the top of the party was extremely vulnerable — as events would later prove.

At midnight, after the crucial vote in the Central Committee, Lenin personally sent a cable to Berlin accepting the German terms for peace proposed at Brest-Litovsk. For several days, however, the enemy's troops continued to advance deep into Russia and the Ukraine without an acknowledgement of Lenin's telegram being made. It seemed quite clear that the Germans had decided to capture Petrograd and overthrow the Bolshevik regime. Lenin now decided to fight — completely reversing his earlier position — and called for volunteers. Military help was sought from the Allies, who were much more concerned to keep Russia in the war than they were with the nature of its government and readily came up with an offer of military aid.* On Lenin's orders, the Bolsheviks

---

* The refusal of the Allies to regard the situation in Russia from anything but the perspective of the war no doubt helped to keep the Bolsheviks in power at this critical moment. The decision of the French government to give the Bolsheviks military aid coincided with its cancellation of support for the Volunteer Army, which was formed to overthrow the Bolshevik regime. The Allied governments were all badly informed of the true situation in Russia, and placed too much faith for far too long in the hope of getting revolutionary Russia to rejoin the war.

prepared for the evacuation of the capital to Moscow, which threw Petrograd into panic. The railway stations were jammed with people trying to escape, while thousands left every day on foot. Law and order broke down altogether, as armed gangs looted abandoned shops and houses and angry workers, faced with the evacuation of their factories, tried to recoup weeks of unpaid wages by pilfering from the factory stores. It was at this point, with the capital sliding into anarchy, that Lenin issued his Decree on 'The Socialist Fatherland in Danger!' which did so much to fuel the Red Terror.

On 22 February the Central Committee reconvened to discuss the question of accepting military aid from the Allies. With the support of Trotsky and Lenin (*in absentia*), the motion in favour of doing so was passed — though only just, for Bukharin and the other advocates of a revolutionary war were violently opposed to taking aid from the imperial powers. When the vote was taken, Bukharin threatened to resign from the Central Committee in protest. 'We are turning the party into a dung-heap,' he complained to Trotsky and then burst into tears.[93]

As it turned out, the question of Allied aid was irrelevant. On 23 February the Germans at last delivered their final terms for peace. Berlin now demanded all the territory which its troops had seized in the course of the war, including those they had occupied in the last five days. This meant, in effect, the German annexation of the Ukraine and most of the Baltic. The Central Committee reconvened at once. Lenin threatened to resign if the peace terms were not accepted. Draconian though the new terms were, they at least left the Bolsheviks in power. 'It is a question', Lenin warned, 'of signing the peace terms now or signing the death sentence of the Soviet Government three weeks later.' Trotsky was not convinced of this, but knew that a divided party, which would result from Lenin's resignation, could not fight a revolutionary war, and on this basis he abstained from the crucial vote on Lenin's proposal, which thus passed by seven votes to four with four members abstaining. Only the Bukharin faction, which was prepared, in the words of Lomov, to 'take power without Ilich [Lenin] and go to the Front to fight', remained in opposition right to the end and resigned from the Central Committee in order to free themselves for a campaign against the peace both among the party rank and file and in the country at large. Later that night Lenin presented the peace proposals to the Soviet Executive, where they were duly passed by 116 votes to 85. Throughout his speech Lenin was heckled with cries of 'Traitor!' and 'Judas!' from the Left SRs and many on the left wing of his own party. In the early hours of the following morning he sent to Berlin an unconditional acceptance of the German terms.[94]

*　*　*

The Treaty of Brest-Litovsk was finally signed on 3 March. None of the Bolshevik leaders wanted to go to Brest-Litovsk and put their name to a treaty which was seen throughout Russia as a 'shameful peace'. Yoffe flatly refused; Trotsky put himself out of contention by resigning as Commissar for Foreign Affairs; Sokolnikov nominated Zinoviev, whereupon Zinoviev nominated Sokolnikov. In the end, the delegation had to be made up of secondary party leaders, including G. V. Chicherin, the grandson of a nobleman and prominent tsarist diplomat who succeeded Trotsky as Commissar for Foreign Affairs.

By the terms of the treaty, Russia was forced to give up most of its territories on the continent of Europe. Poland, Courland, Finland, Estonia and Lithuania were all given nominal independence under German protection. Soviet troops were to be evacuated from the Ukraine. All in all, it has been calculated that the Soviet Republic lost 34 per cent of her population (fifty-five million people in all), 32 per cent of her agricultural land, 54 per cent of her industrial enterprises and 89 per cent of her coalmines.[95] As a European power, Russia, in economic and territorial terms, had been reduced to a status on a par with seventeenth-century Muscovy.

As a direct consequence of the treaty, Germany was able to push on unopposed towards the fulfilment of her imperial ambitions in the east. The Ukraine was immediately occupied by half a million German and Austrian troops. On the whole, they were welcomed by the urban propertied classes, most of whom were Russians and fed up with the nationalist and socialist policies of the Rada government. They looked forward to the cities being run by the 'orderly Germans'. But in the countryside, where the troops were engaged in ruthless requisitioning of foodstuffs for the hungry citizens of Austria, the Ukrainian peasants were bitterly opposed to the German presence. To begin with, the responsibility for collecting the grain had been left to the Rada. It was to despatch 300 truckloads of grain per day — a sort of tribute to Berlin, agreed under the Peace Treaty of 9 February, in exchange for the German troops' protection of the Ukraine's independence against Russia. The Ukrainian peasants had been generally supportive of the Rada parties during 1917; but their nationalism did not include the export of Ukrainian grain to a foreign country. They gradually reduced their sowings and concealed their grain from the Rada agents. As the Rada fell behind with its payment of this tribute, the German troops took it upon themselves to go into the villages and collect the grain. They did so indiscriminately, taking vital stocks of food and seed from many peasant farms and, without the approval of the Rada, punishing the peasants who refused to pay the levy in their military courts. Millions of acres of unsown peasant land were turned over to the former landowners with the aim of punishing the peasant saboteurs. The result was a wave of peasant revolts and guerrilla wars designed to disrupt the German requisitions: bridges and railway lines were destroyed and German units were attacked from the woods. The Ukrainian countryside was thrown into chaos. Most of these peasant activities were organized by the Left SRs — both the Russians and the Ukrainians (who were soon to break away from the Ukrainian SRs and form the Borotbist or SR Fighters' Party). But the Germans blamed the Rada for failing to control the situation. At the end of April, in a coup supported by the Russified landowners, who were equally opposed to these peasant wars, they arrested the Rada government and replaced it with their own puppet regime under Hetman Skoropadsky, a general in one of the first Ukrainianized army corps and one of the Ukraine's richest landowners who had been an aide-de-camp of Nicholas II. He was now to perform an equally servile role for the Ukraine's new masters in Berlin.

Within Russia the treaty guaranteed a privileged status for German economic interests. German property was exempt from nationalization — even land and enterprises confiscated after 1914 could be reclaimed by their German owners. It was also possible under the treaty for Germans to buy up Russian assets and thus exclude them from the Bolshevik decrees of nationalization. Hundreds of Russian enterprises were sold to German nationals in this way, thereby giving them a dominant hold over the private sector. The words *nemets* (German) and 'trader', which had always been linked (and confused with 'traitor') in the minds of the ordinary Russians, were now virtually the same in reality.

For Russian patriots, who had long been obsessed by the thought of the Slavs being subjected to the economic domination of the Teutons, the Brest-Litovsk Treaty was a national catastrophe. Prince Lvov, who was living in Tiumen' at the time, became almost suicidal and, according to his aunt, would not get out of bed for several days. General Brusilov, a stalwart of the pan-Slav cause, was thrown into deep depression by the news. It was uncharacteristic of this great optimist, who had always managed to keep his spirits up, even at the darkest moments of the war. With his leg in plaster, still recovering from the wound inflicted on it during the fighting in Moscow, he lay in bed for days bemoaning Russia's ruin. His wife later claimed that he found solace in religion: God took up the space vacated by the Fatherland in his mental world. It also made him more accepting of what he now saw as 'Russia's tragic destiny'. He was certainly not inclined to join the civil war against the treaty, although the Cheka, which could not understand why such an aristocrat would not join the Whites, later imprisoned him on the assumption that he had done just that. Brusilov's refusal to take up arms against the Soviet regime was based on the conviction, as he put it in a letter to his brother, that 'the people have decided Russia's fate'. Although Brusilov's heart was no doubt with the Whites, he knew only too well that their cause was doomed because they supported the resumption of the war. If there was one thing that Brusilov had learned from the experience of 1917, it was that the Russian people wanted peace at any cost, and that all the talk of the patriotic parties about defending Mother Russia and its borders was entirely alien to them.[96]

Opposition to the treaty was not limited to anti-Soviet circles. The Bukharin faction and the Left SRs were thrown together by their rejection of the 'shameful peace' and combined to form a powerful opposition in the Soviet Executive. The Left SRs resigned from Sovnarkom in protest at the treaty, and later took up terrorist measures, including the assassination of the German Ambassador, in the futile hope of wrecking it and reviving the revolutionary war. The emergence of the Bukharin faction, the Left Communists, grouped around the journal *Kommunist*, split the Bolshevik Party down the middle. Many of these young idealists, if not so much Bukharin himself, linked their support for a revolutionary war with their opposition to the *rapprochement* with the bourgeoisie which Lenin called for in the spring under the programme of 'state capitalism'. They were opposed to the idea of any let-up in the war against the bourgeoisie — either in the form of peace with the imperialists abroad, or of a compromise with the capitalists at home. They saw the revolution as an international crusade against capitalism and, unlike Lenin, believed that this could be sustained through the revolutionary energies of the peasants and the workers within a genuinely democratic and decentralized system of Soviet power.

✳   ✳   ✳

The peace of Brest-Litovsk marked the completion of Lenin's revolution: it was the culmination of October. In his struggle over the treaty, as in his struggle for power itself, Lenin had always been uncompromising. There was no sacrifice he was not prepared to make for the consolidation of the revolution on his own terms. As a result of his intransigence, the Bolsheviks had been isolated from the rest of the revolutionary parties and split down the middle on several major issues. The seizure of power, the closure of the Constituent Assembly and the signing of the Brest-Litovsk Treaty, all of which had been carried out on Lenin's instigation, had plunged the country deeper and deeper into civil war. Russia itself had ceased to be a major power in the world. It was forced to retreat from the continent of Europe, to turn in on itself, and to look towards the east. After the Treaty of Brest-Litovsk there was no real prospect of the revolution spreading to the West. Lenin was quite adamant about this, and all his talk of the 'inevitable revolution in Germany' cancelling out the losses of the treaty was no more than bluff for the sake of party morale and propaganda.[97] True, during 1919 and 1920, Lenin would flirt with the idea of exporting Communism through the Comintern; but this did not amount to much. To all intents and purposes, the 'permanent revolution' had come to an end, and from this point on, in Lenin's famous phrase, the aim of the regime would be limited to the consolidation of Socialism in One Country.

The removal of the capital to Moscow symbolized this growing separation from the West. Petersburg had always been a European city, 'Russia's window on the West'; Moscow, by contrast, was a physical reminder of its Asiatic traditions. The imprisoned Tsar no doubt would have found the move somewhat ironic, for he had always preferred the old capital to Petersburg. The retreat of the Bolsheviks eastwards, into the heartland of Muscovite Russia, had been largely forced on them by the continuation of the German advance after the ratification of the treaty. On 2 March German planes dropped bombs on Petrograd. Lenin was convinced the Germans were planning to occupy the city and remove the Bolsheviks. Allied aid was once again called for — Kamenev was sent to London and British troops landed at Murmansk — whilst the Bolsheviks fled to Moscow.

Lenin and Trotsky soon moved into the Tsar's former quarters in the Kremlin. The musical clock on the Spassky Tower, through which their motor-cars entered the Kremlin, was rebuilt so that its bells rang out the tune of the Internationale instead of 'God Save the Tsar'. Most of the Tsar's former servants were kept on at first. One of them, the aged Stupishin, had served several emperors in his time, and he soon became firmly attached to both Lenin and Trotsky in turn, no doubt having observed, as Trotsky later wrote, 'that we appreciated order and valued his care'. During meals, the neat little manciple would move 'like a shadow behind the chairs' and silently turn the plates this way or that so that the double-headed eagle on the rim was the right side up. Trotsky thought the Kremlin, 'with its medieval wall and its countless gilded cupolas, was an utter paradox as a fortress for the revolutionary dictatorship'.[98] But in fact it was a highly fitting building, even a symbolic one, and not just because the Bolsheviks behaved like the new 'tsars' of Russia. For the civil war regime on which they now embarked was set in many ways to take Russia back to the customs of its Muscovite past.

Part Four

THE CIVIL WAR AND
THE MAKING OF
THE SOVIET SYSTEM
(1918–24)

12 Last Dreams of the Old World

i St Petersburg on the Steppe

In his wonderful novel, *The White Guard*, Mikhail Bulgakov describes the surreal life of Kiev during the spring of 1918, when the city became filled with refugees from the Bolshevik north.

> Among the refugees came grey-haired bankers and their wives, skilful businessmen who had left behind their faithful deputies in Moscow with instructions to them not to lose contact with the new world which was coming into existence in the Muscovite kingdom; landlords who had secretly left their property in the hands of trusted managers; industrialists, merchants, lawyers, politicians. There came journalists from Moscow and Petersburg, corrupt, grasping and cowardly. Prostitutes. Respectable ladies from aristocratic families and their delicate daughters, pale depraved women from Petersburg with carmine-painted lips; secretaries of civil service department chiefs; inert young homosexuals. Princes and junk-dealers, poets and pawnbrokers, gendarmes and actresses from the Imperial theatres.[1]

Kiev was not the only city to be overrun in this way. Bulgakov's description could have been applied to almost any major city in the south. But the presence of the Germans and their puppet Ukrainian government headed by the Hetman Paulo Skoropadsky, which pledged to protect the property of the refugees and gave them employment, certainly made Kiev the place to go. Every house was filled to bursting point. Russian princes slept on floors and divans. The city had an atmosphere of frenzied excitement, with everyone living as if there was no tomorrow. People dined in vast numbers at expensive res-taurants, gambled away fortunes at clubs and casinos, and indulged in wild affairs. Cafés did a brisk business selling cocktails and women. Cabarets and theatres were packed out every night, as people laughed away their fears. Shop windows were crammed with French perfumes and silks, great slabs of sturgeon and caviar, and vintage bottles of Abrau champagne with the double-headed eagle on their labels.

These refugees hated the Bolsheviks with a passion. But very few were inclined to fight them. 'Their hatred', wrote Bulgakov, 'was not the kind of aggressive hatred that spurs the hater to fight and kill, but a passive and cowardly type of hatred.'[2] They muttered words of outrage as they sat in their restaurants over lunch and read about the latest horrors in the north. But they had no intention of giving up these comforts to go off to war. This was a bourgeoisie on the run.

Only the officers — the landowners' sons and students whose studies had been broken off by the war — hated the Reds with the sort of hatred that made them want to fight. These young men had fled their shattered regiments at the Front and risked their lives crossing the country to reach the cities of the south. By day, they roamed the streets penniless and unshaven; at night they slept on people's chairs and floors, using their greatcoats as blankets. This was a dispossessed generation who had nothing to lose in a civil war. Many of them had already seen their families lose their landed estates to the peasantry, or had had their own careers, their hopes and expectations, ruined as a result of the revolution. They drank too much, seethed with anger and thought only of revenge.

One of these student officers, Roman Gul', was passing through Kiev on his way to join the White Guards on the Don during the winter of 1917. In October he had received a telegram from his father: 'The estate is destroyed, ask for leave.' Since then he had been on the run from the Bolsheviks. Travelling through Russia in a third-class railway carriage, Gul' was disgusted by the malice and mistrust on the faces of the peasant troops around him. 'These are the people who smashed our old mahogany chairs,' he wrote to a friend from the train; 'these are the people who tore up my favourite books, the ones I bought as a student on the Sukharevka;* these are the people who cut down our orchard and cut down the roses that mama planted; these are the people who burnt down our home.' It was partly in order to avenge this loss that Gul', like so many young men of his class, had resolved to join the Whites. 'I saw that underneath the red hat of what we had thought of as the beautiful woman of the Revolution there was in fact the ugly snout of a pig. My heart was full of doubts and hesitations, but I convinced myself that in the end, to put all this right, one had to take responsibility, one even had to be prepared to commit the sin of murder.'[3]

Gul's destination, Novocherkassk, was the headquarters of the fledgling Volunteer Army led by Alexeev and Kornilov. After the Bolshevik seizure of power, and Kornilov's release from the Bykhov Monastery, both men had fled to the sleepy town on the steppe, where the Don Cossacks, thought by the

---

* A large flea-market in Moscow.

Whites to be stalwart supporters of the old order, had recently elected General Kaledin as the Ataman of their traditional assembly, the Krug. Taciturn and gloomy, Kaledin was a typical Cossack general of the old school. During 1917 he had sided with Kornilov against the Soviet and at the Moscow Conference in August had called forthrightly for the abolition of all the democratic army organizations.

The Don Krug had declared its independence on 20 November. The basic concern of the Don Cossack leaders was to defend this, but the Volunteers had persuaded them that this could only be achieved by joining forces with them against the Bolsheviks. The latter had mobilized the support of much of the non-Cossack population in the Don — among the Russian peasants (*inogorodnye*), the industrial workers and the sailors of the Black Sea Fleet — for an offensive against Rostov, the major city of the Don. Hence, to begin with, Kaledin welcomed the arrival of the Volunteers — a mere forty officers, calling themselves Alexeev's Organization — on 17 November. His own forces had been fast disintegrating, as the younger and more radical Cossacks, who were in no mood to fight the Reds, returned from the Front and began to campaign against his leadership. Many local Cossacks were afraid that the presence of the Volunteers might make Novocherkassk, the Don capital, a target for the Bolsheviks. Because of this Cossack mistrust of the Whites, Alexeev's officers had had to be hidden in a hospital at first. But as the Reds approached, and it became clear that the Don could not be defended without their support, Kaledin was able to deploy them without serious Cossack objections. At the beginning of December the Red Guards finally captured Rostov. Kaledin imposed martial law and called on the Volunteers to retake the city (his own Cossacks had refused to fight). Alexeev's army, which by this stage had grown to a force of some 500 officers, was quite sufficient to defeat the more numerous but hopelessly indisciplined Red Guards. The six-day battle began on 9 December — St George's Day, the patron saint of Russia. It was the first major battle of the civil war.[4]

The battle for Rostov was typical of the fighting that characterized the first twelve months of the war (October 1917 to September 1918). There were no fixed 'fronts', as such, since neither side had enough men or channels of supply, and the movement of the fighting was extremely fluid. Large towns could be captured by tiny armies hardly worthy of the name. Most troop movements were by rail, and for this reason these early confrontations have become known as 'the railway war'. It became a question of loading a handful of men and some machine-guns on to a train and moving off to the next station — which would then be 'captured' along with the town. The 'fighting' in these battles was often farcical, since many of the rank-and-file soldiers, especially on the Red side, were reluctant to fight at all (many of them had only joined up in order to get an army coat and a daily ration of food). It often happened that the opposing sides would unexpectedly run across each other in a village or some small town and, after a meeting, would agree to retreat rather than engage. The Red soldiers, in particular, would often run away in panic as soon as the first shots were fired; and although the Whites, as 'volunteers', had many fewer problems of this sort, there were many occasions when their officers were also forced to use terror against their own troops. On both sides, officers played down the failures of their men, whilst exaggerating their 'successes', in their operational reports. As Trotsky once complained, every town was captured, or so it was claimed, 'after a fierce battle'; while every retreat was 'only as a result of the onslaught of superior forces'. These absurd aspects of the civil war were best captured by Jaroslav Hašek in his comic novella *The Red Commissar*. Its Schweikian hero orders his troops to retreat to the left when his lines are broken on the right. He then sends a telegram to headquarters announcing a 'great victory' and the encircle-ment of the Whites.[5]

The growth of the Volunteer Army was largely due to the charismatic presence of General Kornilov. He and his followers had fled from the open jail at the Bykhov Monastery after Dukhonin had lost control of Stavka to the Bolsheviks in November. Since this ruled out the possibility of bringing down the Bolsheviks from inside Soviet Russia, and indeed put themselves at risk of execution, the Bykhov generals resolved to flee to the Don. Most disguised themselves and travelled by train through Bolshevik Russia. Lukomsky shaved off his beard and spoke in a German accent; Romanovsky masqueraded as an ensign; Markov as a common soldier. Denikin pretended to be a Polish nobleman and travelled third class: it was here that he witnessed for the first time the 'boundless hatred' of the common people for 'everything that was socially or intellectually higher than the crowd'. Proud as ever, Kornilov, however, refused to hide his identity and instead led his loyal Tekinsky Regiment on a forced march through hostile Bolshevik terrain. They were finally stopped and engaged in battle by a Red armoured train. Kornilov's white horse was shot from underneath him. He managed to escape, and reassembled most of his troops, but they were already too demoralized to go on, and Kornilov, realizing that he could make it only without them, decided to abandon them and complete his journey alone disguised as a peasant. Ironically, he travelled to the Don in a Red Guards' train.[6]

Novocherkassk, which Gul' reached on New Year's Eve, was a microcosm of the old Russia in exile. St Petersburg on the steppe. The fallen high and mighty thronged its muddy streets. 'Here were generals, with their stripes and epaulettes, dashing cavalry officers in their colourful tunics, the white kerchiefs of nurses, and the huge Caucasian fur hats of the Turkomen warriors,' recalled Gul'. Numerous Duma politicians had come to try and direct the White movement: Miliukov, Rodzianko, Struve, Zavoiko, G. N. Trubetskoi, N. N. Lvov, even the SR, Boris Savinkov. Leading intellectuals also made the Don their home, both in the physical and in the spiritual sense. Marina Tsvetaeva, whose husband, Sergei Efron, was one of the first to join the Volunteers, wrote a series of poems, *The Swan's Encampment*, from her Moscow garret, in which she idealized the rebels on the Don as the 'youth and glory' of Russia:

> White Guards: Gordian knot
> Of Russian valour.
> White Guards: white mushrooms
> Of the Russian folksong
> White Guards: white stars,
> Not to be crossed from the sky.
> White guards: black nails
> In the ribs of the Antichrist.

'White Guards', 27 July 1918[7]

For Tsvetaeva, as for so many of her class and background, the Don represented the last hope of saving Russian civilization. It was, as she expressed it, the 'last dream of the old world'.

In Novocherkassk the official clock ran on St Petersburg time — an hour behind local Don time — as if in readiness to resume the work of government in the tsarist capital. Nothing better symbolized the nostalgic attitudes of the Whites. They were, quite literally, trying to put back the clock. Everything about them, from their tsarist uniforms to their formal morning dress, signalled a longing to restore the old regime. In later years, looking back on the civil war, all the most intelligent people on the White side, whether in south Russia or Siberia, acknowledged that this identification with the past was a major reason for their defeat. For however much the leaders of the Whites might have pledged their belief in democratic principles, they were much too rooted in the old regime to be accepted as a real alternative to the Bolsheviks; and this was even more true of the White officers and the local officials who came into contact with the ordinary people and formed their image of the White regime. Astrov, the Kadet who joined the Volunteers, wrote in 1920: 'We, with our dated ploys, our dated mentality and the dated vices of our bureaucracy, complete with Peter the Great's Table of Ranks, could not keep up with the Reds.' Shulgin, the Nationalist, wrote in 1919: 'The counter-revolution did not put forward a single new name ... That was the main reason for our tragedy.' Struve, writing in 1921, stressed how this 'old regime psychology' had prevented the Whites from adopting the sort of revolutionary methods essential to win a civil war:

> Psychologically, the Whites conducted themselves as if nothing had happened, whereas in reality the whole world around them had collapsed, and in order to vanquish the enemy they themselves had to undergo, in a certain sense, a rebirth ... Nothing so harmed the 'White' movement as this very condition of psychologically staying put in previous circumstances, circumstances which had ceased to exist ... Men with this 'old regime' psychology were immersed in the raging sea of revolutionary anarchy, and psychologically could not find their bearings in it ... In the revolutionary storm that struck Russia in 1917, even out-and-out restorationists had to turn revolutionaries in the psychological sense: because in a revolution only revolutionaries can find their way.[8]

It was his dislike of this restorationism — and his wounded leg — which prevented Brusilov from coming to the Don, despite several appeals by his old friend Alexeev. While Brusilov was clearly sympathetic to the Whites, he was convinced that their cause 'was doomed to fail because the Russian people, for better or worse, have chosen the Reds'. There was no point, as he explained to a friend in early April, in trying to put the clock back. 'I consider the old regime as having been abolished for a very long time.' Kornilov's war against the Bolsheviks might have been, as he put it, 'brave and noble', but it was also a 'stupid act' that was 'bound to waste a lot of young men's lives'. No doubt there was a hint of his own dislike for Kornilov in this. But there was also a sense of resignation that made Brusilov reject a civil war — as if, in his mind, the revolution had been planned by God and was part of a divine comedy whose end was not yet clear. As a patriot, Brusilov thought that it was his 'duty to remain on the people's side' — which meant taking no side in the civil war, even if this also meant betraying his own social class and ideology. Meinecke's dictum of 1919 — 'I remain, facing the past, a monarchist of the heart, and will become, facing the future, a republican of the mind' — might just as well have been Brusilov's.[9]

The Volunteer Army was an officers' army. That was its major problem: it never succeeded in attracting the support of the civilian population, not even of private soldiers. When Kornilov was first shown the list of volunteers, he exclaimed in anger: 'These are all officers, but where are the soldiers?' Of the first 3,000 volunteers, no more than a dozen were rank-and-file troops. There has never been such a top-heavy army in the history of warfare. Captains and colonels were forced to serve as privates. Major-generals had to make do with the command of a squadron. Constant squabbling over the command posts caused terrible headaches for the General Staff. Senior generals refused to serve under younger officers promoted strictly on merit; monarchists refused to obey commanders opposed to the Tsar. Some refused to serve below the rank they had held in the imperial army, thinking it beneath their dignity. The cafés were full of these idle officers. They dubbed the Volunteers 'toy soldiers'. Pride in their previous rank and status overcame their desire to fight.[10]

Even the two men at the head of the movement could not stop themselves from petty bickering. Kornilov had been given the command of the Volunteer Army, while Alexeev was placed in charge of political and financial matters. But the division never really worked and both men got in each other's way. Relations became so bad that routine communications between them had to be made through messengers, even though their offices were next door to each other. The atmosphere was poisoned by their continuous squabbles, as Roman Gul' discovered when he tried to enlist at the army's offices in Novocherkassk. Unaware that the enlistment bureau was run by Alexeev's supporters, he named a relative of Kornilov as one of his referees. 'The ensign made a grimace, shrugged his shoulders and said through his teeth: "Look, he doesn't really belong to our organization." ' It was only later that Gul' learned of the 'covert struggle and the secret war between the two leaders'. The split had less to do with ideology than with tactics, style and personal rivalry. Both men had accepted the February Revolution and had pledged to restore the Constituent Assembly. But Kornilov was hostile to the Kadet politicians — and indeed to all politicians — whom Alexeev courted. He also favoured bolder tactics — including terrorism inside Soviet Russia — than the conservative Alexeev. 'Even if we have to burn half of Russia and shed the blood of three-quarters of the population, we shall do it if that is needed to save Russia,' Kornilov once said. Alexeev and the senior generals looked upon Kornilov as a rabble-rouser and a demagogue, who had only risen to the rank of general after the February Revolution. Yet it was precisely this image of the 'self-made man' — an image which Kornilov had cultivated — that made him the idol of the junior officers. It was a clash between the old tsarist principles of seniority and the mass politics of 1917.[11]

As an army of Russian officers, the Volunteers were always bound to have a problem with their Cossack hosts. The White leaders had made the Don their base because they had presumed the Don Cossacks to be stalwart supporters of the old order. But this owed more to nineteenth-century myths than to twentieth-century realities. In fact the Cossacks were themselves divided, both on regional and generational lines. In the northern districts the Cossacks were smallholders, like the local Russian peasants, and generally supported the ideas advanced by the younger and more democratic Cossack officers for a socialist republic that would unite them with the peasantry. The northerners resented the southern districts, both for their wealth and for the pretensions of their elders to speak for the territory as a whole. The younger and war-weary Cossacks from the Front — influenced by the officers risen from their ranks — were more inclined to find some accord with Bolshevik Russia than to fight against it. Thus it was really only in the southern Don — where the Cossacks were more wealthy and more determined to defend their historic landed privileges against the demands of the Russian peasants for land reform — that the Cossacks were prepared to fight the Bolsheviks. Most of the Cossacks of the northern Don, by contrast, rallied behind the Military Revolutionary Council in Kamenskaia led by the officer, Philip Mironov, who had organized the Don Cossack revolt of 1905–6. Mironov's aim was an independent socialist republic uniting the Cossacks with the Russian peasants. But in effect his MRC was to serve as a fifth column for the Bolshevik troops as they invaded the Don from the eastern Ukraine. Meanwhile, in the Don's industrial cities the mainly Russian workers, who were generally supportive of the Bolsheviks, staged a number of protest strikes against the presence of the Volunteers. The workers massacred suspected supporters of the Whites — which in effect meant all the *burzhooi* — while the Whites carried out equally savage reprisals, putting out the eyes and cutting off the noses of hundreds of strikers. In short, there was a spiral of increasing terror as the cities of the Don descended into civil war.

To a growing number of the local Cossacks, all this appeared to be an alien conflict imported from Russia. The younger Cossacks who had spent the past three years at the Front were especially hostile to the idea of fighting for the Whites. So there was a growing split between Cossack fathers and Cossack sons, as the readers of Sholokhov's novel *And Quiet Flows the Don* will recall, and Kaledin's forces fell apart as the younger Cossacks turned their backs on war. The defence of the Don was thus left to the Volunteer Army and a dwindling number of mainly older Cossacks who remained loyal to Kaledin. Without proper supplies or finance — the Rostov middle classes were reluctant to support the Volunteers — they had little chance of holding off the Reds.[12]

On 8 February, six days after a workers' uprising in the city, the Reds captured Taganrog. They were now less than fifty miles from Rostov. Kaledin's government was doomed. The Volunteers, seeing no reason to sacrifice their army in the defence of Rostov, prepared to abandon it and march south to the Kuban, where the Cossacks, worried by the Red advance, might be persuaded to join them. Kaledin resigned as Ataman. The same day he shot himself. Ten days later, on 23 February, the Red Army captured Rostov for the second time in three months. Novocherkassk, the Don capital, fell on the 25th. With the conquest of the Don, the Soviet control of Russia was virtually complete. Only the Kuban remained as a major pocket of resistance. Lenin pronounced the civil war over. But in fact it had only just begun.

*   *   *

The Ice March, as the Volunteers' retreat from the Don to the Kuban came to be known, was *the* heroic epic of the Russian civil war.* The drama of the Ice March became a legend among the Whites and was later retold in countless émigré memoirs. This was the defining moment of the White movement, the moment when the Volunteers became a real army, as if their very survival, against all the odds, bound them together and gave them a strength that far transcended their actual numbers.

On 23 February, as the Soviet forces entered Rostov, Kornilov led off his Volunteers, some 4,000 highly trained soldiers and officers, armed with no more than a rifle each and a few cannons, across the frozen steppelands of the Don. They marched in single file, a thin black line in the vast snow-covered steppe. Their long civilian tail — bankers, politicians, university professors, journalists, nurses and the wives and children of the officers — slowed them down. This was the bourgeoisie of Rostov on the run. They preferred this cruel journey to staying behind and running the risk of falling victim to the Bolsheviks. The Ice Marchers marched by day and night avoiding the railways and the settlements, where the population was likely to be hostile. The wounded and the sick were left behind. Many of them shot themselves rather than run the risk of being captured by the Reds.

General Lukomsky, whose group separated from the main column, was taken captive by the Russian villagers of Guliai-Borisov and brought before a Revolutionary Tribunal. Lukomsky tried to convince the villagers that he was a travelling businessman, but this was hardly likely to win him any friends, and they called for the *burzhooi* to be shot. But Lukomsky was able to escape in the confusion, when just before his scheduled execution the villagers beat to death two Volunteers and began to fight among themselves for their boots. Whilst waiting to be executed, Lukomsky had seen his own grave being dug, and had taken some cyanide pills which he had had with him since his imprisonment in the Bykhov Monastery. Luckily for him, they had no effect.[13]

The deeper the Whites moved into the steppe, the more they resorted to terror against a hostile population. Their Ice March left a trail of blood. It was perhaps unavoidable, given the Volunteers' desperate need for food and the reluctance of the peasants to give it to them. The Whites were stranded in a Red peasant sea. But there was also an element of sheer class war and revenge in their violence, as in so many acts of the White Terror, which was a mirror image of the class resentment and hatred that drove the Red Terror. Terror lay

---

* There was nothing to compare with it on the Red side — except perhaps the long march of the Taman Army, trapped by the White forces in the Taman Peninsula, during August and September 1918. This epic story formed the basis of Serafimovich's famous novel *The Iron Flood*. The Taman Army had a heroic status under the Soviet regime. All the more ironic, then, that Yeltsin should have used it to bombard the parliament building in October 1993.

at the heart of both regimes. The Whites were the avengers of those who had suffered at the hands of the revolution. As Wrangel later wrote, 'we had not brought pardon and peace with us, but only the cruel sword of vengeance'. Most of the officers were landowners' sons, who, like Gul', had lost their inheritance to the peasantry. They had every reason to seek vengeance — not just against the despised peasantry but against the 'Bolshevik' Jews and intellectuals who had stirred them up. One of the worst White atrocities during the Ice March took place in the village of Lezhanka. It was inhabited by Russian peasants well known for their revolutionary sympathies. Roman Gul' watched in horror as his fellow officers brutally slaughtered sixty peasants, many of them old men and women, in a reprisal for the Red Terror in Rostov. Hundreds of peasants were stripped bare and whipped while the Volunteers stood around and laughed. Gul' met one poor peasant woman — she cooked him breakfast in her hut — who had lost her husband and three sons. All of them had been shot as 'Bolsheviks'. This was a rude disillusionment for Gul', who had joined the White movement under the illusion that it was fighting for democratic ideals betrayed by the Bolsheviks. He began to wonder if 'the Whites were in fact any better than the Reds'.[14]

After several weeks wandering across the steppe, fighting off the Reds with their last ammunition, Kornilov ordered the Volunteers to attack Ekaterinodar, capital of the newly established North Caucasian Soviet Republic. On 23 March they had been joined by the Kuban Army, some 3,000 Cossacks led by General Pokrovsky, which had fled Ekaterinodar and somehow stumbled across the Don marchers in the nearby Circassian Hills. At a surreal summit meeting in the hillside village of Shendzhii, with all the formal protocol of the old regime, Kornilov and Pokrovsky united their armies for the recapture of the Kuban. On 10 April, Kornilov, acting as the overall commander, ordered the combined force of 7,000 men to begin the attack on the capital. They met fierce resistance from the Reds, some 18,000 troops in all. Kornilov soon realized that the siege was doomed to fail, threatening the destruction of the whole army, yet still refused to retreat. That, after all, was not in his nature. 'If we do not take Ekaterinodar,' he told Denikin on the 12th, 'there is nothing left for me to do but to put a bullet through my head.'[15]

In the event, Kornilov did pay with his life for his suicidal venture. Early on the following morning a chance shell landed a direct hit on his farmhouse headquarters, burying him in the rubble.* General Denikin, who immediately took over the command, tried to keep the news of his death from the men. Kornilov, to them, was not just a commander, but the very symbol of their cause, and it was bound to shatter their morale at this critical point in the

---

* The Reds later claimed that they had been informed of the whereabouts of Kornilov's headquarters by a defector from the Volunteers.

battle. The great White hero was buried in a modest churchyard in the village of Elisavetinskaya. But the Reds later found the grave and carried off his rotting corpse to Ekaterinodar, where they paraded it through the town before burning it in the main square.

Ironically, Kornilov's death was probably the salvation of the Whites. Had he lived, he would undoubtedly have ordered a final attack on Ekaterinodar, which was almost bound to end in complete defeat. The night before his death, he had refused to heed the advice of his generals to leave the farmhouse, which had been heavily shelled for several days, because it was 'not worth the trouble; tomorrow we'll begin the final assault'.[16] Denikin, who had never been keen on the idea of the siege, ordered the army to retreat quickly to the north, leaving behind some 200 wounded to speed up their march. If the Reds had made a serious effort to pursue them, instead of dancing on Kornilov's grave, they might have won the civil war there and then. But the Volunteers were allowed to flee back to the Don, from where they had launched their grim march. Four thousand set out and at least that number returned. More importantly, they came back with their fighting spirit strengthened.

* * *

The Don to which they returned had, in the ten weeks of their absence, been terrorized by the Bolsheviks. The Don Soviet Republic managed to achieve what Kaledin had always tried but failed to do — to turn the Cossacks against the Reds. After the Bolsheviks captured Rostov, the Red Army rulers instituted a reign of terror over the Don. Soviets were imposed on the Cossack settlements and foodstuffs were requisitioned from them at gunpoint. Punitive levies were extorted from the *burzhoois* and hundreds of hostages were shot at random. The Red Guards, retreating from the German advance towards Taganrog and licensed by the Bolsheviks to 'loot the looters', roamed through the *stanitsas*, or Cossack settlements, reaping bloody havoc. Churches were attacked, priests were executed. One priest had his nose and ears cut off, and his eyes pulled out, in front of the worshippers at an Easter service.

The result was a wave of Cossack uprisings — as much out of fear of what the Reds *might* do as anger at what they had already done — starting in the villages near Novocherkassk. These had always been the richest in the Don and were thus the most exposed to requisitioning and the terror. The Cossacks were driven to revolt by the image of the 'Bolsheviks' as the incarnation of all their worst fears and prejudices about ethnic outsiders and the Russian state. Each *stanitsa* had its own insurgent army, usually organized by the officers and equipped by the Cossack farms. During April these converged on the *stanitsa* of Zaplavskaya, near Novocherkassk, where there was a strong force of officers and men, to prepare for the liberation of the capital. By the end of April, they had 10,000 cavalrymen. With the Reds distracted by the German advance from

Taganrog to Rostov at the start of May, the Cossacks retook Novocherkassk without serious resistance from the exhausted Reds. There they elected a Krug for the Salvation of the Don, led by General Krasnov, their new Ataman, who had led the expedition against Petrograd to restore Kerensky's rule during the October Days.[17]

Krasnov looked every inch the Cossack Ataman. He came from a famous Cossack family and, being a great impresario of the 'Cossack cause', often played on this lineage. He had been a journalist before the war, and later, in exile, he would make a living as a novelist. Both personae were available to Krasnov the politician. There were no bounds to his historical imagination. He filled his speeches with archaic terms, designed to create the illusion of an ancient Cossack nationhood stretching back to the Middle Ages. By focusing on the glories of the Cossack past, he aimed to unite the Cossacks around the idea of their struggle against the Bolsheviks as a war of national liberation. It was a fancy-dress nationalism, based more on myth than on history, but it was powerful all the same. The 'All-Great Don Host', a title which had not been used in official documents since the seventeenth century, was restored on Krasnov's orders. The personal rule of the Ataman, as well as the Cossacks' rights and privileges over the non-Cossack population (now condemned as 'Bolsheviks' to a man), were upheld by the Don Krug's Basic Laws. It was a kitsch attempt to return to the Cossack Golden Age of Russian fairy tales. Public buildings hung out the Cossack flag; schoolchildren were ordered to sing Cossack hymns; there was even a special Cossack prayer.[18]

With the Cossacks in control of the Don, supported by the Germans to the west and the Volunteers to the south, the stage was set for the anti-Bolshevik forces to consolidate their military hold over the whole of the region; this they did between May and August.

By the middle of June, Krasnov's Don Army numbered 40,000 soldiers. It was armed by the Germans in exchange for Cossack wheat. With the Reds stretched on the Volga, it successfully completed the reconquest of the Don and created buffer zones in the north towards Voronezh and Tsaritsyn. Meanwhile, the Volunteer Army was reinforced by the arrival of 2,000 troops from the Romanian Front led by Colonel Drozdovsky. It was now in a position to launch a new offensive: but in which direction? Alexeev and Krasnov both wanted Denikin to strike north towards Tsaritsyn on the Volga: Alexeev to link up with the Czechs and the Komuch forces further up the Volga in Samara; Krasnov to lift the threat on the Don from the Red forces based in Tsaritsyn. Had this been done, the combined forces of the Volunteers, Krasnov's Cossacks, the Czechs and the Komuch might have won the civil war by advancing on Moscow from the vital bridgehead of the Volga. But Denikin stubbornly refused and marched his Volunteers southwards into the wilderness of the Kuban steppe. He wanted to strengthen the White rear by building up an army of Kuban Cossacks. By doing so he missed a vital opportunity to link up with the other anti-Bolshevik armies. Krasnov's Cossacks attacked Tsaritsyn on their own later in the autumn; but they could not take it. By the time Denikin finally reached the Volga, during the following summer, his eastern allies were in full retreat and the chance to combine forces had passed for ever.

On the face of it, the Volunteers should never have had the slightest chance of victory in this Second Kuban Campaign. There were only 9,000 of them, as opposed to 80,000 Reds at the start of the campaign in June. But the Reds were cut off from their depots in the north, surrounded by a largely hostile population, and as a consequence their conscript troops were demoralized. The Volunteers, by contrast, were highly disciplined and spurred on by the memory of the Ice March. One-third of their troops at the start of the campaign were exiled Kuban Cossacks fighting for the liberation of their homelands. This proportion grew as the Volunteers advanced into the Kuban, where the local Cossacks, who had suffered under the Reds, either joined the Volunteers or formed their own detachments to fight alongside them. On 18 August, after several weeks of fighting, they finally captured Ekaterinodar. The Reds fled south to Piatigorsk, in the Caucasian mountains, while the Whites extended their control throughout the northern and western Kuban. By November, they had seized control of Stavropol too. From a tiny force of officers during the Ice March, the Volunteers had grown to an army 40,000-strong with a rich territorial base the size of Belgium from which to launch their crusade against the Bolsheviks.[19]

* * *

General Denikin could not have expected to find himself supreme ruler of these territories. He had only been the Volunteers' commander since Kornilov's death — and Alexeev had remained the political leader of the movement. 'Alexeev's Army' was how the Volunteers were still known. But Alexeev was a sick man, and he died in October, leaving Denikin the undisputed military and political leader of the counter-revolution in the south. The constitution of the Volunteer Army, drawn up after the occupation of Ekaterinodar, gave him the powers of a military dictator: Kornilov's dream had been realized at last. But Denikin was no Kornilov: he lacked the character to play the part of a Generalissimo; and that partly explains the Whites' defeat.

Denikin was a military man: he came from a soldiers' family, and had spent all his life in the army. Politics was a foreign country to him, and he approached it from a narrow military perspective. The Academy of the General Staff had not encouraged him to think beyond the three basic articles of faith: Autocracy, Orthodoxy and Nationalism. 'For the officers', he recalled, 'the structure of the State was a preordained and unshakeable fact, arousing neither doubts nor differences of opinion.' The experience of 1917 — which taught him that the army fell apart when it dabbled in politics — strengthened Denikin's apoliticism. It bred in him, as in many officers, a contempt for all politicians. He wanted, in his own words, to keep it immune 'from the wrangling politicians' and to establish his 'own programme on the basis of simple national symbols that could unite everyone'.[20]

The constitution served Denikin's aim. This verbose charter was a triumph of form over content, full of legal ideals that were quite impracticable in a civil war. It was, in short, just what one would expect from a constitution written by the Kadets. It promised everything to everyone; and ended up by giving nothing to anyone. All citizens enjoyed equal rights; yet 'special rights and privileges' were reserved for the Cossacks. The state was governed by law; yet there were no legal limits on Denikin's dictatorship (they called him 'Tsar Anton'). None of the basic political issues facing Russia was confronted seriously. What form of government should it have? Was the Empire to be revived? Were the rights of the landed gentry to be restored? All these questions were buried in the interests of the military campaign.

Perhaps this was understandable given the divisions at Ekaterinodar. A multitude of groups and factions, from the Black Hundreds on the Right to the radical democrats on the Left, vied with each other for political influence over the White movement. None had a base of popular support; yet all strove for a 'historic role'. They bickered with each other and played at politics. The State Unity Council and the National Centre were the only two groups with any real influence, sharing the posts in Denikin's government. The former was monarchist and denied the legitimacy of the February Revolution. The latter was Kadet and pledged to restore the Constituent Assembly. It is little wonder that Denikin chose to avoid politics. He saw himself surrounded by scheming politicians, each trying to pull him in one direction or another. He tried to steer a middle course, keeping his pronouncements open and vague so as not to offend anyone, and increasingly withdrew into his own narrow circle of right-wing generals — Romanovsky, Dragomirov and Lukomsky being the most crucial — where the main decisions were made. The Special Council was a sorry phantom of a government. It rubber-stamped decisions already taken by the generals, and buried itself under paper decrees on such vital matters as the postal service or the minute details of finance and supply. Much of its time was taken up with the burning question of whether schools should use the old or the new orthography — and of course it opted for the old spelling. Senior politicians, such as Shulgin and Astrov, would not demean themselves with such work; and their absence from the Special Council downgraded its effectiveness even further.[21]

During the early days this neglect of politics did not seem to matter.

It was enough to place the military campaign before everything else, and to concentrate on promoting vague national symbols as an alternative to the Reds' propaganda. But later on, when the Whites could aim not just to conquer Russia but also had to try and rule it, this neglect of politics became a disastrous weakness. Their politics lost them the civil war, at least as much as their reverses on the battlefield.

The White leaders — and this applies to Siberia as much as it does to the South — failed to adapt to the new revolutionary world in which the civil war had to be fought. They made no real effort to develop policies that might appeal to the peasants or the national minorities, although the support of both was essential. They were too firmly rooted in the old Russia. The vital importance of propaganda and local political structures passed them by almost completely: dominated by the narrow outlook of the army, they could not understand the need for mass mobilization in a civil war. It was not until 1919, and then only on the Allies' insistence, that the Whites began to devote any real resources to their own machinery of propaganda. And even then the whole thing was approached in a low-key and amateurish fashion compared with the brilliant propaganda of the Reds. OSVAG, Denikin's propaganda agency, was originally set up within the Department of Foreign Affairs: it saw its main aim as to convince the Allies, rather than the Russian people, of the merits of the White cause, and very little of its material ever reached the factories or the villages. It was grossly under-financed and under-valued by the White leaders, not least because it opposed their Rightist views, and for this reason the generals often claimed that it was staffed by 'draft-dodgers', 'socialists' and 'Jews'.[22]

The Whites, in short, failed to understand the nature of the war in which they were engaged. They assumed that it could be fought in the manner of a conventional nineteenth-century conflict: by placing the army above politics. Yet this was to ignore the basic fact that in any civil or total war the ability of the armies to mobilize the population's resources in the territories which they occupied was bound to determine the outcome of the struggle. Their capacity to do this was precisely a question of politics: terror alone was not enough; it was also a question of tapping mass support or at least exploiting mass opposition to the enemy. This was especially so in the major campaigns of the Russian civil war (in 1919) when both the Reds and the Whites grew from small partisan forces to mass conscript armies which depended on the mobilization of the peasantry and its resources. For neither side could count on the peasantry's support, and they were both weakened by desertion and peasant revolts in the rear which were attributable as much to political failure as to military exactions.

The Whites failed to develop a viable politics for the task of democratic mobilization. On the major policy questions — land and nationalities — they drew up voluminous but non-committal bureaucratic projects for future debate. Everything was put off until the Constituent Assembly had been reconvened; and then, under the pressure of the Rightists, the Constituent Assembly itself was postponed. The Whites could not free themselves from the bureaucratic customs of the old regime. They adopted a dead and legalistic approach to a revolutionary situation that cried out for bold popular reforms. They saw themselves as the representatives of the old Russian state in exile and postponed all politics until military victory had returned them to the old capital; they never understood that victory itself was dependent on forging a new type of state.

✻　✻　✻

One of the Volunteers' most pressing problems was their relationship with the Cossacks. The White generals were Russian centralists. But the Don and Kuban Cossacks both wanted to establish independent states. They even sent their own unofficial representatives to the Versailles Peace Conference in an unsuccessful effort to get the backing of the Western Powers. Given their military dependence on the Cossacks, the Whites should have tried to placate them. Yet they never even came close to satisfying their demands. They looked on the Cossacks as ordinary Russians and dismissed their nationalism as the work of a few extremists. The Kuban government, led in the main by chauvinists and demagogues, flexed its muscles in an effort to behave like a sovereign power. It banned Russian immigration to the Kuban, closed its borders to exports, and took control of the railways. Such actions were a constant thorn in the side of the Volunteers. To keep the army fed and equipped, the Whites were forced to requisition foodstuffs from Cossack settlements, riding roughshod over the local organs of self-rule, all grist to the mill of the Cossack national leaders.

Perhaps the Whites' intransigence was a blessing in disguise: the Cossacks' nationalism in action was not a very pretty sight. The Kuban Cossacks drove out thousands of non-Cossacks (mainly Russians and Ukrainians) from their farms and villages, expelled their children from the local schools, and murdered many hundreds of them as 'Bolsheviks'. The Krug even debated the idea of driving all the non-Cossacks out of the Kuban altogether.* It was a sort of 'ethnic cleansing' based on the idea that the Cossacks were a superior race to the non-Cossack peasantry. The Cossack leaders frequently expressed the opinion that their people were the only Russians of any value and that all the rest were 'shit'. The Krug did nothing to stop the persecutions. In one village a group of Cossack soldiers seized the school mistress, an immigrant Russian who had taught the local Cossack children for over twenty years, and beat her to death.

---

* One Cossack delegate thought this was too kind and said it would be better simply to kill all the non-Cossacks.

None of her Cossack neighbours tried to save her. The Whites had an obvious interest in protecting the non-Cossacks: they represented 52 per cent of the Kuban population. If the Cossacks were left to their devices, the others would be driven into the arms of the Reds. Yet the Whites' intransigence on Cossack independence merely fanned the flames of this racial hatred and led to the steady worsening of relations with the Kuban government. If only the Whites had made some gesture towards the idea of Cossack autonomy, albeit conditionally upon the defeat of the Reds, they might have stopped the rot. But they failed to seek a compromise. Trapped in the nineteenth-century world of the Russian Empire, they were as insensitive to the national aspirations of the Cossacks as they were to all nationalisms other than their own.[23]

The Kuban Cossacks were just as unsuccessful in their campaign to establish an independent army. From a military point of view, this would have been disastrous for the Whites, for the Kuban Cossacks made up most of their troops and virtually all of their cavalry. The Don Cossack Army, moreover, which was independent, was hardly an encouraging example. Its loose detachments, each organized by a separate Cossack settlement, were outside the control of the central command. They fought bravely to defend their own local homelands but were reluctant to move away from them. This became a critical problem as the Whites advanced into central Russia during 1919. The Cossacks did not much care who ruled in Moscow so long as they were left to themselves. 'Russia is none of our business' — thus Denikin summed up their attitude. The failure of the Don Army to take Tsaritsyn, despite a two-month siege at the end of 1918, had already shown the limits of the Cossacks' morale outside their homelands. Once they were let loose on Russian peasant soil, they were always inclined to degenerate into looting; and in Jewish settlements they often indulged in pogroms. This was to be a major reason for the White defeat: the plundering and violence of the Cossack cavalry in 1919 did more than anything to rally the population of central Russia behind the Reds. It was also why Denikin resisted Cossack demands for an independent army. He would not even consider separate Cossack units.[24]

The Whites manifested the same inflexibility towards the demands of the national minorities. 'A Russia Great, United and Indivisible' was the central plank of their ideology. Without any clear social alignment, the Whites relied on the idea of the Russian nation and the Empire to draw together their disparate elements. Their imperial policies owed as much to' the ideas of the Kadets and the Octobrists as they did to the values of the old regime. Miliukov and Struve now defended a Great Russia as firmly as the most reactionary monarchist. This commitment to the Russian Empire was a fundamental weakness in the White movement, because its armies were based mainly in those territories (the Ukraine, the Caucasus and the Baltic) where the non-Russian population favoured at the very least more autonomy and perhaps complete independence from Russia. The Whites failed to see that a compromise with these national aspirations was essential if they were to build a broad base of support among the non-Russian peoples. Instead of making the nationalists their allies, they turned them into enemies.

As an army staffed mainly by sons of the gentry, the Volunteers were even more at odds with the peasants. Although himself the son of a former serf, Denikin never saw the vital need to accept the revolution on the land if his army was to conquer peasant Russia. The Whites assumed they could win the civil war without the support of the peasantry; or, at any rate, they seemed to think that the whole question of land reform could be put off until after victory. Their view of the civil war — that its outcome would be decided by military force alone — ruled out the need to present popular policies as part of their campaign. Not that their agrarian policies could ever have been popular: the dominance of the landowning class among Denikin's followers made it impossible for the Whites in south Russia to advance a programme on the land capable of winning mass peasant support. The two commissions set up by Denikin to make proposals for land reform both stressed the sale of the gentry's surplus land (and then only three years after the end of the civil war) but ruled out any compulsory expropriation. This was basically the minimalist Kadet land programme of 1917. It refused to recognize the fact of the rural revolution and continued to defend — probably as much preoccupied with the sanctity of the law as with the interests of the gentry — the formal property rights of the landowners. Statisticians calculated that if a programme was introduced on the basis of the commissions' proposals, the peasants would have had to give back three-quarters of the land they had seized from the gentry since 1917. Thus the vast mass of the peasantry had every reason to oppose the Whites.[25]

All the more so, since Denikin's armies and his local officials were notorious for helping the squires to reclaim their land in the territories which they reconquered. The policy was often justified on the grounds that gentry-farmed estates were more productive, but this was a flimsy excuse for the restoration of the old order. In any case, most of the land returned to the ownership of the gentry was rented back to the peasantry (usually at a fixed rate of one-third of the harvest). The system of local government in so far as there was one, as opposed to military rule and terror, was turned over to the local squires and the former tsarist police and officials acting in the name of district captains. The inescapable conclusion was that the Whites were seeking to restore the discredited local apparatus of the old regime. The district captains, for example, were remarkably similar to the tsarist land captains, who had ruled the villages like petty tsars. There were several cases of the same land captains returning as district captains to their former fiefdoms, where they took savage revenge on the villagers, executing and flogging their leaders. The efforts of the liberals to restore the volost zemstvos met with stiff resistance from the Rightist elements in Denikin's regime on the grounds that this would undermine the status of the local nobility. The worst form of the gentry's reaction — that which had opposed the volost zemstvos under Stolypin — lived on at the heart of the White regime. As Denikin himself acknowledged, the rural power holders under his regime may have had the advantage of experience:

> but in terms of their psychology and world-view, their customs and their habits, they were so far removed and alienated from the changes that had taken place in the country that they had no idea how to act in the new revolutionary era. For them it was a question of returning to the past — and they tried to restore the past both in form and spirit.[26]

This failure of the Whites to recognize the peasant revolution was the reason for their ultimate defeat. Denikin himself later admitted as much. It was only in 1920, after their failure to penetrate into the rural heart of central Russia, that the Volunteers finally confronted the need to appeal to the peasants; but by then it was too late. Whereas land reform was the first act of the Bolsheviks, it was the last act of the Whites: that, in a peasant country, says it all.

* * *

In November 1918, with the end of the fighting in Europe, the civil war entered a new phase. The rupture of the Brest-Litovsk Treaty after the German defeat and the retreat of German troops from the Baltic, the Ukraine and the Crimea gave the civil war armies the chance to step into the vacuum left by this withdrawal.

The Volunteers had every reason to be optimistic. With the defeat of the Germans, they expected the Allies to increase their support for the White cause in the south. Until then, the Allies had looked at the civil war from the sidelines. Their main interest had been in the north and in Siberia, where they had been hoping to resurrect a Russian army to continue the war against Germany. A few hundred British marines had occupied the Arctic ports of Murmansk and Arkhangelsk to defend Allied military stocks. After the Treaty of Brest-Litovsk they had even become involved in minor skirmishes against the Reds. German occupation of the Ukraine and their control of the Black Sea had made it difficult for the Allies to get military aid to the Volunteers. But all that had now changed. The Allies recognized Denikin as the main White leader in the south and pledged material support, including twelve divisions, to help occupy the Ukraine. They also promised the Volunteers the Allied military supplies left behind by the Russian army on the Romanian Front — if only they could get their hands on them. The height of this wave of euphoria came on 23 November, when an Anglo-French fleet sailed into Novorossiisk. General Poole and Lieutenant Erlich disembarked and were met by vast cheering crowds. They assured them that Britain and France were committed to the same goals as the Volunteers. Everyone expected the Whites to march triumphantly on Moscow, now that the Allies were on their side. They had defeated the mighty German armies; it would surely be a simple task for them to see off the Bolsheviks. Such optimism was further strengthened by the rise of Admiral Kolchak on the Eastern Front.

In fact the promise of Allied aid turned out to be empty. The involvement of the Western powers never amounted to much in material terms and always suffered from a lack of clear purpose or commitment. Western public opinion was divided between the Reds and Whites, while most of those in the middle, weary after four years of total war, were opposed to sending more troops abroad. Most of the Allied politicians were not sure why they should get involved in a foreign civil war now that the World War was over. Many of them knew very little about Russia — Lloyd George, for example, thought that Kharkov was a general rather than a city — and, as always in international matters, ignorance bred indifference. Some politicians, such as Churchill, wanted to launch a Western crusade against Communism, but others feared that a White victory would result in a strengthened Russia with renewed imperial ambitions, and preferred to see Russia Red but weak. The Western leaders wavered schizophrenically between these two views. They could not decide whether to make war or peace with the Soviet rulers — and thus ended up doing both. With one hand they gave military aid to the Whites; with the other they tried to force them into peace talks.*

As so often in these situations, Western policy was one of drift. Once the British gave aid to the Whites, France and the other imperial powers quickly followed suit. It was like a poor man's game of poker: none of the players wanted to be left out of the bidding, since the prize (influence in Russia) was much too great, but none of them would play with very high stakes. The result was that all the major powers (Britain, France, Italy, Canada, Japan and the United States) despatched only small forces — just, as it were, to keep their hand in.

---

* In January 1919 President Wilson and Lloyd George agreed terms with the Bolsheviks for a peace conference on the island of Prinkipo, just off Constantinople. The Bolsheviks offered to honour Russia's foreign debts, to make minor territorial adjustments and to suspend hostile propaganda against the West — although this was later explained by the Soviets as a diplomatic manœuvre. The White leaders would not have anything to do with the conference. They felt betrayed by the Allied suggestion that they should come to terms with the Reds. Churchill and the French backed them. The conference never convened, but Wilson continued peace talks with the Bolsheviks. William Bullitt, his principal foreign policy adviser, was sent on a secret mission to Moscow. Bullitt was favourably impressed by the Soviet experiment and recommended a separate peace, but this was scotched by the British and the French.

The intervention never reached the threatening level later claimed for it by Soviet historians. It was just enough to keep the Whites from defeat but insufficient to give them a real crack at victory. Denikin's forces, for example, received a few hundred khaki uniforms and some tins of jam during the first months of Western aid. British soldiers and tanks arrived in the spring, followed by the French navy, which landed at Odessa. Almost immediately, the sailors mutinied — they had no stomach for a war against the Reds who were at that time advancing on Odessa — and the French ships had to be evacuated.

Because the Whites were getting such meagre aid, Petliura's Ukrainian nationalists were the first to fill the vacuum left by the withdrawal of the German forces from the Ukraine. They were soon forced out of Kiev and pushed deep into the Western provinces by the Reds invading from the north. But the Reds in turn had only a weak hold over the Ukraine, which sank deeper and deeper into chaos. The Bolsheviks' policies in the countryside met with widespread resistance from the peasantry, who rallied to the local nationalists, to the various Green armies that hid out in the woods and to Makhno's anarchists. Meanwhile, the Whites were rallying their own forces. The withdrawal of the Germans had deprived Krasnov's Don Army of its main protector and exposed its left flank to the Reds who were advancing from the Ukraine. The Don Army had already been stretched by its winter campaign against Tsaritsyn. It was falling apart, its Cossacks deserting in droves as the Reds advanced. Krasnov was forced to seek Denikin's aid, knowing that the White leader would demand the subordination of the Don Army to his own command. With the Allies backing Denikin, there was little else that Krasnov could do. On 8 January the Don Army was finally merged with the Volunteers. They were now called the Allied Forces of South Russia — although in reality they were anything but a unified force.

The counter-revolutionary armies of the south were now under the command of men committed to a national campaign. During the following spring they were to break out of their Cossack homelands and occupy south Russia, most of the Ukraine and even threaten Moscow itself. In the process their forces were to grow and develop into a mass conscript army dependent on the recruitment of the peasantry. This was the root of their ultimate downfall: their neglect of politics had not prepared them for the tasks that now confronted them in ruling these newly conquered territories.

ii The Ghost of the Constituent Assembly

By comparison with the bread-starved cities of the Bolshevik north, the Volga city of Samara was a gourmand's delight. Peasant carts laden down with bags of flour and carcasses of meat, milk and vegetables trundled daily into its busy market. Food was plentiful and it showed in the rosy cheeks of the city's residents. Merchants grew fat on the booming trade: they dressed in the finery and jewels that had once belonged to the well-to-do of Petrograd and Moscow. Even the horses looked well fed.

Thousands of so-called 'former people' fled to the Volga city. Among the refugees were the remnants of the shattered Right SRs, seeking a new provincial base after their defeat in Petrograd and Moscow. The Volga region was a stronghold of their party. Its peasant population had voted overwhelmingly for it in the elections to the Constituent Assembly. The SR leaders naturally assumed the people of the Volga would rally behind their struggle against the Leninist dictatorship. If the Bolshevik drive to power had been based on the hunger of the urban masses, then the restoration of the democracy would depend on the well-fed peasantry. Bread and liberty went together.

But the Right SRs were soon to be disillusioned by their pilgrimage to the provinces. Their local party organizations were in total disarray. With the return of the peasant soldiers, many of them radicalized by the army, the Volga Soviets had swung to the far left. Soviet power had taken root in the villages as a system of local self-rule, the Constituent Assembly was now a remote parliament. The peasants had greeted its closure by the Bolsheviks with a deafening silence. It was hardly the outburst of popular indignation the SRs had expected. 'Unless', declared Klimushkin, one of the SR leaders in Samara, at the start of May, 'there is a spur from the outside in the near future, we can give up all hopes of a *coup d'état*.'[27]

By one of those curious accidents of history, that spur came at the end of the same month in 1918 when a legion of Czech soldiers became embroiled in a conflict with the Soviets along the Trans-Siberian Railway. The Czech Legion had been formed by Czech nationalists working inside Russia after the outbreak of the First World War. During the war it was enlarged by Czech and Slovak prisoners of war and deserters from the Austrian army, and by 1917 it was a force of some 35,000, most of them students and officers. As nationalists fighting for independence from the Austro-Hungarian Empire, they had sided with the Russians against the Central Powers. Thomas Masaryk and Eduard Beneš, the Czech Nationalist leaders, had agreed to the Legion's formation as an independent corps of the Russian army on the South-Western Front. After the Treaty of Brest-Litovsk the Legion resolved to continue its struggle as part of the Czech army fighting in France. Rather than run the risk of crossing enemy lines, they decided to travel eastwards, right around the world, reaching Europe via Vladivostok and the United States. On 26 March an agreement was made with the Soviet authorities at Penza, whereby the Czechs were allowed to travel on the Trans-Siberian Railway as 'free citizens' with a 'specified number of weapons for self-defence'.

Had this agreement been adhered to by both sides, the civil war would have taken a very different course. But the passage of the Czechs was marked by increasing mistrust and tension. The trains were held up by the local Soviets, which barraged the Czechs with propaganda and tried to confiscate their weapons. The Czechs, in turn, became suspicious that the Bolsheviks were preparing to hand them over to the Germans — a suspicion increased by the order from Moscow in April for half the Legion to turn around and be evacuated through Arkhangelsk (the irony was that, unknown to the Czechs, the order had been given at the behest of the Allies). The Czechs resolved to fight their way, if necessary, through Siberia to Vladivostok. Events came to a head on 14 May, when the Cheliabinsk Soviet in the Urals arrested some Czechs who had been involved in a brawl with a group of Hungarian prisoners of war. The Czech soldiers occupied the town, released their comrades and disarmed the small Red Guard unit. Moscow ordered the local Soviets to disarm the Czechs in turn. 'Every armed Czech found on the railway', read Trotsky's telegram of the 25th, 'is to be shot on the spot.'[28] It amounted to a declaration of war on the Czechs, and its effect was only to increase their determination to fight their way through to the East. This was a shame from the Bolsheviks' viewpoint, for there had been no real need to alienate the Czechs, and it was in everyone's interests to get them out of Russia as soon as possible. Trotsky's overreaction to the Cheliabinsk incident created a hostile army in the heart of Soviet Russia.

The Czech Legion, broken up into six groups along the entire length of the Trans-Siberian Railway, captured one town after another: Novo-Niko-laesvk on 26 May; Penza and Syzran on the 28th and the 29th; Tomsk on the 31st; Omsk on 6 June; and Vladivostok on the 29th. The Red Army was still not properly organized, and the untrained and ill-disciplined Red Guards, made up of workers from the local towns, who often ran away at the first sign of danger, were no match for the well-trained Czechs.

This was the case with the capture of Samara on 8 June. With the Czechs in the nearby city of Penza, the underground SR leaders in Samara approached them with a request to help them overthrow Soviet power in the Volga capital. This was in contravention of the policy of the Right SRs (passed at the Eighth SR Party Assembly in May) that foreign troops should not be involved in the 'people's struggle' against Bolshevism. But the SR leaders in Samara managed to convince themselves — as did the Czechs themselves, who had declared their own pious intention not to get involved in the Russian civil war — that an intervention could be justified in this case. Their aim of continuing the war against Germany depended on removing the Bolsheviks from power. Certainly, the Allies, seeing how easy was the Legion's victory in Siberia, were coming round to the idea of using the Czechs against the Bolsheviks. Later that summer they would send them aid. Meanwhile, it was the SRs' alleged connections with the French Government — grossly exaggerated, as it turned out — that finally persuaded the Czechs to help them in Samara. The Volga city was in a strike-ridden state of chaos after an uprising by the unruly garrison in the middle of May. The Soviet could muster only 2,000 Red Guards, most of them Latvian workers evacuated during the war, out of a population of 200,000. Such was the ephemeral nature of Bolshevik power in the provincial towns. The Red Guards stood little chance against the 8,000 well-armed Czechs — and most of them ran away as soon as the Legion approached. A mere six Czechs and thirty Red Guards were killed in the 'Battle of Samara'.[29]

The new government took its name and legitimacy from the Constituent Assembly. The Committee of Members of the Constituent Assembly — or Komuch — saw itself as the All-Russian Parliament in provincial exile. It called on all the members of the disbanded Assembly, with the exception of the Bolsheviks of course, to join it. Its five founding members were all SR members of the Constituent Assembly, three of them from Samara itself. By the end of its four-month reign, the ranks of the Komuch had been swelled by 100 members of the dissolved parliament, including Viktor Chernov, the chairman of its one and only session on 5–6 January 1918. This 'leader of the democracy' was treated as a VIP, with an armed guard outside his suite in the National Hotel and a series of banquets arranged in his honour. It was hoped he would become the figurehead of a national crusade.

The Komuch was basically an SR government with the addition of a few representatives from the national minorities (mainly the Tatars and Bashkirs, both quite numerous in the Volga region) and Mensheviks and Kadets who joined it in defiance of their respective Central Committees. Most of the leading Right SRs came to this Citadel of Liberty, including Zenzinov, Avksentiev and Breshko-Breshkovskaya, the 'Grandmother of the Revolution'. It was in many ways a resurrection of Kerensky's government — except that Kerensky himself was by this time in exile in Paris. The Komuch was a ghostly laboratory testing the central principle upon which the Provisional Government had stood and fallen: the idea that the provinces were not ready for Socialism and that the revolution should therefore not go beyond the democratic stage. This was the theoretical obsession which had prevented the SRs and the Mensheviks from establishing Soviet power in 1917; and it would now form the basis of their equally deluded effort to rally the provinces against the Bolsheviks.

'There can be no question of any kind of socialist experiments,' proclaimed the Samara press. The essence of the Komuch was the restoration of democracy, which meant postponing the social revolution until after the reconvocation of the Constituent Assembly, which alone could decide social questions. Like the Provisional Government, the Komuch saw itself as a temporary administration pending the re-establishment of parliamentary rule. All its pronouncements began with such self-limiting formulae as: 'Until the restoration of the legal authorities'; 'Until the return of normal relations'; or words to that effect. Its programme was dressed stiffly in the liberal pretence of political neutrality. Although freedoms of speech, press and assembly were restored, the civil war conditions made it difficult to respect them and the prisons of Samara were soon filled with Bolsheviks. Ivan Maisky, the Menshevik Minister of Labour, counted 4,000 political prisoners. The town dumas and zemstvos were restored and the Soviets, as class organs, barred from politics. The Komuch also declared its support for a 'democratic federation', which won it plaudits from the Bashkir and Tatar communities in the Volga region.[30]

In the industrial field, the Komuch, like the Provisional Government, tried to steer a middle course between labour and capital, and ended up satisfying neither. Class divisions were too strong. The workers rejected the Komuch as 'bourgeois' and passed defiantly Bolshevik resolutions in the Soviet. The factory committees were stripped of their powers and control of the factories was transferred to their former owners or (where they were absent) to government-appointed managers. The banks were returned to private control. Free trade was restored and a Council of Trade and Industry, dominated by industrialists, was set up to help formulate economic policy. But even this was not enough to convince the middle classes that the Komuch was not dangerously 'socialist'. They could see only that the eight-hour day was still guaranteed; that the trade unions and the Soviet were still in operation; and that the red flag still hung from the Komuch buildings. What, they asked, was the point of replacing the Bolsheviks with a 'semi-Bolshevik' regime like the Komuch? Why replace the Reds with these 'Pinks' when you could have the Whites instead?

During the early days of the Komuch the Samara middle classes, thankful for the overthrow of the Soviet, had approved a government loan. But they soon switched their support to the White counter-revolution in the east. The Komuch was forced to raise taxes from the sale of vodka — always unpopular with the workers. It also printed money which fuelled inflation. The peasants reduced their food sales to the cities, as money lost its value, forcing the Komuch to introduce bread rationing. Its urban base collapsed even further. Only the tiny provincial intelligentsia stayed with it to the end. During the August Duma elections the pro-government parties polled a derisory 15 per cent; two-thirds of the electorate did not even bother to vote. Democracy was resoundingly silent.[31]

Despite the SRs' expectations, the Volga peasantry proved no more supportive of their government. Had the SRs been willing to support the peasant revolution, things might have been different. But that would have meant recognizing the peasant Soviets — and the Komuch leaders were not prepared to go that far. They were determined to replace the Soviets with the volost zemstvos, in which all the rural classes, including the nobility, were represented on an equal basis. But as in 1917, the zemstvo elections were boycotted by the mass of the peasants, who were already committed to their Soviets as organs of direct village self-rule. Even where the zemstvos were elected, it was often difficult for them to function because the rural intelligentsia and officialdom had largely disappeared from the villages since the revolution, while the peasant communes refused to pay their taxes. In some villages the Soviet remained in power but referred to itself as the 'zemstvo' in communiqués with the Komuch.* The Komuch was powerless to stamp out this charade, even when it sent in troops. The peasants were too firmly committed to the Soviets as the guarantors of their revolution on the land.

The Komuch was equally reluctant to sanction the peasants' seizures of the gentry's land. True, it upheld the land reform passed at the first and only session of the Constituent Assembly which had recognized the abolition of all landed property. But a subsequent decree, passed on 22 July, enabled the former landowners to reclaim any winter fields which they had sown. This in effect meant reversing one-third of the peasant requisitions of arable land. Troops often had to be called in to enforce the decree. Its aim had been to 'reinforce the rule of law' after the 'anarchic' peasant land seizures during the previous winter and spring, but instead the impression was created, especially among the poorest peasants, who had been given most of the gentry's fields, that the Komuch wanted to restore the old regime on the land. They could be forgiven for this interpretation since some of the local squires saw the decree as a licence to take the law into their own hands. With the help of an army brigade, or their own private militia, they would seize back their property; sometimes they even had the peasant leaders flogged in public to 'teach them a lesson'.[32]

*   *   *

Of all the Komuch's policies, none was more unpopular than the call-up for the People's Army. In any civil war the success of the contenders depends on their relative abilities to mobilize the local population. This test the Komuch failed in no uncertain fashion.

During the summer, the Komuch and Czech forces were able to conquer territory almost at will. The Reds were chronically weak, without food supplies or a proper army. Ufa fell to the Czechs on 6 July; Simbirsk, Lenin's birthplace, on the 22nd; and Kazan, with its huge tsarist gold reserve, on 6 August. Two days later the munitions workers of Izhevsk, 150 miles to the north of Kazan, rose up against the Soviet and declared their sympathy for the Komuch. It was the biggest ever workers' uprising against the Bolsheviks — and a major

---

* Such deception was facilitated by the fact that in 1918 most of the Soviets were still using the old zemstvo stationery.

embarrassment for the regime. The revolt soon spread to the neighbouring countryside, where many of the workers' families still lived. Volunteer detachments were formed to fight the Reds. This was the height of the Komuch's fortunes. It now controlled an area the size of mainland Italy, with a population of fourteen million people.

But the Komuch's military potential was always very fragile. The Czech Legion was unwilling to fight in Russia indefinitely. Its soldiers were tired and wanted to go home, and their morale declined further as the Reds became better organized. By the middle of August, the Czech units were falling apart. Some of the soldiers were socialists and they went over to the Reds, who barraged them with propaganda; others simply gave up fighting and sold off their supplies to the local population. The Czech Legion broke down into bands of petty profiteers.

It was all the more essential, then, that the Komuch should raise its own troops from the Volga population. One of its first acts had been to appeal for volunteers. In the towns some 8,000 people — most of them students and cadets, but also refugees and the unemployed without other means of support — responded to the call. But in the countryside the number of volunteers was tiny: the majority of the peasantry wanted nothing to do with the 'fratricidal' civil war. Whilst they were willing to defend the revolution in their own localities — and for this they formed their own peasant companies — most of them looked on the war as a remote struggle between the urban parties. 'The mood of the peasants is indifferent,' declared a recruiting officer of the People's Army; 'they just want to be left to themselves. The Bolsheviks were here — that's good, they say; the Bolsheviks went away — that's no shame, they say. As long as there is bread then let's pray to God, and who needs the Guards? Let them fight it out by themselves, we will stand aside. It is well known that playing it by ear is the best side to be on.' At the Samara peasant assembly, organized by the Komuch in September, the delegates declared that they would 'not fight their own brothers, only enemies'. They 'refused to support a war between the political parties' and urged the Komuch 'to come to an agreement with the Bolsheviks'. One delegate proposed that 'the continuation of the civil war ought to be decided by a referendum, and until we know the opinion of the whole population we do not have a moral right to vote on this resolution [to support the war]'.[33]

To the mass of the peasants, whose political horizons were limited to the narrow confines of their villages, the national goals of the Komuch were quite alien. The restoration of the Constituent Assembly meant little to them when they already had the land and their freedom. The Komuch's call for the renewal of the war against Germany, six months after the fighting had ceased, clashed with the peasantry's parochial pacifism. 'The war with Germany and all wars are bad,' resolved the peasants of one village. 'If we do not fight, then the

German soldiers will not take our territory,' reasoned the peasants of another. The district police chief of Samara concluded that 'the population is poorly enlightened about the aims of the People's Army ... The idea has taken root that the "bourgeois" have started a new war because the "peace" signed by the Bolsheviks is unfavourable to them; but that the peasantry "has suffered no loss" and will not do so if it allows the bourgeoisie to fight by themselves.'[34]

Such class antagonisms were worsened by the attitudes of the People's Army officers. The fate of the Komuch would have been different had it been able to find its own loyal corps of democratic officers; the army commissars of 1917 would have fitted the bill perfectly. But very few of them were now left: some, like Linde, had been engulfed by the revolution; others, like Os'kin, had joined the Reds. There were no more citizen-patriots of the type who had rallied behind Kerensky; the idea of the 'democratic officer' was now merely oxymoronic.* The Komuch had no choice but to make do with the officers who volunteered for it. Colonel Galkin, a typical military bureaucrat of the tsarist era, was placed in charge of the People's Army. His headquarters became a stronghold of Rightist and monarchist officers, a Trojan horse of White counter-revolution inside the democratic citadel. The Komuch leaders were fully aware of this but, as Klimushkin put it, 'we were so sure of the force of democracy that we were not afraid of the officers' plans'. Under Galkin, the tsarist system of military discipline was restored. Officers even wore a scaled-down version of their epaulettes. Many of them were the sons of local squires and sometimes wreaked a violent revenge on the villages that had seized their familes' estates.[35] No wonder the peasants were not keen on the so-called People's Army.

The poor response to the appeal for volunteers forced the Komuch to resort to conscription at the end of June. Fearful that the older peasants would be infected by the Bolshevism which had swept through the army in 1917, it called up those aged under twenty-one. Yet even they showed the familiar symptoms of insubordination. Only one in three of the conscripted men turned up at the recruiting stations: the rest were 'deserters'. The appearance rate was lowest in the western districts bordering the Front, which says a great deal about the reasons for the Bolshevik victory. In contrast to their opponents, the Bolsheviks were usually able, at least at the critical moments of the civil war, to mobilize the peasantry just behind the Front. However much the peasants disliked the Reds, they feared a restoration of the old landed regime much more. Neither the Komuch nor the Whites were ever able to penetrate the central zone of Soviet power, where the peasant revolution was most firmly rooted.

All the civil war armies suffered from chronic problems of desertion, but the People's Army suffered more than most, largely as a result of having to

---

* The Komuch did make an effort to recruit the services of Brusilov; but this came to nothing.

improvise an army at the Front. Whereas the Bolsheviks had been in power for ten months before the major fighting began, the Komuch was barely ten weeks old when it faced the first Red onslaught. There was never enough time to build up a proper military infrastructure. Too often there were no uniforms or guns for the new recruits. Soldiers received little proper training before being put into battle, so that panic often broke out in the ranks at the first moment of danger. During August and September, the height of the harvest season, thousands of soldiers ran back to their farms, just at the moment when the Reds were launching their offensive. The Komuch tried to stem the desertions by sending punitive Cossack detachments into the villages. Military field courts, reminiscent of Stolypin's notorious tribunals in 1905–6, were given sweeping powers to punish the deserters and their families. Peasant leaders were publicly flogged and hanged; hostages were taken to force the deserters out of hiding; and whole villages were burned to the ground when soldiers failed to give themselves up. To the peasants, all this must have seemed like a return of the old regime with a vengeance.

The effect of repression was merely to strengthen the peasantry's resistance and drive many of them into the arms of the Reds. Villagers formed brigades, often organized by the Soviet, in order to resist the People's Army and its punitive detachments. These village 'armies' went to war with rusty guns, pitchforks and axes, and odd pieces of artillery mounted on peasant carts. Some fought as partisan units alongside the Red Army and later became regular detachments of it. The Domashki village brigade was a classic example. It fought against the Cossacks on the southern steppelands of Samara before becoming the nucleus of the 219th Domashki Rifle Division, a regular detachment of the Fourth Red Army. The Pugachev, Novouzensk, Krasnokutsk and Kurilovo Regiments had similar origins. The soldiers in these regiments were relatives and neighbours. In the Kurilovo Regiment there was a father and six sons. This cohesion was unmatched by any other fighting force in the civil war, with the exception of the Cossack detachments, which were similar in many ways.[36] This was the stuff of the legend of Chapaev, the main Red commander of these partisans, upon which three generations of Soviet children were to be brought up.

* * *

Without an effective army, it was only a matter of time before the Komuch lost its hold on the Volga region. During the summer the Reds had gradually built up their forces for a Volga campaign: it was here that the Red Army took shape as a regular conscript army. Worker detachments were raised in Moscow and the other towns of the central Soviet zone and despatched to the Eastern Army Group on the right bank of the Volga. On Lenin's orders, 30,000 troops were transferred from the anti-German screens in the west. He gambled (correctly, as it turned out) that the Central Powers were too stretched in Europe to exploit the gap. By the beginning of September 1918, the Reds had amassed 70,000 troops on the Eastern Front — an advantage of two to one over the forces of the Komuch. This was the start of the real fighting of the civil war. Up to now only minor units, none numbering more than 10,000 men, had been involved. Kazan was taken by the Reds on 10 September. Colonel Vatsetis, who led the attack, was rewarded by being made the main Commander-in-Chief of the whole Red Army. Defeat would have brought its own kind of reward — Lenin had ordered him to be shot if the crucial city was not taken. Two days later the First Red Army under Mikhail Tukhachevsky broke through to Simbirsk. From this point, the resistance of the People's Army was effectively broken; the Czech forces fell apart. Samara fell on 7 October.

The SRs dissolved the Komuch and fled to Ufa. There they found themselves at the mercy of the White counter-revolution sweeping in from the east. Under the protection of the Czechs several rival power centres had emerged in Siberia: the Eurasian land mass was a patchwork of regional regimes. A Urals Government was based in Ekaterinburg and claimed jurisdiction over Perm. The various Cossack *woiskos*, Orenburg and Ural'sk the most westerly of them, formally recognized the Komuch but conducted themselves as independent 'powers'. The Bashkirs and Kirghiz also had their own 'states', while within the Komuch territory there was also a national government of the Turko-Tatar Tribes. Of all these rival power centres, by far the most important was the Siberian Government based in Omsk. It had been formed by Kadet and SR politicians in the Tomsk Duma before the coming of Soviet power; and reformed by them in Omsk in the wake of the Czech revolt. P. V. Vologodsky, the jurist and advocate of Siberian autonomy, became its head of government on 23 June. Breshko-Breshkovskaya, who passed through Omsk in early July, took a dim view of its new leaders:

> Omsk is dusty and dirty. The government leaders have neither intellect nor any conscience. There is nothing positive or hopeful in the composition of the 'Siberian Government'. Its so-called 'ministers' are nothing but question marks. Talking with them it is clear that they neither believe in themselves nor in the success of their own undertaking.[37]

The Omsk government soon fell under the domination of the Rightist and monarchist officers in the Siberian Army. Lacking a close relationship with the Czechs, it none the less relied on them for military support. By September, the Siberian Army had 38,000 mainly peasant conscripts. Under the flag of Siberia — green for its forests and white for its snows — it had the support of those older Siberian settlers who favoured independence from the rest of Russia. Rightist officers from the Volga also flocked to it as an alternative to the 'socialist' Komuch. The domination of these Rightist elements in Omsk was enough to prevent the Siberian Government from reconvening the Duma. The Rightists wanted nothing less than a dictatorship.

The rivalry between Samara and Omsk had always been intense. It broke out in a customs war and a series of territorial disputes. But there were also growing pressures to find agreement: the military position of the Komuch was steadily weakening; and the Allies were concerned that such petty conflicts should not prevent a combined effort to repulse the advancing Reds. Such an agreement finally materialized at the State Conference held in Ufa from 8 to 23 September. There the Komuch leaders found their voice increasingly drowned out by the Rightists on their own side, who were calling for the sort of dictatorship favoured by the Siberians. The Kazan industrialist Kropotkin called for a 'strong and united military power to save Russia from those politicians [i.e. the socialists] who have ruined it'. According to V. N. Lvov, the power-broker in the Kornilov fiasco, another 'military dictator' was essential.[38]

To appease the Komuch leaders a compromise of sorts was struck. The ultimate sovereignty of the Constituent Assembly, provided it could find a quorum of 250 members, was recognized by the Ufa Conference. But in the meantime the Komuch lost its claim to be the legal government of all Russia. In its place a five-man Directory was set up as the executive arm of the Provisional All-Russian Government based in Omsk. It was an alliance of two SRs (Avksentiev and Zenzinov), two Siberian liberals (Vologodsky and Vinogradov) and General Boldyrev, close to the SRs, who also acted as the Commander-in-Chief. Although the SRs thus had a nominal majority in the new government, they were the real losers. In the fragmented politics of the civil war it would be a Sisyphean task to raise the quorum needed to restore the Constituent Assembly. To all intents and purposes, their citadel of liberty was in ruins.

The Directory was a pale reflection of the French revolutionary government after which it was named. This was a government only on paper. It had no proper structure or means of financing itself. Until near the end of its eight weeks in power, it was accommodated in a railway carriage in a siding a few miles from Omsk, hardly a prestigious 'capital' for what claimed to be the only legal government of Russia. Avksentiev, its chairman, was a dilettante who played at politics. He 'surrounded himself with aides-de-camp, brought back the old titles', and, according to one contemporary, 'created a buffoon sort of pomp behind which there was nothing of any real substance'. It was a throwback to the last days of Kerensky. This Directory had even less authority than the Provisional Government. It did not even command the confidence of the factions it represented. Both the SRs and the Rightist circles plotted against it from the start. Each thought the alliance gave too much power to the other side. Omsk was full of intrigues and rumours of a coup. 'Mexico amidst the snow and ice', was how Boldyrev described it.[39]

The Rightist officers struck first. On 17 November a Cossack detachment broke into a meeting of the SRs in Omsk and arrested several of their leaders, including the two Directors, Avksentiev and Zenzinov. They were accused of plotting the overthrow of the Directory. It is true that the Chernov group had plotted against it from the start. But so too had the Rightists, and they now used the SR plot as a pretext for their own *coup d'état*. The next morning the Directory's Council of Ministers gave its blessing to the coup and invited Admiral Kolchak to become the Supreme Ruler. There were hardly any forces prepared to defend the Directory. The Czechs had lost the will to fight since the declaration of Czech independence on 28 October. All they wanted was to go home. As for the People's Army, it was in a state of advanced decay.

For the next fourteen months Alexander Kolchak was the paramount leader of the counter-revolution, along with Denikin. It is somehow fitting that an admiral without a fleet should have been the leader of a government based in a town 4,000 miles from the nearest port; for Kolchak was one of history's misfits. Small but imposing with dark piercing eyes, he was an oddity, a mining engineer and an Arctic explorer in a tsarist Naval Staff dominated by the landed nobility. In 1916, when he was appointed Commander of the Black Sea Fleet, Kolchak, at only forty-one, was young enough to be the son of most of the other field commanders. In 1917 he refused to go along with the fleet committees and, in a dramatic resignation which made his name politically, broke his sword and threw it overboard. General Budberg described Kolchak as a 'big sick child':

> He is undoubtedly neurotic, quick to lose his temper, and very stormy . . . He is a pure idealist, slavishly devoted to his sense of duty and the idea of serving Russia, of saving her from Red oppression . . . Thanks to this idea he can be made to do anything. He has no personal interests, no *amour propre*, and in this respect is crystal pure . . . He has no idea of the hard realities of life, and lives by illusions and received ideas. He has no plans of his own, no system, no will: he is like soft wax from which his advisers and intimates can fashion whatever they like.[40]

All these characteristics were reflected in Kolchak's behaviour during the overthrow of the Directory. He was a passive — almost accidental — figure in the coup. He merely happened to be in the right place at the right time, giving the conspirators a figurehead. At the time of the Bolshevik seizure of power Kolchak was on a military mission to the United States. After a year in Manchuria he made his way back to Russia on the Trans-Siberian Railway, reaching Omsk in mid-October, where Boldyrev persuaded him to become the Minister of War. There is no evidence to suggest that Kolchak played a direct role in the overthrow of the Directory, although historians to this day still refer to it as 'Kolchak's coup'. From what we now know of this murky episode, it seems that the Rightists in Omsk engineered the coup without Kolchak's knowledge to force him into taking power. Earlier that day several Rightist officers had pleaded with him to become dictator. Kolchak was hardly averse to the idea of dictatorship: his trips to the Front had convinced him of the 'complete lack of support for the Directory'. Nor was he unaware of the general plans for a *coup d'état*: the salons and barracks of Omsk were full of talk about the need for an iron fist; they even talked about it in the offices of the Directory. Kolchak's close ally, General Knox, head of the British military mission in Siberia, also supported a dictatorship.* At first, on 17 November, the Admiral refused to take power: Boldyrev, he said, was the head of the army; and it was not clear if he could win the support of the Siberians and the Allies. But once the officers had taken power for him, Kolchak changed his mind. It seemed to him on the morning of the 18th that some dictator had to fill the vacuum if street violence was to be avoided. At the Council of Ministers he suggested Boldyrev for this role, but Boldyrev was absent and the ministers, in any case, preferred the Admiral to the 'socialist' Boldyrev. Urged by Knox to do his duty, Kolchak agreed and accepted the title of Supreme Ruler.[41]

* * *

This was the end of the Right SRs and their 'democratic counter-revolution', as Ivan Maisky called it. Kolchak had the SR leaders imprisoned and then escorted to the Chinese border, where they were deported. Some of them made it back to Western Europe, where they lived a life of comfortable but regretful exile. Others returned to Russia, where they continued to organize themselves underground, adopting a stance of equal hostility to Reds and Whites. For several weeks after the coup, Kolchak's police carried out a series of bloody reprisals against SR activists. Hundreds were arrested — many as 'hostages' to be executed in the event of SR acts of terror against the dictatorship. Among the hostages in Omsk were twenty SR deputies of the Constituent Assembly, ten of whom were shot in December following a workers' uprising in the town.

Kolchak, meanwhile, defined his regime's purpose in strictly military terms. Like Denikin, he was a narrow soldier: politics were beyond him. Apart from the overthrow of Bolshevism and the 'salvation of Russia' he had no real idea of what he was fighting for. He made some vague pronouncements about

---

* It is doubtful, however, whether Knox played any part in the preparations for the coup. This was the mischievous contention of the French at the time — that Kolchak had been installed by the British as 'their man' in order to build up their influence in Siberia.

the restoration of law and order and the Constituent Assembly, although, judging by his own views, this last was clearly not to be restored in the democratic form of 1917.* But otherwise all politics were to be abolished in the interests of the military campaign. Denikin was to make the same mistake. Politics were themselves a crucial determinant of the military conflict. Without policies to mobilize or at least to neutralize the local population, his army was almost bound to fail. Moreover, by failing to make his own policies clear, Kolchak allowed others to present them for him: both from the propaganda of the Reds and from the conduct of his own Rightist officers, the population of eastern Russia gained the fatal impression that Kolchak's movement aimed to restore the monarchy.

The middle ground between the Reds and the Whites was thus eroded and eventually disappeared. The whole of the country was now engulfed in the civil war. There was no place in it for the fragile democracy whose roots had been laid down in 1917. Russia was too polarized, and the mass of its people too poorly educated, to sustain democratic institutions against enemies on both extremes. The anti-Bolshevik movement would not reassume a democratic form until the autumn of 1920, by which time it was too late to unseat the new autocracy. The tragedy of the Russian Revolution was that the people were too weak politically to determine its outcome.

---

* As Kolchak later acknowledged at his interrogation in 1920: 'The general opinion ... was that only a government authorized by the Constituent Assembly could be a real one; but the Constituent Assembly which we got ... and which from the very beginning started in by singing the "Internationale" under Chernov's leadership, provoked an unfriendly attitude ... It was considered to have been an artificial and a partisan assembly. Such was also my opinion. I believed that even though the Bolsheviks had few worthy traits, by dispersing the Constituent Assembly they performed a service and this act should be counted to their credit.' (Varneck and Fisher (ed.), *Testimony*, 106–7.)

13 The Revolution Goes to War

i Arming the Revolution

It was five years since Dmitry Os'kin had last been in Tula. Then, in 1913, he had been a simple peasant boy fresh from the countryside to sign up as a soldier of the Tsar. Now, in the spring of 1918, he was returning to the same town, a commissar in Trotsky's army, to put steel into the revolution.

The years of war and revolution had been kind to Os'kin. He had risen through the ranks, winning four St George's Crosses on the way, as the old caste of officers was destroyed. During 1917 his fortunes rose as his politics moved to the Left: he rode on the tide of the soldiers' revolution. His SR credentials won him command of a regiment, followed by election to the Central Committee of the Soldiers' Soviet on the South-Western Front. In October he went as an SR delegate to the Second Soviet Congress — one of that 'grey mass' of unwashed soldiers in the Smolny Hall whom Sukhanov had blamed for the Bolshevik triumph. In early 1918, when Trotsky began to build the officer corps of the new Red Army, he turned first to the NCOs, like Os'kin, who had learned their trade in the tsarist army. It was a marriage of convenience between the ambitions of the peasant sons and the military needs of the regime. As Napoleon had once said, every soldier carried in his knapsack the baton of a field-marshal: that was the making of an *armée revolutionnaire*.

One hundred miles south of Moscow, Tula was the arsenal of the revolution. After the evacuation of Petrograd it became the hub of the Soviet Republic's munitions industry. At the height of the First World War its factories employed over 60,000 workers, although by the time of Os'kin's arrival, with the general flight to the countryside, only 15,000 were left. The new military commissar took up his office in the Soviet building, housed in the former Peasant Bank, which, as if to symbolize the new social order, was surrounded by metal factories.[1]

The local Red Guards, which Os'kin had come to reorganize, had been mostly set up by the workers during 1917 to defend their factories against the threat of a 'counter-revolution'. After the Bolshevik seizure of power there had been a great deal of talk about using them to form a new type of 'proletarian army' rather than retaining the remnants of the old (and mainly peasant) one.

The Bolsheviks did not like the idea of a standing army. They thought of the army as a tool of oppression wielded by the old regime against the revolution. A workers' militia would be more egalitarian, and the Red Guards were to be the basis of such a force. They made up the units of the new Red Army, whose establishment was decreed on 15 January. Apart from their ideological objections to the idea of a standing army, the Bolsheviks also had practical reasons for favouring the volunteer principle at this stage: the disintegration of the old army and the complete absence of any apparatus to carry out conscription left them no choice. The only real troops they could rely on were the three brigades of Latvian Rifles, 35,000 strong, which stood alone between them and disaster during the first months of their regime.

At this time, when the workers were fleeing the cities, the new Red recruits were largely made up of unemployed former soldiers, and all those 'vagabond, unstable elements that', in Trotsky's words, 'were so numerous at the time'. Some of them had no doubt come to like the army way of life, or at least preferred it to post-war civilian hardships. But most of them had nowhere else to go — the war left them without home or family. They were stranded in towns like Tula, half-way between the Front and their long-abandoned homes. Many of these migrants signed up with the Red Guards simply to receive a standard-issue coat, or a pair of boots, before running off to sell them and start the whole process over again in some other town. The new Proletarian Militia was a rag-and-bone trade for the down and out.[2]

Naturally, such an army was virtually useless on the battlefield. The image of the Red Guards as disciplined crack troops is the stuff of Soviet mythology. The Red Guards were irregular detachments, motley-clothed and armed, poorly disciplined and very heavy-drinking. The 'committee spirit' of 1917 lived on in their ranks. Officers were elected and their primitive operational plans were usually voted on by a show of soldiers' hands. The military consequences were disastrous. Attacks were launched without proper scouting, often using no more than a school atlas. The soldiers fought in a wild and undisciplined manner, all too frequently breaking up in panic at the first sight of the enemy. Crushing defeats by the Germans in February and March, followed by the Czechs in May and June, made it clear to Trotsky that such methods would not do. With the Soviet regime on the brink of defeat, the Red Army would have to be reformed on the model of the old imperial army, with regular units replacing the detachments, proper discipline in the ranks, professional officers and a centralized hierarchy of command. That reformation was to be Os'kin's task in Tula.

One of Trotsky's first measures was to call on the services of ex-tsarist officers. They were called 'military specialists' rather than officers to dissociate them from the old regime (for the same reason soldiers were now called 'Red

Army servicemen'). Some 8,000 ex-tsarist officers had volunteered to fight for the Bolsheviks after their seizure of power. The soldiers and their committees, for whom the revolution meant above all the ending of officers' authority, greeted them with much hostility. But the shortage of NCOs, as well as the so-called Red Commanders, whose training had only just begun, ensured that brute military needs won the day over revolutionary zeal. Now Trotsky sought to extend the principle with the mass conscription of the ex-tsarist officers, brushing aside the soldiers' objections by simply abolishing their committees. On 29 July he issued his famous Order Number 228, calling up all officers. By the end of the year, 22,000 ex-tsarist officers had been recruited; and in the course of the civil war the number rose to 75,000, not including doctors, vets and other officials. By the end, three-quarters of the senior commanders in the Red Army were drawn from the tsarist officer corps.[3]

What motivated these officers? Some, like Brusilov, who was to join the Red Army in 1920, were moved by a sense of patriotic duty: the country, for better or worse, had chosen the Reds, or so it seemed to them, and their duty was to serve it. Many were also driven by an inbred sense of military duty: these were 'army men' who would serve that institution regardless of its politics. Perhaps some junior officers were also attracted by the prospect of a more senior command in the new army than they might have expected in the old one. But the most common motivation was the simple need to find a job: it was survival, not self-advancement, which drew the officers to the Soviet cause. Most of them had lost their military pension, often their only means of livelihood, and were thus much worse off than the other ruined classes of Old Russia. Amidst the terror of 1918, moreover, they were well advised to make themselves useful to the regime. For as Trotsky was to put it in a memo to Lenin, by employing the ex-tsarist officers 'we shall lighten the load on the prisons'.* The officers who joined were closely supervised by the commissars, like Os'kin, and warned that any acts of betrayal of the Red Army would lead to the arrest of their families. 'Let the turncoats realize', read Trotsky's special order of 30 September, 'that they are at the same time betraying their own families — their fathers, mothers, sisters, brothers, wives and children.'[4]

There was a storm of opposition to the recruitment of these officers. Many soldiers saw it as a return to the old military order, and as a betrayal of Order Number One. They particularly resented the reintroduction of pay differentials based on rank, of compulsory saluting, and of special badges and uniforms, not to speak of rations and privileges, for the officers. The party workers in the army saw it as a challenge to their power, while the NCOs and the Red

---

* At that time (October 1918) there were 8,000 officers sitting as 'hostages' in the Cheka prisons (*Revvoensovet Respubliki*, 36).

Commanders were jealous of the 'men with golden epaulettes' and feared that they might block their own promotion. Os'kin himself was in two minds about the tsarist officers. As a military man, he could see the desperate need for competent commanders. Military efficiency had to be placed before revolutionary equality. The antics of the Left SRs and the Anarchists in Tula — teenage fanatics of the militia principle — had caused enough chaos to convince him of the need for Bolshevik discipline and organization (he joined the party in July 1918). And yet, at the same time, as a peasant-NCO and a man of some ambition, he also resented the privileges of the ex-tsarists. Where he had earned his rank through courage under fire, most of them had gained theirs through birth and education. He felt that their attitudes were unchanged — 'their facial muscles winced whenever they were addressed by the soldiers as "comrade commander" ' — and feared this might lead them to revolt.[5]

The military setbacks of the summer were quickly blamed by Trotsky's critics on the ex-tsarist officers. The loss of Simbirsk to the Komuch in July had indeed been partly brought about by the mutiny of M. A. Murav'ev, a lieutenant-colonel in the tsarist army and the Left SR Commander of the Eastern Front. During the following months a concerted campaign was launched within the party against Trotsky's policies. Two articles in *Pravda* were the catalysts of this conflict. Sorin, a member of the Moscow Party Committee, accused Trotsky of vesting 'too much power' in the ex-tsarist officers, while unfairly making the commissars 'answer with their lives' when the soldiers refused to obey their orders. A commissar named Panteleev had indeed been shot on Trotsky's orders after his detachment had fled from the battle for Kazan. The case became a *cause célèbre* for those determined to defend the independence of the party and its commissars against the commanders. Kamensky, a commissar in Voroshilov's army on the Southern Front, claimed in the other *Pravda* article that the ex-tsarist commanders acted like virtual 'autocrats', while the commissars were merely there to 'append a decorative signature' to their orders.[6]

Kliment Voroshilov, an Old Bolshevik and Red Guard commander, was the leading figure of this Military Opposition, as it soon came to be known. Based in Tsaritsyn, Voroshilov refused to carry out the orders of Trotsky's central command organ, the Revolutionary Military Council of the Republic (RVSR) and its Commander on the Southern Front, the ex-tsarist General Sytin based at Kozlov. Stalin backed Voroshilov, although he always denied belonging to the Military Opposition. This direct challenge to Trotsky's authority from such a senior party comrade was the origin of much of the personal animosity between Trotsky and Stalin in the years to come.

Trotsky turned the criticisms of his policies into a question of the party's general confidence in himself as Commissar for War. He demanded that the editors of *Pravda* be censured for publishing the articles by Sorin and

Kamensky. He also demanded Stalin's recall from the Southern Front, where the Georgian was shooting dozens of officials and creating havoc as a special commissar for food supply. This was a dangerous game for Trotsky to play. The sentiments of the Military Opposition, like those of the Left Communists, from which it had in part originated, were widely shared among the rank and file who had joined the party since 1917. As they saw it, the whole purpose of the revolution was to replace the old 'bourgeois specialists' with proletarians loyal to the party. Theirs was a communism of careerists — one that combined an egalitarian rejection of the old authorities with the demand that they, as Communists, should enjoy a similar position of power and privilege within the new regime. In their eyes, comradeship and class were the only necessary qualifications for military advancement. Battles would be won by the 'revolutionary spirit' of the comrades and their men, not by the outmoded science of the tsarist Military Academy.

Underlying this mistrust of the officers was an instinctive lower-class resentment of all privilege and a deep anti-intellectualism. These same attitudes were also displayed towards the other so-called 'bourgeois specialists' employed by the Soviet regime in the bureaucracy and industry (i.e. Civil Servants, managers and technicians who had held their posts before 1917). Many intellectuals in the party leadership were themselves targets of this demagogic hostility from the rank and file. Trotsky, Kamenev and Zinoviev, Stalin's three great rivals in the 1920s,* suffered particularly on this score. Their Jewish looks no doubt had much to do with it. Most of the Military Opposition came from lower-class families and had had no more than a basic education. Voroshilov was the son of a casual labourer on the railways, and had spent only two years at school. These 'sons of the proletariat' were resentful at having to give way to officers who had enjoyed all the privileges of noble birth and education in the Military Academy. Much of their resentment, as junior commanders, was provoked by what they saw as Trotsky's arrogance and his Bonapartist manners as the head of the Red Army. He always arrived at the Front in his richly furnished train (Trotsky was well known as a gourmet and his train was equipped with its own high-class restaurant). His commissars were always dressed in immaculate uniforms, with expensive leather boots and shiny golden buttons. Perhaps with a little more sensitivity Trotsky might have neutralized the Military Opposition. But he had never been noted for his tact — Trotsky himself once admitted that he was disliked within the party for his 'aristocratism' — and his pride had

---

* Stalin's rise to power was partly dependent on the mobilization of this anti-intellectualism against the Old Bolsheviks (those who had joined the party before 1917) among the rank-and-file Communists. Many of his most important allies in the 1920s were former members of the Military Opposition. Voroshilov, for example, joined the Politburo in 1925.

been wounded by the Opposition's challenge to his position and authority. Trotsky chose to strike back where it would hurt most, ridiculing his critics as 'party ignoramuses'. The odd betrayal by the military specialists, he claimed, was not as bad as the loss of 'whole regiments' through the incompetence of 'semi-educated' Communist commanders who 'could not even read a map'.[7]

The conflict rumbled on through the winter, until March 1919, when, with Kolchak on the Volga, Lenin made an appeal for party unity, and a compromise of sorts was struck at the Eighth Party Congress. Trotsky's employment of the ex-tsarist officers was to be supported on the grounds of military exigency, but the supervisory role of the commissars and the general power of the party in the army were both to be increased, along with the training of Red Commanders for future leadership of the army. This, however, was just to throw a blanket over the dispute. The chain of command in the army became even more confused, with the commanders, the commissars and the local party cells all engaged in a three-cornered struggle for authority.[8] Moreover, the conflict between Trotsky and the Military Opposition was to emerge the following summer, when Stalin relaunched a general attack on the leadership of the army.

✳   ✳   ✳

In the summer of 1918, with the Reds facing defeat on all sides, the Soviet Republic was declared a 'single military camp'. Martial law was imposed throughout the country. The RVSR under Trotsky's leadership became the supreme organ of the state; the whole economy was geared towards the needs of the army; and the country was divided into three main Fronts (Eastern, Southern and Northern), five Army Groups and a Fortified Area in the west. The Bolshevik leaders made fist-banging speeches and the press came out with bold headlines calling on the people to do their duty and defend the Fatherland.

In this desperate situation, Trotsky had no choice but to call for mass conscription. The Red volunteers were many too few and poorly disciplined to counteract the Germans in the Ukraine, the British in the north, the Czechs on the Volga, the Japanese in the Far East and the Whites aided by the Allies on the Don. Mass conscription was Trotsky's second major reform, after the recruitment of the ex-tsarist officers, and it was just as controversial as the first.

Whereas the Red Guards were seen as an army of the working class, mass conscription was bound to produce an army of peasants. Most Bolsheviks saw the peasants as an alien and hostile social force. Conscription on this scale was in their eyes tantamount to arming the enemy. It would 'peasantize' the Red Army and end the domination of the working class within it, an important retreat from the party's principles. But then the revolution was itself in retreat, with the Reds on the brink of defeat. If they were to survive, they had no choice but to mobilize the peasantry.

To begin with, though, most of the conscripts continued to be drawn from the cities. Of the fifteen compulsory mobilizations declared between June and August, eleven applied only to urban workers. With hundreds of factories closing every month, there was no great problem in getting workers to enrol for the army: 200,000 did so from Moscow and Petrograd alone. The local party organs also threw in 40,000 of their own members. Semen Kanatchikov, the Bolshevik worker now turned roving commissar, arrived in Tula to oversee the despatch of Communists to the Eastern Front. Os'kin thought him a 'severe task-master' and expressed his fears that if the best comrades were called up, there would not be enough left in Tula to defend the revolution there. This was a major problem for the provincial party organizations. Many of their most committed members were lost in battle, so that the worst elements, the self-seekers and the corrupt, took control of local party cells.[9]

During these first campaigns, when the Red Army was desperate for recruits, ultimate proof of devotion to the party was shown by fighting for it at the Front. The Bolsheviks had always distinguished themselves with a macho and military self-image. They dressed in leather jackets — a military fashion of the First World War — and all carried guns.* Half a million party members joined the Red Army during the civil war. Trotsky, who compared these Communist fighters to the Japanese Samurai, ensured that they were distributed evenly throughout all the army units. Party members, if not appointed commissars, were certainly expected to lead from the front. Many of them fought with a desperate courage, if only for fear of their own capture (and almost certain torture) by the Whites. The bravery of the Communist soldiers became part of the Reds' civil war mythology. It was what the Bolshevik historian L. N. Kritsman would later call the 'heroic period' of the revolution. And from that romantic image — the image of the party as a comradeship in arms unafraid to advance or conquer any fortress — came many of its basic ruling attitudes.

Mass conscription of the peasantry was one fortress still to be conquered. In 1918 the Soviet regime had no real military apparatus in the countryside. Few volost Soviets had a military committee (*voenkom*), the main organ responsible for carrying out Red Army conscription. Even where there was a military committee its work was usually hampered by the village commune, which alone had a register of peasants eligible for conscription. The first remotely comprehensive military census of the population was not completed until 1919 — which of course meant that until then any conscription was bound in effect to be no more than a voluntary call-up. It was hardly surprising, then, that of the 275,000 peasant recruits anticipated from the first call-up in June, only 40,000 actually appeared.[10]

---

* All party members had the right to carry guns. It was seen as a sign of comradely equality. They were not disarmed until 1935 — after the murder of Kirov.

There were several reasons why the peasants would resist mobilization into the Red Army. The first harvest of the revolution, which coincided with the call-up, was the most compelling. Peasant recruitments and desertions in all the civil war armies fluctuated in accordance with the farming seasons. Peasants joined up in the winter, only to desert the following summer. In the central agricultural regions the weekly rate of desertion was up to ten times higher in summer than in winter. As the Red Army grew on a national scale, such desertions became more common, topping two million during 1919, because the recruits were more fearful of being sent to units a long way from their farms.[11]

During the autumn of 1918 many village communes called on both sides to end the civil war through negotiation. Many even declared themselves 'neutral republics' and formed brigades to keep the armies out of their 'independent territory'. There was a general feeling among the peasants that they had been at war for far too long, that in 1917 they had been promised peace, and that now they were being forced to go to war again. Whole provinces — Tambov, Riazan', Tula, Kaluga, Smolensk, Vitebsk, Pskov, Novgorod, Mogilev and even parts of Moscow itself — were engulfed by peasant uprisings against the Red Army's conscriptions and its all too often coercive requisitioning of peasant food and horses. Os'kin, in Tula, had to deal with one of the largest revolts in November. Bands of peasants armed with harrows, spades and axes marched on the towns, where they ransacked and burned the Soviet's military offices. Many of the rebels had been called up. Others had lost their only horse to the army draft (a catastrophe for any peasant farm). Peasant recruits in the local barracks, disgruntled by the harsh conditions there, often joined the uprisings. Tula was surrounded by a band of 500 peasants. Os'kin and Kanatchikov mobilized the party and 2,000 factory workers, threatening shirkers with instant execution, and, with the help of a Red Army brigade from Moscow, pushed the rebels back to their villages, where they then carried out a series of brutal repressions. Os'kin calmly recalled that 'we shot several hundred peasants'. He sat as judge and jury on the ring-leaders of the uprisings, sentencing dozens of them to public hangings. Such were the powers and the responsibilities of a Bolshevik commissar.[12]

During the first months of 1919 the rate of peasant conscription improved markedly. The slack period of the farming season and the growing threat of a White advance from the Volga and the Don, leading to the loss of the land which the peasants had gained in the revolution, were crucial factors. But the general strengthening of Soviet power in the countryside also played its part. From 800,000 soldiers in January, the Red Army doubled in size by the end of April, the height of Kolchak's offensive in the east. Most of the new recruits came from the Volga region, the Red frontier against Kolchak, where the peasants had most to fear from a White victory.[13]

'We had decided to have an army of one million men by the spring,' declared Lenin in October 1918, 'now we need an army of three million. We can have it. And we shall have it!' And have it they did. The Red Army grew to three million men in 1919, and to five million by the end of the following year. But ironically, the possession of an army on such a scale was a serious handicap to the regime's military potential. For the army grew much faster than the devastated Soviet economy was able to keep it supplied with the instruments of war: guns, clothing, transport, fuel, food and medicine. The soldiers' morale and discipline fell in step with the decline in supplies. They deserted in their thousands, taking with them their weapons and uniforms, so that new recruits had to be thrown into battle without proper training, so that they in turn were even more likely to desert. The Red Army was drawn into a vicious circle of mass conscription, blockages of supply and mass desertion. And this locked the whole economy into the draconian system of War Communism, whose main purpose was to channel all production towards the demands of the army (see pages 612–15, 721–32).

With hindsight, the Bolsheviks might have done better to opt for a smaller army, better disciplined, better trained and better supplied, and not such a burden on the economy. As one Red commander put it to Lenin in December 1918: 'It is a thousand times more expedient to have no more than a million Red Army men, but well-fed, clothed and shod ones, rather than three million half-starved, half-naked and half-shod ones.' Such an army, made up largely of workers, would have been more battle-worthy than the peasant conscripts who barely knew how to handle a gun and ran home at the start of the harvest. The Reds, in practice, had no real fighting chance against the Whites, whose troops were much better trained and disciplined, unless they outnumbered them by four and sometimes even ten to one. For every active Red on the battlefield there were eight others who for lack of training, clothing, health or ammunition could not be deployed.[14] A smaller army, moreover, by placing less pressure on the economy, would not have led to the same excesses — the violent requisitionings, the imposition of labour duty, the militarization of the factories — which did so much to alienate the peasants and workers from the Soviet regime. Yet arguments from hindsight are the luxury of historians: when Lenin made his panic call for a mass army, the regime seemed on the brink of defeat; and it is easy to understand why he opted for safety in numbers.

Watching the parade on Red Square to mark the first anniversary of the October Revolution, Lenin was shocked by the ragtag appearance of the troops. 'Look at them,' he exclaimed, 'they march like bags of sand.' In most of the units there were no standard uniforms, and the soldiers dressed in whatever came to hand. Many wore the uniforms they took from the captured Whites (who in turn wore British Army surplus kit). As for leather boots, they were worn only by the Red Army commanders, the commissars and the cavalrymen. The peasant infantry marched in the crude bast shoes, or *lapti*, manufactured in the villages. But even these were in short supply and there were times when, for lack of adequate footwear, whole regiments had to be confined to barracks. The supply of weapons was not much better. It was largely a question of shells: whereas the army was firing between seventy and ninety million rounds a month, the main arsenal at Tula was producing only twenty million. 'There were times', as Trotsky put it, 'when every one of a soldier's stock of cartridges counted, and when delay in the arrival of a special train bringing ammunitions resulted in whole divisions retreating.'[15]

'Comrades!', a bad-tempered Trotsky warned an army conference in 1919, 'although we have not been brought down by Denikin or Kolchak, we may yet be brought down by overcoats or boots.' In fact, if anything, the Red Army was brought down — quite literally — by illness and disease. More soldiers died from disease than from fighting in the civil war. Typhus, influenza, smallpox, cholera, typhoid and venereal diseases were the main killers, but many more men suffered from lice, stomach bugs, dysentery and toothache. On an average day in an average unit, 10 to 15 per cent of the men would be too ill to fight and had to be abandoned to fortune in the rear. But some units were taken out of action by rates of illness of up to 80 per cent. This was particularly true in 1920, when 30 per cent of the Red Army — that is, over a million men — contracted typhus. The unhygienic conditions of army life, where soap and bath water were not seen for weeks, were the root cause of the problem. But the situation was made much worse by the chronic shortages of doctors and nurses, surgical spirits, bandages and drugs. The rapid to-and-fro movements of the Fronts, so characteristic of the civil war, also made it difficult to set up proper field hospitals or to organize transport to the rear. The sick and wounded could thus be neither properly cared for at the Front, nor easily evacuated to the rear. The agony they must have gone through can only be imagined. Trotsky himself, touring the Southern Front in June 1919, was shocked to see the way the wounded men were treated:

> Transports arrived by rail at Lisky station containing wounded men who were in a frightful condition. The trucks were without bedding. Many of the men lay, wounded and sick, without clothes, dressed only in their underwear, which had long remained unchanged: many of them were infectious. There were no medical personnel, no nurses and nobody in charge of the trains. One of the trains, containing over 400 wounded and sick Red Army men, stood in the station from early morning until evening,

without the men being given anything to eat. It is hard to imagine anything more criminal and shameful![16]

Given such hellish conditions, no one could expect the soldiers to behave like saints. Heavy drinking, brawls and looting were the most common — and least serious — problems of indiscipline. But there were also daily reports of soldiers disobeying orders; refusing to take in new recruits because of the extra burden on supplies; demanding leave and better conditions; and threatening to or actually lynching their commanders. Full-scale mutinies were not uncommon, culminating in the occupation of the Front headquarters, the arrest or murder of the staff and the election of new officers. It was back to the chaos of 1917. Much of the violence was reserved for the well-dressed officers and commissars, especially if they were suspected of corruption in the distribution of supplies. This violence was given a revolutionary edge by the fact that the officers were often seen as *burzhoois* — and an ethnic one by the fact that many of the commissars were Jews. Although anti-Semitism was generally much less widespread than among the Whites or Ukrainian nationalists, it was a definite problem in the ranks of the Red Army. One can only wonder what Trotsky must have felt as he read the reports of his own soldiers' pogroms in the Jewish settlements of the Ukraine, where he himself had grown up as a boy and where some of his relatives still lived.[17]

Desertion was the simplest solution to the soldier's woes. Over a million men deserted from the Red Army in 1918, and nearly four million by 1921. Trotsky said the Red defeats of 1919 — in the east in the spring and in the south in the summer — were a 'crisis of reinforcements', and that is precisely what they were. The Red Army was losing deserters faster than it could replace them with men trained and equipped for battle; and as the quality of the reinforcements fell, so the rate of desertion increased.

The commissars stopped at nothing in their desperate effort to stem the flood of peasant desertions. They sent detachments into the villages behind the Front and punished peasant households suspected of harbouring deserters. Punitive fines were imposed, livestock and property were confiscated, hostages were taken, village leaders were shot, whole villages were burned in an effort to persuade the deserters to return. Os'kin, not to be outdone in this zealotry, even formed a special brigade of Chinese Communists to help him combat the Tula deserters. He assumed that the Chinese would be 'more merciless' than the 'soft-hearted Russians' in taking reprisals against the villagers. Such measures were rarely effective, often merely strengthening the opposition of not only the deserters, but also the entire local peasantry, already embittered by the requisitioning and conscriptions of the Reds. Some deserters formed themselves into guerrilla bands. These were called the Greens partly because they hid out in the woods and were supplied by the local peasants; sometimes these peasant armies called themselves Greens to distinguish themselves from both Reds and Whites. They even had their own Green propaganda and ideology based on the defence of the local peasant revolution. During the spring of 1919 virtually the whole of the Red Army rear, both on the Eastern and the Southern Fronts, was engulfed by these Green armies. In Tambov, Voronezh, Saratov, Penza, Tula, Orel, Nizhnyi Novgorod, Kaluga, Tver and Riazan' provinces peasant bands, sometimes several thousand strong, destroyed the railways, the telegraphs and bridges, ransacked the Soviet military depots and ambushed passing Red Army units. The destruction and chaos which the Greens brought about was to be a crucial factor in weakening the Red Front at a vital moment in the civil war and would lead to the breakthrough of the Whites.[18]

* * *

It may seem odd that a peasant boy like Os'kin should have been so ruthless in putting down the peasants of his native province. But in fact it was not unusual. The Red Army was full of peasant NCOs and commissars like him. It was their School of Communism — transforming them from peasants into comrades — and it was a vital part of their education to learn how to use violence against 'their own'. There was nothing new in this. Military service has always been a form of upward mobility and psychological transformation for the peasantry. The army broadens the peasant's horizons, acquaints him with new technologies and methods of organization, and often teaches him how to read and write. The Russian experience of the First World War was a revolutionizing one in this respect. Most of the peasants called up by the army had, like Os'kin, been educated during the boom in rural schooling between 1900 and 1914. Three out of four peasant recruits into the army in 1914 were registered as literate. They formed a huge pool from which a new class of officers and military technicians would come, replacing the old élite as it was destroyed by the war with the Central Powers. Six out of ten of the military students educated in the officer schools between 1914 and 1917 came from peasant families.[19] These were the radical ensigns, the Os'kins of 1917, who led the revolution in the army and were elected to the soldiers' committees. By educating them, the old regime had sown the seeds of its own destruction.

　　　It also created the foot soldiers of the new regime. Having risen so far through the ranks, it was hard for these peasant sons to return from the war to the dull routines of village life. Their new skills and prestige, not to speak of their own self-esteem, gave them the ambition to aim for something better. For Os'kin, as for so many peasants of that war generation, this could only mean serving the new regime. Joining the party offered them a welcome escape from the narrow village world of their peasant fathers and grandfathers, the old Russia of icons and cockroaches. It gave them entry into the new and urban-centred world of the ruling élite. Most of the Soviet bureaucracy, the provincial commissars and comrades of the 1920s, was drawn from these sons of the peasantry; and for most of them, as for Os'kin, the Red Army was the route to glory.

The Bolsheviks were quick to realize the potential of the Red Army as a school for their future bureaucrats. Compulsory lessons in reading, writing and arithmetic were introduced for all ranks from as early as April 1918. More people learned to read in the barracks and bivouacs of the Red Army than the rest of the country put together during the first years of the Soviet regime. By the end of 1920, there were 3,000 Red Army schools, with over two million books. The first emblem of the Red Army showed a hammer and a sickle with a rifle and a book.[20]

Much of the teaching was inevitably the crudest sort of political indoctrination. It was a marriage between the old socialist and intelligentsia ideals of mass enlightenment and the doctrinal demands of the Bolshevik regime. Primers and textbooks were filled with scenes from everyday life, familiar to the peasants, from which moral and political lessons would then be drawn. These were ABCs of Communism. Dora Elkina recalls how she came to write the first Soviet primer. In 1919 she was sent to the Southern Front to teach the soldiers how to read and write. Having got hold of some old school textbooks, she wrote out the first sentence on the blackboard: 'Masha ate the kasha'. But the soldiers only laughed and heckled. Close to tears, she hit upon the idea of turning the lesson into a political discussion and explained to the soldiers why they could not go home to their Mashas, and why the country was short of kasha. Then she turned to the blackboard and wrote: 'We are not slaves, slaves we are not!' It was a great success among the soldiers, for whom the idea of not being slaves had always been a vital aspect of the revolution. This simple expression of human dignity later became famous as the opening line of her reading book. It was used in primary schools throughout the 1920s and 1930s. For millions of Russians, many of them still alive, it was the first sentence they ever learned to read.[21]

The poet Mayakovsky also wrote and illustrated one of several primers put out by the Commissariat of Enlightenment in the civil war. Clearly rooted in the Lubok tradition — simple picture tales which had sold in their millions in the nineteenth century — it was a brilliant piece of popular satire, with offbeat couplets in the style of a peasant *chastushka*, or rhyming song, and a rude iconoclastic humour that would appeal to the soldiers in the trenches:

B
The Bolsheviks hunt the *burzhoois*
The burzhoois run a mile

K
It's hard for cows (*korovy*) to run fast
Kerensky was Prime Minister

M
The Mensheviks are people
Who run off to their mothers

Ts
Flowers (*tsvety*) smell sweet in the evening
Tsar Nicholas loved them very much[22]

The Red Army was the principal arena of Bolshevik propaganda in the civil war. It aimed to school its soldiers in the principles of Bolshevism — to transform them from peasants into proletarians. 'The main aim of our propaganda in the Red Army', declared one of its pioneers, 'is to fight against the petty-bourgeois, proprietorial psychology of the peasant, and to turn him into a conscious revolutionary fighter.'[23] There were army reading clubs and discussion groups, where the latest newspapers were reviewed; evening concerts and lecture meetings, where various Bolshevik dignitaries appeared; propaganda trains furnished with libraries, printing presses and even cinemas, which toured the Fronts; and Red Army drama groups which entertained the troops with cabarets and plays to drive home the meaning of Soviet power and highlight the evil of its foes.

Half a million Red Army soldiers joined the Bolshevik Party during the civil war. These were the missionaries of the revolution. They carried Bolshevism, its ideas and its methods, back to their towns and villages, where they flooded into the Soviet institutions during the early 1920s. The whole of the Soviet apparatus was thus militarized. Certain Fronts and armies would colonize certain commissariats. Party factions were formed on the basis of the links between veterans of the civil war. The Red Army as a whole, with its centralized command, was seen as a model for the Soviet apparatus. Trotsky often compared the two, likening the need for discipline in industry and society at large to the need for discipline in the ranks. The success of the Red Army increasingly led to the application of military methods throughout the Soviet system. Nothing did more to shape the ruling attitudes of the Bolsheviks than the experience of the civil war. The image and the self-identity of the Soviet regime was based on the mythology of a new order born out of armed struggle against the old; and, rather as in Franco's Spain, this foundation cult of the civil war became a vital mythological propaganda weapon of the Stalinist regime, with its constant demands on the Soviet people to display the same heroic spirit, the same discipline and self-sacrifice, as they had shown in the civil war. Even the language of the Bolshevik regime, with its constant talk of 'campaigns', 'battles' and 'Fronts', of its 'vanguards' and 'fighters' for Socialism, bore the traces of this militarism. The Bolshevism that emerged from the civil war viewed itself as a crusading brotherhood of comrades in arms, conquering Russia and the world with a red pencil in one hand and a gun in the other.

ii 'Kulaks', Bagmen and Cigarette Lighters

In January 1920 Emma Goldman returned to the Petrograd she had known as a teenager in the 1880s. For over thirty years, while the Anarchist had lived in the United States, the 'gaiety of the city, its vivacity and brilliancy' had remained fresh in her memory. But the Petrograd she found in 1920 was a very different place:

> It was almost in ruins, as if a hurricane had swept over it. The houses looked like broken old tombs upon neglected and forgotten cemeteries. The streets were dirty and deserted; all life had gone from them. The population of Petrograd before the war was almost two million; in 1920 it had dwindled to five hundred thousand. The people walked about like living corpses; the shortage of food and fuel was slowly sapping the city; grim death was clutching at its heart. Emaciated and frost-bitten men, women, and children were being whipped by the common lash, the search for a piece of bread or a stick of wood. It was a heart-rending sight by day, an oppressive weight by night. The utter stillness of the large city was paralysing. It fairly haunted me, this awful oppressive silence broken only by occasional shots.[24]

The great cities of the north were the major casualties of the revolution and civil war. They suffered most from its physical destruction, becoming little more than ghost towns. Petrograd was one of the principal victims: the evacuation of the capital to Moscow seemed to deprive it of all life. Gorky, a *Peterburzhets* to the end, saw its decay as a sign of Russia's fall from civilization, its descent from Europe into Asia. 'Petrograd is dying as a city,' he wrote to Ekaterina in 1918. 'Everyone is leaving it — by foot, by horse, by train. Dead horses lie in the streets. The dogs eat them. The city is unbelievably dirty. The Moika and Fontanka are full of rubbish. This is the death of Russia.'[25] Zamyatin, in his story *The Cave* (1922), depicted civil-war Petrograd as an ice-age settlement, peopled by troglodytes who worshipped their 'cave-god', the primus stove, and burned their books to keep themselves alive. The hero of the story, Martin

Martinych, a lover of Scriabin's Opus 74, is reduced to stealing logs from his neighbour.

To the city survivors of these years, it must indeed have seemed as if the urban life of Russia was returning to the prehistoric age. The once bustling city centres were now pervaded by an eerie silence. Shops and restaurants were boarded up; factories were closed. There was so little traffic that weeds began to grow in the deserted streets. 'Petrograd is becoming a cemetery,' Vasilii Vodovozov, an aged professor and liberal activist, noted in his diary during the spring of 1919. 'But the air is as clean as in a village cemetery.' Horses vanished from the city streets, as their owners could no longer feed them, only to reappear as stinking meat in soups and goulashes. 'Civil war sausage' was a euphemism for horsemeat — or even worse (for it was not just horses that disappeared: hunger also wiped out the urban populations of dogs, cats and birds, along with the animals in the zoos). One of the sights of the cities in these years was the emaciated figures of children pulling carts and taxis as human draught animals. Even the Kremlin could not feed its horses — twenty of them died from hunger — so its officials had to travel around in private taxis.[26]

Rats and cockroaches were the only species to thrive. The decay of the housing stock and the sanitation system produced a breeding ground for vermin. Wooden fences disappeared as people ripped them up for firewood. A three-storey house that had been abandoned would be stripped down to its brick foundations within a couple of nights. Three thousand wooden houses were stripped apart in Petrograd alone during 1919–20. People walked away with window-frames, floorboards, doors and wall panels. Whole urban tree populations disappeared as people chopped them down for firewood. In the Ukrainian city of Nikolaev the central boulevards lost all their trees during the two days of January 1920 between the departure of the Whites and the arrival of the Reds. In the freezing winters of the civil war the most valuable gift one could give a friend was a piece of firewood. People were literally prepared to kill for it. They burned their own furniture, their books and letters, just in order to keep the cold away.[27]

As for the sanitary conditions of the cities, they were almost indescribable. Water pipes cracked in the arctic winter frosts. People had to collect water from pumps in the street, and to use the courtyards for toilets. The staircases of apartment blocks always smelled of urine. Without electric light, which was only turned on for two or three hours in the evening, people made their own sort of wick-and-oil lamp out of a bottle filled with fat. It was called a *nedyshalka* (a 'don't breathe'), since it filled the room with a smelly smoke that irritated throats and lungs and blackened all the walls. According to one contemporary, this primitive lamp 'made darkness visible but did not permit reading or writing or even much movement' because it 'went out at the slightest breath'. There was no real system for collecting rubbish because of the shortage of horses. People dumped their rubbish in the streets and squares — which soon attracted vermin. Diseases spread at epidemic rates: cholera, typhus, dysentery and influenza killed people in their thousands every year. The death rate in Petrograd reached an estimated eighty per thousand in 1919. Morgues and cemeteries could not cope, and corpses lay around for months waiting to be buried.[28]

Food, or the lack of it, lay at the heart of the urban crisis. 'Famine in Petrograd has begun,' Gorky wrote in June 1918. 'Almost daily they pick up people who have dropped from exhaustion right in the streets.' Food deliveries to the cities plummeted. Bakeries closed. Even in the Volga city of Saratov, right in the middle of the country's richest grain-producing region, long bread queues would form before 5 a.m., two hours before the bakeries opened. The average worker was consuming fewer than 2,000 calories a day — less than half the recommended intake. Compared with the pre-war years, hardly themselves a golden age, he was eating half the amount of bread and one-third the amount of meat. Food prices rocketed, and workers' wages could not keep up. In 1918 the real value of the average worker's wage was 24 per cent of its value in 1913; and by the end of 1919 its value was as low as 2 per cent. Studies showed that the average worker was spending three-quarters of his income on food, as opposed to less than half in 1913. They also showed that wages accounted for only half the workers' income. In other words, the mass of the workers were forced to feed themselves through the informal or black economy. Ethel Snowden, who came to Moscow in 1920 as a member of the British TUC and Labour Party delegation, asked her guide during a factory tour how much the average worker earned. When she was told what this was, and that it was enough to feed his family for no more than three days, she exclaimed naively: 'Oh! how clever and frugal of the workers to live without any food for the other twenty-seven days of the month. How do they do it?' The answer, of course, was that they traded on the side. They sold their belongings in the flea-markets; travelled to the countryside to barter with the peasants; put their children on the streets to beg; and their wives and daughters on the streets to sell themselves. There were at least 30,000 prostitutes on the streets of Petrograd in 1918, most of whom were teenage girls. Many of them were from 'respectable families'. One study in the early 1920s found that 42 per cent of the prostitutes in Moscow were from the gentry or bourgeois families who had been ruined by the revolution. Emma Goldman found the Nevsky Prospekt lined with nice young girls 'selling themselves for a loaf of bread or a piece of soap or chocolate'.[29]

For the so-called 'former people', without employment or a living ration, the daily hunt for food was soul-destroying. Once mighty scions of the aristocracy were reduced to selling their last precious possessions on the streets. The fat classes became thin. When asked how they were, people would joke: 'It could be worse. At least, I'm managing to lose some weight.' Even the Brusilovs often went hungry, despite the regular gifts of butter, milk, honey and sour cream that were sent to them by loyal peasant veterans of the war. In 1919 Brusilov agreed to accept a position in the archives office of the Red Army Staff to supervise a compilation of Russia's part in the Great War. This paid him a wage of 3,500 roubles a month, which was hardly enough to live on. 'It was painful to see how they lived,' recalled a close friend of the Brusilovs. 'Their main meal was a single dish, usually consisting only of potatoes.'[30]

Gorky took up the cause of the starving intelligentsia. He publicized their desperate plight in his editorials in *Novaia zhizn'*. Professor Gezekhus, the famous physicist, now an old man of seventy-two, was ill in hospital, 'blown up with hunger', like some African famine victim. Vera Petrova, a zemstvo physician, was 'dying of hunger, helpless, dirty, in a dusty awful room'. Glazunov, the famous composer, had grown 'thin and pallid', and lived with his aged mother in two unheated rooms in Petrograd. When H.G. Wells came to visit him, Glazunov begged him to send him some paper so that he could write out his compositions. Even Pavlov, Russia's only Nobel scientist, was forced to spend his time growing carrots and potatoes. Gorky appealed to the Bolshevik leaders for special rations, a better flat and other requirements on behalf of these starving geniuses. Lenin indulged most of his requests: he had always retained a special fondness for Gorky and, perhaps more relevantly, was very aware of his influence abroad. Gorky used this to save as much of the old Russian culture as he could: he became its self-appointed curator (sometimes using his position to buy up works of art cheaply for himself). The threat to culture posed by the revolution had been one of Gorky's constant themes. On the morning of the Bolshevik seizure of power he had headlined his column in *Novaia zhizn'* CULTURE IS IN DANGER! He established a writers' refuge in the former house of Yeliseev, a wealthy merchant, on the corner of the Nevsky Prospekt and the Bolshaia Morskaya. At night the pointed building looked like a boat, so that it became known as the 'ship of fools'. Later Gorky set up a House of Artists too. He also established his own publishing house, World Literature, to publish cheap mass editions of the classics. Its offices employed hundreds of writers, journalists, academics, musicians and artists as translators and copy-editors who would otherwise have been left to fend for themselves. Gorky saw it less as a business than as a charity. And indeed many of the greatest names of twentieth-century literature — Zamyatin, Gumilev, Babel, Chukovsky, Khodasevich, Mandelstam, Shklovsky, Piast, Blok and Zoshchenko — owed their survival through these hungry years largely to the patronage of Gorky. Although in later years many of them condemned Gorky for his close links with the Bolsheviks, they themselves would not have survived the civil war without his contacts.[31]

Gorky turned his enormous flat on the Kronversky Prospekt into a refuge for the penniless and the persecuted victims of the civil war. Compared with the cold and the dampness in which most of the population lived, it was something of a paradise. Viktor Serge described it as 'warm as a greenhouse'. Gorky accumulated various 'wives' and 'sisters', 'daughters' and 'brothers', all of them in some way victims of the terror, whom he allowed to shelter in his home. So many people came to Gorky's flat — at first simply to drink tea and chat but they somehow ended up by staying several years — that the wall between it and the neighbouring flat had to be knocked through and the two apartments made into one. Gorky's mistress, Moura Budberg (then still Baroness Benckendorff), lived in one room, and cooked most of the meals with a girlfriend of the artist Tatlin, who lived in another. There was always an interesting and motley collection of people around the lunch and dinner tables. Famous writers and artists would rub shoulders with the workers and the sailors whom Gorky had picked up on the streets. H. G. Wells stayed when he came to Russia in 1920. Shaliapin was a frequent visitor, and always cursed the Bolsheviks; yet so too were the Bolshevik leaders, Lunacharsky and Krasin, and the deputy head of the Petrograd Cheka, Gleb Bokii, who must have met many of his victims there. There was even a former Grand Duke, Gavril Konstantinovich Romanov, together with the former Grand Duchess and their dog. Gorky had taken pity on them and rescued them from the Cheka jails after Gavril had fallen ill. The couple lived on the top floor, in a room filled with antique furniture and Buddhist statues, and hardly ever left the house for fear of arrest. At meals they would sit in haughty silence. For, as the former Grand Duke later wrote, there were the sort of people at Gorky's table 'that rejoiced at our misery', and 'it was distasteful for us to have to mix in such society'.[32]

It did not take long before the rumour spread that Gorky could help anyone, and he was besieged by begging letters. A certain professor wanted Gorky to procure a special pair of spectacles for him. A poetess begged for a ration of milk for her baby. A provincial doctor needed a new set of premises since the old ones had been requisitioned by the Soviet. A widow wanted a railway ticket to return to her family in the countryside. One old man even wrote with a request for false teeth. Many people wanted Gorky to help them get their relatives released from the Cheka jails — and he did try to intervene on behalf of many (see pages 648–9). But others asked for the impossible. One man, for example, wrote to ask what Gorky was going to do about the fact that he had been robbed. And a prisoner wrote to ask if there would be an amnesty to celebrate the occasion of Gorky's fiftieth birthday — and, if so, if he could be released.[33] Like Rasputin, Gorky had become a sort of *maître de requêtes* for all those who were too powerless to penetrate the offices of the state.

* * *

The urban food crisis was, in the main, a problem of distribution and exchange rather than production. The railway system had virtually collapsed, largely as a result of the economic crisis and the chronic shortages of fuel, and could not cope with the transportation of foodstuffs to the cities. The railway depots were graveyards of broken-down locomotives. More than half the rolling stock was in need of repair, yet the railway workshops were totally run down. The main problem was lack of parts. In one repair shop, for example, the workers were found to be stripping the parts from one engine in order to repair another, so that for every engine that was repaired several others would be even further disrepaired. The railways were thrown into further chaos by the vast crowds of hungry townsmen, soldiers and refugees from the war zones, who stormed every train bound for the countryside, where they hoped to settle or buy up cheap food. Railway officials were easily bribed, and many goods trains were pilfered or diverted. Food wagons which left the countryside full would arrive empty in Petrograd or Moscow.[34]

But the real root of the urban crisis was the peasantry's reluctance to sell foodstuffs for paper money. With the wartime collapse of consumer pro-duction and the huge inflation of prices, peasants could buy less and less with the rouble fortunes they were being offered for their produce. Government efforts to buy the food at fixed prices, going back to 1916, had only encouraged the peasants to withdraw from the market. They reduced their production, shifted to crops not subject to state control, or hid their surpluses from the government's procurement agents. Many peasants used their grain to fatten up the cattle, or sold it to black-market traders from the towns, while many others turned it into vodka.

Cottage industries boomed, largely undetected by statisticians, as the peasants sought to manufacture all those household products they had once bought from the towns but which were now either unavailable or too expensive for them to buy. Rural craftsmen fashioned simple ploughs and sickles out of old scrap iron. Flax and hemp were grown for clothes and rope; timber was cut to make wheels and furniture; reeds were gathered to make baskets; clay was dug for pottery; and oil-producing seeds were grown for fuel. Old rural handicrafts that had gone to the wall in the age of steam were now resurrected. Rural Russia was slowly returning to the methods of the Middle Ages, when, in the words of one official:

Rus' had neither railways nor steamboats, nor steam-mills, nor factories, nor any other 'European invention', when handicraftsmen fed, clothed, and heated the whole of Russia and made all its footwear, when everything was done by them on a tiny scale and very coarsely — with a hand chisel instead of a lathe, with an axe instead of a saw.[35]

THE CIVIL WAR

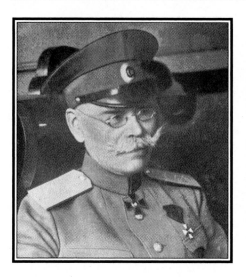

65 General Alexeev – the last chief of staff in the imperial army and, along with Kornilov, the founder of the White movement in south Russia.

66 General Denikin – leader of the White armed forces in south Russia between 1918 and 1920.

67 Admiral Kolchak – the main White leader in east Russia and, thanks to his connections with the Allies, the nominal head of the whole White movement.

68 Baron Wrangel, who led the last White campaign in the Crimea during 1920.

69 The Red Army was no match for the Czech Legion, pictured here during the capture of Vladivostok in June 1918. The aim of the Czechs was to travel eastwards to the United States, and from there return to the European war.

70 The White armies were top-heavy – too many generals and not enough soldiers. A group of White officers await the arrival of Admiral Kolchak during a military parade in Omsk, December 1918.

71 By contrast the Red forces were bottom-heavy – too many infantry and not enough commanders with expertise. The 'committee spirit' of 1917 lived on in the ranks of the Red partisan units such as Makhno's, pictured here in 1920, where tactics were decided by a show of soldiers' hands.

72 Armoured trains like this played a vital role in the civil war.

73 Part of the Red Army, the Latvian Division, passing through a village near the South-Western Front, 1919.

74 Two Red Army soldiers take a break during the fighting on the South-Western Front, 1919.

75-6 The Red Army served as an important channel for the spread of literacy and propaganda. *Above*: soldiers in Tula reading Red Army leaflets, spring 1919. *Below*: the Red Army brings its propaganda to the village. The mobile library of II Cavalry Corps, 1922.

77 Nestor Makhno in 1919. Facing annihilation by the Bolsheviks, Makhno and the remnants of his army left Russian territory in 1921. After brief periods of imprisonment in Romania and Poland, the anarchist leader lived in Paris until his death in 1935.

78-80 Terror was a weapon of all the armies in the civil war. *Above*: the Whites hang a peasant of Kursk province for the possession of an old hunting rifle, September 1919. *Below*: just one Jewish victim of a pogrom by a band of Ukrainian nationalists in Poltava province, 1920. *Overleaf*: the Reds kill a Polish officer during the war against Poland in 1920. The naked man was hanged upside-down, beaten, cut and tortured until he died.

The countryside, in short, was becoming more archaic and more autarkic. It was learning to live without the towns and, on the whole, was doing very well without them. True, there were places where the peasants themselves went hungry during the spring of 1918, especially in the northern regions, which had always been dependent upon importing grain. It was nonsense for the Bolsheviks to claim that any peasant hoarding food was a 'kulak', or capitalist, since many did so to avoid starvation in the winter months. The harvest of 1917 had been small and, with the gentry's extra land now to sow, many of the peasants had no surplus. In Tver, for example, they were said to be eating 'cakes made of linseed oil and straw'. Even Semenov, a model peasant farmer, wrote to a friend in April 1918 that he did 'not have nearly enough grain to eat or feed my cattle'. Like thousands of other peasant communities, Semenov and his fellow villagers of Andreevskoe were forced to mount an expedition to buy up and import grain from the fertile south.[36]

Which is just what the townspeople did as well. Millions fled from the hungry cities and tried to settle in the countryside to be closer to the sources of food. The great industrial cities of the north lost half their populations as Russia returned to its rural past. 'The city is in danger!' declared Viktor Serge. Petrograd lost nearly three-quarters of its population between 1918 and 1920. Moscow's population was more than halved. Railway stations were thrown into chaos as crowds battled to get on to trains bound for the countryside. People travelled on the roofs of the carriages, and hung on to the windows and the brake-pads, risking life and limb. One train left Petrograd so overcrowded that it overbalanced on a bridge and fell into the Neva River, drowning hundreds of passengers.[37]

The nobility fled to what remained of their landed estates. Tanya Kuzminsky, Tolstoy's sister-in-law, travelled from Petrograd to Yasnaya Polyana. Her niece helped her on the way, pleading with the porters to find her a seat on the train: 'She was Natasha Rostova in *War and Peace*.' But this meant nothing to the guards. It was only thanks to a group of commissars that the frail old woman, dressed in her furs, was finally given a wooden box to sit on in one of the goods wagons. Other nobles, without estates, tried their luck in the countryside in any case. The Brusilovs went to stay in a village north of Moscow on the invitation of the peasants. Marina Tsvetaeva, the poetess, went to live in the rural backwaters of Tambov province, where she could trade her last possessions for pork fat, pumpkins and potatoes. Countess Meshcherskaya, a scion of the Russian aristocracy, went with her daughter to the sleepy rural town of Rublev, where they worked in the kitchens of a water-mill and lived in the workers' dormitory. All that she had left of her inheritance — which had once included three huge estates, two palaces and a famous Botticelli — was a china teapot in the rococo style which she donated to the workers' tea-room.[38]

But it was the workers who made up the bulk of those who fled the starving cities. Many of them had been laid off by their factories as a result of the industrial crisis of 1917–18. Although no one knows the precise figure, something like a million workers were unemployed by the spring of 1918. The war industries were the hardest hit, particularly munitions and chemicals, losing in all some half a million workers. The metal industries of Petrograd, in particular, were devastated by fuel shortages, demobilization and the evacuation of the capital. The workforce of these factories declined from a quarter of a million to barely 50,000 during the first six months of 1918. It was a catastrophe for the Bolsheviks. Their once mighty strongholds, the New Lessner and the Erickson plants, each of which had had more than 7,000 workers during the autumn of 1917, were reduced to a skeleton workforce with only 200 workers between them by the following spring. During the first six months of the Bolshevik regime, the number of Bolsheviks in Petrograd fell from 50,000 to a mere 13,000. The Bolshevik Party, in the words of Shliapnikov, was becoming 'the vanguard of a non-existent class'.[39]

According to the Bolsheviks and their historians, it was the skilled and 'class conscious' workers who mainly fled the cities. The depopulation of the cities thus paralleled their 'declassing', to adopt the rather ugly Marxist phrase, meaning the breakdown of the working class. It was important for the Soviet establishment to argue this because it allowed them to depict the growing wave of workers' strikes and protests from the spring of 1918 as the work of 'backward' or 'petty-bourgeois' types stirred up by the Mensheviks and the SRs. How embarrassing it would have been for them to have to admit that the very workers who had helped to bring them to power in October were calling for their downfall six months later. Yet that was more or less what happened. Those most likely to flee to the countryside were those workers who had arrived in the cities last — especially the women who had come during the industrial boom of the First World War — and who thus had retained the closest ties with their native villages. These were the unskilled and semi-rural workers — invariably the first to be laid off by the factory employers — so that the workers who were left in the cities tended to be the most skilled and proletarian (i.e. those who had been born in the cities and who had no real links with the countryside). It was these workers who led the strikes and protests against the Bolsheviks in 1918 (see pages 624–6).

The prospect of a share in the communal land or of setting up in some rural trade was usually enough to lure semi-rural workers back to their native villages. According to a report from the Briansk metallurgical factory in 1920, 'all the workers with a tie to the village want to leave the factory and settle there'. Generally, the peasants welcomed those workers who had relatives in the village or who had some useful trade to contribute (e.g. carpenters and blacksmiths); but they were very rarely willing to give either land or food to those who had neither. These immigrants were usually left to support themselves by casual labour, and their plight was often desperate. One memoirist from Tambov province recalls these workers and their families 'walking across the fields after the rye harvest looking for any ears of grain that had been dropped'.[40]

It was not just the flight of the workers with which the Bolsheviks had to contend. Industry and transport were thrown into chaos by the endless travelling of city people to and from the countryside to buy up stocks of food. Millions of townspeople, from all classes, relied on this petty trade — or 'bagging', as it was called — to feed themselves. They would leave the cities with bags of clothes and household goods to sell or exchange in the rural markets, and return with bags of food. The railways were paralysed by the armies of 'bagmen'. The Orel Station, a major junction *en route* to the south, had 3,000 bagmen pass through it every day. Many of them travelled in armed brigades which hijacked trains, leaving the local authorities powerless. The most popular destinations — Tambov, Kursk, Kazan, Simbirsk and Saratov provinces — were each invaded by something in the region of 100,000 bagmen every month.[41]

For the hungry cities of the north this primitive trade was a universal means of livelihood. Virtually everyone was forced to turn themselves into a part-time trader — workers, officials, even Communists. It was a natural and spontaneous response to the economic crisis and the breakdown of the market between town and country. But it brought chaos to industry. Nearly all the workers were engaged in the bag trade in some form. Many of them travelled into the countryside with tools, fuel and scrap-iron, which they had stolen from their factories. Others fabricated primitive goods in their factories to barter with the peasants. Primus stoves, penknives and cigarette lighters were the most common trade. But shoe soles were also made from conveyor belts; candlesticks from bits of piping; axes and ploughs from iron bars. The whole phenomenon became known as 'cigarette lighterism' (*zazhigolochnichestvo*), one of the longest and hardest words to pronounce in the Russian language. It was not uncommon for factory committees to sanction or at least to turn a blind eye to these spontaneous initiatives. Many of the committees gave their own anarchic gloss to the Decree on Workers' Control, taking it to mean the right of the workers to divide between themselves the products of their labour — or, if there were none, the assets of their factory — just as the peasants had divided up the land. Industry was brought virtually to a halt as most of the workers spent most of their time fabricating these black-market goods and running off to the countryside to barter them for food. On the average day in the average factory 30 per cent of the workforce would be absent. In some metal factories the rate of absenteeism could be as high as 80 per cent.[42]

During their first precarious months in power the Bolsheviks could do very little to stop this 'bagging'. Any restrictions they tried to impose were bound to be evaded by the workers who depended on the bag-trade to survive. The right to travel to the countryside for food was a major demand of the workers' strikes and protests during the spring of 1918. Many of the factories and even some of the district and city Soviets organized this trade on a collective basis. Without recourse to some form of trade, industry would have to come to a complete halt. The factory or the Soviet would make an agreement with a village or a rural Soviet to exchange a certain number of factory goods for an equivalent amount of foodstuffs. A brigade of workers would then be sent to complete the exchange. Try though they did, the Bolsheviks were powerless to prevent this collective bartering. One commissar in Samara province claimed that it was useless trying to stop the bagmen 'since they all travel with passports from their Soviet'. Local rates of natural exchange began to take the place of money. In Kaluga, for example, a yard of cloth was worth a pound of butter, or two pounds of peas; a pound of soap was worth two pounds of millet; and a pair of boots a pound of potatoes. Flour was the gold standard of this medieval system: a pound was worth thirty pounds of kerosene, or three pounds of tobacco, or a winter coat.[43]

The co-operatives played an important part in this local trade, often setting the terms of barter and exchange. The co-operatives had flourished during the war as one of the main means of trade between town and country. By 1918, they claimed to serve the needs of a hundred million consumers (70 per cent of the population).[44] Factories, trade unions, professional groups and resident associations formed themselves into urban co-operatives for the procurement of goods. Peasants joined co-operatives to market their goods and obtain the manufactures they needed in exchange. The rural co-operatives also served as a conduit for agricultural improvements, offering the peasants advanced tools, fertilizers, credit and advice on the latest farming techniques. For Semenov, a pioneer of the co-operative movement in Volokolamsk, this was one of the revolution's main achievements.

*   *   *

Had they not been so hostile to the market, the Bolsheviks might have used this collective barter system to help feed the cities and supply industry. Primitive and chaotic though it was, it would still arguably have been more efficient than the state monopoly of food supply which they began to introduce from May 1918 as the foundation of their planned economy. War Communism, as this system became known, was in many ways a prototype of the Stalinist economy. It aimed to abolish all private trade, maximize the state's control of distribution and the labour market, nationalize all large-scale industry, collectivize agriculture, and at its height in 1920 replace the money system with a universal system of state rationing.

The origins of War Communism have long been a subject of intense debate between historians. To those on the Left it was essentially a pragmatic response to the military exigencies of the civil war; while to those on the Right it was derived directly from Leninist ideology. The argument has broader implications for the nature and development of the Soviet regime. According to the left-wing view, War Communism was no more than a temporary diversion from the mixed economy that Lenin had outlined during the spring of 1918 and to which he returned in the New Economic Policy of 1921. This implies that the 'soft' or pro-market socialism pursued by the Bolsheviks in these two periods was the real face of Leninism as opposed to the 'hard' or anti-market socialism of the War Communist and Stalinist eras. Hence the 'Leninism' proclaimed for Gorbachev's reforms. In the right-wing view, however, the 'hard socialism' of the civil war was directly inspired by the statist methods at the heart of Lenin's revolutionary ideology. The Bolsheviks, in this account, adopted War Communism as a means of introducing socialism by decree, and made concessions to the market only when they were forced to do so. There was thus a logical progression, a historical continuity, between Lenin's programme of 1902, War Communism and the Stalinist planned economy.

While both pragmatism and ideology were relevant factors, neither is sufficient as an explanation of the way in which the world's first planned economy was organized.

The pragmatic argument has fundamental flaws. As a purely pragmatic response to the chaos of the spring, the Grain Monopoly of May 1918 — the first major element of War Communism — was disastrous. Its futile and absurd efforts to stamp out the free market merely caused more chaos, as thousands of commissars and much of the state's resources had to be diverted to the war against free trade. On purely practical grounds, it would have been better to retain the market rather than to try and stamp it out, as Lenin himself recognized in 1921. And indeed at crisis points throughout the civil war the Bolsheviks were forced to lift the bars on private trade in recognition of the fact that the state distribution system was unable to feed the cities. Amongst themselves the Bolsheviks acknowledged that, despite their own anti-market rhetoric, they could not survive without the market.

What about the argument that War Communism was a reponse to the exigencies of the civil war? To be sure, the Bolsheviks, like all the wartime governments in Europe at this time, were trying to control the economy in the military interests of the state (much of the Bolshevik economic programme was modelled on the German war economy). But War Communism was not just a *response* to the civil war; it was also a *means of making civil war*. The civil war was not fought only on the battlefields. It was a fundamental aspect of the Bolsheviks' revolutionary strategy, and was also fought on what they called the 'internal front', in society and the economy, through the policies of War Communism. Unless one acknowledges this fundamental fact — that the policies of War Communism were seen by the Bolsheviks as an instrument of struggle against their social or 'internal' enemies — it is impossible to explain why these policies were kept in place for more than a year after the White armies had been defeated.

The case for War Communism as inspired by ideology is also insufficient. Certainly, the Bolsheviks were all united by a fundamental belief in the possibility of using state coercion to effect the transition to socialism in a backward peasant country such as Russia. This was the essence of their ideology. They also shared a deeply ingrained mistrust of the market which could be defined as ideological. Foreign socialists were shocked by the violence of the Bolsheviks' hatred of free trade. The Bolsheviks did not just want to regulate the market — as did the socialists and most of the wartime governments of Europe — they wanted to abolish it. 'The more market the less socialism, the more socialism the less market' — that was their credo. This crude political economy was no doubt the result of the Bolsheviks' own life experience. Most of the party's rank and file were peasant sons and workers, young men like Kanatchikov, who had suffered from the worst of both rural and urban poverty. Marx had taught them that all this was the result of 'capitalism'. They saw the workings of the market as a simple expression of capitalist exploitation. Even the primitive trade of the bagmen would lead in their view, if unchecked, to the resurrection of the capitalist system. Although the overwhelming majority of the bagmen were trading for consumption rather than profit, the Bolsheviks depicted them as 'speculators', 'profiteers' and 'parasites'. All the social evils of the post-war world, from unemployment to prostitution, were blamed by them on the workings of the market.

It could not be said, however, that this *dirigiste* and militantly anti-market ideology had been expressed in a clear economic strategy before the introduction of War Communism. Indeed, the Bolsheviks were sharply divided over economic policy during 1918. Whereas the Left Communists wanted to move immediately towards the abolition of the capitalist system, Lenin talked of using capitalist methods for the revolutionary reconstruction of the economy. These divisions resurfaced repeatedly throughout the years of the civil war — especially over fiscal policy and the use of 'bourgeois' managers — so that the policies of War Communism had to be chopped and changed in the interests of party unity. Hence, whereas right-wing historians may think of War Communism as a monolithic programme integral to Bolshevik ideology, much of it was in fact improvised.

The introduction of War Communism was essentially a *political* response to the urban crisis of 1918. During that spring the Bolsheviks were obsessed by the example of the Paris Commune. They constantly compared their own position to that of the Parisian revolutionaries of 1871, and debated their own policies by the light of historical analogy, trying to work out whether they might have saved the French revolutionaries from their defeat. The Bolsheviks were all too conscious of the fact that their power base, like that of the Communards, was confined to the major cities, and that they were facing defeat because they were surrounded by a hostile peasantry with whom they had no goods to trade for food. They had convinced themselves that, unless they extended their power to the countryside and launched a crusade against the 'grain-hoarding' peasants, their urban revolution, like that of the Commune, would be destroyed by starvation. The flight of the workers from the cities and their strikes and protests against food shortages were seen as the first signs of this collapse. It was essential, as the Bolsheviks saw it, to seize the peasantry's grain by force, to stem the chaos of the bag-trade and to get a firm grip on industry, if they were to avoid certain defeat.

*   *   *

When Trotsky defended the introduction of the grain monopoly at a Soviet assembly on 4 June, he was heckled from the floor. The Left SRs accused him of 'waging a civil war against the peasantry'. On 9 May the Bolsheviks had indeed declared that all the peasants' surplus grain would henceforth become the property of the state. They were now despatching armed brigades to requisition the grain from the peasantry by force; and their propaganda made it clear that this was to be seen as a 'battle for grain'. Trotsky himself told the meeting on 4 June: 'Our Party is for civil war! Civil war has to be waged for grain. We the Soviets are going into battle!' At this point a delegate had shouted: 'Long live civil war!' No doubt he had meant it as a joke. But Trotsky turned on him and replied with deadly seriousness: 'Yes, long live civil war! Civil war for the sake of the children, the elderly, the workers and the Red Army, civil war in the name of direct and ruthless struggle against counter-revolution.'[45]

For Lenin and most of his followers, civil war was a vital phase in any social revolution. 'Civil war is the same as class war,' declared one of the Bolshevik leaders in Baku. 'We are supporters of civil war, not because we thirst for blood, but because without a struggle the oppressors will not give up their privileges to the people.'[46] As the Bolsheviks saw it, a civil war was no more than a violent form of class struggle. There was no real distinction in their view between the military conflict and the social conflict in every town and village.

As such, in Lenin's view, the civil war was to be welcomed as a necessary phase of the revolution. He had always argued that the civil war had been started by the forces of the Right during the summer of 1917, and that the Bolshevik seizure of power should be seen as the joining of the armed struggle by the proletarian side; the class conflicts of the revolution were unresolvable by political means. Russia was split into two hostile camps — the 'military dictatorship' and the 'Dictatorship of the Proletariat' — and it was a question of which side would prevail. All Lenin's policies, from the October seizure of power to the closure of the Constituent Assembly and the Treaty of Brest-Litovsk, could be seen (and were seen by the opposition) as a deliberate incitement to civil war. Lenin himself was doubtless convinced that his party's best hope of building up its own tiny power base *was to fight a civil war*. Indeed he often stressed that the reason why the Paris Commune had been defeated was that it had failed to launch a civil war. The effects of such a conflict were predictable — the polarization of the country into 'revolutionary' and 'counter-revolutionary' forces, the extension of the state's military and political power, and the use of terror to suppress dissent — and were all deemed by Lenin to be necessary for the consolidation of the dictatorship. Of course Lenin could not have foreseen the full extent of the civil war that would unfold from the following autumn — in April 1918 he had even declared that the civil war was already won — and, if he had, he might have thought again about using civil war to build up his regime. But even so, it is surely true that the Bolsheviks were psychologically prepared for a civil war in a way that could not be said of their opponents. One might compare it to the Spanish civil war: Franco's side was ready — and eager — for a civil war; the same could hardly be said of the Republicans.

The 'battle for grain', the Bolsheviks' civil war against the countryside, was rooted in a fundamental mistrust — bordering on hatred — of the peasantry. As Marxists, they had always viewed the peasantry with something akin to contempt. 'Anarchic', 'backward', 'counter-revolutionary' — thus began their peasant lexicon. The peasants were too illiterate and superstitious, too closely tied to the Old Russia, to play a role in the building of their new society. They were too 'petty-bourgeois' (O most heinous of Marxist sins!), too imbued in the principles and habits of private property and free trade, to become comrades. This contempt for the peasantry was often most marked among those worker Bolsheviks of peasant stock — the Kanatchikovs of the party — who as young men had run away from the crushing poverty and the boredom of the village, from the domination of the priests, and the violence of their heavy-drinking fathers, to roam the cities in search of work. For them the city was a world of progress and opportunity, symbolized by school and industry, whereas the village stood for everything — backwardness, poverty and stupid superstition — they wanted to sweep away. 'I am not village' was the first expression of their adopted working-class identity. And through the proletarian culture of the cities, which had first led them to Bolshevism, they sought to banish their peasant past.

A clear sign of this anti-peasant attitude — which was so vital to the whole development of the Soviet regime — may be found in the small biographies that all Bolsheviks were asked to write about themselves on taking up

Soviet office. A quarter of them came from peasant backgrounds; yet few spoke of their past in positive terms. 'From an early age', recalled one Bolshevik from Vologda, 'education was my only chance to escape from the impoverished and idiotic life of the village. I wanted to run away, anywhere, as far away from the village as possible.'[47]

Marxism gave a pseudo-scientific respectability to this hatred of the peasantry. Its 'laws' of historical development 'proved' that the peasantry was doomed to extinction. The penetration of the market and of capitalist relations into the countryside would inevitably result in the class division of the peasantry. Lenin had shown that the village was becoming divided into two hostile classes — the poor peasants, who were said to be the allies of the proletariat, and the 'kulaks', or 'capitalist farmers', who were said to be its enemies — and this schema became the guiding principle of Bolshevik policy in the countryside. In fact the analysis was pure fantasy: the number of peasant capitalists was very small indeed — certainly not enough to constitute a 'class'. Even the number of peasant households employing regular wage labour had numbered less than 2 per cent before the revolution and declined considerably in 1917. In the vast majority of villages all that distinguished the richest from the poorest peasant was the ownership of an extra horse or cow, or a house made out of brick, as opposed to one of wood, with a raised floor instead of boards laid on the ground.

The peasants whom the Bolsheviks categorized as 'kulaks' were usually no more than the patriarchal leaders of the village. These were the Maliutins of Russia, the white-bearded peasant elders like the one in Andreevskoe who stood in the way of all Semenov's reforms. These, it is true, were often the richest farmers, to whom the rest of the villagers might well have been indebted, either for the use of a horse or for the loan of money. But this did not make them 'kulaks' in the eyes of the peasants — and even Semenov, who had good reason to despise Maliutin, never called him one. Many of the peasants looked up to these elders with a mixture of fear and respect. As the most successful farmers in the village, they were often seen as the natural leaders of the community. They were usually the staunchest upholders of communal traditions, the people who dealt with the outside powers, and their neighbours naturally went to them for advice on agricultural matters. The first peasant Soviets were often headed by these village elders.

The Bolsheviks had given vocal support to the peasant Soviets during the first months of their regime. This enabled them to neutralize the peasants during their struggle for power in the cities. But as a result Soviet power in the countryside had been decentralized — which had made the task of extracting food and soldiers from the peasantry all the harder. The peasant Soviets naturally defended the economic interests of the local population. They tried to block the export of grain to the cities or at least to demand a price high enough to allow them to buy the goods they needed in return. As the urban food crisis deepened, the Bolsheviks increasingly blamed it on so-called 'kulak hoarders'. Their propaganda portrayed the typical 'kulak' as a fat and greedy capitalist who speculated on the hunger of the urban workers. The 'kulak' took his place alongside the *burzhooi* as the 'internal enemy' of 'the revolution'. For the Bolsheviks the 'kulak' was a scapegoat, a means of focusing the anger of the workers against the 'counter-revolutionary' village rather than themselves. The Bolsheviks now claimed that the peasant Soviets were dominated by the 'kulaks' and were being run by them in league with the SRs to starve the revolution out of existence. This was false — and Lenin knew it. The rural Soviets, as he himself had acknowledged, were general peasant bodies. They had merely put their own interests before those of the cities. But the myth of a 'kulak grain strike' gave his party the pretext it needed to launch a civil war against the peasantry.[48]

Lenin gave the battle cry in a speech of astounding violence during the summer of 1918:

> The kulaks are the rabid foes of the Soviet government . . . These bloodsuckers have grown rich on the hunger of the people . . . These spiders* have grown fat at the expense of the peasants ruined by the war, at the expense of the workers. These leeches have sucked the blood of the working people and grown richer as the workers in the cities and factories starved . . . Ruthless war on the kulaks! Death to all of them.[49]

The 'Food Army' led this onslaught on the 'kulak hoarders'. Its armed requisitioning brigades (*prodotriady*) were empowered to occupy the villages and extract their surplus grain by force. Before they left the cities, they would pose for a photograph, like an army going off to battle. The brigades were supposed to consist of the cream of the working class. But in fact, like the first Red Army units, their 76,000 members were made up mainly of the unemployed, the rootless and migrant *lumpen* elements, and former soldiers with nowhere else to go. The provincial provisions authorities constantly complained that the brigades were 'of poor quality and indisciplined', that they 'carried out their work without the slightest plan', that they 'often used coercion against the peasantry', and that they took from them not only surplus grain but vital stocks of seed, private property, guns and vodka. In the words of one provincial commissar, their work amounted to little more than 'organized robbery from the peasants'.[50]

'At times', wrote Tsiurupa, the People's Commissar for Provisions, 'the

---

* No doubt a reference to *Spiders and Flies*, the best-selling pamphlet of 1917 which had done so much to shape the popular myth of the *burzhooi* (see pages 523–4).

food brigades would emulate the methods of the tsarist police.' Sometimes they occupied a village and tortured the peasants in a brutal fashion until the required amount of food and property was handed over. 'The measures of exaction are reminiscent of a medieval inquisition,' reported one official from Yelets, 'they make the peasants strip and kneel on the floor, and whip or beat them, sometimes killing them.' The approach of a food brigade was enough to make the peasants flee in panic. One shocked commissar in Ufa province reported the following incident. He had entered the hut of a peasant woman who, it seemed, had failed to run away when his small platoon, which she had mistaken for a food brigade, had arrived in the village. She began to scream and seized her little boy. 'Cut me down and kill me but don't take my child,' she cried. The commissar tried to calm her down by telling her that she was safe, whereupon the peasant woman said: 'I thought you were going to kill me. I had no idea that there were Bolsheviks who did not murder peasants. All those we have seen are *oprichniki* [the detested henchmen of Ivan the Terrible].' In the Borisoglebsk district of Tambov province — a future stronghold of the Antonov revolt (see pages 753–5) — there was a barbarous brigade leader named Margolin, who stole indiscriminately from the peasants, and raped their women or took away their horses when they could not pay the levy. Many of the peasants were forced to buy up grain from the neighbouring province of Voronezh, or part with their last vital stocks of food and seed, to keep Margolin satisfied. Another local tyrant, a brigade leader named Cheremukhin, turned the southern villages of Balashov, just behind the Red Front against Denikin, into his corrupt private fiefdom. Peasant food and property were requisitioned with brutal force, often leaving the farmers with nothing to eat or sow, and peasant women were routinely raped. The leader of a nearby food brigade left a vivid impression of the peasant mood on passing through one of 'Cheremukhin's villages':

> The peasants mistook us for some of Cheremukhin's assistants and all fell down on to their knees and bowed before us. One could feel that the spirit of the Revolution among the people of this village had been entirely suppressed. The slavery of Tsarism was again clearly visible on their faces. The effect upon us was one of overwhelming demoralization.[51]

Most peasants tried to hide their precious grain stocks from the food brigades. Bags of flour were buried under floorboards, in the lofts of barns, deep in the woods and underground. The brigades assumed that all the villages did this and that the hidden grain was surplus, whereas in fact it often found vital reserves of seed and food. A 'battle for grain' thus began, with the brigades using terror to squeeze out the stocks and the peasants counteracting them with passive resistance and outright revolt. During July and August 1918 there were over 200 uprisings against the food brigades. The Bolsheviks tried to portray them as 'SR-kulak revolts'; but they were in fact general village rebellions, in which the poorest peasants (who were left the hungriest by the requisitions) often played a leading role. These uprisings were violent and spontaneous, usually in response to some atrocity perpetrated by the brigades. In one village of Samara province, where the food brigade had robbed and murdered several villagers, the peasants exacted a savage revenge. One night in November, they decapitated the twelve members of the brigade as they slept in the party offices and placed their heads on poles at the village entrance as a gruesome warning to other brigades. Three weeks later the Red Army bombarded the village with artillery and, when all the villagers had fled to the woods, burned it down.[52]

Inside the village the brigades were supposed to be assisted by the new Committees of the Rural Poor (*kombedy*). Lenin heralded their institution, on 11 June, as the moment when the countryside embarked on the Socialist Revolution. This was to be the peasants' October, when the 'rural proletariat' would join the 'class struggle' against the 'kulaks', the 'rural bourgeoisie'. By helping the brigades to extract their grain, the *kombedy* were to bring about the 'socialist transformation' of the village, replacing the 'kulak Soviets' and completing the expropriation of other 'kulak' property, such as surplus land and livestock. As Sverdlov put it, the aim was to 'split the village into two warring classes' and 'inflame there the same civil war as in the cities'. Upon that depended the survival of the Soviet regime in the countryside.[53]

The *kombedy* failed dismally to ignite this 'class war' in the village. This was where Marxist dogma collapsed under the weight of peasant reality. Most villages thought of themselves as farming communities of equal members related by kin: they often called themselves a 'peasant family'. That was the basic idea (if not the reality) of the peasant commune. As such, they were hostile to the suggestion of setting up a separate body for the village poor. Didn't they already have the Soviet? Most village communes either failed to elect a *kombed*, leaving it to outside agitators, or else set up one which every peasant joined on the grounds, as they often put it, that all the peasants were equally poor. In this case, the *kombed* was indistinguishable from the Soviet. The peasants of Kiselevo-Chemizovka in the Atkarsk district, for example, resolved that a *kombed* was not needed, 'since the peasants are almost equal, and the poor ones are already in the Soviet. The organization of a separate *kombed* would only lead to unnecessary tensions between citizens of the same commune.' The Bolshevik agitators were quite unable to split the peasants on class lines. The poor peasants were simply not aware of themselves as 'proletarians'. Nor did they think of their richer neighbours as a 'bourgeoisie'. They all thought of themselves as fellow villagers and looked at the efforts of the Bolsheviks to split them with suspicion and hostility.[54]

So the *kombed* in many places was set up by elements from outside the commune. These were not the poor peasant farmers but immigrant townsmen and soldiers, landless craftsmen and labourers excluded from the commune. A study of 800 *kombedy* in Tambov province found that less than half their members at the volost level had ever farmed the land; 30 per cent of them were soldiers. In the semi-industrial villages of the north these social types may well have been 'insiders'; but in the agricultural south they were strangers to the village core. Disconnected from the peasant commune, upon which all rural government depended, they were unable to carry out their tasks without resorting to violence. They requisitioned private property, made illegal arrests, vandalized churches and generally terrorized the peasants. They were more like a local mafia than an organ of the Soviet state. In one Saratov volost, for example, the *kombed* was run by the Druzhaev brothers in alliance with the chief of the regional police, comrade Varlamov. They went around the villages extorting money, guns and vodka from the terrified peasants. Livestock was also confiscated and handed over to their henchmen among the 'village poor'. One peasant who could not pay was forced to watch them rape his wife. This state of terror lasted for six months. The villagers petitioned 'comrade Lenin' in the hope of ending it. As one of them put it: 'The people are beginning to say that life was better under the Tsar.'[55]

Along with the food brigades, the *kombedy* sparked a huge wave of peasant revolts. These reached a peak in November, the height of both the 'battle for grain' and the first major Red Army mobilizations. Whole districts of Tambov, Tula and Riazan' were swallowed up by peasant bands armed with pitchforks and guns. Elsewhere the uprisings were more sporadic but no less violent. The peasants lynched and murdered the *kombed* members, the local Bolsheviks and the leaders of the Soviets. The Bolshevik Central Committee member Smidovich, who was sent to report on the Tula revolts, concluded in November that 'the peasants are beginning to feel as if they are being ruled by the arbitrary will of an alien set of masters; they no longer believe in the promises of Soviet Power and only expect bad from it'.[56]

At the Sixth Soviet Congress in November Lenin called for the abolition of the *kombedy*. This was the start of a new policy, endorsed by the Eighth Party Congress the following March, to improve relations with the middle peasantry. It was an admission that the *kombedy* had, as Lenin put it, waged a 'reckless war of destruction against the interests of the peasants'. The whole attempt to divide the village into two hostile classes had, as he admitted, been misconceived, and it was now to be abandoned.[57] But it was surely too late for the Bolsheviks to repair their relations with the peasantry.

A few weeks after the abolition of the *kombedy*, in January 1919, the Bolsheviks also changed their tactics in the 'battle for grain'. The requisitioning of the 1918 harvest, the first carried out by Soviet power, had been nothing less than disastrous. Only a fifth of the levy had been collected by the end of the year. Of course the Bolsheviks blamed it on the 'kulaks'; but in fact the weakness of their own procurement infrastructure was to blame. The food brigades had no effective means of accounting for the harvest. The *kombedy* pursued their own local interests at the expense of the centre, sometimes even keeping the grain for themselves. The collection depots were unable to cope with the volume of grain because of fuel shortages. And the chaos on the railways often meant that grain did not reach the towns. The January reform, known as the Food Levy or *prodrazverstka*, had been intended to reinforce the system. It differed from the grain monopoly of May 1918 in two main respects. First, whereas the grain monopoly had been limited to cereals, all the major foodstuffs, including livestock and vegetables, were subjected to the food levy.* And second, whereas the quotas of the grain monopoly had been set by the local food organs in accordance with the harvest estimates, the quotas of the food levy were set from above, by the central state, in accordance with its general needs and then simply divided among the provincial authorities. Thus the principle, however loosely it may have been applied, that the quotas should match the actual harvest surplus was abandoned altogether. Increasingly, the levies bore no relation to the peasantry's ability to pay. The requisitioning brigades were simply instructed to extract the necessary amounts of food by force, even if this meant taking the peasants' last vital stocks of food and seed. It was assumed, in this terrifyingly ignorant calculus, that an empty barn was a sign that its owner was a 'kulak' hiding food.[58]

And so as the civil war moved towards its climax, during the spring of 1919, the 'battle for grain', that other civil war behind the Red Front, also reached its own insane heights. It became a life-and-death struggle between the Bolsheviks and the peasantry.

*　　*　　*

Stamping out the bagmen was the final element of the Bolshevik 'battle for grain'. Flying brigades (*zagraditel'nye otriady*) were set up to police the roads and railways. They were ordered to confiscate all foodstuffs from the passengers coming into town, leaving them only their legal allowance of one-and-a-half *puds* (hence the bagmen became known as the 'one-and-a-half *puders*'). Trains were stopped and searched, their passengers forced to disembark and open up their luggage. The brigades behaved more like bandits than government officials. They confiscated money, clothes and drink from the passengers. The Cheka

---

* One exception was onions — no doubt the result of a bureaucratic slip. A boom in onion production soon followed, as the peasants sought to exploit this last remaining legal area of free trade.

carried out similar raids on the urban markets, hunting out bagmen from the countryside.

All this of course was a futile exercise. It was impossible to stamp out the market, just as King Canute could not force back the sea. Throughout the period of War Communism the trains continued to be filled by bagmen (it was easy for them to bribe the railway officials). Lenin himself acknowledged that at least half the foodstuffs reaching the towns had been brought in by the bagmen; and at times the figure was much higher. The Bolsheviks had little choice but to tolerate this private trade, without which the workers would have starved. Their policy towards the bagmen vacillated in fact: at critical moments of the civil war, when they needed to keep the railways free for the military, they would clamp down on them and try to ban all passenger transport; but at other times the bagmen were allowed to continue more or less without hindrance. Bolshevik policy on the urban markets was equally fitful. The Cheka would occasionally carry out a raid, seizing goods and arresting vendors, after which business would slow down for a few days, but then the markets would return to normal. The enormous Sukharevka market in Moscow flourished throughout the civil war years, despite constant Cheka raids. Most of the state's own textile factories in the capital purchased their cloth from private salesmen there. The Sukharevka came to symbolize the old world of free trade which the Reds could not conquer. Lenin himself once lamented that in the soul of every Russian there was a 'little Sukharevka'.[59]

Futile though it may have been to try, squeezing out the bag-trade was essential for the Bolsheviks in industry. It was impossible to maintain industrial production if the workers kept running off to the countryside for food. Control of the food supply went hand in hand with the control of labour. The Bolsheviks were adamant on the state's need to control the movement of labour. This was the essence of War Communism — 'the right of the dictatorship', as Trotsky put it, 'to send every worker to the place where he is needed in accordance with the state plan'. To advocate the freedom of labour, as the Mensheviks did, was, in Trotsky's words, the 'milky way to Socialism'. Without the food monopoly or the abolition of the labour market, the economy would be ruined and the working class destroyed by the 'chaotic movement of the workers from one factory to another.' The high road to socialism, in his view, entailed ending all free labour and imposing state control on all large-scale industry. This was to be a completely planned economy.[60]

Throughout the spring of 1918 the Bolsheviks had been moving towards the nationalization of industry. Imposing their own managers in the factories seemed the only way to stop the chaos brought about by the 14 November Decree on Workers' Control, which had been a vital political concession to the factory committees and trade unions. Control by the factories through collegial management boards had helped the Bolsheviks to win the support of many of the workers, and dealt a blow to the factory owners during the regime's struggle for the control of the industrial capitals. But the economic effect of the policy had been catastrophic. The workers' bodies in control of the factories had merely voted themselves huge pay rises, fuelling the inflation. They had also carried out a destructive campaign of terror and violence, often motivated by revenge, against the old managers and technicians, which had disrupted the management of production. The workers' bodies had done very little to stop the decline of labour discipline and the constant thefts of tools and raw materials to make cigarette lighters and other illegal goods for the bag-trade.

Even more importantly, the factory committees and trade unions had become part of a growing workers' protest movement against the Bolshevik dictatorship. The working class remained just as militant as in 1917 — only now their anger was focused on the party that ruled in their name. Strikes and workers' protests engulfed all the country's major industrial districts, including the former Bolshevik strongholds in Petrograd and Moscow, during the spring of 1918. Much of the discontent was of the most basic economic kind. Workers complained about the shortages of bread and the threat of unemployment; they were disgusted that the so-called Workers' State had done nothing to improve their lives. This gave rise to a general disillusionment with politics, often combined with vague hostility towards the Bolsheviks as the ruling party, among many workers. According to Gorky, many 'workers spat whenever they heard the name of the Bolsheviks mentioned'. This sort of cynical — but essentially pre-political — attitude was best summed up by the slogan which began to appear on city walls: 'Down with Lenin and horsemeat! Give us the Tsar and pork!'[61] But for other workers politics still mattered, especially for those with a background of Menshevik or SR activism who had an alternative political vision to counterpose against that of the Bolsheviks; and their reaction to the crisis of the spring was to form themselves into a protest movement, the Extraordinary Assemblies of Factory and Plant Representatives, which was by far the most powerful threat the Bolsheviks ever encountered from the working class.

The Extraordinary Assemblies were a grass-roots workers' movement. Established in March, they had a membership of several hundred thousand workers at the height of their influence in June. The Mensheviks and SRs played a prominent role in their leadership at the national level, and it was often their local activists who were to the fore in factory assemblies. The spring marked a general resurgence of these parties' fortunes in the industrial cities. By establishing an electoral pact they were able to defeat the Bolsheviks in several city Soviet elections. But it does not follow that the workers' assemblies were a protest movement *for* the Mensheviks and the SRs as opposed to one (which happened to include them) *against* the Bolsheviks.[62] True, many of the factories' protest resolutions voiced the same concerns as the Mensheviks and the SRs: they condemned the closure of the Constituent Assembly, the Brest-Litovsk Treaty and the repression of the opposition. But this may only go to show that Mensheviks and SRs wrote these resolutions and either added these demands to those of the workers or else framed the workers' demands in their own terms. In any case, judging from the minutes of the factory meetings, the thing that exercised the workers most was a general feeling that the promise of a 'workers' revolution' — a promise that had led many of them to support the Bolsheviks in the autumn of 1917 — had not been fulfilled. As the striking workers of the Sormovo factory declared in June: 'The Soviet regime, having been established in our name, has become completely alien to us. It promised to bring the workers Socialism but has brought them empty factories and destitution.' This, as far as one can tell, was a general feeling shared by all the politicized workers — including a large proportion of the rank-and-file Bolsheviks, many of whom joined the Extraordinary Assemblies movement. Even the Vyborg district party committee in Petrograd, that bastion of militant Bolshevism in 1917, distributed the propaganda of the Extraordinary Assemblies to its members.[63]

By April 1918, Lenin had come round to the view that industry had to be brought under state control, as opposed to workers' control through collegial boards, with a traditional management structure ('one-man management') capable of restoring labour discipline. In 'The Immediate Tasks of Soviet Power', written that month, Lenin demanded that the working-class offensive against the capitalist industrial system should be halted in the broader interests of economic reconstruction. The expertise of the 'bourgeois' managers had to be tapped in the interests of the state; this, he admitted, meant using capitalist methods to construct the socialist order. It would be necessary to pay the bourgeois managers a high salary, and to restore their authority on the shop-floor, in order to ensure their co-operation with the Soviet regime, even though this went against the egalitarian principles of the Left. But, he argued, since the working class had not yet been trained for the tasks of management, this was a 'tribute' that had to be paid. The ideals of equality had to be sacrificed in the interests of efficiency.[64]

From this point on the Bolsheviks began to encourage the process of nationalization, the second major plank of War Communism after the war against the market. Until then, it had developed largely from below, on the initiative of the local Soviets and workers' organizations, and had assumed the character of a revolution in the factories with the workers using the process to impose their own control on the managers. Now, with Lenin's backing, it was taken over by the central state and its All-Russian Council for the Economy (VSNKh), which used the process to replace the workers' system of factory management with state-appointed ('bourgeois') managers aiming to restore discipline on the shop floor. This in effect meant shifting the centre of industrial power from the factory committees and the trade unions to the managerial apparatus of the party-state.[65]

The change in policy was clearly motivated by the growing threat from the working class. The easiest way to stop the factory organizations from acting as a channel for the workers' opposition movement was to bring them under central dictation. The Sovnarkom Decree of 28 June, by which most of Russia's large-scale industry was nationalized, came just three days before a general strike in Petrograd called by the Extraordinary Assemblies in protest against the Bolshevik regime. Although the decree had been in preparation for several weeks, there is no doubt that its precise timing was largely dictated by the need to pre-empt this strike.* Since 9 May, when the Cheka had opened fire on a crowd of demonstrating workers in the Petrograd suburb of Kolpino, there had been a spiral of strikes and workers' protests, industry had been brought to a virtual halt, and in those cities where free polling was allowed, the Mensheviks and SRs had swept the board. In short, it appeared as if the Petrograd strike, if it was allowed to go ahead, might easily develop into a national strike, perhaps leading to the downfall of the regime. This was also a critical moment in the civil war, with the Czechs and the SRs building up a power base on the Volga and widespread revolts in the Red rear. The Bolshevik Commissar for the Press, Volodarsky, was assassinated by an SR on 20 June. The Bolshevik leadership was afraid that this might be the start of a *coup d'état* by the SRs and the Mensheviks. They thought it was essential to bring the factories under state control and to head off the threat of a general strike in their last remaining stronghold of power.

The Decree on Nationalization transferred the management of the factories from the workers' organizations to the party apparatus. The party bosses used it to threaten the workers with dismissal if they went ahead with their planned strike. The strike organizers were arrested — especially those who were known to be connected with the SRs and the Mensheviks — and dozens of them shot as 'counter-revolutionaries'. Not surprisingly, given this intimidation, very few workers came out on to the streets for the general strike. The Bolsheviks drove home their victory: the Extraordinary Assemblies were outlawed, their leaders imprisoned and the dissident trade unions purged. The Mensheviks and SRs were now expelled from the Soviets, denounced as 'counter-revolutionaries', and driven underground. The last of the opposition newspapers were shut down. Even Gorky's *Novaia zhizn'*, which had helped to organize the Petrograd strike and which had often declared its support for the Extraordinary Assemblies,

---

* Another consideration was that many of the joint-stock companies affected by the decree were German-owned and that under the Brest-Litovsk Treaty any of these companies which were nationalized after 1 July would have to be fully indemnified (Malle, *Economic*, 59–61).

was finally closed on 16 July. 'We are heading for a total civil war,' a despondent Gorky wrote to Ekaterina, 'and it seems that the war will be a savage one . . . Oh, how hard it is to live in Russia! We are all so stupid — so fantastically stupid.'[66]

iii The Colour of Blood

Strange though it may seem, Lenin only became a Russian household name and image in September 1918 — and then only because he had nearly died. During the first ten months of Bolshevik rule, he was rarely seen in public. Shots fired at his car on New Year's Day had left the leader of the world revolution fearful for his life; and after that he seldom ventured out of his closely guarded quarters in the Smolny or the Kremlin. 'Nobody even knew Lenin's face,' Krupskaya wrote of those early weeks. 'In the evening he would often stroll around the Smolny and nobody would ever recognize him, since there were still no portraits of him then.'*[67]

All that changed on 30 August. Lenin had gone to the Mikhelson Factory in the southern Moscow suburbs to deliver a standard harangue to the workers on the need to defend the revolution, as was the custom of the Bolshevik leaders on Friday afternoons. Earlier that day news had reached him that Uritsky, the Bolshevik chief of the Petrograd Cheka, had been killed by an SR assassin, Leonid Kanegiser. Lenin's family had pleaded with him to call off his visit; but Lenin this time chose to go ahead. As he left the factory, a woman named Fanny Kaplan approached him through the crowd and shot three times at him. Lenin fell to the ground, while his bodyguards pursued the assassin. By the time he was brought back to the Kremlin, he seemed on the point of death. One of the bullets had lodged in his neck and he was bleeding profusely. Blood had entered one of his lungs. (It did not stop him from making sure his doctors were Bolsheviks.) For the next few days his life hung in the balance. But then he began to recover and by 25 September was declared well enough to go with Krupskaya to convalesce at Gorki, a village outside Moscow, where an estate had been requisitioned for his private use.

Lenin's quick recovery was declared a miracle in the Bolshevik press. He was hailed as a Christ-like figure, blessed with supernatural powers, who was not afraid to sacrifice his own life for the good of the people. Bukharin, the editor of *Pravda*, claimed fantastically that Lenin had refused help after the shooting and, 'with his pierced lungs still spilling blood', had gone back to work immediately so as to make sure that the 'locomotive' of the revolution did

---

* The first official portrait of Lenin only appeared in January 1918.

not stop. Zinoviev, in a special pamphlet for mass distribution, extolled Lenin as the son of a peasant who had 'made the revolution': 'He is the chosen one of millions. He is the leader by the grace of God. Such a leader is born once in 500 years in the life of mankind.' Dozens of other eulogies appeared in the press during the weeks after the shooting. The workers were said to be concerned only for one thing: that 'their leader' should recover. Lenin's poster-portrait began to appear in the streets. He himself appeared for the first time in a documentary film, *Vladimir Ilich's Kremlin Stroll*, shown throughout Moscow that autumn to dispel the growing rumour that he had been killed. It was the start of the Lenin cult — a cult designed by the Bolsheviks, apparently against Lenin's will,* to promote their leader as the 'people's Tsar'.[68]

The cult was reminiscent in some ways of the ancient cult of the divine Tsar. It went back to the medieval practice of canonizing princes who were prematurely killed whilst serving Russia. But the Lenin cult was new in the sense that it also fed into folklore myths of the popular leaders against the Tsar, such as Stenka Razin or Emelian Pugachev, blessed with magical and Christ-like powers. Here was the mixture of peasant Christianity and pagan myth that had long associated revolution with the hunt for truth and justice (*pravda*) in the popular consciousness. The orchestrators of the Lenin cult consciously played upon this theme. 'Lenin cannot be killed', declared one of his hagiographers on 1 September, 'because Lenin is the rising up of the oppressed. So long as the proletariat lives — Lenin lives.' Thus Lenin as the Workers' Christ. Another propagandist claimed that it had been the 'will of the proletariat' that had miraculously intervened, like some crucifix or a button on his chest, to deflect Kaplan's bullets from causing a fatal wound. Poems were published depicting Lenin as a martyr sent by God to suffer for the poor:

> You came to us, to ease
> Our excruciating torment,
> You came to us a leader, to destroy
> The enemies of the workers' movement.
> We will not forget your suffering,
> That you, our leader, endured for us.
> You stood a martyr . . .

A biography of Lenin for the workers was rushed out after the shooting. With the sort of title that one more readily associates with the cults of Stalin or Mao,

---

* According to Bonch-Bruevich, Lenin disapproved of the cult (Marxist ideology negated the significance of any individual in history) and put a brake on it when he recovered (Bonch-Bruevich, *Vospominaniia o Lenine*, 337–40).

The Great Leader of the Workers' Revolution, it depicted Lenin as supremely wise, a superhuman God-like figure, beloved by all the workers. A similar pamphlet for the peasants, *The Leader of the Rural Poor, V. I. Ul'ianov-Lenin*, was printed in 100,000 copies. It read a bit like the *Lives of the Saints*, the favourite reading of the peasants. All sorts of myths about Lenin, the fighter for truth and justice, began to circulate among the peasantry. Photographs of him appeared for the first time in remote villages. These were often placed in the 'red corner', the 'holy spot' inside the peasant hut where icons and portraits of the Tsar had been traditionally placed.[69]

Lenin's failed assassin, Fanny Kaplan, was a young Jewish woman and former Anarchist turned SR, who told the Cheka that the plot to kill him had been all her own. She said that Lenin had betrayed the revolution, and that 'by living longer, he merely postpones the ideal of socialism for decades to come'. Kaplan was detained in the same Lubianka cell as the British diplomat, Bruce Lockhart, whom the Bolsheviks had also arrested on suspicion of involvement in the plot. He described her entering the cell:

> She was dressed in black. Her hair was black, and her eyes, set in a fixed stare, had great black rings under them. Her face was colourless. Her features, strongly Jewish, were unattractive. She might have been any age between twenty and thirty-five. We guessed it was Kaplan. Doubtless the Bolsheviks hoped that she would give us some sign of recognition.

But she did not. Soon she was removed to the Kremlin, where she was almost certainly tortured before being shot (and her remains destroyed without trace) on 3 September. According to Angelica Balabanoff, soon to become the Secretary of the Comintern, Krupskaya wept at the thought that, in Kaplan, the first revolutionary had been killed by the revolutionary government.[70] One wonders how much she wept for the thousands of other revolutionaries shortly to be killed in revenge for the wounding of her husband.

Although Kaplan had always denied it, she was at once accused of working for the SRs and the Western Powers.* It was yet another 'proof' in the paranoiac theory that the regime was surrounded by a ring of enemies; and that, if it was to survive, a constant civil war had to be waged against them. The Bolshevik press called for mass reprisals. Having drummed up a rage of adulation

---

* It later emerged at the SR Trial in 1922 that Kaplan had been recruited by the SR Combat Organization, an underground terrorist outfit not officially connected with the SR Central Committee (most of whom had moved to Samara by August 1918) but supported by some of its members (e.g. Gots) who remained in Moscow. The Combat Organization assassinated the Bolshevik Commissar Volodarsky on 20 June. It also tried to murder Trotsky on his way to the Eastern Front; but he foiled the plan by changing trains at the last moment.

for the Bolshevik leader, it did not take much to turn this passion into violent hatred for his enemies. The mass circulation *Krasnaia gazeta* set the tone on 1 September:

> Without mercy, we will kill our enemies in scores of hundreds. Let them be thousands, let them drown themselves in their own blood. For the blood of Lenin and Uritsky let there be floods of bourgeois blood — more blood, as much as possible.

Peters, the deputy head of the Cheka, denounced Kaplan's shot at Lenin as an attack on the working class and called on the workers to 'crush the hydra of counter-revolution' by applying mass terror. The Commissar for Internal Affairs ordered the Soviets to 'arrest all SRs at once' and take 'hostages' *en masse* from the 'bourgeoisie and officers': these were to be executed on 'the least opposition'.[71] It was the signal for the start of the Red Terror.

*   *   *

The Red Terror did not come out of the blue. It was implicit in the regime from the start. As Kamenev and his supporters had warned the party in October, the resort to rule by terror was bound to follow from Lenin's violent seizure of power and his rejection of democracy. The Bolsheviks were forced to turn increasingly to terror to silence their political critics and subjugate a society they could not control by other means.

Lenin had always accepted the need to use terror in order to 'defend the revolution'. It was a weapon in the 'civil war'. Of course he was careful to distance himself in public from the institutions of the Terror — others put their signatures to its death warrants — and this helped to fuel the myth that Lenin was a good and gentle 'Tsar' who had nothing to do with the evil actions of his *oprichniki*. But behind the scenes Lenin was a stalwart champion of the Red Terror. On 26 October 1917 the Second Soviet Congress had passed a resolution proposed by Kamenev to abolish the death penalty. Lenin was absent from the session and, when told of it, flew into a rage:

> Nonsense, how can you make a revolution without firing squads? Do you expect to dispose of your enemies by disarming yourself? What other means of repression are there? Prisons? Who attaches significance to that during a civil war?

Lenin looked upon the use of terror as a means of class war against the 'bourgeoisie'. From the start, he had encouraged the mass terror of the lower classes against the rich and the privileged through the slogan 'Loot the Looters!' 'We must encourage the energy and the popular nature of the terror,' he wrote the following June.[72] As we saw in Chapter 11, this mass terror had given the Bolsheviks a strong base of emotional support among those elements of the poor who derived a certain satisfaction from seeing the rich and mighty fall regardless of whether it brought any improvement in their own lot. The early Cheka system was directly shaped by the local initiatives of this mass terror.

Since its establishment in November 1917, the Cheka had grown by leaps and bounds. When it moved into its first headquarters in Petrograd, the Cheka had a tiny staff. Dzerzhinsky, its chief, carried all its records in his briefcase. But by the end of March, when the government moved to Moscow and the Cheka occupied the infamous Lubianka building (formerly occupied by Lloyd's Insurance), it had a staff of more than 600, rising to 1,000 by June, not including the security troops. Provincial Chekas were slower to develop; but nearly all the provinces and most of the districts had a Cheka branch by September, when the order came down to unleash the Red Terror.[73]

The Cheka was a state within a state. There was scarcely any aspect of Soviet life, from the struggle against counter-revolution to the issuing of dog licences, that it did not cover. From the start it worked outside the law. The Commissariat of Justice struggled in vain to subordinate it to the courts. The knock on the door in the middle of the night, interrogations and imprisonment without charge, torture and summary executions — these were the methods of the Cheka. In the words of one of its founders:

> The Cheka is not an investigating commission, a court, or a tribunal. It is a fighting organ on the internal front of the civil war ... It does not judge, it strikes. It does not pardon, it destroys all who are caught on the other side of the barricade.[74]

During the early months of Bolshevik power the Cheka was not as murderous as it would later be. One source counted 884 executions listed in the press between December and July. The presence of the Left SRs — who joined the Cheka in January and remained in it even after they resigned from Sovnarkom in March — had a restraining influence. So too did public protests, especially from the workers, whose strike resolutions nearly always condemned the Terror. The time when the public lived in terror of the Cheka had still not arrived. Take, for example, the famous incident in the Moscow Circus. The humourless Chekists had taken exception to the anti-Soviet jokes of the clown Bim-Bom and burst into the middle of his act in order to arrest him. At first the audience thought it was all part of the act; but Bim-Bom fled and the Chekists shot him in the back. People began to scream and panic ensued. News of the shooting spread, giving rise to public condemnations of the Cheka Terror.

Hundreds turned out for the clown's funeral, which became in effect a demon-stration.[75]

During these early stages of the Terror arrests were often random. This stemmed from the chaotic nature of the newly emergent police state: virtually anyone could be arrested on denunciation by an enemy or on the whim of the local Cheka boss. All sorts of people filled the Cheka jails in these early months. Prince Lvov, who was arrested by the Cheka in Ekaterinburg, described his fellow prisoners in February as a 'very motley public', from princes and priests to ordinary peasants. Even Lenin's cousin, Viktor Ardashev, was arrested and shot by the Ekaterinburg Cheka in January 1918. The Bolshevik leader only found out some months later, when he ordered an official to convey his greetings to Ardashev and was told that he had been killed. It seems he was very fond of his cousin. But the affection was not returned. Ardashev was a prominent Kadet in Ekaterinburg and had organized a Civil Service strike against Lenin's government.[76]

∗   ∗   ∗

Two landmarks stand out in the progress of the Terror: the Left SR uprising and the murder of the imperial family.

The Left SR uprising was one of the most farcical episodes in the history of the revolution. It epitomized the naiveté of the Left SRs. The remarkable thing is that at its crucial moment the Left SRs might have over-thrown the Bolshevik regime: only, it appears, success was not part of their plan. This was not a *coup d'état* but — not unlike the Bolsheviks' own July uprising of 1917 — a suicidal act of public protest to galvanize 'the masses' against the regime. At no point did the Left SRs ever really think of taking power. They were only 'playing' at revolution.

The ideals that had brought the Left SRs into Sovnarkom in December all seemed to them to be in jeopardy by the following June. The freedom of the Soviets had been stifled by the dictatorship. The interests of the peasantry had been trampled on by the grain monopoly and the *kombedy*. Civil liberties had gone down the drain, along with the Left SRs' foolish notion that, by joining the Bolsheviks in government, they might restrain their abuses of power. But the greatest of their disappointments was the Brest-Litovsk Treaty. Like the Left Communists, the Left SRs believed that the treaty had transformed Russia into a vassal of the German Empire, and that it had given up the only hope of spreading socialism to the West through a revolutionary war against the imperial-ists. On the signing of the peace, the Left SRs condemned the Bolsheviks as traitors to the revolution and resigned from Sovnarkom, although they remained in the Soviet Executive and ironically the Cheka. Count Mirbach, the German Ambassador, who arrived in the latter half of April to resume diplomatic relations between Berlin and Moscow,* became a target of terrorist threats from the Left SRs, who were out to disrupt the peace.

Their campaign of noisy opposition reached its peak at the Fifth Soviet Congress, which opened in the Bolshoi Theatre on 4 July. Given the swing away from the Bolsheviks in the Soviets during the spring, the Left SRs had a large delegation, although not as many as they had expected, and it was suspected that the Bolsheviks had packed the congress with their own supporters. The Left SRs claimed to represent 'the masses' who had supported the 'Soviet revolution' but who felt betrayed by the Bolsheviks. Kamkov and Spiridonova, the party's two main leaders, denounced the Bolsheviks' policies. Top of their list was the 'shameful peace', which they said had sold out the workers and peasants of the Ukraine to the German imperialists. They vowed to resume a revolutionary war and waved their fists at the imperial loge, where, symbolically, Count Mirbach was in attendance.

Two days later he was assassinated. This act of terror was supposed to disrupt the peace by provoking Germany to attack Russia. Like the terrorists' bombs of the nineteenth century, it was also meant to spark a popular uprising against the regime. The decision to assassinate Mirbach had been taken by the Left SRs on the evening of the 4th, after the first session of the Congress, when it became clear that they could not win the majority they needed to bring about a change in the government's pro-German and anti-peasant policies. A Left SR motion of no-confidence in the Bolsheviks — designed to win the support of the Left Communists — had been defeated, and the Left SRs had walked out. Spiridonova — who despite her genteel appearance had never wanted for terrorist verve — masterminded Mirbach's murder. She recruited Yakov Bliumkin, a Left SR Chekist suitably placed in charge of counter-espionage against the Germans, and his photographer, Nikolai Andreev, to do the bloody deed. In the afternoon of the 6th they arranged a meeting with the Ambassador on the pretext of discussing the case of a Count Robert Mirbach, believed to be a relative of his, arrested on suspicion of spying. After a brief conversation, the Chekists pulled out revolvers and opened fire. Their shots missed and Mirbach began to escape. But Bliumkin threw a bomb after him, causing fatal injuries. The two men escaped through a window, Bliumkin taking a bullet in the leg, and fled in a waiting car to the Pokrovsky Barracks of the Cheka Combat Detachment, commanded by Dmitrii Popov, another prominent Left SR in the Cheka, which became the headquarters of the uprising. Lenin was at once summoned to the German Embassy to apologize for the murder. Never before in diplomatic history had a Russian head of state been humiliated in this way.

Later that afternoon Dzerzhinsky went to the Pokrovsky Barracks and

---

* Soviet Russia set up its first foreign embassy in Berlin at this time.

demanded that Bliumkin and Andreev be turned over for arrest. But the Cheka Combat Detachment arrested him instead and declared its allegiance to the uprising. The insurgents then occupied the Cheka headquarters at the Lubianka, capturing Latsis, Dzerzhinsky's makeshift replacement. This was not a street uprising but a palace coup inside the Cheka: it owed everything to the uncharacteristic negligence of the Bolsheviks. The Left SRs had been allowed to fill seven of the twenty seats in the Cheka Collegium. Dzerzhinsky had appointed the Left SR Alexandrovich as his own deputy and allowed him to build up the Combat Detachment as an exclusively Left SR unit. On the evening of the 6th Alexandrovich — who according to Spiridonova had known nothing of the plot to murder Mirbach and had only joined the Left SR uprising on the 6th itself — took command of the insurgent troops.

At this point there was virtually nothing to prevent the Left SRs from seizing power. They had 2,000 well-armed troops in the capital compared to the 700 loyal to the regime. The bulk of the Latvian Rifles, the only crack troops in the capital upon which the Bolsheviks could rely, had been celebrating St John's Day at the Khodynka Field — scene of the disaster on the coronation of the last Tsar in 1896 — on the outskirts of the capital. The Latvians were unable to return to Moscow because of fog, torrential rain and thunderstorms. Lenin was in a state of utter panic: like Kerensky in October, he had no troops to defend his regime. Vatsetis, the Latvian commander placed in charge of the government's defence, recalls being summoned to the Kremlin after midnight, where 'the atmosphere was like the Front in the theatre of a war'. Lenin's first question to him was: 'Comrade, can we hold out till morning?'[77]

But the Left SRs showed no inclination to press home their military advantage. They were much less interested in seizing power themselves than they were in calling for a popular uprising to force the Bolsheviks to change their policies. The Left SRs had no idea where this uprising would end up: they were happy to leave that to the 'revolutionary creativity of the masses'. They were the 'poets of the revolution' and, like all poets, were anarchists at heart. At every stage of their relationship with the Bolsheviks, the Left SRs had been outsmarted by them; and even now, when they had them at their mercy, they soon lost the upper hand. Instead of marching on the Kremlin, the Left SR leaders went to the Bolshoi Theatre, where the Soviet Congress was in session. Spiridonova gave a long and characteristically hysterical speech denouncing the Bolshevik regime. Yet while she spoke the guards in charge of security at the congress surrounded the building and sealed off all the exits. The Bolshevik delegates were allowed to leave but all the others were arrested. The Left SRs had walked into a trap.

Later that night the Bolsheviks recaptured the Lubianka. Then, in the small hours of the morning, Vatsetis's forces overcame the Combat Detachment in the Pokrovsky Barracks. Vatsetis was rewarded by the grateful Bolsheviks with

10,000 roubles and the Command of the Eastern Front: in September he was given the command of the whole Red Army. And yet the Left SRs were defeated less by him than they were by themselves. As their own party comrade Steinberg put it, they were beaten 'not because their leaders were not brave enough, but because it was not at all their purpose to overthrow the government'.

Several hundred rebels were arrested. Alexandrovich and twelve other leaders of the Combat Detachment were summarily executed on the 7th. Most of the other Left SR leaders were imprisoned and placed on trial in November, when, given the climate at that time, they received extraordinarily lenient sentences (some of the Bolsheviks did not want to punish them at all) and indeed were later amnestied. Spiridonova was sentenced to a year's imprisonment, and then amnestied, only to be rearrested in February 1919, declared a lunatic and incarcerated in the Kremlin barracks. But she soon escaped, having won the sympathy of her guards. Bliumkin also managed to escape and later joined the Bolsheviks. As a party, the Left SRs were finished after the failed uprising of July. Its activists were forced out of the Soviets and driven underground. Hundreds were imprisoned or executed.[78] Others — who had opposed the July uprising — broke away to form a new party called the Revolutionary Communists. With the removal of the Left SRs, who alone had acted as a brake on the lawlessness of the Cheka, a new wave of terror now began. Ironically, given their involvement in the Cheka, the Left SRs were its first victims.

*   *   *

After his abdication in March 1917, Nikolai Romanov (as he was now called) had been kept under house (or rather palace) arrest along with his family and their retinue at Tsarskoe Selo. Apart from the limitations on their movement, they suffered few privations: the huge costs of feeding and dining all of them were kept from the press for fear of causing public outrage.[79] Their lives in these months were not unlike a long Edwardian house party — only with the difference that the 'house guests' were confined to certain rooms and, instead of the normal hunting, had to limit their exercise to a short walk around the garden supervised by guards.

Nicholas showed no real signs of missing power. Judging from his diaries, these were among the happiest days of his whole life. Liberated from the burdens of office, which he had always unhappily borne, he was free to pursue the private bourgeois lifestyle he had always hankered for. Kerensky, who visited the former Tsar on several occasions at Tsarskoe Selo (the Tsarina insisted on calling him Kedrinsky), later wrote that 'all those who watched him in his captivity were unanimous in saying that Nicholas II seemed generally to be very good-tempered and appeared to enjoy his new manner of life. It seemed as if a heavy burden had fallen from his shoulders and that he was greatly relieved.' Nicholas filled these quiet days with his family in games of dominoes, reading aloud *The Count of Monte Cristo*, gardening, rowing, tennis and prayers. Never before had he slept so well.[80]

This first stage of their captivity came to an end in the middle of August, when the imperial family was evacuated to the Siberian town of Tobolsk. Kerensky was concerned for their personal safety. There had always been the very real danger that an angry crowd might break into the palace and wreak a savage vengeance on the former Tsar: there had been one such attempt back in March by a group of soldiers from Petrograd. This danger seemed to be on the increase after the July Days. It had originally been intended to send the Tsar and his family to England, where George V, Nicholas's cousin, had invited him in March. But the Petrograd Soviet was adamantly opposed to the idea, insisting that the former Tsar should be imprisoned in the Peter and Paul Fortress. Moreover, George V withdrew his invitation for fear of alienating the Labour Party, although this was for a long time covered up by the shamefaced Windsors.* So it was resolved to send them to Tobolsk instead, a provincial backwater far from the influence of the revolution, where they took up a relatively comfortable residence in the house of the former governor. In addition to the numerous ladies and gentlemen of their suite, the imperial family were accompanied by two valets, six chambermaids, ten footmen, three cooks, four assistant cooks, a butler, a wine steward, a nurse, a clerk, a barber and two pet spaniels.[81]

The situation of the former royals took a turn for the worse in the early months of 1918. They noticed it in the growing rudeness of their guards, increased restrictions on their movements and the disappearance of luxuries, such as butter and coffee, which up until now they had taken for granted. The changes were connected with developments in the nearby industrial city of Ekaterinburg. A Soviet Congress of the Urals Region held there in February had elected a Bolshevik presidium led by Fillip Goloshchekin, a veteran Bolshevik and friend of Sverdlov. The Ekaterinburg Bolsheviks were well known for their militancy. They were hostile to the relative comfort in which the Tsar had so far been held and were determined to get him transferred to their own control — some with a view to his imprisonment, others with a view to his execution.

Goloshchekin pleaded with Sverdlov to let him have the Tsar, claiming that in Tobolsk the danger was greater that he might escape. There were rumours of various monarchist plots — some of them real, some imagined, and some invented — to liberate the imperial family. Sverdlov did not say no – the Urals' Bolsheviks were not the sort to mess around – but in fact there was a secret plan, ordered by the Central Committee, to bring the Tsar back to Moscow,

---

* The refusal of the British royal family to visit Russia for the next seventy-five years because of the murder of the Romanovs may thus seem to many readers to contain a large dose of typical British hypocrisy.

where Trotsky was planning a great show trial for him, in the manner of Louis XVI, with himself in the role of chief prosecutor. Trotsky proposed:

> an open court that would unfold a picture of the entire reign (peasant policy, labour, nationalities, culture, the two wars, etc.). The proceedings would be broadcast to the nation by radio; in the villages accounts of the proceedings would be read and commented upon daily.[82]

With this aim in mind, in early April Sverdlov ordered the commissar, Vasilii Yakovlev, to bring Nicholas and, if possible, the rest of his family back to Moscow alive.* Yakovlev was told to travel via Ekaterinburg so as not to arouse the suspicions of the Bolsheviks there who, if they found out his real mission, would have kidnapped and executed the former Tsar. Indeed, in April the Soviet of the Urals Region passed a resolution to that effect; and Zaslavsky, one of the Ekaterinburg commissars, prepared an ambush to kidnap the Tsar. 'We should not be wasting our time on the Romanovs,' Zaslavsky said to Yakovlev on his arrival in Tobolsk, 'we should be finishing them off.'[83]

The journey from Tobolsk to Ekaterinburg was to be full of risks. The spring thaw was just beginning, flooding the roads; and the Tsarevich, whose haemophilia had recently returned, was too sick to be moved. Yakovlev was told by Moscow to leave the rest of the family behind and set off with the ex-Tsar alone. But Alexandra would not be parted from Nicholas,† and in the end the two of them set off together, minus four of the children (who would follow later), in open carts towards Tiumen, the nearest railway junction, 170 miles away. On the way they passed through Pokrovskoe, Rasputin's native village. Alexandra noted in her diary: 'stood long before our friend's house, saw his family & friends looking out of the windows at us'.[84]

Once they had boarded the train at Tiumen, Yakovlev became suspicious of the local Bolsheviks. He had heard that a cavalry detachment was planning to attack the train on its way to Ekaterinburg and kidnap his royal charges — the 'cargo', as he referred to them in his coded messages to Moscow. So he went on a roundabout route via Omsk to the east. This strengthened the suspicions of the Ekaterinburg Bolsheviks that he was planning to save the Tsar, perhaps

---

* Until recently the role of Yakovlev was something of a mystery. It was argued both that he was working for the Bolsheviks and that he was a White secret agent planning to rescue the imperial family. New evidence now puts his role as an agent of Moscow beyond dispute, although it is true that in July, whilst in command of the Second Red Army on the Eastern Front, he defected to the Whites (see Radzinsky, *Last Tsar*, ch. 11).

† The imperial couple were afraid that he would be taken to Moscow and forced to sign the Brest-Litovsk Treaty. The fact that they believed that the Bolsheviks should either need or want his signature for this is a telling sign of how far removed they had become from political reality (see Wilton, *Last Days of the Romanovs*, 206).

taking him to Japan. A battle of telegrams followed, with both Yakovlev and Goloshchekin urging Sverdlov in Moscow to give them sole control of the ex-Tsar. Sverdlov this time gave in to Goloshchekin, ordering Yakovlev to turn back and proceed to Ekaterinburg. It seems that Goloshchekin's assurance that the imperial couple would not be harmed was enough to persuade Sverdlov to let this powerful party leader finally have his way. 'Have come to an agreement with the Uralites,' Sverdlov cabled Yakovlev. 'They have taken measures and given guarantees.' Yakovlev agreed but warned prophetically that, if the ex-Tsar was taken to Ekaterinburg, he would probably never leave alive. Sverdlov made no reply.[85]

The imperial couple arrived in Ekaterinburg on 30 April (the rest of the family followed on 23 May). They were met at the station by an angry mob and imprisoned in a large white house commandeered the day before from Nikolai Ipatev, a retired businessman. The Bolsheviks called it the House of Special Designation — and it was there that the Romanovs would die. The regime in the house was strict and humiliating. A large fence was built around it to prevent communication with the outside world. Later the windows were painted over. The guards were hostile. They accompanied the Empress and her daughters to the lavatory; scrawled obscenities on the walls; and helped themselves to the prisoners' belongings, stored in the garden shed. Except for meals, the prisoners were confined to their rooms. To while away the hours, Nicholas, for the first time in his life, read *War and Peace*.

It was in the first week of July that the decision was taken to execute all the captive Romanovs. Right up until its final collapse, the Soviet regime always insisted that the murder was carried out on the sole initiative of the Bolsheviks in Ekaterinburg. But the evidence that has since emerged from the archives shows conclusively that the order came from the party leadership in Moscow. This in fact had been known in the West from an entry in Trotsky's diary of 1935 in which he recalled a conversation with Sverdlov shortly after the murder:

Speaking with Sverdlov, I asked in passing, 'Oh yes, and where is the Tsar?' 'Finished,' he replied. 'He has been shot.' 'And where is the family?' 'The family along with him.' 'All?' I asked, apparently with a trace of surprise. 'All,' Sverdlov replied. 'Why?' He awaited my reaction. I made no reply. 'And who decided the matter?' I enquired. 'We decided it here. Ilich [Lenin] thought that we should not leave the Whites a live banner, especially under the present difficult circumstances . . .' I asked no more questions and considered the matter closed.[86]

The new archival evidence merely fills in the details. Goloshchekin arrived in

Moscow at the end of June for the Fifth Soviet Congress. His view that the Romanovs should be killed was well known. Consultations with Lenin took place and this idea was accepted in principle without a firm date being set. On 16 July Goloshchekin, having returned to Ekaterinburg, sent a coded telegram to Sverdlov and Lenin via Zinoviev informing them that the execution had to be carried out without further delay 'due to military circumstances'.[87] The Czech Legion had surrounded the city and, with only a few hundred Red Guards at their disposal, the local Bolsheviks saw little chance of safely evacuating the imperial family. Later the same day, Moscow confirmed via Perm that the execution was to go ahead immediately. The confirmation may well have come directly from Lenin himself.[88]

Why did the Bolsheviks change their mind and go ahead with the murder, reversing their earlier decision to put Nicholas on trial in Moscow? The military considerations were certainly real enough, contrary to what many historians have said. The Czechs captured Ekaterinburg on 25 July, eight days after the murder; but they might easily have done so several days before, since the city was surrounded and they had many more troops than the Reds. But it is doubtful that either they, or any of the Whites, would have wanted to make such a sad and discredited figure as Nicholas their 'live banner'. A martyred Tsar was more useful to them than a live one who was politically dead. Both Denikin and Kolchak were intelligent enough to realize that a monarchist restoration was out of the question after 1917, although both had monarchists among their advisers. Perhaps the Bolsheviks did not understand this. Perhaps they were victims of their own propaganda that the Whites were monarchists to a man.

But even so, there is no doubt that the murder was also carried out for other reasons. The party leaders were by this stage having second thoughts about the wisdom of a trial. Not that there was any real prospect of finding the ex-Tsar innocent. Trotsky was a master of the political trial, as his own in 1906 had shown, and he would no doubt show with brilliant logic how, as an autocrat who claimed the right to rule in person, Nicholas was himself to blame for the crimes of his regime. Nor was there any prospect of the ex-Tsar being allowed the legal nicety of able lawyers to defend him: the Russian equivalents of Malesherbes and de Sèze — Louis XVI's lawyers at his trial — were all in prison or exile by this stage. It was rather the more fundamental problem — one raised by Saint-Just against Louis's trial — that putting the deposed monarch in the dock at all was to presuppose the *possibility* of his innocence. And in that case the moral legitimacy of the revolution would itself be open to question. To put Nicholas on trial would also be to put the Bolsheviks on trial. The recognition of this was the point where they passed from the realm of law into the realm of terror. In the end it was not a question of proving the ex-Tsar's guilt — after all, as Saint-Just had put it, 'one cannot reign innocently' — but a question of eliminating him as a rival source of legitimacy. Nicholas had to die so that Soviet power could live.

On 4 July the local Cheka had taken over the responsibility of guarding the Romanovs at the Ipatev House. Yakov Yurovsky, the local Cheka boss who led the execution squad, was one of Lenin's most trusted lieutenants — ruthless, honest, intelligent and cruel. His brother said he 'enjoyed oppressing people'.[89] The Tsar's murderer was also a Jew — a fact for which the Jews would pay in future. On the night of the murder, 16–17 July, at about 1.30 a.m., Yurovsky awoke the Tsar's physician and ordered him to rouse the rest of the prisoners. At 2 a.m. all eleven of them were led down the stairs to the basement. Nicholas carried the Tsarevich, followed by the Empress and her daughters, the Tsar's physician and the rest of the retinue. Anastasia carried the King Charles spaniel Joy. On their request, two chairs were brought in for the Empress and Alexis, who was still recovering from his recent attack of bleeding. None of them seemed aware of what was about to happen: they had been told that there had been shooting in the town and it was safer for them in the basement. After a few minutes, Yurovsky entered the room with the execution squad — six Hungarians, usually described as 'Latvians', and five Russians. Each had been assigned to shoot a particular victim, but when they entered the room it turned out that they were not facing the right person and the room was too small, with murderers and victims practically standing on each other's toes, for the necessary changes to be made: it was this that partly caused the confusion that followed. Yurovsky read out the order to shoot the Romanovs. Nicholas asked him to repeat it: his last words were 'What? What?' Then the firing began. Yurovsky shot Nicholas point blank with a Colt. The Empress also died instantly. Bullets ricocheted around the room, which filled up with smoke. When the firing finished, after several minutes, Alexis lay alive in a pool of blood: Yurovsky finished him off with two shots in the head. Anastasia, who also showed signs of life, was stabbed several times with a bayonet.[90]

Given all the evidence that has come to light, it is inconceivable that any of the Romanovs survived this ordeal.* After the murder the bodies were driven off in a lorry and dumped in a series of nearby mineshafts. These turned out to be too shallow to conceal the bodies and the next day they were removed. But on the way to some deeper mines the lorry got stuck in the mud and it was decided to bury the corpses in the ground. Sulphuric acid was poured on their faces to hide the identity of the corpses should they be discovered. This proved unnecessary — and ineffective. The graves were not discovered until after the collapse of the Soviet regime. But by this time, DNA analysis of the bones,

---

* The only certain survivor was the spaniel Joy.

brought back to Britain in 1992, was enough to establish beyond doubt that they belonged to the Romanovs.[91]

News of the execution reached Lenin the next day during a session of Sovnarkom. The people's commissars were engaged in a detailed discussion of a draft decree for health protection when Sverdlov came in with the news. The brief announcement of the Tsar's death was met with general silence. Then Lenin said: 'We shall now proceed to read the draft decree article by article.'[92]

The official announcement appeared in *Izvestiia* on 19 July. It mentioned only the death of the ex-Tsar, claiming that the 'wife and son of Nicholas Romanov have been sent to a safe place'. The Bolsheviks, it seems, were afraid to acknowledge that they had murdered the children and servants — all of them, after all, innocent people — lest it should lose them public sympathy. But in fact public reaction was remarkably subdued. 'The population of Moscow received the news with amazing indifference,' noted Lockhart. Rumours that the rest of the family had been killed elicited few emotions. Only the monarchists were moved. Brusilov, a monarchist of the heart and a Republican only of the mind, refused to believe that the rumours were true and prayed every night for the 'missing Romanovs'. The lie was kept going until 1926, when the publication of Sokolov's book in Paris, *The Murder of the Imperial Family*, based on the findings of a commission set up by Kolchak, made this no longer tenable. But in the meantime the legend had been born that perhaps not all the Romanovs had died. It is a legend that still lives today, despite the huge weight of evidence against it. All of which merely goes to show that there is more currency — and more profit — in fiction than in history.[93]

Why has the murder of the Romanovs assumed such significance in the history of the revolution? It could be said that they were only a few individuals, whereas revolutions are about the millions. This is the argument of Marxist historians, who have tended to treat this episode as a minor side-show to the main event. E. H. Carr, for example, gave it no more than a single sentence in his three-volume history of the revolution. But this is to miss the deeper significance of the murder. It was a declaration of the Terror. It was a statement that from now on individuals would count for nothing in the civil war. Trotsky had once said: 'We must put an end once and for all to the papist-Quaker babble about the sanctity of human life.' And that is what the Cheka did. Shortly after the murder Dzerzhinsky told the press:

The Cheka is the defence of the revolution as the Red Army is; as in the civil war the Red Army cannot stop to ask whether it may harm particular individuals, but must take into account only one thing, the victory of the revolution over the bourgeoisie, so the Cheka must defend the revolution and conquer the enemy even if its sword falls occasionally on the heads of the innocent.[94]

The Bolsheviks murdered other Romanovs after the execution of the former Tsar.* Six members of the old dynasty were murdered on the following night at Alapaevsk in the northern Urals. But in a sense their deaths were now just one small part of the Red Terror.

*   *   *

One of the most terrifying aspects of the Terror was its random nature. The knock on the door at midnight could come to almost anyone. The Bolsheviks justified the Terror as a civil war against the counter-revolution. But they never made clear who those 'counter-revolutionaries' were. Indeed, in so far as the Terror was driven by the regime's own paranoiac fear that it was surrounded by hostile enemies working together to overthrow it — in this view the Kaplan plot was all part and parcel of the SR and Menshevik opposition, the White Guard reaction, the Allied intervention, Savinkov's uprising in Yaroslavl',† the peasant uprisings and workers' strikes — virtually anyone could qualify as a 'counter-revolutionary'. In this sense the Terror was a war by the regime against the whole of society — a means of terrorizing it into submission. 'Terror', Engels wrote, 'is needless cruelties perpetrated by terrified men.'

A tour of the Cheka jails would reveal a vast array of different people. One former inmate of the Butyrka jail in Moscow recalls seeing politicians, ex-judges, merchants, traders, officers, prostitutes, children,‡ priests, professors, students, poets, dissident workers and peasants — in short a cross-section of society. The Petrograd poetess Gippius wrote that 'there was literally not a single family that had not had someone seized, taken away, or disappear completely' as a result of the Red Terror, and for the circles in which she moved this is almost certainly true.[95]

---

* The Grand Duke Mikhail, Nicholas's brother, had been killed in June.

† Boris Savinkov, Kerensky's Deputy War Minister during the Kornilov episode, led an uprising of army officers in the town of Yaroslavl', to the north of Moscow, on 6 July. It gained the support of the local workers and peasants and spread briefly to the neighbouring towns of Murom and Rybinsk. Soviet troops regained Yaroslavl' on 21 July. They shot 350 officers and civilians in reprisal for the revolt, which was said to be the joint work of the SRs, the White Guards, the Czechs and the Allies. Savinkov's underground organization, the Union for the Defence of the Fatherland and Freedom, was linked with the National Centre in Moscow, which supported the Volunteer Army. It also received money from the Czechs and the Allies — who were both under the illusion that Savinkov's sole purpose was to raise a new Russian army to resume the war against the Central Powers. There is no evidence linking the Allies with Savinkov's plot to overthrow the Bolsheviks.

‡ A government inspection of Moscow jails in March 1920 found that children under the age of seventeen comprised 5 per cent of the prison population (*Izvestiia gosudarstvennogo kontrolia*, 4, 1920: 7–10).

Many of the Cheka's victims were 'bourgeois hostages' rounded up without charge and held in readiness for summary execution in reprisal for some alleged counter-revolutionary act. Of course most of them were not 'bourgeois' at all. The round-ups were much too crude for that, sometimes consisting of no more than the random arrest of people on a stretch of street blocked off at each end by Cheka guards. People were arrested merely for being near the scene of a 'bourgeois provocation' (e.g. a shooting or a crime); or as the relatives and known acquaintances of 'bourgeois' suspects. One old man was arrested because during a general raid the Cheka found on his person a photograph of a man in court uniform: it was the picture of a deceased relative taken in the 1870s. Many people were arrested because someone (and one was enough) had denounced them as 'bourgeois counter-revolutionaries'. Such denunciations often arose from petty squabbles and vendettas. Yakov Khoelson, a military inspector, was arrested in November, for example, when two people jumped ahead of him in the queue for the Moscow Opera. They shouted 'provocation!' and complained to the doorman that Khoelson and two others had jumped the queue. The Cheka was called and Khoelson was arrested. Nikolai Kochargin, a petty official, was arrested in the same month after a dispute with a friend at work who had repaid him a loan in forged coupons. Kochargin went to the Cheka to com-plain — only to find himself arrested the next day when his debtor denounced him as a trader in forged coupons.[96]

Arbitrary arrests were particularly common in the provinces, where the local Cheka bosses were very much their 'own men' pursuing their own civil wars of terror. But the principle urged by Lenin — that it was better to arrest a hundred innocent people than to run the risk of letting one enemy of the regime go free — ensured that wholesale and indiscriminate arrests became a general part of the system. Peshekhonov, Kerensky's Minister of Food, who was imprisoned in the Lubianka jail, recalls a conversation with a fellow prisoner, a trade unionist from Vladimir, who could not work out why he had been arrested. All he had done was to come to Moscow and check into a hotel. 'What is your name?' another prisoner asked. 'Smirnov', he replied, one of the most common Russian names:

'The name, then, was the cause of your arrest,' said a man coming towards us. 'Let me introduce myself. My name too is Smirnov, and I am from Kaluga. At the Taganka there were seven of us Smirnovs, and they say there are many more at the Butyrka . . . At the Taganka they somehow managed to find out that a certain Smirnov, a Bolshevik from Kazan, had disappeared with a large sum of money. Moscow was notified and orders were issued to the militia to arrest all Smirnovs arriving in Moscow and send them to the Cheka. They are trying to catch the Smirnov from Kazan.'

'But I have never been to Kazan,' protested the Vladimir Smirnov. 'Neither have I,' replied the one from Kaluga. 'I am not even a Bolshevik, nor do I intend to become one. But here I am.'[97]

Reading the letters of the victims' families to Dzerzhinsky, one gets a better sense of the human tragedy that lay behind each arrest. Elena Moshkina wrote on 5 November. Her husband, Volodya, aged twenty-seven, an engineer in the Moscow Soviet, had been imprisoned as a 'bourgeois hostage' in the Butyrka because it was alleged he belonged to the Union of Houseowners. Moshkin had joined the union on behalf of his mother; but her house had been sold in 1911 and he had since resigned. Elena pleaded to take his place in jail, since they had two small children to support and only Volodya's salary to live on. They could not pay the 5,000 roubles demanded as a ransom by the local Cheka boss, who had admitted that they had no evidence against her husband and that he was merely 'a hostage of the rich'. Moshkina's letter came to nothing: it was marked in red pencil 'into the archive'.[98]

Liubov Kuropatkina wrote to Dzerzhinsky on 18 November. Her husband, Pavel, had been imprisoned 'as a bourgeois hostage' in Pskov. The soldiers of his regiment had twice elected him as their officer, once after February and once after October, despite his tsarist rank as a corporal and his senior age (sixty-eight). He had led the regiment on the Pulkovo Heights against Kerensky's troops after the Bolshevik seizure of power. For this, the soldiers had allowed him to keep his savings, 50,000 roubles, which he then donated to the Soviet at Krasnoe Selo. In April 1918 Kuropatkin fell ill with malaria and the couple retired to a village near Pskov to farm a small allotment. He had been arrested before the first harvest, and his wife was now left on her own to feed seven small children and her very old father. She had two grown-up sons in the Red Army, and another who had disappeared as a prisoner of war in Hungary. 'My own health has always been poor, I cannot do physical work, and the constant worry for the safety of my husband has broken me. I cannot travel the sixty *versty* to the jail in Kholm to visit him.' Her letter was also marked 'into the archive'.[99]

Nadezhda Brusilova was another letter writer to Dzerzhinsky. Brusilov had been arrested shortly after midnight on 13 August and imprisoned in the Lubianka. His apartment must have been under surveillance because earlier that evening he had been approached by two agents of the Komuch who had offered him a large sum of money to go with them to Samara and help to lead the fledgling People's Army. Brusilov had refused; but this did not prevent him from being arrested (nor the Komuch agents from being shot). During the raid the

Chekists confiscated all Brusilov's medals: it must have been a torment for him to lose these final fragments of his broken past. Brusilov was never charged. Nadezhda was told that he had not even been arrested, but had merely been 'taken prisoner' to prevent him falling into the hands of the regime's opponents. 'His name is too popular,' one Chekist told her. Dzerzhinsky himself explained to Brusilov that he had been detained because they had 'evidence' that Lockhart was planning to stage a coup in Moscow and pronounce the general a 'dictator'. Brusilov replied that he had never met the British agent, whereupon Dzerzhinsky candidly acknowledged: 'All the same, we cannot take the risk, people would rally behind your name.'* When Brusilov asked what he could do to speed up his release, the Cheka leader was just as frank again: 'Write your memoirs on the former army and abuse the old regime.' The old general was finally released in October and placed under house arrest. It is a measure of the suffering he must have gone through, without any medicine for his injured leg, that even this great patriot should beg his captors to let him and his family emigrate from Russia and settle in 'some neutral country'.[100]

Conditions in the Cheka prisons were generally much worse than in any tsarist jail. A government inspection of the Moscow Taganka jail in October 1918, for example, found overcrowded cells, no water, grossly inadequate rations and heating, and sewage dumped in the courtyard. Nearly half the 1,500 inmates were chronically sick, 10 per cent of them with typhus. Corpses were found in the cells. The Peter and Paul Fortress, that great symbol of the tsarist prison state, was now an even more forbidding place. The Menshevik Dan, who had been imprisoned there in 1896, found himself once again behind its bars in the spring of 1921. Whereas before there had been one man to a cell, there were now two or three; and women were imprisoned there for the first time. Dan was held with hundreds of other prisoners in the basement, where the food stores had been previously kept. Four men shared each tiny cell. The walls 'dripped with damp', there was no light and the prisoners, fed only once a day, were never allowed out for exercise.[101] Compared to this the old prison regime in the fortress had been like a holiday camp. Most of its inmates before 1917 had been allowed to receive food and cigarettes, clothing, books and letters from their relatives.

Many of the Cheka's most notorious techniques had been borrowed from the tsarist police. The use of provocateurs, stool-pigeons and methods of torture to extract confessions and denunciations came straight out of the

---

* Brusilov's brother, Boris, was also arrested at this time, along with three other members of his family. They were 'hostages' and were ordered to be executed if Brusilov joined the anti-Bolsheviks. Boris was ill with influenza and had been literally taken from his sick-bed. He died in prison a few days after his arrest. Whilst in jail he received no medical treatment.

Okhrana's book.* This was hardly surprising — and not just because, in Flaubert's words, 'in every revolutionary there is hidden a gendarme'. The Bolsheviks had sat in tsarist jails for years. Literally they had learned the system from the inside. And they now applied it with a vengeance. Dzerzhinsky had spent half his adult life in tsarist prisons and labour camps before he became head of the Cheka. It was not surprising if he set out to inflict on his victims the same cruelty he had suffered in those years. Hatred and indifference to human suffering were to varying degrees ingrained in the minds of all the Bolshevik leaders — and this was no doubt in part a legacy of their prison years.

The ingenuity of the Cheka's torture methods was matched only by the Spanish Inquisition. Each local Cheka had its own speciality. In Kharkov they went in for the 'glove trick' — burning the victim's hands in boiling water until the blistered skin could be peeled off: this left the victims with raw and bleeding hands and their torturers with 'human gloves'. The Tsaritsyn Cheka sawed its victims' bones in half. In Voronezh they rolled their naked victims in nail-studded barrels. In Armavir they crushed their skulls by tightening a leather strap with an iron bolt around their head. In Kiev they affixed a cage with rats to the victim's torso and heated it so that the enraged rats ate their way through the victim's guts in an effort to escape. In Odessa they chained their victims to planks and pushed them slowly into a furnace or a tank of boiling water. A favourite winter torture was to pour water on the naked victims until they became living ice statues. Many Chekas preferred psychological forms of torture. One had the victims led off to what they thought was their execution, only to find that a blank was fired at them. Another had the victims buried alive, or kept in a coffin with a corpse. Some Chekas forced their victims to watch their loved ones being tortured, raped or killed.

Needless to say, there were many sadists in the Chekas. They treated the tortures as sport, vying with each other to perform the most extreme violence. Some victims recall the Chekists standing about and laughing at their torture. There were even 'human hunts'. Most of the sadists were young men in their teens brutalized by war and revolution. Many were out to prove their 'hardness'. There is also evidence to suggest that many of them may have been non-Russians — Poles, Latvians, Armenians and Jews — in so far as they made up a high proportion of the Cheka. Lenin certainly favoured their employment in the Cheka, claiming that the Russians were 'too soft' to carry out the 'harsh measures' of the Terror. Yet many of the Cheka's torture methods were reminiscent of the brutal forms of killing employed by the Russian peasantry.

* During the 1980s the KGB still trained its recruits with Okhrana manuals (see Kalugin, *Vid s Lubianki*, 35).

Women were also not exempt from the perpetration of sadistic violence. Vera Grebennikova, for example, was alleged to have killed over 700 people, many of them with her bare hands, during two months in Odessa. Rebecca Platinina-Maisel in Arkhangelsk killed over a hundred, including the whole family of her ex-husband whom she crucified in an act of savage revenge.

Such was the brutalizing effect of this relentless violence that not a few Chekists ended up insane. Bukharin said that psychopathic disorders were an occupational hazard of the Chekist profession. Many Chekists hardened themselves to the killings by heavy drinking or drug abuse. For example, the notorious sadist Saenko, the Kharkov master of the 'glove trick', was a cocaine addict. To distance themselves from the violence the Chekists also developed a gangster-like slang for the verb to kill: they talked of 'shooting partridges', of 'sealing' a victim, or giving him the *natsokal* (an onomatopoeia of the trigger action).[102]

Executions were the final product of this machinery of terror. Tens of thousands of summary executions were carried out in courtyards and cellars, or in deserted fields on the edge of towns, during the years of the civil war. Whole prisons would be 'emptied' by the Cheka before a town was abandoned to the Whites. At night the cities tried to sleep to the sound of people being shot. The Bolsheviks themselves, however, did not lose much sleep. In 1919, during a session of Sovnarkom, Lenin wrote a note and passed it to Dzerzhinsky: 'How many dangerous counter-revolutionaries do we have in prison?' Dzerzhinsky scribbled, 'About 1,500' and returned the note. Lenin looked at it, placed the sign of a cross by the figure, and gave it back to the Cheka boss. That night, 1,500 Moscow prisoners were shot on Dzerzhinsky's orders. This turned out to be a dreadful mistake. Lenin had not ordered the execution at all: he always placed a cross by anything he had read to signify that he had done so and taken it into account. As a result of Dzerzhinsky's simple error 1,500 people lost their lives.[103]

* * *

The Red Terror evoked protests from all quarters of society. Patriarch Tikhon condemned the violence and climate of fear created by the Bolsheviks, citing the prophecy of St Matthew: 'All they that take the sword shall perish with the sword.' The opposition parties denounced the Terror in their underground news-papers. The famous Anarchist philosopher, Prince Kropotkin, whose daughter had been arrested in August 1918,* denounced the Terror in a long and bitter letter to the Bolshevik leader, who was still recovering from Kaplan's bullets, on 17 September: 'To throw the country into a red terror, even more so to arrest

* She had been on her way to England, where she had good contacts with the Trade Union movement, in order to campaign for food aid to the hungry children of Russia, when she was arrested in Yamburg (GARF, f. 4390, op. 14, d. 57, l. 7).

hostages, in order to protect the lives of its leaders is not worthy of a Party calling itself socialist and disgraceful for its leaders.' Workers also condemned the bloody terror perpetrated in their name. 'Enough blood! Down with Terror!' proclaimed the All-Ukrainian Trade Union Council in September. 'Red is the colour of truth and justice,' declared the railway workers of Kozlov. 'But under the Bolsheviks it has become the colour of blood.'[104]

As the 'conscience of the Revolution', Gorky was by far the most outspoken critic of the Terror. Hundreds of people, from poets to peasants, wrote to him pleading for his help to save their loved ones. Gorky felt a strong moral obligation to do what he could for all of them. 'I am their only hope,' he told Ekaterina. This was the point when the humanist in him got the better of the revolutionary: he was more concerned for the individual than any abstract cause. He bombarded the Bolshevik leaders with countless letters demanding the release of innocent individuals from the Cheka jails. Their tone became increasingly irate. 'In my view,' he wrote to Zinoviev in March 1919 protesting against the arrest of an academic, 'such arrests cannot be justified by any political means ... The disgusting crimes you have perpetrated in Petersburg during the past few weeks have brought shame to the regime and aroused universal hatred and contempt for its cowardice.' The following October he wrote to Dzerzhinsky appealing for the release of Professor Tonkov, President of the Military-Medical Academy: 'All these arrests I see as an act of barbarism, as the deliberate destruction of the best brains of the country and I declare that by such actions the Soviet regime has made an enemy out of me.'[105]

Some of Gorky's protests went straight to Lenin. The Bolshevik leader took an indulgent view of his favourite writer's efforts to save human souls from the furnace of the revolution. He even intervened on some of their behalfs. The writer Ivan Volnyi, for example, gained his release from the Cheka jail in Orel through the combined efforts of Gorky and Lenin.[106] But Lenin would have none of Gorky's general criticisms of the Terror. Responding to the question of Tonkov's arrest, for example, Lenin confessed in a letter to Gorky 'that there have been mistakes'. But he went on to justify the general policy of arresting people like Tonkov, who were suspected of 'being close to the Kadets', in a preventive way. In his letter Lenin spelled out the difference between himself and Gorky. It was also the basic difference — one of means and ends — between the Bolsheviks and the democratic socialists:

Reading your frank opinion on this matter, I recall a remark of yours [from the past]: 'We artists are irresponsible people.' Exactly! You utter incredibly angry words — about what? About a few dozen (or perhaps even a few hundred) Kadet and near-Kadet gentry spending a few days in jail in order to prevent plots ... which threaten the lives of tens of thousands of workers and peasants. A calamity indeed! What injustice. A few days, or even weeks, in jail for intellectuals in order to prevent the massacre of tens of thousands of workers and peasants! 'Artists are irresponsible people.'[107]

Within the party there were also critics — not so much of the Terror itself but of its excesses. Kamenev, Bukharin and Olminsky led the attack on the abuse of Cheka power. Essentially, they were carrying on where the Left SRs in the Commissariat of Justice had left off in July in trying to subordinate the Cheka to the state. Their campaign culminated in November with the demand for the Cheka's abolition and its replacement by a new terror organ directly under the control of the Soviet Executive. But the 'hard men' in the party — Lenin, Stalin and Trotsky — stood firmly behind the Cheka. Later efforts to moderate the Cheka, such as the Statute of February 1919, came to little. Although it was subordinated to the Commissariat of Justice, the Cheka continued to function as before — as a state within a state — circumventing its control. The Bolshevik Central Committee, and from 1919 the Politburo, exercised the only real control over the Cheka. Lenin himself took an intimate interest in its activities and protected it from criticism and reform.

Under Lenin's regime — not Stalin's — the Cheka was to become a vast police state. It had its own leviathan infrastructure, from the house committees to the concentration camps, employing more than a quarter of a million people. These were the Bolshevik *oprichniki*, the detested police of Ivan the Terrible. During the civil war it was they who would secure the regime's survival on the so-called 'internal front'. Terror became an integral element of the Bolshevik system in the civil war. Nobody will ever know the exact number of people repressed and killed by the Cheka in these years. But it was certainly several hundred thousand, if one includes all those in its camps and prisons as well as those who were executed or killed by the Cheka's troops in the suppression of strikes and revolts. Although no one knew the precise figures, it is possible that more people were murdered by the Cheka than died in the battles of the civil war.

14 The New Regime Triumphant

i Three Decisive Battles

Prince Lvov wrote to the American businessman Charles Crane on 12 October 1918:

> Bolshevism has found a fertile soil in the base and anarchistic instincts of the people. It is in this sense a Russian sickness, and can only thus be cured by foreign intervention. The re-establishment of order and of the healthy forces in Russia can only be achieved under the protection of an organized army.

The Prince had long pinned his hopes for Russia's liberation on the United States. Unlike other counter-revolutionaries, he had no illusions of a popular uprising against the Bolsheviks. Four chaotic months at the head of the Provisional Government had made him sceptical about the potential of the Russian people as a constructive democratic force. 'Georgii is very down in the mouth,' Lvov's aunt had noted in her diary after a visit to him in his Cheka jail in Ekaterinburg on 13 March. 'He is convinced that Russia lacks the strength to organize its own salvation, since it has been destroyed and its salvation can only come from the outside.' Lvov did not believe in the Cossack Vendée in the south. He looked instead to Siberia, where there was more hope of an Allied intervention in that spring.[1]

For three months Lvov sat in prison. His Bolshevik jailer, a former piano-maker from Petrograd, took an immediate liking to the Prince and allowed him to put his agricultural knowledge to the benefit of the other inmates by reorganizing the prison farm so that they had meat and fresh vegetables to eat. Even behind bars Lvov carried on with the practical zemstvo-type reforms with which he had always occupied himself. Goloshchekin, the militant Bolshevik leader in Ekaterinburg, wanted Lvov shot for his alleged involvement in a counter-revolutionary plot. But Poliakov, the Left SR Commissar for Justice in the city, had his doubts about the merits of the case, and the judges, who had no evidence, were eventually forced to set Lvov free. There is a story — though it has never been proved — that Lenin had pleaded with the Ekaterinburg leaders to let the former Prime Minister go. After his release Lvov fled to Omsk and attached himself to the Siberian government. It was on its behalf that he left in September for the United States, travelling via Vladivostok, to plead the case for Allied intervention in the White campaign against the Bolsheviks.[2]

So far the story of Allied intervention had been something of a farce. None of the Western powers knew what their aims were in Siberia; but neither did any of them want to be left out. Under the pretext of guarding Allied stores and keeping the Trans-Siberian Railway open, Western troops were landed in Vladivostok. The British were the first to arrive in early July with the Middlesex Battalion led by Colonel Ward, the Labour MP for Stoke-on-Trent. It was a real Dad's Army. Made up of men declared unfit for battle, it was known as the 'Hernia Battalion'. In their smart new khaki uniforms, patently unsuitable for the harsh conditions of Siberia, they soon became an object of ridicule. They were fodder not for cannons but for cartoons. French and US troops arrived soon after, followed by the Japanese, but their purpose remained unclear. The Western powers wanted a stable government in Siberia in order to resurrect the Russian army and reconstitute the Eastern Front against the Central Powers. But the Japanese, who had ambitions to annex Russia's Far East, wanted, on the contrary, instability. Both sought to serve their separate purposes by financing the Cossack warlord, Grigorii Semenov, whose regime in Chita claimed to control the mountainous terrain east of Lake Baikal. In fact Semenov served no one but himself. Like the other warlords of the Far East, Kalmykov and Ungern-Sternberg, Semenov was less a politician than a bandit. His mercenary troops robbed and murdered the local population with quite unspeakable barbarism. Never have the taxes of the Western democracies been so criminally wasted.[3]

With the advent of Kolchak, the Allies at last had a Russian national hero whom they could back with confidence against the Bolsheviks. Thanks to the support of General Knox, the head of the British military mission, Kolchak received more aid from London than any other leader of the Whites. A second British battalion was sent to Omsk in January 1919, along with a small naval detachment which fought the Reds on the Kama River, while Knox himself took over the training of Kolchak's officers in Vladivostok. But it was US support that really mattered, since the other Western powers would undoubtedly follow its lead. 'Everything depends on America,' Lvov wrote to Crane from Tokyo.[4]

On 15 November the Prince finally arrived in Washington. All his hopes for Russia were now focused on a meeting with the President. As the leader of the free world, Woodrow Wilson would surely recognize his moral obligation to promote the cause of freedom in Russia. This of course was a naive dream: with the ending of the world war, the Americans had no intention of sending more troops to Siberia. But, like many of the Russian liberals, Lvov idealized the land of the free. 'I am convinced', he wrote to Crane, 'that the

World War is giving birth to a new world order led by the United States.' Lvov was also convinced that President Wilson would share his liberal ideals: theirs would be a meeting of hearts as well as minds. On 21 November the two finally met. The meeting lasted only fifteen minutes. Wilson was friendly but not prepared to discuss the commitment of further troops. According to one of his aides, all he had to say when the meeting was over was: 'Did you notice what a wonderful beard the Prince has?'[5]

Had Lvov been a normal person, this disappointment would have been enough to shatter his optimism. After three months of travelling around the world, all his hopes had come to naught. But the Prince was not normal. He was as persevering as Pangloss himself, and travelled on to Paris in his moral quest. There Kolchak and Denikin placed him at the head of their delegation — formed from the Russian Political Conference* — to plead their case for Allied aid and diplomatic recognition at the Versailles Peace Conference in January. Recognition did not come: the Allies were determined to maintain the hypocrisy of neutrality in the Russian civil war. But thanks to the Prince and his delegation, they did send large amounts of aid to Kolchak. In the first six months of 1919 his White army received from them: one million rifles; 15,000 machine-guns; 700 field guns; 800 million rounds of ammunition; and clothing and equipment for half a million men. This was roughly equivalent to the Soviet production of munitions for the whole of 1919, and was certainly enough to launch a major campaign against the Reds. Thirty thousand Allied troops (Czechs, Americans, British, Italians and French) defended Kolchak's rear and maintained the 4,000-mile supply route along the Trans-Siberian Railway from Vladivostok to Omsk.[6]

Under their protection, Kolchak built up his forces in preparation for an early spring offensive against the Reds. Some people have suggested that he struck too early, before his armies were really ready, and that he should have waited for the summer, by which time Denikin might have joined him in a combined offensive on the Volga. But at the time there were decisive reasons for an early offensive. Some success was needed to ensure further Allied aid and recognition for the Kolchak regime. The Reds appeared on the brink of collapse. On Christmas Eve Kolchak's troops had captured the vital industrial city of Perm, routing the Third Red Army in the process. This opened up the possibility of pushing on towards Arkhangelsk, where the Allies had installed a White government under the Russian General K. E. Miller. The 'Perm Catastrophe' was obviously the outcome of a chronic breakdown in the Red rear. Soldiers

---

* The other delegates were V. A. Maklakov (Kerensky's Ambassador in Paris), Sazonov (Kolchak's — and Nicholas II's — Foreign Minister) and the veteran Populist N. V. Chaikovsky (head of the Northern Region government based in Arkhangelsk). The Russian Political Conference was a government in exile made up of former diplomats and other public men in Paris. Savinkov, Nabokov, Struve and Konovalov were among its members.

had been hastily thrown into battle without proper training. Lacking enough food or winter clothing to withstand the arctic conditions, they surrendered *en masse* to the Whites. There they told them of the critical situation behind the Red Front. Military conscriptions and requisitionings had sparked a violent wave of peasant uprisings. The Red Terror had murdered thousands of innocent civilians in the cities of the Urals, turning virtually the whole population, including the workers, against the Bolsheviks. Relations were particularly strained with the Tatars and Bashkirs of the Volga-Ural region. The Reds were seen, in the words of one of their commissars, 'as a hostile army of occupation depriving the Muslims of their autonomy and trampling on their customs'.[7]

Kolchak's offensive pushed west on three Fronts. The main attacking force was the Western Army under General Khanzhin, which advanced towards Ufa at the start of March. It was made up from the remains of the Komuch's People's Army and supplemented by peasant conscripts. There were also 10,000 worker-volunteers from the munitions factories of Izhevsk and Votkinsk who had fled to Kolchak on the suppression of their uprising against the Bolsheviks in November. On their right flank was Gajda's Siberian Army, made up mainly of peasant conscripts, which attacked towards Viatka; and on their left the Orenburg and Siberian Cossacks, who fought alongside the Bashkir units under General Dutov. Their aim was to capture Orenburg and to link up with the Whites on the south-eastern steppe. This would cut off the Reds in Central Asia. The total front-line strength of Kolchak's forces was around 100,000 men.

By mid-April Kolchak's forces had advanced more than 200 miles and had captured an area larger than Britain. Their destination, the Volga River, was within a few days' march. Behind their own lines the Reds were meanwhile struggling to cope with the largest peasant uprising until that time — the so-called 'War of the Chapany' (named after the local peasant term for a tunic) which engulfed whole districts of Simbirsk and Samara under the slogan of 'Long live the Soviets! Down with the Communists!'[8] The Whites talked confidently of the 'race to Moscow'. In Paris Lvov saw Kolchak's prestige soar among the Allies. Further huge credits were advanced to Omsk. It seemed that Western diplomatic recognition for the Whites was just around the corner.

But on 28 April the Reds launched a counter-offensive. It was led by Mikhail Frunze, who was later to become a Soviet hero but who at this time was still a relatively unknown Bolshevik. An ex-worker in his early thirties, Frunze's only real experience of war had been at the head of a Red brigade during the struggle for power in Moscow. Thousands of party members were mobilized and despatched to the Eastern Front. The newly organized Komsomol, the Communist Youth League, sent 3,000 of its members. The Soviets were also ordered to recruit ten to twenty conscripts from each volost. Due to the resistance of the peasants, only 13,000 recruits actually appeared — slightly more than two per volost — but it still helped to tip the balance against the Whites. The Reds were also joined by the majority of the Bashkir units which defected from Kolchak's side in May. By mid-June, Frunze's forces had pushed Kolchak's armies back to where they had started from, east of Ufa. After that the cities of the Urals fell to the Reds like dominoes as the Whites fell apart and retreated in panic. Orenburg, Ekaterinburg and the vital railhead at Chelia-binsk had all been lost by the middle of August. There was little to stop the Reds from marching on to Omsk. Kolchak now had fewer than 15,000 soldiers in the field, barely an eighth of his active forces at the height of his advance.[9]

There were a number of military reasons for the collapse of the Kolchak offensive. But behind all of them lay politics. It was a case of military overstretch, where the regime in the rear lacked the political means to sustain the army at the Front.

Take the problem of command. There were very few commanders of any calibre to be found in Kolchak's army. Only 5 per cent of the 17,000 officers had been trained before the war and most were young wartime ensigns. General Lebedev, the *de facto* head of the army, was only thirty-six. He had been a colonel in the tsarist General Staff. Like most of Kolchak's senior commanders, he was more expert in political intrigue than in the science of war. The army leaders, in the words of Baron Budberg, 'thought of themselves not just as a military but also as a political corps'. This, after all, was a military dictatorship. Political factions soon developed among the commanders' supporters, with the result that the army broke up into little more than a disunited collection of separate detachments, each pursuing its own little war. The more the army became politicized, the more its bureaucracy ballooned out of all proportion to the soldiers in the field. At the height of the offensive there were 2,000 officers in the staff at Omsk alone to administer 100,000 soldiers. Even in Semipalatinsk, 1,500 miles from the fighting, there was a staff of over 1,000. Instead of serving at the Front too many commanders sat around in offices and cafés in the rear.[10]

Then there was the problem of supplies. Kolchak's army, even more than Lenin's, suffered from shortages at the Front. It had to resort to feeding itself from the villages near the Front, which often meant violent requisitioning, leading to the alienation of the very population the Whites were supposed to be liberating. Part of the problem was Kolchak's short-sighted economic policies. He would not use the tsarist gold reserves to counteract runaway inflation. Peasants withdrew their foodstuffs from the market as the Omsk banknotes lost their value. Nothing was done to resurrect the chronic state of Siberia's industries: they were simply written off as a bastion of Bolshevik influence. Consumer goods and military supplies had to be brought in by rail from the Pacific, 4,000 miles away. Much of them were held up by bandits east of Lake Baikal, or by peasant partisans. Whole trainloads were also diverted by the railway workers, many of whom were sympathetic to the Reds and all of whom were badly paid. In Omsk itself valuable supplies were often squandered by corrupt officials. The venality of Kolchak's regime was notorious. The staff of Gajda's army was drawing rations for 275,000 men, when there were only 30,000 in his combat units. The Embassy cigarettes imported from England for the soldiers were smoked by civilians in Omsk. English army uniforms and nurses' outfits were worn by civilians, while many soldiers dressed in rags. Even Allied munitions were sold on the black market. Knox was dubbed the Quartermaster General of the Red Army: Trotsky even sent him a joke letter thanking him for his help in equipping the Red troops.[11]

The atmosphere of the Omsk regime was filled with moral decadence and seedy corruption. Cocaine and vodka were consumed in prodigious quantities. Cafés, casinos and brothels worked around the clock. Kolchak himself led by example, living with his mistress in luxury in Omsk while his poor wife and son were packed off to Paris. The Admiral had no talent for choosing subordinates and filled his ministries with third-rate hangers-on from the old regime. 'The company is awful,' he complained to his wife. 'I am surrounded by moral decay, cowardice, greed and treachery.' But Kolchak largely had himself to blame. If he had managed not to alienate the zemstvos, the one local source of administrative talent, things would not have been so bad. Budberg was appalled by the situation he found as Minister of War:

> In the army, decay; in the Staff, ignorance and incompetence; in the Government, moral rot, divisions and the intrigues of ambitious egotists; in the country, uprising and anarchy; in public life, panic, selfishness, bribes and scoundrelism of every sort.

In such a climate little was achieved. The offices responsible for supply were full of corrupt and indolent bureaucrats, who took months to draw up meaningless statistics, legislative projects and official reports that were then filed away and forgotten. 'The whole regime', Budberg concluded, 'is only form without content; the ministries can be compared to huge and imposing windmills, busily turning their sails, but without millstones and most of their internal working parts broken or missing.'[12]

By far the biggest weakness of Kolchak's army was its failure to mobilize the local population. Its offensive came to a halt for want of adequate reinforcements, while far too many conscripts deserted. This was mainly a question of the peasants. True, the White advance was critically weakened by the desertion of the Bashkirs and the Cossacks on the southern flank, which allowed Frunze's army to break through. But the vast majority of the population in Western Siberia and the Volga-Kama region, where the offensive would be made or broken, were either Russian or Ukrainian peasants. On the face of it, there was no reason why the Siberian peasants should be hostile to the Whites. There was no real landownership by the gentry to the east of the Urals, so the major factor binding the peasants to the revolution in central Russia did not come into play here. Most of the older settlers were relatively wealthy mixed and dairy farmers, who, one would have thought, should have had a stake in the Whites' *post bellum status quo* based on private property. Yet the peasants to the east of the Urals proved just as reluctant to join Kolchak's army as those to the west.

It was partly a question of image. Kolchak's regime, rightly or wrongly, was associated with a restoration of the tsarist system. This was communicated by the epaulettes of his officers; and by the tsarist and feudal methods employed by his local officials, who often whipped the peasants when they disobeyed their orders. This was bound to bring them into head-on conflict with the Siberian peasantry, whose ancestors had run away from serfdom in Russia and the Ukraine and whose love of freedom and independence was thus very strong. The whole ethos of the Kolchak regime was alien to the peasants — a feeling expressed in the peasant *chastushka*, or rhyming song:

> English tunics, Russian epaulettes;
> Japanese tobacco, Omsk despots.

The closer the Whites moved towards central Russia the harder it became for them to mobilize the local peasantry. In the crucial Volga region, the furthest point of Kolchak's advance, the peasants had gained more of the gentry's land than anywhere else in Russia and so had most to fear from a counter-revolution. Here Kolchak dug his own grave by failing to sanction the peasant revolution on the land. Like Denikin's regime in the south, where the landowners were equally dominant, Kolchak's government was quite incapable of anything more than a carefully guarded bureaucratic response to what was the vital issue of the civil war. It was a classic example of the outdated methods of the Whites. 'Any future land law', Kolchak's land commission declared on 8 April, would 'have to be based on the rights of private property'. Only the 'unused land of the gentry' would be 'transferred to the toiling peasantry', which in the meantime could do no more than rent it from the government. As one critic put it, such a declaration was 'a marvellous propaganda tool for the Bolsheviks. All they have to do is to print it up and distribute it to the peasantry.'[13]

To mobilize the peasants Kolchak's army resorted increasingly to terror. There was no effective local administration to enforce the conscription in any other way, and in any case the Whites' world-view ruled out the need to persuade the peasants. It was taken for granted that it was the peasant's place to serve in the White army, just as he had served in the ranks of the Tsar's, and that if he refused it was the army's right to punish him, even executing him if necessary as a warning to the others. Peasants were flogged and tortured, hostages were taken and shot, and whole villages were burned to the ground to force the conscripts into the army. Kolchak's cavalry would ride into towns on market day, round up the young men at gunpoint and take them off to the Front. Much of this terror was concealed from the Allies so as not to jeopardize their aid. But General Graves, the commander of the US troops, was well informed and was horrified by it. As he realized, the mass conscription of the peasantry 'was a long step towards the end of Kolchak's regime'. It soon destroyed the discipline and fighting morale of his army. Of every five peasants forcibly conscripted, four would desert: many of them ran off to the Reds, taking with them their supplies. Knox was livid when he first saw the Red troops on the Eastern Front: they were wearing British uniforms.[14]

From the start of its campaign, Kolchak's army was forced to deal with numerous peasant revolts in the rear, notably in Slavgorod, south-east of Omsk, and in Minusinsk on the Yenisei. The White requisitioning and mobilizations were their principal cause. Without its own structures of local government in the rural areas, Kolchak's regime could do very little, other than send in the Cossacks with their whips, to stop the peasants from reforming their Soviets to defend the local village revolution. By the height of the Kolchak offensive, whole areas of the Siberian rear were engulfed by peasant revolts. This partisan movement could not really be described as Bolshevik, as it was later by Soviet historians, although Bolshevik activists, usually in a united front with the Anarchists and Left SRs, often played a major role in it. It was rather a vast peasant war against the Omsk regime. Sometimes the local peasant chieftains were somewhat confused as to what they were fighting for. Shchetinkin, for example, a partisan leader in Minusinsk, issued this comic proclamation:

> It is time to finish with the destroyers of Russia, Kolchak and Denikin, who are continuing the work of the traitor Kerensky . . . The Grand Duke Nikolai Nikolaevich has arrived in Vladivostok and taken power over Russia. He has commanded me to raise the people against Kolchak. Lenin and Trotsky in Moscow have subordinated themselves to the Grand Duke and have been appointed as his ministers. I call on the Orthodox people to take up arms for the Tsar and Soviet Power.

Generally, however, the partisan movement expressed the ideas of the peasant revolution in hostile opposition to the towns. A good example of its ideology is to be found at the First Peasant Congress of Insurgents from the districts of Kansk, Krasnoyarsk and Achinsk which convened in April 1919. It proposed a whole 'constitution of peasant power', with a 'peasant government', communal taxes in accordance with norms set by Congress, and the 'distribution of the riches of the land among the toiling peasantry'. It even passed a 'peasant code' which set sentences of community service for those found guilty of drunken brawls, gambling, catching spawning fish and — an act evidently seen by the peasant delegates on a par with these — rape.[15]

The partisan movement was strongest in those regions — Tomsk and Yenisei provinces in central Siberia, the Altai and Semipalatinsk in the south, and the Amur valley in the east — where the most recent Russian immigrants were concentrated. These were generally the poorer peasants, many of whom had to supplement their income by working on the railways and down the mines. But the movement also spread to the richer farming regions as the repressions of the Omsk regime increased. Peasant deserters from Kolchak's army played a leading role in the partisan bands. They had that little extra knowledge of the outside world which can be enough in a peasant community to catapult a young man into power. The peasant bands fought by guerrilla methods, to which the wild and remote forest regions of the taiga were so well adapted. Sometimes they joined forces with the Red Army units which had been hiding out in the taiga since the Bolsheviks had been forced out of Siberia during the summer of 1918. The partisans' destruction of miles of track and their constant ambushes of trains virtually halted the transportation of vital supplies along the Trans-Siberian Railway to Kolchak's armies for much of the offensive. Thousands of his soldiers had to be withdrawn from the Front against the Reds to deal with the partisans. They waged a ruthless war of terror, shooting hundreds of hostages and setting fire to dozens of villages in the partisan strongholds of Kansk and Achinsk, where the wooded and hilly terrain was perfect for holding up trains. This partly succeeded in pushing the insurgents away from the railway. But since the terror was also unleashed on villages unconnected with the partisans, it merely fanned the flames of peasant war. As Kolchak's army retreated eastwards, it found itself increasingly surrounded by hostile peasant partisans. Mutinies began to spread as the Whites came under fire from all sides: even the Cossacks joined them. Whole units of Kolchak's peasant conscripts deserted as the retreat brought them closer to their native regions. By November 1919, Kolchak's army was falling apart. Once again the Whites had been defeated by the gulf between themselves and the peasantry.[16]

On 14 November Omsk was abandoned by Kolchak's forces as the Reds, who now outnumbered them by two to one, advanced eastwards. It was a classic case of White incompetence, with the leading generals caught in two minds as to whether to defend the town or evacuate it — and in the end doing neither properly. The Reds took the city without a fight, capturing vast stores of munitions that the Whites had not had time to destroy, along with 30,000 troops. Thousands of officers and their families, clerks and officials, merchants, café owners, bankers and prostitutes fled the White capital and headed east. The lucky ones travelled by train, the unlucky ones by horse or on foot. The bourgeoisie was on the run. The wounded and the sick — whose numbers were swollen by a typhus epidemic — had to be abandoned on the way. This was not just a military collapse; it was also a moral one. The retreating Cossacks carried with them huge supplies of vodka and, as all authority disappeared, indulged themselves in mass rape and pillage of the villages along their way. One of the characters in *Doctor Zhivago*, much of which was based on Pasternak's experiences in Siberia, summed up the atmosphere: 'Before there had been obligations of all kinds — sacred duties to the country, the army, and society. But now the war was lost, everything seemed to have been deposed, nothing was any longer sacred.'[17]

Kolchak headed towards his new intended capital in Irkutsk, 1,500 miles east of Omsk. The longest of his six trains, with twenty-nine cars, was taken up by the tsarist gold reserve, which had been captured from the Reds at Kazan and handed over to Kolchak. Three hundred miles from his destination, Kolchak's train was held up by the Czechs, and for most of December it remained stranded in the middle of nowhere. Meanwhile, in Irkutsk, the Political Centre, a coalition of the trade unions, the zemstvos and the left-wing parties took over the city and proclaimed itself the government of Siberia. Kolchak was declared an 'enemy of the people' and ordered to be brought to trial. On 4 January 1920 Kolchak resigned, transferred the command of his army to Semenov and travelled with the Czechs to Irkutsk, where he expected to be handed over to the Allied missions. But somehow he was betrayed and delivered to the Irkutsk Bolsheviks. From what we know, it seems most likely that he and his gold were handed over by the Czechs in exchange for a guaranteed passage to Vladivostok, where at last they could set sail for the United States on their journey round the world to return home. Neither the Political Centre nor the Allied missions did anything to save the Admiral. On 21 January a five-man commission (two Bolsheviks, two SRs and one Menshevik) interrogated him. There were plans to bring him back to Moscow and place him on public trial. But, as with the trial of Nicholas, these plans were aborted and, on 6 February, he was sentenced to execution. Perhaps the Reds feared Kolchak's capture by the remnants of his army, which were assembling just outside the city. Or perhaps the Bolsheviks simply preferred to have him dead.* Early the next morning Kolchak was shot. His body was buried beneath the ice of the Ushakovka River.

---

* There is an order from Lenin to Smirnov, Chairman of the Siberian MRC, instructing him to explain Kolchak's execution as a response to the threat of the Whites (RTsKhIDNI, f. 2, op. 1, d. 24362). But the date of this order is unclear. Richard Pipes believes it was written before 7 February, thus suggesting a plot by Lenin to camouflage the reasons for the execution (*Russia Under the Bolshevik Regime*, 117–18). But there is no corroboration of this.

If Kolchak's final defeat had taken so long, it was largely because the Reds had been forced to divert a large proportion of their troops from Siberia to the Southern Front, where Denikin was threatening to break through during the summer of 1919.*

During March and April, at the height of the Kolchak offensive, Denikin's forces broke out from Rostov to occupy the crucial Donbass coal region and the south-east Ukraine. Some historians have seen this as a critical strategic mistake. Denikin's original plan had been to strike towards Tsaritsyn in order to link up with Kolchak's forces. But this plan was abandoned in late March, when the Reds, who were desperate for coal, invaded the Donbass and the northern Don. Faced with the choice between saving the Don or linking up with Kolchak on the Volga, Denikin opted for the former. He had always given top priority to the defence of his Cossack strongholds. That had been the reasoning behind his preference the previous summer to launch a Second Kuban Campaign rather than attack towards Tsaritsyn; and now those same priorities came into play. Denikin's decision was bitterly opposed by several leading generals, notably Baron Wrangel, the lofty six-foot-six leader of the Caucasian Army, who constantly intrigued against Denikin. Wrangel denounced the decision not to advance towards Tsaritsyn as a 'betrayal of Kolchak's troops', allowing the Reds 'to defeat us one by one'. Given that Kolchak's troops in March were barely 200 miles from Tsaritsyn, perhaps Denikin was wrong not to run the risk of losing the Don to link up with them. The Reds were certain that they would be defeated if the two White armies combined. However, it must be said in Denikin's defence that he was responding to what can only be called a war of genocide against the Cossacks. The Bolsheviks had made it clear that their aim in the northern Don was to unleash 'mass terror against the rich Cossacks by exterminating them to the last man' and transferring their land to the Russian peasants. During this campaign of 'decossackization', in the early months of 1919, some 12,000 Cossacks, many of them old men, were executed as 'counter-revolutionaries' by the tribunals of the invading Red Army.[18]

* This was the first major strategic disagreement among the Bolshevik leadership. Trotsky and Vatsetis, his Commander-in-Chief, argued against pursuing Kolchak beyond the Urals so that troops could be withdrawn to the Southern Front. But Kamenev, the Eastern Front Commander, backed up by Lenin and Stalin, insisted on the need to pursue Kolchak to the end. The conflict went on through the summer, weakening the Red Army leadership at this critical moment of the civil war. It showed, above all, that Trotsky's authority was in decline. His strategy, both on the Eastern and the Southern Fronts, was rejected in favour of Kamenev's, who replaced Vatsetis on 3 July. Trotsky was furious, suspecting that Stalin and the Military Opposition were trying to oust him from the leadership. He wrote a letter of resignation, which was rejected by the Central Committee on 5 July. Trotsky's authority was further weakened by the reconstitution of the RVSR with four new members (Kamenev, Gusev, Smilga and Rykov) who all had differences with its Chairman.

It was the spontaneous Cossack uprising against this terror which enabled Denikin to break through. Thousands of Cossacks joined his troops as they advanced northwards in the spring. The main White force in the Donbass was led by General Mai-Maevsky. A chubby pear-shaped man with small piggy eyes and a pince-nez, he was the most unlikely military hero. 'If he had not worn a uniform,' Baron Wrangel wrote, 'you would have taken him for a comedian from a little provincial theatre.' Mai-Maevsky was notorious for his drunken orgies: by the end of the civil war there were few brothels in southern Russia where he was not known. Yet he was also one of the Whites' most able generals — a brilliant tactician, physically courageous and idolized by his 12,000 'coloured troops' (so-called because of their multi-coloured caps). Under his command the Volunteer Army advanced from the Donbass into the south-east Ukraine, easily defeating Makhno's Red partisans on the way. Kharkov was captured on 13 June, Ekaterinoslav on the 22nd, as the Red peasant conscripts ran away at the first sight of these crack White forces. Meanwhile, in one of the most remarkable campaigns of the civil war, Wrangel's Caucasian Army marched for forty days across the sun-baked south-eastern steppe — and at the end of it captured Tsaritsyn against superior forces on 19 June. The Red defenders of the Volga city fled in panic as soon as they saw Wrangel's British tanks approach. Forty thousand Reds were captured by the Whites along with a huge store of munitions.[19]

Denikin's breakthrough had been facilitated by a number of factors. The Whites had the advantage of superior cavalry and supplies, thanks in large part to the Allies. Despite his own physical immobility, the rotund Mai-Maevsky was a master improviser of the war of movement. He used his British aeroplanes for reconnaissance of enemy terrain and despatched his cavalry by railway to those points where they could inflict the most damage. One unit could fight at three different places in a single day. The Reds, meanwhile, were clearly overstretched by the climax of the fighting on the two main Fronts — the Southern and the Eastern. They were also suffering from a crisis in supplies. According to Trotsky, this was the main reason for the collapse of the Southern Front. 'Nowhere do the soldiers suffer so much from hunger as in the Ukraine,' he told the Central Committee on 11 August. 'Between a third and a half of the men are without boots or undergarments and go about in rags. Everyone in the Ukraine except our soldiers has a rifle and ammunition.' The supply crisis led to indiscipline and mass desertion. In the seven months of Denikin's advance, from March to October 1919, the Reds registered more than one million deserters on the Southern Front. The rear was engulfed in peasant uprisings, as the Reds resorted to the violent requisitioning of horses and supplies, forcible conscription of reinforcements and repressions against villages suspected of hiding deserters.[20]

The south-eastern Ukraine, where Makhno's partisans were in control, became a major region of peasant revolt just at the height of the Denikin offensive. Nestor Makhno was the Pancho Villa of the Russian Revolution. He was born in 1889 in Hulyai Pole, the centre of his peasant insurrection. During 1905 he had joined the Anarchists and, after seven years in the Butyrka jail, returned to Hulyai Pole in 1917, where he formed the Peasant Union — later reformed as the Soviet — and organized a brigade, which carried out the seizure of the local gentry's estates. During the civil war Makhno's partisans fought almost everyone: the Rada forces; Kaledin's Cossacks; the Germans and the Hetmanates; Petliura's Ukrainian Nationalists; the rival bands of Grigoriev and countless other warlords; the Whites; and the Reds. The strength of his guerrilla army lay in the quality and the speed of its cavalry, in the support it received from the peasantry, in its intimate knowledge of the local terrain and in the fierce loyalty of its men. Makhno's alleged exploits, which included drinking bouts of superhuman length, gave him a legendary status among the local peasants (they called him 'Batko', meaning 'father'). It was not unlike the myth of Stenka Razin as a peasant champion of truth and justice who was blessed with supernatural powers. Under the black flag of the Anarchists, Makhno stood for a stateless peasant revolution based on the local self-rule of the free and autonomous Soviets that had emerged in the countryside during 1917. When the Whites advanced into the Ukraine Makhno put his 15,000 men at the disposal of the Reds. In exchange for arms from Moscow, his troops became part of the Third Division under Dybenko, although they retained their own internal partisan organization. Trotsky made a point of blaming their lack of discipline for the Red defeats.* In June he ordered the arrest of Makhno as a 'counter-revolutionary' — his anarchist conception of a local peasant revolution was inimical to the Proletarian Dictatorship — and had several of his followers shot. Makhno's partisans fled to the forests and turned their guns against the Reds. Most of the peasants in the south-east Ukraine supported his revolt.

From Tsaritsyn, on 3 July, Denikin issued his Moscow Directive. The three main White forces were to converge on the capital in a gigantic pincer movement along the main railways, thus cutting off its main lines of supply. Wrangel's Caucasian Army was to march up the Volga from Tsaritsyn to Saratov, and turn in from there to Penza, Nizhnyi Novgorod and on to Moscow; General Sidorin and the Don Army were to advance north via Voronezh; while Mai-Maevsky's Volunteer Army was to march from Kharkov via Kursk, Orel and

---

* It is true that Makhno's partisans often broke down under pressure from the Whites. But given how poorly they were supplied by the Reds, this was hardly surprising. They certainly did not deserve the vilification they received from Trotsky. This in fact had less to do with Makhno than it did with Stalin. By laying the blame for the Red defeats on the guerrilla methods of Makhno's partisans, Trotsky could attack the 'guerrilla-ism' of the Military Opposition and thus reinforce his argument for military discipline and centralization.

Tula. It was an all-or-nothing gamble, counting on the speed of the White cavalry to exploit the temporary weakness of the Reds. Wrangel bitterly opposed the Directive. He called it the 'death sentence' of the White Army. In his view it ran the risk of advancing too far and broadly without adequate protection in the rear in the form of trained reserves, sound administration and lines of supply to maintain the offensive. Wrangel preferred to concentrate the troops and advance more slowly in one sector — namely his own on the Volga. But when he put this to Denikin, the latter exclaimed: 'I see you want to be the first man to set foot in Moscow!'[21]

With hindsight it is clear that the Directive was a disastrous mistake: it cost the Whites the civil war. Denikin himself later admitted that the Front became much too broad, mainly because the cavalry commanders, whom he could not control, took it upon themselves to expand the territory under their occupation. It was a case of too many generals and not enough authority. As the Front grew, so too did the need for fresh troops and supplies. Yet the front-line units were by this stage several hundred miles from their bases in the rear. They resorted to violent requisitioning and conscription from the local popu-lation, thereby alienating the very people they were supposed to liberate. Denikin had always said that the advance on Moscow would depend on a 'national uprising of the people against the Soviet regime'; but the effect of his armies' actions was to rally them behind it.[22]

The offensive started well enough. On 31 July Denikin's forces captured Poltava, followed by Odessa and Kiev in August, as Soviet power in the Ukraine crumbled. Meanwhile, in August, Mamontov's Cossacks, 8,000 strong, broke deep into the Red rear towards Tambov, blowing up munition stores and railway lines and dispersing newly drafted Red recruits. Tambov and Voronezh were both briefly occupied and looted as part of Mamontov's plan to disrupt the rear. During September Mai-Maevsky's advance continued into central Russia. Kursk was taken on the 20th and Voronezh, once again, ten days later. On 14 October the Whites took Orel. Only 250 miles from Moscow, this was the closest they would come to victory. The Bolsheviks were thrown into panic. Precisely at this moment, just as Denikin was threatening to capture Moscow from the south, another White army under General Yudenich was being amassed on the outskirts of Petrograd. For once the Whites had managed to co-ordinate the attacks of their two main armies, and for a few crucial days in mid-October it seemed that this would be enough to defeat the Reds.

Bunkered in the Kremlin, Lenin received hourly telephone reports from his commanders at the two Fronts. Desperate measures were put into action for a last-ditch defence of Moscow: 120,000 workers and peasants were forcibly conscripted into labour teams to dig trenches on the southern approach roads. Meanwhile, the Bolsheviks prepared for the worst. Many of them tore up their party tickets and tried to ingratiate themselves with the Moscow bourgeoisie in the hope of saving themselves when the Whites arrived. Others got ready to go underground. Secret plans were laid for the evacuation of the government to the Urals. Some of the senior party leaders even prepared to flee abroad. Elena Stasova, the Party Secretary, was ordered to procure a false passport and a wad of tsarist banknotes for each member of the Central Committee.[23]

But the signs that the Whites had overstretched themselves soon became apparent. While their armies had more than doubled in size since the spring, they still lacked enough troops to sustain their advance towards Moscow. Denikin's 150,000 soldiers were very thinly spread along the thousand miles of the Southern Front, making them vulnerable to a counter-offensive. In the rear the Whites had left themselves without enough troops to defend their bases against Makhno's partisans, the Ukrainian nationalists and the Chechens in the Caucasus, and at the height of the Moscow offensive they were forced to withdraw vital troops to deal with them. They were also hampered in part by the lack of reinforcements. The Kuban Cossacks, whom Wrangel was counting on to reinforce his campaign against Saratov on the Volga, refused to leave their homelands. It was the old problem of Cossack localism: without guarantees of autonomy for the Kuban — which the Whites were not prepared to give — they would not take part in the fighting in Russia. But the real problem for the Whites — and the single biggest reason why their offensive ran out of steam — was their inability to mobilize enough troops within the newly occupied regions of the Ukraine and Russia. And here the Whites were defeated by their own political failures.

In the Ukraine the Whites were crippled from the start by their Great Russian chauvinism. This guaranteed the opposition of the richer peasants, much of the rural intelligentsia and the petty-bourgeoisie, all of whom were sympathetic to the Ukrainian nationalist cause. Of all the contenders for power in the Ukraine — the Greens, the Blacks, the Reds and the Whites — Denikin was the only one who made no concessions to the nationalists. This was not a mistaken calculation: the need to defend the Great Russian Empire was the essential belief of the White regime. Even if they had been told that without such concessions they could not succeed, the Whites would still have refused to make them. Dragomirov, Lukomsky and Shulgin, the three Kievan Russians who dominated the White movement in the south, were more Russian than the Russians in Russia. Denikin satisfied their nationalist demands. He appointed Russians to all official posts; suppressed the agrarian co-operatives, strongholds of the nationalist movement; and forbade the use of the Ukrainian language in all state institutions including schools. He even denied the existence of a Ukraine — which he called 'Little Russia' in all his pronouncements. His clumsy 'Proclamation to the Little Russian People', in which he pledged to reunite

the Commissars!' became the slogan of the strike. To suppress the strike the Bolsheviks had waged civil war against the workers. Dzerzhinsky himself had been sent by Lenin on 3 April. Special Communist detachments had occupied the factories and up to 1,000 workers had been arrested. Since then relations with the workers had been less embattled — Os'kin had made sure that better food supplies were brought in — but this was now threatened by a renewed strike as food stocks once again became depleted. Given the vital need to keep munitions production going, there was no choice in Os'kin's view but 'to militarize the factories and repress the workers if they went on strike'. None of the Bolsheviks had any illusions about the possibility of negotiating a settlement with the workers: there was not enough time. And, in any case, as Lenin admitted to the Politburo on 15 October, 'the masses in Tula are a very long way from being with us'. In fact, if anything, they were with the Mensheviks, who had led the general strike in the previous spring and who, before that, had held majorities in the city Soviets. Some of the Mensheviks now chose to agitate for the Reds in Tula in order to repel Denikin. It was a measure of the Bolsheviks' desperation, and of the low esteem in which the workers held them, that they had to rely on their deadliest rivals to come to their aid. Os'kin and his comrades were reluctant to do so, fearful as they had been of any other party since the general strike, but Lenin intervened to open up the factory doors to the Mensheviks. Dan told the Tula workers that the victory of the Whites would mean the defeat of the revolution; but the hungry workers seemed only bored by this. The Mensheviks were forced to conclude that the workers were 'extremely hostile to the Communists and no appeal to defend the revolution against Denikin could pacify their mood'.[28]

The need for urgent results also lay behind Os'kin's extraordinary measures for Tula's military defence. Thousands of peasants and 'bourgeois' citizens were forcibly conscripted into labour teams. They worked day and night felling timber to fuel the factories and digging trenches around the city. Hundreds of their relatives were held as 'hostages' — to be shot if the work was not done properly. Os'kin had no qualms about using such measures: they were 'necessary for the defence of the revolution'. Thousands of Red Army reinforcements were despatched to Tula, including the famous Latvian Rifle Division, stalwart supporters of the Bolshevik regime. Os'kin organized the conscription of 20,000 local troops in addition to this. 'The whole of Tula', as he put it, 'was turned into one huge barracks.' Soldiers were billeted in every spare building. The town squares and parks were taken over by tanks and units of soldiers going through their drill. Machine-gun posts were mounted on the tallest buildings along the major roads and mined barricades were erected at the entrance to the town. Throughout the southern districts of the province there were look-out posts, linked by telephone with Tula, to warn of the approach of Denikin's troops.

The gentry's abandoned manors were turned into barracks. One regiment made its home on Tolstoy's former estate at Yasnaya Polyana; while another camped nearby on Prince Lvov's at Popovka.[29]

At this crucial moment, with the outcome of the struggle very finely balanced, hundreds of thousands of peasant deserters were returning to the Red Army. This return was a decisive factor, tipping the balance in favour of the Reds, and it says a great deal about why the Bolsheviks won the civil war. Right-wing accounts of the civil war have tended to present the victory of the Reds as something that was achieved without mass support. The Bolsheviks, so the argument goes, simply had a larger territorial base upon which to draw. They were more systematic than the Whites in their use of terror and coercion to extract the necessary military resources from a civilian population which was essentially hostile to both sides and indifferent to the outcome of their struggle. This is two-thirds right. But the fact that the Bolsheviks could at least claim to stand for 'the revolution' — and they had captured its most important symbols such as the Red Flag — also surely enabled them to mobilize a certain level of support, albeit only a conditional support and as the less bad of two options, from the peasantry, and indeed as we shall see from certain workers too, who feared that a victory of the Whites would reverse their own gains from the revolution.

This is clearly shown by the story of the return of the peasant deserters to the Red Army. Until June, the Reds' campaign against desertion had relied on violent repressive measures against the villages suspected of harbouring them. This had been largely counter-productive, resulting in a wave of peasant revolts behind the Red Front which had facilitated the White advance. But in June the Bolsheviks switched to the more conciliatory tactic of 'amnesty weeks'. During these weeks, which were much propagandized and often extended indefinitely, the deserters were invited to return to the ranks without punishment. In a sense, it was a sign of the Bolshevik belief in the need to reform the nature of the peasant and to make him conscious of his revolutionary duty — thus the Reds punished 'malicious' deserters but tried to reform the 'weak-willed' ones — as opposed to the practice of the Whites of executing all deserters equally. Between July and September, as the threat of a White victory grew, nearly a quarter of a million deserters returned to the Red Army from the two military districts of Orel and Moscow alone. Many of them called themselves 'volunteers', and said they were ready to fight against the Whites, whom they associated with the restoration of the gentry on the land. These were regions where the local peasantry had made substantial land gains in 1917. In Orel the amount of land in peasant use had increased by 28 per cent; while in the Moscow military district the increase was as much as 35 per cent. The threat of a White victory made the peasants fear for the loss of their new land — a fear that the Reds encouraged through their propaganda — and they were prepared to send their sons back to the army to defend this land. However much the peasants might have disliked the Bolshevik regime, with its violent requisitionings and bossy commissars, they would continue to defend it as long — and only as long — as it stood between the Whites and their own revolution on the land.[30]

By October, the Reds had nearly 200,000 troops ready for battle on the Southern Front. This gave them twice as many forces as the Whites. In preparation for a counter-offensive against the Whites, Alexander Egorov was given command of the Southern Front on 11 October. His career pattern was very similar to Os'kin's and indeed typical of the new Red military élite. He had risen to the rank of colonel during the First World War, had joined the Left SRs in 1917, and had defected to the Bolsheviks during the summer of 1918. Egorov was the principal architect of the Red Army victory in the south — although in fact there was very little planning, since the strategy had been changed at the final moment and was largely improvised as it went along.* Os'kin found nothing but panic and chaos at the headquarters of the Southern Front. Nobody even knew for sure 'where our troops were located'.[31]

Despite this confusion, which was characteristic of the whole of the civil war, these large-scale battles of October were very different from the sort of fighting that had typified the earlier stages of the civil war. The battles of 1918 had really been no more than small-scale skirmishes and artillery duels. The small and motley forces had been mostly concerned with self-preservation, there had been no fixed positions or Fronts, and towns and territories had frequently changed hands. It had been like a minor nineteenth-century war. But the battles of October were much heavier and resembled more the fighting of the First World War. Hundreds of thousands of soldiers were involved, millions of cartridges were fired every day, there were tanks and aeroplanes, and armoured cars, and the battles went on through the night. With better command structures in both armies, and their officers under stricter orders not to retreat, thousands of soldiers' lives were expended over insignificant bits of land. Neither side took prisoners.

The Red counter-offensive on the Southern Front had two key strategic elements. The first was a surprise attack by the Striking Group of Latvian Rifles, some 12,000 crack troops situated to the west of Orel, on the left flank of the Volunteer Army as it pushed north towards Tula. After a fierce and bloody battle, in which nearly half the Latvians were slaughtered, the Whites were

---

* The original Red strategy, set in July, had been to attack from the Volga to the Don; but this was changed on 15 October, the day after Orel fell, when the Politburo resolved to concentrate all the Red forces around Tula. Kamenev, the Commander-in-Chief, was not even consulted on the change.

pushed back beyond Orel. At this point the second key element of the counter-offensive was deployed. On 19 October the Red Cavalry suddenly attacked the Cossacks on the left flank of the Whites, eventually chasing them back towards Voronezh. The Cossacks must have been astonished by the Red horsemen, since they had hardly ever been deployed before. Trotsky had always underestimated the strategic advantages of the cavalry in a war of movement like the civil war. It was only the Mamontov Raid that had taught him the slogan 'Proletarians to Horse!'[32]

To build up their cavalry the Reds had turned in 1918 to Semen Budenny. This tall and imposing cavalry officer, complete with a handlebar moustache, was the son of a non-Cossack peasant from the Don region. He had been drafted into the tsarist army in 1903, and after the war against Japan, when his horsemanship had first been spotted, had been enrolled in the Imperial Cavalry Riding School in St Petersburg. By 1914, Budenny had risen to become a sergeant-major in the élite Imperial Dragoons. He was one of the many NCOs to join the Bolsheviks in 1917; and like many of them soon fell in with Stalin and the Military Opposition. In 1918 Voroshilov placed him at the head of a small cavalry force fighting against Krasnov's Cossacks near Tsaritsyn. This First Red Cavalry Corps was largely made up of poor Cossacks and non-Cossack peasants from the northern Don. It was reinforced from these same elements in preparation for the counter-offensive against Denikin. This was the nucleus of Budenny's celebrated Cavalry Army, the one immortalized through Babel's stories, which recounted its adventures in the war against Poland during 1920. Many of Stalin's most honoured commanders, if not the most talented, won their spurs in the 'Konarmiia'. Apart from Marshal Budenny, who was buried in Red Square in 1970, there were Marshal Timoshenko (who led the Red Army into the Second World War) and Marshal Zhukov (who led it to victory in 1945).

Pursued by the Red Cavalry, the White Cossacks fled south to the Don, abandoning Voronezh to the Bolsheviks on 24 October. From this strategic city, Budenny's horsemen advanced towards Kastornoe, a crucial railway junction between Moscow and the Don. They finally captured it on 15 November after several days of bloody fighting against Shkuro's Cossacks. This effectively sealed the fate of Denikin's offensive. The Whites were now threatened with the prospect of complete encirclement by the Reds, and they were forced to beat a hasty retreat south. Never again did they threaten to break through into central Russia.

* * *

October was a double opportunity missed by the Whites. At the height of the fighting at Orel a second major White force, the North-Western Army, advanced to the outskirts of Petrograd.

Given its shortcomings, it is amazing that the North-Western Army ever got so far. It had been formed in Pskov with the help of the German army during 1918. After the defeat of Germany, as the Red Army had advanced westwards, it had retreated into Estonia, then a newly independent state in the grips of its own civil war. There it had been able to build up its forces behind the natural barrier of Lake Peipus. By May 1919, when it re-entered Russia and launched its attack on Petrograd, the army had some 16,000 men, most of them Russian prisoners of war handed over by the Germans and deserters from the Reds.

The army was led by General Yudenich, a small-time hero of the First World War whom Kolchak had recognized as his commander in the Baltic. Aged fifty-seven and weighing eighteen stone, Nikolai Yudenich was both too old and fat to inspire anyone as a leader. With his flabby cheeks, his bald head and his twirling moustache, he looked every bit the unreconstructed Russian aristocrat that he was. Yudenich had never really reconciled himself to the downfall of the Tsarist Empire — and this was to be the cause of his own downfall.

Like all the White generals, Yudenich's instinct was to bury politics in the interests of his military campaign. 'Against the Bolsheviks without Politics' was his slogan. The North-Western Government was a piece of democratic window-dressing to appease the Allies. It had no real intention of governing Russia. Yudenich dismissed the need for a reform programme, and did not count on a popular uprising to pave his army's way to Petrograd: this was to be a military conquest not a winning of the people's hearts and minds. In fact quite the contrary occurred. As soon as his army entered Soviet soil, it met the opposition of the population and its mainly Russian conscripts began to desert. This lack of support within Russia meant that Yudenich was obliged to call on foreign troops. The Allies were luke-warm towards his mission — they were looking to withdraw from the civil war — and only sent him minimal supplies. True, British warships blockaded Petrograd and even attacked Kronstadt; but no Allied land troops were sent to Yudenich. Even if they had been willing to support the Whites in an offensive against Petrograd, Yudenich's connections with the Germans would have been enough to prevent the Allies from supporting him.

Without the support of the Allies the success of Yudenich's offensive against Petrograd would rest on the willingness of Finland to act as a springboard and supply base for his army. The Finnish border was only twenty miles from Petrograd — nearly ten times shorter than the march through Russia via Pskov. Yet even here — with the prize of Petrograd so close to their grasp — the White generals allowed their obstinate commitment to the Russian Empire to get in the way of an accord with the Finns.

The Finnish Defence Corps under General Mannerheim had grown into a major national army since its defeat of the Reds at Helsingfors during the spring of 1918. It was the Finns rather than the Whites whom the Bolsheviks feared most in Petrograd. By June 1919, it was reckoned that there were up to 100,000 Finnish troops around Lake Lagoda. One quarter of them were facing Petrograd. The price of Finland's support for Yudenich was simple: a guarantee of its independence. This should have been a formality: Finland was already, to all intents and purposes, an independent state and was recognized as such by most of the Western powers. Yet the Whites thought that even this small price was still too much to pay. Their simple-minded nostalgia for the Russian Empire, which they were committed to restore, prevented them from making deals with nationalists. 'History will never forgive me if I surrender what Peter the Great won,' Kolchak had declared with typical bombast when urged, as the supreme leader of the Whites, to yield to the Finnish demand. Prince Lvov and the Political Conference in Paris were adamantly opposed to the idea of granting Finland recognition until its status had been finally resolved by the Constituent Assembly in Russia. This was also typical of the Whites' fixation with the legal framework of the past — a fixation which prevented them from engaging with the political realities of the present. Mannerheim was well disposed to the anti-Bolshevik cause. But not even he could persuade the war-weary Finns to support the Whites without a guarantee of recognition. The Reds, on the other hand, had granted Finland recognition eighteen months before. They were now offering a peace accord with the Finns if they remained neutral in the civil war, while threatening them with 'merciless extermination' if they joined the Whites. The Allies urged Yudenich to recognize Finland, realizing that without its support his offensive was doomed to fail. But the White general refused to budge. This gave Mannerheim, facing an election in July, no choice but to wash his hands of the Whites. He refused to give Yudenich troops or to let his army operate from Finnish soil. It was a crucial setback for the Whites, forcing them to advance on Petrograd by the longer and more hostile route through Yamburg and Gatchina.

Yudenich made a last desperate effort to enlist the support of the Estonians. But they were a small nation, and a young and fragile one, and they were unwilling to give the Whites many troops, especially when the latter would not even recognize Estonian independence in return. The Reds were quick to exploit the situation — just as they had been in the Finnish case — offering Estonia a peace accord if it remained neutral in the civil war. The natural inclination of the Estonians to avoid involvement in the civil war thus coincided with their best interests as an independent state forced to live next door to the Soviets.

Left to his own devices, Yudenich ordered a dash for Petrograd on 10 October. He was banking on the Reds being caught short by the fighting on the Southern Front. To begin with, the gamble paid off. The Bolsheviks had indeed transferred units to the south. The 25,000 troops of the Seventh Red Army, left to defend Petrograd, were utterly demoralized and beginning to desert. Aided by Colonel Liundkvist, the Chief of Staff of the Seventh Army who defected to the Whites and supplied them with details of the Red positions, Yudenich's 18,000 troops advanced rapidly. By the 20th they had reached the Pulkovo Heights, overlooking the Petrograd suburbs. 'There was the dome of St Isaac's and the gilt spire of the Admiralty,' one his officers recalled, 'one could even see trains pulling out of the Nikolai Station.' So confident were they of victory on that day that one of their generals even refused the offer of field-glasses to survey the city because, as he put it, they would in any case be walking down the Nevsky Prospekt the next day.[33]

News of the White advance created panic among the Reds. Lenin wanted to abandon Petrograd and concentrate on the Southern Front. But Trotsky was adamant that the birth-place of the revolution should be defended at all costs, even if that meant fighting in the streets, and he persuaded Lenin to change his mind. On 16 October Trotsky was despatched to the old capital to take charge of its defence. Zinoviev, the Petrograd party boss, had completely lost his nerve and could do nothing but lie down on a sofa in the Smolny. This was one of the few occasions in the civil war — much fewer than claimed by his acolytes — when Trotsky's presence at the Front helped to decide the outcome of the battle. At one point he even mounted a horse, rounded up the retreating troops and led them back into battle.

Trotsky's first task was to boost morale — and this he did with his brilliant talent for mass oratory. He urged the soldiers not to give up and made fun of the enemy's British tanks, from which the Reds had run away, describing them as nothing more than boxes 'made of painted wood'. He even ordered the Putilov plant to knock up a few vehicles resembling tanks to give the troops reassurance that they too had these machines on their side. Trotsky's next task was to transform Petrograd into a fortress and prepare its population for a battle in the streets. Martial law was declared in the city and a night-time curfew was imposed. Thousands of workers and bourgeois residents were mobilized to erect barricades on the streets and squares. Lenin urged Trotsky to raise 30,000 people, to 'set up machine-guns behind them and to shoot several hundred of them in order to assure a real mass assault on Yudenich'. The city's sewage system was pulled up and used to build the barricades. Trenches were dug in the southern suburbs and machine-guns were posted on top of all the buildings along the main roads into the centre. Military trucks and motorcycles hurtled around Petrograd by day and night; Bolsheviks in leather jackets stood around at road blocks with guns around their shoulders; and all the major buildings were guarded by teams of worker volunteers.[34]

Although Petrograd, like every other city, had been troubled by frequent strikes, the threat of a White breakthrough seemed to galvanize many workers into defending the Soviet regime. As one of the Whites' spies in Petrograd put it:

> The worker elements, at least a large section of them, are still Bolshevik inclined. Like some other democratic elements, they see the regime, although bad, as their own. Propaganda about the cruelty of the Whites has a strong effect on them ... Psychologically, they identify the present with equality and Soviet power and the Whites with the old regime and its scorn for the masses.

Hundreds of workers armed themselves with rifles and turned out to defend the Smolny. Meanwhile, in the courtyard of the Soviet headquarters, a dozen motorcars were kept ready to whisk away the party leaders should Petrograd fall. Viktor Serge and his pregnant wife abandoned their room in the Astoria Hotel and spent the night in an ambulance parked in the suburbs. With a little case and two false passports, they were ready to flee at a moment's notice.[35]

In their rush to get to Petrograd, the Whites had failed to cut the railway link to Moscow. This crucial blunder allowed the Reds to bring up reinforcements in time for a counter-offensive on 21 October. It was a sign of their desperation that even at the height of the battle against Denikin the Reds were prepared to transfer vital reserves from Tula to Petrograd. Lenin made the crucial decision, directly telephoning Os'kin himself. 'I was literally caught for breath when a voice on the telephone said "Lenin here",' Os'kin later wrote. He promised Lenin a whole brigade of highly disciplined Communist reserves who were to play a vital role in the counter-offensive. Kamenev, the Red Commander-in-Chief, called them 'our Queen of Spades' — the last trump card needed to win the game. Against Yudenich's 15,000 troops, the Reds now had almost 100,000 — enough even by their own wasteful standards to turn the tables against the Whites. After three days of brave and bloody fighting for the Pulkovo Heights — the Reds courageously held off Yudenich's tanks with nothing but their rifles — the Whites were pushed back towards Estonia. Without reserves, their retreat was just as quick as their advance had been. In mid-November the Estonians allowed Yudenich's forces to enter their country, although only after disarming them. Trotsky wanted to pursue the Whites into Estonia ('the kennel for the guard dogs of the counter-revolution'). But this proved unnecessary. Yudenich resigned and his army was disbanded. On New Year's Eve Estonia signed an armistice with Soviet Russia, followed by a peace treaty — Moscow's first with its border states — on 2 February 1920.[36]

To honour Trotsky's role in the defence of Petrograd, he was awarded the Order of the Red Banner, the first such order of its kind. Trotsky attained the status of a hero.* Gatchina, where much of the fighting had taken place, was renamed Trotsk. It was the first Soviet town to be named after a living Communist.

* * *

As Denikin's forces fled southwards they lost all semblance of discipline and began to break up in panic. Napoleon had once remarked about his own retreat from Moscow: 'from the sublime to the ridiculous it is only one step'. Much the same could be said for Denikin's.

It was not just the Reds who had caused the Whites to panic. Makhno's partisans, Petliura's Ukrainian nationalists and various other partisan bands ambushed the White units from all sides as they retreated towards the Black Sea. Denikin's forces were passing through terrain where the local population, in Wrangel's words, 'had learned to hate us'. Then, in late November, came the shocking news that the British were ending their support for the Whites. Coupled with the news of Kolchak's defeat, this had a devastating effect on morale. 'In a couple of days the whole atmosphere in South Russia was changed,' remarked one eye-witness. 'Whatever firmness of purpose there had previously been was now so undermined that the worst became possible. [Lloyd] George's opinion that the Volunteer cause was doomed helped to make that doom almost certain.' The optimism that had so far maintained the White movement — Sokolov compared it to the gambler's desperate belief that his winning card would somehow turn up — now collapsed completely. Soldiers and officers deserted *en masse*. The Cossacks became disenchanted with the Whites. Many of the Kuban Cossacks refused to go on fighting unless Denikin satisfied their demands for a separate state.[37]

There was similar disenchantment within the huge White civilian camp. People no longer believed in victory, and thought only of how to flee abroad. Shops and cafés closed. There was a mad rush to exchange the Don roubles issued by Denikin for foreign currency. In a repeat of the panic scenes in Omsk, thousands of officers and civilians struggled to get aboard trains for the Black Sea ports. The wounded and the sick, whose numbers were swollen by a raging typhus epidemic, were simply abandoned. This could no longer be called a 'bourgeoisie on the run'. Most of the refugees were now penniless, whatever their former fortunes. It was a poor mass of naked humanity fleeing for its life. One witness saw this in the flight from Kharkov:

> As the last Russian hospital train was preparing to leave one evening, in the dim light of the station lamps strange figures were seen crawling along the platform. They were grey and shapeless, like big wolves. They

---

* And his opponents, notably Stalin, warned for the first time of the dangers of Bonapartism.

came nearer, and with horror it was recognized that they were eight Russian officers ill with typhus, dressed in their grey hospital dressing-gowns, who, rather than be left behind to be tortured and murdered by the Bolshevists, as was likely to be their fate, had crawled along on all fours through the snow from the hospital to the station, hoping to be taken away on a train.[38]

In the context of this moral collapse the White Terror reached its climax and the worst pogroms against the Jews were carried out. It was a last savage act of retribution against a race whom many of the Whites blamed for the revolution.

Anti-Semitism was a fact of life in Russia throughout the revolutionary period. Attacks on Jews often played a part in the violence of the crowd. The word pogrom could mean both an attack on the Jews and an assault on property in general. The tsarist regime, in stirring up the one, had always been careful not to let it spill over into the other. The scapegoating of Jews for the country's woes became much more widespread after 1914. The Pale of Settlement was broken down by the war and the Jews dispersed across Russia. They appeared in the major cities of the north for the first time in large numbers. During the revolution Jews entered the government and official positions also for the first time. Not many Jews were Bolsheviks, but many of the leading Bolsheviks were Jews. To large numbers of ordinary Russians, whose world had been turned upside-down, it thus appeared that their country's ruin was somehow connected with the sudden appearance of the Jews in places and positions of authority formerly reserved for the non-Jews. It was a short step from this to conclude that the Jews were plotting to bring about Russia's ruin. The result was mass Judeophobia. 'Hatred of the Jews', wrote a leading sociologist in 1921, 'is one of the most prominent features of Russian life today; perhaps even the most prominent. Jews are hated everywhere — in the north, in the south, in the east, and in the west. They are hated by people regardless of their class or education, political persuasion, race, or age.'[39]

During the early stages of the White movement in the south anti-Semitism played a relatively minor role. There were even Jews in the Volunteer Army, some of them heroes of the Ice March. OSVAG, Denikin's propaganda organ, employed many Jews. But as the Whites advanced into the Ukraine, where the Jewish population was more concentrated than in the Don, their ranks were engulfed by a vengeful hatred of the Jews. The initiative came from the Cossacks and their regimental officers, although Denikin, a passive anti-Semite, did little to resist it and several of his generals encouraged it. Jews were forced out of Denikin's army and administration. White propaganda portrayed the Bolshevik regime as a Jewish conspiracy and spread the myth that all its major leaders were Jews apart from Lenin.* As the head of the Red Army, Trotsky (or Bronstein, as he was parenthesized in the White press) was singled out as a monstrous 'Jewish mass-killer' of the Russian people. The Jews were blamed for the murder of the Tsar, for the persecution of the Orthodox Church and for the Red Terror. Now it is true that the Jews were prominent in the Kiev and other city Chekas. But this was used as a pretext to take a bloody revenge against the Jewish population as a whole. As the Chief Rabbi of Moscow once put it, it was the Trotskys who made the revolutions but it was the Bronsteins who paid the bills. Most of the White leaders, including Denikin, took the view that the Jews had brought the pogroms on themselves because of their 'support' for the Bolshevik regime. The whole of the White movement was seized by the idea that the persecution of the Jews was somehow justified as a popular means of counter-revolution. The Russian Rightist Shulgin, a major spokesman on the Jews' collective guilt, later acknowledged that the pogroms were a White revenge for the Red Terror. 'We reacted to the "Yids" just as the Bolsheviks reacted to the *burzhoois*. They shouted, "Death to the *Burzhoois!*" And we replied, "Death to the Yids!" '[40]

The first major pogroms were perpetrated by Petliura's Ukrainian nationalist bands in the winter of 1918–19. The partisans of Makhno and Grigoriev also carried out pogroms, as did the Poles in 1920, and some units of the Red Army. In all these pogroms, except those of the Poles (which were racially motivated), anti-Jewish violence was closely associated with the looting and destruction of Jewish property. The Ukrainian peasant soldiers hated the Jews mainly because they were traders, inn-keepers and money-lenders, in short the 'bourgeoisie' of the 'foreign' towns who had always exploited the 'simple villagers' and kept them living in poverty. It was common for pogrom leaders to impose a huge revolutionary tax on the Jews — in the belief that they were fantastically wealthy — and then to kill the hostages taken from them when the taxes were not paid. The Bolsheviks employed the same methods during the Red Terror. It was also common for the pogrom leaders to license their soldiers to loot Jewish shops and houses, murdering and raping the Jews in the process, and to allow the local Russian population to help themselves to a share of the spoils, under the pretext that the Jews had grown rich from speculating on the economic crisis and that their wealth should be returned to the people. The Bolsheviks called this looting the looters.

The pogroms carried out by Denikin's troops were largely driven by the same simple instinct to rob, rape and kill a Jewish population which was

---

* The myth gained currency in Western circles. General Holman, for example, the head of the British military mission to Denikin, told a Jewish delegation that of the thirty-six Commissars in Moscow, only Lenin was not a Jew (Shekhtman, *Pogromy*, 298).

seen as wealthy, alien and weak. But in a way that was more apparent than in the earlier pogroms they were also motivated by a racial hatred for the Jews and by a hatred of them, in the words of one White officer, as the 'chosen people of the Bolsheviks'. Whole Jewish towns were burned and destroyed on the grounds that they had supported the Reds (was it any wonder that they did?). Red stars were painted on the synagogues. Jews were taken hostage and shot in reprisal for the Red Terror. Jewish corpses were displayed in the street with a sign marked 'Traitors', or with a Red Star cut into their flesh.[41]

On seizing a town from the Reds, it was common for the White officers to allow their soldiers two or three days' freedom to rob and kill the Jews at will. This was seen as a reward for the troops and a just retribution for the part played by the Jews in supporting the Reds. There were no recorded cases of a White officer ever halting a pogrom, but several cases where even senior generals, such as Mamontov and Mai-Maevsky, ordered them. One of the worst pogroms took place in Kiev, right under the noses of the White authorities. From 1 to 5 October the Cossack soldiers went around the city breaking into Jewish homes, demanding money, raping and killing. The officers and local priests urged them on with speeches claiming that 'The Yids kill all our people and support the Bolsheviks.' Even Shulgin, an ardent anti-Semite, was disturbed by the climate of 'medieval terror' in the streets and by the 'terrifying howl' of the 'Yids' at night 'that breaks the heart'. Yet General Dragomirov, who ruled the city, did not order a stop to the pogrom until the 6th, the day after the orgy of killing had finally burned itself out.[42]

Many pogroms were accompanied by gruesome acts of torture on a par with those of the Red Terror. In the town of Fastov the Cossacks hung their victims from the ceiling, releasing them just before they choked to death: if their relatives, who watched this in terror, could not pay up the money they had demanded, the Cossacks repeated the operation. The Cossacks cut off limbs and noses with their sabres and ripped out babies from their mothers' wombs. They set light to Jewish houses and forced those who tried to escape to turn back into the fire. In some places, such as Chernobyl, the Jews were herded into the synagogue, which was then burned down with them inside. In others, such as Cherkass, they gang-raped hundreds of pre-teen girls. Many of their victims were later found with knife and sabre wounds to their small vaginas. One of the most horrific pogroms took place in the small Podole town of Krivoe Ozero during the final stages of the Whites' retreat in late December. By this stage the White troops had ceased to care about world opinion and, as they contemplated defeat, threw all caution to the winds. The Terek Cossacks tortured and mutilated hundreds of Jews, many of them women and young children. Hundreds of corpses were left out in the snow for the dogs and pigs to eat. In the midst of this macabre scene the Cossack officers held a surreal ball in the town post office, complete with evening dress and an orchestra, to which they invited the local magistrate and a group of prostitutes they had brought with them from Kherson. While their soldiers went killing Jews for sport, the officers and their *beau monde* drank champagne and danced the night away.[43]

Thanks to the newly opened archives, we now have a fuller idea of how many Jews were killed by pogroms in the civil war. The precise number will never be known. Even the pogroms by the Whites, which are the best known, raise all sorts of statistical problems; and there were many other pogroms against Jews (by the Ukrainian nationalists, by Makhno's partisans, by the invading Polish forces and by the Reds) whose victims were never counted at all. But one can say with some certainty that the overall number of Jewish murder-victims must have been much higher than the 31,071 burials officially recorded or indeed the estimates of 50,000–60,000 deaths given by scholars in the past. The most important document to emerge from the Russian archives in recent years, a 1920 report of an investigation by the Jewish organizations in Soviet Russia, talks of 'more than 150,000 reported deaths' and up to 300,000 victims, including the wounded and the dead.[44]

* * *

The fleeing thousands of Denikin's regime all piled into Novorossiisk, the main Allied port on the Black Sea, in the hope of being evacuated on an Allied ship. By March 1920, the town was crammed full of desperate refugees. Dignitaries of the old regime slept a dozen to each room. Typhus reaped a dreadful harvest among the hordes of unwashed humanity. Prince E. N. Trubetskoi and Purishkevich died in the awful conditions of Novorossiisk. No one gave any more thought to the idea of fighting the Reds, whose cavalry encircled the town. Seven years of war and revolution had bred in these people a psyche of defeat — and they now thought only of escape. British guns were thrown into the sea. Cossacks shot their horses. Everyone wanted to leave Russia but not everyone could be taken by the Allied ships. Priority was given to the troops, 50,000 of whom were carried off to the Crimea on 27 March. That left 60,000 Whites at the mercy of the Reds. Amidst the final panic to get on board there were ugly scenes: princesses brawled like fish-wives; men and women knelt on the quay and begged the Allied officers to save their lives; some people threw themselves into the sea.[45]

For Denikin's critics, this botched evacuation was the final straw. A generals' revolt had been steadily gaining ground since the first reverses of the autumn, as it became clear that the Moscow Directive had been a strategic error. On arriving in the Crimea, they now demanded Denikin's resignation. General Wrangel emerged as the clear successor from a poll of the senior commanders. Because of their repugnance at the idea of 'electing' a new leader — that would smack of the democracy that had destroyed the army in 1917 — they prevailed upon Denikin to resign and 'appoint' Wrangel as his successor. This was the final insult for Denikin, who had only recently discharged his rival. He was now obliged to recall him from Constantinople, where Wrangel had been in exile. The same British ship that brought Wrangel back to Russia took Denikin to the Turkish capital. He would never see his fatherland again.

Under General Wrangel the Whites made one last stand against the Bolsheviks. But it was obvious from the start that their task was doomed. The Soviet war against Poland, which diverted Red troops from the Southern Front, briefly enabled the Whites to gain a toe-hold in the Crimea. But it was only a matter of time before the Reds turned their attention to them again: and when they did so the outcome was never really in doubt. To all intents and purposes, the Whites were defeated in April 1920.

What were the fundamental reasons for their failure? The White émigré communities would agonize for years over this question. Historians whose views are broadly sympathetic to the White cause have often stressed the 'objective factors' that were said to have stacked the odds against them.[46] The Reds had an overwhelming superiority of numbers, they controlled the vast terrain of central Russia with its prestigious capitals, most of the country's industry and the core of its railway network, which enabled them to shift their forces from one Front to another. The Whites, by contrast, were divided between several different Fronts, which made it difficult to co-ordinate their operations; and they were dependent on the untrustworthy Allies for much of their supplies. Other historians have stressed the strategic errors of the Whites, the Moscow Directive foremost among them, and the Reds' superior leadership, commitment and discipline.

All these factors were no doubt relevant — and in a conventional war they might well have been enough to explain the outcome. But the Russian civil war was a very different sort of war. It was fought between armies which could count neither on the loyalty of their mostly conscript troops nor on the support of the civilian population within the territories they claimed to control. Most people wanted nothing to do with the civil war: they kept their heads down and tried to remain neutral. As one Jew told Babel, all the armies claimed to be fighting for justice, but all of them pillaged just the same.[47] By 1920, when Russia was reduced to the brink of starvation, many people would no doubt have welcomed any 'tsar' so long as he could provide them with bread. Both the Reds and the Whites were constantly crippled by mass desertion, by the breakdown of supplies, by strikes and peasant revolts in the rear. But their ability to maintain their campaigns in spite of all these problems depended less on military factors than on political ones. It was essentially a question of political organization and mass mobilization. Terror of course also played a role. But by itself terror was not enough — the people were too many and the regimes too weak to apply it everywhere — and, in any case, terror often turned out to be counter-productive.

Here the Reds had one crucial advantage that enabled them to get more soldiers on to the battlefield when it really mattered: they could claim to be defending 'the revolution' — a conveniently polyvalent symbol on to which the people could project their own ideals. Being able to fight under the Red Flag gave the Bolsheviks a decisive advantage. Its symbolic power largely accounts for the fact that the peasants, including hundreds of thousands of deserters, rallied to the Red Army during the Whites' advance towards Moscow in the autumn of 1919. The peasants believed that a White victory would reverse their own revolution on the land. It was only after the final defeat of the Whites that the peasant revolts against the Bolsheviks assumed mass proportions. This same 'defence of the revolution' also helps to explain the fact that many workers, despite their complaints against the Bolsheviks, rallied behind the Soviet regime during Yudenich's advance towards Petrograd.

At the root of the Whites' defeat was a failure of politics. They proved unable and unwilling to frame policies capable of getting the mass of the population on their side. Their movement was based, in Wrangel's phrase, on 'the cruel sword of vengeance'; their only idea was to put the clock back to the 'happy days' before 1917; and they failed to see the need to adapt themselves to the realities of the revolution. The Whites' failure to recognize the peasant revolution on the land and the national independence movements doomed them to defeat. As Denikin was the first to acknowledge, victory depended on a popular revolt against the Reds within central Russia. Yet that revolt never came. Rather than rallying the people to their side the Whites, in Wrangel's words, 'turned them into enemies'.[48]

This was partly a problem of image. Although Kolchak and Denikin both denied being monarchists, there were too many supporters of a tsarist restoration within their ranks, which created the popular image — and gave ammunition to the propaganda of their enemies — that they were associated with the old regime. The Whites made no real effort to overcome this problem with their image. Their propaganda was extremely primitive and, in any case, it is doubtful whether any propaganda could have overcome this mistrust. In the end, then, the defeat of the Whites comes down largely to their own dismal failure to break with the past and to regain the initiative within the agenda of 1917. The problem of the Russian counter-revolution was precisely that: it was too counter-revolutionary.

With the defeat of the Whites the Old Russia of Prince Lvov had finally been buried. 'My heart bleeds', he wrote to Rodichev in November 1920, 'for my distant and unhappy native land. It pains me to think of the torments being suffered there by my friends and relatives — and indeed by all the people.'

In 1918 Lvov had insisted on the need to fight the Reds by military means. He had not believed in the possibility of a democratic movement within Russia. Yet by 1920 even he had come to see that this was wrong. 'We were mistaken to think that the Bolsheviks could be defeated by physical force,' he wrote to Bakhmetev in November. 'They can only be defeated by the Russian people. And for that the Whites would need a democratic programme.'[49]

ii Comrades and Commissars

A shocking report landed on Lenin's desk in September 1919. It showed that the Smolny, citadel of the October Revolution, was full of corruption. 'Money flows freely from the coffers of the Petrograd Soviet into the pockets of the party leaders,' the head of its Workers' Section wrote to Lenin. For several months the Provisions Department had failed to release food to the workers' districts, and yet meanwhile from the back of the Smolny foodstuffs were being sold by the lorry-load to black-marketeers. 'The hungry workers see the well-dressed Tsarinas of the Soviet Tsars coming out with packets of food and being driven away in their cars. They say it's just the same as it was in the old days with the Romanovs and their Fräulein, Madame Vyrubova. They are afraid to complain to Zinoviev [the party boss in Petrograd] since he is surrounded by henchmen with revolvers who threaten the workers when they ask too many questions.' Shocked by this report, Lenin ordered Stalin, as the People's Commissar for State Control, to carry out an 'ultra-strict inspection of the Smolny offices'. He wanted it completed without the knowledge of Zinoviev or his officials. But Stalin refused to 'spy on comrades', claiming this would undermine the work of the party at a crucial moment of the civil war. It was typical of his attitude: the bonds of comradeship and the survival of the party were more important than any evidence of the abuse of power.[50]

 The incident was symptomatic of a general problem in the party: power was breeding corruption. This corruption was much more deep-rooted than the common or garden form of venality that grows in every government. The Bolsheviks were not like any Western party. They were more like a ruling class, similar in many ways to the nobility, with which Lenin himself often compared them. 'If 10,000 nobles could rule the whole of Russia — then why not us?' Lenin had once said. The comrades were indeed stepping into their shoes. Joining the party after 1917 was like joining the nobility. It brought preferment to bureaucratic posts, an élite status and privileges, and a personal share in the party-state. The ethos of the party dominated every aspect of public life in Soviet Russia, just as the ethos of the aristocracy had dominated public life in tsarist Russia. Perhaps this corruption was bound to happen in a party like the Bolsheviks whose own state-building in the civil war rested on the mass recruitment of the lower classes. In a social revolution, such as this, one of the main motives for joining the party was bound to be the prospect of self-advancement. But the problem was intensified by the fact that the Bolsheviks in office acted beyond any real control. It was, in effect, a clientèle system, with powerful cliques and local networks of patronage and power beyond the control of any party organ in the capital. There were times when the Bolsheviks acted more like a local mafia than the ruling party of the largest country in the world.

During the civil war the Bolshevik leaders turned a blind eye to such corruption. This was a time when the comrades were being called on to make great sacrifices for the revolution — many of them worked around the clock and showed a fanatical devotion to the party — and the odd indulgence seemed a small price to pay. In early 1918 Lenin himself had backed a plan to organize a special closed restaurant for the Bolsheviks in Petrograd on the grounds that they could not be expected to lead a revolution on an empty stomach. 'The workers will understand the necessity of it.'[51] Since then the principle had been gradually extended so that, by the end of the civil war, it was also deemed that party members needed higher salaries and special rations, subsidized housing in apartments and hotels, access to exclusive shops and hospitals, private dachas, chauffeured cars, first-class railway travel and holidays abroad, not to mention countless other privileges once reserved for the tsarist élite.

Five thousand Bolsheviks and their families lived in the Kremlin and the special party hotels, such as the National and the Metropole, in the centre of Moscow. The Kremlin's domestic quarters had over 2,000 service staff and its own complex of shops, including a hairdresser and a sauna, a hospital and a nursery, and three vast restaurants with cooks trained in France. Its domestic budget in 1920, when all these services were declared free, was higher than that spent on social welfare for the whole of Moscow. In Petrograd the top party bosses lived in the Astoria Hotel, recently restored to its former splendour after the devastations of the revolution as the First House of the Soviets. From their suites, they could call for room service from the 'comrade waiters', who were taught to click their heels and call them 'comrade master'. Long-forgotten luxuries, such as champagne and caviar, perfume and toothbrushes, were supplied in abundance. The hotel was sealed to the public by a gang of burly guards in black leather jackets. In the evening government cars were lined up by the entrance waiting to take the élite residents off to the opera or to the Smolny for a banquet. 'Grishka' Zinoviev, the 'Boss of Petrograd', often came and went with his Chekist bodyguards and a string of assorted prostitutes.[52]

The top party leaders had their own landed estates requisitioned from the tsarist élite. Lenin occupied the estate of General Morozov at Gorki, just outside Moscow. Trotsky had one of the most resplendent estates in the country: it had once belonged to the Yusupovs. As for Stalin, he settled into the country mansion of a former oil magnate. There were dozens of estates dotted around the capital which the Soviet Executive turned over to the party leaders for their private use. Each had its own vast retinue of servants, as in the old days.[53]

Lower down the party ranks the rewards of office were not as great but the same venal attitude was much in evidence. Of course there were comrades who were motivated by the highest ideals, who lived modestly and who practised the egalitarianism which their leaders preached. Lenin himself lived in three small rooms of the Kremlin and was never motivated by financial gain. But there were bound to be many others for whom such ideals were mere rhetoric and whose motivation was more down-to-earth. Bribe-taking, thefts and the sale of public property were endemic within the party. Almost anything could be purchased from corrupt officials: foodstuffs, tobacco, alcohol, fuel, housing, guns and permits of all kinds. The wives and mistresses of the party bosses went around, in Zinoviev's words, 'with a jeweller's shop-window hanging round their necks'. Their homes were filled with precious objects earned as bribes. One official in the Foreign Ministry had two Sèvres vases and a silver musket which had once belonged to Peter the Great. Not surprisingly, the most venal comrades tended to be found in the Cheka. After all, it was their job to 'squeeze the bourgeoisie'. Rabkrin (the Workers' and Peasants' Inspectorate) reported hundreds of cases where the Chekists had abused their power to extract money and jewels from their victims. Prisoners were often released in exchange for bribes. Even the Lubianka, the Moscow headquarters of the Cheka, was riddled with corruption. Bottles of cognac and other precious items would go mysteriously missing, while well-dressed prostitutes were often seen emerging from the secret buildings where these goods were stored.[54]

Lenin liked to explain the problem of corruption by the idea that impure elements from the petty-bourgeoisie had wormed their way into the Soviet apparatus as it became larger in the civil war. It is true that the lower levels of the state apparatus had many non-proletarians whose commitment to the Bolshevik regime was often mainly one of self-interest. But the problem of corruption was not confined to them. It engulfed the party as a whole, including those who had served it the longest and who tended to remain at its top. In short, the corruption was the result of the unbridled exercise of power.

It was not just a question of the Bolshevik monopoly of power in the Soviets. This had been completed in most of the cities by the summer of 1918 — well before the corruption became endemic. It was also a question of those Soviets being transformed from revolutionary bodies, in which the assembly was the supreme power and controlled the work of the executives, into bureaucratic organs of the party-state where all real power lay with the Bolsheviks in the executives and the assembly had no control over them. The corruption was a result of the bureaucratization just as much as of the monopolization of power.

This dual process involved a number of simultaneous developments within the party-state. There was no master plan. When the Bolsheviks came to power they had no set idea — other than the general urge to control and centralize — of how to structure the institutional relationships between the party and the Soviets. These relationships grew spontaneously out of the general conditions of the revolution. The local Soviets and party organs were highly decentralized and improvised in nature during the early months of 1918. Many of them declared their own local 'republics' and 'dictatorships' which blindly ignored the directives of Moscow. Indeed it had become so common for the rural Soviets to tear up the decrees of the central government for cigarette paper that when Lenin gave his agitators the Decree on Land to take into the countryside he also gave them old calendars to distribute in the hope that these might be torn up instead of the decree.[55] Kaluga Province became proverbial for its resistance to centralized authority in 1918. There was a Sovereign Soviet Republic of Autonomous Volosts in Kaluga. It was the closest Russia ever came to an anarchist structure of power, with the Soviet of each volost empowered to set up border controls in its territory. Thus the agents of the state in Moscow were obliged to obtain a passport from each separate Soviet as they passed from one village to another. Only during the civil war, when they stressed the need for strict centralized control to mobilize the resources of the country, did the Bolsheviks plan the general structure of the party-state.

Their first priority was to win control of the Soviets and other vital organs, such as the trade unions. The Mensheviks and SRs still had a presence in these bodies, albeit as 'non-party' delegates after their parties were banned in the summer of 1918.* All the Communist electoral tactics employed in this century to subvert democratic bodies were first developed in the Russian civil war. The Bolsheviks engaged in widespread ballot-rigging and intimidation of the opposition. Voting at Soviet and trade union congresses was nearly always done by an open show of hands so that to vote against the Bolsheviks was to invite harassment from the Cheka, whose presence was always strongly felt at election meetings. With a secret ballot the Bolsheviks would not have won very many elections. 'Soviets without the Communists!' was increasingly the slogan of the workers and the peasants. But the Bolsheviks did away with this 'convention of bourgeois democracy' on the grounds that a secret ballot was no longer needed in the 'higher form of freedom' apparently enjoyed by the Soviet people.

---

* From 1918 to 1922 the ban on the Mensheviks and the SRs would be briefly lifted from time to time. But even during these periods the Bolsheviks would persecute their activists.

And with the system of open voting — which was the tradition of the Russian village commune — there were very few elections they could lose. Even the artists of the Marinsky Opera, hardly a bastion of Communism, voted unanimously for the Bolsheviks in the Soviet elections of 1919.

The enforcement of voting by party slates also worked to the advantage of the Bolsheviks. As the only legal party within the Soviets, they alone could meet as a caucus to co-ordinate strategy, whereas other parties and factions remained divided on the Congress floor. It meant that, even as a small minority, the Bolsheviks could often win elections in the local Soviets by presenting themselves as the only party capable of being held responsible for the actions of the central government. With a bare majority the Bolshevik slate in its entirety would often form the Soviet executive rather than seats being allocated according to the strength of the different factions. It was a case of winner takes all.

Once in command of the Soviet executives, the Bolsheviks aimed to centralize power under their control. Soviet congresses were seldom called and, in their absence, power was exercised by the Soviet executives along with their permanent departmental staffs, which were appointed in each policy area. The socialist opposition called this the *ispolkomshchina*, or executive dictatorship. During the revolutionary period the Soviet executives had been largely made up of peasant and worker volunteers. But they were now increasingly made up of full-time professional bureaucrats paid by the central party-state and only seldom re-elected. Plough-pushers were giving way to pen-pushers.

Increasingly, the work of the Soviets was driven by the party apparatus. The party was expanding its control into both the administrative and the political branches of the state. Until 1919, the party as such had all but disappeared as its forces entered the Soviets. The Central Committee barely existed — Lenin and Sverdlov did most of its work together on the back of an envelope — and had only the weakest connections with the local party cells. Some Bolsheviks even suggested that the party had served its purpose and could be abolished now that it controlled the Soviets. It seemed to many of the Bolsheviks that the party cells were, in Nikolai Krestinky's words, no more than the 'agitation departments of the local Soviets'. All this changed in the spring of 1919. For one thing, the sudden death of Sverdlov, who had stood at the head of both the party and the Soviet bureaucracies, suggested the need for separation between the two structures. For another, it now appeared to the Bolsheviks, struggling to cope with the chaotic Soviet apparatus in the civil war, that the party structure could be used to introduce more centralized forms of Soviet control.

Following the Eighth Party Congress in March the central party apparatus was built up in preparation to take over control of the Soviets. A five-man Politburo was established (Lenin, Trotsky, Stalin, Kamenev and Krestinsky) to decide party policy. The staff of the Central Committee was increased five-fold during the course of the following year, with nine departments and various bureaux appended to it to formulate policies in various areas, together with a Party Secretariat and a special Organizational Bureau (Orgburo) to allocate party forces throughout the country. A strict centralism was imposed on the local party cells: their members were now told to carry out the orders of the higher party bodies rather than those of the Soviets. Since the chairmen of the local Soviets were invariably party members — and often the chairman of the local party cell — this effectively subordinated the whole of the Soviet apparatus to the party. The Bolsheviks began to talk of the Soviets and other public bodies, such as the trade unions, as 'transmission belts' of party rule. It was a phrase that Stalin would make famous.

The higher party organs tended increasingly to appoint their own special commissars to Soviet positions hitherto elected from below. By 1920, the Central Committee was making about 1,000 such postings a month. The provincial party organs made similar postings at the district and volost level. Os'kin's in Tula was one of the most notorious practitioners of this 'appointmentism'. Its aim was to increase the Centre's control over the local apparatus by sending down its most loyal and trusted comrades to take command of it in military style. But this was sometimes counter-productive. The roaming commissars were prone to alienate the local activists by riding roughshod over their interests. This gave rise to growing protests among the Bolshevik rank and file against the party's 'militarization', which resulted in the atrophy of the local party organizations and their alienation from the leadership. Perhaps even more importantly, the frequent use of such appointments also meant that many Soviets were ruled by party bosses wholly alien to the local region and thus perhaps more inclined to the abuse of power. Semen Kanatchikov was a typical representative of this nomadic commissar class. Although a native of Moscow province, he was appointed by the Central Committee to senior posts in Tomsk, Perm, Sverdlovsk, Omsk, the Tatar Republic and Petrograd during the course of the civil war. For nearly two years, he did not see his wife and two little children, whom he left in hiding in Barnaul. This 'appointmentism' could only add to the growing sense, both among the people and the party rank and file, that Soviet power was something alien and oppressive.[56]

*   *   *

Not surprisingly for a party-state that aimed to control the whole of society, the Soviet bureaucracy ballooned spectacularly during the first years of Bolshevik rule. Whereas the tsarist state had left much in the hands of private and public institutions, such as the zemstvos and the charities, the Soviet regime abolished all of these and assumed direct responsibility for the activities which they had performed. The result was the bureaucratization of virtually every aspect of life in Russia, from banking and industry to education. From 1917 to 1921 the number of government employees more than quadrupled, from 576,000 to 2.4 million. By 1921, there were twice as many bureaucrats as workers in Russia. They were the social base of the regime. This was not a Dictatorship of the Proletariat but a Dictatorship of the Bureaucracy. Moscow, in Lenin's words, was 'bloated with officials': it housed nearly a quarter of a million of them, one-third of the total workforce in the city by the end of 1920. The centre of Moscow became one vast block of offices, as committees were piled on top of councils and departments on top of commissions.[57]

Perhaps a third of the bureaucracy was employed in the regulation of the planned economy. It was an absurd situation: while the economy came to a standstill, its bureaucracy flourished. The country was desperately short of fuel but there was an army of bureaucrats to regulate its almost non-existent distribution. There was no paper in the shops but a mountain of it in the Soviet offices (90 per cent of the paper made in Russia during the first four years of Soviet rule was consumed by the bureaucracy). One of the few really busy factories was the Moscow Telephone Factory. Such was the demand of this new officialdom for telephones that it had a waiting list of 12,000 orders.[58]

This correlation — empty factories and full offices — was not accidental. The scarcer goods were, the harder it became to control their distribution, since the black market thrived on shortages, so that the state increased its intervention. The result was the proliferation of overlapping offices within the economy. Apart from the central commissariats (e.g. food, labour, transport) and their local organs in the Soviets, there was the network of organs subordinate to the VSNKh, the All-Russian Council for the Economy, including its local economic councils, the manufacturing trusts and the special departments for the regulation of individual commodities (Glavki). Then there were also the *ad hoc* agencies set up by the regime for military supply, like the Council of Labour and Defence or such acronymic monsters as Chusosnabarm (the Extraordinary Agency for the Supply of the Army), which in principle could over-rule the other economic organs. Of course, in practice, there was only confusion and rivalry between the different organs. The more the state tried to centralize control, the less real control it actually had. Lower down the scale, at factory level, the bureaucracy proved just as ineffective. For every 100 factory workers there were 16 factory officials by 1920. In some factories the figure was much higher: of the 7,000 people employed at the famous Putilov metal plant, only 2,000 were blue-collar workers; the rest were petty officials and clerks. Such were the material advantages of a white-collar job, not least access to food and goods in short supply, that such parasites were bound to grow in number as the economic crisis deepened. All the strike resolutions of these years complained about factory officials 'living off the backs of the workers'.[59]

Lenin liked to claim that the problem of bureaucratism was a legacy of the tsarist era. It is true that the Soviet bureaucracy inherited the culture of the tsarist one. But by 1921 it was also ten times bigger than the tsarist state. There was some continuity of the personnel, especially in the central organs of the state. Over half the bureaucrats in the Moscow offices of the commissariats in August 1918 had worked in some branch of the administration before October 1917. Many of the central organs also employed armies of young bourgeois ladies, most of whom had never worked before, to do the petty paper work. One eye-witness recalls them walking by their hundreds every morning through the snow from the Moscow suburbs to the centre of the city. There they worked all day in unheated offices, their wet shoes and clothes never drying out, before walking back to the suburbs to help feed their hungry relatives. Otherwise, however, the lower you went down the apparatus the more it was dominated by the lower classes entering officialdom for the first time. The majority of these elements, especially in provincial towns, came from the lower-middle classes — what Marxists called the 'petty bourgeoisie': bookkeepers, shop assistants and petty clerks; small-time traders and artisans; activists of the co-operatives; engineers and factory officials; and all those who might have once worked as technicians or professionals in the zemstvos and municipal organs. As for the workers, in whose name the regime had been founded, they represented a very small proportion of those who entered the Soviet bureaucracy: certainly no more than 10 per cent (based on those with blue-collar occupations before 1917). Even in the management of industry workers made up less than one-third of officials. It is reasonable to conclude that most of these lower-middle strata were attracted to the Soviet regime less by their own revolutionary ideals than by the relatively high wages and short working-hours of its officials. It was certainly a more attractive prospect than the cold and hunger that awaited those from the older bourgeoisie who chose instead to turn their backs on it. The typical day of a Soviet official was spent gossiping in corridors, smoking cigarettes and drinking coffee, or standing in queues for the special rations that went only to the Soviet élite.[60]

In the countryside the influence of the Soviet regime penetrated further than the tsarist had. During the civil war the majority of the Soviet executives at volost level were transformed from democratic organs of peasant revolution into bureaucratic organs of state taxation. In the Volga region, where this process has been studied, 71 per cent of the volost Soviet executives had at least one Bolshevik member by the autumn of 1919, compared with only 38 per cent in the previous spring. Two-thirds of all the executive members were registered as Bolsheviks. This gave the regime a foothold in the volost townships: in the volost Soviet executives, which like their counterparts at the higher level concentrated power in their own hands at the expense of the Soviet congress, the Bolsheviks could count on a more or less reliable body to enforce the food levies and mobilizations. Having lost control of the Soviet, the peasants retreated to their villages, rallied round their communes and turned their backs on the volost Soviet. The growing conflict between the peasantry and party-state was thus fought on the same battle-lines — between the villages and the volost township — as the conflict had been fought between the peasantry and the gentry-state.[61]

The key to this process of Bolshevik state-building was the support of that young and literate class of peasants who had left the villages in the war. Os'kin was a typical example. In the Volga region 60 per cent of the members of the volost Soviet executives were aged between 18 and 35 (compared with 31 per cent of the electorate) and 66 per cent were literate (compared with 41 per cent). This was the generation who had benefited from the boom in rural schooling at the turn of the century and had been mobilized during the war. In 1918 they had returned to their villages newly skilled in military techniques and conversant with the two great ideologies of the urban world, socialism and atheism. The peasants were often inclined to view them as their natural leaders during the revolution on the land. The old peasant patriarchs, like Maliutin in Andreevskoe, were generally not literate enough to cope with the complex tasks of administration now that the gentry and the rural intelligentsia were no longer there to guide them. To many of these peasant soldiers, whose aspirations had been broadened by their absence from the village, the prospect of working in the Soviet appeared as a chance to rise up in the world. After the excitement of the army it could often seem a depressing prospect to have to return to the drudgery of peasant farming and to the 'dark' world of the village. By working in the Soviet and joining the party they could enhance their own prestige and power. They could get a clean office job, with all its perks and privileges, and an entry ticket into the new urban-dominated civilization of the Soviet regime. Throughout the peasant world Communist regimes have been built on the fact that it is the ambition of every literate peasant son to become a clerk.

*   *   *

Peasants made up the majority of those who flooded into the party. From 1917 to 1920, 1.4 million people joined the Bolsheviks — and two-thirds of these came from peasant backgrounds. Joining the party was the surest way to gain promotion through the ranks of the Soviet bureaucracy: fewer than one in five Bolshevik members actually worked in a factory or a farm by the end of 1919. The top official posts were always given to Bolsheviks, often regardless of their skills or expertise. The Ukrainian Timber Administration, for example, was headed by a first-year medical student, while ordinary carpenters, metal workers, and even in one case an organ-grinder, were placed in charge of its departments at the provincial level.[62]

The Bolshevik leaders encouraged the mass recruitment of new party members. With constant losses from the civil war, there was always a need for more party fodder. Special Party Weeks were periodically declared, when the usual requirement for recommendations was suspended and agitators were sent out to the factories and villages to encourage and enrol as many members as they could. The Party Week of October 1919, at the height of the White advance, more than doubled the size of the party with 270,000 new members signing up.[63]

But the Bolsheviks were also rightly worried that such indiscriminate recruitments might reduce the party's quality. The hegemony of the working class within the party — although always actually a fiction since most of the leading Bolsheviks were from the intelligentsia — now seemed under threat from the peasantry. The mass influx of these lower-class members also reduced the levels of literacy, a crucial handicap for a party aiming to dominate the state administration. Less than 8 per cent of the party membership in 1920 had any secondary education; 62 per cent had only primary schooling; while 30 per cent had no schooling at all. Such was the rudimentary level of intelligence among the mass of the local officials that almost any scrap of paper, so long as it carried a large stamp and seal, could be enough to impress them as a government document. One Englishman travelled throughout Russia with no other passport than his tailor's bill from Jermyn Street which he flaunted in the face of the local officials. With the bill's impressive letter heading, its large red seal and signature, no official had dared to question it.[64]

As for the political literacy of the rank and file, this was just as rudimentary. A survey of women workers in Petrograd who had joined the party during the civil war found that most of them had never heard or thought about such words as 'socialism' or 'politics' before 1917. The Moscow Party found in 1920 that many of its members did not even know who Kamenev was (Chairman of the Moscow Soviet). Such ignorance was by no means confined to lower-class Bolsheviks. At a training school for Bolshevik journalists none of the class could say who Lloyd George or Clemenceau were. Some of them even thought that imperialism was a republic somewhere in England.[65]

And yet in an important way this complete lack of sophistication was one of the party's greatest strengths. For whatever the abuses of its rank-and-file officials, their one virtue in the common people's eyes was the fact that they spoke their own simple language, the fact that they dressed and behaved much like them, the fact in short that they were 'one of us'. This gave the Bolsheviks a symbolic appeal, one which their propaganda ruthlessly exploited, as a 'government of the people', even if in fact they betrayed this from the start. For many of the lower classes this symbolic familiarity was enough for them to identify themselves with the Bolshevik regime, even if they thought that it was bad, and to support it against the Whites (who were not 'one of us') when they threatened to break through.

No doubt many of these local Bolsheviks were genuinely committed to the ideals of the revolution: political sophistication and sincerity are hardly correlative in politics, as anyone from the advanced democracies must know. Yet others had joined the party for the advantages that it could bring. Bolshevik leaders constantly warned of the dangers of 'petty-bourgeois careerists and self-seekers' corrupting the party ranks. They were particularly disturbed to find out that a quarter of the civil war members in senior official positions had joined the Bolsheviks from another party, mostly from the Mensheviks and the SRs. The counter-revolution seemed to be invading the party itself. Trotsky called these infiltrators 'radishes' — red on the outside but white inside.

Actually, the Bolshevik leaders had little real idea of what was happening to their own party. They interpreted its growing membership in simple terms of class when the real position was much more complex. The mass of the rank and file were neither peasants nor workers, but the children of a profound social crisis which had broken down such neat divisions. The typical male Bolshevik of these years was both an ex-peasant and an ex-worker. He had probably left the village as a young boy during the industrial boom of the 1890s, roamed from factory to factory in search of work, become involved in the workers' movement, gone through various prisons, fought in the war, and returned to the northern cities, only to disperse across the countryside, during and after 1917. He was a rootless and declassed figure — like the revolution, a product of his times.

In many ways the new Bolsheviks were far more submissive than the old ones had ever been. It resulted from their lack of education. While they were able to mouth mechanically a few Marxist phrases, they were not sufficiently educated to think freely for themselves or indeed to question the party leaders on abstract policy issues. Many of the workers had been educated in adult technical schools or, like Kanatchikov, at evening classes. They were essentially practical men with a strong bent towards self-improvement. All of them were concerned, in one way or another, with the problems of modernization. They sought to abolish the backward peasant Russia of their own past and to make society more rational and equal. There was nothing theoretical or abstract in their Marxism: it was a practical, black-and-white dogma that gave them a 'scientific' explanation of the social injustice they themselves had encountered in their lives, and provided a 'scientific' remedy. The party leaders were the masters of this science and, if they said the peasants were hoarding grain, or that the Mensheviks were counter-revolutionaries, then this must be so. Only this can explain the readiness of the rank and filers to do their leaders' bidding, even when they could see that the result would be disastrous for their own localities. The persistence of the local Bolsheviks with the food requisitions in the Volga region during the autumn of 1920 — in spite of the first signs of impending famine there — is an obvious and depressing example of how this grim and unquestioning obedience, which the Bolsheviks called 'discipline' and 'hardness', had got the better of individual conscience. The good comrade did what he was told; he was content to leave all critical thinking to the Central Committee.

And yet, though docile in terms of politics, the massed ranks of the Bolshevik Party were by no means easy to control. It was partly a problem of corrupt local cliques taking over the provincial party cells. In Nizhnyi Novgorod, for example, everything was run by the local mafia of Bolshevik officials in alliance with the black-marketeers. They defied Moscow's orders and for several months sabotaged the efforts of its agent, a young Anastas Mikoyan, sent down by the Orgburo to impose control. But to a certain extent the whole of the party apparatus had also developed as a clientèle system with many of the leaders at national level each controlling their own private networks of patronage in the provinces or in individual branches of the state. Lunacharsky filled the Commissariat of Enlightenment with his own friends and associates. Even Lenin gave several Sovnarkom posts to his oldest friends and relatives: Bonch-Bruevich and Fotieva, both close associates from his Geneva days, were made secretaries; Krupskaya was appointed Deputy Commissar for Education; Anna Ul'ianova, Lenin's sister, was placed in charge of child welfare; while her husband, Mark Elizarov, was made People's Commissar of Railways. But of all the party patrons, Stalin was by far the most powerful. Through his control of the Orgburo he was increasingly able to place his own supporters in many of the top provincial posts. The effect of all these placements was to transform the party into a loose set of ruling dynasties, each of them organized on their own 'family' or clan lines. It was thus inclined to break up into factions.[66]

Lenin failed to understand the nature of his own party's bureaucratic problem. He could not see that the Bolshevik bureaucracy was fast becoming a distinct social caste with its own privileged interests apart from those of the working masses it claimed to represent. He responded to the abuses of the bureaucracy with administrative measures, as if a few minor technical adjustments were enough to eradicate the problem, whereas what was needed, at the very least, was a radical reform of the whole political system. Most of his measures proved counter-productive.

First, he tried to stop the build-up of corrupt local fiefdoms by ordering the party's leading cadres to be regularly moved by the Orgburo from post to post. Yet this merely widened the distance between the leaders and the rank and file and thus weakened the accountability of the former. It also increased Stalin's private patronage as the head of the Orgburo.

Then Lenin ordered periodic purges to weed out the undesirables who were attracted to the party as it grew. The first purge was carried out in the summer of 1918: it halved the membership from 300,000 to 150,000. During the spring of 1919 a second major purge was implemented which reduced the membership by 46 per cent. And once again, in the summer of 1920, 30 per cent of the members were purged from the party. Most of these purges were carried out at the expense of peasants and non-Russians, who were deemed the weakest link in social terms. The frequent call-up of party members to the Front also served as a form of purge since it encouraged the less than committed to tear up their party cards. The effect of all these purges was to destabilize the party rank and file (only 30 per cent of those who had joined the party between 1917 and 1920 still remained in it by 1922) and this was hardly likely to encourage loyalty.[67]

Finally Lenin ordered the regular inspection of the apparatus. It was reminiscent of the tsarist regime with its own constant revisions which Gogol had satirized in *The Government Inspector.* A whole People's Commissariat known as Rabkrin was constructed for this purpose. Formed in February 1920 with Stalin at its head, it combined the two functions of state inspection and workers' control which had previously been carried out by separate bodies. Lenin's idea was to fight red tape and improve efficiency through constant reviews of all state institutions by the inspectorates of workers and peasants. In this way he thought the state could be made democratically accountable. But the result was just the reverse. Rabkrin soon became a bureaucratic monster (and another base of Stalin's growing patronage) with an estimated 100,000 officials, the majority of them white-collar workers, in its local cells by the end of 1920.[68] Instead of helping to cut down the bureaucracy, Rabkrin had merely increased it.

* * *

'How do I live? — that is not a pleasant tale,' Gorky wrote to Ekaterina in February 1919. 'Only the Commissars live a pleasant life these days. They steal as much as they can from the ordinary people in order to pay for their courtesans and their unsocialist luxuries.' Gorky was not alone in bitterly resenting the privileges of the Communist élite. Popular anecdotes and graffiti ridiculed the Bolsheviks as the real Russian bourgeoisie in contrast to the phantom one of their propaganda. 'Where do all the chickens go?', 'Why are there no sausages?' — there were a hundred variations of the riddle but the answer was always the same: 'The Communists have eaten them all.' The word 'comrade', once an expression of collective pride, became a form of abuse. One woman, addressed as such on a Petrograd tram, was heard to reply: 'What's all this comrade! Take your "comrade" and go to hell!' Senior officials were bombarded with complaints about Communists 'living off the backs of the common people'. Workers roundly condemned the new Red élite. One factory resolution from

Perm demanded that 'all the leather jackets and caps of the commissars should be used to make shoes for the workers'.[69]

The Brusilovs had a special reason to be resentful. They were forced to share their small Moscow apartment with a certain commissar — a former soldier whom the general had once saved from the death penalty at the Front — together with his girlfriend and his mother. Brusilov describes the situation vividly:

> Coarse, insolent and constantly drunk, with a body covered in scars, he was now of course an important person, close to Lenin etc. Now I wonder why I saved his life! Our apartment, which had been clean and pleasant until he came, was thereafter spoiled by drinking bouts and fights, thievery and foul language. He would sometimes go away for a few days and come back with sacks of food, wine and fruit. We were literally starving but they had white flour, butter, and whatever else they cared for. The main thing we resented was their hoard of fuel. That was the freezing winter of 1920, when icicles hung on our living-room walls. The primus had long ceased to work and we were freezing. But they had a large iron stove and as much fuel as they liked.[70]

Complaints about the Bolshevik élite were also heard in the party itself. There was a groundswell of feeling in the lower party ranks that the leadership had become too distant from the rank and file. Many of these criticisms would come to be expressed by the Democratic Centralists and the Workers' Opposition, the two great factions which rocked the party leadership in 1920–I (see pages 731–2). As one Old Bolshevik from Tula wrote to Lenin in July 1919: 'We have cut ourselves off from the masses and made it difficult to attract them. The old comradely spirit of the party has died completely. It has been replaced by a new one-man rule in which the party boss runs everything. Bribe-taking has become universal: without it our Communist comrades would simply not survive.' Writing to Trotsky the following May, Yoffe expressed similar fears about the degeneration of the party:

> There is enormous inequality and one's material position largely depends on one's post in the party; you'll agree this is a dangerous situation. I have been told, for example, that before the last purge the Old Bolsheviks were terrified of being kicked out mainly because they would lose their right to reside in the National Hotel and other privileges connected with this. The old party spirit has disappeared, the spirit of revolutionary selflessness and comradely devotion! Today's youth is being brought up in these new

conditions: that is what makes one fear most for our Party and the Revolution!'[71]

iii A Socialist Fatherland

At the age of sixty-six, when most men are planning to play with their grand-children, Brusilov made the most dramatic change of his entire military career and volunteered to serve in the Red Army. It was no ordinary defection from the old corps of tsarist generals. Brusilov was Russia's most famous soldier, its only hero from the First World War, and as such the last living symbol of a winning aristocratic past. News of his appointment in May 1920 to a Special Conference of Trotsky's Revolutionary Military Council came as a rude shock to all those who looked back with nostalgia to the days before 1917. 'Brusilov has betrayed Russia,' one ex-colonel wrote. 'How can it be that he prefers to defend the Bolsheviks and the Jews rather than his fatherland?' added the wife of an old Guards officer. False rumours circulated that Brusilov had received lavish bribes (two million roubles, a Kremlin apartment) for his services to the Reds. The General collected a drawerful of hate-mail. How, asked one, could a nobleman like him choose to serve the Reds at a time when 'the Cheka jails are full of Russian officers'? It was 'nothing less than a betrayal'. All this weighed heavily on Brusilov's conscience.* 'It was the hardest moment of my life,' he wrote five years later. 'All the time there was a deathly silence in the house. The family walked about on tiptoes and talked in whispers. My wife and sister had tears in their eyes.'[72] It was as if they were mourning for their past.

Brusilov's conversion to the Reds was a case of putting country before class. He had every reason to hate the Bolsheviks, and often called them the Antichrist. They had not only imprisoned him but had also virtually murdered his sick brother and arrested several of his closest friends during the Red Terror. Yet Brusilov refused to join the Whites. Two wounds — his wounded leg and his wounded pride at the White adulation for his old rival Kornilov — stopped him from going to the Don. He was also still convinced that it was his duty to remain in Russia, standing by the people even if they chose the Reds. Bolshevism, in the old general's view, was bound to be a 'temporary sickness' since 'its philosophy of internationalism is fundamentally alien to the Russian people'. By working with the Bolsheviks, patriots like him could redirect the revolution

---

* Brusilov tried to make the release of the officers a condition of his service for the Reds. Trotsky agreed to do what he could but admitted that he himself was 'not on good terms with the Cheka and that Dzerzhinsky could even arrest him'. Brusilov later set up a special office to appeal for the release of the officers — and as a result of its efforts several hundred officers were released (RGVIA, f. 162, op. 2, d. 18).

towards national ends. It was, as he saw it, a question of diluting Red with White — of 'turning the Red Star into a Cross' — and thus reconciling the revolution with the continuities of Russian history. 'My sense of duty to the nation has often obliged me to disobey my natural social inclinations,' Brusilov said in 1918. Although as an aristocrat he clearly sympathized with the Whites and rejoiced when their armies advanced towards Moscow, he always thought that their cause was both doomed and flawed by its dependence upon the intervention of the Allies. The fate of Russia, for better or worse, had to be decided by its own people.[73]

During the past year two things had happened to strengthen his convictions. One was the murder of his only son, a Red Army commander whose cavalry regiment had been captured by the Whites in the battle for Orel in September 1919. No one knew for certain how Alexei died but Brusilov was convinced that he had been executed on Denikin's orders when the Whites found out who he was. Denikin was thought to despise Brusilov for having overseen the 'destruction of the army' during 1917. The fact that Alexei had only joined the Reds in the hope of persuading the Cheka to spare his father's life left Brusilov full of remorse. He blamed himself for Alexei's death and was determined to avenge it.[74] Blood, if not class, had made him Red.

So too had Russian nationalism. The Polish invasion of the Ukraine was the other vital factor behind Brusilov's conversion to the Reds. Since its partition in the eighteenth century, Poland had lived in the shadows of the three great empires of Eastern Europe. But suddenly with the Versailles Treaty it found itself with a guarantee of independence and a great deal of new territory given to it by the victorious Western powers as a buffer between Germany and Russia. It often does not take much for a former nation-victim to behave like a nation-aggressor; and as soon as Poland gained its independence it began to strut around with imperial pretensions of its own. Marshal Pilsudski, the head of the Polish state and army, talked of restoring 'historic Poland' which had once stretched from the Baltic to the Black Sea. He promised to reclaim her eastern borderlands — the 'Lithuania' cherished by Mickiewicz and other Polish patriots of the nineteenth century — that had been lost to Russia in the partitions. These were ethnically intermingled regions — Polish and Jewish cities like Lvov, Polish former landowners and Ukrainian or Belorussian peasants — to which both Russia and Poland had a claim. As the Germans withdrew from the east, Polish troops marched in to the borderlands. Pilsudski led the capture of Wilno in April 1919. During the summer the Poles continued to advance into Belorussia and the western Ukraine, capturing Minsk and Lvov. Fighting halted for a while in the winter as the Poles and Russians haggled over borders. But these negotiations broke down in the spring of 1920, when the Poles launched a new offensive. Largely supplied by the Allies, and having signed a pact with Petliura, Pilsudski led a combined force of Poles and Ukrainian nationalists in a mad dash towards Kiev, then held very tenuously by the Bolsheviks. It was a desperate bid to transform the Ukraine into a Polish satellite state. The roots of this adventure went back to the previous winter, when Petliura, forced out of the Ukraine by the Reds, had settled in Warsaw and signed a pact with Pilsudski. By this agreement Petliura's Ukrainian nationalist forces would help the Poles to re-invade the Ukraine and, once they were re-installed in power in Kiev, would cede to Poland the western Ukraine. It was in effect a Polish Brest-Litovsk. The Poles advanced swiftly towards Kiev, whilst the Reds, who were also facing the Whites in the south, broke up in confusion. On 6 May the Poles took Kiev without much resistance. It was less an invasion than a parade. The residents of Kiev watched their new rulers march into the city with apparent indifference. This, after all, was the eleventh time that Kiev had been occupied since 1917 — and it was not to be the last.*

For Russian patriots like Brusilov the capture of Kiev by the Poles was nothing less than a national disaster. This was not just any other city but the birthplace of Russian civilization. It was inconceivable that the Ukraine — 'Little Russia' — should be anything but Orthodox. Brusilov's ancestors in the eighteenth century had given up their lives defending the Ukraine against the Poles, and as a result the Brusilovs had been given large amounts of land there. Having spent the war and millions of Russian lives defending the western Ukraine from the Austrians, Brusilov was damned if he would now let it pass to the Poles without a fight. He thought it was 'inexcusable that Wrangel should attack Russia at this moment', even more so since the Whites had clearly planned their attack to coincide with that of the Poles. The Whites were placing their own class interests above those of the Russian Empire — something Brusilov had refused to do. On 1 May he wrote to N. I. Rattel, a Major-General in the imperial army and now Trotsky's Chief of Staff, offering to help the Reds against the Poles. 'It seems to me', he wrote, 'that the most important task is to engender a sense of popular patriotism.' The war against Poland, in his view, could only be won 'under the Russian national flag', since only this could unite the whole Russian people:

---

* The twelve changes of regime in Kiev were as follows: (1) 3 March–9 Nov 1917: Provisional Government; (2) 9 Nov 1917–9 Feb 1918: Ukrainian National Republic (UNR); (3) 9–29 Feb 1918: First Ukrainian Soviet Republic; (4) 1 March 1918: occupation by the army of the UNR; (5) 2 March–12 Dec 1918: German occupation; (6) 14 Dec 1918–4 Feb 1919: Directory of the UNR; (7) 5 Feb–29 Aug 1919: Second Ukrainian Soviet Republic; (8) 30 Aug 1919: occupation by forces of Directory of the UNR; (9) 31 Aug–15 Dec 1919: occupation by White forces; (10) 15 Dec 1919–5 May 1920: Third Ukrainian Soviet Republic; (11) 6 May–11 June 1920: Polish occupation; (12) 2 June 1920–: final Ukrainian Soviet Republic.

Communism is completely unintelligible to the millions of barely literate peasants and it is doubtful that they will fight for it. If Christianity failed to unify the people in two thousand years, how can Communism hope to do so when most of the people had not even heard of it three years ago? Only the idea of Russia can do that.[75]

Trotsky at once saw the propaganda victory to be won by getting Brusilov to join the Reds. The next day he announced the general's appointment as the Chairman of a Special Conference in command of the Western Front.* Printed in *Pravda* on 7 May, the announcement was typical of the increasingly xenophobic tone of the Bolsheviks' rhetoric. It called on all patriots to join the army and 'defend the Fatherland' from the 'Polish invaders', who were 'trying to tear from us lands that have always belonged to the Russians'. Trotsky claimed that the Poles were driven by 'hatred of Russia and the Russians'. The Red Army journal, *Voennoe delo*, published a xenophobic article (for which it was later suspended) contrasting the 'innate Jesuitry of the Polacks' with the 'honourable and open spirit of the Great Russian race'. Radek characterized the whole of the civil war as a 'national struggle of liberation against foreign invasion'. The Reds, he said, were 'defending Mother Russia' against the efforts of the Whites and the Allies to 'make it a colony' of the West. 'Soviet Russia', he concluded on a note of warning to the newly independent states, aimed to 'reunite all the Russian lands and defend Russia from colonial exploitation.'[76] It was back to the old imperialism.

The Bolsheviks were stunned by the success of their own patriotic propaganda. It brought home to them the huge potential of Russian nationalism as a means of popular mobilization. It was a potential Stalin later realized. Within a few weeks of Brusilov's appointment, 14,000 officers had joined the Red Army to fight the Poles, thousands of civilians had volunteered for war-work, and well over 100,000 deserters had returned to the Red Army on the Western Front. There were mass patriotic demonstrations with huge effigies of Pilsudski and Curzon which the protesters proceeded to burn. 'We never thought', Zinoviev confessed, 'that Russia had so many patriots.'[77]

But in fact the patriotic motives that had driven Brusilov to join the Reds were shared by many people from the Old Russia. National Bolshevism, as their creed was later called, urged the patriotic intelligentsia to rally behind the Soviet state, now that it had won the civil war, for the resurrection of a Great Russia. It was an echo of the call by *Vekhi* to give up opposition to the

---

* Apart from Brusilov the conference included his two closest friends from the tsarist army, Generals Klembovsky and Zaionchkovsky, as well as his old ally Polivanov, the former Minister of War.

tsarist regime after the 1905 Revolution — and this was reflected in the title of its journal, *Smena vekh* (Change of Landmarks), whose first issue, in November 1921, paid homage to Brusilov. Nikolai Ustrialov, the best-known exponent of National Bolshevism, was a right-wing Kadet who had been a propagandist for Kolchak's regime before defecting to the Reds in 1920 on the grounds that they had won the civil war through the support of the Russian people and their revolution could be redirected towards national goals. 'The interests of the Soviet system will inevitably coincide with Russia's national interests,' he wrote in 1920. 'The Bolsheviks, by the logic of events, will progress from Jacobinism to Napoleonism.' If enough patriots joined the Reds, Ustrialov argued, the Soviet regime would be Russified. It would be turned White from the inside. Ustrialov glorified the Bolsheviks for two main reasons: for what he (and many other intellectuals such as Blok and the Scythians) saw as their Asiatic Slavophilism, uniting the East against the West; and for their restoration of a strong Russian state. He defended the Bolshevik dictatorship as a necessary remedy for the anarchy which had engulfed the country since 1917. He urged the Bolsheviks to recreate the Russian Empire (crushing all those 'pygmy states') and to reassert its power in the world. Such sentiments were widely shared by the intelligentsia. In a sense National Bolshevism was the true victor of the civil war. 'We lost but we won,' the Rightist Shulgin wrote in *1920*. 'The Bolsheviks beat us but they raised the banner of a united Russia.' It was not just a question of the Right, although the old imperialists were among the first to rally round the Red flag of a Great Russia. For the Left, too, it was a short step from the worship of 'the people' and its powers of destruction to the acceptance of the Bolshevik regime as the outcome of that 'national revolution' and the only means of Russia's resurrection. This was the logic that drove many socialists to join the Bolsheviks after the civil war. Even Gorky was swept along by the patriotic tide. Writing to H. G. Wells in May 1920, he was angry with a London *Times* reporter for claiming he had found a human finger in his soup at a restaurant in Petrograd. 'Believe me,' he fumed with national pride, 'I am not unaware of the negative aspects created by the war and revolution, but I also see that in the Russian masses there is awakening a great creative will.'[78]

   This groundswell of patriotism no doubt partly influenced the Bolshevik decision to turn the defensive war against Poland into an offensive one. Having driven the Poles back from Kiev, in mid-July the Reds crossed the Curzon Line — where the Allies drew the Polish-Russian border — and continued to advance towards Warsaw. Since this would not be the last time the Red Army would move across the Russian border into Europe — it did so again in 1945 — it is important, not least for our understanding of the Cold War, to work out the Bolsheviks' motives in this counter-offensive against Poland. Some historians, such as Norman Davies and Richard Pipes, have staked their scholarly reputations on the argument that, if Warsaw had fallen to the Red Army, Lenin would have ordered it to push on to Berlin in preparation for a general assault on Western Europe.[79]

It is true, as Pipes and Davies have both argued, that the Bolsheviks viewed the invasion of Poland as a likely catalyst to the revolution not just in Poland but throughout Europe. Following the Red Army to Warsaw was a Provisional Polish Revolutionary Committee led by Dzerzhinsky, which would hand over power to the Communists once it arrived in the Polish capital. This was the height of the Bolsheviks' optimism in the exportability of Communism. Their expectations had been raised by the Spartacist Revolt in Berlin and the short-lived Soviet Republics in Hungary and Bavaria during 1919. In that spring, when the Comintern was formed, Zinoviev had predicted that 'in a year the whole of Europe will be Communist'. There was a time, he later admitted, when 'we had thought that only a few days or even hours remained before the inevitable revolutionary uprising'. By the summer of 1920 the Comintern had spread its influence throughout the capitals of Europe. Hardly a month went by without some delegation of Western socialists arriving in Russia to inspect and report back on the Great Experiment. Moscow was turned into one vast Potemkin village, with happy groups of workers and lavish banquets laid on for these naive foreign dignitaries, so that they went home full of praise. The Second Congress of the Comintern, which met in Moscow at the height of the advance towards Warsaw, aimed to create a single European Communist Party under Moscow's guidance. The mood of the Congress was expectant. Every day the delegates followed the movement of the Red Army on a great map which was hung on the wall of the Congress hall. Lenin, who had insisted on the invasion of Poland against the advice of both Trotsky and Stalin, was convinced that the European revolution was just around the corner. It was inevitable, in his dogmatic Marxist view, that every other country should reach its October. The Kapp Putsch of March 1920 was a 'German Kornilov affair'; Estonia was 'passing through its Kerensky period'; while Britain, with its Councils of Action, was in 'its period of Dual Power'.[80]

There is no doubt that Lenin's insistence that every other country should follow Russia's road was symptomatic of a general Bolshevik imperiousness. It was that mixture of Russian nationalism and Communist internationalism which later came to characterize the whole dogmatic tone of Soviet foreign policy. The Bolsheviks boasted that Russia led the world when it came to making revolutions and assumed that all foreign Communists should be made to toe the Moscow line. That was certainly the essence of the Comintern Congress and its '21 Conditions' for admission to the new International. The Comintern was a Bolshevik Empire.

But it is a long way from this to argue that Lenin was planning to impose his revolution on Western countries by the bayonet. It was not a question of volition — had it been possible for the Red Army to take Berlin or even Budapest Lenin might well have ordered it do so — but rather one of practicalities. The Bolsheviks were painfully aware that their own peasant army, and even more so their exhausted economy, could not sustain a winter offensive, especially one in a foreign field. That was why they were so quick to make peace with Poland during the autumn of 1920, even though it cost them a territorial foothold in Galicia which, in Lenin's own words, could have 'opened up a straight road of revolution . . . to Czechoslovakia and Hungary'. Why then did they bother to invade Poland at all? A newly published speech by Lenin to the Ninth Party Conference in September 1920 provides the most convincing evidence so far. It suggests that the offensive against Warsaw was not supposed to be the start of an invasion of the West — as Richard Pipes has misleadingly suggested — but on the contrary a deterrent to the West against invading Russia. Lenin believed that Pilsudski's Poland had been built up by the Western powers as a weapon against Soviet Russia. As he saw it, a well-armed Poland fitted in with the general Allied plan to encircle Russia with hostile powers: Warsaw, Washington and Wrangel were connected. By invading Poland, the central pillar of the Versailles Treaty, Lenin aimed to 'shake' the Western system. With Poland Sovietized there would be an increased threat of the revolution spreading to the West, or so at least he believed. This was a form of national self-assertion, a way of warning the capitalist powers that Russia would no longer allow itself to be 'carved up' by them and would fight back when attacked. It was a political offensive against the Western capitals, a declaration of the 'international civil war', but not the start of the invasion of Europe. Naturally, it must be borne in mind that Lenin's speech was given in the immediate aftermath of the Red Army's defeat at Warsaw: there was thus a powerful motive to put on a brave face and boost the party's morale by claiming that in any case the offensive's political aims had been achieved. But, until new evidence proves to the contrary, it remains the most convincing explanation of the Bolsheviks' motives in Poland.[81]

The lessons of the Red defeat in Poland were extremely painful for the Bolsheviks to learn. There had certainly been military errors. Tukhachevsky's Western Army had rushed ahead towards Warsaw, underestimating the determination of the Poles to defend their capital and cutting off his own troops from their supplies. The South-Western Army had failed to support them, continuing to advance in the opposite direction towards Lvov, which Stalin seemed determined to take at all costs. The result was that Tukhachevsky's southern flank became exposed, allowing Pilsudski to launch a counter-offensive and drive the Reds back into Russia, where, with the first snows falling in October, the Front stabilized. But the root of the defeat was political: the Polish workers had failed to rise in support of the invading Red Army but, on the contrary, had rallied to Pilsudski. Nationalism proved a more potent force than international

Communism. Lenin soon admitted his mistake. 'Poland was not ready for a social revolution,' he told the Party Conference in September. 'We encountered a nationalist upsurge from the petty bourgeois elements* as our advance towards Warsaw made them fear for their national survival.' Lenin realized that the same would also hold true for the rest of Europe. Trying to impose Communism from the outside would merely have the effect of turning its potential supporters into nationalists.[82]

Defeat in Poland finally made the Bolsheviks give up their fantasies of a European revolution. The Treaty of Riga, signed with Poland in March 1921, marked the start of a new era of peaceful co-existence between Russia and the West. Moscow recognized an enlarged Poland — and thus by implication the Versailles Treaty — by ceding to it much of Belorussia. Trading was resumed with Britain the same month. No one in the West took the threat of a Soviet invasion seriously any more. The Polish disaster had clearly shown that Russia's peasant army was not strong enough to sustain an offensive against even the smaller Western powers. The lesson for the Bolsheviks was clear: their best chances of exporting Communism lay to the East.

The Asiatic strategy had first been proposed by Trotsky in a secret memorandum written as early as August 1919:

> There is no doubt at all that our Red Army constitutes an incomparably more powerful force in the Asian terrain of world politics than in the European terrain. Here there opens up before us an undoubted possibility not merely of a lengthy wait to see how events develop in Europe, but of conducting activity in the Asian field. The road to India may prove at the given moment to be more readily passable and shorter for us than the road to Soviet Hungary ... The road to Paris and London lies via the towns of Afghanistan, the Punjab and Bengal.

By the summer of 1920 a dual policy had taken shape: revolutionary agitation in the East combined with support for national liberation movements, even of a 'bourgeois' nature, against Western imperialism. Whilst making peace with the British in the West, the Bolsheviks pursued an undeclared war against them in the East. They backed the Afghan rebels and subverted the British protectorate in northern Persia. There is even evidence that Lenin tried to form an army of Central Asian tribes to invade India through Afghanistan.[83]

The Congress of the Peoples of the East, held in Baku in September 1920, was the first attempt to spread Communism into Asia. It was also the last. No doubt the chaos of the Congress floor had much to do with this. With

---

* By which he meant workers and peasants not yet advanced enough for Bolshevism.

1,900 delegates from dozens of countries as far afield as Turkey and Japan, it took ages and a great deal of general babble to translate the speeches into all the languages. Some delegates had dubious credentials: there were various khans and beks who turned out to be traders and who spent the duration of the Congress selling carpets in the markets of Baku. Apart from the delegates, the Congress received hundreds of messages of support from towns and villages across Asia. One of these announced the sacrificial slaughter of a hundred sheep and cattle in honour of the people's liberation, and requested help from the Congress to transport them to Baku. This, in short, was a colourful pageant, 'a Beano', as H. G. Wells, a witness, put it, but 'as a meeting of Asiatic proletarians it was preposterous'. The delegates dressed up in their national costumes and marched in procession through Baku. Effigies of Lloyd George, Millerand and Wilson, got up in court dress, were burned. Speakers declared their undying hatred of British imperialism; while Zinoviev, brushing aside Poland, claimed that 'the real revolution will flare up only when we are joined by the 800 million people who live in Asia.'[84] But in terms of its influence on Asia, the Congress had almost no effect.

*   *   *

The Bolsheviks' support for national-liberation movements in the British Empire contrasted starkly with their opposition to them in former Russian colonies. Lenin had always planned to reconstruct the basic geographic framework of the Russian Empire. His concessions to national self-determination in the programme of 1911 were no more than tactical. He argued that nationalism could be used to destroy the tsarist state and that, after a suitable interlude of 'bourgeois' national rule, the non-Russians would rejoin Russia as a socialist federation. What he meant by this is a different question. Was Lenin genuine in his public professions of support for a free federation of sovereign republics, each by implication with the right of secession, or was he planning, by force if necessary, to make the borderlands rejoin a unitary Russian state? Certainly, in his private letters Lenin was cynical about the idea of a loose confederation. In 1913, for example, he wrote to Gorky that 'the Austrian type of abomination' would not be allowed to happen in Russia. 'We will not permit it. There are more Great Russians here. With the workers on our side we won't allow any of the "Austrian spirit".'[85]

During the civil war this question became lost in the exigencies of military struggle. The Reds conquered the borderlands as they drove the Whites out, and imposed the same forms of centralized control as in the rest of Russia through the party and the Red Army. This could be seen as a conscious strategy to rebuild the Empire under Communist control; there were certainly enough Russian chauvinists among the conquering institutions to support this plan. But in many ways the conquest of the borderlands was much more dependent

81-2 The fuel crisis in the cities. *Above*: Muscovites dismantle a town house for firewood. *Below*: a priest is commandeered to help transport timber. Many horses died for lack of food so human draught was used.

83-4 Selling to eat. *Above*: women of the 'former classes' sell their last possessions on the streets of Moscow. *Below*: a soldier buys a pair of shoes from a group of *burzhooi* fallen on hard times.

85-6 Selling to eat. *Above*: a low-level party functionary haggles over a fur scarf with a female trader at the Smolensk market, Moscow, 1920. The woman on the left has the appearance of a *burzhooika*. *Below*: traders at the Smolensk market, Moscow, 1920. The woman with the string bag and the loaf of bread is almost certainly a prostitute.

87 Putting the gentle classes to work. Two ex-tsarist officers are made to clear the streets under the inspection of a commissar with guards, the Apraksin market in Petrograd, 1918. The main purpose of this sort of forced labour was to humiliate and degrade the privileged classes of the old regime.

88 The Bolshevik war against the market. Cheka soldiers close down traders' stalls on the Okhotnyi Riad (Hunters' Row) in Moscow, May 1919.

89 Requisitioning the peasants' grain.

90 'Bagmen' travelled to and from the countryside exchanging food for manufactured goods. The result was chaos on the railways.

91 The 1 May *subbotnik* ('volunteer' labour on Saturday) on Red Square in Moscow, 1920.

92 By 1920 the state was feeding – or rather underfeeding – thirty million people in makeshift cafeterias like this one at the Kiev Station in Moscow.

93 The new ruling class: delegates of the Ninth All-Russian Party Congress, Moscow, 1920.

94 A typical example of the new bureaucracy: the Agitation and Propaganda Department of the Commissariat for Supply and Distribution in the Northern Region. Note the portrait of Marx, the leathered commissar, and the bourgeois daughters who served in such large numbers as secretaries.

95 The Smolny Institute on the anniversary of the October coup. But it was fast becoming not so much a bastion of the Marxist revolution as one of the corruption of the party élite.

upon local conditions than this would suggest. Under pressure from the native Communists, Lenin came to realize by 1920 that conquest in itself was not enough to control the non-Russian territories — at least not without the constant resistance of the native population. The effective exercise of power necessitated the recruitment of leaders who could speak the native language and give the regime a national veneer. Since the native population was based mainly in the villages, and the regime in the cities, it also demanded a softer approach towards the peasants. In this sense the New Economic Policy was closely linked with the process of state-building in the non-Russian lands. The Tenth Party Congress of March 1921, which introduced the NEP, also passed a resolution calling on the party to foster national cultures. *Korenizatsiia* (indigenization) was the thrust of Bolshevik policy in the 1920s. The domain of the native language was extended into education, publishing and administration. Schools and colleges were rapidly established to train up a native élite. Peasant boys from the native population became clerks in the towns, hitherto dominated by the Russians. In the cultural sphere, at least, the Soviet regime was in many ways continuing the work of nation-building and modernization begun by the nationalists before 1917. Granting cultural and economic freedom largely pacified the native peasantry, leaving what remained of the nationalist intelligentsia without a popular base.

In the Ukraine the nationalist movement had already collapsed by the time the Bolsheviks launched their third and final invasion during the autumn of 1919. The military vicissitudes of 1917–20, when the Ukraine had ten different regimes, were hardly conducive to national unity. Two brief spells of nationalist rule in Kiev — the Rada of March 1917 to February 1918, and the Directory of the following December to February 1919 — were not enough to inculcate a national consciousness into the Ukrainian peasantry, who were largely cut off from and hostile to the towns. Until the end of the nineteenth century, the idea of an independent Ukrainian state had existed mainly in Shevchenko's poetry and Cossack myth. With the exception of the western Ukraine, where the landowners were mainly Poles, the mass of the peasants remained untouched by the intelligentsia's nationalism. The strength of the peasantry's attachment to the idea of the independent village made them hostile to a national state. During 1917, however, the socialist parties in the Rada had built up a mass base of rural electoral support by linking the idea of national independence with the autonomy of the village and a land reform in the interests of the peasants. They succeeded in translating the abstract concept of the nation into social terms which were real to the peasantry. But the promised land reforms were never carried out. The Rada and the Directory were politically paralysed by the growing internal division between nationalists like Petliura, who subordinated social reforms to the national struggle, and those like Vinnichenko, who subordinated nationalism to social change. Without land reform, the peasants had little incentive to fight for an independent Ukraine. Neither the Rada nor the Directory was able to mobilize a truly national force against the invading armies of the Reds or the Whites. Even Petliura was forced to raise his so-called National Army on Polish soil.

The urban head of the Ukrainian national movement was thus cut off from its rural body. What remained was a local peasant nationalism, focused on the idea of the autonomous village, which continued to dominate the Ukraine, making it virtually impossible to rule from the cities, until the early 1920s. This smallholders' nationalism was seen in the *atamanshchina*, the local peasant bands of Makhno, Grigoriev and countless other warlords, who claimed to defend the free Ukrainian village from both Whites and Reds; in the rural economic war against the towns, which the peasants saw as 'foreign' and as the centres of a hostile state; and in the pogroms against Jews as the outward symbols of that alien nature. It was also seen in the mass appeal of the Borotbist Party, formed from the Ukrainian Left SRs, which stressed cultural nationalism as a form of village autonomy, a means of uniting and empowering the peasants in the revolutionary struggle against the Russified urban bourgeoisie.

It was this peasant nationalism which made life so hard for the Bolsheviks in their first two attempts to conquer the Ukraine (during the first three months of 1918 and the first six of 1919). With only the workers and the army on their side, they were reduced to ruling it by terror. The second of these two Red regimes was especially violent. Bulgakov captured its terrible power in his image of the huge Red armoured train in the forest outside Kiev at the end of *The White Guard*. It is a good example of the way that sometimes only a novelist can describe the essence of civil war:

> The locomotive rose up like a black, multi-faceted mass of metal, red-hot cinders dropping out of its belly on to the rails, so that from the side it looked as if the womb of the locomotive was stuffed with glowing coals. As it hissed gently and malevolently, something was oozing through a chink in its side armour, while its blunt snout glowered silently toward the forest that lay between it and the Dnieper. On the last flat-car the bluish-black muzzle of a heavy calibre gun, gagged with a muzzle-cover, pointed straight towards the City eight miles away.

This second invasion of the Ukraine was almost certainly carried out on Stalin's personal authorization but without the knowledge or approval of Lenin. It was led by a group of Bolsheviks who were determined to bring the Ukraine back under Moscow's rule. Many of them were Russians from the Ukraine who had taken up Bolshevism partly as a form of identification with Russia itself. Georgii

Piatakov, who instigated the invasion and became the head of the Bolshevik regime in the Ukraine, was typical of this conquering Soviet élite. His father had been a Russian industrialist in the Ukraine, so it could be said that a certain urban-Russian arrogance towards the native peasants was inbred in him. Like many leading Bolsheviks on the Southern Front — Voroshilov, Kaganovich and Ordzhonikidze also come to mind — Piatakov had close ties with Stalin. The extreme centralism which he imposed on the Ukraine was a thin disguise for his own Great Russian chauvinism. The Ukrainian nationalist intelligentsia were imprisoned in their hundreds during the Red Terror of 1919. 'Bourgeois property' was sent off by the train-load to Moscow. Nearly all the Bolshevik posts in the Ukraine were filled by Russians, who ruled the country like colonial masters. The Ukrainian peasants were subjected to the worst excesses of the Bolshevik requisitioning campaigns. The *kombedy* and the collective farms, both of which had clearly failed in Russia itself, were forcibly imposed on the Ukrainian peasants — and this despite the fact that the traditions of private and inheritable property were much more deeply rooted among the Ukrainian peasants than among the Russian ones.[86]

The result was a wave of peasant revolts against the Bolshevik regime throughout the Ukraine, of which Makhno's was merely the largest. Lenin was furious: the insensitivity of Piatakov's regime had undermined the Reds' control of the Ukraine and opened the door to its conquest by the Whites. During the autumn of 1919, as the Reds once again swept south across the Ukraine, Lenin insisted that this time his comrades should be more sensitive to national sentiment. The 'Federalists' among the Ukrainian Bolsheviks had been calling for this for some time, and their views were now being echoed by senior Bolsheviks such as Ordzhonikidze. 'We must find a common language with the Ukrainian peasant,' he wrote to Lenin on 19 November. These themes were taken up by Lenin in December. At the Eighth Party Conference he spoke out for the first time against the 'primitive Russian chauvinism' displayed by certain Bolsheviks. The resolution on the Ukrainian question recognized the strength of national sentiment, albeit among the 'backward' masses. It called for the use of the Ukrainian language in all Soviet institutions and for a *rapprochement* with the Ukrainian villages.[87]

In March 1920, as the first step towards this, the Borotbists were finally admitted to the Ukrainian Bolshevik Party. Like the earlier alliance with the Russian Left SRs, this was a great political victory for the Bolsheviks: it split the main rival party in the Ukraine and gave them access to the villages. The Borotbists were the only Ukrainian party with a mass peasant following. During the campaigns against the Hetmanate, Petliura and Denikin, the Reds had relied upon them to organize the peasant partisans. The Borotbists espoused a synthesis of cultural nationalism and peasant socialism within a decentralized Soviet federal structure. They were the true heirs of the peasant nationalism which had driven the revolution in the Ukraine during 1917 and 1918. When the Ukrainian Directory abandoned its commitment to a socialist programme, most of the Borotbists (about 4,000 out of 5,000) joined the Bolsheviks. They hoped to moderate the Bolsheviks' Communism and to make them more aware of the national culture of the Ukrainian peasants.[88] Once again, it was nationalism that turned these opponents of the Bolsheviks Red.

Although, in the long run, the Borotbists failed, they did succeed in gaining a decade of relative cultural autonomy for the Ukraine during the 1920s. National sentiments, defeated in the form of the Ukrainian national movement, reappeared within the Ukrainian Bolshevik Party and state apparatus. Both were increasingly taken over by Ukrainians determined to defend the autonomous rights of their republic. Here, then, was another sort of 'national Bolshevik'. In some ways it was a precursor to Tito's nationalist movement in Yugoslavia against Stalinist supercentralism. As in Russia, most of the new Ukrainian élite was recruited from literate peasant sons mobilized by the war and revolution and eager for progress and social advancement. The result was the rapid Ukraini-anization of the Ukraine's towns, which before the revolution had been dominated by the Russians. Between 1923 and 1926 the proportion of Kiev's population which was Ukrainian increased from 27 per cent to 42 per cent. Closely connected with this was the flourishing of Ukrainian culture during the 1920s, especially after 1924, when Olexander Shumsky, the ex-Borotbist leader, was placed in charge of the republic's cultural affairs. The Ukrainian language, which the tsarist rulers had dismissed as a farmyard dialect, was now recognized as an essential tool for effective propaganda in the countryside and the recruitment of a native élite. During the 1920s it spread its domain into schools and offices, street names and shop signs, Soviet documents and ensignia, party congresses, newspapers and journals. More Ukrainian children learned to read their native language in the 1920s than in the whole of the nineteenth century.[89] The nationalist ideal of an independent Ukraine may have been crushed by the new Empire-State, but at least the Ukrainian nation had been given a cultural base.

In the Muslim lands this same pattern — of military conquest by the Reds followed by the fostering of national cultures — was even more marked. In fact here the Bolsheviks did not so much foster existing national cultures as *create new nations* where only tribal entities had existed before 1917.

In the Bashkir and Tatar regions of the Volga-Urals new republics were created as the Red Army moved across the region pursing Kolchak. Moscow opposed the plans of the pan-Muslim intelligentsia for a Bashkir-Tatar state and ruthlessly exploited the ethnic divisions between the two regions. The Red Army, in alliance with Validov, the military leader of the Bashkir pastoralists, set up the Bashkir Autonomous Republic in March 1919. Most of its population was

Tatar. Validov and his troops had defected from the Whites at the height of the fighting on the Eastern Front. He believed that the Reds, unlike Kolchak, would give the Bashkirs independence and the right to expel Russian settlers. But once the conquest of the Urals was completed, the Reds handed power in the region to the Ufa Soviet, which was dominated by Russian workers. Moscow was not prepared to let the vital industries of the Urals region fall into the hands of Bashkir nationalists. In May 1920 it issued a decree abolishing the political autonomy promised to the Bashkirs only fourteen months before: the key institutions of the republic were henceforth to be subordinated to the Moscow authorities. The Bashkir Communists resigned from the government *en masse* and fled into the Urals, where they joined the other Bashkir rebels against Soviet rule. The new republican government had no Bashkirs in it but was made up of Tatars and Russians. Meanwhile, a separate Tatar Autonomous Republic was also established in May 1920 — although, like the Bashkir one, it was autonomous only in name and not even properly Tatar. Three-quarters of the ethnic Tatars in the region were left outside the republic's borders; and even inside them they made up only half the population, compared to the 40 per cent which were Russian.[90] *Divide et impera.*

Moscow's Tatar strategy was supported, however, by an influential group of Muslim intellectuals, who saw in Bolshevism a chance to advance their own ideal of a secular Islamic nationalism. These were the radical *jadids*, the bourgeois modernizers of the nineteenth century who opposed the feudal-clerical élites, the *qadymists* and mullahs. They dominated not only the Tatar professions but also the officer corps of the national units. Mirsaid Sultan-Galiev was their most important theoretician and the leader of the Tatar Republic. In his youth he had been a teacher, a journalist and a *jadid*. He joined the Bolsheviks in 1917 and rose quickly within Stalin's Commissariat of Nationalities. During the civil war on the Eastern Front, when the Reds badly needed Muslim troops, Sultan-Galiev was allowed to pursue a largely independent line. He established an independent Muslim Communist Party and separate Muslim army units with a special badge in gold and green of the Islamic crescent moon and star. But once Kolchak had been defeated, Moscow began to roll back his powers in an effort to centralize control. This prompted the Tatar to revise his Marxism in the light of what he now saw as a persistent problem of colonialism. The Asians, he argued in a series of articles published in 1919 and 1920, would not be liberated by the socialist revolution in the West, since it was in the interests of the new proletarian rulers to perpetuate the empires they had inherited rather than abolish them. The solution was to unite all the colonial peoples, who were 'proletarians' by virtue of their oppression alone, in a worldwide revolution. This of course echoed the Bolshevik strategy towards Asia, as expressed at the Baku Congress. But Sultan-Galiev did not stop there. He argued that for all the Asian peoples, both under Communism and imperialism, the goals of national unity and liberation were more important than the social revolution. The Muslims in the Russian Empire, for example, were more united by their common Islamic way of life (as opposed to their religion) than they were divided by class antagonisms. This meant that the Bolsheviks should seek to root their regime in the Islamic traditions, while attempting to secularize them and modernize Muslim society. It was a cross between Marx and the *jadid*.

In 1923 Sultan-Galiev was expelled from the party and briefly imprisoned for his heresy. Yet for much of the 1920s his ideas continued to influence the Bolsheviks' policies towards the Tatars. The Tatar language was modernized and made less scholastic, as the *jadids* had themselves advocated. This weakened the power of the mullahs and made it easier for the native peasants to learn how to read. Imported Russian words which had crept in under the tsarist policy of Russification were also removed. The Tatar language broadened its domain, entering schools and administration. The native population became better educated and began to enter public office in much larger numbers than under the Tsar. Tatar culture briefly flourished. This, in short, was the start of a national cultural revolution, albeit one that Stalin soon aborted.

Kolchak's defeat also allowed the Reds to complete the conquest of Central Asia. In early 1918 the Russian railway workers and soldiers of Tashkent had established a Turkestan Soviet Republic. But it was cut off from the rest of Russia by the Orenburg Cossacks, who were Kolchak's allies, and its influence was confined to the cities. The cotton-growing regions of the Ferghana Valley were controlled by the native rebels, known as the Basmachis, whose bands united the separate Turkic tribes (Uzbeks, Kirghiz and Tajiks) against the Russian-Soviet regime under the banner of 'Turkestan for the Natives'. Punitive requisitionings from the Muslim population had sparked a dreadful famine during 1918, in which it is estimated that at least a quarter of the population died, and this gave the Basmachis almost universal support in the countryside. Since the divide between town and country was also a political and ethnic division, it was understandable that the Soviet regime was seen as a new form of colonial exploitation; which is largely what it was. When the Red Army arrived in Tashkent at the end of 1919 it set up a special commission to report on the Soviet government. It concluded that it had been dominated by 'colonially nationalistic hanger-on elements' and 'old servants of the tsarist regime' who used 'the camouflage of the class struggle . . . to persecute the native population in a most brutal manner'. The tsarist colonial policy of banishing the Kirghiz pastoralists to the infertile regions and settling Russian colonists on the fertile plain had even been intensified. In the Semirechie region the local Soviet had introduced a slave economy, forcing the Kirghiz natives to work without payment on Russian peasant farms or risk execution. The attitude of the Bolshevik leaders in Tashkent towards this had been one of callous indifference. One of the Bolsheviks had been heard to say that the Kirghiz were 'the weakest race from the Marxist point of view and must die out anyway.'[91]

Under pressure from Lenin, the Tashkent government slowly changed its attitudes after 1920. Land taken from the natives was returned; requisitionings were reduced, and brought to a halt from 1921 under the NEP; bazaars were allowed to reopen; mosques were taken out of Soviet control; and Koranic law, which the Tashkent government had abolished in 1918, was restored for believers. All this helped to quell the Basmachi revolt: by 1923 it had virtually been liquidated and remained only in the isolated eastern mountain regions of Uzbekistan and Tajikstan, where with the aid of the mujahaddin, it continued for several more years. Meanwhile, the Soviet regime pursued its policy of recruiting native élites. Over half the delegates to the Turkestan Party Congress in 1921 were Muslims, many of them from the old secular intelligentsia, or *jadid*, who saw in the regime a modernizing force. And indeed to a large extent it was. The new republics of Central Asia — Uzbekistan, Turkmenistan, Kazakhstan, Kirghizia and Tajikstan — were all, in a cultural sense at least, built up as modern nations in the 1920s. Vast resources were invested in education at all levels, which greatly improved literacy rates. Special efforts were devoted to the training of a native political and technical élite. There was a boom in native-language publications for the new reading public. Most journalists, it is true, had to be recruited from the Volga Tatars, who were culturally more advanced than the Central Asians but not always conversant with the nuances of the local language. Thus one Uzbek daily, *Kyzyl bairak*, appeared for a time with the slogan above its title-head: 'Tramps of the World Unite!'[92] But such mistakes are bound to happen when a national culture is built up from scratch.

International relations complicated the Soviet conquest of the Caucasus. Turkey and Britain both vied with Russia for domination of this vital region after 1918. The Turks had designs on Azerbaijan, to whose population they were ethnically and linguistically related. They also wanted to keep Armenia weak in order to retain their hold on eastern Anatolia, which they had cleared of its Armenian population through the genocide of 1915. As for the British, they saw in the Caucasus a buffer protecting Persia and India from Russia. It was also rich in manganese and oil, which the British, in their best traditions of colonial piracy, were busily exporting from the Baku oil-fields whilst their troops were stationed there as a 'protective force'. The brief independence of the three Caucasian nations (Armenia, Azerbaijan and Georgia) was almost wholly dependent upon the temporary post-war weakness of Russia and Turkey, the traditional powers in the region, and, at least in the case of the last two, the protection of Britain as well. On their own, these nations were much too small and ethnically divided to maintain their independence once Russia and Turkey began to reassert their domination in the region.

Azerbaijan, the first to fall to Soviet Russia, was a typical example of a post-colonial nation ill-prepared for the trials of independent existence amidst all the conflicts of the time. During its brief period of independence, from May 1918 to April 1920, it had no less than five governments. Land reform and ethnic conflict were the main sources of instability. The failure of the Mussavat socialists to push through their land reform against the resistance of the Armenian bourgeoisie enabled the Bolsheviks to pose as the champions of the Muslim rural poor. The economic crisis in Baku, caused by the collapse of its main oil export market in Russia, also gave the Bolsheviks a base of support among the Muslim and Russian unemployed. By February 1920, the Bolshevik Party had 4,000 members in Baku and Tiflis, who were openly agitating in the streets and urging Moscow to send in the troops. The Azeri army was much too weak to put up any serious resistance against the 70,000 troops of the Eleventh Red Army then moving south towards Azerbaijan through the Terek and Dagestan regions. Most of its senior staff, made up of Turks and Georgians, had been infiltrated by the Bolsheviks. But it was Turkey's acquiescence which sealed the conquest of Azerbaijan. By March 1920, when British forces occupied Constantinople, Kemal Ataturk's nationalists were ready to agree to the Soviet take-over of the Caucasus in order to secure Moscow's aid for the Turkish independence movement against Britain. The Caucasus would thus become a channel for the shipment of Soviet weaponry into Turkey. Kemal agreed to start military operations against Armenia to help bring this about. The alliance with Turkey enabled the Reds to win a sizeable fifth column of Turkic-Muslim support in Azerbaijan during their invasion. The Turkish officers of the Azeri army welcomed the northern conquerors, naively believing that they had no intention of ending the independence of Azerbaijan and that their aim was to help the pan-Turk movement. On 28 April the Red Army entered Baku without armed resistance. No one was prepared to defend the Azerbaijan nation. Ordzhonikidze and Kirov, the leaders of the Caucasian Bureau established by the Central Committee in Moscow to Sovietize the Caucasus, arrived the next day and began a reign of terror. Several leaders of the national government were executed and uprisings in the Azerbaijani countryside were brutally put down.[93]

Turkey's involvement was equally vital in the Soviet conquest of Armenia. The whole identity of this tiny and embattled nation was defined by its fear and hatred of the Turk. The Dashnak leaders relied upon this to keep the country united in the face of overwhelming difficulties which it confronted after the declaration of Armenian independence in May 1918. The country was overcrowded with refugees from Anatolia who had fled from the Turkish massacres and this placed a huge strain on the economy. Then there were the bitter territorial disputes with Georgia in the north and Azerbaijan over Nakhichevan, Zangezur and the mountainous region of Nagorno-Karabakh.* Unlike its two neighbours, Armenia had no foreign allies. Britain, in particular, supported Azerbaijan against it. It had always preferred to deal with 'gentlemen Turks' than with 'swarthy Christians', as Arnold Toynbee put it in a biting critique of Whitehall's policies.[94] Britain, after all, was the greatest colonial power in the Muslim world. Isolated internationally and surrounded by hostile powers, it was perhaps natural for the Dashnaks to appeal to Armenian nationalism. They promised to build a new Armenian Empire stretching from the Black Sea to the Caspian. As the first step towards this Armenian forces occupied eastern Anatolia and carried out a series of revenge massacres against the Turkish population. It was a foolish provocation — Kemal's nationalists were bound to fight back — and one can only conclude that the Dashnaks either greatly underestimated Turkish strength or, through their own xenophobia, were temporarily deprived of their senses. Perhaps both.

A war between Turkey and Armenia was just what the Bolsheviks needed. Their own organization in Armenia was minuscule — at the First Party Conference in Erevan only a dozen people turned up — so a Red invasion was not feasible. In May 1920, shortly after the Eleventh Army had occupied Baku, the Bolsheviks in Kars staged a coup in the hope of sparking a Red invasion to help the 'revolutionary masses', but this was easily suppressed and Lenin, who was more concerned with Poland at this stage, instructed Ordzhonikidze to hold off. But six months later, in November 1920, with the Armenians on the brink of a humiliating defeat at the hands of the Turks, Lenin ordered the Reds to march on Erevan. As they did so, the Soviet diplomatic mission in the Armenian capital presented the Dashnak government with an ultimatum to surrender power to a Revolutionary Committee, which was following the Red troops from Azerbaijan. The Dashnaks complied, seeing surrender to the Soviets as a lesser humiliation to defeat by the Turks. They could resist neither. On 29 November the Armenian Soviet Republic was declared. 'Thus one more Soviet Republic,' Ordzhonikidze cabled to Moscow. The Dashnaks entered a coalition with the Bolsheviks but were soon persecuted by their Russian 'allies' and forced into exile, along with many other Armenian nationalists and intellectuals. Meanwhile the Reds carried out a ruthless campaign of requisitioning, carrying off train-loads of food and booty to Russia. The zeal of the new regime was such that

---

* The Nagorno-Karabakh region, which is still the subject of disputes today, was a summer-pasture ground for the Azeri nomads. Armenia claimed the region in 1918. There were Armenian settlements there, from which many of the nation's leading intellectuals had come, and so, like Mount Ararat, the region became a symbol of Armenia. The Armenian government tried to stop the Azeris from coming into the region by setting up border guards. This resulted in bitter local fighting. Both the Soviets and the British favoured giving Karabakh to the Azeris.

even beehives and barbers' instruments were expropriated in the name of the Friendship of the Peoples.[95]

The fall of Armenia left Georgia surrounded by the Reds. Of the three Caucasian nations, this was the most viable as an independent state. The Georgians had a clear sense of their own national history and culture, a large native intelligentsia, and in the Mensheviks a genuine national leadership. During its first six months of independence, from May to November 1918, Georgia had the protection of the Germans, and after that of the British. The Menshevik government, led by Noi Zhordaniia, modelled itself on the German Social Democrats, putting statesmanship before social revolution. This was a reverse of the Mensheviks' dogma which had prevented them from taking power in 1917. But with 75 per cent of the vote in the elections to the National Assembly there was simply no other national party.

Land reform was the basis of their power. By breaking up the larger farms and estates, owned increasingly by Armenians, they won the support of the Georgian peasants, who were allowed to buy most of the land at democratic prices. The land reform consecrated the smallholding peasant as the embodiment of the Georgian nation. It forged a synthesis of national and class solidarity — the Georgian peasants and impoverished nobles against the Armenian bourgeoisie — which enabled the Menshevik government to enjoy two years of relative stability.

Only the ethnic minorities, the Ossetians and Abkhazians, with their demands for self-government, caused serious difficulties. Their high-handed treatment by the government in Tiflis, which was not immune to petty chauvinism, gave the Bolsheviks a real base of support. It was here, among the poor tribes of the northern Caucasus, that they built up their military organization for the subversion of independent Georgia. The Ossetian rebels were trained by the Bolsheviks in Vladikavkaz, just across the border in Russia, and sent across the mountains into Georgia. Within Georgia itself, the Bolsheviks had almost no support. The tiny Georgian police force had no difficulty in suppressing the Bolshevik leadership. In May 1920, when the Tiflis Bolsheviks tried to stage a coup to persuade the Eleventh Red Army (then in Baku) to launch an invasion, it was easily put down. Lenin ordered the Reds to pull back from Georgia: troops were needed on the Polish Front and, at least as Lenin later claimed, Georgia was not yet ripe for Sovietization. On 7 May, the Soviet Government signed a treaty with Georgia recognizing its independence and pledging not to interfere in its internal affairs.[96]

Here the Georgian Mensheviks made a fatal mistake. In a secret clause they agreed to legalize the Bolshevik Party in Georgia. Hundreds of activists were released from jail. No doubt the Mensheviks rationalized this as the price of guaranteeing Georgia's independence. But, as their oldest foes, they should have known better than to trust the Bolsheviks. The Georgian Bolsheviks now became a fifth column of the Red Army based in Baku. Strikes and revolts against the government were planned from the Soviet Embassy in Tiflis with the aim of sparking an invasion. Lenin remained opposed to the military option, favouring a more gradual process of revolutionary subversion. Like Trotsky, he was concerned by the possible reaction of the British and the Germans, with whom the Bolsheviks were hoping to trade, not to mention the reaction of Turkey. The Western Socialist leaders had hailed Georgia as the only truly socialist country in the world. Karl Kautsky and Ramsay MacDonald had made a pilgrimage to Tiflis during 1920 and returned to Europe full of praise. There were also a practical problem. Kamenev, the head of the Red Army, warned that the troops of the Eleventh Red Army were too exhausted for a new offensive. But Ordzhonikidze was impatient for the 'liberation' of his native Georgia and, without Moscow's knowledge, began to build up troops on the Armenian and Azerbaijani borders. Together with Kirov, the Soviet Ambassador in Tiflis, he pleaded with Lenin for immediate intervention. 'One cannot hope for an internal explosion. Without our help Georgia cannot be Sovietized,' the two men wrote on 2 January. Stalin supported them in another letter two days later. Lenin finally agreed. 'Do not postpone,' he wrote on Stalin's letter.[97]

On 14 February 1921 the Politburo ordered the invasion to begin. Neither Kamenev nor Trotsky was informed. Against the 100,000 invaders Georgia's tiny army, which had always been more of a symbol than a shield for the nation, stood no chance. It fought bravely for over a week before surrendering Tiflis on the 25th. Taking advantage of Georgia's collapse, Turkey now invaded it from the south-west with the aim of capturing the port of Batum. This prevented the Menshevik leaders from making a last stand in their old rural stronghold of Guria, as they had intended. On 18 March they finally surrendered to the Reds and boarded an Italian ship bound for Europe. The rest of their organization went underground. It remained a dominant presence in the countryside, where it led the uprising that shook the Soviet Republic of Georgia in 1924.

Lenin was aware of the depth of the Mensheviks' popularity in the countryside and was worried that the 'Great Russian chauvinism' displayed by some Bolsheviks during the invasion might turn Georgia into a bed of nails. On 2 March he had written to Ordzhonikidze urging him to pursue 'a special policy of concessions with regard to the Georgian intelligentsia and small merchants'. This was the time when the NEP was introduced. Lenin saw its concessions to peasant agriculture, the free market and foreign trade as essential for the regime in Georgia. But he worried that the Bolsheviks in Ordzhonikidze's Caucasian Bureau were dangerously caught in the old mentalities of War Communism and Russian centralism. The Caucasus, he explained in a letter to the local Bolsheviks on 14 April, was 'even more peasant than Russia' and this required 'more softness, caution and conciliation' in the transition to socialism than in the rest of Russia. Makharadze's wing of the Georgian Party championed the cause of National Bolshevism and, thanks in part to them, some gains were made by the policy of *korenizatsiia* during the early 1920s. More Georgians entered Soviet office, many of them former Mensheviks. There was a boom of publications in the Georgian language, which began to replace Russian in the public sphere. All this showed that Georgia's subjugation did not have to mean a cultural defeat. In the words of the Georgian poet, Leo Kiacheli, 'the Georgian soul should rule in Georgia'.[98]

Yet there were still some Bolsheviks who were not even prepared to concede this. It was ironic that the foremost among these were two Georgians, Ordzhonikidze and Stalin, whose own Bolshevism had become mixed in a complex way with a sort of Great Russian chauvinism. The conflict rumbled on beneath the surface until 1922, when it suddenly erupted on to the Moscow scene. But that is the story of Lenin's last struggle.

* * *

Brusilov rejoiced in the reformation of the Russian Empire, albeit under the Red Star rather than the Cross. It reconciled him to his own decision to join the Reds and ensured his continued support for them after the war with Poland, when they turned their attention to the Whites in the Crimea. Brusilov was furious with Wrangel for attacking Russia during the war against Poland. It showed, in his view, that the Whites were prepared to betray Russia for their own narrow political ends. Patriotism was Brusilov's main motive for siding with the Reds against these last guardians of the Old Russia. It must have aroused curious emotions; for Brusilov was helping to destroy his own class.

It was fitting that the Whites should make their last stand on the picturesque Crimean peninsula. This Russian riviera, with its palms and cypresses, its vineyards and mountains, had been the playground of the aristocracy, whose summer palaces lined its southern coast. In their noble minds the Crimea was a place of childhood summers, a symbol of the good life in Old Russia, where it was thought the sun would never set. Now, in the summer of 1920, it was the last bit of Russian soil that had not been taken by the Reds. It was the last resort of fallen dukes and generals, of provincial governors and bishops, of landowners without estates, of industrialists without factories, of state officials without appointments, of lawyers without jobs and of actresses without a stage. The bourgeoisie had nowhere else to run to.

At the head of this forlorn cause stood Baron Peter Wrangel, a six-foot scion of the old military aristocracy, who had risen through the élite Imperial Guards. Unlike the 'army man' Denikin, Wrangel was well aware of the need to fight the civil war by political as well as military means. 'It is not by a

The New Regime Triumphant

triumphal march from the Crimea to Moscow that Russia can be freed,' he told his first press conference in April, 'but by the creation — on no matter how small a fragment of Russian soil — of such a Government with such conditions of life that the Russian people now groaning under the Red yoke will inevitably submit to its attractions.' The Whites, Wrangel realized, could never come to power as long as they were seen to be fighting for the restoration of the old regime. They had to pledge their support for radical reforms capable of winning the support of the peasantry, the workers and the national minorities. Wrangel called it 'making leftist policies with rightist hands'.[99]

This was not just an opportunistic response to the weak military position which Wrangel had inherited. It stemmed from a genuine realization that the defeat of Denikin's regime had been brought about as much by its own outdated bureaucratic methods and failure to adapt to the new revolutionary situation as by its military difficulties. But the aim was contradictory: the rightist hands in Wrangel's regime would never make genuine leftist policies and pretending that they would was, in Miliukov's phrase, 'a clumsy attempt to cheat the world with liberal catchwords'. The government and military circles in Sevastopol were filled with figures from the old regime. Krivoshein, the last tsarist Minister of Agriculture, was placed in charge of the interior. His police carried out a massive witch-hunt against suspected 'Bolsheviks', which meant anyone who opposed the regime. Hundreds of liberal journalists and politicians were arrested, while the zemstvo organs were harassed as 'hotbeds of Bolshevik activity'. One zemstvo official complained to Krivoshein — only to be told that 'all the leftists were the same', whether they were Bolsheviks or liberals. Krivoshein's police force was filled with officials from the old regime who used their positions to reap a savage revenge against the peasantry for 1917, or else make themselves rich through bribes and requisitions. The proximity of the Front, which meant that most of the Crimea was placed under the jurisdiction of military field courts, served as a pretext for this White Terror. Thousands of ordinary peasants and workers were imprisoned, and hundreds shot, as suspected 'spies'. Terror by the soldiers — mainly in the form of looting and pogroms — was a major problem, souring relations with the local population, not least because the White officers tolerated and sometimes even encouraged such actions in order to secure the loyalty of their men. After three years of fighting in the field, the White, or Russian Army, as it was now called, had developed a strong caste spirit. Many of the officers saw themselves as an occupying army in a foreign land, and acted with impunity towards the Crimean population. Rather than acting as a model government to promote the White cause in the rest of Russia, Wrangel's 'rightist hands' did more to advance the Red cause in the Crimea.[100]

As with Denikin, the land issue was crucial here. Wrangel recognized the need to pass a land reform capable of winning peasant support. 'The question had to be settled for an important psychological reason: we had to tear the enemy's principal weapon of propaganda from him,' the Baron recalled in his memoirs. 'We had to allay the peasants' suspicion that our object in fighting the Reds was no other than to restore the rights of the great landed proprietors and to take reprisals against those who had infringed these rights.' But the committee which Wrangel appointed to draw up the land reform was dominated by such landed interests. The result was a Land Law, passed on 25 May, that still fell far short of the peasant demands. Its basic aim was to create a class of peasant proprietors by giving them a small plot of land as private property. It was another 'wager on the strong'. Like Stolypin's land reforms, it was to be linked to the establishment of a volost-level zemstvo in which the peasants would be dominant. But the law was full of complex regulations which would have taken years to implement; and there were far too many bureaucratic loopholes which allowed the squires to hold on to their land. The district zemstvos, for example, which set the amount of land to be transferred to the peasants, would still be dominated by them. There was also the problem of compensation: the peasants were to pay for the gentry's land by giving them one-fifth of its harvest (in the three-field system this was equivalent to 30 per cent of the annual harvest). After the revolution and the civil war, when the peasant farms had been severely weakened, this would have been a heavy burden, and would have kept the peasant farmers economically dependent on the squires for perhaps a generation — and that had probably been its aim.[101]

Wrangel's Land Law was a paternalist solution to the peasant question, not a revolutionary one. In the nineteenth century it would have been considered progressive; but after 1917 it was reactionary. It proved that Wrangel's regime was just as caught up as Denikin's in the bureaucratic methods of the past. Nothing better symbolized this than the decision to sell the Land Law for 100 roubles in booklet form (it was assumed that if the peasants had to pay for it, they would value the law more). Compared with the Bolsheviks' simple land decree, which they publicized in millions of leaflets and gave away free to the peasantry, it betrayed a dismal failure to comprehend the propaganda purpose of such laws. Wrangel's regime, like Denikin's, failed to understand that to win the civil war it had to adopt revolutionary methods.[102]

The price the Whites paid was widespread peasant indifference to their cause and, in the districts nearest the Front, where the burden of food and transport requisitioning was at its heaviest, even outright hostility. It meant they could never recruit enough troops to break out from their Crimean base. Even the wealthy farmers of the Tauride region, the first area the Whites would have to cross on entering the mainland, 'looked upon us', in the words of one of their officers, 'as an army of old Olympians, titled generals and their cronies, puffed up with pride and arrogance'. The problem was made all the more acute by the fact that the Cossacks, the mainstay of the Whites, were showing growing signs of disaffection, looting the villages and demanding to return to their homelands. According to one officer, the Don Army had become no more than 'a mob of people, who thought only of their own salvation and material welfare, but certainly not of a struggle with the Reds'. The left wing of the Don Krug, now dominated by younger Cossacks from the front-line units, was actively campaigning for a break with the 'reactionary' Wrangel and for peace negotiations with the Bolsheviks, in the naive hope of securing from them a promise of autonomy for the Don.[103]

To begin with, Wrangel had rejected the idea of an offensive. The British refused to support one and he himself preferred to build up his base on the peninsula. But with the Polish attack on Russia, Wrangel saw his chance. On 6 June he landed troops by boat on the coast of the Azov Sea and during the next few days pushed more land troops north into the Tauride region. This established a bridgehead on the mainland, doubling the size of Wrangel's territory, and gaining in the Tauride a much-needed source of agricultural produce for the swollen population of the Crimea. During August and September Wrangel tried to push north, into the Don and the Kuban. But his forces, hastily conscripted from the Tauride peasants, soon fell apart (it was harvest time) and the Cossacks had to spend most of their energies chasing deserters. By October, with the Polish war completed, the Reds were ready to concentrate on Wrangel. On the 20th they launched their counter-offensive: it took six days for the 130,000 Reds to force the 35,000 Whites back into the Crimea. Makhno's partisans did most of the fighting and took the brunt of the heavy losses on the Red side — for which Trotsky then rewarded them with an order for their capture and execution.[104]

The Whites held off the Red advance into the Crimea, building fortifications at the Perekop Isthmus, whilst preparing to evacuate. No one had any illusions about their ability to hold out for long and virtually everyone who had any connections with the White movement wanted to get on board the Allied ships. There was a mad rush to buy foreign currency: on 28 October 600,000 roubles would buy £1 in Sevastopol; by 1 November the rate had risen to one million roubles; and by the 10th, when the embarkation began, to four or even five million. Given the huge numbers of people involved, the evacuation was a model of good planning. There was none of the panic and disorder that had accompanied the evacuation of Denikin's forces from the Kuban in March. The troops retreated in good order, holding off the Reds for long enough for nearly 150,000 refugees to board a fleet of 126 British, French and Russian ships that took them to Constantinople. Wrangel was among the last to embark on 14 November. His ship was suitably called the *General Kornilov*: the man who had started the White movement took its last leader into exile.[105]

For Brusilov the defeat of the Whites had a tragic end. Shortly before the evacuation he had been approached by Skliansky, Trotsky's Deputy Commissar for Military Affairs, who claimed that a large number of Wrangel's officers did not want to leave Russia and might be persuaded to defect to the Reds if Brusilov put his name to a declaration offering them an amnesty. Skliansky offered him the command of a new Crimean Army formed from the remnants of Wrangel's forces. Brusilov was attracted by the idea of a purely Russian army made up of patriotic officers. It would enable him to Russify the élite of the Red Army, as he had always set out to do, and possibly to save the lives of many officers. He agreed to Skliansky's proposal and prepared, despite his injured leg, to depart for the Crimea. Three days later he was told the plans had been cancelled: Wrangel's officers, Skliansky told him, had not proved willing to defect after all. Brusilov later found out that this was not true. During the final evacuation at Sevastopol the Reds had distributed — dropping by aeroplane in fact — thousands of leaflets offering an amnesty in Brusilov's name. Hundreds of officers had believed it and stayed behind to surrender to the Reds. All of them were shot.

Five years later Brusilov still found it hard to live with his conscience. In 1925 he wrote in his (as yet unpublished) memoirs:

> God and Russia may judge me. The truth I do not know — can I blame myself for this atrocity, if it in fact happened? I have never discovered if it really happened as it was related to me: how true is the story? I only know that this was the first time in my life that I had ever met such fanatical evil and trickery and that I fell into such an unbearably depressed state that, to tell the truth, whoever found themselves in it would find it incomparably easier simply to be shot.
>
> If I was not myself a deeply religious person, I could have simply killed myself. But my belief that every individual is responsible for the consequences of his voluntary and involuntary sins forbad me from doing that. In the revolutionary storm, in the mad chaos, I could not always act logically, foreseeing all the twists of fate: it is possible that I made many mistakes, that I will admit. But I can say with a clear conscience, before God Himself, that I never thought of my own interests, or my own safety, but thought only of my Fatherland.[106]

Nine months later the old General died.

15 Defeat in Victory

i Short-cuts to Communism

After his adventures in the civil war Dmitry Os'kin took over the command of the Second Labour Army in February 1920. Formed from the surplus troops of the Second Red Army after Denikin's defeat, it was set the task of restoring the devastated railways on the Southern Front. Instead of rifles the soldiers carried spades. 'There was a general feeling of anti-climax not to be involved in the fighting any more,' Os'kin later wrote. 'It was a dull life in the railway sidings.' The only compensation for the commissar was the knowledge that the work was essential for the restoration of the economy after the ravages of the revolution and the civil war. The southern railways carried vital supplies of grain and oil to the industrial cities of the north. During the civil war some 3,000 miles of track had been destroyed. There were huge cemeteries of broken-down engines. Travelling from Balashov to Voronezh, Os'kin noted the general ruination: 'The stations were dead, trains rarely passed through, at night there was no lighting, only a candle in the telegraph office. Buildings were half-destroyed, windows broken, everywhere the dirt and rubbish was piled high.' It was a symbol of Russia's devastation. Os'kin's soldiers cleared up the mess, and rebuilt tracks and bridges. Military engineers repaired the trains. By the summer the railways began to function again and the operation was declared a great success. There was talk of using the troops to run other sectors of the economy.[1]

Trotsky was the champion of militarization. On his orders the First Labour Army had been organized from the remnants of the Third Red Army in January 1920. After the defeat of Kolchak, the soldiers had been kept in their battle units and deployed on the 'economic front' — procuring food, felling timber and manufacturing simple goods, as well as repairing the railways. The plan was in part pragmatic. The Bolsheviks were afraid to demobilize the army in the midst of the economic crisis. If millions of unemployed soldiers were allowed to congregate in the cities, or join the ranks of the disenchanted peasants, there could be a nationwide revolt (as there was in 1921). Moreover, it was clear that drastic measures were needed to restore the railways, which Trotsky, for one, saw as the key to the country's recovery after the devastations of the civil war. In January 1920 he became the Commissar for Transport: it was the first post he had actually requested. Apart from their chronic disrepair, the railways were dogged by corrupt officials, who were like a broken dam to the flood of bagmen who brought such chaos to the system. Petty localism also paralysed the railways. Every separate branch line formed its own committee and there were dozens of district rail authorities competing with each other for scarce rolling stock. Rather than lose 'their' locomotives to the neighbouring authority they would uncouple them before the train left their jurisdiction, so trains would be held up for hours, sometimes even days, while new locomotives were brought up from the depot of the next authority. Despite the best efforts of the railway staff, it took a whole week for one of Trotsky's senior officials to travel the 300 miles from Odessa to Kromenchug.[2]

But at the heart of Trotsky's plans there was also a broader vision of the whole of society being run on military lines. Like many Bolsheviks in 1920, Trotsky envisaged the state as the commander of society — mobilizing its resources in accordance with the Plan — just as a General Staff commanded the army. He wanted the economy to be run with military-style discipline and precision. The whole population was to be conscripted into labour regiments and brigades and despatched like soldiers to carry out production orders (couched in terms of 'battles' and 'campaigns') on the economic front. Here was the prototype of the Stalinist command economy. Both were driven by the notion that in a backward peasant country such as Russia state coercion could be used to provide a short-cut to Communism, thus eliminating the need for a long NEP-type stage of capital accumulation through the market. Both were based on the bureaucratic fantasy of imposing Communism by decree (although in each case the result was more akin to feudalism than anything to be found in Marx). As the Mensheviks had once warned, it was impossible to complete the transition towards a socialist economy by using the methods that had been used to build the pyramids.

After its triumphs in the civil war it was no doubt tempting for the Bolsheviks to view the Red Army as a model for the organization of the rest of society. *Po voennomy* — 'in the army way' — became synonymous with efficiency in the Bolshevik lexicology. If military methods had defeated the Whites, why could they not be used to construct socialism? All that had to be done was to turn around the army so that it marched on the economic front, so every worker became a foot soldier of the planned economy. Trotsky had always argued that factories should be run on military lines.* Now, in the spring of 1920, he outlined this brave new world of Communist labour, where the 'headquarters' of the planned economy would 'send out orders to the labour front' and 'every

---

* The same idea was expressed at this same time by Gastev and the other pioneers of the Taylor movement in Soviet Russia (see pages 744–5).

evening thousands of telephones would ring at headquarters to report conquests on the labour front.' Trotsky argued that the ability of socialism to conscript forced labour was its main advantage over capitalism. What Soviet Russia lacked in economic development it could make up through the coercive power of the state. It was more effective to compel the workers than it was to stimulate them through the market. Where free labour led to strikes and chaos, state control of the labour market would create discipline and order. This argument was based on the view, which Trotsky shared with Lenin, that the Russians were bad and lazy workers, that they would not work unless driven by the whip. The same view had been held by the Russian gentry under serfdom, a system with which the Soviet regime had much in common. Trotsky extolled the achievements of serf labour and used them to justify his economic plans. He would have no truck with the warnings of his critics that the use of forced labour would be unproductive. 'If this is so,' he told the Congress of Trade Unions in April 1920, 'then you can put a cross over Socialism.'[3]

At the heart of this 'barracks communism' was the Bolsheviks' fear of the working class as an independent and increasingly rebellious force. Significantly from about this time the Bolsheviks began to talk of the 'workforce' (*rabochaia sila* or *rabsila* for short) rather than of the 'working class' (*rabochii klass*). The shift implied the transformation of the workers from an active agent of the revolution into a passive object of the party-state. The *rabsila* was not a class, nor even an assortment of individuals, but simply a mass. The word for a worker (*rabochii*) was returning to its origins: the word for a slave (*rab*). Here was the root of the Gulag system — the mentality of dragooning long lines of half-starved and ragged peasants onto building sites and into factories. Trotsky epitomized this when he said that the labour armies were made up from a 'peasant raw material' (*muzhitskoe syr'ie*). It was the idea that human labour, far from being the creative force which Marx had extolled, was in fact no more than a raw commodity which the state could use up to 'build socialism'. This perversion was implicit in the system from the start. Gorky had foreseen this in 1917 when he wrote that 'the working class is for a Lenin what ore is for a metalworker'.[4]

The experience of the civil war had done nothing to boost the confidence of the Bolshevik leaders in their relationship with the working class. Shortages of food had turned the workers into petty traders and part-time peasants, shuffling between factory and farm. The working class had become nomadic. Industry was reduced to chaos by the constant absence of half the workers on trips to buy food from the countryside. Those in the factories spent most of their time making simple goods to barter with the peasants. Skilled technicians, in high demand, roamed from factory to factory in search of better conditions. Productivity fell to a tiny fraction of pre-revolutionary levels. Even vital munitions plants were brought to a virtual standstill. As the living standards

of the workers fell, strikes and go-slows became common. During the spring of
1919 there was a nationwide outbreak of strikes. Hardly a city was left
untouched. Everywhere better food supplies topped the list of strikers' demands.
The Bolsheviks answered with repression, arresting and shooting the strikers in
their thousands, many of them on suspicion of supporting the Mensheviks.[5]

Without the stimulus of the market, which they still rejected on ideological grounds,* the Bolsheviks had no means to influence the workers apart
from the threat of force. They tried to stimulate production by offering key
workers high wage bonuses, often linked to piece rates, thus going back on the
egalitarian promise of the revolution to eliminate pay differentials. But since
the workers could not buy much with paper money this had not given them
much incentive. To keep the workers in the factories the Bolsheviks were forced
to pay them in kind — either in foodstuffs or in a share of the factory's
production which the workers could then use to barter with the peasants. Local
Soviets, trade unions and factory boards had bombarded Moscow with requests
for permission to pay their workers in this way, and many had done so on their
own authority. By 1920 the majority of factory workers were being partly paid
in a share of their production. Instead of paper money they were taking home
a bag of nails, or a yard of cloth, which they then exchanged for food. Willy-
nilly, the primitive market was slowly reappearing at the heart of the planned
economy. If this spontaneous movement had been left unchecked, the central
administration would have lost its control of the country's resources and thus
the power to influence production. So rather than trying to stop the movement,
which it had tried but failed to do in 1918–19, it sought instead from 1920
to organize these natural payments, if only to make sure that they went first to
the workers in vital industries. This was the basis of the militarization of heavy
industry: strategic factories would be placed under martial law, with military
discipline on the shopfloor and persistent absentees shot for desertion on the
'industrial front', in exchange for which the workers would be guaranteed a Red
Army ration. By the end of the year 3,000 enterprises, mainly in munitions and
the mining industry, had been militarized in this way. While soldiers were being
turned into workers, workers were being turned into soldiers.

Linked with this was a general shift of power in the factory from the
collegiate management boards, which had been partly elected by the workers, to
the system of one-man management with managers increasingly appointed by the
party hierarchy. Trotsky justified this by comparing it to the transition from

---

* Trotsky did put forward tentative proposals for an NEP-like market reform in February
1920, but these were turned down by the Central Committee. He swung back at once to the
policy of militarization: radical reforms, whether by free trade or coercion, were needed to restore
the economy.

elected to appointed military commanders, claiming that this had been the root of the Red Army's success in the civil war. The new managers thought of themselves as commanders of an industrial army. They saw trade union rights as a nuisance, an unnecessary hindrance to industrial discipline and efficiency, just as the soldiers' committees had been in the army. Trotsky even went so far as to advocate the complete subordination of the trade unions to the party-state apparatus: since this was a 'workers' state' there was no longer any need for the workers to have their own independent organizations.[6]

During 1920 the principle of forced labour was applied in other fields. Millions of peasants were drafted into labour teams to fell and transport timber, to build roads and railways and to collect the harvest. Trotsky envisaged the whole population being mobilized into labour regiments which would double up as a standing army or militia. It was similar to the military feudalism of Count Arakcheyev, the War Minister of the 1820s, who had established a network of colonies combining serf labour with army service on Russia's western borders. Trotsky's plan was the heir to a long line of tsarist 'administrative utopias', stretching back to Peter the Great, which had all looked to the methods of the army to rationalize the irrational Russians, to regimentalize the anarchic peasants, to dress them, drill them and dragoon them for the needs of the absolutist state. Os'kin, like Trotsky, looked forward to the day when 'no foreign power would dare to invade Russia because the whole of its population would be ready, some at the Front with arms in hand, others in industry and agriculture, to defend the Fatherland. The whole country would be one armed camp.' All this was nothing but a bureaucratic dream. The peasant labour teams, like the labour armies, proved fantastically inefficient. It took fifty conscripts one whole day, on average, to cut down and chop up a single tree. Roads built by labour teams were so uneven that, in the words of one observer, they 'looked like frozen ocean waves' and to travel on them was 'worse than an amusement ride'. Desertion from labour duty was so common that in many districts there were more people engaged in chasing the deserters than in performing the duty itself. Villages were occupied, fines were imposed and hostages shot, including the leaders of the Soviet, if they were suspected of hiding deserters. Thousands of peasants were sent to labour camps, set up in every province as 'corrective institutions' for those workers who had been found guilty of violating labour discipline.[7]

Equally ineffective were the *subbotniki*, Saturday labour campaigns, when workers and students were dragooned as 'volunteers' into such noble socialist duties as clearing rubbish from the streets and squares. During the May Day week of 1920 over a million Moscow residents were involved in this 'festival of labour'. From then on it became a permanent feature of the Soviet way of life: not only days but whole weeks were set aside when people were called on to work without pay. The Bolsheviks hailed the *subbotnik* as the crowning achievement of Soviet collectivism. Politically, it probably helped to enforce a sense of discipline, conformity and obedience in the urban population. Not to 'volunteer' for the *subbotnik* was, after all, to invite suspicion and perhaps persecution as a 'counter-revolutionary'. But economically it achieved very little. Professor Vodovozov records his impressions of the mass *subbotnik* held in Petrograd on I May:

> On the square between the Winter Palace and the Admiralty there was a hive of activity. There were really an awful lot of workers, much more than required by the work in hand: they were clearing away the iron railings and piles of bricks that had been lying around for eighteen months since the [palace] fence was broken. Rosta [the Russian Telegraph Agency] proclaimed that at last the ugly fence was gone. But not quite: the bricks were indeed gone but the iron railings had merely been piled up at the far end of the square. And there they remain today. The whole square is still a pile of rubbish. No doubt it cost ten times more to dismantle the fence, albeit incompletely, than it cost to build it in the first place.[8]

One of the effects of the civil war was to depreciate the value of money. During 1918–19 the Bolsheviks were caught in two minds over this. Should they try to maintain the value of the rouble or abolish it? On the one hand, they recognized the need to continue printing money to pay for goods and services. They also knew that the mass of the population would judge their regime by the value of its money. On the other hand, there were some Bolsheviks on the extreme Left who thought that inflation should be encouraged in order to phase out money altogether. They wanted to replace the money system with a universal system of goods allocation on the basis of coupons from the state. They assumed (erroneously) that by getting rid of money they would automatically destroy the market system and with it capitalism, so that socialism would result. The economist Preobrazhensky dedicated one of his books: 'To the printing presses of the Commissariat of Finance — that machine-gun which shot the bourgeois regime in its arse, the monetary system'. By 1920 the left-wingers had got their way: money was being printed at such a furious rate that it was pointless to defend it any longer. The Mint was employing 13,000 workers and, quite absurdly, using up a large amount of Russia's gold reserves to import the dyes and paper needed to print money. It was costing more to print the rouble than the rouble was actually worth. Public services, such as the post and telegraph, transport and electricity, had to be made free because the state was losing money by printing and charging rouble notes for them.[9] The situation was surreal — but then this was Russia.

Left-wing Bolsheviks saw the ration coupon as the founding deed of the Communist order. The class of one's ration defined one's place in the new social hierarchy. People were classed by their use to the state. Thus Red Army soldiers, bureaucrats and vital workers were rewarded with the first-class ration (which was meagre but adequate); other workers received the second-class ration (which was rather less than adequate); while the *burzhoois*, at the bottom of the pile, had to make do with the third-class ration (which, in Zinoviev's memorable phrase, was 'just enough bread so as not to forget the smell of it'). In fact by the end of 1920 there was so little food left in the state depots — and so many people on the rations system — that even those on the first-class ration were receiving only just enough to slow down the rate of their starvation. Thirty million people were being fed, or rather underfed, by the state system. Most of the urban population depended largely on work-place canteens, where the daily fare was gruel and gristle. Yet such were the trials of finding a canteen that was open, and then of standing in line for its meagre offerings, that more energy was probably wasted doing all this than was gained from the actual meal. This was not the only absurdity. In almost every field where rationing was introduced, from food and tobacco to clothing, fuel and books, more time and energy were wasted distributing the product than that product was actually worth. Factories and offices were brought to a standstill while workers stood in line to receive their rations. The average person spent several hours every day traipsing from one Soviet office to another trying to exchange well-thumbed coupons for the goods they promised to deliver but which were so seldom to be found. No doubt they noticed the well-fed and well-clothed appearance of the bureaucrats with whom they had to plead.

The Petrograd professor, Vasilii Vodovozov, a leading liberal of the 1900s and a friend of Lenin's in his youth, describes a typical day in his diary. Readers acquainted with the Soviet Union may find his observations familiar:

3 December 1920
I shall describe my day — not because the minor details are of interest in themselves but because they are typical of the lives of nearly everyone — with the exception of a few bosses.

Today I got up at 9 a.m. There is no point getting up before since it is dark and the house lights are not working. There is a shortage of fuel. I have no servant (why is another story) and have to do the samovar, care for my sick wife (down with Spanish 'flu) and fetch the wood for the stove alone. I drank some coffee (made from oats) without milk or sugar, of course, and ate a piece of bread from a loaf bought two weeks ago for 1,500 roubles. There was even a little butter and in this respect I am better off than most. By eleven I was ready to go out. But after such a breakfast I was still hungry and decided to eat in the vegetarian canteen. It is frightfully expensive but the only place in Petrograd I know where one can eat with relative ease and without registration or the permission of some commissar. It turned out that even this canteen was closed, and would not be open for another hour, so I went on to the Third Petrograd University, in fact now closed as a university but where there is still a cafeteria in which I am registered to eat. There I hoped to get something to eat for myself, my wife and our friends, the Vvedenskys, who are also registered to eat there. But here too I had no luck: there was a long queue of hopeful eaters, tedium and vexation written on their faces; the queue was not moving at all. What was the problem? The boiler had broken down and there would be a delay of at least an hour.

Anyone reading this in the distant future may suppose that these people were expecting a banquet. But the whole meal was a single dish — usually a thin soup with a potato or cabbage in it. There is no question of any meat. Only the privileged few ever get that — i.e. the people who work in the kitchens.

I decided to leave and put off eating until after work. By 1 p.m. the tram had still not come so I returned to the canteen: there was still no food and no prospect of it for at least another half an hour. There was no choice but to go to work hungry.

At the Nikolaev Bridge I finally caught up with a No. 4 tram. There was no current on the line and the tram was stationary. I still don't understand this. All the trams had stopped but why had they started out if they knew that there was not enough fuel to complete their journeys? People remained seated — some at last gave up and got off to walk towards their destinations, while others sat there with Sisyphean patience. Two hours later I saw the trams were running but by 5 p.m. they had all stopped again.

By 2 p.m. I had reached the archive by foot. I stayed for half an hour and then went on to the University, where there was supposed to be a ration of cabbage handed out at 3 p.m. To whom I did not know. Perhaps to professors — it was worth the chance. But again I was out of luck: it turned out that the cabbage had not been delivered and would be given out tomorrow. And not to professors but only to students.

I also found out that there would be no bread ration for a week: some people said that all the bread had already been given out to the Communists who run all the committees.

From the University I went home, saw to my wife, did what was needed and went back to the vegetarian canteen with the hope of eating. Again out of luck: all the food was gone and there would be no more for at least an hour. I decided not to wait but went to the Vvedenskys to ask them if they could queue there later. From there I went back home at 5 p.m. And there I had my first piece of luck of the day: the lights in our sector were switched on [Petrograd was divided into sectors for electricity and because of the power shortage each took its turn to have light in the evening]. That gave me one precious hour to read — the first hour of the day free from running around for meals, bread, or cabbage, or fetching wood. At six I went to the Vvedenskys to eat (at last!), and came back to write these lines. At nine it went dark. Luckily a friend of ours came to look after my wife for a couple of hours in the evening and that gave me more precious time. After nine I lit a candle, put on the samovar, drank tea with my wife, and at eleven went to bed.[10]

The key to this Communist utopia was the control of the food supply: without that the government had no means of controlling the economy and society. The Bolsheviks were painfully aware of the fact that their regime lay at the mercy of a largely hostile peasantry. Their smallholding farms produced little for the market, and in the present climate, when there were no consumer goods to buy and any food surplus was claimed by the state, withdrew further into subsistence production and the autarkic nexus of the village. Lacking goods to trade with the peasants, the Bolsheviks resorted to brute force in the 'battle for grain', sending in armed squads to seize their foodstuffs and sparking peasant revolts across the country. This was another hidden civil war. Although the Bolsheviks were careful to pay lip-service to the smallholding peasant system consecrated by their own Decree on Land — this, after all, was what had brought them the support of so many peasants in the civil war against the Whites — they believed that the future of Soviet agriculture lay in gigantic collective and Soviet farms, *kolkhozy* and *sovkhozy*, producing directly for the state. The troublesome peasant — with his petty proprietary instincts, his superstitions and his attachment to tradition — would be abolished by these socialist farms since all those who worked in them would be recast as *kolkhoz* or *sovkhoz* 'workers'. Miliutin dreamed of 'agricultural factories producing grain, meat, milk and fodder, which will free the socialist order from its economic dependence on the petty-proprietary farms'.

Here again the Bolsheviks were carried away by their utopianism, believing that they could create socialism by decree. The Russian peasant was cautious by nature: it would take decades of gentle education, backed up by visible agronomic proof, to persuade him that large-scale farming with modern technology and collective labour teams was really so advantageous for him that it warranted a break with the traditions — the family farm, the commune and the village — which had sustained his father and grandfather. Yet in February 1919 the Bolsheviks passed a Statute on Socialist Land Organization which, at one stroke, declared all peasant farming 'obsolescent'. All unfarmed land which had belonged to the gentry was now to be turned over to the new collectives, much to the annoyance of the peasantry, which saw its claim to the gentry's estates as a sacrosanct achievement of the revolution. By December 1920 there were over 16,000 collective and state farms with nearly ten million acres of land and a million employees — many of them immigrant townsmen — between them. The largest, the *sovkhozy*, set up by the state, had over 100,000 acres; while the smallest, the various *kolkhozy*, set up by collectives of local peasants, could have fewer than fifty.

Many of the larger collective farms saw themselves as a microcosm of the experimental communistic lifestyle. Families pooled their possessions and lived together in dormitories. People ate and worked in their collective teams. Women did heavy field work alongside the men, and sometimes nurseries were set up for the children. There was also an absence of religious practice. This essentially urban lifestyle, modelled on the factory artel, did much to alienate the local peasantry, who believed that in the collectives not only the land and tools were shared but also wives and daughters; that everyone slept together under one huge blanket.

Even more scandalous to the peasants was the fact that most of the collectives were run by people who knew nothing about agriculture. The *sovkhozy* were largely made up of unemployed workers who had fled the towns; the *kolkhozy* of landless labourers, rural artisans, and the poorest peasants, who through misfortune, too much drinking, or simple laziness, had never made a success of their own farms. Peasant congresses were inundated with complaints about the poor way the collective farms were run. 'They have got the land but they don't know how to farm it,' complained the peasants of Tambov province. Even the Bolsheviks were forced to concede that the collective farms had become 'refuges for slackers' who could not 'stand up to the carping criticism of individual peasant farmers'. Despite their exemption from the food levy and generous state grants of tools and livestock, very few collectives ran at a profit, and many of them ran at a heavy loss. Less than a third of their total income was derived from their own production, the rest coming mainly from the state. Some collectives were so badly run that they had to conscript the local peasants for labour duty on their fields. The peasants saw this as a new form of serfdom and took up arms against the collectives. Half of them were destroyed in the peasant wars of 1921.[11]

✳   ✳   ✳

It was not just the peasantry who rebelled against these Communist experiments. In industry too the policies of militarization gave rise to growing strikes and protests, passive resistance and go-slows by the workers. Policies designed to tighten discipline merely gave way to more indiscipline. Three-quarters of Russia's factories were hit by strikes during the first six months of 1920. Despite threat of arrests and execution, workers in cities across the country marched and shouted in defiance, 'Down with the Commissars!' There was a general sense of anger that, long after the end of the civil war, the Bolsheviks were persevering with their warlike policies towards the working class. It was as if the whole industrial system had become trapped in a permanent state of emergency, that even in peace it was placed on a war footing, and that this state was being used to exploit and suppress the working class.[12]

Within the party too Trotsky's policies were meeting with growing opposition from the rank and file. His high-handed efforts to break up the railway union, which he blamed for the chaos on the railways, and to replace it with a general transport union (Tsektran) subordinated to the state apparatus, enraged Bolshevik trade-union leaders, who saw it as part of a broader campaign to end all independent union rights. The controversy over the role of the unions had been building up since the start of 1919. The party programme of that year had set out the ideal that the trade unions should directly manage the industrial economy — but only when the working class had been educated for this task. Until then, the role of the unions was to be limited to the fields of workers' education and discipline at work. As the trend towards one-man management continued, a growing number of union leaders became concerned that the promise of direct union management was being put off to the distant future. They managed to defeat the efforts of party leaders to impose the principle of one-man management at the Third Trade Union Congress in January 1920. At the Ninth Party Congress in April they forced the leadership to compromise and offer them a share of the managerial appointments in exchange for their acceptance of the principle.

This delicate balance — between the trade unions and the party-state — was upset by Trotsky's plans, put forward in the summer of 1920, to transform the transport unions into a branch of the state bureaucracy. The whole principle of union autonomy was now seen to be at stake. Nor were the union leaders alone in opposing Trotsky; much of the party leadership itself backed them. Zinoviev, a personal rival of Trotsky, denounced his 'police methods of dragooning workers'. Shliapnikov — joined in January by Kollontai — established the so-called Workers' Opposition to defend the rights of the trade unions and, more generally, to resist the spread of 'bureaucratism' which they said was stifling the 'spontaneous self-creativity' of the working class. The Workers' Opposition enjoyed widespread union support, especially from the metalworkers, among whom the sentiments of class solidarity — expressed both in the ideal of workers' control and in the hatred of the 'bourgeois specialists' — were most firmly rooted. It gave voice to widespread class hatred of factory managers and bureaucrats, whom the workers denounced as the 'new ruling class' and the 'new bourgeoisie'. Many of these sentiments were also expressed by the other major opposition faction in the party, the Democratic Centralists. This group of mostly intellectual Bolsheviks was opposed to the bureaucratic centralism of the party and to the demise of the Soviets as organs of direct worker-rule. Some of their more radical comrades in Moscow, where their base was strongest, even opened the doors of the district party executives to the Bolshevik rank and file in an effort to promote *glasnost*, or openness, in local government. They were the first to use the term.

These two controversies — over the unions and the party-state — merged and developed into a general crisis during the autumn of 1920. At a Special Party Conference in September the two opposition factions combined to force through a series of resolutions whose aim was to promote democracy and *glasnost* in the party: all party meetings were to be opened up to the rank and file; the lower party organs were to have more say in the appointment of higher officials; and the higher organs were to be made more accountable to the rank and file. Strengthened by this victory, the opposition factions prepared for battle over the trade unions. At the Fifth Trade Union Congress in November Trotsky threw down the gauntlet by proposing that all union officials should be appointed by the state. This sparked a bitter conflict within the party, with Trotsky pushing for the immediate and, if necessary, forcible merger of the unions with the state apparatus and the opposition factions fighting tooth and nail for the independence of the unions. Lenin supported Trotsky's goal but advocated a less high-handed approach towards its implementation in order to avoid a damaging split within the regime. 'If the party quarrels with the trade unions,' Lenin warned, 'then this will certainly be the end of Soviet power.' The Central Committee was hopelessly divided on the issue, and for the next three months the conflict raged in the party press as each faction tried to mobilize support for the decisive battle which would surely come at the Tenth Party Congress the following March.[13] With the government so patently in crisis, and the whole of the country engulfed by revolts and strikes, Russia was on the verge of a new revolution.

ii Engineers of the Human Soul

In October 1919, according to legend, Lenin paid a secret visit to the laboratory of the great physiologist I. P. Pavlov to find out if his work on the conditional reflexes of the brain might help the Bolsheviks control human behaviour. 'I want the masses of Russia to follow a Communistic pattern of thinking and reacting,' Lenin explained. 'There was too much individualism in the Russia of the past. Communism does not tolerate individualistic tendencies. They are harmful. They interfere with our plans. We must abolish individualism.' Pavlov was astounded. It seemed that Lenin wanted him to do for humans what he had already done for dogs. 'Do you mean that you would like to standardize the population of

Russia? Make them all behave in the same way?' he asked. 'Exactly', replied Lenin. 'Man can be corrected. Man can be made what we want him to be.'[14]

Whether it happened or not, the story illustrates a general truth: the ultimate aim of the Communist system was the transformation of human nature. It was an aim shared by the other so-called totalitarian regimes of the inter-war period. This, after all, was an age of utopian optimism in the potential of science to change human life and, paradoxically at the same time, an age of profound doubt and uncertainty about the value of human life itself in the wake of the destruction of the First World War. As one of the pioneers of the eugenics movement in Nazi Germany put it in 1920, 'it could almost seem as if we have witnessed a change in the concept of humanity . . . We were forced by the terrible exigencies of war to ascribe a different value to the life of the individual than was the case before.'[15] But there was also a vital difference between the Communist man-building programme and the human engineering of the Third Reich. The Bolshevik programme was based on the ideals of the Enlightenment — it stemmed from Kant as much as from Marx — which makes Western liberals, even in this age of post-modernism, sympathize with it, or at least obliges us to try and understand it, even if we do not share its political goals; whereas the Nazi efforts to 'improve mankind', whether through eugenics or genocide, spat in the face of the Enlightenment and can only fill us with revulsion. The notion of creating a new type of man through the enlightenment of the masses had always been the messianic mission of the nineteenth-century Russian intelligentsia, from whom the Bolsheviks emerged. Marxist philosophy likewise taught that human nature was a product of historical development and could thus be transformed by a revolution. The scientific materialism of Darwin and Huxley, which had the status of a religion among the Russian intelligentsia during Lenin's youth, equally lent itself to the view that man was determined by the world in which he lived. Thus the Bolsheviks were led to conclude that their revolution, with the help of science, could create a new type of man.

Lenin and Pavlov both paid homage to the influence of Ivan Sechenov (1829–1905), the physiologist who maintained that the brain was an electro-mechanical device responding to external stimuli. His book, *The Reflexes of the Brain* (1863), was a major influence on Chernyshevsky, and thus on Lenin, as well as the starting point for Pavlov's theory on conditioned reflexes. This was where science and socialism met. Although Pavlov was an outspoken critic of the revolution and had often threatened to emigrate, he was patronized by the Bolsheviks.* After two years of growing his own carrots, Pavlov was awarded a

---

* It is tempting to conclude that Pavlov was the target of Bulgakov's satire, *The Heart of a Dog* (1925), in which a world-famous experimental scientist, who despises the Bolsheviks but accepts their patronage, transplants the brain and sexual organs of a dog into a human being.

handsome ration and a spacious Moscow apartment. Despite the chronic shortage of paper, his lectures were published in 1921. Lenin spoke of Pavlov's work as 'hugely significant' for the revolution. Bukharin called it 'a weapon from the iron arsenal of materialism'. Even Trotsky, who generally stayed clear of cultural policy but took a great interest in psychiatry, waxed lyrical on the possibility of reconstructing man:

> What is man? He is by no means a finished or harmonious being. No, he is still a highly awkward creature. Man, as an animal, has not evolved by plan but spontaneously, and has accumulated many contradictions. The question of how to educate and regulate, of how to improve and complete the physical and spiritual construction of man, is a colossal problem which can only be conceived on the basis of Socialism. We can construct a railway across the Sahara, we can build the Eiffel Tower and talk directly with New York, but we surely cannot improve man. No, we can! To produce a new, 'improved version' of man — that is the future task of Communism. And for that we first have to find out everything about man, his anatomy, his physiology and that part of his physiology which is called his psychology. Man must look at himself and see himself as a raw material, or at best as a semi-manufactured product, and say: 'At last, my dear *homo sapiens*, I will work on you.'[16]

The New Soviet Man, as depicted in the futuristic novels and utopian tracts which boomed around the time of the revolution, was a Prometheus of the machine age. He was a rational, disciplined and collective being who lived only for the interests of the greater good, like a cell in a living organism. He thought not in terms of the individual 'I' but in terms of the collective 'we'. In his two science fiction novels, *Red Star* (1908) and *Engineer Menni* (1913), the Bolshevik philosopher Alexander Bogdanov described a utopian society located on the planet of Mars sometime in the twenty-third century. Every vestige of individuality had been eliminated in this 'Marxian-Martian society': all work was automated and run by computers; everyone wore the same unisex clothing and lived in the same identical housing; children were brought up in special colonies; there were no separate nations and everyone spoke a sort of Esperanto. At one point in *Engineer Menni* the principal hero, a Martian physician, compares the mission of the bourgeoisie on earth, which had been 'to create a human individual', with the task of the proletariat on Mars to 'gather these atoms' of society and 'fuse them into a single, intelligent human organism'.[17]

The ideal of individual liberation through the collective was fundamental to the Russian revolutionary intelligentsia. 'Not "I" but "we" — here is the basis of the emancipation of the individual,' Gorky had written in 1908. 'Then at last man will feel himself to be the incarnation of all the world's wealth, of all the world's beauty, of all experience of humanity, and spiritually the equal of all his brothers.' For Gorky, the awakening of this collective spirit was essentially a humanist task: he often compared it to the civic spirit of the Enlightenment. Russia had missed out on that cultural revolution. Centuries of serfdom and tsarist rule had bred, in his view, a 'servile and torpid people', passive and resistant to the influence of progress, prone to sudden outbursts of destructive violence, yet incapable, without state compulsion, of constructive national work. The Russians, in short, were *nekulturnyi*, or 'uncivilized': they lacked the culture to be active citizens. The task of the cultural revolution, upon which the political and social revolutions depended, was to cultivate this sense of citizenship. It was, in Gorky's words, to 'activate the Russian people along Western lines' and to liberate them from their 'long history of Asiatic barbarism and idleness'.[18]

In 1909 Gorky, Bogdanov and Lunacharsky had established a school for Russian workers at the writer's villa on the island of Capri. Thirteen workers (one of them a police spy) were smuggled out of Russia at great expense and made to sit through a dry course of lectures on the history of socialism and Western literature. The only extra-curricular entertainment was a guided tour by Lunacharsky of the art museums of Naples. Bologna was the venue for a second workers' school in 1910. The object of this exercise was to create a group of conscious proletarian socialists — a sort of 'working-class intelligentsia' — who would then disseminate their knowledge to the workers and thereby ensure that the revolutionary movement created its own cultural revolution. The founders of the school formed themselves into the Vpered (Forward) group and immediately came into bitter conflict with Lenin. The Vperedists' conception of the revolution was essentially Menshevik in the sense that they saw its success as dependent upon the organic development of a working-class culture. Lenin, by contrast, was dismissive of the workers' potential as an independent cultural force and stressed their role as disciplined cadres for the party. The Vpered group also claimed that knowledge, and technology in particular, were the moving forces of history in a way that Marx had not envisaged, and that social classes were differentiated less by property than by their possession of knowledge. The working class would thus be liberated not just by controlling the means of production, distribution and exchange, but by a simultaneous cultural revolution which also gave them the power of knowledge itself. Hence their commitment to the enlightenment of the working class. Finally, and even more heretically, the Vperedists argued that Marxism should be seen as a form of religion — only with humanity as the Divine Being and collectivism as the Holy Spirit. Gorky highlighted this humanist theme in his novel *Confession* (1908), in which the hero Matvei finds his god through comradeship with his fellow men.

After 1917, when the leading Bolsheviks were preoccupied with more pressing matters, cultural policy was left to these former Vperedists in the party. Lunacharsky became the Commissar of Enlightenment — a title that reflected the inspiration of the cultural revolution which it set as its goal — and was responsible for both education and the arts. Bogdanov headed the Proletkult organization, set up in 1917 to develop proletarian culture. Through its factory clubs and studios, which by 1919 had 80,000 members, it organized amateur theatres, choirs, bands, art classes, creative writing workshops and sporting events for the workers. There was a Proletarian University in Moscow and a *Socialist Encyclopedia*, whose publication was seen by Bogdanov as a preparation for the future proletarian civilization, just as, in his view, Diderot's *Encyclopédie* had been an attempt by the rising bourgeoisie of eighteenth-century France to prepare its own cultural revolution.[19]

As with the Capri and Bologna schools, the Proletkult intelligentsia displayed at times a patronising attitude towards the workers they sought to cultivate. Proletkult's basic premise was that the working class should spontaneously develop its own culture; yet here were the intelligentsia doing it for them. Moreover, the 'proletarian culture' which they fostered had much less to do with the workers' actual tastes — vaudeville and vodka for the most — which these intellectuals usually scorned as vulgar, than it had to do with their own idealized vision of what the workers were supposed to be: uncorrupted by bourgeois individualism; collectivist in their ways of life and thought; sober, serious and self-improving; interested in science and sport; in short the pioneers of the intelligentsia's own imagined socialist culture.

*   *   *

The revolution of 1917 came in the middle of Russia's so-called Silver Age, the first three decades of this century when the avant-garde flourished in all the arts. Many of the country's finest writers and artists took part in Proletkult and other Soviet cultural ventures during and after the civil war: Belyi, Gumilev, Mayakovsky and Khodasevich taught poetry classes; Stanislavsky, Meyerhold and Eisenstein carried out an 'October Revolution' in the theatre; Tatlin, Rodchenko, El Lissitsky and Malevich pioneered the visual arts; while Chagall even became Commissar for Arts in his native town of Vitebsk and later taught painting at a colony for orphans near Moscow. This coalition of commissars and artists was partly born of common principles: the idea that art had a social agenda and a mission to communicate with the masses; and a modernist rejection of the old bourgeois art. But it was also a marriage of convenience. For despite their initial reservations, mostly about losing their autonomy, these cultural figures soon saw the advantages of Bolshevik patronage for the avant-garde, not to speak of the extra rations and work materials they so badly needed in these barren years. Gorky was a central figure here — acting as a Soviet patron to the artists and as an artists' leader to the Soviets. In September 1918 he agreed to collaborate with Lunacharsky's commissariat in its dealings with the artistic and scientific worlds. Lunacharsky, for his part, did his best to support Gorky's various ventures to 'save Russian culture', despite Lenin's impatience about such 'trivial matters', from the publishing house World Literature, where so many destitute intellectuals were employed, to the Commission for the Preservation of Historical Buildings and Monuments. Lunacharsky complained that Gorky had 'turned out completely in the camp of the intelligentsia, siding with it in its grumbling, lack of faith and terror at the prospect of the destruction of valuable things under the blows of the revolution'.

The nihilistic wing of the avant-garde was especially attracted to Bolshevism. It revelled in its destruction of the old world. The Futurist poets, for example, such as Mayakovsky, practically threw themselves at the feet of the Bolsheviks, seeing them as an ally of their own struggle against 'bourgeois art'. (The Italian Futurists supported the Fascists for much the same reason.) The Futurists pursued an extreme iconoclastic line within the Proletkult movement which enraged Lenin (a conservative in cultural matters) and embarrassed Bogdanov and Lunacharsky. 'It's time for bullets to pepper museums,' Mayakovsky wrote. He dismissed the classics as 'old aesthetic junk' and punned that Rastrelli should be put against the wall (*rasstreliat* in Russian means to execute). Kirillov, the Proletkult poet, wrote:

> In the name of our tomorrow we shall burn Raphael
> Destroy the Museums, crush the flowers of Art.[20]

This was by and large intellectual swagger, the vandalistic pose of second-rate writers whose readiness to shock far outstripped their own talents.

Stalin once described the writer as the 'engineer of human souls'. The artists of the avant-garde were supposed to become the great transformers of human nature during the first years of the Bolshevik regime. Many of them shared the socialist ideal of making the human spirit more collectivist. They rejected the individualistic preoccupations of nineteenth-century 'bourgeois' art, and believed that they could train the human mind to see the world in a different way through modernist forms of artistic expression. Montage, for example, with its collage effect of fragmented but connected images, was thought to have a subliminal didactic effect on the viewer. Eisenstein, who used the technique in his three great propaganda films of the 1920s, *Strike, The Battleship Potemkin* and *October*, based his whole theory of film on it. A great deal of fuss was made of the 'psychic revolution' which was supposed to be brought about by the cinema, the modernist art form *par excellence*, which, like the psychology of modern man, was based on 'straight lines and sharp corners' and the 'power of the machine'.[21]

As the pioneers of this 'psychic revolution', the avant-garde artists pursued diverse experimental forms. There was no censorship of art at this time — the Bolsheviks had more pressing concerns — and it was an area of relative freedom. Hence there was the paradox of an artistic explosion in a police state. Much of this early Soviet art was of real and lasting value. The Constructivists, in particular artists such as Rodchenko, Malevich and Tatlin, have had a huge impact on the modernist style. This could not be said of Nazi art, or of what passed for art in Stalin's day, the grim monumental kitsch of Socialist Realism. And yet, almost inevitably, given the youthful exuberance with which the avant-garde embraced this spirit of experimentalism, many of their contributions may seem rather comical today.

In music, for example, there were orchestras without conductors (both in rehearsal and performance) who claimed to be pioneering the socialist way of life based on equality and human fulfilment through free collective work. There was a movement of 'concerts in the factory' using the sirens, turbines and hooters as instruments, or creating new sounds by electronic means, which some people seemed to think would lead to a new musical aesthetic closer to the psyche of the workers. Shostakovich, no doubt as always with tongue in cheek, joined in the fun by adding the sound of factory whistles to the climax of his Second Symphony ('To October'). Equally eccentric was the renaming of well-known operas and their refashioning with new librettos to make them 'socialist': so *Tosca* became *The Battle for the Commune*, with the action shifted to the Paris of 1871; *Les Huguenots* became *The Decembrists* and was set in Russia; while Glinka's *Life for the Tsar* was rewritten as *The Hammer and the Sickle*.

There was a similar attempt to bring theatre closer to the masses by taking it out of its usual 'bourgeois' setting and putting it on in the streets, the factories and the barracks. Theatre thus became a form of Agitprop. Its aim was to break down the barriers between actors and spectators, to dissolve the proscenium line dividing theatre from reality. All this was taken from the techniques of the German experimental theatre pioneered by Max Reinhardt, which were later perfected by Brecht. By encouraging the audience to voice its reactions to the drama, Meyerhold and other Soviet directors sought to engage its emotions in didactic allegories of the revolution. The new dramas highlighted the revolutionary struggle both on the national scale and on the scale of private human lives. The characters were crude cardboard symbols — greedy capitalists in bowler hats, devilish priests with Rasputin-type beards and honest simple workers. The main purpose of these plays was to stir up mass hatred against the 'enemies' of the revolution and thus to rally people behind the regime. One such drama, *Do You Hear, Moscow?*, staged by Eisenstein in 1924, aroused such emotions that in the final act, when the German workers were shown storming the stronghold of the Fascists, the audience itself tried to join in. Every murdered

Fascist was met with wild cheers. One spectator even drew his gun to shoot an actress playing the part of a Fascist cocotte; but his neighbours brought him to his senses.

The most spectacular example of revolutionary street theatre was *The Storming of the Winter Palace*, staged in 1920 to celebrate the third anniversary of the October insurrection. This mass spectacle ended the distinction — which in any case had always been confused — between theatre and revolution: the streets of Petrograd, where the revolutionary drama of 1917 had been enacted, were now turned into a theatre. The key scenes were re-enacted on three huge stages on Palace Square. The Winter Palace was part of the set with various windows lit up in turn to reveal different scenes inside. The *Aurora* played a star role, firing its heavy guns from the Neva to signal the start of the assault on the palace, just as it had done on that historic night. There was a cast of 10,000 actors, probably more than had taken part in the actual insurrection, who, like the chorus in the theatre of the Ancient Greeks, appeared to embody the monumental idea of the revolution as an act of the people. An estimated 100,000 spectators watched the action unfold from Palace Square. They laughed at the buffoonish figure of Kerensky and cheered wildly during the assault on the palace. This was the start of the myth of Great October — a myth which Eisenstein turned into pseudo-fact with his 'docudrama' film *October* (1927). Stills from this film are still reproduced in books, both in Russia and the West, as authentic photographs of the revolution.[22]

Art too was taken on to the streets. The Constructivists talked of bringing art out of the museums and into everyday life. Many of them, such as Rodchenko and Malevich, concentrated their efforts on designing clothes, furniture, offices and factories with the stress on what they called the 'industrial style' — simple designs and primary colours, geometric shapes and straight lines, all of which they thought would both liberate the people and make them more rational. They said their aim was 'to reconstruct not only objects, but also the whole domestic way of life'. Several leading avant-garde painters and sculptors, such as Chagall and Tatlin, put their hands to 'agitation art' — decorating buildings and streetcars or designing posters for the numerous revolutionary celebrations and festivals, such as I May or Revolution Day, when the whole of the people was supposed to be united in an open exhibition of collective joy and emotion. The town was literally painted red (sometimes even the trees). Through statues and monuments they sought to turn the streets into a Museum of the Revolution, into a living icon of the power and the grandeur of the new regime which would impress even the illiterate. There was nothing new in such acts of self-consecration by the state: the tsarist regime had done just the same. Indeed it was nicely ironic that the obelisk outside the Kremlin erected by the Romanovs to celebrate their tercentenary in 1913 was retained on Lenin's orders.

Its tsarist inscription was replaced by the names of a 'socialist' ancestry stretching back to the sixteenth century. It included Thomas More, Campanella and Winstanley.[23]

As far as one can tell, none of these avant-garde artistic experiments was ever really effective in transforming hearts and minds. Left-wing artists might have believed that they were creating a new aesthetic for the masses, but they were merely creating a modernist aesthetic for themselves, albeit one in which 'the masses' were objectified as a symbol of their own ideals. The artistic tastes of the workers and peasants were essentially conservative. Indeed it is hard to overestimate the conservatism of the peasants in artistic matters: when the Bolshoi Ballet toured the provinces during 1920 the peasants were said to have been 'profoundly shocked by the display of the bare arms and legs of the *coryphées*, and walked out of the performance in disgust'. The unlife-like images of modernist art were alien to a people whose limited acquaintance with art was based on the icon.* Having decorated the streets of Vitebsk for the first anniversary of the October insurrection, Chagall was asked by Communist officials: 'Why is the cow green and why is the house flying through the sky, why? What's the connection with Marx and Engels?' Surveys of popular reading habits during the 1920s showed that workers and peasants continued to prefer the detective and romantic stories of the sort they had read before the revolution to the literature of the avant-garde. Just as unsuccessful was the new music. At one 'concert in the factory' there was such a cacophonous din from all the sirens and the hooters that even the workers failed to recognize the tune of the Internationale. Concert halls and theatres were filled with the newly rich proletarians of the Bolshevik regime — the Bolshoi Theatre in Moscow was littered every night with the husks of the sunflower seeds which they chewed — yet they came to listen to Glinka and Tchaikovsky.[24] When it comes to matters of artistic taste, there is nothing the semi-educated worker wants more than to mimic the bourgeoisie.

*   *   *

Alongside new art forms the 'dreamers' of the revolution tried to experiment with new forms of social life. This too, it was presumed, could be used to transform the nature of mankind. Or, more precisely, womankind.

Women's liberation was an important aspect of the new collective life, as envisaged by the leading feminists in the party — Kollontai, Armand and Balabanoff. Communal dining halls, laundries and nurseries would liberate women from the drudgery of housework and enable them to play an active role in the revolution. 'Women of Russia, Throw Away Your Pots and Pans!', read

---

* The Socialist Realism of the 1930s, with its obvious iconic qualities, was much more effective as propaganda.

one Soviet poster. The gradual dissolution of the 'bourgeois' family through liberal reform of the laws on marriage, divorce and abortion would, it was supposed, liberate women from their husbands' tyranny. The Women's Department of the Central Committee Secretariat (Zhenotdel), established in 1919, set itself the task to 'refashion women' by mobilizing them into local political work and by educational propaganda. Kollontai, who became the head of Zhenotdel on Armand's death in 1920, also advocated a sexual revolution to emancipate women. She preached 'free love' or 'erotic friendships' between men and women as two equal partners, thus liberating women from the 'servitude of marriage' and both sexes from the burdens of monogamy. It was a philosophy she practised herself with a long succession of husbands and lovers, including Dybenko, the Bolshevik sailor seventeen years her junior whom she married in 1917, and, by all accounts, the King of Sweden, with whom she took up as the Soviet (and the first ever female) Ambassador in Stockholm during the 1930s.

As the Commissar for Social Welfare Kollontai tried to create the conditions for this new sexual harmony. Efforts were made to combat prostitution and to increase the state provision of child-care, although little progress could be made in either field during the civil war. Unfortunately, some local commissariats failed to understand the import of Kollontai's work. In Saratov, for example, the provincial welfare department issued a 'Decree on the Nationalization of Women': it abolished marriage and gave men the right to release their sexual urges at licensed brothels. Kollontai's subordinates set up a 'Bureau of Free Love' in Vladimir and issued a proclamation requiring all the unmarried women between the ages of eighteen and fifty to register with it for the selection of their sexual mates. The proclamation declared all women over eighteen to be 'state property' and gave men the right to choose a registered woman, even without her consent, for breeding 'in the interests of the state'.[25]

Little of Kollontai's work was really understood. Whereas her vision of the sexual revolution was in many ways highly idealistic, she was widely seen to be encouraging the sexual promiscuity and moral anarchy which swept through Russia after 1917. Lenin himself had no time for such matters, being himself something of a prude, and condemned the so-called 'glass-of-water' theory of sexual matters attributed to Kollontai — that in a Communist society the satisfaction of one's sexual desires should be as straightforward as drinking a glass of water — as 'completely un-Marxist'. 'To be sure,' he wrote, 'thirst has to be quenched. But would a normal person lie down in the gutter and drink from a puddle?' Local Bolsheviks were dismissive of 'women's work', nicknaming Zhenotdel the 'babotdel' (from the word 'baba', a peasant wife). Even the women themselves were suspicious of the idea of sexual liberation, especially in the countryside, where patriarchal attitudes died hard. Many women were afraid that communal nurseries would take away their children and make them orphans of the state. They complained that the liberal divorce laws of 1918 had merely made it easier for men to escape their responsibilities to their wives and children. And the statistics bore them out. By the early 1920s the divorce rate in Russia had become by far the highest in Europe — twenty-six times higher than in bourgeois Europe. Working-class women strongly disapproved of the liberal sexuality preached by Kollontai, seeing it (not without reason) as a licence for their men to behave badly towards women. They placed greater value on the old-fashioned notion of marriage, rooted in the peasant household, as a shared economy with a sexual division of labour for the raising of a family.[26]

It was not just in sexual matters that Lenin disapproved of experimentation. In artistic matters he was as conservative as any other nineteenth-century bourgeois. Lenin had no time for the avant-garde. He thought that their revolutionary statues were a 'mockery and distortion' of the socialist tradition — one projected statue depicting Marx standing on top of four elephants had him foaming at the mouth — and he dismissed Mayakovsky's best-known poem, '150,000,000', as so much 'nonsense, arrant stupidity and pretentiousness'. (Many readers might agree.) Once the civil war was over Lenin took a close look at the work of Proletkult — and decided to close it down. During the autumn of 1920 its subsidy was drastically cut back, Bogdanov was removed from its leadership, and Lenin launched an attack on its basic principles. The Bolshevik leader was irritated by the iconoclastic bias of Proletkult, preferring to stress the need to build on the cultural achievements of the past, and he saw its autonomy as a growing political threat. He saw it as 'Bogdanov's faction'. Proletkult certainly had much in common with the Workers' Opposition, stressing as it did the need to overthrow the cultural hegemony of the bourgeoisie, as still manifested in the employment of the 'bourgeois specialists', and indeed shortly later in the NEP itself. There was in this sense a direct link between the anti-bourgeois sentiments of the Proletkult and Stalin's own 'cultural revolution'. From Lenin's viewpoint, closing down the Proletkult was an integral aspect of the transition to the NEP. While the NEP was a Thermidor in the economic field this cessation of the war on 'bourgeois art' was a Thermidor in the cultural one. Both stemmed from the recognition that in a backward country such as Russia the achievements of the old civilization had to be maintained as a base on which to build the socialist order. There were no short-cuts to Communism.

Lenin wrote a great deal at this time on the need for a 'cultural revolution'. It was not enough, he argued, merely to create a Workers' State; one also had to create the cultural conditions for the long transition to socialism. What he stressed in his conception of the cultural revolution was not proletarian art and literature but proletarian science and technology. Whereas Proletkult looked to art as a means of human liberation, Lenin looked to science as a

means of human transformation — turning people into 'cogs' of the state.* He
wanted the 'bad' and 'illiterate' Russian workers to be 'schooled in the culture
of capitalism' — to become skilled and disciplined workers and to send their sons
to engineering college — so that the country could overcome its backwardness in
the transition towards socialism.[27] Bolshevism was nothing if not a strategy of
modernization.

Lenin's emphasis on the need for a narrow scientific training was
reflected in the change in education policies during 1920–I. The Bolsheviks
viewed education as one of the main channels of human transformation: through
the schools and the Communist leagues for children and youth (the Pioneers
and the Komsomol) they would indoctrinate the next generation in the new
collective way of life. As Lilina Zinoviev, one of the pioneers of Soviet schooling,
declared at a Congress of Public Education in 1918:

> We must make the young generation into a generation of Communists.
> Children, like soft wax, are very malleable and they should be moulded
> into good Communists ... We must rescue children from the harmful
> influence of family life ... We must nationalise them. From the earliest
> days of their little lives, they must find themselves under the beneficent
> influence of Communist schools. They will learn the ABC of
> Communism ... To oblige the mother to give her child to the Soviet
> State — that is our task.

The basic model of the Soviet school was the Unified Labour School. Established
in 1918, it was designed to give all children a free and general education up to
the age of fourteen. The practical difficulties of the civil war, however, meant
that few such schools were actually established. During 1920 a number of
Bolshevik and trade union leaders began to call for a narrower system
of vocational training from an early age. Influenced by Trotsky's plans for
militarization, they stressed the need to subordinate the educational system to
the demands of the economy: Russia's industries needed skilled technicians and
it was the schools' job to produce them. Lunacharsky opposed these calls, seeing
them as an invitation to renounce the humanist goals of the revolution which
he had championed since his Vperedist days. Having taken power in the name
of the workers, the Bolsheviks, he argued, were obliged to educate their children,
to raise them up to the level of the intelligentsia, so that they became the
'masters of industry'. It was not enough merely to teach them how to read and
write before turning them into apprentices. This would reproduce the class
divisions of capitalism, the old culture of Masters and Men separated by

---

* Stalin often referred to the people as 'cogs' (*vintiki*) in the vast machinery of the state.

their power over knowledge. Thanks to Lunacharsky's efforts, the polytechnical principles of 1918 were basically retained. But in practice there was a growing emphasis on narrow vocational training with many children, especially orphans in state care, forced into factory apprenticeships from as early as the age of nine and ten.[28]

Lenin's patronage of Taylorist ideas ran in parallel with this trend. He had long hailed the American engineer F. W. Taylor's theories of 'scientific management' — using time-and-motion studies to subdivide and automate the tasks of industry — as a means of remoulding the psyche of the worker, making him into a disciplined being, and thus remodelling the whole of society along mechanistic lines. Lenin encouraged the cult of Taylorism which flourished in Russia at this time. The scientific methods of Taylor and Henry Ford were said to hold the key to a bright and prosperous future. Even remote villagers knew the name of Ford (some of them thought he was a sort of god guiding the work of Lenin and Trotsky). Alexei Gastev (1882–1941), the Bolshevik engineer and poet, took these Taylorist principles to their extreme. As the head of the Central Institute of Labour, established in 1920, he carried out experiments to train the workers so that they would end up acting like machines. Hundreds of identically dressed trainees would be marched in columns to their benches, and orders would be given out by buzzes from machines. The workers were trained to hammer correctly by holding a hammer attached to and moved by a hammering machine so that after half an hour they had internalized its mechanical rhythm. The same process was repeated for chiselling, filing and other basic skills. Gastev's aim, by his own admission, was to turn the worker into a sort of 'human robot' (a word, not coincidentally, derived from the Russian verb to work, *rabotat'*). Since Gastev saw machines as superior to human beings, he thought this would represent an improvement in humanity. Indeed he saw it as the next logical step in human evolution. Gastev envisaged a brave new world where 'people' would be replaced by 'proletarian units' so devoid of personality that there would not even be a need to give them names. They would be classified instead by ciphers such as 'A, B, C, or 325, 075, 0, and so on'. These automatons would be like machines, 'incapable of individual thought', and would simply obey their controllers. A 'mechanized collectivism' would 'take the place of the individual personality in the psychology of the proletariat'. There would no longer be a need for emotions, and the human soul would no longer be measured 'by a shout or a smile but by a pressure gauge or a speedometer'. This nightmare utopia was satirized by Zamyatin in his novel *We* (1924), which inspired Orwell's *1984*. Zamyatin depicted a future world of robot-like beings, the 'we', who are known by numbers instead of names and whose lives are programmed in every detail. The satire was dangerous enough for *We* to remain banned in the Soviet Union for over sixty years.

Gastev's vision of the mechanized society was no idle fantasy. He believed it was just around the corner. *The ABC of Communism*, written by Bukharin and Preobrazhensky in 1919, claimed that a 'new world' with 'new people and customs', in which everything was 'precisely calculated', would soon come into existence. The mechanistic motifs of Proletkult art were supposed to foster this new Machine World. There was even a League of Time, whose 25,000 members in 800 local branches by the time Zamyatin wote *We*, kept a 'chronocard' on which they recorded how they spent each minute of their day ('7.00 a.m. got out of bed; 7.01 a.m. went to the lavatory') so as to be more efficient in their use of time. The crusaders of this clockwork world wore oversized wristwatches (there is still a fashion for them in Russia today). As self-appointed 'Time Police', they went round factories and offices trying to stamp out 'Oblomovism', that very Russian habit of the wastage of time. Another one of their plans to save time consisted of replacing the long words and official titles of the Russian language with shorter ones or acronyms. Politicians were told to cut their verbose comments, and speakers at congresses to keep their speeches short.[29]

* * *

The war against religion played a vital role in this battle for the people's soul. The Bolsheviks saw religion as a sign of backwardness (the 'opium of the masses') and the Church as a rival to their power. In particular, they saw the religion of the peasants as a fundamental cultural gulf between their own Enlightenment ideals and the 'dark' people of the countryside, a people they could neither understand nor ever really hope to convert to their cause. The war against religion was thus an aspect of their broader campaign to conquer the 'otherness' of the peasantry.

Until 1921 the war against religion was fought mainly by propaganda means. The Bolsheviks encouraged the popular wave of anti-clericalism that had swept away the Church lands in 1917. The Decree on the Separation of Church and State in January 1918 aimed to place the clergy at the mercy of the local population by taking away its rights to own property — church buildings were henceforth to be rented from the Soviets — or to charge for religious services. Religious instruction in schools was also outlawed. Bolshevik propaganda caricatured the clergy as fat parasites living off the backs of the peasantry and plotting for the return of the Tsar. Most provincial newspapers had regular columns on the 'counter-revolutionary' activities of the local priests, although in fact most of the parish clergy had either gone or been dragged along with the peasant revolution. Needless to say, the Cheka jails were full of priests.

The aim of Bolshevik propaganda was to replace the worship of God with veneration of the state, to substitute revolutionary icons for religious ones. Communism was the new religion, Lenin and Trotsky its new arch-priests. In this sense the Bolshevik war against religion went one step further than the

Jacobin dechristianization campaigns: its aim was not just to undermine religion but to appropriate its powers for the state.

On the one hand was the Bolsheviks' iconoclastic propaganda. Christian miracles were exposed as myths. Coffins said to hold the 'incorruptible' relics of Russian saints were opened up and found to contain bare skeletons or, in some cases, wax effigies. The celebrated 'weeping icons' were shown to be operated by rubber squeezers that produced 'tears' when an offering was made. The peasantry's attachment to religious and superstitious explanations was ridiculed as foolish: harvest failures and epidemics were to be avoided by agronomic and meteorological science rather than prayer and rituals in the fields. 'Godless acres' were farmed beside 'God's acres' — the former treated with chemical fertilizers, the latter with holy water — to drive home the point. Peasants were taken for rides by aeroplane so that they could see for themselves that there were no angels or gods in the sky. Most of the local press had special columns for this sort of 'scientific atheism'. Hundreds of atheistic pamphlets and stories were also published. Literature and music deemed to be religious were suppressed. The works of Plato, Kant, Schopenhauer, Nietzsche and Tolstoy were all banned on these grounds, as was Mozart's Requiem, nearly all of Bach and the Vespers of Rachmaninov. There was also an atheist art — one especially blasphemous poster showed the Virgin Mary with a pregnant belly longing for a Soviet abortion — and an equally iconoclastic theatre and cinema of the Godless. Then there were study groups and evening classes in this 'science' of atheism (a good grounding in it was essential for advancement in the party-state). A Union of the Militant Godless was established in 1921 with its own national newspaper and hundreds of local branches which held 'debates' with the clergy on the question: 'Does God Exist?' These debates usually involved the staged conversion of at least one priest, who would suddenly announce that he had been convinced that God did not exist, and would call on the Soviet authorities to forgive him his error. Most of these priests must have been tortured in the Cheka jails, or else threatened with imprisonment, in order to make them confess in this way. Even so, the victory of the Godless was by no means assured. In one debate the priest asked the Godless who had made the natural world. When they replied that Nature had made itself through evolution there were hoots of laughter from the peasant audience, to whom such a proposition seemed quite ridiculous, and a victory for the priest was declared.[30]

On the other hand was the Bolshevik propaganda which held up Communism as the new religion. The festivals, rituals and symbols of the Communist state were consciously modelled on their Christian equivalents — which they sought to replace. Soviet festivals were scheduled on the same days as the old religious holidays: there was a Komsomol Christmas and Easter; Electric Day fell on Elijah Day; Forest Day (a throwback to the peasant-pagan past) on Trinity Sunday. May Day and Revolution Day were heavily overladen with religious symbolism: the armed march past the Kremlin, the religious centre of Orthodox Russia, was clearly reminiscent of the old religious procession, only with rifles instead of crosses. The cult of Lenin, which flourished in the civil war, gave him the status of a god. The very symbol of the Communist state, the Red Star, was steeped in religious and messianic meaning deeply rooted in Russian folklore.

A Red Army leaflet of 1918 explained to the servicemen why the Red Star appeared on the Soviet flag and their uniforms. There was once a beautiful maiden named *Pravda* (Truth) who had a burning red star on her forehead which lit up the whole world and brought it truth, justice and happiness. One day the red star was stolen by *Krivda* (Falsehood) who wanted to bring darkness and evil to the world. Thus began the rule of *Krivda*. Meanwhile, *Pravda* called on the people to retrieve her star and 'return the light of truth to the world'. A good youth conquered *Krivda* and her forces and returned the red star to *Pravda*, whereupon the evil forces ran away from the light 'like owls and bats', and 'once again the people lived by truth'. The leaflet made the parable clear: 'So the Red Star of the Red Army is the star of *Pravda*. And the Red Army servicemen are the brave lads who are fighting *Krivda* and her evil supporters so that truth should rule the world and so that all those oppressed and wronged by *Krivda*, all the poor peasants and workers, should live well and in freedom.'[31]

In private life, as in public, religious rituals were Bolshevized. Instead of baptisms children were 'Octobered'. The parents at these ceremonies, which boomed in the early 1920s, promised to bring up their children in the spirit of Communism; portraits of the infant Lenin were given as gifts; and the Internationale was sung. The names chosen for these Octobered children — and indeed for adults who also changed their names — were drawn from the annals of the revolution: Marx; Engelina; Rosa (after Rosa Luxemburg); Vladlen, Ninel, Ilich and Ilina (acronyms, nicknames or anagrams for Lenin); Marlen (for Marx and Lenin); Melor (for Marx, Engels, Lenin and October Revolution); Pravda; Barrikada; Fevral (February); Oktiabrina (October); Revoliutsiia (Revolution); Parizhkommuna (Paris Commune); Molot (hammer); Serpina (sickle); Dazmir (Long Live the World Revolution); Diktatura (Dictatorship); and Terrora (Terror). Sometimes the names were chosen on the basis of a misunderstanding or simply because they were foreign sounding and were thus associated with the revolution: Traviata, Markiza, Embryo and Vinaigrette. Red weddings were another Bolshevik ritual, popular among the Komsomol youth. They were usually held in a factory or some local club. Instead of the altar the couple faced a portrait of Lenin. They made their vows of loyalty both to each other and to the principles of Communism. In his satirical novel *Dog's Wedding* (1925), Brykin reproduced such a vow. 'Do you promise', asks the officiator, 'to follow the path of Communism as bravely as you are now opposing the church and the old people's customs? Are you going to make your children serve as Young Pioneers [the Komsomol organization for younger children], educate them, introduce scientific farming methods, and fight for the world revolution? Then in the name of our leader, Comrade Vladimir Ilich Lenin, I declare the Red Marriage completed.' Finally, there was the Red Funeral, mainly reserved for Bolshevik heroes, which drew on the funereal traditions of the revolutionary movement — with its guard of honour, the coffin set high on a bier draped in red, the dirgelike hymn 'You Fell Victim', the graveside orations and the gunfire salute — originally used at Bauman's burial, that first martyred Bolshevik, in 1905.[32]

From 1921 the war against religion moved from words and rituals to the closure of churches and the shooting of priests. Lenin instigated this totally gratuitous reign of terror. Apart from the Academy of Sciences, the Church was the only remaining national institution outside the control of the party. Three years of propaganda had not undermined it — in many ways the civil war had made people turn to religion even more — so Lenin sought to attack it directly. The famine of 1921–2 gave him the pretext he needed. Although the Church had actively joined in the famine relief campaign, offering to sell some of its non-consecrated valuables to buy foodstuffs from abroad, Lenin found a strategy that enabled him to accuse it of selfishly turning its back on the crisis. He ordered the Church to hand over its consecrated valuables for sale as well, even though he must have known that it was obliged to disobey the order (the secular use of consecrated items was sacrilegious). This provocation would make the Church appear as it was charged — as an 'enemy of the people'. To rally the public against it the press called hysterically for all the Church's valuables to be sold for the famine victims: 'Turn Gold into Bread!' was the emotive slogan. In a last desperate effort to prevent the pillage of his churches, Patriarch Tikhon offered to raise money equivalent to the value of the consecrated items through voluntary subscriptions and the sale of other property; but his offer was refused. Lenin was not interested in the money; he wanted a pretext to assault the Church.

On 26 February 1922 a decree was sent out to the local Soviets instructing them to remove from the churches all precious items, including those used for religious worship. The decree claimed that their sale was necessary to help the famine victims; but little of the money raised was used for this purpose. Armed bands gutted the local churches, carrying away the icons and crosses, the chalices and mitres, even the iconostases in bits. In many places angry crowds took up arms to defend their local church. In some places they were led by their priests, at others they fought spontaneously. The records tell of 1,414 bloody clashes during 1922–3. Most of these were utterly one-sided. Troops with machine-guns fought against old men and women armed with pitch forks and rusty rifles: 7,100 clergy were killed, including nearly 3,500 nuns, but only a handful of Soviet troops. One such clash in the textile town of Shuya, 200 miles north-east of Moscow, in March 1922, prompted Lenin to issue a secret order for the extermination of the clergy. The event was typical enough: on Sunday 12 March worshippers fought off Soviet officials when they came to raid the local church; when the officials returned three days later with troops and machine-guns there was some fighting with several people killed. The Politburo, in Lenin's absence, voted to suspend further confiscations. But Lenin, hearing of the events in Shuya, dictated contrary orders over the phone from his country residence at Gorki with strict instructions of top secrecy. This memorandum, first published in full by a Soviet publication in 1990, reveals the cruel streak in Lenin's nature. It undermines the 'soft' image of Lenin in his final years previously favoured by left-wing historians in the West who would have us believe that the 1920s were a hopeful period of 'Soviet democracy' before the onset of Stalinism. Lenin argued that the events in Shuya should be exploited to link the clergy with the Black Hundreds, to destroy the Church 'for many decades', and to 'assure ourselves of capital worth several hundred million gold roubles . . . to carry out governmental work in general and in particular economic reconstruction'. It was 'only now', in the context of the famine, that the hungry peasants would 'either be for us or at any rate neutral' in this 'ferocious' war against the Church; 'later on we will not succeed.' For this reason, continued Lenin:

> I have come to the unequivocal conclusion that we must now wage the most decisive and merciless war against the Black Hundred clergy and suppress its resistance with such cruelty that they will not forget it for decades to come . . . The more members of the reactionary bourgeoisie and clergy we manage to shoot the better.

It has recently been estimated that 8,000 people were executed during this brutal campaign in 1922 alone. Patriarch Tikhon claimed to know of 10,000 priests in prison or exile, including about 100 bishops. It was only after 1925, under pressure from Russia's Western trading partners, that the persecution came to a temporary halt.[33]

According to Gorky, the Bolsheviks deliberately used the Jews in their ranks to carry out confiscations of church property. He accused them of deliberately stirring up anti-Semitism to divert the anger of the Christian community away from themselves. In several towns, such as Smolensk and Viatka, there were indeed pogroms against the Jews following the confiscation of church property. Meanwhile, the Bolsheviks were closing down synagogues as part of their campaign against religion. The first to be closed were in Chagall's home town of Vitebsk in April 1921. The Soviet authorities claimed that six of the city's eighty synagogues were needed for conversion to Yiddish schools. The Jews quickly occupied those synagogues which had been targeted for closure and held prayer meetings in them. But the authorities removed them with troops, smashing windows, chanting 'Death to the Yids!' and killing several worshippers in the process. None of the synagogues was used as a school: one became a Communist university; several were turned into workers' clubs; one even became a shoe factory. More closures followed in Minsk, Gomel, Odessa and Kharkov. Overall, 800 synagogues were closed down by the Communists between 1921 and 1925.

There was more than just a tinge of anti-Semitism in all this. The lower party ranks were filled, in Gorky's words, with 'old Russian nationalists, scoundrels, and vagabonds, who despise and fear the Jews'. The Military and Workers' Oppositions, which mobilized their support from the lower party ranks, both used the rhetoric of anti-Semitism in their language of class animosity towards the 'bourgeois specialists'. The early years of the NEP, which witnessed a boom in the sort of small-scale trading where Jews were traditionally dominant, strengthened this anti-Semitism. For the lower-class Bolsheviks, in particular, it was galling to see the 'Jewish' traders 'taking over' Moscow. During the civil war these 'speculators' would have been arrested; now they lived better than the party rank and file, while half the Russian workers were unemployed. The revolution, it seemed to them, was in retreat both on the class and the racial fronts. It was in this context that many of the more militant Bolsheviks began to argue, as Marx himself had done, that the Jews as a social group were synonymous with capitalism — that all traders were essentially 'Jews'. Such ideas were prevalent in the Bolshevik campaign against Judaism which took off in 1921. The ultimate insult of this campaign was delivered on the Jewish New Year of 1921 when a mock 'trial' of Judaism was put on for propaganda purposes. It was staged in the same courtroom in Kiev where the innocent Beiliss (also read: Judaism) had been tried in 1913.[34]

* * *

The Bolshevik persecution of religion did little to weaken the hold of this 'opiate' on the minds of the population. Although the 1920s witnessed a decline of religion, especially among the rural youth who went to school or left the countryside for the city, this probably had less to do with the Bolsheviks' efforts than with the secularizing tendencies of modern life. It had been happening in any case for decades. In fact, if anything, the oppressive measures of the Bolsheviks had precisely the opposite effect — of rallying the believers around their religion. Despite the separation of Church and state, the local clergy continued to be supported by the voluntary donations of their parishioners as well as by fees and grants of land from the peasant communes. Ironically it was not that far from the dreams of the nineteenth-century liberal clergy for an organic self-supporting parish. Even those who no longer believed in their religion with the same unquestioning faith often continued not merely to observe but also to show a strong attachment to its rituals. Octobered babies and Red Weddings failed to supplant their religious equivalents (which also happened to be more fun). People continued to bury their dead rather than cremate them, despite the shortages of coffins and graves and the free state provision of cremations, because, in the words of one morgue official, 'the Russians are still either too religious or too superstitious to part from the Orthodox burial traditions'.[35]

As in religion, so in the fields of culture and social life, the attempt by the Bolsheviks to 'make the world and man anew' foundered on the rocks of reality. It was in many ways a utopian dream — one of the most ambitious in history — to believe that human nature could be changed by simply altering the social environment in which people lived. Man cannot be transformed quite so easily: human nature moves more slowly than ruling ideologies or society. This is perhaps the one enduring moral lesson of the Russian Revolution — as it is indeed of the terrible history of this century.

iii Bolshevism in Retreat

A letter from Sergei Semenov:

Andreevskoe, 21 January 1921

Dear Anna,

Life in the village has become unbearable. True, we are much better off than the peasants in the rest of Russia. Neither the food requisitioning nor the labour duty has really yet affected us. But we still suffer from the daily acts of robbery, stupidity and dishonesty by our local bearers of Soviet Power which make normal life impossible. The labouring people, in whose name all this has been done, no longer support the new regime. I will not write another letter of complaint to Kamenev [chairman of the Moscow Soviet]. As the proverb goes, 'There is nothing worse than a deaf man who will neither listen.'

Despite the ending of the war and all the promises to get the country back on to its feet, our population does not believe the current authorities are capable of this. It is so fed up and angry, it is so devoured by the feeling of oppression, that it is incapable of positive thoughts and cannot see a way out of this situation. Many are despairing because Wrangel and the Poles were beaten — and yet nobody wants to admit that the answer to our problems lies not in changing things from the outside but in changing the way we live ourselves.[36]

The sense of anger and despair which Semenov's letter expresses was shared by peasants throughout Russia. All the ideals of the peasant revolution had been destroyed by the Bolshevik regime. The peasant Soviets of 1917, which to a large extent had realized the old ideal of *volia*, of village freedom and autonomy, had been taken over by the Communists. What had been organs of peasant self-rule now became bureaucratic organs of the state. The revolution on the land, which had aimed to make the smallholding peasant farm universal, was now threatened by the collective farms. The gentry's estates which the peasants had thought would belong to them were being transferred to the state. And what sort of state was that? Not one that helped the peasants to prosper. It was one that took away their only sons and horses for the army, one that prolonged the devastations of the civil war, one that forced them into labour teams and robbed them of their food. 'The freedom we were given by the revolution was taken from us by the new regime,' complained one peasant to a foreign journalist in January 1921. 'Life in the village is now like it was under the Tsar.'

By 1921 much of peasant Russia had been brought to the brink of a terrible famine. While the famine crisis of 1921–2 was directly caused by a year of drought and heavy frosts, the worst affected areas were clearly those that had suffered most from the requisitionings of 1918–21. In Samara province, for example, the worst-hit region of the famine crisis, the amount of grain requisitioned during 1919–20 exceeded the actual harvest surplus by 30 per cent with the result that the average peasant household lost 118 kg of food, fodder and seed from its basic stores. In the harsh conditions of 1921 this often proved the difference between life and death. In the Balashov district of neighbouring Saratov province, where Cheremukhin's murderous brigade collected the levy, the amount of requisitioned grain even exceeded the total harvest so that the peasants were forced to pay it from stocks they had accumulated in previous years and in the autumn of 1920 there was, in the words of one official, 'no seed left to sow'. Throughout the grain-producing regions of Russia the Bolsheviks had deliberately set their food levies higher than the estimated harvest surplus on the grounds that the peasants would hide up to one-third of their actual food surplus. On this same basis the requisitioning brigades had indiscriminately seized whatever foodstuffs they could find in the village barns, often shooting peasants who resisted them as 'kulaks', even though, as many Bolshevik officials were forced to admit, these were usually the poorest peasants who would simply starve if they lost their last vital food stocks to the levy. During 1920, as the signs of the imminent crisis became clearer, provincial food officials pleaded with the Centre to call a halt to their disastrous levies. 'There is simply no grain left to take,' warned one official from the German Volga region in September 1920. And yet Moscow pressed for more. In the German Volga region 42 per cent of the paltry 1920 harvest was seized and shipped off to the hungry north.

Villages were ransacked, children held to ransom, peasants whipped and tortured to squeeze their last few grains from them.[37]

To begin with the peasants defended themselves with the usual 'weapons of the weak': passive resistance and subterfuge. They buried their grain beneath the ground, fed it to their livestock, or turned it into moonshine rather than lose it to the Bolsheviks. They also began to take up arms in sporadic local revolts and rebellions of increasing frequency, size and violence. Two thousand members of the requisitioning brigades were murdered by angry peasants during 1918; in 1919 the figure rose to nearly 5,000; and in 1920 to over 8,000. By the autumn of 1920 the whole of the country was inflamed with peasant wars. Makhno's peasant army, still up to 15,000 strong after Wrangel's defeat, roamed across the Ukrainian steppe and, together with countless other local bands, succeeded in paralysing much of the rural Soviet infrastructure until the summer of 1921. In the central Russian province of Tambov the Antonov rebellion was supported by virtually the entire peasant population: Soviet power ceased to exist there between the autumn of 1920 and the summer of 1921. In Voronezh, Saratov, Samara, Simbirsk and Penza provinces there were smaller but no less destructive peasant rebel armies creating havoc and effectively limiting the Bolsheviks' power to the towns. Hundreds of small-scale bandit armies controlled the steppelands between Ufa and the Caspian Sea. In the Don and the Kuban the Cossacks and the peasants were at last united by their common hatred of the Bolsheviks. The rebel armies of the Caucasian mountains numbered well over 30,000 fighters. In Belorussia the nationalist-led peasants took over most of the countryside and forced the Soviets of Minsk and Smolensk to be evacuated. By far the biggest (though least studied) of the peasant revolts broke out in western Siberia: the whole of the Tiumen', Omsk, Cheliabinsk, Tobolsk, Ekaterinburg and Tomsk regions, complete with most of the major towns, fell into the hands of peasant rebels, up to 60,000 of them under arms, and virtually the whole of the Soviet infrastructure remained paralysed during the first six months of 1921. And yet throughout Russia the same thing was happening on a smaller scale: angry peasants were taking up arms and chasing the Bolsheviks out of the villages. Less than fifty miles from the Kremlin, not far from Semenov's Andreevskoe, there were villages where it was dangerous for a Bolshevik to go.[38]

What is remarkable about these peasant wars is that they shared so many common features, despite the huge distances between them and the different contexts in which they took place.

Most of the larger rebellions had started out in 1920 as small-scale peasant revolts against the requisitioning of food which, as a result of their incompetent and often brutal handling by the local Communists, soon became inflamed and spread into full-scale peasant wars. The Tambov rebellion was typical. It had started in August 1920 in the village of Kamenka when a food brigade arrived to collect its share of the new grain levy. At over eleven million *puds* the levy for the province had clearly been set much too high. Even Lenin wondered in September 'whether it should not be cut'. The 1920 harvest had been very poor and if the peasants had paid the levy in full they would have been left with a mere one *pud* of grain per person, barely 10 per cent of their normal requirements for food, seed and fodder. Already in October there were hunger riots. By January, in the words of the Bolshevik Antonov-Ovseenko, sent in to help put down the revolt, 'half the peasantry was starving'. The peasants of Kamenka were relatively wealthy — which meant they starved more slowly than the rest — and an extra levy was imposed on them. They refused to pay this levy, killed several members of the requisitioning brigade, and armed themselves with guns and pitchforks to fight off the Soviet reinforcements sent in from Tambov to put their revolt down. Neighbouring villages joined the uprising and a rudimentary peasant army was soon organized. It fought under the Red Flag — reclaiming the symbols of the revolution was an important aspect of these people's uprisings — and was led by the local peasant SR hero, Grigorii Plezhnikov, who had organized the war against the gentry estates in 1905 and 1917. Meanwhile, a network of Peasant Unions (STKs) began to emerge in the villages — often they were organized by the local SRs — which replaced the Soviets and helped to supply the insurgent army. Over fifty Communists were shot.

The speed with which the revolt spread caught the Bolsheviks in Tambov unprepared. The Soviet and party apparatus in the province had become extremely weak. People had been leaving the party in droves — many of them ex-SRs who soon joined the rebels — as industrial strikes and corruption scandals had made belonging to it a source of both danger and embarrassment. Because of the war against Poland there were only 3,000 Red Army troops, most of them extremely unreliable, in the provincial garrison. They had only one machine-gun for the whole of the insurgent district of Kirsanov. The rebels took advantage of this weakness and marched on the provincial capital. Thousands of peasants joined them as they approached Tambov. The Bolsheviks were thrown into panic. When reinforcements arrived they forced the rebels back and unleashed a campaign of terror in the villages. Several rebel strongholds were burned to the ground, whole herds of cattle were confiscated, and hundreds of peasants were executed. Yet this merely fanned the flames of peasant war. 'The whole population took to the woods in fright and joined the rebels,' reported one local Communist. 'Even peasants once loyal to us had nothing left to lose and threw in their lot with the revolt.' From Kirsanov the rebellion soon spread throughout the southern half of Tambov province and parts of neighbouring Saratov, Voronezh and Penza. It was at this point that the Left SR activist Alexander Antonov took over the leadership of the revolt, building it up by the end of 1920 into what Lenin himself later acknowledged was the greatest threat his regime had ever had to face.[39]

Soviet propaganda portrayed the peasant rebels as 'kulaks'. But the evidence suggests on the contrary that these were general peasant revolts. The rebel armies were basically made up of ordinary peasants, as suggested by their agricultural weapons — pitchforks, axes, pikes and hoes — although deserters from the civil war armies also joined their ranks and often played a leading role. In Tambov province there were 110,000 deserters, 60,000 of them in the woodland districts around Kirsanov, on the eve of the revolt. Many of the rebels were destitute youths — mostly under the age of twenty-five. Popov's peasant army in Saratov province was described as 'dressed in rags', although some wore stolen suits. The bands of the Orenburg steppe were, in the words of the Buguruslan Party, made up of:

> people who have been completely displaced through poverty and hunger. The kulaks help the bandits materially but themselves take up arms only very rarely indeed. The bands find it very easy to enlist supporters. The slogan 'Kill the Communists! Smash the Collective Farms!' is very popular among the most backward and downtrodden strata of the peasantry.

Inevitably, given the general breakdown of order, criminal elements also attached themselves to the peasant armies, looting property and raping women, a factor which later helped the Bolsheviks to divide the rebels from the local population.[40]

The strength of the rebel armies derived from their close ties with the village: this enabled them to carry out the guerrilla-type operations which so confounded the Red Army commanders. What the Americans later learned in Vietnam — that conventional armies, however well armed, are ill-equipped to fight a well-supported peasant army — the Russians discovered in 1921 (and rediscovered sixty years later in Afghanistan). The rebel armies were organized on a partisan basis with each village responsible for mobilizing, feeding and equipping its own troops. In Tambov and parts of western Siberia the STKs, which were closely connected to the village communes, performed these functions. Elsewhere it was the communes themselves. The Church and the local SRs, especially those on the left of the party, also helped to organize the revolt in some regions, although the precise role of the SR leadership is still clouded in mystery.[41]

With the support of the local population the rebel armies were, in the words of Antonov-Ovseenko, 'scarcely vulnerable, extraordinarily invisible, and so to speak ubiquitous'. Peasants could become soldiers, and soldiers peasants, at a moment's notice. The villagers were the ears and eyes of the rebel armies — women, children, even beggars served as spies — and everywhere the Reds were vulnerable to ambush. Yet the rebels, when pursued by the Reds, would suddenly vanish — either by merging with the local population, or with fresh horses supplied by the peasants which far outstripped the pursuing Reds. Where the Reds could travel thirty miles a day the rebels could travel up to a hundred miles. Their intimate knowledge of the local terrain, moreover, enabled them to move around and launch assaults at night. This supreme mobility easily compensated for their lack of artillery. They literally ran circles around the Reds, whose commanders complained they were 'everywhere'. Instead of engaging the Reds in the open, the rebels stuck to the remote hills and forests waiting for the right moment to launch a surprise attack before retreating out of sight. Their strategy was purely defensive: they aimed not to march on Moscow — nor even for the most part to attack the local towns — but to cut themselves off from its influence. They blew up bridges, cut down telegraph poles and pulled up railway tracks to paralyse the Reds. It was difficult to cope with such tactics, especially since none of the Red commanders had ever come across anything like them before. The first small units sent to fight the rebels were nearly all defeated — Tukhachevsky said their 'only purpose was to arm the rebels' — and they soon became demoralized. Many Reds even joined the rebels.[42]

The aims and ideology of the revolts were strikingly uniform and reflect the common aspirations of the peasant revolution throughout Russia and the Ukraine. All the revolts sought to re-establish the peasant self-rule of 1917–18. Most expressed this in the slogan 'Soviet Power without the Communists!' or some variation on this theme. The same basic idea was sometimes expressed in the rather confused slogans: 'Long Live Lenin! Down with Trotsky!' or 'Long Live the Bolsheviks! Death to the Communists!' Many peasants were under the illusion that the Bolsheviks and the Communists were two separate parties: the party's change of name in February 1918 had yet to be communicated to the remote villages. The peasants believed that 'Lenin' and the 'Bolsheviks' had brought them peace, that they had allowed them to seize the gentry's land, to sell their foodstuffs freely on the market and to regulate their local communities through their own elected Soviets. On the other hand, they believed that 'Trotsky' and the 'Communists' had brought civil war, had taken away the gentry's land and used it for collective farms, had stamped out free trade with requisitioning and had usurped their local Soviets.

Through the slogan of Soviet power, the peasant rebels were no doubt partly seeking to give their protest a 'legitimate' form. They sometimes called their rebel organs 'Soviets'. None the less, their commitment to the democratic ideal of the revolution was no less genuine for this pretence. All the peasant movements were hostile to the Whites — and it was significant that none of them really took off until after the Whites' defeat. Many of the rebel leaders (e.g. Makhno, Sapozhkov, Mironov, Serov, Vakhulin, Maslakov and Kolesov) had fought with the Reds, and often with distinction, against the Whites. Others had served as Soviet officials. Antonov had been the Soviet Chief of Police in the Kirsanov district until the summer of 1918, when, like the rest of the Left SRs, he had broken with the Bolsheviks and turned the district into a bastion of revolt. Sapozhkov, who led a rebel peasant army in the Novouzensk district of Samara during the summer of 1920, had formerly been the Chairman of the Novouzensk Soviet, a hero of its defence against the Cossacks and a leader of the Bolshevik underground in Samara against the Komuch. Piatakov, a peasant rebel leader in the neighbouring Saratov province, had been a Soviet provisions commissar. Voronovich, one of the rebel leaders in the Caucasus, had been the Chairman of the Luga Soviet in 1917. He had even taken part in the defence of Petrograd against Kornilov.[43]

The peasants often called their revolts a 'revolution' — and that is just what they aimed to be. As in 1917, much of the rural state infrastructure was swept aside by a huge tidal wave of peasant anger and destruction. This was a savage war of vengeance against the Communist regime. Thousands of Bolsheviks were brutally murdered. Many were the victims of gruesome (and symbolic) tortures: ears, tongues and eyes were cut out; limbs, heads and genitals were cut off; stomachs were sliced open and stuffed with wheat; crosses were branded on foreheads and torsos; Communists were nailed to trees, burned alive, drowned under ice, buried up to their necks and eaten by dogs or rats, while crowds of peasants watched and shouted. Party and Soviet offices were ransacked. Police stations and rural courts were burned to the ground. Soviet schools and propaganda centres were vandalized. As for the collective farms, the vast majority of them were destroyed and their tools and livestock redistributed among the local peasants. The same thing happened to the Soviet grain-collecting stations, mills, distilleries, beer factories and bread shops. Once the rebel forces had seized the installation 'huge crowds of peasants' would follow in their wake removing piecemeal the requisitioned grain and carting it back to their villages. This reclamation of the 'people's property' — in effect a new 'looting of the looters' — helped the rebel armies to consolidate the support of the local population. But not all the rebels were such Robin Hoods. Simple banditry also played a role. Most of the rebel armies held up trains. In the Donbass region such hold-ups were said to be 'almost a daily occurrence' during the spring of 1921. Raids on local towns, and sometimes the peasant farmers, were another common source of provisions. The appearance of these rebel forces, with their vast herds of stolen livestock and their long caravans of military hardware, liquor barrels and bags of grain must have been very colourful. Antonov's partisans made off from Kniazeva in the Serdobsk district with the entire contents of the costumes and props department of the local theatre, complete with magic lanterns, dummies and bustles. One eye-witness described Popov's rebel army in the Volga town of Khvalynsk as a long train of machine-gun carriers each drawn by six horses:

> the carriers were covered with bloodstains and the horses were decorated with brightly coloured ribbons and material. Ten of the carriers also bore gramophones, while others carried barrels of beer and vodka. All day long the bandits sang and danced to the music and the town was taken over by an unimaginable din.[44]

By March 1921 Soviet power in much of the countryside had virtually ceased to exist. Provincial Bolshevik organizations sent desperate telegrams to Moscow claiming they were powerless to resist the rebels and calling for immediate reinforcements. The consignment of grain to the cities had been brought to a virtual halt within the rebel strongholds. As the urban food crisis deepened and more and more workers went on strike, it became clear that the Bolsheviks were facing a revolutionary situation. Lenin was thrown into panic: every day he bombarded the local Red commanders with violent demands for the swiftest possible suppression of the revolts by whatever means. 'We are barely holding on,' he acknowledged in March. The peasant wars, he told the opening session of the Tenth Party Congress on 8 March, were 'far more dangerous than all the Denikins, Yudeniches and Kolchaks put together'.[45] Together with the strikes and the Kronstadt mutiny of March, they would force that Congress to abandon finally the widely hated policies of War Communism and restore free trade under the NEP. It was a desperate bid to stem the tide of this popular revolution. Having defeated the Whites, who were backed by no fewer than eight Western powers, the Bolsheviks surrendered to the peasantry.

* * *

The wave of workers' strikes that swept across Russia during February 1921 was no less revolutionary than the peasant revolts. Given the punishments which strikers could expect (instant dismissal, arrest and imprisonment, even execution), it was a brave act, an act of defiance, to stage a strike in 1921. Whereas earlier strikes had been a means of bargaining with the regime, those of 1921 were a last desperate bid to overthrow it.

'Workers, you have nothing to lose but your chains!' Marx's dictum had never been more true. The militarized factory had enserfed the working class. Lacking enough foodstuffs to stimulate the workers, the Bolsheviks depended on coercion alone. Workers were deprived of their meagre rations, imprisoned, even shot, if their factories failed to meet the set production quotas. With the poor harvest and the growing reluctance of the peasantry to relinquish their grain, food stocks in the cities shrank to dangerously low levels during the winter of 1920–1. The disruption of transport by heavy snows made the situation worse. On 22 January the bread ration was cut by one-third in several industrial cities, including Moscow and Petrograd. Even the most privileged workers were given only 1,000 calories a day. Hundreds of factories across the country were forced to close their gates for lack of fuel. The Menshevik Fedor Dan saw starving workers and soldiers begging for food in the streets of Petrograd. Women queued overnight to buy a loaf of bread.[46] It was reminiscent of the situation on the eve of the February Revolution.

Moscow was the first to erupt. A rash of workers' meetings called for an end to the Communists' privileges, the restoration of free trade and movement (meaning their right to travel into the countryside and barter with the peasants), civil liberties and the Constituent Assembly. White flags were hung in the factories as a traditional mark of working-class protest. The Moscow printers took the lead: they had staged a similar protest in May 1920 and both the Mensheviks and SRs were strong within their union. But such was the general level of discontent that the protest movement needed little encouragement. The Bolsheviks sent emissaries to the factories to try to defuse the situation; but they were rudely heckled. According to one (rather questionable) report, Lenin himself appeared before a noisy meeting of metalworkers and asked his listeners, who had accused him of ruining the country, whether they would prefer to have the Whites. But his question drew an angry response: 'Let come who may — whites, blacks or devils — just you clear out.' By 21 February thousands of workers were out on strike. Huge demonstrations marched through the streets of the Khamovniki district and, after attempts to disperse the crowds had failed, troops were ordered in. But, as in February 1917, the soldiers refused to fire on the crowds and special Communist detachments (ChON) had to be called in which killed several workers. The next day even bigger crowds appeared on the streets. They marched on the Khamovniki barracks and tried to get the soldiers out; but the soldiers were now locked inside and Communist detachments once again dispersed the crowds by force. On 23 February, as 10,000 workers marched in protest through the streets, martial law was declared in the capital.[47]

Meanwhile, the strikes spread to Petrograd. Numerous factories held protest rallies on the 22nd. As in Moscow, the workers called for an end to the privileged rations of the Communists, the restoration of free trade and movement, and, under the influence of the Mensheviks and SRs, free re-elections to the Soviets and the convocation of the Constituent Assembly. Over the next three days thousands of workers came out on strike. All the biggest metal plants — the Putilov, Trubochny, Baltic and Obukhovsky — joined the movement, along with most of the docks and shipyards. It was practically a general strike. On the Nevsky Prospekt and Vasilevsky Island there were clashes between strikers and troops. Some of the soldiers fired on the workers, killing and wounding at least thirty, but several thousand soldiers, including the Izmailovsky and Finland

Regiments, went over to the crowd. Even the sailors of the *Aurora*, that floating symbol of Bolshevik power, docked in the city for winter repairs, disembarked to join the demonstrations.

It did not take a genius to realize that this was exactly the same situation that, four years before to the day, had sparked the mutiny of the Petrograd garrison which led to the downfall of the tsarist regime. The Bolsheviks were petrified of another mutiny and did everything they could to keep the soldiers in their barracks. They even took away their shoes, on the pretext of replacing them with new ones, to stop the soldiers going out. The city was placed under martial law on the 25th. All power was vested in a special Committee of Defence with Zinoviev at its head. The party boss, who was always inclined to panic in such situations, made a hysterical appeal to the workers, begging them to return to work and promising to improve their economic situation. Meanwhile the Cheka was arresting hundreds of strikers — together with most of the leading Mensheviks and SRs in the city — while thousands of others were locked out of their factories and thus deprived of their rations. All of which was bound to exacerbate the strikes. The workers now called openly for the overthrow of the Bolshevik regime. On 27 February, the fourth anniversary of the revolution, the following proclamation appeared in the streets. It was a call for a new revolution:

> First of all the workers and peasants need freedom. They do not want to live by the decrees of the Bolsheviks. They want to control their own destinies.
>
> We demand the liberation of all arrested socialists and non-party working men; abolition of martial law; freedom of speech, press, and assembly for all who labour; free elections of factory committees, trade unions and soviets.
>
> Call meetings, pass resolutions, send delegates to the authorities, bring about the realization of your demands.[48]

That same day the revolt spread across the Gulf of Finland to the Kronstadt naval base: a real revolution now moved one step closer. In 1917 Trotsky had called the Kronstadt sailors the 'pride and glory of the Russian revolution'.* They were the first to call for Soviet power, and they played a key role in the events of October. Yet Kronstadt had always been a troublesome bastion of revolutionary maximalism. Its sailors were Anarchist as much as Bolshevik. What they really wanted was an independent Kronstadt Soviet Republic — a sort of island version of the Paris Commune — as opposed to a

---

* The term had originally been used by the liberal press to describe Kerensky in 1917.

centralized state. Until the summer of 1918 the Kronstadt Soviet was governed by a broad coalition of all the far-left parties. Its executive was chosen for its competence rather than its party, and was strictly accountable to the elected Soviets (or 'toiling collectives') on the naval base. Such democracy was intolerable to the Bolsheviks. They purged the Soviet of all the other parties and turned it into a bureaucratic organ of their state. The sailors soon became disgruntled. Although they fought for the Reds during the defence of Petrograd, in October 1919, they only did so to defeat the Whites, whom they saw as an even greater evil than the Bolsheviks. Once the civil war was over the sailors turned their anger on the Reds. They condemned their treatment of the peasantry. Many of the Kronstadt sailors came from the countryside — the Ukraine and Tambov were especially well represented — and were shocked by what they found there when they returned home on leave. 'Ours is an ordinary peasant farm,' wrote one of the *Petropavlovsk* crew in November 1920 after learning that his family's cow had been requisitioned; 'yet when I and my brother return home from serving the Soviet republic people will sneer at our wrecked farm and say: "What did you serve for? What has the Soviet republic given you?" ' The feudal lifestyle of the Communist bosses was another source of mounting resentment among both the sailors and the party rank and file. Raskolnikov, the Kronstadt Bolshevik leader of 1917, returned to the base in 1920 as the newly appointed Chief Commander of the Baltic Fleet and lived there like a lord with his elegant wife, the Bolshevik commissar Larissa Reissner, complete with banquets, chauffeured cars and servants. Reissner even had a wardrobe of dresses requisitioned for her from the aristocracy. Half the Kronstadt Bolsheviks became so disillusioned that they tore up their party cards during the second half of 1920.[49]

When news of the strikes in Petrograd reached the Kronstadt sailors they sent a delegation to the city to report on their development. When they returned, on 28 February, the crew of the *Petropavlovsk*, previously a Bolshevik stronghold, raised their own banner of revolt with a proclamation calling for free Soviet elections, freedom of speech, press and assembly (albeit only for the workers and peasants, the left-wing parties and the trade unions), 'equal rations for all the working people', and 'freedom for the peasants to toil the land as they see fit' provided they did not use hired labour. Whereas the workers' resolutions called for the reconvocation of the Constituent Assembly, the sailors remained opposed to this. It had been an Anarchist group of Kronstadt sailors who had forcibly closed down the Constituent Assembly in January 1918. Their programme remained strictly Soviet in the sense that they aimed to restore their own multi-party Soviet of 1918. Moreover, unlike the peasant rebels, whose slogan was 'Soviets *without* the Communists!', they were even prepared to accept the Bolsheviks in this coalition provided they accepted the principles of Soviet democracy and renounced their dictatorship. This helps to explain why —

uniquely among the revolts of 1921 — more than half the Bolshevik rank and file in Kronstadt chose to join the mutiny.

Embarrassed by the loss of this former stronghold, the Bolsheviks tried to claim that the Kronstadt rebels were not the same as those of 1917, that the best proletarian sailors had been lost in the civil war and replaced by 'peasant lads in sailors' suits' who brought with them from their village 'anarchist' and 'petty-bourgeois' attitudes. Yet, as Israel Getzler has shown, this was in fact a case of the Bolsheviks being abandoned by their own most favoured sons. The Kronstadt rebels of 1921 were essentially the same as those of 1917. The majority of their leaders were veteran sailors of the Kronstadt Fleet. Some of them, such as the SR-Maximalist Anatolii Lamanov, chief ideologist of the mutiny, had been prominent members of the Kronstadt Soviet in 1917–18. On the two major ships involved in the mutiny, the *Petropavlovsk* and the *Sevastopol*, 94 per cent of the crew had been recruited before 1918.[50] In its personnel, as in its ideology, the mutiny was a return to the revolutionary days of 1917.

Revolutionary anger and excitement spilled on to the streets on 1 March. A mass meeting in Anchor Square attended by 15,000 people, nearly one-third of the Kronstadt population, passed a resolution calling for the Soviet to be re-elected. Kalinin, sent to calm the sailors, was rudely heckled, while Kuzmin, a Bolshevik commissar of the fleet, was booed off the stage. The next day 300 delegates from the various ships and shipyards met to elect a new Soviet. The mutinous Bolsheviks made up a large minority of the delegates. Alarmed by rumours that Communist guards were about to storm the meeting, the delegates chose instead to select a five-man Revolutionary Committee, which hurriedly set about organizing the island's defence. The old spirit of revolutionary improvisation had returned.

Although these rumours turned out to be false, the Bolsheviks in Petrograd were indeed preparing to suppress the mutiny. They could not wait for it to peter out. Revolts in other cities, such as Kazan and Nizhnyi Novgorod, were already being inspired by it. The ice-packed Gulf of Finland, moreover, was about to thaw and this would make the fortress, with the whole of its fleet freed from the ice, virtually impregnable. On 2 March martial law was imposed on the whole of Petrograd province. Troops and artillery were amassed along the coastline opposite Kronstadt. As in the defence of Petrograd against the Whites, Trotsky was despatched to the old capital to take command of operations. He arrived on 5 March and ordered the mutineers to surrender at once. In an ultimatum that could have been issued by a nineteenth-century provincial governor to the rebellious peasants he warned that the rebels would 'be shot like partridges' if they did not give up in twenty-four hours. Trotsky ordered the families of the sailors living in Petrograd to be arrested as hostages. When the head of the Petrograd Cheka insisted that the mutiny was 'spontaneous', Trotsky cabled Moscow to have him dismissed.[51]

The assault began on 7 March. For a whole day the Bolsheviks' heavy guns bombarded the fortress from the north-western coast. It was Women Workers' Day and amidst the noise of the exploding shells the Kronstadt radio sent out greetings to the women of the world. The distant thunder of heavy guns could be heard by Alexander Berkman twenty miles away on Nevsky Prospekt. The American Anarchist, whose faith in the revolution had been suddenly revived by the mutiny, noted in his diary at 6 p.m. that day: 'Kronstadt has been attacked! Days of anguish and cannonading. My heart is numb with despair; something has died within me.' The aim of the shelling was to 'soften' up the fortress in preparation for an assault across the ice. The troops would have to run across a terrifying five-mile stretch of ice exposed to the guns of the Kronstadt boats and forts. Morale was understandably low among the conscript troops and Tukhachevsky, who was put in charge of the operation, had to place special Communist security troops among their units and Cheka machine-guns behind their backs to make sure they did not run away. They moved forward early the next morning: a snowstorm provided them with cover and some of the forward troops were given white sheets. The assault, however, ended in disaster. The heavy guns of the mutineers made channels of water in the ice into which many of the assaulting troops, blinded by the snowstorm, fell and drowned. Two thousand soldiers were mown down by machine-guns from the outer forts. When the snowstorm lifted the huge expanse of ice was revealed to be littered with corpses.[52]

Meanwhile, amidst all this fighting, the mutineers began to carry out their 'revolution'. This was a republic built under fire. In its hectic eighteen days of rule (I–18 March) the Kronstadt Revolutionary Committee dismantled the Communist apparatus, organized the re-elections of the trade unions and prepared for Soviet re-elections. On 8 March its own *Izvestiia* published a statement of 'What we are fighting for'. It was a moving document of protest that summed up for the sailors — and indeed for the Russian people as a whole — what had gone wrong with the revolution:

> By carrying out the October Revolution the working class had hoped to achieve its emancipation. But the result has been an even greater enslavement of human beings. The power of the monarchy, with its police and its gendarmerie, has passed into the hands of the Communist usurpers, who have given the people not freedom but the constant fear of torture by the Cheka, the horrors of which far exceed the rule of the gendarmerie under tsarism . . . The glorious emblem of the toilers' state — the sickle and the hammer — has in fact been replaced by the Communists with the bayonet

and the barred window, which they use to maintain the calm and carefree life of the new bureaucracy, the Communist commissars and functionaries.

But the worst and most criminal of all is the moral servitude which the Communists have also introduced: they have laid their hands on the inner world of the toiling people, forcing them to think in the way that they want. Through the state control of the trade unions they have chained the workers to their machines so that labour is no longer a source of joy but a new form of slavery. To the protests of the peasants, expressed in spontaneous uprisings, and those of the workers, whose living conditions have compelled them to strike, they have answered with mass executions and a bloodletting that exceeds even the tsarist generals. The Russia of the toilers, the first to raise the red banner of liberation, is drenched in blood.[53]

This was the context in which the Tenth Party Congress assembled in Moscow on 8 March. Two critical problems confronted the leadership: the defeat of the Workers' Opposition — and to a lesser extent the Democratic Centralists — with their two dissident resolutions on the trade unions and party democracy; and the resolution of the revolutionary crisis in the country.

Lenin, as always in such situations, was in a rage. He would stop at nothing to ensure the defeat of the Workers' Opposition. Kollontai was targeted for personal abuse. Lenin would not speak to her and threatened those who did. During the debates he used the fact that Shliapnikov and Kollontai were known to have been lovers to ridicule their arguments for proletarian solidarity. 'Well, thank God,' he said to general laughter, 'we know that Comrade Kollontai and Comrade Shliapnikov are a "class united"'. To sly sarcasm Lenin added slander, condemning the Workers' Opposition as a 'syndicalist deviation' and accusing it of sharing the same ideals as the Kronstadt mutiny and the workers' strikes. This was of course false: whereas both groups of protesters were demanding the overthrow of the Bolshevik dictatorship, the Workers' Opposition merely wanted to reform it. But such distinctions were harder to make than they were to blur. In the atmosphere of hysterical panic — which Lenin helped to create at the Congress with his constant warnings that Soviet power could be overthrown at any moment — the Bolshevik delegates were much too frightened to question Lenin's charge. They accepted his demagogic line that strict party unity was called for at this moment and that to tolerate such opposition factions could only benefit the enemy. No doubt, if it had come to a vote, Lenin's position on the trade union question would have received a substantial majority in any case. The 'Platform of Ten', as it was known, offered a welcome compromise between Trotsky's super-centralism and the 'syndicalism' of the Workers' Opposition, effectively restoring the position of the Ninth Party Congress whereby the state would continue to run industry through the system of One-Man Management and consult the unions on managerial appointments. But Lenin's tactics made victory sure. His two resolutions condemning the Workers' Opposition received massive majorities, with no more than thirty of the 694 Congress delegates voting against them.[54]

Lenin now consolidated his victory with one of the most fateful decisions in the history of the Communist Party — the ban on factions. This secret resolution, passed by the Congress on 16 March, outlawed the formation of all party groupings independent of the Central Committee. By a two-thirds vote of the Central Committee and the Control Commission such factions could be excluded from the party. The ban had been proposed by Lenin in a moment of vindictive anger against the Workers' Opposition. It was passed by a Congress which had clearly become bored and impatient with the factional squabbles of the past few months, and which in the present crisis was only too eager to rally round its leader against his opponents in the party. Neither Lenin nor the rank and file fully realized the ban's potential significance. Henceforth, the Central Committee was to rule the party on the same dictatorial lines as the party ruled the country; no one could challenge its decisions without exposing themselves to the charge of factionalism. Stalin's rise to power was a product of the ban. He used the same tactics against Trotsky and Bukharin as Lenin had used against the Workers' Opposition. Indeed it was mainly to enforce the ban and carry out the purge of the Workers' Opposition that Lenin created the office of a General Secretary of the Party, with Stalin as the first 'Gensek', in April 1922. By the Twelfth Party Congress of 1923 that purge was accomplished — as was Stalin's ascendancy in the Central Committee. Shliapnikov and Kollontai, though spared the ignominy of expulsion from the party, were both sent into diplomatic exile — the former to Paris, the latter to Stockholm. Supporters of the Workers' Opposition were removed from their party and trade union posts. Most of them were harassed, some imprisoned, nearly all of them were later shot in Stalin's terror. Shliapnikov was murdered in 1937.

No less monumental than the ban on factions was the second historic resolution of the Tenth Party Congress, the replacement of food requisitioning by the tax in kind. This abandoned the central plank of War Communism and laid the foundations of the NEP by allowing the peasants, once the tax had been paid, to sell the rest of their surplus as they liked, including through the free market. It was a clear attempt to stimulate production: the overall burden of the tax was 45 per cent lower than the levy of 1920 (it was later reduced to a standard rate of 10 per cent of the harvest); there were tax rebates for peasants who increased their sowings and productivity; the individual peasant was made responsible for his own share of the tax, thus abolishing the collective responsibility of the commune; and there was to be a special fund of consumer goods and agricultural tools for exchange with the most productive peasants. Lenin, it seems, had been moving towards this 'new deal' with the peasants for several weeks. A report on the Antonov uprising, delivered by Bukharin to the Politburo on 2 February after his return from a trip to Tambov, had made it clear that it was impossible to continue with the requisitionings in view of the strength of the peasantry's resistance to them there and in many other provinces. There can be no doubt that the timing of the introduction of the tax in kind was determined by the urgent need to pacify these peasant wars, which Lenin feared more than the Whites.[55]

Fearful that the delegates would denounce the tax as a restoration of capitalism, Lenin attempted to limit its discussion by delaying the introduction of the resolution until 15 March, the penultimate day of the Congress, by which time many of the delegates had already left for the Kronstadt Front. Lenin's own lecture on the NEP monopolized the session, leaving little time for any other speakers. He stressed that the tax in kind was desperately needed to quell the peasant revolts and to build a new alliance — the *smychka* — with the peasants, based on the market. Soviet power could not survive without it, since the failure of the revolution in the West left the proletariat without other allies. The policies of the civil war had been a utopian dream — it was impossible to create socialism by administrative fiat — and in a backward peasant country such as Russia there was no other way to restore the economy after the devastations of the past few years, let alone to accumulate the capital for the socialist transformation of the country, than through the market. He dismissed fears that restoring private trade would lead Russia back to capitalism: this was to be a socialized market. The capitalist classes in Russia, including the 'kulaks', had already been destroyed by the revolution. And as long as it controlled the 'commanding heights' of the economy, banking, heavy industry, transport and foreign trade, then the state could regulate the market and use fiscal pressures to encourage the smallholders towards the collective farms and co-operatives. Lenin's tactics clearly worked. His speech had lasted for nearly three hours and by the time he sat down most of the delegates were either too weary or too intimidated to engage in serious theoretical debate. Whereas on other issues there were up to 250 different speakers, there were only four, other than Lenin himself, on the tax in kind. All of them were chosen by the presidium, were strictly limited to ten minutes each, and none had any serious criticisms to make. Neither Trotsky nor Bukharin expressed a desire to speak on the new tax, although both had espoused contrary policies up until that time, and between them had spoken on no fewer than fourteen occasions during the other sessions of the Congress. Even Shliapnikov, who later condemned the tax as a retreat before the peasantry, remained strangely silent after his bruising of the past few days.[56] The defining policy of the 1920s was passed virtually without discussion. The era of the stage-managed Party Congress had arrived.

Meanwhile the Bolsheviks focused their attention on the suppression of the popular revolts. On 10 March 300 delegates at the Tenth Party Congress volunteered to fight on the Kronstadt Front after hearing Trotsky's bleak description of the situation there. Eager to prove their loyalty, members of the Workers' Opposition were among the first to step forward. The delegates arrived in Petrograd the following day bringing news with them of the coming tax in kind to boost the morale of the troops. By this stage, the strikes in Petrograd had petered out: arrests and concessions — including a promise by Zinoviev as early as 27 February that free trade was about to be restored — proved enough to break them. Moscow's strikes followed the same pattern. On 16 March the final assault on the Kronstadt fortress commenced. After several days of heavy artillery shelling from the coast and bombing from the air, 50,000 crack troops advanced across the ice in the dark hours of early morning. The battle raged for eighteen hours. But by midnight on the 17th the rebellion had been defeated and most of the sailors had surrendered. Over 10,000 Red troops were killed, including fifteen delegates of the Tenth Party Congress who had joined in the assault. When the battle was over the government in Helsingfors requested Moscow to have all the corpses cleared away lest they should be washed up on the Finnish coast and create a health hazard following the thaw.

The next morning hundreds of prisoners from the Kronstadt base were marched through Petrograd on their route to prison. Near the centre they saw a group of workers carrying sacks of potatoes on their backs. 'Traitors!' the sailors shouted, 'you have sold our lives for Communist potatoes. Tomorrow you will have our flesh to eat with your potatoes.' Later that night some 500 rebels were shot without trial on Zinoviev's orders: the regular executioners refused to do it, so a brigade of teenage Komsomols was ordered to shoot the sailors instead. Some of the rebels managed to flee to Gorky's flat and tell him of these executions. Gorky was outraged — like many socialists he had supported the rebellion from the start — and at once called Lenin to complain. The Bolshevik leader ordered Zinoviev to explain his actions before a party meeting in Gorky's flat. But at the meeting Zinoviev promptly had a heart attack (Gorky later claimed that it was faked) and the result was that he was only lightly reprimanded for an action which, in any case, Lenin had probably approved. During the following months 2,000 more rebels were executed, nearly all of them without trial, while hundreds of others were sent on Lenin's orders to Solovki, the first big Soviet concentration camp on an island in the White Sea, where they died a slower death from hunger, illness and exhaustion. About 8,000 Kronstadt rebels escaped across the ice to Finland, where they were interned and put to public works. Some of them were later lured back to Russia by the promise of an amnesty — only to be shot or sent to concentration camps on their return.[57]

The suppression of the Kronstadt rebellion had a shattering effect on socialists throughout the world. There could not be a more conclusive proof that the Bolsheviks had turned into tyrants. Alexander Berkman, with 'the last thread of his faith in the Bolsheviks broken', wandered in despair through the streets of Petrograd — the city where the revolution had been born and where it had now died. On 18 March he noted with bitter irony in his diary: 'The victors are celebrating the anniversary of the Commune of 1871. Trotsky and Zinoviev denounce Thiers and Gallifet for the slaughter of the Paris rebels.'[58]

Military might and ruthless terror also held the key to the suppression of the major peasant revolts, although in some places such as the Volga region famine and exhaustion did the job instead. The turning point came in the early summer, when the Bolsheviks rethought their military strategy: instead of sending in small detachments to fight the rebels they swamped the rebel areas with troops and unleashed a campaign of mass terror against those villages that supported the rebels whilst trying to ween away the others through propaganda. The new strategy was first applied in Tambov province, where Tukhachevsky, fresh from his success against Kronstadt, was sent in April to crush the Antonov revolt. By the height of the operation in June the insurgent areas were occupied by a force of over 100,000 men, most of them crack troops from the élite Communist security units and the Komsomol, together with several hundred heavy guns and armoured cars. Aeroplanes were used to track the movement of the bands and to drop bombs and propaganda on to their strongholds. Poison gas was also used to 'smoke the bands out of the forests'. Through paid informers, the rebels and their families were singled out for arrest as hostages and imprisoned in specially constructed concentration camps: by the end of June there were 50,000 peasants in the Tambov camps, including over 1,000 children. It was not unusual for whole village populations to be interned and later shot or deported to the Arctic Circle if the rebels did not surrender. Sometimes the rebel villages were simply burned to the ground. In just one volost of the Tambov district — and it was not even particularly noted as a rebel stronghold — 154 peasants were shot, 227 families were taken hostage, 17 houses were burned down and 46 were torn down or transferred to informers. Overall, it has been estimated that 100,000 people were imprisoned or deported and 15,000 people shot during the suppression of the revolt.[59]

Along with the big stick there was also a small carrot to induce the peasants to abandon their support for the rebels. Villages that passed a resolution condemning the 'bandits' were rewarded from a special fund of salt and manufactured goods. The Bolsheviks were counting on the rebels, once they heard of these resolutions, to take reprisals against the treacherous villages so that they could drive a wedge between them and undermine the rebels' social base. There was also an amnesty for the rebels, although those who were foolish enough to surrender, about 6,000 in all, were nearly all imprisoned or shot. Finally, there was a barrage of propaganda about the benefits of the NEP, although its rather questionable efficacy hardly warrants the claims later made for it by the Bolsheviks. Many peasants, even in the Moscow region, had never heard of the tax in kind, while most of those who had, as Tukhachevsky acknowledged at the time, were 'definitely not inclined to believe in the sincerity of the decree'.[60]

By the late summer of 1921, when much of the countryside was struck down with famine, most of the peasant revolts had been defeated in the military sense. Antonov's army was destroyed in June, although he escaped and with smaller guerrilla forces continued to make life difficult for the Soviet regime in the Tambov countryside until the following summer, when he was finally hunted down and killed by the Cheka. In western Siberia, the Don and the Kuban all but the smallest peasant bands had been destroyed by the end of July, although peasant resistance to the Soviet regime continued on a smaller scale — and in more passive ways — until 1923. As for Makhno, he gave up the struggle in August 1921 and fled with his last remaining followers to Romania, although his strongholds in the south-east Ukraine continued to be a rebellious region for several years to come. To many Ukrainians Makhno remained a folk-hero (songs were sung about him at weddings and parties even as late as the 1950s) but to others he was a bogey man. 'Batko Makhno will get you if you don't sleep,' Soviet mothers told their children.[61]

The Mensheviks and SRs were suppressed along with the rebels. It was axiomatic to Bolshevik propaganda that the peasant revolts and workers' strikes had been organized by these parties. It was certainly true that they had sympathized with them, and in some cases had even supported them. But much more relevant was the fact that, as the popularity of the Bolsheviks had plummeted, so that of the SRs and Mensheviks had grown: they were a threat to the regime. By claiming that the SRs and Mensheviks had organized the strikes and revolts of 1921, the Bolsheviks sought both a pretext to destroy their last political rivals and an explanation for the protests that denied their popular base. The arrest of the 'counter-revolutionary' Mensheviks, some 5,000 in all, during 1921, and the grotesque show trial of the SR leaders the following year, when the whole party was in effect convicted as 'enemies of the people',[62] were last desperate measures by the Bolsheviks to claim a popular legitimacy for their bankrupt revolution.

* * *

The New Economic Policy was originally conceived as a temporary retreat. 'We are making economic concessions in order to avoid political ones,' Bukharin told the Comintern in July. 'The NEP is only a temporary deviation, a tactical retreat, a clearing of the land for a new and decisive attack of labour against the front of international capitalism,' Zinoviev added in December. Lenin also saw it in these terms. The NEP was 'a peasant Brest-Litovsk', taking one step backwards to take two steps forward. But, unlike many of the other party leaders, Lenin accepted that the period of retreat was likely to be long enough — he talked vaguely of 'not less than a decade and probably more' — to constitute not just a tactical ploy but a whole recasting of the revolution. The NEP, he reminded the party in May, was to be adopted ' "seriously and for a long time" — we must definitely get this into our heads and remember it well, because rumours are spreading that this is a policy only in quotes, in other words a form of political trickery that is only being carried out for the moment. This is not true.'[63]

As Lenin saw it, the NEP was more than a temporary concession to the market in order to get the country back on its feet. It was a fundamental if rather ill-formulated effort to redefine the role of socialism in a backward peasant country where, largely as a result of his own party's *coup d'état* in 1917, the 'bourgeois revolution' had not been completed. Only 'in countries of developed capitalism' was it possible to make an 'immediate transition to socialism', Lenin had told the Tenth Party Congress. Soviet Russia was thus confronted with the task of 'building communism with bourgeois hands', of basing socialism on the market. Lenin of course remained full of doubts: at times he expressed fears that the regime would be drowned in a sea of petty peasant capitalism. But in the main he saw the market — regulated by the state and gradually socialized through co-operatives — as the only way to socialism. Whereas the Bolsheviks up till now had lived by the maxim 'The less market the more socialism', Lenin was moving towards the slogan 'The more market the more socialism'.[64]

But, like the leopard with its spots, the Bolsheviks could not easily erase their innate mistrust of private trade. Even Bukharin, who later became the main defender of the NEP, warmed to it only slowly during the course of 1921–3. Many of the rank-and-file Bolsheviks, in particular, saw the boom in private trade as a betrayal of the revolution. What, only months ago, had been condemned as a crime against the revolution was now being endorsed and encouraged. Moreover, once the doors had been opened to the market it was difficult to stop the flood of private trade that was almost bound to follow after the shortages of the previous four years. By 1921 the whole population was living in patched-up clothes and shoes, cooking with broken kitchen utensils, drinking from cracked cups. Everyone needed something new. People set up stalls in the streets to sell or exchange their basic household goods, much as they do today in most of Russia's cities; flea-markets boomed; while 'bagging' to and from the countryside once again became a mass phenomenon. Licensed by new laws in 1921–2, private cafés, shops and restaurants, night clubs and brothels, hospitals and clinics, credit and saving associations, even small-scale manufacturers sprang up like mushrooms after the rain. Foreign observers were amazed by the sudden transformation. Moscow and Petrograd, graveyard cities in the civil war, suddenly burst into life, with noisy traders, busy cabbies and bright shop signs filling the streets just as they had done before the revolution. 'The NEP turned Moscow into a vast market place,' recalled Emma Goldman:

> Shops and stores sprang up overnight, mysteriously stacked with delicacies Russia had not seen for years. Large quantities of butter, cheese and meat were displayed for sale; pastry, rare fruit, and sweets of every variety were to be purchased. Men, women and children with pinched faces and hungry eyes stood about gazing into the windows and discussing the great miracle: what was but yesterday considered a heinous offence was now flaunted before them in an open and legal manner.'[65]

But could those hungry people afford such goods? That was the fear of the Bolshevik rank and file. It seemed to them that the boom in private trade would inevitably lead to a widening gap between rich and poor. 'We young Communists had all grown up in the belief that money was done away with once and for all,' recalled one Bolshevik in the 1940s. 'If money was reappearing, wouldn't rich people reappear too? Weren't we on the slippery slope that led back to capitalism? We put these questions to ourselves with feelings of anxiety.' Such doubts were strengthened by the sudden rise of unemployment in the first two years of the NEP. While these unemployed were living on the bread line the peasants were growing fat and rich. 'Is this what we made the revolution for?' one Bolshevik asked Emma Goldman. There was a widespread feeling among the workers, voiced most clearly by the Workers' Opposition, that the NEP was sacrificing their class interests to the peasantry, that the 'kulak' was being rehabilitated and allowed to grow rich at the workers' expense. In 1921–2 literally tens of thousands of Bolshevik workers tore up their party cards in disgust with the NEP: they dubbed it the New Exploitation of the Proletariat.[66]

Much of this anger was focused on the 'Nepmen', the new and vulgar get-rich-quickly class of private traders who thrived in Russia's Roaring Twenties. It was perhaps unavoidable that after seven years of war and shortages these wheeler-dealers should step into the void. Witness the 'spivs' in Britain after 1945, or, for that matter, the so-called 'mafias' in post-Soviet Russia. True, the peasants were encouraged to sell their foodstuffs to the state and the co-operatives by the offer of cheap manufactured goods in return. But until the socialized system began to function properly (and that was not until the mid-1920s) it remained easier and more profitable to sell them to the 'Nepmen' instead. If some product was particularly scarce these profiteers were sure to have it — usually because they had bribed some Soviet official. Bootleg liquor, heroin and cocaine — they sold everything. The 'Nepmen' were a walking symbol of this new and ugly capitalism. They dressed their wives and mistresses in diamonds and furs, drove around in huge imported cars, snored at the opera, sang in restaurants, and boasted loudly in expensive hotel bars of the dollar fortunes they had wasted at the newly opened race-tracks and casinos. The ostentatious spending of this new and vulgar rich, shamelessly set against the background of the appalling hunger and suffering of these years, gave rise to a widespread and bitter feeling of resentment among all those common people, the workers in particular, who had thought that the revolution should be about ending such inequalities.

This profound sense of plebeian resentment — of the 'Nepmen', the 'bourgeois specialists', the 'Jews' and the 'kulaks' — remained deeply buried in the hearts of many people, especially the blue-collar workers and the party rank and file. Here was the basic emotional appeal of Stalin's 'revolution from above', the forcible drive towards industrialization during the first of the Five Year Plans. It was the appeal to a second wave of class war against the 'bourgeoisie' of the NEP, the new 'enemies of the people', the idea of a return to the harsh but romantic spirit of the civil war, that 'heroic period' of the revolution, when the Bolsheviks, or so the legend went, had conquered every fortress and pressed ahead without fear or compromise. Russia in the 1920s remained a society at war with itself — full of unresolved social tensions and resentments just beneath the surface. In this sense, the deepest legacy of the revolution was its failure to eliminate the social inequalities that had brought it about in the first place.

16 Deaths and Departures

i Orphans of the Revolution

'No, I am not well,' Gorky wrote to Romain Rolland on his arrival in Berlin — 'my tuberculosis has come back, but at my age it is not dangerous. Much harder to bear is the sad sickness of the soul — I feel very tired: during the past seven years in Russia I have seen and lived through so many sad dramas — the more sad for not being caused by the logic of passion and free will but by the blind and cold calculation of fanatics and cowards . . . I still believe fervently in the future happiness of mankind but I am sickened and disturbed by the growing sum of suffering which people have to pay as the price of their fine hopes.'[1] Death and disillusionment lay behind Gorky's departure from Russia in the autumn of 1921. So many people had been killed in the previous four years that even he could no longer hold firm to his revolutionary hopes and ideals. Nothing was worth such human suffering.

Nobody knows the full human cost of the revolution. By any calculation it was catastrophic. Counting only deaths from the civil war, the terror, famine and disease, it was something in the region of ten million people. But this excludes the emigration (about two million) and the demographic effects of a hugely reduced birth-rate — nobody wanted children in these frightful years — which statisticians say would have added up to ten million lives.* The highest death rates were among adult men — in Petrograd alone there were 65,000 widows in 1920 — but death was so common that it touched everyone. Nobody lived through the revolutionary era without losing friends and relatives. 'My God how many deaths!' Sergei Semenov wrote to an old friend in January 1921. 'Most of the old men — Boborykin, Linev, Vengerov, Vorontsov, etc., have died. Even Grigory Petrov has disappeared — how he died is not known, we can only say that it probably was not from joy at the progress of socialism. What hurts especially is not even knowing where one's friends are buried.' How death could affect a single family is well illustrated by the Tereshchenkovs. Nikitin

---

* It also excludes the reduced life expectancy of those who survived due to malnutrition and disease. Children born and brought up in these years were markedly smaller than older cohorts, and 5 per cent of all new-borns had syphilis (Sorokin, *Sovremennoe*, 16, 67).

Tereshchenkov, a Red Army doctor, lost both his daughter and his sister to the typhus epidemic in 1919; his eldest son and brother were killed on the Southern Front fighting for the Red Army in that same year; his brother-in-law was mysteriously murdered. Nikitin's wife was dying from TB, while he himself contracted typhus. Denounced by the local Cheka (like so many of the rural intelligentsia) as 'enemies of the people', they lost their town house in Smolensk and were living, in 1920, on a small farm worked by their two surviving sons — Volodya, fifteen, and Misha, thirteen.[2]

To die in Russia in these times was easy but to be buried was very hard. Funeral services had been nationalized, so every burial took endless paperwork. Then there was the shortage of timber for coffins. Some people wrapped their loved ones up in mats, or hired coffins — marked 'PLEASE RETURN' — just to carry them to their graves. One old professor was too large for his hired coffin and had to be crammed in by breaking several bones. For some unaccountable reason there was even a shortage of graves — would one believe it if this was not Russia? — which left people waiting several months for one. The main morgue in Moscow had hundreds of rotting corpses in the basement awaiting burial. The Bolsheviks tried to ease the problem by promoting free cremations. In 1919 they pledged to build the biggest crematorium in the world. But the Russians' continued attachment to the Orthodox burial rituals killed off this initiative.[3]

Death was so common that people became inured to it. The sight of a dead body in the street no longer attracted attention. Murders occurred for the slightest motive — stealing a few roubles, jumping a queue, or simply for the entertainment of the killers. Seven years of war had brutalized people and made them insensitive to the pain and suffering of others. In 1921 Gorky asked a group of soldiers from the Red Army if they were uneasy about killing people. 'No they were not. "He has a weapon, I have a weapon, so we are equal; what's the odds, if we kill one another there'll be more room in the land." ' One soldier, who had also fought in Europe in the First World War, even told Gorky that it was easier to kill a Russian than a foreigner. 'Our people are many, our economy is poor; well, if a hamlet is burnt, what's the loss? It would have burnt down itself in due course.' Life had become so cheap that people thought little of killing one another, or indeed of others killing millions in their name. One peasant asked a scientific expedition working in the Urals during 1921: 'You are educated people, tell me then what's to happen to me. A Bashkir killed my cow, so *of course* I killed the Bashkir and then I took the cow away from his family. So tell me: shall I be punished for the cow?' When they asked him whether he did not rather expect to be punished for the murder of the man, the peasant replied: 'That's nothing, people are cheap nowadays.'

Other stories were told — of a husband who had murdered his wife for no apparent reason. 'I had enough of her and there is the end of it,' was the murderer's explanation. It was as if all the violence of the previous few years had stripped away the thin veneer of civilization covering human relations and exposed the primitive zoological instincts of man. People began to like the smell of blood. They developed a taste for sadistic forms of killing — a subject on which Gorky was an expert:

> The peasants in Siberia dug pits and lowered Red Army prisoners into them upside down, leaving their legs to the knees above ground; then they filled in the pit with soil, watching by the convulsions of the legs which of the victims was more resistant, livelier, and which would be the last to die.
>
> In Tambov province Communists were nailed with railway spikes by their left hand and left foot to trees a metre above the soil, and they watched the torments of these deliberately oddly-crucified people.
>
> They would open a prisoner's belly, take out the small intestine and nailing it to a tree or telegraph pole they drove the man around the tree with blows, watching the intestine unwind through the wound. Stripping a captured officer naked, they tore strips of skin from his shoulders in the form of shoulder straps, and knocked in nails in place of pips; they would pull off the skin along the lines of the sword belt and trouser stripes — this operation was called 'to dress in uniform'. It, no doubt, demanded much time and considerable skill.[4]

The single biggest killer of these years — it accounted in all for some five million lives — was the famine crisis of 1921–2. Like all famine crises, the great Volga famine was caused in part by man and in part by God. The natural conditions of the Volga region made it vulnerable to harvest failures — and there had been many in recent years, 1891–2, 1906 and 1911 just to name a few. Summer droughts and extreme frosts were regular features of the steppeland climate. Gusting winds in the spring blew away the sandy topsoil and damaged tender crops. These were the preconditions of the Volga famine in 1921: the crop failure of 1920 was followed by a year of heavy frost and scorching summer drought that transformed the steppelands into one huge dustbowl. By the spring it became clear that the peasants were about to suffer a second harvest failure in succession. Much of the seed had been killed off by the frosts, while the new corn stalks which did emerge were weedy in appearance and soon destroyed by locusts and field-rats. Bad though they were, these cracks in nature's moulds were not enough to cause a famine crisis. The peasants were accustomed to harvest failures and had always maintained large stocks of grain, often in communal barns, for such emergencies. What made this crisis so disastrous was the fact that the peasant economy had already been brought to the brink of disaster, even before nature took its toll, by the requisitionings of the civil war. To evade the levies the peasants withdrew into subsistence production — they grew just enough grain to feed themselves and their livestock and provide for seed. In other words they left no safety margin, no reserves of the sort that had cushioned them from adverse weather in the past, since they feared that the Bolsheviks would take them. In 1920 the sown area in the Volga region had declined by a quarter since 1917. Yet the Bolsheviks continued to take more — not just surpluses but vital stocks of food and seed — so that when that harvest failed it was bound to result in the ruin of the peasants.[5]

By the spring of 1921 one-quarter of the peasantry in Soviet Russia was starving. Famine struck not only in the Volga region but in the Urals and Kama basins, the Don, Bashkiria, Kazakhstan, western Siberia and the southern Ukraine. The famine was accompanied by typhus and cholera which killed hundreds of thousands of people already weakened by hunger. The worst affected regions were on the Volga steppe. In Samara province nearly two million people (three-quarters of the population) were said to be dying from hunger by the autumn of 1921: 700,000 of them did in fact die by the end of the crisis. In one typical volost, Bulgakova, with a population of 16,000 in January 1921, 1,000 people had died, 2,200 had abandoned their homes and 6,500 had been paralysed by hunger or disease by the following November. Throughout the Volga region hungry peasants resorted to eating grass, weeds, leaves, moss, tree bark, roof thatch and flour made from acorns, sawdust, clay and horse manure. They slaughtered livestock and hunted rodents, cats and dogs. In the villages there was a deathly silence. Skeletons of people, children with their bellies bloated, lay down quietly like dogs to die. 'The villagers have simply given up on life,' one relief worker noted in Saratov. 'They are too weak even to complain.' Those with enough strength boarded up their ruined farms, packed their meagre belongings on to carts, and fled to the towns in search of food. At the town markets a few loaves of bread would be exchanged for a horse. Many people did not make it but collapsed and died along the road. Huge crowds converged on the railway stations in the vain hope of catching a train to other regions — Moscow, the Don, Siberia, almost anywhere, so long as it was rumoured there was food. They did not know that all transportation from the famine region had been stopped on Moscow's orders to limit the spread of epidemics. This was the scene at the Simbirsk railway station in the summer of 1921:

Imagine a compact mass of sordid rags, among which are visible here and there lean, naked arms, faces already stamped with the seal of death. Above all one is conscious of a poisonous odour. It is impossible to pass. The waiting room, the corridor, every foot thickly covered with people, sprawling, seated, crouched in every imaginable position. If one looks closely he sees that these filthy rags are swarming with vermin. The typhus stricken grovel and shiver in their fever, their babies with them. Nursing babies have lost their voices and are no longer able to cry. Every day more than twenty dead are carried away, but it is not possible to remove all of them. Sometimes corpses remain among the living for more than five days . . .

A woman tries to soothe a small child lying in her lap. The child cries, asking for food. For some time the mother goes on rocking it in her arms. Then suddenly she strikes it. The child screams anew. This seems to drive the woman mad. She begins to beat it furiously, her face distorted with rage. She rains blows with her fist on its little face, on its head and at last she throws it upon the floor and kicks it with her foot. A murmur of horror arises around her. The child is lifted from the ground, curses are hurled at the mother, who, after her furious excitement has subsided, has again become herself, utterly indifferent to everything around her. Her eyes are fixed, but are apparently sightless.[6]

Hunger turned some people into cannibals. This was a much more common phenomenon than historians have previously assumed. In the Bashkir region and on the steppelands around Pugachev and Buzuluk, where the famine crisis was at its worst, thousands of cases were reported. It is also clear that most of the cannibalism went unreported. One man, convicted of eating several children, confessed for example: 'In our village everyone eats human flesh but they hide it. There are several cafeterias in the village — and all of them serve up young children.' The phenomenon really took off with the onset of winter, around November 1921, when the first snows covered the remaining food substitutes on the ground and there was nothing else to eat. Mothers, desperate to feed their children, cut off limbs from corpses and boiled the flesh in pots. People ate their own relatives — often their young children, who were usually the first to die and whose flesh was particularly sweet. In some villages the peasants refused to bury their dead but stored the corpses, like so much meat, in their barns and stables. They often begged relief workers not to take away the corpses but to let them eat them instead. In the village of Ivanovka, near Pugachev, a woman was caught with her child eating her dead husband and when the police authorities tried to take away his remains she shouted: 'We will not give him up, we need him for food, he is our own family, and no one has the right to take him away from us.' The stealing of corpses from cemeteries became so common that in many regions armed guards had to be posted on their gates. Hunting and killing people for their flesh was also a common phenomenon. In the town of Pugachev it was dangerous for children to go out after dark since there were known to be bands of cannibals and traders who killed them to eat or sell their tender flesh. In the Novouzensk region there were bands of children who killed adults for their meat. Relief workers were armed for this reason. There were even cases of parents killing their own babies — usually their daughters — in order to eat their flesh or feed it to their other children.

It is easy to say that such acts were simply a sign of moral depravity or psychosis. But it was often compassion which drove people to cannibalism. The agony of watching one's children slowly die of hunger can spur people to do anything, and in such extreme circumstances the normal rules of right and wrong can seem remote. Indeed when interviewed the flesh-eaters appeared quite rational and had often developed a new moral code to legitimize their behaviour. Many of them argued that eating human flesh could not be a crime because the living soul had already departed from the bodies, which remained 'only as food for the worms in the ground'. Moreover, the craving for human flesh which starving people can easily develop once they have eaten it was not peculiar to any social class. Hungry doctors often succumbed to eating it after long spells of relief work in the famine region, and they too stated that the worst part of the experience was 'the insuperable and uncomfortable craving' which they acquired for human flesh.[7]

Until July 1921 the Soviet government refused to acknowledge the existence of the famine. It was a major embarrassment. As in the crisis of 1891, the press was even forbidden to use the word 'famine'. It continued to report that everything was well in the countryside after the introduction of the NEP. This deliberate policy of neglect was even more pronounced in the Ukraine: although famine was widespread there by the autumn of 1921, Moscow continued to export large quantities of grain to the Volga until the following summer. Of course, this was taking from one hungry region to give to another, even hungrier. But it may also be, as Robert Conquest has argued convincingly for the famine of 1930–2, that Moscow sought to punish the Ukrainian peasants for their opposition to the Bolshevik regime.[8]

As in 1891, it was left to the public and foreign bodies to organize the relief campaign. Gorky took the lead. On 13 July he issued an appeal 'To All Honest People' which later appeared in the Western press:

Tragedy has come to the country of Tolstoy, Dostoevsky, Mendeleev, Pavlov, Mussorgsky, Glinka and other world-prized men. If humanitarian ideas and feelings — faith in whose social import was so shaken by the damnable war and its victors' unmercifulness towards the vanquished — if faith in the creative force of these ideas and feelings, I say, must and can be restored, Russia's misfortune offers a splendid opportunity to demonstrate the vitality of humanitarianism. I ask all honest European and American people for prompt aid to the Russian people. Give bread and medicine. Maxim Gorky.

With a group of other public figures Gorky appealed to Lenin for permission to organize a voluntary body for famine relief. The All-Russian Public Committee to Aid the Hungry, or Pomgol for short, set up as a result on 21 July, was the first and the last independent public body established under Communism. It was partly as a concession to Gorky and partly as a means of securing foreign aid that Lenin agreed to its formation. The seventy-three members of Pomgol included leading cultural figures (Gorky, Korolenko, Stanislavsky); liberal politicians (Kishkin, Prokopovich, Kuskova); an ex-tsarist minister (N. N. Kutler) and a veteran Populist (Vera Figner); famous agronomists (Chayanov, Krondatev) and engineers (P. I. Palchinsky); doctors; and Tolstoyans. There was even a place for Alexandra Tolstaya, the writer's daughter, who had spent the past four years in and out of Cheka jails and labour camps. Pomgol sought to revive the public spirit that had saved the country in 1891: it made appeals to the public at home and abroad to contribute to the relief campaign. Prince Lvov, who had taken part in the relief efforts of thirty years before, collected money and sent off food supplies through the Paris Zemgor organization (even in exile, he continued with his zemstvo work). To make sure that Pomgol did not get involved in politics the Bolsheviks assigned to it a 'cell' of twelve prominent Communists led by Kamenev. Lenin was adamant that the famine crisis should not give rise to the same public opposition as that of 1891 had done.[9]

Responding to Gorky's appeal, Herbert Hoover offered to send the American Relief Administration to Russia. Hoover had established the ARA to supply food and medicines to post-war Europe. Hoover's two conditions were that it should be allowed to operate independently, without intervention by the Communist officials, and that all US citizens should be released from Soviet jails. Lenin was furious — 'One must punish Hoover, one must publicly slap his face so that the whole world sees,' he fumed — yet like any beggar he could not be choosy. Once Pomgol had secured American aid Lenin ordered it to be closed down, despite vigorous protests from Kamenev and Gorky. On 27 August all its public members — except Gorky and Korolenko — were arrested by the Cheka, accused of all manner of 'counter-revolutionary activities', and later sent into exile abroad or to restricted zones in the interior. Even Gorky was pressurized by Lenin to go abroad 'for his health'.[10]

By the summer of 1922, when its activities were at their height, the ARA was feeding ten million people every day. It also despatched huge supplies of medicine, clothes, tools and seed — the last enabling the two successive bumper harvests of 1922 and 1923 that finally secured Russia's recovery from the famine. The total cost of the ARA operation was sixty-one million dollars.

The Bolsheviks received this aid with an astonishing lack of gratitude: never has such a generous gift horse been so shamefully looked in the mouth. They accused the ARA of spying, of trying to discredit and overthrow the Soviet regime,* and constantly meddled in their operations, searching convoys, withholding trains, seizing supplies, and even arresting relief workers. The two conditions of aid set by Hoover — freedom from intervention and the release of all Americans from prison — were thus both blatantly broken by the Bolsheviks. Further outrage was caused in America when it was discovered that at the same time as receiving food aid from the West, the Soviet government was exporting millions of tons of its own cereals for sale abroad. When questioned, the Soviet government claimed that it needed the exports in order to purchase industrial and agricultural equipment from abroad. But the scandal made it impossible to raise extra US funds for the ARA in Russia, and in June 1923 it suspended its operations.[11]

For Gorky the way the Soviet government had handled the famine crisis was both shameful and embarrassing. It was a major factor in his decision to leave Russia. When the worst of the famine was over the Bolsheviks sent a short formal note of gratitude to the American people. But Gorky was more generous in his thanks. In a letter that voiced many of his deepest ideals, Gorky wrote to Hoover on 30 July 1922:

> In all the history of human suffering I know of nothing more trying to the souls of men than the events through which the Russian people are passing, and in the history of practical humanitarianism I know of no accomplishment which in terms of magnitude and generosity can be compared to the relief that you have actually accomplished. Your help will enter history as a unique, gigantic achievement, worthy of the greatest glory, which will long remain in the memory of millions of Russians whom you have saved from death. The generosity of the American people resuscitates the dream of fraternity among people at a time when humanity greatly needs charity and compassion.[12]

One of the saddest legacies of the revolution was the huge population of orphans who roamed the streets of every city. By 1922 there were an estimated seven million children living rough in stations, derelict houses, building sites, rubbish dumps, cellars, sewers and other squalid holes. These ragged, barefoot children,

---

* Hoover's motives are not entirely clear. Intensely hostile to the Soviet regime, he may indeed have sought to use the famine relief as a means of diplomatic leverage and political influence in Russia. But this does not negate a genuine humanitarian concern on Hoover's part. Nor does it merit the Bolshevik charge. See Weissman, *Herbert*, ch. 2.

whose parents had either died or abandoned them, were a symbol of Russia's social breakdown. Even the family had been destroyed.

These orphans of the revolution were a ghastly caricature of the childhood they had lost. The struggle for survival on the streets forced them to live like adults. They had their own jargon, social groups and moral codes. Children as young as twelve got 'married' and had their own children. Many were seasoned alcoholics, heroin or cocaine addicts. Begging, peddling, petty crime and prostitution were the means by which they survived. At stations they swarmed like flies, instantly swooping on any scraps of food thrown to them from the trains. Some child beggars maimed themselves or shamed themselves in public to gain some small gratuity. One boy who lived in the station at Omsk would smear his face with his own excrement if people gave him five kopecks. There was a close connection between them and the criminal underworld. Gangs of children stole from market stalls, mugged pedestrians, picked people's pockets and broke into shops and houses. Those who were caught were likely to be beaten in the street by members of the public, who had very little sympathy for the orphans, but it seemed that even this would not deter them. The following scene in a market square was witnessed by one observer:

I myself saw a boy of about 10 to 12 years of age reach out, while being beaten with a cane, for a piece of bread already covered with grime and voraciously cram it into his mouth. Blows rained on his back, but the boy, on hands and knees, continued hurriedly to bite off piece after piece so as not to lose the bread. This was near the bread row at the bazaar. Adults — women — gathered around and shouted: 'That's what the scoundrel deserves: beat him some more! We get no peace from these lice.'

Nearly all these orphans were casual prostitutes. A survey of 1920 found that 88 per cent of the girls had engaged at some time in prostitution, while similar figures were found among the boys. Some of the girls were as young as seven. Most of the sexual acts took place in the streets, in market-places, in station-halls and parks. The girls had pimps — themselves usually no more than teenage boys — who often used them to rob their clients. But there were also paedophiliac brothels run by so-called 'aunties', who gave the children food and a corner of a room, whilst putting them to work and living off their earnings.[13] For millions of children this was the closest thing they ever had to maternal care.

'There are twelve-year-old children who already have three murders to their name,' Gorky wrote to Lenin in April 1920. Once an orphan of the streets himself, Gorky was one of the first to champion the struggle against 'juvenile delinquency'. That summer he set up a special commission to combat the problem, which provided colonies and shelters for the children and taught them how to read and write. Similar initiatives were undertaken by the League for the Rescue of Children established in 1919 by Kuskova and Korolenko with the approval of Sovnarkom. But with only half a million places in all the institutions put together, and seven million orphans on the street, this could only scratch the surface of the problem. Increasingly, the Bolsheviks turned to penal remedies, despite their own proclaimed principle of 1918 that there should be 'no courts or prisons for children'. Prisons and labour camps contained thousands of children, many under fourteen, the age of criminal responsibility. Another way of dealing with the problem was to allow factories to employ the children as sweated labour. Even in the civil war, when thousands of adult workers were laid off, there was a huge growth of child employment, with some workers as young as six, especially in the smaller factories where exploitative practices died hard. Despite widespread calls to limit the children to six hours of labour, and to make employers provide two hours of schooling, the authorities chose not to intervene, claiming it was 'better to have the children working than living from crime on the streets', with the result that many minors ended up by working twelve or fourteen hours every day.[14]

Children also made excellent soldiers. The Red Army had many young teenagers in its ranks. Having spent the whole of their conscious lives surrounded by the violence of war and revolution, many of them had no doubt come to think that killing people was part of normal life. These little soldiers were noted for their readiness to do as they were told — their commanders often played the role of surrogate fathers — as well as for their ruthless ability to kill the enemy, especially when led to believe that they were avenging their parents' murder. Ironically, many of these children were in fact much better off in the army — which treated them as its own children, clothing and feeding them and teaching them to read — than they would have been living on the streets.

* * *

According to Nina Berberova, Gorky came to Europe angry not only at what had been done in Russia but profoundly shaken by what he had seen and experienced. She recalls a conversation he had with her husband, the poet Khodasevich:

> Both (but at different times) in 1920 went to a children's home, or perhaps reformatory for pre-teenagers. These were mostly girls, syphilitics, homeless from twelve to fifteen; nine out of ten were thieves, half were pregnant. Khodasevich . . . with a kind of pity and revulsion remembered how these girls in rags and lice had clung to him, ready to undress him there on the staircase, and lifted their torn skirts above their heads, shouting obscenities at him. With difficulty he tore himself away from them. Gorky went through a similar scene: when he began to speak about it, horror was on

his face, he clenched his jaws and suddenly became silent. It was clear that his visit shook him deeply — more, perhaps, than his previous impressions of tramps, the horrors of the lower depths from which he took his early subject matter. Perhaps, now in Europe, he was healing certain wounds he himself was afraid to admit to; and at times . . . he asked himself, and only himself: Was it worth it?

Gorky was himself an orphan of the revolution. All his hopes for the revolution — hopes by which he had defined himself — had been abandoned in the past four years. Instead of being a constructive cultural force the revolution had virtually destroyed the whole of Russian civilization; instead of human liberation it had merely brought human enslavement; and instead of the spiritual improvement of humanity it had led to degradation. Gorky had become deeply disillusioned. He described himself in 1921 as 'in a misanthropic mood'. He could not reconcile his own humanist and democratic socialism with the realities of Lenin's Russia. He could no longer 'turn a deaf ear' to the faults of the regime in the hope of doing good and reforming it later: all his efforts had come to naught. If his own ideals had been abandoned in Russia, there was nothing left for him to do but abandon Russia.[15]

    Gorky's decision to emigrate from Russia was preceded by mounting conflict with the Bolsheviks. The mindless terror of the past four years, the destruction of the intelligentsia, the persecution of the Mensheviks and SRs, the crushing of the Kronstadt rebels, and the Bolsheviks' callousness towards the famine crisis — all these had turned Gorky into a bitter enemy of the new regime. Much of Gorky's enmity focused on Zinoviev, the party boss in his own Petrograd. Zinoviev disliked Gorky, he saw his house as a 'nest of counter-revolution', and placed him under constant surveillance: Gorky's mail was opened; his house was constantly searched; and his close friends were threatened with arrest. Gorky's most angry letters of denunciation during the Red Terror were all addressed to Zinoviev. In one he claimed that his constant arrests had made 'people hate not only Soviet Power but — in particular — you in person'. Yet it soon became clear that behind Zinoviev stood Lenin himself. The Bolshevik leader was scathing about Gorky's denunciations. In a menacing letter of July 1919 he claimed that the writer's whole 'state of mind' had been made 'quite sick' by the 'embittered bourgeois intellectuals' who 'surrounded' him in Petrograd. 'I don't want to thrust my advice on you,' Lenin threatened, 'but I cannot help saying: change your circumstances radically, your environment, your abode, your occupation — otherwise life may disgust you for good.'[16]

    Gorky's disillusionment with Lenin deepened during 1920. The Bolshevik leader was opposed to the editorial independence of Gorky's publishing house, World Literature, and threatened to cease supporting it financially. Gorky complained bitterly to Lunacharsky. He rightly suspected that Lenin was trying to bring all publishing under state control — something he found anathema — and claimed (or threatened) that the only way to keep the project going was to run it from abroad. But with the stern Lenin breathing down his neck there was little the commissar could do. In his play *Don Quixote* (1922) Lunacharsky re-enacted the strained triangular relationship between himself (in the part of Don Balthazar), Gorky (Don Quixote) and Lenin (Don Rodrigo). Here are Don Balthazar's parting words to Don Quixote. They summarize the clash between Gorky and Lenin — between the ideals of the revolution and its grim 'necessities':

> If we had not broken the plots in the rear, we would have led our army to ruin. Ah, Don Quixote! I do not wish to aggravate your guilt, but here you played your fatal role. I will not hide the fact that it came into stern Rodrigo's head to bring down the threatening hand of the law on you, as a lesson to all the soft-hearted people who thrust themselves and their philanthropy into life, which is stern and complicated and full of responsibility.[17]

The deaths of two of Russia's greatest poets, Alexander Blok and Nikolai Gumilev, were the last straw for Gorky. Blok had been struck down in 1920 by rheumatic fever as a result of living through the civil war in unheated lodgings and in hunger. But Blok's real affliction was despair and disillusionment with the outcome of the revolution. To begin with he had welcomed its destructive violence as a purgatory for the rotten old world of Europe out of which a new and purer world of Asiatics — the Scythians — would emerge. His epic poem 'The Twelve', written in 1918, had depicted twelve rough Red Guards marching 'in step with the Revolution' through a blinding snowstorm destroying the old world and making the new. At their head, bearing the Red Flag, wreathed in white roses, and walking lightly above the snow, was the figure of Jesus Christ. Blok later noted that while writing this sensational poem: 'I kept hearing — I mean literally hearing with my ears — a great noise around me, a noise made up of many sounds (it was probably the noise of the old world crumbling).' For a while Blok continued to believe in the messianic mission of the Bolsheviks. But by 1921 he had become disillusioned. For three years there was no poetry. Gorky, a close friend, compared him to a 'lost child'. Blok plagued him with questions about death and said that he had given up all 'faith in the wisdom of humanity'. Kornei Chukovsky recalled Blok's appearance at a poetry reading in May 1921: 'I was sitting backstage with him. On stage some "orator" or other . . . was cheerfully demonstrating to the crowd that as a poet Blok was already dead . . . Blok leaned over to me and said, "That's true. He's telling the truth, I'm dead." ' When Chukovsky asked him why he did not write poetry any more, Blok told him: 'All sounds have stopped. Can't you hear that there are no longer any sounds?' That same month Blok took to his death-bed. His doctor insisted that he needed to be sent abroad to a special sanatorium. On 29 May Gorky wrote to Lunacharsky on his behalf. 'Blok is Russia's finest living poet. If you forbid him to go abroad, and he dies, you and your comrades will be guilty of his death.' For several weeks Gorky continued to plead for a visa. Lunacharsky wrote in support to the Central Committee on 11 July. But nothing was done. Then, at last, on 10 August, a visa came. It was one day late: the night before the poet had died.[18]

If Blok had died through despair and neglect, the death of Gumilev, just two weeks later, was much more straightforward. He was arrested by the Petrograd Cheka, jailed for a few days, and then shot without trial. Gumilev was accused of being involved in a monarchist conspiracy — an allegation that was almost certainly false, although he was a monarchist by sentiment. A committee of intellectuals formed at Blok's funeral had petitioned for his release. The Academy of Sciences had offered to guarantee his appearance in court. Gorky was asked to intervene and rushed to Moscow to see Lenin. But by the time he returned to Petrograd with an order for his release, Gumilev had already been shot. Gorky was so upset he coughed up blood. Zamyatin said he had never seen him 'so angry as he was on the night when Gumilev was shot'.[19]

Gumilev was the first great Russian poet to be executed by the Bolsheviks. His and Blok's deaths symbolized for Gorky, as for the intelligentsia as a whole, the death of the revolution. Hundreds of people — 'all that remained of literary Petersburg' in Zamyatin's words — turned out for the funeral of Blok. Nina Berberova, then only a young girl, recalls how on seeing the announcement of Blok's death she was 'seized by a feeling, which I never again experienced, that I was suddenly and sharply orphaned . . . The end is coming. We are lost.' Anna Akhmatova, Gumilev's first wife, similarly mourned, not just for a poet but for the ideals of a generation, at Blok's funeral:

> In a silver coffin we bore him
> Alexander, our pure swan,
> Our sun extinguished in torment.[20]

Two months later, plagued by ill health himself, Gorky left Russia, seemingly for good.

ii The Unconquered Country

Fours years of revolution had not reunited the villagers of Andreevskoe. They remained divided between the two old rivals. On the one side stood Sergei Semenov, progressive farmer and reformer, who dreamt of bringing the trappings of the modern world to this poor and God-forsaken hole. On the other stood Grigorii Maliutin, the heavy-built and heavy-drinking peasant elder, an Old Believer and opponent of all change, who had now resisted Semenov's reform efforts for the best part of thirty years.

The feud between them had begun in the 1890s, when Maliutin's daughter, Vera, had killed her illegitimate baby and buried it in the nearby woods. The police had arrived to investigate, and the rich Maliutin had been forced to buy them off. He accused Semenov of informing the police and began a campaign of intimidation — burning his barn down, killing his livestock, accusing him of sorcery — to drive him from the village. Maliutin finally achieved his aim in 1905 when Semenov established a branch of the Peasant Union in Andreevskoe; this was enough to make him a dangerous revolutionary in the eyes of the local judiciary, and he was sent into exile abroad. But three years later he returned to Andreevskoe as a pioneer of Stolypin's land reforms. He tried to introduce the advanced farming methods he had learned in Western Europe on private plots hived off from the commune. Some of the younger and more progressive peasants joined his enclosure movement. But Maliutin was once again enraged — within the commune he was the boss — and along with the other elders of the village had succeeded in blocking his reforms. 'All my dreams for a better life', Semenov wrote to a friend in 1916, 'have been destroyed by this obstinate and jealous man.'

The revolution tipped the scales in Semenov's favour. The old power structure upon which Maliutin had depended, of the volost elder, the local police and the gentry land captain, was dismantled overnight. Within the village the voice of the younger and more progressive farmers was also becoming more dominant, while that of the old patriarchal leaders like Maliutin, who saw nothing good in the revolution, was increasingly ignored. As a champion of reform, Semenov became a dominant figure at the village assembly. He always spoke out against the old patriarchal order and the influence of the Church. In 1917 he helped to organize the land redivision in Andreevskoe, cutting down Maliutin's farm to half its size. He was active in both the district Soviet land department and the local co-operatives; established associations for the purchase of advanced tools, market gardening, improved dairy farming and flax cultivation; wrote pamphlets and gave lectures on agronomy; campaigned against alcoholism; set up a school and a library in the village; and even wrote plays for the 'people's theatre' which he had established with his schoolteacher friend in the nearby township of Bukholovo. He even drew up plans on how to cover the villages of Volokolamsk with electric and telephone cables which he sent to the Moscow Soviet. Although Semenov's Tolstoyan beliefs prevented him from taking up office in the village or the volost Soviet, there was no doubt, as one local put it, 'that the peasants, not just of Andreevskoe, but of the whole region as well, saw him as their leader and champion'.

Meanwhile, Maliutin and his fellow elders continued to oppose his every move. They claimed that he was a Communist — and that his reforms in the village had merely brought upon it all the evils of the new regime. The local priest accused him of sorcery, and warned that his 'atheism' would lead to the devil. Archdeacon Tsvetkov of Volokolamsk joined in the denunciations, claiming that Semenov was the Antichrist. The new village school, organized by Semenov in 1919, enraged them especially, since it was built from timber taken from the woods that had belonged to Maliutin and the Church before they had been nationalized. Moreover, the school had no religious instruction. In place of the cross on the classroom wall there was the obligatory portrait of Lenin. One night Semenov's barn was burnt; on another his farm tools were taken and sunk in the lake. Anonymous denunciations were sent to the local Cheka claiming that Semenov was a 'counter-revolutionary' and a 'German spy': on more than one occasion Semenov was hauled in by the Cheka to answer for his actions, although a brief call to Kamenev, the Chairman of the Moscow Soviet, whom Semenov vaguely knew, was always enough to release him. During 1921, when Russia was hit by various cattle epidemics, Maliutin and his allies blamed the death of the livestock in the village on Semenov's 'evil reforms'. It was even claimed that he had 'made the cattle ill by sorcery'. Some of the peasants now became confused. Although they knew that throughout Russia cattle were dying from similar diseases, they wanted explanations for their own losses, and some now became suspicious of Semenov.

In the end, Maliutin organized his old rival's murder. On the night of 15 December 1922, as he was walking to Bukholovo, Semenov was ambushed by several men, including two of Maliutin's sons, who suddenly appeared from their sister Vera's house on the edge of the village. One of them shot Semenov in the back. As he turned to face his attackers they fired several more shots, and then, as he lay dead on the ground, blew off his face. They cut the blood-red sign of a cross into his chest.

It had been a cowardly murder. Semenov had always faced his rivals openly and had been fair to their points of view; yet they maligned him and shot him in the back. Later, when the murderers were arrested, they claimed that Semenov had been 'working for the devil' and that he had conjured up the cattle plague. They also confessed that Grigorii Maliutin and the Archdeacon Tsvetkov had ordered them to kill Semenov — 'in the name of God', as the latter had told them. They were all convicted of conspiring to murder and sentenced to ten years of hard labour each in the Arctic north.

Semenov was buried on his own beloved plot of land in Andreevskoe: he became a part of the soil for which he had lived and struggled all these years. Thousands of people from the surrounding villages attended the funeral, including hundreds of schoolchildren whom Semenov had personally taught. 'It is tragic to lose such a life', his friend Belousov said in his address, 'just at the moment when his work and teachings have become so badly needed by the people.' To commemorate Semenov's achievements, the village school was named after him, while his farm was preserved by the state, and run by his son until 1929, as a model farm to show the peasants the benefits of the latest agricultural innovations. Semenov would have been deeply touched: it was something he had dreamed of all his life.[21]

Never known to miss an opportunity for party propaganda, *Pravda* focused on this small provincial tale. It portrayed Maliutin as the evil 'kulak' and Semenov as the poor but politically conscious peasant. All of which was of course nonsense — Semenov was no more poor than Maliutin was a 'kulak', and in any case it was not class that had divided them. What the murder really showed was that less than a hundred miles from Moscow there were villages, such as Andreevskoe, which modern civilization had not yet reached — a world apart where the people still believed in witchcraft and lived as if they were trapped in the Middle Ages. The Bolsheviks had yet to conquer this unknown country. They looked at it with misapprehension, like an army in a foreign land. Early Soviet ethnographers, who set out for the countryside around Moscow like explorers for the Amazon forests, found that many of their fellow Russians still believed the earth was flat, that angels lived in clouds, and that the sun went around the earth. They discovered a strange village culture steeped in archaic and patriarchal ways, a world where time was still measured by the seasons and religious holidays as opposed to months, a world full of pagan rituals and superstitions, of wife-beating, mob law, fist fights and bouts of drinking that went on for days.

The Bolsheviks were unable to understand this world — Marx had said nothing about sorcery — let alone to govern it. Their state infrastructure had only got as far as the volost townships. Most of the villages were still governed by their own commune, whose smallholding 'peasant' nature had been greatly strengthened by the revolution and the civil war. Indeed, Russia as a whole had become much more 'peasant' in the previous few years. The great urban populations had largely disintegrated, industry had been virtually destroyed and the thin veneer of provincial civilization had been swept away by the revolution. The smallholding peasants were all that was left. No wonder so many Bolsheviks felt threatened by the peasant mass. Gorky, who was just as hostile to the 'barbaric peasants', expressed their fears. 'The immense peasant tide will end by engulfing everything,' he told a foreign visitor shortly before his departure for Berlin. 'The peasant will become the master of Russia by sheer force of numbers. And it will be a disaster for our future.'[22] This fear of the peasant was the great unresolved tension of the 1920s — one that led inexorably towards the tragedy of collectivization.

True, rural life was not all dark. Under the NEP some of the trappings of the modern world began to trickle down to the villages. Electric power came. Even Andreevskoe had its first electric cables in 1927, thus finally realizing Semenov's dream. Lenin had extolled the new technology as a panacea for Russia's backwardness. 'Communism equals Soviet power plus the electrification of the entire country,' his famous slogan went. He seemed to equate it with magical powers, once even prophesying that the light bulb — or the 'little Ilich lamps', as they became known — would replace the icon in the peasants' huts. In Soviet propaganda the light bulb became a symbol for the torch of enlightenment: light was a metaphor for everything good, just as darkness was for poverty and evil. Photographs showed the peasants marvelling in almost religious wonderment at the new electric spheres of light. As Lenin saw it, a national grid would integrate the remote village world into the modern culture of the cities. Backward peasant Russia would be led out of darkness by the light of industry, and would come to enjoy a bright new future of rapid economic progress, mass education and liberation from the drudgery of manual labour. Much of this was fantasy: centuries of backwardness could not be overcome by a simple switch. Lenin, for so long the critic of utopianism, had at last succumbed, as H. G. Wells put it, to this 'utopia of the electricians' and, in contravention of all Marxist doctrine, had placed his faith in technology to overcome Russia's deep-rooted social problems.[23]

There were other signs of rural civilization in the 1920s. Hospitals, theatres, cinemas and libraries began to appear in the countryside. The period of the NEP witnessed a whole range of agronomic improvements which amounted to nothing less than an agricultural revolution. The narrow and intermingled arable strips that had made communal farming so inefficient were rearranged or broadened on nearly a hundred million hectares of allotment land. Multi-field crop rotations such as those of Western Europe were introduced on nearly one-fifth of all communal land. Chemical fertilizers, graded seed and advanced tools were used by the peasants in growing numbers. Dairy farming was modernized; and many peasants turned to market crops, such as vegetables, flax and sugar beet, which before the revolution had been grown exclusively by the commercial farms of the gentry. Semenov, who in his own times had pioneered such reforms, would have been no less pleased by the rural co-operatives — both for commodity exchange with the towns and for credit to purchase tools and livestock — which grew impressively in the 1920s. By 1927, 50 per cent of all peasant households belonged to an agricultural co-operative. As a result of these improvements, there was a steady rise in productivity. The 1913 levels of agricultural production were regained by 1926, and surpassed in the next two years. The harvest yields of the mid-1920s were 17 per cent higher than those of the 1900s, the so-called 'golden age' of Russian agriculture.[24]

There were also real gains in literacy, resuming the trend of the 1900s, as more village schools were built in the 1920s. By 1926, 51 per cent of the Soviet population was considered literate (compared with 43 per cent in 1917, and 35 per cent in 1907). The biggest gains were among village youth: peasant sons in their early twenties were more than twice as likely to be literate than their fathers' generation; while young peasant women of the same age were five times more likely to be literate than their mothers'. This growing generation gap was both demographic and cultural. By 1926, more than half the rural population was under the age of twenty, and over two-thirds under thirty. These were by and large the literate peasants. Many of them were acquainted with the world outside the village through their service in the army. They challenged the authority of their peasant elders, rarely went to church and displayed a strong individualist striving reflected in a sharp increase of household partitioning during the 1920s, as these sons broke away from their fathers and set up nuclear households of their own. Peasant sons were also increasingly ousting their fathers as the head of the household and gaining a greater say in the running of the farm.[25] The Russian village was much less split between rich and poor, as the Bolsheviks had mistakenly believed, than it was divided between fathers and sons.

This generational conflict helped the Bolsheviks to build up their influence in the countryside through the organization of its restless youth. The Komsomol grew much more rapidly than the party in the countryside — from 80,000 members in 1922 to well over half a million, three times the number of rural Bolsheviks, by 1925. The Komsomol was a social club for the bored teenagers of the village. It organized them in a crusade against the Church and the old patriarchal order. Its aim was 'to turn the village upside down'. Through its recruitment for the party it also offered these ambitious youths the chance to advance themselves and leave the backward village, which so many of them had come to despise, for the bright lights of the urban world. A survey of the Komsomol in one of the most agricultural districts of Voronezh province during the mid-1920s found that 85 per cent of its members came from peasant families; yet only 3 per cent said that they wanted to work in agriculture. In 1923 a young student of ethnography summarized the attitudes of his contemporaries in his village in Volokolamsk, not far from Semenov's Andreevskoe:

This is what the young people say about their elders: 'The old people are fools. They work themselves to exhaustion and get nothing from it. They don't know anything except how to plough — which is to say they don't know anything . . . Give up the farm. It is not profitable and does not justify the labour spent on it' . . . [The young people want] to get away, to get away as quickly as possible. Anywhere, if one can only get away — to the factory, to the army, to study, or become an officer — it doesn't matter.[26]

Semenov and Kanatchikov had noted the same attitudes thirty years before. The rejection of the village by its youth was, it seems, a constant source of Bolshevik recruitment.

The Red Army, along with the Komsomol, was a means of organizing this restless village youth. Young men who had returned from the army often took the lead in the rural Soviets and in the Komsomol crusade against the old rural order. One group of veterans held a 'congress' in their village to discuss ways to organize a 'struggle against darkness, religion, moonshine and other evils'. Having grown accustomed to the army life, these young veterans soon became bored with the life of the village, where, as one of them put it, 'there are no cultures of any kind'. They despised the old rural ways of the village and, if they did not leave it altogether, sought in every way to set themselves apart by adopting urban and military dress. One source noted that all 'former soldiers, rural activists, and Komsomols — that is all those who counted themselves progressive people — went around in military and semi-military uniforms'. Many of these youths later played an active role in Stalin's campaign of collectivization. They joined the grain-requisitioning squads which resumed the civil war against the village after 1927; set up 'initiative groups' to organize collective farms; took part in the renewed attacks on the Church; helped to suppress peasant resistance; and later became officials or machine operators in the new collective farms.[27]

And yet the fact remained that within the village the Bolsheviks were without real authority. This was the root cause of the failure of the NEP. Unable to govern the countryside by peaceable means, the Bolsheviks resorted to terrorizing it, ending up in collectivization. The events of 1918–21 had left a deep scar on peasant–state relations. Although the civil war between them had come to an end, the two sides faced each other with deep suspicion and mistrust during the uneasy truce of the 1920s. Through passive and everyday forms of resistance — foot-dragging, habitual failure to understand instructions, apathy and inertia — the peasants hoped to keep the Bolsheviks at bay. As the party took over the Soviet administration in the volost townships, the peasants withdrew from the Soviets altogether and regrouped politically in their village communes. The resurrection of the absolutist state thus recreated the ancient division between the volost as the seat of state or gentry power — 'interested only in collecting taxes', as one peasant put it — and the village as the domain of the peasants. Outside the volost townships the Bolsheviks had no authority. Nearly all their members were concentrated there, where they were needed to run the fledgling organs of the state. Very few rural Bolsheviks lived in the villages or had any real ties with the peasantry. Only 15 per cent of the rural party members were engaged in farming; while less than 10 per cent came from the region to which they were assigned. As for the rural party meetings, they were concerned mainly with state policy, international events and even sexual ethics — but very rarely with agricultural matters.

The rural Soviets were just as powerless. Although technically subordinated to the volost administration, their mainly peasant members were reluctant to go against the interests of the village communes, upon whose taxes they depended for their budgets. Indeed the villagers often elected a simpleton or an alcoholic, or perhaps some poor peasant in debt to the village elders, in order to sabotage the Soviet's work. It was an old trick of the peasants and had been applied to the volost administration before 1917. The Bolsheviks, in their usual inept manner, responded by centralizing power, cutting down the number of rural Soviets; yet this made matters worse, for it left the vast majority of the villages without a Soviet at all. By 1929, the average rural Soviet was trying to rule nine separate villages with a combined population of 1,500 people. Without telephones, and sometimes even without transport, the Soviet officials were rendered impotent. Taxes could not be properly collected, Soviet laws could not be enforced. As for the rural police force, it was minuscule, with each policeman on average responsible for 20,000 people in eighteen or even twenty villages.[28] A decade after 1917 the vast majority of the countryside had yet to experience Soviet power.

There was a common assumption among those Bolsheviks who wrote about the NEP — Bukharin was a classic example — that the growing affluence and cultural advancement of the countryside would somehow dissolve this political problem. This was mistaken. Under the smallholding system of the NEP the political culture of the village became even more distinctly 'peasant', in fundamental opposition to the state, and no amount of propaganda or education could ever hope to bridge this gap. Why, after all, should a better-educated peasant be more susceptible to Communist control or indoctrination? The rural intelligentsia, who alone could have played an intermediary role between the peasantry and the regime, was a tiny island in this peasant ocean, with its own distinct urban culture and, by all accounts, increasingly mistrusted by the peasants.[29] The longer the NEP went on, the greater the disjunction became between the ambitions of the Soviet regime and its impotence in the countryside. Militant Bolsheviks were increasingly afraid that the revolution would degenerate, that it would sink in the 'kulak' mud, unless a new civil war was launched to subjugate the village to the town. Here were the roots of Stalin's civil war against the village, the civil war of collectivization. Without the means to govern the village, let alone to transform it on socialist lines, the Bolsheviks sought to abolish it instead.

iii Lenin's Last Struggle

The first signs that Lenin was unwell became apparent in 1921 when he began to complain of headaches and exhaustion. Doctors could not diagnose the illness — it was as much the result of a mental breakdown as a physical one. For the past four years Lenin had been working virtually without a break for up to sixteen hours every day. The only real periods of rest had been in the summer of 1917, when he was on the run from Kerensky's government, and during the weeks of recuperation from Kaplan's assassination attempt in August 1918. The crisis of 1920–I had taken a heavy toll on Lenin's health. The physical symptoms of 'Lenin's rage', as Krupskaya once described it, sleeplessness and irritation, headaches and depressed exhaustion, returned to dog him during his bitter struggles with the Workers' Opposition and the revolts in the country at large. The Kronstadt rebels, the workers and the peasants, the Mensheviks, the SRs and the clergy, who were all arrested and shot in large numbers, became victims of his rage. By the summer of 1921, Lenin had once again emerged victorious; yet the signs of his mental exhaustion were clear for all to see. He showed lapses of memory, speech difficulties and erratic movements. Some doctors put it down to lead poisoning from Kaplan's two bullets, which were still lodged in Lenin's arm and neck (the one in his neck was surgically removed during the spring of 1922). But others suspected paralysis. Their suspicions were confirmed on 25 May 1922, when Lenin suffered his first major stroke, leaving his right side virtually paralysed and depriving him for a while of speech. Lenin now realized, in the words of his sister, Maria Ul'ianova, who was to nurse him until his death, 'that it was all finished for him'. He begged Stalin to give him poison so that he could kill himself. 'He doesn't want to live and can't live any longer,' Krupskaya told him. She had tried to give Lenin cyanide but lost her nerve, so the two of them had decided to ask Stalin instead as a 'firm and steely man devoid of sentimentality'. Although Stalin would later wish him dead, he refused to help him die; and the Politburo voted against it. For the moment, Lenin was more useful to Stalin alive.[30]

During the summer of 1922, as he recovered at his country house at Gorki, Lenin concerned himself with the question of his succession. This must have been a painful task for him since, like all dictators, he was fiercely jealous of his own power and evidently thought that no one else was good enough to inherit it. All Lenin's last writings make it clear that he favoured a collective leadership to succeed him. He was particularly afraid of the personal rivalry between Trotsky and Stalin, which he realized might split the party as he withdrew from the scene, and sought to forestall this by balancing the one against the other.

Both men had virtues in his eyes. Trotsky was a brilliant orator and administrator: he more than anyone had won the civil war. But his pride and arrogance — not to speak of his past as a Menshevik or his Jewish-intellectual looks — made him unpopular in the party (both the Military and the Workers' Oppositions had to a large extent been against him personally). Trotsky was not a natural 'comrade'. He would always rather be the general of his own army than a colonel in a collective command. It was this which gave him the position of an 'outsider' to the rank and file. Although a member of the Politburo, Trotsky had never held a party post. He rarely attended party meetings. Lenin's feelings towards Trotsky were summarized by Maria Ul'ianova: 'He did not feel sympathy for Trotsky — he had too many characteristics that made it extraordinarily hard to work collectively with him. But he was an industrious worker and a talented person, and for V. I. that was the main thing, so he tried to keep him on board. Whether it was worth it is another question.'[31]

Stalin, by contrast, seemed at first much more suited to the needs of a collective leadership. During the civil war he had taken on himself a huge number of mundane jobs that no one else had wanted — he was the Commissar for Nationalities, the Commissar of Rabkrin, a member of the Revolutionary Military Council, of the Politburo and the Orgburo, and the Chairman of the Secretariat — with the result that he soon gained a reputation for modest and industrious mediocrity. Here was the 'grey blur' whom Sukhanov had described in 1917. All the party leaders made the same mistake of underestimating Stalin's potential power, and his ambition to exercise it, as a result of the patronage he had accrued from holding all these posts. Lenin was as guilty as the rest. For a man of such intolerance, he proved remarkably tolerant of Stalin's many sins, not least his growing rudeness towards himself, in the belief that he needed Stalin to maintain unity in the party. It was for this reason that, on Stalin's own urging, and apparently backed by Kamenev, he agreed to make Stalin the party's first General Secretary in April 1922. It was to prove a crucial appointment — one that enabled Stalin to come to power. Yet by the time Lenin came to realize this, and tried to have Stalin removed from the post, it was already too late.[32]

The key to Stalin's growing power was his control of the party apparatus in the provinces. As the Chairman of the Secretariat, and the only Politburo member in the Orgburo, he could promote his friends and dismiss opponents.

During the course of 1922 alone more than 10,000 provincial officials were appointed by the Orgburo and the Secretariat, most of them on Stalin's personal recommendation. They were to be his main supporters during the power struggle against Trotsky in 1922–3. Most of them came, like Stalin himself, from very humble backgrounds and had received little formal education. Mistrusting intellectuals such as Trotsky, they preferred to place their trust in Stalin's wisdom, with his simple calls for proletarian unity and Bolshevik discipline, when it came to matters of ideology.

Lenin had gone along with Stalin's growing powers of 'appointmentism' from Moscow as an antidote to the formation of provincial opposition factions (the Workers' Opposition, for example, remained strong in the Ukraine and Samara until 1923). As the Chairman of the Secretariat, Stalin spent much of his time rooting out potential troublemakers from the provincial party apparatus. He received monthly reports from the Cheka (renamed the GPU in 1922) on the activities of the provincial leaders. Boris Bazhanov, Stalin's personal secretary, recalls his habit of pacing up and down his large Kremlin office, puffing on his pipe, and then issuing the curt command to remove such and such a Party Secretary and send so and so to replace him. There were few party leaders, including members of the Politburo, whom Stalin did not have under surveillance by the end of 1922. Under the guise of enforcing Leninist orthodoxy, Stalin was thus able to gather information about all his rivals, including many things they would rather have kept secret, which he could use to secure their loyalty to himself.[33]

While Lenin recovered from his stroke Russia was ruled by the trium-virate — Stalin, Kamenev and Zinoviev — which had emerged as an anti-Trotsky bloc during the summer of 1922. The three met before party meetings to agree their strategy and instruct their followers on how to vote. Kamenev had long had a soft spot for Stalin: they had been together in exile in Siberia; and Stalin had sprung to his defence when Lenin tried to have him kicked out of the party for his opposition to the October coup. Kamenev had ambitions to lead the party and this had led him to side with Stalin against Trotsky, whom he considered the more serious threat. Since Trotsky was Kamenev's brother-in-law, this meant putting faction before family. As for Zinoviev, he had little love for Stalin. But his hatred for Trotsky was so all-consuming that he would have sided with the Devil so long as it secured his enemy's defeat. Both men thought they were using Stalin, whom they considered a mediocrity, to promote their own claims to the leadership. But Stalin was using them, and, once Trotsky had been defeated, he went on to destroy them.

By September Lenin had recovered and was back at work. He now became suspicious of Stalin's ambitions and in an effort to counteract his growing power proposed to appoint Trotsky as his deputy in Sovnarkom. Trotsky's followers have always argued that this would have made their hero Lenin's heir. But in fact the post was seen by many people as a minor one — power was concentrated in the party organs rather than the government ones — and no doubt for this reason Stalin was happy to vote for Lenin's resolution in the Politburo. Indeed it was Trotsky who was most opposed, writing on his voting slip: 'Categorically refuse'. He claimed that his objections were on the grounds that he had already criticized the post in principle when it had been introduced the previous May. Later he also claimed that he had turned the post down on the grounds that he was a Jew and that this might add fuel to the propaganda of the regime's enemies (see pages 803–4). But his refusal was probably as much because he thought it was beneath him to be merely a 'deputy chairman'.

This does not mean that Lenin shared this dim view of the Sovnarkom job. Nor does it mean that he offered it to Trotsky, in the words of Lenin's sister, as merely a 'diplomatic gesture' to compensate for the fact that 'Ilich was on Stalin's side.' Lenin had always placed a higher value on the work of Sovnarkom than on that of the party itself. Sovnarkom was Lenin's baby, it was where he focused all his energies, even to the point where, amazingly, he became ignorant of party life. 'I am admittedly not familiar with the scale of the Orgburo's "assignment" work,' he confessed to Stalin in October 1921. This was Lenin's tragedy. During his last months of active politics, as he came to grapple with the problem of the growing power of the leading party bodies, he increasingly looked to Sovnarkom as a means of dividing the power between the party and the state. Yet Sovnarkom, as Lenin's personal seat of power, was bound to decline as he became ill and withdrew from politics. Even with Trotsky standing in for him as chairman, it was almost certainly too late to halt the shift in power to the party organs in Stalin's hands, and Trotsky must have known this.[34]

Lenin's suspicions of Stalin deepened when, in October, Stalin proposed to expel Trotsky from the Politburo as a punishment for his arrogant rejection of the Sovnarkom post. It became clear to Lenin, as he acquainted himself with the activities of the triumvirate, that it was acting like a ruling clique and intended to oust him from power. This was confirmed when Lenin discovered that as soon as he retired from the Politburo meetings, which he often had to leave early because of exhaustion, the triumvirate would pass vital resolutions which he would only learn about the next day. Lenin now ordered (on 8 December) that Politburo meetings were not to go on for more than three hours and that all matters left unresolved were to be put off to the following day. At the same time, or so Trotsky later claimed, Lenin approached him with an offer to join him in a 'bloc against bureaucracy', meaning a coalition against Stalin and his power base in the Orgburo. Trotsky's claim is credible. This, after all, was on the eve of Lenin's Testament, which was mainly concerned with the problem of Stalin and his hold on the bureaucracy. Trotsky had already criticized the party bureaucracy, Rabkrin and the Orgburo in particular. And we know that Lenin shared his opposition to Stalin on both foreign trade and the Georgian issue. In sum, it seems that towards mid-December Lenin and Trotsky were coming together against Stalin. And then suddenly, on the night of 15 December, Lenin suffered his second major stroke.[35]

Stalin at once took charge of Lenin's doctors and, on the pretext of speeding his recovery, obtained from the Central Committee an order giving him the power to keep him 'in isolation' from politics by restricting visitors and correspondence. 'Neither friends nor those around him', read a further order of the Politburo on 24 December, 'are allowed to tell Vladimir Ilich any political news, since this might cause him to reflect and get excited.' Confined to his wheelchair, and allowed to dictate for only '5 to 10 minutes a day', Lenin had become Stalin's prisoner. His two main secretaries, Nadezhda Alliluyeva (Stalin's wife) and Lydia Fotieva, reported to Stalin everything he said. Lenin was evidently unaware of this, as later events were to reveal. Stalin, meanwhile, made himself an expert on medicine, ordering textbooks to be sent to him. He became convinced that Lenin would soon die and increasingly showed open contempt towards him. 'Lenin kaput,' he told colleages in December. Stalin's words reached Lenin through Maria Ul'ianova. 'I have not died yet,' her brother informed her, 'but they, led by Stalin, have already buried me.' Although Stalin based his reputation on his special relationship with Lenin, his real feelings towards him were betrayed in 1924, when, having had to wait a whole year for him to waste away and die, he was heard to mutter: 'Couldn't even die like a *real* leader!' Actually, Lenin might have died much sooner. Towards the end of December he became so frustrated with the restrictions on his activities that he once again requested poison so that he could end his life. According to Fotieva, Stalin refused to supply the poison. But he no doubt soon came to regret it, since in the brief spells when he was allowed to work Lenin now dictated a series of notes for the forthcoming Party Congress in which he condemned Stalin's growing power and demanded his removal.[36]

These fragmentary notes, which later became known as Lenin's Testament, were dictated in brief spells — some of them by telephone to a stenographer who sat in the next room with a pair of earphones — between 23 December and 4 January. Lenin ordered them to be kept in the strictest secrecy, placing them in sealed envelopes to be opened only by himself or Krupskaya. But his senior secretaries were also spies for Stalin and they showed the notes to him.[37] Throughout these last writings there is an overwhelming sense of despair at the way the revolution had turned out. Lenin's frenzied style, his hyperbole and obsessive repetition, betray a mind that was not just deteriorating through paralysis but was also tortured — perhaps by the realization that the single goal on which it had been fixed for the past four decades had now turned out a monstrous mistake. Throughout these last writings Lenin was haunted by Russia's cultural backwardness. It was as if he acknowledged, perhaps only to himself, that the Mensheviks had been right, that Russia was not ready for socialism since its masses lacked the education to take the place of the bourgeoisie, and that the attempt to speed up this process through the intervention of the state was bound to end up in tyranny. Was this what he meant when he warned that the Bolsheviks still needed to 'learn how to govern'?

Lenin's last notes were concerned with three main problems — with Stalin in each as the principal culprit. The first of these was the Georgian affair and the question of what sort of union treaty Russia should sign with the ethnic borderlands. Despite his own Georgian origins, Stalin was the foremost of those Bolsheviks whom Lenin had criticized during the civil war for their Great Russian chauvinism. Most of Stalin's supporters in the party were equally imperialist in their views. They equated the colonization of the borderlands, the Ukraine especially, by Russian workers, and the suppression of the native peasant population ('petty-bourgeois nationalists'), with the promotion of Communist power. As the Commissar for Nationalities, Stalin proposed in late September that the three non-Russian republics that had so far come into being (the Ukraine, Belorussia and Transcaucasia) should join Russia as no more than autonomous regions, leaving the lion's share of power to the federal government in Moscow. The 'autonomization plan', as Stalin's proposals came to be known, would have restored the 'Russia united and indivisible' of the Tsarist Empire. It was not at all what Lenin had envisaged when he had assigned to Stalin the task of drawing up the plans for a federal union. Lenin stressed the need to pacify what he saw as the justified historical grievances of the non-Russians against Russia by granting them the status of 'sovereign' republics (for the major ethnic groups) or 'autonomous' ones (for the smaller ones) with broad cultural freedoms and the formal right — for whatever that was worth — to secede from the union.

Stalin's plans were bitterly opposed by the Georgian Bolsheviks, whose attempts to build up their own fragile political base depended on the concession of these national rights. Already, in March 1922, Stalin and his fellow-Georgian, Ordzhonikidze, head of Moscow's Caucasian Bureau, had forced Georgia, much against its leaders' will, to merge with Armenia and Azerbaijan in a Transcaucasian Federation. It seemed to Georgia's leaders that Stalin and his henchman were treating Georgia as their fiefdom and riding roughshod over them. They rejected the autonomization plan and threatened to resign if Moscow forced it through.*

---

* The opposition of the other republics was more circumspect: the Ukrainians refused to give their opinion on Stalin's proposals, while the Belorussians said that they would be guided by the Ukraine's decision.

It was at this point that Lenin intervened. To begin with he took Stalin's side. Although his proposals were undesirable — Lenin forced them to be dropped in favour of the federal union that later became known as the Soviet Union Treaty ratified in 1924 — the Georgians had been wrong to issue ultimatums and he told them so in an angry cable on 21 October. The next day the entire Central Committee of the Georgian Communist Party resigned in protest. Nothing quite like it had ever happened before in the history of the party. From late November, however, when Lenin was generally beginning to turn against Stalin, his position changed. New evidence from Georgia made him think again. He despatched a fact-finding commission to Tiflis, headed by Dzerzhinsky and Rykov, from which he learned that during the course of an argument Ordzhonikidze had beaten up a prominent Georgian Bolshevik (who had called him a 'Stalinist arsehole'). Lenin was outraged. It confirmed his impressions of Stalin's growing rudeness and made him see the Georgian issue in a different light. In his notes to the Party Congress on 30–1 December he compared Stalin to an old-style Russian chauvinist, a 'rascal and a tyrant', who could only bully and subjugate small nations, such as Georgia, whereas what was needed from Russia's rulers was 'profound caution, sensitivity, and a readiness to compromise' with their legitimate national aspirations. Lenin even claimed that in a socialist federation the rights of 'oppressed nations', such as Georgia, should be greater than those of the 'oppressor nations' (i.e. Russia) so as to 'compensate for the inequality which obtains in actual practice'. On 8 January, in what was to be the final letter of his life, Lenin promised the Georgian opposition that he was following their cause 'with all my heart'.[38]

Lenin's second major concern in his Testament was to check the growing powers of the party's leading organs, which were now under Stalin's control. Two years earlier, when his own command had been supreme, Lenin had condemned the proposals of the Democratic Centralists for more democracy and *glasnost* in the party; but now that Stalin was the great dictator Lenin put forward similar plans. He proposed to democratize the Central Committee by adding 50 to 100 new members recruited from the ordinary workers and peasants in the lower organs of the party. To make the Politburo more accountable he also suggested that the Central Committee should have the right to attend all its meetings and to inspect its documents. Moreover, the Central Control Commission, merged with Rabkrin and streamlined to 300 or 400 conscious workers, should have the right to check the Politburo's powers. These proposals were a belated effort (similar in many ways to Gorbachev's *perestroika*) to bridge the widening gap between the party bosses and the rank and file, to make the leadership more democratic, more open and efficient, without loosening the party's overall grip on society.

The final issue of Lenin's last writings — and also by far the most explosive — was the question of the succession. In his notes of 24 December Lenin voiced his worry about a split between Trotsky and Stalin — it was partly for this reason that he had proposed to enlarge the size of the Central Committee — and, as if to underline his preference for a collective leadership, pointed out the faults of the major party leaders. Kamenev and Zinoviev were compromised by their stand against him in October. Bukharin was 'the favourite of the whole Party, but his theoretical views can only be classified as Marxist with reserve'. As for Trotsky, he 'was personally perhaps the most capable man in the present Central Committee, but he has displayed excessive self-assurance and shown excessive preoccupation with the purely administrative side of work'. But it was for Stalin that Lenin's most devastating criticisms were reserved. Having become the General Secretary, he had 'accumulated unlimited power in his hands, and I am not sure that he will always know how to use this power with sufficient caution'. On 4 January Lenin added the following note:

Stalin is too rude and this defect, although quite tolerable in our midst and in dealings between Communists, becomes intolerable in a General Secretary. For this reason I suggest that the comrades think about a way to remove Stalin from that post and replace him with someone who has only one advantage over Comrade Stalin, namely greater tolerance, greater loyalty, greater courtesy and consideration to comrades, less capriciousness, etc.[39]

Lenin was making it clear that Stalin had to go.

Lenin's resolve was further strengthened at the start of March, when he learned about an incident which had taken place between Stalin and Krupskaya several weeks before but which had been kept secret from him. On 21 December Lenin had dictated to Krupskaya a letter to Trotsky congratulating him on his successful tactics in the battle against Stalin over the foreign trade monopoly. Stalin's informers told him of the letter, which he seized upon as evidence of Lenin's 'bloc' with Trotsky against him. The next day he telephoned Krupskaya and, as she herself put it, subjected her 'to a storm of coarse abuse', claiming she had broken the party's rules on Lenin's health (although the doctors had authorized her dictation), and threatening to start an investigation of her by the Central Control Commission. When she put the phone down, Krupskaya apparently went pale, sobbed hysterically and rolled around on the floor. Stalin's reign of terror had begun. When Lenin was finally told about this incident, on 5 March, he dictated a letter to Stalin demanding that he should apologize for his 'rudeness' or else risk a 'breach of relations between us'. Stalin, who had become completely arrogant with power, could hardly mask his contempt for

THE REVOLUTIONARY INHERITANCE

96-7 The people reject the Bolsheviks. *Above*: Red Army troops assault the mutinous Kronstadt Naval Base, 16 March 1921. *Below*: peasant rebels ('Greens') attack a train of requisitioned grain, February 1921.

98-100 The famine crisis of 1921-2. *Above*: Bolshevik commissars inspect the harvest failure in the Volga region, 1921. The crisis was largely the result of Bolshevik over-requisitioning. *Below*: the victims of the crisis; an overcrowded cemetery in the Buzuluk district, 1921. *Opposite*: cannibals with their victims, Samara province, 1921.

101-3 Orphans of the revolution. *Above*: street orphans in Saratov hunt for food remains in a rubbish tip, 1921. *Opposite above*: orphans were ripe for political indoctrination. This young boy, seen here giving a speech from the agit-train *October Revolution*, was the Secretary of the Tula Komsomol. He was part of the generation which, a decade later, pioneered the Stalinist assault on old Russia. *Opposite below*: orphans also made good soldiers: a national unit of the Red Army in Turkestan, 1920.

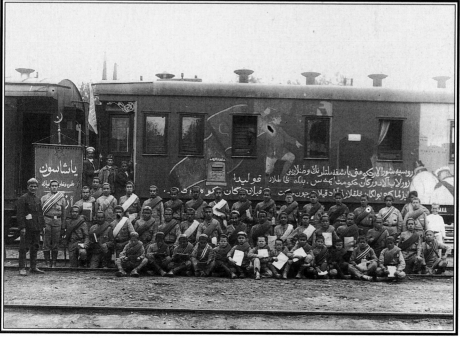

104 The war against religion: Red Army soldiers confiscate valuable items from the Semenov Monastery in Moscow, 1923.

105-6 The revolution expands east. *Above*: the Red Army arrives in Bukhara and explains the meaning of Soviet power to the former subjects of the Emir, September 1920. *Below*: two Bolshevik commissars of the Far East.

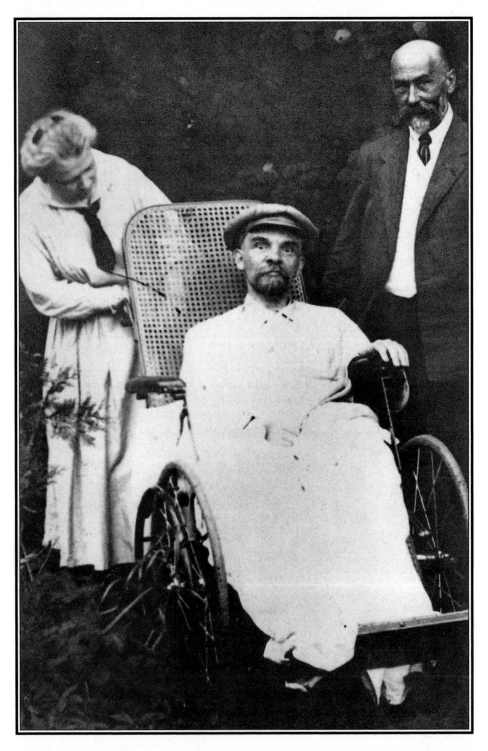

107 The dying Lenin, with one of his doctors and his younger sister Maria Ul'ianova, during the summer of 1923. By the time this photograph was taken, Stalin's rise to power was virtually assured.

the dying Lenin in his ungracious reply.* Krupskaya, he reminded him, 'is not just your wife but my old Party comrade'. In their 'conversation' he had not been 'rude' and the whole incident was 'nothing more than a silly misunderstanding ... However, if you consider that for the preservation of "relations" I should "take back" the above words, I can take them back, although I fail to understand what all this is supposed to be about, or where I am at "fault", or what, exactly, is wanted of me.'[40]

Lenin was devastated by the incident. He became ill overnight. One of his doctors described his condition on 6 March: 'Vladimir Ilich lay there with a look of dismay, a frightened expression on his face, his eyes sad with an inquiring look, tears running down his face. Vladimir Ilich became agitated, tried to speak, but the words would not come to him and he could only say: "Oh hell, oh hell. The old illness has come back." ' Three days later Lenin suffered his third major stroke. It robbed him of the power to speak and thus to contribute to politics. Until his death, ten months later, he could only utter single syllables: '*vot-vot*' ('here-here') and '*s'ezd-s'ezd*' ('congress-congress').[41]

In May Lenin was moved to Gorki, where a team of doctors was placed at his disposal. On fine days he would sit outside. There a nephew found him one day 'sitting in his wheelchair in a white summer shirt with an open collar ... A rather old cap covered his head and the right arm lay somewhat unnaturally on his lap. [He] hardly noticed me even though I stood quite plainly in the middle of the clearing.' Krupskaya read to him — Gorky and Tolstoy gave him the most comfort — and strove in vain to teach him how to speak. By September, with the help of a cane and a pair of orthopaedic shoes, he was just able to walk again. Sometimes he pushed his wheelchair round the grounds. He began to read papers sent from Moscow and, with Krupskaya's help, learned to write a little with his left hand. Bukharin visited in the autumn and, as he later told Boris Nikolaevsky, found Lenin deeply worried about who was to succeed him and about the articles he could not write. But there was no question of him ever returning to politics. Lenin, the politician, was already dead.[42]

*   *   *

Getting Lenin out of the way was just what Stalin needed. Through his spies Stalin had learned of Lenin's secret letter to the Twelfth Party Congress. If he was to survive in office, he had to prevent it from being read out there. On 9 March Stalin used his power as the General Secretary to put off the Congress from mid-March until mid-April. Trotsky, although he stood to gain most from Stalin's likely downfall at the Congress, readily agreed to its delay. He even reassured Kamenev that, whilst he agreed 'with Lenin in substance' (i.e. on the Georgian question and party reform), he was 'for preserving the status quo' and

* It was not published until 1989.

'against removing Stalin' provided there was a 'radical change' of policies. Trotsky concluded with the hope that: 'There should be no more intrigues but honest co-operation.' The outcome of this 'rotten compromise' — just what Lenin had warned him not to make — was that the Party Congress witnessed Stalin's triumph rather than his final defeat. Lenin's notes on the nationality question and the reform of the party were distributed among the delegates, discussed, and then dismissed by the leadership. Most of the delegates, in any case, probably shared the view expressed by Stalin that at a time when unity was needed in the party above all else there was no need to waste time discussing democracy. The urge to silence Trotsky, and all criticism of the Politburo, was in itself a crucial factor in Stalin's rise to power.[43] Lenin's notes on the question of the succession, including his demand that Stalin be removed, were not read out at the Congress and remained suppressed until 1956.*

It is difficult to explain Trotsky's conduct. At this crucial moment of the power struggle, when he could have won a major victory, he somehow engineered his own defeat. Among the forty members of the new Central Committee, elected at the Congress, he could count only three supporters. Perhaps, sensing his growing isolation, especially after Lenin's stroke, Trotsky had decided that his only hope lay in trying to appease the triumvirate. His memoirs are filled with the conviction that he had been brought down by a conspiracy of its three leaders. There was certainly a very real danger that, if he had opted to defy them, Trotsky would have been accused of 'factionalism' — and after 1921 this was a political death sentence. But there is also some truth in the claim that Trotsky lacked the stomach for a fight. There was an inner weakness to his character, one that stemmed from his pride. Faced with the prospect of defeat, Trotsky preferred not to compete. One of his oldest friends tells the story of a chess game in New York. Trotsky had challenged him to a game, 'evidently considering himself a good chess player'. But it turned out that he was weak and, having lost the game, went into a temper and refused to play another game.[44] This small episode was typical of Trotsky: when he came up against a superior rival, one who was able to out-manœuvre him, he chose to retreat and sulk in glorious isolation rather than lose face by trying to confront him on disadvantageous terms.

This was, in a sense, what Trotsky did next. Rather than fight Stalin

---

* The contents of the Testament were made known to the delegates of the Thirteenth Party Congress in 1924. Stalin offered to resign but his offer was rejected on the suggestion of Zinoviev to 'let bygones be bygones'. The conflict with Lenin was put down to a personal clash, with the implication that Lenin had been sick and not altogether sound in mind. None of these last writings was fully published in Russia during Stalin's lifetime, although fragments appeared in the party press during the 1920s. Trotsky and his followers made their contents well known in the West, however (Volkogonov, *Stalin*, ch. 11).

in the highest party organs he took up the standard of the Bolshevik rank and file, posing as the champion of party democracy against the 'police regime' of the leadership. It was a desperate gamble — Trotsky was hardly known for his democratic habits and he ran the deadly risk of 'factionalism' — but then he was in desperate straits. On 8 October he addressed an Open Letter to the Central Committee in which he accused it of suppressing all democracy within the party:

> The participation of the party masses in the actual formation of the party organization is becoming increasingly marginal. A peculiar secretarial psychology has been established in the past year or so, its main feature is the belief that the [party] secretary is capable of deciding every and any question, without even knowing the basic facts ... There is a very broad stratum of party workers, both in the government and party apparatus, who completely abnegate their own party opinion, at least as expressed openly, as if assuming that it is the apparatus of the secretarial hierarchy which formulate party opinion and policy. Beneath this stratum of abstainers from opinion lies the broad party masses, for whom every decision already comes down in the form of a summons or command.

Support for Trotsky came from the so-called 'Group of 46' — Antonov-Ovseenko, Piatakov and Preobrazhensky were the best known — who also wrote in protest to the Central Committee. The climate of fear in the party was such, they claimed, that even old comrades had become 'afraid to converse with one another'.[45]

Predictably, the party leadership accused Trotsky of instigating a dangerous 'platform' which could lead to the creation of an illegal 'faction' in the party. Without responding to his political criticisms, the Politburo issued a vicious personal attack on Trotsky on 19 October. Trotsky was arrogant, considered himself above the day-to-day work of the party, and acted by the maxim 'all or nothing' (i.e. 'Give me all or I'll give you nothing'). Four days later Trotsky addressed a defiant rebuttal of the charges of 'factionalism' to the Plenum of the Central Committee. On 26 October he appeared at the Plenum itself.

Until recently it was thought that Trotsky had not attended this crucial meeting. Deutscher and Broué, his two main biographers, both have him absent with the flu. But he did attend and, indeed, put up such a powerful defence that Bazhanov, Stalin's secretary, who was charged with transcribing Trotsky's speech, buried the records of it in his personal files. They were found there in 1990. Trotsky's speech was a passionate denial of the allegations of 'Bonapartism' which he claimed had been levelled against him. It was at this point that he raised the question of his Jewish roots. To prove that he lacked ambition Trotsky cited two occasions when he had turned down Lenin's offer of high office — once in October 1917 (Commissar of the Interior) and once again in September 1922 (Deputy Chairman of Sovnarkom) — on the grounds that it would not be wise, given the problem of anti-Semitism, to have a Jew in such a high post. On the first occasion Lenin had dismissed this as 'trivial'; but on the second 'he was in agreement with me'.[46] Trotsky's implication was obvious: opposition to him in the party — and Lenin had acknowledged this — stemmed partly from the fact that he was a Jew. It was a tragic moment for Trotsky — not just as a politician but also as a man — that at this turning point in his life, standing condemned before the party, he should have to fall back on his Jewish roots. For a man who had never felt himself a Jew, it was a mark of how alone he now was.

Trotsky's emotional appeal made little impression on the delegates — most of whom had been picked by Stalin. By 102 votes to two the Plenum passed a motion of censure against Trotsky for engaging in 'factionalism'. Kamenev and Zinoviev pressed for Trotsky to be expelled from the party; but Stalin, always eager to appear as the voice of moderation, thought this was unwise and the motion was rejected.[47] Stalin, in any case, had no need to hurry. Trotsky was finished as a major force and his expulsion from the party — which finally came in 1927 — could await its time. The one man capable of stopping Stalin had now been removed.

*   *   *

The public had not been told that Lenin was dying. Right until the end the press continued to report that he was recovering from a grave illness — one from which any mortal man would have died. By inventing this 'miracle recovery' the regime sought to keep alive the cult of Lenin upon which it now increasingly depended for its own sense of legitimacy. The term 'Leninism' was used for the first time in 1923: the triumvirate sought to present themselves as its true defenders against Trotsky, the 'anti-Leninist'. The same year saw work commence on the first edition of his collected works (the *Leninskii sbornik*), the holy scriptures of this orthodoxy, and the establishment of the Lenin Institute (formally opened in 1924), complete with an archive, a library and a museum of Leninania. There was a spate of hagiographies whose main aim was to create myths and legends — Lenin as a poor peasant, or a worker, Lenin as the lover of animals and children, Lenin as the tireless worker for the people's happiness — which might help to make the regime more popular. It was also from this time that huge portraits of Lenin began to appear on the façades of public buildings — one Moscow park even had a 'living portrait' of him made up of bedding plants — while inside many factories and offices there were 'Lenin Corners' with approved photographs and artefacts to illustrate his achievements.[48] As Lenin the man died, so Lenin the God was born. His private life was nationalized. It became a sacred institution to consecrate the Stalinist regime.

Lenin died on 21 January 1924. At 4 p.m. he had a massive stroke, fell into a deep coma and died shortly before 7 p.m. Apart from his family and attendant doctors, the only witness to his death was Bukharin. In 1937, pleading for his own life, he claimed that Lenin had 'died in my arms'.[49]

The announcement was made by Kalinin the next day to the delegates of the Eleventh Soviet Congress, which was then in session. There were screams and sobbing noises from the hall. Perhaps because of its unexpectedness, the public showed signs of genuine grief: theatres and shops closed down for a week; portraits of Lenin, draped in red and black ribbons, were displayed in many windows; peasants came to his rest home at Gorki to pay their last respects; thousands of mourners braved the arctic temperatures to line the streets of Moscow from the Paveletsky Station to the Hall of Columns, where Lenin's body was brought to lie in state. Over the next three days half a million people queued for several hours to file past the bier. Thousands of wreaths and mournful declarations were sent by schools and factories, regiments and naval ships, towns and villages throughout Russia. Later, in the months following the funeral, there was a mad rush to erect monuments and statues of Lenin (one in Volgograd had Lenin standing on top of a giant screw), and to rename streets and institutions after him. Petrograd was renamed Leningrad. Whole factories pledged to join the party — one agitator said that this 'would be the best wreath on the coffin of the deceased leader' — and in the weeks following his death 100,000 proletarians were signed up in this so-called 'Lenin enrolment'. Many Western journalists saw this 'national mourning' as a 'post-mortem vote of confidence' in the regime. Others saw it as a cathartic release of collective grief after so many years of human suffering. People sobbed hysterically, hundreds fainted, in a way that defies rational explanation. Perhaps it shows that the cult of Lenin had already cast its spell: that however much they may have hated his regime the people still loved the 'Good Lenin', just as in the old days they had despised the boyars but loved the 'Father Tsar'.

Lenin's funeral took place on the following Sunday in arctic temperatures of minus 35° centigrade. Stalin led the guards of honour who carried the open coffin from the Hall of Columns to Red Square, where it was placed on a wooden platform. The Bolshoi Theatre orchestra played Chopin's Funeral March, followed by the old revolutionary hymn, 'You Fell Victim', and the Internationale. Then, for six hours, column after column, in all an estimated half a million people, marched past the coffin in gloomy silence, lowering their banners as they passed. At precisely 4 p.m., as the coffin was slowly lowered into the vault, sirens and factory whistles, cannons and guns, were sounded across Russia, as if letting out a huge national wail. On the radio there was a single message: 'Stand up, comrades, Ilich is being lowered into his grave.' Then there was silence and everything stopped — trains, ships, factories — until the radio broadcast once again: 'Lenin has died — but Leninism lives!'

In his will Lenin had expressed the wish to be buried next to his mother's grave in Petrograd. That was also the wish of his family. But Stalin wanted to embalm the corpse. If he was to keep alive the cult of Lenin, if he was to prove that 'Leninism lives', there had to be a body on display, one which, like the relics of the saints, was immune to corruption. He forced his plan through the Politburo against the objections of Trotsky, Bukharin and Kamenev. The idea of the embalmment was partly inspired by the discovery of Tutankhamun's tomb in 1922. Lenin's funeral was compared in *Izvestiia* to those of 'the founders of the great states in ancient times'. But it probably owed as much to Stalin's Byzantine interpretation of the Russian Orthodox rites. Trotsky, who was horrified by Stalin's plan, compared it to the religious cults of the Middle Ages: 'Earlier there were the relics of Sergius of Radonezh and Serafim of Sarov; now they want to replace these with the relics of Vladimir Ilich.' At first they tried to preserve Lenin's body by refrigeration. But it soon began to decompose. A special team of scientists (known as the Commission for Immortalization) was appointed on 26 February, five weeks after Lenin's death, with the task of finding an embalming fluid. After working round the clock for several weeks, the scientists finally came up with a formula said to contain glycerine, alcohol and other chemicals (its precise composition is still kept a secret). Lenin's pickled body was placed in a wooden crypt — later replaced by the granite mausoleum which exists today — by the Kremlin wall on Red Square. It was opened to the public in August 1924.[50]

Lenin's brain was removed from his body and transferred to the Lenin Institute. There it was studied by a team of scientists, charged with the task of discovering the 'substance of his genius'. They were to show that Lenin's brain represented a 'higher stage of human evolution'. It was sliced up into 30,000 segments, each stored between glass plates in carefully monitored conditions, so that future generations of scientists would be able to study it and discover its essential secrets. The brains of other 'undisputed geniuses' — Kirov, Kalinin, Gorky, Mayakovsky, Eisenstein and Stalin himself — were later added to this cerebral collection. They formed the beginnings of the Institute of the Brain, which still exists in Moscow today. In 1994 it publicized its final autopsy on Lenin: his was a perfectly average brain.[51] Which just goes to show that ordinary brains can sometimes inspire extraordinary behaviour.

* * *

What would have happened if Lenin had lived? Was Russia already set on the path of Stalinism? Or did the NEP and Lenin's last writings offer it a different departure? Historians should not really concern themselves with hypothetical questions. It is hard enough to establish what actually happened, let alone to prophesy what might (or in this case might not) have happened. But the consequences of Lenin's succession are perhaps large enough to warrant a few words of speculation. After all, so much of the history of the revolution has been written from the perspective of what happened inside Stalin's Russia that one may well ask whether there was any real alternative.

On the one hand it seems clear that the basic elements of the Stalinist regime — the one-party state, the system of terror and the cult of the personality — were all in place by 1924. The party apparatus was, for the most part, an obedient tool in Stalin's hands. The majority of its provincial bosses had been appointed by Stalin himself, as the head of the Orgburo, in the civil war. They shared his plebeian hatred for the specialists and the intelligentsia, were moved by his rhetoric of proletarian solidarity and Russian nationalism, and on most questions of ideology were willing to defer to their Great Leader. After all, they were the former subjects of the tsars. Lenin's last struggle for the 'democratic' reform of the party was never likely to succeed in its attempt to change this basic culture. His proposed reforms were purely bureaucratic, concerned only with the reform of the internal structure of the dictatorship, and as such were incapable of addressing the real problem of the NEP: the strained political relationship between the regime and society, the unconquered countryside in particular. Without a genuine democratization, without a basic change in the ruling attitudes of the Bolsheviks, the NEP was always doomed to fail. Economic freedom and dictatorship are incompatible in the long term.

On the other hand, there were fundamental differences between Lenin's regime and that of Stalin. Fewer people were murdered for a start. And, despite the ban on factions, the party still made room for comradely debate. Trotsky and Bukharin argued passionately with each other about the strategy of the NEP — the former favoured squeezing the foodstuffs from the peasantry whenever the breakdown of the market system threatened to slow down industrialization, whereas Bukharin was prepared to allow a slower pace of industrialization so as to maintain a market-based relationship with the peasantry — but these were still intellectual debates, both men were supporters of the NEP, and, despite their differences, neither would have dreamt of using these debates as a pretext to murder one another or to send their opponents to Siberia. Only Stalin was capable of this. He alone saw that Trotsky and Bukharin had become so blinded by their own political debates and rivalry that he could use the one to destroy the other.

In this sense Stalin's personal role was itself the crucial factor — as was, by his absence, Lenin's role as well. If Lenin's final stroke had not prevented him from speaking at the Congress in 1923, Stalin's name today would occupy a place only in the footnotes of Russian history books. But that 'if' was, if you will, in the hands of providence, and this is history not theology.

Conclusion

'I do not believe that in the twentieth century there is such a thing as a "betrayed people",' Gorky wrote to Romain Rolland in 1922. 'The idea of a "betrayed people" is nothing but a legend. Even in Africa there are only peoples not yet organized and therefore powerless politically.'[1] Gorky's view of the Russian Revolution denied that the people had been betrayed by it. Their revolutionary tragedy lay in the legacies of their own cultural backwardness rather than the evil of some 'alien' Bolsheviks. They were not the victims of the revolution but protagonists in its tragedy. This may be a painful lesson for the Russian people to learn at the end of the twentieth century. Seventy years of Communist oppression might well be thought to have earned them the right to see themselves as victims. But Russia's prospects as a democratic nation depend to a large extent on how far the Russians are able to confront their own recent history; and this must entail the recognition that, however much the people were oppressed by it, the Soviet system grew up in Russian soil. It was the weakness of Russia's democratic culture which enabled Bolshevism to take root. This was the legacy of Russian history, of centuries of serfdom and autocratic rule, that had kept the common people powerless and passive. 'And the people remained silent' was a Russian proverb — and it describes much of Russian history. To be sure, this was a people's tragedy but it was a tragedy which they helped to make. The Russian people were trapped by the tyranny of their own history.

'We are slaves because we are unable to free ourselves,' Herzen once wrote. If there was one lesson to be drawn from the Russian Revolution it was that the people had failed to emancipate themselves. They had failed to become their own political masters, to free themselves from emperors and become citizens. Kerensky's speech of 1917, in which he claimed that the Russian people were perhaps no more than 'rebellious slaves', was to haunt the revolution in succeeding years. For while the people could destroy the old system, they could not rebuild a new one of their own. None of the democratic organizations established before October 1917 survived more than a few years of Bolshevik rule, at least not in their democratic form. By 1921, if not earlier, the revolution had come full circle, and a new autocracy had been imposed on Russia which in many ways resembled the old one.

To explain this failure of democracy one must go back into Russian history. Centuries of serfdom and autocratic rule had prevented the ordinary people from acquiring the consciousness of citizens. One can draw a direct line from this serf culture to the despotism of the Bolsheviks. The abstract concept of the 'political nation', of a constitutional structure of civic rights, which had underpinned the French Revolution, remained largely alien to the Russian peasantry, confined in their isolated village worlds. The popular notion of power in Russia continued to be articulated in terms of coercive domination and quasi-religious authority derived from the traditions of serfdom and autocracy rather than in terms of a modern law-based state distributing rights and duties between citizens. The everyday power that the peasant knew — the power of the gentry captain and the police — was arbitrary and violent. To defend himself from this despotism he relied not on appeals to legal rights — indeed he replicated this despotic violence in his brutal treatment of his wife and children — but on the evasion of officialdom. Power *for* the peasant meant autonomy — it meant freedom from the state — which in itself was almost bound to give rise to a new coercive state, not least because the effect of this anarchic striving was to make the village virtually ungovernable. Indeed there were times in 1917 when the peasants themselves called for a 'master's hand', a 'popular autocracy' of the Soviets, to bring order to the revolutionary village.[2] The anarchism of the peasant was often wrapped in a cocoon of authoritarianism. Russian culture was one in which power was conceived not in terms of law but in terms of coercion and hegemony. It was a question of masters and men, of which side would prevail and dominate the other. Lenin once described it as 'who whom?' In this sense the revolution was the 'serfs' revenge', as Prince Lvov put it in the violent summer of 1917, and it led to the mass terror of the civil war.

The outcome could have been different. During the last decades of the old regime a public sphere was emerging which, given enough time and freedom to develop, might have transformed Russia into a modern constitutional society. The institutions of this civil society — public bodies, newspapers, political parties — were all growing at enormous speed. Western concepts of citizenship, of law and private property, were starting to take root. Not even the peasants were left untouched, as the story of Semenov's reform efforts in the village of Andreevskoe shows. To be sure, the new political culture was fragile and confined largely to the tiny urban liberal classes; and, as the events of 1905 showed, it was always likely to be swept away by the bloody violence of the 'serfs' revenge'. But there were enough signs of modern social evolution to suggest that Russia's power question might have been resolved in a peaceful way. Everything depended on the tsarist regime's willingness to introduce reforms. But there was the rub. Russia's last two Tsars were deeply hostile to the idea of a modern constitutional order. As Russia moved towards the twentieth century, they sought to return it to the seventeenth, ruling Russia from the court and trying to roll back the modernizing influence of the bureaucracy. The archaic privileges of the noble estate were increasingly defended by the court and its supporters against the logic of a modern social order based on the ownership of property, which Stolypin had tried to introduce. As a result a violent peasant revolution became almost inevitable. The civil liberties and parliamentary rights extracted from the Tsar in October 1905 were successively withdrawn by the autocracy once the revolutionary danger passed, with the result that a constitutional resolution of the power question became virtually impossible. Time and time again, the obstinate refusal of the tsarist regime to concede reforms turned what should have been a political problem into a revolutionary crisis: decent-minded liberals like Prince Lvov were forced into the revolutionary camp by the regime's idiotic policy of blocking the initiatives of patriotic public bodies such as the zemstvos; self-improving workers like Kanatchikov, deprived of the right to defend their class interests through legal parties and trade unions, were forced into the revolutionary underground; and those non-Russians who had wanted more rights for their national culture were driven by the tsarist policies of Russification to demand their nation's independence from Russia. The tsarist regime's downfall was not inevitable; but its own stupidity made it so.

The First World War was a gigantic test of the modern state, and as the only major European state which had failed to modernize before the war it was a test which tsarist Russia was almost bound to fail. The military establishment was too dominated by the court's own loyal aristocrats for more competent generals like Brusilov to assume command of the country's war effort; the military-industrial complex, to adopt a Cold War phrase, was too closely (and corruptly) linked with the bureaucracy to create a competitive war economy; while the tsarist regime was far too jealous of its powers to allow the sort of public war initiatives from which other powers derived so much strength. But the regime's overwhelming shortcoming was its utter failure to muster the patriotism of its peasant soldiers, who for the most part felt little obligation to fight for the Russia beyond their own native region, and even less to fight for the Tsar. This was the ultimate proof of the regime's failure to build a modern state: the ordinary peasant did not feel that he was subject to its laws. The tsarist regime paid the price for this with its own downfall — as, in their own way, did the democratic leaders of 1917. They also tied their fortunes to the war campaign in the naive belief that the 'patriotic masses' might at last be called upon to carry out their duty to the nation now that it was free. But their belief in the 'democratic nation' turned out to be equally illusory; and the summer offensive, just like all the previous fighting, underlined the fact that there were two Russias, the privileged Russia of the officers and the peasant Russia of the conscripts, which were set to fight each other in the civil war.

1917 was all about the shattering of misplaced ideals. Liberals like Lvov placed all their faith in the rule of law. They believed that all Russia's problems could be resolved peacefully by parliamentary means. This was to hope against all hope — even for an optimist like Lvov. Russia's brief experience of parliamentarism between 1906 and 1914 had done little to convince the common people that a national parliament could work for them. They were much more inclined to place their trust in their own local class organizations, such as the Soviets, as the SRs found out when the people failed to rally behind the defence of the Constituent Assembly after January 1918. The constitutional phase of the revolution had essentially been played out by 1914: the liberal Duma parties had failed to satisfy the demands of the workers and peasants for social reforms; their electoral base was in terminal decline; and the left-wing parties which based their appeal on a militant rejection of a Duma coalition with the bour-geoisie increased their support after 1912. As the reactionary but no less visionary minister Durnovo had warned the Tsar in 1914, conceding power to the Duma, which would be the cost of a defeat in the war, was almost bound to end up in a violent social revolution since the masses despised the liberal bourgeoisie and did not share their belief in political reforms. The social polarization of the war made this prophecy even more compelling. To the Okhrana it was obvious by the end of 1916 that the liberal Duma project was superfluous, and that the only two options left were repression or a social revolution. And yet, despite all the evidence, the liberal leaders of 1917 and the democratic socialists who forced them into power continued to believe that a Western constitutional settlement might be imposed upon Russia and, even more improbably, that it might be expected to hold firm and provide a viable structure for the resolution of the country's problems in the middle of a total war and social breakdown. How naive can politicians be?

Lenin might justifiably have called this the 'constitutional illusion' of the liberals. It was to place an almost mystical faith — one held religiously by Prince Lvov — in Western ideals of democracy that were quite unsuited to revolutionary Russia. And liberal efforts to impose the disciplines of statehood upon the Russia of 1917, to make it fit the patterns of 1789, only accelerated the collapse of all authority, as the common people, in reaction, carried out their own local revolutions: the attempt to carry through a military offensive led to the disintegration of the army; the attempt to regulate property relations through national laws merely had the effect of speeding up peasant land seizures. This social revolution against a state that was increasingly seen to be 'bourgeois' was the main appeal of Soviet power, at least in its early stages before the Bolsheviks took over the local Soviets. It was the direct self-rule of the workers in their factories, of the soldiers in their regiments, and of the peasants in their villages; and it was the power which this in turn gave them to dominate their former masters and class enemies.

Only a democracy that contained elements of this social revolution had any prospect of holding on to power in the conditions of 1917. The Soviet leaders, because of their own dogmatic preconceptions about the need for a 'bourgeois revolution', missed a unique chance to set up such a system by assuming power through the Soviets; and perhaps a chance to avert a full-scale civil war by combining the power of the Soviets with that of the other public bodies, such as the zemstvos and the city dumas, under the Constituent Assembly. This sort of resolution would have been acceptable to Bolshevik moderates such as Kamenev, to left-wing Mensheviks such as Martov and to any number of left-wing SRs. Undoubtedly, this would have been a precarious resolution: neither Lenin nor Kerensky would have accepted it; and there was bound to be armed opposition to it from the Right. Some sort of civil war was unavoidable. But such a democratic settlement — one which satisfied the social demands of the masses — was perhaps the only option that had any chance of minimizing the scale of that civil war. It alone could have stopped the Bolsheviks.

Bolshevism was a very Russian thing. Its belief in militant action, its insistence, contrary to the tenets of Hegel and Marx, that a revolution could 'jump over' the contingencies of history, placed it firmly in the Russian messianic tradition. Its call for All Power to the Soviets, which in the first months of Bolshevik rule entailed the direct self-rule of the peasantry, the soldiers and the workers, legitimized the anarchic tendencies of the Russian masses, and institutionalized a new *pugachevshchina*, a merciless rebellion against the state and its civilization which Gorky, like Pushkin a hundred years before, looked upon with horror as an expression of Russian barbarism. The Bolshevik Terror came up from the depths. It started as part of the social revolution, a means for the lower classes to exact their own bloody revenge on their former masters and class enemies. As Denikin noted, there was an almost 'boundless hatred' of ideas and of people higher than the crowd, of anything which bore the slightest trace of abundance, and this feeling expressed an envy and a hatred that had been accumulated by the lower classes not only over the past three years of war but also over the previous centuries. The Bolsheviks encouraged (but did not create) this hatred of the rich through their slogan 'Loot the looters!' They used it to destroy the old social system, to mobilize the lower classes against the Whites and the imperialists, and to build up their terror-based dictatorship. It in turn provided them with a powerful source of emotional support among all those downtrodden and war-brutalized people who gained satisfaction from the knowledge that the wealthy classes of the old regime were being destroyed and made to suffer, as they themselves had suffered, regardless of whether it brought any improvement in their own lot.

As a form of absolutist rule the Bolshevik regime was distinctly Russian. It was a mirror-image of the tsarist state. Lenin (later Stalin) occupied the place of the Tsar-God; his commissars and Cheka henchmen played the same roles as the provincial governors, the *oprichniki*, and the Tsar's other plenipotentiaries; while his party's comrades had the same power and privileged position as the aristocracy under the old regime. But there was a crucial difference between the two systems: whereas the élite of the tsarist regime was socially alien to the common people (and in the non-Russian borderlands was ethnically alien as well), the Soviet élite was made up for the most part of ordinary Russians (and by the natives in the non-Russian lands) who spoke, dressed and acted much like everybody else. This gave the Soviet system a decisive advantage over the Whites in the civil war: it enabled it to hold on to the emotive symbols of 'the Revolution', the Red Flag above all else, and thus to present itself as the champion of the people's cause. The 'old regime' image of the Whites, which was largely merited by their old regime mentality, and their obstinate refusal to endorse the peasant revolution on the land or to recognize the break-up of the Tsarist Empire, strengthened the Bolsheviks' propaganda claim. The emphatic rejection of the Whites by the peasantry and the non-Russians determined the outcome of the civil war.

During the first five years of the Soviet regime over one million ordinary Russians joined the Bolshevik Party. Most of these were peasant sons, literate young men like Kanatchikov and Os'kin, who had left the village to work in industry or to join the army before 1917, and who in the process came to reject the 'dark' and 'backward' ways of the old peasant Russia. Some of them returned to their native villages and were recruited by the Bolsheviks as part of the emerging rural bureaucracy. For the most part, they were committed to a cultural revolution that would bring the village closer to the towns: peasant agriculture would be modernized; the trappings of modern civilization, such as schools, hospitals and electric light, would be brought to the countryside; and the Church's influence would be reduced. The albeit very gradual spread of Bolshevism in the countryside during the 1920s was based on this revolt by the younger peasants against the old — and still largely dominant — patriarchal village; and it was in many ways a continuation of the type of reforms which peasants like Semenov had been pioneering for the past thirty years. But the majority of these peasant sons, including Os'kin and Kanatchikov, were drawn into Bolshevism from outside the village — either through the army or through industry — and it was not so much the reform of the old peasant Russia as its abolition which attracted them to the party's cause. Their allegiance to Bolshevism was intimately linked with their own self-identity as 'proletarians', which in their eyes (and in the rhetoric of the party) meant first and foremost that they were *not peasants*. They saw Bolshevism as a force of progress, both for Russia and for themselves, as a means of wiping out the brutal village world from which they had come and of replacing it with the urban culture of school and industry through which they themselves had risen to become a part of the official élite. Virtually the whole of the party's self-identity and ideology was to become based on the militant rhetoric of industrial progress, of overcoming drunkenness and superstition, and of getting Russia to catch up with the West.

This drive to overcome backwardness was the kernel of Stalin's 'revolution from above', the forcible drive towards industrialization during the first of the Five Year Plans (1928–32). As Stalin himself put it in an impassioned speech of 1931, Russia had been beaten throughout its history because it was backward, it had been beaten by the Mongol khans, the Swedish feudal lords, the Polish-Lithuanian pans, the Anglo-French capitalists, the Japanese and German imperialists: 'We are fifty to one hundred years behind the advanced countries. We must cover this distance in ten years. Either we do this, or they will crush us.' This great leap forward had a powerful appeal for all those lower-class Bolsheviks who as young men had run away from the backwardness of the Russian peasant world and who saw the revolution as a national revolt against this inheritance of poverty. By the 1920s the party rank and file had become dominated by these semi-educated types. Most of them had joined the party in the civil war and, in one form or another, owed their allegiance to Stalin's apparatus. They had little understanding of Marxist theory, and the arguments of Lenin, Trotsky and Bukharin, the three great intellectuals of the party, about the NEP's finer strategies left most of them cold. The NEP in general seemed a retreat to them after the great advances of the civil war — and in this sense the failure of the NEP was rooted in the party's own political culture. One of Stalin's shock-workers recalls how the party's youth was frustrated with the NEP:

> The Komsomols of my generation — those who met the October Revolution at the age of ten or younger — harboured a grudge against our fate. When we became politically conscious and joined the Komsomol, when we went to work in the factories, we lamented that there was nothing left for us to do because the spirit of the revolution had gone, because the harsh but romantic years of the civil war would not return, and because the older generation had left to us a boring mundane life without struggle or excitement.[3]

Stalin's revolution against the NEP promised a return to the 'heroic period' of the civil war when the Bolsheviks had conquered every fortress and pressed ahead on the road towards socialism without fear or compromise. It promised a resumption of the class war against the 'kulaks' and the 'bourgeois specialists', before whom the NEP had been in retreat, combined with a militant (if mendacious) rhetoric of proletarian hegemony.

Stalin always portrayed his revolution as a continuation of the Leninist tradition, the belief that the party vanguard's subjective will and energy could overcome all adverse objective contingencies, as Lenin himself had argued during the October seizure of power. And in a way Stalin was correct. His drive towards industrialization, sweeping aside the market and the peasantry, was in essence no different from Lenin's own drive towards Soviet power which had swept aside democracy. One could argue that the command system was itself an inevitable outcome of the contradiction of October — a proletarian dictatorship in a peasant country — a contradiction with which Lenin himself came to grapple in his final tragic years. Soviet Russia's international isolation, which stemmed directly from October, and which as a result of Allied intervention in the civil war gave rise to xenophobic paranoia about Russia's 'capitalist encirclement', reinforced the argument of the Stalinists that the 'peasant-cart-horse pace' of industrialization favoured by Bukharin under the NEP would be much too slow for Russia to catch up with — and defend itself against — the West. The social isolation of the civil war regime, which stemmed equally from October, forced it to adopt the command system, which, although relaxed briefly in the 1920s, was almost bound to be taken up again in view of the party's problems with the peasantry and the growing reluctance of its rank and file to sacrifice the ideal of rapid industrialization to the market relationship with it. Finally, there was the problem of the party's culture which haunted Lenin in his final years. Having taken power in a backward country, its lower-class recruits were bound to lack the technical expertise to take over the running of the state and industry; and yet its rhetoric of equality which had attracted them to it in the first place was also bound to set them up in opposition to the 'bourgeois specialists' upon whom the party-state was forced to depend. The NEP in this sense was a precarious and perhaps impossible balance between the revolution's need to preserve the old culture and to learn from it — what Lenin called its 'school of capitalism' — and the proletarian initiative to destroy it which, more than anything else, lay at the heart of Stalin's cultural revolution.

* * *

'Russia has changed completely in the past few years,' wrote Prince Lvov to Bakhmetev in November 1923.

> It has become a completely new Russia. The people and the power are, as usual, two different things. But Russia more than ever before belongs to the people . . . To be certain, the government is hostile to the people and their national feelings, standing as it does for international goals, it deceives the people and turns them into slaves, but nonetheless it still receives the support of this oppressed and enslaved people. They would still defend

the regime if it was attacked by an intervention or by an organization within Russia fighting under the old slogans or in the name of a restoration . . .

The people supports Soviet power. That does not mean they are happy with it. But at the same time as they feel their oppression they also see that their own type of people are entering into the apparatus, and this makes them feel that the regime is 'their own'.

The Prince's recognition of the Soviet regime was an extraordinary volte-face for a man who only five years earlier had confidently told the US President that the Russian people would rally to the Whites. His mind had been changed by the Whites' defeat — a defeat which, as he now recognized, had been brought about 'by the choice of the people' — and by the introduction of the NEP, which in his view had satisfied the main demands of his beloved peasants. 'The land question', Lvov wrote to Bakhmetev, 'has still not been resolved, it will still give rise to bloody conflicts, but in the mind of the ordinary peasant it has been decided once and for all — the land now belongs to him.'

For the exiled Prince, living now in Paris, the revolution had come full circle. In 1923 he received a letter from Popovka in Russia telling him that the peasants had divided up the land of the Lvov estate. The same peasants who forty years before had helped the young Prince and his brothers to restore its run-down farm economy had now taken possession of the estate themselves. It would surely not be over-generous to assume that Lvov was not unpleased by this news. All of his long life in public service had been dedicated to the peasantry. Even now, in his final years, he commuted every day from his small apartment in Boulogne-sur-Seine into Paris, where he worked for a Russian aid committee that collected money for the victims of the famine and helped place Russian refugees. It was a sort of Zemgor in Paris.

One Friday night in March 1925 Lvov returned from Paris feeling ill. He went to bed — and died of a heart attack in his sleep. The funeral was held at the Russian Orthodox church in rue Daru in Paris. The whole émigré community was in attendance, and the press was full of tributes to this 'sincere servant of the people'.[4]

In a more settled and peaceful country a man of Prince Lvov's background and talents might have expected to serve for many years as a minister for agriculture or, say, education. In England he would have served in the Liberal government of Gladstone or Lloyd George, and today there would no doubt be a statue to him in one of London's many parks and squares. But in the Russia of Lvov's own lifetime figures like him were destined not to last in the revolutionary storm; and today his statue does not stand in any Russian city.

Great Russian nationalism did for Brusilov what the NEP had done for Prince Lvov: it reconciled him, despite his hostility to Communism, with the Bolshevik regime. For Brusilov the collapse of the Russian Empire rather than the downfall of the monarchy had been the real tragedy of 1917; and now that the Empire had been reconstructed, with the loss of only Poland, the Baltic lands and Finland, he could rest assured that the Russian national spirit would also be restored. 'Bolshevism will one day pass away,' the General liked to prophesy, 'and all that will be left will be the Russian people and those who remained in Russia to direct the people on the correct path.' This was the basis of his National Bolshevism — that Russian patriots like him could redirect the revolution towards national ends if sufficient numbers of them joined the Red regime to turn it White from the inside.

After the campaigns against the Poles and Wrangel, the old General was put to work in the People's Commissariat of Agriculture, where he was responsible for increasing the stock of pedigree horses for the cavalry. It was a thankless task — most of the Red so-called 'military experts' seemed to think that one could mount the cavalry on peasant cart-horses — and he was relieved to be soon transferred to the Chief Inspectorate of Cavalry, where his expertise from the élite tsarist Guards was much better employed. During the latter half of 1921 Brusilov's health began to decline sharply: his wounded leg had developed gout; he was kept awake at night with chronic bronchitis; and his modest salary was not enough to keep his small flat warm. Over the next three years he constantly petitioned to be allowed to retire — he turned seventy in 1923 — but his Soviet masters would not grant him this. It was only in 1924, when Budenny was eager to purge the cavalry of all its 'White bones', that he was finally released.

To recuperate from his growing list of ailments Brusilov and his wife Nadezhda spent the following spring in the Czech town of Karlsbad, where there was a famous sanatorium. The war hero of 1916 was welcomed by the Czechs; President Masaryk, an old friend, laid on a special dinner for him in Prague Castle and (perhaps more importantly) gave him an allowance which enabled him to overcome the shock of how expensive things had become in post-war Europe. Brusilov found it 'extremely pleasant to be once again among civilized Europeans' after the long years of civil war in Russia which had done so much to sour personal relations. Indeed the only hostility he met was from the Russian émigré community, which would not forgive him for having joined the Reds. Perhaps it was this that finally convinced him to return to Russia, despite Masaryk's presidential promise that the Czechs would adopt him as their own. The émigrés, as Brusilov saw it, were the real traitors for they had placed their own class interests above those of Russia, and, even if they were to accept him, he could not bring himself to live among them. Later that summer he and his wife returned to Moscow. As Nadezhda later explained, 'he wanted to be buried in Russian soil'.[5]

Brusilov died quietly in his sleep on 17 March 1926. The funeral was a grand affair, which was only fitting for a national war hero. Red Army delegations lined the Moscow streets, military bands played the funeral march, and church choirs sang as his coffin was carried on the shoulders of six soldiers to the Novodechie Monastery, where he was laid to rest in the cemetery. Hundreds of veterans from the First World War came to Moscow for the funeral from as far afield as Nizhnyi Novgorod and Tver, and the main church was too small to contain all the mourners. The three Red Army chiefs, Voroshilov, Egorov and Budenny, each read an address in praise of Brusilov, although they refused to bow before the priests or to take part in the prayers. It was a strange mixture of the old and the new — Soviet emblems mixed with icons and crosses — as perhaps befits this strangely mixed-up man. Nadezhda thought that the whole thing was symbolic: 'the new Russia was burying the old'.[6]

Dmitry Os'kin was a son of the new Russia. He joined Brusilov's army in the First World War as an ordinary private; and yet by the time of the General's death this peasant lad was a senior figure in the Soviet military establishment. After his command of the Second Labour Army during 1920 Os'kin was given command of the Soviet Republic's Reserve Army, an important post which placed him in charge of nearly half a million men. He was held up by the regime as a shining example of a Red Commander whom it had always promised to promote from the ranks of the peasants and workers joining the Red Army in the civil war. Here was a soldier who had carried in his knapsack the baton of a general, if not of a field-marshal, and it was on the basis of this self-image as a likely peasant lad that he wrote his trilogy of military memoirs in the 1920s. Os'kin's last years are obscure. During the later 1920s he became a military bureaucrat in Moscow. He died in 1934, possibly a victim of Stalin's terror, at the tender age of forty-two.

That was certainly Kanatchikov's fate. Like Os'kin, he was a son of the new Russia whose service to the party in the civil war brought him steady promotion through the ranks. It was only fitting that this peasant-son-cum-worker whose conversion to the cause had been so bound up with his own political education should concentrate his party career in that field. In 1921, at the age of forty-two, he was appointed to the rectorship of the Communist University in Petrograd, a prestigious post which he held for the next three years. In 1924 he became the head of the Central Committee's Press Bureau; and in the next year he took over its Department of Historical Research. Not bad for a man with only four years' schooling. Kanatchikov became one of the party's leading publicists in its campaign against the Trotskyites: his *History of a Deviation* (1924) became the standard anti-Trotsky diatribe; and throughout the 1920s he produced a long line of similar hack works. But this did not save him from Stalin's firing squads in his war against the Old Bolsheviks. In 1926

Kanatchikov sided with the 'left opposition' of Zinoviev and Kamenev, who criticized the policies of Stalin and Bukharin on the grounds (and this was significant for Kanatchikov) that they were too soft on the peasantry. For this 'deviation' Kanatchikov was punished with a posting in Prague as a TASS correspondent. Two years later he was allowed to return to Russia after he had written a grovelling letter to the Central Committee in which he confessed his 'political mistakes'. His ardent support for collectivization — the logical conclusion of his rejection of the old peasant Russia — earned him a temporary 'rehabilitation'. In 1929 he was made the editor of the newly founded *Literary Newspaper*, the weekly publication of the Soviet Writers' Union. During the next few years he wrote a string of party pamphlets in support of Stalin, for which he was rewarded with a larger flat, all the usual party perks and a steady increase in his salary. But in Stalin's Russia every party member was haunted by his past and when, from the end of 1935, Stalin moved to wipe out the 'Zinovievites', Kanatchikov's star fell once again. He was arrested in 1936 and sentenced to eight years' hard labour in the Gulag. Like so many Bolshevik victims of the Great Terror, he pleaded with Stalin to intervene and grant him mercy without realizing that it was Stalin himself who had ordered his arrest. Kanatchikov had served out half his sentence by the time he died in 1940.[7]

Exile for Gorky was a form of torture. While he could not bear to live in Soviet Russia, nor could he bear to live abroad. For several years he wavered in this schizophrenic state, homesick for Russia yet too sick of it to return home. From Berlin, Gorky wandered restlessly through the spa towns of Germany and Czechoslovakia before settling in the Italian resort of Sorrento. 'No, I cannot go to Russia,' he wrote to Rolland in 1924. 'I feel like a person without a homeland. In Russia I would be the enemy of everything and everyone, it would be like banging my head against a brick wall.'

It was not so much the nature of the Soviet regime as its hostile policy towards the arts and its friendly policies towards the peasantry which kept him in exile during the NEP years. Although he had always opposed the rise of the Bolshevik dictatorship, he had also found a means of justifying it as a necessary antidote to the instinctive anarchism of the peasantry. Gorky was nothing if not contradictory. His rationalization of the Soviet regime became even more marked after Lenin's death, which filled him with remorse. Gorky had both loved and hated Lenin, and their relationship could not now be resolved. 'Yes, my dear friend,' Gorky wrote to Rolland, 'Lenin's death has been a very heavy blow for me. I loved him. I loved him with wrath.' Nina Berberova, who knew Gorky well during his years in Berlin and Marienbad, later wrote that Lenin's death had made him 'very tearful' and that he did not stop crying throughout the next weeks as he wrote his eulogistic *Memories* of him. 'Gorky was overwhelmed with repentance,' Berberova recalled. He 'reassessed his attitude to the October

Revolution and the early years of Bolshevism, to the role of Lenin, to his being right and Gorky being wrong . . . Quite sincerely he believed that Lenin's death had left him orphaned with the whole of Russia.' Gorky's *Memories* of Lenin were the first step towards his reconciliation with Lenin's successors in the Kremlin. In 1926, on Dzerzhinsky's death, he even wrote in praise of the Cheka leader ('a gifted man with a sensitive heart and a strong sense of justice'). And yet he was still not ready to return to Russia. No doubt he was frightened about what he might find there. For the Russia in his mind was always much rosier than the Russia of reality, and even Gorky, despite his ability to deceive himself, must have been aware of this. Certainly, his life-long attachment to the principles of individual liberty and human dignity was still strong enough to hold him back, especially as a creative artist whose own ability to continue to write had become increasingly dependent on the freedoms and the comforts he could enjoy only in the West. His work was flourishing in Europe, with *The Artamonov Business*, followed by the first two volumes of *The Life of Klim Samgin*, his two great didactic novels, written between 1925 and 1928. Meanwhile, in Russia the Soviet regime had drawn up an index of 'counter-revolutionary' books — which included Plato, Kant, Ruskin, Nietzsche and Tolstoy — to be withdrawn from all public libraries. Gorky was outraged by this censorship and began to write a letter to the government renouncing his Soviet citizenship. But then in anger he tore the letter up: however much he might despise the Soviet regime's 'spiritual vampirism', he could not bring himself to cut his links with it.[8]

In the end, as with Brusilov, it was good old-fashioned Russian nationalism that persuaded Gorky to return home. For one thing, he could not abide the Russian émigrés — and they could not abide him. 'To us Russians,' wrote one Paris exile in 1922, 'Gorky is one of those who are morally and politically responsible for the great calamities that the Bolshevik regime has brought to our country. Years will pass, but he will never be forgotten.'[9] The more anti-Soviet the émigrés became, the more Gorky reacted by aligning himself with the Soviet regime. Moreover, the rise of Fascism in his adopted homeland of Italy made Gorky reject all his earlier ideals — ideals that had formed the basis of his opposition to the Bolsheviks — about Europe as a historic force of moral progress and civilization. The more disillusioned he became with Fascist Europe the more he was inclined to extol Soviet Russia as a morally superior system. No doubt this was wishful thinking but in the context of the times it is understandable.

Gorky went back to Russia in 1928. After five summer trips he settled there for good in 1932. His return was hailed by the Soviet regime as a great victory in its propaganda war against the West. The prodigal son was showered with honours: the Order of Lenin was conferred on him; he was given Riabushinsky's house in Moscow, a masterpiece of the *style moderne* which he filled with treasures at the state's expense; a trilogy of films was made about his life; Tverskaia Street in Moscow became Gorky Street; and his native city of Nizhnyi Novgorod was renamed Gorkii. All these honours were designed to buy Gorky's political support. The Soviet regime to which he had returned was deeply split between Stalin's supporters and the Rightists, such as Bukharin, Rykov and Tomsky, who opposed Stalin's extreme policies on collectivization and industrialization. To begin with, Gorky occupied a place between the two, and this made him a valuable target for both sides. On the one hand Gorky saw Stalin's policies as the only way for Russia to escape its backward peasant past. Yet on the other he did not like Stalin as a human being (whereas he was close friends with Bukharin and Rykov) and opposed his policies on literature. Between 1928 and 1932, as far as one can tell from the sketchy sources, Gorky lent his support to Stalin while attempting to restrain his extreme policies. It was the same role that he had played with Lenin between 1917 and 1921. Gorky secured the release of many people from the labour camps, and, it seems likely, persuaded Stalin to write his famous article 'Dizzy with Success' in March 1930, in which the leader condemned the excesses of his local officials for the first murderous campaign of collectivization.[10]

To his former comrades, to those socialists who had made a stand against the Bolsheviks or had made a complete break with Soviet Russia, Gorky's return to Moscow seemed like a betrayal. Viktor Serge, who saw Gorky in 1930, later recalled him as a tragic figure, a once outspoken critic of the Soviet regime who had somehow allowed himself to become silenced:

What was going on inside him? We knew that he still grumbled, that he was uneasy, that his harshness had an obverse of grief and protest. We told each other: 'One of these days he'll explode!' And indeed he did, a short while before his death, finally breaking with Stalin. But all his collaborators on the *Novaia zhizn'* of 1917 were disappearing into jail and he said nothing. Literature was dying and he said nothing . . . I happened to catch a glimpse of him in the street. Leaning back alone, in the rear seat of a big Lincoln car, he seemed remote from the street, remote from the life of Moscow, reduced to an algebraic cipher of himself. He had not aged but rather thinned and dried, his head bony and cropped inside a Turkish skull-cap, his nose and cheekbones jutting, his eye-sockets hollow like a skeleton's.

But the truth was more complex — and in this was Gorky's final tragedy. Shortly after his return in 1932 he began to think that perhaps he was mistaken to remain in Russia. He found himself increasingly opposed to the Stalinist regime — but at the same time he could not escape it. He had become a Soviet institution, everywhere he went the public adored him, and although he felt himself a prisoner of this, he would or could not run away again. For one thing, his sales in Europe had declined, and he had become financially dependent on the Soviet regime. For another, Stalin would not let him go abroad.[11]

During these last years of his virtual imprisonment in Soviet Russia Gorky became a thorn in Stalin's side. He objected to the Stalinist cult of the personality and, after much prevarication, finally summoned the courage to refuse a commission to write a hagiographic portrait of Stalin, as he had once done for Lenin. Reading between the lines of Gorky's public writings one can detect a growing cynicism towards the Stalinist regime — his essays against Fascism, for example, could be read as a condemnation of all types of totalitarianism, whether in Europe or the USSR — while in what remains of his private writings one cannot miss his contempt for Stalin. After Gorky's death a large oil-skin notebook was found in his belongings in which he compared Stalin to a 'monstrous flea' which 'propaganda and the hypnosis of fear have enlarged to incredible proportions'. There is evidence to suggest that by 1934 Gorky had become involved in a plot against Stalin with the two Rightists, Rykov and Bukharin, along with Yagoda, the chief of the NKVD, and Kirov, the party boss of Leningrad, who was assassinated in 1934. This would account for the murder of Gorky's son Maxim, almost certainly on Stalin's orders, since Maxim had been acting as a messenger between his father and Kirov. It may also account for Kirov's murder — also most likely on the orders of Stalin — and perhaps for the murder of Gorky himself.[12]

The circumstances of Gorky's death remain a mystery. His health had been in decline for several years. Along with the old problem of his lungs there was a growing list of ailments, including heart disease and chronic influenza. By 1936 it had become a race to finish his great epic *The Life of Klim Samgin* before he died. 'End of the novel, end of the hero, end of the author,' Gorky said in June. Shortly after, on the 17th, he went into a fever, started spitting blood and died the next day. Those who were with him in his final days testify that Gorky died a natural death. But two years later, during the show trial of March 1938, two of Gorky's doctors were found guilty of his 'medical murder' (i.e. administering fatal doses of improper medicines) on Yagoda's orders as part of the 'plot against Soviet Power' of which Bukharin and Rykov were said to be the ringleaders. Now it may well be that Stalin merely used what in fact had been the writer's natural death as a pretext to destroy his enemies. But Gorky's involvement with the opposition makes it just as likely that Stalin murdered him. Certainly, his death came at a highly convenient time for Stalin — just two months before the show trial of Zinoviev and Kamenev which Gorky had intended to expose as a lie — and we all know what the butcher in the Kremlin did with people who got in his way. Many years later it was claimed that the doctors involved in Gorky's autopsy had found traces of poison in the corpse. Ekaterina, Gorky's widow, was quite certain that her former husband had been murdered when she was asked about this in 1963; and many Russians now agree with her.[13] The truth will probably never be known.

Gorky was buried with full Soviet honours, with Stalin himself leading the funeral procession. There was a march past in Red Square and the writer's ashes were placed in a niche in the Kremlin wall behind the Lenin Mausoleum. Thus Gorky became a Stalinist institution.

* * *

The Russian Revolution launched a vast experiment in social engineering — perhaps the grandest in the history of mankind. It was arguably an experiment which the human race was bound to make at some point in its evolution, the logical conclusion of humanity's historic striving for social justice and comradeship. Yet born as it was of the First World War, when Europe had been brought to the brink of self-destruction, it was also one that many people believed was essential at that time. By 1918 most European socialist parties subscribed to the view that capitalism and imperial competition had been the fundamental causes of the war and that to prevent another war like it they would somehow have to be swept away. It seemed to them, in short, that the old world was doomed, and that only socialism, in the words of the Internationale, could 'make the world anew'.

The experiment went horribly wrong, not so much because of the malice of its leaders, most of whom had started out with the highest ideals, but because their ideals were themselves impossible. Some people might say that it failed because Russia in 1917 had not been advanced enough for socialism, at least not on its own without the support of the more advanced industrial societies. Thus, in their view, it was Russia's backwardness and international isolation that led it down the path of Stalinism rather than the logic of the system itself. This is no doubt in part true. None of the Bolsheviks of 1917 had expected Soviet Russia to be on its own — and even less to survive if it was. Their seizure of power in October had been predicated upon the assumption that it would provide the spark for a socialist revolution throughout Europe, and perhaps throughout the colonial world. When this revolution failed to come about, they almost inevitably felt themselves bound to adopt a strategy that, if only in the interests of defence, put industrialization before all else. And yet since the Soviet model has so often led to the same disastrous ends — despite having been applied in different local forms and in such diverse places as China, south-east Asia, eastern Europe, sub-Saharan Africa and Cuba — one can only conclude that its fundamental problem is more to do with principles than contingencies.

The state, however big, cannot make people equal or better human beings. All it can do is to treat its citizens equally, and strive to ensure that their free activities are directed towards the general good. After a century dominated by the twin totalitarianisms of Communism and Fascism, one can only hope that this lesson has been learned. As we enter the twenty-first century we must try to strengthen our democracy, both as a source of freedom and of social justice, lest the disadvantaged and the disillusioned reject it again. It is by no means a foregone conclusion that the emerging civil societies of the former Soviet bloc will seek to emulate the democratic model. This is no time for the sort of liberal-democratic triumphalism with which the collapse of the Soviet Union was met in many quarters in the West. Reformed (and not-so-reformed) Communists may be expected to do well electorally — and may even be voted back into power — as long as the mass of the ordinary people remain alienated from the political system and feel themselves excluded from the benefits of the emergent capitalism. Perhaps even more worrying, authoritarian nationalism has begun to fill the vacuum left by the collapse of Communism, and in a way has reinvented it, not just in the sense that today's nationalists are, for the most part, reformed Communists, but also in the sense that their violent rhetoric, with its calls for discipline and order, its angry condemnation of the inequalities produced by the growth of capitalism, and its xenophobic rejection of the West, is itself adapted from the Bolshevik tradition.

The ghosts of 1917 have not been laid to rest.

Notes

Full details of titles are given in the Bibliography, pages 862–94.

I The Dynasty

1 *Novoe vremia*, 17, 18, 20–8 Feb 1913; Romanov, *V mramornom*, 174–7; Taneeva, *Stranitsy*, 98–101; Buchanan, *Dissolution*, 36–7.

2 *Novoe vremia*, 18–28 May 1913; *Niva*, 24, 1913, 477–9; Mossolov, *At the Court*, 240–1; Romanov, *V mramornom*, 178; Kokovtsov, *Out*, 361.

3 Whelan, *Alexander III*, 32–3.

4 'Dnevnik A. A. Polovtsova' (1902), 3, 1923: 136; Iswolsky, *Memoirs*, 264–5; Wortman, 'Moscow and St Petersburg', 253–4; Verner, *Crisis*, 79.

5 Wortman, *Scenarios*, 381–7; Wortman, 'Moscow and St Petersburg', 250–1; Spiridovitch, *Les Dernières*, 2: 253–62.

6 Wortman, 'Moscow and St Petersburg', 254–7, 260–2.

7 Rodzianko, *Reign*, 75–7.

8 Kokovtsov, *Out of My Past*, 361; Miliukov, *Political Memoirs*, 236.

9 Wortman, 'Invisible Threads', 397–8.

10 Elchaninov, *Tsar*, 148; Wortman, 'Invisible Threads', 392–3.

11 Elchaninov, *Tsar*, 2–3, 121.

12 Massie, *Nicholas*, 227; *The Times*, 22 Feb, 6 March 1913; *British Documents on Foreign Affairs*, I, A, 6: 323.

13 *Memoirs of Count Witte*, 201, 710–13; Serge, *Ville en danger*, 37.

14 Pasternak Slater (ed.), *Vanished Present*, 185–7.

15 Romanov, *Once a Grand Duke*, 168; *Memoirs of Count Witte*, 95; Zaionchkovsky, *Russian Autocracy*, 18–19.

16 Gurko, *Tsar*, 8; Wolfe, 'Autocracy', 68; Essad-Bey, *Nicholas*, 26.

17 Iswolsky, *Memoirs*, 248–50; Romanov, *Once a Grand Duke*, 178; Ferro, *Nicholas*, 16.

18 Wolfe, 'Autocracy', 66–7; Romanov, *Once a Grand Duke*, 168–9.

19 Salisbury, *Black Night*, 50–8; Iswolsky, *Memoirs*, 259–60.

20 Massie, *Nicholas*, ix; Pares, *The Fall*, 57.

21 Pares (ed.), *Letters of the Tsaritsa*, 409; Chernov, *Great Russian*, I; Trotsky, *History*, 73–4; Gurko, *Tsar*, 23–4.

22 Rogger, *Russia*, 20; Verner, *Crisis*, 64–7; Lieven, *Nicholas*, 113; Wolfe, 'Autocracy', 72.

23 Pares, *The Fall*, 157; Verner, *Crisis*, 45–59; Lieven, *Russia's Rulers*, 287–9; Lieven, *Nicholas*, 105–6, 115–16.

24 Buchanan, *Dissolution*, 36.

25 Romanov, *Once a Grand Duke*, 169; Mossolov, *At the Court*, 31; Romanov, *V mramornom*, 60; de Jonge, *Life and Times*, 110; Pares (ed.), *Letters of the Tsaritsa*, xii.

26 Chernov, *Great Russian Revolution*, 16; Gurko, *Tsar*, 69–70; Gilliard, *Thirteen Years*, 50, 83.

27 Gurko, *Tsar*, 34, 48–9; Pipes, *Russian Revolution*, 60.

28 Gilliard, *Thirteen Years*, 52.

29 Smitten, 'Poslednyi', 10: 119–20; de Jonge, *Life and Times*, 36, 45, 54; Kotsiubinskii, 'Sekret', 2 Dec 1994; Curtiss, *Church and State*, 175–7; Graham, *With the Russian Pilgrims*, 180.

30 Fuhrmann, *Rasputin*, 13–14; de Jonge, *Life and Times*, 64–5.

31 Fuhrmann, *Rasputin*, 94–8; de Jonge, *Life and Times*, 214–15.

32 Massie, *Nicholas*, 318.

33 Kotsiubinskii, 'Sekret', 2, 9 and 16 Dec 1994; de Jonge, *Life and Times*, 78, 224; Fuhrmann, *Rasputin*, 35; Pipes, *Russian Revolution*, 259–60.

34 Fuhrmann, *Rasputin*, 51, 119–20; Lockhart, *Diaries*, I: 128–9.

35 de Jonge, *Life and Times*, 204. On Marie Antoinette see Hunt, *Family Romance*, ch. 4.

36 de Jonge, *Life and Times*, 187, 201–2.

37 Simanovich, *Rasputine*, 23–4; *Moscow News*, 9, 1991; Gilliard, *Thirteen Years*, 64–5; Gurko, *Tsar*, 90; Mamantov, *Na gosudarevoi sluzhbe*, 233.

2 Unstable Pillars

1 'Dnevnik A. A. Polovtsova'; *Memoirs of Count Witte*, 88–9, 199.

2 Becker, *Nobility and Privilege*, 64; Lieven, 'Russian Civil Service', 371; Zaionchkovskii, *Pravitel'stvennyi*, 223; Raeff, 'Bureaucratic Phenomena', 401–2; Raeff, *Understanding*, 608; Mosse, 'Bureaucracy', 605–6; Ferro, *Nicholas*, 15.

3 Pipes, *Russia Under the Old Regime*, 286–7; Lieven, *Russia's Rulers*, 125–9.

4 Lieven, *Russia's Rulers*, 198–9.

5 Raeff, 'Bureaucratic Phenomena', 403–4; Verner, *Crisis*, 51–9; Rieber, 'Sedimentary Society', 358–9; Lieven, *Russia's Rulers*, 133–6; Pearson, *Russian Officialdom*, 14–15; Trubetskaia, *Kniaz*, 38.

6 Lincoln, *In the Vanguard*, 107; Whelan, *Alexander III*, 83–7.

7 Saunders, *Russia*, 213.

8 Whelan, *Alexander III*, 91; Lieven, *Russia's Rulers*, 192; Wcislo, 'Bureaucratic', 382–3.

9 Lieven, *Russia's Rulers*, 68–72, 185–92, 385.

10 Whelan, *Alexander III*, 32–3.

11 Urussov, *Memoirs*, 1, 12; Robbins, *Tsar's Viceroys*, 1–2.

12 Urussov, *Memoirs*, 96; Judge, 'Urban Growth', 48–50.

13 Clowes, Kassow, West (ed.), *Between Tsar and People*, 3–27, 41–56, 75–89; Pipes, *Struve: Liberal on the Left*, 195.

14 Chekhov, *Plays*, 322; Urussov, *Memoirs*, 100; Bok, *Reminiscences*, 100.

15 Urussov, *Memoirs*, 98; Rogger, *Russia*, 52–3.

16 Robbins, 'His Excellency', 76; *Padenie*, I: 33, 49; Robbins, *Tsar's Viceroys*, 244–5. For a contrary view on the governors, stressing their subordination to the central ministries, see Yaney, *Systematization*, 330.

17 Pipes, *Russian Revolution*, 68; Polner, *Zhiznennyi*, 55–6.

18 Rogger, *Russia*, 49; Robbins, *Tsar's Viceroys*, 183–4; Weissman, 'Regular', 46–50, 56–8; Yaney, *Systematization*, 333–7.

19 Manning, *Crisis*, 9–10; Shanin, *Russia as a 'Developing Society'*, 147.

20 BA, Bakhmeteff Collection, Box 39, Lvov, 'Moi vospominaniia', 2–4, 10, 13, 15–16, 83; Polner, *Zhiznennyi*, 24–30.

21 *Dni*, 21 March 1925; Polner, *Zhiznennyi*, 62; Obolenskii, *Moia zhizn'*, 373–4.

22 Mackenzie Wallace, *Russia*, 2: 249.

23 'Dnevnik A. A. Polovtsova' (1901), 3, 1923: 97; McKenzie, 'Zemstvo'; Stone, *Europe*, 204; Tyrkova-Williams, *To, chego*, 253.

24 Yaney, *Urge*, 51, 98, 102–8; Macey, 'Land Captains'; Semenov, *Dvadtsat'*, 86; *A Radical Worker*, 151–2.

25 *Polnoe sobranie zakonov*, 14, 1894: 11,014.

26 Keep, 'Military Style'; Verner, *Crisis*, 22–3; Elchaninov, *Tsar*, ch. 8.

27 Bushnell, *Mutiny*, 1–2.

28 Fuller, *Civil-Military*, 49, 144–53; Bushnell, *Mutiny*, vii, 15–21.

29 Wildman, *End*, I: 33–5; Bushnell, *Mutiny*, 10–11.

30 McNeal, *Tsar and Cossack*; Rieber, 'Landed', 36; Bushnell, *Mutiny*, 110–11.

31 Oberuchev, 'V dni', 60; BA, Brusilov Collection, mss. 'Gazeta "Dni" '; Grondijs, *La Guerre*, 84, 263; Shabanov, 'Kratkii', 5–9; GARF, f. 5972, op. I, d. 21a, l. 11–12; op. 3, d. 70, l. 148.

32 Brussilov, *A Soldier's Notebook*, 17.

33 Ibid., 9–10.

34 Cherniavsky, *Tsar and People*, 111–16, 119–20, and ch. I on saintly princes; Billington, *Icon*, 47, 64.

35 Curtiss, *Church and State*, 3–32, 71–2, 345–6; Freeze, 'Handmaiden'.

36 Morrison, 'Church Schools', 193; Curtiss, *Church and State*, 186.

37 Waldron, 'Religious Toleration', 104–15; Freeze, 'Handmaiden', 89–90; Freeze, 'Bringing Order'; Engelstein, *Keys to Happiness*, 27–8, 34, 51–2.

38 Freeze, ' "Going" ', 215–32; Dixon, 'Church's Social Role', 167–92.

39 *A Radical Worker*, 27–34.

40 Gorky, *My Universities*, 122; Matossian, 'Peasant Way of Life', 19–20; Belinskii, *Izbrannye*, 2: 516.

41 Lewin, *Making*, ch. 2; Ramer, 'Traditional Healers'.

42 Stepniak, *Russian Peasantry*, 372; Freeze, *Parish Clergy*; Belliutsin, *Description*, 189.

43 Curtiss, *Church and State*, ch. 5; Freeze, *Parish Clergy*, 330f, 389f; Meyendorff, 'Russian Bishops'; Simon, 'Church', 206–12.

44 Curtiss, *Church and State*, 237ff, 405.

45 Gellner, *Nations*, 6 and passim.

46 Lenin, *PSS*, 25: 66.

47 Hofer, 'Creation of Ethnic Symbols'; Anderson, *Imagined Communities*; Gellner, *Nations*, 57–8.

48 Hofer, 'Creation of Ethnic Symbols', 124.

49 Hobsbawm, *Nations*, 54; Uustalu, *History*, 121–4.

50 Davies, *God's Playground*, 2: 6–7, 19–27, 37, 352–7.

51 Seton-Watson, *Russian Empire*, 411; Reshetar, *Ukrainian*, 6–10; Shevelov, 'Language Question', 74–9, 92–3.

52 Suny, *Making*, chs 4–6; Swietochowski, *Russian Azerbaijan*, 23–6.

53 Hobsbawm, *Nations*, 48–9; Slomka, *From Serfdom*, 171.

54 Suny, 'Nationality', 232; Swietochowski, *Russian Azerbaijan*, 11.

55 Suny, *Making*, 116ff; Swietochowski, *Russian Azerbaijan*, 21; Rorlich, *Volga Tatars*, ch. 8.

56 Himka, *Galician*, xxii, chs 2–4.

57 Guthier, 'Popular Base'; Krawchenko, *Social*, 21; Shevelov, 'Language Question', 79; Guthier, 'Ukrainian Cities', 158–9; Himka, *Galician*, 158–75.

58 Krawchenko, *Social*, 264; Himka, *Galician*, 36–40.

59 Himka, *Galician*, 199–202; Trotsky, *History*, 898.

60 Maynard, *Russian Peasant*, 379.

61 Davies, *God's Playground*, 84; Rogger, *Jewish Policies*, 106.

62 *Pervaia vseobshchaia perepis'*, 1–19.

63 Pares, *Fall*, 64; Krawchenko, *Social*, 26; Lehovich, *White*, 25.

64 Rogger, *Jewish Policies*, 16, 29, 30–2; Aronson, *Troubled*, esp. 67–81, 145–60. See also Klier and Lambroza (ed.), *Pogroms*.

65 *The Diaries of Theodor Herzl*, 395; Rogger, *Russia*, 203; Rogger, 'Russian Ministers', 42.

3 Icons and Cockroaches

1 Gorky, *My Universities*, 101; Troyat, *Tolstoy*, 789.

2 Wortman, *Crisis of Russian Populism*, 10; Engelstein, *Keys to Happiness*, ch. 5.

3 Gorky, *My Universities*, 107–9, 124–5, 134, 140–50.

4 Herzen, *From the Other Shore*, 166; Dostoevsky, *Polnoe sobranie sochinenii*, 22: 44. On this whole question see also Frierson, *Peasant Icons*.

5 Aksakov, *Polnoe sobranie sochinenii*, 1: 292; Fanger, 'Peasant in Literature', 252–6.

6 Wortman, *Crisis of Russian Populism*; Glickman, 'Alternative View', 693–704; Pipes, *Russian Revolution*, 113.

7 Gorky, *Letters*, 54.

8 Dal', *Poslovitsy*, 404–5.

9 Rittikh, *Krest'ianskoe*, 135.

10 Frierson, 'Razdel', 80, 83; 'Peasant Family Divisions', 309–10.

11 Brooks, *When*, 4; Rashin, 'Gramotnost' ', 46; Eklof, *Russian*, 285, 287.

12 Eklof, *Russian*, 423.

13 Rashin, 'Gramotnost' ', 37.

14 Mironov, 'Russian Peasant Commune', 450–1; Matossian, 'Peasant Way of Life', 14–16; Engelstein, *Keys to Happiness*, 118–19, 180.

15 Matossian, 'Peasant Way of Life', 4–8; *Some Notes on Social Conditions*, 7; Gatrell, *Tsarist Economy*, 33.

16 Frank, 'Popular Justice'; Frierson, 'Crime and Punishment'.

17 Gorky, 'On the Russian', 25; Frieden, *Russian Physicians*, 189–90.

18 Gorky, 'On the Russian', 17–18; Worobec, 'Victims', 199; Gorky, *My Universities*, 119.

19 Czap, 'Peasant-Class Courts'; Frierson, 'Rural Justice'; Burds, 'Social Control', 56–9, 70–81.

20 Pipes, *Russian Revolution*, ch. 3; Herzen, *From the Other Shore*, 180.

21 Pakhman, *Obychnoe*, 1: 7–8; Efimenko, *Issledovaniia*, 2: 55–62.

22 Efimenko, *Issledovaniia*, 2: 139–41, 153–9; Pakhman, *Obychnoe*, 2: 209–11.

23 Semenov, *Dvadtsat'*, 35–40; Efimenko, *Issledovaniia*, 2: 176–9.

24 Gorky, 'On the Russian', 12; Stites, *Revolutionary Dreams*, 15–16.

25 Tsytovich, *Sel'skoe obshchestvo*, 64.

26 Pipes, *Old Regime*, 157.

27 Berberova, *Italics Are Mine*, 12–13.

28 For a classic statement of the traditional view — that the peasants were reduced to destitution by over-population, inefficient farming methods and increases in indirect taxation — see Gerschenkron, 'Agrarian Policies'. For the main 'revisionist' argument — that the rise in government receipts from indirect taxation reflected the growing spending power of the peasants, resulting from their greater productivity — see Simms, 'Crisis in Russian Agriculture'. Simms has also attacked the traditional view that the 1891 famine crisis was due to soil exhaustion and backward farming methods: 'Crop Failure'. His arguments are loosely supported by Gregory in 'Grain Marketings' and 'Russian Living Standards'. On regional variations see Wheatcroft, 'Crises and the Condition'.

29 Kushner (ed.), *Selo Viriatno*, 24; Semenov, *Dvadtsat'*, 1; Stepniak, *Russian Peasantry*, 55.

30 Shanin, *Russia as a 'Developing Society'*, 93–102.

31 Gatrell, *Tsarist Economy*, 50–1; Robinson, *Rural Russia*, 94–7; Figes, *Peasant Russia*, 11–12.

32 Shanin, *Awkward Class*, 48.

33 Polner, *Zhiznennyi put'*, 38; Shanin, *Russia as a 'Developing Society'*, 137, 147; Anfimov, *Zemel'naia arenda*, 15.

34 Mixter, 'Peasant Collective Action', 196–7; Manning, *Crisis*, 20–1.

35 Semenov, *Dvadtsat'*, 67.

36 Rashin, *Formirovanie*, 327. This was the annual number of internal passports issued to peasant migrant labourers. It probably does not account for all the five million 'peasants' registered as living in the cities by the 1897 census.

37 Koenker, 'Urbanization', 85–90; Bater, *St Petersburg*, 47, 308–9; Smith, *Red Petrograd*, 15–23.

38 *A Radical Worker*, 4, 6. See also the excellent discussion of the themes thrown up by Kanatchikov's story in Zelnik, 'Russian Bebels'.

39 Semenov, *Dvadtsat'*, 5–6; Tsarev, *Samouchka*, 17.

40 Brooks, *When*, 13, 55–6.

41 Johnson, *Peasant and Proletarian*; Bradley, *Muzhik and Muscovite*, 16–18, 27; von Laue, 'Russian Labour', 48; *A Radical Worker*, 21.

42 *A Radical Worker*, 9; Bonnell, *Roots of Rebellion*, 124; Bradley, *Muzhik and Muscovite*, ch. 6; Glickman, *Russian Factory Women*, 11–14; McKean, *St Petersburg*, 39.

43 Zelnik, *Labour and Society*, 241; Bater, *St Petersburg*, 342–4, 352–63.

44 *A Radical Worker*, 8, 21.

45 von Laue, 'A Secret Memorandum', 71; Glickman, *Russian Factory Women*, 145.

46 Tugan-Baranovsky, *The Russian Factory*, 324; McDaniel, *Autocracy*, 171.

47 This was the argument of Soviet historians, determined to show that the revolution had been supported by a genuine 'proletariat', one born in the cities and fully 'class conscious'. Most Western historians have agreed, to a greater or lesser extent, that it was the most urbanized workers who were the most militant. See, e.g., the works of Bonnell, Koenker, Smith and McKean.

48 The classic statement of this view is Haimson, 'Problem of Social Stability'. The argument was originally developed by the Mensheviks to explain why they had apparently lost ground in the cities to the Bolsheviks after 1905. It was claimed that, whereas the Mensheviks had retained support among skilled and unionized workers, the Bolsheviks had found a receptive audience for their more militant propaganda among the young and impulsive peasant-workers, who had flooded into the cities during the industrial boom. The implication was that the Bolsheviks were not supported by the genuine working class, but by a turbulent half-peasant mass susceptible to sporadic outbursts of violence and demagogic appeals.

49 See, e.g., Brower, 'Labour Violence'. For some telling criticisms see the contributions at the end of this article by Johnson, Suny and Koenker.

50 *A Radical Worker*, 59, 63, 71.

51 Babushkin, *Recollections*, 51; *A Radical Worker*, 102.

52 *A Radical Worker*, 105.

53 Gorky, *My Childhood*, 9; *A Radical Worker*, 129.

54 *A Radical Worker*, 115.

55 Sapronov, *Iz istorii rabochego dvizheniia*, 35.

56 Zelnik, 'Russian Bebels', 443; Shapovalov, *Po doroge k marksizmu*, 53–4.

4 Red Ink

1 Gernet, *Istoriia*, 3: 169; 4: 43, 45, 139.

2 Custine, *Empire*, 334; Rogger, *Russia*, 69.

3 Gernet, *Istoriia*, 5: 260–1, 306; Galili, *Menshevik*, 195; Trotsky, *History*, 812; Zelnik, 'Fate', 21.

4 Haimson (ed.), *Making*, 189.

5 Berdyaev, *Origin*, 3–5, 48–9; Tyrkova-Williams, *To, chego*, 98.

6 Hamburg, *Politics*, 14; Geifman, *Thou*, 173. I am indebted to Boris Kolonitskii for the Dubois story.

7 Berlin, *Russian Thinkers*, 122–5.

8 Szamuely, *Russian*, 201–2; Raeff, *Origins*, 123–4.

9 Blok, 'People', 359; Kelly, *Bakunin*, 97; Berdyaev, *Origin*, 32–3; Szamuely, *Russian*, 222–3.

10 Belinskii, *Polnoe sobranie sochinenii*, 10: 217–18; Lotman, 'The Poetics of Everyday Behaviour' and 'The Decembrists in Daily Life'.

11 Matthewson, *Positive Hero*, 74–7; Besancon, *Intellectual*, 118–19.

12 Ulam, *Bolsheviks*, 65; Gleason, *Young*, 296; Szamuely, *Russian*, 288; Valentinov, 'Chernyshevskii', 194; Valentinov, *Encounters*, 67–8.

13 Gleason, *Young*, 75; Szamuely, *Russian*, 321–5; Pipes, *Russia Under the Old Regime*, 271; Kelly, *Bakunin*, 94; Venturi, *Roots*, 136.

14 Koz'min, 'Molodaia Rossiia', 92, 103–4.

15 Gleason, *Young*, 341; *Pravitel'stvennyi Vestnik*, 11 July 1871; Steklow, *Bakunin*, 3: 542.

16 Malia, *Herzen*, 396, 407–8; Berlin, *Russian Thinkers*, 199.

17 Venturi, *Roots*, xxvi.

18 Bogucharskii, *Aktivnoe*, 128–9.

19 Tkachev, *Izbrannye*, 3: 64–85; Szamuely, *Russian*, 388–95.

20 Geifman, *Thou*, 21.

21 'Karl Marks', 6–10; Resis, '*Das Kapital*', 221–2.

22 Knizhnik, 'Poliakov', 76–7; Haimson (ed.), *Making*, 33; Resis, '*Das Kapital*', 226 (n. 22).

23 Haimson (ed.), *Making*, 31–3, 458; Valentinov, *Encounters*, 23; Pipes, *Struve: Liberal on the Left*, 57, 59, 61.

24 Kerensky, *Crucifixion*, 13; Volkogonov, *Lenin*, 6, 8–9, 13.

25 RTsKhIDNI, f. 2, op. 2, d. 125, l. 1; Volkogonov, *Lenin*, xxxvii, 6, 52; Valentinov, *Maloznakomyi*, 34.

26 Valentinov, *Encounters*, 107; *NZh*, 7 Nov 1917.

27 Ulam, *Bolsheviks*, 12, 162; Gorev, *Iz partiinogo*, 10; Potresov, *Posmertnyi*, 21.

28 Potresov, *Posmertnyi*, 294; Ulam, *Bolsheviks*, 118.

29 McNeal, *Bride*, 65.

30 Krupskaia, *Vospominaniia*, 35.

31 Lenin, *PSS*, 6: 9; Haimson (ed.), *Making*, 103, 105, 126.

32 Ulam, *Bolsheviks*, 178, 186; Valentinov, *Encounters*, 112–14; Haimson (ed.), *Making*, 170–1.

33 Valentinov, *Encounters*, 40.

5 First Blood

1 Robbins, *Famine*, 1–2, 11–12, 59–64, 171; Simms, 'Crop Failure', 237.

2 Bogdanovich, *Tri Poslednikh*, 149; Petrunkevich, 'Iz zapisok', 275.

3 Wildman, *Making*, 6–7; Polner, *Zhiznennyi put'*, 52; Frieden, *Russian Physicians*, ch. 6; Petrunkevich, 'Iz zapisok', 276.

4 *Letters of Anton Chekhov*, 237.

5 Tolstoi, *Pis'ma L. N. Tolstogo k zhene*, 208, 363; Semenov, 'Vospominaniia o L. N. Tolstogom', 55–6.

6 Robbins, *Famine*, 177–83; Frieden, *Russian Physicians*, ch. 6; Balzer, 'Problem of Professions', 189–90; Seregny, *Russian Teachers*, 10–11.

7 Haimson (ed.), *Making*, 101.

8 Simms, 'Famine and the Radicals', 16; Martov, *Zapiski*, 94, 137.

9 Haimson (ed.), *Making*, 68.

10 Freeze, 'Soslovie', 11–36; Haimson, 'Problem of Social Identities', 1–20.

11 Kassow, *Students*, 16, 22.

12 For an excellent discussion of the problems confronting the formation of a middle-class identity see Clowes, Kassow and West (ed.), *Between Tsar and People*.

13 Galai, *Liberation*, 54.

14 Manning, 'Zemstvo and Politics', 139–40; Emmons, 'Zemstvo', 433–7; Galai, *Liberation*, 24–55.

15 Kerensky, *Crucifixion*, 78–9.

16 *Istochnik*, 3, 1994: 5; GARF, f. 1807, op. I, d. 382, l. 14.

17 GARF, f. 1807, op. I, d. 382, l. 56.

18 Svobodov, 'Gor'kii i studencheskoe', 71; Pipes, *Struve: Liberal on the Left*, 271–2; Tyrkova-Williams, *Na putiakh*, 72–3; Ivanov-Razumnik, *Memoirs*, 3.

19 *Memoirs of Count Witte*, 369; White, *Diplomacy*, 78–81.

20 *Memoirs of Count Witte*, 384; Pasternak Slater (ed.), *Vanished Present*, 88; Ascher, *Revolution*, 47; Galai, *Liberation*, 198–205; Polner, *Zhiznennyi'*, 67.

21 *Memoirs of Count Witte*, 382–3.

22 Bar-Yaacov, *Handling*, 70; Owen, *Capitalism*, 69; Petrunkevich, 'Iz zapisok', 343; Gurko, *Figures and Features*, 253.

23 Ascher, *Revolution*, 54.

24 'Dnevnik kn. Ekateriny Alexeevny Sviatopolk-Mirskoi', 243, 251; Verner, *Crisis*, 115–17.

25 Galai, *Liberation*, 214–19; Manning, *Crisis*, 74–5, 83–5; Gor'kii, 'Pis'ma k E. P. Peshkovoi' 132.

26 Verner, *Crisis*, 137–40; *Memoirs of Count Witte*, 399; Gurko, *Figures and Features*, 304.

27 Sablinsky, *Road to Bloody Sunday*, 222.

28 McDaniel, *Autocracy*, 64–89; Sablinsky, *Road to Bloody Sunday*, 103–5.

29 Sablinsky, *Road to Bloody Sunday*, 126, 344.

30 Ibid., 212–13, 218.

31 Ibid., 241–3.

32 *M. Gor'kii v epokhu revoliutsii 1905–1907*, 30.

33 Sablinsky, *Road to Bloody Sunday*, 251–2, 273.

34 *M. Gor'kii v epokhu revoliutsii 1905–1907*, 33; Gippius, *Dmitrii*, 132; Ascher, *Revolution*, 98.

35 Gor'kii, 'Pis'ma k E. P. Peshkovoi', 148.

36 Gogol, 'Maksim Gor'kii', 7–19.

37 Levin, *Stormy*, 98–100; Gorky, *Letters*, 32; *NZh*, 25 April 1917.

38 GARF, f. 1807, op. I, d. 382, l. 250; Pasternak Slater (ed.), *Vanished Present*, 110; Ascher, *Revolution*, 94.

39 Galai, *Liberation*, 245–8; Stites, *Women's Liberation*, 198; Balzer, 'Problem of Professions', 191–3; Ascher, *Revolution*, 129.

40 *M. Gor'kii v epokhu revoliutsii 1905–1907*, 55; Gorky, *Letters*, 13.

41 Perrie, 'Russian Peasant', 123–55; Bok, *Reminiscences*, 122–5; Shanin, *Russia, 1905–7*, 94; Mixter, 'Peasant Collective Action', 215; Manning, *Crisis*, ch. 8.

42 Seregny, 'Peasants and Politics', 341–77; Mixter, 'Peasant Collective Action', 194; Shanin, *Russia, 1905–7*, 99–119.

43 Pavlov, *Markovskaya*, 13–14, 18–22, 44, 53; Shanin, *Russia, 1905–7*, 109–11; TsGALI, f. 66, op. I, d. 296, l. 2; d. 312.

44 Bushnell, *Mutiny*, 52.

45 Ibid., 55–6, 60–5; Ascher, *Revolution*, 170–2.

46 Ascher, *Revolution*, 157, 159–60; Galai, *Liberation*, 205–6.

47 *Memoirs of Count Witte*, 406–7; Sablinsky, *Road to Bloody Sunday*, 277–8, 280–1; Verner, *Crisis*, 163; Ascher, *Revolution*, 112.

48 Verner, *Crisis*, 179–80; GARF, f. 1807, op.I, d. 382, l. 202.

49 Gor'kii, 'Pis'ma k E. P. Peshkovoi', 162.

50 Suhr, *1905*, 342–4; Ascher, *Revolution*, 132.

51 For a brilliant discussion of the relationship between 'revolutionary violence' and 'hooliganism' in 1905 see Neuberger, *Hooliganism*, ch. 2.

52 Ascher, *Revolution*, 211–17; Engelstein, *Moscow*, 123; 'Khar'kov v oktiabre'; Lvov–Roga-chevskii, 'Oktiabr'skie dni', 80.

53 Ascher, *Revolution*, 217–21; Trotsky, *My Life*, 186. There is some disagreement over whether Lenin ever spoke in the Petrograd Soviet of 1905. A number of sources state that Lenin spoke there once or twice but there is no definite corroboration.

54 Trotsky, *My Life*, 172–4; Haimson (ed.), *Making*, 324.

55 Verner, *Crisis*, 227; *Letters of Tsar Nicholas and the Empress Marie*, 188.

56 *Memoirs of Count Witte*, 515.

57 Petrunkevich, 'Iz zapisok', 410.

58 Obolenskii, *Moia zhizn'*, 373–4; Polner, *Zhiznennyi*, 97, 110.

59 Emmons, *Formation*, 41–4, 62–72, 146–7; Rosenberg, *Liberals*, 12–24.

60 Emmons, *Formation*, 147, 217–22.

61 *Memoirs of Count Witte*, 501–2; Gurko, *Figures and Features*, 404–5.

62 Miliukov, *Political Memoirs*, 65.

63 Rawson, *Russian Rightists*, 21–33, 46–72, 142–8.

64 Ibid., 137–8; Lambroza, 'Pogroms', 227–8, 233–7; Weinberg, 'Pogrom', 262, 268–9; *Letters of Tsar Nicholas and the Empress Marie*, 190–1.

65 Haimson, (ed.), *Making*, 180–3; Engelstein, *Moscow*, 140; Baring, *A Year in Russia*, 29–30.

66 Zenzinov, *Perezhitoe*, 225; Gul', 'Byloe'.

67 Haimson, (ed.), *Making*, 203; Gor'kii, 'Pis'ma k K. P. Piatnitskomu', 193.

68 Engelstein, *Moscow*, 205, 222; Ascher, *Revolution*, 315–22.

69 'Dnevnik A. A. Polovtsova', (1906), 4, 1923: 99; Bing (ed.), *Secret Letters*, 206;

Manning, *Crisis*, 173; Shanin, *Russia, 1905–7*, 95; Ferro, *Nicholas II*, 118–19; Gurko, *Figures and Features*, 446.

70 Gor'kii 'Pis'ma k E. P. Peshkovoi', 170.

71 Troyat, *Gorky*, 100–6.

72 Gor'kii, 'Pis'ma k pisatel'iam', 132; Pasternak, *Stikhotvoreniia*, 204.

73 Pares, *My Russian Memoirs*, 161–2.

74 Miliukov, *Political Memoirs*, 42; Trotsky, *My Life*, 194–5; Deutscher, *Prophet Armed*, 148.

75 Deutscher, *Prophet Armed*, 168.

76 Naumov, *Iz ustelevshikh*, 2: 72; Manning, *Crisis*, 146; Neuberger, *Hooliganism*, 114, 118–19. See also Weissman, 'Rural Crime'.

77 Shanin, *Russia, 1905–7*, 198; Polner, *Zhiznennyi*, 110–11; BA, Polner Collection, Box 2, Death of Lvov.

78 Neuberger, *Hooliganism*, 237 (and chs 4 and 5); Bely, *Petersburg*, 11; Engelstein, *Keys to Happiness*, 240, 257–60.

79 *Russkie vedomosti*, 16 Nov 1905.

80 *M. Gor'kii v epokhu revoliutsii*, 52.

81 Kelly, 'Self-Censorship', 201; *Vekhi*, 89.

82 Lenin, *PSS*, 41: 8–9.

6 Last Hopes

1 Obolenskii, *Moia zhizn'*, 338–9; Kokovtsov, *Out of My Past*, 129–31.

2 Szeftel, *Russian Constitution*, 119–20, 177–8, 260; Verner, *Crisis*, 300–2.

3 Gurko, *Figures and Features*, 23–5, 27–30. For a more positive assessment of the State Council see Lieven, *Russia's Rulers*.

4 Obolenskii, *Moia zhizn'*, 350.

5 Kryzhanovskii, *Vospominaniia*, 81–2; TsGALI, f. 66, op. 1, d. 324.

6 Baring, *What I Saw in Russia*, 255.

7 Obolenskii, *Moia zhizn'*, 341.

8 Manning, *Crisis*, 199, 218; Hosking and Manning, 'What Was the United Nobility?'; Atkinson, *End*, 53.

9 BA, Polner collection, Box 2, Lvov's Death; Rosenberg, *Liberals*, 17–38.

10 Pares, *Fall*, 111.

11 Bok, *Reminiscences*, 122–5.

12 Ibid., 128.

13 Stolypine, *L'Homme*, 144.

14 Pares, *Memoirs*, 126; Kryzhanovskii, *Vospominaniia*, 210, 219.

15 Leontovitsch, *Geschichte*, 400.

16 Pares, *Memoirs*, 139.

17 Hosking, *Constitutional Experiment*, ch. 4.

18 Edelman, *Gentry Politics*, 10.

19 Korros, 'Landed Nobility', 134–8; Weissman, *Reform in Tsarist Russia*, 198–202; Edelman, *Gentry Politics*, 118–23; Bok, *Reminiscences*, 263.

20 Kokovtsov, *Out of My Past*, 267–8; Miliukov, *Political Memoirs*, 229–30.

21 BA, Kryzhanovsky Collection, Box 2, mss. on Stolypin; Serebrennikov, *Ubiistvo*, 191; Bok, *Reminiscences*, 278–80.

22 Haimson, 'Social Stability', I: 619–42. For a rather different view of working-class politics in these years see McKean, *St Petersburg*, esp. chs 4–5.

23 Semenov's story is based on his own account in 'Legko'; 'Novye khoziaeva'; 'Obnovlenie'; *Dvadtsat' piat' let*; and on his personal papers in TsGALI.

24 TsGALI, f. 200, op. I, d. 80, l. 3.

25 Ibid., f. 2226, op. I, d. 13, l. 354, 360; *Narodnyi pisatel'*, 7.

26 TsGALI, f. 66, op. I, d. 312, l. 4–5.

27 Ibid., f. 200, op. I, d. 80, l. 3; f. 2226, op. I, d. 1067; f. 66, op. I, d. 296, l. 5; f. 122, op. 3, d. 13, l. 5–7; Semenov, 'Legko', 253.

28 Robinson, *Rural Russia*, 194.

29 TsGALI, f. 122, op. I, d. 1197, l. 42.

30 *Agrarnoe dvizhenie v Rossii v 1905–1906*, 151.

31 Figes, *Peasant Russia*, 57–61; Macey, 'Peasant Commune', 221–8; Yaney, *Urge*, 178–84.

32 Yaney, *Urge*, 156–60. The statistics of the reforms are notoriously difficult. The best general survey is Atkinson, 'Statistics'. For a more recent survey at the local level see Pallot and Shaw, *Landscape*, ch. 7.

33 Sternheimer, 'Administering', 286–98; Macey, 'Peasant Commune', 228–30.

34 Danilov, 'Ob istoricheskikh', 106. Earlier figures, which tended to be rather higher, were, Danilov shows, based on computational errors.

35 Semenov, 'Novye khoziaeva', 275.

36 Samuel, *Blood Accusation*, 17.

37 Cohn, *Warrant for Genocide*, 90–8, 108–25; Pipes, *Russia Under the Bolshevik Regime*, 255–7; Engelstein, *Keys to Happiness*, 299–300, 321–6; *Diaries of Theodor Herzl*, 394.

38 Tager, *Decay*, 29; Samuel, *Blood Accusation*, 26–7.

39 Tager, *Decay*, 39–40, 206; Samuel, *Blood Accusation*, 55.

40 Rogger, *Jewish Policies*, 40–55; Gruzenberg, *Yesterday*, 107; Tager, *Decay*, 147–65, 178.

41 Hosking, *Constitutional Experiment*, ch. 7; Haimson, 'Social Stability', I: 619–42; McKean, *St Petersburg*, 149.

42 Edelman, *Gentry Politics*, 176–7; Rogger, *Jewish Policies*, 208–9; Rawson, *Russian Rightists*, 65–72.

43 Pares, *Fall*, 122.

44 Rogger, *Russia*, 168.

45 Hosking, *Constitutional Experiment*, 233; Struve, 'Velikaia Rossiia', 144–6; Seletskii, 'Obrazovanie', 32–48.

46 Lieven, *Russia and the Origins*, 37, 131–3; *Novoe vremia*, 6 March 1914; Hutchinson, 'Octobrists', 225.

47 Lieven, *Russia and the Origins*, 71–2, 92–101; Brussilov, *A Soldier's Notebook*, 38.

48 Lieven, *Russia and the Origins*, 65; Kerensky, *Crucifixion*, 172.

49 Golder, *Documents*, 21.

50 Bark, 'Iiul' 1914', 22; Spring, 'Russia and the Coming of War', 66.

51 Sazonov, *How the War Began*, 46–7; Paléologue, *An Ambassador's Memoirs*, I: 43–4.

52 Brussilov, *A Soldier's Notebook*, 40–1; Gilliard, *Thirteen Years*, 111.

53 Gippius, *Siniaia kniga*, 9; *Russian Schools*, 166–7; Troyat, *Gorky*, 123.

54 Pearson, *Russian Moderates*, 12–13, 15–16.

7 A War on Three Fronts

1 GARF, f. 5972, op. 1, d. 26, ll. 3–5.

2 Stone, *Eastern Front*, 13–14.

3 RGVIA, f. 162, op. 1, d. 17, l. 97; d. 4, l. 108–10; Gourko, *Memories*, 11; Oberuchev, *V dni revoliutsii*, 62; Sokolov, 'Aleksei', 83; BA, Brusilov Collection, mss. 'Gazeta dni'.

4 Lincoln, *Passage*, 83; GARF, f. 5972, op. 3, d. 70, l. 11–13.

5 Stone, *Eastern Front*, 61–8; Lincoln, *Passage*, 63–6, 69–78; Ironside, *Tannenberg*, 245.

6 Knox, *With the Russian Army*, 1: 90.

7 Golovin, *Russian Army*, 45–74; Brussilov, *A Soldier's Notebook*, 93–4.

8 Denikin, *Ocherki*, 1: 19; Heenan, *Russian*, 90; Brussilov, *A Soldier's Notebook*, 37, 39.

9 Brussilov, *A Soldier's Notebook*, 98; Lincoln, *Passage*, 124.

10 Stone, *Eastern Front*, 52; Knox, *With the Russian Army*, 1: 42, 46.

11 Brussilov, *A Soldier's Notebook*, 133, 330.

12 Ibid., 143.

13 Knox, *With the Russian Army*, 1: xxv; Lincoln, *Passage*, 71–2; Os'kin, *Zapiski soldata*, 259–60; Brussilov, *A Soldier's Notebook*, 64–5; Stone, *Eastern Front*, 50–1, 148, 167–8.

14 Sidorov, *Ekonomicheskoe*, 11–12; Lincoln, *Passage*, 106; Knox, *With the Russian Army*, 1: 220; Chaadaeva (ed.), 'Soldatskie pis'ma', 127–8.

15 Brussilov, *A Soldier's Notebook*, 126–7; Lincoln, *Passage*, 105; Chaadaeva (ed.), 'Soldatskie pis'ma', 124–5.

16 GARF, f. 5972, op. 3, d. 70, l. 13–14; Rodzianko, *Reign of Rasputin*, 115–17.

17 Wildman, *End*, 1: 100–2.

18 RGVA, f. 37976, op. 9, d. 4218.

19 Os'kin, *Zapiski soldata*, 143–4, 171, 212–13, 218–21, 243–5.

20 Chaadaeva (ed.), 'Soldatskie pis'ma', 158; Os'kin, *Zapiski soldata*, 223.

21 Chaadaeva (ed.), 'Soldatskie pis'ma', 126–7.

22 Lincoln, *Passage*, 127; Denikin, *Ocherki*, 1: 2: 29–30; Knox, *With the Russian Army*, 1: 317–18; 2: 410.

23 GARF, f. 5972, op. 3, d. 70, l. 82.

24 Lemke, *250 dnei*, 223–55; Knox, *With the Russian Army*, 1: 324–8.

25 Lincoln, *Passage*, 152; Iakhontov, 'Tiazhelye dni', 33, 37, 74.

26 Os'kin, *Zapiski soldata*, 234; RGVIA, f. 162, op. 1, d. 18, l. 4; d. 17; Pireiko, *Na fronte*, 35–6.

27 Golovin, *Russian Army*, 121–2; Os'kin, *Zapiski soldata*, 276–302, 318–33; Lincoln, *Passage*, 146–7.

28 Brussilov, *A Soldier's Notebook*, 170–1, 185.

29 Iakhontov, 'Tiazhelye dni', 54, 98.

30 RGVIA, f. 162, op. 1, d. 15, l. 6; HLRO, 206: Stow Hill Papers. DS 2/2, Box 8, O. L. Kerenskaia, 'Obryvki vospominaniia', 2.

31 Polner, Obolenskii and Turn (ed.), *Russian Local Government*, 54ff, 100–1; Gleason, 'All-Russian', 365–82; Cherniavsky (ed.), *Prologue*, 228.

32 Polner, *Zhiznennyi*, 174–88; Obolenskii, *Moia zhizn'*, 374.

33 Grave (ed.), *Burzhuazia*, 29–31; Polner, Obolenskii and Turn (ed.), *Russian Local Government*, 300–3; Polner, *Zhiznennyi*, 210.

34 Stone, *Eastern Front*, 156, 199–202; Siegelbaum, *Politics of Industrial Mobilization*, 38; Pearson, *Russian Moderates*, 24–47.

35 Pearson, *Russian Moderates*, 46–53; Hamm, 'Liberal Politics'; Rosenberg, *Liberals*, 39–42.

36 Pares (ed.), *Letters of the Tsaritsa*, 125; Iakhontov, 'Tiazhelye dni', 107–36.

37 Grave (ed.), *Burzhuazia*, 59–60; Pares (ed.), *Letters of the Tsaritsa*, 100, 166.

38 *Russkie vedomosti*, 27 Sep 1915.

39 Grave (ed.), *Burzhuazia*, 62–3.

40 Pares (ed.), *Letters of the Tsaritsa*, 114, 152, 221, 409.

41 Pares, *Fall*, 317; Rodzianko, *Reign of Rasputin*, 178.

42 Knox, *With the Russian Army*, 2: 412; Pares (ed.), *Letters of the Tsaritsa*, 134, 301.

43 Knox, *With the Russian Army*, 2: 416.

44 Stone, *Eastern Front*, 234; Brussilov, *A Soldier's Notebook*, 199–200.

45 Brussilov, *A Soldier's Notebook*, 215; GARF, f. 5972, op. 3, d. 70, l. 80.

46 Stone, *Eastern Front*, 235.

47 Sokolov, 'Aleksei', 213–14; Golovin, 'Brusilov Offensive', 577–81.

48 GARF, f. 5972, op. 3, d. 70, l. 49, 155; Stone, *Eastern Front*, 249; RGVIA, f. 162, op. 1, d. 17, l. 159–60.

49 Hindenburg, *Out of My Life*, 158; Brussilov, *A Soldier's Notebook*, 238–51, 267; Pares (ed.), *Letters of the Tsaritsa*, 346.

50 Brussilov, *A Soldier's Notebook*, 256; Pares, *Fall*, 364–70; Lincoln, *Passage*, 257–8.

51 RGVIA, f. 162, op. 1, d. 10; Brussilov, *A Soldier's Notebook*, 248, 272.

52 Knox, *With the Russian Army*, 2: 466–7, 472.

53 RTsKhIDNI, f. 75, op. 1, d. 14; Golovin, *Russian Army*, 246.

54 CUL, Templewood Papers, XXI: I: 24; Pares, *Fall*, 301–2.

55 Katkov, *Russia 1917*, 157–60; Massie, *Nicholas*, 152, 299, 346–7; Kerensky, *Crucifixion*, 196–8.

56 Florinsky, *End*, 141; Pearson, *Russian Moderates*, 109–10; Katkov, *Russia 1917*, 218.

57 Pares (ed.), *Letters of the Tsaritsa*, 394; BA, Brusilov collection, Memoirs, 3: 46; Pares, *Fall*, 381.

58 Pearson, *Russian Moderates*, 117–18. I am indebted to Boris Kolonitskii for the point about the teachers.

59 Voeikov, *S tsarem*, 185.

60 Pearson, *Russian Moderates*, 122, 137; Hasegawa, *February*, 182.

61 GARF, f. 5972, op. 1, d. 219, l. 161. On the historiography of these plots see Hasegawa, *February*, 187–8.

62 Kotsiubinskii, 'Sekret', 27, 29 Dec 1994; Purishkevich, *Ubiistvo*, 81; Purishkevich, *Dnevnik*, 141.

63 Romanov, *V mramornom*, 307; Lincoln, *Passage*, 310–11.

64 Trotsky, *My Life*, 276; Deutscher, *Prophet Armed*, 241.

65 Serge and Sedova, *Life and Death*, 30.

66 Trotsky, *My Life*, 283.

67 Ibid., 219.

68 Cohen, *Bukharin*, 22; Trotsky, *My Life*, 243; Kollontai, *Iz moei zhizni*, 146; Clements, *Bolshevik Feminist*, 84.

69 Ermanskii, *Iz perezhitogo*, 119.

70 Gankin and Fisher (ed.), *Bolsheviks and the World War*, 322.

71 Dazhina and Tsivlina, 'Iz arkhiva A. M. Kollontai', 1: 227; 2: 227.

72 Trotskii, *Sochineniia*, 8: 66–7; Deutscher, *Prophet Armed*, 216–23.

73 Trotsky, *My Life*, 280; Dazhina, 'Amerikanskie dnevniki'; Ziv, *Trotskii*, 67; Draper, *Roots*, 77.

74 Shliapnikov, *On the Eve*, 27–8, 38; Burdzhalov, *Russia's Second Revolution*, 26; McKean, *St Petersburg*, ch. 12.

75 RGIA, f. 806, op. 5, d. 10313, ll. 12–13; Voronov, 'Analiz', 56–7; Minor, *Novye formy*, 1–16; Mendel'son, *Itogi*, 22–4; Binshtok and Kaminskii, *Narodnoe pitanie*, 45–52.

76 Antsiferov et al (ed.), *Russian Agriculture*, 140, 151–2; Anfimov, *Rossiiskaia derevnia*, 241–2, 280ff.

77 Antsiferov et al (ed.), *Russian Agriculture*, 222.

78 Leiberov and Rudachenko, *Revoliutsiia i khleb*, 17–20.

79 Strumilin, *Izbrannye proizvedeniia*, 5: 187; McKean, *St Petersburg*, 337–8; Koenker, *Moscow Workers*, 84–7; Hasegawa, *February Revolution*, 67–9; Binshtok and Kaminskii, *Narodnoe pitanie*, 24–35; Gernet, *Moral'naia statistika*, 97; Gor'kii, 'Pis'ma k E. P. Peshkovoi', 176.

80 Shliapnikov, *On the Eve*, 75, 94; Hasegawa, *February Revolution*, 87ff; Smith, *Red Petrograd*, 48–53; Koenker, *Moscow Workers*, 88–90; McKean, *St Petersburg*, chs 13–14; Strumilin, *Izbrannye proizvedeniia*, 5: 186–7.

81 Siegelbaum, *Politics of Industrial Mobilization*, ch. 7; Hasegawa, *February Revolution*, 123–32.

82 Ivanov, 'Volnenie', 171–2.

83 Hasegawa, *February Revolution*, 159–68; Shklovsky, *Sentimental Journey*, 8.

84 Wildman, *End*, I: 105ff; Chaadaeva, *Armiia nakanune*, 65–9; 'Soldatskie pis'ma', 134–59; Brussilov, *A Soldier's Notebook*, 282.

85 Sidorov, *Revoliutsionnoe*, 221.

8 Glorious February

1 Balk, 'Poslednie', 28; Hasegawa, *February Revolution*, 199; Heald, 'Witness', 45; *Trudy tsentral'nogo*, 7: I: 252; Gor'kii, 'Pis'ma k E. P. Peshkovoi', 192.

2 Lih, *Bread*, 12; Balk, 'Poslednie', 28; Hasegawa, *February Revolution*, 200.

3 Balk, 'Poslednie', 26–9; Hasegawa, *February Revolution*, 21–4.

4 Hasegawa, *February Revolution*, 232–8; Balk, 'Poslednie', 31; LRA, MS 790/20 (letter by Marguerite Bennet, 15 March 1917); BC, Ransome Papers, Telegraph 50, 10 March 1917; RGIA, f. 1282, op. 1, d. 741, l. 41–2.

5 Hasegawa, *February Revolution*, 247–53; Balk, 'Poslednie', 35–6.

6 BA, Finland Regiment Collection, Box 10, D. I. Khodnev, 'Fevral'skaia revoliutsiia

1917 g. i zapasnyi battalion leib-gvardii finlandskogo polka'; Hasegawa, *February Revolution*, 253–5; RGIA, f. 1282, op. I, d. 741, l. 89.

7 Balk, 'Poslednie', 39–42; Sukhanov, *Russian*, 5; Hasegawa, *February Revolution*, 258.

8 *Padenie*, I: 190.

9 Hasegawa, *February Revolution*, 267–9; Martynov, *Tsarkaia armiia*, 85; Kirpichnikov, 'Vosstanie', 7–9.

10 Cherniaev, 'Vosstanie'; Martynov, *Tsarskaia armiia*, 87–9; *Padenie*, I: 195–200.

11 Kirpichnikov, 'Vosstanie', 10–15.

12 Kantorovich, 'Fedor Linde', 221–38; *Kievskaia mysl'*, 3 Sep 1917; Sokolov, *White Nights*, 21–2.

13 Balk, 'Poslednie', 45; Hasegawa, *February Revolution*, 404–5; Kantorovich, 'Fedor Linde', 239.

14 Jones, *Russia in Revolution*, 105–6; Shklovsky, *Sentimental*, 15.

15 Kantorovich, 'Fedor Linde', 238; Romanov, *V mramornom*, 318; Gorky, *Fragments*, 167; Bulgakov, 'Revoliutsiia', 9–10; Jones, *Russia in Revolution*, 123–4; Raskolnikov, *Kronstadt*, 4; Shklovsky, *Sentimental*, 16.

16 Jones, *Russia in Revolution*, 108; Zenzinov, 'Fevral'skie dni', 5: 219–20; Gorky, *Fragments*, 164; Berkman, *Bolshevik Myth*, 203.

17 Balk, 'Poslednie', 55; Shulgin, *Dni*, 162–7; *Petrogradskii sovet*, I: 34–5, 46.

18 Sukhanov, *Russian*, 16; *The Times*, 17 March 1917; Jones, *Russia in Revolution*, 127; Bulgakov, 'Revoliutsiia', 28.

19 BA, Finland Regiment Collection, Box 10, D. I. Khodnev, 'Fevral'skaia revoliutsiia 1917 g. i zapasnyi battalion leib-gvardii finlandskogo polka', 63.

20 On the body language of the crowds see my forthcoming book (with Boris Kolonitskii), *Interpreting the Russian Revolution: Essays on the Language, Rites and Symbols of 1917*.

21 Pitcher (ed.), *Witnesses*, 14; *The Times*, 16 March 1917.

22 RGIA, f. 1278, op. 10, d. 7, l. I; Bulgakov, 'Revoliutsiia', 7, 9–10; Jones, *Russia in Revolution*, 134.

23 Jones, *Russia in Revolution*, 119; GARF, f. 102, op. 341, d. 57, l. 24–9; f. 5849, op. 2, d. 33, l. 4–5; Bulgakov, 'Revoliutsiia', 14–17; *RPG*, I: 140; Anet, *Révolution*, I: 129–30.

24 Sukhanov, *Russian*, 78, 95; Gor'kii, 'Pis'ma k E. P. Peshkovoi', 194.

25 See, for example, Simon Schama's condemnation of crowd violence (and thus by implication the whole revolution) in *Citizens: A Chronicle of the French Revolution*, London, 1989. Richard Pipes's approach in *The Russian Revolution* is coloured by the same prejudice against violence.

26 Sukhanov, *Russian*, 96.

27 Sorokin, *Leaves*, 14–16; Bulgakov, 'Revoliutsiia', 19; Jones, *Russia in Revolution*, 163.

28 Mstislavskii, *Five Days*, 23; Sukhanov, *Russian*, 21; Krupskaia, *Vospominaniia*, 271; Aronson, *Rossiia*, 4.

29 Sukhanov, *Russian*, 43, 177; Trotsky, *History*, 18.

30 Hasegawa, *February Revolution*, 330–45, 380; Sukhanov, *Russian*, 59–62, 83–7; Zenzinov, 'Fevral'skie dni', 215–18.

31 Hasegawa, *February Revolution*, 348–59; *RPG*, I: 45–7; Shulgin, *Dni*, 179.

32 Mstislavskii, *Five Days*, 30–I; Shklovsky, *Sentimental*, I5–16; Bulgakov, 'Revoliutsiia', 2I; Nabokov, *Provisional*, 43–4.

33 Jones, *Russia in Revolution*, 165–6; NLW, Lord Davies Papers, C3/23.

34 Pipes, *Russian Revolution*, 303; *RPG*, I: 47–8; Cantacuzène, *Revolutionary Days*, 147–9.

35 Zenzinov, 'Fevral'skie dni', I: 237–9.

36 *RPG*, 2: 846–9; *Petrogradskii sovet*, I: 49–50; Sukhanov, *Russian*, 113.

37 *RPG*, 3: 1223–4.

38 Mstislavskii, *Five Days*, 64–5.

39 Hasegawa, *February Revolution*, 410–16; Sukhanov, *Russian*, 116–25; *RPG*, I: 135–6.

40 *RPG*, I: 136; Mstislavskii, *Five Days*, 65.

4I Trotsky, *History*, 201; Sukhanov, *Russian*, 140–4; *RPG*, I: 128–9.

42 Kolonitskii, 'Zagadka', 164–7; Wilcox, *Russia's Ruin*, 191; Nabokov, *Provisional Government*, 75; Gippius, *Peterburgskie*, 15.

43 'Dnevnik Nikolaia Romanova', 136; Mordvinov, 'Otryvki', 86; Hasegawa, *February Revolution*, 274.

44 Kokovtsov, *Out of My Past*, 408; Paléologue, *Ambassadors' Memoirs*, 3: 151–2.

45 Hasegawa, *February Revolution*, 434–40.

46 *Padenie*, I: 203–7; Balk, 'Poslednie', 54–5; Martynov, *Tsarskaia armiia*, 107–8; Benckendorff, *Last Days*, 6–9.

47 Hasegawa, *February Revolution*, 473–9; Martynov, *Tsarkaia armiia*, 144–5.

48 *RPG*, I: 83–9; Hasegawa, *February Revolution*, 495–502.

49 Hasegawa, *February Revolution*, 503–5; *RPG*, I: 95–6.

50 Mordvinov, 'Otryvki', 113.

5I Pares, *Fall*, 420–I; Paley, *Memories*, 26.

52 *Perepiska Nikolaia i Aleksandry*, 5: 225; Hasegawa, *February Revolution*, 510; Shulgin, *Dni*, 269.

53 Shulgin, *Dni*, 270–I; *Padenie*, 6: 265–8.

54 Paley, *Memories*, 60–I; Benckendorff, *Last Days*, 16–17.

55 Sukhanov, *Russian*, 146–7; Hasegawa, *February Revolution*, 531–3.

56 Miliukov, *Istoriia*, I: 53–5; Kerensky, *Catastrophe*, 70; *Padenie*, 6: 266–8; Hasegawa, *February Revolution*, 556–60.

57 Nabokov, 'Provisional Government', 18–20, 46–55; Hasegawa, *February Revolution*, 561–3.

58 *Izvestiia*, 4–16 March 1917; Kornakov, 'Simvolika', 360; Paustovsky, *Story*, 474–5; TsGASP, f. 1000, op. 74, d. 13, l. 64; TsGAVMF, f. 2023, op. I, d. 7, l. I.

59 Iusupov, *Pered izgnaniem*, 187; *War, Revolution and Peace*, 50; RGIA, f. 1278, op. 10, d. 4, l. 241–2.

60 *1917 god v derevne*, 40, 64; TsGASP, f. 8558, op. I, d. 5, l. 30; RGIA, f. 1278, op. 10, d. II, l. 332.

6I Kornakov, 'Simvolika', 361.

62 Heald, 'Witness', 64–6; Stites, 'Iconoclastic', 7–9; Sukhanov, *Russian*, 74; Nazhivin, *Zapiski*, 32–3; Bulgakov, 'Revoliutsiia', 24, 28–9.

63 RGIA, f. 1412, op. 16, d. 534, l. 4. See also d. 101–12, 529–44.

64 Kolonitskii, 'Kul't vozhdia', 17–18; Swift, 'Kul'turnoe', 403.

65 RGIA, f. 1278, op. 10, d. 4, l. 242; *RPG*, I: 216–21; 2: 803–19, 862–5; Buryshkin, *Moskva*, 319; Peshekhonov 'Pervye nedeli', 290–1; Silver, *Russian Workers'*, 38.

66 Trotsky, *History*, 193.

67 Buchanan, *My Mission*, 2: 86, 114; *War, Revolution and Peace*, 46; Kolonitskii, 'Kul't vozhdia', 24–6.

68 Pyman, *Life*, 2: 243, 247; Zhukovskii-Zhuk, 'Kogda', 64; Schweitzer, *Tsvetaeva*, 138.

69 Kolonitskii, 'The "Russian Idea" ', 4, 9, 13–14; TsGAVMF, f. r-2063, op. I, d. 7, l. 12; Oberuchev, *V dni*, 49; Sorokin, *Chelovek*, 228; *Gubernskii*, 54; TsGASP, f. 7384, op. 9, d. 76, l. 23–4; Kolonitskii, 'Kul't vozhdia', 7.

70 Paustovsky, *Story*, 474; NLW, Lord Davies Papers, C3/23; BC, Ransome Papers, Telegraph 53, 15 March 1917.

71 Polner, *Zhiznennyi*, 245.

9 The Freest Country in the World

1 Nabokov, 'Provisional Government', 44.

2 Hoare, *Fourth Seal*, 256; BA, Polner Collection, Box 2, Death of Lvov; Tsereteli, *Vospominaniia*, 2: 63–4; Gor'kii, 'Pis'ma k E. P. Peshkovoi', 195.

3 IM, f. 454, op. 3, d. 70; Tsereteli, *Vospominaniia*, I: 63–4; Nabokov, 'Provisional Government', 84; Bublikov, *Russkaia*, 33–4.

4 Polner, *Zhiznennyi*, 231–45; Tsereteli, *Vospominaniia*, I: 114; IM, f. 454, op. 3, d. 70.

5 Kerensky, *Memoirs*, 227–8.

6 Chernov, *Great Russian*, 103; Shlapentokh, 'Images', 34–5; Sorokin, *Leaves*, 39; Heald, *Witness*, 89–90; IM, f. 454, op. 3, d. 70.

7 *RPG*, I: 191–242; Polner, *Zhiznennyi*, 247.

8 Shliapnikov, *Semnadtsatyi god*, 2: 236.

9 Sukhanov, *Russian*, 145; Schapiro, 'Political Thought', 106–7; Nabokov, 'Provisional Government', 135–6; Rosenberg, *Liberals*, 146–7; *RPG*, I: 435–47, 451.

10 TsGALI, f. 66, op. I, d. 312, l. 8.

11 Ibid., f. 122, op. 3, d. 13; Tsarev, *Samouchka*, 37–8.

12 TsGALI, f. 66, op. I, d. 312; f. 122, op. 3, d. 13; f. 200, op. I, d. 80.

13 Figes, *Peasant Russia*, 56–61.

14 GARF, f. 393, op. 3, d. 359, l. 202; Figes, *Peasant Russia*, 47–56, 122–4.

15 Chernov, *Rozhdenie*, 313; Galynskii, *Ocherki*, 116.

16 GARF, f. 398, op. 2, d. 144, l. 158–9; Galynskii, *Ocherki*, 117, 141, 172.

17 GARF, f. 1791, op. 2, d. 144, l. 82; RGIA, f. 1278, op. 10, d. 4, l. 270–2.

18 IM, f. 454, op. 3, d. 70.

19 Figes, *Peasant Russia*, 33–7, 40–6; GARF, f. 406, op. 2, d. 237, l. 133, 160; Trotsky, *History*, 882.

20 Koenker and Rosenberg, *Strikes*, 82, 87, 156, 229.

21 Keep, *Russian Revolution*, 69; Smith, *Red Petrograd*, 65–8; Koenker, *Moscow Workers*, 107–9; *RPG*, 2: 712–13.

22 Koenker and Rosenberg, *Strikes*, 102, 137–9, 172–3, 231; BC, Ransome Papers, Telegram 91, 3 April 1917; Ferro, *Russian Revolution*, 112–13.

23 Pitcher (ed.), *Witnesses*, 101–2; Reed, *Ten Days*, 40; Paustovsky, *Story*, 481. On the idea of 'fêtes de libération' see M. Perrot, *Les Ouvriers*, Paris, 1974, 2: 548.

24 *Ekonomicheskoe polozhenie*, 2: 201; Smith, *Red Petrograd*, 80–98, 139–67.

25 Wade, *Red Guards*, 80–114, 173–82; Dune, *Notes of a Red Guard*, 51–7.

26 Rosenberg, 'Social Mediation', 173–8; Hogan, 'Conciliation', 49–66; Galili, *Menshevik Leaders*, 119–23.

27 Rosenberg, 'Social Mediation', 181–3; Galili, *Menshevik Leaders*, ch. 6; Koenker and Rosenberg, *Strikes*, 200–2.

28 *RPG*, 1: 317; Radkey, *Agrarian Foes*, 40, 216–18.

29 Suny, *Revenge*, 29–30, 45, 54, 63, 75; Guthier, 'Popular Base', 40.

30 Reshetar, *Ukrainian*, 320–1; Suny, *Revenge*, 48.

31 Khrystiuk, *Zametky*, 1: 46; Bociurkiw, 'Rise', 222–4; Frenkin, *Russkaia armiia*, 211–56.

32 RGVIA, f. 162, op. 1, d. 18.

33 *RPG*, 1: 334–5; Upton, *Finnish Revolution*, chs 1–6; Ketola, 'Russkaia', 293–6; *Den'*, 12 May 1917.

34 *RPG*, 1: 344–55; *NZh*, 21 July 1917.

35 *RPG*, 1: 374–7, 383–8; Stojko, 'Ukrainian', 9ff; Tsereteli, *Vospominaniia*, 2: 89.

36 *RPG*, 1: 389–92; Reshetar, *Ukrainian*, 57; IM, f. 454, op. 3, d. 70.

37 RGVIA, f. 162, op. 1, d. 17, l. 199; GARF, f. 5972, op. 1, d. 21a, l. 12.

38 Wildman, *End*, 1: 228–45; BA, Brusilov Collection, mss, 'Gazeta "Dni" '; RGVIA, f. 162, op. 2, d. 18.

39 'Iz ofitserskikh pisem', 200; Kal'nitskii, *Ot fevralia*, 43.

40 RGVIA, f. 162, op. 2, d. 18; Polovtsov, *Glory*, 206; Heenan, *Russian*, 97–8; Ferro, *October*, 84–5; GARF, f. 1791, op. 2, d. 629, l. 73.

41 *Trud*, 27 May 1917.

42 *RPG*, 2: 1044–6, 1077–8, 1098; Wade, *Russian Search*, 26–38.

43 *NZh*, 23 April 1917; Kantorovich, 'Fedor Linde', 242–3; *Kievskaia mysl'*, 3 Sep 1917; *RPG*, 3: 1242–4.

44 Roobol, *Tsereteli*, 133; Galili, *Menshevik Leaders*, 134–40, 179–85.

45 *RPG*, 3: 1241–2, 1267–9; Rosenberg, *Liberals*, 109–13; Wade, *Russian Search*, 47; IM, f. 454, op. 3, d. 70.

46 *RPG*, 3: 1276–8; Roobol, *Tsereteli*, 123–4; IM, f. 454, op. 3, d. 70.

47 Sukhanov, *Russian*, 269–70; Service, *Lenin*, 2: 154–5.

48 Karpinskii, 'Vladimir', 105–6; Valentinov, *Encounters*, 21.

49 For the latest (inconclusive) evidence on this subject see Volkogonov, *Lenin*, 109–28.

50 Getzler, *Martov*, 147–8; Service, *Lenin*, 2: 151–3.

51 Gorky, *Lenin*, 35; Service, *Lenin*, 2: 187; *NZh*, 10 Nov 1917.

52 Lenin, *PSS*, 31: 9–59, 99–100; Sukhanov, *Russian*, 274–5.

53 Sukhanov, *Russian*, 285–8; Lenin, *PSS*, 31: 113–16; Service, *Lenin*, 2: 155–60, 165–6; Lenin, *Leninskii sbornik*, 7: 307–8; RTsKhIDNI, f. 72, op. 3, d. 687, l. 2; Shub, *Lenin*, 109.

54 Trotsky, *History*, 300–7; Zelnik, 'Fate', 6; Rabinowitch, 'Bol'sheviki', 116–19.

55 Valentinov, *Encounters*, 148; Besançon, *Intellectual*, 193–6; Volkogonov, *Lenin*, 62.

56 Struve, 'My Contacts', 593; Volkogonov, *Lenin*, 35–49; Fischer, *Life*, 329.

57 Valentinov, *Encounters*, 50.

58 Gul', 'Byloe'; *RPG*, 2: 1209.

59 Voline, *Unknown*, 244; Rolland, *Journal*, 1168; Valentinov, *Encounters*, 148–51.

60 Trotsky, *History*, 303, 558; 'Pis'ma moi', 11: 35.

61 Fischer, *Life*, 57–8; Aronson, *Rossiia*, 47–52; Valentinov, *Encounters*, 42.

62 Service, *Lenin*, 2: 169–77, 185; Rabinowitch, *Prelude*, 46–7; Trotsky, *History*, 340.

63 Rabinowitch, *Prelude*, 42–5. For the view that the Central Committee had been planning a putsch see Pipes, *Russian Revolution*, 401–5.

64 Mawdsley, *Baltic Fleet*, 6–7, 21, 34, 51–3; *RPG*, 3: 1296–9; Raskolnikov, *Kronstadt*, 34.

65 Rabinowitch, *Prelude*, 260.

66 Rabinowitch, *Prelude*, ch. 3; Sukhanov, *Russian*, 402–6; Lenin, *PSS*, 31: 267.

67 *RPG*, 3: 1322–6; Sukhanov, *Russian*, 415–19.

68 AG, Pg-Rl, 30–19–603 (published here for the first time).

69 *NZh*, 18, 20 April, 18 May 1917; AG, Pg-Rl, 30–19–603.

70 Trotsky, *Military Writings*, 1: 215; Agursky, *Third Rome*, 171–2; Pyman, *Life*, 2: 268–305.

71 *NZh*, 27 April, 9 May, 18 May 1917; Taneeva, *Stranitsy*, 292; RGIA, f. 794, op. 1, d. 4, l. 4.

72 AG, Pg-Rl, 30–19–601 (published here for the first time).

73 *NZh*, 7 Dec 1917.

74 RTsKhIDNI, f. 75, op. 1, d. 67, l. 1–3 (published here for the first time).

75 Gor'kii, 'Pis'ma k E. P. Peshkovoi', 196.

76 *NZh*, 25 April, 18 May 1917; AG, Pg-In.

77 Gorky, 'On the Russian Peasantry', 25; AG, Pg-Rl.

78 *NZh*, 18 April, 19 Nov, 6 Dec, 7 Dec 1917.

79 Gorky, *Lenin*, 30.

80 *NZh*, 23 April 1917.

81 AG, Pg-Rl, 30–19–601.

82 *NZh*, 20 April 1917; AG, Pg-Rl, 30–19–603.

10 The Agony of the Provisional Government

1 Kerensky, *Memoirs*, 278–9.

2 Ibid., 271.

3 RGVIA, f. 162, op. 1, d. 18; BA, Pronin Collection, Box 1, 'Miting generala Brusilova'.

4 RGVIA, f. 162, op. 1, d. 17, l. 202.

5 *RPG*, 2: 925–6, 927–8; Heenan, *Russian*, 38–42, 44.

6 *RPG*, 3: 1739; Lockhart, *Memoirs*, 180.

7 Kolonitskii, 'A. F. Kerenskii', 98; Tsvetaeva, *Stikhotvorenie*, 2: 63 ('To the Tsar at Easter [21 May 1917]').

8 Stepun, *Byvshee*, 2: 33–5; Kerenskii, *Izdaleka*, 204; Heenan, *Russian*, 103; RGVIA, f. 162, op. I, d. 18.

9 *RPG*, 2: 913–15.

10 Rosenberg, 'Russian Municipal', 161; AG, PG-Rl, 30–19–603; Rougle, 'Intelligentsia', 72; *RPG*, 2: 486–7.

11 Paustovsky, *Story*, 486.

12 Pares, *My Russian Memoirs*, 459.

13 Botchkareva, *Yashka*, 151–68.

14 *RPG*, 2: 880–3; RGVIA, f. 162, op. I, d. 18; Wildman, *End*, 2: 22–3.

15 Abraham, *Kerensky*, 199–200; Farmborough, *Nurse*, 269–70.

16 Kerensky, *Memoirs*, 274, 282.

17 RGVIA, f. 162, op. I, d. 17, l. 200; BA, Pronin Collection, Box I, 'Miting gen. Brusilova'.

18 RGVIA, f. 162, op. I, d. 18.

19 RGVIA, f. 162, op. I, d. 18; Wildman, *End*, 2: ch. 2.

20 Stepun, *Byvshee*, 2: 10; Brussilov, *Soldier's Notebook*, 290–1, 307–8, 340.

21 Golovin, *Russian Army*, 197; Heenan, *Russian*, 97–8.

22 RGVIA, f. 162, op. I, d. 18; Bauermeister, *Spies*, 128–37.

23 RGVIA, f. 162, op. I, d. 18.

24 Wildman, *End*, 2: 89ff; Stankevich, *Vospominaniia*, 155–6, 160.

25 Botchkareva, *Yashka*, 208–18.

26 Miliukov, *Russian*, I: 195.

27 Polner, *Zhiznennyi*, 254; IM, f. 454, d. 3, l. 70.

28 Trotsky, *History*, 518.

29 Heenan, *Russian*, 54–5; Kerensky, *Catastrophe*, 207–10.

30 IM, f. 454, d. 3, l. 47–67.

31 Rabinowitch, *Prelude*, 117–18, 121–2.

32 Rabinowitch, *Prelude*, 122–40; *Pravda*, 4 July 1917; *RPG*, 3: 1338–40.

33 *RPG*, 3: 1335–6; Trotsky, *History*, 529–30; Sukhanov, *Russian*, 429–30; Buchanan, *Petrograd*, 134; Blok, *Sobranie sochinenii*, 7, 273.

34 Sukhanov, *Russian*, 431; Trotsky, *History*, 525.

35 'Pis'ma moi', 2: 35; *RPG*, 3: 1339–44; Rabinowitch, *Prelude*, 167–70; Sukhanov, *Russian*, 431–2; Woytinsky, *Stormy*, 300.

36 Sukhanov, *Russian*, 432; Buchanan, *Petrograd*, 135–6.

37 Rabinowitch, *Prelude*, 174–6.

38 Pipes, *Russian Revolution*, 419; Rabinowitch, *Prelude*.

39 Sukhanov, *Russian*, 479; *Krasnaia Gazeta*, 16 July 1920; Zinoviev, 'Lenin', 62.

40 Buchanan, *Petrograd*, 139; Raskolnikov, *Kronstadt*, 153–72; Pares, *My Russian Memoirs*, 465.

41 Sukhanov, *Russian*, 441–2; *Rabochy i soldat*, 26–7 July 1917; Rabinowitch, *Prelude*, 181–4.

42 Krupskaia, *Vospominaniia*, 166 and passim.

43 AG, PG-Rl, 30–19–605 (published here for the first time).

44 Woytinsky, *Stormy*, 301–2; *RPG*, 3: 1356.

45 Sukhanov, *Russian*, 444–7; Raskolnikov, *Kronstadt*, 166–7.

46 Sukhanov, *Russian*, 448–9; Woytinsky, *Stormy*, 305–6. The 176th Regiment had in fact been loosely aligned to the Inter-District Group of Social Democrats.

47 *RPG*, 3: 1347.

48 Sukhanov, *Russian*, 450.

49 Nikitine, *Fatal Years*, 155–7; Sukhanov, *Russian*, 462–4.

50 Sukhanov, *Russian*, 455.

51 *RPG*, 3: 1364–5; Nikitine, *Fatal Years*, 119–22; Zeman (ed.), *Germany*, 94–5; Rabinowitch, *Prelude*, 206–7.

52 Polovtsov, *Glory*, 258.

53 Trotsky, *History*, 570; Sukhanov, *Russian*, 469–70.

54 *NZh*, 15 Aug 1917.

55 Zinoviev, 'Lenin', 70.

56 Lenin, *PSS*, 32: 433–4.

57 AG, PG-RI, 30–19–605 (published here for the first time).

58 *NZh*, 9 July 1917.

59 *RPG*, 3: 1350.

60 Polovtsov, *Glory*, 259–60; IM, f. 454, d. 3, l. 18; Polner, *Zhiznennyi*, 258.

61 Kolonitskii, 'A. F. Kerenskii', 98–106.

62 Krasnov, 'Na vnutrennom fronte', 106. The following account of Linde's death is compiled from pages 105–12 of Krasnov, 'Na vnutrennom'; and Sokolov, *White Nights*, 15–40. The incident is also related, with a good deal of artistic licence, in Pasternak's *Doctor Zhivago* (Chapter 5).

63 Kantorovich, 'Fedor Linde', 251; *Kievskaia mysl'*, 3 Sep 1917; Gippius, *Siniaia kniga*, 169–71; *RPG*, 3: 1390–1.

64 Cantacuzène, *Revolutionary Days*, 30; Rabinowitch, *Bolsheviks*, 39–42.

65 Brussilov, *A Soldier's Notebook*, 317; RGVIA, f. 162, op. 1, d. 4, l. 79, 83.

66 Vertsinskii, *God*, 18; Bogaevskii, *Vospominaniia*, 39; Katkov, *Kornilov*, 39–41; Brussilov, *A Soldier's Notebook*, 100–2, 321; Grondijs, *La Guerre*, 264.

67 GARF, f. 5849, op. 2, d. 35, l. 2–3.

68 White, 'Kornilov', 187–9; Katkov, *Kornilov*, 138–9.

69 Martynov, *Kornilov*, 16–20.

70 Abraham, *Kerensky*, 255; Stepun, *Byvshee*, 2: 144–5.

71 Brussilov, *A Soldier's Notebook*, 320; *RPG*, 2: 989–1010.

72 Martynov, *Kornilov*, 33–4; Savinkov, *K Delu*, 13–14.

73 Martynov, *Kornilov*, 20; PRO, FO 371, 3015, N 165148/17, 93–4; Stepun, *Byvshee*, 2: 143–4.

74 Katkov, *Kornilov*, 56–7, 171–2; Botchkareva, *Yashka*, 225; Lukomskii, *Vospominaniia*, 228.

75 Vladimirova, *Kontrrevoliutsiia*, 84; Stepun, *Byvshee*, 2: 162–3; *RPG*, 3: 1510–15.

76 Gippius, *Siniaia*, 162, 164.

77 Katkov, *Kornilov*, 50–1, 74–9, 84–8, 136–7, 159; *RPG*, 3: 1558–71.

78 *NZh*, 3 Sep 1917; *RPG*, 3: 1574–5; Katkov, *Kornilov*, 92.

79 Katkov, *Kornilov*, 97; Martynov, *Kornilov*, 110–11.

80 Pipes, *Russian Revolution*, 459–60; RGVIA, f. 162, op. 1, d. 4, l. 53.

81 Rabinowitch, *Bolsheviks*, 132–44.

82 Ibid., 144–50; *RPG*, 3: 1586–9.

83 Denikin, *Ocherki*, 2: 86; Katkov, *Kornilov*, 130–4.

84 Trotsky, *My Life*, 331.

85 HLRO, 206, Stow Hill Papers, DS 2/2, Box 8, O. L. Kerenskaia, 'Obryvki vospominanii', 8.

86 McCauley (ed.), *The Russian Revolution*, 36–7.

87 Smith, *Red Petrograd*, 110–16, 160–7; Koenker, *Moscow Workers*, 194–5, 198–200, 222–4.

88 Rosenberg, 'Russian Municipal', 159–61.

89 Keep, *Russian Revolution*, 146.

90 Rabinowitch, *Bolsheviks*, 174–5; Trotsky, *History*, 804–6; Sukhanov, *Russian*, 528.

91 Ziv, *Trotskii*, 69–74; Deutscher, *Prophet Armed*, 284–5; Lunacharsky, *Revolutionary*, 65.

92 Rabinowitch, *Bolsheviks*, 154–8.

93 Smith, *Red Petrograd*, ch. 7; Koenker, *Moscow Workers*, 184–6, 320–5; Koenker and Rosenberg, *Strikes*, 254–60, 280–6; *RPG*, 3: 1640–52.

94 *Delo derevni*, 27 Aug 1917; Lutskii, 'Krest'ianskoe', 49–78.

95 TsGANKh, f. 478, op. 1, d. 149–50; d. 202, l. 7–8; Edwards, *Sonya*, 466.

96 Figes, *Peasant Russia*, 61–84.

97 Galili, *Menshevik*, 384; Radkey, *Agrarian*, 403ff; Raleigh, *Revolution*, 235–7, 267–70.

98 Lenin, *PSS*, 32: 433–4; 33: 5–120; 34: 10–17.

99 Ibid., 34: 133–9.

100 *RPG*, 3: 1684–91, 1714–21; Trotsky, *History*, 916–17.

101 Haimson (ed.), *Making*, 18; Galili, *Menshevik*, 302, 327–8, 336–7.

102 Trotsky, *History*, 1156; Gorky, *Lenin*, 46.

103 Lenin, *PSS*, 34: 239–41.

104 Ibid., 34: 214–28, 242–7, 272–83.

105 Sukhanov, *Russian*, 556; Rabinowitch, *Bolsheviks*, 202; RTsKhIDNI, f. 17, op. 1, d. 33.

11 Lenin's Revolution

1 Sukhanov, *Russian*, 498–9; Reed, *Ten Days*, 54–5, 87.

2 Rabinowitch, *Bolsheviks*, 209–16, 219; Lenin, *PSS*, 34: 264–8.

3 RTsKhIDNI, f. 17, op. 1, d. 34, l. 1–15.

4 Ibid., l. 16–17; *NZh*, 18 Oct 1917; Lenin, *PSS*, 34: 423–7.

5 Rabinowitch, *Bolsheviks*, 215.

6 *Russkaia revoliutsiia glazami Petrogradskogo chinovnika*, 15 Oct 1917; PRO, War Office, 158/964: 6; FO 371, 2997, N 142922, 126; Reisner, *Izbrannye*, 489–90; CUL, Hardinge Papers, 35: 27; HLRO, 206: Stow Hill Papers, DS 2/2, Box N18: 15–16; Ferro, *October*, 285; Gippius, *Siniaia*, 175, 187.

7 PRO, FO 371, 3016, N 205925: 542–5; N210021: 582; N 208373: 577–8; 3017 N 209501: 10–11; N 208214: 567–70; N 210844: 572–3; Nabokov, *Ispytaniia*, 97, 99–100, 102, 139–40.

8 Gippius, *Siniaia*, 210; RGVIA, f. 162, op. 1, d. 18.

9 Nabokov, 'Provisional Government', 78.

10 Rabinowitch, *Bolsheviks*, 253–4.

11 TsGASP, f. 131, op. I, d. 8, l. 6; f. 54, op. I, d. 2, l. 48; f. 148, op. I, d. 24, l. 1; Startsev, 'Voenno-revoliutsionnyi komitet', 134; Ignat'ev, 'V noch' ', 314.

12 Melgunov, *Bolshevik*, 81.

13 Rabinowitch, *Bolsheviks*, 272; *Izvestiia TsK KPSS*, 1989, 1: 226.

14 Rabinowitch, *Bolsheviks*, 274–81; Lenin, *PSS*, 35: 1.

15 Kostiukov, 'Kak my opozdali', 32–7; *Oktiabr'skoe*, 2: 346; Rabinowitch, *Bolsheviks*, 282; Trotsky, *History*, 1108–9; Blagonravov, 'Fortress', 206.

16 Rabinowitch, *Bolsheviks*, 290–1.

17 GARF, f. 543, op. I, d. 1, l. 24–5; Sukhanov, *Russian*, 617–18; Melgunov, *Bolshevik*, 58–61.

18 GARF, f. 3348, op. I, d. 149, l. 2; Melgunov, *Bolshevik*, 68–70; Pal'chinskii, 'Poslednye chasy', 137; Reed, *Ten Days*, 92–3.

19 Sinegub, 'Zashchita', 152; Melgunov, *Bolshevik*, 76; GARF, f. 3348, op. I, d. 149, l. 3.

20 Reed, *Ten Days*, 106–7, 110–11.

21 Maliantovich, 'V zimnem', 120–1; Reed, *Ten Days*, 112; Melgunov, *Bolshevik*, 80; Buchanan, *My Mission* 2: 208.

22 Reed, *Ten Days*, 98–9; Sukhanov, *Russian*, 616, 635 and passim; *Oktiabr'skoe*, 2: 353; Pipes, *Russian Revolution*, 498.

23 *Vtoroi vserossiiskii s'ezd*, 2–4, 33–5.

24 Cited in Rabinowitch, *Bolsheviks*, 294.

25 *Vtoroi vserossiiskii s'ezd*, 43–4; Getzler, *Martov*, 163.

26 *Vtoroi vserossiiskii s'ezd*, 43–4; Rabinowitch, *Bolsheviks*, 297.

27 GARF, f. 3348, op. I, d. 149, l. 2–3; Melgunov, *Bolshevik*, 89–91; Rabinowitch, *Bolsheviks*, 299–301.

28 *Vtoroi vserossiiskii s'ezd*, 47–54; Reed, *Ten Days*, 113–16.

29 Trotsky, *History*, 1140; Startsev, *Ocherki*, 195; Mawdsley, *Baltic Fleet*, 112–13.

30 Trotsky, *History*, 1079; Korenev, 'Chrezvychainaia', 29; Melgunov, *Bolshevik*, 67; Reed, *Ten Days*, 94–5, 106; Averbakh, 'Revoliutsionnoe', 25–6.

31 TsGASP, f. 131, op. I, d. 7, ll. 2, 7, 13, 24; d. 8, ll. 6, 17, 22, 54, 57, 59.

32 GARF, f. 1236, op. I, d. 1, l. 70, 81, 83–5, 119, 136, 147, 154, 157; d. 12, l. 14, 153–4; d. 13, l. 56; d. 37, l. 6; d. 39, ll. 5, 20, 28; f. 1791, op. 2, d. 594, 596; TsGASP, f. 131, op. I, d. 8, l. 54; Bonch-Bruevich, 'Strashnoe', 180–92; Korolenko, 'Iz dnevnikov', 378–80.

33 *NZh*, 11 Jan 1918.

34 *NZh*, 18 Oct 1917.

35 GARF, f. 1236, op. I, d. 1, ll. 28, 53–4, 58, 62; d. 12, l. 77; Koenker, *Moscow Workers*, 345; Mandel, *Petrograd Workers*, 328–32; *Znamia truda*, 2 Nov 1917.

36 RGVIA, f. 162, op. I, d. 18.

37 RTsKhIDNI, f. 17, op. I, d. 39.

38 Bone (ed.), *Bolsheviks*, 136–42; Trotskii, *Stalinskaia shkola*, 123.

39 Clements, *Bolshevik Feminist*, 124–6; Bunyan and Fisher (ed.), *Bolshevik*, 226; Iroshnikov, *Sozdanie*, 161–7.

40 Bunyan and Fisher (ed.), *Bolshevik*, 323.

4I Melgunov, *Bolshevik*, I27–8, I70, I80–I; 'Pis'ma moi', 2: 43.

42 *NZh*, 7 Nov I9I7.

43 Liubovitch, 'Kak', 65–9; Rigby, *Lenin's*, 45–5I, 62–3.

44 Rigby, *Lenin's*, I4–I9, 30ff; Bunyan and Fisher (ed.), *Bolshevik*, I85–6; Liberman, *Building*, I3.

45 *The Debate on Soviet Power*, 68–89, I40–2, 200–I.

46 GARF, f. I236, op. I, d. I, ll. 59, I02, I04, I07–8; Sorokin, *Leaves*, I05–6.

47 Radkey, *Election*, appendix; Radkey, *Sickle*, 248–9, 28I–306.

48 *The Debate on Soviet Power*, I47.

49 Bunyan and Fisher (ed.), *Bolshevik*, 356–62; Dolgorukov, *Velikaia*, 57ff; *NZh*, 6 Dec I9I7; *The Debate on Soviet Power*, I74, I77.

50 Gippius, *Peterburgskie dnevniki*, 365.

5I Leggett, *Cheka*, I7.

52 AG, Pg-Rl, 30–I9–6I6 (published here for the first time).

53 *The Debate on Soviet Power*, I54.

54 Lenin, *PSS*, 35: I62–6, 22I–3; *Nash vek*, 6 Jan I9I8.

55 Bunyan and Fisher (ed.), *Bolshevik*, 369–70; *NZh*, 9 and II Jan I9I8.

56 Sorokin, *Leaves*, I25; Sokolov, 'Zashchita', 67; Roobol, *Tsereteli*, I80–I; Bonch-Bruevich, *Na boevykh*, 250.

57 *Vserossiiskoe uchreditel'noe*, II0–II.

58 Sokolov, *White Nights*, 2I0.

59 Sokolov, 'Zashchita', 24, 26, 32–3.

60 AG, Pg-Rl, 30–I9–6I7 (published here for the first time).

6I On this see my forthcoming article, 'The Russian Revolution of I9I7 and Its Language in the Village', *Russian Review*.

62 Figes, *Peasant Russia*, 68; Sokolov, 'Zashchita', I6.

63 Denikin, *Ocherki*, 2: I47–8; *Izvestiia vserossiiskogo soveta krest'ianskikh deputatov*, 28 May I9I7; *Pravda*, I Jan I9I9.

64 Kolonitskii, 'Antibourgeois', I90; Nazhivin, *Zapiski*, I5, 28; GARF, f. 55I, op. I, d. I08, l. 2.

65 Kolonitskii, 'Antibourgeois', I84–5, I9I; Libknecht, *Pauki*, 4; TCL, Margoulis Collection, 'Protokoly fabzavkoma', 8.

66 Lenin, *PSS*, 35: 204.

67 Ibid., 327; *NZh*, I6 March I9I8.

68 Stites, *Revolutionary Dreams*, I27; GARF, f. I236, op. I, d. I, l. 47, 67; Krasnov, 'Iz vospominanii', I62–5; Melgunov, *Red Terror*, II3ff; Obolenskii, 'Krym', 2I6.

69 Bunyan and Fisher (ed.), *Bolshevik*, 324; Meshcherskaya, 'Trudovoe', 205–6.

70 GARF, f. 393, op. 2, d. 59, l. 35–8.

7I Clements, *Bolshevik Feminist*, I3I–3; Bunyan and Fisher (ed.), *Bolshevik*, 587; GARF, f. I30, op. 2, d. I55, l. 22; d. I67, l. 3.

72 Gor'kii, *Polnoe sobranie sochinenii*, I7: 2I2; Lenin, *PSS*, 35: 203; Trotskii, *Sochineniia*, I7, I: 290–I.

73 Arbenina (Meyendorff), *Through Terror*, 102; Pozner, *Dela*, 26–7; RGVIA, f. 162, op. I, d. 18; Wrangel, *From Serfdom*, 301–4.

74 Nazhivin, *Zapiski*, 14.

75 Figes, *Peasant Russia*, 101ff, 132–5; Channon, 'Tsarist Landowners', 584; Rudnev, *Pri vechernykh*, 112–29.

76 GARF, f. 4390, op. 14, d. 80, I. 8–10.

77 *NZh*, 19 Nov 1917.

78 GARF, f. 1791, op. 2, d. 629, l. 18; Karich', 'O narodnom', 23–32; GARF, f. a-353, op. 3, d. 59, 60, 91, 95, 99, 108; Bunyan and Fisher (ed.), *Bolshevik*, 289–91; *Narodnoe pravo*, 3–4, 1918: 209–10; Speranskii, 'Narodnoe', 25–30.

79 Lenin, *PSS*, 35: 357–8. Recently discovered evidence suggests Trotsky wrote the Decree (see *Moscow News*, 12: 1991).

80 *Izvestiia*, 23 Aug 1918.

81 *Materialy narodnogo kommissariata iustitsii*, I: 29.

82 Melgunov, *Red Terror*, 22–3.

83 *NZh*, 17 Jan 1918; Steinberg, *In the Workshop*, 145.

84 Reed, *Ten Days*, 133.

85 Trotsky, *My Life*, 355; Reed, *Ten Days*, 132; Kennan, *Russia Leaves the War*, 75–6.

86 Fokke, 'Na stene', 15–17, 36–8.

87 Trotsky, *My Life*, 378; Deutscher, *Prophet Armed*, 366.

88 RTsKhIDNI, f. 17, op. I, d. 405, l. 1–13.

89 Fokke, 'Na stene', 207.

90 RTsKhIDNI, f. 17, op. I, d. 409.

91 Hoffman, *War Diaries*, I: 206–7.

92 RTsKhIDNI, f. 17, op. I, d. 410, l. 3–17.

93 Trotsky, *My Life*, 406.

94 RTsKhIDNI, f. 17, op. I, d. 412, l. 9; Wheeler-Bennett, *Brest-Litovsk*, 258–62.

95 Wheeler-Bennett, *Brest-Litovsk*, 269.

96 *Istochnik*, I, 1994: 26; RGVIA, f. 162, op. I, d. 5, l. 136.

97 RTsKhIDNI, f. 4, op. 2, d. 3734, l. 1–2.

98 Trotsky, *My Life*, 366–9.

12 Last Dreams of the Old World

I Bulgakov, *White Guard*, 51–2.

2 Ibid., 54.

3 Gul', *Ledianoi pokhod*, 8–10.

4 Kenez, *First Year*, 41–2, 55–64.

5 Trotsky, *HRA*, 2: 287–8; Hašek, *Red Commissar*, 23.

6 Denikin, *Ocherki*, 2, I: 94–100; Bogaevskii, *Vospominaniia*, 23–7; Suvorin, *Za rodinoi*, 15.

7 Gul', *Ledianoi pokhod*, 15; Tsvetaeva, *Selected Poems*, 62.

8 Bechhofer, *In Denikin's Russia*, 78; *Moscow News*, 16 April 1922; Pipes, *Russia Under the Bolshevik Regime*, 14.

9 Grondijs, *La Guerre*, 262–6; RGVIA, f. 162, op. 1, d. 18. Meinecke's dictum from Faulenbach (ed.), *Geschichtswissenschaft*, 69.

10 Kenez, *First Year*, 100–1.

11 Gul', *Ledianoi pokhod*, 16–17; Nesterovich-Berg, *V bor'be s bol'shevikami*, 97.

12 Holquist, 'Russian Vendée', 131ff; Kenez, *First Year*, 89–92; Medvedev and Starikov, *Mironov*, 45; Suvorin, *Za rodinoi*, 21, 29–30.

13 Denikin, *Ocherki*, 2, 1: 224; Lukomskii, *Vospominaniia*, 1, 156–64.

14 Wrangel, *Memoirs*, 185; Denikin, *Ocherki*, 2, 1: 237; Gul', *Ledianoi pokhod*, 65–9, 72–4, 145–7.

15 Kenez, *First Year*, 103–13; Denikin, *Ocherki*, 2, 1: 295.

16 Denikin, *Ocherki*, 2, 1: 298.

17 Holquist, 'Russian Vendée', 211–26; Kenez, *First Year*, 119–27.

18 Kenez, *First Year*, 141.

19 Ibid., 169–71; Skobtsev, *Tri goda*, 144.

20 Denikin, *Staraia*, 2: 89; *Ocherki*, 3: 128.

21 Kenez, *Defeat*, 55–8, 80–4.

22 Sokolov, *Pravlenie*, 93–115; Denikin, *Ocherki*, 4: 233; Dolgorukov, *Velikaia*, 129–30.

23 Kenez, *Defeat*, 112–20.

24 Denikin, *Ocherki*, 3: 61; Krasnov, 'Vsevelikoe', 223–7, 232–5; Kenez, *First Year*, 166–75.

25 Denikin, *Ocherki*, 4: 221–4; Sokolov, *Pravlenie*, 187–8, 286–7; Pokrovskii, *Denikin-shchina*, 173–5; Kin, *Denikinshchina*, 82, 89, 95–109.

26 Kenez, *Defeat*, 60–2; Lehovich, *White*, 331; Denikin, *Ocherki*, 4: 218.

27 Maiskii, *Demokraticheskaia*, 46.

28 *Khronika grazhdanskoi voiny v Sibiri*, 168.

29 Figes, *Peasant Russia*, 163–4.

30 Maiskii, *Demokraticheskaia*, 72–4, 84, 178–80.

31 Ibid., 84–8, 92–3, 126–31, 144–6.

32 Figes, *Peasant Russia*, 167–72.

33 Ibid., 175–8.

34 *Krasnaia byl'*, 3: 53; *Vestnik komiteta uchreditel'nogo sobraniia*, 23 Aug 1918.

35 Mel'gunov, *Tragediia*, 1: 99; Petrov, *Ot Volgi*, 50; Figes, *Peasant Russia*, 179.

36 Figes, *Peasant Russia*, 178–82.

37 GARF, f. 5975, op. 1, d. 13, l. 9.

38 Maiskii, *Demokraticheskaia*, 141–2; Melgunov, *Tragediia*, 1: 206.

39 Gins, *Sibir'*, 1, 1: 259; Churchill, *Aftermath*, 97.

40 Budberg, 'Dnevnik', 15: 331–2.

41 Varneck and Fisher (ed.), *Testimony*, 173.

13 The Revolution Goes to War

1 RGVA, f. 37976, op. 9, d. 4218; Os'kin, *Zapiski voenkoma*, 5–7.

2 Trotsky, *HRA*, 1: 5; Figes, 'Red Army', 174–5.

3 Kavtaradze, *Voennye*, 175–8; Hagen, *Soldiers*, 23–6.

4 *Trotsky Papers*, I: 149; Trotsky, *HRA*, I: 196.

5 Benvenutti, *Bolsheviks*, 66–8, 70, 76; Os'kin, *Zapiski voenkoma*, 118–19.

6 *Pravda*, 29 Nov and 25 Dec 1918.

7 Trotsky, *HRA* I: 199–210, 220–6.

8 Benvenutti, *Bolsheviks*, 92–108.

9 Figes, 'Red Army', 176–7; Os'kin, *Zapiski voenkoma*, 147.

10 Figes, 'Red Army', 177–9.

11 Ibid., 199–202.

12 GARF, f. 130, op. 2, d. 120, l. 45, 54; d. 277, l. 175–86; Os'kin, *Zapiski voenkoma*, 113.

13 Figes, 'Red Army', 182–6.

14 *Trotsky Papers*, I: 797; Figes, 'Red Army', 183–4.

15 White, *Growth of the Red Army*, 118; Figes, *Peasant Russia*, 293; Trotsky, *HRA*, I: 13.

16 Trotsky, *HRA*, 2: 109, 298; Figes, 'Red Army', 193.

17 Figes, 'Red Army', 195–8.

18 Ibid., 198–206; Os'kin, *Zapiski voenkoma*, 147–50; RGVIA, f. 7, op. 2, d. 483, l. 2; Brovkin, *Behind*, 145–55; *Antonovshchina*, 45–6.

19 Wildman, *End*, I: 101.

20 GARF, f. 2314, op. 9, d. 2, l. 15–16.

21 Elkina, 'Likvidatsiia', 52–6.

22 Maiakovskii, *Polnoe sobranie sochinenii*, 2: 92–5.

23 GARF, f. 2313, op. 3, d. 26, l. 27.

24 Goldman, *My Disillusionment*, 8–9.

25 AG, Pg-Rl, 30–19–619 (published here for the first time).

26 GARF, f. 539, op. 1, d. 3190, l. 24, 29–30, 35–6; *Izvestiia gosudarstvennogo kontrolia*, 5, 1919: 20; *NZh*, I June 1918; Pozner, *Dela*, 41; GARF, f. 551, op. 1, d. 20, l. 19.

27 GARF, f. 539, op. 1, d. 3190, l. 18; Pozner, *Dela*, 42; Sorokin, *Leaves*, 209, 217–18; Berkman, *Bolshevik Myth*, 266.

28 Sorokin, *Leaves*, 219–20; *Materialy po statistike Petrograda*, I, 1920: 10; McAuley, *Bread*, 276–8.

29 *NZh*, I June 1918; Babine, *Diary*, 33; Strumilin, *Zarabotnaia plata*, 5, 17–18; Strumilin, 'Prozhitochnoi', 4–8; Strumilin, 'Biudzhet', 1–5; McAuley, *Bread*, 280; Stites, *Women's*, 372; Goldman, *My Disillusionment*, 11.

30 Harrison, *Marooned*, 99; GARF, f. 5692, op. 1, d. 101, l. 23.

31 *NZh*, 21 May, I June 1918; Levin, *Stormy*, 203; Wolfe, *Bridge*, 77–8, 88–92; Scherr, 'Notes', 260–1; Rozhdestvenskii, *Stranitsy*, 264; Fitzpatrick, *Commissariat*, 132–3.

32 Khodasevich, *Nekropol*, 231–2; Berberova, *Italics*, 169–70; Romanov, *V mramornom*, 357–8.

33 Levin, *Stormy*, 206, 210.

34 GARF, f. 5469, op. 2, d. 50, l. 116; Figes, *Peasant Russia*, 255–7.

35 *Kooperativnaya mysl'* (Saratov), no. 4 (35), 19 Jan 1919; Figes, *Peasant Russia*, 284–95.

36 GARF, f. 130, op. 2, d. 441, l. 35; TsGALI, f. 66, op. 1, d. 913, l. 9.

37 Serge, *L'an 1*, 119; McAuley, *Bread*, 89.

38 Edwards, *Sonya*, 447–50; GARF, f. 5972, op. I, d. I0I, l. 29; Schweitzer, *Tsvetaeva*, 162–3; Meshcherskaia, 'Trudovoe kreshchenie'.

39 Isaev, *Bezrabotitsa*, 6; Kleinborg, *Istoriia*, 285; McAuley, *Bread*, 88–9, 188; Rabino-witch, 'Bol'sheviki', 124–5; *Odinnadtsatyi s'ezd RKP(b)*, 103–4.

40 Koenker, 'Deurbanization', 90–5; Brower, ' "City" ', 62–3; Figes, *Peasant Russia*, 138–44; Okninskii, *Dva goda*, 176.

41 GARF, f. I30, op. 3, d. 443, l. 35, 36, 55, 93, 98.

42 Chase, *Workers*, 19–20; Brower, ' "City" ', 72–3; 24; GARF, f. 545I, op. 3, d. 475.

43 TsGANKh, f. 1943, op. 4, d. II6. l. 17; GARF, f. 5451, op. 4, d. 148, l. 175; f. 3429, op. I, d. 305, l. I4I; *Izvestiia samarskogo gubprodkomiteta*, 7–8, 1918: 22–3; Figes, *Peasant Russia*, 95–6; Vaisberg, *Den'gi i tseny*, 109–13.

44 Kabanov, *Oktiabr'skaia*, 210–II.

45 Trotsky, *HRA*, I: 85.

46 Suny, *Baku*, 208.

47 GARF, f. 393, op. II, d. 199, l. 60.

48 Figes, *Peasant Russia*, 66–7, 81–3, 188.

49 Lenin, *PSS*, 37: 40–I.

50 GARF, f. I30, op. 2, d. 442; d. 443, ll. 22, 38, 52, 75, 122.

51 TsGANKh, f. I943, op. I, d. 448, l. 70; op. 6, d. 376, l. 85; GARF, f. 4390, op. 2, d. 327, l. 38; f. I30, op. 2, d. 443, l. 53; GAVO, f. 503, op. I, d. 49, l. 24.

52 GAKO, f. 7, op. I, d. 535, l. 23.

53 *Protokoly zasedanii*, 294.

54 Figes, *Peasant Russia*, 188–99.

55 Aver'ev (ed.), *Komitety*, I: 21–2; GARF, f. 393, op. 3, d. 336, l. 285.

56 GARF, f. I30, op. 2, d. 277, l. 177.

57 *Leninskii sbornik*, 18: I44, 206.

58 Figes, *Peasant Russia*, 249–6I.

59 Harrison, *Marooned*, 150–7; Banerji, 'Commissars', 271.

60 Trotskii, *Sochineniia*, I2: 136–7.

61 AG, Pg-Rl, 30–I9–62I; McAuley, *Bread*, 280.

62 For the view that the workers consciously supported the opposition parties see Brovkin, 'The Mensheviks' Political Comeback'. For the opposite (and generally more persuasive) view that the workers' protest movement was not politicized in party terms see Rosenberg, 'Russian Labor'.

63 GARF, f. I30, op. 2, d. 616, l. 2; Rabinowitch, 'Bol'sheviki', I26–7.

64 Lenin, *PSS*, 36: 175–84.

65 Malle, *Economic*, ch. 2.

66 Gor'kii, 'Pis'ma k E. P. Peshkovoi', I99.

67 *O Lenine*, 54.

68 *Pravda*, I Sep 1918; Tumarkin, *Lenin Lives!*, 82–90.

69 Tumarkin, *Lenin Lives!*, 83–5, 91–5; Seifullina, 'Muzhitskii'.

70 *Proletarskaia Revoliutsiia*, 6–7, 1923: 284; Lockhart, *Memoirs*, 320; Balabanoff, *My Life as a Rebel*, 209.

71 *Krasnaia gazeta*, I Sep 1918; *Izvestiia*, 3 Sep 1918; *Ezhenedel'nik chrezvychainykh komissii*, I, 1918: II.

72 Trotskii, *O Lenine*, 101; Ferro, *October*, 265.

73 Leggett, *Cheka*, 30–4.

74 Latsis, *Chrezvychainye*, 8.

75 Melgunov, *Red Terror*, 27–8; Peters, 'Vospominaniia', 9.

76 GARF, f. 1236, op. I, d. 5; Polner, *Zhiznennyi*, 262; *Moscow News*, 14–21 June 1992.

77 *Piatyi vserossiiskii s'ezd*, 5–37; Rabinowitch, 'Maria', 426–7; Leggett, *Cheka*, 72–6.

78 Hoover, Steinberg, 'The Events of July 1918', 22; Rabinowitch, 'Maria', 429.

79 Benckendorff, *Last Days*, 88.

80 Kerensky, *Catastrophe*, 268–9.

81 Massie, *Nicholas*, 449.

82 Trotskii, *Dnevniki i pis'ma*, 100–1.

83 Radzinsky, *Last Tsar*, 239.

84 Ibid., 248.

85 GARF, f. 601, op. 2, d. 32, l. 71; *Sovetskaia Rossiia*, 12 July 1987.

86 Trotskii, *Dnevniki i pis'ma*, 100–1.

87 GARF, f. 130, op. 2, d. 653, l. 12.

88 Radzinsky, *Last Tsar*, 313–15.

89 *Literaturnaia Rossiya*, 28 Sep 1990.

90 Radzinsky, *Last Tsar*, ch. 15; Steinberg and Khrustalev, *Fall*, 357–60.

91 For the story of the bones see Massie, *Romanovs*.

92 Miliutin, 'Stranitsy iz dnevnika', 10.

93 *Izvestiia*, 19 July 1918; Lockhart, *Memoirs*, 304; GARF, f. 5972, op. I, d. 22b, l. 365; Sokolov, *Ubiistvo*.

94 Carr, *Bolshevik*, I: 174; Radzinsky, *Last Tsar*, 278; Radek, *Portrety*, I: 50.

95 *Cheka*, 47, 90–1, 158–63; *Pamiat'*, 4: 379.

96 Peshekhonov, 'Pered', 205; GARF, f. 130, op. 2, d. 67, l. 525, 546.

97 Peshekhonov, 'Pered', 205–6.

98 GARF, f. 130, op. 2, d. 67, l. 20.

99 Ibid., l. 263f.

100 Ibid., f. 5972, op. 3, d. 121, l.2; d. 350; RGVIA, f. 162, op. I, d. 18, l. 42–3.

101 *Izvestiia gosudarstvennogo kontrolia*, I, 1919: 16–17; Dan, *Dva goda skitanii*, 126–33.

102 Melgunov, *Red Terror*, 162–200; Steinberg, *In the Workshop*, 145.

103 Gul', 'Byloe'.

104 GARF, f. 130, op. 2, d. 751, l. 151; f. 1129, op. 2, d. 105, l. 16–17; Bunyan, *Intervention*, 253–7.

105 AG, Pg-Rl, 16–40–1; Pg-Rl, 13–51–2.

106 GARF, f. 4390, op. 14, d. 133.

107 Lenin, *PSS*, 51: 47–8.

14 The New Regime Triumphant

1 GARF, f. 6028, op. 1, d. 20, l. 9–10; *Istochnik*, 1, 1994: 24.

2 Polner, *Zhiznennyi*, 259–65; *Rus'*, 19 March 1925.

3 Fleming, *Fate*, 92–4, 105–6.

4 GARF, f. 6028, op. 1, d. 10, l. 5.

5 Ibid., d. 20, l. 8; Polner, *Zhiznennyi'*, 272.

6 GARF, f. 6028, op. 1, d. 17; *Grazhdanskaia voina*, 229.

7 Kiriukhin, *Iz dnevnika*, 71–2.

8 Figes, *Peasant Russia*, 324–33.

9 Ibid., 313–14; Lincoln, *Red*, 261–5; Fleming, *Fate*, 139.

10 Budberg, 'Dnevnik', 15: 281, 290, 326.

11 Graves, *America's*, 200; Budberg, 'Dnevnik', 14: 225.

12 Fleming, *Fate*, 136; Budberg, 'Dnevnik', 14: 262.

13 Gins, *Sibir'*, 2, 2: 151–7.

14 Graves, *America's*, 147, 153–5, 160–1.

15 Mel'gunov, *Tragediia*, 3, 1: 167–8; Maksakov (ed.), *Partizanskoe*, 1: 129–43.

16 GARF, f. 1805, op. 1, d. 12; Maksakov (ed.), *Partizanskoe*, 1: 145–72, 289.

17 Fleming, *Fate*, 157.

18 GARF, f. 439, op. 1, d. 108, l. 58; Medvedev and Starikov, *Philip Mironov*, 110–15; Brovkin, *Behind*, 101–6; Holquist 'Russian Vendée', ch. 5.

19 Kenez, *Defeat*, 27–34; Malet, *Makhno*, 30–2; Wrangel, *Memoirs*, 88.

20 Kenez, *Defeat*, 20–1; Mawdsley, *Russian*, 170; *Trotsky Papers*, 2: 650; Figes, 'Red Army', 182, 188.

21 Wrangel, *Memoirs*, 89.

22 Denikin, *Ocherki*, 5: 118.

23 *Revvoensovet respubliki*, 177; Stankevich, *Vospominaniia*, 149; Soloman, *Sredi krasnykh vozhdei*, 214–18; *Istochnik*, 1, 1994: 3.

24 Kin, *Denikinshchina*, 115–16, 142–6; Friedgutt, *Iuzovka*, 2: 373.

25 Denikin, *Ocherki*, 4: 86–8.

26 Rakovskii, *V stane belykh*, 25, 38; Lehovich, *White*, 324–5; Denikin, *Ocherki*, 4: 93–4; Sokolov, *Pravlenie*, 192–4; GARF, f. 439, op. 1, d. 108, l. 59.

27 Trotsky, *My Life*, 473.

28 GARF, f. 130, op. 3, d. 363; Brovkin, *Behind*, 73–7, 167–8; Os'kin, *Zapiski voenkoma*, 179; *Revvoensovet respubliki*, 180; Hoover, Martov Collection, 'Oborona revoliutsii i sotsial-demoktariia', 3.

29 *Revvoensovet respubliki*, 177; Os'kin, *Zapiski voenkoma*, 187, 202–3.

30 GARF, f. 130, op. 3, d. 198; Danilov, 'Pereraspredelenie', 284–7; Figes, 'Red Army', 206–9.

31 Egorov, *Razgrom*, 144; Os'kin, *Zapiski voenkoma*, 233.

32 Trotsky, *HRA*, 3: 412–14.

33 Ruhl, *New Masters*, 109; Mannerheim, *Memoirs*, 221.

34 Trotsky, *My Life*, 440–8, 473–4; Serge, *Memoirs*, 93; *Trotsky Papers*, 1: 718–19.

35 McAuley, *Bread*, 255; Serge, *Memoirs*, 91–3.

36 Os'kin, *Zapiski voenkoma*, 237; *Vospominaniia o . . . Lenine*, 2: 262.

37 Bechhofer, *In Denikin's Russia*, 121; Sokolov, *Pravlenie*, 191.

38 Bechhofer, *In Denikin's Russia*, 101.

39 Pipes, *Russia Under the Bolshevik Regime*, 99–114; Maslov, *Rossiia*, 2: 37.

40 Knei-Paz, *Trotsky*, 546; Shulgin, *1920 god*, 28.

41 GARF, f. 6764, op. 1, d. 775, l. 19.

42 Ibid., l. 20–23; Poliak, 'Zhutkie dni', 17–36; Shekhtman, *Pogromy*, 368.

43 Maleev, *Tridtsat' dnei*; GARF, f. 6764, op. 1, d. 775.

44 GARF, f. 6764, op. 1, d. 775, l. 3–4.

45 Sokolov, *Pravlenie*, 253; Miliukov, *Russia Today and Tomorrow*, 230.

46 See e.g. Pipes, *Russia Under the Bolshevik Regime*, 9–14.

47 Babel, *1920 Diary*, 7.

48 Wrangel, *Memoirs*, 185.

49 BA, Bakhmeteff Collection, Box 5.

50 GARF, f. 4390, op. 13, d. 38.

51 Fischer, *Lenin*, 121.

52 GARF, f. 551, op. 1, d. 20, 21, 27, 29, 39; Pascal, *En Communisme*, 93–6.

53 GARF, f. 551, op. 1, d. 59.

54 RGVA, f. 33987, op. 3, d. 46, l. 142–3; GARF, f. 4085, op. 1, d. 14; f. 130, op. 2, d. 71, l. 332; f. 4390, op. 2, d. 327; op. 4, d. 109; *Deviataia konferentsiia RKP(b)*, 168; Harrison, *Marooned*, 124.

55 Bonch-Bruevich, *Na boevykh postakh*, 115.

56 Rigby, *Lenin's Government*, 176–8, 184–5; Service, *Bolshevik*, 120–2; Zelnik, 'Fate', 26–7.

57 Pipes, *Russia Under the Bolshevik Regime*, 446; Sakwa, *Soviet Communists*, 49–53, 191–3; Lenin, *PSS*, 52: 65.

58 GARF, f. 5469, op. 2, d. 50, l. 81.

59 *Struktura i sostav organov*, 68; Goldman, *My Disillusionment*, 54.

60 Solomon, *Sredi*, 222–7; Orlovsky, 'State', 185–92; *Struktura i sostav organov*, 79.

61 Figes, *Peasant Russia*, ch. 5.2.

62 Adelman, 'Development', 93; Rigby, *Political Elites*, 49; Rapoporta, 'Poltora goda', 103.

63 Kitaev, 'Stroitel'stvo', 104.

64 Rigby, *Political Elites*, 28–9; Dukes, *Red Dusk*, 23.

65 Sakwa, *Soviet Communists*, 154; GARF, f. 539, op. 1, d. 3190, l. 53.

66 Rigby, *Political Elites*, 47–61.

67 Adelman, 'Development', 93, 96–8.

68 GARF, f. 4085, op. 1a, d. 139, l. 30.

69 AG, Pg-Rl, 30–19–630; Sorokin, *Sovremennoe*, 52; GARF, f. 130, op. 3, d. 158, l. 414; *Petrogradskaia pravda*, 19 Jan 1919.

70 RGVIA, f. 162, op. 2, d. 18.

71 GARF, f. 130, op. 4, d. 245, l. 397–8; RGVA, f. 33987, op. 3, d. 46, l. 143.

72 Arbatov, 'Ekaterinoslav', 113; GARF, f. 5972, op. 1, d. 101; op. 3, d. 170, l. 3–4; RGVA, f. 33987, op. 1, d. 278; RGVIA, f. 162, op. 2, d. 18.

73 BA, Brusilov Collection, Manuscripts 'Gazeta "Dni" ', 42; RGVIA, f. 162, op. 2, d. 18; Grondijs, *La Guerre*, 265.

74 GARF, f. 5972, op. 1, d. 226, l. 208–10.

75 RGVIA, f. 162, op. 2, d. 18; RGVA, f. 33988, op. 1, d. 267, l. 1–2.

76 GARF, f. 5972, op. 3, d. 170, l. 1; Trotsky, *HRA*, 3: 158; *Pravda*, 11–12 May 1920.

77 GATO, f. 1832, op. 1, d. 834, l. 9; Stites, *Revolutionary*, 95–6; Arbatov, 'Ekaterinoslav', 113.

78 Agursky, *Third Rome*, 185ff; Burbank, *Intelligentsia*, 219–25; Ustrialov, *V bor'be*, 13; Gor'kii, *Perepiska A. M. Gor'kogo s zarubezhnymi*, 67.

79 Davies, *White Eagle*, 187; Pipes, *Russia Under the Bolshevik Regime*, 182.

80 *Kommunisticheskii internatsional'*, 1 May 1919; Zinoviev, *Sochineniia*, 15: 281; Carr, *Bolshevik*, 3: 180–1, 192.

81 *Istoricheskii arkhiv*, 1 1992: 12–30.

82 Ibid., 16–17.

83 *Trotsky Papers*, 1: 623, 625; Agabekov, *OGPU*, 16.

84 Wells, *Russia in the Shadows*, 99; *Congress of Peoples of the East*, 34.

85 Lenin, *PSS*, 48: 163.

86 Bulgakov, *White Guard*, 266; Graziosi, 'Piatakov', 121–4.

87 Ordzhonikidze, *Stat'i i rechi*, 1: 106–7; *Resolution and Decisions of the Communist Party*, 2: 102.

88 Majstrenko, *Borot'bism*, 191.

89 Krawchenko, *Social Change*, 55; Mace, *Communism*, 69.

90 Rorlich, *Volga Tatars*, 138.

91 Pipes, *Formation*, 182; Park, *Bolshevism in Turkestan*, 36.

92 Becker, *Russia's Protectorates*, 299–301; Park, *Bolshevism in Turkestan*, 133–4, 375.

93 Gokay, 'Turkish'; Swietochowski, *Russian Azerbaidzhan*, 147ff.

94 PRO, FO 371/3404.

95 Hovannisen, *Republic*, 2: 249–50, 291.

96 Suny, *Making*, 192–9, 205–6.

97 Pipes, *Russia Under the Bolshevik Regime*, 164.

98 Suny, *Making*, 210; Lenin, *PSS*, 42: 367; 43: 199; Jones, 'Establishment', 623–8.

99 Wrangel, *Memoirs*, 171–5.

100 Miliukov, *Russia Today and Tomorrow*, 181; Obolenskii, 'Krym', 27, 31–2, 35, 41–2; Rakovskii, *Konets*, 84–5, 147–50.

101 Wrangel, *Memoirs*, 175, 191; Obolenskii, 'Krym', 11–15, 30–2; Miliukov, *Russia Today and Tomorrow*, 178–9; Gukovskii (ed.), 'Agrarnaia', 52–3, 69–72.

102 Valentinov, 'Krymskaia', 15–16.

103 Kalinin, *Pod znamenem*, 104; Rakovskii, *Konets*, 9, 158.

104 Wrangel, *Memoirs*, 274–5; Obolenskii, 'Krym', 17; Rakovskii, *Konets*, 82–4.

105 Valentinov, 'Krymskaia', 85–6; Bechhofer, *In Denikin's*, ch. 7; Kenez, *Defeat*, 306–8.

106 RGVIA, f. 162, op. 2, d. 18.

15 Defeat in Victory

1 Os'kin, *Khoziaistvennaia*, 16–20, 24; TsGANKh, f. 3429, op. I, d. 1527, l. 16, 190.

2 TsGANKh, f. 3429, op. I, d. 1487, l. 25; d. 1527, l. 5; f. 1884, op. 28, d. I; *Doklad ot narodnogo komissara putei soobshcheniia*, 5–9; *Narodnyi komissariat putei soobshcheniia*, 6; Rosenberg, 'Social Background', 364–7.

3 *Krasnoarmeets*, 16–20, Feb 1920, 8; *Tretii Vserossiiskii s'ezd professional'nykh soiuzov*, I: 87–90, 97.

4 *Deviatyi s'ezd RKP(b)*, 94; *NZh*, II Nov 1917.

5 GARF, f. 5451, op. 3, d. 336; op. 4, d. 148, 289; f. 382, op. 4, d. 477; f. 130, op. 3, d. 363; TsGANKh, f. 1637, op. I, d. 359, 361; f. 3429, op. I, d. 857; Brovkin, *Behind*, ch. 2.

6 *Dva goda deiatel'nosti TsK po snabzheniiu rabochikh*; Malle, *Economic*, 123–35, 182–4.

7 Trotsky, *HRA*, 3: 47–52, 65–7; GAKO, f. 193, op. 2, d. 159, l. 102; Stites, *Revolutionary*, 19–24; Os'kin, *Khoziaistvennaia*, 78–9; Donskii, 'Ot Moskvy', 208; GARF, f. 130, op. 5, d. 1037, l. 19–20; op. 3, d. 104, l. 30, 68; TsGANKh, f. 3429, op. I, d. 1527, l. 1–6; d. 857, l. 148; Bunyan (ed.), *Origin*, 71–4.

8 Chase, 'Voluntarism', 115; GARF, f. 539, op. I, d. 3190, l. 30.

9 Banerji, 'Commissars', 264; Ransome, *Six Weeks*, 88–92; Malle, *Economic*, 153–85.

10 McAuley, *Bread*, 286–95; Sorokin, *Leaves*, 220; GARF, f. 539, op. I, d. 3190, l. 12–15.

11 Figes, *Peasant Russia*, 295–308; TsGANKh, f. 478, op. 3, d. 1157, l. 58; op. 4, d. 69, l. 60; Kabanov, *Krest'ianskoe*, 240–73.

12 GARF, f. 130, op. 3, d. 414; Brovkin, *Behind*, 287–99.

13 Rosenberg, 'Social Background'; Schapiro, *Origin*, 256–92; Fitzpatrick, *Cultural Front*, 25–30; Sakwa, *Soviet*, 216–60.

14 Sokolov, *White Nights*, 67–72.

15 Burleigh, *Death*, II.

16 Joravsky, *Russian Psychology*, 53–63, 207–13; Trotskii, *Sochineniia*, XXI: 110–12.

17 Stites, *Revolutionary*, 32–3; Bogdanov, *Red Star*, 60–77, 196.

18 Gor'kii, *Polnoe sobranie sochineniia*, 24: 18–19; AG, Pg-In.

19 Scherrer, 'Écoles', 265; RTsKhIDNI, f. 17, op. 60, d. 43, l. 19; Read, *Culture*, 113–14.

20 Mally, 'Intellectuals'; Read, *Culture*, 89–90, 111–33; Fitzpatrick, *Commissariat*, 129–33; Stites, *Revolutionary*, 70–I; McClelland, 'Utopianism', 411.

21 Michelson, 'Wings', 61–9; Taylor, *Politics*, 36.

22 Stites, *Revolutionary*, 94–5, 136; Pipes, *Russia Under the Bolshevik Regime*, 305–8.

23 Bowlt, 'Constructivism', 204; Stites, *Revolutionary*, 90.

24 Harrison, *Marooned*, 125–6; Chagall, *My Life*, 137; Pethybridge, *Social*, 149; Donskii, 'Ot Moskvy', 199.

25 Clements, 'Effects', 105.

26 Stites, *Women's*, 362, 377; Goldman, *Women*, 7; Farnsworth, 'Village', 246; Fitzpatrick, 'Sex', 268–9; Goldman, 'Working-Class', 129–30, 134–9.

27 Bonch-Bruevich, *Vospominaniia*, 380; Pipes, *Russia Under the Bolshevik Regime*, 299.

28 Zenzinov, *Deserted*, 27; Fitzpatrick, *Commissariat*, 31–3, 67, 218; McClelland, 'Utopianism', 119–24.

29 Stites, *Revolutionary*, 146–57; Toller, *Which*, 114; Gastev, 'O tendentsiiakh', 44–5; *ABC*, 75.

30 GARF, f. 130, op. 2, d. 153, l. 12; d. 163, l. 60; Stites, *Revolutionary*, 105–9; *Moscow News*, 19–26 August, 1990; Karpov, 'Po volnam', 40–1; Hindus, *Red*, 275–6.

31 Stites, *Revolutionary*, 110; Tumarkin, *Lenin*, 71–2.

32 Stites, *Revolutionary*, 111–13; Kolonitskii, 'Revolutionary Names', 211–12, 223; Stites, *Women's*, 364.

33 Pipes, *Russia Under the Bolshevik Regime*, 347–9; Vasil'eva, 'Russkaia', 43–4; RTsKhIDNI, f. 5, op. 2, d. 48, l. 29, 81–2; *Izvestiia TsK*, 4, 1990, 190–3; *Moscow News*, 19–26 August 1990.

34 Agursky, *Third Rome*, 266–7; Pipes, *Russia Under the Bolshevik Regime*, 356; Yodfat, 'Closure'; GARF, f. 353, op. 3, d. 755, l. 125–31, 167–9, 201–2, 237–9; Gitelman, *Century*, 118.

35 Figes, *Peasant Russia*, 147–50; GARF, f. 4390, op. 12, d. 40, l. 17, 24.

36 TsGALI, f. 552, op. 1, d. 3827, l. 49.

37 *Volia Rossii*, 18 Jan 1921; Figes, *Peasant Russia*, 269–72.

38 GARF, f. 5556, op. 1, d. 35a, 50; f. 130, op. 3, d. 414, l. 7–8; op. 5, d. 712, l. 53; *Volia Rossii*, 22 March, 27 July 1921; *Trotsky Papers*, 2: 386–7.

39 *Trotsky Papers*, 2: 492–5; RGVA, f. 7, op. 2, d. 483, l. 8; f. 235, op. 5, d. 63, l. 5, 6, 9, 10, 19–21, 25, 37, 38; d. 217, l. 15; GATO, f. 1832, op. 1, d. 631, l. 16, 26, 84; *Antonovshchina*, 95–6, 150–9; Radkey, *Unknown*, 38, 139–43, 192–6; Trifonov, *Klassy*, 37, 246; BA, Lidin Collection, 'Antonovshchina', 6.

40 GATO, f. 1832, op. 1, d. 834, l. 9; GARF, f. 130, op. 3, d. 414, l. 35, 61; Figes, *Peasant Russia*, 329, 349.

41 *Antonovshchina*, 198–210; Brovkin, *Behind*, 363–8; *Trotsky Papers* 2: 46–51; Figes, *Peasant Russia*, 326, 348–9.

42 *Trotsky Papers*, 2: 504–7; GARF, f. 130, op. 5, d. 712, l. 34; Trifonov, *Klassy*, 80, 111; *Krasnaia armiia*, 3–4, 1921, 35–9.

43 Figes, *Peasant Russia*, 329–31, 334, 339, 344; GARF, f. 130, op. 5, d. 712, l. 27; *Trotsky Papers*, 2: 404–5; *Volia Rossii*, 21 Dec 1920.

44 *Trotsky Papers*, 2: 480; Figes, *Peasant Russia*, 346–7, 351; Radkey, *Unknown*, 319–20; Gorky, *Russian*, 18; GARF, f. 130, op. 5, d. 712, l. 23.

45 Lenin, *PSS*, 43: 18, 82.

46 *Pravda*, 22 Jan 1921; Dan, *Dva*, 104–5.

47 *New York Times*, 6 March 1921; Sakwa, *Soviet*, 244–5.

48 Brovkin, *Behind*, 391–4; Dan, *Dva*, 106; *Kronshtadtskii miatezh*, 26.

49 Sukhanov, *Russian*, 446; Getzler, *Kronstadt*, 173–6, 209–11; Radkey, *Unknown*, 404; *Pravda o Kronshtadte*, 145.

50 *Pravda o Kronshtadte*, 46–7; Getzler, *Kronstadt*, 205–8, 218–19, 223–9.

51 *Volia Rossii*, 17 March 1921; Avrich, *Kronstadt*, 76–87; *Kronshtadtskii miatezh*, 146–7; Pipes, *Russia Under the Bolshevik Regime*, 382.

52 Avrich, *Kronstadt*, 151–4; Berkman, *Bolshevik*, 303.

53 *Pravda o Kronshtadte*, 82–4.

54 Balabanoff, *Impressions*, 97–8; Balabanoff, *Life*, 252; Lenin, *PSS*, 43: 41.

55 Carr, *Bolshevik*, 2: 280–6; Schapiro, *Origin*, 307, 309; *Antonovshchina*, 109–10, 307; RTsKhIDNI, f. 17, op. 3, d. 128, l. 1.

56 *Desiaty s'ezd*, 403–15; Mikoian, *Mysli*, 156.

57 Avrich, *Kronstadt*, 46–51, 202–16; Sakwa, *Soviet*, 245–6; Sorokin, *Leaves*, 268–9; Levin, *Stormy*, 210; RTsKhIDNI, f. 76, op. 3, d. 167.

58 Berkman, *Bolshevik*, 303.

59 Esikov and Protasov, ' "Antonovshchina" ', 52; RGVA, f. 235, op. 2, d. 82, l. 40; op. 5, d. 133, l. 70; f. 33988, op. 2, d. 315, l. 256; *Trotsky Papers*, 2: 537; *Volia Rossii*, 27 July 1921.

60 *Trotsky Papers*, 2: 482, 518, 529; *Volia Rossii*, 28 April 1921.

61 Arbatov, 'Batko', 112.

62 Schapiro, *Origin*, 205; Jansen, *Show*, 128.

63 *New Economic*, 58; Pipes, *Russia Under the Bolshevik Regime*, 369; Lenin, *PSS*, 43: 27, 329.

64 Lenin, *PSS*, 43: 25; 44: 163; 45: 82, 387–8.

65 Cohen, *Bukharin*, 138–41; Goldman, *My Further*, 23.

66 Barmine, *One*, 124–5; Goldman, *My Further*, 201–2; Ball, *Russia's*, 16.

16 Deaths and Departures

1 *Correspondence*, 26: 56.

2 Mawdsley, *Russian*, 285–7; Pipes, *Russia Under the Bolshevik Regime*, 508–9; Fisher, *Famine*, 83; TsGALI, f. 552, op. 1, d. 3827, l. 48; GARF, f. 130, op. 4, d. 245, l. 174–80.

3 Donskii, 'Ot Moskvy', 205; Sorokin, *Sovremennoe*, 229–32; Shklovsky, *Sentimental*, 170; *Izvestiia gosudarstvennogo kontrolia*, 3–4, 1919, 33; GARF, f. 4390, op. 12, d. 40, l. 17, 24, 53.

4 GARF, f. 5972, op. 1, d. 21a, l. 65; *Cheka*, 11; Fisher, *Famine*, 97; Gorky, 'On the Russian', 16, 18.

5 Figes, *Peasant Russia*, 267–73, 274–6.

6 *Kniga o golode*, 7, 16, 38–42, 48–53, 119, 123; *Volia Rossii*, 28, 29 Sep 1921; BA, ARA, Information Relative to Relief Work in Russia, Memo April 1922; Fisher, *Famine*, 90.

7 *Itogi bor'by*, 196; *Kniga o golode*, 52, 131–2, 140; Zenzinov, *Deserted*, 72–4; Fisher, *Famine*, 98; Raleigh (ed.), *Russian*, 209–10.

8 Conquest, *Harvest*.

9 AG, Pg-In; BA, Polner Collection, Box 1, Letter from Lvov to F. Rodichev, 10 Sep 1921; Wolfe, *Bridge*, 108–9; Heller, 'Premier', 131–44.

10 *PSS*, 53: 110–11; Heller, 'Premier', 147ff; Wolfe, *Bridge*, 112.

11 Fisher, *Famine*, 195–210, 308–32, 553, 557.

12 *ARA Bulletin*, ser. 2, 28: 6.

13 Ball, 'Survival', 34, 36–7, 41–2, 47; Ball, *And Now My Soul*, chs 1–3; Sorokin, *Sovremennoe*, 66.

14 *Lenin and Gorky*, 163; Zenzinov, *Deserted*, 10–17; Juviler, 'Contradictions', 263–5;

Serge, *Memoirs*, 98; *Biulleten' otdela sotsial'nogo obezpecheniia i okhrana truda*, I, 1919: 17, 44–5.

15 Berberova, *Italics*, 188–9; Shub, 'Maksim', 244.

16 Khodasevich, *Nekropol*, 233–4; Khodasevich, *Belyi koridor*, 227–34; RTsKhIDNI, f. 75, op. I, d. 149; *Lenin and Gorky*, 145–8.

17 AG, Pg-Rl, 23–44–35; RTsKhIDNI, f. 75, op. I, d. 70; Fitzpatrick, *Commissariat*, 131.

18 Pyman, *Life*, 2: 274, 290–I, 374–5; Gorky, *Fragments*, 142–3; Vogel (ed.), *Alexander*, 75; AG, Pg-Rl, 23–44–3; Rg-P, 46–I–40.

19 Khodasevich, *Nekropol*, 113–40; Wolfe, *Bridge*, 121–2. Nadezhda Mandelstam, hostile to Gorky, claims he did nothing to intervene on behalf of Gumilev (*Hope Abandoned*, 88).

20 Pyman, *Life*, 2: 379; Berberova, *Italics*, 123.

21 TsGALI, f. 200, op. I, d. 80, l. 3; f. 2226, op. I, d. 1067; f. 66, op. I, d. 296, l. 5; d. 312, l. 4–5; d. 324, l. I–2; d. 913, l. 18; f. 122, op. 3, d. 13, l. I, 5–7.

22 *Pravda*, 11 Jan 1923; Morizet, *Chez*, 241–2.

23 Lenin, *PSS*, 42: 159; Liberman, *Building*, 60; Stites, *Revolutionary*, 48–50; Wells, *Russia*, 135.

24 Danilov, *Rural*, 160–72, 271–91; Danilov, *Sovetskaia*, 212.

25 Mironov, 'Gramotnost' '; Danilov, *Rural*, 42–4, 231–43.

26 Shanin, *Awkward*, 189–90; Kenez, *Birth*, 173, 186; *Ocherki byta*, 10–12.

27 Hagen, *Soldiers*, 300–2, 314–15; Fitzpatrick, *Stalin's*, 36.

28 Iakovlev, *Derevnia*, 74; Khataevich, 'Partiia', 106; Iakovlev, *Nasha*, 33, 163; Male, *Russian*, 93–4; Weissman, 'Policing', 179.

29 GARF, f. 130, op. 4, d. 245, l. 377; Gorky, 'On the Russian', 23, 74; *Izvestiia TsK*, 2, 1989: 204.

30 Volkogonov, *Lenin*, 425–7; *Izvestiia TsK*, 12, 1989: 198.

31 *Izvestiia TsK*, 12, 1989: 197.

32 Volkogonov, *Stalin*, 69; Antonov-Ovseenko, *Time*, 25–6.

33 Fainsod, *How*, 182; Pipes, *Russia Under the Bolshevik Regime*, 462; Antonov-Ovseenko, *Time*, 27–9.

34 Pipes, *Russia Under the Bolshevik Regime*, 467; *Izvestiia TsK*, 12, 1989: 198; Lenin, *PSS*, 53: 300.

35 Naumov, '1923 god', 36; Lenin, *PSS*, 45: 327; Trotsky, *My Life*, 498–9.

36 RTsKhIDNI, f. 5, op. 2, d. 27, l. 88; Lenin, *PSS*, 40: 710; Volkogonov, *Stalin*, 80; Valentinov, *Novaia*, 185–7; Antonov-Ovseenko, *Time*, 23; *Moscow News*, 23 April 1989.

37 Fotieva, *Iz zhizni*, 279; *Moscow News*, 22 Jan 1989.

38 *Izvestiia TsK*, 9, 1989: 191, 196, 199–200, 205–6; Lenin, *PSS*, 45: 211–13, 356–62, 557–8; 54: 299–300, 330; *Pravda*, 12 Aug 1988.

39 Lenin, *PSS*, 45: 344–6.

40 Pipes, *Russia Under the Bolshevik Regime*, 478; Lenin, *PSS*, 45: 327–30; 54: 674–5; *Izvestiia TsK*, 12, 1989: 193, 198.

41 *Izvestiia Tsk*, 4, 1990: 109; Pipes, *Russia Under the Bolshevik Regime*, 479; Volkogonov, *Lenin*, 428–9.

42 Weber and Weber, *Lenin*, 197; Nikolaevsky, *Power*, 12.

43 This emerges clearly from the recently published *Stalin's Letters to Molotov.*

44 Deutscher, *Prophet Unarmed*, 106; Trotsky, *My Life*, ch. 40; Ziv, *Trotskii*, 76.

45 *Izvestiia TsK*, 5, 1990: 169–70; 6, 1990: 190. The phrase 'police regime' was borrowed from Bukharin (*Izvestiia TsK*, 10, 1990: 168).

46 *Izvestiia TsK*, 5, 1990: 178–9; 7, 1990: 176–89; Deutscher, *Prophet Unarmed*, 118; Broué, *Trotsky*, 373; *Voprosy Istorii KPSS*, 5, 1990: 35–7.

47 *Izvestiia TsK*, 10, 1989: 188–9; Pipes, *Russia Under the Bolshevik Regime*, 485.

48 Tumarkin, *Lenin Lives!*, 119–33.

49 *New York Times*, 15 June 1992.

50 Tumarkin, *Lenin Lives!*, 139–49, 160–4, ch. 6.

51 *Argumenty i fakty*, 576, Nov 1991, 1; *The Times*, 19 Jan 1994.

Conclusion

1 AG, PG-In.

2 *Delo derevni*, 20 Sep, 3 Nov 1917.

3 Kuromiya, *Stalin's*, xi; Vorobei, *Odin*, 13.

4 BA, Bakhmeteff Collection, Box 5; *Poslednie novosti*, 8 March 1925.

5 GARF, f. 5972, op. 1, d. 21a, l. 22–4; RGVIA, f. 162, op. 1, d. 18; BA, Brusilov Collection, mss. 'Gazeta "Dni" '.

6 GARF, f. 5972, op. 1, d. 219, l. 197–215.

7 *A Radical Worker*, 389–91; RTsKhIDNI, f. 72, op. 3, d. 687; Zelnik, 'Fate', 9–11.

8 AG, Pg-In; Berberova, *Italics*, 189; Troyat, *Gorky*, 156, 160; *Moscow News*, 25 Jan 1990.

9 Troyat, *Gorky*, 154.

10 Ivanov, 'Pochemu', 105–6, 109–10, 116, 129; Spiridonova, 'Gorky and Stalin', 417–18.

11 Serge, *Memoirs*, 268; Ivanov, 'Pochemu', 101–2, 127–8, 131.

12 Spiridonova, 'Gorky and Stalin', 418–23; Ivanov, 'Pochemu', 120–6. For a different view of Maxim's death see Shentalinsky, *The KGB's Literary Archive*, 262–6.

13 Tucker, *Stalin in Power*, 362–5; Conquest, *Great Terror*, 387–9; Ivanov, 'Pochemu', 133.

Bibliography

Archives in Russia

AG	Gorky Archive, Institute of World Literature, Moscow
GAKO	State Archive of Kuibyshev Oblast'
GARF	State Archive of the Russian Federation, Moscow
GATO	State Archive of Tambov Oblast'
GAVO	State Archive of Voronezh Oblast'
IM	Historical Museum, Moscow
RGAE	Russian State Archive of the Economy, Moscow
RGIA	Russian State Historical Archives, St Petersburg
RGVA	Russian State Military Archive, Moscow
RGVIA	Russian State Military History Archive, Moscow
RTsKhIDNI	Russian Centre for the Preservation and Study of Documents of Most Recent History, Moscow
TsGALI	Central State Archive of Literature and Art, Russia
TsGASP	Central State Archive of St Petersburg
TsGAVMF	Central State Archive of the Military Naval Fleet, St Petersburg

Archives in Europe and the USA

BA	Bakhmeteff Archive, Columbia University, USA
BC	Brotherton Collection, University of Leeds, England
CUL	Cambridge University Library, Manuscripts Room, England
HLRO	House of Lords Record Office, Historical Collection, London
Hoover	Hoover Institution on War, Revolution and Peace, Stanford, California, USA
LRA	Leeds Russian Archive, England
NLW	National Library of Wales, Department of Manuscripts and Records, Aberystwyth
PRO	Public Records Office, London
TCL	Trinity College Library, Cambridge, England

Contemporary Newspapers

Delo derevni
Den'
Izvestiia
Izvestiia gosudarstvennogo kontrolia
Izvestiia vserossiiskogo soveta krest'ianskikh deputatov
Kievskaia mysl'
Krasnaia armiia
Krasnaia byl'
Krasnaia gazeta
Krasnoarmeets
Narodnoe pravo
Narodnyi pisatel'
New York Times
Novaia zhizn' [NZh]
Novoe vremia
Pamiat'
Petrogradskaia pravda
Poslednie novosti
Pravda
Pravitel'stvennyi vestnik
Proletarskaia revoliutsiia
Rabochii i soldat
Rus'
Russkie vedomosti
Sovetskaia Rossiia
The Times
Trud
Vekhi
Vestnik komiteta uchreditel'nogo sobraniia
Volia Rossii
Znamia truda

Books and Articles

ABC of Communism, The, Ann Arbor, 1966.
Abraham, R., *Alexander Kerensky: The First Love of the Revolution*, London, 1987.
Adelman, J. R., 'The Development of the Soviet Party Apparatus in the Civil War: Centre, Localities and the National Areas', *Russian History*, 9, 1, 1982.
Agabekov, G., *OGPU, The Russian Secret Terror*, New York, 1931.

Agrarnoe dvizhenie v Rossii v 1905–1906 gg., St Petersburg, 1908.

Agursky, M., *The Third Rome: National Bolshevism in the USSR*, Boulder, 1987.

Aksakov, K. S., *Polnoe sobranie sochinenii*, 2 vols, St Petersburg, 1861.

Anatomiia revoliutsii. 1917 god v Rossii: massy, partii, vlast', St Petersburg, 1994.

Anderson, B., *Imagined Communities*, London, 1983.

Anet, C., *La Révolution Russe*, 4 vols, Paris, 1927.

Anfimov, A. M., *Zemel'naia arenda v Rossii v nachale XX veka*, Moscow, 1961.

Anfimov, A. M., *Rossiiskaia derevnia v gody pervoi mirovoi voiny*, Moscow, 1962.

Antonov-Ovseenko, A., *The Time of Stalin: Portrait of Tyranny*, New York, 1983.

Antonovshchina: Krest'ianskoe vosstanie v Tambovskoi gubernii v 1919–1921 gg. Dokumenty i materialy, Tambov, 1994.

Antsiferov, A. N. et al., *Russian Agriculture During the War*, New Haven, 1930.

Arbatov, Z., 'Ekaterinoslav 1917–1920 gg.', *Arkhiv russkoi revoliutsii*, 12, Berlin, 1923.

Arbatov, Z., 'Batko Makhno', *Vozrozhdenie*, 29, Paris, 1953.

Arbenina, S. (Baroness Meyendorff), *Through Terror to Freedom*, London, 1929.

Aronson, G., *Rossiia v epokhu revoliutsii*, New York, 1966.

Aronson, I. M., *Troubled Waters: The Origins of the 1881 Anti-Jewish Pogroms in Russia*, Pittsburgh, 1990.

Ascher, A., *The Revolution of 1905: Russia in Disarray*, Stanford, 1988.

Atkinson, D., 'The Statistics on the Russian Land Commune, 1905–1917', *Slavic Review*, 4, 1973.

Atkinson, D., *The End of the Russian Land Commune, 1905–1920*, Stanford, 1983.

Averbakh, V. A., 'Revoliutsionnoe obshchestvo po lichnym vospominaniiam', in *Arkhiv russkoi revoliutsii*, 14, Berlin, 1924.

Aver'ev, V. N. (ed.), *Komitety bednoty: Sbornik materialov*, 2 vols, Moscow-Leningrad, 1933.

Avrich, P., *Kronstadt 1921*, Princeton, 1970.

Babel, I., *1920 Diary*, London, 1995.

Babine, A., *A Russian Civil War Diary: Alexis Babine in Saratov, 1917–1922*, ed. D. J. Raleigh, Durham, 1988.

Babushkin, I., *Recollections (1893–1900)*, Moscow, 1957.

Bakhtin, M. M., *The Dialogic Imagination*, Austin, Texas, 1981.

Balabanoff, A., *My Life as a Rebel*, London, 1938.

Balabanoff, A., *Impressions of Lenin*, Ann Arbor, 1964.

Balk, A. P., 'Poslednie piat' dnei tsarskogo Petrograda (23–8 fevralia 1917 g.)', *Russkoe proshloe*, 1, 1991.

Ball, A., *Russia's Last Capitalists*, Berkeley, 1987.

Ball, A., 'Survival in the Street World of Soviet Russia's *Bezprizornye*', *Jahrbücher für Geschichte Osteuropas*, 39, 1, 1991.

Ball, A., *And Now My Soul Is Hardened: Abandoned Children in Soviet Russia, 1918–1930,* Berkeley, 1994.

Balzer, H., 'The Problem of Professions in Imperial Russia', in E. Clowes et al. (ed.), *Between Tsar and People.*

Banerji, A., 'Commissars and Bagmen: Russia during the Civil War, 1918–1921', *Studies in History,* 3, 1987.

Baring, M., *A Year in Russia,* London, 1907.

Baring, M., *What I Saw in Russia,* London, 1927.

Bark, P., 'Iiul' 1914', *Vozrozhdenie,* 22, Paris, 1959.

Barmine, A., *One Who Survived: The Life Story of a Russian Under the Soviets,* New York, 1945.

Bartlett, R. (ed.), *Land Commune and Peasant Community in Russia: Communal Farms in Imperial and Early Soviet Society,* London, 1990.

Bar-Yaacov, N., *The Handling of International Disputes by Means of Inquiry,* London, 1974.

Bater, J. H., *St Petersburg: Industrialization and Change,* London, 1976.

Bauermeister, A., *Spies Break Through: Memoirs of a German Secret Service Officer,* London, 1934.

Bechhofer, C. E., *In Denikin's Russia,* London, 1921.

Becker, S., *Russia's Protectorates in Central Asia: Bukhara and Khiva, 1865–1924,* Cambridge, Mass., 1968.

Becker, S., *Nobility and Privilege in Late Imperial Russia,* DeKalb, Illinois, 1985.

Belinskii, V. G., *Izbrannye filosofskie sochineniia,* Moscow, 1948.

Belinskii, V. G., *Polnoe sobraniie sochinenii,* Moscow, 1953–6.

Belliutsin, I. S., *Description of the Clergy in Rural Russia,* Cornell, 1985.

Bely, A., *Petersburg,* Harmondsworth, 1983.

Benckendorff, Count Paul, *Last Days at Tsarskoe Selo (March–August 1917),* London, 1927.

Benvenutti, F., *The Bolsheviks and the Red Army, 1918–1922,* Cambridge, 1988.

Berberova, N., *The Italics Are Mine,* London, 1991.

Berdyaev, N., *The Origin of Russian Communism,* Glasgow, 1937.

Berkman, A., *The Bolshevik Myth: Diary, 1920–1922,* London, 1925.

Berlin, I., *Russian Thinkers,* London, 1978.

Besançon, A., *The Intellectual Origin of Leninism,* Oxford, 1981.

Billington, J., *The Icon and the Axe: An Interpretative History of Russian Culture,* New York, 1966.

Bing, E. J. (ed.), *The Secret Letters of the Last Tsar,* New York, 1938.

Binshtok, V. I., and Kaminskii, L. S., *Narodnoe pitanie i narodnoe zdorov'e,* Moscow, 1929.

Blagonravov, G. I., 'The Fortress of Peter and Paul, October 1917', in *Petrograd: October 1917,* Moscow, 1957.

Blok, A., *Sobranie sochinenii v vos'mi tomakh*, Moscow-Leningrad, 1960–3.

Blok, A., 'The People and the Intelligentsia', in M. Raeff (ed.), *Russian Intellectual History: An Anthology*, New Jersey, 1978.

Bociurkiw, B., 'The Rise of the Ukrainian Autocephalous Orthodox Church, 1919–1922', in G. Hosking (ed.), *Church.*

Bogaevskii, A. P., *Vospominaniia 1918 goda*, New York, 1963.

Bogdanov, A. A., *Red Star: The First Bolshevik Utopia*, ed. L. Graham and R. Stites, Bloomington, 1984.

Bogdanovich, A. V., *Tri poslednikh samoderzhtsa. Dnevnik*, Leningrad, 1924.

Bogucharskii, V., *Aktivnoe narodnichestvo semidesiatykh godov*, Moscow, 1912.

Bok, M., *Reminiscences of my Father, P. A. Stolypin*, New Jersey, 1970.

Bonch-Bruevich, V. D., 'Strashnoe v revoliutsii', in V. D. Bonch-Bruevich, *Na boevykh postakh fevral'skoi i oktiabr'skoi revoliutsii*, Moscow, 1930.

Bonch-Bruevich, V. D., *Vospominaniia o Lenine*, Moscow, 1969.

Bone, A. (ed.), *The Bolsheviks and the October Revolution: Minutes of the Central Committee of the RSDLP(b), August 1917–February 1918*, London, 1974.

Bonnell, V. E., *Roots of Rebellion: Workers' Politics and Organization in St Petersburg and Moscow, 1900–1914*, Berkeley, 1983.

Botchkareva, M., *Yashka: My Life as a Peasant, Soldier and Exile*, London, 1919.

Bowlt, J. E., 'Constructivism and Early Soviet Fashion Design', in A. Gleason et al. (ed.), *Bolshevik Culture.*

Bradley, J., *Muzhik and Muscovite: Urbanization in Late Imperial Russia*, Berkeley, 1965.

British Documents on Foreign Affairs: Reports and Papers from the Foreign Office Confidential Print, Part I, Series A, vol. 6, University Publications of America, 1983.

Brooks, J., *When Russia Learned to Read: Literacy and Popular Literature, 1861–1917*, Princeton, 1985.

Broué, P., *Trotsky*, Paris, 1988.

Brovkin, V., 'The Mensheviks' Political Comeback: The Elections to the Provincial City Soviets in Spring 1918', *Russian Review*, 42, 1983.

Brovkin, V., *Behind the Front Lines of the Civil War: Political Parties and Social Movements in Russia, 1918–1922*, Princeton, 1994.

Brower, D., 'Labour Violence in Russia', *Slavic Review*, 11, 1982.

Brower, D., ' "The City in Danger": The Civil War and the Russian Urban Population', in D. P. Koenker et al. (ed.), *Party, State, and Society.*

Brower, D., *The Russian City between Tradition and Modernity, 1850–1900*, Berkeley, 1990.

Brussilov, A., *A Soldier's Notebook, 1914–1918*, London, 1930.

Bublikov, A. A., *Russkaia revoliutsiia: vpechatleniia i mysli ochevidtsa i uchastnika*, New York, 1918.

Buchanan, G., *My Mission to Russia and Other Diplomatic Memories*, 2 vols, London, 1923.

Buchanan, M., *Petrograd: The City of Trouble, 1914–18*, London, 1918.

Buchanan, M., *The Dissolution of an Empire*, London, 1932.

Budberg, A., 'Dnevnik', *Arkhiv russkoi revoliutsii*, 12–15, Berlin, 1923.

Bulgakov, M., *The White Guard*, Harmondsworth, 1973.

Bulgakov, V., 'Revoliutsiia na avtomobiliakh (Petrograd v fevrale 1917 g.)', *Na chuzhoi storone*, 6, Berlin-Prague, 1924.

Bunyan, J. (ed.), *The Origin of Forced Labour in the Soviet State, 1917–1921: Documents and Materials*, Baltimore, 1967.

Bunyan, J. (ed.), *Intervention, Civil War, and Communism in Russia: April–December 1918: Documents and Materials*, New York, 1976.

Bunyan, J., and Fisher, H. (ed.), *The Bolshevik Revolution, 1917–1918: Documents and Materials*, Stanford, 1961.

Burbank, J., *Intelligentsia and Revolution: Russian Views of Bolshevism, 1917–1922*, Oxford, 1986.

Burds, J., 'The Social Control of Peasant Labor in Russia: The Response of Village Communities to Labor Migration in the Central Industrial Region, 1861–1905', in E. Kingston-Mann and T. Mixter (ed.), *Peasant Economy*.

Burdzhalov, E. N., *Russia's Second Revolution*, Bloomington, 1988.

Buryshkin, P. A., *Moskva kupecheskaia*, New York, 1954.

Burleigh, M., *Death and Deliverance: 'Euthanasia' in Germany, 1900–1945*, Cambridge, 1994.

Bushnell, J., *Mutiny Amid Repression: Russian Soldiers in the Revolution of 1905–1906*, Bloomington, 1985.

Cantacuzène, Princess, *Revolutionary Days*, London, 1920.

Carr, E. H., *The Bolshevik Revolution, 1917–1923*, 3 vols, London, 1950.

Chaadaeva, O. A. (ed.), 'Soldatskie pis'ma v gody mirovoi voiny (1914–1917 gg.)', *Krasnyi Arkhiv*, 65–6, 1934.

Chaadaeva, O. A., *Armiia nakanune fevral'skoi revoliutsii*, Moscow-Leningrad, 1935.

Chagall, M., *My Life*, London, 1965.

Channon, J., 'Tsarist Landowners After the Revolution: Former Pomeshchiki in Rural Russia During NEP', *Soviet Studies*, 39, 1987.

Chase, W. J., *Workers, Society and the Soviet State: Labor and Life in Moscow, 1918–1929*, Urbana, 1987.

Chase, W. J., 'Voluntarism, Mobilization and Coercion: Subbotniki, 1919–1921', *Soviet Studies*, 41, 1989.

Cheka: materialy po deiatel'nosti chrezvychainykh komissii, Berlin, 1922.

Chekhov, A., *Plays*, Harmondsworth, 1972.

Chekhov, A., *Letters of Anton Chekhov*, selected by S. Karlinsky, London, 1973.

Cherniaev, V., 'Vosstanie pavlovskogo polka 26-go fevralia 1917 g.', in *Rabochii klass Rossii, ego soiuzniki i politicheskie protivniki v 1917 godu. Sbornik nauchnykh trudov*, Leningrad, 1989.

Cherniavsky, M., *Tsar and People: Studies in Russian Myths*, New Haven, 1961.

Cherniavsky, M. (ed.), *Prologue to Revolution*, Englewood, 1967.

Chernov, V., *Rozhdenie revoliutsionnoi Rossii (fevral'skaia revoliutsiia)*, Paris-Prague-New York, 1934.

Chernov, V., *The Great Russian Revolution*, New Haven, 1936.

Churchill, W. S., *The Aftermath*, London, 1929.

Clements, B., *Bolshevik Feminist: The Life of Alexandra Kollontai*, Indiana, 1979.

Clements, B., 'The Effects of the Civil War on Women and Family Relations', in A. Gleason et al. (ed.), *Bolshevik Culture*.

Clowes, E., Kassow, D., and West, J. (ed.), *Between Tsar and People: Educated Society and the Quest for Public Identity in Late Imperial Russia*, Princeton, 1991.

Cohen, S., *Bukharin and the Bolshevik Revolution*, Oxford, 1980.

Cohn, N., *Warrant for Genocide*, New York, 1966.

Congress of Peoples of the East: Baku, September 1919: Stenographic Report, London, 1977.

Conquest, R., *The Harvest of Sorrow*, London, 1986.

Conquest, R., *The Great Terror: A Reassessment*, London, 1990.

Correspondence Romain Rolland, Maxime Gorki, in *Cahiers Romain Rolland*, Paris, 1991.

Curtiss, J., *Church and State in Russia: The Last Years of the Empire*, New York, 1940.

Curtiss, J., *The Russian Church and the Soviet State, 1917–1950*, Boston, 1953.

Custine, Marquis de, *Empire of the Tsar: A Journey through Eternal Russia*, New York, 1989.

Czap, P., 'Peasant-Class Courts and Peasant Customary Justice in Russia, 1861–1912', *Journal of Social History*, I, 1967.

Dal', V., *Poslovitsy russkogo naroda*, Moscow, 1957.

Dan, F., *Dva goda skitanii*, Berlin, 1921.

Danilov, V. P., 'Ob istoricheskikh sud'bakh krest'ianskoi obshchiny v Rossii', *Ezhegodnik po agrarnoi istorii*, vyp. 6, *Problemy istorii russkoi obshchiny*, Vologda, 1976.

Danilov, V. P., 'Pereraspredelenie zemel'nogo fonda Rossii v rezul'tate velikoi oktiabr'skoi revoliutsii', in *Leninskii dekret o zemle: sbornik statei*, Moscow, 1979.

Danilov, V. P., *Sovetskaia dokolkhoznaia derevnia: sotsial'naia struktura, sotsial'nye otnosheniia*, Moscow, 1979.

Danilov, V. P., *Rural Russia Under the New Regime*, London, 1988.

Davies, N., *White Eagle, Red Star: The Polish-Soviet War, 1919–1920*, London, 1972.

Davies, N., *God's Playground: A History of Poland*, 2 vols, London, 1981.

Dazhina, I. M. (ed.), 'Amerikanskie dnevniki A. M. Kollontai (1915–1916 gg.)', *Istoricheskii arkhiv*, I, 1962.

Dazhina, I. M., and Tsivlina, R., 'Iz arkhiva A. M. Kollontai (Dnevniki, pis'ma, stat'i 1915–1917 gg.)', *Inostrannaia Literatura*, 1–2, 1970.

The Debate on Soviet Power: Minutes of the All-Russian Central Committee of Soviets, Second Convocation, October 1917–January 1918, ed. J. Keep, Oxford, 1979.

de Jonge, A., *The Life and Times of Grigorii Rasputin*, New York, 1982.

Delmas, J., 'Légionnaire et diplomate: Le capitaine Z. Peshkoff', *Revue historique de l'Armée*, 10, 1968.

Denikin, A. I., *Ocherki russkoi smuty*, 5 vols, Paris, 1921–6.

Denikin, A. I., *Staraia armiia*, Paris, 1929–31.

Desiaty s'ezd RKP(b). Stenograficheskii otchet, Moscow, 1963.

Deutscher, I., *The Prophet Armed: Trotsky, 1879–1921*, Oxford, 1954.

Deviataia konferentsiia RKP(b). Protokoly, Moscow, 1972.

Deviatyi s'ezd RKP(b). Protokoly, Moscow, 1960.

The Diaries of Theodor Herzl, ed. Marvin Lowenthal, London, 1958.

Dixon, S., 'The Church's Social Role in St Petersburg', in G. Hosking (ed.), *Church*.

'Dnevnik A. A. Polovtsova', *Krasnyi arkhiv*, 3–4, 1923; 33, 1929; 46, 1931; 67, 1934.

'Dnevnik Nikolaia Romanova', *Krasnyi arkhiv*, 20–22, 1927.

'Dnevniki kn. Ekateriny Alekseevny Sviatopolk-Mirskoi za 1904–1905 gg.', *Istoricheskie zapiski*, 77, 1965.

Doklad ot narodnogo komissara putei soobshcheniia, Moscow, 1919.

Dolgorukov, Prince P. D., *Velikaia razrukha, 1916–1926*, Madrid, 1964.

Donskii, R., 'Ot Moskvy do Berlina', *Arkhiv russkoi revoliutsii*, I, Berlin, 1923.

Dostoevskii, F. M., *Polnoe sobranie sochinenii v tridtsati tomakh*, Leningrad, 1980–4.

Draper, T., *The Roots of American Communism*, New York, 1967.

Dukes, P., *Red Dusk and the Morrow*, London, 1922.

Dune, E., *Notes of a Red Guard*, Urbana, 1993.

Dva goda deiatel'nosti tsentral'noi komissii po snabzheniiu rabochikh i ee mestnykh organov (1919–1921gg), Moscow, 1921.

Edelman, R., *Gentry Politics on the Eve of the Russian Revolution: the Nationalist Party, 1907–1917*, New Brunswick, 1980.

Edwards, A., *Sonya: The Life of Countess Tolstoy*, London, 1981.

Efimenko, A., *Issledovaniia narodnoi zhizni*, 2 vols, Moscow, 1884.

Egorov, A. I., *Razgrom Denikina 1919*, Moscow, 1931.

Eklof, B., *Russian Peasant Schools: Officialdom, Village Culture and Popular Pedagogy, 1861–1914*, Berkeley, 1986.

Ekonomicheskoe polozhenie Rossii nakanune velikoi oktiabr'skoi sotsialisticheskoi revoliutsii, Leningrad, 1967.

Elchaninov, A., *Tsar Nicholas II*, London, 1913.

Elkina, D., 'Likvidatsiia negramotnosti v Krasnoi Armii na frontakh grazhdanskoi voiny', *Narodnoe obrazovanie*, 12, 1957.

Emmons, T., *The Formation of Political Parties and the First National Elections in Russia*, Cambridge, Mass., 1983.

Emmons, T., 'The Zemstvo in Historical Perspective', in T. Emmons and W. Vucinich (ed.), *The Zemstva*.

Emmons, T. and Vucinich, W. (ed.), *The Zemstva in Russia: An Experiment in Local Self-Government*, Cambridge, Mass., 1982.

Engelstein, L., *Moscow 1905: Working Class Organisation and Political Conflict*, Stanford, 1982.

Engelstein, L., *The Keys to Happiness: Sex and the Search for Modernity in Fin-de-Siècle Russia*, Cornell, 1992.

Ermanskii, O. A., *Iz perezhitogo*, Moscow-Leningrad, 1927.

Esikov, S. and Protasov, L., ' "Antonovshchina": novye podkhody', *Voprosy istorii*, 6/7, 1992.

Essad-Bey, M., *Nicholas II: Prisoner of the Purple*, London, 1936.

Fainsod, M., *How Russia Is Ruled*, Cambridge, Mass., 1963.

Fanger, D., 'The Peasant in Literature', in W. Vucinich (ed.), *The Peasant*.

Farmborough, F., *Nurse at the Russian Front*, London, 1977.

Farnsworth, B., 'Village Women Experience the Revolution', in A. Gleason et al. (ed.), *Bolshevik Culture*.

Faulenbach, B. (ed.), *Geschichtwissenschaft in Deutschland*, Munich, 1974.

Ferro, M., *The Russian Revolution of February 1917*, London, 1972.

Ferro, M., *October 1917: A Social History of the Russian Revolution*, London, 1980.

Ferro, M., *Nicholas II: The Last of the Tsars*, London, 1991.

Figes, O., *Peasant Russia, Civil War: The Volga Countryside in Revolution (1917–1921)*, Oxford, 1989.

Figes, O., 'The Red Army and Mass Mobilization during the Russian Civil War', *Past and Present*, 129 (1990), 206–9.

Fischer, L., *The Life of Lenin*, London, 1965.

Fisher, H., *The Famine in Soviet Russia, 1919–1923*, New York, 1927.

Fitzpatrick, S., *The Commissariat of Enlightenment: Soviet Organization of Education and the Arts under Lunacharsky*, Cambridge, 1970.

Fitzpatrick, S., 'Sex and Revolution: An Examination of Literary and Statistical Data on the Mores of Soviet Students in the 1920s', *Journal of Modern History*, 50, 1978.

Fitzpatrick, S., *The Cultural Front: Power and Culture in Revolutionary Russia*, Cornell, 1992.

Fitzpatrick, S., *Stalin's Peasants: Resistance and Survival in the Russian Village After Collectivization*, Oxford, 1994.

Fitzpatrick, S., Rabinowitch, A. and Stites, R. (ed.), *Russia in the Era of NEP: Explorations in Soviet Society and Culture*, Bloomington, 1991.

Fleming, P., *The Fate of Admiral Kolchak*, London, 1963.

Florinsky, M., *The End of the Russian Empire*, New Haven, 1931.

Fokke, D. G., 'Na stene i za kulisami brestskoi tragikomedii', *Arkhiv russkoi revoliutsii*, 20, Berlin, 1930.

Fotieva, L., *Iz zhizni Lenina*, Moscow, 1959.

Frank, S., 'Popular Justice, Community and Culture among the Russian Peasantry, 1870–1900', *Russian Review*, 46, 1987.

Freeze, G., ' "Going to the Intelligentsia": the Church and its Urban mission in Post-Reform Russia', in E. Clowes, S. Kassow and J. West (ed.), *Between Tsar and People*.

Freeze, G., *The Parish Clergy in Nineteenth-Century Russia: Crisis, Reform, Counter-Reform*, Princeton, 1983.

Freeze, G., 'Handmaiden of the State? The Church in Imperial Russia Reconsidered', *Journal of Ecclesiastical History*, 36–1, 1985.

Freeze, G., 'The Soslovie (Estate) Paradigm and Russian Social History', *American Historical Review*, 91, 1986, 11–36.

Freeze, G., 'Bringing Order to the Russian Family: Marriage and Divorce in Imperial Russia, 1760–1860', *Journal of Modern History*, 62, 1990.

Frenkin, M., *Russkaia armiia i revoliutsiia 1917–1918*, Munich, 1978.

Frieden, N. M., *Russian Physicians in an Era of Reform and Revolution, 1856–1905*, Princeton, 1981.

Friedgutt, T., *Iuzovka and Revolution*, 2 vols, Princeton, 1989, 1993.

Frierson, C., 'Rural Justice in Public Opinion: The Volost' Court Debate, 1861–1912', *Slavonic and East European Review*, 64, 1986.

Frierson, C., 'Crime and Punishment in the Russian Village: Rural Concepts of Criminality at the End of the Nineteenth Century', *Slavic Review*, 46, 1987.

Frierson, C., 'Razdel: The Peasant Family Divided', *Russian Review*, 46, 1987.

Frierson, C., 'Peasant Family Divisions and the Commune', in R. Bartlett (ed.), *Land*.

Frierson, C., *Peasant Icons: Representations of Rural People in Late 19th Century Russia*, Oxford, 1993.

Fuhrmann, J., *Rasputin: A Life*, New York, 1990.

Fuller, W., *Civil-Military Conflict in Imperial Russia, 1881–1914*, Princeton, 1985.

Galai, S., *The Liberation Movement in Russia 1900–1905*, Cambridge, Mass., 1973.

Galili, Z., *The Menshevik Leaders in the Russian Revolution: Social Realities and Political Strategies*, Princeton, 1989.

Galynskii, T., *Ocherki po istorii agrarnoi revoliutsii Serdobskogo uezda, Saratovskoi gubernii*, Serdobsk, 1924.

Gankin, O. and Fisher, H. (ed.), *The Bolsheviks and the World War: The Origins of the Third International*, Stanford, 1940.

Gatrell, P., *The Tsarist Economy, 1850–1917*, London, 1986.

Geifman, A., *Thou Shalt Kill: Revolutionary Terrorism in Russia, 1894–1917*, Princeton, 1993.

Gellner, E., *Nations and Nationalism*, Oxford, 1983.

Gernet, M. L., *Istoriia tsarskoi tiur'my*, 5 vols, Moscow, 1961–2.

Gernet, M. L., *Moral'naia statistika*, Moscow, 1972.

Gerschenkron, A., 'Agrarian Policies and Industrialization in Russia, 1861–1917', in *Cambridge Economic History of Europe*, 6/2, Cambridge, 1965.

Getzler, I., *Martov: A Political Biography of a Russian Social Democrat*, London, 1967.

Getzler, I., *Kronstadt, 1917–1921: The Fate of a Soviet Democracy*, Cambridge, 1983.

Gilliard, P., *Thirteen Years at the Russian Court*, London, 1921.

Gins, G. K., *Sibir', soiuzniki i Kolchak: povorotnyi moment russkoi istorii 1918–1920 gg.*, Peking and Kharbin, 1921.

Gippius, Z., *Siniaia kniga*, Belgrade, 1929.

Gippius, Z., *Dmitrii Merezhkovskii*, Paris, 1951.

Gippius, Z., *Peterburgskie dnevniki (1914–1919)*, New York, 1982.

Gitelman, Z., *A Century of Ambivalence*, New York, 1988.

Gleason, A., *Young Russia*, New York, 1980.

Gleason, A., Kenez, P. and Stites, R. (ed.), *Bolshevik Culture*, Bloomington, 1985.

Gleason, W., 'The All-Russian Union of Zemstvos and World War I', in T. Emmons and W. Vucinich (ed.), *The Zemstva*.

Glickman, R., 'Alternative View of the Peasantry', *Slavic Review*, 32, 1973.

Glickman, R., *Russian Factory Women: Workplace and Society, 1880–1914*, Berkeley, 1988.

Gogol', D., 'Maksim Gor'kii v petropavlovskoi kreposti', *Katorga i ssylka*, 8/9, 1932.

Gokay, B., 'Turkish Settlement and the Caucasus (October 1918–March 1921)', paper presented to University of Birmingham, 1993.

Golder, F., *Documents on Russian History, 1914–1917*, New York, 1927.

Goldman, E., *My Disillusionment in Russia*, Garden City, 1923.

Goldman, E., *My Further Disillusionment in Russia*, Garden City, 1924.

Goldman, W., 'Working-Class Women and the "Withering Away" of the Family: Popular Responses to Family Policy', in S. Fitzpatrick et al. (ed.), *Russia in the Era of NEP*.

Goldman, W., *Women, the State and Revolution: Soviet Family Policy and Social Life, 1917–1936*, Cambridge, 1993.

Golovin, N., *The Russian Army in the World War*, New York, 1931.

Gorev, B., *Iz partiinogo proshlogo. Vospominaniia, 1895–1905*, Leningrad, 1924.

Gor'kii, A. M., 'Pis'ma k K. P. Piatnitskomu', in *Arkhiv A. M. Gor'kogo*, vol. 4, Moscow, 1954.

Gor'kii, A. M., 'Pis'ma k E. P. Peshkovoi, 1895–1926', in *Arkhiv A. M. Gor'kogo*, vol. 5, Moscow, 1955.

Gor'kii, A. M., 'Pis'ma k pisatel'iam i I. P. Ladyzhnikovu', in *Arkhiv A. M. Gor'kogo*, vol. 7, Moscow, 1959.

Gor'kii, A. M., *Perepiska A. M. Gor'kogo s zarubezhnymi literatorami*, Moscow, 1960.

Gor'kii, A. M., *Polnoe sobranie sochinenii*, Moscow, 1968.

A. M. Gor'kii v epokhu revoliutsii, 1905–1907 gg. Materialy, vospominaniia, issledovaniia, Moscow, 1957.

Gorky, M., *Letters*, Moscow, 1964.

Gorky, M., *My Childhood*, Harmondsworth, 1966.

Gorky, M., *My Universities*, Harmondsworth, 1966.

Gorky, M., *Lenin*, Edinburgh, 1967.

Gorky, M., *Fragments from My Diary*, London, 1972.

Gorky, M., 'On the Russian Peasantry', in R. E. F. Smith (ed.), *The Russian Peasantry 1920 and 1984*, London, 1977.

Gourko, G., *Memories and Impressions of War and Revolution in Russia, 1914–1917*, London, 1918.

Graham, S., *With the Russian Pilgrims to Jerusalem*, London, 1914.

Grave, B. B. (ed.), *Burzhuazia nakanune revoliutsii*, Moscow, 1927.

Graves, W. S., *America's Siberian Adventure, 1918–1920*, New York, 1941.

Grazhdanskaia voina na Volge v 1918 godu. Sbornik pervyi, Prague, 1930.

Graziosi, A., 'G. L. Piatakov (1890–1937): A Mirror of Soviet History', *Harvard Ukrainian Studies*, 14, 1990.

Gregory, P., 'Grain Marketings and Peasant Consumption, Russia, 1885–1913', *Explorations in Economic History*, 17, 1980.

Gregory, P., 'Russian Living Standards During the Era of Industrialisation, 1885–1913', *Review of Income and Wealth*, 26, 1980.

Grondijs, L.-H., *La Guerre en Russie et en Sibérie*, Paris, 1922.

Gruzenberg, O., *Yesterday: Memoirs of a Russian-Jewish Lawyer*, Berkeley, 1981.

Gubernskii s'ezd krest'ianskikh deputatov Tomskoi gubernii, Tomsk, 1917.

Gukovskii, A. I. (ed.), 'Agrarnaia politika Vrangelia', *Krasnyi Arkhiv*, 26, 1928.

Gul', R., 'Byloe', *Ogonek*, 7 February 1992.

Gul', R., *Ledianoi pokhod*, Berlin, n.d.

Gurko, V. I., *Figures and Features of the Past: Government and Opinion in the Reign of Nicholas II*, Stanford, 1939.

Gurko, V. I., *Tsar i Tsaritsa*, Paris, n.d.

Guthier, S., 'The Popular Base of Ukrainian Nationalism in 1917', *Slavic Review*, 38, 1979.

Guthier, S., 'Ukrainian Cities During the Revolution and Inter-War Period', in I. Rudnytsky (ed.), *Rethinking Ukrainian History*, Edmonton, 1981.

Guthier, S., 'The Roots of Popular Ukrainian Nationalism: A Demographic, Social and Political Study of the Ukrainian Nationality to 1917', Ph.D. diss., Univ. of Michigan, 1990.

Hagen, M. von, *Soldiers in the Proletarian Dictatorship: The Red Army and the Soviet Socialist State, 1917–1930*, Ithaca and London, 1990.

Haimson, L., 'The Problem of Social Stability in Urban Russia, 1905–1917', *Slavic Review* 23–4, 1964–5.

Haimson, L. (ed.), *The Politics of Rural Russia, 1905–1914*, Bloomington, 1979.

Haimson, L. (ed.), *The Making of Three Russian Revolutionaries: Voices from the Menshevik Past*, Cambridge, 1987.

Haimson, L., 'The Problem of Social Identities in Early Twentieth-Century Russia', *Slavic Review*, 47, 1988.

Hamburg, G., *Politics of the Russian Nobility, 1881–1905*, New Brunswick, 1984.

Hamm, M., 'Liberal Politics in Wartime Russia: An Analysis of the Progressive Bloc', *Slavic Review*, 53, 1974.

Harrison, M. E., *Marooned in Moscow*, New York, 1921.

Haségawa, T., *The February Revolution: Petrograd 1917*, Seattle, 1981.

Hašek, J., *The Red Commissar*, London, 1983.

Heald, E., 'Witness to Revolution: Letters from Russia, 1916–1919', Kent State University Press, 1974.

Heenan, L. C., *Russian Democracy's Fateful Blunder: The Summer Offensive of 1917*, New York, 1987.

Heller, M., 'Premier avertissement: un coup de fouet. L'histoire de l'expulsion des personnalités culturelles hors de l'Union Soviétique en 1922', *Cahiers du monde russe et sovietique*, 20–I, 1974.

Herzen, A., *From the Other Shore*, Oxford, 1979.

Himka, J.-P., *Galician Villagers and the Ukrainian National Movement in the Nineteenth Century*, New York, 1988.

Hindenburg, P. von, *Out of My Life*, London, 1920.

Hindus, M., *Red Bread*, Bloomington, 1988.

Hoare, S., *The Fourth Seal*, London, 1930.

Hobsbawm, E. J., *Nations and Nationalism since 1870: Programme, Myth, Reality*, Cambridge, 1990.

Hofer, T., 'The Creation of Ethnic Symbols from the Elements of Peasant Culture', in P. Sugar (ed.), *Ethnic Diversity and Conflict in Eastern Europe*, Santa Barbara, 1980.

Hoffman, M. von, *War Diaries and Other Papers*, London, 1929.

Hogan, H., 'Conciliation Boards in Revolutionary Russia: Aspects of the Crisis of Labor-Management Relations in 1917', *Russian History*, 9, 1982.

Holquist, P., 'A Russian Vendée: The Practise of Revolutionary Politics in the Don Countryside, 1917–1921', Ph.D. diss., Columbia, 1995.

Hosking, G., *The Russian Constitutional Experiment: Government and Duma, 1907–14*, Cambridge, 1973.

Hosking, G. and Manning, R. T., 'What Was the United Nobility?', in L. Haimson (ed.), *The Politics of Rural Russia*.

Hosking, G. (ed.), *Church, Nation and State in Russia and Ukraine*, London, 1991.

Hovannisen, R., *The Republic of Armenia*, 2 vols, Berkeley, 1971, 1982.

Hunt, L., *The Family Romance of the French Revolution*, London, 1992.

Hutchinson, J. F., 'The Octobrists and the Future of Russia as a Great Power', *Slavonic and East European Review,* 50, 1972.

Iakhontov, A., 'Tiazhelye dni', *Arkhiv russkoi revoliutsii,* 17, Berlin, 1926.

Iakovlev, Ia., *Derevnia kak ona est',* Moscow, 1924.

Iakovlev, Ia., *Nasha derevnia: Novoe v starom i staroe v novom,* Moscow, 1924.

Ignat'ev, A., 'V noch' na 25 oktiabria 1917 goda', *Krasnaia letopis',* 6, 1923.

Ironside, E., *Tannenberg: The First Thirty Days in East Prussia,* London, 1925.

Iroshnikov, M., *Sozdanie sovetskogo tsentral'nogo gosudarstvennogo apparata,* Moscow-Leningrad, 1966.

Isaev, A., *Bezrabotitsa v SSSR i bor'ba s neiu, 1917–1924,* Moscow, 1924.

Iswolsky, M., *Memoirs,* London, 1920.

Itogi bor'by s golodom v 1921–1922 gg. Sbornik statei i otchetov, Moscow, 1922.

Iusupov, F., *Pered izgnaniem, 1887–1919,* Moscow, 1993.

Ivanov, A., 'Volnenie v 1916 g. v 181-om zapasnom pekhotnom polku', *Krasnaia letopis',* 10, 1924.

Ivanov, V. V., 'Pochemu Stalin ubil Gor'kogo?', *Voprosy literatury,* 1993, no. 1.

Ivanov-Razumnik, V. R., *The Memoirs of Ivanov-Razumnik,* Oxford, 1965.

'Iz ofitserskikh pisem c fronta v 1917 g.', *Krasnyi Arkhiv,* 50–1, 1932.

Jansen, M., *A Show Trial under Lenin,* The Hague, 1982.

Johnson, R., *Peasant and Proletarian: The Working Class of Moscow in the Late Nineteenth Century,* New Brunswick, 1979.

Jones, S., *Russia in Revolution, Being the Experience of an Englishman in Russia during the Upheaval,* London, 1917.

Jones, S., 'The Establishment of Soviet Power in Transcaucasia: The Case of Georgia, 1921–1928', *Soviet Studies,* 40, 1988.

Joravsky, D., *Russian Psychology: A Critical History,* Oxford, 1989.

Judge, E. H., 'Urban Growth and Anti-Semitism in Russian Moldavia', in L. H. Judge and J. Y. Simms (ed.), *Modernization and Revolution.*

Judge, E. H. and Simms, J. Y., *Modernization and Revolution: Dilemmas of Progress in Late Imperial Russia: Essays in Honor of Arthur P. Mendel,* New York, 1992.

Juviler, P., 'Contradictions of Revolution: Juvenile Crime and Rehabilitation', in A. Gleason et al. (ed.), *Bolshevik Culture.*

Kabanov, V. V., *Oktiabr'skaia revoliutsiia i kooperatsiia (1917–mart 1919),* Moscow, 1973.

Kabanov, V. V., *Krest'ianskoe khoziaistvo v usloviiakh 'voennogo kommunizma',* Moscow, 1988.

Kalinin, I., *Pod znamenem Vrangelia,* Leningrad, 1925.

Kal'nitskii, Ia., *Ot fevralia k Oktiabriu: Vospominaniia frontovika,* Khar'kov, 1924.

Kalugin, O., *Vid s Lubianki,* Moscow, 1990.

Kantorovich, V., 'Fedor Linde', *Byloe,* 24, 1924.

'Karl Marks i tsarskaia tsenzura', *Krasnyi Arkhiv,* 1933, I.

Karpinskii, V. A., 'Vladimir Il'ich za granitsei v 1914–1917 gg.', *Zapiski Instituta Lenina*, vol. 2, Moscow, 1927.

Karpov, U., 'Po volnam zhiteinogo moria. Vospominaniia', *Novyi mir*, I, 1992.

Kassow, S., *Students, Professors and the State in Tsarist Russia*, California, 1969.

Katkov, G., *Russia 1917: The February Revolution*, London, 1967.

Katkov, G., *The Kornilov Affair: Kerensky and the Break-up of the Russian Army*, London, 1980.

Kavtaradze, A., *Voennye spetsialisty na sluzhbe Respubliki Sovetov 1917–1920 gg.*, Moscow, 1988.

Keep, J. L. H., *The Russian Revolution: A Study in Mass Mobilization*, London, 1976.

Keep, J. L. H., 'The Military Style of the Romanov Rulers', *War and Society*, I, 2, 1983.

Kelly, A., *Mikhail Bakunin: A Study in the Psychology and Politics of Utopianism*, Yale, 1987.

Kelly, A., 'Self-Censorship and the Russian Intelligentsia, 1905–1914', *Slavic Review*, 46, 1987.

Kenez, P., *Civil War in South Russia, 1918: The First Year of the Volunteer Army*, Berkeley, 1971.

Kenez, P., *Civil War in South Russia, 1919–1920: The Defeat of the Whites*, Berkeley, 1977.

Kenez, P., *The Birth of the Propaganda State*, Cambridge, 1985.

Kennan, G. F., *Russia Leaves the War*, Princeton, 1956.

Kerenskii, A. F., *Izdaleka*, Paris, 1922.

Kerensky, A. F., *The Catastrophe: Kerensky's Own Story of the Russian Revolution*, London, 1927.

Kerensky, A. F., *The Crucifixion of Liberty*, London, 1934.

Kerensky, A. F., *The Kerensky Memoirs: Russia and History's Turning Point*, London, 1965.

Ketola, E., 'Russkaia revoliutsiia i nezavisimost' Finlandii', in *Anatomiia*.

'Khar'kov v oktiabre 1905 g. (pis'mo uchastnika sobytii)', *Katorga i ssylka*, 19, 1925.

Khodasevich, V. F., *Nekropol: Vospominaniia*, Brussels, 1939.

Khodasevich, V. F., *Belyi koridor. Vospominaniia*, New York, 1982.

Khronika grazhdanskoi voiny v Sibiri, Moscow-Leningrad, 1926.

Khrystiuk, P., *Zametki i materialy do istorii ukrainskoi revoliutsii, 1917–1920 gg.*, 2 vols, Vienna, 1921.

Kin, D., *Denikinshchina*, Leningrad, 1927.

Kingston-Mann, E. and Mixter, T. (ed.), *Peasant Economy, Culture, and Politics of European Russia, 1800–1921*, Princeton, 1991.

Kiriukhin, N., *Iz dnevnika voennogo komissara: grazhdanskaia voina, 1918–1919 gg.*, Moscow, 1928.

Kirpichnikov, T., 'Vosstanie I-go volynskogo polka v fevrale 1917', *Byloe*, 27–28, 1917.

Kitaev, M., 'Stroitel'stvo sel'skikh partiinykh organizatsii v gody grazhdanskoi voiny', *Voprosy istorii KPSS*, 7, 1975.

Kleinborg, L., *Istoriia bezrabotitsy v Rossii, 1857–1919 gg.*, Moscow, 1925.

Klier, J. and Lambroza, D. (ed.), *Pogroms: Anti-Jewish Violence in Modern Russian History*, Cambridge, 1992.

Knei-Paz, B., *The Social and Political Thought of Leon Trotsky*, Oxford, 1978.

Kniga o golode, Moscow, 1922.

Knizhnik, I., 'N. P. Poliakov — izdatel' "Kapitala" Karla Marksa', *Voprosy istorii*, 6, 1947.

Knox, A., *With the Russian Army, 1914–1917*, 2 vols, London, 1921.

Koenker, D. P., *Moscow Workers and the 1917 Revolution*, Princeton, 1981.

Koenker, D. P., 'Urbanization and Deurbanization in the Russian Revolution and Civil War', *Journal of Modern History*, 57, 1985.

Koenker, D. P., Rosenberg, W. G. and Suny, R. G. (ed.), *Party, State and Society in the Russian Civil War: Explorations in Social History*, Bloomington, 1988.

Koenker, D. P. and Rosenberg, W. G., *Strikes and Revolution in Russia, 1917*, Princeton, 1989.

Kokovtsov, Count V. N., *Out of My Past: The Memoirs of Count Kokovtsov*, Stanford, 1935.

Kollontai, A. M., *Iz moei zhizni i raboty*, Moscow, 1974.

Kolonitskii, B., 'A. F. Kerenskii i Merezhkovskie v 1917 godu', *Literaturnoe obozrenie*, 3, 1991.

Kolonitskii, B., ' "Revolutionary Names": Russian Personal Names and Political Consciousness in the 1920s and 1930s', *Revolutionary Russia*, 6, 1993.

Kolonitskii, B., 'Antibourgeois Propaganda and Anti-"Burzhui" Consciousness in 1917', *Russian Review*, 53, 1994.

Kolonitskii, B., 'Zagadka Kerenskogo', *Zvezda*, 6, 1994.

Kolonitskii, B., 'Kul't vozhdia', unpublished ms.

Kolonitskii, B., 'The "Russian Idea" and the Ideology of the February Revolution', unpublished ms.

Korenev, S. A., 'Chrezvychainaia kommissiia po delam byvshikh ministrov', *Arkhiv russkoi revoliutsii*, 7, Berlin, 1922.

Kornakov, P., 'Simvolika i rituly revoliutsii 1917 g.', in *Anatomiia*.

Korolenko, V. G., 'Iz dnevnikov 1917–1921 gg.', in *Pamiat'. Istoricheskii sbornik*, 2, Paris, 1979.

Korros, A. S., 'The Landed Nobility, the State Council and P. A. Stolypin, 1907–1911', in L. Haimson (ed.), *The Politics of Rural Russia*.

Kostiukov, 'Kak my opozdali ko vziatiu zimnego dvortsa', *Krasnyi balteets*, 6, 1920.

Kotsiubinskii, A., 'Sekret liubvi Grigorii Rasputina', Smena, 2, 9, 16, 23, 27, 29 December 1994.

Koz'min, B., 'Molodaia Rossiia', in B. Koz'min, P. G. Zaichnevskii i 'Molodaia Rossiia', Moscow, 1913.

Krasnov, P., 'Na vnutrennom fronte', Arkhiv russkoi revoliutsii, I, Berlin, 1922.

Krasnov, P., 'Vsevelikoe voisko donskoe', Arkhiv russkoi revoliutsii, 5/8, Berlin, 1922–3.

Krasnov, V., 'Iz vospominanii o 1917–1920 gg.', Arkhiv russkoi revoliutsii, 8, Berlin, 1923.

Krawchenko, B., Social Change and National Consciousness in Twentieth-Century Ukraine, New York, 1985.

Kronshtadtskii miatezh: sbornik statei, vospominanii i dokumentov, Leningrad, 1931.

Krupskaia, N., Vospominaniia o Lenine, Moscow, 1968.

Kryzhanovskii, S., Vospominaniia, Berlin, 1938.

Kuromiya, H., Stalin's Industrial Revolution: Politics and Workers, 1928–1932, Cambridge, 1988.

Kushner, P. (ed.), Selo viriatno v proshlom i nastoiashem, Moscow, 1958.

Lambroza, S., 'The Pogroms of 1903–1906', in J. D. Klier and S. Lambroza (ed.), Pogroms.

Latsis, M., Chrezvychainye komissii po bor'be s kontrrevoliutsiei, Moscow, 1921.

Laue, T. von, 'A Secret Memorandum of Sergei Witte on the Industrialization of Imperial Russia', Journal of Modern History, 26, 1954.

Laue, T. von, 'Russian Labour between Field and Factory, 1892–1903', California Slavic Studies, 3, 1964.

Leggett, G., The Cheka: Lenin's Political Police, Oxford, 1981.

Lehovich, D., White Against Red: The Life of General Anton Denikin, New York, 1974.

Leiberov, I. P. and Rudachenko, S. D., Revoliutsia i khleb, Moscow, 1990.

Lemke, M. K., 250 dnei v tsarskoi stavke, Petrograd, 1920.

Lenin, V. I., Polnoe sobranie sochinenii, Moscow, 1958–65 [PSS].

Lenin, V. I., Leninskii sbornik, 39 vols, Moscow-Leningrad, 1924–80.

Lenin and Gorky: Letters, Reminiscences, Articles, Moscow, 1973.

Leontovitsch, V., Geschichte des Liberalismus in Russland, Frankfurt-am-Main, 1957.

Leslie, R., Reform and Insurrection in Russian Poland, London, 1963.

Letters of Tsar Nicholas and the Empress Marie, ed. E. Bing, London, 1937.

Levin, D., Stormy Petrel, London, 1967.

Lewin, M., The Making of the Soviet System, New York, 1985.

Liberman, S., Building Lenin's Russia, Chicago, 1945.

Libknecht, V., Pauki i mukhi, Samara, 1917.

Lieven, D., 'The Russian Civil Service Under Nicholas II: Some Variations on the Bureaucratic Theme', Jahrbücher für Geschichte Osteuropas, 29, 1981.

Lieven, D., Russia and the Origins of the First World War, London, 1983.

Lieven, D., *Russia's Rulers Under the Old Regime*, New York, 1989.

Lieven, D., *Nicholas II: Emperor of All the Russias*, London, 1993.

Lih, Lars T., *Bread and Authority in Russia 1914–1921*, Berkeley, 1990.

Lincoln, W. B., *In the Vanguard of Reform: Russia's Enlightened Bureaucrats 1825–1861*, Dekalb, Ill., 1982.

Lincoln, W. B., *Passage Through Armageddon: The Russians in War and Revolution*, New York, 1986.

Lincoln, W. B., *Red Victory: A History of the Russian Civil War*, New York, 1989.

Liubovich, A., 'Kak organizovalsia i rabotal narodnyi kommissariat pocht i telegrafov v pervyi period oktiabr'skoi revoliutsii', *Proletarskaia revoliutsiia*, 5, 1926.

Lockhart, R. H. B., *Memoirs of a British Agent*, London, 1933.

Lockhart, R. H. B., *The Diaries of Sir Robert Bruce Lockhart*, London, 1973.

Longley, D. A., 'Some Historiographical Problems of Bolshevik Party Unity', *Jahrbücher für Geschichte Osteuropas*, 22, 1974.

Lotman, Iu., 'The Decembrists in Daily Life', in Iu. Lotman and B. Uspenskii, *Semiotics*.

Lotman, Iu., 'The Poetics of Everyday Behaviour', in Iu. Lotman and B. Uspenskii, *Semiotics*.

Lotman, Iu. and Uspenskii, B., *The Semiotics of Russian Culture*, Ann Arbor, 1984.

Lukomskii, A. F., *Vospominaniia*, 2 vols, Berlin, 1922.

Lunacharsky, A. V., *Revolutionary Silhouettes*, London, 1967.

Lutskii, E. A., 'Krest'ianskoe vosstanie v Tambovskoi gubernii v 1917 g.', *Istoricheskie zapiski*, 2, 1938.

L'vov-Rogachevskii, 'Oktiabr'skie dni 1905 goda v Khar'kove', *Katorga i ssylka*, 19, 1925.

McAuley, M., *Bread and Justice: State and Society in Petrograd, 1917–1922*, Oxford, 1991.

McCauley, M. (ed.), *The Russian Revolution and the Soviet State, 1917–1921: Documents*, London, 1988.

McClelland, 'Utopianism versus Revolutionary Heroism in Bolshevik Policy: The Proletarian Culture Debate', *Slavic Review*, 39, 1980.

McDaniel, T., *Autocracy, Capitalism and Revolution in Russia*, Berkeley, 1988.

Mace, J., *Communism and the Dilemmas of National Liberation: National Communism in Soviet Ukraine, 1918–1933*, Cambridge, 1983.

Macey, D. J., 'The Land Captains: A Note on their Social Composition, 1889–1913', *Russian History*, 16, 1989.

Macey, D. J., 'The Peasant Commune and the Stolypin Reforms: Peasant Attitudes, 1906–14', in R. Bartlett (ed.), *Land Commune*.

McKean, R. B., *St Petersburg Between the Revolutions: Workers and Revolutionaries, June 1907–February 1917*, New Haven, 1990.

McKenzie, K. E., 'Zemstvo Organizations and Their Role within the Administrative Structure', in T. Emmons and W. Vucinich (ed.), *The Zemstva*.

Mackenzie Wallace, D., *Russia*, 2 vols, London, 1905.

McNeal, R. H., *Bride of the Revolution: Krupskaya and Lenin*, Ann Arbor, 1972.

McNeal, R. H., *Tsar and Cossack, 1855–1914*, New York, 1967.

Maiakovskii, V., *Polnoe sobranie sochinenii*, Moscow, 1955–61.

Maiskii, I., *Demokraticheskaia kontrrevoliutsiia*, Moscow, 1923.

Majstrenko, I., *Borot'bism: A Chapter in the History of Ukrainian Communism*, New York, 1954.

Maksakov, V. (ed.), *Partizanskoe dvizhenie v Sibiri*, Moscow-Leningrad, 1925.

Male, D., *Russian Peasant Organization Before Collectivization*, Cambridge, 1971.

Maleev, A. F., *Tridtsat' dnei evreiskogo pogroma v mestechke Krivoe Ozero*, Moscow, 1921.

Malet, M., *Nestor Makhno in the Russian Civil War*, London, 1982.

Malia, M., *Alexander Herzen and the Birth of Russian Socialism, 1812–1855*, Harvard, 1961.

Maliantovich, P. N., 'V zimnem dvortse 25–26 oktiabria 1917 goda', *Byloe*, 12, 1918.

Malle, S., *The Economic Organization of War Communism, 1918–1921*, Cambridge, 1985.

Mally, L., 'Intellectuals in the Proletkult: Problems of Authority and Expertise', in D. P. Koenker, W. G. Rosenberg and R. G. Suny (ed.), *Party*.

Mamantov, V. I., *Na gosudarevoi sluzhbe*, Tallinn, 1926.

Mandel, D., *The Petrograd Workers and the Soviet Seizure of Power*, New York, 1984.

Mandelstam, N., *Hope Abandoned*, London, 1974.

Mannerheim, C. G. E., *The Memoirs of Marshal Mannerheim*, New York, 1954.

Manning, R. T., *The Crisis of the Old Order in Russia: Gentry and Government*, Princeton, 1982.

Manning, R. T., 'The Zemstvo and Politics, 1904–1914', in T. Emmons and W. Vucinich (ed.), *The Zemstva*.

Martov, Iu., *Zapiski sotsialdemokrata*, Berlin, 1922.

Martynov, E. I., *Kornilov: Popytka voennogo perevorota*, Leningrad, 1927.

Martynov, E. I., *Tsarskaia armiia v fevral'skom perevorote*, Leningrad, 1927.

Maslov, S. S., *Rossia posle chetyrekh let revoliutsii*, 2 vols, Paris, 1922.

Massie, R. K., *Nicholas and Alexandra*, London, 1968.

Massie, R. K., *The Romanovs: The Final Chapter*, London, 1995.

Materialy narodnogo kommissariata iustitsii, I, Moscow, 1918.

Materialy po statistike Petrograda, I, Petrograd, 1920.

Matthewson, R. W., *The Positive Hero in Russian Literature*, Stanford, 1975.

Matossian, M., 'The Peasant Way of Life', in W. Vucinich (ed.), *The Peasant*.

Mawdsley, E., *The Russian Revolution and the Baltic Fleet: War and Politics, February 1917–April 1918*, London, 1978.

Mawdsley, E., *The Russian Civil War*, London, 1987.

Maynard, J., *The Russian Peasant and Other Studies*, London, 1942.

Medvedev, R. and Starikov, S., *Philip Mironov and the Russian Civil War*, New York, 1978.

Melamed, S. M., 'St Paul and Leon Trotsky', *Reflex*, Nov 1927.

Melgunov, S. P., *The Red Terror in Russia*, London, 1925.

Mel'gunov, S. P., *Tragediia Admirala Kolchaka*, Belgrade, 1930.

Melgunov, S. P., *The Bolshevik Seizure of Power*, Oxford, 1972.

Mendel'son, A. L., *Itogo prinuditel'noi trezvosti i novye formy p'ianstva*, Leningrad, 1916.

Meshcherskaia, E., 'Trudovoe kreshchenie', *Novyi mir*, 4, 1988.

Meyendorff, J., 'Russian Bishops and Church Reform in 1905', in G. Hosking (ed.), *Church*.

Michelson, A., 'The Wings of Hypothesis', in *Montage and Modern Life, 1919–1942*, Boston, 1992.

Mikoian, A., *Mysli i vospominaniia o Lenine*, Moscow, 1970.

Miliukov, P. N., *Istoriia vtoroi russkoi revoliutsii*, Sofia, 1921.

Miliukov, P. N., *Russia Today and Tomorrow*, London, 1922.

Miliukov, P. N., *Political Memoirs, 1905–1917*, Ann Arbor, 1967.

Miliukov, P. N., *The Russian Revolution*, 3 vols, Florida, 1987.

Miliutin, V., 'Stranitsy iz dnevnika', *Prozhektor*, 4, 1924.

Minor, A. S., *Novye formy p'ianstva denaturom i spirtosoderzhashchimi zhidkostiami*, Moscow, 1915.

Mironov, B., 'The Russian Peasant Commune After the Reforms of the 1860s', *Slavic Review*, 44, 1985.

Mixter, T., 'Peasant Collective Action in Saratov Province, 1902–1906', in R. Wade and S. Seregny, *Politics and Society in Provincial Russia: Saratov, 1590–1917*, Columbus, Ohio, 1989.

Mordvinov, A., 'Otryvki iz vospominanii', *Russkaia letopis'*, 5, 1923.

Morizet, A., *Chez Lénine et Trotski à Moscou*, Paris, n.d.

Morrison, J. D., 'The Church Schools and Seminaries in the Russian Revolution of 1905', in G. Hosking (ed.), *Church*.

Mosse, W. E., 'Bureaucracy and Nobility in Russia at the End of the Nineteenth Century', *Historical Journal*, 24, 1981.

Mossolov, A. A., *At the Court of the Last Tsar*, London, 1935.

Mstislavsky, S., *Five Days Which Transformed Russia*, London, 1988.

Nabokov, K. D., *Ispytaniia diplomata*, Stockholm, 1921.

Nabokov, V. D., 'The Provisional Government', in U. D. Medlin and S. L. Parsons (ed.), *V. D. Nabokov and the Russian Provisional Government, 1917*, New Haven, 1976.

Narodnyi komissariat putei soobshcheniia za dva goda revoliutsii. Otchet VII-my vserossiiskomu s'ezdy sovetov, Moscow, 1919.

Narodnyi pisatel' Sergei Terent'evich Semenov, Moscow, 1968.

Naumov, A. N., *Iz ustelevshikh vospominanii, 1868–1917,* 2 vols, New York, 1954.

Naumov, V., '1923 god: sud'ba leninskoi al'ternativy', *Kommunist,* 5, 1991.

Nazhivin, I., *Zapiski o revoliutsii,* Vienna, 1921.

Nesterovich-Berg, M. A., *V bor'be s bol'shevikami,* Paris, 1931.

Neuberger, J., 'Stories of the Street: Hooliganism in the St Petersburg Popular Press, 1900–1905', *Slavic Review,* 48, 1989.

Neuberger, J., *Hooliganism: Crime, Culture and Power in St Petersburg, 1900–1914,* Berkeley, 1993.

New Economic Policies of Soviet Russia, The, Chicago, 1921.

Nikitine, B. V., *The Fatal Years,* London, 1938.

Nikolaevsky, B. I., *Power and the Soviet Elite: 'The Letter of an Old Bolshevik' and Other Essays,* New York, 1965.

Oberuchev, K., *V dni revoliutsii: vospominaniia uchastnika velikoi russkoi revoliutsii 1917 goda,* New York, 1919.

Obolenskii, V. A., 'Krym pri Vrangele', *Na chuzhoi storone,* 9, 1925.

Obolenskii, V. A., *Moia zhizn', moi sovremenniki,* Paris, 1988.

Ocherki byta derevenskoi molodezhi, Moscow, 1924.

Odinnadtsatyi s'ezd RKP(b). Stenograficheskii otchet, Moscow, 1922.

Okninskii, A., *Dva goda sredi krest'ian: vidennoe, slyshannoe, perezhitoe v Tambovskoi gubernii s noiabria 1918 goda do noiabria 1920 goda,* Newtonville, Mass., 1986.

Oktiabr'skoe vooruzhennoe vosstanie v Petrograde: Dokumenty i materialy, ed. G. N. Golikov et al., Moscow, 1957.

O Lenine: sbornik statei i vystuplenii, Moscow, 1965.

Orlovsky, D. T., 'State-Building in the Civil War: The Role of the Lower-Middle Strata', in D. P. Koenker et al. (ed.), *Party.*

Ordhonikidze, F. K., *Stat'i i rechi,* Moscow, 1956.

Os'kin, D. P., *Khoziaistvennaia rabota 2-oi osoboi armii,* Moscow, 1926.

Os'kin, D. P., *Zapiski soldata,* Moscow, 1926.

Os'kin, D. P., *Zapiski voenkoma,* Moscow, 1931.

Os'kin, D. P., *Vospominaniia o Vladimire Il'iche Lenine,* Moscow, 1957.

Owen, T. L., *Capitalism and Politics in Russia: A Social History of the Moscow Merchants, 1855–1905,* Cambridge, 1981.

Padenie tsarskogo rezhima, 7 vols, Leningrad, 1924–7.

Pakhman, S. V., *Obychnoe grazhdanskoe pravo v Rossii,* 2 vols, St Petersburg, 1877, 1879.

Pal'chinskii, P. I., 'Poslednye chasy vremennogo pravitel'stva v 1917 godu', *Krasnyi Arkhiv,* I, 1933.

Paléologue, M., *An Ambassador's Memoirs,* vol. I, London, 1923.

Paley, Princess, *Memories of Russia, 1916–1919,* London, n.d.

Pallot, J. and Shaw, D., *Landscape and Settlement in Romanov Russia, 1613–1917,* Oxford, 1990.

Pamiat': istoricheskii sbornik, Paris, 1981.

Pares, B. (ed.), *Letters of the Tsaritsa to the Tsar,* London, 1923.

Pares, B., *My Russian Memoirs,* London, 1931.

Pares, B., *The Fall of the Russian Monarchy,* London, 1939.

Park, A. G., *Bolshevism in Turkestan, 1917–27,* New York, 1957.

Pascal, P., *En Communisme: Mon journal de Russie, 1918–1921,* Lausanne, 1977.

Pasternak, B., *Stikhotvoreniia i poemy,* Moscow-Leningrad, 1965.

Pasternak Slater, Ann (ed. and trans.), *A Vanished Present: The Memoirs of Alexander Pasternak,* Oxford, 1994.

Paustovsky, K., *Story of My Life,* New York, 1964.

Pavlov, I., *Markovskaia respublika,* Moscow, 1926.

Pearson, R., *The Russian Moderates and the Crisis of Tsarism, 1914–1917,* London, 1977.

Pearson, T., *Russian Officialdom in Crisis,* Cambridge, 1990.

Perepiska Nikolaia i Aleksandry Romanovykh, vol. 5, Moscow-Leningrad, 1927.

Perrie, M., 'The Russian Peasant Movement of 1905–1907: Its Social Composition and Revolutionary Significance', *Past and Present,* 57, 1972.

Perrot, M., *Les Ouvriers en grève: France, 1871–1890,* Paris, 1974.

Peshekhonov, A. V., 'Pered krasnym terrorom', *Na chuzhoi storone,* 2, 1923.

Peshekhonov, A. V., 'Pervye nedeli (iz vospominanii russkoi revoliutsii)', *Na chuzhoi storone,* I, 1923.

Peters, 'Vospominaniia o rabote v VChK v pervyi god revoliutsii', *Proletarskaia revoliutsiia,* 10, 1924.

Pethybridge, R., *The Social Prelude to Stalinism,* London, 1974.

Petrogradskii sovet rabochikh i soldatskikh deputatov v 1917 godu. Dokumenty i materialy, vol. I, St Petersburg, 1993.

Petrov, P. P., *Ot Volgi do Tikhogo Okeana v riadakh belykh (1918–1922 gg.),* Riga, 1930.

Petrunkevich, I. I., 'Iz zapisok obshchestvennogo deiatelia', *Arkhiv russkoi revoliutsii,* 21, Berlin, 1934.

Piatyi vserossiiskii s'ezd sovetov rabochikh i kazachikh deputatov. Stenograficheskii otchet, Moscow, 1918.

Pipes, R., *The Formation of the Soviet Union: Communism and Nationalism, 1917–1923,* Harvard, 1954.

Pipes, R. (ed.), *Revolutionary Russia,* Harvard, 1968.

Pipes, R., *Struve: Liberal on the Left,* Cambridge, Mass., 1970.

Pipes, R., *Russia Under the Old Regime,* London, 1982.

Pipes, R., *The Russian Revolution, 1899–1919,* London, 1990.

Pipes, R., *Russia Under the Bolshevik Regime, 1919–1924,* London, 1994.

Pireiko, A., *Na fronte imperialisticheskoi voiny,* Moscow, 1925.

'Pis'ma moi k tebe, konechno, istoricheskie', *Voprosy istorii KPSS*, 2, 1991.

Pitcher, H. (ed.), *Witnesses of the Russian Revolution*, London, 1994.

Pokrovskii, G., *Denikinshchina*, Berlin, 1923.

Poliak, V., 'Zhutkie dni na Ukraine', *Evreiskaia letopis'*, 2, Moscow, 1923.

Polner, T. I., *Zhiznennyi put' kniazia G. E. Lvova*, Paris, 1932.

Polner, T. I., Obolenskii, V. and Turn, S. (ed.), *Russian Local Government During the War and the Union of Zemstvos*, New Haven, 1930.

Polovtsov, Gen. P. A., *Glory and Downfall: Reminiscences of a Russian General Staff Officer*, London, 1935.

Potresov, A. N., *Posmertnyi sbornik proizvedenii*, Paris, 1937.

Pozner, V., *Dela i dni Petrograda: vospominaniia i razmyshleniia, 1917–1921*, Berlin, 1923.

Pravda o Kronshtadte, Prague, 1921.

Protokoly zasedanii vserossiiskogo tsentral'nogo ispolnitel'nogo komiteta (4 sozyva), Moscow, 1920.

Purishkevich, V. M., *Dnevnik*, Riga, 1924.

Purishkevich, V. M., *Ubiistvo Rasputina*, Paris, n.d.

Pyman, A., *The Life of Alexander Blok*, vol. 2, *The Release of Harmony, 1908–1921*, Oxford, 1980.

Rabinowitch, A., *Prelude to Bolshevism: The Petrograd Bolsheviks and the July 1917 Uprising*, Bloomington, 1968.

Rabinowitch, A., *The Bolsheviks Come to Power: The Revolution of 1917 in Petrograd*, New York, 1978.

Rabinowitch, A., 'Bol'sheviki, nizy i sovetskaia vlast': Petrograd, fevral' 1917–iiul' 1918', in *Anatomiia*.

Rabinowitch, A., 'Maria Spiridonova's "Last Testament" ', *Russian Review*, 54, no. 3, 1995.

Radek, K., *Portrety i pamflety*, Moscow, 1933.

Radical Worker in Tsarist Russia, A: The Autobiography of Semen Ivanovich Kanatchikov, ed. R. E. Zelnik, Stanford, 1986.

Radkey, O. H., *The Election to the Russian Constituent Assembly of 1917*, Cambridge, Mass., 1950.

Radkey, O. H., *The Agrarian Foes of Bolshevism*, New York, 1958.

Radkey, O. H., *The Sickle Under the Hammer: The Russian Socialist Revolutionaries in the Early Months of Soviet Rule*, New York, 1973.

Radkey, O. H., *The Unknown Civil War in Soviet Russia*, Stanford, 1976.

Radzinsky, E., *The Last Tsar: The Life and Death of Nicholas II*, London, 1992.

Raeff, M., *Origins of the Russian Intelligentsia: The Eighteenth-Century Nobility*, New York, 1966.

Raeff, M., 'The Bureaucratic Phenomena of Imperial Russia', *American Historical Review*, 84, 1979.

Raeff, M., *Understanding Imperial Russia: State and Society in the Old Regime*, Columbia, 1984.

Rakovskii, G. N., *V stane belykh (ot Orla do Novorossiiska)*, Constantinople, 1920.

Rakovskii, G. N., *Konets belykh (ot Dnepra do Bosfora)*, Prague, 1921.

Raleigh, D. J., *Revolution on the Volga: 1917 in Saratov*, Cornell, 1986.

Ramer, S. C., 'Traditional Healers and Peasant Culture in Russia, 1861–1917', in E. Kingston-Mann and T. Mixter (ed.), *Peasant Economy*.

Ransome, A., *Six Weeks in Russia in 1919*, London, 1919.

Rapoporta, Iu. K., 'Poltora goda v sovetskom glavke', *Arkhiv russkoi revoliutsii*, 2, 1921.

Rashin, A., 'Gramotnost' i narodnoe obrazovanie v Rossi v XIX i nachale XX v.', *Istoricheskie zapiski*, 37, 1951.

Rashin, A., *Formirovanie rabochego klassa Rossii*, Moscow, 1958.

Raskolnikov, F. F., *Kronstadt and Petrograd in 1917*, London, 1982.

Rawson, D., *Russian Rightists and the Revolution of 1905*, Cambridge, 1995.

Read, C., *Culture and Power in Revolutionary Russia*, London, 1990.

Reed, J., *Ten Days that Shook the World*, London, 1977.

Reisner, L., *Izbrannye proizvedeniia*, Moscow, 1958.

Reshetar, J., *The Ukrainian Revolution, 1917–1920*, Princeton, 1950.

Resis, A., '*Das Kapital* Comes to Russia', *Slavic Review*, 24, 1970.

Resolutions and Decisions of the Communist Party of the Soviet Union, vol. 2, *The Early Soviet Period*, Toronto, 1976.

Revvoensovet respubliki, Moscow, 1991.

Rieber, A., 'Landed Property, State Authority, and Civil War', *Slavic Review*, 47, 1988.

Rieber, A., 'The Sedimentary Society', in E. Clowes et al. (ed.), *Between Tsar and People*.

Rigby, T. H., *Lenin's Government: Sovnarkom, 1917–1922*, Cambridge, 1979.

Rigby, T. H., *Political Elites in the USSR: Central Leaders and Local Cadres from Lenin to Gorbachev*, Aldershot, 1990.

Rittikh, A. A., *Krest'ianskoe pravoporiadok*, St Petersburg, 1902.

Robbins, R., *Famine in Russia, 1891–1892*, New York, 1975.

Robbins, R., *The Tsar's Viceroys: Russian Provincial Governors in the Last Years of the Empire*, Cornell, 1987.

Robbins, R., 'His Excellency the Governor: The Style of Russian Provincial Government at the Beginning of the Twentieth Century', in *Imperial Russia, 1700–1917: State, Society, Opposition*, de Kalb, Ill., 1988.

Robinson, G. T., *Rural Russia Under the Old Regime*, London, 1932.

Rodzianko, M. V., *The Reign of Rasputin: An Empire's Collapse*, London, 1927.

Rogger, H., 'Russian Ministers and the Jewish Question, 1881–1917', *California Slavic Studies*, 8, 1975.

Rogger, H., *Russia in the Age of Modernization and Revolution, 1881–1917*, London, 1983.

Rogger, H., *Jewish Policies and Right-Wing Politics in Imperial Russia*, Berkeley, 1986.

Rolland, R., *Journal des années de guerre*, Paris, 1952.

Romanov, Grand Duke A. M., *Once a Grand Duke*, London, 1932.

Romanov, Grand Duke G. K., *V mramornom dvortse*, New York, 1955.

Roobol, W. H., *Tsereteli — A Democrat in the Russian Revolution: A Political Biography*, The Hague, 1976.

Rorlich, A.-A., *The Volga Tatars: A Profile in National Resilience*, Stanford, 1986.

Rosenberg, W. G., 'The Russian Municipal Duma Elections of 1917: A Preliminary Computation of Returns', *Soviet Studies*, 21–2, 1969.

Rosenberg, W. G., *Liberals in the Russian Revolution: The Constitutional Democratic Party, 1917–1921*, Princeton, 1974.

Rosenberg, W. G., 'The Social Background to Tsektran', in D. P. Koenker, W. G. Rosenberg and R. G. Suny (ed.), *Party*.

Rosenberg, W. G., 'Russian Labor and Bolshevik Power: Social Dimensions of Protest in Petrograd after October', *Slavic Review*, 44, 1985.

Rosenberg, W. G., 'Social Mediation and State Construction(s) in Revolutionary Russia', *Social History*, 19, 2, 1994.

Rougle, C., 'The Intelligentsia in Russia, 1917–1918', in Nils A. Nilsson (ed.) *Art, Society, Revolution: Russia, 1917–1918*, Stockholm, 1979.

Rozhdestvenskii, V. A., *Stranitsy zhizni: iz literaturnykh vospominanii*, Moscow, 1974.

RPG: see *Russian Provisional Government*.

Rudnev, S., *Pri vechernykh ogniakh: vospominaniia*, Newtonville, Mass., 1978.

Ruhl, A., *New Masters of the Baltic*, New York, 1921.

Russian Provisional Government 1917, The: Documents, ed. R. G. Browder and A. F. Kerensky, 3 vols, Stanford, 1961 *[RPG]*.

Russian Schools and Universities in the World War, New Haven, 1929.

Russkaia revoliutsiia glazami petrogradskogo chinovnika. Dnevnik 1917–1918, Oslo, 1986.

Sablinsky, W., *The Road to Bloody Sunday: Father Gapon and the St Petersburg Massacre of 1905*, Princeton, 1976.

Sakwa, R., *Soviet Communists in Power: A Study of Moscow During the Civil War, 1918–1921*, London, 1988.

Salisbury, H. E., *Black Night, White Snow: Russia's Revolutions, 1905–1917*, New York, 1978.

Samuel, M., *Blood Accusation*, London, 1966.

Sapronov, T., *Iz istorii rabochego dvizheniia*, Newtonville, Mass., 1976.

Saunders, D., *Russia in the Age of Reaction and Reform*, London, 1992.

Savinkov, B. S., *K delu Kornilova*, Paris, 1919.

Sazonov, J. D., *How the War Began in 1914*, London, 1925.

Schapiro, L., *The Origin of the Communist Autocracy: Political Opposition in the Soviet State, First Phase, 1917–1922*, London, 1977.

Schapiro, L., 'The Political Thought of the First Provisional Government', in R. Pipes (ed.), *Revolutionary Russia*.

Scherr, B., 'Notes on Literary Life in Petrograd, 1918–22: A Tale of Three Houses', *Slavic Review*, 36, 1977.

Scherrer, J., 'Les Écoles du parti de Capri et de Bologne: La formation de l'intelligence du parti', *Cahiers du monde russe et sovietique*, 19, 1978.

Schweitzer, V., *Tsvetaeva*, London, 1988.

Seifullina, L., 'Muzhitskii skaz o Lenine', *Krasnyi nov'*, I, 1924.

Seletskii, V., 'Obrazovanie Partii Pogressistov', *Vestnik moskovskogo gosudarstvennogo universiteta, Istoricheskaia Seriia*, 5, 1970.

Semenov, S. T., 'Legko li u nas vydeliat'sia iz obshchiny?', *Sovremennik*, 5–6, 1911.

Semenov, S. T., *Vospominaniia o L. N. Tolstogo*, St Petersburg, 1912.

Semenov, S. T., 'Novye khoziaeva', *Sovremennik* 10, 1913.

Semenov, S. T., *Dvadtsat' piat' let v derevne*, Petrograd, 1915.

Semenov, S. T., 'Obnovlenie chernozema', *Russkaia mysl'*, 2 and 4, 1917.

Senn, A., *The Emergence of Modern Lithuania*, Princeton, 1959.

Serebrennikov, A., *Ubiistvo Stolypina: svidetel'stva i dokumenty*, New York, 1986.

Seregny, S. J., 'Peasants and Politics: Peasant Unions During the 1905 Revolution', in E. Kingston-Mann and T. Mixter (ed.), *Peasant Economy*.

Seregny, S. J., *Russian Teachers and Peasant Revolution: The Politics of Education in 1905*, Bloomington, 1989.

Serge, V., *La Ville en danger: Petrograd l'an II de la révolution*, Paris, 1924.

Serge, V., *Memoirs of a Revolutionary, 1901–1941*, Oxford, 1967.

Serge, V., *L'an I de la révolution*, Paris, 1971.

Serge, V. and Sedova, N. S., *The Life and Death of Leon Trotsky*, London, 1973.

Service, R., *The Bolshevik Party in Revolution: A Study in Organizational Change, 1917–1923*, London, 1979.

Service, R., *Lenin: A Political Life*, 3 vols, London, 1985, 1991, 1995.

Seton-Watson, H., *The Russian Empire, 1801–1917*, Oxford, 1967.

Shabanov, V., 'Kratkii Biograficheskii Ocherk', unpublished ms.

Shanin, T., *The Awkward Class*, Oxford, 1972.

Shanin, T., *Russia as a 'Developing Society'*, vol. I, *The Roots of Otherness: Russia's Turn of Century*, London, 1985.

Shanin, T., *Russia, 1905–7: Revolution as a Moment of Truth*, vol. 2, *The Roots of Otherness: Russia's Turn of Century*, London, 1986.

Shapovalov, A. I., *Po doroge k marksismu: vospominaniia rabochego revoliutsionera*, Moscow, 1922.

Shekhtman, I. B., *Pogromy dobrovol'cheskoi armii na Ukraine*, Berlin, 1932.

Shentalinsky, V., *The KGB's Literary Archive*, London, 1995.

Shevelov, G., 'The Language Question in the Ukraine in the Twentieth Century (1900–1941)', *Harvard Ukrainian Studies*, 10, 1986.

Shklovsky, V., *Sentimental Journey*, Ithaca, 1970.

Shlapentokh, D., 'The Images of the French Revolution in the February and Bolshevik Revolutions', *Russian History*, 16-1, 1989.

Shliapnikov, A., *On the Eve of 1917: Reminiscences from the Revolutionary Underground*, London, 1982.

Shliapnikov, A., *Semnadsatyi god*, 4 vols, Petrograd, 1923.

Shub, D., 'Kropotkin and Lenin', *Russian Review*, 12, 1953.

Shub, D., 'Maksim Gorkii i kommunisticheskaia diktatura', *Mosty*, 1, 1958.

Shub, D., *Lenin*, London, 1966.

Shulgin, V. V., *Dni*, Leningrad, 1926.

Shulgin, V. V., *1920 god*, Leningrad, 1927.

Sidorov, A. L., *Revoliutsionnoe dvizhenie v armii i flote v gody pervoi mirovoi voiny 1914–fevr. 1917*, Moscow, 1966.

Sidorov, A. L., *Ekonomicheskoe polozhenie Rossii v gody pervoi mirovoi voiny*, Moscow, 1973.

Siegelbaum, L. H., *The Politics of Industrial Mobilization in Russia, 1914–1917: A Study of the War-Industry Committees*, London, 1983.

Silver, B., *The Russian Workers' Own Story*, London, 1938.

Simanovich, A., *Rasputine*, Paris, 1930.

Simms, J. Y., 'The Famine and the Radicals', in E. H. Judge and J. Y. Simms (ed.), *Modernization*.

Simms, J. Y., 'The Crisis in Russian Agriculture at the End of the Nineteenth Century: A Different View', *Slavic Review*, 36, 1977.

Simms, J. Y., 'The Crop Failure of 1891: Soil Exhaustion, Technological Back-wardness, and Russia's "Agrarian Crisis" ', *Slavic Review*, 41, 1982.

Simon, G., 'Church, State and Society', in G. Katkov et al. (ed.), *Russia Enters the Twentieth Century*, London, 1971.

Sinegub, A., 'Zashchita zimnego dvortsa v den' 25 oktiabria 1917', *Arkhiv russkoi revoliutsii*, 4, 1922.

Skobtsev, D. E., *Tri goda revoliutsii i grazhdanskoi voiny na kubany*, Paris, n.d.

Slomka, J., *From Serfdom to Self-Government: Memoirs of a Polish Village Mayor*, London, 1941.

Smith, S. A., *Red Petrograd: Revolution in the Factories, 1917–1918*, Cambridge, 1983.

Smitten, B. N., 'Poslednyi vremenshchik poslednego tsaria. Materialy chrezvychai-noi sledstvennoi komissii vremennogo pravitel'stva o Rasputine i razlozhenii samoderzhaviia', *Voprosy istorii*, 10, 12, 1964; 1, 2, 1965.

Sokolov, B. F., 'Zashchita vserossiiskogo uchreditel'nogo sobraniia', *Arkhiv russkoi revoliutsii*, 12, 1924.

Sokolov, B. F., *The White Nights: Pages from a Russian Doctor's Notebook*, London, 1959.

Sokolov, Iu. V., 'Aleksei Alekseevich Brusilov', *Voprosy istorii*, II, 1988.

Sokolov, K. N., *Pravlenie generala Denikina (iz vospominanii)*, Sofia, 1921.

Sokolov, N. A., *Ubiistvo tsarskoi sem'i*, Paris, 1925.

Solomon, G. A., *Sredi krasnykh vozhdei: Lichnoe perezhitoe i vidennoe na sovetskoi sluzhbe*, 2 vols, Paris, 1930.

Some Notes on Social Conditions in Soviet Russia, London, 1925.

Sorokin, P., *Sovremennoe sostoianie Rossii*, Prague, 1922.

Sorokin, P., *Leaves from a Russian Diary*, New York, 1924.

Sorokin, P., *Chelovek, tsivilizatsiia, obshchestvo*, Moscow, 1992.

Speranskii, 'Narodnye zasedateli', *Proletarskaia revoliutsiia i pravo*, 5, 1918.

Spiridonova, L., 'Gorky and Stalin. (According to New Materials from A. M. Gorky's Archive)', *Russian Review*, 54, no. 3, 1995.

Spiridovitch, A., *Les Dernières Années de la cour de Tsarskoe Selo*, 2 vols, Paris, 1928–9.

Spring, D. W., 'Russia and the Coming of War', in R. J. W. Evans and H. Pogge von Strondmann (ed.), *The Coming of the First World War*, Oxford, 1988.

Stalin's Letters to Molotov, ed. L. T. Lih, O. V. Naumov and O. V. Khlevniuk, New Haven, 1995.

Stankevich, V., *Vospominaniia, 1914–19 g.*, Berlin, 1920.

Startsev, V. I., 'Voenno-revoliutsionnyi komitet i krasnaia gvardiia', in *Oktiabr'skoe vooruzhennoe vosstanie v Petrograde: sbornik statei*, Moscow-Leningrad, 1957.

Startsev, V. I., *Ocherki po istorii Petrogradskoi krasnoi gvardii i rabochei militsii*, Moscow-Leningrad, 1965.

Steinberg, I. N., *In the Workshop of the Revolution*, New York, 1953.

Steinberg, M. D. and Khrustalev, V. M., *The Fall of the Romanovs: Political Dreams and Personal Struggles in a Time of Revolution*, New Haven, 1995.

Steklow, G., *Mikhail Bakunin*, Stuttgart, 1913.

Stepniak (Kravchinskii), S. M., *The Russian Peasantry: Their Condition, Social Life, and Religion*, London, 1905.

Stepun, F., *Byvshee i nesbyvsheesia*, 2 vols, New York, 1956.

Sternheimer, S., 'Administering Development and Developing Administration: Organizational Conflict in Tsarist Bureaucracy, 1906–1914', *Canadian-American Slavic Studies*, 9, 1975.

Stites, R., *The Women's Liberation Movement in Russia: Feminism, Nihilism and Bolshevism, 1860–1930*, Princeton, 1978.

Stites, R., *Revolutionary Dreams: Utopian Vision and Experimental Life in the Russian Revolution*, Oxford, 1989.

Stites, R., 'Iconoclastic Currents in the Russian Revolution: Destroying and Preserving the Past', in A. Gleason et al. (ed.), *Bolshevik Culture*.

Stolypine, A., *L'Homme du dernier tsar*, Paris, 1931.

Stojko, W., 'Ukrainian National Aspirations and the Russian Provisional Government', in T. Hunczak (ed.), *The Ukraine, 1917–1921: A Study in Revolution*, Harvard, 1977.

Stone, N., *The Eastern Front, 1914–1917*, London, 1978.

Stone, N., *Europe Transformed, 1878–1918*, London, 1983.

Struktura i sostav organov VSNKh v tsentre i na mestakh v 1921 g., Moscow, 1922.

Strumilin, S. G., 'Prozhitochnoi minimum i zarabotki chernorabochikh v Petrograde', *Statistika truda*, 2–3, 1918.

Strumilin, S. G., 'Biudzhet moskovskogo rabochego', *Statistika truda*, 1–4, 1919.

Strumilin, S. G., *Zarabotnaia plata i proizvoditel'nost' truda v russkoi promyshlennosti v 1913–1922 gg.*, Moscow, 1923.

Strumilin, S. G., *Izbrannye proizvedeniia*, vol. I, Moscow, 1963.

Struve, P. B., 'Velikaia Rossia: iz razmyshlenii o probleme russkogo moguchestva', *Russkaia mysl'*, 28, 1908.

Struve, P. B., 'My Contacts and Conflicts with Lenin', *Slavic Review*, 12, 1933–4.

Stulov, P. M., 'Pervyi pulemetnyi polk i iiulskie dni 1917 g.', *Krasnaia letopis'*, 3, 1930.

Suhr, G., *1905 in St Petersburg: Labor, Society and Revolution*, Stanford, 1989.

Sukhanov, N. N., *The Russian Revolution: A Personal Record*, ed. J. Carmichael, Princeton, 1984.

Suny, R. G., *The Baku Commune, 1917–18*, Princeton, 1972.

Suny, R. G., *The Making of the Georgian Nation*, Indiana, 1988.

Suny, R. G., 'Nationality and Class in the Revolutions of 1917: A Re-examination of categories', in N. Lampert and G. Rittersporn (ed.), *Stalinism: Its Nature and Aftermath*, London, 1992.

Suny, R. G., *The Revenge of the Past: Nationalism, Revolution, and the Collapse of the Soviet Union*, Stanford, 1993.

Suvorin, B., *Za rodinoi: geroicheskaia epokha dobrovol'cheskoi armii*, Paris, 1922.

Swietochowski, T., *Russian Azerbaijan, 1905–1920: The Shaping of a National Identity in a Muslim Community*, Cambridge, 1988.

Swift, A., 'Kul'turnoe stroitel'stvo ili kul'turnaia razrukha? (Nekotorye aspekty teatral'noi zhizni Petrograda i Moskvy v 1917 g.)', in *Anatomiia*.

Svobodov, A., 'A. M. Gor'kii i studencheskoe dvizhenie 1901 goda. (Po delam arkhiva Nizhegorodskogo gubernskogo zhandarmskogo upravleniia)', *Katorga i ssylka*, 6, 1927.

Szamuely, T., *The Russian Tradition*, London, 1988.

Szeftel, M., *The Russian Constitution of April 23, 1906*, Brussels, 1976.

Tager, A. B., *The Decay of Czarism: The Beiliss Trial*, Philadelphia, 1935.

Taneeva (Vyrubova), A., *Stranitsy iz moei zhizni*, Berlin, 1923.

Taylor, R., *The Politics of the Soviet Cinema, 1917–1929*, Cambridge, 1979.

Tkachev, P., *Izbrannye sochineniia na sotsial'no-politicheskie temy*, Moscow, 1932.

Toller, E., *Which World? Which Way?*, London, 1931.

Tolstoi, L. N., *Pis'ma L. N. Tolstogo, 1848–1910 gg.*, Moscow, 1910.

Tolstoi, L. N., *Pis'ma L. N. Tolstogo k zhene, 1862–1910 gg.*, Moscow, 1915.

Tretii vserossiiskii s'ezd professional'nykh soiuzov, Moscow, 1921.

Trifonov, I., *Klassy i klassovaia bor'ba v SSSR v nachale NEPa*, Leningrad, 1964.

Trotskii, L. D., *O Lenine*, Moscow, 1924.

Trotskii, L. D., *Sochineniia*, Moscow, 1925–7.

Trotskii, L. D., *Stalinskaia shkola falsifikatsii*, Berlin, 1932.

Trotskii, L. D., *Dnevniki i pis'ma*, ed. Iu. G. Fel'shtinskii, New Jersey, 1986.

Trotsky, L. D., *My Life*, Harmondsworth, 1975.

Trotsky, L. D., *The History of the Russian Revolution*, trans. M. Eastman, London, 1977.

Trotsky, L. D., *How the Revolution Armed*, in *The Military Writings and Speeches of Leon Trotsky*, 5 vols, trans. B. Pearce, London, 1979 [*HRA*].

Trotsky Papers The, ed. J. M. Meijer, 2 vols, The Hague, 1964, 1971.

Troyat, H., *Tolstoy*, Harmondsworth, 1980.

Troyat, H., *Gorky*, London, 1991.

Trubetskaia, O., *Kniaz S. N. Trubetskoi (vospominaniia sestry)*, New York, 1953.

Trudy tsentral'nogo statisticheskogo upravleniia, 7, 1, Moscow, 1921.

Tsarev, B., *Samouchka pisatel' S. T. Semenov*, Moscow, 1925.

Tsereteli, I. G., *Vospominaniia o fevral'skoi revoliutsii*, 2 vols, The Hague, 1963.

Tsvetaeva, M., *Stikhotvorenie i poemy*, 5 vols, New York, 1982.

Tsvetaeva, M., *Selected Poems*, trans. D. McDuff, Newcastle, 1987.

Tsytovich, N., *Sel'skoe obshchestvo kak organ mestnogo upravleniia*, Kiev, 1911.

Tucker, R. C., *Stalin in Power: The Revolution from Above, 1928–1941*, New York, 1990.

Tugan-Baranovsky, M. I., *The Russian Factory in the Nineteenth Century*, Homeward, Ill., 1970.

Tumarkin, N., *Lenin Lives! The Lenin Cult in Soviet Russia*, Cambridge, Mass., 1983.

Tyrkova-Williams, A. V., *Na putiakh k svobode*, New York, 1952.

Tyrkova-Williams, A. V., *To, chego bol'she ne bydet*, Paris, n.d.

Ulam, A., *The Bolsheviks*, New York, 1965.

Upton, A., *The Finnish Revolution, 1917–1918*, Minneapolis, 1980.

Urussov, S. D., *Memoirs of a Russian Governor*, London, 1908.

Ustrialov, N. I., *V bor'be za Rossiiu*, Kharbin, 1920.

Uustalu, E., *The History of the Estonian People*, London, 1952.

Vaisberg, R. E., *Den'gi i tseny (podpol'nyi rynok v period 'Voennogo Kommunizma')*, Moscow, 1925.

Valentinov, A. A., 'Krymskaia epopeia (po dnevnikam uchastnikov i po dokumentam', *Arkhiv russkoi revoliutsii*, 5, 1922.

Valentinov, N., 'Chernyshevskii i Lenin', *Novyi zhurnal*, 26, 1951.

Valentinov, N., *Encounters with Lenin*, London, 1968.

Valentinov, N., *Maloznakomyi Lenin*, Paris, 1972.

Valentinov, N., *Novaia ekonomicheskaia politika i krizis partii posle smerti Lenina. Gody raboty v VSNKh vo vremia NEP: vospominaniia*, Stanford, 1971.

Varneck, E. and Fisher, H. (ed.), *The Testimony of Kolchak and Other Siberian Materials*, Stanford, 1935.

Vasil'eva, D. Iu., 'Russkaia pravoslavnaia tserkov' i sovetskaia vlast' v 1912–27 gg.', *Voprosy istorii*, 8, 1993.

Venturi, F., *Roots of Revolution: A History of the Populist and Socialist Movements in Nineteenth Century Russia*, New York, 1960.

Verner, A., *The Crisis of Russian Autocracy: Nicholas II and the 1905 Revolution*, Princeton, 1990.

Vertsinskii, E. A., *God revoliutsii: vospominaniia ofitsera general'nogo shtaba za 1917–18 gg.*, Tallinn, 1929.

Vladimirova, V., *Kontrrevoliutsiia v 1917 g. (Kornilovshchina)*, Moscow, 1924.

Voeikov, V. N., *S tsarem i bez tsaria*, Helsingfors, 1936.

Vogel, L. (ed.), *Alexander Blok: An Anthology of Essays and Memoirs*, Ann Arbor, 1982.

Voline, *The Unknown Revolution*, New York, 1975.

Volkogonov, D., *Stalin: Triumph and Tragedy*, London, 1992.

Volkogonov, D., *Lenin: Life and Legacy*, London, 1994.

Vorobei, K., *Odin za vsekh, vse za odnogo*, Leningrad, 1961.

Voronov, D. N., 'Analiz derevenskogo alkogolizma i samogonnogo promysla', *Voprosy narkologii*, I, Moscow, 1926.

Vserossiiskoe uchreditel'noe sobranie, Moscow-Leningrad, 1930.

Vtoroi vserossiiskii s'ezd sovetov rabochikh i soldatskikh deputatov, Moscow, 1957.

Vucinich, W. (ed.), *The Peasant in Nineteenth-Century Russia*, Stanford, 1968.

Wade, R., *The Russian Search for Peace, February–October 1917*, Stanford, 1969.

Wade, R., *Red Guards and Workers' Militias in the Russian Revolution*, Stanford, 1984.

Waldron, P., 'Religious Toleration in Late Imperial Russia', in O. Crisp and L. Edmondson (ed.), *Civil Rights in Imperial Russia*, Oxford, 1989.

War, Revolution, and Peace in Russia: The Passages of Frank Golder, 1914–1927, ed. T. Emmons and B. Patenaude, Stanford, 1992.

Wcislo, F. W., 'Bureaucratic Reform before World War I', *Russian History*, 16, 1989.

Weber, G. and Weber, H., *Lenin: Life and Works*, London, 1980.

Weinberg, R., 'The Pogrom of 1905 in Odessa: A Case Study', in J. Klier and D. Lambroza (ed.), *Pogroms*.

Weissman, B., *Herbert Hoover and Famine Relief to Soviet Russia*, Stanford, 1974.

Weissman, N., 'Rural Crime in Tsarist Russia: the Question of Hooliganism', *Slavic Review*, 37, 1978.

Weissman, N., *Reform in Tsarist Russia: the State Bureaucracy and Local Government, 1900–9*, New Brunswick, 1981.

Weissman, N., 'Regular Police in Tsarist Russia, 1900–1914', *Russian Review,* 20, 1985.

Weissman, N., 'Policing the NEP Countryside', in S. Fitzpatrick, A. Rabinowitch and R. Stites (ed.), *Russia in the Era of NEP: Explorations in Soviet Society and Culture,* Indiana, 1991.

Wells, H. G., *Russia in the Shadows,* London, 1920.

Wheatcroft, S. G., 'Crises and the Condition of the Peasantry in Late Imperial Russia', in E. Kingston-Mann and T. Mixter (ed.), *Peasant Economy.*

Wheeler-Bennett, J., *Brest-Litovsk: The Forgotten Peace,* New York, 1938.

Whelan, H. W., *Alexander III and the State Council,* New Brunswick, 1982.

White, D. D. F., *The Growth of the Red Army,* Princeton, 1944.

White, J. A., *The Diplomacy of the Russo-Japanese War,* Princeton, 1964.

White, J. D., 'The Kornilov Affair: A Study in Counter-Revolution', *Soviet Studies,* 20, 1968.

Wilcox, E. H., *Russia's Ruin,* London, 1919.

Wildman, A., *The Making of a Workers' Revolution: Russian Social Democracy, 1891–1903,* Stanford, 1967.

Wildman, A., *The End of the Russian Imperial Army,* 2 vols, Princeton, 1980, 1987.

Wilton, R., *Russia's Agony,* London, 1918.

Wilton, R., *Last Days of the Romanovs,* London, 1920.

Witte, S. I., *The Memoirs of Count Witte,* trans. and ed. S. Harcave, London, 1990.

Wolfe, B. D., *The Bridge and the Abyss: The Troubled Friendship of Maxim Gorky and V. I. Lenin,* London, 1967.

Wolfe, B. D., 'Autocracy Without an Autocrat', in *Revolution and Reality: Essays on the Origin and Fate of the Soviet System,* Chapel Hill, 1981.

Worobec, C. D., 'Victims or Actors? Russian Peasant Women and Patriarchy', in E. Kingston-Mann and T. Mixter (ed.), *Peasant Economy.*

Wortman, R., *The Crisis of Russian Populism,* Cambridge, 1967.

Wortman, R., 'Moscow and Petersburg: The Problems of Political Center in Tsarist Russia, 1881–1914', in S. Wilentz (ed.), *Rites of Power: Symbolism, Ritual, and Politics Since the Middle Ages,* Philadelphia, 1985.

Wortman, R., 'Invisible Threads: The Historical Imagery of the Romanov Tercentenary', *Russian History,* 16, 2–4, 1989.

Wortman, R., *Scenarios of Power: Myth and Ceremony in Russian Monarchy,* Princeton, 1995.

Woytinsky, W. S., *Stormy Passage,* New York, 1961.

Wrangel, N., *From Serfdom to Bolshevism: The Memoirs of Baron N. Wrangel,* London, 1927.

Wrangel, P. N., *The Memoirs of General Wrangel,* London, 1929.

Yaney, G., *The Systematization of the Russian Government,* Urbana, 1973.

Yaney, G., *The Urge to Mobilize: Agrarian Reform in Russia, 1801–1930,* Urbana, 1982.

Yodfat, A. Y., 'The Closure of Synagogues in the Soviet Union', in *Soviet Jewish Affairs,* 3, 1973.

Zaionchkovsky, P. A., *The Russian Autocracy Under Alexander III,* Gulf Breeze, 1976.

Zaionchkovskii, P. A., *Pravitel'stvennyi apparat: samoderzhavnoi Rossii v XIX v.,* Moscow, 1977.

Zelnik, R. E., *Labor and Society in Tsarist Russia: The Factory Workers of St Petersburg, 1855–90,* Stanford, 1971.

Zelnik, R. E., 'Russian Bebels: an Introduction to the Memoirs of Semen Kanatchikov and Matvei Fischer', *Russian Review,* 3–4, 1976.

Zelnik, R. E., 'The Fate of a Russian Bebel: Semen Ivanovich Kanatchikov, 1905–1940', *The Carl Beck Papers in Russian and East European Studies,* 1105, Pittsburgh, 1995.

Zeman, Z. (ed.), *Germany and the Revolution in Russia, 1915–1918,* London, 1958.

Zenzinov, V., *Deserted: The Story of the Children Abandoned in Soviet Russia,* London, 1931.

Zenzinov, V., 'Fevral'skie dni', *Novyi zhurnal,* 34–3, 1953.

Zenzinov, V., *Perezhitoe,* New York, 1953.

Zhukovskii-Zhuk, 'Kogda otkrylis' t'iuremnye dveri', *Katorga i ssylka,* 15, 1925.

Zinoviev, G. E., 'Lenin i iiul'skie dni', *Proletarskaia revoliutsiia,* 8–9, 1927.

Zinoviev, G. E., *Sochineniia,* Leningrad, 1923–9.

Ziv, G., *Trotskii: po lichnym vospominaniiam,* New York, 1921.

Zozulia, *Tsar' (cherez god),* Petrograd, 1918.

1917 god v derevne: vospominaniia krest'ian, Moscow-Leningrad, 1929.

Index

BODLEY
HEAD

THE HISTORY OF THE BODLEY HEAD

The Bodley Head was founded in 1887 by John Lane and Elkin Matthews.
Initially trading in antiquarian books in London, in 1894 Lane and Matthews
began to publish works of 'stylish decadence', including the notorious literary
periodical *The Yellow Book*. The Bodley Head became a private company in 1921
and in the 1970s formed a publishing group with Jonathan Cape and
Chatto & Windus. It was bought by Random House in 1987
and ceased trading as an adult imprint in 1990.

2008 saw the launch of an exciting and entirely new imprint within
Random House's VINTAGE division with the revival of the distinguished
Bodley Head name. In its new incarnation The Bodley Head is devoted to
excellence in non-fiction in all fields. Its two principal strands are books
of impeccable scholarship in the humanities and sciences, and books which
directly address the intellectual and cultural issues of our times.

For more information on books published by The Bodley Head please visit:
www.vintage-books.co.uk

For updates and news follow us on Twitter @TheBodleyHead